TWENTY PLAYS

for Young People

A COLLECTION OF PLAYS FOR CHILDREN

Selection and Foreword

by

WILLIAM B. BIRNER

THE ANCHORAGE PRESS

Anchorage, Kentucky

1967

i

CONTENTS

iii

FOREWORD

When I first approached the publishers of this anthology, crying for a collection of dramatic literature for children, I felt sure that others also felt this need. I was quite surprised by their reaction. "There are not enough good children's plays to make a book about." "What do you mean, a wide-spread need?" "What plays would you include?" This last made me pause. There are so many plays, but what limitations would be made? What criteria would be used in choosing them? Asked to draw up a list of the plays I would include, I returned home dejected by the thought either that I could be so wrong, or even if right, that I could not be convincing. I was reassured, therefore, when the publishers themselves uncovered evidence of the need for this book, and agreed to undertake the project.

Excitingly and suddenly, I realized that I had not simply suggested a project for others, but was quickly becoming personally involved in it. And very difficult questions had to be answered. What should a new anthology do? What should children's theatre do? I knew what my personal needs were — a source book. But what were the needs of others? It seemed that three valid approaches could be taken. We could stop, look back, and almost historically see where we had been. We could pause, open our eyes, and look to see where we really were. We could slow down, look ahead, try to ascertain where we were going, and possibly ask where we should be going. Might not all of these things be accomplished?

These were the needs that presented themselves. No major children's theatre anthology had been published since 1932, and since that time broad changes had taken place in the repertoire. We are growing more aware of the needs of our audience, their sophistication, interests, capabilities. Our newest plays reflect the mass media, the contemporary theatre, the international repertoire. There is a new theatre public seriously in need, not of just a source book, but of a working acquaintance with a representative body of dramatic literature for children. New artists of the future will be developing from this public. They will need a foundation to grow from, and a direction to move in. If this anthology can trace the development of the current literature, indicate the trends toward which it is leading us, and suggest, implicity or explicity, the necessary questions for the future, it will answer the immediate need. That is what this volume attempts to do. It is hoped that it will be read by many lay persons, including children, for pure pleasure; that it will fill a gap in the libraries of general theatre people; that it will be useful to serious theatre producers wishing to extend their knowledge of the children's theatre repertoire; and that in its broadest aim, it will acquaint the general public with a representative body of children's theatre literature.

As in any anthology, the selection of plays is bound to please some, and disturb others. As needs and aims grew more clear, the list changed many times before reaching its present form. While instructive and pleasurable, the selection process was one of the most difficult tasks I have ever had to face — examining beliefs, rationalizing, defending, convincing both myself and others. One really learns his feelings toward a play as he adds, subtracts, and balances, and screening out, narrows down a list, never really convinced that other plays should not have been considered, and possibly some deleted. Never, in choosing individual plays for production, have I felt as personally involved with a playscript as I now do with each of these.

The titles collected here were chosen, not necessarily to offer the best scripts for current production, but rather to represent the development of a young but growing body of literature. Several criteria were used. For purely practical purposes, the list was limited to twenty plays. For copyright reasons, the selection was confined to plays from the Anchorage Press list. This is acknowledged a limitation, but not a serious one, since this list, while certainly not containing every significant play, reflects an honest cross-section of those scripts identified with the American children's theatre movement since 1935.

To be most valuable and relevant, all of the plays chosen bear some role in the currently-produced repertoire. The total selection attempts to represent the relative contributions of some of the best-known children's theatre playwrights, and follow the growth of their work in literary and chronological order. The list is indicative of types of plays and types of sources, and hopefully indicates some potentialities to be further explored for the future. The play choices have been limited to "full-length" plays (in children's theatre terms), and indicate the Anchorage Press' "first" successful ventures toward increasingly complex meanings and forms. In each case, the dates referred to are those of publication, rather than of premiere production.

In surveying the twenty plays, one thing becomes increasingly clear. In striving to achieve the "increasingly complex meanings and forms", the children's theatre has been accustomed to use the conventions developed by the contemporary adult theatre, and has so far failed to advance original conventions of its own. Thus, while there is nothing inherently wrong in drawing upon the devices, and sometimes the talents, of the adult art world, it would seem that children's theatre personnel have either been hesitantly lacking in confidence, or lacking in that imaginative perception so necessary to a vital, creative art. Not that theatre for children is a separate art from theatre for adults—but as a part of the theatre family, children's theatre should be able to contribute to its advancement, rather than settle into a position of perennial dependency.

If the mechanics, the forms, the values of theatre are changing, it is because the society and environments of the life it reflects are changing — and the greater the change in our society, the greater is the difference likely to be in the theatre of the future. And if the environment of adults is changing, the change will be even more radical for the child. Better than 75% of the children in school today will probably live to work at jobs that do not presently exist. Their children will likely be involved with individualized, computerized instruction, three dimensional television, some unpredictable art forms of the future. Too long children's theatre has shrunk from holding the mirror up to nature as it is, presenting instead nature as we would like to see it, a platonically-idealized concept of the world around us. Changing environments, however, are interacting with changing ideals — and like it or not, we cannot claim relevance to future generations unless our mirror reflects an awareness of this real, actual, wonderful, shocking world. We have learned this from the adult theatre, and recent children's

vii

theatre playwrights have come to grips with it, marking a giant step forward. But the children's theatre cannot continue to depend on the adult theatre to blaze the trail. For the sake of an audience that cries out to be pointed toward the future, the children's theatre must seek its own new forms, styles, techniques, levels of meaning, terms of expression.

What of the current repertoire? Is it likely, from its past development, that it can grow to meet the needs of the future? I am very hopeful of this. It is interesting to note that the current repertoire has developed in a clear pattern of logical, if not conscious, steps toward meeting modern requirements. If we are not quite at the level where we would wish to be, we might remind ourselves that the contemporary adult theatre is dissatisfied too, even after 2500 years of change, trial, success, and failure, primarily evolving from other art forms, and not really innovating until recently; while children's theatre has had the benefit of little more than half a century of development.

The curiously logical, if indirect, progression that brings a *Jack and the Beanstalk* forward to a *Trudi and the Minstrel,* that brings a *Tom Sawyer* to a *Don Quixote of La Mancha,* that brings an *Indian Captive* to an *Abe Lincoln of Pigeon Creek,* and that brought us from dramatizations and adaptations to original plots, may possibly bring us, before long, to more shining achievements. How many further steps it will take to advance children's theatre to a truly mature literature, encompassing the original and the adapted, the contemporary and the historical, the realistic, fantastic, abstract, the perfectly simple, can only be guessed. As children's theatre discovered romanticism half a century late, epic techniques a few decades late, and the principles of the absurd late but while the movement was still with us, so it may not be long before it can join the truly avant garde, in its best and broadest sense.

Knowing where we stand, and surveying the enticing avenues that beckon ahead, it should now prove enlightening to take pause, and see where our literature came from.

Aside from such nineteenth century productions as *Uncle Tom's Cabin* and *Rip Van Winkle,* plays for children are predominantly a twentieth century phenomenon. In what might be considered a "golden age", the first two decades of this century gave us such fine productions as James Barrie's *Peter Pan,* Maurice Maeterlinck's *The Blue Bird,* Jessie B. White's *Snow White and the Seven Dwarfs,* and Jules Goodman's *Treasure Island.* These "early" plays in fact still provide valuable contributions to the current repertoire. However, the same economic factors which plague the professional children's theatre today halted further expansion of these early ventures. The ensuing gap in dramatic entertainment for children was filled by the widely-touring companies of Clare Tree Major. From this touring program, children's theatre in America became a national movement, growing rapidly in the 1930's. Its appetite was insatiable, and many different kinds of plays were required to meet its varying needs. As the movement became largely an amateur one, there were never enough plays, and producers were often willing to accept inferior scripts, just for the sake of variety.

The major growth of the children's theatre in the United States has taken place since the 1930's, and the progress made during this period, in the evolution of the repertoire, is noticeable. It is this development over some thirty years that provides the material for this anthology.

A few words should be said about categorization of plays for discussion. A work of art, no matter how naive or sophisticated, cannot be sorted like the morning mail. No matter what categories are chosen, a system will not always work. Categories are arbitrary pigeon-holes, nothing more. Some plays are difficult to join with others, some insist on suiting several categories. We thought of two categories — originals and adaptations. This system only tells us source, neglecting form and content. The four popular categories advanced by Dr. Kenneth Graham — fantasies, literary adaptations, histories, modern stories — allow us to classify plays for examination and comparative purposes. By combining the dissimilar in such clusters, however, much of the development of the literature does not show. For purposes of elucidation, I undertook to increase the categories to seven, by separating out folk material, nonsense, and formal comedy. The results served only to confuse, rather than clarify. And so it is with conviction (and a little chagrin) that I abandon categories, and leave any necessary pigeon-holing to individual readers, teachers, producers, allowing their personal dictates to take precedence over mine.

For developmental purposes the plays do have to be considered in sequential groups. Playwrights do not, however, write in regard to past and present time-tables, so that while the sequences are basically chronological and generally parallel, there are deviations. The historical placement of a single, individual play is not of major importance, except as it relates to the overall picture. An accurate chronological listing of the twenty plays included in this book, may be found in the table of contents.

The first play in this chronology, and in this volume, is Charlotte Chorpenning's *Jack and the Beanstalk* (1935). As one of the long-time favorite fairy-tales, its primary position is fitting. From the folk and fairy tales come the later fantasies and comedies, sometimes in modern forms — and this part of the literature accounts for a disproportionate share of the productions each year. Chorpenning has drawn her dramatization from one of the earliest fairy-tales most obviously laden with pagan and Christian symbols. Using the simplest of dialogue, she has drawn her characters in clear-cut, black-and-white terms. From the lazy Jack of the fairy tale, she creates Jack the devoted son, who is obliged to earn his good fortune. Otherwise, she is religiously faithful to the story, but extends its morality by introducing the character of Frihol, and the Man in the Moon, who draw up the rules for proving Jacks' moral fortitude.

Published the same year, 1935, Sara Spencer's *Tom Sawyer* is characteristic of another type of play written in this period — the simple, straight literary adaptation. Without dilution or elaboration, Spencer set out to bring to the stage this seemingly aimless, meandering portrait of boyhood. Less organic in form than some of Twain's other novels, *Tom Sawyer* does not lend itself readily to dramatic treatment — as indeed other authors have found, before and since, including Mark Twain himself. It has no plot. The Spencer adaptation (which has had the benefit of several revisions since its first version), does not attempt to supply this lack, making no more of it than a succession of episodes, lifted almost verbatim from the novel. This format permits only a visual portrayal of the queer enterprises Tom and his friends engaged in. It does not reveal how they felt and thought. This is its failure. Its achievement is that it was the first, and remains one of the very few, children's plays that does not depend upon a story line.

On a similar plane with *Jack and the Beanstalk* and *Tom Sawyer,* Chorpenning's 1937 play, *The Indian Captive,* was the first historical play of the period, and took a brave turn toward originality. Based on the true story of a young girl captured by the Seneca Indians in and around Pennsylvania, the author was obliged to research the incident, the period, and the pioneer and Indian living habits; select the characters needed to present the story, and breathe life into them; place her own interpretation on the historical facts; and devise her own plot, dialogue, and theme, without benefit of any other source material than history books. The play is marked by the same Spartan literalness that characterized other children's plays of the period. Its story is lean, its message overstated. But it led the repertoire into another subject area, and laid the foundation for later, more ambitious historical works.

The last play from the decade of the 1930's is Rosemary Musil's *The Ghost of Mr. Penny.* This 1939 "mystery-comedy" is included in this volume as one of the first original, contemporary realistic plays written for children. It is the only play of its kind included, because it is representative of the plays which might be grouped with it. While there is great demand for the "today play", little improvement has been made in this area since *Mr. Penny* was written. *Mr. Penny* is a weak script, by later standards, reminiscent of the melodramatic radio scripts popular in its time. Its situation is contrived, its major characters are unbelievable, its denouement is far-fetched. It still amuses contemporary children, and ranks among the best of its type. Progress is sorely needed here.

These plays point to the 1930's as an interesting decade, characterized by the adaptation to dramatic form of popular types of children's literature, by dramatic treatment of historical material, and by early strivings toward original contemporary drama which have failed to bear fruit in ensuing years. The plays were written with intense literalness, made to serve moralistic purposes, in a plain, honest, two-dimensional style. The characters seem somehow less than real, their dialogue and motivations reduced to the utmost obviousness.

It was not until 1944, with *Rumpelstiltskin*, that Chorpenning began to draw characters more nearly resembling people, and use them to mask her direct moralities. Although Rumpel is evil incarnate, he has human weaknesses that eventually lead to his destruction. Although the heroine is beautiful, good, and brave, she is also tricky enough to weasel out of her bargain. Although her father is foolishly proud, he is no more so than other fathers might be with such a daughter. The complexities of human behavior begin to creep in, filling out the flat, picture-book figures.

A year later, in 1945, Martha Bennet King's *Peter Peter, Pumpkin Eater* advanced character development in children's theatre considerably. This play contains the rustic folk flavor of nineteenth century Americana. The story is King's invention of a situation which might revolve around the well-known Mother Goose rhyme. Within this story, the playwright presents a depth and truth in characterization rarely found in a children's story. Easily mistaken as a childish, single-level story, *Peter Peter* can speak to every youth today, with unique eloquence. Underneath its nursery quality, it deals with a young man's pursuit of independence from the family community. The family, remaining totally unaware of Peter's real needs, makes no attempt to achieve understanding or communication. On another level, however, this is a play about marriage and responsibility — and as Peter learns to accept his obligation to a personal relationship, one wonders how many adults might be surprised were they to reinterpret their thoughts on the child's level.

In 1947, an element of style was introduced into the repertoire, with Madge Miller's Chinese-manner play, *The Land of the Dragon*. Without pretending to authenticity, this play makes skillful and comic use of the outward conventions of the Chinese theatre. Although the story of the play is wholly original, the basic plot is as old as the classic fairy-tales, the characters appropriately stylized, the theme literal, and the diaolgue rhythmic with Oriental-type imagery. For a later treatment of the Oriental style, one might wish to examine Beaumont Bruestle's *The Wonderful Tang* (1953). *Tang* is more reminiscent of Chinese fairy-tales. *

In the turn from the 1940's to the 1950's, two plays marked advancing steps for the repertoire, rounding out a cycle of growth. If, as appears likely, Mark Twain himself was more interested in Huck Finn than in Tom Sawyer, Frank Whiting and Corinne Rickert had more in their favor, in their 1949 adaptation of *Huckleberry Finn*, than Spencer did with *Tom Sawyer*. Not only was Twain more successful with the characters of Huck and Jim, but the story is more tightly written. The adapters have retained this, and managed to co-relate the sequential incidents more naturally. Whereas *Tom Sawyer* can most readily be accepted on a literal level, *Huckleberry Finn* works more profoundly as the drives for freedom give meaning to the action on many levels.

Keith Engar's 1952 play, *Arthur and the Magic Sword,* completes the second cycle, as the originally simple types of plays have first been given literal treatments, and then more ambitious, multiple-level examples. The legends surrounding the real, quasi-real, unreal figures of epic history have long intrigued adult and child since Homer's *Odyssey*. From such sources as *Mort d'Arthur, Song of Roland,* Bullfinch's *Mythology,* playwrights have conjectured possible, if not necessarily probable, incidents from the lives of these characters. Engar offers us the classic tale of how Arthur, as a young lad, retrieved Excalibur from the rock, proved his heritage, and won his kingdom. Similarly, Anne Nicholson made a study of Charlemagne and the characters around him, and collaborating with Chorpenning to write *The Magic Horn,* (1951) gave us a picture of the knightly boy Roland in the Emperor's court. In both cases, the playwrights show us epic heroes as high-minded youngsters faced with plots and intrigues against them. We see them work out solutions, and win the victories or trials — and this justifies their later elevation to legend. In both of these plays, broad license is taken, in adapting material from sources. The result seems to bring these figures more meaningfully close to the contemporary child.

In the matter of dramatic license in children's theatre, no one has made wiser, more effective use of it than British playwright Nicholas Stuart Gray. In 1951, Gray added characters, situations, and motivations to the basic plot of *Beauty and the Beast,* and by sheer inventiveness expanded the meaning and the charm of the original story. In this play, we are offered the personal contribution and comment we expect from mature playwrights. Such plays as these served to bridge the gap between the literal authenticity of *Rumpelstiltskin* and the worldly wit of *Niccolo and Nicolette,* between the stoic accuracy of *The Indian Captive* and the conjectural character study of *Abe Lincoln of Pigeon Creek.*

The plays of the 1940's and early 1950's marked more pretentious treatment of the fairy-tales and classics. In these tales the playwrights found and projected more advanced levels of meaning. Some trial (and error) was made of comedy and historical manipulation. Probably most important, some originality began to make its appearance, in the creation of characters and stories.

These early indications of growth began to assemble into a trend, starting in the late 1950's. Alan Cullen's *Nicollo and Nicolette* was imported from England in 1957, and this addition to the repertoire brought the original fantasy to a new level of sophistication. Retaining the format of the classic fairy-tale-fantasy, Cullen invented a play that, while still showing the marks of a "children's theatre syndrome", came closer to a mature respect for the child audience — possibly because Cullen addresses his plays to a wider public than children. As children's theatre developed in the 1960's, the playwrights grew more quizzical, and began to take source material as a point of departure, now using it as a vehicle for ideas, not just plot. New levels of complexity appeared, and the old cliches were studiously avoided. The new plays actually demonstrated some irreverence for the old forms — such as Cynthia Zievers' 1964 fairy-tale spoof, *Dr. Graymatter's Dilemma,* with its ugly princess, its lazy prince, and its "beat" dragon.

Cullen took fantasy several steps further, mixing it with nonsense in *King Patch and Mr. Simpkins* in 1964, and advancing toward actual absurdity with *Trudi and the Minstrel* in 1966. While still

xiv

sharing some relationship with *Peter Pan* and *The Blue Bird, Trudi* has just as much in common with *Through the Looking Glass,* Dr. Seuss, and *Oh Dad, Poor Dad, Mamma's Hung You in the Closet and I'm Feeling So Sad.* And while some of *Trudi's* characters originated in *Cinderella* and *Beauty and the Beast,* the Baroness clearly belongs in the cast of *Oh Dad.* From Lewis Carroll to Frank Baum, respectable nonsense has been favored by children. But if nonsense were the only contribution from Cullen's work, it would offer nothing newer than *Alice in Wonderland.* Nonsense, however, is most frequently marked by lack of plot. This is never true of Cullen, whose plot-lines are strong and straight, and whose inimitable nonsense characters generate theatrical presence.

Another English playwright, Alan Broadhurst, also made a substantial contribution to the advancement of this period. His play, *The Great Cross-Country Race* (1966), applies current theatre mechanics and practices to an old fable, and succeeds not only in presenting a dramatic account of the race between the Hare and the Tortoise, but also in making a wry comment on the human types who intrude into the animal world. Both Broadhurst and Cullen use some of the devices of nonsense to develop an organic story. Derived from nonsense, *King Patch, Trudi,* and *Cross-Country Race* move with gathering assurance into the realm of absurdity. They include elements of the existential, the epic, the absurd. Within the context of an unbelievable tale, each emphasizes, to varying degrees, that things are not what they seem; absolutes appear to be lacking; communication between individuals is deliberately oblique; and "heroes" Patch, Trudi, and the Tortoise seem to achieve their ends almost incidentally.

These three plays are each written to be staged in a frankly presentational style. Each is episodic, somewhat mad, highly theatrical. Cullen's characters are capable of the most incredible actions. Broadhurst makes liberal use of spectacular effects and tear-rounds. Neither playwright asks the audience to suspend disbelief, and while their plays remain effective throughout, no audience can sustain involvement in them without remembering where they are. All three heroes are unheroic — Patch and Trudi more acted upon than acting, the Tortoise simply plodding along in his customary, homely way. The antagonists (it is difficult to consider them villains) are either bumbling incompetents, or all-powerful schemers brought low by innate human errors — and all take themselves too seriously to be serious.

Thus fantasy began to lean toward spoof, and inevitably led to satire. For many years there was an unwritten law that satire for children was forbidden, but the playwrights of the 1960's found a way to lead the repertoire into this direction. No one would wish to abandon the beautiful, sumptuously-staged fantasies that bring stars to the eyes of children, and leave their innocence untouched. May we always have them with us! But the real world is not all sweetness and light. It is bitterness and darkness too, and a repertoire that aims to hold the mirror up to nature must reflect all of nature's hues.

Eugene Schwartz' play, *The Dragon,* is a satire, in the most biting political sense, of totalitarianism. Brought to the United States from Russia in 1963, it has yet to be absorbed into the main stream of the children's theatre repertoire. But it is here, and its astringent note has seeped into our consciousness.

It was a Belgian author, however, who exercised the most profound influence on the changing American taste. While Cullen and Broadhurst were moving the children's theatre toward the maturity of the contemporary theatre, Arthur Fauquez started to move it toward what can only be regarded as a maturity of truthfulness. Through satirical characterization, *Reynard the Fox* (1962) comments upon humanity as it is, rather than as it is usually idealized to be for children. By offering the first substantial rogue-hero (quite different from the laissez-faire "wickedness" of Huck Finn), Fauquez implies that children are capable of understanding what Orlin Corey has called "a concept of human behavior which may be at variance with the philosophical diet upon which they have often been fed." Fauquez also implies, by expecting children to interpret satire, that the child is sensitively aware of man's foibles. In production *Reynard* has proved this. Contrary to one popular opinion, *Reynard the Fox* is a moral play. It speaks of casting first stones, of courage of conviction, of truth to self. Only improve the hunters' aim, and Reynard would be a voluntary martyr, even if remaining a realist.

xvi

Fauquez' second play, *The Man Who Killed Time* (1964), is a very different play from *Reynard*. Rather than the more general satire, it is a romantic comedy, depending strongly upon mood and local color for effectiveness. This play allows its central character to develop through a natural sequence of events, and we are more concerned with this than with the simple plot within which he operates. Ambrosio is an exaggerated character, larger than life. Instead of fighting personified villains, his antagonist is time — society's mechanized devices for "dividing my life into pieces, and cutting the hours into minutes like little 'o's', and seconds into grains of sand". While drawing a hero who is not exactly "swashbuckling", Fauquez gives Ambrosio a bell tower as challengeable as Don Quixote's windmill.

As a culmination, to date, of many years of learning the art of literary adaptation, Fauquez' *Don Quixote of la Mancha* (1967) stands high. Cervantes' epic of the knight of the kitchen utensils is acknowledged one of the great works of fiction. It is also one of the longest ones. One must grant either foolhardiness or courage to the playwright undertaking to concentrate the sensational adventures of this beloved Hidalgo into the few moments allowed onstage. The Belgian playwright's success is attested to by Orlin Corey, who staged the American premiere:

> "*Don Quixote of la Mancha* is indeed true to Cervantes. Notwithstanding the incredible achievement of compression, and the difficult demands of the dramatic form, this play has very few of the faults and almost all the virtues of the original."*

Each character is real, is true. With the exception of a stilted translation of Sancho Panza's illiterate grammar, the dialogue and action are sharp and fluent. These characters progress as they should with a certain inevitability, each to his own destiny — Don Quixote to his death. It is not a sad or unhappy ending. It is a natural ending, accomplished without the contrivances usually presented to conclude plays for young people. I cannot believe that children would leave the theatre depressed or disheartened. Rather would they feel lifted for having witnessed the trials of this gentle crusader.

*See INTRODUCTION to *Don Quixote of La Mancha*, Page 1058.

Combining the truthful character studies of Fauquez, and the conjectural history of earlier plays like *The Magic Horn* or *Arthur and the Magic Sword,* William E. Wilson's 1962 play, *Abe Lincoln of Pigeon Creek,* loosely uses some of the incidents and characteristics of young Abe that are recorded. Rather than emphasizing historical values, or focusing on a moment of victory, Wilson "reconstructs" ten years from the life of a boy as he grows into a young man, tracing the slow process of ripening that shaped a character. Only in the title does the author suggest that this was a character that would later captivate most of a nation. This character development is unmatched in any other play for young people, and the depth of characterization is equalled only by *Don Quixote.* To discover how far the repertoire has come, in its treatment of Americana, we need only compare *Abe Lincoln of Pigeon Creek* to the stilted, history-book treatment of *Daniel Boone* by Leona Baptist, in 1940.

As with *Reynard* and *Don Quixote,* there are those who would question the appropriateness of *Abe Lincoln of Pigeon Creek* for children — for the very reasons that make them good theatre and good literature. They are real. There is no reason we should be afraid to show children that which they already know — that people are born, they live, they may or may not do worthwhile things, and they die. People are not all good, and not all bad, they judge each other, grow, err, and learn. If this is where our recent plays are heading, they are finally moving toward the sincerity required of art.

Another play which is respectful of this sincerity, and of the capabilities of its audience, combines these attributes with the symbols of the fantastic. Joseph Golden's *Johnny Moonbeam and the Silver Arrow* (1962) is not really a play in the conventional sense, but remains an interesting vehicle of theatre, as it essays a unique and adventurous form. Instead of using dialogue, the author tells his story in dance mime, and the narration is spoken by an Olympian if colloquial figure, who spurs Johnny on through his quest, shares his anxiety with the audience, and occasionally thrusts himself into the stage action on Johnny's behalf. "He is a vivid, earthy character, but he can consort with moonbeams, moving nimbly among them, because he spins the dreams common to all boys." Without gimmicks, extraneous humor, superfluous incidents, this play quickly epitomizes man's most dramatic conflict — that of a single human being alone against everything greater than himself, and eventually against his own self. Because of its symbolic and partially abstract form, the work cannot present Johnny as a fully-developed character. But he is real. So real that if one did not know this to be an original invention of Golden's, he could be easily convinced that it might have been taken from American Indian folklore — its honesty is that authentic.

Because of its allegiance to the fable, Aurand Harris' *Androcles and the Lion* (1964) might also be regarded as "folk". Coming from this source, it is not surprising that this play is morally didactic — this is the nature of fable. But considering the slapstick and trickery contained in the plot, Harris only accepts the moral presence in its fable form, and the directness native to the Commedia del'Arte style. The philosophy that the children's audience will accept this difference is a new concept in playwriting for children. Harris uses the necessary action, which must be spontaneous and effectively surprising for the plot to work, and shapes it in the most impromptu style of theatre. The improvised comedy of the Italian sixteenth century theatre disallows the spectacle usually considered paramount for children. It is as theatrical and "alienating" as the devices by which Brecht reminds his audience that they are in a theatre watching a play. Children's audiences accept, respect, and enjoy it. One of the obvious reasons for this success is that the real, the probable, the necessary, all depart and are sacrificed for laughter. In the nature of pure farce, *Androcles* depends upon much physical by-play and bodily assault. As Phyllis Hartnoll notes, farce retains its concern with humanity, while depicting the grosser faults of mankind, and the relationship between his sometime stupidity and his natural environment. By using the simplicity of the fable, the style and slapstick of Commedia, and the rough-and-tumble business of farce, Harris compactly achieves the ability to make palatable some of the most direct moralizing regarding man's inhumanity in the face of the fundamental goodness of nature.

In 1966, Harris repeated this success in a different form, with another "moralistic" play, *Rags to Riches,* a musical treatment of the Horatio Alger dime-novel or "pulp". This broad adaptation of an earlier genre is not the spoof that we find in some of the contemporary fairy-tales. It is a straight-faced, earnest presentation of nineteenth-century melodrama. Frequently, modern companies erroneously play *The Drunkard* or *Ten Nights in a Barroom* with tongue in cheek, and by making fun of themselves, negate the serious belief that the Victorian audience had in the morality of the play. Companies which retain the period style, and play these melodramas straight, allow the audience to see humor in style, while coincidentally discerning the contemporary values in the message. This is the strength of *Rags to Riches* — and in this respect it parallels *The Dragon,* in which Schwartz treated the fairy-tale in dead earnest. Both playwrights revert to an earlier style to make their point, and in both cases actors who attempt to ridicule this style, court disaster.

Aad Greidanus' 1965 play, *Two Pails of Water,* from Holland, is not really related to any other play in this volume, except as it is a distinct form of comedy — judicious comedy, more concerned with the development of thought than with the character. Intellectually remote from reality, this type of comedy takes as its purpose the correction of social absurdities. Greidanus, while not reaching to Moliere's comedy of ridicule, gives us a play which, for all its old comedy lightness, and almost silly surface quality, plays on more subtle levels with the above criteria. The style and plot of *Two Pails* hold us removed from reality, almost lifting the ridiculous in stage business to the sublime in theme. Drawing upon a farcical style of playing, the old idea of mistaken identities, comedy of coincidence, and pure folly, Greidanus' story speaks humorously but sharply of materialism, and from the overly-lazy to the overly-industrious, he questions the value we place on work, and the acquisition of the good life.

The early 1960's began to spoof the same tired cliches which the 1950's began to escape from. During this decade, playwrights began to introduce serious efforts toward satire, nonsense, and absurdity; enlarged their treatment of adaptation and folk material; and undertook new and expanding adventures in the old area of original fantasy. Importantly, in a few cases, they began learning to draw truly three-dimensional characters with dramatic scope and theatrical meaning.

With these steps the children's theatre, for the first time, began to join the contemporary theatre.

It is only realistic to point out that while these seem to be real trends, they are only potentialities. The development of the repertoire is far from fait accompli. The twenty plays cited here seem to trace a pattern of progress, but they have been carefully selected for this purpose, from among more than two hundred titles in the total repertoire, some of which might have led us far astray. On the basis of this thirty-year study, the future holds risk, as well as promise.

The important "today play" remains unwritten. Television has done it, with such programs as "Father Knows Best" and "Leave it to Beaver". Cinema has done it, with such films as "The Island of the Blue Dolphins" and "To Kill a Mockingbird". The theatre has dragged its feet.

It is intended that this anthology reflect the changes that have taken place in over thirty years of playwriting for young people. Certainly this is not all of dramatic literature for this audience, and any serious study of the total literature should be more widely inclusive and encompassing. For those who wish it, a suggested supplementary list of plays is appended in the back of this volume. As with the plays collected in these covers, it is not expected that this list will please everyone. It will do for a start.

—William B. Birner
School of Theatre
Ohio University
Athens, Ohio

July, 1967

Jack and the Beanstalk

by

CHARLOTTE B. CHORPENNING

Copyright, 1935

THE CHILDREN'S THEATRE PRESS

Cloverlot, Anchorage, Kentucky

1

JACK AND THE BEANSTALK

By Charlotte B. Chorpenning

THE ANCHORAGE PRESS
Cloverlot
Anchorage, Kentucky 40223
U. S. A.

Jack and the Beanstalk

CAST

(in the order of their appearance)

JACK
BOSSY, his cow
WIDOW BESS, his mother
FRIHOL, the Magic Maker
RAFE HEYWOOD
NICHOLAS
JOAN
OLD TYB
GAVIN
ANNOT
GIANT'S WIFE
GIANT
HARP
MAN IN THE MOON

ACT ONE

ACT TWO

ACT THREE

The first production of this play was given in 1933 by the Goodman Memorial Theatre, in Chicago, Illinois, under the direction of Charlotte B. Chorpenning.

Jack and the Beanstalk

ACT ONE

The scene is the garden in front of Widow Bess's house. It is a small house of peasant type. Stage right, and across the back, a stone wall, with a gate opening onto a street or common, near the upper corner. Left, the cottage, with a practical door and a small doorstep. Below it, a stone well, with curb broad enough for sitting.

A rough bench stands against the wall, left. A garden table, with stools on either side, is left of center. This table is rigged for magic lights.

The curtain rises on the cow, stretching over the fence, and Jack stretched full length on the back wall, dreamily waiting for his mother to appear. The cow moos pitifully, and as Jack pays no heed, grows more insistent. Jack finally looks up with a laugh, leaps down, runs to the well, catches up a pail of water, and runs across to offer her a drink. The cow refuses, tossing her head.

JACK: Oh, you're not thirsty! You're hungry.

COW *(agreeing sadly)*: Moo-oo.

JACK: Poor Bossy! It's terrible to be hungry. I'm hungry too.

COW *(sympathetic)*: Moo! Moo!

JACK: Mother will be home soon. She'll bring us something to eat.

COW *(delighted)*: Moo-oo!

JACK: You must be a very grateful cow, and give us lots of milk. Just to get us something to eat, Mother's gone to sell the thing she cares most about in all the world, except you and me.

COW *(questioning)*: Mooou-oo?

JACK: Don't you know what it is? It's the big silver candlestick. It's the very last of the things father left when he died. It made Mother cry to think of selling it. But she had to sell it—or sell you.

COW *(alarmed and protesting vigorously)*: Moo! Moo-oo!

JACK *(laughing and throwing his arms around her)*: We couldn't sell you, could we, Bossy?

COW *(emphatic, tossing her head)*: Moo! Moo-oo-oo! *(The Widow enters through the gate, carrying the silver candlestick. She pauses to look sadly at Jack as he pets the cow, then goes on toward the cottage, wiping her eyes. Jack turns and sees her.)*

JACK: Mother! . . . Why, you've brought back the candlestick.

WIDOW: Nobody wanted it. They said a candle stuck on a piece of wood gave just as much light.

JACK *(crestfallen)*: Oh! Then you didn't bring anything to eat.

WIDOW: Yes I did. I brought you an oatcake and some cheese.

JACK: Hurrah! (*He seizes the parcel she holds out to him, and takes a famished bite. Then he stops.*) Where's yours, Mother?

WIDOW: I don't want any, son.

JACK: You said that at breakfast.

WIDOW: Eat, lad.

JACK: I'll leave you a piece.

COW: Moo-oo . . . (*Jack starts to give the cow a bite, but is checked by a sudden thought.*)

JACK: Mother! . . . Where did you get the money to buy this cake?

WIDOW: Never mind now, Jack. Eat it.

JACK: (*frightened, insisting*): Where did you, Mother? Where did you get the money?

WIDOW: I'll tell you when you finish eating.

JACK: You've sold Bossy-cow!

WIDOW: There, there now.

JACK: (*throwing down the food*): I don't want it! I don't want it!

WIDOW: Be a man, Jack. Think of poor Bossy-cow. She's hungry. We have nothing for her to eat. We have no money to buy anything. It's cruel to let her go hungry. I have sold her to the richest man in town. He can give her all the hay and meal she needs.

JACK: The richest man in town?

WIDOW: Yes.

JACK: That's Rafe Heywood. He's cruel to his beasts. He flogs his donkey! He kicks his dog! He shan't have Bossy-cow! He'll club her. He'll prod her with his pitchfork, the way he did his poor sick horse. (*He rushes to throw his arms around the cow.*) He shan't have you! He shan't have you!

COW: (*appealingly*): Moo-oo. Moo-oo.

WIDOW (*drawing Jack away*): S-h-h. Come inside, lad. Rafe Heywood may come for her in a minute. There, there now. Hush, Jack. Hush, lad. Come. (*She leads him in, protesting and sobbing. As they disappear, Frihol appears outside the wall, seemingly leaping out of the ground. He is dressed in green and brown. His cap is the shape of a bean leaf, twisted around his head. The bottom of his tunic has points like the tips of bean leaves. He is radiant, and almost seems to grow taller as one looks at him. He looks about with an air of secrecy, then leaps over the wall into the garden. The cow lows at him very softly.*)

FRIHOL (*crossing to stroke the cow*): What's the matter, old girl? You look worried.

COW: Moo-oo-oo-oo!

FRIHOL: Oh, I see! And you don't want to be sold?

COW: Moo! Moo!

FRIHOL: What's the matter with Rafe Heywood? He's rich enough to feed you better than Jack.

6

COW: Moo—oo—oo!

FRIHOL: Oh, he's that kind, is he? Well, rest easy, old fellow. He shan't have you.

COW *(excitedly bobbing her horns toward the gate)*: Moo! Moo-moo! Moo-moo! Moo! *(Rafe Heywood enters. He is an arrogant man, pretentiously dressed.)*

RAFE: Hey! What are you doing with my cow?

FRIHOL *(suddenly assuming the look and bearing of a frail old man)*: I didn't know it was your cow, sir.

RAFE *(thrusting him away roughly)*: I've just come to finish paying for it. Let it alone.

COW *(threateningly)*: Moo-oo-oo-oo!

RAFE: Back, there! Back! *(The cow tosses her head and lowers her horns. Rafe jumps back, but blusters to cover up his cowardice.)* Ugly, are you? Show me your horns, will you? Wait till you are snug tied up in my barn.

FRIHOL: Kind sir, I have a request to make of you.

RAFE: If you want money, be off. I've no money to waste on beggars. And if you want work, be off too. I want strong men. I can't have shaking carcasses around my place. You'd eat more than you were worth.

FRIHOL: Nay, good sir. All I want is this cow.

RAFE: H'mmm. What will you pay for her?

FRIHOL *(piercing him with his keen glance)*: What price are you giving the Widow?

RAFE: That's no business of yours. How much money have you?

FRIHOL: I have no money, sir. But I have some wonderful beans that are better than coin.

RAFE: Beans! For money? Ha, ha, ha, ha, ha, ha! *(A group of villagers going by pause at the sound of his mirth, and draw near the gate.)*

NICHOLAS: What's the joke, Rafe Heywood?

RAFE: This old crack-wit wants to use beans for money!

JOAN: With Rafe Heywood? Ha, ha, ha, ha, ha, ha! *(They all laugh, in an effort to flatter the richest man in town.)*

FRIHOL *(holding out the beans)*: They are more beautiful than money. *(Another burst of laughter.)*

RAFE: Beautiful! Bah! Get along, old fool!

FRIHOL: Look, dame! Look, Master! See all the little stripes and sprinkles of color in them!

NICHOLAS *(shoving him away roughly)*: Crazy!

FRIHOL: Here are dots like violets and peach bloom in the spring. And lines as green as grass in summertime. And white, as shining as new snow at Christmas. See, here's the brown of the earth and the blue of the sky all the year around! Give me the cow for mv

7

beans. They are worth all the gold in the world.

OLD TYB (*who has edged forward to look at the beans*): Hear the simpleton! His silly snow at Christmas time! Beans with colors in them worth more than gold!

FRIHOL: It's true, Dame. They have wonders in them.

OLD TYB (*sneering*): Aye! There's a man in the moon!

FRIHOL: Aye! How did you know that?

OLD TYB: My granny told me before I cut my teeth. And the stars are out all day! She told me that, too. Ha, ha!

FRIHOL: Aye! They're all shining up there now . . . if you could only see them.

OLD TYB: Ninny! Mooncalf!

RAFE: Get the old loon out of my way!

GAVIN: Hey, gaffer, get along!

JOAN: March, or we'll cuff you soundly!

RAFE: Drive him out of town!

NICHOLAS (*striking him so that he falls*): Off with you, addlepate! Get your crazy headpiece out of our sight!

FRIHOL: My beans! Spare me! You spill my beans! Masters, dames, have mercy! My beautiful beans! (*Jack has entered at the sound of the tumult, closely followed by his mother.*)

RAFE: Give the fool a taste of your cudgel, Nicholas.

NICHOLAS (*currying favor*): Aye, Rafe Heywood. Aye, sir . . . Stir your stumps, old one, or I'll warm the soles of your feet with this.

JACK (*leaping between Nicholas and Frihol*): Leave him alone!

NICHOLAS: Out of my way!

JACK: Drop your cudgel then! You shan't strike him!

NICHOLAS: We'll see.

JACK: You're a coward, to flog an old man!

RAFE: Suppose Rafe Heywood told him to?

JACK: He shan't do it!

RAFE: Then you shall do it yourself. Here, ancient! This young cockerel will practice his cudgel on you.

FRIHOL: Pity, young sir.

JACK: Don't be afraid.

RAFE: Give the old lack-wit ten stout blows.

JACK: No. I won't!

RAFE: You won't, eh?

JACK: No!

RAFE (*seizing his arm and twisting it*): Now—will you do what Rafe Heywood says?

JACK: I won't hurt him!

RAFE: There's not a boy in this town—nor man either—can say "I won't" to Rafe Heywood, and not be sorry for it. Give me that cudgel.

8

WIDOW *(in distress)*: Nay, sir, hold your hand, I pray you! He's but a lad! Jack, Jack! Why do you anger good Rafe Heywood so?

JACK: He's wicked! I hate him! I told you not to sell Bossy to him! He'll hurt her!

RAFE: So, young spitfire! So you've a liking for the cow I've just bought. In, Dame, and we'll count out the money for her. *(The Widow goes into the cottage with Rafe. There is an instant's pause, everyone feeling the relief from Rafe's presence.)*

GAVIN: Well, ancient, if you know what's good for you, you'll be off before Rafe Heywood comes out of there.

FRIHOL *(struggling to get up)*: My knees fail under me.

JACK *(assisting him)*: Sit on the well-curb there.

ANNOT: Come on, Nicholas. There's fine dancing on the green.

NICHOLAS: I'll dance a jig with you, Annot, and be back again before Rafe Heywood finishes with the Widow. *(Nicholas and Annot skip off, hand in hand.)*

JOAN: Aye, that's safe. Rafe Heywood takes his time about a bargain.

GAVIN: He never lets a penny slip through his fingers through haste or hurry.

OLD TYB: Magic beans! Ha, ha, ha, ha! *(The villagers, one by one, disappear, and Jack runs to the cow.)*

JACK: Never mind, Bossy. I won't leave you with him long. I'll earn pennies and buy you back again.

FRIHOL *(who has been watching him throughout with delight)*: I'll buy your cow.

JACK: You? Have you money?

FRIHOL: I have what is better than money. See? *(He spreads the beans on the table.)*

JACK: Oh-h! What beautiful beans! How smooth they are! What shining colors! Oh, I like them!

FRIHOL: Take them, and let me have your cow.

JACK: Oh, I want them, but I can't give you Bossy for them. We have nothing to eat. You can't buy bread with these few beans.

FRIHOL *(telling a secret)*: Yes, you can.

JACK: The baker wants three pennies for one little loaf.

FRIHOL: The beans will bring you pennies, and silver pieces, and gold.

JACK: Enough to buy butter for our bread, like Rafe Heywood?

FRIHOL: Enough to buy anything you want.

JACK: Oh! Could I have a cake as big as that?

FRIHOL: You can have anything you imagine in your mind.

JACK: Oh-h!

FRIHOL: Now tell me. What would you like?

JACK: I'd like butter on our bread every day. And apples, and grapes. And greens for Mother, like the lettuce and carrots they set for the king. Oh yes! I'd like a gown for Mother! Silk, like a queen's, and blue as the sky! And music—something that makes its own music, to make Mother laugh, the way she did when Father used to play his fiddle.

FRIHOL: You can have them all, for your cow. The beans will bring them to you.

JACK: These?

FRIHOL: They're magic.

JACK: Oh! But Mother says there isn't any magic.

FRIHOL: You know better.

JACK: Do you believe in magic?

FRIHOL: Watch! *(He goes to the table on which the beans are spread out, moves his hands over them mysteriously. His movements have the lines of a growing plant.)*
Beans who lay in the brown, brown earth,
Beans who looked in the face of the sun,
Beans who drank of the rain and the dew,
Have you magic enough for a blue silk gown, for a boy to give his mother?
(A brilliant blue light glows on his outstretched hand and mysterious face. Jack appears to see and handle the blue silk gown.)

JACK: O-h-h!

FRIHOL: Have you magic for garden greens, that a mother may eat like a king? *(A green light.)*

JACK *(softly)*: Mother! See the carrots—and lettuce!

FRIHOL: Have you magic for red, red apples? And grapes. *(A red light. Jack pantomimes the eating of apples and grapes.)*

JACK: M-m-m-m! And music?

FRIHOL: And music, to make a lonely woman laugh? *(There is utter stillness, and then faint but clear chords of a harp. Jack gets slowly to his feet, rapt. When the music ceases, he leaps toward the cottage door.)*

JACK: Mother! . . .Rafe Heywood!

FRIHOL *(reaching him in one bound)*: They don't believe in it! Keep them away!

JACK: But I can't sell Bossy unless they say I may. Rafe Heywood's giving money to Mother for her now.

FRIHOL: You can give Rafe Heywood double his money, back again.

JACK *(tempted)*: Oh-h-h.

FRIHOL: And I'd be good to Bossy-cow.

JACK: And Rafe Heywood will kick her and flog her.

FRIHOL: I'll give her fresh green grass the whole year round, and the finest meal. And I'll brush her coat till it shines like silk. We like each other, don't we?

COW *(assenting, friendly)*: Moo-oo!

JACK *(throwing his arms around Bossy)*: Good-bye, Bossy. Good-bye.

10

Take her quickly, before Rafe Heywood comes out of the house.

FRIHOL: Pick up the beans before I go. Be sure to believe in them.

JACK *(Jack turns to pick up the beans, but stops):* What shall I say to get the money? You didn't tell me the charm. *(Getting no anwser, he turns back, but both Frihol and the cow are gone.)* Where are you? Where did you go? *(He runs about, looking over the wall, down the street. He vaults the wall where the cow stood, calling:)* Where are you? I don't know the charm! I don't know how to get the money! *(He returns to the table, looking down at the beans.)* What if they shouldn't work! *(He makes passes over them, as nearly like those of Frihol as he can.)* Please give me the money to pay Rafe Heywood. *(Nothing happens. He stares at the beans in terror.)* They don't work! *(He gathers them up and puts them on the ground.)* I know! *(He makes a circle around the beans, then chants in imitation of Frihol.)*

Beans who lay in the brown, brown earth,
Beans who looked in the face of the sun,
Beans who drank of the rain and the dew,
Give me the money to pay Rafe Heywood.

(Nothing happens.) Suppose it only works for him? Oh dear . . . what will Mother say? *(Rafe and the Widow enter. Jack snatches up the beans and sinks onto the bench waiting for the lightning to strike.)*

RAFE: Well, you've got the money now. The cow's mine.

WIDOW: Jack will drive her home for you, won't you, son?

RAFE: Well, speak up! Why, where's your cow gone? Go fetch her!

WIDOW: Why, where is she, Jack?

JACK: She's gone.

RAFE: I can see that for myself. Where?

JACK: I sold her.

RAFE *(shouting):* What?

JACK *(standing up to him):* I sold her.

RAFE: That cow was mine. Your mother sold her to me.

JACK: I sold her first.

RAFE: You stole her from me! You're a thief!

JACK: I'm not a thief! *(Crosses to Mother.)* Mother, I sold Bossy to a kind old man, who paid much more for her than Rafe Heywood did. And I'll pay Rafe Heywood back every penny.

WIDOW: Then count the money into his hand. Quickly.

JACK: I have to get it, first.

WIDOW: Jack! Surely you didn't let him take the cow away without leaving you the money!

JACK: Oh no! He left me these.

WIDOW: Beans!

RAFE: Ha, ha, ha! The old fool played his trick on the booby!

11

JACK: They're magic.

WIDOW: Oh, Jack!

JACK: They are, Mother. I can get all the money I want from these.

WIDOW (coming down to door step): God-a-mercy! The lad has lost his wits!

JACK: No, I haven't, Mother. They are magic. Only he went without telling me the charm. (The villagers have been stopping by to listen, and now guffaw with derision.) I'll find out the charm, Mother.

WIDOW: There's no such thing as magic, my poor boy.

JACK: He showed me magic! I don't know what to say to get the money, but I know that these beans are magic!

WIDOW: Oh, Jack, Jack! What have you done? Here is your money, Rafe Heywood. The cow is gone.

RAFE: I don't want the money. I'll have the cow, or I'll put this young rogue in jail.

WIDOW: He meant no harm, sir.

RAFE: He'll learn not to meddle with Rafe Heywood. Step along, thief.

WIDOW: Nay, sir, he'll behave. He's all I have in the world. Take the money and leave me my poor lad!

RAFE (taking the money bag from her outstretched hand): Where are the pennies I gave you in the market place, to bind the bargain?

WIDOW: I spent them for food.

RAFE: So! Spent my money and stole my cow! No! I want full value for the cow, and a pretty sum besides, to buy this thieving rascal out of jail.

WIDOW: I have no sum of money.

RAFE: What have you left to sell?

WIDOW: Nothing except the roof over my head. Will you take my cottage, and let the boy go free?

RAFE: It is not enough . . . I'll take your land and cottage and everything on it.

WIDOW: You are a hard man.

JACK: Where will we sleep?

RAFE: That's not my affair.

JACK: Mother can't sleep on the road, like a gypsy.

RAFE: You should have thought of that before you stole my cow. Well, Widow? Is the house mine, or shall I march this imp to jail?

WIDOW: Take the cottage, and let my boy alone.

RAFE: And the land?

WIDOW: And the land.

RAFE: And everything on it?

WIDOW: And everything on it. If it must be.

RAFE: Done! Which of you will be witnesses to this bargain for me? (The villagers fairly fall over themselves in their eagerness to oblige Rafe.)

12

ANNOT: I will! I, Rafe Heywood!

NICHOLAS: Nay, let me! 'Tis a man's place!

JOAN (*thrusting Annot aside*): I make a good witness, sir. I forget nothing!

GAVIN: I'll be proud to witness a bargain for Rafe Heywood.

OLD TYB: It's my right, sir. I'm the oldest.

RAFE: Well, Widow, here are five good witnesses to our bargain.

GAVIN: She'll never dare to break a bargain made before us all.

WIDOW: I do not break bargains. My word binds me more fast than a hundred bargains.

RAFE: Here are the points of our bargain. To make up for the price of the cow her son stole from me, and sold for a handful of beans, the Widow gives me certain things. One, this cottage. Two, everything in her cottage. Three, all her land.

WIDOW: Oh, sir, leave me that little strip over the wall to work, that we may keep from starving.

RAFE: Go out and beg to keep yourselves from starving. It is all your land, or no bargain at all!

WIDOW: Very well.

RAFE: You hear. All five of you. The Widow gives me all the land on both sides of the wall, and everything that stands or grows on it. Do you consent to that, Widow?

WIDOW: I consent.

RAFE: This week, I must go to the cattle fair in the next town. This day next week, I will come to take possession. Be ready to go away at once. Keep the bargain well in mind, neighbors. Lose no point of it. (*He goes out, followed by the neighbors, gabbling incoherent flattery of him. "You have made a fine bargain, sir," etc.*)

OLD TYB (*as a parting shot*): Magic beans! Ha, ha, ha, ha!

WIDOW: Oh, Jack, Jack! See what you have done to us. (*She flings herself down at the table and bursts into tears.*)

JACK: Don't cry, Mother. Rafe Heywood shan't have our cottage. I'll find the charm. There's a whole week to find it. Mother, don't cry! Oh, what shall I do? (*He takes out the beans and looks at them desperately.*) Beans . . . beans . . . magic beans . . .

WIDOW: Beans! Beans! Beans! Jack, be still. I can't bear the word!

JACK: I'm trying to find the charm, Mother. Lift up your head, so I can put them where the old man had them.

WIDOW (*flinging the beans over the wall*): Take them out of my sight, the foolish things!

JACK (*running to look after them*): Oh, where did they go? Where are they? They're gone! Mother! My beans are gone!

WIDOW: Good riddance of them.

JACK: They're magic, and you threw them away!

13

WIDOW: Don't say such foolish things. How could a handful of beans be magic? *(She sinks onto the well-curb in despair.)*

JACK: They are magic! I know they are! I know it! I know it! *(Jack flings himself on the bench, sobbing faintly. The same harp music that we heard earlier in the scene is heard now. A bean tendril comes wavering up above the wall, and grows upward, its leaves getting stouter and stouter. Both Jack and his mother lift their heads to hear the music, then slowly look around. Jack sees it first.)* It's the music . . . Mother! Look! It's growing! It came from my beans!

WIDOW: God-a-mercy! It's magic, sure enough! Come into the house!

JACK: It will give me money to pay Rafe Heywood!

WIDOW: Keep away from it, lad.

JACK *(at the foot of it)*: It will lead me to the money.

WIDOW: It's going clean above the clouds!

JACK: It's pointing up! The money will be up there!

WIDOW: Jack! What are you doing?

JACK: I'm going up! *(He springs to the bean stalk. He has no need to climb, as the growth of the bean stalk carries him up.)*

WIDOW: No, son! Don't think of such a thing! . . . Jack!

JACK: I'm not afraid. Goodbye, Mother! I'm going for the money.

WIDOW *(as Jack goes higher and higher)*: Jack! . . . Jack! . . . Jack!

CURTAIN

14

JACK AND THE BEANSTALK

ACT TWO

SCENE 1

The scene is the Giant's kitchen. A huge wide window back, with nothing but the sky seen through it. The sky is not blue, like ours. The light is not the light of earth.

There is a fireplace with a side oven, large enough to hold a little boy, with a door which opens onto the stage. There is a kettle, also large enough for a little boy. There is a two-piece door, like a Dutch door, which opens to the outside, and another ordinary door opening into a cupboard which holds the harp. Near the outer door is a dresser, and on it the golden hen on its nest, and a basket of golden eggs. The Giant keeps these last near the door, to have them handy to throw at his wife when he comes in.

The Giant's wife is seated, preparing a large carrot. Suddenly she lifts her head in alarm and sniffs. She looks around at the window, sniffs again, drops her carrot in consternation.

WIFE *(sniffing):*　Earth!　Someone from the earth!　*(She runs to the window and leans out, sniffing.)*　Something is growing up!　Something is on it!　A little boy!　Oh dear, oh dear!　*(She shakes her fist toward the outer door.)*　You shan't have him!　You shan't. *(She shuts the window swiftly, runs to the dresser and takes a great knife, tries to hide it one place and another, then hurries across to put it on the top of the oven, thrusting it back into the corner. She returns to her vegetables, much perturbed. The door opens stealthily, the top only moving, and the Giant looks in, a grin on his face. He must be more grotesque than terrible, or small children will be frightened. He reaches around and gathers up several golden eggs, chuckling soundlessly, then begins pelting her. She is on her feet, bobbing up and down behind the protection of the chair.)*

GIANT:　Sniffing again.　As soon as my back is turned, you squeeze water out of your eyes like the people down on earth.　What's the matter now?

WIFE:　You are so hard to please.　You throw golden eggs at me.

GIANT:　Well, why do you let tears run down your face when I've told you not to?

WIFE:　I can't help it.　They come.

GIANT:　What makes them come, when I've told them not to?

WIFE:　You don't like me.　Whenever I think of that, they come.

15

GIANT *(crossing to his chair)*: I don't like anybody.

WIFE: You're all I have. If you don't like me, nobody will like me. And I can't get over wanting to be liked. I suppose it's because my grandmother lived down on earth.

GIANT: Why did I ever take a wife with a lot of silly human feelings! . . . Where's my dinner?

WIFE *(much afraid)*: It's . . . it's nearly ready.

GIANT *(sniffing)*: All I smell is roots and herbs. Where's that little lamb I brought you to kill?

WIFE *(averting her face)*: It—it got away.

GIANT *(striding slowly to her and turning her averted face to him)*: Got away?

WIFE *(averting her face on the other side)*: Y . . . yes. *(Giant swings around to probe her face from that side, and she averts her face again. This continues, his voice louder, hers fainter, with every turn, until he finally looks into her eyes, and she is then unable not to tell the truth.)*

GIANT: Got away?

WIFE: Y-y-yes.

GIANT: Got away?

WIFE: Uh . . . yes.

GIANT: G-o-t a-w-a-y!

WIFE: Uh . . . h . . . y-y-yes.

GIANT: G-o-t a-w-a-y!

WIFE *(in a whisper)*: I let it go.

GIANT: You let my dinner go?

WIFE: It looked at me so friendly. It had such big eyes. It rubbed against—

GIANT: I'll teach you! . . . *(Wife ducks behind chair expecting eggs.)* Why is that window shut?

WIFE *(backing away from table)*: Uh . . . h . . . I was cold.

GIANT: Cold?

WIFE: Yes.

GIANT: Cold?

WIFE: Y-yes . . .

GIANT: C-o-l-d !

WIFE: No.

GIANT: Ha! Open that window! *(She does, and he sniffs the air.)* Fee, fi, fum! I smell the blood of an Englishman! Where is he?

WIFE: I don't know.

GIANT: Did you look for him?

WIFE: Yes.

GIANT: That's why you closed that window! You didn't want me to know he was near. Did you see him?

WIFE: No.

GIANT *(looking into her eyes)*: No?

WIFE *(decisively)*: No.

GIANT: Well, you're telling the truth this time. *(He leans out the window and sniffs.)* Ha! He's getting near. It's a little boy! Ha! That'll be a dinner. Is the knife sharp?

WIFE: You made it sharp for the lamb.

GIANT: I'll make it sharper for the little boy. *(Giant looks for the knife in the cupboard, turns on her furiously, at which she jumps nervously. Then he looks in another place, repeating interplay with her. Finally he sees it on the oven. He gets it, whets it to the tune of "Fee, fi, fo, fum, etc.")*

Fee, fi, fo, foy, I smell the blood of a little boy! One stroke of this of this will chop off his head. Here, let me see you swing it. *(She takes it gingerly, and makes the least little movement with it. He growls at her, and she makes a larger one. He growls, and she makes a complete swing. The beanstalk appears. She sees it and whimpers in nervous excitement.)* What are you crying about?

WIFE: I don't want to kill a little boy.

GIANT: I've had enough of your whining and squeezing out tears. You shall dance until you can't stand up!

WIFE: No! No! No! Don't make me dance again!

GIANT: Will you kill the boy when he comes up?

WIFE: I can't, Giant. I get feelings that stop me.

GIANT: Harp!

HARP *(with the strain heard in the first act)*: Master!

GIANT: Come out. *(The Harp comes out of the cupboard. It is a harp on the order of the ancient Irish ones, with the actor's head for the ornamental head at the top. Behind them, the tendril of the beanstalk comes wavering up, and grows until the leafy top is out of sight. Only the Wife notices it.)*

Can you dance men down?

HARP: I can dance men down,
I can dance men up.
I do my master's bidding.

GIANT: Dance her down, down! *(The music plays. The Wife dances, pleading as she does so.)*

WIFE: No, no, no! No more! Stop it! *(The Giant laughs, spreading out his arms for the Wife to dance under and around.)* I'll kill him if I find him!

GIANT: You will kill him?

WIFE: Yes, yes!

GIANT: Harp, be still. Go in. *(The Harp stops playing, and goes into the cupboard. The Wife stands reeling, holding onto the table to steady herself.)* You will kill him this time?

WIFE: Yes.

GIANT: That's what you said about the lamb.

WIFE: It looked at me so trustingly.

GIANT *(crossing to dresser)*:   A boy from the earth might do that.   You have such a soft, silly face.   Anyone would trust it.

WIFE: Next time, I won't see his eyes.   I'll turn my head away when I strike.

GIANT *(throwing an egg or two at her)*:   And miss him!   You have to look, to strike a good blow.

WIFE: I'll come up behind him, where I can't see his eyes.

GIANT: What if he turns around?

WIFE: I'll give him something to eat.   Then he won't look around.

GIANT   How do you know he'll be hungry?

WIFE: Little boys are always hungry.

GIANT *(sniffing with delight)*:   Well, set out food for him.   And I'll go and get wood to build up the fire and get the oven hot.   *(He goes out singing "Fe, fi, fo, fum!" She wrings her hands. Jack appears on the beanstalk and looks in, eager, excited. He leaps lightly down to the floor.)*

JACK: Oh, what a wonderful house!   *(Wife jumps high off the floor, where she has been listening at the keyhole for the Giant. Jack doffs his hat.)*   Is this where the money is?

WIFE: Oh, how did you come here?

JACK: I climbed the beanstalk.   It grew from my beans .They're magic.

WIFE *(nervously)*:   Are you hungry?

JACK: Why, yes I am!   I haven't had anything to eat today.

WIFE *(swallowing sobs, but seating him at the table)*:   Well, here's some bread and jam, and some cake, and candy.

JACK: Oh, thank you . . . How big everything is!

WIFE *(getting the knife and trembling to touch it herself)*:   Eat.   *(She stands behind him in position to swing the knife, but is interrupted various times by Jack's looking around.   Whenever he does, she hides the knife quickly behind her.)*

JACK *(looking around)*:   How did you know I was hungry?   *(Wife hides knife.)*

WIFE: Little boys are always hungry.

JACK *(turning back to food)*:   That's what my mother says.

WIFE *(drawing knife slowly out)*:   Don't look around like that.   Eat your bread and jam.

JACK *(turning around, Wife hides knife)*:Um-m-m-m.   This is good. I'm going to save some to take down to my mother.

WIFE *(as Jack turns back, Wife draws out knife again)*:   I'll give you more for your mother.

JACK: Oh, how good you are!

WIFE *(working herself up to it)*:   Don't look around.

JACK: Why not?   Are you doing magic?

18

WIFE *(getting knife higher)*: Yes.

JACK: You can do it when I'm looking. The old Magic Maker that gave me the beans did.

WIFE *(higher)*: I can't do it when you're looking. Watch your plate!

JACK: I like people who do magic.

WIFE *(in position)*: Be still now. Don't talk.

JACK: You don't sound happy. *(He turns, full of sympathy, in time to check the downward stroke.)* Why aren't you happy? What's the matter? . . . Why, you're crying! *(He throws his arms around her.)* Don't cry. *(The knife goes clattering on the floor.)*

WIFE: I won't hurt you! I'll never hurt you! Here, put that nasty thing away!

JACK *(unconscious that he has been in danger)*: What a big knife!

WIFE: Put it on the oven there.

JACK: Ooh, it's sharp! What do you do with it?

WIFE: I . . . I cut up the Giant's meat.

JACK *(delighted)*: Oh, does a Giant live here?

WIFE: Yes.

JACK: I've never seen a Giant. Is he magic too?

WIFE: He's bad and cruel. He eats little boys. You must go right away, before he comes back.

JACK: I can't go without the money.

WIFE: What money?

JACK: The Magic Maker said the beans would give me money to take care of my mother. So I came for it.

WIFE: Oh!

JACK: You must be the person that's going to give it to me.

WIFE: Must I?

JACK *(full of confidence)*: Well, aren't you?

WIFE: Why, yes! There's money enough. The Giant hasn't counted it yet, so he won't miss it. *(She goes to the money-box, which he helps her to take to the table.)* Hold out your hands.

JACK: I can't carry it in my hands. I need them to climb with.

WIFE: Haven't you a pocket?

JACK: It isn't big enough.

WIFE: Here, then. The Giant has eight bagsful counted. I'll fill another from the box before he comes back. Go now! Quick!

JACK: Oh, thank you! Thank you!

WIFE: Hurry!

JACK *(loath to go)*: Well, Mother doesn't need the money for a week. I don't know how long it took me to get here, but it didn't seem a very long time.

WIFE: Time! There isn't any time up here. It might be a week or a year down on earth already!

JACK: A week already? I must hurry to take the money down!
(*The Giant's voice comes near and clear.*)
GIANT *(offstage)*: Fee, fi, fo, fum . . . I'll have a feast on that little boy!
WIFE: Oh, it's too late now. Here he comes. You'd better hide.
JACK: Where shall I go?
WIFE *(opening the door to the harp)*: Here . . . Oh, no, he might call for the Harp.
JACK *(darting under the table)*:Here!
WIFE: No, no! He often kicks over the table when he's angry. *(Jack runs to the dresser.)* No, no, no! He might want to sharpen the knife!
JACK: Where, then?
WIFE *(running to open the oven door)*: The oven! Here, quick! *(She shuts the oven door on him.)* There!
JACK *(opening the door)*: I can't breathe.
WIFE: Leave the door open a crack . . . so. *(She sits primly in front of the oven as the Giant enters.* . . . . . .
GIANT *(sniffing)*: Aha! You caught him!
WIFE: No, no. I didn't catch anybody.
GIANT *(snorting and sniffing with joy)*: He's here.
WIFE: Where?
GIANT: I'll find him! *(He looks under the table.)* That cloth is crooked. And what is my money-box doing on the table?
WIFE: I . . . I was going to fill another bag.
GIANT: What for?
WIFE: Why—why . . .
GIANT: You have stolen a bag of my money!
WIFE: No, no, I haven't.
GIANT: Bring me my bags! *(As she hesitates, he roars so that she jumps and runs for them.)* Bring me my money bags! *(She fetches them all and sets them on the floor. The Giant lifts them, one in each hand, counting as he does so, and sets them on the table beside him.)* Two! . . . Four! . . . Six! *(He holds the last one up with a flourish.)* Seven! Aha! There is one gone!
WIFE: Uh . . . You counted wrong.
GIANT *(fixing her with an accusing eye)*: What have you done with it?
WIFE: You must have made a mistake.
GIANT: I never make mistakes.
WIFE: Count them again.
GIANT Um . . . m. Well . . . *(She stands behind him, and he repeats his performance, lifting the bags from the table and putting them on the floor. As he turns back to the table after putting down the count of four, she hooks a bag from the floor, and when he turns back to the floor, she puts it on the table. Thus he finds two on the table at the end.)* Two . . . Four . . . Six . . .

20

WIFE: Eight!

GIANT: That can't be. There were only seven.

WIFE: I told you you made a mistake.

GIANT: How could I, when I never do? . . . You're up to tricks!

WIFE: No one could trick you, Giant. Anyone as clever as you.

GIANT: That's so. Well, I'll soon catch you if you are. Stand over there where I can see you. I'll not take my eyes off you. Not for a second. Now don't move. Count. *(He keeps his eyes on her, reaching behind himself and groping for the bags. He gets two at each count as before.)* How many?

WIFE: Two.

GIANT *(grimly)*: Two!

WIFE *(as he holds up the next two)*: Four.

GIANT: Four!

WIFE *(twisting her hands in an agony of apprehension)*: Six.

GIANT: Six! *(Jack has softly pushed open the oven door and held up his bag as a sign to the Wife. He now climbs noiselessly out and creeps up behind the Giant, ready to put his bag in position to be picked up.)* Keep your hands still!

WIFE: Yes, Giant.

GIANT: What are you trembling for?

WIFE: I'm afraid I'll make a mistake. You never make mistakes, but I sometimes do. *(The Giant is groping around, having found the last bag. Jack is carefully trying to put it within his reach without being caught.)*

GIANT: See that you don't make any now. *(He holds up the single one.)* How many? Aha! How many?

WIFE *(at a signal from Jack)*: There's one on the floor.

GIANT: I felt everywhere. You're just trying to make me look around.

WIFE *(as Jack draws away hastily)*: No, no! Don't look around. Just stretch hard. *(The Giant does, keeping his eyes glued on the Wife. Jack shoves the bag against his hand, then keeps pulling it just out of his reach. The Giant stretches so far to grasp it, that a final touch on the round of the chair from Jack sends him sprawling. Jack gets back in the oven in a flash. The Giant stares at the bag in amazement.)* Eight!

GIANT: Be quiet! Wait till you're asked.

WIFE: Yes, Giant. Shall I put away the money?

GIANT: No! Don't touch it! *(In getting up, he turns toward the oven and sniffs furiously.)*
Fee, fi, fum! He's very near. *(Sniff, sniff.)* Get everything ready. I'll build up the fire, so the even will be hot.

WIFE: No! Don't do that!

GIANT: Don't do that! Don't do that! What a wife! Shut the window. The draft is wrong. Shut it tight.

WIFE: It's too soon to build up the fire. I want to cook him in the pot. *(Giant piles on wood and blows furiously. The fire glows brilliantly.)*

GIANT *(between puffs)*: Yes, if I want to cook him in the oven, you want to cook him in the pot. Be quiet, or I'll throw golden eggs at you. *(Wife swiftly takes basket of golden eggs, and empties them out of the window.)*

WIFE: I won't be quiet. It's too soon to build up the fire.

GIANT: Be quiet!

WIFE *(putting the empty basket safely in place)*: It's too soon to build up the fire.

GIANT: Will you be quiet?

WIFE: It's too soon to build up the fire!

GIANT *(striding to the egg basket)*: I'll quiet you! . . . What's happened to my golden eggs?

WIFE: You must have thrown them all at me.

GIANT: I'll soon get more. Keep the fire up! Fee, fi, fo, fum! He ought to be here any minute now.

WIFE: Yes, Giant.

GIANT: My fingers itch to throw eggs at you. *(He takes the hen and sits in the large chair. The Wife kneels by the fire, gradually putting the fire out. Smoke rises from it. The Giant strokes the hen and croons to it.)*
Little hen, so old, so old,
Give me eggs of shining gold.
One, two, three, four,
Lay me these and lay me more.
Five, six, seven, eight,
Lay them early, lay them late..
Nine, ten—
(He has grown sleepy from the smoke, but rouses himself.)
The fire is smoking. Blow on it!

WIFE *(blowing hard, away from the fire)*: It has stopped now.

GIANT *(again crooning, going off to sleep)*:
Little hen so old, so old.
Give me eggs . . . of shining . . . gold,
One, two . . . three . . .
(He is deep asleep. The Wife opens the oven door. Jack steals out, starts to sneeze, but the Wife catches him just in time. He is dripping with perspiration. Together they steal to the Giant to lift the hen from his lap. He stirs and rearranges himself just as they are about to take it. Finally, each lifts one of his heavy arms carefully off the hen, the Wife fastens it onto Jack's shoulder by a strap, gives him his bag of gold, and hurries him out of the window. He disappears down the beanstalk, waving a hand at the Wife after his face is out of sight.)

WIFE *(carried away by her feelings)*: Oh, bless him! Bless him!

22

GIANT *(stirring)*: Gr-r-r-rump?

WIFE: Nothing.

GIANT: I heard you say something.

WIFE: You dreamed it.

GIANT: Always contradicting. *(He reaches for an egg, and misses the hen.)* Where is my hen?

WIFE: It . . . it flew right out that door. I tried to catch it, but it got away.

GIANT *(striding to look into her eyes)*: Got away?

WIFE *(avoiding his eyes)*: Yes.

GIANT: Got away?

WIFE: Yes . . .

GIANT: Got away!

WIFE: Y-y-yes . . .

GIANT *(holding her face)*: G-o-t a-w-a-y?

WIFE: No.

GIANT *(flinging her away)*: What happened to it?

WIFE: I . . . I don't know.

GIANT *(striding to her again)*: Don't know?

WIFE *(trembling)*: Do know.

GIANT: Aha! What?

WIFE: Well, I—

GIANT: You what?

WIFE *(wringing her hands)*: I . . .

GIANT: Well?

WIFE: Well . . .

GIANT: Well!

WIFE *(backward on her toes with the stress of her emotion)*: I won't tell!

GIANT *(setting her on the toes of his great boots)*: What!

WIFE: I won't tell!

GIANT: You will!

WIFE: I won't!

GIANT: Harp!

HARP: Master!

GIANT: Come out! *(Harp enters.)* Can you dance her to death?

HARP: I can dance men to death, I can dance men to life, I can do my master's bidding.

GIANT: Dance her to death! *(The Harp begins to play, and the Wife to dance. After a minute:)* What happened to my golden hen?

WIFE *(dancing more and more madly)*: I . . . Won't . . . Tell! ! !

CURTAIN

ACT TWO

Scene 2

On the beanstalk, between earth and sky. The sweep of blue space back of the beanstalk, which rises out of clouds, and is cut off from sight by the proscenium. Only the glittering moon, with the Man in the Moon curled up in its crescent, keeps the beanstalk company in the silence and solitude. There is a definite time of silence when the scene is first revealed.

Frihol sits on a stem of the beanstalk, peering out from among the leaves, in deep thought. He is still, and so little noticeable, in his green garments, that he will probably not be noticed in the first instant.

After a time, the Man in the Moon stretches, and opens his eyes. He suddenly leans forward.

MAN IN THE MOON: Hello! There's the Maker of Magic!

FRIHOL: Hello! Hello! There's the Man in the Moon! Did you know they don't believe in you down on earth?

MAN IN THE MOON (*laughing heartily, a silver tinkle*): Well, I believe in myself. That's the important thing.

FRIHOL: Oh, but think of the fun they lose by not believing in us.

MAN IN THE MOON: What are you doing with that great beanstalk?

FRIHOL (*mysteriously*): I'm bringing something about!

MAN IN THE MOON: You're always bringing something about.

FRIHOL: I'm always trying to. Things don't come about easily.

MAN IN THE MOON: What are you trying to do now?

FRIHOL: I'm trying to find someone to take my magic things away from a great Giant who lives at the top of the beanstalk. I want someone to bring them down to earth.

MAN IN THE MOON: How will you ever find anyone brave enough, and strong enough, to do that?

FRIHOL: Did you ever notice a little boy down on earth, called Jack?

MAN IN THE MOON: Of course. I often peep through his window at night.

FRIHOL: I grew this beanstalk so that he could go up to the Giant's house and get my magic things. Now I must find out if he is fit to be trusted with them down on earth. You see, the hen will give him all the gold he wants. The Harp will do his will, no matter what it is. One must have courage and good wits to be trusted with such power as that.

MAN IN THE MOON: How can you tell whether he is to be trusted?

FRIHOL: I have a test for him. If he does not pass the test he will

24

never reach the earth at all. The beanstalk will vanish away like a light that has gone out, and that will be the end of Jack.

MAN IN THE MOON: What is your test?

FRIHOL: Up there, the Giant is dancing his wife to death because Jack brought away the hen that laid the golden eggs. Down there, Rafe Heywood is driving Jack's mother out of the house, penniless and alone. Unless Jack uses his wits to save them both, I shall have to take my magic things away from him, and give them to a boy who will make better use of them.

MAN IN THE MOON: But how will Jack know that they both need help?

FRIHOL: Sh . . . h . . . h! He's coming! Watch! *(Jack comes climbing down, the two bags of gold and the hen over his shoulder. He stops when he gets opposite the Moon, and stares in amazement.)*

JACK: Why! . . . It looks like the Man in the Moon!

MAN IN THE MOON: It is.

JACK: Oh! You can even talk!

MAN IN THE MOON: That's because you believe in me.

JACK: How did you know I believed in you?

MAN IN THE MOON: I peep into all the children's windows at night. I can hear all their thoughts scurrying and scampering around in their heads.

JACK: Oh! Did you look into my room last night?

MAN IN THE MOON: Yes. Your bed was empty. Your Mother was crying about it.

JACK: Was she? Oh, I must go down, right away! *(He starts down in a hurry.)*

FRIHOL: Wait!

JACK: *(looking all about him)*: What was that?

FRIHOL: What have you there on your back?

JACK *(joyful)*: It's the magic man! Look, sir, look! It all came true! See, here is money to pay Rafe Heywood. And here is a hen that lays golden eggs.

FRIHOL: Where did you get that?

JACK: The Giant's wife gave it to me.

FRIHOL: Oho! And what will the Giant do to his poor little wife for that?

JACK: I didn't think of that.

FRIHOL: Think of it now.

JACK: Oh! He won't like it. He'll be angry. He's cruel when he's angry. Perhaps I'd better take it back. *(He starts up the beanstalk.)*

FRIHOL: What will your mother do, if Rafe Heywood comes before she gets the money?

JACK: Oh, I didn't think of that.

FRIHOL: Think of it now.

JACK: He'd drive her out. He'd be ugly to her. He shan't! *(He looks up, then down.)* I don't know which way to go. I wish I knew what was going on.

FRIHOL: Would you like to hear what they are saying?

JACK: Who?

FRIHOL: The Giant. And Rafe Heywood. The Giant is talking to his wife. And Rafe Heywood is talking to your mother.

JACK *(astonished)*: How do you know?

FRIHOL: I can hear them. Would you like to hear them too?

JACK: Voices can't come so far.

FRIHOL: Yes they can. They're already here—if you could only hear them.

JACK: Can you make me hear them?

FRIHOL: Listen! *(He makes signs, as for the music in Act One.)*
Beanstalk roots, in the brown, brown earth,
Beanstalk leaves, in the rain and the dew,
Beanstalk stem which climbs to the sun,
Have you magic enough for a faraway boy to hear the voice of his mother?
(Silence for a space, then the Widow's voice, from below.)

WIDOW: Not tomorrow, good Rafe Heywood. Do not drive me out tomorrow.

RAFE: Have you the money for the cow?

WIDOW: No, not yet. My boy—

RAFE: Then keep your bargain!

WIDOW: Let me stay a little longer. Only till my boy comes home.

RAFE: Not a day! Tomorrow was the day we named in the bargain. Tomorrow you go!

WIDOW: I can't leave my home alone. I have no place to go.

RAFE: The road is wide, and you have two feet.

WIDOW: But Jack won't know where to find me.

RAFE: What's that to me? Be gone when I come again tomorrow, or my men will beat you off the place with cudgels.

JACK *(starting down the beanstalk)*: You . . . !!!

FRIHOL: Wait!

WIDOW: Good sir, come back. Come back and hear me.

RAFE: Bah! I'll come back tomorrow! *(The Widow weeps.)*

JACK: Mother! . . . Mother! . . . I've got the money! . . . Mother! . . . She doesn't hear me. Good-bye. I'm going down.

FRIHOL: Wait! Stop!
Beanstalk far from the brown, brown earth,
Climbing above the rain and the dew,
Looking down on the face of the sun,
Have you magic enough for a faraway boy to hear the voice of the Giant?

26

(Harp music.)

GIANT *(above)*:   What happened to my golden hen?

WIFE: I . . . won't . . . tell!

GIANT: You will tell, or I'll throw this table at you!

WIFE: I . . . won't . . . tell!

JACK: Don't hurt her!   I took it!

GIANT: Take that!   *(Crash!)*   And that!   *(Another crash!)*

OLD TYB'S VOICE *(below)*:   Well, Widow, so you've got to leave your home.

WIDOW *(weeping)*:   He will not listen to me at all.   Unless Jack comes tonight, I shall be driven away, alone!   Oh, if Jack would only come with the money!

JACK: Here it is, Mother!   *(He unfastens a bag of gold and holds it far out, then drops it, leaning out to listen.   The Widow's sobbing continues, but otherwise everything is silent for a space.   The plop of the bag dropping on the earth is heard presently.   Jack leans down even further in his eagerness.)*

OLD TYB: Look, Widow!   Lift your head.   Something fell from the beanstalk.

WIDOW: It is gold!

OLD TYB: Let me see.   So it is, sure enough!

WIDOW: Jack must have dropped it.   He is safe!

OLD TYB: Your home is saved, too.

WIDOW: Yes, my home is saved!

GIANT: *(above)*:   What happened to my golden hen?   Will you tell me?

WIFE *(faintly)*:   No!!   No!   No.

GIANT: Harp, play me a jig.   Play a wild jig!   I will beat a drum to it. I will go out and make a great cudgel.   It shall be my drumstick. And you, my wicked wife, who will not tell, you shall be my drum!

JACK *(climbing furiously)*:   You shan't!   You shan't!   You shan't! *(Curtain on Frihol, laughing with satisfaction.)*

ACT TWO

Scene 3

The Giant's house again. The Wife is lying over an overturned chair, the table is upset, and other things indicate the source of the noises heard in the preceding scene. The Wife is still moving faintly to the music of the Harp, who stands just as we saw her last, her expression tragic.

The beanstalk begins to quiver, and the Wife wearily raises her head, sniffing. In alarm, she drags herself, still dancing, over to the window.

WIFE: Go back, little Earth man. Go back! Go back!

JACK *(appearing at the window)*: I came back to save you from the Giant. Where is he?

WIFE: He's gone out to get a cudgel. Go back down your beanstalk. He'll kill you.

JACK: I must save you first. Stop dancing around and think of a plan.

WIFE: I can't stop dancing. I must dance as long as the Harp plays.

JACK: Why?

WIFE: The Giant ordered the Harp to dance me to death.

JACK: Then I'll make the Harp stop playing.

WIFE: You can't. The Harp will obey nobody but its master.

JACK: I'll be its master. Harp!

HARP: Master!

JACK: Stop playing! *(The Harp stops, then bows to Jack.)*

WIFE *(arrested from dancing, at last)*: It did stop! You are its master!

JACK: The Magic Maker said that the beans would bring me music.

WIFE: Make it play the Giant asleep. Then we can get away.

JACK: Harp!

HARP: Master!

JACK: Can you play the Giant dead asleep?

HARP: I can play him dead asleep,
   I can play him wide awake,
   I do my master's bidding.

JACK: Play the Giant dead asleep, the very next time you see him.

HARP *(triumphantly)*: I will play the Giant dead asleep, the very next time I see him.

JACK: Do not wait to be told again. Begin the very minute you see him.

HARP: I will not wait to be told again. I will begin the very minute I see him.

GIANT *(offstage)*: Fee, fi, fo, foy—*(Jack darts off to hide in the oven.)*

28

WIFE: Make the Harp go in, quick!

JACK *(as he climbs in the oven)*: Harp!

HARP: Master!

JACK: Go in! *(The Harp goes into the cupboard. The Giant enters with his cudgel.)*

GIANT: Why are you not dancing?

WIFE: The Harp stopped playing.

GIANT: Who made it stop? There is somebody here! I'll find him! Take the cover off that kettle!

WIFE: The kettle?

GIANT: The kettle, the kettle, the kettle! Yes, the kettle! *(Wife lifts the lid of the kettle, and the Giant leans way in, burning his face with steam. Wife laughs.)* Be still! Where have you hidden him?

WIFE: He isn't here.

GIANT: You are playing tricks on me.

WIFE: No one could play tricks on you, Giant. Anyone as clever as you.

GIANT *(scratching his head, pleased)*: That's true. Still . . . I will look under the table. *(He bumps his head under the table-top.)* Ouch! . . . Open that door to the dresser.

WIFE: There is no one in the dresser.

GIANT: Open the door! *(Wife does, and he looks, pinching his finger as he closes it.)* Ouch! . . . *(He suddenly thinks of the oven, stops, pointing at it.)* Open that door!

WIFE *(swallowing hard)*: Yes, Giant. Yes. *(She moves part way toward it, then stops, pointing to the cupboard.)* Uh . . . we'll skip this door, of course. You don't want to look in there.

GIANT *(suspicious at once, as she meant him to be)*: Who said I didn't?

WIFE: There is no one in there but the Harp.

GIANT: Oh, there isn't, eh? Open that door!

WIFE: Why should you look in there?

GIANT: Open that door!

WIFE: Yes, Giant . . . Nobody could be hiding behind the Harp.

GIANT: We'll soon see. Harp! . . . Harp! Why don't you answer?

WIFE: Perhaps the Harp has a new master, Giant.

GIANT: We'll see about that. Harp, come out . . . come out! I'll fetch you! *(The Giant lifts his cudgel over his shoulder to aim a blow at the Harp. Jack, who has been watching this scene from a crack in the oven door, now leaps onto the window sill, and seizes the end of the club. Giant swings the club around and sees Jack. Meanwhile, the Harp has begun to play.)* Oh, there you are! *(Jack runs around the room, and takes a flying leap over the table, leaping onto it, and off it, in one stride. The Giant follows, getting one foot on the table and falling off it. He yawns. Jack leaps over him as he sprawls on the floor, and takes refuge in the corner, right back. The Giant corners him, spreading his arms wide and coming in on him closer*

29

and closer, smacking his lips and snorting. Jack dodges under one of his arms and escapes. Jack takes refuge behind the fallen chair. The Giant swings his club, trying to hit him, Jack dodging each stroke in perfect rhythm. The Giant finally hits himself with the club on a back-swing, and Jack escapes during his roar of pain. Jack takes refuge in the corner, back left, and the Giant closes in on him again, shouting, "Now I've got you!" He spreads his legs wide and lifts his club for a straight-down blow. Jack runs between his legs and escapes. The Giant loses his balance by the swing of the club between his legs. He falls heavily and leans back against the wall, yawning and rubbing his eyes.) Curse you! Why are my eyes so full of sleep?

WIFE: The Harp is playing you to sleep, Giant.

GIANT: *(swaying to the music):* I don't want to go to sleep.

WIFE *(musically chanting):* You will go. You will go.

GIANT *(drowsily):* Harp . . . play me wide awake . . .

HARP: I am playing you asleep,
Deep, deep, deep asleep,
Deep, deep, deep asleep.

JACK *(peeping out from under the overturned table):* Deep, deep, deep asleep. *(With one final drowsy burst of strength, the Giant lunges after him on hands and knees, and catches hold of Jack's ankle. But his chin gets caught above the table, so that he cannot move, and the Wife runs to pull on Jack. Jack finally wriggles free, the Giant falls back on the floor motionless, asleep. There is an instant's silence as they watch him.)* Let us go. Harp!

WIFE: Wait! The Giant will wake as soon as the music stops, and will come down after us.

JACK: Then we must tie him up. Have you any rope?

WIFE *(running to the dresser):* Plenty of it.

JACK: *(as she brings it):* Tie his hands . . . Now his feet. *(They do, drawing the rope back with all their might, one on each side.)* Tie him to the back of the chair! *(They do.)*

WIFE: There!

JACK: Now we must go.

WIFE *(leaping over the Giant's outstretched feet and going for the knife):* Wait! Take this.

JACK: What for?

WIFE: The Giant is very strong. Suppose he broke the ropes and came down after us. This is the only knife that will cut him. It will cut anything. Be careful of it. It might cut the beanstalk.

JACK: You can't cut the beanstalk. I tried it, coming up.

WIFE: This will cut it. You must be careful.

JACK *(trying it on a tendril):* So it will! . . . Harp!

HARP: Master.

JACK: Can you lead me down to my mother?

30

HARP: I can lead men up, I can lead men down,
I do my master's bidding.
JACK: Lead me down to my mother. *(The Harp goes ahead, and Jack
follows. The music dies away slowly, and the Giant stirs out of his
sleep. The Giant's wife is on the window sill.)*
GIANT *(in the throes of waking up)*: Wife!
WIFE *(full of mischief)*: Yes, Giant?
GIANT: What is the matter with my hands? What is the matter with
my feet?
WIFE: Someone has tied you up, Giant.
GIANT: Untie me, quick!
WIFE: I will not untie you, Giant. I will leave you tied up forever!
I am going away. I am going down to the earth to find my Granny
Tyb! She will like me! *(She begins to climb down.)*
GIANT: Wife!
WIFE: Good bye, Giant. I shall never come back any more.
GIANT: Untie me, Wife! Come back!
WIFE *(now out of sight, her voice disappearing)*: Good bye! *(The
Giant struggles with his bonds, falling over his chair, finally gnawing
the ropes on his arms in two, then twisting till he gets his legs free.
He starts for the window with the chair still fastened to his back,
discovers it, works it off with rage, and starts down the beanstalk
as the curtain falls.)*

CURTAIN

ACT THREE

The Widow's garden as in Act One, except that evidences of prosperity replace those of poverty. The Harp is just leaving the beanstalk. She makes a movement of her head, and music sounds at the end of her line.

HARP: I can make men blind, I can make men see,
I am seen by none till my master calls.
(She stops behind the beanstalk, where she cannot be clearly seen. The door opens, and Widow Bess enters, going eagerly to look up the beanstalk. She wears the dress "as blue as the sky." While she is peering up, as if the very intensity of her desire might bring Jack back to her, Old Tyb comes slowly through the gate, followed by Annot and Joan.)

OLD TYB: Always looking up there. That's the way I did when my grandchild went away. . . . She never came back.

WIDOW *(reassuring herself)*: He will come. I am sure he will. Everything is ready for him. And this is his birthday.

ANNOT: What a fine dress you are wearing.

WIDOW: It is to please my boy. He always wanted me to wear a gown like a piece of the sky. Feel its softness, only.

ANNOT: Silk! You have gold enough for that?

WIDOW: It seems strange. But I have gold enough and to spare.

JOAN: The folk were saying down in the village, that you had fine woven linen, and carven silver cups for your table.

WIDOW: So I have. I have always dreamed of a fine cup for my boy to drink from, and now I have one. See for yourself. *(She throws open the cottage door. They look in, exclaiming with delight.)*

OLD TYB: Aye, that is a fine cup, sure enough.

ANNOT: What beautiful bright cushions!

JOAN: What shining copper pans for your cooking!

OLD TYB *(turning away to sit on the well-curb)*: When I was young, I believed such things could happen.

WIDOW: And now you see they can.

OLD TYB: There is something queer about it. It never happened to me.

WIDOW: It was Jack who did it.

OLD TYB *(ominously)*: Aye, Widow. And where is Jack?

WIDOW *(turning hopefully to the beanstalk)*: He went up . . . up . . .

OLD TYB: And where does it end?

ANNOT: Aye, Widow. Where does it end?

WIDOW: Don't! Don't! He must come back! He wouldn't leave his mother here alone. He's all I have in the world.

32

OLD TYB: That's what I used to think when my grandchild went away. She was all I had in the world, but she left me here alone.

WIDOW: Don't say such things! Please be quiet. Oh, why did I let him go?

NICHOLAS (at the gate with Gavin): Why should she be weeping? Hasn't she all the gold she wants?

ANNOT: Her little boy climbed up above the clouds, and he has never come back.

NICHOLAS: And he never will.

JACK (very far above): Mother!

WIDOW: Jack! Jack! . . . I hear him! . . . Jack! Jack! Jack!

JACK: I'm coming. Catch! (A bag of gold comes hurtling down.)

CROWD: Money! Money!

WIDOW (holding it to her as if it were her boy): More gold! My boy sent it!

JACK (above, nearer): Mother!

WIDOW: I see him. Up! Up! Just a speck!

OTHERS (in great excitement): I see him too! . . . It moves! . . . Yes, there he is!

JACK (always nearer): Catch! Catch! (Handfuls of gold come flying down. All but the Widow, who stands waiting for Jack, arms upstretched, scramble madly for the gold. They bump into each other, they snatch from each other. Nicholas puts his foot on a coin, as Gavin tries to pick it up, and as they face each other in fury, Annot slips the gold into her own pocket. Etc.)

CROWD (scrambling): Money! Gold pieces! Coppers! Silver pieces! Gold! (As they stand, each counting his own prize, Jack comes in sight, and leaps down to throw his arms about his mother.)

JACK: Mother!

WIDOW: Jack! Jack! (They stand embraced, the stage suddenly silent.)

OLD TYB: When I was young, I believed such things could happen.

JACK: See what I brought you. Here is money.

CROWD (gasping at sight of the money bags): Look at it!

JACK: And here is a hen that will lay us golden eggs.

CROWD: Golden eggs!

JACK: And here is a knife that will cut anything in the world.

NICHOLAS (testing it, and showing it to Gavin): Feel, how sharp!

GAVIN: Young man, you have riches now. Could you spare a little for a man with many mouths to feed?

JACK (swinging the bag from his shoulder onto the table): Give Gavin a handful, Mother. (The Widow pours a double handful into Gavin's open waiting palms.)

ANNOT (teetering with hope): Oh-h! If I could have a silken gown, like the one your Mother wears!

JACK (*digging into the bag to get money for her*):   Get yourself one.

NICHOLAS: Just five, no more, of those large coins, would buy the bit of land I need to make me a free man.

JACK: Here!   And here's some more to buy your seed.

JOAN: Oh, you're a fine young master.   Let me have enough to stock my kitchen shelves with fine copper pans, such as your mother has bought herself.

JACK: Give her just what you paid for yours, Mother.

WIDOW: Now we shall have everything we want.

JACK: Except Old Tyb.   She didn't ask for anything.

WIDOW: Isn't there anything you would like to have, neighbor Tyb?

JACK: What is it you want?

OLD TYB (*lost in her dreams*):   When I was younger, I had a little grandchild, with shining eyes.   Her name was Tyb.   And I'd say to little grandchild Tyb, "Where did you get your shining eyes?" And she'd answer, "My mother's eyes were just like that, and her mother's, and hers, way back in a row."   Just as I taught her.   That was many years ago.

JACK (*softly*):   But isn't there anything you want now?

OLD TYB (*with bitter sarcasm*):   Yes!   I want my heart to be young, as it was once.

JACK: Oh, I can give you that . . . Harp!

HARP: Master!

JACK: Come here.   (*The Harp comes out from behind the beanstalk, and through the gate.*)

ANNOT: God-a-mercy!

NICHOLAS: What thing is this?

WIDOW: Jack!

JACK: Don't be afraid.   Watch! . . . Harp, can you play Old Tyb young in heart?

HARP: I can make men young, I can make men old,
   I do my master's bidding.

JACK: Make Old Tyb young in heart.   Make Mother too.   Make everybody!   (*The Harp begins to play. At first, all are motionless, a spell falling over them.   Then they move slightly, their bodies dropping the tension of years and relaxing to the music. Then the joy bubbles up in them, and they sway to the music, turning to each other and getting ready to dance. Old Tyb is the first to move in dance rhythm, laughing in surprise, first softly, then more freely, until she gets up and dances. She begins slowly, but soon gets wildly hilarious, shouting with laughter, leaping high in the air with both feet, holding her skirts up to do so.   It is a comic dance, of course, but she never loses the surprised and wondering quality with which the dance began, each shout of laughter being a fresh greeting of the miracle of joy growing within her. At the same time, Nicholas and*

34

Joan, Gavin and Annot, join hands and prance off, then make a circle. They, too, are laughing deliciously as they spin around. Jack and his mother dance together, bowing to each other, swinging with locked arms, etc., bubbling over with joy. In the midst of it, the Giant's wife appears on the beanstalk, and laughs from her perch. She stands on the wall, feeling the rhythm of the music until Nicholas sees her, and dances over to swing her off the wall. She spins with one and another, ending with Old Tyb, with whom she is dancing, center, when Jack, breathless, swings across to shout to the Harp to stop. The others fall panting and laughing onto the bench and in chairs, but Tyb and the Wife slow down gradually, and stand looking at each other.)

OLD TYB *(in breathless hope)*:   Where did you get those shining eyes, pretty one?

WIFE: My mother's eyes were just the same, and her mother's, and hers, way back in a row.

OLD TYB: What is your name?

WIFE: My name is Tyb, and my mother's, and her mother's, way back in a row.

OLD TYB: My name is Tyb.   I'm looking for my grandchild.

WIFE: I'm looking for my granny!

OLD TYB: I've found my grandchild!

WIFE: I've found my granny!   *(They fling their arms around each other in ecstasy.   The others laugh with sympathy, and spring to their feet, flinging gold coins up in the air for pure playfulness. Rafe Heywood enters.)*

RAFE: What are you doing with my gold coin?   *(They shrink back from him.)*

NICHOLAS: The boy gave us the coin.

WIDOW: Nay, sir, it is not your coin they sport with.   I have yours ready, all counted and tied up.

RAFE: So that's your game!   I have been hearing how you were wasting my coin, dressing yourself in silk, like a rich man's wife.

JACK: It's not your gold.   I brought it down the beanstalk.

RAFE: The beanstalk is mine! . . . The cottage and the land, and everything that stands or grows on it.   Do you mind the points of the bargain, neighbors?   Was that the bargain?

NEIGHBORS *(mumbling)*:   It was.

RAFE: Is the gold in the garden, or not? . . . Speak up!   All of you! . . . Friend Nicholas?

NICHOLAS: The gold is yours, but—

RAFE: Empty your pockets of what is mine!   *(Nicholas gives up his gold. Rafe passes before each in turn, holding out his hand, and each reluctantly gives up his remaining treasure.)*

ANNOT: Only enough to buy a bright silk gown.

RAFE: What are your gowns to me!

GAVIN: It is such a small part of what you have, good sir. My sons—

RAFE: What do I care for your sons? Did I bring them into the world?

JACK: You have no right to take away their gold. I gave it to them!

WIDOW: Give us just a small sum to start with, sir.

RAFE: Not a copper!

JACK (taking up the hen): Never mind, mother. We'll have enough without the money.

RAFE: So that's the hen that lays the golden eggs. Put it down. (Jack is defiant.)

WIDOW: Put it down, lad. I made the bargain. (Jack, after a struggle with himself, puts it down.)

RAFE (looking the Harp over): This is a pretty toy. I'll make good use of this.

JACK: You can't! It won't play for you. You are not its master.

RAFE: We'll see whether I am or not.

JACK: I'll show you. Harp!

HARP: Master.

JACK: Come here. (The Harp obeys, to the amazement of the on-lookers.)

RAFE: 'Tis an obedient piece of metal.

JACK: Now, Rafe Heywood, I can ask for any music that I wish, and the Harp will play it. See if it will play for you.

RAFE: Harp! . . . Harp!

ANNOT: It answered Jack.

RAFE: Be still! . . . Harp!

JACK: Tell it to play us deep asleep.

RAFE: Harp! Play us deep asleep! (The Harp looks at him, defiant.) Play us deep asleep! Play us deep asleep! (The neighbors laugh, pointing at him.) Be quiet!

JACK: See, that shows who is master. It will not do your will. It will do mine.

RAFE: If it will do your will, let me see it happen. Tell it to play us deep asleep yourself.

JACK: I will. Harp!

HARP: Master!

JACK: Can you play us deep asleep?

HARP: I can play men deep asleep, I can play men wide awake, I do my master's bidding.

JACK: Play us deep asleep.

HARP (playing): I am playing you asleep. Deep, deep asleep. (All feel the spell, and begin to sink into sleep.)

RAFE (struggling against sleep): Wait! Wait! Here, this is enough! Stop it! Stop it!

HARP (triumphant): I am playing you asleep,

36

Deep, deep, deep asleep . . .
Deep asleep . . . asleep . . . asleep . . .

RAFE: No one can play me asleep against my will.

HARP: Deep, deep, deep, asleep . . .

RAFE: No more!

HARP: I am playing you asleep . . . *(Rafe collapses, leaning against the gate, back. The others have already sunk onto benches, etc. Jack is on the stool, center, his head on the table. His mother is opposite him.)*

OLD TYB *(out of her dreams, as quiet settles over all)*: Lullaby, pretty one . . .

ANNOT *(murmuring in a dream)*: A scarlet feather and silver shoes . . .

NICHOLAS: A soft slope in the warm sun . . .

JACK *(dreaming also)*: Mother . . .

WIDOW: Hush lad. Your father is playing his fiddle.

GIANT *(very far away)*: Fee, fi, fo, fum! I smell the blood of an Englishman. Be he live or be he dead, I'll grind his bones to make my bread. *(The Harp looks anxiously up the beanstalk, which is shaking with the weight of the Giant, but continues to play. Jack stirs uneasily in his sleep as the Giant begins.)*

JACK: Mother!

GIANT *(a little nearer)*: Fee, fi, fo, foy—I'll steal that little boy. I'll climb down so fast that none shall hear, And none shall know that I am near.

JACK *(dreaming)*: Harp!

HARP *(pleased)*: Master! *(Jack mumbles in his dream, and the Harp goes to him, anxious, and repeats at his side:)* Master!

JACK *(dreaming)*: Can you play us, play us, wide awake . . .

HARP: I am playing you awake!
Wide, wide, wide awake!
Awake! Awake! I am playing you awake!
(Rafe is the first to lift his head. He looks at the shaking beanstalk in wonder and dread. The Giant's voice has ceased. Jack rubs his eyes and then remembers.)

JACK: There, Rafe Heywood, are you master of the Harp, or am I?

RAFE: H'm-m-m. Where did you get this Harp that calls you master?

JACK: It was up there, with the money and the hen.

ANNOT: Oh, I'm going up!

CROWD: I too! So am I! etc. *(There is a general rush toward the beanstalk, but Rafe bars the way at the gate.)*

RAFE: Keep away, all of you. The beanstalk is mine! What is at the top is mine! I shall be the one to go up.

JACK: No! No! There is a Giant up there! *(Rafe is climbing, but he pauses to look down and speak.)*

37

RAFE: So! You have a tricky head, haven't you? You think you can scare me away with talk of a Giant? I see through that. I'm going up!

WIFE: Oh, there is a Giant up there, earth man!

RAFE: So you would like to go up too! What would you like—a magic harp or a golden hen? *(He climbs on up. The Giant's boots show, coming down. The people on the ground see them and shout warnings to Rafe. He laughs, looking down to scoff at them as he climbs up, so that he does not see the Giant who is not looking down at him. Finally, the Giant sees him, and reaches down to catch Rafe by the hair. There is pandemonium below as they fight. The Giant shakes him, and he hangs by his knees, dead.)*

GIANT *(trying him)*: You are too tough to be worth eating. Aha! There is the boy I want! *(He sees his wife.)* Aha! And there you are! I'll go back and get the rope to tie you up this time. You'll never get untied. I'll sling one over each shoulder, and up you'll go. Um . . . m . . . m. *(He climbs up, laughing and snorting. Meantime, the men have caught Rafe, and lift him off the beanstalk. The others gather around awed, back of well.)*

GAVIN *(incredulous)*: Rafe Heywood is dead.

WIDOW: We need fear him no more.

NICHOLAS: He thought there was nothing as powerful as he.

CROWD: We all thought so.

OLD TYB *(looking up the beanstalk)*: Now we know there is.

WIDOW: But, Jack, the Giant said he would come back to get you.

NICHOLAS: Tear down the beanstalk. *(They all try, but it does no good. The Giant speaks again, faint, but approaching.)*

GIANT: Fee, fi, fo, foy! *(The Widow has run into the house and brought out an axe, which she gives to Jack. He swings it against the beanstalk with no effect.)*

GAVIN: Let me try! *(He also fails. The Giant is very near, roaring and snorting and laughing. They shout and cry, Nicholas snatching the axe, but to no avail.)*

WIFE: Jack! The knife! The Giant's knife!

JACK: Yes, where is it? *(They search madly. Finally Nicholas and Annot, beyond the wall, see it under the table, point and shout above the din. Jack catches it up and leaps up onto the wall, just in time to shout to the Giant before he gets near enough to reach him.)* Go back! Go back, or I'll cut you down!

GIANT: Do you think I am afraid of a little boy? *(As the Giant takes another step down and stretches out his arm to snatch at Jack's head, Jack swings the knife. There is lightning, blackness, lightning again, as the beanstalk sways and comes crashing down, the Giant with it. The neighbors scream in terror. The Giant tries to rise, but staggers forward again, and falls dead. There is a sudden dead silence after

38

the uproar, then Jack approaches cautiously, and puts a foot on the Giant's chest, triumphant. All gather near, silent but safe. Behind the wall, Frihol suddenly appears, with a magic gesture, and is gone. The cow looks over the wall, and moos softly. Jack runs to throw his arms around the cow's neck, laughing with joy.)

CURTAIN

Tom Sawyer

ADAPTED FROM MARK TWAIN

By

SARA SPENCER

*A Play for Old and Young
With or Without Music*

TOM SAWYER

By Sara Spencer

THE ANCHORAGE PRESS
Cloverlot
Anchorage, Kentucky 40223
U. S. A.

TOM SAWYER

Characters

TOM SAWYER

SID SAWYER

ALFRED TEMPLE

BEN ROGERS

JIM HOLLIS

HUCKLEBERRY FINN

JOE HARPER

AMY LAWRENCE

JANIE HARDIN

GRACIE MILLER

SUSAN HARPER

BECKY THATCHER

AUNT POLLY

MRS. THATCHER

SCHOOLMASTER

MUFF POTTER

INJUN JOE

DR. ROBINSON

PREACHER

SHERIFF

TOM SAWYER

Musical Numbers

Music and Lyrics by Barbara Burnham

For producers wishing to present a musical version of this play, the following songs are provided:

ACT ONE
"When Monday Comes"
    Solo: Tom Sawyer
"Come Along You All"
    Duet: Muff Potter and Chorus of children
"Now Will You Promise"
    Duet: Tom Sawyer and Becky Thatcher

ACT TWO
"I'm A-Feared"
    Duet: Tom Sawyer and Huckleberry Finn
"Oath"
        Duet: Tom Sawyer and Huckleberry Finn
"Whitewash Song"
    Two-Part Chorus, with Solos: All the Boys
"Who Done it"
    Chorus, with Solos by Sheriff and Muff Potter
"Pirate Song"
    Trio: Tom Sawyer, Joe Harper, and Huckleberry Finn

ACT THREE
"I'm Homesick"
    Solo: Joe Harper
"Dirge"
    Various Solos, with underlying mourning by Chorus

ACT FOUR
"He's a Goner"
    Chorus, with various Solos
"Aw Becky Don't Cry" (Reprise of "Now Will You Promise")
    Duet: Tom Sawyer and Becky Thatcher
"Halleloo"
    Chorus
"Square Dance"
    Chorus. Square Dance called by Preacher

Lyrics for the above numbers are included in the separate play-book only. Music score is available from the publisher, at extra cost.

TOM SAWYER

Scenes

ACT ONE

ACT TWO

ACT THREE

ACT FOUR

45

AUTHOR'S NOTE

Tom Sawyer is not tailored to fit the needs of any known theatrical company. It requires twelve young people, in leading roles. It also requires eight adults. And since this is a play about the difference between the two, a sharp contrast between the generations is necessary.

Young people are rarely accomplished actors. And it is difficult for the most accomplished actor to simulate the miracle that is childhood. So the author of this play presents the producer with a near-impossible task, and has no advice to offer.

Nevertheless, I entrust this play to producers with the fervent hope that they will find the means to address it to all humanity. For although my play, like Mark Twain's book, is intended mainly for the entertainment of boys and girls, I hope it will not be shunned by men and women on that account. Part of my plan, like Mark Twain's, has been to pleasantly remind adults of what they once were themselves, and of how they felt, and thought, and talked, and what queer enterprises they sometimes engaged in.

—The Playwright

46

TOM SAWYER

ACT ONE

SCENE 1.—Tom's bedroom. A double bed, a wash-stand, a motto
on the wall.

*(Tom and Sid are asleep, Tom snoring vociferously, Sid snoring
like a steam whistle.)*

AUNT POLLY *(offstage).* Tom! Oh, Tom! Monday!

TOM *(opens his eyes dazedly, yawns, then comes alert).* Monday!

*(He sighs drearily, then begins to plan. Feels around over his
body for ailments, coughing experimentally, rejecting a loose
tooth, etc. If desired, Song No. 1, "When Monday Comes", may
be used here. Finally he unties the rag around his sore toe, and
falls to groaning.)*

Oh-h-h!

(But Sid snores on.)

Ohh-h-h-h! Oooh-h-h-h!

(No response from Sid. Tom reaches over and shakes him.)

Sid! Sid! Ohhhhh-h-h-h! Ooooh-h-h-h!

SID *(waking up).* Tom! Say, Tom!

TOM. Ohhhhhh-h-h-h-h! Oooooooh-h-h-h!

SID *(shaking him).* Here, Tom. Tom! What's the matter, Tom?

TOM. Oh, don't, Sid. Don't joggle me.

SID. Why, what's the matter, Tom? I must call Auntie.

TOM. No, never mind. It'll be over by and by, maybe. Don't call
anybody. Ohhhhhhhhh-h-h-h-h-h!

SID. But I must. Don't groan so, Tom. It's awful! How long you
been this way?

TOM. Hours. Ouch! Don't stir so, Sid. You'll kill me. Ohhhhhh-
h-h-h!

SID. Tom, why didn't you wake me sooner? Oh, Tom, don't! It makes
my flesh crawl to hear you.

TOM. I forgive you everything, Sid. Ohhh-h-h-h-h! Everything you
ever done to me.

SID. Oh, Tom, you ain't dying, are you? Don't, Tom. Oh, don't!
Maybe—

47

Tom. I forgive everybody, Sid. Tell 'em so, Sid. And Sid, you give my brass knob and my cat with one eye to Joe Harper. And tell him—Ohhh-h-h-h!

Sid (*making for the door*). Oh, Aunt Polly! Come quick! Tom's dying!

Aunt Polly (*offstage*). Dying?

Sid. Yes'm. Don't wait. Come quick!

Aunt Polly (*still offstage*). Rubbage! I don't believe it.

(*But she rushes in, just the same, and finds Tom on the bed, writhing.*)

You, Tom! Tom, what's the matter with you?

Tom. Oh, Auntie, I'm—Oh-h-h-h!

Aunt Polly. What's the matter? What is the matter with you, child?

Tom. Oh, Auntie—my sore toe's mortified!

Aunt Polly (*sinking on the bed with relief, and chuckling*). Tom, what a turn you did give me! Now you shut up that nonsense and climb out of this.

Tom (*quite subdued*). Aunt Polly, it seemed mortified. And—and it hurt so, I never minded my tooth at all.

Aunt Polly. Your tooth, indeed. What's the matter with your tooth?

Tom. One of 'em's loose, and it aches perfectly awful. Oh-h-h-h-h!

Aunt Polly. There, now, don't begin that groaning again. Open your mouth. Well, your tooth is loose, but you're not going to die about that. Sid, get me a hot iron off the kitchen stove.

(*Sid gleefully rushes off, as Aunt Polly pulls a spool of thread from her apron pocket, and attaches one end of it to the bed-post. The other end she attaches to Tom's tooth.*)

Tom (*shrinking away*). Oh, please, Auntie, don't pull it out. It don't hurt any more. I wish I may never stir if it does. Please don't, Auntie. I don't want to stay home from school.

Aunt Polly. Oh, you don't, don't you? So all this was because you thought you'd get to stay home from school and go a-fishing. Oh, Tom, you'll be the death of me yet. Here, Sid.

(*Sid has re-entered with the iron, and gives it to her, gloating at Tom's misery. Aunt Polly thrusts the iron close to Tom's face. Tom jerks back, and the tooth is dangling by the bed-post.*)

Sid. Goody, that's what you get.

AUNT POLLY. Now you boys get your clothes on, and come on here to breakfast. I have an errand for you, Tom, before you go to school.

(Aunt Polly goes out.)

SID *(pulling on his pants, underneath his night-shirt).* Didn't you think you was smart now?

TOM *(peeling off his night-shirt and disclosing himself fully dressed underneath).* You go to grass.

SID. A lot of good it did you.

TOM *(experimenting).* I can spit!

SID. You better not spit in here. I'll tell Auntie on you.

TOM *(detaching the tooth from the bed-post).* All right, tattle-tale. You're just riled because I can spit and you can't.

SID. What you goin' to do with that tooth?

TOM. Keep it awhile. Then I'll trade it.

SID. What'll you take for it?

TOM. Nothing you got, sissy. Maybe I'll trade it to Ben Rogers for that window-sash of his.

SID. Go ahead and do it. See if I care.

AUNT POLLY *(offstage).* Tom! Come on here. You'll be late.

TOM. Yes'm, Aunt Polly. I'm comin'.

(He turns for a last word to Sid.)

Smarty.

(And goes out, dodging the pillow that Sid throws.)

ACT ONE

SCENE 2. A village street. A white board fence. A barrel.

(School bell is heard, off. Ben Rogers enters, walking carefully as he balances books, slate, and dinner pail on his head.)

(Sid Sawyer comes in behind him, deliberately jostles him, knocking the things to the ground.)

(Amy Lawrence enters, jumping rope.)

(Susan Harper and Becky Thatcher enter, admire Amy's jumping rope. May take a few trial jumps.)

(Gracie Miller and Jane Hardin enter. Jane proudly exhibits a bandaged finger, and enjoys a momentary fame, as all the girls cluster around.)

(Jim Hollis enters, balancing a straw on his nose.

(Tom Sawyer dashes in, pointing off to a vision behind him.

(The vision enters, Alfred Temple, walking primly, and wearing a hat, shoes, and spectacles. The girls are impressed, the boys either envious or resentful. Tom yanks his jacket as he passes. Alfred turns in umbrage.

(From the opposite direction, Muff Potter enters, the town tramp, fishing pole over his shoulder. If desired, Song No. 2, "Come Along You All", may be used here. Some of the children may reflect the town's opinion of this low character.

(During the above scene, ad-libbed conversation may be used if the producer feels the need. Preferably, however, the scene should be covered by indistinguishable school-child chatter.

(The second school bell is heard off, insistently. Muff Potter shambles off toward the river. The children bustle off toward school. As Alfred Temple starts out, Tom purposely slings his books so as to strike Alfred in the small of the back. Alfred turns to glare at him.)

ALFRED. That's the second time.

TOM. I can lick you.

ALFRED. I'd like to see you try it.

TOM. Well, I can do it.

ALFRED. No you can't, either.

TOM. Yes I can.

ALFRED. No you can't.

TOM. I can.

ALFRED. You can't.

TOM. Can!

ALFRED. Can't!

TOM. What's your name?

ALFRED. 'Tisn't any of your business maybe.

TOM. Well, I 'low I'll make it my business.

ALFRED. Well, why don't you?

TOM. If you say much, I will.

ALFRED. Much, much, much! There, now.

TOM. Oh, you think you're pretty smart, don't you? I could lick you with one hand tied behind me, if I wanted to.

50

ALFRED. Well, why don't you? You say you can do it.

TOM. Well, I will—if you fool with me.

ALFRED. Oh, yes. I've seen whole families in the same fix.

TOM. Smarty! You think you're some now, don't you? Oh, what a hat!

ALFRED. You can lump that hat if you don't like it. I dare you to knock it off. And anybody that will take a dare will suck eggs.

TOM. Say, if you give me much more of your sass, I'll light into you.

ALFRED. Oh, of course you will.

TOM. Well, I will.

ALFRED. Well, why don't you do it, then? What do you keep on saying you will for? Why don't you do it? It's because you're afraid.

TOM. I ain't afraid.

ALFRED. You are.

TOM. I ain't!

ALFRED. You are!

TOM. Get away from here.

ALFRED. Go away yourself.

TOM. I won't!

ALFRED. I won't either!

(Joe Harper enters on the run, late for school, but stops to watch this drama.)

TOM *(drawing a line on the path with his toe)*. I dare you to step over that, and I'll lick you till you can't stand up. And anybody that would take a dare will steal sheep.

ALFRED *(stepping over it promptly)*. Now you said you'd do it. Let's see you do it.

TOM. Don't you crowd me. You better look out.

ALFRED. Well, you said you'd do it. Why don't you do it?

TOM. By jingo, for two cents, I would do it.

ALFRED *(holding out two pennies)*. There, mister. There's your two cents.

(Tom strikes the two pennies to the ground, and the two boys come to grips. The fight does not last long. In a few moments Tom is astride of the new boy, pounding him with both fists.)

TOM. Holler 'nuff.

51

ALFRED (*struggling and crying*). I won't.

TOM (*pounding on*). Holler 'nuff!

ALFRED. 'Nuff! 'Nuff!

TOM (*letting him go*). There, that'll learn you. Better look out who you're fooling with next time.

ALFRED (*crying, as he brushes himself off*). Never you mind, mister. You just see what I do to you the next time I catch you out.

(*He starts off to school, snuffling, but when Tom's back is turned, he picks up a stone and flings it at Tom, then takes to his heels as Tom makes a show of starting off in pursuit.*)

JOE. Hey, watch out! Gee whillikers, Tom, what was that all about?

TOM. I didn't like his airs.

JOE. Well—you better come on. It's late.

TOM (*flushed with victory*). It's too hot to hurry.

(*The final bell is heard, off.*)

JOE (*bolting off*). There's the bell!

(*He exits.*)

TOM. Wait for me, Joe!

(*Automatically, Tom starts to bolt off after Joe, and turns to pick up his books. But just at this point, Huckleberry Finn meanders in, swinging a dead cat by the tail. Tom is lost in admiration.*)

Huckleberry!

HUCK. H'lo.

TOM. What's that you got?

HUCK. Dead cat.

TOM. Lemme see him, Huck. My, he's pretty stiff. Where'd you get him?

HUCK. Bought him off'n a boy.

TOM. What'd you give?

HUCK. I give a piece of lickerish, and a bladder that I got at the slaughter-house.

TOM. Say—what is dead cats good for, Huck?

HUCK. Good for? Cure warts with.

TOM. Cure warts with? I know other ways—but how do you cure them with dead cats?

52

HUCK. Why, you take your cat, and go and get in the graveyard about midnight, where somebody that was wicked has been buried. And when it's midnight, a devil will come—or maybe two or three. But you can't see 'em. You can only hear 'em. And when they're takin' that feller away, you heave the cat after 'em and say, "Devil foller corpse, cat follow devil, wart foller cat, I'm done with ye!" That'll fetch any wart.

TOM. Sounds right. When you going to try it, Huck?

HUCK. Tonight. I reckon they'll come after old Hoss Williams tonight.

TOM. But they buried him on Saturday. Didn't the devils get him Saturday night?

HUCK. Why, how you talk! How could their charms work till midnight, and then it's Sunday. Devils don't slosh around much of a Sunday, I don't reckon.

TOM. That's so, I bet. Hey, lemme go with you.

HUCK. All right—if you ain't afeared.

TOM. Feared? 'Tain't likely. Will you meow under my window?

HUCK. Yes. And you meow back if you get the chance.

TOM. I will—if Aunt Polly ain't awake. Well, so long, Hucky.

HUCK. You ain't goin' to school now, are you? You'll get a lickin' for bein' late.

TOM. I have to.

HUCK. Why?

TOM. Sid'll tell on me if I don't.

HUCK (*drawing something from his pocket with a great show of unconcern*). Suit yourself.

TOM. What's that?

HUCK. Nothing but a tick.

TOM. Where'd you get him?

HUCK. Out in the woods.

TOM. What'll you take for him, Huck?

HUCK. I don't know. I don't want to sell him.

TOM. Oh, all right. It's a mighty small tick anyway.

HUCK. Oh, anybody can run down a tick that don't belong to you. I'm satisfied with it. It's a good enough tick fer me.

TOM. Sho, there's ticks a-plenty. I could have a thousand of 'em if I wanted to.

HUCK. Well, why don't you? Because you know mighty well you can't, that's why. This is a pretty early tick, I reckon. It's the first one I've seen this year.

TOM. Say, Huck, I'll give you my tooth for him.

HUCK. Less see it.

TOM (showing it proudly). There!

HUCK. Is it genuwyne?

TOM. Genuwyne? Watch!

(And showing the cavity, he spits through it.)

HUCK. All right. It's a trade.

TOM (sadly). I haven't even had the chance to show that tooth to anybody yet.

HUCK. You can show 'em the hole.

TOM. That's so. Well, so long, Huck. I might as well go on and get my lickin'.

HUCK. Don't forget tonight.

TOM (going off). I won't.

(He leaves.)

HUCK. So long.

(He watches Tom off, then looks the tooth over appreciatively, and pockets it. He looks down at the dead cat on the ground.)

Here, kitty, kitty.

(He gathers the cat up by the tail, and swings off with it.)

ACT ONE

SCENE 3. The schoolroom. Two long benches on each side. The master's desk. A hat-rack, hung with bonnets, hats, and dinner pails.

(The girls are seated on one side of the room, the boys on the other.)

MASTER. Fourth Reader!

(Amy Lawrence, Gracie Miller, and Ben Rogers approach the Master's desk.)

Amy Lawrence, you may recite.

AMY (sing-songing it off). Shameful Death.
> There were four of us about that bed.
> The mass-priest knelt at the side—

54

MASTER. You may not go on, Amy, until you can deliver that piece with the proper expression.

AMY (*using broad gestures*). There were four of us about that bed.
> The mass-priest knelt at the side.
> I and his mother stood at the head.
> Over his feet lay the bride.
> We were quite sure that he was dead,
> Though his eyes were open wide.
> He did not die in the night,
> He did not die in the day,
> But in the morning twilight—

(*But Tom Sawyer appears at the door, and all action is suspended.*)

MASTER. Thomas Sawyer!

TOM. Sir?

MASTER. Come up here. Now, sir, why are you late again, as usual?

TOM. I — uh — I —

MASTER. Speak up.

TOM. Well — uh — I — I — (*defiantly*) — I stopped to talk with Huckleberry Finn!

MASTER (*horrified*). You — you did what?

TOM. Stopped to talk with Huck Finn.

MASTER. Thomas Sawyer, this is the most astounding confession I have ever listened to. No mere ruler will answer for this. Take off your jacket.

(*Tom does. The Master takes up a switch from the desk, and goes to the door.*)

Now, come here, sir.

(*They go out, and we hear the switching off stage, while the children flock to the doorway to see it. But when the Master comes back, they are all sitting primly in their seats again. The Master returns, propelling Tom ahead of him.*)

Now, sir, go and sit with the girls! And let this be a warning to you.

(*The room titters, and Alfred Temple looks justified, as Tom takes a seat beside Becky Thatcher.*)

The Fourth Reader will continue with its lesson. Amy Lawrence, you will finish learning the poem for tomorrow. Benjamin Rogers!

BEN. It was the schooner Hesperus—

MASTER. You will announce the title of your piece, Benjamin.

BEN. The Wreck of the Hesperus.
It was the schooner Hesperus
That — that —

MASTER *(prompting)*. That sailed.

BEN. That sailed — that sailed — that sailed the windy sea.

MASTER. The wintry sea.

(While the recitation continues in pantomime, Tom puts a peach in front of Becky Thatcher. She thrusts it away. He puts it back.)

TOM. Please take it. I got more.

(Becky pretends to be absorbed in her book.)

I'll draw you a picture.

BEN. Blue were her eyes — blue were her eyes—

MASTER *(prompting)*. As the.

BEN. Blue were her eyes as the —

MASTER. Zero, Benjamin. You may spend the rest of the hour studying the poem. Grace Miller!

GRACIE. A Lament.
O world! O time! O life!

MASTER *(correcting)*. Oh world, o life, o time.

GRACIE. O world! O life! O time!
On whose last steps I climb —

(This continues silently, while we hear Tom's conversation with Becky.)

BECKY *(trying to see Tom's slate)*. Let me see it.

TOM *(showing it)*. It's not much.

BECKY. It's nice. Make a man.

TOM *(dashing off a man in a few strokes)*. All right.

BECKY. It's a beautiful man. Now make me coming along.

TOM. Here you are. Only that's not pretty enough.

BECKY. Silly, it's ever so nice. I wish I could draw.

TOM. It's easy. I'll learn you.

BECKY. Oh, will you? When?

TOM. At recess. Do you go home for dinner?

BECKY. I'll stay if you will.

TOM. Good. That's a whack.

BECKY. What are you drawing now?

TOM. I'm not drawing. I'm writing.

BECKY. What are you writing?

TOM. Oh, it ain't anything.

BECKY. Yes it is.

TOM. No it ain't. You don't want to see.

BECKY. Yes I do. Please let me.

TOM. You'll tell.

BECKY. No I won't. Deed and double deed I won't.

TOM. You won't tell anybody at all? Ever, as long as you live?

BECKY. No, I won't ever tell anybody. Now, let me.

TOM. Oh, you don't want to see.

BECKY. Now that you treat me so, I will see!

(She pulls the slate away from him, but is overcome with shyness when she reads it.)

Oh, you bad thing!

(The master at this point bears down on Tom, and leads him by the ear to his own seat, beside Joe Harper.)

MASTER. Now, Thomas Sawyer, we'll see if you can behave yourself a little better in your own seat. Fifth Reader!

(Susan Harper, Jim Hollis, and Alfred Temple approach the Master's desk.)

James Hollis, what is the capital of the state of Missouri?

JIM. The capital of the state of Missouri is—the capital of the state of Missouri—

MASTER. Zero. Susan Harper, what is the capital of the state of Missouri?

SUSAN. Saint Louis.

MASTER. Zero. Alfred Temple.

ALFRED. The capital of the state of Missouri is Jefferson City.

MASTER. Correct. There, boys and girls, is an example of how a question should be answered. James Hollis, name another important city in the state of Missouri.

(While this goes on in pantomime, Tom at his seat pulls out his tick. Joe Harper is promptly interested.)

JOE. What's that you got, Tom?

TOM. It's a tick. What'd you think it was?

JOE. What you going to do with him?

TOM. Just play with him.

JOE. Suppose he crawls away from you.

TOM (*placing the tick on his slate*). I'll turn him back with my pencil.

JOE. He's coming over my way.

TOM. Don't let him go off, Joe. Turn him back.

JOE. Mighty lively little tick, ain't he?

TOM. Sure is. He's the first one this year, too. Quit proddin' him. Let him come over to my side.

JOE. Let me play with him a little.

TOM. Tell you what. I'll draw a line. Now as long as he's on your side of the slate, you can stir him up, and I'll leave him alone. But if you let him get away and get on my side, you're to leave him alone as long as I can keep him from crossing over.

JOE. All right. Go ahead. Start him up.

(*The tick scene proceeds in pantomime.*)

MASTER. James Hollis, what are the chief products grown in the state of Missouri?

JIM. The chief products grown in the state of Missouri are — are — fishing —

MASTER. Susan Harper, what are the chief products grown in the state of Missouri?

SUSAN. Corn.

MASTER. Corn and what else?

SUSAN. Just corn.

MASTER (*with a bland assurance that here at last will come the exemplary answer*). Alfred Temple, what is produced in the state of Missouri besides corn?

ALFRED. Whiskey.

MASTER. Ahem! Will you all open your books to page 165, and read just what it says.

(*The Fifth Reader turns pages industriously, while our attention is drawn to Tom and Joe again.*)

JOE. Tom, you let him alone.

58

Tom. I only want to stir him up a little, Joe.

Joe. No sir, it ain't fair. You just let him alone.

Tom. Blame it, I ain't going to stir him much.

Joe. Let him alone, I tell you.

Tom. I won't.

(The whole room is watching the tick scene now, for the Master is descending on the two boys.)

Joe. You shall. He's on my side of the line.

Tom. Look here, Joe Harper, whose is that tick?

Joe. I don't care whose tick he is. He's on my side of the line, and you shan't touch him.

Tom. Well, I just bet I will, though. He's my tick, and I'll do what I blame please with him, or die.

(But here the Master interferes, and both boys receive a sounding whack across the shoulders.)

Master. What is that thing?

Tom. Only just a tick.

(The Master, after one helpless, horrified glance, gingerly picks up the tick, and throws it out the door.)

Master. Let that be the end of that nonsense, Thomas Sawyer. Now. Everybody will get out your copy books. Open them to the page you have prepared for today.

(Everybody does, and the Master passes from one to the other, looking them over as he goes.)

Alfred Temple—ah! I should like to show the whole room just what a perfect page can look like. Compare that, for example, with this one. Thomas Sawyer, there are five big blots on this page, three words misspelled, and the writing is very irregular. You will remain during the recess period, and rewrite the whole lesson. The rest of you may put away your books. We now adjourn for recess.

(There is a general rush for the dinner pails, and then the door. Tom joins the movement, and whispers to Becky.)

Tom. Put on your bonnet and let on you're going home. Then when you get to the corner, give the rest of 'em the slip, and come back through the lane.

Becky. All right.

MASTER. Thomas Sawyer! Come back here. You are to spend your recess period working on your writing lesson, while the rest of the school is out playing. Now get out your book, sir, and go to work.

(Tom goes through the motions. The Master goes to the door.)

If you finish before the time is up, you may step outside for a few minutes of fresh air.

(The Master leaves, and the room is empty, except for Tom. He works feverishly on his writing lesson, closes the book, and gets up, going to the door to look for Becky. Then, going behind the Master's desk, he is elated to find the key in the drawer, and looking carefully around, he opens the drawer, slips a book out, and starts looking through it. Hearing a step outside, he hastily slips it back. Becky comes in.)

TOM. Becky! What a turn you did give me! I thought you were old Dobbin. Look!

(He shows her the key to the drawer.)

BECKY. What is it?

TOM. Old Dobbin's left the key in his drawer.

BECKY. What's in it?

TOM. His book. The Book of Mystery. He never has let anyone look at it. Shall we peep?

BECKY. I'm 'most scared to, Tom.

TOM. Oh, all right. I'd rather talk to you, anyway. Do you love rats?

BECKY. No! I hate them!

TOM. Well, I do too—live ones. But I mean dead ones, to swing around your head on a string.

BECKY. No, I don't care much for rats anyway. What I like is chewing gum.

TOM. I should say so. Wish I had some now.

BECKY. Do you? I've got some. I'll let you chew it awhile, but you must give it back to me.

TOM. Thanks. We'll take turns. Was you ever at a circus, Becky?

BECKY. Yes, and my pa's going to take me again sometime, if I'm good.

TOM. I'm going to be a clown in a circus when I grow up.

BECKY. Oh, are you? That'll be nice. They're so lovely—all spotted up.

Tom. Yes, and they get slathers of money—'most a dollar a day, Ben Rogers says. Say, Becky, was you ever engaged?

Becky. What's that?

Tom. Why, engaged to be married.

Becky. No.

Tom. Would you like to be?

Becky. I reckon so. I don't know. What is it like?

Tom. Like? Why, it ain't like anything. You only just tell a boy you won't ever have anybody but him—ever, ever, ever,—and then you kiss, and—and that's all. Anybody can do it.

Becky. Kiss? What do you kiss for?

Tom. Why, that, you know, is to—well, they always do that.

Becky. Everybody?

Tom. Why, yes, everybody that's in love with each other. Do you remember what I wrote on the slate, Becky?

Becky. Ye — yes.

Tom. What was it?

Becky. I — I shan't tell you.

Tom. Shall I tell you?

Becky. Ye — yes — but some other time.

Tom. No. Now.

Becky. No, not now. Tomorrow.

Tom. Oh no, now. Please, Becky. I'll whisper it. I'll whisper it ever so easy.

(Becky hangs her head, and Tom softly whispers in her ear.)

Now you whisper it to me—just the same.

Becky. No, Tom.

Tom. Yes, Becky.

Becky. Well, you turn your face away, so you can't see, and then I will. But you mustn't ever tell anybody, will you, Tom? Now you won't, will you?

Tom. No, indeed. Indeed I won't, Becky. Now!

(Becky leans toward him timidly, and whispers.)

Now, Becky, it's all done—all but the kiss.

61

(Becky covers her face with her hands.)

Aw, don't you be afraid of that. It ain't anything at all.

(Gently, he tugs her hands away, and kisses her. If desired, Song No. 3, "Now Will you Promise", may be used here.)

And you ain't ever to love anybody but me, Becky. And you ain't ever to marry anybody but me, never, never, and forever. Will you?

BECKY. No, I'll never love anybody but you, Tom, and I'll never marry anybody but you—and you ain't ever to marry anybody but me, either.

TOM. Certainly. Of course. That's part of it. And always coming to school, or when we're going home, you're to walk with me—when there ain't anybody looking. And you choose me, and I choose you at parties. Because that's the way you do when you're engaged.

BECKY. It's so nice. I never heard of it before.

TOM. Oh, it's ever so gay! Why, me and Amy Lawrence—

BECKY *(shocked)*. Tom!

TOM. I mean—

BECKY *(crying)*. Oh, Tom! Then I ain't the first you've ever been engaged to!

TOM. Oh, don't cry, Becky. I don't care for her any more.

BECKY *(sobbing)*. Yes you do, Tom. You know you do.

(Tom tries to comfort her, but she shakes him off.)

TOM. Becky, I—I don't care for anybody but you. Honest.

(Becky sobs. Tom pulls a brass and iron knob out of his pocket, and looks at it sadly.)

Becky, this is the very best thing I've got. Please, Becky, won't you take it?

(Becky strikes it to the floor. Tom gathers up his pride, and marches out through the door. Becky cries on for a minute, then lifts her head, and looks all about. No Tom. She runs to the door.)

BECKY. Tom! Tom! Come back, Tom!

(No response. Her heart is broken, and she falls to sobbing again, laying her head on the Master's desk. In the midst of her tears, her attention is drawn to the key in the drawer. Drying her eyes, but still sobbing spasmodically, she opens the drawer and gets out the Book of Mystery. She has just opened it when Tom rushes in the door. In her haste to hide the book, she tears a page.)

TOM. Did you call me, Becky?

BECKY (*wailing*). You made me tear it! I hate you, Tom Sawyer!

TOM. Becky!

BECKY. You're just as mean as you can be, to sneak up on a person like that.

TOM. How could I know you was looking at old Dobbin's book? I was clear down the road, and thought I heard you call me.

BECKY. You ought to be ashamed of yourself, Tom Sawyer. You know you're going to tell on me, and oh, what shall I do? I'll be whipped, and I never was whipped in school!

TOM. Never been licked in school? Shucks, what's a licking?

BECKY. Be so mean if you want to. I hate you. I hate you!

TOM. Who cares, Miss Smarty?

(*And he flings out, with his head held high, retrieving his precious knob as he goes. Becky's misery is now complete. She sinks to the floor beside the Master's desk, rocking with a despair too great for utterance. Alfred Temple peers cautiously into the room, and finding it apparently empty, makes a beeline for Tom's seat, where he spatters ink in his copy-book. Becky looks up in time to see him.*)

BECKY. Alfred Temple, what are you doing?

ALFRED. Oh-h! Uh—nothing.

BECKY. You are so, too. You're splattering ink on somebody's copy-book.

ALFRED. Well—what of it?

BECKY. It's the meanest thing a boy can do—that's what of it. And I've a good notion to tell on you.

ALFRED. Oh, don't tell on me, Becky. He had it coming to him. He gave me a licking this morning.

BECKY. Who?

ALFRED. Tom Sawyer.

BECKY. Is that Tom Sawyer's copy-book?

ALFRED. Yes. He has it coming to him.

BECKY. He certainly has something coming to him.

ALFRED. Then you won't tell, will you, Becky?

BECKY. I'm not promising.

ALFRED. You must like Tom Sawyer.

BECKY. I don't! I hate him!

ALFRED. Here comes old Cross-Patch. Recess is over, I guess. Remember, don't tell.

(Alfred leaps for his books, and when the Master enters, he is deep in study. Becky is in her own seat.)

MASTER. Well, Master Temple. This is very fine—very fine indeed, to see you spend even your recess time in studying.

ALFRED. Yes, sir. Books are my only companions.

MASTER. That is a very elevated thought. Becky, school is about to take in. Have you had any fresh air?

BECKY. Yes sir.

MASTER. Well, perhaps you can do me a favour by rounding the rest of the school in.

(The Master rings the bell, and Becky goes to summon the children.)

Alfred, since you are such an interested student, perhaps you would like to write a composition, and deliver it before the parents at the Examination Exercises.

ALFRED. I am always glad to do anything to improve my mind, sir.

MASTER. If you will speak to me about it at recess tomorrow, we may decide upon a subject for the composition.

(By this time, the pupils have all returned, hung up their dinner pails, and seated themselves.)

You may have the next fifteen minutes for a study period. Thomas Sawyer, have you completed that work in your copy-book?

TOM. Yes sir.

MASTER. Bring it up here.

(Tom presents the book with some show of assurance, but when the Master opens the book, his expression changes.)

Is this the work you call completed?

TOM *(gaping at it)*. I didn't leave it that way, sir.

MASTER. That's very likely, isn't it? Hold out your hand, sir.

(Tom takes his punishment with the ruler.)

Now, sir, you will stay this evening, after school, and rewrite that whole lesson twenty times. Sit down, sir, and I hope I shall not have to speak to you again today.

(Tom returns to his seat.)

JOE. Less see it, Tom. Craminee! Tom, you are the messiest boy I ever did see. How anybody could make that much mess with just a little old pen—

TOM (*scratching his head, puzzled*). I don't remember doin' it, Joe. Honest Injun, I don't.

MASTER (*with a roar—he has just opened his Book of Mystery*). Ahem!!! Who Tore This Book?

(*Dead silence.*)

Benjamin Rogers, did you tear this book?

BEN. No sir.

MASTER. Joseph Harper, did you?

JOE. No sir.

MASTER. Amy Lawrence, did you tear this book?

AMY. No sir

MASTER. Gracie Miller?

GRACIE. No sir.

MASTER. Susan Harper, did you do this?

SUSAN. No sir.

MASTER. Rebecca Thatcher, did you—no, look me in the face—did you tear this book?

(*Becky cannot speak.*)

TOM. I done it!

(*An electric silence lasts for a moment.*)

MASTER (*with gathering wrath*). You again, Master Sawyer! Come up here, sir. School is dismissed for the day!

(*The Master is rolling up his sleeves as the scene ends.*)

END OF ACT ONE

SCENE 1.   The graveyard. Three or four tombstones. An eerie light.

(Tom and Huck creep stealthily in, carrying their dead cat. An owl hoots mournfully. A dog howls offstage.)

TOM.   Here's the grave, Hucky.

HUCK.   We have to hide, though. The devils won't come if they see any humans around. Here.

(They settle themselves behind one of the tombstones.)

TOM.   Hucky, do you believe the dead people like it for us to be here?

HUCK.   I wish I knowed. It's awful solemn-like, ain't it?

TOM.   I bet it is. Say, Hucky, do you reckon Hoss Williams hears us talkin'?

HUCK.   O' course he does. Least, his sperrit does.

TOM.   I wisht I'd said *Mister* Williams. But I never meant any harm. Everybody called him Hoss.

HUCK.   A body can't be too partickler how they talk about these dead people, Tom.

TOM.   Sh-h-h!

HUCK.   What is it?

TOM.   Listen!

HUCK.   Oh, my! What a turn you did give me. That ain't nothin' but the wind.

TOM.   Oh, I'm mighty glad to hear it. I thought it was the sperrits.

HUCK.   Don't go grabbin' me so sudden like that, Tom.

TOM.   Sh-h-h! There it is again. Didn't you hear it?

HUCK.   I —

TOM.   There! Now you hear it!

HUCK.   Lord, Tom, they're comin'! They're comin' sure! What'll we do?

TOM.   I dunno. Think they can see us?

HUCK.   Oh, Tom, they can see in the dark, same as cats. I wisht I hadn't come.

TOM.   If we keep perfectly still, maybe they won't notice us.

HUCK.   I'll try to, Tom. But Lord, I'm all of a shiver!

TOM.   Look! See there? They've got a light. What is it, Hucky?

66

HUCK. It's devil-fire. Oh, Tom, this is awful.

(If desired, Song No. 4, "I'm A-Feared", may be used here.)

TOM. Here they come!

HUCK. It's the devils, sure enough! Three of 'em! Lordy, Tom, we're goners! Can you pray?

TOM. I'll try, but don't you be afeared. Now I lay me down to sleep—

HUCK. Sh-h-h-h!

TOM. What is it?

HUCK. They're humans! One of 'em is, anyway. One of 'em's old Muff Potter's voice.

TOM. No, 'Tain't so, is it?

HUCK. I bet I know it. Don't you stir nor budge. He ain't sharp enough to notice us.

TOM. Is he drunk again?

HUCK. Ain't he always? The old rip.

TOM. All right. I'll keep still. Now they're stuck. Can't find it. Here they come again. Now they're hot. Red hot! They're pointing right this time. Say, Huck, I know another of them voices. It's Injun Joe!

HUCK. That's so—that murderin' half-breed. Lordy, Tom, I'd druther they was devils a dern sight. What kin they be up to?

TOM. And the third one is young Dr. Robinson. He took dinner with us last Sunday. What's he doing with them two?

(The three men come in. Dr. Robinson is carrying a lantern. Injun Joe is carrying two spades. Muff Potter is pushing a wheelbarrow containing a rolled-up blanket.)

DR. ROBINSON. Here it is. Now. Muff, spread the blanket out on the ground.

MUFF. It's tied.

DR. ROBINSON. Cut the rope.

(Muff fumbles through his pockets for his knife, but lurches as he tries to cut the rope.)

Damn you, Muff Potter! Did you have to spend the whole evening in the tavern?

INJUN JOE. Here, Potter. Give me the knife.

(He takes Potter's knife, quickly cuts the rope, and spreads the blanket on the ground.)

67

DR. ROBINSON. Now hurry and get to work, men. The moon might come up at any moment.

MUFF. I'm not a-diggin' up no ghosts, Sawbones, without more pay. You'll just out with another five, or there she stays.

INJUN JOE. That's the talk!

DR. ROBINSON. Look here, what does this mean? You required your pay in advance, and I've paid you.

INJUN JOE. Yes, and you done more than that. Five years ago, you drove me away from your father's kitchen one night, when I come to ask for something to eat. You said I warn't there for no good, and when I swore I'd get even with you if it took a hundred years, your father had me jailed for a vagrant. Did you think I'd forgot? The Injun blood ain't in me for nothin'. And now I've got you, and you've got to settle, you know.

(He shakes his fist in the Doctor's face. The Doctor knocks him to the ground.)

MUFF. Here, now, don't you hit my pard.

(Muff lurches toward the Doctor, and grapples with him, but after a few rounds the Doctor knocks him out. Injun Joe has Muff's knife in his hand, and has been creeping, catlike and stooping, around the combatants, seeking an opportunity to use it. Now, as the Doctor flings himself free of Muff, Injun Joe springs on him, and drives the knife into the Doctor's breast. The Doctor gasps, reels, then falls, partly upon Potter, and lies still.)

INJUN JOE. That score is settled, damn you.

(He stoops, to rifle the Doctor's pockets, transferring the money to his own. Then, seeing Muff still unconscious, he puts the fatal knife in Muff's right hand, sinks back on his heels to wait a few moments, then begins to rouse Muff.)

Potter! Here, Potter!

(Muff begins to stir and groan. He sits up quickly, pushing the body from him, and taking in the dreadful scene.)

MUFF. Lord, how is this, Joe?

INJUN JOE. It's a dirty business. What did you do it for?

MUFF. I? I never done it.

INJUN JOE. Look here. That kind of talk won't wash.

MUFF. You mean I stabbed the Doctor?

INJUN JOE. It's your knife, ain't it? And it's in your hand.

MUFF *(casting the knife away from him)*. I thought I'd got sober, Joe. I'd no business to drink tonight. But it's in my head yet—worse than when we started. Can't recollect anything of it hardly. Tell me, Joe—honest, now, old feller—did I do it? I never meant to. 'Pon my soul and honour, I never meant to. Tell me how it was, Joe. Oh, it's awful! And him so young and promising.

INJUN JOE. Why, you two was scuffling, and he fetched you an awful blow under the chin, and you fell flat. Then up you come, all reeling and staggering like, and snatched the knife and jammed it into him, just as he fetched you another clip. And here you've laid, dead as a wedge till now.

MUFF. Oh, I didn't know what I was a-doing. I wish I may die this minute if I did. It was all on account of the whiskey, I reckon. I never used a weepon in my life before, Joe. I've fought, but never with weepons. They'll all say that. Joe, don't tell. Say you won't tell, Joe—that's a good feller. I've always likd you, Joe, and stood up for you. Don't you remember? You won't tell, will you, Joe?

INJUN JOE. No, you've always been fair and square with me, Muff Potter, and I won't go back on you now. There now, that's as fair as a man can say.

MUFF. Oh, Joe, you're an angel! I'll bless you for this the longest day I live.

INJUN JOE. Here, now, that's enough of that. This ain't any time for blubbering. You be off yonder way, and I'll go this. Move now, and don't leave any tracks behind you.

MUFF. I will, Joe. I will. I never meant to do it. 'Pon my soul, I didn't.

(He starts trotting off, then exits running.)

INJUN JOE *(watching him off)*. If he's as fuddled as he looks, he won't think of the knife until too late. Chicken-heart!

(He goes out in the opposite direction. The two boys, who have watched this scene with frozen horror, peer cautiously out from their hiding place, and are pulled irresistibly to the dead body.)

TOM. Is he dead, Hucky?

HUCK. Dead as a door-nail.

TOM. Are you sure?

HUCK. Ain't a spark of life in him, Tom.

TOM. Huckleberry, what do you reckon'll come of this?

HUCK. I reckon hangin'll come of it.

TOM. Do you, though?

HUCK. Why, I know it, Tom.

Tom. Who'll tell? Us?

Huck. What are you talking about? Suppose something happened, and Injun Joe didn't get hung. Why, he'd kill us some time or other, just as sure as you live.

Tom. That's just what I was thinking to myself. Hucky, are you sure you can keep mum?

Huck. Tom, we got to keep mum. You know that. That Injun devil wouldn't think any more of drownding us than a couple of cats, if we was to squeak about this, and they didn't hang him. Now look-a-here, Tom, less take and swear to one another—that's what we got to do. Swear to keep mum.

Tom. I'm agreed. Would you just hold hands and swear that we—

Huck. Oh, no, that wouldn't do for this. That's good enough for little rubbishy things, but there orter be writing about a big thing like this—and blood!

Tom. That's just what I think. Hand me that shingle there.

(And taking a piece of charcoal from his pocket, Tom laboriously writes the oath on a piece of pine shingle.)

Huck. Gee, Tom, I didn't know you could write that good. What's it say?

Tom *(reading as he writes)*. Huck Finn and Tom Sawyer swears they will keep mum about this, and wish they may drop down dead in their tracks if they ever tell and rot.

(If desired, this oath may be sung, instead of spoken, using Song No. 5, "Oath".)

Huck. Now we got to sign it in blood.

(He pulls a pin from his lapel, and starts to prick his finger.)

Tom. Hold on. Don't do that. A pin's brass. It might have verdigrease on it.

Huck. What's verdigrease?

Tom. It's p'ison, that's what it is. You just swallow some of it once. You'll see. Here, use a needle.

(Both boys prick their finger with Tom's needle, and make their mark on the shingle.)

Huck. Tom, does this keep us from ever telling—always?

Tom. Of course it does. It don't make any difference what happens, we got to keep mum. We'd drop down dead—don't you know that?

Huck. Yes, I reckon that's so.

70

(A dog howls offstage.)

Tom! Listen to that dog! Which of us does he mean?

Tom. I dunno. Peep out and see. Quick!

Huck. No, you, Tom.

Tom. I can't—I can't do it, Huck.

Huck. Please, Tom. There it is again.

Tom *(as the dog howls again)*. Oh, Lordy, I'm thankful! It's Mr. Harbison's bulldog. I know his voice.

Huck *(much relieved)*. Oh, that's good. I tell you, Tom, I was scared to death. I'd a bet anything it was a stray dog.

(The dog hows again.)

Oh, my, that ain't no Harbison's bulldog! Do look, Tom. I just know it's a stray dog!

Tom *(screwing up his courage, and peering off in the direction Muff Potter took)*. Oh, Huck, it is!

Huck. Quick, Tom! Which of us does he mean?

Tom. Huck, he must mean us both. We're right together.

Huck. Oh, Tom, I reckon we're goners.

Tom. It's a sure sign, Huck.

Huck. I reckon there ain't no mistake about where I'll go. I been so wicked.

Tom *(beginning to sniffle)*. Dad fetch it! This comes of playing hookey, and doing everything a fellow's told not to do. I might 'a been good, like Sid, if I'd 'a tried. But no, I wouldn't, of course. But I lay, if I ever get off this time, I'll just waller in Sunday schools!

Huck *(sniffling too)*. You bad? Confound it, Tom Sawyer, you're just old pie, alongside of what I am. Oh, Lordy, Lordy, I wisht I only had half your chance.

Tom. Look, Hucky, he's got his back to us!

Huck. Well, he has, by Jingoes! Did he before?

Tom. Yes, he did. But I, like a fool, never noticed. Oh, this is bully, you know. Now who can he mean?

Huck. Tom, Muff Potter went off that way.

Tom. Geeminy! It's him!

Huck. And a stray dog don't mean just bad luck, Tom. It means sure death.

Tom. Huck, let's get home.

HUCK. Keep mum.

TOM. You just bet I'll keep mum.

HUCK. Sh-h-h-h!

TOM. Sh-h-h-h!

(Giving the dead body a wide berth, they go off together.)

ACT TWO

SCENE 2. A village street. A high board fence. A barrel on one side.

(Tom appears with a bucket of whitewash and a long-handled brush. Surveying the endless reaches of fence, he sighs despairingly, then dips his brush and passes it along the topmost plank once or twice. Comparing the insignificant whitewashed streak with the far-reaching continent of unwhitewashed fence, he sits down on the barrel, discouraged. Aunt Polly marches in briskly, takes in the scene.)

AUNT POLLY *(whacking Tom on the seat with her slipper)*. Is this the way you paint the fence?

(Tom leaps to his feet, and starts whitewashing with vigour.)

TOM. I was just gettin' ready to start.

AUNT POLLY. Remember, this is only the first coat.

TOM *(stopping his exertions)*. First coat?

AUNT POLLY. I want three coats on this fence, Tom.

TOM. Aunt Polly, this is a holiday. Can't a boy play on a holiday?

AUNT POLLY. When you finish your work.

TOM. All the other boys are playin' this morning. We was goin' to have a big battle over on Cardiff Hill. Joe Harper's army and mine.

AUNT POLLY. You heard what I said, Tom.

TOM. Well, can't I paint the inside today, 'stead of the outside?

AUNT POLLY. What difference does that make?

TOM. Everybody in tarnation'll see me here on the sidewalk.

AUNT POLLY. Well, what of it?

TOM. I just told you, none of the other boys have to work on a holiday.

AUNT POLLY *(going)*. You wouldn't either, if you'd do your work on other days. Three coats, now.

(She leaves.)

Том. Jeehosophat! And look comin'!

(Out of his despair is born an inspiration. He falls to whitewashing with elaborate care, handling the brush with an artist's touch, then standing back to get the full effect of it. Alfred Temple comes in.)

ALFRED *(chewing on an apple)*. Hee-eee! Lookit Tom Sawyer! Tom has to paint his Aunt Polly's fence on a holiday! Hee-eee! Tom's up a stump, ain't you, Tom? You got to work, haven't you, Tom?

Том *(turning around to look at him with an air of surprise)*. Why, it's you, Alfred. I warn't noticin'.

ALFRED. I'm going swimming, I am. Don't you wish you could? But of course you'd rather work, wouldn't you? 'Course you would.

Том. What do you call work?

ALFRED. Why, ain't that work?

Том. Maybe it is, and maybe it ain't. All I know is, it suits Tom Sawyer.

ALFRED. Oh, come now, you don't mean to let on you like it?

Том. Like it? Well, I don't see why I oughtn't to like it. Does a boy get a chance to whitewash a fence every day?

ALFRED. Well, no, I guess he doesn't.

Том. Well, then.

ALFRED. Say, Tom, let me whitewash a little.

Том. No—no. I reckon it wouldn't hardly do, Alfred. You see, Aunt Polly's awful partickler about this fence—right here on the street, you know.

ALFRED. Oh, come, now. Lemme try. Only just a little.

Том. Alfred, I'd like to, honest Injun. But Aunt Polly's so partickler. If you was to tackle this fence, and anything was to happen to it—

ALFRED. Oh, shucks, I'll be just as careful. Now lemme try. Say, I'll give you the core of my apple when I finish eating it.

Том. Well—no. No, Alfred. Now don't. I'm afeared—

ALFRED. I'll give you all of it, Tom.

Том *(taking the apple)*. Well, all right. I'll let you brush for just a minute. Now be mighty careful.

ALFRED. I will.

Том. Go slow around the edges now. I can't have any splatters on my fence.

ALFRED. Is that all right?

73

Tom (*his mouth full of apple*). Better. Be sure to fill in all those cracks. Well, here comes Joe Harper. Hi, Joe! Lookin' for me?

Joe (*entering*). You're a fine commander. Don't even come to your own battle.

Tom. That's so. We were goin' to fight today weren't we?

Joe. You don't mean to say you forgot?

Tom. Well, I sort of thought of it early this morning, but when Aunt Polly said she wanted me to paint this fence, why, everything else just sort of slipped my mind.

Joe. You mean you wanted to paint this fence?

Tom. 'Course. It's very partickler work. I'm just lettin' Alfred work on it for a few minutes.

Joe. What you givin' him for doin' your work?

Tom. You mean what'd he give me for lettin' him? He gave me this apple.

Joe (*impressed, watches Alfred a moment*). Tell you what. I got a kite I'll give you if you'll let me paint awhile.

Tom. Aren't you goin' to have the battle?

Joe. We've already had it. Beat your army to pieces.

Tom. Well I tell you, Joe. I wasn't aimin' to let anybody else work on that fence, but now that I let Alfred—your home-made newspaper kite, without any string?

Joe. I'll help you make the string.

Tom. Well, I guess maybe you can take a few strokes, soon as Alfred gets through. You have to be awful careful, you know, Joe, on account of this is the front fence, right on the sidewalk, and Aunt Polly said—

(*Ben Rogers and Jim Hollis burst in.*)

Ben. Hey, Tom, why didn't you come to the battle?

Jim. How do you expect us to fight without any general?

Ben. The boys want to get another general.

Jim. Well, by hokey, lookit Alfred Temple. What's he doin', Tom?

Tom. He's just paintin' until Joe Harper gets his turn.

Ben. No! Is it fun?

Tom. Fun? It's fun enough for Tom Sawyer to miss a battle on account of.

Jim. No—really? Is that why you didn't come to the battle, Tom?

74

Tom. I reckon it is.

Ben. Let me have a turn, Tom, after Joe.

Jim. Ah, no. Let me. I'm your adjutant general.

Ben. Tom, you owe me a good turn. I let you copy my 'rithmetic last week.

Tom. Wait a minute. Don't you think I want to paint a little myself?

Jim. Well, you might just let us try it, mightn't you?

Tom. No—no. I don't think I better. Why, you all might ruin that fence.

(If desired, Song No. 6, "Whitewash Song", may be used here.)

Jim. Please, Tom.

Ben. You let Alfred and Joe paint on it, didn't you?

Tom. Well—Alfred give me an apple for his turn. And Joe give me his kite.

Ben. Oh.

Jim *(ransacking his pockets for treasure)*. I'll give you a handle off a leather grip.

Ben. I'll give you a key, Tom. It won't fit nothin', but it's brass. And I'll throw in a piece of blue bottle glass to look through.

Tom. Oh, all right. But see what you boys have let me in for. If anybody else comes along, I won't get a chance to paint myself.

(Sid rushes in, breathless.)

Sid. Hey, fellows, listen! You know young Doc Robinson? He's been found killed over in the graveyard!

(The boys drop everything, and mill around him. Tom hangs nervously on the edge, where Huck Finn has slipped in unobtrusively, and joined him.)

Joe. Sid, you don't mean it!

Jeff. How'd it happen?

Alfred. Who killed him?

Ben. Did you see it?

Sid. I saw the Sheriff go by, with a bunch of men, on their way to the graveyard. So I went along. And when we got there—

Mrs. Harper *(offstage)*. Joe! Joe!

Joe. Ma'am?

Mrs. Harper *(off)*. You come right here this minute!

JOE. Oh, Mom, I can't. I'm busy.

MRS. HARPER *(off)*. You march yourself right home, young man. Or I'll come and get you!

JOE *(going reluctantly)*. Now what have I done?

BEN. Go on, Sid. What happened?

SID. There was a big crowd standin' around. Everybody was there. But I pushed around till I saw it—and oh, it was awful! The grass was all over blood. He'd been stabbed with a knife!

JIM. Don't they know who done it?

SID. It was Muff Potter's knife!

BOYS. Old Muff Potter?

SID. And then the Preacher he spied Muff Potter kind of skulkin' behind a tree, and the Sheriff went and got him, and he was a-shakin' all over, and when they made him look at the dead doctor, he just covered up his face and cried.

BEN. Didn't he say nothin'?

SID. No, he just cried. And then the Sheriff told Injun Joe to put the body in the wagon, and—and—

ALFRED. What?

BEN. Go on.

SID. And—and just as he picked it up, the wound bled a little!

(There is a horrified hush from the little group.)

TOM. Don't that kind of look like Injun Joe did it?

HUCK *(intensely, to Tom)*. Sh-h-h!

SID. Listen. The body was in three feet of Muff Potter when it done it!

BOYS. How awful!

ALFRED. Well—what can you expect of a low character like that?

JIM. He's onery, all right—but I wouldn't have figgered him for a killer.

BEN. And why would he want to kill the doctor?

SID. Look! Here they come!

TOM. Hucky, the Sheriff's got him!

HUCK. And that half-breed, Injun Joe, right behind 'em.

(The Sheriff enters, ostentatiously leading a cringing Muff Potter by the arm, and followed by the townspeople in an angry mood, Injun Joe among them.)

76

MUFF (*sobbing*). I didn't do it, friends, 'Pon my word and honour, I didn't. I never done it.

(*If desired, Song No. 7, "Who Done It?", may be used here.*)

SHERIFF. This is a serious business, Potter.

MUFF. Oh, Sheriff, it's awful! But I didn't do it.

SHERIFF. Who's accused you?

MUFF. Oh, Joe, you promised me you'd never—

SHERIFF. Is that your knife?

MUFF. Oh, Lordy! I shouldn't have left it there. Tell 'em, Joe. Tell 'em. It ain't any use any more.

INJUN JOE. Do you want me to, Muff?

MUFF. Yes. Tell 'em. No use tryin' to keep it down now.

INJUN JOE. Well, Sheriff, you see, the young Doctor, he asked me to help him do a little job. I didn't know what kind of a job it was, but I'll do anything to turn an honest penny. Well, he told me to bring some help, and I rounded up Muff Potter. Last night, when we met him, he give us spades and a wheelbarrow, and we all started out for the graveyard. When I finally found that he wanted us to rob Hoss Williams' grave, I stood right up and said I wouldn't do it. And then the young Doctor he doubled up his fists and knocked me down. But I heard Potter here say, "Don't you hit my pard!" And when I got up, the young Doctor was lying on the ground, and Potter had his knife out, dripping blood.

SHERIFF. Will you say all this on oath, Joe?

INJUN JOE. Yes sir.

SHERIFF. Come along to the courthouse.

(*The little procession moves off, followed by all but Tom and Huck.*)

TOM (*gasping for breath*). Did you hear Injun Joe tell that whopper, Huck? And it didn't even thunder and lightning!

HUCK. You know why?

TOM. No. Why?

HUCK (*mysteriously*). He's sold himself to the devil!

TOM. No! Is that so?

HUCK. Old Mother Hopkins says so. And she's a witch.

TOM. Huck, have you told anybody about that?

HUCK. 'Course I haven't.

Tom. Never a word?

Huck. Never a solitary word, so help me.

Tom. They couldn't anybody get you to tell, could they, Huck?

Huck. Get me to tell? Why, if I wanted that half-breed Injun to kill me, they could get me to tell maybe. They ain't no different way.

Tom. Are you sure, Huck?

Huck. 'Course I'm sure. Long as I'm in my right mind. What's the matter with you, Tom?

Tom. Huck, Sid says I talk in my sleep!

Huck. Tom!

Tom. Aunt Polly won't let me sleep by myself.

Huck. Tom, you better leave home.

Tom. Where would I go?

(Joe Harper marches in, with vengeance in his eye. The boys spring apart, guiltily.)

Joe. Tom, I just wanted to tell you boys good-bye.

Tom. Good bye? Where you goin'?

Joe. I'm going to run away. It's very plain that my mother is tired of me, and wants me out of the way. Tell her I hope she'll be happy, Tom, and never be sorry that she drove me out into the great world.

Tom. Joe, where you goin'?

Joe. I don't know. But don't forget me, Tom. Nor you either, Huck.

Tom. Forget you? I'm comin' along. And so is Huck. Ain't you, Huck?

Huck. Sure, I'll come. Where to?

Joe. You mean you fellows want to run away too?

Tom. Sure, it's just the ticket. Only yesterday Aunt Polly whacked me for feedin' the cat some medicine I was supposed to take. Maybe when she doesn't have me here to fuss at, maybe then she'll be sorry.

Huck. This'll be fun. Where'll we go?

Joe. Let's go out in a desert somewhere, and be hermits, and live in a cave. And after while, we'll die of cold and hunger, and then they'll be sorry. And maybe next time, Mother won't whip her boy for drinkin' cream that he never even saw.

Tom. I got a better idea than that. Let's be pirates, and lead a life of crime!

78

HUCK. What's pirates?

TOM. They're a kind of robber gang that holds up ships and things. Listen, let's sneak out a raft and go over to Jackson's Island. That's about three miles down the river. We better take a few supplies with us. Can you get anything, Joe?

JOE. I'll try. Anyway, we can always catch fish over on Jackson's Island.

HUCK. I can bring some tobacco.

TOM. We'll meet at the old wharf at midnight. And we better have a password, so's to 'dentify each other.

HUCK. A password? What you want a password for?

TOM. Why, pirates always have to have a password. Now everybody think.

(They all think hard for a minute.)

I know! Blood!

JOE. That's good!

HUCK. Say, what's the use to put on all that stuff? Everbody'll be down in the village tonight for the fireworks. There won't be anybody at the wharf.

TOM. How you talk! If we're goin' to be pirates, we got to act like pirates, don't we?

HUCK. How do pirates act?

TOM *(dramatizing it)*. They go—"Hist! If the foe stirs, let him have it to the hilt, for dead men tell no tales!"

(If desired, Song No. 8, "Pirate Song", may be used here.)

Now, let's swear allegiance.

(They cross hands in a mysterious way, known only to them.)

I, Tom Sawyer, the Black Avenger of the Spanish Main—

JOE. I, Joe Harper, the Terror of the Seas—

HUCK. I, Huck Finn, the—the—

TOM *(prompting him)*. Huck Finn the Red-Handed—

HUCK. Huck Finn the Red-Handed—

ALL THREE. Swear to be a faithful pirate to the death! . . . Blood!

(And they go off in different directions, with many piratical gestures to keep mum.)

END OF ACT TWO

ACT THREE

SCENE 1. Jackson's Island. A practical hollow-tree-stump, two or three rocks, some practical bushes and loose branches, a camp-fire. Afternoon light.

(The three boys are sitting contentedly around the fire, Huck smoking a corn-cob pipe.)

JOE. Ain't it gay?

TOM. It's nuts! What would the boys say if they could see us?

JOE. I reckon they'd just die to be here, eh, Hucky?

HUCK. I reckon so. Anyways, I'm suited.

TOM. It's just the life for me. Ain't you glad you decided to be a pirate, Joe, 'stead of a hermit?

JOE. Oh, a heap sight. I'd a good deal rather be a pirate, now that I've tried it.

HUCK. What do pirates have to do?

TOM. Oh, they have just a bully time—take ships and burn 'em, and get the money and bury it. And kill everybody on the ships— make 'em walk the plank.

JOE. And they carry off the women. They don't kill the women.

TOM. No, they don't kill the women. They're too noble. And the women's always beautiful, too.

JOE. And don't they wear the bulliest clothes! All gold and silver and diamonds!

HUCK. Who?

JOE. Why, the pirates.

HUCK *(looking at his own bedraggled appearance)*. I reckon I ain't dressed fitten fer a pirate, but I ain't got none but these.

TOM. Oh, the fine clothes will come fast enough, after we begin our adventures.

JOE. These clothes'll do to start with, though rich pirates generally start with the regular costume.

TOM. Listen!

(A deep, sullen boom is heard in the distance.)

JOE. What is it?

TOM. I wonder.

HUCK. 'Tain't thunder, because thunder—

Tom. Hark! Listen, don't talk!

Joe. Let's look. It's on the river.

(They all strain off, in the direction of the river. Tom gets up on the tree-stump, to see better.)

Tom. It's the ferry-boat. Look at all the people on it.

Huck. Is there a picnic or something?

(The boom is heard again.)

Tom I know! Somebody's drownded!

Huck. That's it! They done that last summer when Bill Turner got drownded. They shoot a cannon over the water, and that makes him come to the top.

Tom. Yes, and they take loaves of bread and put quicksilver in 'em, and set 'em afloat. And wherever there's anybody that's drowned, they'll float right there and stop.

Joe. Yes, I've heard about that. I wonder what makes the bread do that.

Tom. Oh, it ain't the bread so much. I reckon it's mostly what they say over the bread before they start it out.

Huck. But they don't say anything over it. I've seen 'em, and they don't.

Tom. Well, that's funny. But maybe they say it to themselves.

Joe. That must be so, because how could an ignorant lump of bread find a drowned person, unless it had a spell set on it to send it to the very place?

Huck. Who do you reckon is drownded?

Tom *(looking off toward the boat again)*. By jings, I wish I was over there now.

Huck. I do too. I'd give heaps to know who it is.

Joe. Nobody was drownded before we left last night, was they?

Huck. It must have happened this morning.

Tom. Boys! I know who's drownded! It's us!

Huck. Us? We ain't drownded.

Joe. But they think we are. Glory be!

Huck. Shucks, sure enough?

Tom. Of course it is. Who else could it be? They've just had time to miss us.

Joe. Just think, to get the big ferry-boat out, just for us!

Tom. Let's celebrate! What shall we do?

Joe. I know. Let's smoke!

Tom. Bully. Will you give us a pipe, Huck?

Huck. Sure. Plenty of corn-cobs, and I've got a whole sheaf of leaf tobacco.

Tom. I smoked a cigar made out of grapevines onct.

Huck. Shucks, that ain't nothin' to a corn-cob pipe. Here, light up.

(*The two boys, with awed spirits, light their pipes at the fire.*)

Joe (*coughing a little*). The smoke tastes kind of hot, but I like it.

Tom. Why, it's just as easy. If I'd a knowed this was all, I'd 'a learnt long ago.

Joe. So would I. It's just nothing.

Tom. Why, many a time I've looked at people smoking, and thought, "Well, I wish I could do that." But I never thought I could.

Joe. That's just the way with me, ain't it, Huck? You've heard me talk just that way, haven't you, Huck? I'll leave it to Huck if I haven't.

Huck. Yes, heaps of times.

(*He looks off toward the ferry-boat.*)

They're followin' the shore pretty close. Reckon they thought we got drownded in swimmin'.

Tom. They haven't missed the raft yet, I guess.

Joe. I believe I could smoke this pipe all day. I don't feel sick.

Tom. Neither do I. I bet I could smoke all day. But I bet you Ben Rogers couldn't.

Joe. Ben Rogers? Why, he'd keel over with just two draws.

Tom. 'Deed he would. Say, Joe, I wish the boys could see us now.

Joe. So do I.

Tom. Say, boys, don't say anything about it. And some time when they're around, I'll come up to you and say, kind of loud—"Joe, got a pipe?" And you'll say, kind of careless-like, as if it warn't anything, you'll say—"Yes, I got my old pipe, and another one, but the tobacco ain't very good." And I'll say—"Oh, that's all right, if it's strong enough." And then you'll out with the pipes, and we'll light up, just as calm. And then, just see 'em look.

Joe. By jings, that'll be gay. I wish it was now.

Tom. So do I. And when we tell 'em we learned when we was off pirating, won't they wish they'd been along!

82

JOE. I just bet they will.

(But neither Tom nor Joe is feeling quite so easy now, and after a few agonized glances offstage—)

I've lost my knife. I reckon I better go and find it.

TOM. I'll help you. You go over that-a-way, and I'll hunt around by the spring.

HUCK. I'll come along if you want.

JOE. No, never mind.

HUCK. We can find it.

(And Joe and Tom vanish rather suddenly, leaving Huck alone by the camp-fire, puffing away on his corn-cob pipe. The lights dim out on this scene.)

ACT THREE

SCENE 2. On the Island, the fourth day out. Early morning.

(A frying-pan is on the camp-fire. Huck is up on the tree-stump, shading his eyes, and looking off toward the river. Joe's voice can be heard offstage, calling for Tom.)

JOE *(off)*. Tom! Tom!

(Huck, unsuccessful in his search, goes to tend the fish. Joe comes in.)

Where would he go? In four days on this island, we've explored all the places. Huck, do you reckon he's deserted?

HUCK. No. Tom's true-blue, Joe. He wouldn't desert. That'd be a disgrace for a pirate.

JOE *(thoughtfully)*. I don't know.

HUCK. It is awful lonesome.

JOE. It sure is. Fish ready?

HUCK. Almost.

JOE. Tom left his rubber ball, and three fish-hooks, and a while alley. I reckon they are ours, aren't they?

HUCK. The writin' says they are if he ain't back in time for breakfast.

(Tom strides grandly in.)

TOM. Which he is!

HUCK. Tom!

JOE. What have you been up to, Tom Sawyer?

83

Tom. I'll tell you when I've had some breakfast.

Huck. Fish is 'most ready.

Joe. I hate fish.

Tom. Smells good. Oh, ain't this gay?

Joe. Tom, your hair's wet. Have you been over to mainland?

Tom. Been swimmin'. Here Huck, I'll help you.

Joe. Breakfast is about over, I reckon, over there.

Tom. Not such a breakfast as this. Just look.

Joe. I want to go home.

(If desired, Song No. 9, "I'm Lonesome", may be used here.)

Tom. Ah, Joe, you don't mean it. Why, home ain't shucks to pirating.

Huck. Fish is ready, Joe. Here, you can have the biggest one.

Joe. Oh, boys, let's give it up. I want to go home.

Tom. Ah, Joe, eat some breakfast. You'll feel better by and by.

Joe *(blinking back the tears)*. It's so lonesome.

Tom. Just think of the fishing that's here.

Joe. I don't care for fishing. I want to go home.

Tom. But Joe, there ain't another such swimming place anywhere.

Joe. Swimming's no good. I don't care for it, somehow, when there ain't anybody to say I shan't go in. I mean to go home.

Tom. Oh, shucks. Baby! You want to see your mother, I reckon.

Joe *(snuffling)*. Yes, I do want to see my mother. And you would too, if you had one. I'm no more Baby than you are.

Tom. Well, we'll let the little cry-baby go home to his mother, won't we, Huck? Poor thing—does it want to see its mother? And so it shall. You like it here, don't you, Huck? We'll stay, won't we?

Huck *(without conviction)*. Well—I reckon so.

Joe *(openly crying now)*. I'll never speak to you again as long as I live. There, now, Tom Sawyer.

Tom. Who cares? Nobody wants you to. Go 'long home and get laughed at. Oh, you're a fine pirate. Huck and me ain't cry-babies. We'll stay, won't we, Huck? Let him go if he wants to. I reckon we can get along without him, perhaps.

Joe. Never you mind, Tom Sawyer. Just wait till I get my things.

(He stamps off.)

Tom (*to his departing back*). Go ahead, Smarty.

(*But Huck too has picked up Joe's mood, and is quietly whistling, while he eyes Joe's preparations offstage.*)

Don't worry, Huck. We don't need him.

(*Huck, still whistling, rises to keep Joe under observation offstage.*)

Here, let's divide this fish.

(*Huck declines with a gesture, without interrupting his whistling. Tom eats the fish without appetite.*)

Anyway, Joe'll change his mind, I expect, by the time he gets dressed.

Huck (*breaking his ominous silence*). What if he don't?

Tom. Well—but he will.

Huck (*after a painful pause*). I want to go too, Tom.

Tom. What?

Huck. Oh, Tom, it's gettin' so lonesome, and now it'll be worse, with Joe gone. Let's us go too, Tom.

Tom. I won't. You can all go, if you want to. I mean to stay.

Huck. Tom, I better go.

Tom. Well, go along. Who's hendering you?

Huck. I wisht you'd come too, Tom.

Tom. Well, you wish wrong, that's all.

(*Huck turns sorrowfully away, and starts off toward Joe, but stops at Tom's exclamation.*)

Listen!

Huck. What is it?

Tom. Sh-h-h-h! There, hear it? That ain't Joe, is it?

Huck. No. Joe went off that-a-way. Oh, my!

(*Tom gets up on the tree-stump, and looks toward the river.*)

Who is it, Tom?

Tom. It's a man. He's getting out of a boat. Cover up the fire, Hucky. He's comin' this way.

(*They hide the pan of fish under a pile of leaves, and cover the fire with green branches.*)

Huck. Come on, Tom. Let's run.

Tom.   Keep still. We'll be safer under this bush.

Huck.   But Tom, suppose Joe was to march right onto him?

Tom.   Craminee! That's so. Let's run!

Huck (*pulling him down under the bush*).   Too late. Here he comes.

Tom.   Huck, look. It's Injun Joe! We should 'a run, like you said.

Huck.   Lordy! I wisht we was out of this.

Tom.   Sh-h-h! Don't breathe.

(*Injun Joe enters, looks back toward the river, then spits scornfully.*)

Injun Joe.   Pesky town!

(*He looks searchingly all around him.*)

Now, which tree-stump was it? 'Twas more inland than this. Ah!

(*He strides purposefully off.*)

Tom.   He's lookin' for a tree-stump.

Huck.   I'm glad it warn't that one.

Tom.   But suppose he finds Joe. He'd kill him.

Huck.   I'll try to crawl out, and warn him.

Tom.   We dassen't. Here he comes back.

(*Injun Joe re-enters, still searching.*)

Injun Joe.   That's funny. Maybe 'twas this one, after all.

(*He goes directly to the tree-stump the boys have been using all along, reaches into a hollow-place in it. A look of satisfaction spreads over his face.*)

Ah-h-h!

(*He draws out a bag that clinks cheerfully, as he holds it up in exaltation.*)

Six hundred dollars!

(*He hugs it to him, gloating, then sobers as he thinks back to the hollow in the stump.*)

Wait a minute.

(*He peers back into the stump.*)

Hello. What's this?

(He reaches inside with one hand, and feels. Then he goes to work seriously with both hands, tugging and struggling, finally lifts out a heavy old wooden box.)

Man!

(Drawing out his knife, he goes to work prying the box open, then gasps.)

It's money!

(He dumps out a mound of gold coins.)

Gold money! There must be thousands of dollars here! Part of the swag from Murrell's gang, I reckon. Tree, you sure know how to keep a secret.

(He starts scooping the gold back into the box, then eyes the tree-stump again.)

Reckon you're the safest hiding place, after all.

(He starts to put the heavy box back into the hollow, then stops as he sniffs.)

I smell fire.

(Covering the box and the money-bag with his jacket, he begins looking for the camp-fire. The boys, who have watched this scene with bulging eyes, are now frozen with terror. Injun Joe locates the camp-fire, and kicks the branches off.)

There's somebody on this island. Somebody's camping here.

(Drawing his knife, he searches all around, circling the bush where the boys are hidden. He peers into the far distance in all directions, then shrugs, and puts his knife away.)

Well, let them. They'll never know I've been here. But old tree, I'm not leaving the money here, for them to find. Not exactly.

(Straining, as he picks up the heavy treasure box, and the money-bag.)

Old tree, you've been a good friend. But now, this'll be safer in the cave.

(He carries his burden off toward the river. The boys crouch close, listening for his departure. Finally, Tom ventures out, and climbs cautiously on the tree-stump to look off.)

HUCK. Is he gone?

TOM. He's puttin' the treasure box in the boat. Don't move yet. He's coverin' it up with his jacket. Now he's got in. He's pushin' off. He's gone.

HUCK *(creeping out into the open)*. Whew, that was close! By jings, Tom, why didn't we think to look in that holler?

Tom. Ain't that the rottenest luck! Here we been playin' around over that stump every day. He's out in the current now.

(Climbs down from his perch. Huck is examining the hollow in the stump.)

Huck. Don't reckon there could be anything more in here.

Tom. Nah, 'tain't likely. Huck, did you hear him say he was goin' to put that money in the cave?

Huck. Yes—and there ain't but one cave around here, and that's MacDougall's.

Tom. Yes, but that cave is five miles long. And there's parts of it nobody's ever been into.

Huck. I'd hate to go in there lookin' for it, and run into him.

Tom. Oh, Lordy, Huck, don't say it.

Huck. I'd ruther be poor, a dern sight.

(Joe enters, his trousers pulled over his trunks, ready to swim for the mainland. He carries a partially-consumed ham.)

Joe. Well, good-bye, Huck.

Tom. You can't go yet, Joe. 'Tain't safe.

Joe *(pointedly ignoring Tom)*. I'm leavin' this for you, Huck.

Huck. Wait till that boat gets across. Look.

Joe *(mounting the tree-stump, looks toward the river)*. What of it? I don't care if he sees me. The whole town'll see me soon enough.

Tom. Joe, that's Injun Joe in that boat.

(Joe is impressed, but ignoring Tom, He looks to Huck.)

Huck. Really.

Joe. No!

Huck. If you'll wait till he gets away, Joe, I'll come with you.

Tom. Hucky!

Huck. Oh, come on, Tom. Let's all go back.

Tom. No!

Huck. You think it over, Tom. We'll wait for you when we get to shore.

Tom. Well, you'll wait a blame long time, that's all.

Joe. Come on, Huck. Let him be stubborn if he wants to.

(Huck slowly rolls up his over-long pants.)

We can lay low in the sand till Injun Joe is out of sight.

(He stamps off. The tension between Tom and Huck is terrible. Tom is torn, but his pride will not let him back down.)

Huck *(sadly)*. So long, Tom.

(He departs after Joe.)

(Until now, Tom has made a great show of unconcern. But left by himself, his inner turmoil becomes painfully evident. All is very lonely and still. If desired, the strains of Song No. 9, "I'm Lonesome", may be repeated here. Tom dashes his sleeve across his eyes, then hardens himself.)

Tom. I won't! They won't have the nerve to go through with it, anyway.

(He climbs up on the stump, to follow their progress.)

They're wadin' out!

(Pride loses.)

Hey, fellows, wait, wait!

(He dashes off, in their direction.)

(Off). I want to tell you something!

Huck *(off)*. Joe! Hold on! Tom's a-comin'!

Tom *(off)*. Come back! I got somethin' to tell you!

Joe *(off)*. What?

Tom *(off)*. Something big. Hurry!

(Tom pulls a reluctant Joe in, followed by Huck.)

Joe. Looky here, Tom Sawyer. You ain't a-holdin' me here. I mean to go home.

Huck. Me, too.

Tom. And so do I. But we can't go now!

Huck. What's to keep us?

Joe. Why not?

Tom. 'Cause they think we're drownded, and they're goin' to have a funeral for us, that's why!

Joe. What?

Huck. A funeral? For us?

Joe. How can they?

Huck. It makes you feel right creepy. You ain't makin' this up, are you, Tom?

JOE. Listen, Tom Sawyer, how do you know this?

TOM (a little ashamed). Last night, after you fellows went to sleep, I slipped off and hooked a ride over to the mainland.

HUCK. Tom, you didn't!

JOE. I knew you was up to something.

HUCK. Didn't they see you?

TOM. 'Course not. What do you take me for? I hid.

JOE. Then how'd you find out about the—the funeral?

TOM. I crawled under Aunt Polly's bed, and I heard 'em talk about it. Now, listen, fellows. I'll tell you my plan. And if you don't think it's the best you ever heard, I'll go back with you right now.

(The scene begins to fade out.)

They plan to have the funeral Sunday morning. Now this being Friday—

(The scene closes on three plotting pirates.)

ACT THREE

SCENE 3. The village church. A pulpit, pews, a stained-glass window.

(The school children are clustered together, talking of the tragedy. While they talk, the pews fill up with other townspeople.)

AMY. And I was a-standin' just so—just as I am now. And as if you was him, I was as close as that. And he smiled just this way, and he said, "Never you mind. You just wait. I know something that's going to happen." And I never thought what he meant.

BEN. I got a busted balloon that I traded Joe onct for a fish-hook.

GRACIE. I got some writing of Tom's in one of my books.

BECKY. Could I see it, Gracie, if I come over to your house today?

JANE. My brother's got an old stick of Joe Harper's, that they used to play war with.

JIM. Onct I played hookey with Huck Finn. And Tom and me, we stole a watermelon last summer.

ALFRED. Well, Tom Sawyer, he licked me once!

(They all scoff.)

BEN. Most of us can say that.

AMY. Sh! Here comes the families.

(The children yield place to the chief mourners. Aunt Polly and Sid come in together, followed by Mrs. Harper and Susan. The two women are sobbing.)

SID. Don't take on so, Aunt Polly. I hope Tom's better off where he is, but if he'd been better in some ways—

AUNT POLLY. Sid! Not a word against my Tom, now that he's gone. He was the best-hearted boy that ever was, though he tormented the life out of me, almost.

MRS. HARPER. It was just so with my Joe. Always full of mischief, but just as unselfish and kind as he could be.

AUNT POLLY. Oh, Sereny, I don't know how to give Tom up. He was such a comfort to me.

MRS. HARPER. It's hard—oh, it's so hard. Only last Saturday, my Joe busted a firecracker right under my nose, and I knocked him sprawling. Little did I know then how soon—Oh, if it was to do over again, I'd hug and bless him for it.

AUNT POLLY. I know just how you feel, Sereny. Just the day before he left, my Tom took and filled the cat full of Pain-Killer medicine, that I gave him to take himself, and I thought the cat would tear the house down. And—God forgive me!—I cracked Tom's head with my thimble. Poor boy—poor, dead boy. But he's out of all his troubles now. And the last words I ever heard him say was—

(She breaks down. If desired, Song No. 10, "Dirge", may be used here.)

SID. Sh, Aunt Polly. Here comes the Preacher.

(The Preacher enters, and stalks ponderously to his pulpit. A hush falls over the congregation, and the weeping is subdued. But as the Preacher's address proceeds, fresh sobs break out, and all are so preoccupied with their grief that nobody notices three bedraggled pirates creep in to listen.)

PREACHER. My friends, we are met here to mourn together over the passing of three young souls that have departed from our midst in the past week. Never before has this village suffered such a blow as now, in the loss of these three high-minded, brave, fearless young boys. Oh, my friends, a great orator once said, "The good that men do in this world is oft interred with their bones, but the evil lives after them." Let that not be true of these three young boys. Let us recall only the sweet, generous natures that led them to do noble and beautiful deeds, and let us ask forgiveness for the hard thoughts we have nourished against them, in their moments of innocent pleasure and fun. My friends, Joe Harper was once known to give away some tokens to a poor German lad that enabled him to earn a Bible. And before their tragic disappearance, Tom Sawyer and Huckleberry Finn visited the county jail, to bring comfort and cheer to the unhappy prisoner, Muff Potter, who is held there for murder. Pardon me, my friends, I cannot hold back a tear—

(But by this time, the whole church is reduced to muffled sobs. The moment has come for the three boys to reveal themselves. As they creep forward, the minister raises his streaming eyes, and stands transfixed, then other eyes follow his.)

AUNT POLLY. Oh, me! I can even see his sperrit in the broad daylight.

MRS. HARPER. I can see my Joe too—just as plain as if he was alive.

BEN. Is it real?

ALFRED. It's ghosts, that's what it is!

BECKY. Tom!!!

TOM. Hello, Becky.

PREACHER. They're alive!

(The boys are suddenly surrounded, everybody shouting at once.)

AUNT POLLY. Tom! What a turn you do give a body! I thought I'd never see you alive.

MRS. HARPER. Joe! Is it really you? I'd given you up.

AUNT POLLY. Tom, I don't care what new mischief you've been into —oh, Tom!

TOM. Aunt Polly, it ain't fair. Somebody's got to be glad to see Huck.

AUNT POLLY. And so they shall. I'm glad to see him, poor thing.

(And poor Huck, who was just about to escape to freedom, is hauled back and kissed, just like any civilized child.)

Huck Finn, you shall come straight home with us to dinner. And Sid, you run ahead and tell Mary to put some ice cream in the freezer.

PREACHER *(shouting above the hubbub)*. Praise God! Sing! And put your hearts in it!

(He leads off with "Old Hundred", in which the congregation joins heartily.)

END OF ACT THREE

ACT FOUR

SCENE 1.   Outside the Courthouse, adjoining the jail. A flight of steps leading to the Courthouse entrance. A brick wall, with barred window, set at an angle to it. A barrel.

(Tom, in thoughtful mood, is sitting on the Courthouse steps. Sheriff enters from the direction of the jail.)

SHERIFF.   Why, Tom, you here again?

TOM.   Yes sir.

SHERIFF.   Well, you can't sit here on the Courthouse steps. People will be coming for the trial.

TOM.   Yes sir. I know. Sheriff, are they going to hang Muff Potter?

SHERIFF.   It looks mighty bad for him, Tom. And he don't deny the killing. Just says he can't remember doin' it.

TOM.   Sheriff, Muff Potter ain't never hurt anybody.

SHERIFF.   That's not for us to decide, my boy. Run along now. I have to open up the Courthouse.

(Sheriff unlocks the door, and goes inside the Courthouse. Tom waits till he is safely out of earshot, then crosses to the barrel.)

TOM.   You can come out now, Huck.

HUCK *(climbing out of the barrel, somewhat more disreputable than usual).* By jings, Tom, I don't mind when they throw their potato peels over me—but some joker tumped in a bucket of clinkers.

TOM.   Did you bring the tobacco?

HUCK.   I got it.

TOM.   Come on. The Sheriff'll be out in a minute.

(They cross to the barred window of the jail.)

Pss-s-st! Muff! Muff Potter!

(No answer. The boys exchange apprehensive glances.)

HUCK.   You don't reckon they've already taken him away, do you?

TOM.   Muff! Muff! Are you there?

(Muff's head appears at the window.)

MUFF.   Is that you, boys? Oh, bless you. You ain't forgot poor old Muff.

TOM.   Hucky here, he's brought you something.

HUCK.   It's only a little tobacco.

TOM. And here's some lucifer matches.

MUFF. Boys, you've been so good to me.

HUCK. Oh, shucks, it ain't nothin'.

MUFF. Yes it is. It means a big lot to a man in trouble, when everybody else has turned against him.

TOM. Oh, Muff, don't say so!

HUCK. You never killed anybody, Muff.

MUFF. Oh, boys, you're the only friends I got. Get up on one another's backs, and let me shake your hands. That's it. Yourn'll come through the bars, but mine's too big. Little hands and weak, but they've helped me a power—and I know they'd help me more if they could. Yes, if they could.

(Sheriff comes out of the Courthouse.)

SHERIFF. Here, you boys, what are you doing there talking to the prisoner? Get down from there!

TOM. Yes sir. We was only—

SHERIFF. Get along home now. It's nearly time for Court. Muff, are you ready?

MUFF. I'm ready, Sheriff. Good bye, boys. You've been mighty good to me, and I won't forget it. I know you'd help me if you could.

SHERIFF. Go along now—and don't let me catch you lurking around this jail again.

(The boys make a show of leaving, and Sheriff goes off in direction of the jail.)

TOM *(close to tears)*. Did you hear what he said, Huck?

HUCK. I heerd.

TOM. He said he knew we'd help him if we could—and Huck, we can!

HUCK. Jee-hosophat! What are you a-thinkin' of, Tom? We wouldn't be alive two days if we told.

TOM. Well, he won't be alive two days if we don't.

HUCK. But Tom, we swore. Don't you know that if you tell, you'll drop down dead and rot?

TOM. Oh, Hucky, what are we goin' to do?

(Janie Hardin skips in, gay and excited, followed shortly by Ben Rogers and Jim Hollis.)

JANIE. We're going on a pick-a-nick! We're going on a pick-a-nick! Tom! Tom! We're all invited on a picnic!

94

BEN. Shucks, what's a picnic?

(Becky Thatcher, Susan Harper, and Gracie Miller enter, chattering animatedly.)

JIM. We been on picnics before, I reckon.

(Joe Harper enters.)

GRACE. But this is a big, all-day picnic, down the river, on the ferry-boat!

JOE. On the ferry-boat?

SUSAN. You tell them, Becky.

BECKY. My ma's going to let me give a picnic party next Saturday. And you are all invited.

BEN. Are we really going on the ferry-boat, Becky?

BECKY. Yes. Down the river, all the way to MacDougall's Cave.

TOM. MacDougall's Cave?

BECKY. Yes. That's where we'll have our lunch.

JOE. By Jings! And after lunch, we can go exploring in the cave.

(Tom and Huck exchange significant glances. Amy Lawrence and Alfred Temple enter.)

AMY. You ought to be ashamed of yourself, Alfred Temple. And if you're going to say such things, I won't listen to you.

ALFRED. All I said was he's the bloodiest-looking villain in the country.

JIM. Who?

(Aunt Polly enters, with Sid.)

ALFRED. Why, Muff Potter. It's a wonder he wasn't hung long before now. The whole town says so.

AUNT POLLY. Well, I don't say so, young man. I've known Muff Potter all my life, and I never knew him to harm a fly.

(Mrs. Harper enters with Preacher and Schoolmaster.)

SID. But Aunt Polly, Injun Joe saw him kill the doctor.

AUNT POLLY. Mph! I don't believe that sneaky Injun. How do, Brother Walters, Mr. Dobbin. Oh, Sereny, ain't it awful?

BEN. My pa said if he was to get loose, they'd lynch him.

JOE. And I bet they would, too.

MRS. HARPER. Joe Harper, you just hush right up with that kind of talk.

JOE. Gee Whillikers, Mom, I—I—

MRS. HARPER. Many's the time you boys have been glad enough to go off fishing with Muff Potter, whenever you got the chance.

JOE. Well, Jiminee, how was I to know he was a killer?

JANIE (beginning to cry). He ain't a killer. He mended my dolly.

ALFRED. He is too a killer—ain't he, Mr. Dobbins?

SCHOOLMASTER. There is good reason to believe that he did kill the young doctor, ladies.

AUNT POLLY. On the say-so of that heathen Injun?

SCHOOLMASTER. Well, not entirely. Ahem. I have evidence of my own to support Injun Joe's testimony. And so has Brother Walters here.

AUNT POLLY. Preacher!

MRS. HARPER. You don't mean it, Brother Walters!

PREACHER. Sister Harper, it is like you soft-hearted ladies to pity anybody in trouble. It is the nature of women, God bless them. And Muff Potter needs pity, poor wretch—yes, and prayer, too. For there is no question in any reasonable mind, that under the influence of that demon drink, he did kill young Dr. Robinson.

AUNT POLLY. Oh, Preacher, how can you be so sure?

PREACHER. Aunt Polly, I saw him that night with my own eyes.

MRS. HARPER. You saw the killing?

PREACHER. Not the killing. But I saw him wash off the blood-stains in the branch.

AUNT POLLY. No!

PREACHER. It was about midnight, and bright moon, and I was on my way home from visiting the sick-bed of Brother Hopkins, up the branch. Muff Potter came slipping out from behind the trees, kind of moaning to himself. I thought he was just drunk as usual. And he knelt down beside the water, and washed his hands.

SCHOOLMASTER. Now why would he do that, unless they had blood on them?

BEN. 'Tain't like Muff Potter to wash hisself, I reckon.

ALFRED. Unless he's got a reason.

PREACHER. And in the bright moonlight, I could see dark splotches on his shirt.

ALFRED. You see? He done it all right.

JOE. If he didn't do it, Mom, why don't he say so?

AUNT POLLY. Oh, Preacher, you wouldn't think harsh of a man for washin' himself, would you?

MRS. HARPER. And he's always got splotches on his shirt.

PREACHER. But ladies, that's not all. Mr. Dobbin here can identify the knife.

JOE. The knife?

SCHOOLMASTER. Yes, ladies. I've been called to testify to this point in court. Ahem. The day before the murder, I was addressing an envelope in the post office when my pencil point broke. Muff Potter was loafing around there, and I borrowed his knife to sharpen it.

PREACHER. It was the same knife that killed the doctor, ladies.

SCHOOLMASTER. It was a distinctive knife. I'd know it anywhere. It was the same one.

MRS. HARPER. If that's so, he's as good as gone.

PREACHER. Yes, I'm afraid he's a goner.

(If desired, Song No. 11, "He's a Goner", may be used here. Injun Joe enters, and crosses silently toward the Courthouse. The children shrink from him in fear, whispering to each other about him. The adults hold themselves aloof. In this hostile climate, the Preacher confronts him at the Courthouse steps.)

My man, what you are about to swear to, in that Courthouse, may send an unfortunate man to his death. Are you prepared to have this on your conscience?

INJUN JOE. Milksop!

(Sheriff enters, leading Muff Potter, from the jail.)

SHERIFF. Stand back, folks, and let the prisoner come through. Come along, Muff.

(Muff is chained, and downcast. He shrinks from the accusing and pitying faces, as he makes his way to the Courthouse steps. There, he turns to face them.)

MUFF. Oh, folks, I done an awful thing, but I beg you not to think so hard of me. I didn't do it a-purpose. I liked the young doctor. I liked all my neighbors, and I loved their chillun, and tried to befriend 'em what I could. It was the drink that did it, friends, and I reckon I'm a-going to pay for it. It's only right I should. But when I'm dead, folks, don't forget me. You bring your chillun to my grave, and you warn 'em about the evils of drink. And tell 'em what happened to poor Muff Potter. And Preacher, you pray for my soul.

(All are visibly moved. Muffled sobs are heard.)

SHERIFF. That'll do, Muff. Come along now.

TOM. I can stop this hangin'—and by Jings, I a-goin' to!

(Pulling away from the terrified Huck, he makes his way to the Courthouse steps. Huck moves as far away as possible from Injun Joe, but eyes him watchfully throughout the scene.)

Sheriff! Muff Potter never done it. I saw it happen!

SHERIFF. What?

(Sensation in the crowd. Injun Joe stands staunch, staring Tom down.)

TOM *(losing his nerve)*. Y-y-yes sir. I saw the killin'. I was there.

SHERIFF. Where?

TOM *(timidly)*. In—in—in the graveyard.

SHERIFF. The night of the murder, around midnight?

TOM. Y-y-y-yes sir.

INJUN JOE. He's lying.

SHERIFF. Were you anywhere near Hoss Williams' grave?

TOM. Yes sir.

SHERIFF. How near?

TOM. Near as I am to you. But I was hid.

SHERIFF. Where?

TOM. Behind the next tombstone.

(Injun Joe eyes the crowd, for an avenue of escape.)

SHERIFF. Why?

TOM. Well—we—I—I—

SHERIFF. Speak up, my boy, if you are telling the truth.

TOM. We—ah—I—I was aimin' to bury a dead cat.

SHERIFF *(thundering)*. A dead cat?

TOM *(whispering)*. Y-y-yes sir.

(A ripple of mirth in the crowd.)

SHERIFF. And what happened?

TOM. Well, sir, we dropped the cat. I reckon its carcass is still there. But we saw it all, Sheriff. And Muff Potter never done it. Muff was knocked out cold. But he took Muff's knife and—

(He points a finger toward Injun Joe.)

—and he done it!

SHERIFF. Catch him!

(But Injun Joe has sprung through the crowd. Huck, ever so innocently, trips him. And Preacher and Schoolmaster make a show of grabbing at him. But shaking them off easily, he is up and gone, pursued by the Sheriff, Preacher and Schoolmaster. Tom is making to join in the pursuit, but is hauled back abruptly by Huck. The rest of the crowd swarms affectionately around Muff Potter.)

HUCK. They'll never catch him, Tom. Them Injuns can go like the wind, and leave no tracks. He'll come back and kill us, sure.

TOM. How can he, Huck? If they catch him, he'll be locked up. And if he gets away, he won't dare show his face around here again.

HUCK. He's got treasure hid somewheres around here. He ain't goin' to leave here without that.

TOM. That's so. Lordy, Huck, what'll we do?

HUCK. Stay out of sight, I bet you.

(He starts sneaking away.)

TOM. Wait for me!

(Becky breaks away from the group surrounding Muff Potter.)

BECKY. Oh, Tom, how could you be so brave!

AUNT POLLY. Tom, you done the right thing, for once. I'm proud of you.

(An admiring public gathers around the frightened boy.)

ACT FOUR

SCENE 2. MacDougall's Cave. Rocky silhouettes. Stalactites and stalagmites. A high boulder, which must be practical. Dim light. The sound of water dripping slowly.

(Injun Joe enters, panting. Flattens himself against the boulder, and listens.)

INJUN JOE. Drat those kids! All through the cave, curse 'em. But they won't have the nerve to venture this far, I reckon.

(He listens a moment, then climbs the boulder. At the top, he stands precariously balanced on a narrow ledge, but lights a candle, improving the light.)

Good thing I had one of those lucifer matches.

(Carrying the candle, he locates a position, and tugs at a loose rock, which he finally removes.)

Ah-h-h-h!

(He draws out of hiding the wooden money-box, and lets a few coins filter through his fingers. His eyes glisten with greed.)

Money! If Injun Joe has to go, he takes you with him.

(At the sound of a shout offstage, he claps the box shut, and turns quickly.)

Tom *(offstage).* Yoo—oo—oo! *(Echo.)*

Becky *(offstage).* Yoo—oo—oo! *(Echo.)*

(In his haste, Injun Joe loses his balance on the narrow ledge. He tries to catch himself, but too late. We see him fall to the ground. He writhes a few moments, then lies still. Tom and Becky grope their way in, carrying candles.)

Tom. This must be an entirely new part of the cave, Becky. None of the others have been here at all.

Becky. Tom, it seems ever so long since I heard any of the others.

Tom. Come to think, Becky, we're way down below them, and I don't know how far north or south or east, whichever way it is. We couldn't hear them here.

Becky. I wonder how long we've been here, Tom. We better start back.

Tom *(looking for possible exits).* Yes, I reckon we better. Perhaps we better.

Becky. Can you find the way, Tom? It's all a mixed-up crookedness to me.

Tom. I reckon I could find it—but then the bats. If they put out our candles, it will be an awful fix. Let's try some other way, so as not to go through there.

Becky. Well, but I hope we won't get lost. It would be too awful.

Tom *(groping in different directions).* Oh, it's all right. This ain't the way, but we'll come back to it right away.

Becky. Oh, Tom, never mind the bats. Let's go back that way. We seem to get worse and worse off.

Tom. Listen. Yoo—oo—oo! *(echo).*

Becky. Oh, don't do that again, Tom. It's too horrid.

Tom. It is horrid, but I better, Becky. They might hear us, you know.

Becky. Tom, you didn't make any marks, to trace our way back by!

Tom. Becky, I was such a fool. Such a fool! I never thought we might want to come back. No, I can't find the way. It's all mixed up.

BECKY. We're lost. We're lost! We can never get out of this awful place! Oh, why did we ever leave the others?

TOM. Don't cry, Becky. It's all my fault.

BECKY. Don't say that, Tom. Let's try again.

TOM. We mustn't go far. Here, Becky. Let me blow out your candle. We may need it, later.

BECKY. Tom!

TOM. Maybe not, though. We'll look some more.

BECKY. Oh, Tom, it's not a bit of use.

TOM. 'Course it is, Becky. Don't give up. We'll find a way.

BECKY. No we won't, Tom. We never will. Oh Tom, last night I dreamed of the most beautiful country you ever saw. I reckon we are going there, Tom.

TOM. Maybe not. Cheer up, Becky. Here, sit down and rest a minute.

BECKY. Oh no, Tom. Let's move on and look some more.

TOM. Becky, can you bear it if I tell you something?

BECKY. I'll try to, Tom. What is it?

TOM. Well, then, Becky, we must stay here, where there's water to drink. This is our last bit of candle.

BECKY. Tom!

TOM. I'm sorry, Becky.

BECKY. Well, all right. We might as well stay here as anywhere. We're going to die anyway, and it doesn't make much difference where.

TOM. Becky, don't talk like that. We're not going to die.

BECKY. Yes we are, too. I know we're going to die, and I'm all ready for it.

TOM. Becky, here. I've got a kite-line in my pocket. Now you hold one end of it, and I'll take the other and explore some of the side-passages. If you get scared waiting here, just give a little pull on this string, and I'll come a-running.

BECKY. All right, Tom. But it's not a bit of use. I'll just wait here and die. It won't take long. But Tom, come back every once in a while and speak to me. And when the awful time comes, stay by me and hold my hand till it's over, will you, Tom?

TOM. 'Course I will. But don't you worry, Becky. We ain't goin' to die in here.

(If desired, Song No. 12, "Aw, Becky, Don't Cry", may be used here, reprise of Song No. 3, "Now Will you Promise".)

Now here. I'll be back in a little while. Wait for me.

(Leaving Becky, he fumbles his way around by candle-light, toward the boulder. He almost stumbles over Injun Joe's body.)

Lordy! It's Injun Joe!

(He turns to flee, then stops, and returns fearfully, holding his shaking candle so as to see better.)

That's funny. That ain't no natural way to sleep.

(Cautiously, he kneels to look closer, then after a false start, brings himself to touch the body. When there is no response, he musters his courage to feel the heart.)

Craminee! He's dead!

(Awed, he stands up, and extends his candle to explore the location, spies the ledge at the top of the boulder. He gropes his way to climb the boulder, by the route Injun Joe used earlier, but does not venture to stand on the narrow ledge.)

By Jings, the treasure! So this is where he's been hidin' out.

(With sudden resolution, he climbs back down, takes off his jacket and covers the dead face, then hastily gropes his way back to Becky.)

Becky, I—I—

BECKY. Tom, what's the matter? You're shaking! Where's your jacket? What is it, Tom?

TOM. Becky, I—I think we better explore somewhere else. We don't want to stay here.

BECKY. But what about the water, Tom?

TOM. We'll have to find some in another place. We can't stay here. Come on.

BECKY. Tom, they'll miss us, won't they?

TOM. Yes, they will. Certainy they will.

BECKY. Maybe they're hunting for us now, Tom.

TOM. Why, I reckon maybe they are. I hope they are.

BECKY. When would they miss us, Tom?

TOM. Why, when they got back to the boat, I reckon.

BECKY. Tom, it might be dark then. Would they notice we hadn't come?

Tom. I don't know. But anyway, your mother would miss you, soon as they got home.

Becky. Oh, Tom! She thinks I'm staying all night with Susie Harper!

Tom. Good Lord, Becky!

Becky (crying). Oh, Tom! Tom, we'll never be found! We're in here forever and ever!

Tom. Aw, don't cry, Becky. Let's get away from this fearsome place.

(As the scene ends, two frightened children are groping their way off.)

ACT FOUR

Scene 3. The village church.

(The Preacher is just dismissing the congregation. If desired, he may say, "Let us praise the Lord with a song. Hallelujah", and Song No. 13, "Halleloo", may be used here. The Preacher lifts his hand in benediction.)

Preacher. Amen.

(The people rise and break up into little groups. Preacher comes down from the pulpit to greet his flock.)

Mrs. Harper. Good morning, Mr. Dobbin.

Aunt Polly. Good morning, Sheriff.

Sheriff. Morning, Aunt Polly.

Aunt Polly. Good morning, children. I'm glad to see the picnic didn't keep you from comin' to church this morning.

(The children mumble greetings.)

Ben. No'm. Ma made me.

Aunt Polly. That's more than I can say for my Tom.

Preacher. I didn't see your Tom in Sunday School this morning, Aunt Polly.

Aunt Polly. Oh, he turned up missing from the picnic, Preacher. I reckon he stayed with the Harpers last night, and now he's afraid to come to church. I've got to settle with him.

Mrs. Harper. Good morning, Aunt Polly.

Aunt Polly. Good morning, Sereny. Is my Tom going to sleep all day at your house?

Mrs. Harper. Your Tom?

Aunt Polly. Yes. Didn't he stay with you last night?

103

Mrs. Harper. Why, no. Was he supposed to?

Aunt Polly (anxious). Well, where else could he be?

Mrs. Harper. I was expecting Becky Thatcher for the night, but Susan came home without her. Reckon she changed her mind, and went home.

Gracie. Becky ain't home, Mrs. Harper. I stopped by for her this morning, and her mother said she was spending the night at your house.

Mrs. Harper (alarmed). But she didn't. Oh, my!

(Their concern spreads through the congregation in whispers. All attention is focused on the two women.)

Aunt Polly. Joe Harper, have you seen my Tom this morning?

Joe. No'm.

Aunt Polly. When did you see him last?

Mrs. Harper. When did you see Becky last, Susan?

Joe and Susan (scared). I don't remember.

Sheriff (taking charge). Look here, didn't they come back on the ferry-boat with the rest of you?

Joe. I don't remember seein' 'em.

Susan. It was dark when we got on, and we were so tired goin' through the cave—

Sheriff (to the children, who are thinking startled thoughts). Do any of you children remember seeing them on the ferry-boat?

(The children answer him with dumb silence.)

Did they go into the cave?

Joe. Yes sir. We all went into it together. And then we got to chasin' through some of the side passages, and—and—

Sheriff. Yes, go on.

Joe. Well, sir, Tom and Becky had a candle apiece, and they took a different turning from us, 'cause they said they was goin' to find something new.

Preacher. Oh, Sheriff, could it be—is it possible they—they are still in the cave?

(Aunt Polly falls to crying, and wringing her hands. Mrs. Harper tries to comfort her. The children are frozen with horror.)

Sheriff. Joe, you run as fast as you can to the town hall and ring the bell. Tell all the men to meet me at the ferry-boat landing in ten minutes. Ben, you find old Mr. Harrison, and tell him to open up the store, and let you have all the candles he has in stock. We'll need twine, too, to track our own way through the cave. You men come with me to the wharf, and we'll arrange for boats to carry us over. Don't fear, Aunt Polly. If they are in the cave, we'll find them.

(*All are rushing about on one errand or another, as the scene closes.*)

ACT FOUR

SCENE 4. A village street. Board fence. Covered barrel.

(*Aunt Polly enters, downcast, carrying a pan of trash. Stops to stroke the board fence, wipes away a tear, then carries the trash to the barrel. As she lifts the lid, she gasps.*)

AUNT POLLY. Huckleberry Finn!

(*Huck's head appears.*)

HUCK. Yes'm.

AUNT POLLY. You climb right out of there.

(*Meekly Huck climbs out. Aunt Polly empties the trash, and sets her pan on the lid of the barrel.*)

Just look at you! After all the Widow Douglas has done to make a nice, clean, respectable boy of you!

HUCK. Yes'm.

AUNT POLLY. Why are you skulking around like this anyway? . . . Don't stop to think up one of your fibs now. What have you done wrong?

HUCK. Aunt Polly, ain't they found Tom yet?

AUNT POLLY. Oh, Huck, no! Nor Becky neither. They've about give up. They say nobody could be alive in that cave after three days.

HUCK. Tom could. Tom's smart.

AUNT POLLY. Two hundred men have searched that cave, day and night, and all they found was Becky's hair-ribbon. Now most of them have come home.

(*Joyful shouting is heard off, followed by a wild peal of bells.*)

Mercy on us! Who's ringing the town bell?

VOICES (*off*). Turn out! Turn out, everybody! They're found! They're found!

HUCK (*bounding off*). It's Tom! It's Tom and Becky! Tom!

(*Aunt Polly stands trembling, adjusting her spectacles. Schoolmaster runs in.*)

SCHOOLMASTER. Aunt Polly! They're found! They're found!

AUNT POLLY. I can't believe it. Tom! Tom! Becky!

SCHOOLMASTER (*shouting in all directions*). Turn out! Turn out, everybody! They're found!

(Muff enters, bearing Tom on his shoulder. Preacher follows with Becky on his, both children looking a little the worse for their experience. Accompanied by Janie, Jim, Gracie and Ben, all shouting, waving, blowing toy horns, etc. Huck tags along shyly, on the fringe.)

AUNT POLLY (*seizing Tom as Muff sets him down*). Tom, boy! Tom!

(Joe and Susan Harper rush in, followed by Sid.)

SUSAN. Oh, Becky! Oh, Tom!

(Sid picks up Aunt Polly's pan and bangs on it.)

JOE (*shouting everywhere*). Turn out, everybody! Here they are! They're found! They're found!

(Mrs. Harper enters, followed by Alfred.)

MRS. HARPER. Well, bless my soul! Becky, child!

AUNT POLLY. Becky, your mother is nearly dead from grief. We made sure you two had fallen into one of them crevices in the cave.

PREACHER. The Sheriff has gone to tell your mother, Becky.

SCHOOLMASTER. Your father is still in the cave, with the searching party.

(Sheriff enters.)

BECKY. Searching party?

SHERIFF. We've sent a skiff over to the cave, to take the news to the searching party.

TOM. We never saw any searching party.

AUNT POLLY. Tom, you don't mean—how did you ever get out, then?

TOM. Well, Aunt Polly, we'd been in there a week or so, I guess. Maybe more. And Becky, she was all wore out. So I left her resting a minute, while I went on explorin' a little bit. I had my kite-line along, and I made her hold one end of that, while I followed a little path as far as the line would reach. I tried that out on three different alleys, and I was just about to give up and turn back, when I thought I saw a tiny speck, way off, that looked like daylight. I dropped the kite-line, and pushed my way toward it, and first thing you know, I was lookin' right out on the river.

106

BEN. Craminee!

JOE. Tom! Just suppose it'd been night.

TOM. Don't think it, Joe. And then I went back for Becky, and told her.

BECKY. He was wonderful, Aunt Polly. I didn't do anything but cry. But Tom just kept looking for new places, and if it hadn't been for him, we never would have got out, I reckon.

AUNT POLLY (all choked up). Becky, child!

TOM. Aw, shucks, that warn't nothin'. But when I showed Becky the little speck of daylight, she nearly died of joy. And then we climbed out of the hole, and were just sittin' there cryin' for gladness when some men came by in a skiff. We told them who we were, but they wouldn't believe us at first, because they said we were five miles down the river below the cave. But anyway they took us aboard, and rowed us to their farm, and gave us some breakfast. And then the old man brought us here in his spring wagon.

CHILDREN. Hoo—ray! 'Ray for Tom, and 'Ray for Becky!

SCHOOLMASTER. Let's have a parade! (Or a Square Dance.)

(If desired, Song No. 14, "Square Dance", may be used here, ending with formulating a parade, and all but Huck marching off to shouting, banging, horn-blowing, etc. But as Huck hangs back, the hero of the parade stops to coax his friend.)

TOM. Come on, Huck. Join the fun.

HUCK. I can't, Tom. I'm layin' low.

TOM. What for?

HUCK. The Widow Douglas wants to adopt me. For keeps. And make me wash, and educate me, and everything. And I can't stand it, Tom.

TOM. Hucky, you don't need it. You're rich. I found the treasure!

HUCK. Tom! Where?

TOM. It's in the cave, and when we get the chance, you and me'll snake over there and get it.

HUCK. And run onto Injun Joe? Not me.

TOM. Hucky, you don't ever need to worry about Injun Joe any more. He's dead.

HUCK. Dead? Lordy! Are you sure?

TOM. Sure. He fell off'n a high ledge where the treasure is. I run onto him in the cave, all spraddled out, dead.

HUCK. Geeminy!

TOM. Now come on. We've got something to parade about!

(They start off together.)

HUCK. Tom, what'll we do with all that money?

TOM. We'll play robbers, of course. Tom Sawyer's Gang—don't that sound splendid? And we'll buy swords and pistols and things that a robber has to have—and waylay people . . .

(And the play ends while we are still caught up in the dreams of childhood—oh, how beautiful they are, and how perishable.)

END OF THE PLAY

THE INDIAN CAPTIVE

by

Charlotte B. Chorpenning

This play was given its premiere production in
1936 at the Goodman Theatre in Chicago, under
the direction of the author.

Copyright, 1937 by

THE CHILDREN'S THEATRE PRESS

"CLOVERLOT"
Anchorage, Kentucky

109

THE INDIAN CAPTIVE

By Charlotte B. Chorpenning

THE ANCHORAGE PRESS
Cloverlot
Anchorage, Kentucky 40223
U. S. A.

CHARACTERS

THOMAS LYTELL, eight or nine years old.

ELEANOR LYTELL, eleven or twelve.

MRS. LYTELL, their mother.

DEBORAH, about Eleanor's age. (Can be doubled with Shining Leaves).

THE OLD QUEEN, an old Indian woman; lean and dignified.

CORNPLANTER, a young Indian Chief.

FALLING LEAVES, an Indian warrior.

MANY BEARS, another Indian warrior.

EAGLE FEATHER, Cornplanter's wife, young, violent.

REDBILL, an Indian boy, about twelve.

SHINING LEAVES, an Indian girl. (Can be doubled with Deborah).

◆

SCENES

ACT ONE

A clearing in the forest, near Plum Creek, Pennsylvania, 1779.

ACT TWO

Near the Lookout Rock, outside Cornplanter's village.

ACT THREE

The same, eight months later.

THE INDIAN CAPTIVE

◆

It may be of interest to an audience to know that this play is based on the authentic story of the captivity among Senecas of Eleanor Lytell, who was later the wife of John Kenzie, of Chicago. Her friendship with the Indians saved her family in the great Chicago Massacre.

Much of the dialogue is taken from the records of her captivity. Cornplanter's closing speech, for example, is authentic. The Old Queen and the jealous Wife, with her attempt at poisoning Eleanor, are historically accurate. Seneca customs have been adhered to throughout the play. Eleanor's Indian name, Ship-under-full-sail, was given her on her adoption for the reason used in the play—"because her spirit is strong and swift."

The Indian Captive

◆

ACT ONE

The balsams are arranged back and at one side, so as to afford screens for the Indians. On the other side, somewhat back, is the indication of the house. The brewing tub is near it, more center and down stage. A gun target with holes, on one tree.

Eleanor and Thomas are scrubbing out the tub, which stands on its side. They stand back and look at it, proudly.

ELEANOR: There! won't mother be surprised when she finds the brewing tub all clean?

THOMAS: Let's turn it down, to dry.
(They do so, laboriously, for it is heavy for them. Just as it is level and ready to be let down, a call like the whistle of a quail is heard. Thomas drops his side of the tub so suddenly that they have to leap back to save their toes.)

ELEANOR *(as they work)*: Hold hard, Thomas. Don't let it go down too fast, or it will pinch you. Here. Let me come around a little.

THOMAS *(dropping it at the bird call)*: Listen!

ELEANOR: Look out! You nearly smashed my foot!

THOMAS: I heard an Indian.

ELEANOR: Where?

THOMAS: In the woods. He whistled like a quail.

ELEANOR: That was just a bird.

THOMAS: Indians whistle like birds, to signal each other.

ELEANOR: There aren't any Indians around, now.

THOMAS: Don't you remember, mother told us we mustn't follow a quail's call into the woods? She said it might be an Indian.

ELEANOR: That was last summer, when the Seneca Indians were picking berries upon Plum Creek. They went away long age.
(Another whistle, answered from a greater distance, by two more.)

THOMAS: There's another!—Listen! They're answering each other!
(Eleanor starts toward the balsam clump to investigate. Thomas runs to hold her back.)
Don't go there! They might be hiding behind trees or bushes.

ELEANOR: I'm not afraid.
(She goes to the edge of the stage, looking off in various directions, and peering around the trees.)
There aren't any in sight, anyway.

THOMAS: I wish mother would come.

(Eleanor looks up and off.)

ELEANOR: It's way past noon by the sun. Mother promised to be home by noon.

THOMAS *(beginning to cry)*: What if the Indians have taken mother?

ELEANOR: Don't cry, Thomas. Mother'll come. I know she will.

THOMAS: But why is she so late?

ELEANOR: I suppose the new settlers were in trouble. Mother would stay if they needed help. She always helps people when they are in trouble.

THOMAS: It's been so long!

ELEANOR: Mother wouldn't like to hear you cry, Thomas. Let's run down to the edge of the clearing and see if she's in sight.

THOMAS: I'm afraid.

ELEANOR: I'll get my gun. We'll go till we meet her. Maybe we can help the new settlers, too. There must be lots to do, or mother would be home by now.

(She goes into the house. Thomas follows her to the door, and stands waiting, back to the balsam clump. Cornplanter, an Indian chief, appears, back, then hides again. A call from Mrs. Lytell, at some distance.)

THOMAS *(jumping up and down)*: There she is! There she is!

ELEANOR: Mother!—I'll beat you to her, Thomas!

THOMAS: Wait! Wait!—

(She comes back and takes his hand and they run off together. Cornplanter comes out from behind the tree. He looks after the children. He is pleased, and murmurs to himself.)

CORNPLANTER: Hoah—

(He peers through the window. He examines the gun, sets it down again, and whistles like a quail. He is answered twice from a distance. He answers in turn, and this keeps up until two other Indians come onto the stage. All wear tunics and leggins and the Seneca head-dress, which is a broad band with a single feather. Cornplanter's eagle feather marks his rank. He points after the children.)

A white woman. And a boy. And a girl.

FALLING LEAVES *(listening)*: They come this way.

MANY BEARS: Shall we take them, Cornplanter?

CORNPLANTER: We will watch and see.

FALLING LEAVES: A white captive would not please the Old Queen, your mother.

MANY BEARS: It would please her more than returning to her with no captive at all.

FALLING LEAVES: The Old Queen sent us to capture a boy, full of courage. He must take the place in her lodge of the brother of Cornplanter, who was killed. He must be adopted into the Seneca tribe. The Old Queen will not adopt a white captive.

114

CORNPLANTER: Indian or white is all one. It is the spirit that looks out of the eyes that counts.

FALLING LEAVES: Has the white boy the spirit of your brother?

CORNPLANTER: The white boy is afraid. He shakes like a young aspen tree when the north wind blows. He makes the sound of a wood mouse when the owl brother has him in his beak.

MANY BEARS: We shall have to return without any captive.

CORNPLANTER: The white *girl* is not afraid.

FALLING LEAVES: What bird told you that?

CORNPLANTER: My eyes told me. She sped straight and free, like a ship under full sail.

MANY BEARS: A swift runner would please the Old Queen. But it was your brother who was killed, not a sister.

CORNPLANTER: Courage went out of our lodge when my brother was killed. If the white girl brings courage into it, she will make a good captive.

(Falling Leaves suddenly lifts a warning finger. They all "freeze". The sound of Mrs. Lytell and the children laughing comes from off.)

Take cover. I will watch. If I wish to take the white child, I will call as the quail calls.

(They disappear swiftly and silently, Cornplanter behind a balsam on the stage, the others off. Mrs. Lytell enters, hand in hand with the children.)

MRS. LYTELL *(stopping to look round)*: Where is my surprise? *(The children laugh with glee.)*

THOMAS: Find it, mother! Find it!

ELEANOR: We'll say warmer when you go near it, and colder when you go away.

MRS. LYTELL: I wonder if Eleanor has made a cake for supper all by herself.

(She starts into the house, passing the tub on the way.)

THOMAS *(as she draws near the tub)*: You're getting warm—warmer—

ELEANOR *(as she passes the tub)*: Colder—colder—

MRS. LYTELL *(stopping at the door)*: Dear me——It can't be in the house at all.

(She takes a step away from the house).

CHILDREN: Warmer—*(She goes back)*. Colder! Colder!

MRS. LYTELL *(coming center a little)*: Is it where I can see it?

(The children shout with laughter).

ELEANOR: You could if you looked.

MRS. LYTELL: Oho! You've hidden it! Let me see. Is it behind a balsam tree, I wonder?

(She goes to the clump which conceals Cornplanter, passing the tub on the way.)

ELEANOR: Very warm—

CHILDREN: Colder—colder—

(As she starts around the clump they run to her, shouting).

ELEANOR: Colder!
(Cornplanter slips around, keeping out of their sight. He is very still. He takes off his head dress that it may not protrude as he peers.)
MRS. LYTELL: Colder?
(She comes on around the clump, front, the children with her. Cornplanter slips back.)
CHILDREN: Warmer—*(as she starts around on this second side)* colder—
MRS. LYTELL: Dear me—
(She comes front a few steps which is also toward the tub, Cornplanter slipping back.)
CHILDREN: Warmer—
(Mrs. Lytell starts back on that side, Cornplanter of course moving with her.)
Colder—
MRS. LYTELL*(on one side, Cornplanter on the other)*: Then it isn't back of the balsams. Is it under something?
ELEANOR *(giggling)*: Sort of.
MRS. LYTELL: It must be inside of something.
THOMAS: It's inside of itself!
(She walks forward. Cornplanter disappears.)
MRS. LYTELL: Let me see, now. Sort of under something—And inside of itself—
CHILDREN *(as she approaches the tub)*: Warmer—Very warm!—Hot!
(She sits down on the tub. They double up with laughter.)
ELEANOR: You're burning up!
THOMAS: Your feet will catch on fire!
MRS. LYTELL: My feet?—I know! It's under the tub.
(She lifts the tub. The children spring to help her. They are very proud of their work. Cornplanter peers out, interested.)
Well, well! The brewing tub is all clean and scrubbed! What fine workers I have in my home! What strong arms and backs! Did Thomas lift a side of this heavy tub?
ELEANOR: Yes!
THOMAS *(shamefaced)*: I—I dropped my side, mother. I almost hurt Eleanor's toes.
ELEANOR *(defending him)*: It was only beause you were afraid. We can put it down ourselves all right, mother. Show her, Thomas. See?
(They tip the tub down again.)
MRS. LYTELL: Why were you afraid, son?
THOMAS: I heard quail calling in the woods. I thought it was Indians. I—I cried because you didn't come.
MRS. LYTELL: Cried? A boy who can lift that tub?
ELEANOR: Thomas is a fraid-cat.
MRS. LYTELL: Not a bit of it. Wait till he's a little older and he'll be the bravest boy in the wilderness. You were afraid a year ago, too.

116

THOMAS: You'd be afraid now, if the Indians came.

MRS. LYTELL: Sit down here by me, both of you. I have something important to tell you. *(The children crowd close.)* You are children of pioneers. Do you know what that means?

ELEANOR: I do. It means we have come to a new land.

MRS. LYTELL: That's right. And in a new land there are many things that are hard to do, and many things that are dangerous. That is why pioneers must stand by each other.

ELEANOR: You mean like staying to help, the way you did today?

MRS. LYTELL: Yes. If a neighbor needs help, a pioneer must leave his own home and go to help him. He must stay as long as he is needed. And nobody must cry about it.

THOMAS: I'm not crying!

MRS. LYTELL: Good! And pioneers must face dangers every day. And they must never be afraid.

THOMAS: Not of Indians, even?

MRS. LYTELL: Prick up your ears, now, for you must never forget this.

ELEANOR *(excited by her tone)*: Go on!

MRS. LYTELL: Indians do not like cowards. If ever you see an Indian, you must not act afraid.

THOMAS: They steal people! They hit them with clubs. They tie them to trees and light fires under them.

MRS. LYTELL: Do you know why they do that?

THOMAS: They are bad.

MRS. LYTELL: They are giving their captives a chance to show how brave they are. A brave Indian sings when the fire is under him.

ELEANOR: Oh! What do they sing?

MRS. LYTELL: They sing songs like this: *(In a high monotonous chant like an Indian)* "I am brave. I am not afraid. Life is nothing at all to one who is not afraid."

ELEANOR *(imitating her)*: "I am brave. I am not afraid. Life is nothing at all to one who is not afaird." *(She claps her hands.)* I like it! I am never going to be afraid again!

MRS. LYTELL: When a captive sings, the Indian knows he is strong and has courage. Sometimes they put out the fire and adopt him into their tribe.

THOMAS: Would they do that to us, if they caught us?

MRS. LYTELL: If you did not act afraid, they would not have to put fire under you. They would know you were brave without it.

THOMAS: I don't want to be adopted by an Indian. I want to stay with you!

MRS. LYTELL: If ever an Indian captured you, I would come and find you. You could be sure of that.

THOMAS: How would you know where they took us?

MRS. LYTELL: I'd find out. It might take a long time, but I would.

ELEANOR: How could you talk to them? They don't talk like us.

MRS. LYTELL: When your father was alive, he learned the Seneca talk, so he could trade with them. I could learn it, too.

(Deborah, off, is calling and crying. They all leap to their feet, listening.)

THOMAS: Someone's crying!

ELEANOR: It sounds like a girl.

MRS. LYTELL: I believe it's the little girl from Plum Creek. The new settlers have a little girl about as old as you, Eleanor. Her name is Deborah.

(She goes to look off, down the trail, where she entered.)

Deborah!—Deborah—

DEBORAH *(off, approaching)*: Mrs. Lytell—Come, quick—quick—

ELEANOR: I'll go to meet her—

MRS. LYTELL: Do. Run—*(calling, as Eleanor runs off)* What is it?

(The crying grows louder, and the two enter. Eleanor has her arms around Deborah, leading her. Deborah is stumbling with exhaustion and terror.)

Thomas, bring a dipper of water.

(She takes Deborah in her arms.) There now. There, there. What has happened?

DEBORAH: Father! Come quick or he'll die! *(She pulls at her hand.)* Come!

MRS. LYTELL: Tell me plainly, first. What is it?

DEBORAH: They were raising a log to the roof, and the rope broke. It fell on father. We can't lift it! He can hardly breathe! Mother says, Bring something to put on the hurt, and something to eat. All our things were broken and crushed by the log when it fell!

MRS. LYTELL: Here. Thomas has brought you some water. Drink it. Thomas, put the roll of linen strips and the medicine bottles in a little basket.

(Thomas runs off.)

ELEANOR: What can I do, mother?

MRS. LYTELL: Pack some deer's meat and meal and butter and salt and maple sugar in a basket.

(Eleanor runs off.)

You must stop crying, Deborah, so you will be strong to hurry back. That's it. Father will be all right. I know how to lift a log by making a pulley for a rope. You will learn these things, too, when you have been long in the new country.

THOMAS *(comes running out with a small basket)*: I put in everything in the medicine box mother.

MRS. LYTELL: That's right. And here's Eleanor with the food.

ELEANOR: I put in the last of the pound cake, mother. I thought maybe Deborah would like some.

MRS. LYTELL: Good. Now we're off, Deborah, to lift the log.

ELEANOR: Thomas and I are strong, mother. Shan't we go too, to help lift it?

MRS. LYTELL: No, dear. There isn't food enough for all of us. And there would be no place for you to sleep.

THOMAS *(alarmed)*: Won't you be home when it is dark, mother?

MRS. LYTELL: I'll be home as soon as I can, son. But it may not be tonight. Eleanor will take care of you. She knows how to make supper, and how to bar the door when it's dark. You will help her do that.

THOMAS: I'll take care of Eleanor, mother.

ELEANOR: And I'll take care of Thomas.

MRS. LYTELL: Stand your gun near your bed tonight, Eleanor, the way I always do. Goodbye, my little pioneers. Mother will come back to you as soon as she can.

ELEANOR *(calling after them as they start)*: Goodbye, Deborah. Come and play with us when your father is well.

DEBORAH: I will.

THOMAS: Oh, mother. You forgot to give us something to think of you by.

MRS. LYTELL: So I did. Wait, Deborah. Now let me see. I know. Look up. Both of you.

THOMAS: Way up in the sky?

MRS. LYTELL: There's something up there we can all of us see, no matter how far apart we are.

ELEANOR: The little daytime moon!

MRS. LYTELL: Yes. I'll give you a little daytime moon. And if you wake up in the night and I'm not home yet, you peek out of the window and see it shining in at you for me.

THOMAS: Oh, mother, that's the nicest thing you ever gave us.

MRS. LYTELL: And now we're off. Goodbye, my little pioneers.

THOMAS *(calling)*: Goodbye mother.

MRS. LYTELL *(off)*: Goodbye, pioneer.

THOMAS *(fighting back tears)*: I didn't cry.

ELEANOR *(still gazing up)*: It makes me feel as if mother were still here. Now I tell you what let's do.

THOMAS: What?

ELEANOR: Let's have a special feast for supper.

THOMAS: Oh, goody! What shall we have?

ELEANOR: I think mother wouldn't mind if I made a cake. We could keep part of it for her, tomorrow.

THOMAS: Can you make one all by yourself?

ELEANOR: I made the last one. Mother was there, but I didn't have to ask a single question.

THOMAS: Can I help stir?

ELEANOR: Yes. You go and gather up some little twigs to make the fire start quick, and I'll be measuring out the flour and sugar and things.

THOMAS (*uneasy*): Where'll I find the twigs?

ELEANOR: Oh, around, under the balsam trees. Right in that clump will be enough.

THOMAS: All right.

(*Eleanor goes into the house. Thomas stands looking after her. Cornplanter leaves the balsam where he has been out of sight and moves back, his back to the audience, showing plainly. Thomas speaks with bravado, not seeing Cornplanter*):

I'm not afraid.

(*He starts back to the balsam clump. He is startled by the quail call which Cornplanter gives. It is answered from a distance, twice. Thomas sees Cornplanter, who moves back a step or two further without turning. He darts noiselessly to the door and whispers*):

Eleanor—

(*Cornplanter disappears behind a balsam tree. Eleanor comes out and Thomas points to where Cornplanter was. He whispers.*) He's gone.

I saw—

ELEANOR (*also in a whisper*): Listen. Do you hear that?

THOMAS: I heard a rustling.

ELEANOR: Perhaps it was a squirrel.

(*Cornplanter's feather shows above a balsam branch.*)

THOMAS: Look. What is that?

(*It disappears as they look.*)

ELEANOR: It looked like a fawn popping up its head.

(*Two whistles come from near, off. Cornplanter steals off, without looking around at the children.*)

THOMAS: They're coming here.

ELEANOR: He's gone to meet them.

THOMAS: Bar the doors.

ELEANOR: There's no use in that. They can break the doors if they want to. We must hide.

THOMAS: Where?

ELEANOR: They'll look in the house—There's no place there to hide. I know—Help me, Thomas! Quick! Get under the tub.

(*Thomas helps her lift it, and starts to crawl under. He stops.*)

THOMAS: There isn't room for both of us.

ELEANOR: I have my gun. Quick! Quick! (*A little whistle and answer, very soft, from Cornplanter.*) I promised mother! Duck your head! I'm going to let it down!

(*She does. He tries to lift it. His fingers show.*)

THOMAS: Eleanor—

ELEANOR: Sh-h-h Don't be afraid—Keep still.—Keep very still. I'll be all right.

(*She snatches up her gun and sits on the tub with it, ready, facing where the Indian was last seen. She is erect and mistress of herself. This should be so arranged as to give a clear side view of her, gun in hand, chin lifted, waiting. After a pause Falling Leaves appears at the side front, behind Eleanor, peering. He turns and beckons and the other two appear. Cornplanter steals up behind her. With one hand he covers her mouth, with the other he wrests the gun from her. The other two leap in front of her at the same instant and gesture for silence, finger on lips and tomahawks raised. Eleanor, who has sat quiet after the first surprise, nods her head. Cornplanter slowly removes his hand, all three ready to attack if she makes a sound. She smiles at Cornplanter as he moves around front, his hand withdrawn; she puts her finger on her own lips and nods at him. He is delighted with this. He holds out his hand to her, pointing off, not the way Mrs. Lytell went. She rises and takes his hand. Falling Leaves and Many Bears have looked into and around the house with swift movements. It must be plain that Eleanor does not understand their words.)*

FALLING LEAVES *(softly)*: Where is the boy?

MANY BEARS: He has gone into the air, like smoke from a fire.

CORNPLANTER: Let him go. We have a good captive. I will take her to our village. I will give her to the Old Queen, my mother. She shall take the place of my brother in our lodge.

(They go off swiftly, Eleanor marching staunchly by the side of Cornplanter who still holds her hand. After an instant Thomas lifts the tub a little.)

THOMAS *(in a whisper)*: Eleanor—Eleanor—— *(He gets it up on its side with difficulty, and emerges.)*
Eleanor—Eleanor! Eleanor!!

(He dashes to the house, to the edges of the stage, as he calls. He gets himself together, suddenly courageous, as he sees the Indian head dress under the balsam. He picks it up.)

This will show mother what tribe they were—

(He puts it on the tub, cups his mouth with his hands, and calls with all his strength, turning this way and that.)

We'll find you—We-e-ll f-i-n-d you-u—We-ll f-i-n-d you-u—We-ll f-i-n-d you-u--u——

ELEANOR *(From a distance comes Eleanor's voice, faint and growing fainter, but joyous and strong in its quality)*: I am brave. I am not afraid. Life is nothing at all to one who is not afraid—

(Curtain closes before the song is quite finished.)

——CURTAIN——

ACT TWO

The space around an outdoor fire, in Cornplanter's village. The ever-greens are rearranged to change the locality. If it is wished to be accurate in suggesting a dwelling, it should not be a tepee, as the Senecas, to whom Cornplanter historically belonged, used long lodges, built of bark. It is not necessary to have any dwellings at all. The villages were enclosed in high pickets, which could be shown if desired, but would probably only confuse the children, who are not used to think of Indians in that way. Instead, the word Seneca could be changed and tepees used if desired. Three logs around the fire, a tripod for a large kettle, and a large rock are all that is absolutely required. To the rock are fastened leather thongs, or rather, the rings to hold them.

The Old Queen is sitting alone, pounding the drum, or the ground, and singing. Her singing is full voiced and highly dramatic in tone, though she sits stiff and motionless except for her drumming. The last word of each couplet is held into a singing resonance.

OLD QUEEN *(singing)*:

Six moons ago I had two sons,
Now I have one, now I have one.

I mourn the power my lodge has lost,
My son was brave, my son was brave.

(A boy and a girl, about twelve, steal on running, and stop to watch her. They are secret about it, afraid she will see them. She drums without singing for a little space, then her attitude changes. She seems to enlarge and grow stronger.)

His brother brings a captive home,
To take his place, to take his place.

I wait a captive proud and fierce,
To be my son, to be my son—

The torture fire, the gauntlet's blows
He laughs to scorn, he laughs to scorn.

(Redbill, the boy, is drawn slowly forward, stirred by the words about the captive. She stops drumming and points in front and at one side of her.)

122

OLD QUEEN: It's a poor hunter that forgets his shadow.
(Redbill stops, frozen. The Old Queen continues without moving her head.) I think it is Redbill who tries to creep up on the Old Queen.
(Redbill, encouraged by her bantering tone, comes to her.)
REDBILL: How can you tell me from my shadow?
OLD QUEEN: You must learn to see what you look at, Redbill. *(The girl has been slipping toward them.)* Come forward, Shining Leaves. Why are you afraid?
(She comes, laughing, shamefacedly.)
REDBILL: Your song had the sound of the Dance of the Dead, and I knew that dance belongs only to women, and I should be punished if I saw it.
SHINING LEAVES: But there were no women dancing. So I whispered in his ear, "Stay." We wanted to ask you something.
REDBILL: Then when your words made me see a captive laughing at the fire, it made my heart beat hard and I forgot my shadow, to hear you better.
OLD QUEEN: You must learn to keep a cool head when your heart is hot, Redbill. What did you wish to ask?
SHINING LEAVES: Why do you sit alone and sing the song of the dead when there are no women to dance?
OLD QUEEN: I came out from the village to watch for Cornplanter, my son, and to welcome him with my drum. But his brother who was slain rose up in my heart, and I sang.
REDBILL: Will Cornplanter surely come tonight?
OLD QUEEN: He promised to be here before the moon of ripe seeds grew smaller. This is the last night the round moon walks in the sky. Cornplanter does the thing he says. He will come.
SHINING LEAVES: That's what the wife of Cornplanter says. She is watching, too. I saw her standing alone on the lookout rock, there.
(pointing off and back.)
REDBILL: She is running this way!
SHINING LEAVES: She has seen him!
OLD QUEEN: We would hear his warcry before he came in sight.
REDBILL: From the lookout rock, you can see warriors go past the gap, before their warcry comes.
(Eagle Feather, Cornplanter's wife, enters, running. She is a brooding, violent-natured woman, still young.)
WIFE: They have passed the gap. We shall hear their warcry soon!
OLD QUEEN: Redbill, run swift as an arrow from my son's bow. Tell the warriors in the village the queen commands them to stay inside the pickets when the warcry sounds. It is Cornplanter's lodge which waits for a captive. The wife of Cornplanter and his mother will look on the captive here. We will lead him to the village, singing. If he pleases us, we will sing of courage come into our lodge again. Then let the old men come out to meet us, in the dance of adoption. If he does

not please us, we will sing of the torture. Then let the young men come out with war whoops and war dance and lead him to his death. Go into—

REDBILL *(starting)*: I will be swift to tell them.

OLD QUEEN: Redbill! Was the Old Queen through speaking?

REDBILL: I thought you had finished your speaking.

OLD QUEEN: You must learn to watch the face of one who speaks, Redbill. Then you will know when the last work has come past his lips. Go into my lodge and fetch here the kettle of hominy I have ready. My son will want food. He has not eaten for many days.

REDBILL: I think you have finished your speaking.

OLD QUEEN: I have finished.

(Redbill darts off.)

SHINING LEAVES: Why do you say he has not eaten? Can't they shoot game to eat, on the march?

OLD QUEEN: You are a woman, Shining Leaves. You must learn to track out the meaning in what men do, as a hunter tracks the deer through the forest. Cornplanter's word was that he would be here before this moon grew less. These are the last hours he could keep that word. We would not stop for hunting game when his time was short. He will be very hungry.

(A warcry comes from off. It electrifies the three. It is from far away.)
My son!

SHINING LEAVES: They are here! They are here!

OLD QUEEN *(sharply)*: Stand quiet and listen! How can we hear them shout for captives?

(They stand listening intently, fingers raised for counting.)

WIFE: They do not shout. Has Cornplanter returned without any captive at all?

(A sharp shout of the three men off.)

CORNPLANTER, FALLING LEAVES, MANY BEARS: Hoah!!

ALL THREE WOMEN *(with a motion of their fingers)*: One——

(There is an expectant pause.)

WIFE: One. He has brought one captive, and no more.

OLD QUEEN: It will be a good captive! My son would not bring only one, unless he knew his heart was strong and full of courage.

(She seizes the drum. She does not lose her unshakable self mastery, but her emotion rises high within it. Her voice is full and dramatic. Her posture is immovable, except for the intensity of it and a growing enlargement of her whole attitude. She pounds.)
Dance, Eagle Feather! This is the last time the Dance of the Dead will be made for my son who was slain. Tonight his place will be empty no more! A captive comes, to fill it!

(Wife takes a dramatic pose, moving into it slowly.)

SHINING LEAVES: May I dance, too? I have learned the steps from watching the women.

124

OLD QUEEN: You will soon be old enough to dance with the women. You may follow her and learn.

(Shining Leaves jumps up and follows after the Wife in her movements. The dance is a series of postures, intensely expressive of the emotions of the song. The postures are separated by dancing steps, the simple shuffling step always used by the women. By this means the dancers circle around the singer. These postures were not, historically, a set thing, but created by the leader who originated them to express what passed. The song was also composed every time except for the opening couplet. Therefore it is perfectly legitimate to have the dancers create their postures in the play, always remembering that there must be no "fancy" movements, nothing but grim, straightforward, slow expression of primitive emotion. The rhythm is continuous, whether they are stepping ahead, moving into or out of the postures, or holding them through a definite number of beats, which is always the same. The rhythm is a simple one, two, three, four, with marked growth or lessening in loudness, according to the feeling of the singer. There are more complex Indian rhythms, but this simple one is perfectly effective, and was often used by the Indians. The posture may illustrate what is said of the son, if desired—e.g. his keen eye, or his courage. Or it may express the feelings of the dancer.

OLD QUEEN:

Spirits of those who are gone away,
Behold the dance of the dead.

Six moons ago I had two sons,
Now I have one, now I have one.

A place is empty in my lodge,
My son was slain, my son was slain.

My lodge has lost a seeing eye
His sight was keen, his sight was keen.

My lodge has lost a warcry clear.
His voice rang high, his voice rang high.

My lodge has lost a courage high,
My son was brave, my son was brave.

(A warcry comes from off, not far, first Cornplanter alone, then the three men together. The three women "freeze", at the first sound. After the triple cry, the Old Queen leaps to her feet. The three stand like statues, looking toward the voices, waiting, except that Shining Leaves' excitement gets the better of her once or twice, and she makes childish gestures of excitement.)

125

SHINING LEAVES *(craning forward and seeing them first)*: It is a girl!
(A sudden shock passes through the little group, the Old Queen drawing herself up tall and intent, the Wife drawing back, dark-browed, staring, the child crying out involuntarily, then covering her mouth shamefacedly. Cornplanter enters, leading Eleanor by the hand, followed by Many Bears and Falling Leaves. They greet each other by the uplifted hand.)

CORNPLANTER: My mother, I bring to you a child, to take the place of my brother who was slain, six moons ago. She shall dwell in our lodge, and be to me a sister.

WIFE *(furiously)*: Why does my husband bring here that beetleheart, like a captive of worth?

CORNPLANTER: She has an eagle's heart!

WIFE: She is white!

CORNPLANTER: She has the sinews of an Indian maid! She has marched night and day and her strength has not failed!

WIFE: It is a girl. How can she take your brother's place?

CORNPLANTER: She has the spirit of my brother. See. She is not afraid.

WIFE: You chatter like a crow on the top of a dead tree! Caw, caw! Will a white girl go on the warpath to take vengeance on the white man who killed my father?

CORNPLANTER: I do not want my sister to go on the warpath.

WIFE: Your brother would have done it! From the time he was as old as Redbill, I nursed the hate of the white man in his heart! From the day we blackened our faces for sorrow at his death, I have waited for the captive to take his place, and carry out the vow of vengeance your brother made. And you bring me a girl! You bring me a white poison flower! Send her away! I do not like her!

OLD QUEEN *(stern)*: You are letting a lie come past your lips. My son who was slain made no vow of vengeance.

WIFE: He made it to me! In secret he made it! Cornplanter my husband would not go out and kill for me, and I taught vengeance to his brother, secretly!

CORNPLANTER: My mother, the Old Queen forbade me! Her word rules the Senecas.

OLD QUEEN: I forbade your father to raid the white man's home. The warriors will not take vengeance for one who disobeys me. You are like a snake that hisses in the grass and wishes to strike. I will hear no more of this vow. It is as far from the captive who takes my son's place as the rising of the sun is from his setting.

WIFE *(to Queen)*: Will you take into the Senecas one whose courage has not been tested?

CORNPLANTER: She is brave. I have seen.

WIFE: What have you seen? How have you tested her? By a rabbit in the bush? By a smile in your eye? Did you lead her by the hand, all the way.

126

OLD QUEEN: Test her, wife of my son.

WIFE *(viciously, to Eleanor)*: Come here!

(Eleanor looks at her, wondering, and half smiles at her, in uncertainty. The Wife stamps her foot and screams.)

Come here!

OLD QUEEN: Foolish one. A maid can teach you to see what you look at. Why does the captive not obey, Shining Leaves?

SHINING LEAVES: The captive does not understand her words. The speech of her tribe is not ours.

OLD QUEEN: Learn from a child, Eagle Feather. How can she make the captive understand, Shining Leaves?

SHINING LEAVES: If she makes signs, the captive will understand.

OLD QUEEN: The child has given you wisdom. Call the captive to you.

(The Wife gets the better of her rage with difficulty, and makes a gesture to Eleanor. Eleanor looks up at Cornplanter questioningly, and he nods. She goes to the Wife steadily looking into her eyes without flinching. The Wife snarls at her, and lifts a hand as if to strike pointing off at the same time.)

WIFE: Go away from here! I hate you! Go or I will choke the breath of life from you. *(She threatens this with her hands, one on each side of Eleanor's throat. Eleanor still looks into her eyes steadily, though her breath comes fast.)*

Go! *(Pointing again.)*

(Eleanor looks around at Cornplanter. He shakes his head, "no". Eleanor looks back at the Wife and shakes her head. The Old Queen nods, pleased. Falling Leaves and Many Bears burst into loud laughter. Shining Leaves glows.)

MANY BEARS: Why don't you frighten her, Eagle Feather? Glare and snarl like a panther ready to spring!

FALLING LEAVES: Shout and scream a little. Surely you can be more terrible than this!

WIFE: Bring wood for the torture fire, Many Bears! Let her feel the flame! That will try her!

CORNPLANTER: My sister shall not feel the flame!

WIFE: She will not need to feel it! Let her only look on it. That will be enough! Her knees will fail, and she will cry out, like the captive who was put to death last moon, as soon as she sees the fire made ready for her.

OLD QUEEN: Prove your captive, my son.

CORNPLANTER: If her spirit is firm when she sees the fire made ready around her, is that enough?

OLD QUEEN: That is enough.

CORNPLANTER: Pile the brush, as Eagle Feather said. If her spirit fails, you may drive her into the wilderness. If it is firm, she shall dwell with us. But no one shall light the fire.

(The two Indians bring bundles of firewood from behind the rock. The Wife signs to Eleanor to go there. She looks to Cornplanter for con-

firmation. He nods, and after a breathless pause, she walks unflinch-ingly to the rock. The two Indians fasten her hands to the rings with leather thongs.)

WIFE *(to Queen)*: Tell my husband to stand out of her sight. His eyes comfort her.

OLD QUEEN. Turn from the captive, my son.

(Cornplanter looks away from Eleanor. Her lips quiver and her hands move, then she is more erect and still than ever.)

WIFE *(exultant)*: Her hands are trembling!

OLD QUEEN: Her eye does not waiver.

WIFE: I will show her the fire!

(She snatches up a stick and holds it into the fire, front. A red glow at the end of the stick shows that it has caught fire. This effect may be gained by placing a small battery in a hollow groove of the stick. Eleanor's eyes widen and her bosom swells. She looks up. She is praying. Suddenly she begins to sing. It is the tune of the song the mother taught her in the first act. The words should not be used, on account of the supposed difference in language here. Her voice gathers strength as the song goes on. The men shout approbation, exultant. They have grown to love her on the journey. The Wife brandishes the burning brand and rushes at her. Cornplanter snatches it from her, and hurls her back. He puts the fire out with his foot. Many Bears and Falling Leaves loosen her hands. Cornplanter leads her to the Old Queen. She is barely able to keep erect and to smother the hysterical laughter of relief, but manages well enough to prevent disaster.)

CORNPLANTER: My mother, receive your adopted daughter.

(The Old Queen takes her in her arms and presses her close. Eleanor answers her in kind, an outburst of affection expressing her gratitude and her overwhelming emotions. Cornplanter watches this with complacence, nodding to the other two men, who are also pleased with it.)

OLD QUEEN *(as she releases Eleanor)*: Shining Leaves, fetch me Seneca garments for the captive. She shall wear them into the village.

(Shining Leaves runs off. Cornplanter leads Eleanor to the Wife.)

CORNPLANTER: Eagle Feather, my wife, receive your adopted sister.

WIFE: She is bad! She is white! *(covers her eyes.)* I will not look upon her.

CORNPLANTER: She is to me a sister. Treat her so.

WIFE: Your heart is white!

CORNPLANTER: Your words are to me like the wind in my face when I run. They are nothing to me.

WIFE: I will not have her in our lodge!

CORNPLANTER: She dwells with us.

WIFE: May the earth never give you corn again! May the flesh dry from your bones! I will sharpen a knife for the girl-child's heart! I will brew strong poison from the roots in the forest for her drink!

CORNPLANTER: Enough talk!

(Redbill enters with a huge earthen bowl, decorated, of hominy.)

OLD QUEEN: My son, one who has fasted through a long march is like a hollow reed that breaks in the strong wind. Here is food to give you strength before we dance into the village.

CORNPLANTER, MANY BEARS, and FALLING LEAVES: Hoah!

(The Old Queen hands the bowl to Cornplanter.)

OLD QUEEN: This hominy is the gift of the Corn Spirit to the Senecas. Give thanks to the Great Mystery for the warmth of the sun, and the cool of the rain, and the magic of the earth, that drew the tall corn from the ground.

CORNPLANTER: We give thanks to our mother, the Earth, which sustains us. We give thanks to the corn, and to her sisters, the beans and the squashes, which give us life. We give thanks to the bushes and trees, which provide us with fruit. We give thanks to the moon and the stars which give us their light when the sun has lain down to rest. We give thanks to our grandfather Heno, who has given us rain to cheer our plants. We give thanks to the maple, which gives us sweet waters for the good of man.

(Cornplanter lifts the bowl high, and all present, except Eleanor, "say grace"—a prolonged exclamation on a high key from Cornplanter, followed by a swelling chorus from the rest on a lower note. The Old Queen takes the bowl again, and holds it before Eleanor. She does not understand what to do, and stands uncertain after the Queen has spoken.)

OLD QUEEN: With this food we give you our hearts. May the friendship be strong between us forever.

(The Indians frown, and the Wife snarls, as Eleanor, not seeing any spoon, and not knowing what to do, draws back a little. Redbill slips up to her, takes her hand, and puts it into the bowl. Her face lights up as she understands. She takes some of the hominy in her fingers and puts it into her mouth. The Indians are delighted. They call out "Hoah!")

MANY BEARS: Her heart is one with ours!

FALLING LEAVES: She accepts our lodge!

(The Queen puts the bowl in Eleanor's hands. They all come around the bowl and dip in their fingers, taking a bit in turn. Each lifts it toward Eleanor before tasting it. It is a ceremonial. Shining Leaves comes in with the garments in time to share in it. The Wife tries to withdraw from the circle, but Cornplanter pulls her in. She refuses the hominy, but when Cornplanter makes a threatening sign, she takes a few grains in her hand. She removes it from her lips, however, as soon as Cornplanter looks away.)

OLD QUEEN: We will adopt her into our tribe, and give her a Seneca name, according to the customs and usages of our tribe.

CORNPLANTER: She shall be called Ship-Under-Full-Sail, because her spirit is strong and swift.

OLD QUEEN: Shining Leaves and Eagle Feather, help me to dress her as a Seneca maid.

WIFE: I do not wish to see her so.

(The men have squatted on the ground with the hominy bowl, and are scooping up large mouthfulls with eager hunger. The Old Queen turns to Eleanor with the garments, assisted by Shining Leaves. They take off her dress, which is torn from the march, and put on the Seneca tunic over her underslip. Then they put on the leggings, beaded head band, and belt. Eleanor soon understands what is going on, and helps. During this business, comedy can be developed from the famished eating of the men, if needed.)

OLD QUEEN: Lead the captive into the village. The song is rising in me as the floods rise in the spring rains!

(She seizes the drum and starts the song to the same rhythm as the dance of death. Her voice is strong and exultant. Cornplanter takes Eleanor by the hand, and leads her after the Queen, the other two men following, the two children, much excited, bringing up the rear. The Wife stands aside, looking after them with malignant fury.)

OLD QUEEN *(singing):*

My lodge is strong and whole again.
My child has come, my child has come.
I lead her to the council fire.
The warriors wait, the warriors wait.
I show the captive strong and brave,
They dance with joy, they dance with joy.

(Etc. This is probably enough to cover the exit. If more is needed it is easily added in kind. The voice dies away in the distance, the drumming fading with it. The wife lifts her hand with its bit of hominy. Throws it down.)

WIFE *(low, vicious):* I did not take food with her!

(She stands, a statue.)

—— CURTAIN ——

ACT THREE

The scene is the same as Act Two. If it is possible to show the crescent moon, cloudlike in color, that will be an addition, but it is not necessary. It can be done on a dome with a projector, a moving picture machine, or a strong light blocked out with black except where the crescent is cut out. This opening should be covered with frost gelatine.

Eleanor sits alone, looking up at the visible or invisible moon. She is so absorbed in her thoughts that she does not at first notice the call from off. She is not at all sad, however. Only dreamy.

REDBILL *(off)*: Ship-under-full-sail! Ho-o-ah! Ship-under-full-sail!
SHINING LEAVES *(off)*: Ho-o-a-a-ah—!
(Eleanor rouses and waves her hand at the moon.)
ELEANOR: Goodbye, little day-time moon. I'll peek through the opening in the lodge tonight, to see you shine.
(The children run on. Redbill carries birch bark and a bundle of colored quills. Shining Leaves carries a little stack of birchbark canoes, fitted one inside of each other. They are about a foot and a half in length and wide in proportion. Eleanor is eager and intrigued, at once.)
Oh, what is that?
REDBILL: The Old Queen is going up into the hills tonight, to see the women working at the maple sugar camp. She says we may go too.
SHINING LEAVES: We are making canoes to hold the sugar the women make from the sweet waters of the maple tree. We thought you might like to make some, too.
ELEANOR: Oh, yes! Show me how!
REDBILL: Here is bark from our sister the birch tree. And here are quills from our brother the porcupine. The women have colored them bright as the berries in the woods in the moon of shining leaves, and softened them in water.
SHINING LEAVES *(illustrating)*: You fold them, so, and fasten them with the quills, so. This little piece of bone will smooth the path for them.
ELEANOR: Why, it's like a——what name did we give it—a needle!
SHINING LEAVES: What picture shall you make on yours, Ship-under-full-sail? I am making the sky-blue water. See.
(This is the zigzag pattern used in Indian work among the Iroquois. If it is not large enough to show in the sized auditorium being used, she should trace it with a large enough movement to show. They all go to work.)
ELEANOR: I'll make the little day-time moon.
REDBILL: Mine are big. They hold much sugar. Where have you been since the Old Queen finished telling us the story of the West Wind?

131

ELEANOR: I have been·here.

SHINING LEAVES: What were you doing?

ELEANOR: I was talking to my mother—my white mother. My mother the Old Queen thinks I have forgotten her. But I always talk to her when I am alone. *(She chuckles over this last.)* She'll be surprised when she sees I can make canoes!

(The other two put down their work, disturbed.)

REDBILL: What bird will tell her you can make canoes?

ELEANOR: She will come for me, sometime.

SHINING LEAVES: That would be a bad thing.

ELEANOR: It will make me happy.

(The Old Queen and Cornplanter and the Wife enter, and Eleanor jumps up and runs to them. She throws her arms around the Old Queen, who is greatly pleased, and presses her close. The Wife is angered.)

I am giving you thanks, because you take me into the hills to see the women make maple sugar.

CORNPLANTER: What words are these? The sugar camp is far away. Our lodge will be empty without my sister.

OLD QUEEN: It was Redbill and Shining Leaves I promised to take. I did not speak of Ship-under-full-sail.

REDBILL: Ship-under-full-sail is always with us!

SHINING LEAVES: Why should we speak of her? We go nowhere without our sister! She is in all our games and dances!

ELEANOR *(begging)*: I am making a canoe, to fill with sugar. See?

(Many Bears enters, from the other side.)

MANY BEARS *(lifting his hand to greet Cornplanter)*: Hoah.

CORNPLANTER: Hoah. Have you seen something from the lookout rock?

MANY BEARS: We saw someone pass the gap. We went to meet him. It was a white woman.

ELEANOR *(overjoyed)*: Oh!

CORNPLANTER *(angry)*: Send her away!

OLD QUEEN: What white woman dares to come among the Senecas?

WIFE: It is the white child's mother! Speak! Say it is true!

MANY BEARS: She asks if there is a white girl captive in our village.

CORNPLANTER *(harshly)*: There are only Senecas! Tell her so.

WIFE: My husband is not one to let a lie pass his lips! The white girl is by his side!

CORNPLANTER: Do not call her white! She was adopted into our lodge! She is a Seneca!

WIFE: She is white.

CORNPLANTER: She is a Seneca.

OLD QUEEN: She is adopted into our lodge.

WIFE: It does not change her blood to call her that!

MANY BEARS: The white woman is very tired. She begs to sleep in our village tonight. She begs to dip her fingers in our pot of corn with us. She has been many moons going from village to village among the Senecas, looking for her child.

CORNPLANTER: I do not like to hear about that woman. It makes my heart strange.

WIFE: Did you tell her the white child was here?

MANY BEARS: I did not tell her anything about it. I did not say yes. I did not say no. Falling Leaves remained by her side, till I returned with Cornplanter's answer to her prayer.

CORNPLANTER: Tell her to go away.

MANY BEARS: She says she will not go away till she has spoken with the chief.

CORNPLANTER: I will not hear a word!

WIFE: My husband, look at the face of the white girl! What do you see? She trembles with longing for her white home.

CORNPLANTER (without looking at Eleanor): This is her home. She thinks of no other.

WIFE: She is among the Senecas like the dead tree in the forest, which has no roots, and can easily be moved. Her roots are where her white kin are. If you do not send her back to them, she will die.

CORNPLANTER: You have listened to bad birds! She has not grieved for her white kin since the first snow of her stay with us.

WIFE: She is grieving now.

CORNPLANTER: Your words are false! She goes with my mother the Old Queen to the sugar camp, as laughing and strong as a young sapling in the sun.

WIFE: You are blind to what you do not wish to see.

CORNPLANTER: I do not hear you.—Many Bears, tell the white woman to go far from here. If she does not go away, I will take her scalp!

(Eleanor darts to Many Bears and checks him.)

ELEANOR: Oh, wait!

(He turns uncertainly to Cornplanter, who looks away from them all, his arms folded. Eleanor runs between Cornplanter and the Old Queen, catching a hand of each.)

Will my mother let me speak?

OLD QUEEN: Speak.

ELEANOR: Will my brother hear me?

CORNPLANTER (without looking at her): You must not speak of leaving me. I do not like to hear such talk.

ELEANOR: I won't speak a word of that.

CORNPLANTER: You must not even hide the thought in your mind.

ELEANOR: I won't even think about it.

CORNPLANTER: Your eyes must not ask me to go.

ELEANOR: My eyes will not ask anything at all. Your thoughts are in them, like shadows in a pool. Look and see.

(He turns slowly to look at her. She looks up at him steadfastly.)

CORNPLANTER: I will hear your words.

133

ELEANOR: If my brother kills my white mother, he will kill his sister too. She will blacken her face, and mourn till her life is gone out.

CORNPLANTER: If I do not kill her, you will leave me and go to her.

ELEANOR: I will not leave my brother, unless he says, Go.

CORNPLANTER: She will steal into our village. You will see her face. You will hear her voice. Strange feelings will come into you. You do not know now what you will do then. It is better for her to be dead.

ELEANOR: Try me! Oh, my brother, try and see! Bring my white mother where I am. I will show you you can trust me. I will be like an arrow in your hand. I will go or stay at your will.

CORNPLANTER: I do not understand your talk. I would not know what you said together.

ELEANOR: We will not talk at all. We will be as silent as hunters who stalk the deer.

CORNPLANTER: She will beg me to take you. There will be tears in her eyes. I do not like to see them! I do not want her to look at you.

ELEANOR: I am brown from the sun and wind. I wear our Seneca garments. My white mother would not know me from the others.

CORNPLANTER: Your hair is like the cornsilk. Ours is not. She would know by that.

ELEANOR: I will cover it with the skin cap my mother the Old Queen has made me. Oh, my mother, speak to my brother for me! Tell him he can trust my word. Tell him I will not ask to leave him. Tell him to try me. Let me prove my word, and save my white mother's life.

OLD QUEEN. There are tears in your sister's eyes, my son. Will you let them fall?

CORNPLANTER: The tears are for the white woman. I do not like that woman. I am waiting for her death.

(Eleanor throws her arms around Cornplanter.)

ELEANOR: Hear me, my brother!

(Cornplanter thrusts her away.)

CORNPLANTER *(very harshly)*: Bring the white woman, Many Bears. If my sister makes any sign at all while she is here, kill that woman!

ELEANOR: I thank my brother!

CORNPLANTER: Bring your skin cap. Sit with Redbill and Shining Leaves, and do not look at the woman when she comes.

ELEANOR: I will be swift to bring it! *(to the Old Queen)*: My mother, if I do not make any sign at all, will you give my white mother food and rest, before she returns to her own home?

OLD QUEEN: I will go with you. We will bring food for her.

ELEANOR: I thank you. I thank you both!

(She goes off, with the Old Queen.)

CORNPLANTER *(looking after her, speaks sadly, deeply)*: She is glad.——I will not give her up.

(He goes off, toward the lookout rock. The wife, who has sat still and dark-browed throughout this scene, rises. She looks cautiously at Redbill and Shining Leaves, who are back, working on the canoes,

which they take up when the interest of the scene which has held them spellbound, is relaxed. They seem not to see her, though they watch her as soon as her back is turned. She takes some roots from her bosom, and stares at them. She strikes a flint and makes a fire, where it was in the preceding act. She drops the roots into a small pot which stands on the log by the fire. She rises and goes off, back.)

WIFE *(as she goes)*: Do not touch the pot I have set on the fire. I brew strong medicine.

(The children watch her out of sight. Redbill steals up and peers into the pot.)

REDBILL *(low, as Shining Leaves comes to him)*: The wife of Cornplanter brews poison.

SHINING LEAVES: What bird told you that?

REDBILL: I followed her all morning, so silently she did not see me. She gathered the most deadly roots and herbs.

SHINING LEAVES: What is she doing now?

REDBILL *(peering, at the edge of the stage)*: She is plucking baneberry leaves where the moonlight falls at night. Baneberry in the light of the moon is the most deadly poison in the woods. One who drinks it sleeps his life away. He fades and falls like the mayapple when the moon of flowers is gone.

SHINING LEAVES: Why does the wife of Cornplanter brew strong poison.

REDBILL: I think I know.

SHINING LEAVES: I think I know, too.

REDBILL: Let it come past your lips.

SHINING LEAVES: It is not safe to let it out into the day.

REDBILL: She is far out among the trees. She cannot hear.

SHINING LEAVES: I think she brews poison because she hates our white sister.

REDBILL: Something dark is plain to me.

SHINING LEAVES: Share it with me.

REDBILL: Eagle Feather is always watching for a chance to rid herself of our white sister. She will give her this brew to drink. She will tell Cornplanter it is longing for her white home that makes Ship-under-full-sail fade.

SHINING LEAVES: Sh-h-h——

(They slip back to their work. The Wife enters, sits by the pot, drops leaves into it. Eleanor runs on, her skin cap in her hand. She puts it on. The Wife stirs the pot. She lifts it and blows on it to cool it.)

ELEANOR: Look, Redbill. Tell me if you can see any of my hair.

REDBILL: There is a lock.

ELEANOR: Put it under for me, Shining Leaves. If my mother should see it, she would know me. She would cry out, and Cornplanter would tell them to take her scalp. Is it all under—are you sure? Look again. Not a hair must be outside the cap.

SHINING LEAVES: You are trembling, Ship-under-full-sail. Are you afraid?

ELEANOR: I am afraid for my white mother. My knees will not hold me still. My eyes are stinging. I swallow tears. They would anger Cornplanter. It is bad of the tears to come. My white mother is not safe when I have tears on my cheeks.

WIFE: Little sister.

ELEANOR: What is your will, wife of my brother?

WIFE: I have brewed you a medicine, which will drive the tears far from you. It will give your knees back their strength. You will not feel fear after you have taken it. Drink.

(Eleanor goes to her and takes the bowl. Relbill and Shining Leaves make wild motions for her not to drink, unseen by the Wife.)

ELEANOR *(quick-witted)*: My strength has come again, Eagle Feather. My knees do not shake under me at all.

WIFE: Drink, and your strength will stay by you when your white mother comes.

ELEANOR: I will keep my strength, for my mother's sake. I do not need your drink. I have no thirst, now. Set the bowl down. When I have seen my mother, the thirst will come upon me. Then I will drink it.

WIFE: You shall not wait. Drink!

ELEANOR: No!

(Wife holds her and tries to force it through her lips. Redbill darts to them and strikes the bowl to the ground. The Wife cries out in fury. Shining Leaves runs off shrieking.)

WIFE: You spill my brew!

SHINING LEAVES *(running)*: Ho-ah! Old Queen! Ho-a-h!

REDBILL *(snatching up the bowl)*: Cornplanter shall know! Cornplanter! Hoah!

(The Wife tries to snatch the bowl from Redbill. They struggle over it. She tries to empty it.)

WIFE: It is mine. Let me have it!

REDBILL: There is poison in it! You shall not turn it down! You shall not spill the poison! I will show it to Cornplanter and the Queen!

(The Queen with a bowl of food and Shining Leaves enter from one side, Cornplanter almost as soon from the other in great haste. Redbill darts to him with the bowl.)

See what this evil one has given your sister to drink!

(The Queen takes the bowl, sniffs at it, turns on the Wife with stately anger.)

OLD QUEEN: What is this you did?

WIFE: I did what is in my heart. I hate the white child.

CORNPLANTER: Wicked one! Why do you go against your husband?

WIFE: I told you to send her away! If you had listened to my word, I would not have given her the poison bowl! Let her go to her white mother, or she will die!

CORNPLANTER: She did not drink it.

WIFE: There are many ways to make her sicken and die. Send her out of my sight.

OLD QUEEN: Eagle Feather, hear my words. You have plotted the death of a Seneca.

WIFE: She is not a Seneca!

OLD QUEEN: Do not let that lie pass your lips again! One who plots death for one of his own tribe, must be punished. Go to the cave under the lookout rock, where we make offering to the Great Mystery, and wait. When we have made our talk with the white woman, I will bring the old men to the cave. We shall learn what your punishment must be. Don't speak! Do not stay. Take the path to the cave. I am the Queen of the Senecas. Obey my word.

(Wife turns sullenly and starts off. She meets Many Bears, Falling Leaves, and Mrs. Lytell, entering. Mrs. Lytell lifts her hand in Indian greeting as she comes. The Wife flings herself in her path.)

WIFE *(violently)*: They will tell you she is not here! Do not believe them!

(Cornplanter, the Queen, and the other men shout in anger.)

CORNPLANTER, AND OTHERS: Hoah!——

OLD QUEEN: Do not say that!

WIFE: I will say it! It is the truth! I will show you your child, white woman!

(Cornplanter leaps to her side and covers her mouth. Falling Leaves and Many Bears hold her to prevent her pointing. Eleanor sits very still, her work arrested in her hands. The other two children drop theirs and turn to watch. Eleanor should be so placed that her back is to them, her face to the audience.)

OLD QUEEN: Set her on the path to the cave. My son and I will watch her going from the lookout rock.

(They go off, Many Bears and Falling Leaves forcing the Wife, the Queen and Cornplanter following. Mrs. Lytell gets in front of Cornplanter.)

MRS. LYTELL: Will my brother hear what I came to say?

CORNPLANTER *(without pausing or looking at her)*: There is time for that.

(He stalks off. Mrs. Lytell stands, uncertain. She looks at the children and slowly approaches them. Eleanor's hand trembles, but she goes steadily on with her work.)

MRS. LYTELL: If you are Seneca children, you will understand what I say.

(Redbill and Shining Leaves exchange glances, excited and a little frightened. Cornplanter enters silently, upstage, and stands watching them, unseen by any of them.)   . . . .

Do not be afraid. I am a friend of the Senecas. I have learned to speak their tongue that I may talk to them as brothers.

(The children make no response. She comes a little closer.)

Speak to me, Seneca boy. I wait for the sound of your voice.

REDBILL: I have no word to speak to you.

MRS. LYTELL *(touching Shining Leaves)*: Will you speak a word of welcome to me, Seneca maid? I had a daughter who has seen as many summers as you. Eight moons ago, I came to my lodge and found it empty as a nest the birds have left last summer. My daughter had been taken away. I have walked night and day asking at every Seneca village: Do my brothers know of any white captive? Many have said to me, We have heard of a white girl who dwells in Cornplanter's village. I have come here, searching for news of her.

REDBILL: We have no news to give you.

MRS. LYTELL: Have you never heard anyone speak of a captive, in the village yonder?

REDBILL: The Old Queen says to us: Talk flies about the campfire like the wind that blows this way and that. Pay no heed to it.

MRS. LYTELL: Who are you? Your dress is Seneca. Do you live in Cornplanter's village?

REDBILL: My name is Redbill.

MRS. LYTELL *(touching Shining Leaves)*: And this maid?

SHINING LEAVES: My name is Shining Leaves.

MRS. LYTELL: What pretty names. And what are you called, busy one who will not look up from her work?

(Eleanor bends her head still lower, keeping on with her work. Cornplanter is deeply interested.)

Won't you tell me your name?

REDBILL: Her name is Ship-under-full-sail. She won't tell it, because she does not like white people.

(Eleanor is disturbed by this, but swallows it without a sign, except the face.)

MRS. LYTELL: Why not? *(eagerly)* Did you ever know a white child? Won't you tell me, Ship-under-full-sail?

(Eleanor starts to gather up her work.)

REDBILL: You are making her go away.

MRS. LYTELL: Never mind, busy maid. I'll not talk to you. What pretty things you're making, Shining Leaves.

SHINING LEAVES: I'm making the sky blue water on mine. Ship-under-full-sail is making the little day-time moon. See?

MRS. LYTELL *(picking it up)*: The little day-time moon. Ah! Do you suppose my daughter has learned to make such pretty things as this?

SHINING LEAVES *(in a burst of enthusiasm)*: She can make the finest bead work and quill work of us all!

(She suddenly covers her mouth with her hand.)

MRS. LYTELL: What?! What did you say?!

REDBILL *(to Shining Leaves, angrily)*: You make a trail with your words, like the mole who lifts his burrow plain in the earth for the hunter to see!

MRS. LYTELL: You know her! You have seen her! Take me to her! I will give you many gifts if you will take me to her.

138

REDBILL: That is not for us to do.

MRS. LYTELL: I will ask your chief. At last I have found her! Is she well? Is she strong?

SHINING LEAVES: She beats all of us in the races for the girls.

MRS. LYTELL: Are they kind to her?

REDBILL: She is a sister to Cornplanter, the chief, and a daughter to the Old Queen, his mother. The best pieces in the pot of meat Cornplanter fishes out to give her.

SHINING LEAVES: She has the finest garments in the village. The Old Queen makes them herself.

MRS. LYTELL: Is she happy? Does she grieve for her home? Does she long for her mother?

REDBILL: When she came, she grieved much. She went often alone and let her tears fall in secret. She thought we did not know, but we followed her like hunters on the trail, and saw.

(This is the first time Eleanor has heard this.)

SHINING LEAVES: But now she does not do that. She doesn't want to go away.

MRS. LYTELL: She would want to go with me!

REDBILL: You speak foolish words. She is among the Senecas like our sister the birch-tree that gave us this bark, whose roots are in our earth and will not let her be moved.

(Cornplanter is very delighted with this. Eleanor moves uneasily, but is quiet again.)

MRS. LYTELL: She cannot have forgotten her brother. She cannot have forgotten her mother so soon. We have thought of her day and night. We knew she was waiting for me to come.

REDBILL: You have listened to bad birds. She does not wish you to come.

MRS. LYTELL *(to herself)*: Oh—if that were true—

(She turns away. Eleanor looks up at her. Her hands move as if she were about to speak. She puts them down again, resolutely, and returns to her work. Cornplanter looks at the Old Queen, nodding with satisfaction. They come forward.)

CORNPLANTER: You may go now.

MRS. LYTELL: Is my brother the chief whose name I have heard from many villages? Do I speak to Cornplanter, and his mother, the Old Queen?

CORNPLANTER: I am Cornplanter. I do not wish to talk. My mother will give you food from our pot to make you strong for your journey back to your own people.

(The Old Queen brings her the bowl of hominy. Mrs. Lytell dips her fingers into it and puts a bit into her mouth. She waits for the others to do likewise.)

OLD QUEEN: Take the bowl. Eat till your hunger is ended.

MRS. LYTELL: Do not the Senecas take the food they offer a friend?

OLD QUEEN: We do not eat with you.

CORNPLANTER: We do not call you friend. We wish you to go away. We give you food that your knees may not be weak on the trail. These two *(indicating Falling Leaves and Many Bears)* will guide you to the fort built by the white men where the waters pour over the rocks. There you will find many of your own people. Stay with them. Do not come here again.

MRS. LYTELL: My brother, I came in search of my daughter, who has been many moons among the Senecas.

CORNPLANTER: I do not wish to hear of her.

(The Wife comes stealing back of them.)

MRS. LYTELL: I will give many gifts, if I may take my daughter back with me. I cannot live without her. I have come far from my home. I have——

CORNPLANTER *(very harsh)*: Let that woman look the other way! I do not like to see her.

(Falling Leaves turns her away from Cornplanter.)

MANY BEARS: Did our sister speak of gifts?

MRS. LYTELL: I will give you much cloth and many beads and much corn if you will send my daughter back to me.

MANY BEARS: Cloth and beads are a small gift.

FALLING LEAVES: We have corn in plenty.

MANY BEARS: Horses are a good gift.

FALLING LEAVES: Guns are pleasing to the Senecas.

MRS. LYTELL: I will give you ten fine horses and twenty guns.

CORNPLANTER: Do not talk of gifts!

MRS. LYTELL: I will double the gift.

CORNPLANTER: I have heard enough words about gifts! You let bad talk come past your lips when you spoke that word, Many Bears! And you, too! Get out of my sight, both of you! Do not come before me again till you have left the white woman behind you at the fort.

(The two move off. Mrs. Lytell stands, desperate. Many Bears turns back at exit.)

MANY BEARS: We are waiting for you, white woman.

MRS. LYTELL: Go ahead on the path. I will come. I must speak to Cornplanter first——

CORNPLANTER: I will not hear you!

(The Wife suddenly darts to Eleanor, seizes her arm, jerks her to her feet, and snatches off her cap. Her golden hair comes tumbling down on her shoulders. Mrs. Lytell gives a piercing cry. All eyes are on Eleanor. She stands gazing at her mother an instant, then turns resolutely to Cornplanter, walks to his side and takes his hand, looking up at him. He looks away from both, holding her hand, fast.)

MRS. LYTELL: Eleanor!

OLD QUEEN *(to the Wife)*: I will not wait for the old men to judge you, wicked one! Go before me to the village. Redbill and Shining Leaves shall run ahead and call to the women to be ready. They shall dance you out of it, forever. You shall go to the farthest field and

140

dig the earth and hoe the corn forever. Never look into my lodge again! Never dance or work or sit or sing with the Senecas again! *(Old Queen points ahead. The two children run off, the Wife goes very sullen, the Old Queen follows, stately and implacable.)*

ELEANOR *(softly)*: I kept my word.

CORNPLANTER: Your hand trembles.

(Eleanor tries to straighten even more. Mrs. Lytell who has stood overwhelmed, since Eleanor turned from her to Cornplanter, stretches out her arms to her.)

MRS. LYTELL *(pleadingly)*: Eleanor.

(Eleanor looks up at Cornplanter, her face working)

CORNPLANTER *(after a pause)*: Go to her.

ELEANOR *(a glad cry)*: Mother!

(She rushes into her mother's arms. They laugh and cry together, kissing each other, hugging each other. Mrs. Lytell finally holds her close, stroking her hair, and looking up in a silent prayer of thanks.)

CORNPLANTER: She shall go. The mother must have her child again. I will go back alone.

(He goes off.)

—— CURTAIN ——

(Tableau curtain, on Eleanor and her mother.)

The Ghost of Mr. Penny

by

Rosemary Gabbert Musil

The premiere production of this play was given in
March, 1939, by the Children's Theatre of Evanston,
Illinois, under the direction of Miss Winifred Ward.

THE GHOST OF MR. PENNY

By Rosemary Gabbert Musil

THE ANCHORAGE PRESS
Cloverlot
Anchorage, Kentucky 40223
U. S. A.

The Ghost of Mr. Penny

by Rosemary Gabbert Musil

❧

CAST

BILL, a tramp, good-natured, easy-going, lovable

LEWIS, twelve years old, whose ambition is to be a "tough guy"

TOMMY, his friend and pupil

SALLY, their playmate, a gallant and spirited girl

ELLEN, another playmate, rather prim and cautious

PHINEAS, an awkward boy of eighteen or so

MR. JENKINS, a fussy little middle-aged man

MR. SIMMONS, Ellen's father, and the neighborhood policeman

SCENES

ACT ONE:

SCENE: The abandoned coach-house of the old Penny estate, late one afternoon in autumn.

ACT TWO

SCENE: The living room of the old Penny house, after dark, that evening.

ACT THREE

SCENE: The coach-house, the next morning.

145

To

SKIPPY

and his pals

THE GHOST
OF
MR. PENNY

by

ROSEMARY G. MUSIL

ACT ONE

Scene: The abandoned coach-house of an old estate.

There are three openings in the set—the outside door up right center,
the wooden casement window up left center, and a door down left which
leads into the harness room. There is a manger filled with straw at right.

The room looks dusty and neglected. Just below the window is a
gas plate with boxes piled high upon it, and the plate itself protected by an
oil-cloth. A rickety old table occupies the center of the stage, and there
are two matching chairs piled up against the door, which is locked and
barred. An old rusty lantern hangs over the manger.

At the rise of the curtain, the stage is empty, but outside the window,
someone can be heard approaching. The window swings open, revealing
a man with a battered felt hat set on the back of his head.

Bill is evidently a sailor of sorts, for he wears parts of a sailor cos-
tume. He is big and athletic-looking, though lazy, and in his prime of life.
He may be thirty-five or forty-five. It is hard to tell, for he enjoys life,
and his sense of humor and kindliness have kept him young. He is neat,
in spite of the battered felt hat, and a two-days' growth of beard. He
opens the window cautiously, looks inside, and expresses his delight in a
long, low whistle.

He throws a leg over the sill, steps onto the boxes, and into the room.
He is carrying some provisions tied up in a bandana handkerchief. He

147

pushes the window to, and looks about him with pleasure, giving out a big sigh of contentment. Then he begins a more detailed examination of the premises.

He peeps into the harness-room, finding everything to his taste. Then he crosses to center, and tries the table for dust, testing it with a gingerly finger. He brushes his hands off with elaborate care, then spotting the manger at right, he crosses and punches the straw to test it for bedding.

It all suits him down to a T, and he begins to make preparations for a formal supper. Taking a handful of straw, he dusts the table efficiently, then unstacks the two chairs, and dusts them, arranging them at the table, as for a banquet. Then, spying the oil-cloth, he pulls it out and spreads it over the table, straightening it daintily. He puts his bandanna on the table and opens it up, taking out spoon, knife, and fork. Placing these carefully, he casts a critical eye over the whole, and decides something is missing. Then he snaps his fingers and springs out the window, returning almost instantly with a handful of goldenrod, which he crams down into the neck of an old bottle which is found among the boxes and debris.

Surveying his handiwork with pride, Bill beams happily, and draws a can from his bandana. Then he pulls a can-opener from his pocket, and starts to tackle the can. The can-opener offers difficulties, and Bill is still trying to make it work, when a voice is heard outside calling, and he stops to listen attentively.

TOMMY *(outside)*: Lewis! Hey Lewie! I shot you. You're dead! Leeeewie!

(The voice grows fainter, but a scuffling at the window warns Bill, who hastily puts the can-opener in his pocket, gathers up his things, and piles into the manger. The window opens as he does so, and Lewis, a little boy about twelve, climbs in, carrying a home-made shotgun. He squats down beside the table, waiting. The voice of his pursuer comes closer.) Lewie! . . . Leewwie! Quit your hidin' and come on back here! You're dead! . . . Lew . . . I bet I know where you're hidin' at! (Tommy climbs up on a box from outside, opens the window and crawls in. He is about the same age and size of Lewis, and carries a toy pistol.)

LEWIS: Bang! Bang! . . . I got ya!

(He runs out from behind the table.)

TOMMY: Ah, you did not. I got you outside by the house. You were dead before you came in here!

LEWIS: I was not. You just got me in the shoulder.

(Sally "yoo-hoo's" from back in the deep yard surrounding the coach house.)

SALLY *(offstage)*: Leeeewis! . . . Tommieeee! Hey, Tommy, I want to play too!

LEWIS: It's Sally! Quick, shut the window! We don't want any ole

148

girls playing in here. *(The boys slam the windows shut, and pull the bar across it.)*

SALLY *(at the window)*: Tommy Tommy Higgins! . . . I saw you slam this window. Open it up. I want to play in the coach house too.

TOMMY: Ah, go away.

LEWIS: We're playin' G-Men. Girls can't be G-men.

SALLY: I'll be a G-woman then.

(The boys think this remark terribly funny. They go off into gales of derisive laughter.

BOYS: Ha, ha, ha! She'll be a G-woman. Silly old girls think they can be G-women!

SALLY *(outside)*: I've got as much right in there as you have.

TOMMY: Ah, go cook a radish!

(Overcome with this brilliant retort, the boys howl with laughter, and slap each other on the back.)

SALLY: You open this window! The coach house doesn't belong to you.

LEWIS: It doesn't belong to you either.

SALLY: Well, anyway, you let me in!

TOMMY *(whispering)*: Don't answer, and maybe she'll go away.

SALLY: You let me in, or I'll—I'll bust the door down!

LEWIS: She'll bust the door down! Ha! Ha! That's good!

TOMMY: Ho! Ha! Ole doors got about a million bolts in it, I reckon, but she's gonta bust it in! That's good!

SALLY: All right. I'll show you.

(Sally throws her weight against the door. The boys are surprised at her attempt.)

TOMMY: She's tryin' it!

LEWIS: Of all the silly . . .

(The rusty old door, weak in the hinges, suddenly gives way, and Sally falls headlong upon it, into the coach house. For a moment, no one can speak, so surprised are they. Then Sally gets up slowly, rubbing certain parts.)

SALLY: Gee, I did it!

TOMMY: Gosh!

LEWIS: She busted the door in!

SALLY: I told you I would.

(The boys examine the door. Sally smooths her dress and hair.)

TOMMY: Look, the hinges were rusty and they busted right off!

LEWIS: Yeah . . . Hey, hadn't we better set up the door?

(Sally has taken off her shoe and is hopping about trying to find the paper she lost out of it.)

TOMMY: I say we had. What if somebody saw it busted in! Come on, Sally, help us put the door back.

SALLY: Wait a minute, I've got to find the paper out of my shoe.

LEWIS: Paper out of your shoe?

SALLY: Yes, there's a hole in the sole, and I'll ruin my stocking if I don't keep a paper in it.

LEWIS (*picking up folded paper*): This it?

SALLY: Yes . . . Thanks! (*She sits on chair and puts paper back in shoe.*) Now! . . . Do you think we can pick it up?

TOMMY: Grab hold of here and shove it as you raise it! (*The children set the door up, and wonder of wonders, it jams into the doorway and stands by itself.*) Gee! It sticks by itself!

SALLY: Careful, it might fall down!

(*The children hold their hands out for a minute, then breathe easier as they see it is going to stand.*)

LEWIS: Nope, she really sticks . . . Can't even tell it was knocked down!

SALLY: We'd better get away, in case the wind blows it over, or something! (*They back off and turn to the table, leaning on it, and Sally sits in one of the chairs.*)

TOMMY (*examining the table suddenly*): Hey look!

SALLY: What?

TOMMY: There's oil cloth on the table!

LEWIS: Gee, yes, and the chairs are drawn up too, just like somebody had put them there! I never noticed that before!

SALLY: Do you suppose somebody's been here besides us?

LEWIS: Who could have?

TOMMY: Maybe it was the ghost!

SALLY: The ghost!

LEWIS (*derisively*): What ghost?

TOMMY (*lowering his voice and looking about him*): The ghost of Mr. Penny!

SALLY: Of all the silly things! There isn't any such thing as ghosts!

LEWIS: I don't know. They say the big house is haunted.

TOMMY: Yeah, and old Mr. Penny's ghost walks up and down the steps at night, looking for his little boy that shot himself accidentally with a gun!

SALLY: Oh, that's too silly for words! Mr. Penny isn't even dead!

TOMMY: No? Then where is he?

SALLY: Nobody knows. After his little boy shot himself, Mrs. Penny died from shock, and Mr. Penny just wandered away and went to sea.

TOMMY: Well, people have seen his ghost wandering about the big house at night, so he must be dead!

SALLY: The idea! If there'd been a ghost wandering around old Mr. Herman would have seen him, wouldn't he? And Mr. Herman says Mr. Penny isn't dead and that he's coming back some day. That's the reason he stays on there in the big house, waiting for Mr. Penny to come back!

LEWIS: If Mr. Herman saw that ole ghost wanderin' around, he'd have him arrested fer trespassin'!

SALLY: Shh! Somebody's calling!

(*Children listen.*)

ELLEN *(outside window)*: Sally, are you in there?

SALLY: It's Ellen! *(Opens window.)* Hello, Ellen, come on in!

ELLEN *(standing at the window)*: I don't want to climb in the window, I'll get my dress dirty *(superiorly)*.

LEWIS *(mischievously)*: Then why don't you come in by the door?

ELLEN: Is the door open?

LEWIS: Sure it is! Sally came in that way!

ELLEN: Well for pity sakes, why didn't you say so, Sally?

SALLY: Oh, but Ellen, you—

(Ellen starts to turn toward the door, and Lewis puts his hand over Sally's mouth to keep her from telling.)

LEWIS: Just push against the door real hard!

SALLY *(jerking free from Lewis)*: Don't you do it, Ellen!

(Lewis grabs her again and keeps her from talking.)

ELLEN: Well, I guess I can do it if you did, Sally Andrews!

LEWIS: Sure you can! Push real hard!

(Ellen pushes, the door falls in, and the boys howl with laughter. Ellen is mad as a wet pussy cat, and Sally runs to her solicitously to help her up.)

ELLEN: You think you are funny, don't you, Lewis Bleck?

LEWIS *(laughing)*: No! I think you are!

SALLY: I tried to tell you, Ellen!

ELLEN: Well, I came over here to tell you something exciting, but if you're going to act mean— *(She starts out the door, but Sally brings her back.)*

SALLY: Oh, don't pay any attention to the old boys, Ellen!

LEWIS *(helping Tommy lift the door back into place)*: Sure, we're sorry. What's doing?

TOMMY: Did your father capture a bandit or somethin'?

ELLEN: No. Mr. Herman's dead!

CHILDREN: Mr. Herman!

SALLY: Oh, when did it happen?

ELLEN: Sometime yesterday, I guess. My mamma went over to the big house at supper time to take him some hot soup, and he was lying on the table. He'd had a heart attack. He'd been writing, the papers were scattered all over. . . . Mamma went over and swept them all up in the fireplace!

SALLY: For goodness sake!

TOMMY: Gee!

LEWIS: Poor old Mr. Herman can't have us arrested for trespassin' now, I reckon!

ELLEN: And that isn't the worst of it!

SALLY: No?

ELLEN: My mother went back over there late last night, intending to burn the papers she'd swept up in the fireplace . . . and she . . . *(her voice breaks with the weight of her horrible tale)* she took my father's

flashlight and went into the old house, and right away . . . right away
. . . . (her voice breaks again)

TOMMY: Yeah, go on!

ELLEN: She saw it!

SALLY: What?

ELLEN: The ghost, of course!

SALLY: Aw, that's silly!

ELLEN: Yes? Well, maybe you think my mamma would tell a story. Maybe you think . . .

TOMMY: Gosh, Ellen, what was it like?

ELLEN: It was a kind of head hanging in space, and pink cheeks, and purple . . .

LEWIS: Whiskers!

ELLEN: Whiskers . . . er . . . (The spell is broken, the children laugh at Ellen's story.) It did not! It had whiskers, though . . . and a purple tie!

LEWIS: A pink ghost with purple whiskers! Ha, ha!
(Children laugh at her, and Ellen is angry.)

ELLEN: All right, smarties, laugh all you please, but I guess my mamma knows what she saw. She was too scared to even burn the papers!

SALLY: Poor Mr. Herman. All these years, he's kept that house open, waiting for Mr. Penny to come back. And now—he's dead.

LEWIS: Gosh, it gives me the creeps.

TOMMY: Let's don't think about it. Let's play G-men. You girls go away now. We want to play G-men.

SALLY: We'll be G-women, and play too.

LEWIS: Of all the silly—there isn't any such thing as G-women! (Disgustedly) G-women!

TOMMY: Why don't we play Secret Service? They got girls in that.

SALLY: Sure! Let's do!

LEWIS: Ah, we don't want to play with girls! (He throws his gun down on the table, and looks disgusted.)

ELLEN: You'd better treat Sally nice, cause she's got to go to the orphan asylum tomorrow, and you won't get a chance to play with her any more.
(The children all look at Sally pityingly. Sally is serious, too.)

LEWIS: Gee, Sally, do you haff to go tomorrow?

SALLY: I—I reckon so.

TOMMY: Gee, Sally, I'm sure sorry.

SALLY (rallying and attempting to make light of it): Oh, it's . . . it's just a temporary arrangement, Uncle Jim says . . . I'm just going to stay long enough for Uncle Jim to get well, then he's going to get me back again. Besides, it really isn't an orphan asylum, Ellen . . . It's a boarding house for children, and it's got swings and slides, and everything.

(The children are sad, they love Sally.)

TOMMY *(impulsively)*: Here, you can have my gun, Sally.

LEWIS: Mine too.

SALLY *(lighthearted once more, for she has learned to take her troubles a step at a time)*: Thanks . . . but what will Ellen do?

ELLEN *(airily)*: Oh, I could have a real gun if I wanted it!

TOMMY: Gee, Ellen, you mean your father's policeman's gun?

SALLY: Ellen, you wouldn't!

ELLEN: I could if I wanted to. I saw where he keeps it, last night!

LEWIS: Gosh, is it loaded?

ELLEN: Of course. Policemen always keep their guns loaded.

TOMMY: Gee! Go get it, Ellen!

ELLEN: All right, wait here a minute!

(She turns and goes to the window to climb out of it, but the tramp can not stand by now. He hurries out of the stall, crosses quickly to the window, shuts it and bars the way.)

BILL: Oh, no! No. no, Princess! Don't do it! *(The children scream, and scramble together in a heap downstairs at left.)* Guns is bad medicine fer children . . . er anybody fer that matter!

ELLEN: Who—who are you?

TOMMY: You'd better let us out of here!

LEWIS: Yeah, her father's a policeman.

ELLEN: And he'll arrest you for trespassing!

BILL: Aw, shucks! Don't be afraid of me. . . . I wouldn't hurt no one, and I like kids! I wouldn't 'a let you know I was here, but shucks, I couldn't stand by and let the Princess here get her pappy's loaded gun. . . . Why, you kids might of shot each other! That would have been awful!

ELLEN: You were hiding in there! *(pointing to the stall)*

BILL: Aw, now!

TOMMY: Yes, and you'd better get out of here!

BILL: Aw, shucks, I'm not a goin' to hurt nothin' er nobody; I wasn't goin' t' stay long nohow. I'll go now if you say so. But, listen, kids, about guns—guns don't do nobody any good ever! Not even grown up people, let alone kids!

LEWIS: Yeah? Well, I'll bet they do G-men some good!

BILL: G-men? Why, they don't even use 'em most of the time!

TOMMY: Aw, like fun they don't!

(The boys have forgotten to be afraid, and come out and speak boldly with the gentle Bill.)

BILL: Naw, they don't. They use their brains to catch crooks! Take this here feller at the head of the G-men . . . you know what he says?

LEWIS: What?

(The children relax perfectly now, grouping themselves about Bill who is at the table.)

BILL: Well, he says only cowards use guns . . . you know, people who

153

are afraid! And he never uses a gun 'ceptin' in self-defense, 'cause he's seen so many cowardly people dependin' on guns to make 'em brave, that he's downright ashamed t' have a gun!

LEWIS: Honest?

BILL: Sure, that's what he says . . . and me, I never like guns! I don't even like to see kids play with toy guns, 'cause I've seen too much grief they've caused in the world.

TOMMY: You mean like in wars?

BILL: Sure, and in peace times too. So don't ever fool with your pappy's loaded gun, Princess. Why, didn't that poor little Penny boy get killed playin' with his pappy's gun? Just like you were goin' t' do!

(Sally looks at him and catches her breath in sudden excitement. Maybe this tramp is Mr. Penny come back!)

SALLY: Why! How did you know that?

BILL *(unconsciously contributing to her thought)*: Oh, I know a lot of things that would surprise you!

ELLEN: You're just a tramp, that's all, and you can't boss us around! I'll tell my father . . . he's a policeman, and he'll have you—

BILL *(patiently)*: Yeah, I know . . . arrested fer trespassin' . . . but first we got to sort of figure out which one of us is trespassin', ain't we?

ELLEN: Which one of us? Why, you are, of course!

BILL: Well, that depends. Now this here coach house don't belong to you kids, does it?

ELLEN: It doesn't belong to you either! It belongs to Mr. Penny, only he's dead!

SALLY *(quickly)*: No, he isn't dead, either!

BILL *(amused)*: Now, you see there? You don't know much about it after all, do you? Why, for all you know, maybe I own the place!

SALLY: Oh! Oh, are you . . . .

ELLEN: Own the place! Why, you're just a tramp!

TOMMY: Are you?

BILL: Am I what?

TOMMY: Just a tramp like Ellen says?

BILL: Me a tramp? Shucks, Matey, I'm a sailor!

TOMMY: A sailor?

SALLY *(suddenly sure of herself)*: Of course he is!

(Bill looks at her surprised.)

ELLEN: Oh, what do you know about it? If you aren't a tramp, why were you hidin' over there in the manger?

BILL: I just stopped in the manger there to take a little seesta!

LEWIS: A what?

BILL: Seesta! You know . . . a beauty nap. I was kinda tired when I got off the train this morning, so . . .

ELLEN: I knew it! You're just a tramp that comes off of freight trains. My papa's arrested them plenty of times. He'll arrest you, too!

154

BILL: Aw now, Princess!

SALLY: Her name's Ellen.

BILL: Is it now? She's the very spittin' image of a Princess I onct knowed in the South Sea islands, time I got wrecked off the coast of Singapore.

TOMMY: Gee, are you a sailor sure enough?

BILL: Me a sailor? Why shucks, Matey, look here!

(He rolls up his sleeve, and the children crowd about him, even Ellen.)

TOMMY: Gee! Look at the tatooes!

BILL: Look at this here one.

(He doubles up his fist and the lady on his arm dances.)

LEWIS: Look! The lady's dancin'!

TOMMY: Yes, sir! Boy, look at her go!

BILL: And look at this here one!

(Rolls up other sleeve and displays arm.)

TOMMY: Gee, look at the swell snake.

LEWIS: Have you really been shipwrecked?

BILL: Shipwrecked? He asks me have I been shipwrecked! Why Matey, I've been shipwrecked more times than you got fingers er toes! Why, man and boy I sailed the six seas fer . . .

ELLEN *(triumphantly)*: I knew you weren't a sailor!

BILL: Huh?

ELLEN: You said you'd sailed the six seas . . . they're seven! I learned that in geography!

BILL: Yeah, but hadn't you heard? One of 'em died.

ELLEN: Which one?

BILL: Ain't you never heard of the dead sea?

(Rest of children laugh at Ellen's angry face.)

TOMMY: Ha, ha! . . . I get it. They're seven seas, but one of 'em is the dead sea . . . so that leaves six!

ELLEN: I don't think it's funny at all. I don't believe you ever saw the sea!

BILL: What? Me not saw the sea? Why Princess!

SALLY *(slyly looking at Bill as she tries out this next remark on him)*: Mr. Penny was a sailor! Did you know him?

BILL: Sure, I know all about him. His little boy got shot, and his wife died, and he went away and never came back . . . at least not up to now.

(Bill loves children, and he plays their game, talking seriously to them, and giving them the courtesy of answering all their questions in detail. But this answer to Sally is just about perfect to confirm her suspicions that Bill is Mr. Penny himself.)

SALLY: I knew you'd know!

(She smiles knowingly at Bill, who looks at her a little puzzled.)

ELLEN: I'll bet when my father sees you, you'll get out of here mighty quick!

BILL: Aw now Princess, you wouldn't give me away, would you? I haven't hurt nothin' . . .

ELLEN: You're a trespasser and—

SALLY: He is not!

ELLEN: He is too! Anybody that is on property that don't belong to them is a tres—

SALLY: Well, this property belongs to him!

(She tosses her head triumphantly. The children and Bill look at her in amazement.)

ELLEN: Have you gone crazy?

SALLY: Certainly not. This man you've been calling a tramp is just Mr. Penny come back, that's all! *(Airily)*

LEWIS and TOMMY: Mr. Penny come back?

SALLY: Of course he is! Don't you see? He's a sailor, isn't he? Well, Mr. Penny was a sailor, too, after he ran away! Mr. Herman said so!

LEWIS: Gee!

SALLY: And he knows all about the little boy shooting himself with a gun.

TOMMY: Gosh!

(The boys look at the dazed Bill in awe. Bill looks a little uncomfortable. He doesn't want to sail under false colors, but he doesn't want to let Sally down. He finally decides she is just tormenting Ellen, and so he backs her up as best he can without deliberately committing himself.)

ELLEN: Well, that's just about the silliest thing you ever made up, Sally Andrews! He looks like Mr. Penny, doesn't he? Sneaking around the coach house and hidin' in the hay!

TOMMY: Yes, if he's Mr. Penny, why didn't he go right to the big house, and walk in the front door?

SALLY: How you talk! Suppose your wife and little boy had died in that house years ago, and you had gone away trying to forget your troubles. And then you came back, after years of wandering, and found that your faithful old servant had just died there too. Would you feel like bouncing right up to the front door, and walkin' in just like a—a heathen?

TOMMY: Well—maybe not. But—

SALLY: Think of it! *(She uncorks her fertile imagination, and fairly revels in her fanciful tale of the heart-broken Mr. Penny. The boys are immensely impressed. Bill has to put his hands over his mouth, to keep from laughing. Ellen is about to explode with growing indignation.)* Poor Mr. Penny! Too grief-stricken with memories, he hides out here in the coach house, unable to go back and return to the— *(She reaches for the proper expression, then comes through with a flourish.)* the scene of his former triumph!

ELLEN *(snorting in her disgust)*: If that isn't about the . . . You got that out of one of your Uncle Jim's books, Sally Andrews! *(She takes Bill in her confidence, so disgusted is she that she forgets he is an enemy.)* She's always making things like that up! Her uncle writes stories and she's got too big an imagination!

SALLY: I have not!

ELLEN: You have so! I guess even my mother said so! Talking about going to a boarding school for children . . . when everybody knows it's just a plain old orphan asylum!

SALLY *(yelling)*: It is too a boarding house for children!

ELLEN: It is not! My mamma said so!

. . *(Sally begins to cry, and Bill takes a hand.)* . . .

BILL: Here, here. *(He soothes Sally.)* Of course it's a—boarding house. *(He puts his arms about her protectingly and she sobs against him.)*

SALLY: It's got swings and slides and little tents!

BILL: Of course it has, and anybody says it hasn't is crazy! Don't you pay any attention to the Princess here. She just wound up her tongue and let it fly!

ELLEN: I did not! I'm telling the truth. . . . She even makes it up when she says Mr. Andrews is her Uncle Jim. He's not really her Uncle!

SALLY: He is too my Uncle Jim!

ELLEN: He is not! He found you on his doorstep when you were a little baby. He's no relation of yours at all! *(To Bill)* And now he's sick and has to go to a sanitorium and Sally has to go to a—

BILL *(glaring)*: WHERE?

ELLEN *(backing away frightened)*: To a—a boarding house!

BILL: That's better!

SALLY: It's only for a short time, Mr. Penny, and when Uncle Jim is well again he'll write more stories and—

BILL: And he'll make so much money that you'll have a big red automobile and silk dresses and servants and—

SALLY *(happy right away when someone can play her own game)*: And ice cream every day!

BILL: You bet! With chocolate sauce!

SALLY: And nuts!

ELLEN *(under her breath)*: Nuts is right!

SALLY: But you're rich already, aren't you, Mr. Penny?

BILL: Who? Me?

ELLEN: He looks it!

SALLY: Of course! You've got the big house and all the furniture, and the land is VERY valuable!

BILL: You don't say!

LEWIS: Yeah, and I heard you had money hid in the big house too, Mr. Penny.

TOMMY: Yeah, everybody talks about that. Did you hide some money in the big house, Mr. Penny?

BILL: Why, I—er . . . *(He looks at Sally for a cue, but she seems just as interested as the boys, and Bill hesitates about lying.)*

MR. JENKINS *(outside with Phineas)*: Now stand back, Phineas, my boy, while I try to open the door. These keys may not work in this rusty lock without a great deal of pushing and pulling.

(The children and Bill get to their feet, electrified motionless for a second. Then they all scamper with one accord to safety.)

TOMMY: Gosh, somebody's coming!

SALLY: They'll find we busted the door down!

LEWIS: Hide in the harness room, quick!

(The children hide in the harness room, and Bill scoots back into his stall.)

PHINEAS *(outside)*: Maybe I'd better haul off and give it a kind of running push when you put the key in the lock.

MR. JENKINS: Yes, yes, Phineas, that's a good idea!

(Phineas makes a flying tackle against the door, and comes down with it to the floor with a bang. Shocked and surprised, he stares up at Mr. Jenkins with mouth wide open.

PHINEAS: The door fell down!

MR. JENKINS *(sarcastically)*: Do tell!

PHINEAS: Guess I don't know my own strength! *(Gets up stiffly and sets the door against the wall.)* I'm awfully sorry, Mr. Jenkins . . . I didn't go to do it!

MR. JENKINS: Well, no matter now! We haven't time for apologies!

(Mr. Jenkins is a fussy, prissy little nervous man, never smiling and easily annoyed. Phineas is a tall, overgrown boy of eighteen who takes himself quite seriously, though he is not very bright. He is quite important to himself, but good-natured too.)

Hummmm! *(He inspects the table.)* This place looks as if it had been occupied recently.

PHINEAS *(knowingly)*: It's those kids. They play in here lots of times. They come in at the window.

MR. JENKINS: Dear, dear. Something will have to be done about that. I can't have children running all over my property.

PHINEAS: Is the property all yours now, Jenkins?

MR. JENKINS *(inspecting the gas plate)*: Oh yes. I am the closest of kin, and the property will all come to me. My, my! Such gross negligence! The gas is still turned on.

PHINEAS: What kin are you?

(Mr. Jenkins is peering into the manger. He starts, draws back, thinking he saw something. He looks again, then decides he is mistaken.)

MR. JENKINS: Eh—eh—what's that?

PHINEAS: I said—what kin are you?

MR. JENKINS: Oh! Mr. Penny was my brother-in-law.

PHINEAS: Brother-in-law, eh?

MR. JENKINS: That's right.

(Mr. Jenkins is prissing around, examining chairs, table, and peering into corners. Phineas, with his hat pushed back on his head, is lounging against the wall, conversationally inclined.)

PHINEAS: If you're Mr. Penny's brother-in-law, why didn't you turn up here a long time ago, when he first disappeared?

MR. JENKINS: I live a good piece away from this town, Phineas, and I did not keep in touch with the Pennys, and until last night, nobody ever troubled to inform me that the Penny family was all dead.

PHINEAS: Well, they do say that Mr. Penny himself ain't dead.

MR. JENKINS: Nonsense!

PHINEAS: Old Mr. Herman always thought Mr. Penny would come back.

MR. JENKINS: That's ridiculous. It's been established by law that he died at sea in a shipwreck. What's in here, Phineas?
(He has his hand on the knob of the harness-room door.)

PHINEAS: There's an old carriage and some harness. That's all.
(There is a loud scuffling sound, as the children scurry about to find a better hiding place.)

MR. JENKINS *(terrified)*: I heard a noise in there!

PHINEAS *(listens, then nods his head knowingly)*: Yeah—rats. There's lots of 'em out here in the coach house.

MR. JENKINS: Oh my! Oh my! How terribly embarrassing! I have a phobia about rats.

PHINEAS: A what?

MR. JENKINS: A phobia.

PHINEAS: Oh, a fobula. Is it a kind of trap?

MR. JENKINS: Is what a kind of trap?

PHINEAS: That fobula thing you said you had fer rats.

MR. JENKINS: Certainly not! A phobia is a—well, it's a fear! I'm afraid of rats, if you want to know. Well— *(looking about)* I don't see anything more here—

PHINEAS: Say, Jenkins, if you're Mr. Penny's brother-in-law, why, I reckon you might want to keep this. It's a picture I found this morning up at the big house, when I was goin' around with them lawyer fellers.

MR. JENKINS: A picture?

PHINEAS: Yep. It was throwed away, in the old fireplace, in the living room. I thought nobody'd want it, and the lady was kinda purty—

MR. JENKINS: Why, this is a picture of my brother-in-law and his family. There's Penny with his little boy, just as I knew him. And there's his wife and—why, whose baby is this in the picture?

PHINEAS: I wouldn't know. I didn't even know who the lady was, but she looked so purty. But then you bein' a relation, I reckon it's only right you should have it.

MR. JENKINS *(thinking aloud, and suddenly very much upset)*: He didn't have another child. He just had a little boy. The one that shot himself with the gun. *(Sharply:)* Phineas!

PHINEAS *(jumps)*: Uh huh?

MR. JENKINS: Phineas, did anyone ever say my brother-in-law had another baby

PHINEAS: Heck, nobody round here even knew Mr. Penny 'ceptin' maybe Jim Andrews.

MR. JENKINS: Jim Andrews?

PHINEAS: Yeah, he lives back in the woods, and when Mr. Penny built his house Jim was the only one lived hereabouts. It was the Andrews that found the baby on their doorstep, you know, just 'bout the time Mr. Penny left.

MR. JENKINS (angrily, and with great suspicion that all is not well): Confound it, Phineas, I don't know anything about this neighborhood. I told you I haven't heard of my brother-in-law these past fifteen years . . . Now out with it . . . what about this baby left on a doorstep? When did it happen?

PHINEAS: About ten years ago, I reckon; Sally's ten years old now.

MR. JENKINS: Sally? You mean this baby that was found on the doorstep is still around here?

PHINEAS: Yep. Sure, she's Sally . . . Sally Andrews, they call her. . . . Only she won't be around here long. She's going to an orphan asylum tomorrow.

MR. JENKINS (relieved): She is? Then this Andrews fellow must be dead.

PHINEAS: Nope, but he's sick, and Sally ain't got nobody to stay with 'cause Jim has to go to the sanitarium.

MR. JENKINS (to himself): What luck!

PHINEAS: Yeah. Bad luck, ain't it?

MR. JENKINS: Eh? Oh, yes, yes, of course. Very sad.

PHINEAS: Yep, you bet. Everybody likes little Sally. (There is a loud scuffling noise here. Mr. Jenkins is petrified with fear. Uttering a little scream, he drops the picture in his hand, and flees. Phineas looks at him in astonishment, and goes after him, talking reassuringly. As Phineas stands in the doorway, his back to the audience, an arm reaches out of the manger, and picks up the picture Mr. Jenkins has just dropped.) Hey, Jenkins. It's just rats.

MR. JENKINS (from outside, peeping in gingerly): Are—are they gone?

PHINEAS: Well, not very far, I reckon. But rats won't hurt you. Rats is fun.

MR. JENKINS (shuddering): Fun? Ugh! Phineas, I dropped that picture over there somewhere. You bring it along, and let's get out of here.

PHINEAS (looking around): Where'd you drop it?

MR. JENKINS: Why, I don't know. Isn't it there?

PHINEAS: Don't see it anywhere.

MR. JENKINS: I was standing right there by the manger. It couldn't have gone far.

PHINEAS: Well, don't that beat all! Reckon the rats could have got it?

MR. JENKINS: Phineas! Don't mention it!

PHINEAS: I've known 'em to get away with bigger things than that. If you say so, I'll look for their nest, and find it.

MR. JENKINS: No, no! Let them have the picture! So long as it's out of the way, I don't care what happens to it.

PHINEAS: It's kind of a shame. That lady was so purty.

MR. JENKINS: Phineas, there wasn't anything else in that fireplace, was there?

PHINEAS: There's lots of papers and things stuck back in there.

MR. JENKINS: Papers! We'll have to get them out of there!

PHINEAS: Oh, no sir! Them lawyers said absolutely nothing was to be taken off the place.

MR. JENKINS: But the place is mine, Phineas. I've got a right to dispose of my own property.

PHINEAS: Yes, sir. But I got instructions to keep everything just like it is, till the lawyers are through with it.

MR. JENKINS: But those old papers, Phineas. It's dangerous to keep things like that around. Why, anything might happen!

PHINEAS: Anything! 'Tain't likely, is it?

MR. JENKINS: Why, with those old papers scattered around in the fireplace, mice or rats might get in, and somehow start a fire. And that old house would go up, just like that!

PHINEAS: Gee, I never thought of that! They've hired me to keep watch there tonight, and I wouldn't like to get burned up!

MR. JENKINS: Phineas, you take my advice, and burn those papers, before they catch fire.

PHINEAS: Oh, I'd be scared to, Jenkins. Them lawyers said—

MR. JENKINS: Phineas, you burn those papers, and I'll give you five dollars.

PHINEAS: But them lawyers said I—five dollars!

MR. JENKINS: That's what I said.

PHINEAS: What fer?

MR. JENKINS: Why, for burning the papers.

PHINEAS: Five dollars fer burnin' some papers?

MR. JENKINS: Yes. It's worth that much to me to see the property protected.

PHINEAS: But what if those lawyer fellers finds out?

MR. JENKINS: Don't worry. They won't find out. I won't tell them. And I'm sure you won't.

PHINEAS: Jenkins, tell you what. I couldn't take the responsibility of burning them papers myself. But—fer five dollars I'll let you into the house tonight, since it's your own property, and you can burn them yourself.

MR. JENKINS: That's a very good idea, Phineas.

PHINEAS (putting out his hand, importantly): It's a deal!

MR. JENKINS (looking down at his hand in astonishment): A what?

PHINEAS: A deal. Put her there, Jenkins!

MR. JENKINS: Oh! Yes, indeed.

(Phineas pumps his hand down with a bang, and Mr. Jenkins groans.)

PHINEAS: Yes, sir. It's a deal.

MR. JENKINS: Well, let's get away from here. Do you think you can set up that door, Phineas, till it can be fixed?

PHINEAS: Yep, sure. You go on out. I'll take it like this, and—

(He turns about with the door, pulling it up to the opening with him outside. As he tries to put it in place, his long foot gets caught in it. He picks it up again, and comes back into the coach house with it. This time, his hands get caught, as he tries to fix it up into the frame. Finally, he succeeds in propping it upright, but then finds himself inside the coach house, instead of outside. He gives up, and climbs out the window. When he is safely gone, Bill climbs out of the manger, looks through the crack in the door, then takes the picture downstage, to examine it with great eagerness. He looks from it to the harness room, where Sally is. The door of the harness room opens cautiously, and Tommy peeps out.)

TOMMY: They gone?

BILL *(startled, hastily puts the picture in an inner pocket)*: Huh? Oh, sure. Sure they've gone. You can come out now.

TOMMY *(to Lewis, behind him)*: They've gone. Tell the girls.

LEWIS: Hey, you all can come out now.

(The four children appear, somewhat the worse for hay, cobwebs, etc.)

SALLY: Whew! That was a close call. It's a good thing he was afraid of rats.

LEWIS: Rats nothin'! That was Tommy rollin' all over the bottom of the carriage.

TOMMY: Yeah, you'd have wriggled too, if somebody's foot had been in your mouth.

ELLEN: Now I know you're not Mr. Penny, or you wouldn't have run and hid.

TOMMY: Yeah, that was strange!

SALLY: Why so? You don't think he wants to meet people around here yet, do you?

ELLEN: Of course not. They'd arrest him for trespassing.

SALLY: Trespassing? When he owns all this property, and has all that money?

ELLEN *(scornfully)*: What money?

SALLY: The money that's hidden in the big house.

ELLEN: Well, if he's got money there, why don't he go and get it, 'stead of hiding out here in a barn? I don't think there's any money hidden in the house at all. And you're not Mr. Penny, either. You're just a tramp!

SALLY: He is too Mr. Penny! Aren't you, Mr. Penny?

BILL *(uncomfortable)*: Well, you see, I—
(He hardly knows what to say.)
ELLTN: If you're Mr. Penny, where's your key to the big house?
BILL: The key?
ELLEN: Certainly. If you own the house, you must have a key to it, haven't you?
(Bill looks at Sally blankly, but she only encourages him to produce.)
SALLY: Go on, Mr. Penny. Show her the key.
BILL: Well, now, you know—a key's a mighty easy thing to lose.
ELLEN *(triumphantly)*: Aha!
SALLY: Oh, but you wouldn't lose that key, Mr. Penny. I bet it's right in your pocket. *(She plunges her hand into his coat pocket, and brings out the can opener.)* There! Now what do you say!
(The children cluster around to look at it closely.)
ELLEN *(skeptically)*: It's a very funny key.
SALLY: Well, it's a very funny door!
BILL *(weak with relief)*: My, my! I don't see how you do it, lassie.
TOMMY: Gosh! The key to the big house! Will it really open the big house, Mr. Penny?
BILL *(broadly)*: Why, sure!
ELLEN: Like fun it will! Come on up to the big house, and let's see you try it!
SALLY: Ellen, don't you have any feelings at all? If you don't, I do. Mr. Penny, I'm ever so sorry about all the troubles you've had, and I know you haven't got the heart to go near the big house yet, or meet any people. But you'll feel better in a little while. And in the meantime, you can just stay right here in the quiet, and we won't breathe a word.
LEWIS: Sure you can. And if Ellen looks like she's going to tell her father, I'll bop her one.
TOMMY: And if you want anything, why just tell us. We'll fix you up.
BILL: Well, now, that's real thoughtful of you.
SALLY: Is there anything you want, Mr. Penny?
BILL *(fingering the picture, and looking furtively from it to Sally)*
Well,—yes. There is something I want. But it's up at the big house and I don't much like—
SALLY: Is it something we can get for you, Mr. Penny?
BILL: Well—yes. I reckon you could. But—
TOMMY: I bet I know what it is! The hidden money!
SALLY: The treasure? Oh, Mr. Penny, is it? How wonderful!
LEWIS: Sure, we can get that for you, Mr. Penny—if you'll just tell us where it is.
BILL: Now here, hold on. I didn't say I wanted any hidden money, did I?
TOMMY: No, but you do, don't you?
BILL: I didn't even say there was any hidden money there, did I?

SALLY: No. But there is, isn't there?

BILL: Lassie, there may be. And there may not be. I didn't put any there myself, but it's quite likely Mr. Herman did. And as far as I'm concerned, you're perfectly welcome to look for it.

LEWIS: Let's do!

SALLY: All right, we will! We'll go tonight!

BILL: Listen, lassie. You be careful. There'll be a night watchman there tonight. Named Phineas.

ELLEN: Yes. My father is hiring Phineas to guard the place.

TOMMY: Oh pooh! Who's afraid of Phineas? Anybody could get by Phineas.

BILL: Anybody?

LEWIS: Yeah. Anybody. Why, you could get by Phineas yourself, if you wanted to.

BILL: You think I could?

TOMMY: Why, sure. Phineas is scared of his own shadow.

LEWIS: If he saw you coming, he'd hide.

SALLY: Well, just the same—we won't risk it. We'll go early, before Phineas gets there.

ELLEN: We'll have to go before eight o'clock then. Phineas gets there at eight.

SALLY: Oh, Ellen, you do believe he is Mr. Penny now, don't you?

ELLEN: I didn't say so.

SALLY: But you're going!

LEWIS: Sure, she's afraid she'll miss out on something.

BILL: How'll you get in?

SALLY (holding up the can opener): We've got your key!

BILL (uneasily): Ellen here says it won't work.

ELLEN: I just said maybe it wouldn't work.

SALLY: Well, it will work!

TOMMY: Even if it won't—there's the pantry window!

BILL: What about the pantry window?

LEWIS: The catch is broken. We'll get in, all right.

BILL: Well—yes. It looks like there's a way to get in, all right.

SALLY: And when we do, Mr. Penny, what is it you want us to get for you?

BILL: Oh, never mind, Sally girl. It—it's not important.

SALLY: Are you sure? We'd be glad to get it for you.

BILL: No, don't bother. Just forget it.

SALLY: Oh. Well, I wish we could do something for you, Mr. Penny.

BILL: Aw, don't worry about me. I'll be all right.

PHINEAS (outside the window): Hey, you kids in there! You gotta get out. Open the window.

SALLY: It's Phineas!

BILL (making for the manger): Don't tell on me, will you?

LEWIS: Of course not.

164

SALLY: Let's tell Phineas about the ghost!

TOMMY: Let's do! He'll be scared polka-dotted.

PHINEAS *(outside)*: I know you're in there now. Open up this window, or I'll get old man Simmons.

LEWIS: Aw, keep your shirt on, Sill. We're a-comin'.
(Waiting till Bill is well concealed, he opens the window.)

PHINEAS: Well, it's about time. You kids can't play in here any more. I made a deal with old man Jenkins to keep you out of here.

LEWIS: Say, Phineas, did you see the ghost when you were in the big house this afternoon?

PHINEAS: Now come on, you kids, cause I . . . huh! Ghost?

LEWIS: Sure . . . The Ghost of old Mr. Penny.

TOMMY: Yeah, it's got pink cheeks and purple whiskers.
(Boys snicker.)

PHINEAS: Aw, you're just tryin' t' scare me.

ELLEN: I guess my mamma wouldn't tell a story!

PHINEAS: Who? Old lady Simmons? Did she see it?

ELLEN: She certainly did! She went in there to burn the papers in the fireplace, and—

PHINEAS: Yeah, I know!

ELLEN: Well, she saw it. It was a kind of pink face with white whiskers and a purple tie!

PHINEAS *(impressed)*: Gosh!

SALLY: If I were you, Phineas, I sure wouldn't sleep in that old house tonight.

PHINEAS *(impressed)*: Gosh, no. You're right. I'll . . . say! *(suddenly catching on)* How'd you know I was goin' t' sleep there t'night? *(Sally puts her hands over her mouth, realizing she's made a slip.)* Huh, I see now! You kids were just tryin' t' scare me so's you could play 'round there and nobody 'ud bother you! Well, you can't now, see? Now come on and git outta here . . . come on!
(The two girls go submissively to the window, but the boys taunt him.)

TOMMY: Put us out!

LEWIS: Yeah!

PHINEAS: Don't you think I can't!

TOMMY: You got to catch us first!

(Round and round the table they go, the boys laughing, Phineas muttering. The door falls down. Phineas trips over it and falls flat. The boys laugh and run out. Phineas gets up grumbling, shakes his fist after the kids, rubs his hips, and sets the door back up as before.)

PHINEAS: Those crazy kids, tryin' t' scare a feller outta a deal just when he's gettin' in the money. . . . Hope ole man Jenkins don't go charging me fer the door! I didn't go to do it! I'm jest too strong!

CURTAIN

ACT TWO

Scene: The living room of the old Penny house.

The room is long and narrow, and furnished in late Victorian ginger-bread fashion. Downstage right is the front door of the house, leading out of doors. Up left is the first flight of a stairway leading to the upper regions of the house, and down left is the fireplace, containing the fateful scraps of paper. Equally spaced across the back are two high old-fashioned windows, hung with faded draperies. Between them a Victorian sofa sits against the wall and directly over it hangs an old chromo of a man with a white beard and pink cheeks. Down right from the sofa is a table with a comfortable chair beside it, and there is another chair near the fireplace. All the furniture is covered with big white sheets for protection, which gives a rather ghostly effect. Two old swords are crossed over the fireplace, and the andirons, fire-screen, poker and broom are on the hearth.

The stage is quiet for a moment, then the children's voices are heard approaching.

TOMMY *(outside)*: Hey, Sally, have you got the key?

SALLY *(outside)*: I don't need it. Look, the door's not locked!

(She opens the door wide, and the four children are seen standing together on the threshold, all peering into the room.)

TOMMY: Gee, I wonder if old Phineas is here already.

LEWIS: It isn't eight yet.

ELLEN: Go see, Sally.

SALLY: Well, don't push me! *(Sally enters on tip-toe, flashing her light about cautiously. The white sheets over the furniture, and the ghostly moonlight through the back windows, give all the children a thrill.)* No, he's not here. Come on in.

(The children enter, almost holding their breath. Their lights are directed straight ahead at first, and the light all goes one way.)

TOMMY: Gee, look!

LEWIS: Boy!

ELLEN: I—I think I'm going home!

SALLY: Oh Ellen, they're just white sheets.

ELLEN: But the ghost!

SALLY: Now in the first place there aren't any ghosts, and if they were, you said yourself, they don't come out till midnight . . . and it's only eight o'clock!

TOMMY: Just the same, I'm a-gonta go kinda slow!

(The children are in the room well up front now, flashing their lights

about. Suddenly Ellen's light falls on the picture of the old man hanging above the sofa. She utters a shriek and dashes for the door. The boys hear and dash with her. In the doorway, they fight to get through all at once, and are stuck tightly.) Let me outta here!

ELLEN: Oh! Oh!

LEWIS: Get outta my way!

SALLY: Stop it! What's the matter?

ELLEN: The ghost! I saw the ghost!

SALLY: Where?

ELLEN: Up there!

SALLY: On the wall? *(She flashes her light on the picture.)* You mean that thing?

ELLEN *(reassured)*: Oh!

SALLY: It's just a picture of an old man!

ELLEN: But it had pink cheeks and a purple tie, and . . .

SALLY: Yes, and that's what your mother saw when she came in here the other night, too. There aren't any such things as ghosts!

TOMMY: Of all the silly fraid-cats!

LEWIS: Yeah, you did your share of runnin', boy!

TOMMY: Aw, she hollered so loud she scared me!

SALLY: Look, there's the fireplace!

LEWIS: Gee, and look at the old swords, would you!

(Their lights on the fireplace reveal the trash within, and the crossed swords above the mantel. Lewis quickly sets his light upon the mantel and pulls up a chair, climbs up and gets the swords down.)

TOMMY: Are they swell, though! Real swords!

SALLY: You haven't any right to take them down, Lewis. Leave them alone.

LEWIS: Aw, we just want to see what they're like. Here, Tommy!

TOMMY: Yeah, we won't hurt 'em. I'm Robin Hood! Look!

(He brandishes his sword.)

LEWIS: Robin Hood nothin'. . . . He had a bow. *(He jumps down and assumes a ferocious pose.)* Out of me way, you landlubbbers . . . Captain John Silver speaks!

TOMMY: Yeah! Treasure Island! *He begins to stomp about the room, brandishing his sword and chanting in rhythm with his step:)* Fifteen men on a dead man's chest! Yo-ho-ho and a bottle of rum!

(Lewis runs to him, puts his hand on his shoulder and joins the chanting and stomping.)

BOYS: Drink and the devil have done for the rest! Yo-ho-ho and a bottle of rum!

(Sally is delighted.)

SALLY: Oh, come on, Ellen! We're all pirates hunting buried treasure!

(They line up with hands on each other's shoulders and in big hoarse voices stomp about the room and repeat the chant.)

ALL: Fifteen men on a dead man's chest! Yo-ho-ho and a bottle of rum!

Drink and the devil have done for the rest! Yo-ho-ho and a bottle of rum!

ELLEN: But where's the treasure?

SALLY: Yes, we'd better hurry and find it before old Phineas gets here. Put the swords up, boys, and let's go get it.

LEWIS: Where?

SALLY: Where what?

LEWIS: Where'll we go to find it?

TOMMY: Where do they hide money in houses, Sally?

SALLY: In books, there's usually a map to guide you.

ELLEN (sarcastically): Now wouldn't you just imagine Mr. Herman would have made a map and left it around?

TOMMY: Aw, he might, to show Mr. Penny where to look.

SALLY: Oh, the fireplace! They nearly always hide things in fireplaces. (The children turn to the littered fireplace.)

TOMMY: There's enough junk here! What's this thing? (He picks up a piece of paper and reads: "To whom it may concern . . . "

ELLEN: Oh, I know what that is! (She takes it from Tommy, casually looks at it, then tosses it aside.) It's a reference. We had them in grammar and they always start out, "To whom it may concern . . ."

SALLY: Look, could this be a map? (She has a rectangular piece of crumpled paper. The children all inspect it.)

LEWIS: Oh, that's the thing they have in hospitals when babies are born. My mom has one in my baby book. Those are the baby's footprints, and see, there's the baby's name and the doctor and nurse and—

ELLEN: Well for goodness sakes, did we come here to read or find money? We've got to hurry! (She takes it and tosses it aside.)

SALLY: Wait a minute. (She stops, picks up the paper and folds it.) I've got to have some more paper for my shoe. (She sticks the paper in, tries the shoe, finds it's too thin, and picks up the letter also which has been tossed aside. All this time Tommy has been poring over a blueprint he has found.)

TOMMY: Hey, is this thing a map? Look, it's got drawings of floors and things.

LEWIS: Naw, that's a blueprint to a house!

ELLEN: Oh, there's nothing but trash here, let's look somewhere else!

TOMMY: Look, here's something on the back! (Children crowd around.) It's a drawing of some stairs, with a little arrow leading up it . . .

SALLY: Do you suppose that means to go up the stairs? Maybe it is a map!

LEWIS: Yeah, and see that little box like thing at the head of those three flights of stairs? Know what that is?

TOMMY: Sure, that's the little cupola up on top of the house!

SALLY: Oh, do you suppose the money's hid up there?

ELLEN: Why not? That would be the best place for it.

TOMMY: Come on, let's get goin'! Up the stairs, me hearties! *(He still has his sword, which he brandishes.)*

SALLY *(catching the spirit of the thing)*: Men—up yon hill, a treasure awaits us. Fall in!

ALL: Fifteen men on a dead man's chest,
Yo-ho-ho, and a bottle of rum!
Drink and the devil have done for the rest,
Yo-ho-ho, and a bottle of rum!

(They line up as before, and start up the stairs, chanting and stomping, As they disappear from view, another light wavers across the stage, and Bill comes in cautiously, carrying the old lantern that he found in the stable. He goes quickly to the fireplace and begins searching. Suddenly he hears two people approaching the house. He gathers up the trash on the hearth quickly and stuffs it down his shirt, then hides behind the chair at the fireplace.

Enter: Phineas and Officer Simmons. The policeman is carrying a lantern type flashlight. Mr. Simmons' entrance is brisk and cheerful, but Phineas takes one look at the ghostly place and his knees begin to tremble.)

SIMMONS: Well, here you are, Phineas. . . . See, there's a soft sofa you can sleep on if you want to. The lawyers won't care. They just want somebody in the place until they . . . hey, what's the matter with you?

PHINEAS: Th-hose white things ! ! ! !

SIMMONS: You mean these sheets? *(He picks one off the chair and puts it back again.)* Don't be silly. They're just to cover the furniture to keep it from getting dirty. Mrs. Simmons put them on when she cleaned up yesterday.

PHINEAS: They sure look like ghosts or something.

SIMMONS: Well, they're not. They're just sheets! Well, Phineas, as I said, make yourself comfortable, I've got a beat to patrol, so I'll be going. Good night!

(Phineas turns quickly and grabs his coattail.)

PHINEAS: Hey, Mr. Simmons!

SIMMONS: Yes?

PHINEAS: Did—did you . . . er . . . did you ever hear of ghosts with pink whiskers.

SIMMONS: Ghosts with pink whiskers? Ha, ha! That's good, yes sir! Well, good night, Phineas!

(He leaves and Phineas stares dumbly for a minute, then streaks after him.)

PHINEAS: But Mr. Simmons, Mr. Simmons! *(He realizes the policeman is gone.)* Gosh!

(Phineas stands uncertain for a moment, then takes the lantern off the mantel where the policeman has placed it, and walking on tip-toe, as if he were treading egg-shells, he looks under every sheet. His method of doing this is to give a quick look behind him just as he

169

takes the sheet in hand, then to stoop and glance quickly with the lantern. He looks under everything, coming to Bill's chair last of all. He is startled for a moment, as he seems to see something. His knees tremble, then cautiously and very slowly he starts around the chair. As he comes, Bill slides around it behind him. Phineas makes a complete circle around the chair, without catching sight of Bill, and while he stops to scratch his head, Bill seizes the opportunity to glide behind the fire screen. Phineas reverses direction and goes around the chair again. Then, greatly relieved, he mops his perspiring brow.)
Whew! For a moment there, I thought I saw sumepun!
(He takes the lantern now, and inspects the sofa.)
Well, the bed's soft. That's somepun'!
(He puts the lantern on the table near the sofa, unlaces his shoes and drops them to the floor with a thump. While he is absorbed in this task, Bill picks up the fire screen, and holding it for a shield, glides up towards the back window. Phineas does not notice at first, but when he does, his hair simply stands on end. He makes a dive for the table, and waits for the roof to fall. Bill peeps out above the fire screen, but ducks back as Phineas peeps out above the table. Finally Phineas emerges, quaking. The fire screen is quietly behaving itself up by the window. Phineas looks it over from a safe distance.)
Funny! I thought that thing was over in front of the fireplace.
(He starts to lie down again on the sofa, but then decides to make provision for easy escape, if necessary. He makes sure the outside door is unlocked, places the table right nearby the sofa, and pantomimes his intention to dive under the sheet-covered table, scoot it over to the door, and crawl out, in case of trouble. As he starts to lie down again, the searchlight in his hand flashes on the awful picture! With a yell, he makes for the table, bumps his head, and sits on the floor moaning. Then he sees it is just a picture, and is disgusted with himself.)
Dern them kids! Tellin' me about ghosts.
(He puts the light on the table and lies down determinedly on the sofa again. But he is no sooner settled than there is a loud thump above him, and the picture falls down on the couch, right on Phineas' feet. He jumps up, yells, dives under the table, then sees it is only the picture. He climbs out sheepishly.)
Doggone the doggone old picture. The wire's busted! *(He throws it onto the floor by the door.)* Stay there on the floor, you crazy old mutt. They oughtta have things like that in the museum—or the zoo. He looks like an old walrus, with that—
(He freezes upright on the sofa in a listening position. The children are heard descending the stairs, chanting their pirate tune in deep, awful tones. Phineas is too paralyzed to move. Slowly, and with quaking knees, he makes for the table, and gets under it.)
It's them! It's the ghosts! They've come to get me! Oh! Oh!
(With trembling fingers, he puts up a hand, and draws the flashlight

*under the table with him. Then he walks the table toward the outer
door, but bumps into the chair at right. Confused, he turns the table
around, and starts the other way. He stops right in the children's line
of march, and as the children enter the room, he can go no further.
Bill arranges his fire screen to look as innocent as possible.)*

CHILDREN *(entering)*: Fifteen men on a dead man's chest,
Yo-ho-ho, and a bottle of rum!
Drink and the devil have done for the rest,
Yo-ho-ho, and a bottle of rum!

*(Tommy, leading the march, and coming up to the table, pretends it is
an enemy blocking their path. He draws his sword and cries out in
a hoarse voice.)*

TOMMY: So, ye traitorous dog! Ye will seek to block me path, eh?
Take that, and that— *(hitting his sword on the table as if he were
cutting his enemy)* and . . .

*(He stops and the children stare in horror. The table is walking!
Phineas walks it over to the doorway, sneaks out from underneath
and runs outside . . . but the children, naturally, do not see his escape.
They think it must be the work of the ghost! They scream and bunch
together downstage at left.)*

ELLEN: It's the ghost!

SALLY: The table's walkin'!

TOMMY: Oh! Oh!

LEWIS: Help!

ELLEN: I wish I was home!

TOMMY: Me—me too!

SALLY: We've got to get out of here!

LEWIS: We can't! It's in the way.

ELLEN: Isn't there a back door?

TOMMY: It'ud be locked.

ELLEN: Oh dear!

SALLY: Maybe there wasn't anbody under the table! Maybe the
table just scooted when Tommy hit it.

LEWIS: Is—is somebody under there?

(Pause while children listen breathlessly for an answer.)

SALLY: That's what it was! The table just slid when Tommy kinda
pushed it with his sword. We—we're sillies to be so scared!

*(She isn't as brave as she sounds. She's talking to bolster up their
courage.)*

TOMMY: Yeah . . . I'll bet you're afraid to look.

ELLEN: Oh, don't! It might be something awwwwwful!

LEWIS: Go on, Sally, you're not afraid!

SALLY: Of course I'm not! *(She is, though; her knees are shaking.)*

TOMMY: Let's see you do it then.

SALLY: All right! *(But she makes no move, just stares fascinated at
the table. Tommy gives her a shove toward it. She draws back.)*

Don't! Stop shoving me! I'm going! *(Cautiously, she slides a step at a time nearer to the table . . . then with lightning speed, she snatches the cloth off and runs back with it to the group. Once there, she stoops, looks under the table and is reassured.)* There! I told you there was no one there! *(She takes the sheet back and puts it . . . on the table with assurance. The children look, and are reassured. Tommy swaggers about.)*

TOMMY: Shucks, I knew it all the time! I was just trying to scare the rest of you!

LEWIS: Oh yeah? Boy, you're sure a good actor!

ELLEN: Yes, but what was it doing in the middle of the floor?

SALLY: What was it doing? Why, what does any table . . . *(She stops, remembering the table wasn't there at first.)*

LEWIS: It wasn't there when we came in! Somebody's been here!

SALLY: Yes it was! *(Affirming it to make it so, but as she looks at the others, she's not sure either.)* Or wasn't it?

ELLEN: It was not!

TOMMY: Are you s-s-s-s-sure?

ELLEN: Of course I'm sure!
(She flashes her light to the picture, and sees it is gone from the wall.)
It—it's gone!

LEWIS: What's gone?

ELLEN: Him! The ghost! . . . I'm getting out of here!

TOMMY: Me too!

SALLY: But we haven't found the treasure yet.

TOMMY: You can have the whole blame treasure, for all I care.

ELLEN: There isn't any treasure, Sally Andrews. And Mr. Penny is dead! And that can in the coach house is just a tramp! And I'm going to tell my father about him the first thing in the morning.
(At this, the fire-screen topples slightly, then falls over with a crash. The children all scream at once, and Ellen and Tommy fly out the door. Lewis follows close behind, and Sally after him. Bill, looking quite lost without his screen, slips behind the drapery at the window. Sally on her way to the door, stumbles into the picture.)

SALLY: Lewis! Lewis, come back here. Look what I found.

LEWIS *(poking a wary head in)*: What?

SALLY: Remember when you and Tommy fell up there on the floor, when you were in that bedroom upstairs?

LEWIS: Yeah.

SALLY: Well, your fall jarred this old picture, and broke the wire. See, here it is. There aren't any such things as ghosts, honest there aren't. Uncle Jim says there's a reason for everything.

LEWIS: Yeah—but what about that table?

SALLY: Oh, that was nothing. It was—

LEWIS: Oh yeah? And what about that noise?

SALLY *(suddenly terrified)*: Lewis! Lewis, look!

LEWIS: What is it?

SALLY *(pointing to Phineas' shoes, peeping out from under the sheeted couch)*: There's a man under there! *(Lewis just gives one big gulp, and starts for the door. Sally grabs him.)* Lewis, don't you **dare go** and leave me!

LEWIS: Hang on, then.

SALLY: Lewis, let's capture him! We're two to one.

LEWIS: We haven't any weapons.

SALLY: Here's your sword. And I'll hit him with the picture. *(They stand quaking, but armed, and challenge the invisible figure.)* Come on out of there, you!

LEWIS: We g-got you c-c-covered!

(Nothing happens. The feet do not move. Sally and Lewis look at each other.)

SALLY *(suddenly, in a terrified whisper)*: Lewis! Maybe it's a dead man! *(Lewis yells, drops the sword instantly, and breaks away. The sword, in falling, strikes one of the shoes, knocking it over, and Sally calls Lewis back.)* Lewis, it's only a pair of shoes!

LEWIS: Shoes? Whose shoes?

BOTH CHILDREN *(suddenly remembering)*: Phineas! It's Phineas' shoes!

SALLY: Of course! Lewis, you know what?

LEWIS: What?

SALLY: I'll bet— *(she giggles)* I'll bet old Phineas was down here when we were upstairs!

LEWIS: Golly! I'll bet he was!... Oh! and it was him under the table!

SALLY: Yes. Remember how we came down yelling about "dead men"? I'll bet old Phineas thought we were ghosts!

LEWIS: Yeah, and when Tommy hit the table with his sword . . .

SALLY *(she is giggling fit to kill)*: He ran! Ha, ha, ha!

LEWIS *(laughing)*: Boy, that's it! Ha, ha! I'll bet old Phineas thought a herd of elephants were after him! Gee, we were silly to get so scared.

SALLY: Uncle Jim says there's nothing to ever be scared of!

LEWIS: I wish he was here. I'll bet he could think of places to look for the treasure. Where do they hide treasure in your Uncle Jim's books?

SALLY: Oh, in fireplaces and . . .

LEWIS: We looked there.

SALLY: And in hollow panels . . . Oh, we could do that!

LEWIS: What?

SALLY: Knock on the walls with something to see if any of them are hollow. Come on, we'll try it. Here's the poker, and I'll take this thing . . .

(She hands Lewis the poker and she takes a little broom used to sweep the fireplace.)

LEWIS: How do you do it?

SALLY: You just knock . . . like this *(she knocks)* . . . and listen to see if it's hollow. It'll kinda echo if it's a hollow panel.

LEWIS: We ought to do it all over . . . upstairs too.

SALLY: All right . . . come on, we'll start upstairs, then try down here next.

(Sally and Lewis go up the stairs, knocking on the walls as they go. As the sound gets fainter and fainter, Bill creeps out from behind the draperies, and comes down to the table. He pulls the papers out of his shirt, and starts to look through them, but he hears someone coming. He scoops up the papers, and starts to dodge behind the chair. A voice calls softly outside the door.)

MR. JENKINS *(outside)*: Phineas! Phineas, my boy—are you in there?

(Bill recognizes the voice, and suddenly decides to hide in the chair. He climbs under the sheet, and covers himself and the chair completely. Mr. Jenkins enters cautiously, flashing his light about.)

Phineas! I say, Phineas, where are you? *(He looks all about, but the only trace he finds of Phineas is the shoes, which he picks up and puts on the table.)* That's strange!

(He picks up the fallen portrait, and props it against the chair where Bill is hidden. Then he crosses directly to the fireplace. Just as he stoops to look for the papers there, Bill knocks over the picture with a crash. Mr. Jenkins straightens up, frozen with fright. When he finally nerves himself to look around, and sees only the fallen picture, he is vastly relieved, and puts his hand over his heart, to stop its racing. Then he bends to the fireplace again. Suddenly, from upstairs, is heard a dull, rhythmic pounding. Mr. Jenkins raises his head and listens, stricken dumb with fright. Then he rises silently, and with a minimum of wasted effort, makes his way toward the door. When he gets as far as Bill's chair, the pounding suddenly stops, and Mr. Jenkins, holding his heart again, sinks into the chair with relief. Immediately, Bill folds his sheeted arms about him gently. Mr. Jenkins looks at the arms about him, and begins to tremble. His eyes pop out, his mouth hangs open, and slowly he slides off onto the floor. Quickly picking himself up, he scurries out, squeaking like a frightened mouse. Bill follows, waving his sheet about like a ghost. Then, sure that Jenkins is gone, he takes the sheet off, and laughs to himself.)

BILL: Nice work, Bill, me jolly old ghost. *(He starts to spread the sheet back on the chair, but stops when he hears more voices coming.)* Oh! Oh! *(Again he sits in the chair, and pulls the sheet over it. Mr. Simmons appears at the door, followed somewhat shakily by Phineas.)*

SIMMONS: Fine night watchman you are! The next time I get you a job, you'll know it! Seeing ghosts! Why, Phineas, I'm ashamed of you! *(Phineas comes in cautiously, peering about.)* Well, now that we're in here, where's the ghost?

PHINEAS *(doggedly)*: They come down the stairs, and they had clubs

174

and things. . . . First they tried to bean me with the picture, and then they ganged up on me. . . . I fit 'em this way and that way *(he shadow boxes)* but they was too many fer me!

SIMMONS: Oh yeah? Well, there's not even a mouse in here now! How do you account for that? Now, what am I going to do with you? I promised the lawyers this place would be protected tonight.

PHINEAS: Maybe you'd like to do it, Mr. Simmons. *(Hopefully:)* The bed's nice and soft!

SIMMONS: Just like your head! The idea of a grown man seeing ghosts!

PHINEAS: I didn't see 'em . . . I heerd 'em!

SIMMONS: Now if you had been a woman . . . my wife, for instance . . . I'd understand this silliness . . . but a grown man!

PHINEAS: I tell you they come down the stairs . . . they had clubs . . .

SIMMONS: Yes, and just now you said you didn't even see them. Now, Phineas, you just had a nightmare, that's all. You go on back there and forgot all about it. *(He waves his hand toward the sofa. Phineas is almost convinced. He goes over to the sofa and sits on it, looking up at Mr. Simmons, almost persuaded.)*

PHINEAS: You think I could a' dreamed it?

SIMMONS: Of course you did!

PHINEAS *(laughing shakily)*: Well—m-maybe I did.

SIMMONS: Now you just lie back down there and stop having nightmares. I've got a beat to patrol tonight, boy. I can't play nursemaid to an eighteen-year-old fraid-cat.

PHINEAS: Sure, sure, I know. I'm sorry, Simmons. Them crazy kids just got me jittery, I reckon. And then the picture dropping off the wall and—

SIMMONS: Of course! You just heard the wind. See, the table's right where you left it. The sheet's on it, and everything.

PHINEAS *(grinning sheepishly)*: Sure, sure.
(He is easily reassured.)

SIMMONS: All right now. Go to sleep and forget it. So long! *(He goes out.*

PHINEAS *(waving his hand airily)*: So long Simmons . . . Gosh, I sure am ashamed of myself, I am. *(All at once, he looks under the couch and notices his shoes are missing.)* Where's my shoes? My shoes! Hey Simmons! Simm— *(But on his way to the door, he finds his shoes sitting peacefully on the table. His new confidence is decidedly shaken by his discovery.)* I don't care what Simmons says, I ain't a-goin' to sleep again. I'll set right down in this chair, where I can see if any gho— *(He sits on Bill, and at once realizes something is wrong. He lets a feeble ejaculation escape from him, but he cannot move.)* Whoa-ho-ho—

BILL *(putting his arms about Phineas)*: Comfortable, dearie?

PHINEAS *(galvanized)*: Wahoo! Let me outta here! Simmons! Hey, Simmons!

SIMMONS *(answering outside)*: Now what?

PHINEAS *(outside)*: They're back!

SIMMONS: Who's back?

PHINEAS: The ghosts! Inside! *(Sally and Lewis are heard continuing their rythmic pounding as they come down the steps. Bill, stranded center stage, realizes there is only one thing to do, to escape discovery. Throwing the sheet over the chair, he springs quickly to the window up left, throws it open, and vanishes. The pounding grows louder—and nearer—as Simmons rushes inside, with Phineas in his wake.* Look! The window! *(Mr. Simmons rushes to the window, and looks out.)* Listen!

(Mr. Simmons whirls around from the window, and listens intently to the pounding. Phineas, shaking and trembling, slides over to the door, takes one quick look behind him, and runs for all he's worth. Mr. Simmons locks the window quickly, draws his gun, and slips behind the chair, where he can command the stairway. The knocks come closer and closer, as Sally and Lewis come down the steps. Finally the pounding ceases, and they come into the room. With a shock Mr. Simmons recognizes the ghosts.)

SALLY: It's no use, I reckon, Lewis. We've tapped all over.

LEWIS: I guess we might as well give up.

(Mr. Simmons rises up behind the chair, and both children shriek, and cling together.)

SIMMONS: Sally! What are you and Lewis doing here?

SALLY: Gee, Mr. Simmons, you scared us!

LEWIS: Boy! I never did think I'd be so glad to see a policeman!

SIMMONS: What are you two doing in this old house? Don't you know you could be arrested for prowling around in old houses like this? How did you get in?

LEWIS: Oh, we had a key.

SIMMONS: A key? Let's see it.

SALLY: Here it is. Only we didn't have to use it, because the door was already open.

(Simmons looks at the can opener, and grins, spreading his feet wide apart. He looks down at Sally, amused in spite of himself.)

SIMMONS: Sally, you're some girl!

SALLY: Am I, Mr. Simmons?

SIMMONS: Yeah, but you be careful, or that imagination of yours will get you into trouble.

SALLY: But that is the key, isn't it? Of course the door was open, but—

SIMMONS: Yes, I left the door open—for Phineas. . . . This is a can opener!

LEWIS: A can opener! *(He looks at Sally.)* And you said that guy was Mr. Penny, eh?

SALLY: Oh, Lewis, really and truly—he is!

176

SIMMONS: Now, Lewis, you ought to know better than to believe Sally's stories. You know she's always making up things.

SALLY: But Mr. Simmons, really and truly—

SIMMONS *(laughing)*: Now, now, now! Don't go tryin' any of your stories on me! You've scared the liver out of poor Phineas. Now I don't have any night watchman for this house. Come on, get out of here. You two got to go to bed! *(He shoos them out the door, inserts the key in the lock, then turns and flashes his light all about the place.)* Well, ghostie, if you're in here—you'll stay in! *(The key is heard turning in the lock as—*

CURTAIN

ACT THREE

Setting: The old coach house, same as Act One.
There is a faint snoring at the rise of the curtain, to indicate that Bill is asleep in the manger. Outside Sally is calling.

SALLY: Mr. Penny! Mr. Penny! *(Snoring stops.)* Mr. Penny! It's Sally! Please let me in. I have something to tell you!

BILL: Eh? What's that? Who is it? Sally?

SALLY: Yes, open the window, please, Mr. Penny. I've got something to tell you. It's important.

BILL: Sure . . . sure, just a minute . . . *(He hurries out of the stall, suspenders dangling about his hips, his shoes and shirt off. He is so sleepy that at first he doesn't realize he's not presentable. He hurries across the stage, then remembers as he looks at his dangling suspenders.)* Oh! *(To Sally:)* Hey, Princess, wait just a minute, won't you? I got to perform my morning ablutions.

SALLY: You got to do what?

BILL: Got to get dressed. . . . Won't take but a minute, though. Can you wait?

SALLY: Oh! Yes, I'll wait, but hurry, won't you?

BILL: Sure . . . sure . . . *(He slips on his shirt, pulls his middy tie over his head all ready knotted, then puts on his shoes.)* Won't take but just a minute! Almost through now! *(He knots his other shoe.)* There! Now I'm ready! *(He crosses the floor, opens the window, and just as Sally gets up to come through, thinks of something else and closes it again quickly.)* Oh! 'Scuse me, I forgot something! Just a minute! Just a minute! *(He dances on tiptoe hurrying over to the gas plate where he has a can of water and an old pan. He pours some water out in the pan, dips in fingertips cautiously, makes a circle about both his eyes, and his mouth . . . puts his fingers in and shakes them . . . then dries it all on a bandanna out of his pocket. Then he takes out a mirror and pocket comb from his pocket and combs the straw out of his hair.)*

SALLY: Are you hurrying, Mr. Penny?

BILL: Sure, sure! I'm almost through . . . There! *(He puts mirror and comb back in his pocket, turns to the window, opens it with a great flourish.* Good mornin' to you, Princess. You're an early riser!

SALLY: Oh, Mr. Penny, I had to come early because there's not much time! *(She climbs in over the window sill. She is still carrying the blueprint they found the night before.)* Uncle Jim and I are going away this morning.

178

BILL: Gee, Princess, I'm awful sorry.
SALLY: I wanted to show you this. Is this a map?
BILL: This?
(He takes the blue print, and looks at it.)
SALLY: I thought maybe that was a map pointing to the treasure that
  Mr. Herman hid for you. But we looked all over the house, Mr.
  Penny, and we didn't find it.
BILL: Yeah. I know.
SALLY: You know?
BILL: Yeah. I—I went in too.
SALLY: Oh, did you, Mr. Penny?
BILL *(very uncomfortable)*: Sally.
SALLY: Yes, Mr. Penny?
BILL: Don't call me Mr. Penny.
SALLY: But why not, Mr. Penny?
BILL *(worried)*: Sally . . . you—you didn't really think I was Mr.
  Penny, did you?
SALLY *(horrified)*: *Think* you were Mr. Penny?
BILL: Naw. You were just foolin' that little smarty Ellen, weren't you?
SALLY: But you said you were Mr. Penny. And you gave us the key—
BILL: Now, now, now!
SALLY *(she knows what he means)*: Yes, but you—well, anyhow, when
  I said you were Mr. Penny, you let me think it.
BILL: Listen here, Sally. Yesterday when you kids were here, I thought
  you were just—well, kinda stringin' that Ellen along by makin' out I
  was the Mr. Penny feller. Remember, I never said I was him. Not
  once. I don't tell lies. But you got such a big imagination—and you
  seemed to like to pretend so well—that I didn't think it'd do no harm
  to help you put one over on the kids.
SALLY: But if you're not Mr. Penny, who are you?
BILL: Aw, Sally, I'm just an old sailor, like I said. I'm on my way to
  the East coast to catch a ship. I don't amount to much, but I'm not
  a bad feller. Looky here, Sally, I got something to show you.
SALLY: What?
BILL *(taking out the picture)*: See this here picture?
SALLY: Why, it's a picture of a man and his wife and little boy and
  baby, isn't it?
BILL: That man is Mr. Penny. And that lady is his wife. And that's
  his little boy and girl baby.
SALLY: But Mr. Penny didn't have a girl baby did he?
BILL: Yes, Sally. I think maybe he did.
SALLY *(puzzled)*: But—
BILL: Look at that lady in the picture, Sally.
SALLY: She's pretty. She has an awful sweet smile. She looks kind of
  like somebody I've seen somewhere.
BILL: I reckon she does. She's the very spittin' image of you!

SALLY: Me?

BILL: Here, hold this. (*He hands her his pocket mirror.*) Now look, when I pile your hair up on your head like this—see?

SALLY: I do look like her!

BILL: Sure you do. And Sally, I got a big imagination too, and—you know what I think?

SALLY: What?

BILL: I think the baby in this picture is you!

SALLY: Me?

BILL: Um hum.

SALLY: You mean—I'm Mr. Penny's little girl, and this lady is—

BILL: I think so.

SALLY: Oh, that would be wonderful!

BILL: And I'll tell you something else. Listen. That brother-in-law of Mr. Penny's—this Jenkins guy—he thinks you're the little Penny girl too. And he is afraid all this property would go to you instead of him. So last night, he fixed it all up with Phineas to burn any possible proof that this baby was ever born.

SALLY: Why, the meany!

BILL: But I went up to the big house last night to try to get those papers before he did.

SALLY: Did you find them?

BILL: I got all the papers there were, Sally—but no proofs. And without proofs—we can't do a thing.

SALLY: Oh!

BILL: I'm awful sorry, honey.

SALLY (*trying not to show her disappointment*): Oh, that's all right. Thank you for trying, Mr.—Mr.—

BILL: Just call me Bill, Sally.

SALLY: Mr. Bill.

BILL: Even if you're not the little Penny girl, you're my idea of one swell girl!

SALLY (*through her tears*): Thank you, Mr. Bill.

BILL: (*to keep from crying himself*): Sally girl, I gotta be goin'. First thing you know, they'll be lockin' me up for trespassin', and if I don't get that train outta here this afternoon, I'll miss my boat.

(*While he is talking, he is putting things back where he found them—shoving the table back, covering up the gas plate, getting his bundle out of the manger. Sally watches him dolefully.*)

SALLY: I wish you were going to stay here, Mr. Bill.

BILL: Me, with my disposition? Don't try to fool me. Well . . . (*He looks about him.*) I guess things are just like I found 'em so I better be sayin' good bye. It sure was nice knowin' you, Sally. (*He stands there a little awkwardly, his whole heart aching for her disappointment.*)

SALLY: Yes, it's been nice knowing you too, Mr. Pen—Mr. Bill.

BILL: Gosh, honey, I wish I had some money. Do you have to go to that—er—boarding house?

SALLY: I'm afraid so, Mr. Bill. They're coming for Uncle Jim and me this morning.

BILL: Gosh! *(He gets out his handkerchief and blows his nose lustily. Then realizing there is nothing more he can do for her, he squares his shoulders and starts for the window.)* Well, good bye, honey. Keep your chin up.

SALLY: Good bye, Mr. Bill. *(Bill swings his foot over the window ledge, but he stops and looks back. The pause is fatal. Sally flings herself at him, sobbing wildly.)* Oh, Mr. Bill, don't go! Don't go!

BILL *(holding her close)*: Now, now, Sally girl.

SALLY: It's not a boarding house, Mr. Bill. It's an orphan asylum. And I'm so scared Uncle Jim won't get well.

BILL: Aw now, honey . . . Gosh! Look what you got me doing.

SALLY: What?

BILL: Bawlin' like a big overgrown calf after his mammy, that's what!

SALLY: You mean crying? I guess maybe it was my fault. I guess I just sort of hated to see you go, I guess.

BILL: Sure, that's what's the matter with me too, I guess. Here. Blow. *(He holds his handkerchief to her nose. Sally blows her nose hard.)* Now. The storm's all over, isn't it? *(Sally nods.)* All right, let's see the sunshine come out. *(Sally smiles.)* There now, that's more like it. That's fine!

(Sally steps back, and as she does so, she reaches for her offending shoe.)

SALLY *(taking the shoe off)*: Oh!

BILL: What's the matter now?

SALLY: My other shoe's got a hole in it now, and I haven't any paper to put in it.

BILL: Say, I can fix shoes!

SALLY: Doesn't it cost a lot of money?

BILL: Doesn't cost a cent. Here, give 'em to me. I can make some soles to fit inside 'em, out of tree bark.

SALLY *(taking them off and handing them to him)*: But have you got time?

BILL: Sure, and I'll take time, by golly. I wish my knife was sharper.

SALLY: There's a grind stone out there, around the corner of the coach house.

BILL: Is there now? Well, whaddya know? Here, hold my bag, and I'll just find me some soft tree bark, and—

(He is out of the window, and Sally climbs up after him.)

SALLY *(calling after him)*: There's an old mallet there, too, you can use for a hammer. I'll show you.

BILL *(from outside)*: No, you just stay there, lassie. You'll catch cold without your shoes. I'll find it.

SALLY: It's around the corner, by the rain barrel. *(Sally sits in the*

*window ledge, cheerfully humming a tune. All at once, she stiffens in
alarm, as she sees the enemy approaching. She tries to warn Bill.)*
Mr. Bill! Mr. Bill! *(But Bill is out of sight, and out of earshot.
Sally wrings her hands helplessly.)*

MR. JENKINS *(at a distance):* I see you! I see you, you little scamp!
*Sally leaps inside the room, and bars the window. She stands there
uncertainly for a moment, then notices Bill's bandanna in her hand,
and shoves it down her dress. It bulges out ludicrously, and she tries
to pat it down, but failing to conceal it, she sits up close to the table,
so it will not show. She shuts her eyes tightly and prays)* Please
don't let him find Mr. Bill! Please don't let him find Mr. Bill!
*Meanwhile, Mr. Jenkins has reached the door of the coach house.
He speaks to the policeman outside.)* I saw one of those children
climb in here, officer. It's trespassing, that's what it is! Tres—
(The door suddenly falls down, and Mr. Jenkins with it.)

SIMMONS *(helping him up):* Don't be in such a hurry, Jenkins.

MR. JENKINS: Confound that door! There! *(He points to Sally
dramatically.)* There she is!

SIMMONS: Yes, I see her. Well, Sally, I seem to find you in all sorts
of unexpected places, lately.

MR. JENKINS: Well, ask her where that tramp is.

SIMMONS: Where is he, Sally?

SALLY: Where is who?

MR. JENKINS: You know who we mean!

SIMMONS: Ellen told us all about him, Sally. That fellow who went
around here yesterday calling himself Mr. Penny. Has he gone?

SALLY: Oh! Yes, he—he's not here any more.

MR. JENKINS: I don't believe her. He's hiding in there! *(He crosses
swiftly to the harness room, and throws open the door.)* Come out of
there, you! *(Nothing happens).* He isn't there . . . I know! The
manger! That's where I heard that noise yesterday when— *(He
darts over to the manger, and grabs up the hay.)* I've found you!
I've got you! I've—he's not there!

SALLY: I told you he wasn't here.

MR. JENKINS: *(pointing to Sally):* She knows where he is! Arrest her!

SIMMONS: Now, Jenkins, keep your shirt on. Sally, this property
belongs to Mr. Jenkins here now, and you'll have to stay out of it,
understand?

SALLY: Y-yes sir.

SIMMONS: All right now, Sally. Come on and clear out.

MR. JENKINS: She ought to be arrested, and put under lock and key.

SIMMONS: Never mind, Jenkins. You won't have to worry about Sally
any more. She's going away today. Come on, Sally.

MR. JENKINS: I'll board this place up. That's what I'll do.

SIMMONS *(as Sally sits still):* Sally, didn't you hear me? I said come on.

SALLY: I—I can't.

SIMMONS: You can't? Why not?

SALLY: I—I haven't got any shoes on.

(She sticks her feet out from under the table.)

SIMMONS: Where are they?

SALLY: They—they got mud on 'em, and Phineas took 'em off to clean 'em.

(Mr. Simmons stares at her in amazement. Outside, Bill begins to hammer. The two men look at each other, and Jenkins rushes toward the harness room.)

MR. JENKINS: He's in here. *(But he looks in and sees nothing. To Simmons:)* Didn't you hear that, too? *(Sally is kicking the table.)*

SALLY: You mean this? Like I was swinging my feet?

MR. JENKINS *(annoyed)*: Oh! Then don't do it!

SIMMONS: How long is Phineas going to be, Sally?

SALLY: Oh, he'll be back in a minute. You don't have to wait, Mr. Simmons. I'll leave here just as soon as I get my shoes.

SIMMONS: *(suddenly suspicious of Sally)*: I think maybe I'd better wait. *(Bill starts working the grindstone industriously outside, and the noise penetrates the room. The men are alert, and instantly Sally begins a buzzing noise with her teeth.)*

SALLY: Bzzzz! I'm a bee! Bzzz! Bzzz! *(The men say nothing, but look at each other understandingly, and rush into the harness room together. Sally springs up and runs to the window, calling softly.)* Mr. Bill! Mr. Bill! *The two men rush out, and she jumps away from the window, guiltily.)*

MR. JENKINS: That tramp's still around here, and she knows where he is!

SIMMONS: Sally, you mustn't protect this tramp. If you know where he is, say so.

MR. JENKINS: What's that inside her dress? Whats' that inside her—

SIMMONS *(disgustedly)*: The tramp, no doubt! Sally, honey, what's this all about? What have you there?

SALLY: It's—it's just some old things we—we—

(At this moment, Bill lets out a wild war whoop, and comes bounding through the window, everything else temporarily forgotten. Mr. Jenkins grabs him by the collar, but Bill doesn't even see him. He shakes him off as he would a flea, and Jenkins staggers back, protesting.)

BILL: Sally! Sally honey! I've found a real treasure! Look what I found in your shoes!

SALLY: Oh, Mr. Bill, why didn't you stay hidden?

BILL: Look, Sally, you're rich!

MR. JENKINS: It's the tramp, and he's gone crazy. *(To Simmons:)* Do something quick!

SIMMONS *(collaring Bill)*: Come on, you. We've been looking for you.

BILL: Hey, hold on a minute. Listen, Officer, that feller's a crook!

MR. JENKINS: Why, you—you—how dare you call me names, you—

BILL: Because I got the goods on you, that's why.

MR. JENKINS: Officer, lock him up. He's a tramp, and a dangerous character.

SIMMONS: Yeah? *(To Bill:)* And what's your side of the story?

BILL: Listen, Officer. Yesterday I came in here to rest a bit before I continued my journey, and—

MR. JENKINS: See, he admits it. He's been trespassing on my property. Why do you stand there—

SIMMONS: Just a minute, Jenkins. *(To Bill:)* Go on.

BILL: Well, this feller came in here with a guy named Phineas, and Phineas had this here picture. It's a picture of Mr. Penny and his wife and little boy—and baby.

SIMMONS: Baby? I didn't know he had a baby.

BILL: Neither did anybody else, seems like. But there it is.

SIMMONS: But then, in that case—

MR. JENKINS *(indignantly)*: He didn't have a baby! That picture is a forgery! Officer, would you take the word of a tramp against mine?

BILL: You don't have to take my word. Those papers there prove it, in black and white!

MR. JENKINS: Those papers? You stole them out of house, you rascal!
(He makes a lunge toward Sally, to seize the papers, but Mr. Simmons intercepts and takes the papers himself.)

SIMMONS: Now hold on here, Jenkins. These papers came out of the big house, you say?

BILL: Yes, they did! This here's the footprints and birth notice of a baby girl born the time of Sally here, and read this!

SIMMONS *(looking at it)*: It's a letter written by—written by Mr. Herman, Penny's old servant that just died.

BILL: And this Jenkins offered Phineas five dollars to let him into the house last night, so that he could burn those papers. Because they prove that Sally there is heir to the whole Penny estate!

MR. JENKINS: That's not true! I'm the heir to this estate. He's made this all up. Give me those papers!
(He grabs the papers out of Mr. Simmons' hand, and tears them. Bill makes a dive for him, brings him to the ground, wrenches the papers away and gives them to Mr. Simmons. Then he sits on Mr. Jenkins.)

BILL: Here now, read it.

MR. JENKINS: Get off of me! You're killing me!

BILL: Well, I ain't yet, but if you don't keep still—
(He swings his fist. Mr. Jenkins subsides, and Mr. Simmons sits at the table and reads the letter, with Sally at his side.)

SIMMONS *(reading)*: "To whom it may concern: Feeling at last that my master will never return home, and afraid this heart attack will be my last . . ." He was having a heart attack when he wrote this letter! He died of a heart attack!

BILL: Go on.

SIMMONS *(reading)*: " . . . will be my last, I am writing this letter to tell the real story of this tragic household." *(Simmons reads slowly, and with many significant pauses, as if this revelation were too much for him to digest in a hurry.)* "This picture, taken after the birth of the baby girl, shows the baby of whom I alone know the fate. Her name is Nancy Bell Penny, and she has been raised by a neighbor, Jim Andrews, and is now called Sally Andrews" . . . Sally!

BILL. Sure. Sure, I told you! This Herman feller put her on Mr. Andrews' doorstep when Mr. Penny left, because her mother was dead, and he didn't know what to do with her. It tells it there in the letter. And that other thing is her birth certificate and everything to prove it.

MR. JENKINS: It's not so! It's a frame-up! Let me up from here!

SIMMONS *(eyeing Mr. Jenkins coldly)*: If it's not so, then why did you try to destroy these papers?

MR. JENKINS: It's a frame-up, I tell you! Let me up, you ruffian! You're stuffing the breath out of me! You're going to kill me!

BILL *(spitting on his fist significantly)*: That's not a bad idea!

SIMMONS: Sally, the little Penny girl! I can't get over it! It—it's fantastic!

SALLY: Mr. Simmons, does it mean that—that I own the house and property?

SIMMONS: Well, I just guess you do, honey! Why, Sally—er—Nancy, maybe I should say—you're rich! Do you realize that? Rich!

SALLY: And then I won't have to go the orphan asylum?

SIMMONS *(laughing)*: Orphan asylum? I should say not! Why, you can build one, if you like.

SALLY: But will Uncle Jim have to go away?

SIMMONS: You just bet he won't! We'll go tell him about it right away. You can have doctors and nurses, and get him well in no time!

SALLY: Oh, Mr. Bill!

(She throws herself down on Bill's lap, sobbing in her happiness. Mr. Jenkins gives a grunt, and cries out at the extra weight.)

MR. JENKINS: *(panting)*: Officer, you get me up from here before they kill me. I demand my rights!

SIMMONS *(squinting down at him significantly)*: Oh yes, your rights! Well, you let him up, Bill—and give him his rights!

BILL *(understanding)*: Sure, if you say so, Officer. Jump up, honey. I gotta give him his rights.)

(As Jenkins rises to his feet, Bill plants a good solid kick in his pants. Mr. Jenkins squeals.)

SIMMONS: Now, that's your first right. And when I get you down at the police station, and tell the Chief about you, you crooked swindler, you're going to get some more rights that belong to you. Come along now, march outta here.

(He takes him out by the collar, Mr. Jenkins protesting feebly all the while. Sally throws herself into Bill's arms.)

SALLY: Mr. Bill! Oh, Mr. Bill!

BILL: Shhh!

(He pushes her away gently, then putting his finger to his lips for silence, tip-toes over to the door, and looks anxiously after the departing men.)

SALLY *(whispering)*: What is it?

BILL *(whispering back)*: They forgot to arrest me!

SALLY: Oh!

BILL *(wiping his forehead with relief, and sitting weakly at the table)*: They forgot me! Whew! I just have to make that boat this week.

SALLY *(sitting on his knee)*: But Mr. Bill, you don't now.

BILL: No?

SALLY: Of course not! I'm rich now and I got all this big house and everything, and you can stay with Uncle Jim and me!

BILL: And what 'ud I be doin' t' pass the time away?

SALLY: Oh! *(thinking)* Well, you could fix my shoes!

BILL: No, Sally girl, it wouldn't work! I gotta get back t' a ship! I been sailin' too long t' sprout land legs at my age! *(Gets up and gets his bandanna.)*

SALLY: But you will come back, won't you?

BILL: Well, I tell you, Princess, I never like t' make promises like that! A seaman's life is kinda at the mercy of a ship, you know, an' . . .

SALLY: Oh, but you got to come back!

BILL: Well, sir, I tell you what! Remember that story about Cinderella and how the prince got back t' Cinderella?

SALLY: Of course; he kept her slipper and...*Oh!* *(She grabs up her shoes off the table where Bill laid them and shoves them in his hand.)* Take both of them, Mr. Bill, and then you'll be sure to come back!

BILL: You bet I will! I reckon I can't fail now! *(Sticks them in his pocket.)* It's all set then! I'll come back soon as my ship gets in . . . long about next Christmas time, I reckon. *(Moves toward door.)*

SALLY: That will be wonderful! I'll hang up a stocking for you!

BILL: All right now . . . Don't say goodbye then . . . cause goodbye means forever!

SALLY: What'll I say, then, Mr. Bill?

BILL: They's a French name fer saying goodbye fer just a short time. You say "Over the river," see? *(Stoops and kisses her on the cheek. She hugs him tightly.)* Well, "Over the river." *(With a wave of his hand, he's gone out the door. Sally runs to the door and stands there waving.)*

SALLY: Over the river, Mr. Bill . . . Over the river till next Christmas!

CURTAIN

RUMPELSTILTSKIN

by

Charlotte B. Chorpenning

RUMPELSTILTSKIN

By Charlotte B. Chorpenning

Cast For

RUMPELSTILTSKIN

(in the order of their appearance)

RUMPELSTILTSKIN

MOTHER HULDA

MILLER'S DAUGHTER

MILLER'S WIFE

MILLER

GOTHOL

INGERT

KING

KING'S SON

KAREN

NURSE

TWO LADIES IN WAITING

PAGES

Synopsis

ACT ONE

    SCENE 1. At the Edge of the World.

    SCENE 2. In the Queen's garden.

ACT TWO

    SCENE: The Queen's spinning-room, the next morning.

ACT THREE

    SCENE: Same as Act One, a year later.

189

This play was given its premiere production at the Goodman Memorial Theatre, of Chicago, under the direction of the author, Charlotte B. Chorpenning.

The pictures used in this play-book are taken from the Goodman production, and are reproduced here by courtesy of Mrs. Chorpenning.

190

Act One, from "Rumpelstiltskin"

RUMPELSTILTSKIN

ACT ONE

SCENE: *On the Edge of the World.*

At the back, for some width—(enough for Rumpel's dancing)— is a level considerably higher than the forestage. Rumpel is circling his pot and chanting.

RUMPEL *(Dancing around pot)*:
> Today I brew, tomorrow I bake.
> I stamp my foot, and the world doth shake.
> And no one knows from whence I came,

> Or that Rumpelstilskin is my name.
> Oh, show me east, and show me west,
> Till I find the child that suits me best.
> Show me north and show me south—

(During this, a woman's tall figure comes up over the edge of the world; she watches him. Her eyes twinkle, and she laughs silently, but at this point, she shakes her head, and taps him on the shoulder sharply. He stops chanting, and backs away from her. He is afraid of her.)

MOTHER HULDA: Rumpeelstiltskin—
RUMPEL: Eh-h?
MOTHER HULDA: What are you doing?
RUMPEL: I am boiling my pot.
MOTHER HULDA: What are you doing that for?
RUMPEL: It is showing me this place and that in the world.
MOTHER HULDA: Now, now, now! Why do you want to see this place and that?
RUMPEL: I am looking for something to put in my pot.
MOTHER HULDA: Something new?
RUMPEL: Yes.
MOTHER HUDLA: Something different?
RUMPEL: Yes.
MOTHER HULDA: What?
RUMPEL: Something.
MOTHER HULDA: What? . . . Stand still. Look at me. Straight into my eyes. What do you want to put in your pot?
RUMPEL: A baby. A King's baby.
MOTHER HULDA: A King's baby!
RUMPEL: Then, you see, when I boil my pot, I can rule the thoughts of men.
MOTHER HULDA: Why do you want to rule the thoughts of men?
RUMPEL: I want to make an end of them. I want the whole world to myself.
MOTHER HULDA: You told me that before.
RUMPEL: I know it.
MOTHER HULDA: Haven't I given you every power you asked for?
RUMPEL: Yes.
MOTHER HULDA: Why don't you use them?
RUMPEL: When I stamp my foot, the earth shakes, and hurls all men's work to the ground. But they only build it up again.
MOTHER HULDA: That isn't the only thing I let you do.
RUMPEL: When I blow my breath, and my pot sends hot winds to burn men's crops in the field, or cold ones to freeze them in the ground, or floods to wash them away, they only plant the field again. There's something I've found out.
MOTHER HULDA: What?
RUMPEL: You can never make an end of men by sending them trouble. They only learn things from it.
MOTHER HULDA: I knew that all the time. That is why I let you try it.
RUMPEL: But if I can rule their thoughts, I can fill them as full of greed as a night is full of dark when there are no stars. Theen they will make an end of each other.
MOTHER HULDA: For once you've found out something important.

192

RUMPEL: A King's child. A little King's son! *(He runs to the pot and flings something into it. It flames up.)* Today I brew—

MOTHER HULDA: Now, now!

·RUMPEL *(continuing)*: . . . Tomorrow I bake—

MOTHER HULDA: I didn't say you could.

RUMPEL *(continuing)*: Show me a King's son I can take—

MOTHER HULDA *(following him and giving him a spank)*: Stop it!

RUMPEL: For nobody knows from whence I came—*(Mother Hulda snatches him away from the pot by the seat of his trousers.)*

MOTHER HULDA: Rumpelstiltskin! You bad little thing! I didn't say you could put a King's son in your pot.

RUMPEL: I wasn't. I was only making it show me palaces and King's gardens, where a queen might be walking with her baby.

MOTHER HULDA: However would you get the baby if the pot did show one?

RUMPEL: That's easy. I have only to go three times around my pot backward, and my little door will open onto any place in the world I tell it to. When it is dark, and the world is asleep, I can go through my door and steal the baby away.

MOTHER HULDA: Nothing of the sort! If you want your pot to make men greedy, you must bargain for the baby.

RUMPEL: Bargain? Queens don't bargain their babies away.

MOTHER HULDA: You must get a queen to give you her child in exchange for gold.

RUMPEL: No mother in the world would do that.

MOTHER HULDA: Then you can never make men quite greedy enough to make an end of each other.

RUMPEL: There might be one. Or maybe I can trick one into it. I'll keep looking. May I keep looking?

MOTHER HULDA: Oh, yes. You may look. *(Rumpel skips to his pot, and flings something in.)*

RUMPEL:

> Today I brew, tomorrow I bake,
> I search the earth for a child to take.
> And nobody knows from whence I came,
> Or that Rumpelstiltskin is my name.
>
> Boil scarlet and gold, and show me a hall
> Where queens and princes dance at a ball.
> Boil—

MOTHER HULDA: You'll never see a baby at a ball.

RUMPEL: That's so. I'll change.

> Boil green, and show me a garden fair,
> Where a queen walks soft in fragrant air—

(The lights, green at first, then sunny daylight, come up on the garden

below. The Miller's Daughter is discovered. She has just slipped through the gate, and stands drinking the fragrant air, her hand lifted in wonder. She is in brilliant peasant holiday dress.) That's not a queen.

MOTHER HULDA: Sh-h-h! The pot knows.

DAUGHTER: How sweet the air is in a King's garden. But the sun has no more gold than at my father's mill.

RUMPEL: It's just a Miller's daughter.

MOTHER HULDA: Wait a while. *(Rumpel settles down to listen. The Miller's Wife, who has peered in at the gate from the beginning of the Daughter's speech, thrusts her head farther in.)*

WIFE: What are you doing, Daughter?

DAUGHTER: I just tried to see through the gate, and it came open, so I came in.

MILLER *(following his wife in)*: You will get us all killed.

DAUGHTER: I can't help going in when a gate opens. Something seems to call to me—"Find out!" . . . It's wonderful here.

WIFE: No one is allowed to enter the King's garden unless a servant opens the gate.

DAUGHTER: But there wasn't any servant.

WIFE: You'd better knock now.

MILLER: I'll knock very loud.

WIFE: No, don't go way back to the gate. Knock here at the palace.

MILLER *(knocks timidly at palace)*: Do you hear anybody?

WIFE: Not yet.

MILLER and WIFE *(going out the gate, to Daughter)*: Come out! Come back!

DAUGHTER: It's silly to pretend I'm out when I'm in.

WIFE *(entering to pull at her)*: What will happen to us?

DAUGHTER: Don't cry. *(The Miller comes in a step, too, to hustle them both out. The gate is closed tightly from outside. Ingert, a courtier, enters and crosses to the gate. He throws the gate open. The Miller and his Wife and Daughter enter.)*

INGERT: Who are you who come knocking so loudly on the gate of the King's garden?

MILLER: I am the Miller who grinds the King's grain. I have brought a gift of fine new flour to the King. You can't find flour like it anywhere.

WIFE: And I am the Miller's wife. I have brought a gift of fine pies made from our flour. You will never taste such pies in the world.

INGERT: And who is this pretty maid?

DAUGHTER: I am the Miller's daughter, sir.

INGERT: What have you brought?

DAUGHTER: Nothing. I have nothing good enough.

WIFE: I bade you bring a spindle of your fine spinning.

DAUGHTER: It is not perfect enough for a King.

WIFE: It is better than the work of any maiden in this valley.

MILLER (to Ingert): There is no one who can spin as our daughter can.

WIFE: She is the cleverest lass. You can't think!

DAUGHTER (ashamed): I'm not really clever, sir. My parents only think I am.

INGERT: But can you spin at all?

DAUGHTER: Of course, sir. All the girls are taught to do that. But my thread is not as smooth and fine as the thread I can see in my mind. Nothing but the best one can think of is good enough for a King.

MILLER: She spins perfect thread.

DAUGHTER: Oh no! I should have to sit all day at my wheel, and think of nothing else, to do that. And I like too well to walk in the forest and the fields. Then when I am spinning, I shut my eyes and remember how the clouds turned the brook to silver, and the sun turned the grain in the field to gold, and I pretend the whirr of my wheel is music, and I sing:
The world spins, and I spin.
I spin flax into thread for the King to use.
The clouds spin the brook into silver for the moon to walk on.
The sun spins straw into gold.
And knots come into my threads because I am not watching. I am a very bad spinner.

INGERT: All the same, I think the King would like a gift of your spinning, and to hear your song about turning straw into gold. Send your daughter to fetch some of her work, Miller. I will tell the King you are here with your gifts. (Ingert exits.)

DAUGHTER: Now see what you have done. My spinning is only like everyone else's and I must show it to the King.

MILLER: Go quickly, quickly. The King will come out to us soon. You are ordered to bring your work to the King. My daughter is called by the King!

WIFE: Run like a fox, daughter. Tell everyone as you go—"The King sent for my spinning!"

DAUGHTER (going): I should be ashamed to tell it.

WIFE (calling after her): Don't let your feet touch the ground. Hurry! Haste!

MILLER (looking out the gate after her): She goes like an arrow. Oh, what a daughter we have! No one can come near her swiftness.

WIFE: How her feet twinkle in the grasses.

MILLER: If she keeps on like that, she will meet herself going when she comes back.

WIFE: I never heard of that.

MILLER: Our daughter can do it if anyone can.

WIFE: The King himself wishes to see her spinning! What will the neighbors say to that? Ah—get down. The King is coming!

(The King enters. They kneel, holding out their gifts, as the King

enters. The King is an old man, greed written on every line of him.
He is preceded by Ingert and Gothol, two courtiers, and followed by
his son, and daughter, Karen, and her lady-in-waiting. All are ex-
cited and looking eagerly around, except the King's son, who is
skeptical of what he has heard.)

MILLER: Your Majesty, here is the flour from my fine new wheat—

WIFE: And two pies made out of it—

KING *(waving their gifts aside)*: Yes, yes. You are good subjects.
But where is the wonderful spinner Ingert told me about?

MILLER: That is our daughter.

WIFE: She is the most wonderful girl in the world.

KING: Is it she who sang of spinning straw into gold?

WIFE: Oh, yes, King. She sings more sweetly than a nightingale!

MILLER: No one in the village has a voice like hers. The birds in
the forest gather to listen to her.

KING: Straw into gold! Straw is easy to get. I will fill a room with
it. Gothol, fill the three secret rooms with straw.

GOTHOL and INGERT: Straw? . . . Straw?

KING: Why not? Haste! If she can do what you say, she shall marry
my son, and be queen of the land. Straw into gold! Gold! Gold!
What a wife for you, son!

SON: Nay, King, my father, this cannot be true.

KING: Why not? Why not? All my life I have wanted more gold. I
have looked for ways to make more and more. No end to more!
Now I have found it. No long digging by a thousand men. No hours
of waiting while it is cooked and heated in a crucible. A maid who
can spin straw into gold. Where is she? Fetch her to me! She shall
come to dwell in the palace, straightway. There is not her like in
the land!

WIFE: *(to Miller)*: Even the King says there is not her like. Wait till
the neighbors hear that!

MILLER: Our daughter will dwell in the palace!

WIFE: She is going to be queen!

KAREN: Surely, good Miller's wife, your daughter is not as wonderful
as all this—

WIFE: She is most beautiful, and most kind and gentle—

KAREN: But her spinning—

MILLER: Nothing like it has ever come off a wheel.

WIFE: It is as fine as a spider's web when she wants it to be. And
she makes her threads of this color and that—

SON: But Ingert said she told him sometimes it knotted—

MILLER: She is so modest. She never believes anything fine about
herself.

WIFE: Don't ask her what she can do. She will say no, to everything.
But there is nothing she cannot do! If you could taste the cakes she
bakes! If you could sip the ale she brews, or see her planting a fur-

row in the spring. Everything grows that she has to do with. Everything she makes is perfect. It isn't only her spinning. She can weave, and sew a seam, and—and she can dance like birch leaves in the wind; and sing like a brook, or a thrush—

SON: Ah, yes, but can she spin gold?

MILLER: She can spin anything! You should see her at the wheel—

SON *(seeing her approach)*: Ah-h-h-h— *(They all turn to the gate. The Daughter enters, carrying spindles of colored threads. She looks around taken aback by the splendid court folk. After a scrutiny of the company, she goes to the King's son, and kneels with grace, but simply.)*

DAUGHTER: They bade me bring my most fine-spun thread to the King.

SON: I am not the King. I am the King's son.

KING: I am the King. *(The Daughter kneels again, after gazing at him in manifest disappointment and surprise, and lays her spindles at his feet, as she speaks.)*

DAUGHTER: Here is the best of my work, your Majesty. The best is not worthy a King.

KING: Where is the gold one?

DAUGHTER: It is not beautiful enough to bring. The gold thread is never bright enough to please me. I want it to be bright like the sun, and it never is. But this spindle-full is the color of the sky. And this one has the green of leaves in April, when the sun falls through them. And this is like wild roses, along the wayside. All the threads have rough spots, where I fell a-dreaming. But they are brave colors.

KING: Yes, yes. The colors do very well. But it's the gold one I want.

DAUGHTER: I made a bad choice, then. I'm sorry, King. Shall I fetch the gold spindle?

KING: Never mind now. You can make plenty more, can't you?

DAUGHTER: Yes, King. There is plenty of color left in the pot, and plenty of flax on the distaff.

KING: What's that? What do you mean?

WIFE: She means she can have the gold thread spun very quickly, if you want many more spindles-ful.

KING: Good. Get up! It is not fitting that you should kneel to me now, for I have a surprise for you. You are going to marry my son, and dwell in the palace. *(The Miller and his Wife gurgle with delight, in spite of themselves.)*

WIFE: Thank the King, Daughter. Don't gape like that.

MILLER: You are honored. Show your manners. Say "Thank you, King."

DAUGHTER: The King's son will be King some day.

KING: That day will come soon enough . I am an old man, and the crown is heavy on my head. Now that I have all the gold I want, I shall pass the crown on to my son. The day you are wed, he shall be King, and you shall be Queen.

DAUGHTER: But I am just a miller's daughter. I don't know how to be Queen.

KAREN: I will teach you. You please me. You shall be my sister.

DAUGHTER: Then I am not afraid.

KING: Son, take the chain from your neck, and the ring from your finger, and exchange betrothal rights with this maid.

SON: Miller's daughter, take my chain and give me yours, as has been done as a sign of betrothal by King's sons in our line, from the early days. *(Wife pulls at Daughter's skirt, and she kneels. The King's son puts his chain on her.)* It shall be a token and a bond between us.

DAUGHTER *(lifting her flower chain off)*: This is only field flowers I gathered on my way here.

SON: They please me more than gold and jewels.

DAUGHER: But tomorrow they will be dry and dead.

SON: Tomorrow you shall make me another. And every tomorrow after. Take my ring and give me yours, as has been done in token of betrothal by King's sons in our line, from early days.

DAUGHTER: Mine is only plaited grass.

SON: I shall keep it as long as you keep mine. The rings are a token between us also.

KING: Karen, lead her in. And give her garments such as my son's betrothed shall wear.

SON: I will lead her. Karen may come too. *(Ingert, Karen, Daughter, and Son go off. The pages, headed by Gothol, enter, bearing armfuls of straw. They are disdainful and amazed as they go toward the palace)*

KING: That's not enough.

GOTHOL: There is no more at the threshing place, your Majesty.

KING: Miller! Get all the pages and fetch all the straw from the field and mill. Fetch it to the Queen's spinning room. Have you straw enough to fill a room?

WIFE and MILLER: Yes! Oh, yes!

KING: Could you fill two rooms?

WIFE and MILLER: Yes, of course! Oh, yes!

KING: Here are three doors. They open into three rooms for storing the Queen's spinning. Fill those rooms full. I will order them emptied of all else this instant. Three roomfuls of straw! I shall have gold enough. *(King exits.)*

MILLER: The King has ordered all our straw for the palace!

WIFE: We shall be carrying straw under the moon, and in the white dawn.

MILLER: We shall be going in and out of the palace as if we were at home there!

WIFE: Husband! After this night, we shall be as much at home in the palace as in our own mill.

MILLER: Of course! For our daughter is to be Queen.

WIFE: I always told you she was not like other girls.

MILLER: It is good we spoke up for her. She would never speak up for herself. She is so modest.

WIFE: Without her mother and father, she would not be where she is today.

198

MILLER: I always knew she would come to something great, but to be the bride of the King's son, I never thought of.

WIFE: It will go beyond that, too. Some day, she will hold a little King's son in her arms.

MILLER: She will really be the mother of a little King's son!

WIFE: We have done this for her.

MILLER: It is our work.

WIFE: Come. Let us begin our trips to the palace before the neighbors are off the streets. *(Miller and Wife exeunt.)*

RUMPELSTILTSKIN *(laughing with glee, on his high perch)*: Ho, ho! Ho-ho-o-o-o! *(He rises and throws something into the pot, circling. The lights change as he sings, coming up on him, and down on the garden scene.)*
Boil, purple and blue, and dim and grey.
The garden shall fade and fade away.
And nobody knows from whence I came,
Or that Rumpelstiltskin is my name!
(He is so full of triumph and self-importance that he shouts his name louder and louder.)
Rumpelstiltskin!R-u-m-p-e-l-s-t-i-l-t-s-k-i-n! RUMPELSTILTSKIN!

MOTHER HULDA: Now, now, now!

RUMPEL: It is my name.

MOTHER HULDA: Why do you shout it so loud?

RUMPEL: I can't help it. I feel like it.

MOTHER HULDA: Suppose someone hears you?

RUMPEL: How could that happen? No one ever comes to the edge of the world. They are all afraid.

MOTHER HULDA: Now, now! Didn't I say, when I gave you this place, that if anyone in the rest of the world was brave enough, he could get here? *(Rumpel sulks away from her.)* Why don't you answer me?

RUMPEL: I'm not listening.

MOTHER HULDA: Yes, you are. Why don't you answer?

RUMPEL: I don't like to think about it.

MOTHER HULDA *(giving him a spank)*: Tell me what I said.

RUMPEL: I've forgotten.

MOTHER HULDA: Nothing of the sort!

RUMPEL: I've forgotten. *(Mother Hulda catches him by the seat of the trousers, and sets him down.)*

MOTHER HULDA: Rumpelstiltskin, you bad little thing! Tell me what I said.

RUMPEL: You said anyone in the world who was brave enough could come here.

MOTHER HULDA: And what else did I say?

RUMPEL: Nothing!

MOTHER HULDA: Now, now, now, now! What else did I say?

RUMPEL: Nothing!

MOTHER HULDA: What?

RUMPEL: You didn't say anything at all.

MOTHER HULDA: Sit still! Look at me. I am going to say it again.

RUMPEL: No, no, no, no!

MOTHER HULDA: Come back.

RUMPEL: I don't want to hear it.

MOTHER HULDA: Why not?

RUMPEL: I don't like it to be true.

MOTHER HULDA: I will do it whether you remember it or not. So you'd better stop shouting our name to the sky. You'd better even stop singing about it. Someone might come this way.

(He sulks away from her, muttering. A thought strikes him. He points a finger at her, laughing immoderately.)

RUMPEL: Ho, ho! Ha, ha!

MOTHER HULDA: What are you laughing at?

RUMPEL: You.

MOTHER HULDA: Take care. Take care.

RUMPEL: I know a joke on you.

MOTHER HULDA: Are you sure?

RUMPEL: You think someone will find out my name, and there isn't going to be anyone left in the world to find out. I know how I can get a King's son to put in my pot, and get the whole world to myself.

MOTHER HULDA: Now! What will you do to get a King's son for your pot?

RUMPEL: Something!

MOTHER HULDA: What?

RUMPEL: Something.

MOTHER HULDA *(goes to him)*: You must tell me.

RUMPEL: Will you let me do it?

MOTHER HULDA: If I think best.

RUMPEL: The Miller's daughter thinks she is going to be Queen.

MOTHER HULDA: Yes.

RUMPEL: The King ordered a roomful of straw to be carried into the palace.

MOTHER HULDA: Yes.

RUMPEL: The King thinks the Miller's daughter can spin all that into gold.

MOTHER HULDA: I know.

RUMPEL: She can't

MOTHER HULDA: Of course not.

RUMPEL: What will the King do when he finds out she can't?

MOTHER HULDA: I suppose he will order her put to death.

RUMPEL: Ho! I will go down there and make a bargain with her. I will offer to turn the straw into gold for her, if she will give me the first child born to her when she is Queen. . . . I must make haste.

(Rumpel runs to circle the pot, singing:)

200

Three times backward round my pot,
Then I'll be where I am not.
Three times backward—

MOTHER HULDA: Now, now! I didn't say you could go down now.

RUMPEL: Three times backward round my pot—

MOTHER HULDA: Stop it!

RUMPEL: Then I'll be where I am not.

MOTHER HULDA: Do not take another step. *(Rumpel slinks down, but obeys.)* There is no use in going down to the palace until I give you the rule.

RUMPEL: I know it already.

MOTHER HULDA: What do you know already

RUMPEL: The rule for turning straw into gold.

MOTHER HULDA: Oh? What is it?

RUMPEL: Before I can make gold out of straw, I must get the one I do it for to give me something that was dug from deep under the ground, and something that sprang from the soil.

MOTHER HULDA: That is right.

RUMPEL: Well! The gold in the chain which the King's son put on the Miller's daughter was dug from deep in the ground. And the flowers in the chain she gave him sprang from the soil. So there! I can bargain to turn her straw into gold for the chains. Then I can do it, can't I?

MOTHER HULDA: That will give you the chains. But it will not give you the King's child. *(Rumpel mutters, very sulky.)* Will it? *(Rumpel turns his back.)* What is the rule for that? *(Rumpel folds together, more sulky than ever.)* Oh, well, if you know already, you don't need me to tell you. *(She starts off. Rumpel is up like a shot, obstructing her way.)*

RUMPEL: I don't know it. Tell me. Will you tell me?

MOTHER HULDA: Oh yes, I'll tell you. Sit down. Before you can spin straw into gold, in exchange for a Queen's child, you must make two other bargains with her.

RUMPEL: Why must I bargain twice?

MOTHER HULDA: Because once isn't enough.

RUMPEL: Well, what bargains must I make?

MOTHER HULDA: Twice you must get her to bargain away something else she loves—something that was given to her by another, as a token and a bond between them.

RUMPEL: Twice?

MOTHER HULDA: Twice.

RUMPEL: Once she might do it without thinking. But she'd never do it twice. Let me spin the gold for one bargain.

MOTHER HULDA: Nothing of the sort. It must be twice.

RUMPEL: Perhaps she would rather bargain than die! I'll go down and try. May I go down and try?

MOTHER HULDA: Oh yes, you may try.

RUMPEL:

> Three times backward round my pot,
> Then I'll be where I am not.
> Three times backward, and my door
> Will be where there was none before.
> Three times backward, here I go
> To bargain with a Queen below!

(He leaps down and out of sight.)

CURTAIN

Act Two, from "Rumpelstiltskin"

ACT TWO

SCENE: *The Queen's spinning room.*

(On one side, three doors, growing larger from downstage to back.)

WIFE: To think that I have spent the whole night before my daughter's
   wedding carrying straw!

MILLER: *(Throwing his onto the top of the heap)*:   This is the last of it.
   The room won't hold another load. There! That is the end of what
   I brought.

WIFE: This will be the end of mine.

MILLER: Don't try to take so much at once.

WIFE: Don't you hear the bells? They are calling people to see our daughter made Queen. I must be tidied up in time to go into the church.

MILLER: It will be quicker to make two of it.

WIFE: One is enough.

(She is carried across the room by her efforts.)

MILLER: Now, if you made two loads—

WIFE: One is enough.

MILLER: I am the father of the most wonderful girl in the world, and
   I say it would be quicker to make two.

WIFE: I am her mother, and I say, one is enough.

MILLER: I say two is better! And my daughter can spin straw into gold! *(He turns to the wheel with a wide gesture, but stops short. He gulps and stands staring at the wheel. He touches the straw on the spindle. His jaw drops. Wife goes to the door and succeeds finally in getting her load to stay on, and with some difficulty steers herself to the straw pile. She makes a number of preparatory swings of her shoulders, and then pitches the stray up onto the pile. It comes back into her face. She gasps and whirls, looking quickly to see if her husband has caught her, but seeing him engrossed in the wheel, recovers her dignity, gathers up the straw, and gets it onto the pile. She tries to shut the door on it, and has plenty of difficulties, the straw falling out every time she tries it, but eventually gets it shut. The bells stop toward the end of this.)*

WIFE: What are you doing over there?

MILLER: I'm looking at this wheel.

WIFE: It's just a spinning wheel.

MILLER: Yes. It's large, but it would spin.

WIFE: This room is made for it. The King called this the Queen's spinning room.

MILLER: It will be our daughter's spinning room.

WIFE: Yes, for she is to be queen.

MILLER: And this will be her wheel.

WIFE: That's why it is so fine. It is a queen's wheel.

MILLER: The King has put straw on the distaff.

WIFE: I didn't notice that. *(They look at each other, and then away.)*

MILLER: Of course our daughter can spin more beautifully than any-one—but what if the King should say to her—"Sit right here and spin this very straw into gold for me."

WIFE *(touching it)*: It's just ordinary straw.

MILLER: Yes. It's strange.

WIFE: What is strange?

MILLER: That we didn't think of that before.

WIFE: Spinning straw into gold has such a beautiful sound. It seemed as if she could. I felt sure she could. The feeling rose right up in me.

MILLER: Aye, I felt that way too. But I was only thinking of how wonderful she was. I wasn't thinking about a wheel you could touch. with straw from the harvest field on the distaff.

WIFE: No, that seems different, somehow.

MILLER: It would be terrible if we brought our daughter harm.

WIFE: I would rather die.

MILLER: I can't bear to look at it.

WIFE: No, it spoils everything. Anyway she will be queen. She can do as she likes.

MILLER: Why, yes, of course! Queens needn't spin at all if they don't wish!

WIFE: And the King is pleased with her. He wouldn't let her out of his sight.

MILLER: Is there anyone who isn't pleased with her? Didn't the King's son smile on her, and lead her in himself? And the King's daughter called her sister in the first breath. There never was a girl like that! To be made queen all of a sudden!

WIFE: O, what a daughter we have!

MILLER: She will make the King forget all about spinning straw into gold.

WIFE: I wouldn't be surprised if she *could* spin straw into gold, if she set her mind to it.

MILLER: She's clever enough. She'd find a way.

WIFE: And then how the people will worship her!

MILER: There will be shouting and trumpets, and flowers flung under her feet every time she goes abroad.

WIFE: What will the neighbors say then?

(*A page enters, bearing a tray or basket pileed with field flowers. The King's son follows, with Gothol and Ingert. Miller bows, and Wife curtsies.*)

SON: Gothol, tell the Miller's daughter I have brought fresh flowers for the chain.

WIFE: Do you remember us, King's son? It is our daughter who will become your queen.

MILLER: We are her parents.

WIFE: She is our daughter. Is it almost time to set out for the wedding? I heard the bells calling just now.

SON: Those were the bells to call the people from the country, and the far edges of the town. Theere will be bells again before we set out from the palace.

MILLER: Yesterday we came in our holiday togs, but the night's work for the King has put dust in our hair and down our necks. Do you think there will be time for us to go back to the mill and make ourselves fresh?

WIFE: It would never do for us to be a shame to our daughter.

SON: There is no need for you to go back to your mill. Follow this gentleman. Ingert, call one of the serving men to attend the Miller and make him fresh for the wedding. And call one of the serving women to wait on the Miller's wife.

(*Ingert leads the way off. They follow in ecstasy.*)

MILLER: We are to be tended by the servants in the palace.

WIFE: Why not? Is not our daughter to be over them all?

(*Gothol enters, with Karen leading in the Miller's daughter. She is beautifully clad in satin, trimmed with a border of jewels, and wears the chain the King's son put on her in Act One. She is radiant with joy. She makes a court curtsey to the King's son, doing it carefully with delight as she rises from it, clapping her hands. He has bowed to her at the same time. Karen sets the head-dress and the long train on the bench.*)

DAUGHTER: You see, I have learned how to bow to a King already! Of course it wasn't perfect. I suppose it will never be. I am only a girl of the common folk. But I am not afraid to be queen any more, King's son. Shall I tell you why?

SON: Yes. Tell me why.

DAUGHTER: Yesterday, I was afraid. At the very thought of it, my heart beat like a wild bird. Karen tried to teach me how to walk like a queen, and how to dance your way, in the palace, instead of our way on the green. And I grew more frightened all the time. At night, when they left me alone in the great queen's room, I couldn't sleep. I sat at the window, and saw the moon climb up the sky, and over it, and down again. And I said to myself: "The moon looks down on all the folk who will call me Queen. And all at once, I seemed to see them all, and hear them. There were so many who were sad, and so many very poor, and so many crying out for someone wise enough to tell them what to do, that tears fell on my hand, and I called out loud to the night. If only I could help them! And all of a sudden a thought came like a song into my mind. I will be queen, and I can. And when I thought about all that, it seemed quite easy to walk like a queen. Yes, and to dance like one, too! If there were music, I would show you how easy it is. *(Music is heard.)*

SON: There is music. Have them play for us, Gothol. *(They dance. She stops in the middle of a strain.)*

DAUGHTER: Here I am, so full of joy in being queen, I forgot you wanted me to weave you another chain.

SON: Here are the flowers, ready.

DAUGHTER *(putting her face to them)*: They are from my fields! The dew is on them still.

SON: I gathered them myself. *(He takes out three or four.)* Use any but these. These I climbed high to gather. They are to fasten your bride's head-dress.

KAREN: It is custom to fasten that with a great jewel from the royal treasure-room, brother.

SON: Which will you have, Miller's daughter? A costly jewel from the treasure-room or my gift of flowers.

DAUGHTER: I will take your flowers. A jewel from the king's treasure-room is only a sign of riches. Flowers you climbed high to gather are a sign of kindness.

SON: I am glad you choose them. All my life, I have imagined a queen who would choose like that.

DAUGHTER *(working on the chain)*: I will measure your chain by this. *(She touches the gold chain she wears. The King enters, with retinue. Miller and Wife follow all.)*

SON: You will have to make your chain small. The King has come to tell us to set out.

KING: It is not time to set out yet. Before we do that, I must have proof of this maiden's skill in spinning.

DAUGHTER: I told you there are often knots in my thread. *(King throws open the first door.)*

KING: How long will you need to spin this into gold?

DAUGHTER *(to King)*: I do not understand your jest.

KING: I am not jesting. In the night, I thought to myself: "Her father said she could spin straw into gold, and her mother, too. But parents' word is not always the one to listen to. I will see it done with my own eyes."

DAUGHTER: Straw into gold Why should anyone wish to do such a thing? Straw is for the comfort of beasts, to bed them soft and warm, and for helping the soil in our fields when it is turned under the furrow. Who would waste it, giving it the hardness of gold?

KING: What trick are you trying on me now? You want to keep your gold to yourself, is that it?

DAUGHTER: I have no gold.

KING: I do not believe you. I *will not* believe you. I have set my heart on the gold you spin, and I will not give it up. Begin, now. Spin!

DAUGHTER: I cannot.

KING: To the wheel. There is straw ready, on the distaff.

DAUGHTER: Give me flax, and I will spin you thread, ordinary thread. That is all the spinning I know.

KING: I will not hear such words! They tear me to pieces! Give me gold—a roomful of gold. Your father said you could. Your mother praised you for it. They brought straw all night long, for your spinning. Begin!

DAUGHTER: Nay, but King—

KING: Do not say nay. Do not dare say "Nay"! Spin!

DAUGHTER: That would be to work a wonder. I am a simple girl from the mill. I cannot work wonders.

KING: Your mother said you could. Your father boasted about it. I believed them, and I will not be robbed of my belief. Gold out of straw. All night I dreamed about it. I have built my hopes high on it. You shall bring them true, or die. Spin! *(General outcry.)* Be quiet! All! Spin, or I will have you put to death!

SON: No!

DAUGHTER *(to parents)*: I cannot . . . Look what you have done now.

MILLER: Try, Daughter. Try. Surely you can find some way.

WIFE: See, there's the wheel. Spin. Do not stand there so dull and blank. Try! Only try. Find a way. I cannot bear to see you stand like that. I could never look in the face of the sun or the moon, if things go like this. You cannot die! Take courage. You must live. Live!

MILLER: There must be a way. Don't despair like that. You break our hearts. We cannot live without you. Find a way. Find it. Find it!

KING: Let her alone. Maid, will you spin that straw into gold, or die?

WIFE *(kneeling to King)*: Do not punish her for our words. Our tongues went fast. Forgive us. Do not harm our child.

KING: If you deceived your King—
MILLER: We did not mean to deceive you, King. We said only what we felt.
KING: What you said, she must pay for. I will not eat my heart out with bitter disappointment. I will have gold . Rooms full of of it! *(Opens a casement window.)* Come here *(Daughter goes to him. He points out the window.)* I will give you till the shadow of that tree touches this door, to spin this straw on the distaff into gold. If you do it, the bells shall ring for your wedding, and you shall be queen. If you do not, you shall be put to death, and the bells shall toll for your funeral.
SON *(to Daughter)*: Do not tremble so. My father shall not do this to you.
KING: Are you my son?
SON: I have been dutiful all my life. But I will not see this thing done.
KING: I am old, but I have not given over my crown to you.
SON: For all that, you shall not harm this maid.
KING: Let her keep the promise that was made for her, and she shall come to honor, and not harm.
SON: You heard her say that she cannot. Are you mad, to command such a thing?
KING: I may be mad, but I am King. Miller's daughter, the sun's rays are moving on the grass. I shall wait beyond that door. When you have spun this much straw into gold, knock on the door. That much will prove your parents did not lie. If there is no knock before the time is up, I shall send guards to lead you to your death.
SON: I forbid it.
KING: You will forbid the King's guards to do my will?
SON: They shall not lay a hand on her.
KING: You will be King. If you would rule, you must first obey. I bid you to go to the dungeon room and wait, alone, till this maid spins, or dies.
SON: I will not leave her side.
KING: Take his sword from him, Ingert, Gothol.
INGERT: Two against one?
KING: Do not harm him. Take his sword. *(They fight.)* You use your sword as a King's son should. Yet if two can't take you, twenty can.
SON: They will have to slay me first.
KING: Not a hair of your head shall be harmed, if it takes a hundred men.
SON: A thousand men cannot take me alive.
KING: This maid has turned your heart from me. But know this. If you lift your sword against my guard, you lift it against her. She shall pay with her life without waiting to spin, if you defy me.
DAUGHTER: Go, King's son, for my sake. Go, and let me spin the gold.
SON: Can you spin gold?
DAUGHTER: Let me try.
SON: That I must know. For her sake I will do your bidding, King, my father, if you give me your word to let me know whether the gold is spun before you order her death.

KING: You shall know. *(Son goes, under guard.)* So you can spin it, after all!
DAUGHTER: No. It was to save him I said it. I cannot spin straw into anything at all. Believe me.
KING: We shall see. And do not trust to my son's help. I gave my word to tell him. Not to set him free. The bolts shall be drawn on the dungeon room. He shall not come forth till I have the gold. Or your life. Spin!
PARENTS: Have mercy!
KING: Let her spin!
(The Parents go out, the King after them. The Daughter stands an instant, then gathers up some flowers and buries her face in them, weeping. Rumpel pushes open the little door, and comes out. He dances around her silently in delight before he speaks.)
RUMPEL: Why do you weep?
DAUGHTER: Oh! . . . Who are you?
RUMPEL: Someone.
DAUGHTER: Who?
RUMPEL: Someone who wonders why such a pretty maid should weep.
DAUGHTER: I must spin straw into gold, or be put to death. I do not even know how to begin.
RUMPEL: What will you give me to spin all that into gold before the sun on the wall moves the breath of a hair?
DAUGHTER: No one can spin straw into gold.
RUMPEL: I can.
DAUGHTER: Oh, will you?
RUMPEL: If you give me what I ask.
DAUGHTER: What do you ask?
RUMPEL: Something!
DAUGHTER: What?
RUMPEL: Two things.
DAUGHTER: What are they?
RUMPEL: Will you give them to me?
DAUGHTER: Tell me what they are, and I can answer. *(Rumpel skips and rubs his hands together, then comes close to her, touching the chain she wears.)*
RUMPEL: This.
DAUGHTER: No! I cannot give you that. The King's son put it around my neck for a betrothal token.
RUMPEL: *(dancing to touch the flowers the King's son chose for her headdress)*: And this.
DAUGHTER: I can't give you that, either. The King's son climbed high to gather those, as a sign of kindness.
RUMPEL: *(sulking, cross-legged on the floor)*: Very well.
DAUGHTER: I'll give you jewels far finer than those.

209

RUMPEL: I do not want jewels.

DAUGHTER: But I can't give you my betrothal chain.

RUMPEL: Very well.

DAUGHTER: Here are other flowers, just as beautiful.

RUMPEL: I do not want other flowers.

DAUGHTER: But how can I give you the gift the King's son brought me?

RUMPEL: Very well. *(Daughter weeps. Rumpel peeps at her. The sun on the wall is moving.)*

DAUGHTER: I do not want to die!

RUMPEL: Give me what I ask, and you need not die.

DAUGHER: Why will you not take other flowers?

RUMPEL: I want those.

DAUGHTER: But they are the only ones that matter to me.

RUMPEL: Very well.

DAUGHTER: I will give you jewels far finer than any you ever saw.

RUMPEL: I want the chain.

DAUGHTER: But it's the dearest thing in the world to me, for the sake of the one who gave it to me.

RUMPEL: Very well. *(She weeps. He watches, rocking back and forth.)*

DAUGHTER: What shall I do?

RUMPEL: Give me the chain! Give me the flowers! And the straw will be gold in the wink of an eye.

DAUGHTER: I cannot give you those. *(Rumpel stamps his foot, and shakes his arms and fists, running around and jumping up and down in rage, squeaking and chittering in fury. When the gust of temper passes:)*

RUMPEL: Don't put me in a temper. I shall fly to pieces.

DAUGHTER: I only said I can't. *(Rumpel repeats the outbreak worse.)*

RUMPEL: I can't stand this . . . Good bye!

DAUGHTER: Don't go.

RUMPEL: *(cocking his head on one side)*: Will you give me what I ask?

DAUGHTER *(fingering chain, touching flowers)*: Whatever shall I do?

RUMPEL: The sun is moving very fast.

DAUGHTER *(runs to the window and looks out.)*: It is almost to the door.

RUMPEL: Shall I spin the straw into gold?

DAUGHTER: Yes!

RUMPEL: My bargain?

DAUGHTER: Yes!

RUMPEL: Shall I have the chain, and the three small flowers?

DAUGHTER: Yes, yes! Only haste!

(Rumpel dances up to the wheel, chuckling and capering on the way. He dances around it; turning spinning movements into magic. Lights flash, and the wheel whirls faster and faster. He suddenly holds quiet, as if listening intently.)

RUMPEL: It is done! *(He prances to the door, and opens it.)* Look and see. *(Daughter is overwhelmed at the mass of shining gold.)*

DAUGHTER: It is really true!

RUMPEL: Is not that worth a chain, and few field flowers?

DAUGHTER: Alas, what will the King's son say? I have given away his tokens. *(Rumpel begins to prance about her, his eyes on her hand, chuckling and squeaking.)*

RUMPEL: This is once.

DAUGHTER: What are you thinking of?

RUMPEL: I am thinking of twice.

DAUGHTER: Twice? What do you mean? Twice as much gold? It would please the King.

RUMPEL: I will turn more straw into gold. For something.

DAUGHTER: For what?

RUMPEL: Something.

DAUGHTER: What?

RUMPEL *(darting and touching her ring)*: That!

DAUGHTER: My ring? No! That is the last of the things the King's son gave me. I will not part with that.

RUMPEL: Another room full of gold. Twice as large!

DAUGHTER: All the gold in the world is not worth this.

RUMPEL *(stamping his foot. It sticks in the floor, but he gets it out.)* I want the ring!

DAUGHTER: You shan't have it.

RUMPEL *(stamping his foot so hard, it sticks again.)*: The chain is no good to me without it.

DAUGHTER: Then give it back to me.

RUMPEL *(gets his foot free, and wheedles)*: Give me the ring, Miller's daughter. Give me the ring for double the gold. Make a bargain, Queen. Much gold for a silly ring.

DAUGHTER: Do not call it silly. The King's son gave it to me as a token, and he lies in a locked room for my sake.

RUMPLE: Give me your token for gold—for a world full of gold. Bargain with me, Miller's daughter. Bargain with me, Queen.

DAUGHTER: I have said no. Go away! I am tired of you. The King will come soon. *(Daughter runs to look out of the window.)*

RUMPEL: Give the ring first.

DAUGHTER: I will never give it to you. The sun is touching. It is time. Go away from here. Go away, and never come back.

RUMPEL: Very well. *(He opens the little door.)*

KING *(off stage)*: Go in and take her. *(Guards strike on the door)*

RUMPEL *(sticking his head through the little door)*: If you tell anyone I spun the gold, it will turn back to straw. *(He whisks the door shut, as guards enter, letting the King come between them. Karen follows.)*

KING: Gold! It is true! Gold! Yellow gold! See it shine! *(He rushes to touch it, to take a bit in his hands, feeling its weight, and tapping to hear the sound of it.)* All this is out of straw from the fields. What a wonderful girl. You shall be queen this hour. Every day, you shall spin again. Karen, bid them set the bells ringing.

DAUGHTER: Nay, King! Nay Karen! Do not start the bells till I explain. I cannot spin gold every day, King. This is all the gold I can ever spin, ever in all my life.

KING: What?

DAUGHTER: I haven't skill to do it again.

KING: If you can do it once, you can do it twice.

DAUGHTER: No. I cannot do it again. You do not believe me, but I cannot.

KING: That is what you said before.

DAUGHTER: If I could, I would.

KING (throwing open the second door): Perhaps you would rather die than do it again? We shall see. You shall spin this before you take a step toward the church. You shall spin it before my son comes out of the dungeon. You shall spin it before the sun moves to here, or those two shall put you to death. (He stalks off, motioning for the guards to go ahead.)

KAREN (stops to whisper to Daughter): Do it for my brother's sake. (Karen follows after her father.)

DAUGHTER: I wish I hadn't sent the little spinning man away. (She tries to open the little door.) How did he get out of there? (She knocks on the door.) Little man! (There is no response. She goes to the pile of flowers.) I will finish the chain for the King's son. (She works a bit, her tears coming faster. She puts it aside, and runs to look out of the window.) How fast the sun moves! (She goes back to the chain.) This is like one of those he chose for me. I will try to fasten them together in the chain for my bride's head-dress. And this is another. And this. I will put them together. Will he know I was thinking of him, when he sees it after they have put me to death, I wonder? . . . I shall never be queen now. (She sobs bitterly, her face in her hands. Rumpel peeps out, and then skips around her silently. He peers at the rings on her hand, chuckling to himself, and finally darts a finger out to touch it.)

RUMPEL: Why are you weeping so bitterly?

DAUGHTER: The King has ordered me to turn more straw into gold, all that room full. Will you do it again?

RUMPEL: Will you give me the ring?

DAUGHTER: It is better to let you have this ring, than to have him lie in a dungeon. He would not want me to die for a ring. I will give it to you.

RUMPEL: I must have one thing more.

DAUGHTER: Whatever it is, I must give it to you. (Rumpel takes the flower chain she was working on, and puts it over his head. Then he dances to the third door.)

RUMPEL: How much is there this time?

DAUGHTER: That is not the right door.

RUMPEL: There is straw in here.

DAUGHTER (opening second door): This is the room he bade me spin.

RUMPEL: There is no use in spinning this one room full. The King will only order you to spin this other.

DAUGHTER: That is true! The more gold he has, the more he wants. It will surely end in his putting me to death.

RUMPEL: What will you give me to spin all that into gold, too?

DAUGHTER: After all, the King may not order this one.

RUMPEL: But if he does, what will you give me?

DAUGHTER: I have nothing left to give.

RUMPEL: Then give me a promise.

DAUGHTER: Promise?

RUMPEL: Something!

DAUGHTER: What?

RUMPEL: Something.

DAUGHTER: What?

RUMPEL: Something!

DAUGHTER: Tell me quickly. The sun has a very little way to go.

RUMPEL: Promise me the first child born to you when you are Queen.

DAUGHTER: That isn't likely ever to happen.

RUMPEL: Will you promise me?

DAUGHTER: If the King orders me to spin this great room full, will you come and spin it?

RUMPEL: If you will give me that promise.

DAUGHTER: I will give it. Begin on this, or there will not be time. *(Rumpel dances joyfully around the wheel, as before, except that the lights and sounds are more brilliant. He stops and listens, as before.)*

RUMPEL: It is done. *(She opens the door to the second room. The straw is gold. Then opens the door to the last room. It is still straw.)*

DAUGHTER: You will not forget about this room full?

RUMPEL: I will not forget.

DAUGHTER: But how will you know whether he orders it or not? You may be far away.

RUMPEL: I shall know. *(The door is flung open. Rumpel leaps into the door of the last room, closing the door after him. The King enters, with the guards and Karen. The door of the second room is open, showing the shining gold. Karen runs to throw her arms around the daughter. The Miller's wife has also entered. Voices off. Daughter runs to meet the King at railing.)*

DAUGHTER: It is all finished, King. Call your son.

KING: You did it, then!

MILLER: She is saved!

WIFE: I told you she would find a way. My darling, my daughter, my wonderful child!

DAUGHTER: Now will you set him free? Your son?

KING: Suppose, my clever lass, you do just one thing more, before I do that. Here is one more room full of straw. Why not just spin it into gold before we start to the church?

DAUGHTER: I will make a bargain with you, King. I will spin this one more room full into gold, if you will promise never to ask me to spin gold again.

KING: That's a poor bargain, Miller's daughter.

DAUGHTER: Why should I go on making gold all my life? Look at all there is here.

KAREN: You can never use it all, even now.

DAUGHTER: And if you will let this be the end, I'll make all this room full more.

KING: But tomorrow—

DAUGHTER: No, I will not do any more tomorrow. I will not go on spinning straw all my life.

MILLER: Hush, daughter. Don't anger the King.

WIFE: He will think of putting you to death again.

DAUGHTER: Well, if I must do this or die, I may as well die today as after awhile. So if it is your will that I should be put to death, King, let it be now. Then you will never have gold for this straw. You will lose it all.

KING: It would make a great deal. Well, then, turn all this gold, as you did the rest, and I will never ask you to spin again.

DAUGHTER: Leave me alone a little while. It will not take long.

KING: This is a wonderful thing you do. I should like to see it happen.

MILLER and WIFE: Yes, yes, let us watch.

DAUGHTER: No. I could not do it if I were watched.

MILLER: Hear her. The most modest maid. Come, daughter. Sit at the wheel.

WIFE: What a sight it will be. Our daughter, spinning straw into gold!

KING: That is right. Take her to the wheel.

MILLER: Come, modest one. Don't make your father push you so.

KING: Come. The King himself will lead you.

DAUGHTER: I must be alone.

KAREN: Don't be afraid of our eyes. Sit down, now, and begin.
(They push her onto the stool, and stand back, expectant.)

WIFE: Put your hand on the wheel. *(Wife lifts it herself, in spite of the daughter's shrinking away from her. The wheel starts to turn at the touch of her foot, and the lights play. They stand amazed, and ecstatic. While the wheel is spinning, noise is heard in the hall without. Shouts, clash of swords, etc.)*

SON: *(off stage)*: Out of my way!

INGERT *(as he comes flying in)*: He fights like a hundred— *(Ingert is overcome by the sight of the wheel. Gothol and Son enter immediately after him, fighting. Both are halted by what they see. Daughter goes to Son with cry of joy.)*

DAUGHTER: You are safe! *(Cry from all, as she leaves the wheel.)*

KING: Stay at your spinning!

DAUGHTER: I forgot—*(Daughter goes back to the wheel. It runs down.)*

WIFE: Why do you stop!

DAUGHTER: It stops when it is done.

KING: It can't be done as soon as this, can it?

DAUGHTER *(breathless)*: I don't know. *(The third door is opened.)*

KING: How foolish you would have been to die! You shall be served as never queen was served before. There has never been your equal among queens. Gold! Gold! Gold!

MILLER *(at second door)*: Our daughter did it!

WIFE *(at first door)*: It is her work!

SON *(to Daughter)*: I don't know how you have done this, but you are more wonderful than any of them know.

DAUGHTER: I am not wonderful. They only think I am.

SON: Now you are more wonderful than ever . . . Where is my chain?

DAUGHTER: I bargained for the gold with it. Are you angry?

SON: You are my queen. What does a chain matter? . . . The people are waiting, King. Shall we set forth? *(They go out in procession, the bells pealing. The last door opens stealthily. Rumpel comes out, and skips joyfully about.)*

RUMPEL:

> For a million years I brew and bake.
> I stamp my foot, and the world doth shake.
> And nobody knows from whence I came,
> Or that Rumpelstiltskin is my name.
>
> For a million years, I bake and brew.
> I blow my breath, and the winds blow too.
> And nobody knows from whence I came,
> Or that Rumpelstiltskin is my name.
>
> For one year more, I brew and bake,
> And then I shall a King's son take,
> And nobody'll know from whence I came,
> Or that Rumpelstiltskin is my name!

CURTAIN

Act Three, from "Rumpelstiltskin"

ACT THREE

SCENE 1: *In the King's garden, a year later.*

(Rumpelstiltskin is nowhere visible. The Edge of the World is dim and unobtrusive, above. The Miller's Daughter, now the Queen, is seated beside the royal cradle, gazing in still delight on her baby son. The nurse also sits near, singing. The Pages, Miller, Wife, the King, the King's son, Karen, Gothol, Ingert, and the ladies-in-waiting are all watching the child. Ingert is accompanying the Nurse on his guitar. It is a tableau, all eyes bent on the child in adoration.)

DAUGHTER: He is sound asleep. *(To the Pages:)* Carry him over there, where the light is soft and dim.

WIFE: We will carry him.

KING: No, He shall be carried by the King himself.

MILLER: He is our grandson.

KING: So is he mine. *(The three near the cradle.)*

WIFE: A little King's son. And our daughter is his mother. Look! A smile passed over his face just then! He is dreaming. What a wonder-child, to dream, when he is so tiny and so small!

MILLER: He is not small. He grows like grain that was sown in the moon. See how round his arm is! He will be the strongest man in the whole kingdom, in his day! That little arm will lift a mill-stone as if it were a bit of thistle-down, bye and bye.

WIFE: He will have nothing at all to do with mill-stones! He will be King over wide lands. Oh, daughter, what a child you have brought into this world!

KING: See, his little fingers curl around my big one, even in his sleep.

MILLER: So will they around mine.

KING: My great, tall son was like this once. I had forgotten that. My mind was so full of gold.

NURSE: You'll awaken him, between you.

DAUGHTER: Yes, let him sleep

MILLER: We will carry him in.

DAUGHTER: The attendants will do it better.

WIFE: No, they will not be as careful as we.

MILLER: You lift your end too high.

WIFE: No, yours is too low.

KING: Neither of you hold it level. This is how it should be.

NURSE: He is stirring, with all your fuss.

DAUGHTER: You are more careful, but they are more steady.

WIFE: We do it for love.

DAUGHTER: Yes, but they know how.

KING: We are spoiling his sleep. Gothol, Ingert, take him.
(Pages lift the cradle. Very slowly they move, toward the palace door, to music.

DAUGHTER: Do not take him from my sight. Leave the cradle here, by the steps.
(Exeunt all but Son and Daughter.)
How happy they are to have a baby in the palace.

SON: The old King, my father, even forgets his gold, to wonder at him.

DAUGHTER: No one is as happy as I! To please them all in the court, I go quiet and like a Queen. But if I did what I feel like doing, my feet wouldn't touch the ground for joy. Hark! They are dancing by the mill.

SON: They are safe within, all of them. We will please no one but ourselves. *(He swings her up. They do this, laughing. She runs to baby.)*

DAUGHTER: It's good you don't see how wild we are! That is because we are mad with joy about you, little King's son. Are you warm enough? Do you think he should have just a little more to cover him?

SON *(lifting flowers from the bench)*: Use these.

DAUGHTER: No I am weaving these for you.

SON: The fields are purple and white with bloom outside the gate. I'll bring him some. *(Son goes. Daughter settles down to weave the rest of the almost-finished flower chain. Rumpel pushes open the little door, and enters. He moves noiselessly to her. He sits beside her, watching her intently, smiling triumphantly. She rises to look at the baby. Turning back, she sees Rumpel. She screams.)*

DAUGHTER: Who are you? *(Rumpel laughs silently, his eyes unwavering.)* What—what do you want? *(Rumpel laughs.)* Oh, go away! I didn't think it would ever happen.

217

RUMPEL: I have come for my bargain.

DAUGHTER: That was so long ago. It couldn't still be true. I had forgotten all about it.

RUMPEL: Things do not end because you forget them. Fetch the baby.

DAUGHTER: Oh, no! I can't give you my baby!

RUMPEL: There's no use in saying that. This was not a common bargain, such as men make and break. It was made with me! I did what cannot be done. I turned straw into gold. I can do more! I can stamp my foot, and the earth will shake, and this whole place will fall on your head and break your baby into bits.

DAUGHTER: I didn't know that.

RUMPEL: Very well. Fetch the child.

DAUGHTER: He can't do without his mother. He is too little.

RUMPEL: It won't be long he'll need you.

DAUGHTER: What do you mean to do with him?

RUMPEL: Something.

DAUGHTER: Oh, what?

RUMPEL: Something.

DAUGHTER: Will you be good to him?

RUMPEL: Never mind.

DAUGHTER: You have some terrible plan in your mind. I can tell by the sound of your voice. I can tell by the way you laugh. I can tell by the way you walk.

RUMPEL: You must keep your bargain, for all that.

DAUGHTER: I will give you back your gold! I will give you everything I have. The young King, my husband, will give you broad lands and heaped-up treasure.

RUMPEL: I'd rather have a living thing than all the gold in the earth and stars. *(He stamps.)* Come. I have waited long enough.

DAUGHTER: Don't take him from me.

RUMPEL: Fetch him!

DAUGHTER: Take me, instead. Do anything you want to me. Flog me, torture me, kill me, tear me to pieces! Only let my little son stay safe with his father. Go away and let him be. Go away. Go away!

RUMPEL: Don't do that! Don't do it any more. It upsets me.

DAUGHTER *(exhausted)*: Go away—

RUMPEL: Don't do it! It makes me want to say—"You can keep your child."

DAUGHTER: Say it! Say it!

RUMPEL: No, no, no, no, no, no, no! I only want to say it; I don't want to do it! Don't look at me. I don't like to feel like this.

DAUGHTER: You feel sorry. You will have mercy. You will not take him away.

RUMPEL: Yes, I will! Don't look at me!

(Rumpel covers his eyes and jumps up and down.)

DAUGHTER: I am looking at you. I shall keep looking at you till you

promise me. Look! Look! *(She kneels and stretches out her arms.)*
Make me a promise. Say you will leave me my little King's son. Little
man! Little spinning man! I don't know your name. I don't know
what to call you—

RUMPEL *(laughs when she says she doesn't know his name, then uncovers
his eyes)*: I will make you a promise.

DAUGHTER: Yes—

RUMPEL: I have the strangest name in the world. I give you three
guesses. Three times three guesses. If you can tell me my name, I
will not make you keep your bargain.

DAUGHTER: Three times three guesses!

RUMPEL: Now I feel the way I like to feel.

DAUGHTER: Now let me see. I have heard of the three kings who jour-
neyed over mountains and deserts from very far away. Their names
were strange. Never have I heard of them in these parts. But
which, I wonder, is the strangest?

RUMPEL: Why not try them, one at a time? You have plenty of
guesses more.

DAUGHTER: So I have. Well, are you called Casper?

RUMPEL: That is not my name.

DAUGHTER: Are you called Melchior?

RUMPEL: That is not my name.

DAUGHTER: Are you called Balthazar?

RUMPEL: That is not my name! Go on. Guess some more,
Miller's daughter. Guess some more, Queen.

DAUGHTER: You must give me time to think. I was wrong to waste
my guesses without thinking.

RUMPEL: I didn't say I'd give you time. Come, what is my name?

DAUGHTER: I must ask my husband, the young King, for help. I must
ask Karen, and my ladies, and my father, and all of them. You will not
deny me time for that! *(Rumpel turns his back.)* I am begging you.

RUMPEL: Very well. Ask your husband. And his sister, and all the fine
folks in the palace—*(He stamps.)* You have been too slow. I hear
someone coming. Give me the baby. *(He starts for it. She blocks
him, as the young King's voice, singing, draws near. Rumpel whips
out his little door. Daughter runs to meet the son.)*

DAUGHTER: Will you help me!

SON *(puts the chain on)*: Help you? How?

DAUGHTER: You must think. Think hard! What is the strangest
name you konw? *(Son laughs).* Don't laugh. Tell me! It must
be a very strange name.

SON: What is the matter, little Queen? You are frightened. Why do
you cling to me so?

DAUGHTER: You must not ask me questions. You must tell me names.
Quick, now. You have been about the world. What is the strangest
name you have ever heard?

SON: In far-away places, I have heard many names that sounded strange to me. But they did not sound strange to those who used them. I suppose a name isn't really strange unless it sounds so to those who use it.

DAUGHTER: Still, you must have heard one that sounded queer to you.

SON: Not after I thought about it. One name is as good an another.

DAUGHTER: Then call my father and mother, and Ingert and Gothol. They go about among the people. They will surely know names to tell me.

SON: Whatever you wish, little Queen.

DAUGHTER: Don't leave me alone!

SON: Shall I not fetch the others?

DAUGHTER: Call them. Stand here and call.

SON: Ingert! . . . Bring the Miller and his Wife, and Gothol, into the garden.

DAUGHTER: They mustn't ask me why.

SON: I'll see to that. Now laugh a little. I do not like to see you sober and afraid.

DAUGHTER: I can't laugh yet.

WIFE (entering, followed by the others): What do you want?

SON: We are trying to think of strange names. Whoever can think of the strangest name will have a reward. Now, Gothol. Speak.

GOTHOL: Well, once, when I was journeying in a land where alligators blinked on the banks of the streams, and parrots flew in twos high in the sky, I met a man named after a river, and the river's name was: Pappaloappaloapam.

DAUGHTER: Poppaloappalo—what comes next?

MILLER: Pappaloappaloappaloappaloppale—

INGERT: No, no, no. Pappaloappaloapam.

MILLER: Why do you cut me short?

INGERT: Because it is time you stopped.

MILLER: What ground have you for saying such a thing?

INGERT: Enough is enough. More is too much.

MILLER: Why should you say "enough" to me? What have you done in this world? I have brought a daughter up to be Queen, and not a Queen like other Queens, either, but one who has spun straw into gold! And one who is the mother of a little King's son whose like is not to be found in the land!

WIFE: What do you say about that?

DAUGHTER: Oh, hush, father! Hush—

MILLER: Do you say hush to me, Daughter? Do you take sides against us, who have set you so high? Was it not your mother and I who told the King you could make gold out of straw?

WIFE: And wasn't it that very thing that brought about all the rest?

DAUGHTER: Ah, yes, Alas!

MILLER: Would your little son be sleeping in a royal cradle now, if we had not told the King how wonderful you were? And now you say

220

hush to us, and side with Ingert.

DAUGHTER: No, no, no, father. I do not side with anyone. I want more names, that's all. Ingert! It is your turn.

INGERT: Well, when I was wandering in our own village the other day, I heard one man say to another, "Now that the Miller's daughter is Queen, I suppose he lines his stomach with fine wines and roasted meats. And just then the Miller passed by, and the man said—"There goes Roast-Ribs now." I call that a very strange name. Roast-Ribs.

MILLER: Are you making a laughing-stock of me?

DAUGHTER: Roast-Ribs! That is surely a strange name.

MILLER: Before my own daughter!

WIFE: Will you laugh at your own father, child?

DAUGHTER: It is a funny name.

MILLER: Roast-Ribs! What do you mean by calling me that?

INGERT: I called you nothing. I was only saying what I heard. I suppose, perhaps, the man who said it meant you looked as if your ribs were padded well with roasted meats.

WIFE: And what if they are? It's well enough he has some weight to him. What sort of job would he make, running a mill and grinding meal for a kingdom, if he were a reed blown in the wind, like you. You pipestem!

MILLER: You yardstick!

WIFE: Are you the father of a Queen! You—You—

MILLER: Are you the grandsire of a King's son?

WIFE: You sheepshanks!

DAUGHTER: Sheepshanks!

WIFE: You spindleshanks!

DAUGHTER: Spindleshanks! Oh, these are the very strangest names I ever heard! You shall all have rewards, for one name is as strange as another. Take them in, and let them choose each a jewel from my casket.

SON: Lead the way, Spindleshanks. Come, Roast-Ribs. (They go. Rumpel enters behind their backs, and is sitting grinning at the Daughter when she turns around.)

RUMPEL: Pappaloapappaloapam! Pooh!

DAUGHTER: That isn't one of my guesses.

RUMPEL: Pipestem! Pooh!

DAUGHTER: I didn't guess that, either.

RUMPEL: Well, what is my name?

DAUGHTER: Is it Roast-Ribs?

RUMPEL: No! It is not Roast-Ribs.

DAUGHTER: Is it Sheepshanks!

RUMPEL: No! It is not Sheepshanks.

DAUGHTER: Is it Spindleshanks?

RUMPEL: No, it is not Spindleshanks! Guess again! What is my name? What is my name? What is it? What is it? What is it?

221

DAUGHTER: Keep still. I can't guess so soon. I have only three guesses left.

RUMPEL: A thousand guesses would be no better. Nobody knows from whence I came. Nobody's ever heard my name.

DAUGHTER: Not even where you live?

RUMPEL: Nobody ever comes there!

DAUGHTER: Where is it?

RUMPEL: Somewhere.

DAUGHTER: Oh, tell me where!

RUMPEL: Somewhere.

DAUGHTER: Which way is it from here?

RUMPEL: There is a long way, and a short way. If you go east till you come west, or west till you come east, that is the long way. If you go round and round, and say the right words, the door is where you want it. That is the short way.

DAUGHTER: What are the right words?

RUMPEL: Never mind.

DAUGHTER: Do you know them?

RUMPEL: Yes.

DAUGHTER: Who else knows them?

RUMPEL: No one.

DAUGHTER: How long does the long way take from here and back?

RUMPEL: Half a year, and a day besides.

DAUGHTER: How long does the short way take?

RUMPEL (wheeling): Like that.

DAUGHTER: Can nobody but you go the short way to where you live?

RUMPEL: Not unless I leave the door open.

DAUGHTER: What door?

RUMPEL: Never mind.

DAUGHTER: Tell me what door you could leave open.

RUMPEL: It doesn't matter, because I never will. And even if I should, you wouldn't come, because you'd be afraid.

DAUGHTER: What should I be afraid of?

RUMPEL: As soon as you put a finger, or a hair of your head through the door, you'd feel a wild wind. If you went on, it would whirl you round and round, till you came to a high hill, and on it a little house. And before the house a fire burning, and around the fire, you'd see me dancing and maybe shouting my name to the sky and the air.

DAUGHTER: Why do you shout your name?

RUMPEL: Because nobody knows it, and I feel full of myself.

DAUGHTER: Let me see—let me see—

RUMPEL: Now, Mrs. Queen, what is my name?

DAUGHTER: Let me see—

RUMPEL: It's no good hunting in your mind for it. You've never heard it.

DAUGHTER: I'm not.

RUMPEL: Yes you are. You are thinking up names.

DAUGHTER: No, I'm thinking up ways to make you feel sorry for me again.

RUMPEL *(stamping his foot)*: I won't feel sorry for you again.

DAUGHTER *(seizing his hand)*: I will make you. My tears are on your hand.

RUMPEL: No, no, no, no! I will not give up the child! I won't! I won't!

DAUGHTER: That isn't what I'm asking you to do.

RUMPEL: What is it you are asking?

DAUGHTER: Only a little more time.

RUMPEL: I've given you twice already.

DAUGHTER: But I must have more. Your name is very hard to find. I didn't know at first it would be so hard. I must have a long time.

RUMPEL: What's the use of that? You'll never find my name. And when that time is up, you'll come crying and praying and going on your knees again.

DAUGHTER: No. Give me half a year and a day besides, and I'll never ask for time again.

RUMPEL: In half a year and a day besides you'll promise to give me your child without any fuss?

DAUGHTER: If I don't find out your name.

RUMPEL: You won't drop tears on my hand?

DAUGHTER: I'll keep all my tears in my heart.

RUMPEL: Your eyes won't look at me so I'll want to give him up?

DAUGHTER: I'll shut my eyes.

RUMPEL: You won't tremble and shake and kneel at my feet?

DAUGHTER: I will stand like a Queen.

RUMPEL: No! I shall know how you feel, for all that, and I shall feel queer. You must come to meet me as if I were the young King your husband, and say "Here you are again."

DAUGHTER: I will come like that, if you will give me half a year and a day besides.

RUMPEL: Very well! Cover your eyes. I am going away. For half a year and one more day, I am going away, I am going away!

DAUGHTER: Are you gone?

RUMPEL *(opening the door)*: Not yet.

DAUGHTER: I am going to look.

RUMPEL: No!

DAUGHTER: I can't keep from looking much longer. *(Rumpel scrambles through backward. He thrusts his face out, and is about to speak, when she lowers her arm.)* I will look when I count five. *(Rumpel pulls the door to, but shuts it on his finger. He opens it in a temper, making faces at it.)* One, two, three, four, five—*(As she reaches five, he shuts the door. It does not go quite shut. She sees it move, or she would not know it.)* Are you gone? He has left it open. That must be the short way. *(She puts out a hand to open it more, hesitates, then goes ahead. She thrusts her hand in a little way, cries out.)* Oh-h-h! Shall I leave

my baby here? Suppose I never come back. No. I'll try the long
way first. *(Runs to palace door.)* Gothol! Ingert! I must have all
the strange names in the whole world. Ingert, ask in every town and
hamlet, on the top of every hill, and in the hollow of every valley. And
ask among the palm trees and orange groves. And Gothol, you must
go east until you come west, and Ingert, go west until you come east.
In half a year and one day more, you must be back with names for
me. *(They bow, and go.)* Half a year and one day more.

*(The curtain closes, but open immediately on the same scene. It is dark
in the King's garden below. Rumpel, on the Edge of the World, is
circling his pot and singing.)*

RUMPEL:

>Today I bake, tomorrow I brew,
>And half a year is almost through.
>My name, my name, I shout and shout.
>For no one's here to find it out.

*(Rumpel leaps from one side to the other, and front, shouting "Rum-
pelstiltskin!" He breaks into laughter, so hard that he fairly rolls.)*
Now it is time to blow up my fire. Burn, fire burn. Boil, pot, boil.
The half year is up. In only one day more I shall bring you something.
Something new! Something different! *(Mother Hulda appears as he
bends over the fire.)*

MOTHER HULDA: So you haven't learned not to shout your name? *(He
scrambles away from her, still afraid of her. Then he recovers himself.)*

RUMPEL: I will shout my name if I want to. Rumpelstiltskin! I feel
like shouting it, because I have won my bargain. I am the head of
everything. I can do as I like in the world. I shall make an end of
men. I have a little King's son to put in my pot.

MOTHER HULDA: Where is he? *(Rumpel turns his back.)* Where is he?

RUMPEL: He is in the Queen's garden. *(recovering spirit.)* He's waiting
for me. I gave the Queen time. But now the time is up.

MOTHER HULDA: Why did you give the Queen time

RUMPEL: Because.

MOTHER HULDA: Why?

RUMPEL: Because, because, because!!!!!

MOTHER HULDA: Why?

RUMPEL *(stamping)*: I don't want to tell.

MOTHER HULDA: Take care. One day you will stamp too hard.

RUMPEL: I will stamp when I feel like it. I feel like it when you say
I must tell why I gave the Queen time.

MOTHER HULDA: Then tell, and have it over with. Come . . . come
. . . . come!

RUMPEL *(spitting)*: I felt sorry for her.

MOTHER HULDA: Ah . . .

RUMPEL: I couldn't take the baby when I felt sorry for her. The feeling stopped me from it *(Brightening)*: I bargained with her for half

224

a year and one day more, that she couldn't make me feel sorry when I came again.

MOTHER HULDA: But you did feel sorry for her.

RUMPEL: I don't any more. I never will again.

MOTHER HULDA: You might.

RUMPEL: No! *(Rumpel stamps so hard that his foot sticks. He has a hard time getting it free. He feels very sheepish, his eyes sideways on Mother Hulda. When he gets free, his swagger returns.)* I have forgotten how it feels to be sorry.

MOTHER HULDA: Perhaps you will remember it when you go to take the baby away from its mother.

RUMPEL *(flying into a fury)*: No, no, no, no, no, no, no, no!

MOTHER HULDA: Now, now, now. What did I tell you about getting into a temper?

RUMPEL: Nothing.

MOTHER HULDA: Yes I did.

RUMPEL: I've forgotten.

MOTHER HULDA: No you haven't. Look at me. *(He starts to cower, as before, but recovers.)* I am going to tell you again.

RUMPEL: I don't care if you do, I don't believe it.

MOTHER HULDA: It is just as true when you don't believe it, as when you do. I said if you let your temper get the best of you, you will fly to pieces. *(Rumpel struggles between his defiance and his awe of her, then bursts out laughing, pointing at her.)* Rumpelstiltskin, you bad little thing. Why do you laugh at me?

RUMPEL: You said I would fly to pieces. I've been in lots of tempers. I've been in frightful tempers, and I never flew to pieces in my life. I don't care about you. I don't care about anything. I will shout my name if I want. I will be just as mad as I please. I will never be sorry again. I will laugh when I take the King's son from his mother. I will put him in my pot, and make an end of men! *(He laughs in triumph.)*

MOTHER HULDA: Very well. Only be sure you do not make an end of yourself, instead.

RUMPEL: I won't listen to you any more. I don't like to hear the things you say. I'd rather hear myself. I'd rather feel full of myself, and shout my name to the sky.

MOTHER HULDA *(going)*: Very well. *Rumpel flies to shout after her, then to the other side, then front.)*

RUMPEL: Rumpelstiltskin! R-u-m-p-e-l-s-t-i-l-t-s-k-i-n! RUMPEL-STILTSKIN! *(He circles he pot, singing)*

> Boil, purple and red and gold and green,
> Boil every color that ever was seen.
> For something different, something new,
> This very same hour I'm bringing to you.
> For soon my bargain I shall win.
> For my name is—

(During this, Ingret on one side, and Gothol on the other, have come, wandering, up the hill. They see each other, and make signs of silence. At the word "name," each takes an eager step forward, and this calls Rumpel's attention to them. He sees the nearest first.)
What are you doing on my hill?

GOTHOL: I was coming east through the woods of the world, and I heard a great shout, and I followed it up, and I found myself here—

INGERT: I was coming west over the wastes of the world, and I heard a shout, and I followed it here—

RUMPEL: What was the word you heard?—*(They are on the edge of recalling it, but finally give it up.)*

INGERT: Why—it was—

GOTHOL: Oh yes. Ah ... it was—let me see—

INGERT: I don't remember.

GOTHOL: Nor I. It was a word I had never heard before. Was it you who shouted?

RUMPEL: Yes.

GOTHOL: What did you say?

RUMPEL: Something.

INGERT: To whom were you shouting?

RUMPEL: Nobody.

INGERT: What a strange little man. What is your name?

GOTHOL: What are you called? *(Rumpel laughs some more.)*

INGERT: You do not seem to know who we are. We are from the King's court.

GOTHOL: Men do not laugh when we ask them questions. *(Rumpel laughs more.)* What is your name?

RUMPEL: I won't tell you.

INGERT: You had better tell us. The Queen sent us.

RUMPEL: What for?

INGERT: To find out all the strange names we could, to tell her.

RUMPEL: You will never tell her mine! I don't want her to know it.

GOTHOL: It doesn't matter what you want. Make an end of this nonsense. Tell us your name.

RUMPEL *(stamping)*: No!

INGERT: You might as well, first as last. We shall make you before we go.

RUMPEL *(in a temper, flies first at one, then at the other)*: Get off my hill! Get off my hill!

INGERT: Mind your manners, and tell us your name.

RUMPEL: Go away! *(Gothol takes him and lifts him on one arm, holding him horizontally.)*

GOTHOL: What is your name?

RUMPEL: Stand at the edge of the hill, where you came up, and I will sing you a song about my name. *(Gothol and Ingert go to the edge of the hill. Rumpel circles his pot backwards.)*

226

> Three times backward round my pot,
> Then you shall be where you are not—

INGERT: You said you'd tell us your name.

RUMPEL: It's at the end of the song.

> Three times backward, and a door
> Shall open where you were before.

INGERT: I feel strange.

GOTHOL: He's working a spell on us.

RUMPEL: Three times backward.

GOTHOL: Stop!

INGERT: Stop!

RUMPEL: There you go!

GOTHOL: Hold him!

RUMPEL: Whirling to your place below! *(They are caught by the spell at once, and whirl and disappear. Rumpel dances and smirks, full of airs. He puts his hands to his mouth, and calls his name down after each, in a tiny voice.)* Rumpelstiltskin . . . RUMPELSTILTSKIN!. . . I wonder what the little Queen will say to them . . . I'll look *(He runs to his pot.)*

> Boil green, and show me the garden fair,
> Where the Queen walks in the fragrant air.
> For nobody knows from whence I came,
> Or that *(whispers)* Rumpelstiltskin *(loud)* is my name.

(The lights come up on the garden. Daughter, entering from the palace, is listening. Rumpel's voice now sounds far away. He runs to look down on the edge of the hill.)

SON *(entering from the palace)*: What are you doing all alone in the garden, little Queen?

DAUGHTER: I am looking for Gothol and Ingert. It is past time for Ingert and Gothol to return. I must have a name. I must have one! *(The little door flies open, and Ingert whirls out, then Gothol. Both are dazed, and look about in teror.)* Did you find it? *(They nod, gasping.)* The hill on the edge of the world? *(They nod.)*

GOTHOL: As I passed through the woods at the edge of the world, I came to a high hill, and on it was a little house. And before the house burned a fire, and round the fire danced a comical little man, and he hopped on one foot and sang. Just as he came to his name, he saw us, and he drove us away.

INGERT: He put a spell on us, and we knew nothing till we were here.

DAUGHTER: Why didn't you get his name?

INGERT: He would not tell it.

DAUGHTER: You must go back, at once, and get it.

GOTHOL: No. Queen, no. I can never go there again.

INGERT: You had better send us to our death.

GOTHOL: Do not send me up that hill.

SON: I will go for you, little Queen. Tell me the way.

GOTHOL: Do not let the young King go. He will never come back.

SON: You came back again, afraid. But I am not afraid.

DAUGHTER: You must not go. I do not want you to go. Rise, Gothol. Think nothing more about it. Go in, all of you. *(Rumpel laughs, gets up, stretches, yawns, curls on steps. To the Son:)* Call the others, to sit by my son. I wish to walk in my field, as I used to. *(Son goes into palace, to summon ladies-in-waiting. Daughter crosses to cradle, for a loving look at her baby.)*

I am going to save you, little King's son. I am going to find the name myself.

(The ladies enter from the palace.) Do not leave his side until I am here again. Promise me to stay fast.

FIRST LADY: We will stay fast. *(Daughter runs to the door, pulls it open, shrinks away.)*

DAUGHTER: Watch him carefully. *(She gives a muffled cry as she goes out the door. The ladies do not see her go.)*

FIRST LADY: I wish we did not have to stay in this garden. There is dancing down by the mill.

SECOND LADY: If we could slip away, we could dance to their music. *(Ingert and Gothol enter.)* Oh, Ingert, will you do something for me?

INGERT: Say what I can do, and it is done.

SECOND LADY: Stay with the King's son, while we run to the mill and back.

INGERT: If that will please you.

FIRST LADY: It will.

SECOND LADY: You must not leave him till we come again.

FIRST LADY: Promise to stay fast.

INGERT: We will stay fast. *(First and Second Lady exeunt.)*

GOTHOL: What do you think draws them away with so much laughter?

INGERT: I'd like to follow and find out. *(Karen enters.)*

KAREN *(to baby)*: Is he well covered?

INGERT *(at a nudge from Gothol)*: Princess Karen, will you sit beside the little King's son, while we stroll to the mill and back?

KAREN: Very gladly. Do not be long.

GOTHOL *(at exit)*: You will not leave him till we come again?

KAREN: I will not leave.

INGERT: You promise to stay fast?

KAREN: I wil lstay fast. *(Ingert and Gothol exeunt.)* I wonder what goes on they wish so much to see. I'd like to follow them and find out. *(The King enters.)*

KING: Is he awake?

KAREN: King, my father, will you stay with the baby while I go to the mill and back?

KING: Take as long as you like.

KAREN: You will not leave his side? You will stay fast?

KING: I will stay fast. *(She goes.)* She runs off with a will. I wonder what draws her down to the mill. I'd like to follow her and find out. *(Miller and his Wife enter.)* Miller, will you and your wife stay with our grandson here, while I go over the hill to your mill?

MILLER: Go as soon as you like.

KING: You must not leave his side an instant.

WIFE: Do you tell me how to care for my daughter's child?

KING: You must stay fast.

WIFE: Who should stay as fast as we? *(The King goes.)*

MILLER: Why do you think the King goes to our mill?

WIFE: There is dancing on the grass there. It is likely he has gone to hear how the people praise his little grandson.

MILLER: It would be that.

WIFE: All the neighbors will be saying fine things of the child.

MILLER: It would be good to hear them.

WIFE: It wiuld not take long to get there and back.

MILLER: The child is safe in the garden here.

WIFE: No one can enter from without, except by knocking at the gate.

MILLER: We will not be gone but a short while.

WIFE: We will hasten our steps. *(They go.)*

(The Daughter climbs up the hillside of the edge of the world, above. Rumpel is fast asleep. She looks about in fear and amazement.)

DAUGHTER: There is no one here. *(Rumpel stretches and yawns.)*

(Daughter leaps soundlessly back out of sight. Rumpel goes to the edge of the hill, front, and looks down into the garden.)

RUMPEL: Aha! Now is the time! *(He circles the pot, singing.)*

> Today I brew, tomorrow I bake,
> And now I shall the King's child take.
> For nobody knows from whence I came,
> Or that—

(Rumpel burns his finger, and hops around shaking it and sucking it. He returns to the pot and sings again.)

> For nobody knows from whence I came,
> Or that RUMPELSTILTSKIN is my name!
> Three times backward round my pot,
> Then I shall be where I am not.
> Three times backward, and my door
> Will open where was none before.
> Three times backward, here I go,
> To fetch the baby from below!

(He whirls down. Daughter runs to look after him, when he is well out of sight.)

DAUGHTER: What shall I do?

(She returns and mimics Rumpel's charm. It works. She cries out, and disappears. Just as she does so, Rumpel is seen coming through the

door, looking at the baby in the cradle. He claps his hands and hops with satisfaction. He lifts the baby and starts to the little door, but stops at the sound of people approaching, leaps back, alert. The voices offstage grow stronger. Rumpel disappeears with the baby.)

FIRST LADY *(entering)*:   Are you sure it was Ingert you saw?

SECOND LADY: And Gothol with him!

FIRST LADY: It is true! They are not here!

SECOND LADY: The child is alone!

FIRST LADY: What will the Queen say? *(First Lady runs to the cradle and gives a scream of terror. The others rush over.)* He is gone!

SECOND LADY: No, no! He can't be! *(They rush about, looking. One lifts the cradle, looking behind. One rushes to the palace door.)*

FIRST LADY *(Going in)*:   Maybe someone carried him in!

GOTHOL *(offstage)*:   Are you sure it was Karen you saw?

INGERT: There could be no mistake. Hasten! Make haste!

(They stop with relief as they enter.)

FIRST LADY: We left the child with you.

SECOND LADY: You promised to stay fast. And now he is gone!

FIRST LADY *(entering)*:   He is nowhere within.

KAREN *(offstage)*:   Is someone there? . . . Oh, thank Heaven! He is not alone.

GOTHOL *(to Karen)*:   We left the child with you.

INGERT: You promised to stay fast.

BOTH: And now the child is gone.

KAREN *(to cradle)*:   Gone? Gone!

KING *(offstage)*:   Miller . . . Ah! The child is not alone.

KAREN: King, my father, I left the child with you.

KING: Well? Well? Get up! Why are you like this?

KAREN: You promised to stay fast.

KING: Why do you weep Why do you cry out? Where is my grand-child?? ? Speak! Speak! *(He strides to the cradle.)*

KAREN: Now he is gone!

KING: Gone!

MILLER *(offstage)*:   Run! Run! You stayed too long.

WIFE: It was you who wouldn't come.

BOTH: It was you. It was not I!

KING *(as they enter)*:   You! YOU! YOU! I left the child with you!

MILLER: Why do you shout at us? What has come to pass?

WIFE: King!

KING: The child is gone! Gone!

EVERYONE *(to the appropriate person)*:   You promised to stay fast. And now the child is gone! *(The Daughter has entered by the little door, unseen because she was covered by the crowd. She breaks through them.)*

DAUGHTER: What do you say? *(Silence. She looks into their faces, turns to the cradle. They all turn away. She is silent and still.)*

I am too late. *(They move toward her. She motions them away.)*
Where is the young King, my husband?

KAREN: I will tell him you have returned. *(They all go in, leaving her motionless. She covers her face with her hands. Rumpel appears, grinning, the baby in his arms. He prances around her. Finally he laughs aloud. She looks up and cries out, then remembers her bargain.)*

DAUGHTER: Oh-h-h-h!... Well, here you are again. *(Rumpel swaggers to lay the child in the cradle.)*

RUMPEL: Guess your guess, Mrs. Queen. What is my name?

DAUGHTER: Is it—Henry?

RUMPEL: Ho! Ho! Ho! That is not my name.

DAUGHTER: Is it—John?

RUMPEL: Ho! Ho! Ho! That is not my name.

DAUGHTER: Is it—is it, perhaps—RUMPELSTILTSKIN?

(He flies into a terrible rage, stamping, screaming, spitting, and running about the stage. Finally, he stamps with one foot in the cradle. The bottom goes through, and he has a furious time getting free of it, rushing, screaming through his little door, up his hill, stamps himself off at the edge, flying to pieces as he does so. This is of course done with dummy arms and legs, wig and cap, trunk, etc. Daughter clasps her baby close.)

CURTAIN

231

Peter, Peter, Pumpkin Eater

by

Martha B. King

The Children's Theatre Press

Anchorage, Kentucky

PETER, PETER, PUMPKIN EATER

By Martha B. King

PETER, PETER, PUMPKIN EATER

by Martha B. King

Cast

PETER

His GRANDMOTHER

His MOTHER

His sister, PRUELLA

His sister, DAHLIA

ELLEN

JOE BARNES

Joe's wife, ROSIE

Setting

ACT ONE: The side lawn of Peter's farm home on Bean Blossom Hill.

Time: Late afternoon in August.

ACT TWO: Same as Act One.

Time: The following morning.

ACT THREE: Same as Act One. Pumpkin house added.

Time: One month later.

This play was presented for the first time
by the Goodman Theatre of Chicago, under
the direction of Charlotte B. Chorpenning.

PETER, PETER, PUMPKIN EATER

by

Martha B. King

ACT ONE

Peter's family has lived on Bean Blossom Hill for generations. Their home is old, slightly fantastic in design, changing in appearance under different lights. Two doors lead to the parlor and to the kitchen. A practical balcony is reached from an upstairs window. Opposite the house is a tree with a bench built around it. A low fence runs across back stage. In the distance is a cornfield. Between the rows of corn Peter has planted his pumpkins.

The life pattern of the four women living in the house encompasses nothing beyond the conventions of a small, gossipy community and the ever recurring round of domestic details. As the scene opens, they are preparing food for a community dance in the evening. A table has been placed on the lawn where they may mix and beat with more elbow room than in the kitchen. Pruella stands by the table stirring dough in a large bowl. Ma sits on the bench paring apples. Dahlia sits near her, pinching fancy edges on the pie crusts which she has lined up on the bench. Grandma sits in her rocking chair, knitting. All four silently go through the motions of their tasks in time to the theme song (though it is not heard). This rhythm is felt whenever the women are together, symbolic of the mould of their lives. They are distinct individuals, yet caught in the mould. If they were sure that Peter could also be "frozen" in the pattern they would be completely content. But Peter has inherited from his dead father eyes that see the stars.

> *Curtain . . . silence . . . patterned movement.*
> *As the song ends, Grandma looks up.*

GRANDMA: Where's Peter? (*No one answers.*) Where is Peter?

PRUELLA: He went in the house, Grandma.

GRANDMA: He's mighty quiet if he's in there.

MA: I'm glad he's quiet for a minute. Goodness knows he's been under our feet all day.

GRANDMA: I'd like to know where he is for sure. (*Starts to rise.*)

PRUELLA: Leave him alone, Grandma. We never will get off to the dance tonight.

DAHLIA: How many do you think will come to the dance, Ma?

MA: Everybody'll be there. But nobody will bring better food than we're fixing.

DAHLIA: And nobody has a brother can dance better than Peter.

GRANDMA: I'll just see if he is in there. Ever since he ran away last month I haven't felt easy about him. *(Goes to door.)* Peter!

PRUELLA: I still don't see what made him do it . . . running away from a good home like this.

MA: With four women tending to his every need and want.

DAHLIA: I guess he's just restless 'cause all the other boys are working.

MA: There's no call for Peter to work yet, Praise Be.

GRANDMA: He isn't in there.

(*Arrested motion from all.*)

MA: Land sakes, where is he then?

GRANDMA: Run off again. Somebody ought to watch him.

PRUELLA: He's most likely gone down to see those everlasting pumpkins of his.

(*All turn toward the distant field and call. Their manner of calling is to be repeated many times. They use notes of theme song. Ex:*)

MA

DAHLIA

PRUELLA

GRANDMA

(Repeat in different key, ex:)

MA

DAHLIA

GRANDMA

PRUELLA

MA: Why doesn't he answer?
DAHLIA: What if he isn't there?
 (Women repeat the call.)
PRUELLA: Humpf. He's just trying not to hear us.
MA: We ought to be able to see him.   Peter!
DAHLIA: The corn's standing too high.
PRUELLA: He's probably lying on the ground talking to the pumpkin
 vines.
GRANDMA: For all the world like his Pa, always dreaming.

PRUELLA: I'll wake him up. Peter!

(Peter is heard singing, off. The women pause, then flounce back to their work.)
DAHLIA: Hear that? He's coming.
PRUELLA: What a nuisance.
MA: Always worrying us.
PETER *(full of the exuberance of all outdoors. Leaps fence on last note of theme song.)*
"My pumpkins grow a foot each day
They're going to stretch a mile away."
MA: Where have you been, son?
PETER: You ought to see my pumpkins. I'll bet they're going to be the biggest ones in the country.
DAHLIA: That's what you say every year. They never are.
PETER: But I planted special seeds this year. Don't you remember?
PRUELLA: They certainly were special. One dollar and seventy-five cents each. EACH. Five dollars and twenty-five cents for three seeds. More cash money than we get in a week.
PETER: Grandma gave me the money.
(Grandma rocks hard in embarrassment.)
PRUELLA: She did, did she? Well, that doesn't keep everybody in town from saying you're a sucker.
PETER: I am not a sucker. The man said those seeds came from a pumpkin that grew bigger'n a house.
MA: Oh, Peter. *(The haven't-I-told-you-not-to-lie kind of voice.)*
PETER: Honest, Ma. *(Dahlia prevents his sitting on pies on bench.)* The vine it grew on stretched for miles and miles over the country. All the neighbors complained at first 'cause it tangled up their corn and ran over their fences, but when they saw the size of that pumpkin they were glad enough to have seeds from it. The man sold me the ones he got cheap.
PRUELLA: Cheap. He must have nearly laughed himself sick when he was telling you that.
PETER: Well, they're growing . . . faster than any I've ever seen. Come down and see them.
PRUELLA: With six dozen pies to make? I'm too busy.
PETER: You come then, Dahlia.
DAHLIA: I have all these pies to trim. I'm too busy.
PETER: Then you come, Ma. The blossoms are on all the vines.
MA: We're all too busy now, dear.
PETER: But you haven't been down once. I've been there every day. When the corn was high as my shoulder I planted the seeds. I walked between the rows of corn in the soft earth. I took a hoe and made

240

a mound of dirt. I dropped the seeds one by one. That night it rained, a soft warm rain and all the seeds began to sprout. I watched the vines begin to grow. One grew faster than all the rest. It went across the rows of corn. It went right through the pasture fence. It grew and grew and now . . . It's coming right straight up this hill. *(The women watch with a distressed air.)*

GRANDMA: I told you the boy'd have a sunstroke if he didn't wear a hat.

MA: Sit here and rest, dear, while we finish our work. *(Pushes him to bench.)*

PETER: Aw, who wants to rest?

MA: Now sit there, like a good boy. We'll be ready to go to the dance soon. You'll like that.

PETER: No I won't.

MA: You will when the time comes.

(The women renew their work. Dahlia moves back to the bench.)

PETER: Dahlia, I know where a big black snake has his hole.

PRUELLA: Black snake? Did you kill it?

PETER: It wasn't doing me any harm.

PRUELLA: Then I'll kill it. *(Grabs Dahlia's knife and starts.)*

PETER: No, Pruella. You can't do that.

PRUELLA: Yes, I can. Where is it?

PETER: I was only fooling you. Anyway, it would be gone by now.

PRUELLA: You know where its hole is.

PETER: Listen. *(A bird calls . . . record. Peter times his speech to fit the pause in its call.)* What kind of a bird is that? What is it? I heard it three times but I couldn't see it. What do you think it is, Ma?

MA: I didn't hear it.

PETER: I've never heard it before and I know all of the birds around here. It must be a new one. Probably a rare one. What do you think, Pruella?

PRUELLA: Probably a sparrow.

PETER: Maybe it's a strange bird that spends its summers far in the north. It's staring south early. That's what. Let's find it, Pruella.

PRUELLA: I've told you I'm busy.

PETER: Hurry!

MA: Peter. Don't go away.

PETER: You've made me lose it. It's gone. You don't like anything out-doors, do you?

PRUELLA: Of course, I do. But I haven't time to go galavanting around after birds and snakes.

PETER: I love snakes. I wish I could go slipping through the grass the way a snake does.

(Moves with the running, gliding, twisting motion of a snake.)

MA: Stay right here, Peter. Find something to do.

PETER: I know. *(notices the table and crosses. Scoops his finger through the dough and eats it.)*

PRUELLA: Keep your fingers out of that dough. *(Peter sticks another finger full in her open mouth. Dough is a marshmallow mixture.)*

PETER: Let's have a picnic. *(Tries to take a pie.)*

PRUELLA: You can't have one of those pies now.

PETER: This is a picnic.

PRUELLA: Who said it was a picnic? This food's going to the dance and you know it. Now run along.

(Peter sits down at Grandma's feet.)

PETER: We can play we're having a picnic. Here's the sky and sunshine and people and lots of food and pumpkin pie. *(Reaches for pie.)*

MA: Keep your hands away.

PETER *(singing theme tune)*. "I'm as hungry as a bear
Because I've had so much fresh air.
I'd like to eat a pumpkin pie
That stretched from here up to the sky."

Come on, Pruella. Sit down and have a picnic.

PRUELLA: *(counting pies)* One ... two ... three ... Oh, hush. Now you've made me forget how many. Can't you think of something besides stuffing yourself?

PETER: There's nothing else to do. Nobody ever plays with me.

MA: Why, Peter. We play with you.

PETER: Will you go fishing with me? *(Takes pole from behind tree.)*

MA: Mercy. Not today.

PETER: I've got worms.

MA: I can't go fishing, Peter. You can see I have my hands full.

PETER: They're always full. You come Dahlia.

DAHLIA: I wouldn't go fishing for ten million dollars. *(Crosses with a pie in each hand. Peter stops her and they dodge back and forth.)*

PETER: You wouldn't have to fish. You could just keep me company. I'll bet I can catch a whole basket full in half an hour.

DAHLIA: Well, who cares? You'll be all smelly for the dance. *(Exit to kitchen.)*

MA: Stop bothering Dahlia, Peter. Can't you find something to do with yourself?

PETER: I've been doing something with myself for days and days. I want someone to do it with me.

(Still holding his fishing pole, he has an inspiration, eyes the table, and then the balcony and suddenly disappears through back door to reappear at upstairs window. Women fail to see him and he prepares to fish for pies.)

PRUELLA: There. I do believe we're almost ready. I wonder if I can carry some pies in this basket?

242

(Holds up a small one just big enough for a ten cent size pie.)
MA: It looks kind of small.
PRUELLA: It'll do all right. There's one. *(Puts a pie in.)*
GRANDMA: Where's Peter? Pruella, where is Peter?
PRUELLA: He's right . . . *(Looks around.)* Well, of all things.
GRANDMA: If you don't keep an eye on him he won't be here when you want to start.
PRUELLA: Has he gone back down to that pumpkin field?
   (Women start to hunt, calling "Peter" as before. Pruella and Dahlia remain back stage looking off.)
MA: He can't be gone anywhere. He hasn't had time. *(Knocks a pan, from table. It contains small pieces of carrots which roll all over.)* Oh, now see what I've done. I declare that boy will drive me to distraction. *(Ad lib freely as she picks up pieces.)*
GRANDMA: He must be in the house. *(Goes in.. Peter fishes for pie, using rod, line with large piece of wire for hook. End is carefully blunted to prevent injury to any of the cast. He hooks the basket, raises it, takes out pie, lowers basket and steps inside window just as Grandma comes out of house and Ma finishes picking up her carrots.)* He's not in the house.
DAHLIA: He's probably hiding just to tease us. *(Goes off back.)*
GRANDMA: The boy seems restless. You should have gone with him to see his pumpkins, Pruella.
PRUELLA: As if I didn't have enough to do geting all this food ready.
MA: I thought I put a pie in this basket. *(Grandma looks in.)*
GRANDMA: There isn't one there now.
MA: I'm sure I put one in.
GRANDMA: If there isn't one there, you didn't put one in.
MA: Well, here's another one. Oh, Peter, where are you? *(Goes toward tree.)* If you're hiding any place, dear, please come out.
GRANDMA: Come out Peter. Pruella will give you a piece of pie.
PRUELLA: I will not.
GRANDMA: You should have given him some in the first place.
PRUELLA: He didn't need anything to eat and he won't get anything till he gets to the dance.
   (Peter hooks another piece of pie, and returns the basket. Sits on window ledge eating and watching the women with delight.)
DAHLIA: I've looked down the road and he's not there.
GRANDMA: If you folks had eyes in your head he wouldn't be getting away all the time.
PRUELLA: He's probably right in the house.
GRANDMA: I looked there.
PRUELLA: I'll look myself. I'd like to catch him. *(Goes in back door, Comes out front, catching her hair in the hook Peter has left dangling. Note: Before each performance, Peter makes a knot in the line to*

243

indicate where it should hang, and notches the rail of balcony as a resting place for knot. Pruella can see hook from door and catches it with her hand just as it apparently catches in her hair. The line is pulled far out.) Help. Something's got me. *(Women see Peter.)*

DAHLIA: Peter!

GRANDMA: Land a mercy, look at him.

MA: Get down before you fall.

PRUELLA: Help. Help . . . I say, help. *(ad lib.)*.

MA: Hold still. I'm trying to get it out.

(Peter drops pole. Jumps from balcony.)

PETER: I didn't mean to hurt you, Pruella, honest I didn't. *(Pruella, freed, puts hand on hips and glares at him. He backs off.)* I only thought I could get you to play.

PRUELLA: A fine way to play. Making other people get behind in their work.

PETER: I'll help you. What can I do? *(begins stirring in bowl.)*

PRUELLA: There's nothing you can do. Just find something to do with yourself. QUIETLY. *(All women nod "yes" emphatically. Peter sits on bench. Music, off "Pop Goes Weasel," Victor No. 20447-B.)* Is that the music for the dance already?

GRANDMA: We're going to be late.

PRUELLA: Not if we hurry.

GRANDMA: It's Pop Goes the Weasel. I hate to miss it.

(Peter runs across and swings her.)

PETER: You don't have to miss it, Grandma.

(The women stand in positions to mark three corners of a square, shaking their fingers furiously at Peter and Grandma. They ad lib freely. Peter leaves Grandma and swings each woman in turn. Music gets louder.)

PRUELLA: Peter. You're wasting time. How do you think . . . *(he swings her.)*

DAHLIA: Peter, will you stop   *(Peter grabs her.)*

PETER: Grand right and left.

MA: Peter, what am I going to do with you?

(As he skips to her she turns her back, but he swings her anyway.)

PETER: Swing her 'round. *(Returns to Grandma.)* Back again, Grandma.

PRUELLA: Peter, we'll never get off.

(This time he swings her clear off her feet. She screams.)

PETER: Swing that girl. *(Moves to Dahlia.)* That pretty little girl. *(Moves on to Ma.)* The girl I left . . . *(Back to Grandma.)* behind me. *(Both Peter and Grandma shout "Pop Goes the Weasel" as music ends. Three women move at them, scolding. Music goes on. Peter puts his fingers in his ears to shut out their scolding. They ad lib, indicating they want him to sit down and let them talk to him. He stands*

*still. * All seize him and try to take him to chair. He is strong enough
to swing them all around. Does so twice. At last they force him to sit
down, increasing their scolding and pantomiming freely. They pause
and pull his fingers from ears.)*
PETER: I thought you wanted to dance.
*(They begin talking again and his fingers go back. The entire movement
is patterned. As music comes to a climax, they issue their last orders
to sit there until they are ready to go, and file into the house according
to height. Grandma, who is shortest, joins the end of the line shaking
her head over a good dance come to a bad end. Peter is left alone.
The music fades. Joe calls off stage.)*
JOE BARNES: Peter. Peter.
PETER: Joe. Joe Barnes. *(He crouches behind tree.)* Somebody to
   play with.
*(Joe and Rosie run on. Peter rushes at Joe and throws him to ground.
Rosie indignantly tries to pull him off.)*
JOE: Hey you. Let me up.
PETER: Go ahead and get up. Get up why don't you?
JOE: You let me up. I'll fix you.
PETER: Yes, you will. You can't even get up. Go ahead and try. *(Joe
   succeeds.)*
JOE What do you think I am anyway? *(Rosie helps brush him off.)*
PETER: Don't you want to play?
JOE: No.
PETER: You always used to play.
ROSIE: He has responsibilities now.
JOE: Yes. I have a wife to take care of.
PETER: Looks like there'll never be anybody to play with again. *(Sits
   down.)*
ROSIE: You're coming to the dance with us, aren't you?
*(Ma and Dahlia come out of kitchen door, Pruella and Grandma from
front.)*
JOE: We stopped to take you with us.
PETER: I'm not going.
DAHLIA: Well, why not?
PETER: Well . . . I'm just not going.
ROSIE: Oh, why Peter?
PETER: I got reasons.
MA: Land sakes, what are they?
PETER: I got them.
PRUELLA: Speak up or you haven't got them.
DAHLIA: Please tell, Peter.
PETER: I'm just not going, that's all.
DAHLIA: You have to. You're the best dancer in town.
PETER: What's the good of being the best dancer if there's nobody
   to dance with.

PRUELLA: Nobody to dance with? What do you mean?

PETER: All the other boys have wives to dance with.

MA: It that all? Well, you have two sisters and a mother and a grand-mother.

PETER: I want a wife.

JOE: If you had a wife you couldn't keep her.

ROSIE: Oh, Joe. He could too.

PRUELLA: What could a wife do for you I'd like to know?

PETER: She could . . . she could

ROSIE: She could cook for you, Peter. *(Peter agrees eagerly.)*

PRUELLA: Haven't I been doing his cooking for years and years?

ROSIE: She could bake your pies . . . your pumpkin pies.

MA: After all the pies I've made for him . . . *(Sits on bench, weeping.)*

PETER: Nobody in the country can make finer pies than you, Ma. But a wife . . .

ROSIE: She could darn your socks.

GRANDMA: I've sat in this chair and darned his socks since the day he was born and I'd like to see the girl could do'em better.

PETER: Nobody could do'em better, Grandma.

PURELLA: Well?

PETER: *(Forgetting all of them and seeing his wife clearly.)* I want a wife to play with . . . *(they laugh)* to go fishing with me . . . to walk beside me down the road . . . to sing songs and listen to the birds . . . to hunt for snakes and hopping toads and lizards . . . I want a wife to watch my pumpkins grow. *(Laughter at each pause.)*

JOE: Say. How are those special pumpkin seeds by now?

PETER: Getting bigger and bigger.

JOE: I suppose they'll get too big for hauling down to the county fair. Everybody'll just have to come up here to stare at them.

MA: Dear me, I'd forgot those foolish seeds.

JOE: How big is the vine by now?

PETER: Big enough to be growing up this hill.

JOE: Whoops . . . that's a fast moving vine.

PETER: Come down and see for yourself. *(Tries to pull Joe and Rosie down.)*

JOE: I'd be scared too . . . *(winks at the women)* why, first thing you know, that vine'll be walking right up over this hill and down to the other side.

(Women laugh heartily.)

PETER: You can laugh all you like.

JOE: Wait till it gets to moving in and out of people's fences. Will they be mad?

ROSIE: The way you talk. *(adoringly.)*

JOE: But when it gets to moving real fast . . . chasing the cows and scattering the pigs and scaring the horses . . . LOOK OUT.

PETER: Well, I know it's growing. (*Leans on table, back to them all.*)

JOE: I wouldn't doubt it for a minute. (*He grabs a chair and stands on it in the manner of a Fair Barker. The women cluster around, laughing.*) Step right up folks. Looking's free. See the famous travelling pumpkin vine—fastest moving object in the country. Going to move right out of this farm—out of this county . . . out of this state . . . right down to the White House to call on the President.

ROSIE: Isn't he wonderful? That's my Joe.

(*She has gasped "Oh Joe" after each of his elaborate statements.*)

JOE: Step right up folks . . . nothing costs . . . but the seeds.

(*A pumpkin vine with enormous yellow blossoms is seen creeping slowly through the fence and down to center. It is pulled by a wire.*)

ROSIE: Joe. Look.

(*All jump. Dahlia gets on bench.*)

JOE: Jumpin' Jupiter . . . a pumpkin vine!

PETER: I told you so . . . I told you so. Look at that. Look at it. Did you ever see a bigger blossom?

ROSIE: Look at it grow. it's moving, Joe. It's moving right under my eyes . . . right while I'm looking at it.

DAHLIA: It makes me feel kind of creepy.

JOE: It ain't natural. It ain't.

PETER: Look at its blossom . . . big and yellow. It'll be beautiful in the moonlight. I dropped the seed in the ground myself. I watched it grow. I saw the vine start climbing this hill. I'm going to have the most wonderful pumpkin that ever grew.

PRUELLA: Not in this front yard.

GRANDMA: I should say not.

MA: Oh, no, Peter dear.

PETER: Look at that blossom—prettier than any flower.

JOE: Folks will just swarm to see this. We'd better be getting down to the dance to tell them, Rosie.

ROSIE: Come on, Peter.

PETER: No, Rosie. I'm going to stay and watch this vine grow.

ROSIE: Oh, please come.

MA: You run right along, Rosie. He'll be there. (*Joe and Rosie run.*) What's got into you, anyway, son?

PETER: Nobody ever had a pumpkin vine like this. Somebody stay with me and watch it grow.

DAHLIA: Miss a dance to watch a pumpkin vine grow? Oh, Peter!

PETER: Maybe it'll grow faster when it gets dark and the moon shines on it. Maybe it will grow a long way. I'm going to follow it.

PRUELLA: You're going to do no such thing. You're coming with us.

PETER: No. Pruella, I couldn't leave it. If nobody will stay with me, I'm going to stay alone.

GRANDMA: Folks will talk worse than ever if you don't come Peter.

PRUELLA: And wouldn't we look foolish prancing in without you?

DAHLIA: Everybody'd be saying "Where's Peter? How come he isn't around?"

PRUELLA: And we'd be saying "Oh, he's staying home tonight to watch his pumpkin grow."

DAHLIA: And then the things they'd say.

MA: We'll be objects of curiosity, that's what.

GRANDMA: We've always done our best to live right. *(Goes in house.)*

MA: We'll be disgraced.

PRUELLA: Indeed we won't be. Where's that knife? *(Takes one from table. Peter leaps up to stop her.)*

PETER: Pruella, you wouldn't cut it.

PRUELLA: I'd do anything to stop folks talking.

PETER: It's mine.

PRUELLA: Why don't you keep it where it belongs then?

PETER: I will. I'll do anything you want me to Pruella. I'll go to the dance.

PRUELLA: Get out of my way.

PETER: Please. It's going to be my biggest pumpkin. Come on. I want to dance. I want to dance with you.

PRUELLA: Look out.

PETER: Please come. Pruella . . . Please, come . . .

PRUELLA: Nobody's going to laugh at us.

PETER: Stop, Pruella, You can't cut it. You mustn't. Pruella . . . *(They struggle.. Peter with back to audience, hides Pruella's hands as she cuts the vine. The wires are joined with adhesive tape. There is a sudden silence as she cuts it and stands up).* You've done it.

PRUELLA: Well . . . *(She brushes her hands, a little self- conscious, but sure she's in the right.)* That foolishness is stopped.

MA: There'll be no call for folks to come swarming up here now.

DAHLIA: If they start asking silly questions we'll say we don't know what they're talking about. There is no vine.

PETER: The biggest pumpkin anybody ever had. *(The women work briskly. Grandma comes from house with their bonnets.)*

GRANDMA: Here's your bonnet. *(Hands one to each.)*

MA: Come on, Peter. *(Peter does not answer.)*

PRUELLA: Oh, stop your moping. Come along and help carry these baskets.

DAHLIA: I want to dance with you first, Peter.

PETER *(to himself)*: It'll be no fun staying around here any more. I'm going away.

MA: What's that you're saying?

PETER: Nothing.

PRUELLA: Come on.

PETER: I'm not going.

MA: Now, don't start that all over again.

PETER: I won't go.

MA: You'll have a good time once you get there.

PETER: I'm not going any place. She cut it.

DAHLIA: Don't be silly, Peter. It's nothing but an old pumpkin vine. *(The women are standing in a semi-circle behind him, bonnets on, baskets ready.)*

PETER: It was mine. You can go on without me.

PRUELLA: I never in my life . . .

MA: Leave him alone, Pruella. He'll get over it. *(Music comes in softly. "Dan Tucker.")*

PRUELLA: Take this basket then.

MA: We'll walk on ahead, dear. You can follow. *(Exit single file.) (The light has been fading steadily. The music changes to "World Garden." Peter silently takes the cut blossom and goes to bench, sadder than he's ever been in his life. The music fades, blends, comes in again as Ellen's theme song "Chillicothe." Ellen runs on, following the vine. As she reaches the end, an owl hoots.. She is frightened, runs to knock on door, hesitates, hides under table, sees Peter, runs silently across and behind tree, looks around tree at him, moves around behind, sits on bench and reaches out her hand to touch him, sad for his sadness.)*

ELLEN: Hello.

PETER: *(He is startled and does not look at her because of tears.)* How did you get here?

ELLEN: I followed that vine, but it doesn't go any farther.

PETER: Here's the rest of it. *(Hands her blossom, still not looking at her.)*

ELLEN: It's beautiful. What is it?

PETER: A pumpkin blossom.

ELLEN: Oh, I like it.

PETER: Do you really? *(He looks at her in amazement.)*

ELLEN: Oh, yes.

PETER: What's your name?

ELLEN: Ellen. What's yours?

PETER: Peter.

ELLEN: Peter. I like that name. .

PETER: Do you like to play?

ELLEN: Of course I like to play.

PETER: Do you like to fish?

ELLEN: Yes, I like to fish . . . though I've never been fishing, really.

PETER: Oh ho. Where do you live?

ELLEN: Union town.

PETER: Then how did you get over here?

ELLEN: I'm visiting my Uncle. I started out for just a little walk and

I lost myself following that. *(Points to vine.)*

PETER: You couldn't lose yourself around here.

ELLEN: Oh, yes, I could, I'm lost now.

PETER: No, you're not. You're on Bean Blossom Hill.

ELLEN: Bean Blossom Hill. What a nice name. I'd like to live always on Bean Blossom Hill. *(she sits down beside table. Peter kneels.)*

PETER: Please do. I'm glad you got lost.

ELLEN: I could have found my way home but it got dark all of a sudden.

PETER: That's nothing. It always gets dark that way.

ELLEN: But there were strange noises and things flew at me.

PETER: Nothing would touch you.

ELLEN: Why not?

PETER: Things that fly at night have eyes to see with. *(Owl hoots. Owl and following animal sounds are made by a person offstage.)*

ELLEN: Oh, there it is again. What is it?

PETER That's a hoot owl. He's an old friend of mine. He's lived around here a long time. He talks to me in the evening. *(Owl HOO ... HOO ... HOO?)* How are you this evening, Owl? *(Owl: HOO ... HOO?)*

ELLEN: He's saying something. *(Owl Hoo ... hoo hoo?)*

PETER: What's that? *(Owl: who?)* Oh, you want to know who's here with me? This is Ellen. *(Owl: who?)* She's never been on Bean Blossom Hill before and I think you frightened her a little. *(Owl: hoot!)* Oh, yes you did, too. Say something to him, Ellen. *(Ellen is reluctant.)* Go ahead. Don't be afraid.

ELLEN: Good evening, Mr. Owl. You'll have to excuse me for being afraid but I live in a city and the country's very different. *(Owl: Hoots in a scornful way.)* Maybe you'd be afraid in the city. *(Owl: hoot!)* Oh, yes you might ... with all the lights and loud noises and people. *(Owl: laughs almost. A croak from a bull frog interrupts.)* Oh, what's that?

PETER: That's only a bull frog. Listen. *(Croak, croak.)*

ELLEN: He's croaking.

PETER: Don't insult him. That bull frog is singing. He's sitting out there in the pond with a whole circle of lady frogs listening to him. He's puffing out his throat till it's as big as a yellow balloon. *(Croak, croak ... croak.)*

ELLEN: I wish I could see him. Do the lady frogs like him?

PETER: They think he's wonderful. Listen. *(Croak ... croak ... croak.)* Try it yourself. *(PETER tries croaking ... Ellen imitates. They burst out laughing. Then Ellen jumps.)* You aren't still afraid, are you?

ELLEN: Well, not exactly. But I wish things wouldn't move around so much.

PETER: Let's play a game. Pretend you're something that walks in the night. First look up at the friendly stars. *(Ellen looks up, back to audience.)* Feel the soft wind blowing your hair. *(She throws her head back.)* Now . . . Be a rabbit, hopping down low. *(He drops down, sitting on feet, using hands for ears. She follows hopping.)* Hop through the grass and stand still . . . So. You're looking for food that is tender and green and you love the night when you'll not be seen. *(They hop through last line.)* Now . . . *(Peter stands up, thinking. Suddenly holds out his arms like a bat's wings and starts to swoop about.)* Be a bat, swooping down low, flying high and flying low, flying in dips and swoops and circles, hoping the night will last forever . . . for in the daytime the light will blind you. *(They come face to face.)* Now be a dog baying at the moon. *(Both drop down. Peter bays, Ellen yaps like a terrier. They fall on the ground in a gale of laughter.)* Pretend and pretend but don't be afraid. Night in the country is always friendly.

ELLEN: I didn't know the night was like this. I'll never be afraid again. I'll be too busy listening.

(Music "Old World Garden" . . . very soft. Stars come out. In a moment, the music changes to "Chillicothe".)

PETER: I wish you could listen with me always.

ELLEN: So do I. But now I must be going.

PETER: Where?

ELLEN: I'm going to the dance.

PETER: You mustn't do that.

(Music grows louder.)

ELLEN: Why not?

PETER: Because I'm the best dancer in the county and I'm right here. *(Bows. Ellen joins his dance, which has the delicacy of a minuet. Use entire record 20638-A. They end by holding hands, leaning back and whirling as hard as they can. As they separate, they are so dizzy that it causes them to stagger about in the exaggerated manner of children, saying "Oh, I'm dizzy. Where are you? etc." They sink to the ground, feigning fatigue. A radiant light suddenly features the house. Ellen is delighted. Gets up.)*

ELLEN: What a beautiful house, Peter. Is it yours!

PETER: Yes, that's my house.

ELLEN: It looks like a play house, so lovely in the moonlight. I wish I lived in a house like that.

PETER: What would you do in a house like that?

ELLEN: I'd plant flowers all around. Iris and lilies and forget-me nots and dandelions.

(Peter gets up.)

PETER: You don't have to plant dandelions. They just grow.

ELLEN: Then I'd have them everywhere, whole fields of them with bright yellow sunshine on them.

PETER (*Picks an imaginary one*): Then I'd hold a dandelion under your chin and say "Do you like butter?"

ELLEN: Of course I like butter.

PETER: Can you make butter?

ELLEN: Who can make butter?

PETER: Anyone, if she knows how.

ELLEN: How?

PETER: Take milk from the cows, skim off the cream, put it in a churn, push it up and down, push it up and down. See? It's turned to butter. (*Ellen pretends to dip her finger in and taste the butter.*) Now put it in a dish, bake a loaf of bread, cut a great big slice, spread it thick with butter and eat it as fast as you can.

ELLEN: I shall learn to make butter tomorrow. Oh, how can I? I haven't any house.

PETER: Haven't you any house?

ELLEN: Not one of my own. I've always just lived with uncles and aunts, and aunts and uncles, and uncles and aunts.

PETER: Don't you like them?

ELLEN: I like them very much but when you live in someone's else house you have to do everything their way and I want to do things my way.

PETER: So do I. (*Sits down on bench, reminded of the women.*)

ELLEN: Do you have a mother?

PETER: Yes.

ELLEN: Do you have a grandmother?

PETER: Yes.

ELLEN: Do you have any brothers and sisters?

PETER: I have two sisters.

ELLEN: Do you have any wife?

PETER: Pruella says there's nothing a wife could do for me.

ELLEN: Why, Peter. A wife could do so many nice things for you.

PETER: What for instance?

ELLEN: She could keep your house so clean it would glisten like copper.

PETER: Is *that* all?

ELLEN: She could cook and bake and sweep and wash.

PETER: Is that all?

ELLEN: She could make so many flowers grow that the birds and bees would come for miles around just to smell them.

PETER: Go on. (*His interest is revived.*)

ELLEN: She would dance with you in the moonlight.

PETER: Go on.

(*Ellen takes his hand and walks.*)

ELLEN: She would walk all up and down the country roads with you.

PETER: Yes. Yes. Go on. Tell me more.

ELLEN: She would follow your pumpkin vine . . . and fish in the lake. She would tell you stories and sing you songs.

PETER: What kind of songs?

ELLEN: Glad songs and sad songs; slow songs and fast songs; skipping songs and running songs; baking and sweeping and washing songs; wind in the tree songs; rain on the roof songs; stars in the sky songs; and going to sleep songs.

PETER: Can you do all those things?

ELLEN: I could ... if I had a house of my own.

(He turns with a sweeping gesture to offer her his house ... then he remembers.)

PETER: My grandmother wouldn't like it.

ELLEN: Like what?

PETER: My two sisters wouldn't like it at all.

ELLEN: Peter what are you talking about. Wouldn't like what?

PETER: For me to have a wife.

ELLEN: Oh, Peter. When you had a wife, they'd love her.

PETER: Do you think so?

ELLEN: Yes. And now I am going.

PETER: Where?

ELLEN: Back to my uncle's, and tomorrow to another uncle's.

PETER: Couldn't you stay here?

ELLEN: Here? In this house?

PETER: Yes. We could play games and sing songs and walk out in the sun and listen to the night sounds and grow the biggest pumpkins in all the world. Will you stay?

ELLEN: And have a house of my own?

PETER: Yes.

ELLEN: It's a very nice house.

PETER: Then you'll stay. Right now. And never go away?

("Chillicothe" music ... softly.)

ELLEN: I'll stay forever ... starting tomorrow.

PETER: Then tomorrow we'll be married. The very first thing in the morning. When will you be ready?

ELLEN: Seven o'clock.

PETER: Then I'll take you home now so that I'll know where to call for you in the morning.

(Joins the music, saying "seven o'clock." They both sing.)

BOTH:
"Seven o'clock, seven o'clock
Seven o'clock in the morning
We'll be married ... we'll be married.
Seven o'clock in the morning."

(Exit, skipping and holding hands.)

CURTAIN

ACT TWO

A large pumpkin has grown (two dimensional, four feet high). The table is gone. A stool and rocking chair remain. It is seven o'clock in the morning. The shades in the house are drawn. Peter and Ellen run on to the music of "Chillicothe." Ellen wears a long bridal veil and carries a diminutive suitcase.

ELLEN: At last I have a house of my own. Mine. Mine alone. But Peter, it looks so different. Last night in the moonlight, I thought it was a small house. In the sunlight it is a very big house. But it's all mine and nobody lives here but us. I can hardly believe it.

(During her speech, Peter has grown more and more overwhelmed with the enormousness of his act and with a growing fear of the women inside. He'd prefer not facing them.)

PETER: Neither can I.

ELLEN: I didn't think I'd ever have a house like this. It's beautiful. I want to see what it looks like inside. *(Runs to door.)*

PETER: No, Ellen, not yet.

ELLEN: Why not?

PETER: Let's just look at it outside for awhile. *(Pulls her back.)*

ELLEN: All right. Peter, why did you leave all the blinds down?

PETER: I didn't.

254

ELLEN: The house looks as if its eyes were closed. You ought to open the blinds first thing every morning to let the sunshine in.

PETER: My grandmother can't sleep if the sun comes in.

ELLEN: That doesn't mean we have to keeep the sun out of *our* house. I can hardly wait for your mother and your grandmother and your two sisters to come to see us.

PETER: They'll come soon enough.

ELLEN: Then we'd better see that our house is all straightened up.

PETER: Please wait.

ELLEN: I've waited so long already. I can't wait another minute.

PETER: You haven't even looked at my pumpkin yet. *(Pushes her toward it.)* Look at the size of that pumpkin. *(He listens inside door.)*

ELLEN *(amazed)*: *It wasn't here last night.*

PETER: It grew in the night while I was asleep. *(Tiptoes over.)* I found it first thing this morning.

ELLEN: It can't be a real pumpkin. Pumpkins don't grow that big.

PETER: You haven't seen anything yet. That's only a little one. Come on down to the field and I'll show you some really big ones.

ELLEN: After I've seen my house, I'll go with you. *(Starts in.)*

PETER: Ellen, wait.

ELLEN: Why?

PETER: Well, well *(stumbles over words hunting for an excuse to delay.)* You're got to give a house more time to get used to you before you go in for the first time. *(Sighs with relief, sits on bench.)*

ELLEN: Little house. Look at me. Do you like my veil? This veil belonged to my mother. I've kept it in a trunk for years and years. Oh, and do you like my locket? It has my name on it. And do you think you'll like me? Peter, I'm sure the house likes me. I'm going in. *(He has been beaming at her and recovers just in time to stop her.)*

PETER: Ellen.

ELLEN: What's the matter?

PETER: Come here. *(He's desperate. Begins to examine tree trunk very closely.)*

ELLEN: What for?

PETER: You can't see from way over there. Come over here.

ELLEN: What is it? *(She edges over reluctantly to the tree.)*

PETER: Ants.

ELLEN: Ants?

PETER: You've never seen anything so interesting in your life. Look at them. Thousands of ants walking in a straight line up the tree. *(Watches the house over shoulder.)*

ELLEN: Of course, they're interesting but . . .

PETER: They're all carrying something white. Eggs. Yes, sir. Something must have disturbed their old house and they're moving into a new one.

ELLEN: Yes.
(She steps up on bench and follows the imaginary line of ants with her finger.)
PETER: I like to watch ants. They seem like people.
ELLEN: Yes, they do.
PETER: They do everything in order. I wish I could understand their language. I wonder who tells them what to do?
ELLEN: Peter, how can you be so interested in ants when I haven't seen my own house? *(Jumps from bench.)*
PETER: Ellen. Let's go down and get Joe and Rosie. They ought to be here to go into the house with us.
ELLEN: I don't know Joe and Rosie.
PETER: They can stay for breakfast and we'll all go fishing afterwards.
ELLEN: I'm not going any place till I've seen inside of my house.
PETER: Sh . . . they might hear you.
ELLEN: Who might?
PETER: They . . .
ELLEN: There aren't any neighbors near enough to hear us.
PETER: Not the neighbors.
ELLEN: Peter, you seem to be afraid of something.
PETER: I am.
ELLEN: What are you afraid of?
PETER: Of them . . .
ELLEN: Who? *(Peter gesticulates vaguely toward the house.)* Oh ho. Last night you kept me from being afraid in the dark. This morning I'm going to keep you from being afraid in the sunshine. Take a deep breath. *(Peter has been standing with sunken chest. Ellen taps his arm.)* Take a deep breath . . . and we'll walk right in. *(Takes his hand and almost leads him in.)*
PETER: No . . . I've got something to tell you first.
ELLEN: Something nice?
PETER: Not exactly.
ELLEN: Then I won't listen. *(Sits in rocker.)*
PETER: I should have told you last night, but I was afraid you wouldn't come.
ELLEN: I won't listen if it isn't nice.
PETER: It's about the house. The house isn't . . .
ELLEN: It's a beautiful house. Don't say anything against it.
PETER: I'm not. Only, the house isn't . . . the others are . . . *(He groans.)*
ELLEN: I'm only going to listen to nice things today. It's the happiest day I've ever had in my whole life. *(Music: "Chillicothe", softly. Ellen hums with it . . . takes suitcase to bench, takes off veil, folds it in time to music, removes a tiny organdie apron from case and puts veil in. Ties apron and walks toward door.)* Now, I'm going in.
PETER: Ellen, my mother, my grandmother . . .

256

ELLEN *(in doorway)*: Are you still afraid they won't like me? Why, I'll be ever so nice to them. Wait and see how happy I'll make them when they come to visit us.

(She whirls in and closes door. Peter is in a frenzy of fear, runs off behind pumpkin, races back to door calling Ellen, runs off to jump fence, returns, runs around tree, back to door, and finally gets on knees behind tree with fingers in ears. Music is louder. Ellen comes back from back door, looks for him, sees him, walks up behind him. He jumps in terror as she touches him.)

Are you still afraid? Why didn't you tell me there were so many rooms? I'll just have to close some of them off.

PETER: Did you look all over the house?

ELLEN: Oh, yes.

PETER: Did you look upstairs?

ELLEN: Goodness, yes. How did you ever happen to have so many beds? I counted five. Do you sleep in a different bed every night?

PETER: Didn't you see anybody?

ELLEN: Who could be in our house?

PETER: Where are they then?

ELLEN: Where are who?

PETER: Pruella, my mother . . .

ELLEN: Didn't you say they'd come soon?

PETER: Something must have happened to them.

ELLEN: It's too early in the morning for them to go visiting.

PETER: That's it.

ELLEN: I'm glad they haven't come yet. I have so much work to do.

PETER: Work? What doing?

ELLEN: First, I must get breakfast. Aren't you hungry? *(Peter nods "no" and sits down.)* Then I must sweep the house and put flowers in a blue pitcher. I shall go to market with a great big basket on my arm and bring home cakes and cookies and bread and pies.

PETER: You don't get pies in a store. Pruella makes them.

ELLEN: We could make dozens and dozens of pies from that pumpkin, Peter.

PETER: Dozens and dozens.

ELLEN: Let's have a party, right away this evening.

PETER: This evening?

ELLEN: Your mother and your grandmother and your two sisters and all of your friends will come.

PETER: We'd better ask my mother first.

ELLEN: We'll surprise her.

ELLEN: I guess we'll surprise her all right, all right.

ELLEN: We'll hang lanterns from all the branches.

PETER: Dahlia never does that.

ELLEN: They will look like fireflies. We'll put a table right here in the yard.

PETER: I don't know about that.

ELLEN: I'll cover it with a cloth of linen and lace. I shall use blue and white dishes. We'll have ice cream and candy and lemonade with pieces of ginger.

PETER: Lemonade with pieces of ginger? *(He's postive they won't get by.)*

ELLEN: I shall put mint leaves in the lemonade and red cherries. The cakes will have pink icing and yellow icing and green icing.

PETER: Pruella never has that kind of cakes.

ELLEN: I shall wear my veil and walk about saying, "Please will you have some tea? Would you like a white cake with pink icing or a brown cake with yellow icing or a yellow cake with green icing?"

PETER: What will my mother say?

ELLEN: Thank you, Peter's grandmother, I think it is nice being married.

PETER: What will my grandmother say?

ELLEN: Yes, thank you Dahlia. Thank you dear Pruella. We like our house very much.

PETER: Oh, what will my sisters say?

ELLEN: Yes, Mrs. Rosie. I planted the daisies myself but the lilacs were growing a long time ago when Peter's grandmother lived here . . . and the dandelions? Oh, they just grow everywhere. *(She picks an imaginary one, holds it under Peter's chin, then runs to the pumpkin and to the house.)* Do you like butter? A little. Mr. Pumpkin, do you like butter? A little more. Big little house, do you like butter? Oh, you like it most of all. I shall make you some butter. Oh, Mr. Joe, have you seen Peter's pumpkin? It's going to be the biggest pumpkin in all the world. Peter planted it himself. He watched it grow before I came but I'm going to look at it first thing every morning and last thing every night. Isn't it beautiful, Mr. Joe? Isn't it beautiful, everybody?

PETER: I don't care what they say. We're going to have a party.

ELLEN: Of course we are.

PETER: We'll have someone play the fiddle.

ELLEN: Yes.

PETER: We'll dance all night.

ELLEN: Yes. And everybody will see my new house.

PETER: Everybody will see my new wife. I won't tell them a word about you. I'll just surprise them. Joe Barnes will be so surprised he won't know what to say. *(Pretends Joe is sitting on bench.)* Take a look, Joe Barnes. That's my wife.

ELLEN: Oh, Peter. What fun to surprise them.

PETER: Yes, sir. I'll show them. You stay right here till I get back. *(He vaults the fence. "Chillicothe" music comes in softly.)*

ELLEN: My very first party in my very own house . . . and nobody knows I'm here.

(She takes a broom from behind tree and sweeps into the house in time

258

to music. Music changes to "Dan Tucker." The women come on in line, so tired they can hardly drag their feet. They drop into chairs. Grandma is last. She stands swaying in the center.)

DAHLIA: Get Grandma a chair, quick.

(Ma practically carries her to one.)

MA: There now, mother. You're going to be all right. You should have come home to bed last night.

DAHLIA: Nobody could rest till we found Peter.

GRANDMA: Out all night. Think of us. Out all night.

PRUELLA: And we haven't even found a trace of him.

Dahlia sees pumpkin.)

DAHLIA: Pruella. It's grown again.

PRUELLA: It hasn't. *(She's past believing anything.)*

DAHLIA: There it is—plain as the nose on your face.

PRUELLA: I cut it off.

MA: I saw you.

DAHLIA: It's another vine.

MA: Look at the size of it.

GRANDMA: You see? Those seeds are worth every cent the cost. Wait till Peter sees this.

PRUELLA: He isn't here to see it.

DAHLIA: He must come back.

MA: Somebody'll have to find him.

PRUELLA: Who? Hasn't the whole town been looking for him all night? I drove him off. Oh, why did I do it? Why did I cut his vine?

MA: Now, Pruella. You've been talking that way all night. It's no use. How could anybody know his heart was so set on a pumpkin vine?

PRUELLA: I should have known it. He'll hate me forever.

DAHLIA: No, he won't, Pruella. Not when he sees this.

PRUELLA: If he'll only come back. I'll do anything for him . . . anything. I'll bake him twenty pies a day. He can let his pumpkins grow wherever he likes.

MA: Sakes yes. There's not one of us will say a word even if he has pumpkins all over the front yard.

DAHLIA: If only we could find him.

PRUELLA: If we don't I'm going to go crazy.

MA: Me too . . . my little boy . . . all alone . . . out in the night.

GRANDMA: There, there. He'll be back for you to look after him. He doesn't know how to do a blessed thing for himself. You'd better thank your stars he ran away instead of doing what he talked about.

(Women look up, startled.)

MA: What did he talk about?

GRANDMA: Getting himself a wife.

ALL: A wife! *(Loud gasp from all.)*

GRANDMA: Yes. What if we'd come home to find Peter had a wife?

MA: Oh, Pruella. What if you'd driven Peter to bring home a wife?

259

PRUELLA: Well. I pity any wife who comes strutting around this house.
(Ellen swishes dust cloth out of upstairs window. They all jump.)
MA: What was that?
GRANDMA: What?
MA: That noise.
GRANDMA: I didn't hear any noise.
DAHLIA: I did. It came from right up there.
(Ellen starts to sing.)
MA: There. Hear that?
PRUELLA: Somebody's in there.
(Dahlia pulls Grandma over to the others. They line up and listen.)
ELLEN: *("Chillicothe" tune)*: "At seven o'clock I'll sweep my house
At seven o'clock in the morning
I'll set the table
And put on the kettle
At seven o'clock in the morn—*(steps out, gulps)*—ing."
Oh, I didn't know anybody was out here. You frightened me a little. You must be friends of Peter's.
MA: Friends of Peter's?
ELLEN: How stupid of me. I know who you are. You're Peter's mother. *(Curtsey.)* And you're his grandmother, and you're his sister . . .
PRUELLA: Pruella.
ELLEN: And that makes you his sister, Dahlia.
GRANDMA: Who are you?
ELLEN: I'm Ellen.
DAHLIA: Ellen? Where do you live?
ELLEN: I live here now.
GRANDMA: Did she say she lived here?
ELLEN: Yes, I'm Peter's wife.
MA: Peter's wife. *(She sits down suddenly on bench.)*
DAHLIA: Peter's wife. *(She sits down beside Ma.)*
PRUELLA: Say that again. *(She sits down.)*
ELLEN: I'm Peter's wife.
GRANDMA: Peter's wife. *(She sits down. Ellen retreats to pumpkin.)*
ELLEN: Didn't Peter tell you about me?
GRANDMA: Didn't Peter tell us? *(She stands up.)*
PRUELLA: Indeed he didn't. *(Stands up.)*
DAHLIA: We haven't seen Peter. *(Stands up.)*
MA: Where is Peter? *(Stands up.)*
ELLEN: He went down to see you. It's nice of you to visit us so early in the morning. Won't you sit down and make yourselves at home? Peter will be right back as soon as he's invited folks to the party.
MA: Party? What party?
ELLEN: The nicest party anybody ever had.

PRUELLA: Where?

ELLEN: Here. In this yard.

PRUELLA: Here?

MA: Is Peter inviting folks to a party in this yard?

ELLEN: Yes, won't it be fun?

MA: He can't invite folks here without asking us.

ELLEN: He wants to suprise you. He's going to suprise everybody.

MA: He's done it.

ELLEN: I wish he would come.

PRUELLA: So do I.

ELLEN: There's a great deal to do before dark. First, I want him to hang lanterns in all the trees.

DAHLIA: What for?

ELLEN: For the party tonight.

PRUELLA: Tonight? Does he think we're going to get a party ready for tonight?

DAHLIA: There isn't time.

GRANDMA: I'm all tuckered out. I couldn't get a party ready if my life depended on it.

MA: We'll have to. Peter's inviting everybody.

ELLEN: It's nice of you to want to help but I can fix everything myself, thank you.

PRUELLA: If there's going to be a party in my house, I'll do the fixing.

ELLEN: *(still uncomprehending)*: The party's going to be in my house.

PRUELLA: Your house?

ELLEN: Peter said it was my house.

PRUELLA: He must have forgotten about us living here.

ELLEN: Didn't you come here to visit us?

DAHLIA: We live here.

ELLEN: Oh, you can't live here. It's mine. It's the first house I've ever had.

GRANDMA: It was the first house I ever had too. I've lived here since the day I was married.

MA: I've lived here since the day I was born.

PRUELLA: So have I.

DAHLIA: So have I.

ELLEN: Do you live here with Peter? *(Sits down slowly.)*

MA: Peter lives here with us.

ELLEN: Then the house isn't mine.

PRUELLA: Of course it isn't.

ELLEN: Then there won't be any party.

MA: There'll be a party all right.

PRUELLA: If Peter's invited folks to a party there's going to be a party.

MA: We might as well get to work.

PRUELLA: All right. I'll get out the best dishes. Grandma, you polish the silver. Mother, you start the pies. Dahlia, you get our Sunday dresses out. *(She marches in house.)*

DAHLIA *(to Ellen)*: What have you got to wear?

ELLEN: Only this.

DAHLIA: What did you get married in?

ELLEN: My veil.

DAHLIA: Where is it?

ELLEN: In the house.

MA: Pruella . . . bring out her veil.

PRUELLA: This? *(Waves veil from door.)*

GRANDMA: Put it on her. Let's see how she looks.

(They put the veil on and lead her to Grandma.)

MA: I guess she'll look all right. Now, she mustn't get the veil mussed up.

PRUELLA: She'd better sit down in that chair.

ELLEN: No . . . I . . . I . . .

PRUELLA: Where's your trousseau? Folks'll want to see that too, you know.

ELLEN: I haven't any trousseau.

DAHLIA: Didn't you bring any sheets or towels or bonnets or dresses?

ELLEN: I brought my housekeeping apron. *(Holding out the organdie one.)*

PRUELLA: How do you expect to do any work in an apron like that?

ELLEN: It doesn't matter. I'm not going to stay here.

ALL: What?

ELLEN: I'm not going to stay here.

PRUELLA: You can't go away. You're Peter's wife.

ELLEN: I won't stay here.

DAHLIA: Where will you go?

ELLEN: I don't know *(sobbing)* but I'll get my suitcase and I'll go someplace . . . *(runs into house)*

GRANDMA: Oh, now, what will Peter say if she isn't here?

DAHLIA: He'll make a terrible fuss.

MA: He will at first but he'll get over it.

DAHLIA: What will people say when they come to the party to see his wife?

(Pruella has been standing looking after Ellen. Suddenly she turns with finger to lips.)

PRUELLA: Sh . . . they don't know about his wife. He's going to surprise them.

ALL: Sh . . . *(Each says it to the other who puts a finger on her lips and elaborately passes it on.)*

MA: Then maybe it will be the best thing if she does go away.

DAHLIA: She'd better go before Peter comes or he won't let her go.

PRUELLA: Let's help her get off.

(They move toward the door stealthily, in line . . . Grandma, Pruella, Dahlia, and Ma. As they reach the door, Joe calls off stage. They whirl about as if caught stealing.)

262

JOE: Hello.

ROSIE: Hello. *(They run on.)*

JOE: Do you know what folks are saying?

ROSIE: It's all over town that Peter is married.

JOE: Rosie believes it too. *(Joe is much too smart to fall for things.)*

ROSIE: Everybody says so.

GRANDMA: Who told them? Peter?

ROSIE: No. The girl in the post office told them.

(Ma sits down.)

JOE: What does she know about anything? *(Turns to Ma.)* Is Peter married? Listen, Rosie. Do you think Peter's mother would let him get married when the whole town was out looking for him?

ROSIE: Why would the girl in the post office say so?

JOE: Look at Pruella. Why, if Peter were married, Pruella would be getting the biggest wedding supper in town ready . . . wouldn't you, Pruella?

PRUELLA: I suppose so.

ROSIE: Something must have started folks talking.

JOE: Where would Peter find a wife? Dahlia, do you think Peter could find a wife to hunt for snakes and hopping toads and lizards?

DAHLIA: Oh, Joe!

ROSIE: It does seem queer, but the girl in the post office said she saw them . . .

JOE: Grandma, will you please tell Rosie that Peter isn't married?

PETER: *(singing "Chillicothe" song, off)* "I got married

I got married
Seven o'clock in the morning
I got married
I got married . . ."

(He jumps fence . . . sees everybody . . . and jumps right back again . . . long pause.) Well? Have you seen her?

JOE: Seen whom?

PETER: My Wife?

ROSIE: He does have a wife, Joe.

PETER: Yes, I do. *(He steps over fence carefully and goes to Ma.)* I'm sure you'll like her, Ma, honest you will.

MA: Peter, how could you? *(She goes into house, weeping.)*

PETER: She's beautiful, Dahlia. *(Dahlia bursts into loud wails and goes.)* She can do all kinds of things, Pruella.

PRUELLA: Dance and sing and play games? *(Exits haughtily.)*

PETER: She likes my pumpkins, Grandma. *(He kneels by her chair. She hesitates, then breaks into sobs and goes.)* You'll like her, Rosie.

ROSIE: Yes, I will.

JOE: So will I . . . but where are you keeping her?

PETER: I'll show you. Will you come to our party tonight?

ROSIE: Party tonight?

PETER: Everybody's coming. I'm going to surprise them about my wife.

JOE: I'm kind of surprised myself all right.

PETER: I fooled you that time, Joe Barnes . . . there she is. *(Ellen appears at door with suitcase, and there is a long silence while everyone stares.)*

PETER: Well, what do you think of her? That's my wife.

JOE: Where's she going?

PETER: Ellen, what are you doing with that suitcase?

ELLEN: I'm going away.

JOE: *(whistles)* I wondered how you could keep a wife.

PETER: What are you going away for?

ELLEN: We have to find another house, Peter.

PETER: What's wrong with this house?

ELLEN: It isn't mine. Why didn't you tell me they lived here?

PETER: I tried to. You wouldn't listen.

ELLEN: I know. I was so happy.

PETER: I like you when you're happy. Be happy now. Come on. Let's take Joe and Rosie fishing. We'll go past the field where the pumpkins are growing. I'll show you a lake in the middle of the woods.

ELLEN: Oh, Peter, how can I play when there's crying in my heart?

PETER: You mustn't cry.

ELLEN: There isn't going to be any party.

ROSIE: Yes there is, Ellen. Peter's invited everybody.

ELLEN: I'm not going to stay.

ROSIE: That's no way for a wife to do. A wife must stay by her husband always. Isn't that so, Joe?

JOE: That's right, Ellen.

ELLEN: It isn't right for me, I have to go.

ROSIE: You mustn't. Who will darn Peter's socks?

ELLEN: His grandmother.

ROSIE: Who will bake his pies?

ELLEN: His mother.

ROSIE: Who will wash and cook for him?

ELLEN: Dahlia and Pruella.

(By this time, Peter's family have emerged silently from the house.)

ROSIE: No, Ellen. You're his wife. You must do all these things for him.

ELLEN: I can't in that house. It isn't mine.

PETER: I'll get you a house.

JOE: How will you get a house?

PETER: I'll build one.

JOE: You can't build a house.

PETER: Yes, I can.

DAHLIA: I pity anyone who has to live in a house you build.

PETER: *(to Ellen)*: I'll build you a house all right.

JOE: Listen to him, Rosie . . . Peter's going to build a house. First

264

thing he's ever built in his whole life. Let me show you the kind of a house he'll build . . . *(He takes three boards from behind tree and sits on a bench. Rosie sits on ground and holds two of them. Joe holds the third.)* Here are the boards. Now Rosie, you help. Here. You hold this wall. Now here's another wall . . . and here's the third wall.

ROSIE: Where's the roof, Joe?

JOE: Roof? Oh, Peter wouldn't want a roof. If he had a roof he couldn't see the stars.

ROSIE: What if it rains?

JOE: Oh, it won't rain . . . very often.

PETER: Go right on building your house. I'll buy one.

JOE: Buy one? Man, that takes money. *(Pushes boards off.)*

PETER: I'll get the money.

JOE: Will Grandma give it to you?

ELLEN: Peter will work for his money.

JOE: What can Peter do? He's never done any work.

ELLEN: What will you do, Peter?

PETER: I'll . . . I'll *(pause)* I don't know exactly . . . just this minute.

ELLEN: You can work in a store.

GRANDMA: Peter work in a store?

JOE: *(turns politely to Rosie)*: Good morning, Madame. Would you care to buy some nice ripe pumpkin seeds today? They're rare and ripe. Nice seeds for the garden . . . only one dollar and seventy-five cents each.

PETER: Never mind. I'm not going to work in a store.

ELLEN: You can be a policeman.

MA: Not a policeman!

JOE: A policeman. Ho ho. What would he do when somebody said, "Oh, Mr. Policeman, there's a great big pumpkin sitting in my front yard"? *(Goes over to the pumpkin.)* "You're under arrest. Get along there now. Step lively. Down to the jail with you."

PETER: I'm not going to be a policeman.

ELLEN: Maybe you could be a fireman.

PRUELLA: Nobody has fires around here.

JOE: Peter would make a good fireman. No work to do.

ELLEN: You must work at something, Peter. Think of something.

JOE *(counting buttons)*: Rich man—poor man—beggarman—thief—

ELLEN: You can't get me a house unless you work . . .

PETER *(desperate)*: I'll find some kind of work. *(Leads her to house.)* You stay in the house till I come back . . . promise? *(Ellen shakes her head . . . no.)* You can't go away. *(She nods head . . . yes.)* You can't look at me and say you're going away.

ELLEN: No, I can't look at you and say it.

PETER: Good. Then you stay right here and I'll be back for the party. *(Puts Ellen inside, closes door, sees Pruella wearing a hat and cape leaving back door.)* Pruella, where are you going?

PRUELLA: I'm going to market.

PETER: I need you to stay here and take care of Ellen.

PRUELLA: Can't you take care of her yourself?

PETER: I'm going to find work.

PRUELLA: Down in the pumpkin field?

JOE *(bursts out laughing)*: That's a good one!

PETER: That's enough from you, Joe Barnes. I'm tired of listening to your kind of talk . . . go on home.

JOE: Peter. I'm a friend of yours.

PETER: You aren't any more. You laughed at me and made Ellen want to go away. Well, if she does it's your fault. *(The women have all stepped upstage quietly to listen.)* And you . . . all of you . . . you make Ellen happy and keep her here till I get back or I'll take her away and never speak to any of you as long as I live . . . I'll never speak to you again . . . I mean it . . . remember . . . *(Jumps fence and runs off.)*

PRUELLA: Well. I've never heard Peter talk that way before.

JOE: Neither have I.

PRUELLA: I guess I won't go to market just now.
(Ellen is seen walking off behind fence.)

MA: There goes Ellen.
(All women call . . . Joe rushes off and brings her back.)

JOE: Take her suitcase, Rosie. *(Rosie does.)*

ROSIE: Ellen, you promised you wouldn't run away.

ELLEN: I didn't promise.

PRUELLA: It doesn't make any difference. Peter told us to take care of you and we're going to.

ELLEN *(very sweetly, with a few ideas of her own underneath)*: Are you?

JOE: Yes, we are.

PRUELLA: You watch her, Joe. The rest of us had better go on fixing the party. Come on, Rosie.

ROSIE: Be sure to watch her, Joe.

JOE: Trust me. I don't want Peter any madder at me than he is.
(Joe and Ellen stand stiffly.)

ELLEN: Can't we sit down, Joe?

JOE: I guess so.
(They sit. Joe stares ahead. Ellen thinks . . . finger on forehead . . . she has an idea.)

ELLEN: Let's talk about something.

JOE: About what?

ELLEN: What are you going to do at the party?

JOE: I'm not going to do anything.

ELLEN: Aren't you going to do any tricks?

JOE: I don't know any.

266

ELLEN: Look, can you do this one? *(She takes his large white handkerchief and goes center.)* I'll drop your handkerchief on the ground . . . now, you hold your right foot behind you with your left hand . . . no, behind you *(ad lib)*. Now hold your left ear with your right hand . . . Now pick up the handkerchief with your teeth. *(As he struggles to bend his knee, she tiptoes off. Joe gets the handkerchief and catches up with her. Note: handkerchief can be made to stand like a small tent or cone.)*

JOE: I did it. *(Puts handkerchief back in pocket.)*

ELLEN *(laughing with forced gaiety)*: Oh, Joe. That's wonderful . . . I . . . I know another one.

JOE: I don't want to see it.

ELLEN: Oh, yes, you do . . . you can do it to somebody else at the party . . . *(Goes to kitchen door.)* Rosie, will you give me two glasses of water?

JOE: What do you want water for.

ELLEN: You'll see. Here. Put your hand on this bench. *(Joe kneels beside a log stool, turning hands palms up.)* No . . . turn the other side up. That's right. *(Rosie hands her two glasses.)* Thank you, Rosie. Now, I'll put a glass of water on the back of each hand and you try to get them off without spilling the water. *(Rosie exits. The glasses have small pieces of adhesive on the bottom which stick when Ellen presses them down.)*

JOE: How do you get them off? Say—this is a good trick . . . I'll do it to Peter. Ellen— *(Ellen moves off, laughing, believing she has him stumped.)* Ellen . . . Help . . . help . . . Ellen's going . . . help! *(Rosie and Dahlia fly out of the kitchen door and off after Ellen. Joe goes through all kinds of contortions with the glasses, afraid to throw them off . . . trying to get them off with a foot, etc . . . finally achieves it just as they return with Ellen, by catching one in his teeth, taking the other with the free hand. He shakes Ellen as if he'd caught her.)* Don't you know you haven't got a chance of getting away with all of us watching?

ROSIE: And we'll be watching . . . out of the windows . . . even if we are working. And don't do any tricks this time, Joe . . . be careful. *(Exit Rosie and Dahlia.)*

ELLEN: Shall we sit down again, Joe?

JOE: No. I'm tired. You'd better go in the house . . .

(He pushes her in though she leans backward heavily, pretending not to want to. They look out alternately several times. She looks out of door . . . and tiptoes out. Joe tiptoes after her. She walks around the pumpkin and back to the tree. He mimics everything she does with cautious elborateness. She stoops to pick up something and realizes Joe is there. She pretends to have been searching for her locket . . . Joe silently puts her back in the house. Then sits on the bench and in a minute puts his feet up and leans on his elbows, falling

267

asleep. Grandma watches from the back door . . . Ellen appears at the front door wearing Pruella's cape and hat.. As she walks out she meets Grandma but begins to run. All the women pour out . . . ad lib freely . . . Joe sleeps on . . . Ellen dodges them all . . . running back and forth over stage, finally running in back door with all after her in line, Joe last. Shouts heard outside . . . Ellen comes out of front door, frantically takes off hat and cape, puts them on stool, hears someone and hides behind pumpkin, just as Pruella comes out of front door.)

PRUELLA: So! there's my coat! *(Puts them on and moves off just as Joe comes on. He sees her—sneaks up behind her and captures her, thinking he has Ellen.)*

JOE: I've got her. Come on, everybody. I've got her.

(They whirl around and around. Pruella talking indignantly. All rush on stage.)

ROSIE: Joe, it's Pruella.

JOE: I thought she had your coat.

(Ellen seen trying to escape. All shriek and follow her. She runs opposite house. As all are off, she reappears, jumps fence and goes in kitchen door. All follow, jumping fence. Grandma dashes up last, balks like a horse, and runs around end of fence. Crowd uses both doors of house in order not to trip over one another. Ellen appears on balcony, throws a rope down which is fastened inside, slides down and runs off, shouting continues inside. All come out, search yard, and stop, not knowing where to go next.)

PRUELLA: She couldn't get out of that house, I tell you.

DAHLIA: Well, she's done it.

MA: Didn't anybody see her?

ROSIE: She's not in sight on the road.

DAHLIA: Where shall we look now? Let's run . *(All start. Grandma stops at door.)*

GRANDMA: What's the good of running if you don't know where you're going?

(There in front of her nose is the rope. They all see it. Peter cries off, then runs on.)

PETER *(so excited he fails to notice their agiation)*: Listen, everybody. I don't have to look for work. I have it. Right in my own front yard. I can sell pumpkin seeds . . . if I have bigger pumpkins than anybody else, everybody'll want to buy my seeds, won't they? I have big ones now but I'm going to put fertilizer in the soil and dig ditches for the water to run through. I'll use a hoe and a plow and I'll grow the biggest pumpkins in all the world. Then I'll sell the seeds for two dollars and seventy-five cents each. There are over a hundred seeds in every pumpkin and that will make . . .

(All start their individual varieties of mental arithmetic . . . one writes in air with finger, another on ground with stick, another counts on

her fingers. All ad lib at once. Ex: two times zero is zero . . . five times two is ten, put down the zero, carry one . . . etc., etc. After much effort, Peter arrives at-the answer.)
One hundred times two dollars and seventy-five cents . . . let me see
. . . *ad lib)* two hundred and seventy-five dollars . . . and there are at least one hundred pumpkins in the field . . . *(All gasp and start over.)* That's one hundred times two hundred and seventy-five dollars
. . . *(long ad lib.)*

ALL: Two thousand seven hundred and fifty dollars.

PETER: More money than I can ever use. Ellen can have her house. She can have everything she wants . . . Ellen, oh, Ellen! *(He can be heard calling through the house; all on stage seem to collapse. Peter returns.)* Where is she? She isn't in there! Her suitcase isn't in there, either. Where is she? What happened? You said you'd take care of her . . . Somebody tell me where she is . . . She's gone. She's run way . . . you let her get away. How can I ever find her? *(He runs back.)* It's your fault. You let her get away . . .

MA: We'll help you find her. *(All make an eager gesture.)*

PETER: I don't want any help . . . Go away. I never want to speak to any of you again. Go away. Everybody go away . . . leave me alone . . . Oh, leave me alone.

(He drives them all into the house. There is a long silence. Slowly he walks across to the bench and sits down. The music of "Chillicothe" floats in softly.)
Ellen's gone.

CURTAIN

ACT THREE

Same scene, but an enormous pumpkin house fills center and back stage. Peter is working behind it, whistling and singing.

PETER *(theme tune)*: "I've built a house from a pumpkin shell
        I'm sure that Ellen will like it well
        And when she sees it she will say
        Oh Peter why did I ever go 'way?"
(Goes inside. Joe and Rosie look in, timidly.)
JOE: He's finished the house.
ROSIE: He ought to change those signs or Ellen won't know about it.
    (A large placard is fastened on the tree saying, "Ellen, come back and I'll get you a house. Peter.")
JOE: He sounds happier today.
ROSIE: As soon as he comes out, speak to him.
JOE: He won't answer.
ROSIE: He'll answer you, Joe.
JOE: We've been up here every day and he never does.
ROSIE: You haven't spoken to him, either. Somebody has to speak first.
PETER *(comes out singing, doesn't see them till end . . . theme tune)*:
    "Here is a window. Here is a door.
    Hurry up, Mrs. Ellen, put a rug on the floor.
    Did you ever think a pumpkin could be
    As big as a house right under this tree?"

(Sees Joe. Goes in, pretending to close door.)

ROSIE: Peter. Wait.

JOE: See? He always shuts the door.

ROSIE: Well, why didn't you speak to him?

JOE: How could I?

ROSIE: How could you? Just open your mouth and say "hello".

JOE: Hello.

ROSIE: That's right. Only say it when Peter can hear you.

JOE: He wouldn't answer. He isn't speaking to his mother or his grandmother or his sisters.

ROSIE: I'll make him speak to you. Peter.

(Peter hammers whenever she speaks.)

JOE: I'll go and look for Ellen some more. If I find her, he'll speak.

ROSIE: You've been looking for Ellen every day. He's going to speak to you now. Peter. I want to talk to you, Peter.

JOE: He thinks I made her go away.

ROSIE: You didn't.

JOE: Maybe I did laugh at him, but it was only a having-fun kind of laugh.

ROSIE: Don't worry any more. Everything will be all right if you'll say hello.

JOE: I can't. Not if he doesn't want to say it.

ROSIE: You're his friend, aren't you?

JOE: I say I am. *(Meaning that Peter doesn't say so.)*

ROSIE: Then do something. It's a very silly thing for friends not to speak to each other. Peter. *(Hammer, hammer, hammer.)* Peter, please come out. Friends are friends and they have to keep on being friends no matter what happens. What fun is it to go around saying, "Oh, how do you do" to people you don't even like and saying nothing at all to the friends who love you? It's no fun. It's not right. I won't have it. PETER! *(He hammers away, ignoring her.)*

JOE: Come on home, Rosie.

(She sits down beneath a window and motions to Joe to keep quiet.)

ROSIE: I'm not going home till Peter speaks to me, even if I stay here all night.

JOE: Well, I'm going.

(He exits. Rosie thinks hard. Peter looks out of window, then out of door. When he sees Rosie he goes back in house. Rosie sings.)

ROSIE: "I know something, I won't tell
　　　Peter's in a pumpkin shell
　　　He's lost his tongue and cannot say
　　　Hello to Ellen if she comes this way."

(Getting no response, she tries something else. Crossing to bench, she picks up small stick from behind tree, ties her handerchief to one end for a flag of truce. She stoops beneath one window and waves it. Just before Peter looks out she runs around pumpkin to wave it at

271

the other window. Eluding him she waves it across the door. Peter
appears.)
The enemy would like to speak to you. Mr. Peter.
(He silently goes behind pumpkin. Rosie pretends to fall and hurt
herself.)
Peter. Help . . . help . . . my arm . . .Oh, my arm. I've hurt myself.
(Peter runs around. Lifts her arm up and down. She ad libs freely.
Suddenly she smiles. He is furious. Grabs his hammer and sits down
in the doorway and pounds. She in turn feigns anger, rushes to the side
of the house, picks up an ax, raises it over her head ready to smash
The pumpkin. Peter catches her arm.)
PETER: What are you doing with that ax?
ROSIE: I'm going to put another window in your house.
PETER: It doesn't need another window.
ROSIE: It must be dark inside. Ellen likes lots of sunshine.
PETER: Ellen— Have you seen her?
ROSIE: Not yet, but I'm going to.
PETER: When?
ROSIE: I can't tell you the exact minute. Joe's gone to look for her.
PETER: Joe. *(Sits down in rocker in disgust.)*
ROSIE: Oh, Peter. Joe wants to help you. He's been looking for Ellen
every day. Why don't you look with him?
PETER: I can look by myself.
ROSIE: It's not so lonely when you look with somebody else. Besides,
four eyes are sharper than two.
PETER: I don't care.
ROSIE: Of course you care. You can't live alone in a pumpkin shell
without speaking to folks forever.
PETER: I'm not going to speak to anyone again till I find Ellen.
ROSIE: You've been speaking to me. Please talk to your other friends
PETER: I haven't any friends.
ROSIE: Yes, you have. They've all been so sad waiting for you to talk
to them again. Joe and your mother and your grandmother and
Dahlia and Pruella.
PETER: They let Ellen get away.
ROSIE: They've been trying to find her again.
PETER: No, they haven't. They've been trying to keep her from
seeing my sign.
ROSIE: How could they? Those signs are on every tree in the county
almost.
PETER: Somebody keeps taking them down.
ROSIE: Who would do a thing like that?
PETER: Pruella would. All of them would. They think if the signs
are gone I'll never find her. Well, I'm going to find her. Nobody can
stop me. I've made her a house and I'm going to find her.
ROSIE: Peter, maybe Ellen herself has been taking those signs down.

PETER: She hasn't even seen them. They've been taking them down.

ROSIE: Ellen wouldn't come back even if she did see your signs.

PETER: She wanted a house, didn't she? I've made her one.

ROSIE: How can she tell you have a house?

PETER: I've told her on all the signs.

ROSIE: That sign doesn't say you have a house.

PETER: *(walking across to read it, looking back at Rosie to see what she's up to, reads)*: "Ellen, come back and I'll get you a house." That's right, Rosie. It doesn't say I have a house. I'll have to make new ones.

ROSIE: You'd better hurry. If she sees the old ones she might not come.

PETER: Will you help me, Rosie? We can make them fast.

ROSIE: I'll ask all the others to help, too.

PETER: Yes . . . No! I don't want their help.

ROSIE: We could make hundreds of signs so fast.

PETER: I don't need any help.

ROSIE: Never say you don't need help. You need help from everybody.

PETER: I won't let them come in. I won't talk to them. I don't want them to know about my new signs. And when I put them up they'd better not touch them.

ROSIE: You'll be sorry about not letting your friends help.

PETER: I'm letting you help.

ROSIE: Where's some paper?

PETER: I haven't any.

ROSIE: Then I'll run home and get some.

PETER: I'll finish polishing the walls.

(Rosie runs. "Chillicothe" music begins. Peter goes inside. Starts polishing window ledges with a cloth. He stoops down and is out of sight when Ellen comes on timidly. She takes the sign from the tree and writes something on the back of it, watching the house fearfully. She puts the sign back and goes without seeing the pumpkin house. Pruella and Dahlia look cautiously out of the front door . . . move to the pumpkin and each look in a window.)

DAHLIA: Hello, Peter.

(Peter sees them and puts his fingers in his ears. He deliberately leans in the doorway. They sit down sadly.)

PRUELLA: I can't stand this much longer.

DAHLIA: We used to have a good time around here.

PRUELLA: I used to be busy all the time cooking for him. Now he won't touch a thing I cook for him.

DAHLIA: He was always so happy.

PRUELLA: Always into something.

DAHLIA: Always teasing us to do things for him.

PRUELLA: He's never under our feet any more.

DAHLIA: I'd give anything to hear him sing again.

PRUELLA: He's wearing himself out hunting all over the country.

Where on earth could that girl be?

DAHLIA: How could she miss seeing some of his signs? *(Reads the one on tree with weary gesture of doing it for the hundreth time.)* Pruella. This isn't Peter's sign. It's from Ellen. *(Pruella crosses, takes the sign, rushes at Peter who goes in house.)*

PRUELLA: Peter. It's from Ellen . . . Ma, Grandma, come quick. *(Ma and Grandma run out.)* It's from Ellen . . . a note . . . she's coming! *(They all run to the window in line, move around back of pumpkin and appear at opposite window. They beg Peter to come out and listen. He obstinately keeps fingers in ears.)*

MA: Dear me. He won't listen. Go on and read it, Pruella.

PRUELLA: "If you can get me a house right away, put a note on this tree. If I don't find a note I'm going away forever. Ellen. P. S. I have my trousseau."

MA: She must have been here. *(Turns to Peter.)* She didn't see your pumpkin house, Peter.

PRUELLA: Peter. Will you listen to us? Ellen's been here.

DAHLIA: She's coming back.

GRANDMA: Make him listen. *(Pruella and Dahlia drag him out, but he keeps fingers in ears.)* Can't you see we're trying to tell you something?

PETER: Talk all you like. I'm not going to listen. I can't hear a word you say. I've listened to you since the day I was born. You've never listened to anything I wanted you to listen to. Now I won't listen to anything you want me to listen to.

PRUELLA: Ellen's coming back. What are you going to do about it?

PETER: You made Ellen go away. You let her run away from your house. Well, I've built her another house and you can't stop me from finding her.

GRANDMA: For gracious sakes, stop this nonsense.

PETER: I won't talk. I won't listen. Just chatter away all you like.

PRUELLA: Read this, will you? *(Waves the sign in his face again.)*

PETER: That's my sign, all right. I knew you were taking them down. I knew you were trying to keep me from finding her. Well, you can't do it. She's coming back. We're going to have a party too . . . lemonade with pieces of ginger . . . white cake with pink icing, brown cakes with yellow icing, yellow cakes with green icing. You've never had parties like that. Where's Rosie? Why doesn't she come with that paper? Go right on talking. You're talking to yourselves, I can't hear you. Just chatter, chatter chatter . . . I'm going to find Ellen.

(All through this scene the women ad lib. Peter goes off, still talking away. Rosie runs on with the paper but he is gone.)

ROSIE: Peter. Wait, Peter. I have the paper.

MA: He won't be able to find her.

PRUELLA: She'll be back any minute.

DAMLIA: He won't be here when she comes.

ROSIE: Peter. *(Starts after him, then sits down in doorway of pumpkin)*: It will serve him right.

MA: Poor Peter. If he had only listened he would have known she was coming right here.

DAHLIA: I don't see how she missed seeing his house.

PRUELLA: She must have seen it. Of course, she did.

GRANDMA: Then she didn't like it.

MA: Bless her heart. She's just like us. She wants a regular house.

ROSIE: Oh, dear. *(Each echo "oh, dear" in turn.)*

MA: Poor thing. Well, you wouldn't want to live in a pumpkin.

DAHLIA: He hasn't any other house. She'll come and go right away again.

PRUELLA: We mustn't let her.

DAHLIA: What can we do?

MA: She can live in our house.

(All gasp. Music "Dan Tucker" begins softly. All move in rhythm to Ma who sits on bench.. Music continues.)

PRUELLA: Yes. She can say the house is hers. She can do anything she wants to do in it.

MA: We'll give her a room all her own.

GRANDMA: There aren't enough rooms for that.

(This stumps them. All cross arms. Each taps cheek or lips or forehead with finger, trying to find solution.)

PRUELLA: I know. Dahlia can move in with me and give Ellen her room.

DAHLIA: I like my room but I'll do it for Peter.

MA: I'll let her bake Peter's pies.

PRUELLA: She can do his cooking for him.

GRANDMA: She can darn his socks.

DAHLIA: She can do everything her way.

PRUELLA: Let's get her room ready.

DAHLIA: What if she comes?

ROSIE: I'll watch out of the window.

(Music goes up. Go single file into the house. "Dan Tucker" fades into Chillicothe. Ellen runs on eagerly, carrying boxes. She goes out several times to return with packages, boxes, her little suitcase, and a huge pile of pie tins. She counts them all, then turns to read her sign. It is gone. She can hardly believe her eyes. Rosie looks out of the window. Ellen sinks to bench, crying. The women come out, single file, with elaborate gestures, emphasizing the music with steps and hand motions. Ma, who leads, turns with finger to lips to hush the one behind her. That one passes the sh . . . on.. Grandma, who is last, is so in the spirit of the surprise that she turns to hush somebody behind her, does it, realizes there is no one there, and looks again, shaking her head furiously at herself. They surround Ellen on bench.)

MA: There, there, dear. Don't cry.

ELLEN: I didn't mean to cry.

MA: I know just how you feel. I've had disappointments myself.

GRANDMA: Everything's going to be all right. I'm glad you've come back.

DAHLIA: So am I. We were afraid we'd never find you.

PRUELLA: We've looked everywhere for you.

MA: We've found you now and the house is all ready for you.

ELLEN: House? What house?

MA: You're going to live with us.

GRANDMA: The house will be yours same as it was mine once.

PRUELLA: We have your room all ready.

DAHLIA: You're going to have my room.

ELLEN: Oh, I'm not going to stay here.

MA: Of course you are, dear. We *want* you to live with us.

ELLEN: Thank you very much, but I couldn't do that. I have to go now.

ROSIE: No. Peter's coming right back. Think how surprised he'll be to see you.

PRUELLA: He hasn't been happy once since you left.

DAHLIA: He's hunted every day for you.

ELLEN: I saw his signs. *(Picks up a great roll from her bundles.)* I couldn't carry them all. Some of them dropped.

ROSIE: You did take his signs. Why did you do it?

ELLEN: They were for me. I didn't want anybody else to read them.

ROSIE: Why didn't you come right away when you found them?

ELLEN: I wanted to get all my trousseau ready.

ROSIE: I'll run and get Joe. He'll make her stay. *(Runs off.)*

MA: You come right on in the house and get yourself settled before Peter comes.

ELLEN: It's very nice of you to want me to live with you, but I need a house of my own. I only came back because I thought Peter was getting me one.

GRANDMA: He will someday.

MA: He tried. He just didn't know how.

DAHLIA: He did the best he could.

PRUELLA: Goodness knows he worked hard enough.

MA: Men are queer. They never do understand about the kind of a house a woman wants to live in.

ELLEN: Peter knew I wanted a small little house *(almost in tears)*.

MA: There, there, child. He didn't mean to disappoint you. He just loved that pumpkin so much he thought it would do.

PRUELLA: We kept telling him you couldn't live there.

ELLEN: Where?

ALL: There. *(Pointing to pumpkin.)*

ELLEN: In a pumpkin? *(She is bursting with pleasure.)*

PRUELLA: Yes. *(A "can-you-imagine-that" yes.)*

276

ELLEN: Is it a house?

MA: He thought he was making a house.

ELLEN: Did he think he was making a house for me?

PRUELLA: He meant well. Poor boy.

ELLEN: It is a house. *(She has been examining it all around, now goes in, completely enchanted.* It is a house. It has a door. I can walk in. It is a house . . . a real house. Peter did make me a house. Why didn't he tell me? A house for me . . . a house of my own . . . I can walk in and out of my own front door. I can look out of my own front window. I can plant flowers in my own front yard, iris and lilies and for-get-me-nots and dandelions. I can work all day or not work at all, just as I please. I can bake and cook and sweep and wash. I will hang the clothes out in the sun to dry. I will go to market with a great big basket on my arm. I will invite all of my friends in for tea. Oh, I can hardly believe it . . . it's mine. It's beautiful.

DAHLIA: Do you mean you like it?

ELLEN: Oh, yes.

MA: Do you mean you're going to live in it?

ELLEN: Yes, of course.

PRUELLA: In a pumpkin house?

GRANDMA: Are you going to keep house in it?

ELLEN: Forever and forever. Peter made it himself. Nobody else has ever had a house quite like it.

PRUELLA: No, I guess not.

ELLEN: It's right in your front yard . . . Peter shouldn't have put it here. As soon as he comes home, I'll ask him to move it.

MA: No, don't do that. We're—we're glad to have you here. What good is a front yard if nobody lives in it?

ELLEN: Peter will like living near you.

MA: Do you think so?

ELLEN: I will too.

MA: You will?

ELLEN: I haven't had a mother for a very long time *(suddenly kisses ma).* Nor a grandmother *(runs to kiss Grandma)* and I've never had any sisters at all. *(Runs across stage to Dahlia who meets her. They kiss.)*

DAHLIA: You have one now.

PRUELLA: You have two. *(She has watched all this in an embarrased way. She looks so forbidding that Ellen moves to her with some hesitance. Suddenly she tosses her fears to the winds, runs behind Pruella and kisses her on the top of the head.)*

ELLEN: Of course, you've all seen inside of my house.

PRUELLA: Well, no. Peter hasn't been showing the house off much.

ELLEN: Please excuse me. Won't you come in?

MA: I've never seen inside a pumpkin house. *(Goes in.)*

ELLEN: Isn't it pretty? The walls are like satin.

MA: So they are. My, my. Take a look in here, Pruella. *(Pruella hesitates.)*

ELLEN: Please do, Pruella. *(Pruella nods and dashes in.)*

PRUELLA: It's bigger than I thought.

ELLEN: It's just the right size. Please, Dahlia.

DAHLIA: It's the nicest house I've ever seen.

ELLEN: Oh, Grandma, please. *(Grandma scurries across to door.)*

GRANDMA: It's a house. Sure as you're alive. I bought this house. One pumpkin seed. Pretty good house for the money.

DAHLIA: Look at the furniture. Where did it come from?

PRUELLA: Peter must have made it.

MA: A real little chair, well, I declare. *(Carries chair outside.)*

ELLEN: Won't you sit down, Grandma?

(Grandma starts to accept, decides it looks too small and retires. Pruella proudly sits on it.)

GRANDMA: I'll just sit on my own chair, thank you. I'm more used to it.

ELLEN: Let's set the table. When will Peter be coming ?

PRUELLA: It's hard to tell.

ELLEN: I want the house all furnished when he comes back.

DAHLIA: We'll help you unpack. *(They start untying boxes.)*

ELLEN: Here are the curtains. See how they'll look, Pruella.

PRUELLA: New? Think of having new curtains. I've always just fixed up old ones.

MA: How did you know the size of your curtains?

ELLEN: I knew Peter would get me a small house. Here are the dishes. Here is the cloth of linen and lace. Dahlia, will you set the table? Here is a rug. I'll put it down. *(Goes in.)*

PRUELLA: How are the curtains going to look, Ma? *(Holding them up inside window.)*

MA: They're lovely.

PRUELLA: No bride in this town has ever had prettier ones.

DAHLIA: Here are the pie tins. *Carries the great pile inside.)*

MA: Mercy on us, what's this? *(Holds up an enormous apron.)*

ELLEN: That is my housekeeping apron.

DAHLIA: Look at the table. *(Carries it from pumpkin, all set.)*

MA: It looks like a party.

ELLEN: Let's have a party. *(Sits down on small chair beside table.)*

DAHLIA: Right away this evening.

ELLEN: Let's surprise Peter.

PRUELLA: Let's suprise everybody.

GRANDMA: Is there time?

PRUELLA: Of course there's time.

ELLEN: Everybody will see my new house.

MA: Everybody will see my new daughter.

DAHLIA: We'll hang lanterns from all the trees.

ELLEN: They'll look like fireflies.

DAHLIA: We'll use blue and white dishes.

ELLEN: We'll have lemonade *(all join her saying)* with pieces of ginger.

MA: What kind of cakes shall we have?

PRUELLA: White cakes with pink icing . . . brown cakes with yellow icing . . . and yellow cakes with green icing.

ELLEN: Pruella, I didn't know you ever made cakes like that.

PRUELLA: I've always wanted to.

ELLEN: Peter's going to be surprised . . . Peter's going to be surprised.

    (Peter is heard singing off.)

PETER: "I am Peter, Pumpkin Eater
      I had a wife
      But I couldn't keep" *(minor key)*

ELLEN: Peter! Oh, Peter! *(Starts to run off . . . Pruella stops her)*

PRUELLA: Wait, Ellen. We're going to surprise him.

ELLEN: I forgot. Put everything in the house.

    (They fumble everything, dropping packages, holding the suspense of Peter's coming. He sings on.)

DAHLIA: I'll go and invite folks to the party.

MA: Go inside, Ellen. *(She goes in.. Others compose themselves.)*

PRUELLA: Act as if nothing's happened.

MA: He probably won't speak to us.

PETER: *(dropping on bench, finishing song, too sad to go on . . . sees women)*: Hello.

MA: Hello, dear.

GRANDMA: Did you find Ellen?

PETER: No. And I'm sorry I haven't been speaking to you.

MA: That's all right, dear.

PETER: You see, I thought you were taking my signs down. I was wrong.

MA: Who did it?

PETER: Ellen. Rosie said maybe Ellen was taking them but I didn't believe her. I didn't think Ellen would do a thing like that.

GRANDMA: How do you know she did?

PETER: Look what I found. *(Hands his mother a locket.)*

MA: Ellen's locket. It has her name on it. Where did you find it?

PETER: Under a tree. Two signs were laying beside it. She tore them down and stepped on them.

PRUELLA: That was horrid of her. *(Grins at Ellen in window.)*

MA: Maybe she didn't understand about your house, dear.

PETER: When she saw the signs why didn't she come and talk to me?

GRANDMA: Folks have queer notions about when they will and won't talk. *(Pruella and Ellen point to house.)*

PRUELLA: Poor boy. You look tired. I'll you get something to eat.

PETER: Thanks, Pruella. I couldn't eat anything.

PRUELLA: I'll get you something anyway. You help me, Ma.
(Pantomimes to Ellen. There is a pause. Just as Ellen is about to step out, Joe and Rosie run on. Peter doesn't look up.)
ROSIE: There he is, speak to him, Joe.
(Joe moves timidly. Rosie gestures, keeping him going. He struggles, makes many false starts, looks back for reassurance. At last he speaks.)
JOE: Hello.
PETER: Hello.
JOE: Did you find her? *(He can't understand Peter speaking.)*
PETER: No.
JOE: Then why did you speak to me?
PETER: I'm speaking to everybody now.
JOE: Haven't you found any trace of her?
PETER: No.
JOE: Maybe it's a good thing you haven't found her yet. It'll give you time to fix up another kind of a house.
PETER: Why?
JOE: She'd never like—that house. No woman would care about living in a pumpkin.
PETER: I thought Ellen would.
JOE: No. Women want their things to be exactly like other folk's things especially dresses and aprons and curtains and parties and houses . . . especially houses. They like for houses to be all alike. Nobody around this town has a pumpkin house.
PETER: I thought Ellen was different. She liked to play. She could make up songs about everything she was doing. She was a good listener after she got over being afraid, and she said she liked my pumpkins.
JOE: She was probably just saying that.
PETER: I thought she would like that house. I like it. I made a roof, too.
JOE: You did?
PETER: When the stars are out I can take it off and when it rains I can put it on again. Ellen would have liked that.
JOE: Maybe, but it doesn't sound so very steady. She might like a regular roof better.
PETER: Regular things aren't fun.
JOE: Well maybe she'd come back if you had a regular house.
PETER: Then I wouldn't want her to come back. If she doesn't like my pumpkin house she doesn't like me. Oh, what's the use? I might as well be regular myself . . . walk on the sidewalk and never feel the soft earth . . . shut up my ears and never hear the birds sing . . . sleep in the house and never see the stars . . .JUST BE REGULAR.
JOE: She might come back then.
PETER: I'll go to work like everybody else. I'm not going to sell any more seeds. I'm not going to grow any more pumpkins. I never

want to see another pumpkin as long as I live. I made her a house.
She wouldn't even look at it. I'll tear it down. I'll break it up. I'll
knock it into seventy-five pieces.
(The women have come out of the big house and are grinning.)
Laugh all you like. You can all make pies . . . pies and pies and pies.
I'll break the pumpkin into a hundred million pieces . . . Where's
the ax?
(He rushes in the big house. Ellen jumps out of the pumpkin.)
JOE: Jumpin' Jupiter . . . Peter!
ROSIE: Sh . . . It's a suprise . . . Hide, everybody.
PRUELLA: Turn on the lights, Ellen.
*(Ellen turns a switch and the pumpkin is lighted up. The rest of the
stage has grown dark. All hide. Ellen gets behind a tree. Peter
rushes out with the ax.)*
PETER: I'll smash it into a million pieces . . . There isn't going to
be any house . . . *(Hold ax in mid-air, amazed.)* Ellen, Ellen . . .
Where are you? Where are you?
*(Rushes around the pumpkin and back into big house, calling. Ellen gets
in pumpkin and leans out of window. As Peter comes out of the
women's house, he sees her, and stops speechless. The others have
gathered on the far side of the pumpkin and begin to sing.)*
ELLEN: Hello.
(All sing:)
Theme Song:
Peter, Peter, Pumpkin Eater
Had a wife and couldn't keep her
Put her in a pumpkin shell
And there he kept her very well.
*(As they break into theme song, all join hands and gaily circle the
pumpkin, Peter leading.)*

CURTAIN

The Land of The Dragon

A Chinese Fantasy

by

Madge Miller

....

This play was given its premiere production
in 1945, by the Children's Theatre of Pitts-
burgh, under the direction of Miss Grace Price.

....

283

THE LAND OF THE DRAGON

By Madge Miller

THE LAND OF THE DRAGON

Cast

JADE PURE, Princess of the Southern Kingdom

PRECIOUS HARP, Aunt to Jade Pure

TWENTY-FIRST COUSIN ⎫

TWENTY-SECOND COUSIN ⎬ Maids to Jade Pure

TWENTY-THIRD COUSIN ⎭

ROAD WANDERER, A Student

COVET SPRING, Chancellor of the Southern Kingdom

TWENTY-FOURTH COUSIN, A Farmer

SMALL ONE, A Dragon

THE STAGE MANAGER

THE PROPERTY MAN (non-speaking)

NOTE: If a larger cast is desired, guards, townspeople, etc., indicated as voices offstage, may be played on-stage by additional actors.

TIME: In those days

PLACE: The Land of the Dragon

285

Synopsis

PART ONE

Scene 1. Jade Pure's apartment.

Scene 2. A distant field.

Scene 3. Royal garden, outside the Princess' window.

Scene 4. A grassy meadow.

Scene 5. A city street.

Scene 6. Jade Pure's apartment.

Scene 7. Royal Garden.

INTERMISSION

PART TWO

Scene 1. A lonely field.

Scene 2. Before the palace wall.

Scene 3. A dungeon.

Scene 4. Jade Pure's apartment.

Scene 5. The royal throne-room.

Scene 6. A lonely field.

THE LAND OF THE DRAGON

PART ONE

(The curtains remain open throughout. The stage is completely empty. A handsome curtain, black with a red-and-gold dragon painted on it, is hung without folds across the back.

Chinese music—recorded—is played for several minutes before the lights come up on stage, indicating the beginning of the play. The Stage Manager enters right. He is gorgeously dressed, carries an ornamental fan which he uses gracefully, and hops, rather than walks, with short bobbing steps.)

SCENE ONE

STAGE MANAGER *(bowing).* Greetings, Exalted Audience. You are most welcome. May the humble efforts of our actors to please you meet with flowery success. I am the Stage Manager, here to introduce to you each scene as it unfolds. You must pay no attention to me, for to a POLITE audience I am invisible!

(The Property Man has entered with a small black bench which he places center stage. He—or she—is dressed entirely in black, including black gloves. He shuffles with maddening slowness; his face is vacant and sleepy-looking.)

This lazy fellow is our Property Man. He, too should be invisible as he prepares the stage. The first scene takes place in the apartment of the lovely and gracious Jade Pure, Princess of the Southern Kingdom. There is the door, as you can plainly see . . .

(The Property Man opens an imaginary door, steps through it, and closes the door after him.)

And there the window . . .

(The Property Man opens an imaginary window, thrusts his head out and in again, then closes the window and shuffles offstage.)

But our play begins. Approaching us is the Princess Jade Pure herself. I bow to you, and respectfully withdraw.

(He bows and steps to the extreme downstage right of the stage, where he stands throughout the play. Jade Pure, charmingly but simply dressed in lavender and silver, enters, crosses to center stage, turns to face the audience.)

JADE PURE. I am Jade Pure, Princess of the Southern Kingdom. The death of my father, the Emperor, some years ago, left me an orphan, and alone. Sorrowfully I seat myself to await the coming of my cousins and the start of another lonely day.

(As she is seating herself, the three Cousins enter right, one fol-

287

lowing another, the tallest first. They come down center stage, turn to face the audience in the same movement, hiding the Princess from view in their speeches. They are richly dressed; Twenty-First Cousin's costume is predominantly green, Twenty-Second Cousin's, blue; Twenty-Third Cousin's, orange.)

COUSINS *(in unison).* We are . . .

TWENTY-FIRST *(bowing).* Twenty-First Cousin . . .

TWENTY-SECOND *(bowing).* Twenty-Second Cousin . . .

TWENTY-THIRD *(bowing).* Twenty-Third Cousin . . .

COUSINS. Honorable Ladies in the service of Her Highness, the Princess Jade Pure.

(leaning forward, fingers to lips) What we really think of her, you will learn most promptly.

(Twenty-First Cousin and Twenty-Second Cousin step to the left, Twenty-Third Cousin to the right, and bow to the Princess. They remain bent over until she speaks to them. Their attitude toward her is one of thinly-veiled insolence).

Good morning, Your Most Gracious Augustness . . .

TWENTY-FIRST. Daughter to the Sun . . .

TWENTY-SECOND. Sister to the Moon . . .

TWENTY-THIRD. Cousin to each dazzling star!

JADE PURE *(stretching out her hands).* Good morning, dear cousins.

TWENTY-FIRST *(circling to her left to stand behind the bench).* Will this unworthy one be granted the inestimable privilege of arranging Her Highness' hair?

TWENTY-SECOND *(taking Jade's left hand).* And I, the care of the five nails on this, the Princess' left hand?

TWENTY-THIRD *(taking her right hand).* And I, the five remaining here?

JADE PURE. Yes, yes, yes. Begin, I beg of you. And cheer my heart with some gay tale, for I am bitterly unhappy.

(The Cousins arrange her hair, buff her nails with imaginary equipment, as they speak).

TWENTY-FIRST *(pretending astonishment).* Unhappy? You, the Princess of the Southern Kingdom?

TWENTY-SECOND. How can this be so?

TWENTY-THIRD *(with a titter).* And why?

JADE. You know as well as I!

FIRST *(nodding wisely).* Ah, yes, to be sure.

288

SECOND. In just one week you celebrate your eighteenth birthday.

FIRST. If you are not wed, when the clock strikes noon that day, you shall lose all claim to the throne.

THIRD. And Lady Precious Harp, sister to your father, shall ascend it.

JADE *(sighing deeply)*. Yes.

SECOND. Empress you cannot be unless you first become a wife.

THIRD. But no man yet has sought your hand, because . . . *(pausing deliberately)*.

JADE. Because?

FIRST. You ask?

SECOND *(maliciously)*. All know the reason why.

THIRD. Does not the Princess?

JADE. Yes, yes. Because my face is ugly. Do not hesitate to say it.

COUSINS *(scornfully)*. Ugly, ugly, ugly!

JADE *(springing up)*. Cruel, hateful word!

COUSINS *(drawing back)*. We have offended you?

JADE *(her hands over face)*. You have! You have!

FIRST *(haughtily)*. You have offended us, Your Highness!

SECOND. First you bid us speak—

THIRD. And then you storm!

(With quick mincing steps they have lined up, facing rigidly front).

JADE. Ah . . . pardon, cousins.

COUSINS *(turning with one motion to the door, starting forward)*. We go!

JADE *(placing herself between them and the exit)*. O, do not! I have no one else to talk to. Well I know you speak the truth. My aunt, Lady Precious Harp, and Covet Spring, the Chancellor, say it too. They and you say that I am ugly, and I see no one else. And yet . . . come near, dear cousin.

(She takes Twenty-First Cousin's hand and draws her close; with the other hand she touches lightly the girl's eyelids and eyebrows, and then her own).

You have eyes set so . . . and brows above them. So do I!

FIRST *(pulling away quickly)*. But they are not the same!

JADE *(turning to Twenty-Second Cousin)*. And see . . . your nose is fashioned so . . . and mine feels very like.

SECOND. Oh, nothing like!

JADE *(following the same procedure with Twenty-Third)*. Mouths cannot be so very different, when their sizes are so nearly one. And what else is there? Skin . . . but mine is soft; my fingers tell me. Hair . . . you dress it well.

FIRST *(her back to the Princess)*. Extremely well!

JADE *(going to her)*. Then let me see for myself! Bring me a mirror, cousins . . .

(to Twenty-First, who, back turned, shakes her head vigorously) . . . *(to Twenty-Second, who duplicates her sister's action)* . . .

dear cousin

(to Twenty-Third, who does likewise).

It is my coiffure I wish to see . . . truly that is all!

COUSINS *(turning to face her, arms folded primly, in unison)*. No, no, no! "By order of the Lady Precious Harp, Her Highness Princess Jade Pure shall not be permitted—"

JADE. I know. "Shall not be permitted to possess a mirror." But, I beg you, cousins, tell me why.

FIRST. We have told you, many times.

SECOND. It is for your sake alone.

THIRD *(Mockingly)*. You are much too ugly!

JADE. Shall I never marry then?

SECOND. You have had no suitors.

FIRST. None could ever love you.

JADE *(moving restlessly to the imaginary window)*. Shall I stay in here forever, with no mirror and no suitors, never to go outside to the garden I see from my window?

THIRD *(with a derisive titter)*. No doubt!

JADE. But then I am a prisoner, no better off than my tiny caged bird here!

(The Property Man has shuffled on with a gilded cut-out bird-cage which he holds aloft; Jade touches it lightly as she speaks to the imaginary bird inside).

Do you hate it too, poor thing? Why, where are your seeds! almost gone? And very little water! Cousins, you have not been kind to him;

(They ignore her).

I shall go to bring fresh water and seeds myself.

(She exits left).

FIRST (*flouncing down on the bench*). Let her, then!

(*She extends her hands to her sisters standing at either end of the bench; they buff her nails just as they have done Jade Pure's*).

SECOND. How restless she becomes!

THIRD. There is no chance of her escaping?

FIRST. None. A guard stays at the door.

SECOND. The window is too high.

THIRD. And she has no friends to help.

FIRST. Our vigil will be ended soon. In just a week Lady Precious Harp becomes Empress. Ouch!

(*She pulls her hand away from Twenty-Third Cousin, glaring at her and then at her fingers. The Property Man who, listing to the right, is about to doze off, pulls himself upright with a start*).

SECOND. Will she reward us as she promised?

THIRD. Can we trust her? She is crafty.

FIRST. We can be as sly as she. But truly, she is clever. Who else would have thought of such a scheme?

SECOND. To spread word throughout the kingdom that Jade Pure is very ugly . . .

THIRD. So that she will not be wed before her eighteenth birthday . . .

FIRST. And so that Precious Harp herself can claim the throne as next in line! A clever woman!

SECOND. What if someone learns of the Princess' beauty?

FIRST. Stupid! How? There is no way.

THIRD. What if Jade Pure learns of it herself?

FIRST. She never can, with no one near to tell her, and no mirror. Ouch!

(*She pulls her hand away from Twenty-Second Cousin, regards her nails tenderly. The Property Man, who has listed to the left, again jerks upright, awakened by her shriek*).

That is why she cannot go outside into the garden. There are pools and streams of water there.

SECOND. She might see her face in one of them.

THIRD. Or see a gardener.

FIRST. Exactly. (*rising quickly*) Hush . . . someone is coming.

SECOND (*looking off right*). Lady Precious Harp . . .

THIRD. And Covet Spring.

(They enter right. Lady Precious Harp, a coldly handsome woman in her thirties, is exquisitely costumed in royal yellow, bright with gold and jewels. Covet Spring, a corpulent wheezing ancient, wears red, and carries a huge fan which he flutters affectedly. The Property Man sighs deeply, and rests the bird-cage on his hip, assuming a comfortable position).

COUSINS *(bowing).* Most hearty greetings to Her Exalted Ladyship.

PRECIOUS HARP *(arrogantly).* I, Lady Precious Harp, sister to the dear departed Emperor, graciously accept your unworthy greetings.

COUSINS *(bowing).* We bow in welcome to His Mighty Excellency.

COVET SPRING *(also arrogantly).* I, Covet Spring, Chancellor of the Southern Kingdom, nod in reply.

PRECIOUS HARP *(after glancing about, in sudden alarm).* Where is the Princess, my niece? Where is she? Speak!

COVET SPRING. She has not escaped?

FIRST. No. She has gone to fetch water for that wretched bird.

PRECIOUS HARP. Do not leave her unattended for a moment!

(to Twenty-third Cousin, who exits)

You—run quickly to watch her. "A single false move loses the game."

COVET SPRING. She might find a pane of glass in which to see her face, or a polished kettle.

(fanning himself violently) That would be a tragedy!

PRECIOUS HARP. It would indeed. For, knowing her own beauty, she might prove troublesome. I should much regret using violence until after I am Empress.

FIRST. Have no fear. We shall watch her diligently, mindful of the generous reward you have promised my sisters and me.

SECOND *(pointedly).* The most generous reward!

PRECIOUS HARP *(coldly).* Reward . . . ah, yes.

FIRST. You had not forgotten?

PRECIOUS HARP. Indeed not. Faithful servants should be fittingly repaid, and so you will be—most fittingly, when I ascend the throne.

FIRST. *(boldly).* And not a moment later!

(aside to her sister) I mistrust her tone of voice.

292

PRECIOUS HARP *(aside to Covet Spring)*. Fittingly repaid indeed! They know too much!

COVET SPRING *(to her, his fan vibrating vigorously)*. Impertinent maids!

PRECIOUS HARP *(ducking, touching her hair disturbed by the breeze)*. Only take care that your tongue does not wag too saucily, girl, when speaking to your betters.

FIRST *(aside)*. Old witch!

SECOND *(aside)*. Fat rogue!

COVET SPRING. Here is the Princess.

(He and Precious Harp bow slightly as Jade re-enters with imaginary cups of water and seeds; Twenty-Third Cousin follows).

JADE. Welcome, worthy aunt and noble Chancellor.

PRECIOUS HARP *(falsely sweet)*. Sweet child, good-day. How is my niece?

JADE *(busying herself at the cage which the Property Man quickly holds up in position again)*. In good health, thank you. And you?

PRECIOUS HARP. Well enough, well enough. But my thoughts are sorrowful when they dwell on you. Dear child, your eighteenth birthday draws near.

COVET SPRING. And still no husband! Not one suitor even! What a pity!

PRECIOUS HARP. My poor ugly pet, I grieve for you. The throne is yours if you but marry. Think—if this birthday comes, and you remain unwed, I must be Empress! I who dislike intensely any pomp and show. I who loathe power, and have no wish to rule the land!

COVET SPRING. She who is but a simple soul content to paint on silk, and stroll the garden paths!

(Jade has turned from the cage to them; the Property Man exits with it, yawning).

JADE. I should be glad to change the name of Princess then for yours, to be allowed to go outdoors. May I slip out for just an hour or two? There is no one near to be frightened by my ugliness. Please . . . just an hour!

PRECIOUS HARP *(coldly)*. My sweet niece, no.

COVET SPRING. Be guided by your aunt, your father's sister, in whose charge he placed you.

PRECIOUS HARP *(as Jade Pure turns sorrowfully away, placing a hand gingerly on her shoulder)*. There! I shall be generous. Come with us as we leave, and you may glance just once out of the door. For just a moment it will be held open, for your single look. Come, child.

JADE *(following her as she exits)*. Oh, thank you, thank you!

COVET SPRING *(as he exits)*. Lady Precious Harp is ever gracious!

(The Cousins, who have bowed as the others exited, now straighten and look at each other).

THIRD. Ugh! What a dreadful pair!

SECOND. Such arrogance!

FIRST *(furious)*. Servants! We are of the royal blood as well as she!

SECOND. But only distantly related.

THIRD: Do you know, I almost wish a suitor might arrive in time to wed the princess.

(giggling) Then old Precious Harp would howl!

FIRST. Why should she have the throne?

SECOND. How can we stop her?

FIRST *(suddenly)*. Sisters, I have a plan of plans! A suitor shall arrive!

SECOND. But who?

FIRST. Our brother, Twenty-Fourth Cousin!

THIRD. Our Farmer-brother?

SECOND. That simple-minded lout?

THIRD *(with a titter)*. Without two coins in his ragged smock!

SECOND *(also tittering)*. A suitor to the Princess?

FIRST *(sharply)*. Be still and listen. True, he is nothing as he is, but what is to prevent our buying splendid robes, and teaching him court manners?

THIRD *(giggling)*. But a suitor to Jade Pure!

FIRST *(clutching her arm)*. Think! Is there any other who seeks her hand? Where are his rivals?

SECOND *(slowly)*. Why . . . why, there is not a one!

FIRST. Exactly! Since there is no other, he will be crowned Emperor.

THIRD. But what of us?

FIRST. We shall rule through him, the poor weak thing. He has no mind or spirit of his own!

SECOND. But do you think it will succeed? She might refuse him!

294

FIRST. What? Refuse a foreign prince bedecked in jewels, dazzling as a peacock, bringing costly gifts? Come, we must send for Twenty-Fourth Cousin.

SECOND. Dear brother!

THIRD. Dear, dear brother!

(They exit right, hastily, in great excitement).

JADE *(entering right, looking back).* Where do my cousins go so hastily? Just see, they walk out through the door as if it were a simple thing. But I, the Princess, may not leave!

(at the window) They cross the garden when they please, but I remain shut up day after day.

(A bird trill is sounded from offstage; the Property Man runs tardily in with the cage, to which Jade goes).

Will you sing in your cage, little bird? I cannot sing in mine.

(suddenly) But there is something I can do; I can set you free, poor prisoner. Here, perch upon my finger . . .

(The Property Man shuffles off with the cage) . . .

carefully now . . . I shall bring you to the open window. There . . . slip between the bars . . . go free!

(a second trill from offstage)

I must remain!

(She exits left, hands to her face. The Property Man enters to carry off the bench; the Stage Manager steps forward, bows, and speaks).

SCENE TWO

STAGE MANAGER: For the next scene of our illustrious play, we are transported to this distant field. The sun shines hot upon the earth; the farmer with his plow draws near.

(He steps back, as Twenty-Fourth Cousin enters right, plowing his field with an imaginary handplow. He is a meek little man, guileless and cheerful in appearance; his costume is a drab brown and gray, and quite shabby; a large hat rests on the back of his head. When he reaches center stage he stops, straightens, draws a hand across his forehead, removes his hat, and holding it in front of him, turns to the audience).

TWENTY-FOURTH. I am, as you see, a simple farmer, yet Twenty-Fourth Cousin to the ugly Princess Jade Pure, whom my sisters serve. They are fashionable ladies accustomed to court life, but I have no desire to go to the City. I am a farmer. Now you see me plowing my field.

(And he begins again, taking no notice of happy whistling offstage. Road Wanderer enters right; he is a sturdy handsome young man, carelessly dressed in bright if tattered clothes: patches of all colors are splashed over them).

ROAD WANDERER *(to the audience, modestly).* I am Road Wanderer, the humble hero of this play. You will learn more of me as I talk with the good farmer.

TWENTY-FOURTH *(who has straightened, and is watching him).* Good-day, sir.

ROAD WANDERER. Good-day to you, sir.

(calling offstage) Go back, Small One, and wait. Mrograff . . . uzcark!

TWENTY-FOURTH *(his eyes wide, but politely).* You are with a friend?

ROAD WANDERER. Why, yes. My—my watch dog.

TWENTY-FOURTH *(eagerly).* I have a great fondness for dogs, sir. May I perhaps see this one of yours?

ROAD WANDERER *(doubtfully).* He is . . . of an unusual type: Tell me, friend, how do you call yourself?

TWENTY-FOURTH. Twenty-fourth Cousin . . . that is, twenty-four times removed from the royal family. I am a farmer, as you see.

ROAD WANDERER *(sitting down, pretending to lean against a tree).* I do. Is this your tree that I sit down beneath, and lean my back against?

(The Property Man has shuffled in with a tree branch, stylized, which he waves languidly over Road Wanderer's head).

TWENTY-FOURTH. It is.

(proudly) All this is mine,

(pointing) and that small cottage . . . O, it is little enough. My sisters say that it is nothing. They are elegant ladies who serve the ugly Princess Jade Pure in the palace.

ROAD WANDERER. Indeed! What would they say of me who has no more than Small One, and my health?

TWENTY-FOURTH. You have no house?

ROAD WANDERER. I want no house. I am a student who wanders here and there, to and fro.

TWENTY-FOURTH. See here, how do you live? What do you eat?

ROAD WANDERER. That is simple, very simple. I have many friends.

TWENTY-FOURTH. Oh?

296

ROAD WANDERER. They bring me the ripest fruits from the topmost branches, the tenderest roots from below the ground, the sweetest honey, the choicest nuts.

TWENTY-FOURTH *(pushing his hat back on his head)*. What are these friends of yours? Magicians?

ROAD WANDERER. No. They are the birds, the insects, the creatures that climb and dig and swim . . . in short, all animals known to me.

TWENTY-FOURTH. They are all your friends? But why? How?

ROAD WANDERER. I know a secret. I am one who can speak and understand their many languages.

TWENTY-FOURTH *(scratching his head in bewilderment)*. My ancestors! Whose languages?

ROAD WANDERER. Why, the languages of my friends, the animals. The speech of every smallest one of them is known to me.

TWENTY-FOURTH. Ho! That I cannot believe. You are joking with me.

ROAD WANDERER *(sitting up)*. I swear it is the truth. I learned it in my wanderings. Show me the creature I cannot converse with.

TWENTY-FOURTH *(looking about)*. But . . . but there is no creature here. Ah, wait . . . I have it! Your pet—your dog! Call him here!

ROAD WANDERER *(rising hastily)*. No, no . . . not Small One.

TWENTY-FOURTH. A-ha! You dare not try!

ROAD WANDERER. It is for your sake that I—

TWENTY-FOURTH. You shall prove what you say!

(calling offstage) Here, Small One! Come, boy, come!

ROAD WANDERER. Wait! It is no dog!

TWENTY-FOURTH. Good Dog! Come here!

(his voice raising to a shriek of terror) Oh . . . oh . . . oh!

(Small One, a medium-sized highly-colored dragon, enters with a bound and a roar)

A dragon! Help! A dragon! Save me!

(For a moment there is a lively chase: Twenty-Fourth Cousin finally collapses on his knees, clinging to Road Wanderer).

ROAD WONDERER. There! Do you see? Small one, araf . . . err-gad.

TWENTY-FOURTH *(moaning)*. Oh . . . oh . . . oh . . .

ROAD WANDERER (*Good-humoredly*). Cease wailing, man; Do you not see that he is harmless if you are my friend?

(*stroking the dragon*) Yes, this is Small One, my fond watch-dog.

TWENTY-FOURTH (*fearfully, getting to his feet*). Dog, indeed! Who would have guessed a dragon was your pet? Is he—are you certain he is tame, kind sir?

ROAD WANDERER. He will obey me. You need have no fear. Mowta . . . kagota . . . harsk.

TWENTY-FOURTH. What? What do you say!

(*as dragon starts for him*) He comes!

ROAD WANDERER. Wait! Wait! I have told him to approach, and bow to you.

TWENTY-FOURTH. (*staring, open-mouthed, as the dragon attempts a bow*) You spoke to him?

ROAD WANDERER. Have I not told you that I can? Will you see further proof?

(*indicating the hat*) There is your hat, dropped as you ran. Small One shall be told to take it to you. Quirtech . . . mowta harrad.

(*Small One goes obediently to the hat; Twenty-Fourth Cousin finally nerves himself to accept it from the dragon*).

TWENTY-FOURTH. But he obeys! My head is spinning!

(*The dragon turns to Road Wanderer, growling gutturally. Road Wanderer throws back his head and laughs heartily*).

ROAD WANDERER. Small One, that is not polite.

TWENTY-FOURTH (*approaching cautiously*). See . . . you laugh. What has he said?

ROAD WANDERER. Eh? Nothing.

TWENTY-FOURTH. Nothing?

(*The dragon mutters again*).

ROAD WANDERER (*laughing as he strokes its head*). Oggaruk . . . murraf.

TWENTY-FOURTH. I will believe it, truly, that you talk together if you tell me what the monster said. Was it about me?

ROAD WANDERER. Well, . . . yes. He merely asked me . . .

TWENTY-FOURTH (*still closer*). What?

ROAD WANDERER. Who the foolish-looking dunce was I was speaking to, and remarked—

TWENTY-FOURTH: Oh, he did, did he? What else?

ROAD WANDERER. That you might serve as dinner for him, but appeared too lean and stringy!

TWENTY-FOURTH (*leaping away in fright as Small One snaps playfully at his ankles*). Aaaahhh!

ROAD WANDERER. Come back! He meant no harm. But do you now believe my power with animals?

TWENTY-FOURTH. Oh, yes! Indeed I do! You will forgive this humble toiler for his doubts? Such knowledge is beyond belief; that is, it seemed—

(*A bird trill sounds from offstage*).

ROAD WANDERER. Hush! Listen!

TWENTY-FOURTH. What do you hear?

ROAD WANDERER (*indicating the branch which the Property Man holds*). That small bird in the tree. She tells of a prisoner . . . I will call her closer.

(*He trills, holding up a finger as if inviting a bird to alight upon it; the Property Man exits, yawning, with the tree-branch*).

TWENTY-FOURTH. Why, she comes to sit upon your finger!

(*a trill from offstage*)

Listen to her song!

ROAD WANDERER (*listening*). Hush . . . she tells me of a girl . . . a lovely maiden . . . shut up in a tower . . .

TWENTY-FOURTH. But how does she know this?

ROAD WANDERER (*after listening to another trill*). She was a caged bird in the prisoner's room . . . until her young mistress set her free.

TWENTY-FOURTH. And the girl?

ROAD WANDERER. Is a prisoner still. She longs to run about the garden in the sun, and through the meadows . . . but is not permitted . . .

TWENTY-FOURTH. What a cruel fate!

ROAD WANDERER (*after another trill from offstage*). Ah . . . the little bird asks me to free her mistress . . . help her escape from the tower.

TWENTY-FOURTH. Good! "To help another helps yourself."

ROAD WANDERER. But it is no concern of mine. I want no gratitude, no gifts, no one to care for and look after.

TWENTY-FOURTH (*as a particularly loud twittering sounds*). How the bird does chirp!

ROAD WANDERER. She scolds me for my words . . . and doubtless she is right. Well, then, I shall go to see this prisoner, to learn if she is worthy. Then, perhaps . . . Good-bye, friend Cousin; may we meet again!

TWENTY-FOURTH. I wish the same.

(wistfully) A lovely prisoner . . . oh, but I must stay here with my farm. How will you find her?

ROAD WANDERER. On the back of Small One, who can fly— like all dragons, I shall follow this small bird.

(He tosses his hand into the air, as if to send off an imaginary bird, and trills once more; there is an answer from offstage).

Now she will lead us there. Farewell!

(Small One has already waddled off; Road Wanderer follows. Twenty-Fourth Cousin pushes his hat back and gazes up, waving a hand forlornly).

TWENTY-FOURTH. Farewell! May your shadow not grow less!

(awed) Why, there my friend goes, on the dragon's back!

(wistfully) Such a life of high adventure, while to this poor wretch no moment of excitement comes. Alas, I still must plow . . .

(gazing off-stage in the opposite direction) But look! Drawing near my cottage door . . . a messenger, in handsome dress. From whom? What message does he bring?

(calling) I come—I come!

(hurrying off) Perhaps adventure knocks with him!

SCENE THREE

(The Property Man enters with a high box, painted gray and black to simulate a section of stone wall, which he places right center).

STAGE MANAGER *(stepping forward)*. Our scene has changed now to the royal garden outside Princess Jade Pure's window. Here in this stone tower she stays a prisoner, looking down from her high window.

(He steps back as Jade Pure enters; the Property Man assists her to mount the box, after which he exits. The Princess is dressed as before, but now wears a silver headdress with flowing drapery which may be brought forward to serve as a veil. She places her hands on either side of an imaginary window-frame).

JADE. Alas, I am forlorn! Not even my sweet caged bird to cheer my loneliness! While there below me stretch the beauties of the country-side, which I shall never know. Why am I so ugly? Why? If it were not so, I should marry and escape this hateful prison.

(Road Wanderer enters cautiously left, followed by Small One, who puffs and sighs from his recent exertions).

What was that? I see nothing. No . . . it was the sighing of my heart . . . no more.

ROAD WANDERER. Softly, Small One, softly. That must be her window there.

(Jade sighs) Ah, now I hear a voice.

JADE. On the road which leads to the City I see people . . . many people, but they cannot see me. There is no one who can help me.

ROAD WANDERER *(coming closer)*. What a lovely voice. But I cannot see her face.

JADE *(drawing back)*. Who is there? Is there someone there below my window?

ROAD WANDERER. I am here . . . he who is called Road Wanderer.

JADE *(frightened)*. Why have you come, Road Wanderer?

ROAD WANDERER. To set you free. Will you climb down now?

JADE. Free? You will help me to escape?

(aside) Oh, no, for he might see my face!

ROAD WANDERER. What are you saying? You do not want to come outside?

JADE. Oh, yes! I think of nothing else!

ROAD WANDERER. So your small bird told me.

JADE. My Bird?

ROAD WANDERER. The bird you freed. I understood her song.

JADE. But what a mighty gift! To understand the speech of birds!

ROAD WANDERER. Of all animals! I shall tell you more when you descend. But come, a guard may pass by soon.

JADE. Yes, yes, I shall try to climb down if you will help me, but . . . wait . . .

ROAD WANDERER. For what?

JADE *(aside, adjusting her vail)*. My veil . . . I first must veil my face, so that he will not be frightened.

ROAD WANDERER. What? I cannot hear you.

JADE. Now . . . now I am ready.

(thrusting a foot forward timidly, drawing it back) But afraid!

ROAD WANDERER. Have no fear. Just give me your hand, and I will catch you . . . so!

301

JADE (in delight). Oh . . . oh, I am free, and here, outside!

ROAD WANDERER. Remove your veil so that you may better see the world.

JADE. No, no, I cannot! Do not ask me—

(Small One makes a friendly bounce toward her; she screams and rushes to Road Wanderer).

Oohh!

ROAD WANDERER. Hush! Will you call the guards?

JADE. Behind you—

ROAD WANDERER (laughing). That is only Small One, my dragon. He is gentle, and a friend.

JADE (as Small One, making friendly noises, rubs his head against her skirt, timidly touching his head).

Why, yes, he is! I am not afraid of him. I am not afraid of anything!

ROAD WANDERER. Come along. I know a nearby field if it is flowers you want to see—

JADE. And trees . . . and streams of clear, calm water!

ROAD WANDERER. All that. Take my hand and come!

JADE (taking his hand and going off with him). Yes, Yes!

(The dragon skips about playfully for a moment, then, realizing he has been left behind, dashes off with a howl. The Property Man enters to remove the box, returns at once with a roll of blue cloth).

SCENE FOUR

STAGE MANAGER. And so our hero and our heroine run off to find a grassy meadow.

(with a sweeping gesture) That is it. Here is a tree . . . and there, flowers . . . here a pool of fresh spring water.

(He indicates the blue cloth which the Property Man unrolls and places on the stage down right; the Property Man shuffles off as Jade Pure and Road Wanderer re-enter still hand in hand. She breaks and runs about like a child in her joy).

JADE. It is more beautiful than I dreamed! I want to see and hear and touch everything at once!

(stooping to pluck an imaginary flower, then whirling about) What a lovely flower! Just see that small white cloud shaped like a fish!

302

(embracing an imaginary tree) And this slim tree whose fragrant blossoms—oh! You are laughing at me!

ROAD WANDERER *(gently)*. I am laughing with you, because you are so happy. See, even Small One laughs!

(The dragon capers about, roaring happily).

JADE *(stopping, suddenly serious)*. Happy . . . that is so. I am happy! I have never been happy before.

ROAD WANDERER *(stretching out his hand)*. Take off your veil now.

JADE *(covering her face with her hand)*. No, no!

ROAD WANDERER. Why . . . what have I said to grieve you?

JADE: Nothing. You are kind. I shall be ever grateful. Look— is that a pool of water?

ROAD WANDERER. Yes. As clear as crystal. Drink from it if you like.

JADE *(softly)*. A pool that is very like a mirror . . . I may see my face.

(to him) Please, will you be so kind as to stand over there?

ROAD WANDERER. There? Why should I?

JADE. I—I cannot tell you yet. But please, stand there . . . away from me, and do not look in this direction.

ROAD WANDERER *(puzzled)*. If you wish it.

JADE *(kneeling beside the imaginary pool stage right))*. Now . . . I shall remove my veil and look! Oh, no . . . I am afraid! . . . But I have said I was afraid of nothing. This must be the test.

(slowly) And so—I lift my veil.

(She stares for a moment into the water, speechless).

Why . . . why, can my eyes be trusted? I am—I am—

(calling) Road Wanderer! Road Wanderer!

ROAD WANDERER *(hurrying to her, raising her to her feet)*. What is it? What have you found?

JADE. I have found myself! Tell me, is my face displeasing to you?

ROAD WANDERER *(dazed)*. Why . . . you are beautiful! More beautiful than any maiden I have ever looked upon!

JADE. Oh, thank you!

ROAD WANDERER. I am speechless . . . I can find no words; forgive me.

JADE. I am in your debt forever. You have given me this new face!

ROAD WANDERER. I?

JADE. How am I to repay you? Anything you ask—

(Bells are rung excitedly offstage)

Those bells! What can have happened?

ROAD WANDERER. Does it matter? They are ringing in the City.

JADE. But you do not understand! They ring only when some disaster befalls the royal family!

ROAD WANDERER. And I still ask you, does it matter now?

JADE. It does to me! What can it be? We must go back at once!

ROAD WANDERER. To the City?

JADE. Yes!

(running off)

Please hurry!

ROAD WANDERER. But I—

JADE *(imperiously)*. Come!

(Road Wanderer, with a shrug, takes one of Small One's fore-paws, and they hurry off after her. The Property Man enters, rolls up the blue cloth, tucks it under his arm, and exits).

SCENE FIVE

STAGE MANAGER *(stepping forward)*. Our scene is changing once again. I stand now on a city street. But where are the illustrious citizens?

(looking off) Oh, there they are, crowding around that city official who is about to read a Royal Proclamation.

(He steps back. The bells ring again; there is the sound of many voices offstage. Twenty-Fourth Cousin backs on right, on the fringe of an imaginary crowd. He continues to look offstage).

TWENTY-FOURTH. Here! Cease shoving! And back and back they push me, to the edge of the crowd! This city life does not agree with me! Why have my sisters sent such an urgent message bidding me to come? There is something queer about all this. But before I go to the palace, I shall learn why the bells ring, and what that city official has to say.

JADE *(entering right, running)*. What is it? Have they shouted it yet? Oh, good sir, can you tell us?

TWENTY-FOURTH. I? I do not—

(noticing Road Wanderer, who has also entered)—why, it is my friend, Road Wanderer!

ROAD WANDERER *(still concerned about Jade's conduct)*. My respects to you.

TWENTY-FOURTH. Many thanks! And this . . . this must be the lovely prisoner.

JADE *(who has been peering offstage)*. Why were the bells rung? Why?

VOICE OFFSTAGE. Royal Proclamation—

JADE *(as Twenty-Fourth Cousin opens his mouth to reply)*. Listen, listen!

VOICE OFFSTAGE. "Know, subjects of the Southern Kingdom, that your princess, Her Highness, Jade Pure, has mysteriously vanished away, no doubt carried off by the evil demons."

(There are murmurs and exclamations of surprise from offstage).

JADE *(angrily)*. Demons!

TWENTY-FOURTH. Think of that!

VOICE. Silence! "Her Aunt, the Lady Precious Harp, sister of the late Emperor, has therefore graciously consented to ascend the throne and to assume the title of Empress"

(There are feeble cheers, boos, offstage).

JADE *(stamping her foot)*. No! No, no, no!

ROAD WANDERER. What is wrong?

JADE. She shall do no such thing! I, Princess Jade Pure, am very much alive!

TWENTY-FOURTH. Princess Jade Pure!

ROAD WANDERER. You—a princess?

TWENTY-FOURTH. But you are . . . you are—

JADE. Yes! Beautiful!

(looking offstage) Subjects, my aunt would have you believe that I am ugly. Now you see for yourselves.

VOICE OFFSTAGE. Is she really the Princess?

JADE *(holding her hand out imperiously)*. See—the royal ring upon my right hand. Can you doubt it? Bow before your Princess!

(Twenty-Fourth Cousin bows low; Road Wanderer, completely ignored by Jade Pure, whose back is to him, stands straight and stiff).

305

VOICE OFFSTAGE. But how beautiful she is!

SECOND VOICE. There is none more beautiful!

THIRD VOICE. I shall court her!

FIRST VOICE. And I!

JADE. Ring the bells joyously to announce my return! Let Lady Precious Harp know that her plot has failed.

(To Twenty-Fourth Cousin) For I am beautiful, am I not?

TWENTY-FOURTH *(overcome)*. Yes, indeed, Your Highness . . . yes!

JADE *(to Road Wanderer)*. Am I not beautiful?

ROAD WANDERER *(coldly)*. Yes, Your Highness.

JADE *(whirling about, enchanted wtih her triumph)*. Thank you, my good fellow! My very good fellow!

(Road Wanderer turns away with an exclamation of anger).

Why—where are you going?

ROAD WANDERER. To resume my wandering. I have already stayed too long here.

JADE. But I thought . . . that is——

ROAD WANDERER *(bitterly)*. A Princess! More than that, a thoughtless and ungrateful minx!

JADE. How dare you!

ROAD WANDERER. You seek new admirers and forget me!

JADE. Oh!

TWENTY-FOURTH. My friend——

ROAD WANDERER. Eternal gratitude! Your beauty and your throne are all that interest you! You shall not make sport of me a second time.

(He stalks off angrily; Twenty-Fourth Cousin is aghast; Jade Pure suddenly becomes aware of her feelings toward him).

JADE *(calling off)*. Wait, please! Do come back!

VOICE *(offstage)*. How beautiful she is!

SECOND VOICE *(offstage)*. When angry!

THIRD VOICE *(offstage)*. When sad!

JADE. What does it matter now! I have lost Road Wanderer!

(The Property Man enters with two elaborate handkerchiefs, one in each hand. Jade Pure takes one from him, bursts into tears, and exits drying her eyes. Twenty-Fourth Cousin, shaking his head sorrowfully, goes off right).

306

SCENE SIX

STAGE MANAGER *(stepping forward)*. Yes, it is indeed an unhappy moment for the beauteous Jade Pure.

(He takes the second handkerchief from the Property Man who continues to stand motionless with face blank and expressionless, gracefully touches his eyes, and hands it back to the Property Man, who exits).

But do not weep too hard, Kind Audience, for our play has a joyful ending. Others are unhappy in the Royal Palace too. Here in this room, we find the three deceitful Cousins.

(He steps back. Twenty-First, Twenty-Second, and Twenty-Third Cousins sail in, wringing their hands in despair).

TWENTY-FIRST. What a dreadful calamity!

TWENTY-SECOND. All is lost!

TWENTY-THIRD. O unhappy day!

FIRST. We should have watched her every minute!

SECOND. Now all know of Jade Pure's beauty!

THIRD: Suitors are arriving by the dozens! She can marry if she likes this very day!

FIRST. And Twenty-Fourth Cousin . . . no, there is no hope.

SECOND. Shall he not still be a suitor?

FIRST *(pacing back and forth)*. Have you seen those who have come? Kings, princes, nobles of every rank and degree! With unbelievable wealth! Handsome and young and elegant! And our brother—pah!

THIRD. Alas!

SECOND. But you have sent for him, and he will come.

FIRST. Then he must go away again.

(Twenty-Fourth Cousin, who has entered timidly, tries to nerve himself to rap at an imaginary door).

SECOND. Do not be hasty, sister.

(The knock is sounded offstage).

FIRST. Hear! A knock—it must be he. Let him in, but quietly.

THIRD *(opening an imaginary door)*. Come in.

(As Twenty-Fourth Cousin, clutching his hat, hesitates and clears his throat). Come in, quickly.

TWENTY-FOURTH *(whom she has pulled inside by the sleeve)*. Thank you, gracious lady. I—I am looking for my—

FIRST. Brother, can you fail to know us?

FOURTH. What! Those robes, this splendor—are you my three sisters?

FIRST. Of course. Do not speak so loudly.

SECOND. You have had your trip in vain, it seems.

FOURTH. Oh? How is that? Why did you send for me?

THIRD. You were to marry the Princess!

FOURTH. I—what?

FIRST. When it was thought that she was ugly, there were no suitors for her hand. You, brother, as the only prince to ask her hand, would win it.

FOURTH (*his eyes wider than ever*). A prince! But I am not a prince!

SECOND. With handsome robes and borrowed jewels you might have posed—

FIRST (*impatiently*). Enough! Her suitors throng the halls. Such a one as you can stand no chance.

(*pulling him one way*) Just see his shape! It is not regal!

THIRD (*pulling him another*). And the nose—in profile very bad!

SECOND (*pulling his queue*). That queue! It is too short. Not nearly twenty inches!

FIRST. Such feet! So large and flat! The feet of a prince are dainty.

SECOND (*taking one and holding it up*). The hands show callouses and stains, the marks of work!

FOURTH (*feebly*). I am a farmer, sisters!

THIRD (*just realizing it*). Without a fan he comes here to the palace!

SECOND. Yes, without a fan!

FIRST (*turning her back on him and folding her arms*). Begone! We have no use for you.

SECOND (*doing the same*). Begone!

THIRD (*doing the same*). Begone!

FOURTH. Sisters, I— I—

COUSINS (*wheeling about in the same motion, each extending an arm stiffly toward the door*). Begone!

FOURTH (*gulping, bowing and shaking hands solemnly with himself*). I take my leave; good day, my sisters.

(*He exits, after closing the imaginary door behind him. Lady*

308

Precious Harp and Covet Spring enter from the other side, behind the Cousins).

PRECIOUS HARP. Aha!

(The Cousins, startled, turn quickly, their hand to their mouths, then bow).

So there you are! Stupid creatures! Have you left the Princess unattended again?

FIRST. Only for one small moment. Your Ladyship.

SECOND. But not alone. She was occupied in interviewing suitors.

THIRD *(maliciously).* Some of the many who came.

PRECIOUS *(sourly).* Ah, yes.

FIRST *(sweetly).* Her ladyship is doubtless overjoyed at the numbers of young men who have proposed.

SECOND. The Princess soon will marry.

THIRD. And dear Lady Precious Harp need not assume the cares of state!

PRECIOUS. Silence!

COVET SPRING. Impudent servants! Begone at once!

PRECIOUS. Attend your mistress!

COVET. Leave us!

COUSINS *(bowing and exiting quickly).* Yes, Your Ladyship . . . Your Excellency.

(Precious Harp and Covet Spring, left alone, begin to pace from opposite sides of the stage, passing and repassing each other center stage).

COVET. So! All is lost! Spilt water cannot be gathered up.

PRECIOUS. Those simpering bunglers shall pay dear for the failure of our plan. If Jade Pure had been guarded every moment—ah!

COVET. Alas! All know her beauty now. And she will marry. You have lost the throne!

PRECIOUS *(stopping suddenly).* Not yet! Her birthday comes within the week.

COVET *(also stopping).* That is so. That is quite so.

PRECIOUS. The stroke of noon that marks her eighteenth birthday still may find her single. No suitor seems to please her.

COVET *(beginning to pace again).* But she will wed, if just to spite you. Mark my words!

PRECIOUS. I am not beaten! Come!

(Covet Spring does not heed her; she catches his arm, pulling him off-balance).

Come I say. We shall lay new and better plans!

(They exit. The Stage Manager steps forward).

SCENE SEVEN

STAGE MANAGER. Again we change our scene, this time going outside into the Royal Garden. The day is warm and clear. Butterflies come to light upon fragrant lilies. Everything about us is bright and beautiful. But the fair Princess who approaches has no welcoming smile.

(He steps back; Jade Pure enters, protesting to someone offstage).

JADE. No, no. Leave me, I beg of you. Guards, hold them back!

(walking slowly across the stage) I am weary of suitors, and would be alone to rest and think. Let me wander through the garden paths . . .

(The Property Man hastily brings the bench out to place directly behind her).

perhaps to sit a moment on this bench. Strange . . . Strange . . . I am still lonely. Beauty is not happiness. What good are suitors if Road Wanderer be not among them?

(voices offstage)

Voices—who has followed me here? Ah, the Cousins . . . whom I can no longer trust.

TWENTY-FIRST *(entering, bowing).* My Princess, fairer than a day in spring—

TWENTY-SECOND *(entering, bowing).* More lovely than fragile flowers.

TWENTY-THIRD *(entering, bowing).* Whose voice is sweeter yet than the nightingale's song—

JADE. Stop! I have heard enough! What do you want of me?

FIRST. Nothing but to serve you, regal cousin.

SECOND. Who are the most beloved of Princesses.

THIRD. Whose suitors number in the thousands.

FIRST. Who is now the happiest of mortals.

JADE. Ah!

FIRST. What? She sighs?

310

SECOND. She comes to sit alone.

THIRD. Do not her suitors please her?

JADE. No! I have dismissed them, everyone who came today.

FIRST. But your marriage—

JADE. It shall not take place, unless the right one comes.

SECOND (*aside to the others*). Good! She has chosen no one yet.

THIRD. Perhaps our brother should return!

FIRST. Wait . . . I shall question her about the man of her choice. Now mark down what she answers.

> (*to Jade Pure*) Sweet Princess, tell us of the man you wait for. First, of what height should he be?

JADE (*remembering*). Why, half a head as tall as I.

> (*The Property Man has shuffled in to hand a parchment and a brush to Twenty-Second Cousin, exiting immediately*).

SECOND (*marking with the brush on the parchment, which rests on her sister's back*). Our brother must wear thick-soled shoes!

THIRD (*bent double, serving as a desk*). Or walk on stilts!

FIRST. His hair next—of what color should it be?

JADE. Black as a raven's wing, and long.

THIRD. Very long and black!

FIRST. And features?

JADE. Great dark eyes, a fine straight nose—

SECOND. Alas, his nose! What can be done with it?

JADE. Delightful smile, and such a voice!

THIRD. Aha! Our brother has a voice!

SECOND (*despairingly*). But such a voice!

FIRST. What else? What qualities of mind?

JADE. Why, he must know how to be gay . . .

SECOND. Brother shall laugh ho-ho at all he hears.

JADE. And must love nature and all animals . . .

THIRD. Ah, Good! A farmer can do that!

JADE (*dreamily*). All animals, and dragons too . . . such a sweet small dragon he had!

FIRST (*misunderstanding*). What? He must have a dragon?

SECOND. Impossible!

THIRD (*straightening abruptly*). That cannot be!

JADE. But I once knew—

FIRST. You'll have no suitors left if this is known!

SECOND. What man can bring a dragon to you?

JADE (*thoughtfully*). What man indeed!

THIRD. Ridiculous!

FIRST (*conferring with them*). Why, sisters . . .

JADE (*rising, delighted*). Of course, Possession of a dragon! Who but my dear Road Wanderer can meet such a requirement. I must send decrees throughout the kingdom.

FIRST (*to her again*). Surely Your Highness cannot mean—

SECOND. A dragon!

JADE. I do indeed.

THIRD. Dragons! Pah!

PRECIOUS HARP (*entering with Covet Spring*). What is this? What do I hear?

COVET SPRING. Dragons? Dragons? W-where?

FIRST. Incredible!

JADE (*gaily*). My respects to Her Ladyship and His Excellency.

PRECIOUS. Do not stand on ceremony, niece, but tell us: what has caused this uproar?

JADE. Most venerable aunt, I have come to a decision about my marriage.

PRECIOUS (*caught off guard*). Oh, no!

JADE. Let a proclamation be cried throughout the land.

COVET. Too late, too late!

JADE. And this is my royal decision: the suitor who wins my hand must possess a dragon.

PRECIOUS. Why—

COVET. Why—

JADE. That is my only condition. The dragon must, of course, be brought before me by its owner.

PRECIOUS. But this will simply mean—

COVET. Do I understand—

FIRST. How can a—

312

JADE. Just one thing more! If two dragon-owners should appear, it shall be my privilege to select whichever dragon pleases me most.

COVET. Why, I cannot believe—

PRECIOUS. She is mad! How fortunate for us!

JADE (aside). Surely Road Wanderer will hear of my decision and come back to me!

PRECIOUS (slyly). But, see here, niece, what if no dragon-owner appears?

JADE (calmly). Then I shall marry no one.

PRECIOUS. Splendid! Er—that is—

JADE. But have no fear upon that score.

(reseating herself) At least one dragon will be entered.

(The two groups, one on either side of her, talk among themselves. All carry fans. Each group, on finishing its line of dialogue, freezes in conference behind its fans, while the other group says its sequence. This continues to the end of the scene).

FIRST (to her sisters). How can she be so certain?

COVET (to Precious). This is perfect! She will never marry with such a requirement.

PRECIOUS. I wonder.

SECOND. Does our brother own a dragon, do you think?

FIRST. Nonsense!

THIRD. There will be no suitors left once this decree is read.

COVET. We need only wait until her birthday comes and goes.

PRECIOUS. But see how she smiles . . . she does not fear the outcome. Why not? Does she know of a dragon?

FIRST. There must be a dragon somewhere. If our brother could present it—

SECOND. See how the Princess smiles. She knows . . .

THIRD. Knows what?

COVET. She must know something. If there is a dragon, we have lost again. "Out of the wolf's den into the tiger's mouth!"

PRECIOUS. Listen to me. Our course is plain. We must enter a dragon, too!

FIRST. Yes, there can be no other way. We must discover a dragon at once!

SECOND. But where?

313

THIRD. They are surely all dead!

PRECIOUS. Do you know where to find such a thing?

COVET. Ah, that is the problem. A live dragon . . .

PRECIOUS. Do you suppose—ah, but it might not work . . .

FIRST. A live dragon! It is true we may not find . . . I wonder!

SECOND. What?

THIRD. Have you a plan?

COVET. What thought has come to you?

PRECIOUS. Need it be a live dragon?

COVET. But—I see! I see!

FIRST. Why not a make-believe dragon?

SECOND. Oh!

THIRD. Of course! Of course!

PRECIOUS. A cleverly contrived disguise would do. We must find someone whom we can trust to wear a dragon costume.

COVET. Good!

FIRST. A costume made with skill and care—

SECOND. But who would put it on?

THIRD. Whom can we trust in such a risky business?

PRECIOUS. Who shall it be?

COVET. But, more important, who shall be the suitor who presents it?

PRECIOUS. Why, I overlooked that point.

COVET (smugly). But I have not!

FIRST. Our brother!

SECOND. Yes!

THIRD. But wait—he cannot be both suitor and dragon!

PRECIOUS. Well then?

COVET. I shall seek the Princess' hand!

PRECIOUS. You?

COVET. Of course! And you shall play the dragon!

FIRST. I have it!

(indicating both of them)

314

You shall play the dragon!

PRECIOUS. Preposterous!

SECOND. Not I, sister!

THIRD. Nor I!

COVET. But think, Your Ladyship! The plot is dangerous at best; we two must work it out alone.

FIRST. You must! We have no choice!

SECOND. But why not you?

FIRST. I must coach our brother, and prepare his speeches for him.

PRECIOUS. But I—a dragon!

COVET. There is much to gain: a throne!

PRECIOUS. Then if you win Jade Pure, she must be done away with.

COVET. Agreed! And you shall be my Empress.

(aside) And the next to die.

PRECIOUS *(aside)*. He shall not live long after.

FIRST. Come, let us go to find a costume that you two may don.

SECOND. But the Princess?

FIRST. She is dreaming, and will take no notice.

PRECIOUS. Ugh! A dragon! But it must be so. Come now, a costume must be made at once.

COVET. The Princess?

PRECIOUS. Leave her to her dreams. We go to find a dragon!

(And they exit).

THIRD *(who has tiptoed up to the princess to look)*. Yes, her thoughts are far away.

FIRST. Twenty-Four Cousin must be sent for too. But first, we go to find a dragon!

(And they exit off the opposite side of the stage. Jade Pure, who has been oblivious to the hushed conversation, now stirs and sighs happily).

JADE. Of course! The dragon was the answer. Who but the Road Wanderer can bring one to me?

(rising) Yes, he will return . . . I feel it . . . and my happiness with him. I go now to fold my hands and wait . . . for the coming of my dragon!

315

(she exits happily. The Property Man enters to remove the bench. The Stage Manager steps forward).

STAGE MANAGER. Thus ends the first act of our worthy play, most gracious Audience. The noble actors will now rest a moment, sip their tea, and don new costumes. But have patience; they will soon return. And that your wait may be more pleasant,

(clapping his hands) Music shall be played.

(He bows and exits. Chinese music—recorded—is played softly throughout the intermission).

PART TWO

SCENE ONE

(The Stage Manager enters, bows, and speaks).

STAGE MANAGER. Again, our greetings, O-most-gracious Audience! We thank you for your kind attention thus far, and promise you much laughter and excitement in what follows. The stage is now a lonely field far from the palace.

(looking offstage) But the worthy actors are approaching; I once more become invisible.

(He bows again, and withdraws to his corner of the stage. Covet Spring tiptoes cautiously in, looks back offstage, and beckons).

COVET SPRING. Hsst! We are alone, Your Ladyship.

PRECIOUS HARP *(entering in dragon costume, puffing and groaning).* Alas! O woe! That I should come to this! Ancestors, have mercy!

COVET. Yes, this is a place where none will spy us out. And you, Your Ladyship, may practice both your walk and roar.

PRECIOUS *(straightening up).* No, no, Covet Spring! This is too much! My senses must have left me when I gave consent!

COVET. But, my dear Precious Harp, how else can we obtain the throne? It is a prize worth any risk!

PRECIOUS. But oh, the shame—the gross indignity of Precious Harp impersonating a dragon!

COVET *(smoothly).* Her Ladyship cannot appreciate the beauty of the costume and the brilliance of her own portrayal half so well as I. You are a dragon beyond all others, I assure you! Come now, roar again, and let me see that graceful walk.

PRECIOUS *(crouching on all fours).* Alas! But if it must be so, it must.

(She attempts a feeble roar).

COVET. A-ha! Good, good! But if Her Ladyship could roar somewhat more loudly—

(He roars vigorously, frightening her).

PRECIOUS *(leaping away in fright).* Covet Spring! How dare you? But it was a most impressive roar . . . I shall try one . . . now then . . .

(and she roars)

COVET. Ah, good! Better! Yes, much better! Now, the walk; I lead you—so, with this gold chain, and we approach Jade Pure.

317

(They circle the stage rather rapidly, Precious Harp grunting and gasping, resembling an unwilling dog at the end of a leash).

PRECIOUS. Ugh! Stay . . . you move too swiftly . . . stop, I say!

COVET *(stopping)*. A thousand pardons! You are right; a stately pace will give us dignity. As we walk, a roar or two might add—

PRECIOUS. A roar! Ugh . . . oh . . . my breath is all but stopped!

COVET. And when we reach the throne, we both shall bow, and I shall make my speech.

PRECIOUS *(as he begins to pull her along)*. Wait! Let us practice singly, you your speech, and I my roars. Ah, what a sorry business!

COVET. Very well, I shall go over here.

(They stand on opposite sides of the stage).

Princess Jade Pure *(a roar from Precious Harp)*, I come before you *(roar)*

not as your Chancellor today, *(roar, Covet Spring grimaces)* but as a suitor with a dragon

(another roar; Covet Spring glares; suddenly Precious Harp begins to cough and choke).

PRECIOUS. Eh . . . oh! I shall choke! Covet Spring—

COVET *(trying helplessly to thump the dragon on the back)*. What is it? How am I to—

PRECIOUS. Oh, my throat! It is dry as dust, and rough with roaring! *(straightening)* I can stand no more!

COVET *(taking her arm)*. Let us find a brook where we may quench our thirst. There will be time to practice later.

PRECIOUS. Yes, yes! I shall lose this hateful dragon's head with pleasure!

(They exit, Lady Precious Harp beginning to tug at her head. Almost immediately Twenty-First and Twenty-Fourth Cousins enter. The latter is now costumed in gorgeous robes of a variety of colors, and carries an enormous fan; he looks, and is, extremely uncomfortable).

TWENTY-FIRST. Yes, this field will do quite well. We shall have space to practice. Our two sisters are now putting on the costume.

TWENTY-FOURTH *(jerking at his robes and headress)*. But—but, I tell you, I protest again—all this is not what I should like to—

FIRST. Oh, be still! And do not twitch about so! Hold your fan like this.

FOURTH. But I never wanted to hold a fan at all! I want to get back to my farm. Why have you brought me here?

FIRST *(forcibly readjusting his robe)*. You know why, stupid one!

FOURTH *(as she jams his headdress down at a slightly different angle)*. Ouch! Be merciful, sister!

FIRST. What shall I do with you? Nothing is right—nothing! Turn your toes out . . . out, I say!

(Pushing him, as he teeters, toes turned out) Let me see you walk. No. No! Not huge, long strides, but dainty steps! Like this . . .

FOURTH *(starting off)*. No, sister, I regretfully refuse—

FIRST *(seizing him by the shoulders, turning him, and hissing in his ear)*. You will do as I say, little brother! Now, walk! Walk, do you hear?

(He walks, watching his feet) Your head erect.

(pulling his queue from behind) erect! Nose pointed to the sky! But now you have forgotten the fan—flutter it! Flutter it gracefully! Watch . . . toes out, small steps . . .

FOURTH *(thoroughly bewildered)*. I cannot . . . remember . . . so many things at one time . . .

FIRST. You must! Now bow before the Princess.

FOURTH *(becoming himself again)*. The Princess? Where?

FIRST. Not here, idiot of idiots! Bow as you will bow that day before her.

FOURTH. Oh! A bow, you say . . . I am not sure how . . . does it go like this?

(He bows awkwardly, glancing anxiously toward Twenty-First Cousin. A dragon's head is seen moving on stage on the same level as Twenty-Fourth Cousin's head).

FIRST. No, no, no . . .

FOURTH *(turning his head, gazing into the dragon's eyes)*. What do I do then—

(terrified, dashing across to his sister) A d-d-dragon! Look out! Let us flee! Come quickly!

FIRST. Be still!

(A large, awkward-looking dragon, occupied by the two sisters, enters and advances on Twenty-Fourth Cousin, roaring fiercely).

TWENTY-SECOND *(gruffly)*. We have come, little brother—

TWENTY-THIRD. To eat you!

FOURTH *(starting off again)*. Farewell!

319

FIRST. Come back! These are your sisters in their dragon costume.

FOURTH. My sisters?

FIRST (as the dragon preens itself). Is it not a splendid disguise? So realistic!

FOURTH (shuddering). Yes!

FIRST. Come, sisters, walk about a little.

SECOND (starting off in one direction). Very well.

THIRD (moving in the other). I shall be happy—eh!

FIRST. What has gone wrong now?

SECOND. Sister, move with me in this direction!

THIRD (turning). But I cannot see! How can I tell which way to go?

(The dragon begins to turn in a circle, faster and faster, both girls exclaiming in dismay).

FIRST. No, no! You are moving in a circle!

FOURTH. All this will never work! Never! I want no part of it!

SECOND. Oh, sister, stop! My head is spinning!

THIRD. I am giddy too! Oh! Oh!

(Both ends of the dragon sit down abruptly with wails and groans).

FIRST (attempting to get the front end of the dragon on its feet). See here, get on your feet again . . . heavy creature! Brother . . . help your other sister! We must try again—a thousand times if need be! A throne depends on it!

SECOND. No more of this, I beg you!

THIRD. My bones are surely broken, every one!

FIRST (when both are standing again). Enough! Now, brother, stand away. And dragon, listen to me carefully. I am here, holding your shoulder, younger sister . . .

SECOND (the front half). Yes, elder sister.

FIRST. You will move as I command you. Youngest sister, you also will follow my voice.

THIRD (unhappily). Yes, eldest sister.

FIRST. Now, brother! Take hold of the silken cord about the dragon's neck.

(He does so).

We are ready at last. March forward . . . left foot, right foot, left foot . . . brother! This one is your left! . . . left and right—roar now, sisters . . .

320

(they roar feebly) . . . louder . . . left foot, right foot, left foot—
roar now! Brother, head back . . . hold the fan high, and flutter
it in time to left and right and—

*(They have circled the stage and now march off, the dragon
roaring, Twenty-First Cousin still counting. As if in answer to a
particularly loud roar from their side of the wings, a shrill roar
comes from the other side of the stage. There is a moment of
dead silence).*

FOURTH *(offstage, quavering)*. Sister, what was that?

FIRST *(offstage)*. Why . . . I do not know.

PRECIOUS *(offstage)*. Yes, I heard it too.

COVET *(backing on)*. What can it be?

FOURTH *(backing on opposite side of the stage, whispering)*. It
sounded very like a . . . like a dragon!

FIRST *(backing on with the dragon, whispering)*. A dragon? Nonsense!

COVET *(whispering)*. Such a fearful sound!

PRECIOUS *(backing on)*. We must not be discovered!

FIRST. I see no one!

FOURTH *(somewhat louder)*. Let us go away!

COVET. Hark! Voices!

FIRST. Hush! A voice!

PRECIOUS *(continuing to back)*. Come! Let us slip away!

FIRST. You may be right . . . it does seem best to leave! But
silently . . .

COVET. But quietly . . . ssshhh!

FOURTH. Ssshhh!

*(The two groups, backing slowly and elaborately on tiptoe, meet
center stage: Twenty-Fourth Cousin and Covet Spring collide, as
do the two dragons. There is general panic, and the stage is
cleared in a moment).*

COUSINS *(dashing off)*. Dragon! Dragon!

PRECIOUS AND COVET *(dashing off)*. Dragon! Dragon!

*(There is silence. Then Twenty-First Cousin peeps in, comes
cautiously on, pulling her extremely reluctant brother by the
sleeve).*

FIRST. O, come along! There is no one about. I want to see—

FOURTH. But I—I do not want to see! Ah, what an ill-fated wretch
am I, doomed to—

FIRST. Silence! There was something strange about the dragon, I tell you. And I heard a woman's scream, of that I am certain. Here, hold aside these bushes.

(The Property Man has shuffled on, and holds up two cut-out branches, crossed. Twenty-Fourth Cousin spreads them apart for Twenty-First Cousin).

Ah-a!

FOURTH *(Jumping)*. Eh? What do you see?

FIRST. Just as I suspected! That dragon was no dragon at all!

FOURTH. Not a dragon?

FIRST. I see Precious Harp, Her August Ladyship, even now stepping out of the disguise.

FOURTH *(still dazed)*. Disguise?

FIRST *(turning on him angrily)*. Where have your wits fled? Precious Harp and Covet Spring have done the same as we. They will enter a fraudulent dragon, too.

(The Property Man exits with the branches).

FOURTH *(brightening)*. Ah, well, then ours can never win. I shall go back home.

FIRST *(pulling him back)*. You will do nothing of the sort! We shall win! Ours is far larger and handsomer than theirs.

FOURTH. Alas!

FIRST. And if by further trickery our dragon is not chosen, we can denounce their creature as a fraud and them as traitors. What a stroke of luck!

(exiting with him)

Our sisters must be told of it!

(They exit. Lady Precious Harp peeps in cautiously, then enters; Covet Spring follows, staggering under the weight of the dragon costume).

PRECIOUS. No, there is no sight of anything . . . nor sound.

COVET. My ears still ring with the roaring of the beast!

PRECIOUS. But did you mark its size? Far larger than our dragon, and more handsome.

COVET. And more real. How can a costume dragon triumph now?

PRECIOUS. That miserable treacherous girl, Twenty-First Cousin! Where could she have found such a thing?

COVET. Who can tell? I know only that our plot has failed. "Spilt water cannot be gathered up."

PRECIOUS. What if we should steal it?

COVET. What?

PRECIOUS. Their dragon!

COVET. No, not I. I would not go near it!

PRECIOUS *(pacing)*. No, it will be hidden well, there are too many caves to search. Tomorrow is the day . . .

(throwing back her head, her fist pressed against her forehead) tomorrow . . .

(suddenly) Covet Spring!

COVET. Yes? Yes?

PRECIOUS. Look up! What is that—in the sky? Do I dream?

COVET *(also staring up)*. I see it too . . . a large bird, flying now above the city . . . growing larger as it comes toward us . . .

PRECIOUS. Bird—it is too large! A dragon, Covet Spring! I know it is a dragon!

COVET. Flying . . . but then, it is a real one!

PRECIOUS. Yes! An authentic live dragon! Keep your eyes upon it! We must catch it at all costs!

COVET. But look! Upon its back—a man! I see him clearly!

PRECIOUS. They are heading for the palace! Come!

(They circle the stage, running, several times. The Property Man enters with a rod around which is wrapped gray cloth or canvas).

SCENE TWO

STAGE MANAGER *(stepping forward)*. The Lady Precious Harp and Covet Spring run rapidly, and soon draw near the palace walls.

(indicating the Property Man). That lazy fellow is to represent the wall, if he can but stay awake!

(The Property Man has seated himself crosslegged on the stage, holding the rod at arm's length above his head, and now permits the canvas to unroll to the floor, hiding him from view).

COVET SPRING *(winded)*. Oh . . . oh . . . I can go no further.

PRECIOUS HARP. Faster! It is flying low! The palace walls are just ahead!

COVET. But the man . . . its master . . .

PRECIOUS. Shall be done away with!

323

(approaching the "wall," looking over it offstage) See—the thing is circling, coming back to alight inside the walls!

(She seizes a whistle suspended from her sash by a gold cord, and blows several shrill blasts).

Guards! Guards! Capture that creature and its master!

COVET *(also peering over the "wall")*. We shall remain outside!

(roars and shouts come from offstage. Covet Spring leans heavily on the rod; the wall sags but straightens quickly as the Property Man makes an effort to hold it upright).

PRECIOUS. How it struggles! Watch its scales, and do not scratch them!

COVET. Not a large dragon, though. Rather a small one.

PRECIOUS. But real—that is the thing! Aha! They have it now.

COVET. And the young man too.

PRECIOUS. Guards! Take the dragon to the stable in the south field, and secure it there.

VOICE *(offstage)*. It shall be done, Your Ladyship.

PRECIOUS. See that it has food and water in abundance, and the softest straw to lie upon.

VOICE *(offstage)*. We run to do your bidding.

COVET. What of the young man?

PRECIOUS. Ho, guards; Fling that young man, its master, into the darkest dungeon to await execution!

VOICE *(offstage)*. All shall be carried out, Your Gracious Ladyship.

PRECIOUS. He is a traitor dangerous to the safety—

COVET. Hsst! Lady Precious Harp, someone approaches!

PRECIOUS. Go, guards, quickly, with your prisoners. Your silence shall be handsomely rewarded.

COVET. A lady comes.

(The Property Man lowers the wall to rest his arms).

PRECIOUS. Why, Covet Spring, it is my niece, Jade Pure.

COVET. The Princess!

JADE *(who has entered, throwing back her veil)*. Greetings, noble aunt and august chancellor. What do you do here outside the palace walls?

(She looks pointedly at the Property Man, who raises the wall to its proper position again).

324

PRECIOUS. My child, where have you been?

COVET. Alone and unattended?

PRECIOUS. A Princess—walking the highway?

COVET. Such a shocking breach of court decorum! Why,—

PRECIOUS. Exactly! Jade Pure, how do you explain—

JADE. One moment! How can I explain if you refuse to listen? Now then, I have been to the City; I went alone because I could not find my three Cousins. But no one could recognize me in my heavy veil, and thus no harm was done!

PRECIOUS. Perhaps not, but for what purpose did you go!

JADE. Why, to hear news of Road—that is, to learn if any have come with dragons to enter in the contest for my hand.

COVET. Ah! And have any such come—with dragons?

JADE. Not a one. All my former suitors, being dragonless, have returned to their homes. The townspeople question my decision openly, saying that no dragon still exists! But I am not convinced.

PRECIOUS. Nor I!

COVET. Nor I!

PRECIOUS. Rest assured that you shall have at least one dragon!

COVET (muttering). Very likely two.

JADE. You know this? You are certain? But how?

PRECIOUS. Be patient till tomorrow. Covet Spring, accompany me; there are matters to take up.

COVET (as they exit). Good-day, your Highness.

JADE. Farewell, both.

(after they have gone) My mind starts up in fear again! Tomorrow is to be my marriage day, and if a dragon is presented to me, I must wed its owner. Ah, Road Wanderer, why have you not yet come?

(She exits in great agitation. The Property Man rises, rolls up the wall, and tucks it under his arm, exiting yawning).

SCENE THREE

STAGE MANAGER (stepping forward). Alas, kind listeners, our next scene is a dungeon.

(The Property Man re-enters with a bench which he places center stage).

Light can enter through the bars of that strong door . . .

(glaring at the Property Man who has sunk down on the bench) which all of you can see quite clearly.

(He claps his hands impatiently, and the Property Man stands, goes to stage left, sketches a door in pantomime, and takes hold of the imaginary bars and shakes them. He then opens the door, steps out, locks it carefully, and exits).

Who is the prisoner here? If you cannot guess it, wait with patience, for the dismal noise of chains will soon announce his coming.

(The clank of chains begins offstage. Road Wanderer enters, an imaginary ball-and-chain hindering his walking; the chains clank in accompaniment to his steps. He seats himself on the bench).

ROAD WANDERER. A prisoner! And in chains! Is this the order of the Princess? Who wants my death? And where is my dragon, Small One?

(Footsteps sound offstage; Road Wanderer springs up and looks through the imaginary bars of the imaginary cell door).

Guard! Guard! Where is Small One?

GUARD *(offstage)*. Small One?

ROAD WANDERER. My dragon. What have you done with him?

GUARD *(offstage)*. The dragon? It is being fed and washed and polished. They tell me that tomorrow it is to be entered in the contest for the hand of the Princess Jade Pure.

ROAD WANDERER. But—but that cannot be! The dragon is mine! I planned to enter it.

GUARD *(offstage)*. Ah, but you will not be its owner long. The headman's knife will see to that!

ROAD WANDERER. Does the Princess Jade Pure know that I am here?

GUARD. That I cannot say. But my duties call me elsewhere. Farewell.

ROAD WANDERER. Wait! Will you carry a message to the Princess for me?

GUARD. What? Not I!

ROAD WANDERER. But she knows me. She will see to my release!

GUARD. I will carry no messages from one condemned by Lady Precious Harp. I value my own neck too highly. Your misfortune is not mine, poor fellow. Farewell!

ROAD WANDERER. Guard! He is gone, and in a few short hours they will behead me. But what of Jade Pure? She will wait for me, not knowing. I must find some way to tell her. I must send a message somehow. Why, of course . . . an animal can be my messenger! I who speak their language must find some tiny creature nearby who will serve me. True, the Princess cannot understand its speech, but still may guess that it has come from me.

(Striding about the cell, he examines walls and floor and ceiling).

Friends . . . friends . . . hear me. It is I, Road Wanderer! Who will go to fetch the Princess? . . . Not a sound. I hear no creature stirring. Have they too deserted me?

(whirling about) What was—ah! A mouse! A tiny mouse here in my cell.

(stooping to pick up an imaginary mouse) Come, small friend. We shall talk together, you and I; then out between the bars you go to take my message to the Princess!

(He walks off, stroking the mouse; the clanking of chains accompanies his exit. The Property Man enters to remove the bench).

SCENE FOUR

STAGE MANAGER *(stepping forward).* You will come away with me most gladly, I am certain, to a room more pleasant. Look about you—do you recognize once again the elegant apartment of the soon-to-be wedded Princess Jade Pure?

(He steps back. Jade Pure dashes in; she wears an elaborate costume of cloth-of-gold. Twenty-First Cousin, running after her, rearranges her robe and headdress. The Princess continues to walk quickly to and fro, the maid following).

JADE. Look graciously upon me, august ancestors! For this must be my wedding day! What shall I find when I descend to the throne room? Many suitors with dragons, or none?

TWENTY-FIRST. There will be one . . . or two, I think.

JADE. Hurry, dear cousin . . . make haste! I cannot wait to know much longer!

FIRST. But if Her Highness would remain still just one moment, I could—

JADE. All is ready for the ceremony. The temple attendants await my coming. It will take but a few short moments. Make your fingers fly more swiftly! Where are your sisters who should help you?

FIRST. My sisters? A strange sickness has come over them most suddenly. Indeed, they are so changed that Your Highness would not recognize—

(catching sight of something on the floor) Eeeeee!

327

JADE. What is it?

(looking in the direction of Twenty-First Cousin's pointing finger)
Ohh! A mouse!

FIRST. A mouse! It runs toward you!

JADE *(in horror)*. No. no! A bench . . . a chair . . . oh, quickly!

(The Property Man shuffles in with a bench; both girls make a leap for it almost before he sets it down; he exits yawning).

FIRST. It comes closer!

JADE. Hurry! Hurry!

(as they leap up) Ah . . . we have escaped!

(The mouse's squeaking sounds from offstage).

FIRST. But look! It will not leave!

(hands to her ears) That horrid squeaking!

JADE. Back and forth . . . and back and forth again it runs below us!

FIRST. Hateful creature!

JADE *(thoughtfully)*. Looking up, as if at me!

FIRST *(Striking out with her fan)*. Go! Run away! Be silent!

JADE. Listen, cousin! How it squeaks . . . as if it tries to tell us something.

FIRST. It can tell me nothing!

JADE. Look! It runs now to the door . . . now back to me . . .

FIRST. And to the door once more. The thing is mad!

JADE. Or else it tries to tell me to come also. But I wonder why—

(clapping her hands) Road Wanderer! He has come back, and sends it as a joke! Perhaps he waits for me already in the throne room!

(leaping down) Come!

FIRST *(as Jade Pure runs out)*. No, no! Do not leave me here; I dare not set a foot down! Cursed day! This is an omen surely . . . a bad omen!

(The Property Man has shuffled in to remove the bench).

No! I will not leave this bench! I—no, no! Ohhhhhh!

(As he stolidly takes hold of either end of the bench, tipping it forward slightly, she squeals, gathers up her skirts, and makes a dash for the door. The Property Man calmly removes the bench, and brings in a gilded chair which he places center stage, exiting immediately after).

SCENE FIVE

STAGE MANAGER *(who has stepped forward)*. Our slothful servant is placing there the gilded chair in which the Princess Jade Pure sits in state. For this is now the exalted Royal Throne Room, and the ruler of this great kingdom approaches, in considerable haste.

(He steps back, as Jade Pure runs in, stops short).

JADE. No one! But Road Wanderer must be here! He has sent the mouse—I know it!

(after a moment) Oh—perhaps he hides, and waits for me to find him! I shall search each room!

(She runs off the opposite side of the stage. A roar or two is heard from offstage; Lady Precious Harp and Covet Spring back on, both tugging at ropes tied around the kidnapped dragon's neck. Small One emerges reluctantly; they leap back as he snaps at their ankles).

COVET SPRING *(in what he hopes is a soothing tone)*. Now then, take care! We are your loving friends!

PRECIOUS HARP. Ugly vicious brute! How dare it snap at me?

COVET. It can be disposed of once Jade Pure is won. But its young master, this . . . this Road Wanderer—

(At the mention of the name the dragon roars and lunges. They tug frantically at the ropes).

PRECIOUS *(after they have somewhat subdued Small One)*. Fool! See that you do not name his name aloud again! The beast must know it. There is no young man, and never was.

COVET. Oh, no!

PRECIOUS *(prompting him)*. The dragon's master is, without a doubt—?

COVET. Why, I, of course. I am its master.

PRECIOUS. So!

(whispering) The—person whom you spoke of I shall cause to lose his head just after the marriage ceremony.

COVET *(loud)*. Good!

(then whispering) But why not sooner? If he should escape, the head that falls will not be his!

PRECIOUS. Escape? I do not think it possible. Still, it might be best to post a second line of guards.

(handing him her end of the rope) Take care that Small One does not run away.

329

COVET (*as she exits*). You leave me with this—Precious Harp. I cannot—!

(*gazing fearfully at the dragon*) O, unhappy fate! And I, afraid of house cats!

FIRST (*entering from the other side*). Through this arch, now. Guide the beast with care, brother!

(*Twenty-Fourth Cousin enters unhappily, leading their dragon, which swishes about coquettishly*).

FOURTH. Yes, I come, I come.

(*sighing deeply*) But with a heavy heart, and still no liking for this—

FIRST. Hush!

(*indicating Covet Spring whose hands are full keeping his dragon under control*) Old Covet Spring is here!

(*with a titter behind her fan, indicating Small One, who looks to be asleep*) And there is Precious Harp!

(*Their dragon prances near to get a better look, then darts back, giggling in a most un-dragonlike manner. Twenty-Fourth Cousin does not laugh, but stares fixedly at the dragon entered by the opposition*).

FOURTH (*suddenly*). But that is—

FIRST (*tapping their dragon smartly with her fan*). Sisters, you forget yourselves! A dragon must not laugh.

SECOND. But Precious Harp—

THIRD. In that!

(*All three girls giggle; Twenty-First Cousin quickly becomes business-like again*).

FIRST. Enough! Forget that you are girls now. If you must speak, roar!

SECOND and THIRD. Yes, sister.

(*They roar obediently. Small One lifts his head and looks at them. Covet Spring starts, gazes in mingled scorn and alarm at the rival dragon, takes a firmer hold on Small One's leash, and turns his back haughtily on the others*).

FIRST (*jovially*). You are solemn, brother. Is it that you do not find her laughable, the haughty Precious Harp, inside a dragon's costume?

FOURTH. That dragon—I have seen it once before!

FIRST. Of course.

330

FOURTH. No, not then in the field, but at my farm.

(going closer to the dragon, then to her again) Yes! That is Small One!

FIRST *(dreamily)*. Much smaller than our dragon, I agree! And not one-tenth so handsome or so real!

FOURTH *(following, pulling her sleeve)*. You do not understand!

(The Cousin's dragon has edged playfully closer and closer to Small One, who watches warily; Covet Spring also watches nervously, the cord in his hand twitching violently; suddenly the Cousin's dragon makes a rush at Small One, roaring, then skips away; Small One crouches, roars in reply).

FIRST *(surprised)*. Why, what a splendid roar she has! I should not have thought—

FOURTH *(in desperation)*. That is not Precious Harp, I tell you, but Small One! A dragon! A live dragon!

FIRST. Nonsense!

(Growing still bolder, the Cousin's dragon darts up, stamps on Small One's toes, puffs derisively in his face, and leaps away. But Small One, angered, gives chase, pulling the frightened Covet Spring along after him. Twenty-Fourth groans, covers his eyes with his hand. Only the Cousins inside the dragon, and Twenty-First Cousin fail to take the case seriously).

COVET. Oh—oh—oh! Stop! Stop! I beg you!

FIRST *(laughing)*. Lady Precious Harp, who scrambles on the floor —my eyes stream tears of laughter!

FOURTH *(going to her again)*. No, not Precious Harp! That is not Precious Harp inside!

FIRST. But I have seen her! Seeing is believing, foolish one!

FOURTH *(suddenly pointing to the far door)*. Then look!

(Lady Precious Harp stands there, gazing at the scene in consternation).

FIRST *(aghast)*. Precious Harp!

PRECIOUS. Covet Spring! Take care! Our dragon—bring him here!

SECOND and THIRD *(stopping short)*. Lady Precious Harp?

FIRST. It is a dragon! A live dragon!

(With screams of fright, the Cousin's dragon begins to run in earnest, unfortunately, they dash in opposite directions so determinedly that the dragon costume divides. The two sections run wildly about, then discover that they are separated, and try to fit themselves together, Twenty-First Cousin assisting. Lady Pre-

cious Harp goes to the aid of Covet Spring, and helps him to pull Small One back to a neutral corner. In the excitement no one immediately notices Jade Pure who enters quietly, looking worried; what she sees both astonishes and amuses her, but she does not yet become aware of Small One).

SECOND. Save me!

THIRD. Save yourself! I cannot!

PRECIOUS *(to Covet Spring).* Hold him back!

COVET. Do I not struggle?

FOURTH. We are doomed! Alas!

FIRST *(chasing first one half, then the other).* Sisters! Sister, come back!

PRECIOUS. What? Does their dragon divide itself?

COVET. Why, it is not a dragon after all!

PRECIOUS. Ho! Treason!

FOURTH. O woe!

SECOND. Look! The Princess!

PRECIOUS and COVET *(bowing).* The Princess . . .

ALL COUSINS *(bowing even lower).* The Princess . . .

(There is silence as Jade Pure crosses slowly to the gilded chair and sits down; all hold their bent-over poses, motionless).

JADE. I thank you for your salutations. Do not stand on ceremony, but look up now.

PRECIOUS *(stepping forward).* Your Radiant Highness, I would bring a charge against—

COVET *(breaking in excitedly).* There stand the traitors!

FIRST *(falling to her knees).* Mercy! Spare us, O Most-Gracious Sovereign!

SECOND and THIRD *(also kneeling awkwardly).* Mercy! Mercy!

JADE *(smothering a smile).* What are those creatures?

PRECIOUS. A bogus dragon, brought to trick Your Highness.

COVET. Inside are that wretch's sisters!

PRECIOUS. I demand that they be put in dungeons, charged with treason.

COVET. Yes, and that false prince who is their brother.

FOURTH *(removing his headdress and robe).* Then if I must die, I die the simple farmer that I am.

JADE. Why, now I know you! You are his friend—the friend of my Road Wanderer!

(The dragon, with a happy roar, pulls away from his captors and rushes to her, resting its head on her knee).

And—yes, it is Small One, his dragon!

(stroking the dragon's head) I had feared that we should never meet again!

PRECIOUS. The dragon pleases you?

JADE *(delighted)*. He does! Indeed he does! I have decided, this one is my choice, and I shall wed his master. Bring him now before me.

COVET *(stepping forward)*. I am he, Your Highness, the fortunate owner of this worthy beast.

JADE. You? Oh, no!

FOURTH. Indeed, no!

JADE. You are not he, for I know him well!

COVET *(turning to Precious Harp, in confusion)*. Your Ladyship—

PRECIOUS *(smoothly)*. Ah, but Your Highness, Covet Spring is surely the present owner. That young man you speak of willingly parted with the dragon for a sum of gold, saying that he had no wish to marry.

JADE. He sold Small One?

COVET *(picking up his cue)*. Er—yes, to me! Then since this dragon is your choice, I shall become your husband.

PRECIOUS. Exactly! You have pledged your royal word.

JADE. But—Covet Spring!

(low, sinking back) It is not he I love!

COVET. Your word is law. I go at once to prepare for the happy ceremony.

JADE. No! No, I will not marry him! That hateful sly old man!

PRECIOUS *(triumphantly)*. You have made your choice, niece.

(To Covet) Let us see to that beheading now.

COVET. I agree, I agree. Delay may still prove dangerous. Your Highness, we beg leave to withdraw.

(Jade gestures permission).

We leave you to judge these unworthy traitors.

(They exit).

COUSINS *(timidly)*. Your Highness . . .

JADE. Go. Later I shall judge you. Please go and leave me.

FIRST *(scrambling to her feet and backing out, bowing)*. Yes, great and glorious Princess.

SECOND *(following suit)*. We thank you.

THIRD *(following suit)*. We most gratefully thank you.

(Twenty-Fourth Cousin remains, fidgeting nervously, gathering courage to speak.

JADE. So, Small One, he has left you too! And now, deserted, I must marry Covet Spring.

FOURTH. Ahem!

JADE. Still here? Why have you waited?

FOURTH. Why to tell you—

JADE. Speak!

FOURTH. That I do not believe it!

JADE. What?

FOURTH. I still do not believe that Small One's master sold him to these villians! Nor do I believe he willingly has stayed away.

JADE. But then, where is he?

FOURTH. Something is afoot, I fear. If Small One there could talk, we should know what it is.

JADE. Oh, Small One, try to tell us! Where is he? Where is Road Wanderer?

(The dragon roars, dashes toward the door, then returns, pointing off with a paw, pulling Jade by the skirt).

FOURTH. He knows the name!

JADE. He means that we should follow!

(To Twenty-Fourth Cousin) Come with me! Now, lead us, Small One, to Road Wanderer!

(They exit, following Small One. The Property Man enters, removes the gilded chair, then brings on a small wooden block which he puts downstage, left, exiting).

SCENE SIX

STAGE MANAGER *(who has stepped forward)*. And none too soon they go forward to find Road Wanderer, for in a lonely field not far from the palace, a dreadful deed will soon be done, unless The Princess comes in time. For is that not a headman's block?

And is that not Road Wanderer who comes to kneel before it? Ah, alas!

(He steps back, as Precious Harp and Covet Spring enter steathily, in haste).

PRECIOUS HARP. There is no time to spare. This spot will do as well as any.

COVET SPRING. Yes, My mind will not rest while he is alive. Jade Pure might learn of it.

PRECIOUS *(calling offstage)*. Ho, guards! Send forth the prisoner.

VOICE *(offstage)*. Prisoner, go forward.

ROAD WANDERER *(entering)*. Are you the Lady Precious Harp who has imprisoned me?

PRECIOUS. That is my name.

ROAD WANDERER. Of what crime am I guilty? Can you tell me that?

COVET. She cannot!

(confused) Er, that is—

PRECIOUS *(smoothly)*. It is enough that I condemn you. Go to kneel before that block.

COVET. Yes, go!

ROAD WANDERER. Does Jade Pure know of this? Does she too wish my death?

PRECIOUS *(quickly)*. She knows of it, certainly, and she approves.

COVET *(prompted by a poke)*. Why, yes ... approves most heartily!

ROAD WANDERER *(bitterly)*. She knows! Then her ingratitude is now complete. I go to kneel before the headman's block with bitter pleasure!

(He goes to the block, kneels before it, facing the audience, and places his head on it).

COVET. Good!

PRECIOUS *(stretching out her hand imperiously)*. Bring me the great beheading sword.

(The Property Man shuffles in with a large curved sword; she takes it, seemingly unaware of his presence; he exits).

COVET. What a fine broad blade! Is it quite sharp?

PRECIOUS. We soon shall see. First, I pluck a hair from your gray beard—

(plucking an imaginary hair)—so!

335

COVET *(clutching at his beard)*. Ouch! Ouch!

PRECIOUS. And next, test the edge against it.

(She holds up the hair, brings the blade against it).

Ah! I have dropped the hair. Another one will do as well.

COVET *(as she plucks another)*. Ouch! Ouch!

ROAD WANDERER. Why do you mock my misery with these delays? Dispatch me quickly.

PRECIOUS. He is right. We must make haste.

COVET *(rubbing his chin)*. Then give the sword to me.

PRECIOUS. To you? What do you want with it?

COVET *(taking it from her)*. I myself shall deliver the fatal blow.

PRECIOUS *(taking it back)*. Ah, no! That privilege is mine.

COVET *(snatching it away)*. You are a woman!

PRECIOUS *(snatching it back)*. But my right arm has more strength than yours!

COVET *(struggling for possession of it)*. That is not so!

ROAD WANDERER. The death blow! Come!

COVET *(as she wrests it away)*. Well then, I give it up to you.

(slyly as she takes a few practice swings) What a pity! That is such a lovely robe!

PRECIOUS *(stopping abruptly)*. My robe? Why do you speak of it?

COVET *(shrugging)*. His blood will stain it, doubtless. But no matter.

(moving away) I shall stand here and watch.

PRECIOUS. My silken gown stained with his . . . no!

(going after him) Covet Spring, I yield the right to you.

COVET *(refusing the sword)*. I should not dream of so depriving you! No, no . . .

PRECIOUS. Come! Take the sword.

COVET *(shaking his head vigorously)*. No. You may strike.

(with a wave of his hand) His neck awaits you!

PRECIOUS. Covet Spring, I must insist that you perform the deed!

ROAD WANDERER *(raising his head and looking at them)*. Good Covet Spring, I beg you, end my heart-ache!

COVET *(smugly)*. Then, since you both insist, I shall make ready.

(He tucks his robe up higher under his sash, pulls his head-dress down more firmly about his ears, painstakingly rolls his sleeves to his elbows. Precious Harp taps her feet impatiently; Road Wanderer sits back on his heels and views the proceedings gloomily).

PRECIOUS *(impatiently)*. Do you intend to strike or not? Someone may come.

ROAD WANDERER. Have mercy, and act swiftly!

PRECIOUS. Or I may yet forget my gown!

COVET. I am ready now. Give me the sword.

(He stands by Road Wanderer, who obligingly places his head on the block again, rests the blade lightly on his neck, then raises it for a mighty swing).

ROAD WANDERER. Good-bye, false Princess!

COVET. Now!

PRECIOUS *(catching his arm as it descends)*. Stop! You are holding the blade upside-down! The sharp edge faces the sky!

COVET. So it does, so it does!

(changing its position to the correct one and swinging it aloft) This time I shall not fail!

ROAD WANDERER. Let nothing stop you.

COVET. Nothing! Prepare to meet your doom!

(Jade Pure, Twenty-Fourth Cousin, and Small One run in left, in that order).

JADE *(horrified)*. No. no!

TWENTY-FOURTH. Stop!

JADE. Put down that sword!

PRECIOUS. Strike quickly!

COVET *(dropping his sword as Small One makes a rush at him)*. Save me, save me!

(The dragon, roaring fiercely, backs Precious Harp and Covet Spring off into a corner; Jade Pure and Twenty-Fourth Cousin go to Road Wanderer, remove the imaginary bonds that secure his hands behind his back, help him to rise).

ROAD WANDERER. Jade Pure!

FOURTH. My friend!

JADE *(tenderly)*. My poor Road Wanderer.

337

PRECIOUS. Guards! Guards!

FOURTH. They all ran off when the dragon approached.

COVET *(his teeth chattering)*. M-miserable cowards!

JADE. What a near escape from death!

ROAD WANDERER. Then you did not order my beheading?

JADE. I? Never! It was all her doing!

COVET. We are lost!

JADE *(severely)*. You are lost indeed! Your plot has failed. Road Wanderer, the true owner of this dragon, shall become my husband and be the Emperor.

(The first of a series of slow chimes sounds from offstage).

PRECIOUS. Listen! The great clock in the square is striking noon! At the twelfth stroke you will reach your eighteenth year, and I shall claim the throne.

(jubilantly) We have won, Covet Spring, we have won!

COVET. At last!

PRECIOUS *(to him)*. Come to the square with me! Let us stand beneath the clock and at its final stroke you shall proclaim me Empress!

(They hurry out left).

FOURTH. Alas! Three . . . four . . .

JADE *(despairingly)*. What can we do now? Five . . . six . . . I am not yet married!

ROAD WANDERER. There may be a way!

(He faces offstage and gives two shrill whistles, fingers between his teeth).

FOURTH. What now? Have his senses left him?

JADE *(wringing her hands)*. Listen! Eight . . . nine . . .

FOURTH. But the strokes are slower!

(Road Wanderer gives several short whistles).

JADE and FOURTH. Ten . . . . . eleven . . . . .

JADE. But the twelfth—it does not strike!

FOURTH. What can have happened. I shall run to see!

(He runs off left).

JADE. Road Wanderer, have you done this?

338

ROAD WANDERER. Not I, but the dragon-flies which come at my call. They are clinging by the thousands to the hammer of the great clock so that it may not strike twelve!

JADE *(clapping her hands)*. Oh, wonderful! Then you have saved the kingdom!

ROAD WANDERER. But you are not wed! Where is a temple and a holy man to marry us?

JADE. All is ready.

ROAD WANDERER. Let us run swiftly!

FOURTH *(reentering)*. O sorry day!

(as he looks at them) Where are you going?

JADE. To be married so that I may claim the throne.

FOURTH. Too late! Precious Harp and Covet Spring are coming with my sisters! They are riding horses, and will overtake you!

JADE *(anxiously)*. Road Wanderer—

ROAD WANDERER. Riding horses, are they? But all animals obey me! Shall I teach you what to say to stop their horses?

FOURTH. Well...

JADE. Oh, yes!

ROAD WANDERER. Then listen; meh-neh cho-po tee-ka.

FOURTH. Many choppy—what?

ROAD WANDERER. No, no! Listen, man, once more; meh-neh cho-po tee-ka.

FOURTH. I do not know ...

ROAD WANDERER. They will run in a circle till I bid the dragon-flies to let the clock strike twelve.

JADE *(looking offstage)*. Road Wanderer! I see them! We must hurry to the temple!

FOURTH. But the words ... If I cannot remember ...

ROAD WANDERER. You must remember! Me-neh cho-po tee-ka!

FOURTH. Meh-neh cho-po tee-ka. Of course! I have it now!

(horses' hoofbeats sound faintly offstage left).

Hoofbeats! They are coming! But the horses cannot hear me from this distance. I shall wait. Meh-eh po-co ... these are not the right words! What are they? Ma-ny tea-cups ... I forget! I do not know them!

(hoofbeats louder)

339

They are nearer! I must try!

(running to look offstage left and shouting) Chop-sticks! Ma-ny chop-sticks!

(running back) But they do not stop!

(from center stage, shouting above the hoofbeats) Teacups! Choppy teacups! Many choppy teacups! and still they come!

(thumping his forehead) The words, the words!

(Precious Harp, Covet Spring, and the three Cousins gallop in on imaginary horses. Twenty-Fourth Cousin makes a last desperate effort, almost backed offstage right)

Meh-neh cho-po tee-ka! Meh-neh cho-po tee-ka!

(The "horses" rear and begin galloping in a circle, their riders hanging on frantically, slapping the reins, and attempting to stop them).

PRECIOUS *(to her "horse")*. No, no! That way!

COVET. What affects the horses?

FIRST. Mine must be bewitched!

SECOND. Mine will not turn!

THIRD. Mine runs away! Oh, oh!

FOURTH *(jubilantly)*. I have remembered! And the horses heard me! See them trotting in a circle!

(beginning to chuckle) See my sisters . . .

(laughing harder as he watches) . . . Lady Precious Harp . . . and Covet Spring! Go faster, horses, horses, faster!

(repeating rapidly) Meh-neh cho-po tee-ka!

PRECIOUS *(jolted)*. He—gallops—faster!

COVET. But—I cannot—stay astride—

FIRST. Brother—what have—you said to them?

SECOND. Have mercy, brother!

THIRD. Make them—stop, I beg—of you!

FOURTH. I cannot, for I do not know the words!

(laughing) Oh, what a most delightful sight! My haughty sisters . . . wicked Lady Precious Harp . . .

COVET. Then—must we—ride forever?

FOURTH. You must ride until the twelfth stroke sounds. And then . . .

(scratching his head) I cannot say!

340

PRECIOUS *(hope stirring)*. The—twelfth stroke?

(Two shrill whistles sound from offstage; there is a pause, then the clock strikes once).

FOURTH *(anxiously)*. It is noon!

PRECIOUS *(suddenly)*. My horse . . . he throws me off!

COVET. And mine!

FIRST. And mine!

(with wails of despair each "rider" is bucked off in turn, around the circle; they sprawl in grotesque positions).

PRECIOUS *(dazed but determined)*. But it is noon; then I must be the Empress!

(Bells peal joyfully from offstage).

FOURTH *(who has run to look offstage, jubilantly)*. Not so! Listen to the joyful bells! Listen, and bow down to the Emperor and Empress, newly crowned, of the mighty Southern Kingdom!

(Stately Chinese music is played as background from here to the end. To its strains Jade Pure and Road Wanderer reenter; he is now dressed in a gorgeous robe slipped over his original costume; both wear elaborate crowns. Small One follows on his hind legs, strutting importantly; he wears a small crown cocked rakishly over one eye. The five conspirators scramble to their feet, the three Cousins to the royal couple's right, Precious Harp and Covet Spring to their left; Twenty-Fourth Cousin stands with the last-named pair. Twenty-First and Twenty-Third, Precious Harp and Twenty-Fourth bow simultaneously; then Twenty-Second and Covet Spring. The alternate bowing continues to the end).

JADE. I, Empress Jade Pure, salute my worthy—

(then with a frown at the conspirators nearest her; who clasp their hands over their heads in supplication)

and my unworthy subjects!

ALL. Long live our glorious Empress Jade Pure!

ROAD WANDERER. I, Emperor Road Wanderer, salute my royal—

(with a frown at the conspirators nearest him, who also clasp their hands over their heads)

and my soon-to-be-imprisoned subjects!

ALL. Long live our matchless Emperor Road Wanderer!

(All turn simultaneously to face the audience; there is a peal of bells. The Stage Manager and the Property Man take their places between Jade Pure and Road Wanderer).

341

STAGE MANAGER. These, the illustrious actors of our play, and this modest helper salute each most polite and generous spectator!

ALL (*except the Property Man, who appears to be asleep*). Long live this gracious and exalted Audience! The End!

(*The curtain falls slowly as the music plays, the bells ring out again, and those on stage bob merrily up and down. If several curtain calls are taken, the Property Man may slump lower with each, until at last, he is seated cross-legged on the floor, snoring*).

FINIS

HUCKLEBERRY FINN

ADAPTED FROM MARK TWAIN

by

FRANK M. WHITING

and

CORINNE RICKERT

This play was presented for the first time by the University of Minnesota Theatre, in Minneapolis, under the direction of Dr. Frank M. Whiting. The pictures and production notes used in this book were taken from this production, and are reproduced here by courtesy of Dr. Whiting.

HUCKLEBERRY FINN

By Frank M. Whiting and Corinne Rickert

Huckleberry Finn

345

The authors gratefully acknowledge the assistance of those who have helped in countless ways to make a play of HUCKLEBERRY FINN, but are especially indebted to Sara Spencer for advice, encouragement, and assistance in composing the final version of HUCK, and wish to dedicate the finished product very affectionately

To kids—everywhere.

HUCKLEBERRY FINN

Adapted from Mark Twain

by

FRANK M. WHITING

and

CORINNE RICKERT

ACT ONE, SCENE 1.

Overture: Mark Twain Suite, Side 2, "March, Civil War"

*(The house lights fade to darkness, music cross fades into Mark Twain
Suite, Side 1, "Hannibal Days". The lights come on the forestage
revealing Huckleberry Finn, sprawled against a mossy rock, asleep.
His straw hat is over his eyes, willow fishing pole cocked between his
knees, line dangling in orchestra pit. In time with the lazy theme of
the music, he brushes away a fly, then stretches back into dreams. On
the first note of the "Steamboat theme", there is a nibble on the line.
As the theme is repeated, the nibble is repeated. Then, as the music
breaks into its exciting climax, Huck comes to his senses, jumps to his
feet, sets the hook, and for a few minutes, there is a wild tussle, ending
in a kick of disappointment as the line breaks. Suddenly, Huck becomes aware of young voices and laughter. Peering into the misty
darkness, he sees the hundreds of bright eyes that fill the auditorium,
and shows wild alarm.)*

HUCK: Jee-hosophat!
   *(He dives quickly behind the rock, then after a moment peers over the
   top)*: You don't know who I am, do you?

347

AUDIENCE *(who never miss their cue. Have one or two posted, though, just in case)*: Huckleberry Finn!

HUCK *(alarmed)*: Sh-h-h-h! Don't holler out like that! Do you want everybody in tarnation to hear you? *(He glances furtively over his shoulder.)* Aunt Sally Phelps is a-lookin' all over these woods for me. She wants to adopt me, and sivilize me, and I can't stand it. I been there before. Now, listen. You be real quiet now, and don't you tell on me, and maybe I'll tell you how come I get myself in such a fix. If you want me to? 'Course, if you don't —

(He starts to gather up his things and go offstage.)

AUDIENCE: Come back! Yes Yes!

HUCK: Sh-h-h-h! Blame if I don't think you'll get me in trouble yet, Well—*(He comes around and settles down comfortably on the rock. Music creeps in under his narration.)* I reckon you know about me on account of readin' a book called "The Adventures of Tom Sawyer". That book was made by Mr. Mark Twain, and he told the truth, mainly. There was things which he stretched, but mainly, he told the truth. Now the way that book winds up is—the Widow Douglas adopted me, and vowed she'd sivilize me, and she come mighty nigh to doin' it too. She made me wash. They combed me all to thunder. I had to wear shoes all day Sunday, and go to church, and sweat. I couldn't catch a fly in there. I couldn't chaw. I couldn't cuss. I couldn't smoke. I couldn't yawn, nor stretch, nor scratch in front of folks. But I tried it. It come near to killin' me, but I did it. *(Music —Grofe's Mississippi Suite, Side 2, "Old Creole Days" creeps in under narration.)* But every once in a while, I'd slip down to the slave cabins and have a good smoke with the Widow's negro slave, Jim. Jim was a first rate darky, and he knew all kinds of bad-luck signs, and one night, when he conjured for me with his hair-ball, he told me that bad luck was a-headin' my way. And sure enough, the next day, my old Pap laid for me, and he catched me. He took me up the river about three mile in a skiff, where it was woody, and there warn't no houses but an old log hut, and the timber was so thick, you couldn't find it if you didn't know where it was. Well, Pap kep' me with him all the time, and I never got a chanct to run off. He'd lock me up in that cabin, and go off for two or three days at a spell, and I reckon, if I hadn't 'a found an old rusty woodsaw without any handle, I'd be there yet.

(The music swells up to cover the opening of the curtain. Then the background lights creep up, revealing the silhouette of huge, overhanging trees on Jackson's Island. A bit of the great river can be seen between the branches. Down right is the back wall of a log cabin. Up center is a large rock. A tree stump down left. As the audience grows quiet, the sound of sawing wood is heard. Directly, it stops, and we see one of the logs of the cabin, neatly sawed out, be pushed outward from inside the cabin, leaving an opening large enough for a boy to crawl

348

through. Huck climbs out through this opening, with considerable difficulty, carrying an old rusty saw blade, quite small.)

HUCK *(puffing with his exertions)*: Whew!

(He eyes the saw ruefully, rubbing his aching arm and hand. Then, suddenly alert, he steps lightly up on the tree stump, and looks intently out toward the river. Apparently satisfied that he is alone on the island, he whistles a few notes of the Mark Twain theme, then thrusting the saw into his belt, he begins to go to work. Crawling back into the cabin through the opening he has made, he reappears a moment later, with a gallon jug, which he sets outside on the ground, then disappears again. There is a rustling in the bushes up left, and a face peers cautiously out, followed by a body. It is a huge negro, who moves as furtively as Huck, as if in fear of pursuit. He too steps up on the tree stump to look out over the river, then feeling more secure, he steps down, and looks about him with satisfaction. Spying the gallon jug, he seizes it, and drinks thirstily, without noticing the log sawed out of the cabin. Then, still carrying the jug with him, he steps up right, and around the cabin, out of sight. Huck reappears at the opening, with an old battered coffee pot, which he sets outside, then disappears again. Jim reappears down right of the cabin, finds the coffee pot, and picks it up.)

JIM: Funny, Ah didn' see dat befo'.

(He notices the opening for the first time, and the log on the ground. Then, hearing Huck begin to whistle inside the cabin, his eyes bulge, and he stoops down to peer inside. Appalled by what he sees, he clasps the jug and the coffee pot, and steps noiselessly across to the tree stump, where he hides the things and watches, as Huck pokes an old iron skillet out of the opening, and a side of bacon. Huck notices the coffee pot and the gallon jug missing, and takes alarm. He vanishes instantly, inside the cabin. Jim takes advantage of his absence to slip across and appropriate the skillet, then stands at upstage corner of the cabin, with skillet poised to bring down with force on Huck's head. But a moment later, instead of Huck's head, the barrel of a shotgun comes out through the opening. Jim backs around the upstage corner of the cabin, and reappears a few moments later down right, still holding his skillet in a menacing position. By this time, Huck has crawled out, cocked his gun, and starts circling the cabin in Jim's direction. Jim hastily reverses his direction, and reappears at the upstage corner of the cabin, then noiselessly slips across and crouches behind the rock, up center. Huck reappears at upstage corner with his gun, baffled.)

HUCK *(eyeing the ground, where he left his things)*: Those dad-blame goats! Blame if I thought they'd eat an iron skillet! *(Reassured, he crawls back into the cabin, taking his gun with him. Jim once more, steps across to the upstage corner of the cabin, and raises his skillet. This time, it is a fifty-pound bag of cornmeal that Huck pushes through the opening, but it is too late to stop the downswing of Jim's skillet, which descends squarely on the bag of cornmeal.)* That ain't no goat!

(Jim leaps for the shelter of the rock again, as Huck wriggles quickly out of the cabin, with his gun cocked. He stands for a moment, listening and watching. Jim, in suspense, peeps cautiously up over the top of the rock, then ducks back again, but he has been too slow. Huck quietly creeps toward the rock, and crouches on the opposite side. Both hold their breath a minute, then simultaneously, unable to bear the suspense, both raise their heads. For a moment, they stare at one another, too scared to move. Then Huck breathes the word "Jim!"—and at the same time, Jim gasps "Huckleberry Finn!"—and both burst into a spasm of half-embarrassed, half-relieved laughter.)

JIM: Huckleberry Finn: Ho, ha, ha, if you warn't de mos' ska'dest person Ah evah did see!

HUCK: Maybe so, but you was plenty scared yourself.

JIM: Who, me? Aw, Ah 'uz jes' foolin'.

HUCK: Like fun you was!

JIM: Well, if I wuz a little bit sca'd, I had a right to be. Ah thought you 'uz one of de men dat's after me.

HUCK: After you? Who's after you, Jim? What you done?

JIM: Ah—Ah—Ah better not tell.

HUCK: Why

JIM: Well, dey's reasons. But eff'n I wuz to tell—

HUCK: Jim, I won't tell on you, no matter what you done, blamed if I will. Honest Injun—I'll sign in blood if you want me to.

JIM: Nemmine, Huck, Nemmine de blood. Ah'll believe you.

HUCK: Well, then?

JIM *(looking cautiously about)*: Ah—ah done run away, Huck!

HUCK: Jim!

JIM: But mind, you said you wouldn't tell on me.

HUCK: Well, I won't, I said I wouldn't, and I'll stick to it. But how'd you come to do it, Jim?

JIM: Well, Huck, see, it 'uz dis way. Las' night, I heered 'em talkin'—Old Missus and dat slave-trader from New Orleans. I heered 'im say he'd gib her eight hund'd dollahs for me, an' Missus she 'low dat's a big stack of money, an' she say she'll think it over. Well, I never wait to hear no mo'. I lit out for de river—didn't wait to fin' no raf'—no nothin'—jes' jumped in and swum out to dis yer island. I thought dey wouldn' fin' me here.

HUCK: But Jim—you ran away! Now you can't ever get your freedom!

JIM: Yes Ah will, Huck. Dey's places in dis country where all de folks is free—black and white. An' I'm gwine fin' one, if it's de las' thing Ah ever do. So don't you tell on me, Huck.

HUCK: Tell on you? Why, Jim, I'll help you!

JIM: Oh no, Huck, you better not. You know what happen to white folks dat helps a slave run away.

HUCK: That don't make no difference, Jim. I'm good and wicked already. Wickedness is in my line. And I'm bound to go to the bad place for it, so as long as I'm in, and in for good, I might as well go the whole hog.

JIM: But Huck—

HUCK: And anyway, Jim—I'm runnin' away myself!

JIM: You runnin' away?

HUCK: Yep. Pap's had me locked up here for two month or more, and he's gone half the time, and it's too lonesome. And when he gets back, he licks me till I'm all over welts—so I'm fixin' to run away.

JIM *(alarmed)*: Is your Pap here too?

HUCK: Not now he ain't. He rowed over to town yesterday, and'll likely be gone two or three days. I found me an old rusty saw-blade, and 'lowed I'd saw my way out first chanct I got. I been sawin' on that blame log most all night long, and just now got out.

JIM: But Huck, how is you gwine run away? This island ain't three mile long.

HUCK: I got me a raft!

JIM: A raf'? How come you got yo'se'l a raf', when you'se locked up?

HUCK: Come floatin' down the river in the high water this spring. I found it one evenin' when Pap sent me down to fish. And I hid it in some bushes where he hain't found it.

JIM: Huck, you sho' is a bright boy.

HUCK: Shucks, that ain't nothin'. I'm aimin' to fix it so Pap won't even come lookin' for me.

JIM: Why Huck, he's boun' to look fo' you, when he fin's you gone.

HUCK: Not if he thinks I'm dead, he won't.

JIM: Thinks you's daid?

HUCK: Sure. He'll think robbers broke in and killed me. Here, you go load up the raft, while I fix things up.

JIM: How is you gwine fix things up?

HUCK: You'll see. Here, load up this truck, while I get out the rest of it. He'll think the robbers got in and cleaned out the place.

(Jim takes bacon, skillet, coffee pot, gallon jug, and Huck's gun. He leaves the cornmeal for later use.)

JIM: Where Ah gwine fin' dis raf'?

HUCK *(pointing off, up left)*: Down there, in that clump of willows. And stay on the grass, so you don't leave no track.

(Jim carries his load off. Huck goes into the cabin again, and sets a variety of things outside—a blanket, an old bed quilt, a bucket and gourd, a lantern, fish lines, a sack of sugar, a few other odds and ends. Finally, he climbs out with an empty gunny sack. Jim returns, transported with joy.)

JIM: Huck, dat sho' is a mighty pretty little ol' raf'.

HUCK: It ain't much on looks, Jim.

JIM: Oh Huck, it's beautiful! It's de Promised Lan'! It's gwine make a free man out of ol' Jim!

HUCK: Well, it ought to carry us down to Cairo, where the free states begin.

JIM: If dat ol' raf' take me to Cairo, I'll get right down and kiss every plank in it, I'll be so thankful!

HUCK: Now here, Jim, carry this stuff down, and pick me up some rocks on your way back—all you can carry.

JIM: What you want wid rocks, Huck?

HUCK: I want to put 'em in this gunny sack, that's what. Go on now, and don't fool around. I've got to cover up these tracks.

JIM: Yassuh, boss, I'se gwine.

(He goes off with his load, up left. Huck fits the log into place in the cabin, and props it there with two rocks, so it looks undisturbed. A shot is heard off, in Jim's direction. Huck stiffens, looks toward the river, and edges over behind the rock. Jim shouts from offstage.) Huck! Huck, look! *(Huck rises behind the rock, and looks warily out toward Jim)* I got 'im, Huck! I got 'im!

HUCK: Jim! Is that you?

JIM *(running on excitedly, carrying a dead pig)*: Look, Huck! Look! A wild pig! I got 'im right between the eyes!

HUCK *(feeling it)*: Jee-hosophat! Nice, fat one, too!

JIM: He come up on me in de bushes, an' Ah jes' retch for yo' gun, an'—

HUCK: Jim, that's just what I need. Go get me the axe from the woodpile.

JIM: He's already daid, Huck. What you want wid de axe?

HUCK: I want him to bleed, that's what, inside the cabin.

JIM: But Huck, ain' we gwine eat him?

HUCK: No. We're goin' to make out that robbers broke into the cabin and killed me, and splashed blood around. Go get the axe. Woodpile's down there. *(Down right.)*

JIM: Huck, you sho' is a smaht boy. *(He starts off for the axe.)* But you's wastin' a mighty good little pig.

(Huck pulls the log out again, and crawls into the cabin with the pig, as Jim returns.)

Huck, Whar is you?

HUCK: Here. *(Jim jumps.)* Hand it to me. Now you go get these rocks, and put 'em in this sack.

JIM: Yassuh. You is de boss.

(He goes, and the stage is empty for a moment, but Jim returns a moment later, with his arms full of rocks, which he puts in the gunny sack.) What is dese rocks for, Huck?

HUCK *(crawls out with pig wrapped up in his jacket)*: There! Left a good trail of blood in the cabin. Here, take this pig, and put him in the bag with those rocks.

JIM: Huck, yo' jacket sho' is a sight!

HUCK: Is it? Jee-hosophat, that's bully! Give it back to me. Now here, Jim, you take and smash in the cabin door with the axe, so it'll look like robbers done it. Then we'll drag this sack of rocks from the cabin down to the water, and leave plenty of tracks, so's they'll think the robbers killed me and dragged me down there, and threw me in. And we'll drop my jacket on the way, so's it'll look like an accident. Go ahead now, and chop the door in.

JIM *(admiringly)*: Huck, Tom Sawyer hisself couldn't 'a thought up no better plan.
(He goes off right with the axe, and a moment later, we hear the sound of chopping and wood-splintering, as he hacks the door in. Huck fits the log back into the cabin, and props it there with the rocks. Then he scuffs the ground with his foot, and scatters loose dust around, to cover up tracks. Jim comes back with the axe.)
Ah done it, Huck. And robbers couldn't a done no better.
HUCK: That's the ticket. Here, give me the axe. *(He pokes the blade of the axe into the gunny sack.)* We'll bloody it up good.
JIM: Sho' do look like somebody's been killed.
HUCK: Now Jim, pull me out some hair.
JIM: What for, Huck?
HUCK: To stick into the axe. Pull now. *(Huck winces, as Jim pulls.)* Ouch! *(He plants a few wisps of hair on the axe blade, and props it up against the cabin, blade down. Then he decides to prop it blade up. Jim looks at it, and shudders.)*
Now then, we done a good murder. And nobody couldn't 'a done no better 'thout 'n a corpse.
JIM: Ah sho' is glad we ain't got no corpse.
HUCK: Now Jim, listen. We want to leave tracks for 'em to foller, but we don't want 'em to foller down the river, the way we're a-goin'. Now there's a little lake over that-a-way—*(points down right)*—past the wood-pile, about a hundred yards, that's plenty deep, and about five mile wide, and full of rushes. A creek leads out of it on t'other side that goes miles away, I don't know where, but it don't go to the river. That's the way we want 'em to think the robbers went.
JIM: Is dat where you wants to make de trail, Huck?
HUCK: That's the way. Now you carry this gunny sack around front, and don't set it down till you get inside. Then put it down, and drag a heavy trail with it right down to the lake, and heave it in. And be sure it sinks out of sight.
JIM: I'll make a trail dey cain't miss, Huck.
HUCK: And wait a minute. I got another idea. If I wuz to take and rip a hole in this bag of cornmeal—
JIM: Why Huck, it'll spill.
HUCK: That's just what I want it to do—spill a little track all the way over to the lake. Then they'll know it was done by robbers, and the robbers went that way.
JIM: Doggone if dat ain't so!
HUCK: Now you go ahead with the gunny sack, and I'll foller along with the meal.
JIM: Huck, anybody as smaht as you is, dey ought to be president.
(He goes off, down right, with the gunny sack. Huck steps up to get the bag of corn meal, but glimpses something through the branches that arouses his suspicion. He steps up on the tree stump, and looks toward the river.)

HUCK: Jim! Jim, hurry up! Pap's a-comin'! He's half-way across!

JIM (off right): Lawsy me! I'se-a-runnin', Huck!

(Working at frantic speed, Huck pulls the bag of cornmeal center, and starts to rip a hole in it with his saw. He is kneeling there, with one bare foot behind the rock. Suddenly, he drops the cornmeal, and grabs his foot, howling with pain.)

HUCK: Ow-w-w-w!

(Glancing behind the rock, he becomes terrified.)

Jee-hosophat! Jim! Jim, come quick! A rattlesnake!

(He hops up on one foot, and aims at the snake with his saw, but misses.)

Jim!

JIM (rushing in): I'se a-comin', Huck!

HUCK: Rattlesnake! Behind that rock! Don't miss him, Jim! Look out! He's fixin' to spring again!

(Jim grabs a stout stick, and begins to belabor the snake behind the rock.)

JIM: Dar you is! You ain gwine bother nobody no mo'! (Holds up dead snake.)

HUCK: He bothered one too many already.

JIM (noticing Huck's leg): Huck! He done bit you!

HUCK (tries to put weight on his foot): He bit me good! Ow-w-w!

JIM: Don't try to step on it. Here, let ol' Jim carry you.

(He lifts him up, and carries him to the tree stump.)

HUCK: Jim, it ain't no use. Pap's on his way. He'll be here in fifteen minutes.

JIM (peering toward the river): Lawsy, Huck, what we better do?

HUCK: One of us could get away, Jim. But not two of us, and me with a lame foot. Now you go jump on that raft, and slide!

JIM: Me? Why, Huck, is you crazy? What'll yo' Pappy do, when he fin' you here, an' all dat wrack in dah?

HUCK: Oh, he'll lick me, I reckon, but that ain't nothin'. I been licked before. Now don't fool around, Jim. Pap's a-gettin' closer. Go ahead and take the raft, and row!

JIM: Huck, yo' foot is p'isoned wid dat snake-bite. An' ain't nobody know how to cure a snake-bite like ol' Jim. You's a-gwine with me.

HUCK: Don't talk like a crazy man, Jim. I can't even walk.

JIM: Ol' Jim'll tote you.

HUCK: But Jim, you can't tote me, and make a track with that corn meal, and load up the rest of the stuff, and get out of sight before Pap gets here. And anyway, there ain't no cure for a rattlesnake bite. You die of a rattlesnake bite!

JIM: You ain' gwine die, Huck. You's gwine live. Ol' Jim's gwine make you live.

(Starts to pick him up.)

Res' easy now, ah don't want to joggle you none.

HUCK: Jim, you may be a slave, and have a black skin, but you're white inside.

JIM: You's talkin' out of yo' haid, Huck.

HUCK: I ain't, nuther. You're a-savin' my life, dad blame it!

JIM: Ah hopes so, Huck. Ah hopes so. You is de only frien' ol' Jim got in de whole worl'.

HUCK: Jim, if it's the last thing I do, I'm goin' to get you to a free state. and make you a free man. Get going, now!

(The lights fade quickly, music swells—Mark Twain Side 4. Beginning of record, and fade out on quiet interlude—and the curtain closes.)

ACT ONE, Scene 2.

(Almost immediately, Huck is before the curtain again, telling his story. The music fades under narration.)

HUCK: We got away from there slick and clean. Jim worked like lightnin' makin' the cornmeal track, and loadin' up the raft, and then we stayed hid on the raft long enough to see Pap land, and find the tracks we'd made. Pap warn't long figgerin' out just what we aimed for him to, and then you should ' seen him jump in his skift and row back to town to get help. Soon as he was out of sight, we slid the raft out, and made down the river. We kept in the rushes, and laid low, so's nobody could see us, and by dark we was way out of reach. My foot was swole up somethin' terrible, but Jim he knowed what to do He sucked the p'iscn out, and he burned the place with a taller candle, and he kep' puttin' poultices on, and he said conjur-words over 'em, and that's what brought me through, I reckon. I was out of my head most of the time, *(Music cross fades to Mark Twain, Side 3, middle of record.)* but he was awful good to me, Jim was. He could 'a got to Cairo in a week, and been out of danger, but no, he hid the raft in a bunch of bushes, and stayed there four days and nights to nuss me. By that time, the swellin' was all gone, and my leg was good as new, though I warn't much account, and Jim was plumb wore out with nussin' me. So we drifted down the river a piece, and hid up the raft in a quiet little cove, where we could rest a day. We was good and lazy that day, fishin'. sleepin', and arguin'. You never heard anybody argue like ol' Jim. *(As Huck's spot-lights fade, we hear Huck's laugh, and Jim's "It ain't so, Huck. I tells you it ain't so." The music fades out.)*
The stage lights blend in to reveal the raft and the runways anchored against the shore, in a little cove. It is a lazy day. Sunlight filters through the leaves. Jim stretched on the raft, punctuates his arguments by swatting at persistent flies with his willow switch. Huck's energies are divided between his arguments with Jim, and his whittling.)

JIM: I tells you, I don' like kings. They never do nothin' useful.
HUCK: Well, there was Solomon. He done somethin' useful.
JIM: Like what?
HUCK: Well, he married about a million wives, I reckon.
JIM: Humph! I wouldn't want to be him, an' keep a bo'd'n house for all dose women.
HUCK: Well, there's Looie the Sixteenth. You wouldn't 'a minded bein' him, I bet.

JIM: What he do?

HUCK: Oh, he had more money, and palaces, and beautiful women that loved him—and he finally got his head cut off—

JIM *(sits up in abrupt disgust)*: What Ah want to be him for?

HUCK: Well, think of the adventure, Jim. An' there was his little boy the dolphin, that would 'a been king, but they took an 'shut him up in jail, and some say he died there.

JIM *(sympathetically)*: Aw, de po' little boy!

HUCK: But some say he got away, and come to America.

JIM: What he gwine do in America? We ain't got no kings here. How he gwine get a job?

HUCK: Well, some Frenchmen get jobs teachin' people how to speak French.

JIM: Why, don' de French people talk de same as we does?

HUCK *(dogs bark distantly)*: No, 'course not. Sh-h-h! Did you hear a noise?

JIM *(alert)*: Seem lak I heard dogs a-barkin'.

HUCK: Sounded like a pack of hounds.

JIM: Dey's chasin' some po' little ol' fox, I reckon, way ovah dare.

HUCK: Well, anyway, Jim, French people talks mighty different from us. You couldn't understand a word they said.

JIM: Well now, I be ding-busted! How do dat come?

HUCK: I don't know, but it's so. I got some of their jabber out of a book. S'pose a man was to come to you and say Polly voo fanzy—what would you think?

JIM: I wouldn't think nothin'. I'd take an' bust him over de head—dat is, if he warn't white. I wouldn't 'low no darky to call me dat.

HUCK *(delighted and amazed)*: Shucks, it ain't callin' you anything. It's only sayin' "Do you know how to talk French?"

JIM: Well, then, why couldn't he say it?

HUCK: Why, he is a-sayin' it. That's a Frenchman's way of sayin' it.

JIM: Well, it's a blame ridicklous way, an' I don't want to hear no mo' about it. Dey ain't no sense to it.

(He dismisses the whole subject, and returns to resting.)

HUCK: Jim, looky here, does a cow talk like we do?

JIM *(fixing his sack for a pillow)*: No, dey don't.

HUCK: Well, does a cat?

JIM: No, a cat don't nuther.

HUCK: Does a cat talk like a cow, or a cow talk like a cat?

JIM: No, dey don't.

HUCK: It's natural and right for 'em to talk different from each other. ain't it?

JIM: 'Course.

HUCK: And ain't it natural and right for a cat and a cow to talk different from us?

JIM: Why, mos sho'ly it is.

HUCK: Well, then, why ain't it natural and right for a Frenchman to talk different from us? You answer me that. *(Sits.)*

JIM *(bored at having to explain anything so simple, sighs, and rises to a sitting position)*: Is a cat a man, Huck?

HUCK: No.

JIM: Well, den, dey ain't no sense in a cat talkin' like a man. Is a cow a man? Or is a cow a cat?

HUCK: No, she ain't neither of them.

JIM: Well, den, she ain't got no business to talk like either one or the yuther of 'em. Now, is a Frenchman a man?

HUCK: Yes.

JIM: Well, den! Dad blame it, why don' he talk like a man? You answer me dat!

(Huck, unable to answer, just gasps like a fish. The pause is interrupted by the shouting of men, and the wild barking of dogs, very near, off down right.)

Huck! Dat ain' no fox hunt!

HUCK *(standing up to peer off, down right)*: It's a man hunt! There's a pack of hounds runnin' after two men!

JIM: Let's get out of here!

(They seize the poles and start to shove off.)

HUCK: Look out! Here they come! Hide, Jim!

(Jim ducks into the big box with one end knocked out, that serves as a cabin on the raft, just as the King and the Duke dash in, down right, carrying carpet bags, and head toward the raft.)

DUKE: Take us on! Take us on!

KING: Save us! Save us from the dogs!

(The noise of barking, and the shouting of pursuing men grows louder.)

HUCK *(trying to shove off)*: You can't come on here! You can't —

(But the King and the Duke have already piled on.)

KING: It's all right. Shove off, boy. Shove off, before those men and dogs get here.

(The lights black out, and the confusion of dogs and voices fades into music—Mark Twain Side 4—which continues under narration.)

ACT ONE, Scene 3.

(Almost before we know it, the curtain is closed, and spot lights come up, revealing Huck once again before the curtain.)

HUCK: There warn't nothin' to do but head into the open river. The current was swift, and in a few minutes we couldn't hear the dogs any more. Those two men laid down flat behind the cabin, so's they couldn't be seen from shore, and I was in a sweat for fear they'd spy Jim, for the cabin warn't hardly big enough to hide him. But he stayed quiet, and they was so feared for their own skins, that they never thought of nothin' else. So we got away all right, and finally I judged it was safe to talk. *(Music swells, curtain opens, daytime on the river. Jim is still hidden, Huck is poling the raft, King and Duke stretched out flat, trying to conceal themselves. The music fades out.)* You kin set up now.

DUKE: Is it safe?

HUCK: There's about a mile of woods between us and the dogs.

DUKE: Whew, that was a close shave, pardner.

KING: Another minute, and those dogs would have had us.

DUKE: And those men would have dragged us back to town, and tarred and feathered us.

HUCK: Tarred and feathered you? What you all done?

KING: Oh, nothing, my boy.

DUKE: Just a little misunderstanding on the part of those yokels, back there.

KING: Right decent raft you got here, son.

HUCK: 'Tain't big enough. I'll put you all out soon's we find a place to land.

KING: Well, I don't know, now. I was just thinking—

DUKE: Might be a right handy place to work from, eh, King?

KING: Very handy. Land at a town, put on one of my camp-meetin's—

DUKE: Or one of my shows—

KING: Make a quick getaway, and on to the next town.

HUCK: What are you all a-talkin' about?

KING: We are considerin' makin' our home with you on this raft, my boy.

HUCK: Looky here, you two can't stay aboard this raft!

DUKE: Why not?

KING: Young man, do you realize to whom you speak?

HUCK *(he loses some of his starch, over-awed by their tone)*: N-n-no, sir.

KING: Tell him your tragic story, Bilgewater.

DUKE: I am the eldest son of the Duke of Bridgewater, heir to millions, and by rights, I am a Duke.

HUCK: A duke?

DUKE: But torn from hy high estate, hunted of men, despised by the cold world, I serve the river towns in my humble way, as theater-actor—tragedy, you know; selling patent medicines sometimes—anything to earn my humble way.

KING: Yes, and Bilgewater here ain't the only one with a secret birth, young feller.

HUCK: No.

KING: No. Can I trust you.

HUCK: Sure. Yes sir.

KING: Well, I am the late Dauphin of France.

HUCK: What?

KING: Yes. You see before you, in blue jeans and misery, the wanderin', exiled, trampled-on and sufferin' rightful King of France.

HUCK: Gee—a—a king!

KING: Oh, but even a King in these ignorant times, must earn a living. So I have devoted myself to bringing the gospel to the river towns, temperance lectures and such. I've done considerable in the doctorin' way in my time, too. Layin' on o' hands is my best holt—for cancer and paralysis and sich things. Anything I can to benefit these poor benighted little river towns, and turn a little cash. What'd we make on that last haul, pardner!

DUKE: Ain't had time to count it yet, but we're better'n four hundred dollars altogether.

HUCK: Looky here, what were those men chasin you for, back there?

KING: Well, we made a slight miscalculation there, my friend.

DUKE: Yes. We stayed in that town one night longer than we ought.

HUCK: I don't believe you are any King and Duke at all!

KING: Would you doubt our word? Ah, Bilgewater, it is always the way!

HUCK: I believe you're just low-down rascals and liars, and for two cents I'd put you off this raft right here, in the middle of the river!

DUKE: Even in such companionship, on a raft, King, these here gray hairs is disbelieved and dishonored.

KING: Such is the fate of the noble-born, Bilgewater, to be always unappreciated and repudiated and dispised!

HUCK: Well, I'll try to find a piece of shore where I can land you, without gettin' you wet.

(One of Jim's big feet is seen protruding from the cabin.)

KING: Thank you, my boy. Hey! What's behind here?

(He starts to pull the burlap covering back from the cabin entrance.)

HUCK: Don't go in there!

KING: Why not? What have you —

(He catches a glimpse of Jim, and jumps back, grabbing up the first handy object for his defense.)

Well, we have company. Come out of there, you.

(Jim crawls out of the cabin.)

360

Who are you, an what are you doing here?

JIM: N-n-nothin' your Majesty.

HUCK: You leave him alone. He's my friend. We're travelin' down river together.

DUKE: You wouldn't be a runaway slave, would you?

HUCK: Him? No!

JIM *(at the same time)*: Me? N-n-n-no suh!

HUCK: He's just my friend Jim. Besides, would a runaway slave be headin' south?

KING: He might, if he was tryin' to get to one of the free states.

DUKE: Ah—how much do you figger he'd be worth—if he was a slave, of course.

HUCK: Oh, he ain't worth much. He's got—he's got the palsy.

(Kicks Jim, who begins to do a thorough job of shaking.)

JIM: Yassuh! Ah done got de palsy!

HUCK: It comes over him in fits sometimes.

DUKE: The palsy, eh? That's too bad about the palsy, my man. *(He swings on him suddenly.)* What's your name?

JIM *(frightened by his suddenness)*: Jim, yo, honuh.

KING: I thought so. I know all about you, Jim. You're a runaway slave from St. Petersburg, Missouri. And there's posters about you, all up and down the river.

JIM: Lawsy me!

KING: There's big reward out for you. You're wanted for murder.

HUCK: Murder?

JIM: Ah ain' murdered nobody.

KING: Yes you did. You murdered a white boy, by the name of Huckleberry Finn. You robbed him and you murdered him, and threw his body in the water. They found your tracks on an island right opposite St. Petersburg.

JIM: Oh lawsy, Huck, I'm a goner!

HUCK: Looky here, Jim ain't murdered Huck Finn!

DUKE: We saw the posters.

HUCK: I don't care if you saw a hundred posters. Jim didn't murder Huck Finn.

KING: You seem to know an awful lot about it.

HUCK: I know all about it. 'Cuz I'm Huckleberry Finn, that's why!

DUKE: You?

KING: Huckleberry Finn?

HUCK: Yes, me. And I ain't murdered, nuther. But I'd a ben dead by now, of a snakebite, if Jim hadn't 'a saved by life.

DUKE: But how did you—they think you're dead!

HUCK: I know they do. I fixed it up so's they would think so, and Jim helped me. He's a runaway slave, all right, but he ain't done no murder.

KING *(to Jim)*: Rightfully, my man, we should turn you in.

JIM: Oh, please, yo' honuh, I'll be sold South, sure.

HUCK: Looky here, if you all'l promise not to tell on Jim, I— I'll—you kin stay on this raft!

KING *(thoughtfully)*: H'mmmm. What do you think, Bridgewater?

DUKE: Well, it's a proposition. *(Beckons King down to him, and speaks in a low voice.)* Bet we could get forty dollars for him.

KING: We'll have to get to a town first . . . Well, Jim, the Duke and I have decided to travel with you and this lad a while.

JIM: Yassuh. Yassuh, thank you, suh.

DUKE: That is, if you will perform some small services for us.

JIM: Oh, Jim would be mos' honored to death to do suhvice to yo' worship, his mos' royal highness. *(He kneels.)*

KING: Excellent. Excellent.

DUKE: That's fine, Jim, and if you don't mind, you can begin right now by scratching my back.

(Jim, with an enthusiasm born of awe and gratitude, begins to scratch the Duke's back, as the lights fade out, music comes up—Mark Twain Side 4—and the curtain closes.)

ACT ONE, Scene 4.

(Music fades, and spotlights pick up Huck, standing before the curtain.)

HUCK: Well, it didn't take me no time at all to figger out those two rascals and swindlers were just out to play any kind of a trick they could on those little river towns, and what's more, were just watchin' for a chanct to sell out ol' Jim. But I never said nothin' more. If I never learnt nothin' else from my Pap, I learnt that the best way to get along with them kind of people is to let 'em have their way. Besides, I knowed, if we angered 'em any, they might turn in Jim at any town on the river, and get the reward for him. There warn't nothin' for it. We had to stay with 'em till we figgered out some way to shake 'em loose. When we was far enough down the river to be safe, we pulled into shore, and tied up in some bushes. They was a little village about a mile down river, but 't'warn't safe to land any closer. The King slid off into the village to smell out the lay of the land, and see what kind of a swindle they could try there.

(Music blends into scene, then out. The curtain opens on the raft, anchored against some bushes. Jim's long legs are seen sticking out of the cabin, with their bare feet. Duke is scrabbling through his carpetbag. Huck looks idly at some of his literature that spills out.)

DUKE: Here is another one of my favorites. "The world-renowned Shakespear'een actor, Garrick the Youngest, of Drewey Lane Theayter, London —"

HUCK: Did you know him, yer Grace?

DUKE: Know him? I am him! Ah, fallen Grandeur! 'Course, the King thinks we'd ought to stage a nice, rousin' revival. And it might raise consid'able cash.

HUCK: Yes, sir. Would you and the King be gone long?

DUKE: Oh, it would take three of us, Huck. The King to preach, and me to tell how I've lived a life of sin, but aim to reform from now on. And then we'd need you to pass the hat.

HUCK: Oh—but I couldn't leave Jim alone on the raft. What if somebody was to come along and —

DUKE *(gazing at him with calculating eye)*: That's so. We couldn't afford to lose Jim. Well, we could chain him to the raft—and maybe disguise him. Let me look.

(He starts to rummage through his bag again, and draws out a long white nightgown, with white ruffled boudoir cap. Holds it up.)

This is Juliet's costume, from the eternal love story of the immortal bard. "Ah, speak again, bright angel!" . . . No, I'm afraid this is hardly the thing.

(Lays it aside. Huck has pulled out of the bag a Scottish outfit.)
HUCK: What's this?
DUKE: Ah, my poor, unenlightened friend, in these kilts I once danced a highland fling before his Majesty the Royal King — ah — Duncan himself.
HUCK: Dance it for us, yer Grace.
DUKE: My unfortunate lad, what would I do for an orchestra?
HUCK: Jim could play with his mouth organ.
(The Duke snorts with indignant contempt.)
He plays mighty well, yer Grace.
DUKE: Alas, who would have thought that the great Bridgewater would ever be reduced to the mournful accompaniment of a one-piece band. But I must keep in practice. Get your instrument, friend.
(Jim pulls his mouth organ from his belt, and tootles a few notes while the Duke dons the kilted suit.)
JIM: Yassuh! *(The bushes behind the raft move suddenly.)*
HUCK: Hey! What's that? *(King climbs through the bushes, and comes aboard.)*
KING: I got it, Bilgewater! Richest thing we've ever struck!
DUKE: What's up, Majesty?
KING: Man just died in the village down there, and left a flock of money to two brothers nobody ever saw.
DUKE: That's the ticket!
KING: One of 'em's a preacher from Sheffield, England— that's me. And t'other's a deef-and-dumb brother that lives with him. How are you on the deef-and-dumb, Bilgewater?
DUKE: Trust me for that. I've played the deef-and-dumb on the histrionic boards.
KING: We'll have to hail a steamboat coming down from Cincinnati, and arrive in style. We'd ought to have a servant with us. Huck'll do for that. My hat, please, Adolphus!
HUCK: Who you mean? Me?
KING: You, my ignorant friend.
(Huck, finding no other hat handy, hands him Juliet's cap.)
I'm afraid you don't look the part very well. Reckon we'll have to buy him some store clothes. We'll all need a black suit for the mournin'.
(Glances at the white ruffled cap in his hand.)
What's this? What are you doin' in them kilts?
HUCK: His grace was just commencin' to dance for us, yer Majesty.
KING: Nonsense!
DUKE: Puhlease! Let us dance, my friend, to celebrate the launching of a bold new enterprise! Music, there!
(Jim starts to play, and the Duke begins—a poker-faced, burlesqued highland fling, his legs flying in rhythm with almost no relationship to his doleful countenance and torso. The king, caught by the rhythm of Jim's music, begins to clap for the down beats.)

364

KING: Faster! Faster, Duke! Give me a costume!
(Grabbing up the Juliet gown, he struggles into it, and joins the Duke in the dance.)
Whoop it up, Duke! We're goin' to make a killin'!

(The dancing grows to a hilarious climax, as Jim's music gets louder and wilder, and Huck claps and sways to the contagious rhythm of the music.

This scene can be hilarious, if played with the right combination of skill, spirit, and restraint. The line between the sublime and the ridiculous is very thin. The King and the Duke must take themselves very seriously. They must be fools, but should always appear that they are trying not to be. Both the dance and the acting should verge on being excellent. Crude, unskilled antics are always in bad taste, and seldom very funny. You can do anything, if you make it seem that the character cannot help doing it.)

(At the height of it, the curtain closes, and the house-lights come up to indicate the close of Act One.)

ACT TWO, Scene 1.

(After an intermission, music, Mississippi Suite Side 2 "Huckleberry Finn" begins and plays for about 15 seconds before Huck enters, then fades under his narration. Huck is wearing shoes and store clothes.).

HUCK: Look at the clothes they bought me! Jeehosophat, they're oncomfortable—don't seem to git no air through 'em somehow! Cost nearly four dollars, but the King said it was worth it, considerin' the killin' he intended to make on the investment. All the time they was buyin' the clothes, I kep' wishin' I could slip out on 'em, get back to Jim, and head down the river, leavin' 'em stranded, but there warn't a chance. Pretty soon, I was in it for fair. Them two swindlers marched right up to the dead man's house, bold as brass, and knocked on the door.

(The lights fade as we hear the King knocking at the door, then the stage lights come up to reveal a modest sitting room, with a large doorway leading to the parlor, where burning candles indicate that a corpse lies in state. The music fades out, then slowly disappears. As the King's knock is repeated, a kindly little woman in black hurries quietly across the stage to meet them in the wing off left.)

WIDOW BARTLEY: Yes, sir?

KING: Is this where Mr. Peter Wilks lives?

WIDOW *(comes into view down left, having turned away from the King in a struggle to gain control of her tears. The King follows her on)* I'm sorry, sir, but the best I can do is tell you he did live here—until yesterday evening.

KING: Is he — gone? *(Widow nods, holding back her tears. King falls on her shoulder, and cries down her back.)* Alas, alas, our poor brother gone, and we never got a chance to see him. Oh, it's too, too hard! *(He masters himself, and makes deaf-and-dumb signals to the Duke, who appears, followed by Huck, and on receipt of the King's message, also bursts into tears.)*

WIDOW: Oh, you must be Mr. Wilks' two brothers from England!
(King nods tearfully.)
Oh, come in, gentlemen, do! I'll call his two girls.
(She hastens to the parlor door.)
Mary Jane! Susan! Your two uncles is come!
(The two girls appear.)
These is his two orphans, Susan and Mary Jane. Your Uncle Harvey, dears. And your Uncle William.

MARY JANE: Oh, Uncle Harvey!
(Falls on his shoulder, and bursts into tears.)
And Uncle William! Oh Susan, here they are!

366

SUSAN: Oh, Uncle Harvey! I'm so glad you've come!

KING: Poor things! To be left alone in the cold world so!

SUSAN (crying): Oh Uncle Harvey, he did so want to see you before he died!

KING: Where — ah — is he?

MARY JANE: In here, Uncle Harvey. You come too, Uncle William.

KING: May my servant bring in the bags?

MARY JANE: Oh, of course! I'm so thoughtless—come in, won't you?
 (Huck enters, carrying carpet bags)

KING: Adolphus, carry the bags. Miss Susan will tell you where to put them.
 (Mary Jane and Widow Bartley lead Duke and King off to the parlor.)

SUSAN (snuffling back her tears): I reckon you'll have to put those in my room. We don't have a reg'lar spare room.

HUCK: Yes'm.
 (He holds the bags, and waits for her to show him the way.)

SUSAN: Oh, but don't go up there yet. I'll have to move my frocks out. What's your name?

HUCK: Hu — Dolphus.

SUSAN: Dolphus? Did you come from England too?

HUCK: Sure did.

SUSAN: Did you ever see the King?

HUCK: Who—William Fourth? Well, I reckon I have. He goes to our church.

SUSAN: What—regular?

HUCK: Yes, regular. His pew's right over opposite our'n—on t'other side of the pulpit.

SUSAN: I thought he lived in London.

HUCK: Well, he does. Where would he live?

SUSAN: But I thought you lived in Sheffield.

HUCK (choking): I mean—I mean he goes to our church regular when he's in Sheffield. That's only in the summertime, when he comes there to take the sea baths.

SUSAN: Why, how you talk! Sheffield ain't on the sea!

HUCK (choking again): Well, who said it was?

SUSAN: Why, you did.

HUCK: I didn't, nuther.

SUSAN: You did.

HUCK: I never said nothing of the kind.
 (Mary Jane appears at the parlor door.)

SUSAN: I don't believe you anyway.

MARY JANE: Susan! It ain't right nor kind for you to talk so to him, and him a stranger, and so far from his people. How would you like to be treated so?

SUSAN: Why, Maim, he said —

MARY JANE: It don't make any difference what he said, you just ask his pardon.

SUSAN *(apologetically)*: Dolphus, I'm right sorry for what I said, and I hope you won't hold it against me.

HUCK *(quickly, with furtive glances toward parlor door)*: Miss Susan, Miss Mary Jane, there's somethin' I'd ought to tell you —

(But King and Duke appear at parlor door, wiping away their tears.)

KING: Ah, it's a sore trial for us to lose our brother, and to miss seeing him alive, after the long journey of four thousand mile.

MARY JANE: Oh, Uncle Harvey, he tried to last till you came, truly he did. But last night, he knew he couldn't hold out any longer, and he wrote you a letter—all about his property, it was. Here it is.

(She draws a sealed letter out of a desk drawer.)

The neighbors all saw him sign it, so they know it's done proper.

KING: Oh Mary Jane, how can you bear to think of property at a time like this! Here, let me see it.

(She gives him the letter.)

"To my dear brothers, Harvey and William." Oh, it's too sad!

(He cries again, on Duke's shoulder, but masters himself, and opens the letter.) "I am not leaving any will, but I leave my two darling daughters to your care—" Oh, Mary Jane! Susan!

(He folds them both in his arms, and weeps afresh.)

Adolphus, a fresh handkerchief, there!

(Huck looks non-plussed, goes through his own empty pockets, then stands at a loss until Susan passes him hers. He passes it on to the King.)

"I give this dwelling house, and three thousand dollars in gold, to my two girls, Mary Jane and Susan — "

(Mary Jane and Susan weep.)

That's as it should be, my dears. Ah—"My tanyard, which is doing a good business, I leave to Harvey and William, to dispose of as they see fit. Also, three other houses in the south end of town, and fifty-four acres of land, all worth about seven thousand dollars. Also—three thousand dollars in gold. The money you will find hidden in a bag, behind the fourth brick in the fireplace."—What fireplace? Do you know which fireplace, child?

MARY JANE *(weeping)*: This one, Uncle Harvey.

KING: See to it, William. *(He remembers just in time to make deaf-and-dumb signs to Duke, and Duke goes to fireplace.)*

MARY JANE: Oh, I can't bear to see it! Come, Susan, let's fix up the room for Uncle Harvey and Uncle William.

KING: That's right my dears. We'll fetch the money out for you, and when you get back, we'll have it all counted. We want everything square and above-board now.

(Mary Jane and Susan go out, down right, handkerchiefs to their eyes. Duke has pulled out the money-bag.)

DUKE *(letting money fall through his fingers)*: Oh, this ain't bully nor nothin'! Look at this, King!

KING: Here' let's count it. Stack it up in thousands, Huckleberry.
(They all start counting, stacking it up in six piles.)
. . . eight hundred, nine hundred, here's one thousand. It ain't no use talkin', bein' brothers to a rich dead man is the line for you and me, Bilge. Two thousand. How much you got there?

DUKE *(indicating his two piles)*: Three thousand, four thousand.

HUCK: This yer's five thousand, and I'm still countin'. Four hundred. five hundred, and eighty-five dollars.

DUKE: That don't make six thousand.

KING: It says here—three thousand to the girls, and three thousand to us. *(Duke goes back to counting.)*

HUCK: You listen here! You all hain't got no right to rob these poor orphans of their money that rightly belongs to 'em.

KING *(grabbing him by the collar)*: You listen to me, you rat-faced monkey, you keep your head shet! Don't you fergit that, do you hear? Or I might spill that you've got a runaway slave hid down on that raft!

DUKE: We could make a pile, turnin' him in!

KING: So if you know what's good for you, you'll play our game, young man. and mum's the word! *(Shakes him loose.)*

DUKE: There's four hundred and fifteen dollars short.

KING: Dern his skin, I wonder what he done with that four hundred and fifteen dollars.

DUKE: Well, he was a pretty sick man, and likely he made a mistake. Let's let it go. We can spare it.

KING: Shucks, Yes, we can spare it. It's the count I'm thinking about. We want to be awful square and open and above board here, you know.. And when the dead man says there's six thousand dollars —

DUKE: Hold on! Let's make up the deffisit.
(He begins to take money out of his pocket.)

KING *(counting out money from his own pocket)*: It's a most amazin' good idea, Duke. You have got a rattlin' clever head on you sometimes.

DUKE: Leaves me most busted.

KING: Me too. Nothing left but two dollars. But don't worry, my boy. We'll get it back. With interest.

DUKE: Say, I got another idea. Let's take and give this money to the girls!

KING: Good land, lemme hug you, Duke! It's a dazzlin' idea. We'll have to steal it back, of course.

DUKE: Trust me for that.

KING: Oh, this is the boss dodge! Let 'em be suspicious now. This'll lay 'em out. Go and fetch the girls, Huck. Here, Duke, help me gather it up. *(They put the money back in the bag again. Huck goes out, down right, to summon the girls.)*

DUKE: King, maybe we better glide out of this, and clip it down the river with what we've got. We could turn in Jim, too, and maybe add forty of fifty dollars to the till.

KING: What? And not sell the rest of the property? March off like a passel of fools, and leave eight or nine thousand dollars worth of property layin' around just sufferin' to be scooped in? How you talk!

DUKE: Well, I tell you, it's resky.

KING: Just you leave it to me, old chap, and we'll make enough money here to retire on. And don't worry about Jim. I turned him in this morning.

DUKE: You did?

KING: Farmer's got him now. Give me fifty dollars for him. You've got it in there now. But we don't want to leave here till we've got the rest of it. Sh-h-h, now, here they come.

(He makes deaf-and-dumb signs, as Mary Jane and Susan enter, followed by Huck.)

MARY JANE: Oh, Uncle Harvey!

KING: There, there, my dear. Don't cry. Here's the money now, and if we could just have in some witnesses—

SUSAN: There's Widow Bartley and Dr. Robinson in the parlor.

KING: Have 'em in, my dear. We want this to be all fair and square, you know.

MARY JANE: Call them, Susan. *(Susan goes up to beckon to those in the parlor)*. Oh, Uncle Harvey, I just can't tell you—

KING: There, there, my dear. Don't cry.

SUSAN *(leading Widow Bartley and Dr. Robinson in from parlor)*: This here's the Widow Bartley.

KING: Pleased to meet you, ma'am. I've read your name often in my poor brother's letters.

WIDOW: Thank you, sir.

MARY JANE: And this is Dr. Robinson.

KING: Is it my poor brother's dear good friend and physician? I —

DOCTOR: Keep your hands off me. You talk like an Englishman, don't you? You Peter Wilks' brother! You're a fraud, that's what you are!

MARY JANE: Why, Doctor!

WIDOW: Doctor Robinson, I was here when they come. You got no right—

KING: Make no matter, Mrs. Bartley, Mary Jane. What I have to say will change his mind, no doubt. First of all, Mrs. Bartley, since you at least have some confidence in us, I want you to take this two dollars, and buy the finest bunch of flowers you can buy for my poor brother's funeral. Of course, it ain't much—I'm just one of the Lord's poor servants, and I don't have much to give. But what there is, I want to see my poor brother have the best I can afford, as a last mark of respect.

MARY JANE *(weeping afresh)*: Oh, Uncle Harvey!

WIDOW: God bless you, sir. I'll see it's put right where all the neighbors'll see it, an'll know your goodness, sir. (*Looks at Doctor Robinson*) Even though there's those that don't appreciate it.

KING: Thank you, my good woman. Now, friends all, my poor brother that lies yonder has done generous by them that's left behind him in this vale of sorrows. He has done generous by these yer poor little lambs that he loved and sheltered, and that's left fatherless and motherless. Yes, an' we that knows Him knows he would 'a done more generous by 'em if he hadn't been afeared of woundin' his dear William and me. Well, then, what kind of brothers would it be that'd stand in his way at sech a time? And what kind of uncles would it be that'd rob—yes, rob—sech poor sweet lambs as these 'at he loved so at sech a time? If I know William—and I think I do—he—well, I'll jest ask him.

(*He makes deaf-and-dumb signals to the Duke. The Duke does not appear to understand at first, then suddenly seems to catch his meaning, hugs the King warmly, goo-gooing for joy.*)

I knowed It. I reckon that'll convince anybody the way he feels about it. Here, Mary Jane. Here, Susan. Take the money. Take it all! It's the gift of him that lays yonder, cold but joyful.

SUSAN: Oh, Uncle Harvey! (*She and Mary Jane embrace him.*)

WIDOW: Oh, you dear good souls! Oh, how lovely!

MARY JANE: Oh, Uncle Harvey, how could you—

WIDOW: There, Doctor Robinson. What do you have to say now?

DOCTOR: Mary Jane, Susan, I was your father's friend, and I'm your friend, and I warn you, as a friend, and an honest one, to turn your backs on those two scoundrels, and have nothing to do with them. They are the thinnest kind of impostors, and they have fooled you—yes, and fooled your friends, too, who ought to know better. Mary Jane Wilks, you know me for your friend, and for your unselfish friend, too. Now listen to me. Turn these two ignorant rascals out—I beg you to do it. Will you?

MARY JANE (*drawing herself up proudly*): Doctor Robinson, I'm surprised at you. Here is my answer.

(*She puts the bag of money into the King's hands.*)

Take this six thousand dollars, and invest it for me and my sister any way you want to, and don't give us no receipt for it.

(*Susan and Widow applaud. King holds up his head and smiles proudly.*)

DOCTOR: All right. I wash my hands of the matter. But I warn you that a time's coming when you're going to feel sick whenever you think of this day.

KING (*as Doctor goes out down left*): All right, Doctor. When they get sick, we'll try and get 'em to send for you.

(*Music first 15 seconds of Mississippi Suite, Side 4, blends in. As the curtain closes, the three women are all showing their sympathy to the King.*)

ACT TWO, Scene 2.

(Music swells for a moment, then spotlights come up, revealing Huck once more standing before the curtain.)

HUCK: Well, the way those two frauds took on about that dead tanner, you'd 'a thought they'd lost the twelve disciples. If I ever struck anything like it, I'm a Chinaman. It was enough to make a body ashamed of the human race. They had the money hid in the straw tick of their feather-bed, and that night, *(Music, Mark Twain, Side 3, begins 35 seconds from start, creeps in and under.)* while they wuz downstairs, whoopin' up the mournin', I snaked up and stole it out of there. I didn't know where to hide it—but I judged I better hide it outside the house somewheres, because if they missed it, I knowed they give the house a good ransackin'. So I waited till daylight, and I crup downstairs to slide outdoors and give it a good hidin'. All the watchers in the parlor was sound asleep, and nobody heered me, so I thought the coast was clear.

(Spotlights fade, and music swells to cover the opening of the curtain, revealing the sitting-room in early morning light. The candles are still burning up center, and standing in the middle of the parlor door is a large spray of flowers, propped up on a stand. Huck enters stealthily, from door down right, and creeps up to the parlor entrance with the money bag. Peering off into the parlor, and seeing everybody asleep, he tiptoes across to the outside door, down left, but finds it locked. He wrestles with it a minute, and searches for the key, but without success. Suddenly hearing a noise at the door down right, he looks wildly around for a hiding place, and finding no better place at hand, he slips the money-bag into the spray of flowers, where it is completely hidden, and he himself ducks down behind the flowers. Mary Jane enters from down right, handkerchief to her eyes. She crosses to the parlor, and goes in. Huck waits a moment, then rises up behind the flowers, and tries to make his escape, but just as he is about to move, Mary Jane comes back in, dissolved in tears, and falls on a chair, sobbing. Huck listens a minute, then creeps out.)

Miss Mary Jane, I can't a-bear to see you in trouble.

MARY JANE: Oh, Adolphus, you are such a kind boy!

HUCK: I'd like to help you, Miss Mary Jane.

MARY JANE: Oh, it's just foolishness, Adolphus. I hain't no right to take on this way. Uncle Harvey knows best, of course. But Pa was so good and kind, and had so many friends here, and they all loved him so— and I just can't bear to leave!

HUCK: Leave? Leave this town?

MARY JANE: Yes. Uncle Harvey's fixed it all up. He's going to take me and Susan back with him to England. And he's going to sell everything here, soon as the funeral's over—the tan yard and the house, and even the darkies. Oh, dear, to think I ain't never going to see them any more.

HUCK: But you will, Miss Mary Jane, and I know it!

MARY JANE: Oh, Adolphus, say it again! Say it again!

HUCK: Yes'm, it's so.

MARY JANE: How do you know it, Adolphus?

HUCK: Well, let me study a minute. I'm blessed if it don't look to me like the truth is better, and actually safer than a lie.

MARY JANE: Oh yes, Adolphus, it always is!

HUCK: Well, to begin with, ma'am, my name ain't Adolphus. It's Huckleberry Finn, and I'm no more a servant to them two than you are.

MARY JANE: Why, Adol — Huckleberry!

HUCK: No'm, I ain't. Miss Mary Jane, if I tell you somethin', will you keep mum about it?

MARY JANE: Why, of course, Huckleberry.

HUCK: All right. I don't want nothing more out of you than just your word. I'd ruther have it than another man's kiss-the-Bible. If you don't mind, I'll shut the door—and bolt it.

(He goes to bolt the door down right. Mary Jane tiptoes up center, and peeps into the parlor.)

MARY JANE: It's all right. They're all asleep. What is it, Huckleberry?

HUCK: Now don't you holler. Jest set still and take it like a man. I got to tell you the truth, and you want to brace up, Miss Mary Jane, 'cuz it's not a nice kind, and it's goin' to be hard to take, but there ain't no help for it. These uncles of your'n ain't no uncles at all. They're a couple of frauds—regular deadbeats. There, now, we're over the worst of it. You can stand the rest middlin' easy.

MARY JANE: Why—the brutes! Come, don't waste a minute, Huckleberry—not a second. We'll go straight and have it out with them!

HUCK: Wait a minute, ma'am. We got other things to think about too. and anyway, you promised not to tell, remember?

MARY JANE: Oh, what am I thinking about? Don't mind what I said, Huckleberry. Please don't. You won't now, will you? You tell me what to do, and whatever you say, I'll do it.

HUCK: Well, it's a rough gang, them two frauds, and I'm fixed so's I got to stick with 'em a while longer, 'cuz there's another person you don't know about, named Jim, who'd be in big trouble. Well, I got to save him before we can blow on them, you see.

MARY JANE *(listening)*: Huckleberry! They're comin'! They're comin' down to breakfast!

HUCK: Jee-hosophat! Here, I'll unbolt the door, Miss Mary Jane. You skeet in there, and wake up the watchers. And don't you let on.

(Mary Jane runs into the parlor. Huck unbolts door, and runs to flowers,

but has no time to take out the money. King and Duke enter from down right.)

KING: Huckleberry!

HUCK: Y-y-yes sir?

KING: Was you in my room last night?

HUCK: No, yer Majesty.

DUKE: Honor bright now, no lies.

HUCK: Honor bright, yer Grace. I hain't been a-near your room since I took the bags up.

DUKE: Have you seen anybody else go in there?

HUCK: No, yer Grace. Not as I remember, I believe.

KING: Stop and think.

HUCK: Well, I seen one of the darkies come out of there, last night.
   (King and Duke both jump.)

KING: Which one??

HUCK: The fat one. The cook.

DUKE: When was that?

HUCK: Last night, when you all was down here with the watchers.

KING: What'd she do? How'd she act?

HUCK: She didn't do nothin'. And she didn't act anyway much as fur as I could see. 'Course she had on those big starched skirts—she did look oncommon big to me—but she tiptoed away, so I jest figgered—

KING *(To Duke)*: Great guns, this is a go!

DUKE: So the cook got it, eh?

HUCK *(timidly)*: Is somethin' gone wrong?

KING *(whirling on him)*: None o' your business. You keep your mouth shut, you hear! *(To Duke)* We got to swaller it for now, and say nothin' till after the funeral. But then—we'll have it out of the cook!

DUKE: Leave her to me, King.
   (Mary Jane and Widow Bartley enter from parlor.)

KING: Ah—good morning, my dear. Good morning, Mrs. Bartley.

WIDOW: Good morning, sir.

KING: I trust you are not worn out with your long vigil.

WIDOW: Oh no, sir. I was glad to have the privilege of settin' up with him, sir—and if you think of anything else I can do —

KING: Well, since you offer, I'd take it as a kindness if you would do one more thing for me, ma'am.

WIDOW: Oh yes sir, anything.

KING: Since you have provided such a lovely bouquet for us, and since it represents the last poor tribute we can pay to our poor, dear brother. I'd like to ask you to put it in his arms, ma'am.
   (Huck is electrified, Mary Jane uneasy.)

WIDOW: You mean—under the lid?

KING: Under the lid, Mrs. Bartley. Let him go down to the earth, clasping our poor flowers close to his heart.

WIDOW: Yes, sir. *(She moves up center, picks up the bouquet, and carries it off to parlor.) Huck is nearly dancing a jig, but can do nothing.)*

374

MARY JANE: But—Uncle Harvey—

KING: There, there, my dear. I know how you feel. But I know he'll appreciate it, from his place in Heaven.

MARY JANE: But—don't you think—

KING: It's only his due, my dear.

(The Widow appears, up center.)

WIDOW: I put it in, sir. Right on his breast, like you said. And it does look uncommon nice, Mr. Harvey.

KING: Thank you, Mrs. Bartley.

WIDOW: Would you like to come and see, sir? The undertaker's getting ready to screw down the lid.

KING: I don't believe I could stand it now, ma'am. Thank you kindly.

WIDOW *(steps up to parlor door, and speaks to those inside)*. He says to go ahead and screw the lid down. *(To King).* They're takin' him to the church, sir, for the funeral.

KING: Yes, of course. We must all go and have some breakfast now, so as to be ready for the sad ordeal ahead of us.

(They all start for the door right down, but are arrested by the entrance of a neighbor, Mr. Lot Covey, with two nice-looking gentlemen—an older one, and a younger one, with his arm in a sling. They enter from down left.)

COVEY: Here's your opposition line! Here's two sets of heirs to old Peter Wilks—and you pays your money, and you takes your choice!

KING: What do you mean, sir?

COVEY: These here two men just come off the early steamboat, and they claim to be Peter Wilks' two brothers from Sheffield, England. That's what I mean!

(Doctor Robinson enters hastily from the parlor.)

DOCTOR: Here, here, what's all this shouting? Have you no respect for a house of death?

HARVEY *(with an English accent)*: We beg your pardon, sir.

DOCTOR: Bow your heads while they carry out the last remains of Peter Wilks.

(They all bow for a moment.)

Now, then, what's the trouble here?

HARVEY: Well, sir, this is a surprise to me which I wasn't expecting, and I'll acknowledge frankly I'm not very well situated to meet it and answer it, for my brother and I have had misfortunes. He has broken his arm, and our baggage was put off at a town above here last night by mistake. I am Peter Wilks' brother Harvey, and this is his brother William, who can't hear nor speak, and can't even make signs to amount to much, now that he has only one hand to work with.

KING: Broke his arm—very likely, ain't it? And very convenient, too, for a fraud that's got to make signs, and ain't learnt how. Lost their baggage! That's mighty good, and mighty ingenious—under the circumstances!

HARVEY: Sir, we are who we say we are, and in a day or two, when I get the baggage, I can prove it. But up till then, I won't say anything more, but go to the hotel and wait.

DOCTOR (stopping him): Just a minute, sir.

COVEY (to King): Say, looky here. If you are Harvey Wilks, when'd you come to this town?

KING: Yesterday, friend.

COVEY: What time o' day?

KING: In the evenin'—about an hour or two before sundown.

COVEY: How'd you come?

KING: I come down on the Susan Powell from Cincinnati.

COVEY: Well, then, how'd you come to be up at the p'int in the mornin'?

KING: I warn't up at the P'int in the mornin'.

COVEY: It's a lie!

(Everybody gasps. Widow Bartley rushes to King's defense.)

WIDOW: Ain't you ashamed, Lot Covey, to talk that way to an old man, and a preacher.

COVEY: Preacher be hanged. He's a fraud and a liar. He was up at the P'int yesterday morning. I live up there, don't I? Well, I see him there. He come in a canoe, an' he made a deal with ol' Silas Phelps to turn in a runaway slave name o' Jim.

HUCK: What? What'd you say?

COVEY: He shore did, and there's witnesses to prove it. He told Si Phelps he'd found a runaway slave with a two-hundred-dollar price on his head—

HUCK (to King and Duke): You turned in Jim? You dirty cheats and swindlers!

COVEY: And he said he had to leave town shortly, and wouldn't have time to stay and collect the reward. So Phelps gave him fifty dollars for his share in the darky, and he found the darky hid on a raft about a mile above town.

KING: Gentlemen, this whole story is a lie, from start to finish.

COVEY: A lie, is it? I reckon ol' Si Phelps don't have that darky locked up in the wood-shed on his place, waitin' fer his owner to come and claim him. I reckon—

KING: That may be, sir. But it warn't me that sold it to him. There's been a mistake in identity, that's all.

DOCTOR: Neighbors, I don't know whether the new couple is frauds or not—but if these two ain't frauds, I'm mighty much mistaken. Now if you two ain't frauds, you won't object to sendin' for that money, and lettin' us keep it till you prove you're all right. Ain't that so?

KING: Gentlemen, the money ain't there. You can send and see if you want to. But it ain't there.

DOCTOR: Where is it, then?

KING: It's been stole, gentlemen. We hid it in the straw tick on our bed, and this morning it was gone.

DOCTOR: So that's the way of it, is it?

KING: I wish the money was there, for I ain't got no disposition to hinder a fair, open, out-and-out investigation. But it's gone.

DOCTOR: Will you sign a statement to that effect?

KING: Certainly, sir. *(The Doctor scribbles a statement on his pad.)* I'll swear it on oath, if necessary.

DOCTOR: That won't be necessary. There, just sign your name to that, if you please. *(The King signs. Doctor hands paper to Duke.)* And, you, sir.

(Duke pretends not to understand.)

SIGN!

(Duke signs. Doctor carries the paper to the newly-arrived brothers.) Now, would you and your brother please write a line or two, and sign your names?

HARVEY: I will, gladly, sir. But I'm afraid my brother can't do it—not with his arm in a sling. *(He signs.)*

DOCTOR: H'mph! You would go and break your right arm now, wouldn't you?

(He takes the paper from Harvey.) Now Mary Jane, do you have one of your Uncle Harvey's or your Uncle William's letters handy?

MARY JANE: I—I think so, Doctor. Pa always kept 'em.

(She looks in the desk drawer.) Here—here they are.

DOCTOR *(comparing the letters with the samples of handwriting)*: H'mmm. These old letters is from Harvey and William Wilks, and anybody can see they didn't write 'em. Now, here's this old gentleman's handwriting, and—what do you think, Mary Jane?

MARY JANE: It—it's the same! Oh, Uncle—

DOCTOR: Now, now, wait a minute, Mary Jane. We ain't proved it yet.

KING: No you haven't. That was no fair test. My brother William is the cussedest joker in the world, and he didn't try to write. I could see he was going to play one of his jokes when he picked up that pen.

DOCTOR: Is that so? Well now—answer me this. Lot Covey and I helped to lay out Peter Wilks' body for buryin'. Perhaps this gentleman can tell me what was tatooed on his chest.

KING *(fumbles for a bit, then speaks defiantly)*: Why—why—that's a very tough question, ain't it? Yes, sir, I can tell you what was tatooed on his chest. It was just a small thin blue arrow—that's what it was. And if you don't look clost, you can't see it. Now what do you say?

DOCTOR: Covey, did you see any such mark on his chest?

COVEY: No, sir. I didn't.

DOCTOR: All right, sir, what was tatooed on his chest?

HARVEY: There was nothing tatooed on his chest.

DOCTOR *(shakes hands with him)*: Mr. Harvey, sir, right you are. Mary Jane, this is your Uncle Harvey.

MARY JANE *(flies to his arms)*: Oh, Uncle! Uncle Harvey!

DOCTOR: Now, as for you two scoundrels, you'll cough up that money before sundown, or you'll be tarred and feathered good and proper before you're put in jail—if you're not lynched first.

DUKE: But we don't have it!

DOCTOR: Oh, you can talk, can you?

COVEY: Let's duck 'em. Let's drown 'em! Let's ride 'em on a rail!

DOCTOR: Let 'em dig up that money first, Lot.

KING: Oh Doctor, let us off, from the tar and feathers. Please, Doctor! *(He falls on his knees to the doctor.)*

DOCTOR *(shaking him by the collar)*: Where is that money, you rascal?

KING: The money's stole, I tell you. It's gone—unless—*(he eyes Duke)* —unless he knows where it is!

DUKE: Me? Why, you double-crossin'—do you take me for a blame fool? Don't you reckon I know who stole that money?

KING: Yes, sir, I reckon you do know, because you done it yourself!

DUKE *(seizes King by the throat)*: It's a lie!

KING: Take yer hands off! Leggo my throat!

COVEY: Stop that, you! If anybody's goin' to do any chokin' around here, it ain't goin' to be you.

DOCTOR *(shoving King and Duke toward door down left)*: Get out of here. Call the neighbors, Lot. These's two's going to get what's comin' to 'em!

(They all go out, pushing and shoving the two scoundrels, and shouting "Take 'em to the river! Fling 'em in!, etc." Mary Jane is left onstage alone with Huck.)

HUCK: Oh Miss Mary Jane, you don't reckon they're goin' to kill 'em, do you?

MARY JANE: Huckleberry, the way I feel right now, it would serve 'em right if they did!

HUCK: Oh, please, Miss Mary Jane, don't let 'em do it. They ain't got the money.

MARY JANE: Why, Huckleberry, do you know something about the money?

HUCK: Yes'm, I do. I—I—I'm awful sorry, Miss Mary Jane. I'm just as sorry as I can be—but I done the best I could. I did, honest.

MARY JANE: Why, Huckleberry! Do you have the money?

HUCK: No'm, I don't. I did have it. I stole it from them to give to you— —but I come nigh gettin' caught, and I had to shove it in the first place that come handy, and—and—I'm afraid it's not in a very good place, now!

MARY JANE: Why, where is it?

HUCK: I'd rather not tell you where it is, Miss Mary Jane—if you don't mind lettin' me off, but I'll write it for you on a piece of paper. Do you reckon that'll do?

MARY JANE: Why of course, Huck. Here's the paper.

HUCK: And you can read it after I'm gone.

MARY JANE: Gone? Gone where?

HUCK: Can you tell me how to git to Mr. Silas Phelps' place?

MARY JANE: Yes, it's two miles below here, through the woods, in the back country. Is that where you're goin'?

HUCK: Yes'm—but Miss Mary Jane, don't you let on. I'm a-goin' there to steal a runaway slave. He belongs to the Widow Douglas, and I'm a-helpin' him to run away and git to a free state.

MARY JANE (astounded): But—Huckleberry!

HUCK: Yes'm, and he ain't only just a runaway slave. He's wanted for murder besides!

MARY JANE: Murder!

HUCK: Yes'm. Here's your paper, Miss Mary Jane—an' good bye!
(He starts for the door, down left.)

MARY JANE: But Huckleberry—who did he kill?

HUCK (pausing at the door): Me!
(He vanishes quickly out the door, leaving Mary Jane gasping. Then he pokes his head back around the door, to say—)
But don't you let on!

(The lights black out, the curtain closes, and after a moment of appropriate music—final chords of Mark Twain Side 4—the house lights come up slowly for a second intermission.)

The Phelps' back yard, from Act Three of HUCKLEBERRY FINN

ACT THREE, Scene 1

(After intermission, the house-lights fade one-half, music, Mississippi Suite Side 3, sets the mood. After about 15 seconds the house lights go out, and Huck appears before the curtain, still in his store suit. He looks tired and worried. The music is sad and nervous)

HUCK: Well, I left town in a hurry, before they could remember about me bein' hooked up with them two rascals. Last I saw of 'em, they was in the middle of a ragin' rush of people, and an awful whoopin' an' yellin', and bangin' tin pans and blowin' horns, and they had the King and the Duke a-straddle of a rail, and a big barrel of tar handy, and a monstrous pile of feathers. I didn't wait to see it. I felt sorry for 'em someway. But I snaked on by, through the alley, and struck out for the back country. *(Music cross fades to Mississippi Suite, Side 2, "Old Creole Days".* I didn't have no partickler plan, but I was bound I had ot find Jim, or bust. I finally run onto a road, and follered it till I come to Phelps' place. 'Twas one of them little one-horse cotton plantations, and I 'lowed I could hide around and spy out till I could find out where they had Jim locked up.

(Lights fade, music up, cross fade into chickens, bees, barnyard noises. The curtain opens on back yard of Phelps' farm. Running up stage right is the back wall of the house, showing the kitchen door and stoop. There is an old shed or log-cabin up left of center, with its door, facing the audience, padlocked. A rail fence runs across the back, with a rustic gate. An old farm dinner bell stands near the house. When the lights come up, an old colored woman is seen, sitting just outside the kitchen door, churning drowsily. After a moment, Huck sneaks in behind the rail fence, and looks all about him. A dog barks offstage, Huck whirls in alarm, another dog sets up a howl. Several dogs are heard, barking furiously. The colored woman jerks upright, sees Huck, and runs up to the rail fence to call off the dogs. Huck is stranded in the middle.)

LIZE: You, Tige! Back thah, sah! Back, Spot! Begone, you dogs!
(She throws a stick after the dogs, then opens gate for Huck. The dogs subside.)
Come in, young gen'lman.
AUNT SALLY *(calling from the house)*: What's the matter, Lize? What's the dogs a-hollerin' about?
(She appears at the kitchen door, and sees Huck.)
Lan' sakes! It's you at last, ain't it!
HUCK *(gulping)*: Yes'm.
AUNT SALLY: Well, well. You don't look as much like yer mother as I reckoned you would, but lan' sakes, I don't care for that. I'm so glad to see you, seems like I could eat you up. Matilda Angelina Araminta, come out here, it's your cousin Tom. Thomas Franklin Benjamin Jefferson Elexander, it's your cousin Tom. Come and tell him howdy.
(Matilda, about ten, and Elexander, about eight, come out of the house and look at Huck, but duck their heads, put their finger in their mouths, and hide behind Aunt Sally's skirts.)
Lize, hurry up and get him a hot breakfast right away—or did you get your breakfast on the boat?
HUCK: I—I got it on the boat, ma'am.
AUNT SALLY: Well, set down and let me have a good look at you. We been expectin' you a couple of days or more. Your uncle's been gone up to town every day to fetch you. And he's gone again—not more'n an hour ago. You must 'a met him on the road, didn't you? Oldish man, with a —
HUCK: No'm, I didn't see nobody, ma'am.
AUNT SALLY: Well, I don't know how he missed you. He's met every boat, reg'lar. What kep' you? Boat get aground?
HUCK: Yes'm. She—
AUNT SALLY: Don't say yes'm. Say Aunt Sally. Where'd she get aground?
(Huck points up the river, then changes his mind and points down, then decides to be neutral.)

381

HUCK: I—the—it—well, the groundin' didn't keep us back much. 'Twas the cylinder-head blowin' out that done it.

AUNT SALLY: Good gracious! Anybody get hurt?

HUCK: No'm. I mean—no, Aunt Sally.

AUNT SALLY: Well, that's mighty lucky. Well, you hain't told me a word about Sis. Now I'll rest a little and let you do the talkin'.

HUCK: Yes'm.

AUNT SALLY: How are they all?

HUCK: Well, I don't know what to tell you ma'am.

AUNT SALLY: Just tell me everything—what they're doing, how they are, what they told you to tell me. Just start at the beginning.

HUCK: Aunt Sally, ma-am—that is—there's something I ought to tell you. Whoever you think I—that is, I ain't who you think—oh, gee whillikers, what I mean is—

AUNT SALLY: Here he comes! Here, get behind the chair. I'll play a joke on him. Children, don't you say a word!

(Uncle Silas comes around the corner of the house.)

Well, has he come?

UNCLE SILAS: No, he hain't.

AUNT SALLY: Goodness gracious! What can have become of him?

UNCLE SILAS: I can't think. And I must say it makes me dreadful uneasy.

AUNT SALLY: Uneasy? I'm ready to go distracted! He must 'a come, and you've missed him along the road.

UNCLE SILAS: Why Sally, I couldn't miss him along the road!

AUNT SALLY: But oh dear, dear, what will Sis say? He must 'a come!

UNCLE SILAS: I don't know what to make of it, Sally. I'm at my wit's end. Something must 'a happened to the boat.

AUNT SALLY: Why, Silas, Look yonder! Up the road! Ain't that somebody comin'?

(Uncle Silas runs up to the fence to look out, and Aunt Sally pulls Huck out from behind the chair. When the old gentleman turns around, Huck is standing meekly by the chair.)

UNCLE SILAS: Why, who's that?

AUNT SALLY: Who do you reckon it is?

UNCLE SILAS: I hain't no idea. Who is it?

AUNT SALLY: Silas Phelps, use the brain God gave you. That's your nephew, my sister Polly's boy from St. Petersburg, that you went to fetch from the boat. It's Tom Sawyer!

(Hucks mouth opens like a trunk, and stays so for a minute. The children repeat "Tom Sawyer", Uncle Silas repeats it in joy, Aunt Sally repeats it in affirmation, and Huck finally repeats it in sheer amazement and delight.)

UNCLE SILAS: Why Tom, how'd you get here?

AUNT SALLY: You missed him, Silas, just like I told you, and he walked here, mostly through the woods, I reckon.

UNCLE SILAS: But—why—where's your luggage, son?

HUCK: I left it on the wharf.

AUNT SALLY: Why, child, it'll be stole!

HUCK: Not where I hid it, I reckon it won't.

AUNT SALLY: Silas, you hitch right up, and drive back to town, and get this poor child's baggage. Lize, you go straight and kill the fattest chicken you can find for dinner. Come along, children, we'll fix up a blackberry cobbler.

(She sends Lize and the children scurrying. Huck is left alone onstage with Uncle Silas.)

UNCLE SILAS: Well, Tom, if you'll just wait till I catch the mare, and hitch up again—

HUCK: Oh no sir, I couldn't bother you to do that. Why, I could walk back there and get it, while you're hitchin' up.

UNCLE SILAS: Well, that's about the truth. There's a short-cut through this way. *(down left)*

HUCK: Yes, sir.

UNCLE SILAS: And I better go see that the darkies get out to that south field.

HUCK: Yes, sir.

UNCLE SILAS: You go ahead now—but mind you're back here in time for that big dinner your Aunt Sally's fixin' for you.

HUCK: Yes, sir.

(Uncle Silas goes off around the house. Huck watches him off, takes a few steps toward short cut, then doubles back, and starts to climb the fence. Tom Sawyer walks on down left, carrying two bags. He sees Huck at the fence, and drops his baggage. Huck whirls and sees him.)

Hold on! Tom Sawyer!

(Tom's mouth opens and shuts, then he swallows.)

TOM *(weakly)*: Huck!

HUCK: Stay where you are!

TOM: I hain't never done you no harm. You know that. So then, what you want to come back and ha'nt me for?

HUCK: I hain't come back. I hain't been gone.

TOM: Don't you play nothin on me, because I wouldn't on you.

HUCK: I hain't a-playin' nothin' on you, Tom.

TOM: Honest Injun, you ain't a ghost?

HUCK: Honest Injun, I ain't.

TOM: I can't somehow seem to understand it. Looky here, warn't you murdered?

HUCK: No, I warn't murdered. I played it on them. Come and feel of me if you don't believe it.

(Tom approaches cautiously, and feels with a finger, then with his whole hand. A big grin spreads over his face.)

TOM: Hucky! How'd you do it?

HUCK: I ain't got time to tell you, Tom. Listen, your Aunt Sally thinks

I'm you. I walked in here, and she called me Tom, and I didn't tell her the difference. And I got to stay here, Tom.

TOM: Why?

HUCK: Promise you won't tell—ever? Honest Injun?

TOM: Honest Injun.

HUCK: They've got Widow Douglas' darky Jim here, and I'm helpin' him to run away.

TOM: Hucky! Why, Jim is—

HUCK: I know. He's wanted for murder 'cuz everybody thinks he killed me. But he didn't—see? He ain't a murderer at all! It'd be a swell adventure to rescue him, now, wouldn't it? Come on, Tom, say you'll help me.

TOM: It would be sort of adventuresome, wouldn't it?

HUCK: Sure it would. So please, Tom?

AUNT SALLY: Lan' sakes, Tom, you back a'ready? Why, who's this?

HUCK: Why—uh—

(Tom runs across and kisses Aunt Sally.)

AUNT SALLY: Why—you owdacious puppy!

TOM: I'm surprised at you, ma'am.

AUNT SALLY: You're s'p—why, what do you reckon I am? Silas! Silas! Come up here! *(turning back to Tom)* I've a good notion to take and—say, what do you mean by kissing me?

TOM *(humbly)*: I didn't mean nothing, ma'am. I didn't mean no harm. I—I thought you'd like it.

AUNT SALLY: Why, you born fool! What made you think I'd like it? Silas!

TOM: Well, I don't know. Only, they—they told me you would.

AUNT SALLY: They told you I would? Whoever told you's another lunatic. I never heard the beat of it. Who's they?

TOM: Why everybody. They all said so, ma'am.

(Uncle Silas comes around the corner of the house.)

AUNT SALLY: Silas, this young upstart just up and kissed me.

TOM: I'm sorry, sir. They all told me to. They all said—kiss her, and said she'd like it. But I'm sorry, ma'am, and I won't do it no more— I won't honest.

UNCLE SILAS: You won't won't you? Well, I sh'd reckon you won't!

TOM: No sir. I'm honest about it. I won't ever do it again—till she asks me.

AUNT SALLY: Till I ask you! Well, I never see the beat of it in my born days! I lay you'll be seven hundred years old before I ever ask you.

TOM *(turning to Huck)*: Tom, didn't you think Aunt Sally'd open out her arms and say, "Sid—Sid Sawyer—"

AUNT SALLY: My land! Sid! It's Tom's brother Sid!

(She makes a rush for him to hug him, but Tom fends him off.)

TOM: No, not till you've asked me first.

AUNT SALLY: Oh, please, please, Sid, give me a kiss and a hug!

UNCLE SILAS: Well, Sid, I'm mighty glad to have you here, along with Tom.

AUNT SALLY: I never see such a surprise. We warn't lookin' for you at all—only Tom.

TOM: I know, but I begged and begged, and at the last minute, Aunt Polly let me come too. And Tom and me thought it would be a first rate surprise to not let on about me at first. But I reckon it was a mistake.

AUNT SALLY: You'd ought to had your jaws boxed, Sid Sawyer. I hain't been so put out since I don't know when. But I don't care. I'd be willin' to stand a thousand such jokes to have you here.

LIZE *(at the kitchen door)*: Missus, I got de chickum on, an' Massa, if you'll le' me have de key, I got a big pan of greens and co'n pone for —for—

UNCLE SILAS: Oh yes, Lize.

(He gives her a big key from his pocket.)

Well, boys, it's time for you two to come take off them city clothes, and clean up for dinner.

AUNT SALLY: Lan' sakes, yes. Come right along, you two. Matilda Angelina Araminta, you and Thomas Franklin Benjamin Jefferson Elexander carry these grips up to the spare room.

(They all file into the house, but a moment later, Lize comes out carrying a tray of food across to the cabin. She unlocks the padlock, and goes inside. Tom and Huck poke their heads out of the door and watch.)

TOM: Huck, who do you reckon those vittles is for?

HUCK: I thought they were for a dog.

TOM: Well, they ain't for a dog.

HUCK: Why?

TOM: 'Cause part of it's watermelon.

HUCK: That's so. A dog don't eat watermelon.

TOM: I bet he don't. Them vittles is for a man, and a man locked up.

HUCK: Jim! That's Jim in there!

(He rushes across to the cabin. Tom catches him.)

TOM: Hold on! You can't just bust in there.

HUCK: But Tom, we got to find out, don't we?

(Lize comes out of the cabin, empty-handed.)

TOM: Sh-h-h-h! What you got in there? A dog?

LIZE *(giggling)*: Yassuh, Marse Sid. Cur'us dog, too. Does you want to look at 'im?

TOM: Sure.

HUCK *(nudging him)*: Not right here in daybreak! That ain't the way!

TOM *(whispering back)*: It's the way now, all right.

LIZE *(throwing the door open)*: Come here, you.

(Jim appears at the door, a big chain around his leg, and dragging behind.)

385

JIM: Why, Huck! En' good lan'! Ain't dat Marse Tom?
(Tom signals Jim to keep mum.)
LIZE: Why, de gracious sakes! Do he know you gen'lmen?
TOM: Does who know who?
LIZE: Why, dis yer runaway slave.
TOM: I don't reckon he does. What put that into your head?
LIZE: What put it dar? Didn' he just dis minute sing out like he knowed you?
TOM: Who sung out? When did he sing out? What did he sing out? Tom, did you hear anybody sing out?
HUCK: No. I ain't heard nobody say nothin'.
TOM *(to Jim)*: Did you sing out?
JIM: No sah. I hain't said nothin' sah.
TOM: Not a word?
JIM: No, sah. I hain't said a word.
TOM: Did you ever see us before?
JIM: No, sah, not as I knows on.
TOM *(to Lize)*: What do you reckon's the matter with you, anyway? What made you think somebody sung out?
LIZE: Ah don' know, Marse Sid. 'Deed ah don'.
TOM: I know. It's witches. That's what it is!
LIZE: Witches?
TOM: Yes, it's those dad-blame witches. They make you see all kind of things that ain't there. And hear 'em too. Yessir, they pester you somethin' awful. They're tryin' to witch you!
LIZE: Oh, Marse Sid, I don't want to be witched! What you reckon Ah better do?
TOM: I reckon you better go get some white thread, and tie your wool all up in little bunches with it. And you better not lose any time about it.
LIZE: Will it keep 'em off, fo' sure, Marse Sid?
TOM: For sure. And every minute you wait, they got that much more power over you.
LIZE: Oh, lawsamighty, I'm a-goin'! Witches! And me just baptized las' summer!
(She hastens off to the house, holding her head as she goes.)
HUCK: Jim, I'm mighty glad we found you.
JIM: So is I, Huck.
TOM: Don't you ever let on to know us, Jim. We're goin' to make a real splendid, mixed-up plan to set you free.
HUCK: Well, Tom, the door's open. Let's get him out now!
TOM: Oh, there wouldn't be any adventure in that!
HUCK: Well, Tom, there's a square window-hole, with a board nailed across. It'd be big enough for Jim to get through if we wrench off the board.
TOM: I should hope we can find a way that's a little more complicated than that, Huck Finn.

HUCK: Complicated? I don't want no complicated. I want to get Jim
    out of there.

TOM: If we're goin' to get him out of there, we've got to do it with style.
    What's the good of a plan that ain't no more trouble than that?

HUCK: Well, then, how'll it do to saw him out?

TOM: That's more like. It's real mysterious and troublesome. But I bet
    we can find a way that's twice as hard. I know! Let's dig him out!

HUCK: Dig him out?

TOM: Sure, we'll dig him out. It'll take at least a week!

JIM: But Marse Tom, what you gwyne do about dis chain?

HUCK: Chain?

JIM: Dey's got me chained to de bed. *(Both boys rush to look.)*

TOM *(delighted)*: Sure enough! Wonderful!

HUCK: But look, Tom, the end is just slipped around the leg of the bed.
    All we have to do is lift the bed and slip it off.

TOM: Oh no! We'll saw the leg of the bed in two. Then we'll put it back
    together again, and eat the sawdust.

HUCK: But why do we have to—

TOM: Huck Finn, you ought to know enough to know that a respectable
    rescue has to be a little bit complicated. We'll saw the leg off and eat
    the sawdust—unless—

JIM: What is it, Massa Tom?

TOM: I know a better way—but no, there ain't necessity enough for it.

HUCK: For what?

TOM: Why, to saw Jim's leg off, of course!

JIM: Massa Tom!

HUCK: Good land! What would you want to saw his leg off for?

TOM: Well, 'twould be real adventuresome. But never mind. There ain't
    enough necessity. But don't think you two can make this into a little
    one-horse rescue. We've got to steal some sheets, and make him a
    rope ladder.

JIM: Mist' Tom, what Ah want wid a rope ladder?

TOM: To leave for a clue, of course. And we'll smouch one of Uncle Silas'
    white shirts, for Jim to write a journal on.

HUCK: Journal your granny—Jim can't write.

TOM: Well, he can make marks on the shirt, can't he. If we make him a
    pen out of an old pewter spoon?

HUCK: Well, then, what'll we make him the ink out of?

TOM: Many prisoners in the books made it out of iron rust and tears. But
    the best way is to use blood.

JIM: Whose blood?

TOM: Yours, of course.

HUCK: But Tom—

TOM: You got any spiders in there, Jim?

JIM: No sah, thanks to goodness I hain't, Marse Tom.

TOM: All right, we'll get you some.

JIM: But bless you, honey, I don't want none.

TOM: You got to have 'em,they all do. We'll get you some rats, too.

JIM: But Marse Tom, I don' want no rats. I'd jes' as soon sleep wid a rattlesnake.

TOM: That's a prime idea. Where could you keep it?

JIM: Keep what?

TOM: Why, the rattlesnake!

JIM: Marse Tom! You bring a rattlesnake in here, an' I bus' right out through dat wall!

HUCK: What does Jim want with a rattlesnake? What could he do with it?

TOM: He could tame it. A prisoner's got to have some kind of dumb pet.

JIM: No sah!

HUCK: Tom, maybe we could catch some garter snakes, and let on they're rattlesnakes. We could tie buttons on their tails.

TOM: All right then, that's what we'll have to do, use garter snakes. And we'll have to make a file, to file off the chain. And we'll dig the tunnel with our bare hands. And there'll be nonimous letters. Oh, it'll be bully! We'll let on it took us thirty-seven years! Lock up the prisoner, Huck. There'll be real trouble before we get him out!

(Lights out, and music Mississippi Suite, Side 2, start 15 seconds from beginning—fades in and continues under first half of Huck's narration.)

388

ACT THREE, Scene 2.

(Huck stands before the curtain, now in his own regular costume.)

HUCK: We did all Tom said, and a lot more besides. In a week's time, we had the tunnel dug, from the old tool-house right up under Jim's bed, where the counterpin hung down and hid it. We slipped him an old rusty blade to file the chain off with—Tom wouldn't let us use a file. There was nobody like Tom Sawyer for thinkin' up dangers and difficulties. I'd 'a had Jim out of there, easy as tit-tat-toe, if I'd ben doin' it by myself. But Tom's plans was worth fifteen of mine for style, and would make Jim just as free as mine would, and maybe get us all killed besides. We did give Aunt Sally a worrisome time, though. *(The spotlights black out, and music comes up—Mississippi Suite No. 1 —to cover opening of the curtain. Aunt Sally, Uncle Silas, Huck and Tom are grouped together in the back yard.)*

UNCLE SILAS: It's most uncommon, cur'us, Sally. I know perfectly well I took it off, because—

AUNT SALLY: Because you hain't got but one on. I know you took it off. It was on the clo's line two days ago. But it's gone now. A body'd think you would learn to take some care of your shirts, at your time of life.

UNCLE SILAS: I do try all I can, Sally. But I don't see 'em except when they're on me. And I don't believe I've ever lost one off of me.

AUNT SALLY: Well, you'd 'a done it if you could, I reckon. And the shirt ain't all that's gone, nuther. Thar's a spoon gone. And that ain't all. There was ten, and now there's only nine. The calf got the shirt, I reckon, but the calf never took the spoon, that's certain.

UNCLE SILAS: Why, what else is gone?

AUNT SALLY: There's six candles gone, that's what. The rats could 'a got the candles, and I reckon they did. They ben all over the place the last few days. But you can't lay the spoon on the rats, and that I know.

LIZE *(at the kitchen door)*: Missus, dey's a sheet gone.

AUNT SALLY: A sheet gone? Well, for the lan's sake!

UNCLE SILAS: I'll stop up them rat-holes today.

AUNT SALLY: Oh, do hush, Silas. I s'pose the rats took the sheet? Where's it gone, Lize?

LIZE: 'Clah to goodness, I hain't no notion, Miss Sally. She wuz on de clo's line las' time Ah wash, but she ain' dah no mo' now.

AUNT SALLY: I reckon the world is comin' to an end. A shirt, a sheet, and a spoon, and six can—

LIZE: An' Missus, dey's a brass cannelstick miss'n.

AUNT SALLY: Cler out from here, you Lize, or I'll—

UNCLE SILAS (*drawing a spoon out of his pocket, where Tom has planted it during dialogue*). Why, Sally, look-a-here. Here's yer spoon. Now how do you reckon that got into my pocket?

AUNT SALLY: So you had it in yer pocket all the time! An' like as not you've got the other things in there too. Fetch out my cannelstick.

(*She helps him go through his pockets. Tom takes the spoon basket and starts counting. He slips one to Huck.*)

UNCLE SILAS: No, that's all I find.

AUNT SALLY: Well, how'd the spoon get there?

UNCLE SILAS: I really don't know, Sally, or you know I would tell.

AUNT SALLY: Oh, for the lan's sake, git along now, and don't come nigh me again till I've got my peace of mind.

(*Uncle Silas goes around the corner of the house.*)

Anyway, I've got my ten spoons back.

TOM: Why, Aunt Sally, there ain't but nine spoons yet.

AUNT SALLY: Go 'long to your play, and don't bother me. I know better, I counted 'em myself.

TOM: Well, I've counted 'em twice, Aunt Sally, and I can't make but nine.

AUNT SALLY: I reckon you just can't count, Sid. Here. One, two, three, four, five, six, seven, eight — I declare to gracious, there ain't but nine! Plague take the things, I'll count 'em again.

(*Huck slips back the spoon he has. Aunt Sally counts.*)

Hang the troublesome rubbage. There's ten now.

TOM: But Aunty, you counted one of 'em twict. I don't think there's ten.

AUNT SALLY: You numbskull, didn't you see me count 'em?

TOM: I know, but—

AUNT SALLY: I'll count 'em again. One, two, three—

(*Tom smouches one out into his pocket.*)

Seven, eight, nine. Oh, mercy. I'm so addled, I can't count anything. Clear out of here, and let me have some peace, and don't come botherin' back here till dinner!

(*Uncle Silas comes around the house.*)

UNCLE SILAS: Sally! Sally!

AUNT SALLY: Don't Sally me!

UNCLE SILAS: But Sally, look—

AUNT SALLY: Silas Phelps, don't tell me there's anything more. I can't stand it!

UNCLE SILAS: But look what I found tacked to the front door.

AUNT SALLY: Tacked to the front door?

UNCLE SILAS: That's where it was. And no name signed to it.

AUNT SALLY: What is it?

UNCLE SILAS: It's a letter. It says—"Don't betray me, I wish to be your friend. There is a desperate gang of cut-throats from over in Injun Territory going to steal your runaway slave tonight. I am one of the gang, but have got religion, and wish to quit and lead an honest life, so I am betraying their plot. They are big fellows, and all armed, so beware. I do not wish any reward but to know I have done this right thing. Signed, Unknown Friend."

AUNT SALLY: Silas, you go straight, and round up all the neighbors.

UNCLE SILAS: We better set an all-night watch, I reckon.

AUNT SALLY: I reckon! Don't you stop for nothin', Silas. And be sure that each one brings his gun.

UNCLE SILAS *(going)*: We'll turn the dogs loose too.

TOM *(delighted, whispering to Huck)*: Ain't it bully?

HUCK: But Tom—

AUNT SALLY: You boys! You run call the darkies in from the field.

TOM: You want the women too, Aunt Sally?

AUNT SALLY: Oh, mercy me, I don't know. I'm about to lose my mind! *(Matilda screams, inside the house.)*

MATILDA: Ma! Ma!

AUNT SALLY: Lan' sakes, what's the matter now?

MATILDA *(rushing out the kitchen door)*: Ma! There's a snake on my bed!

AUNT SALLY: What?

LIZE *(rushing out of the kitchen, screaming)*: Missus, I see two snakes a-slitherin' out from behind de stove!

AUNT SALLY: Snakes? In my house?

LIZE *(gibbering)*: Yas'm. Dey's all ovah de place! *(Elexander runs out of the house, carrying a snake.)*

THOMAS: Ma, look what I found in the parlor!

AUNT SALLY *(screaming)*: Take it away! Take it away!

HUCK: Here, that's my snake! Where'd you get him?

AUNT SALLY: Your snake? Have you two boys—

TOM: We had a sack full of 'em, Aunt Sally—and we went to a lot of trouble to get 'em—

AUNT SALLY: A sack of 'em? Where?

TOM: In our room. Tom, you must 'a left the sack open. *(Lize and Matilda start screaming. Aunt Sally is at the breaking point.)*

AUNT SALLY *(to Lize and Matilda)*: You stop that. And if you two heathens don't get those snakes out of my house, I'll—eeeeek! *(A snake has dropped from the eaves of the house, squarely down her back. Aunt Sally goes into hysterics. The boys rescue the snake. Aunt Sally sinks sobbing into a chair.)*

HUCK: We're sorry, Aunt Sally, honest. I—I can't see why you mind snakes so.

TOM *(with superior understanding)*: It ain't snakes, Huck. It's the idea of snakes. Look— *(Tom picks up a feather, and strokes it lightly across the back of Aunt Sally's neck. She emits a wild whoop, and dashes for the house.)* See, all women are like that, Huck. Must just be somethin' wrong with 'em. *(Lights black out, and music comes up, covering the closing of the curtain. Mississippi Suite, Side 2, Start 10 seconds from beginning.)*

ACT THREE, Scene 3.

HUCK (*before the curtain*): That was a time, I tell you. 'Long about sun-down, fifteen farmers come pilin' up to the house, and every one of 'em had a gun. They all went into the parlor, and set down, all of 'em fidgety and uneasy, and tryin' to look like they warn't. Aunt Sally locked me and Tom in our room, but we climbed out the window, and shinned down the lightnin' rod in no time. I was feelin' right uneasy myself.

(*Spotlights out, and music up to cover curtain opening. The lights come up on the same set, in night light. The two boys are alone on the stage.*)

Tom, listen. They've found out somehow that tonight's the night of the escape. We better ditch it—anyway for tonight.

TOM: Huck Finn, don't be so chicken-hearted. We've worked a whole week getting everything ready, and now you want to call the whole thing off.

HUCK: But Tom—these men! They've got guns! They've found out!

TOM: Course they've found out. What do you think I tacked that letter on the door for?

HUCK: Did you do that?

TOM: 'Course. You couldn't have a respectable rescue without shootin', could you?

HUCK: But Tom, there's a house full of men in there. With guns!

TOM: I know. Ain't it bully? If I had it to do over again, I bet I could fetch two hundred!

HUCK: Tom, use some sense. They're in there now, layin' plans. In a few minutes, they'll have men posted all around the place. Let's slip Jim out now, and shove off while there's still a chance. I don't want to get mixed up with no buckshot.

TOM: All right. Let's go. We'll snake him out of the tunnel, and—
(*Jim appears at his shoulder.*)

JIM: Marse Tom —

TOM (*jumps violently*): Jim! Hang it! Don't come up on me so sudden!

HUCK: Did you cover up the tunnel, Jim?

JIM: Yassuh Ah did. Ain't it time, Marse Tom?

TOM: Yes, we're all ready. Now, Jim, listen, when they start chasin', don't you run. You just drop down in the bushes, and wait till they're gone, and wait till the dogs go by, and then we'll strike out the other way.

HUCK: It's a noble plan, Jim.

TOM (*as kitchen door opens*): Sh-h-h-h! Duck down!
(*They conceal themselves in the shadows down left, below the cabin.*)

UNCLE SILAS *(at kitchen door)*: Now, Lot, you watch the cabin, and you two take the gate. I'll set the others along the other fence.

COVEY: Don't worry, Silas. If any slave-stealers show up tonight, they'll wish they'd never been born.

(Uncle Silas goes back into the house, and the three men take their posts. One of them props his gun against the gate. The three boys slip past the first guard, who is looking intently off right. They pause in the shadows, unable to think how to get past the two guards at the gate. Tom, as usual, has the inspiration. He picks up a pebble, and tosses it into the bushes down right. The men all whirl to investigate.)

DOCTOR: Who's there?

COVEY: Answer, or I'll shoot!

(They all three make a rush down right, ready for action. The three adventurers slide over the fence, and into some bushes. As Tom goes over last, he reaches back through the gate, and pulls the trigger of the gun propped there. The three men whirl instantly, in time to catch a glimpse of Tom, as he dives out of sight.)

FARMER: There he is, men!

COVEY: I've got him! *(He shoots.)*

DOCTOR: They went over the fence. After 'em boys!

FARMER *(as they all scramble to get over the fence)*: They're breakin' for the river! Shoot!

(They all shoot in the direction of the fugitives. Bedlam breaks loose. There is much shouting and shooting, and barking of dogs, as they all rush out after the three fugitives. As soon as the men are out of sight, the three boys crawl out from their bushes, and climb back over the fence.)

TOM: There they go! Now! Run! That a-way!

(Jim and Huck start to run, but Huck looks around, and sees Tom still by the fence.)

HUCK: Ain't you a-comin', Tom?

TOM: Can't seem to make it, someway.

JIM: Marse Tom! You's been shot!

TOM: Run, Jim! Run! This is your chance to get away! Hurry!

JIM: But Marse Tom, I cain't leave you here shot!

TOM: I'll get a rag and tie it up. Don't stop now. Don't fool around here, right when the escape's goin' so glorious. Get away, Jim!

(Huck and Jim look at each other.)

HUCK: Say it, Jim.

JIM: Huck, if it 'uz him dat 'uz bein' set free, would he say "Go on en save me, nemmine 'bout a doctor fo' to save dis one"? Would Tom Sawyer say dat? You bet he wouldn'. Well, den, is Jim gwyne to say it? No sah! I don' budge a step 'dout we git a doctor.

TOM: But Jim, they'll find you here. You won't get free!

JIM *(quietly)*: I'd never feel free, Marse Tom, if I lefted you alone when you's hurt.

HUCK: Jim, you run for it. I'll stay with Tom.

JIM: You cain't tote him, Huck. En Ah kin.

(He lifts Tom up gently in his arms.)

TOM *(howling with pain)*: Ow-w-w-w! You put me down, Jim, and run for it. Ow-w-w-w!

JIM *(carrying him toward the house)*: Open up de do', Huck.

HUCK *(desperate)*: Jim, you can't go in there, right when you've got a chance to get free!

(Aunt Sally opens the door, and peers out with a lantern. The two children are, as usual, hanging on to her skirts.)

Oh, dad-blame it! We're done for now!

AUNT SALLY: Mercy on us! What's this?

(She sees Jim)

Why, you—you—ain't you chained up in the cabin?

MATILDA: It's Sid, Ma! It's Sid, all bloody!

JIM: He's hurt, Missus. He's hurt bad. He got to have a doctor.

AUNT SALLY: Sid! Oh, he's dead, he's dead! I know he's dead!

TOM: I ain't dead! Ow-w-w-w! Put me down, Jim, hang it!

AUNT SALLY: Oh, he's alive, thank the Lord! And that's enough! Ease him down here, in the chair. Tom, you run ring the dinner bell, and call the men back. Doctor Robinson's with 'em.

HUCK *(running to the bell)*: Yes'm.

AUNT SALLY: Elexander, run get the footstool. We'll try to make him easy. Oh, Sid!

(Elexander runs into the house.)

TOM: I'm all right, Aunt Sally.

AUNT SALLY: Matilda, you hang onto this runaway. I don't know how he got his chain off, and got out of the cabin, but the men'll fix him.

(Elexander brings the footstool.)

Here, Sid, rest your foot here, and don't put any weight on it. The doctor's a-comin'!

(Uncle Silas, Covey, Farmer and Dr. Robinson rush in with their guns.)

UNCLE SILAS: What is it? Did you catch 'em? Great Jumpin' Jupiter!

AUNT SALLY: Here, Doctor. Look at him.

(Doctor kneels by Tom.)

UNCLE SILAS: Sid! Why, Sally, what's the matter here?

DOCTOR: He's got a bullet in his leg, that's what's the matter?

AUNT SALLY: Oh, Sid, don't die! Oh, please don't die, Sid!

DOCTOR: He'll be all right, ma'am. Don't you worry.

UNCLE SILAS: But—but what's happened here?

TOM: Oh, Uncle Silas, we had it planned so beautiful. And now it's all spoiled. You've no idea the trouble we went to, to make it into a grand rescue. We worked every night for a week, diggin' the tunnel, and the trouble we went to, catchin' rats and snakes to keep Jim company—

AUNT SALLY: Sid, what are you talkin' about?

TOM: Why, how we planned to set Jim free!

AUNT SALLY: Sid! Oh, good land! He's out of his head! Doctor!

TOM: No, I ain't out of my head. I know what I'm talking about. And don't call me Sid, neither. Sid Sawyer couldn't think up an escape like this one in a million years.

AUNT SALLY: Not Sid?

UNCLE SILAS: Well, if you're not Sid, then who are you?

TOM: I'm Tom, that's who!

AUNT SALLY: Tom? Tom Sawyer?

TOM: Yes'm.

AUNT SALLY: Well, then—who's this?

TOM: That's my pal, Huck Finn. And he helped me dig the tunnel, and—

UNCLE SILAS: Then you two boys—

COVEY: There's the low-down darky that caused this trouble!

UNCLE SILAS: Leadin' young boys on to scare the life out of this countryside, are you?

FARMER: It's about time we set an example around here!

COVEY: If that boy dies, we ought to lynch him!

UNCLE SILAS: By glory! I got a good notion to—

(Covey and Farmer seize Jim, and drag him across toward gate. Huck breaks in desperately.)

HUCK: No, you don't! You let him go! Jim is the best friend I ever had, even if he is black! He's white inside! He could have got away from you all easy, if he wanted to, but no—he's too white inside to go off and leave a friend with a bullet in his leg. He resked his life for Tom, and he's resked his life for me. And if I ever earn the money, I'm goin' to set him free!

TOM: Don't talk so crazy, Huck. You can't set him free.

HUCK: Why not, I'd like to know?

TOM: Because he's already free! He ain't no slave. He's as free as any cretur that walks this earth!

AUNT SALLY: What does the child mean?

TOM: Widow Douglas set him free a month ago. Said she was sorry she ever thought of sellin' him down the river, and she set him free!

HUCK: Tom! You mean to say we went to all that trouble to set a free slave free!

TOM: Why, sure!

HUCK: But why?

AUNT SALLY: Yes, Tom, why?

TOM: Well, that is a question, I must say. And just like a woman! Why. I wanted the adventure of it, that's what I wanted. And I'd 'a waded neck-deep in blood for the adventure of it!

(Huck and Jim stare at one another, and echo "The adventure of it!" while the rest gaze in flabbergasted amazement.)

HUCK: The adventure of it? Well, I've had enough of the adventure of it. I'm goin' to take the first boat, and go back home, and—

AUNT SALLY: Oh, no you're not.

395

HUCK: Ma'am?

AUNT SALLY: You're a-goin' to stay right here with me!

TOM: Aunt Sally!

UNCLE SILAS: Sally, are you out of your head?

AUNT SALLY: Silas, you know very well you need a bright boy like this around the place. And here's this poor, motherless child, without any home to go to, and I'm just goin' to adopt him, and bring him up like my own boy!

(She advances toward Huck with loving arms. Huck looks about desperately for some source of rescue, but finds none in the astonished faces around him.)

HUCK: Well, now, I'll tell you, ma'am—thank you kindly, but—

AUNT SALLY: And we'll send him to school, and church, and when we get him all civilized, and washed, and combed up—he'll be so different, you just won't even know him!

HUCK *(deciding now to take refuge in flight)*: Yow-w-w-w!

(He is over the fence before anybody can stop him. He halts his rush just long enough to wave his arm, and say—)

So long, Tom!

(And then he is off. The lights black out quickly. The audience starts to applaud, but Huck steps through the curtains to quiet them. Music —Mark Twain No. 2—carries under first part of narration.)

Well — so that's how it all happened. They sent Jim back up home on a steamboat, and I ben tryin' to get a steamboat too — but they watch the wharf too clost. Tom he's well now, and got the bullet rigged up for a watch fob, though he hain't got no watch to hang it on. So I reckon there ain't nothin' more for me to tell about, and I'm rotten glad of it. If I'd 'a knowed what a trouble it was to make a play, I wouldn't 'a tackled it. But it's over now. You was bully to listen like you did.

(Music cross fades to Mark Twain, Side 1, beginning. Huck yawns, reaches for his fishing pole, and begins to sink.)

Jee-hosophat, I'm tired!

(BLACKOUT)

Arthur and the Magic Sword

by

KEITH M. ENGAR

ARTHUR AND THE MAGIC SWORD

By Keith M. Engar

Arthur and the Magic Sword

by KEITH M. ENGAR

CAST

(in order of appearance)

MERLIN
SIR LOT OF ORKNEY
MARGAWSE, his wife, step daughter of King Pendragon
PAGE
SIR URIENS
MORGAN LE FAY, his wife, sister to Margawse
SIR LEODOGRANCE
THE EARL OF BAGDEMAGUS
PAGE
THE ARCHBISHOP OF CANTERBURY
KING UTHER PENDRAGON
SIR LUCAN
FOUR KNIGHTS
LADY IN WAITING
KAY ⎱
ARTHUR ⎰ Children of Sir Hector and Lady Lenore
MARION ⎰
SIR HECTOR
LADY LENORE
MESSENGER
MORDRED, Lot's son

SYNOPSIS OF SCENES

TIME: The sixth century
PLACE: Britain

ACT ONE

SCENE: The great hall of King Pendragon's castle at Camelot.

ACT TWO

SCENE 1. Sir Hector's courtyard, fourteen years later.
SCENE 2. Sir Lot's castle.
SCENE 3. Sir Uriens' castle
SCENE 4. Sir Hector's courtyard, four weeks later.

ACT THREE

SCENE: Church yard in London Town, shortly after.

399

FOREWORD

With the exception of Mordred, the relationships between all characters in this version are fairly consistent with the Arthurian legends, as recorded finally by Malory. Of course there are anachronisms involved in such a character as the Archbishop of Canterbury, but such anachronisms are inherent in the legends themselves. Arthurian tales revolve around a central character who presumably lived in the misty fifth or sixth century, who was given a pseudo-historical treatment by Geoffrey of Monmouth in the twelfth century, whose "history" was highly romanticized and elaborated upon by twelfth to fifteenth century French characters investing such characters as Lancelot, and whose tale was finally set down in Middle English by Sir Thomas Malory in the fifteenth century. Thus, in Malory's Arthurian legends we are not reading about the life and codes of the fifth or sixth century, but of the late Medieval period, twelfth century forward. It naturally follows that we think of Arthur as a late medieval knight, instead of the fur-girthed trial chieftain with the painted tummy that he probably was, and of his retinue as a medieval court.

Considering the above anachronisms, it took no great courage for the writer to perpetrate one of his own, and to have the characters speak in a language that is close to the audience. It did not seem inconsistent to change Middle English to Modern American, any more than it was inconsistent for Malory to change stories written in Latin and French about a Celtic chieftain, into Malory's own contemporary tongue. In both instances, the object was to make the story understandable and alive. Arthur, it is to be hoped, will seem closer to a child in the audience because he speaks in familiar terms.

Grateful acknowledgement is hereby proclaimed for the invaluable suggestions of Dr. Kenneth L. Graham, who directed the premiere performance of ARTHUR AND THE MAGIC SWORD. at the University of Minnesota. in April, 1950.

For Amy, who banished King Lot.

The premiere production of this play was given in 1950 by the University of Minnesota Theatre, at Minneapolis, under the direction of Dr. Kenneth L. Graham.

The pictures used in this book are taken from this production, and are reproduced here by the courtesy of Dr. Graham.

ARTHUR
and the
MAGIC SWORD

by

KEITH M. ENGAR

Copyright, 1967, by

ACT ONE

The scene is the great hall of King Pendragon's castle at Camelot. The setting for this play should be a unit set, merely suggestive of a castle. Realistic representation is not recommended. A stylized treatment would catch the spirit of the play. Essentials are a traveller curtain, which can close to enable shifts to go on backstage, while action is carried on in front of the false proscenium; entrances on either side of the stage, and one behind the dais where the throne sits; a dais and throne; benches on either side of the stage.

Just as the house lights start to dim, music fades up. This music should be suggestive of a primitive mood. (Moussorgsky's "Boris Goudonov", Side 3 of Columbia Album M-516, is appropriate for the purpose.) Also a portent that something powerful is about to happen. After the lights are dimmed, and the music reaches a climax, there should be some spectacular flash of light, a puff of smoke, (ordinary flash powder), and Merlin the Magician appears as though he came out of thin air. He is a rather venerable old gentleman with a long white beard, and a twinkling eye, dressed in a necromancer's costume: long pointed hat, flowing robes covered with mysterious markings such as stars and moons—just what you'd imagine Merlin to look like. Lights come up on Merlin immediately after the flash.

MERLIN: Greetings, you of the twentieth century! I am Merlin the Magician, and I have come fourteen hundred years out of the past, from the seventh century. I've come to take you with me back in time, fourteen hundred years, to the days when knights and fair ladies lived in England. I told you I'm a magician. I can do tricks like this by myself—

(He performs some trick, such as making fruit appear, or a ball disappear. Any novelty shop has simple tricks which will suffice. At the climax of the magic, a slide whistle and a cymbal crash.)

But taking a whole group of people back in time fourteen hundred years is a big trick, so you've got to use your imagination. One thing I will do for you—you see, if I didn't make some magical hocus-pocus, you wouldn't be able to understand the people we're going to see. They didn't speak the same language in those days that you do. They spoke a funny language called Celtic. But I'll fix it so they seem to talk just like you. So now—hold on to your seats, and I'll repeat the magic formula. Ready?

(Lights start to flash crazily, as he croons the formula. Music should reinforce the lights. Suggest "Song of Bernadette", Side E of Decca Album, DA-365.)

Abbali, dabbili, sis boom bah!

We're going back to England, ha ha ha!

Dabbili, mabbili, save those tears!

(Music and lights reach climax, there is a flash, or a cymbal crash, and the curtain opens, as Merlin waves his hand.)

We've just made a trip of fourteen hundred years!

(The stage is dark. Sir Lot is seated on the throne. Only Merlin is set in lights. As Merlin turns to look, music might be faintly heard. Suggest Glasounoff's "Middle Ages", Victor Album DM-1222, Side 4. Lights come up very slowly, during the following speech:)

Well, here we are, in the castle of the ancient King of Britain! Something very important is about to happen. King Pendragon is very sick, and believes he is going to die, so he has called a meeting of the important barons in the land to tell them who should be the next king. But let's see what's going on. The person you see on the throne isn't the King. His name is Sir Lot, and he wants to be King very badly—but let's watch.

(Merlin exits, as the lights on stage reveal Sir Lot sitting on the throne. He is imagining that he is King, commanding people, stroking the throne fondly and possessively. He laughs smugly to himself. Hear-

404

ing a noise from off left, he quickly gets out of the throne, and hides himself in the shadows. As he does, Margawse enters. She is Lot's wife, step-daughter of King Pendragon, very proud and ambitious, but easily cowed by her husband. She is very agitated, and crosses swiftly to the other side of the room. She has a scroll in her hand.)

MARGAWSE *(muttering)*: Where is he?

LOT: Are you looking for me, Margawse?

MARGAWSE: Lot!

LOT *(steps from shadows)*: Yes, dear wife. Why aren't you with your beloved stepfather, the King?

MARGAWSE *(pointing to dais)*: What are you doing there?

LOT *(sits again in the throne)*: Daydreaming. I was pretending I was already "His Majesty, King Lot!!!

MARGAWSE: It's bad luck to be so sure of yourself.

LOT *(snapped back to reality)*: What's disturbed you? *(She involuntarily tries to hide the scroll.)* Give me that scroll.

MARGAWSE *(as Lot starts toward her)*: I—it's just a little song.

LOT *(cutting her off)*: Give it to me! *(Reaches her and snatches the scroll.)*

MARGAWSE: Read it, then. I hope it makes you sweat. *(Lot has unrolled the scroll during her speech. She sits.)*

LOT: How crude, my dear. Well, it's from your sister, Morgan le Fay. *(He reads.)* "Sister, our mother is not away from the castle. She has been kept hidden at Camelot for months." *(Lot is astounded.)* "Find out what you can. I will see you soon. Morgan." . . . How long have you had this?

MARGAWSE: An hour. I've tried to find you.

LOT: This worries me. Why would King Pendragon keep your mother hidden from us?

MARGAWSE: If he's harmed her, I'll kill him!

LOT: Why haven't you known of this before? Is the King too foxy for you?

MARGAWSE *(rises)*: I'm through helping you! *(As she starts to cross in front of him, he grabs her wrist.)*

LOT: Oh, no, you're not! *(As Lot seizes Margawse, a Page enters right,)*

PAGE *(may be a boy, or one of the knights)*: Sir Uriens, and his wife, Morgan le Fay! *(He stands at attention.)*

MARGAWSE *(in a low voice)*: Let go of me! *(Uriens enters, followed by Morgan. He is very flippant in manner and speech, though capable of serious thought and action. His wife is a dark, lithesome thing, who must have something of a hypnotic quality about her. She has pretensions that she is a sorceress.)*

LOT: Greetings, Sir Uriens. Lady Morgan.

URIENS: Sir Lot, as I live and breathe! And his charming wife, Margawse. So nice!

MORGAN: Sister! How are you? *(The Page exits.)*

MARGAWSE: My dear Morgan!

URIENS: Well, my dear Lot, your long waiting will soon be over.

LOT: Waiting?

URIENS: Yes, my astrologer tells me that some great event will happen today. What else could he mean, but the crowning of Sir Lot as King?

MORGAN: Be quiet, you fool!

URIENS: Don't be such a forward hussy, my dear wife, or I shall be obliged to silence you by more direct methods. *(They glare at each other, a split second.)* Anyway, I wasn't addressing you.

LOT: Your good wishes are welcome, but I wouldn't believe your astrologer too closely.

URIENS: Has something happened?

LOT: Hasn't Morgan told you? *(Morgan gestures frantically to Lot to hush.)*

URIENS: Told me what? *(He turns in time to see his wife's gestures. Very icily:)* Is there something I don't know, dear wife—that you've been keeping from me?

MORGAN: Be quiet. Someone is coming. *(Page enters, right, and stands at attention.)*

PAGE: Sir Leodegrance, Baron of Cameliard, and the Earl of Bagdemagus'! *(Pronounced Leo' De Grance'; Cam ee' Leoard; Bag' De Mag' us.) (Leodegrance strides in, a bluff, hearty fellow. Earl of Bagdemagus is timid, a polite gentleman of the old school, well-mannered but slightly ridiculous. With such a name, can you blame him?)*

LEODGRANCE: Well, look who's here, will you? *(He bows.)* Greetings, fair ladies . . . Sir Uriens . . . *and Sir Lot! (Lot bristles. We must see at once that these two fellows dislike each other. The ladies curtsey very formally.)*

URIENS: Greetings right back at you, Sir Leodegrance. Hello, Sir Bag!

BADGEMAGUS *(reserved. Resents the familiarity.)* Pleasure. *(Page exits. Leodegrance and Bagdemagus are grouped stage right, the others stage left.)*

LEODEGRANCE: How are you feeling on this most important day, Sir Lot?

LOT *(very sullen)*: I'm fine, thank you.

LEODEGRANCE: Your broken arm healed?

LOT *(almost snarling)*: Yes. No thanks to you.

URIENS: My dear Lot, let bygones go. If you insist on trying to joust with this madman, you might as well get used to having your body bashed. He's better than you are.

LOT *(violently)*: No one is peaking to you.

MARGAWSE: Husband. Please control your temper.

LEODEGRANCE: Excellent advice. I'll give you a chance for revenge at the next tournament, Sir Lot.

URIENS: Revenge, Sir Leodegrance? Why "revenge"? You beat Sir Lot fairly, didn't you?

LEODEGRANCE: No. I should have fought him with one hand tied behind me.

LOT *(furious)*: You —— *(Margawse restrains him.)*

BAGDEMAGUS: I say, must we have all this? Especially today?

LEODEGRANCE: You're quite right, Sir Bag. I apologize, Sir Lot. One should always be solemn for an important occasion.

LOT: Perhaps you'll soon have reason to be very solemn.

LEODEGRANCE: Yes, if King Pendragon should pass his crown to you, the whole country will have reason to be solemn. But there's no danger. He knows you too well.

LOT: He knows me for what I am—a devoted son-in-law, and servant of the entire kingdom.

URIENS: Everyone knows of the great deeds of Sir Lot. King Pendragon——

MORGAN: Husband, you talk too much.

URIENS: My comfort and joy, be quiet: *(They glare until Uriens composes himself.)* As I was saying, King Pendragon will be wise to make Sir Lot heir to the crown.

LEODEGRANCE: Well, if King Pendragon doesn't, I'll be glad to crown you, Sir Lot—with my sword.

URIENS. Whom do you suggest as a worthy successor to the King? Your noble self, Sir Leodegrance?

LEODEGRANCE: The King's first cousin is named Bagdemagus.

URIENS: Him, King? Fa!

BAGEDEMAGUS: I say, Is there anything terribly wrong with the idea?

URIENS: You can't even rule your own wife.

BAGDEMAGUS: Well, I suppose that's true enough. But what man can? You?

LOT: Try and answer that, Sir Urieus.

MORGAN: Yes, Sir Uriens. Answer that.

URIENS: I should like very much to answer that, my dear wife, by filling your mouth with cold mashed turnip greens. *(Second Page enters from left. May double as a Knight.)*

SECOND PAGE: The Archbishop of Canterbury. *(The Archbishop enters. Page exits. The Archbishop is a venerable gentleman, austere and dignified. All bow deferentially, and murmur "greetings, Your Grace", as the Archbishop mounts the dais.)*

ARCHBISHOP: His Majesty is on his way. I don't have to tell you how sick he is. Any excitement will make him much worse. So I appeal to your conscience to control your tempers on this important day.

MORGAN *(piously)*: Your Grace, you know that we would do nothing to hurt his Blessed Majesty. *(Page enters. Trumpets blare. Suggest Shostakowich' "Symphony No. 5", Side 12, Victor Album DM-619.)*

PAGE: His Majesty, King Pendragon, Monarch of the British Isles! *(Fanfare continues. All on stage kneel. A Guard of Knights enters,*

*carrying banners or spears. All on stage face toward royal entrance,
as the King enters. He is Uther Pendragon, brother of Ambrose, and
father of Arthur. He is suffering from what we call tuberculosis, and
is very thin and wan. He is supported by Sir Lucan, the butler, a gentleman with a drooping moustache. The King seats himself, as the
music ends. Sir Lucan signals one of the Knights to tap the floor
twice with his spear. The crowd stands. Morgan and Margawse rush
solicitously to either side of the throne.)*

MARGAWSE: Why didn't you let me help you, Your Majesty?

KING *(slightly ironical)*: You're very kind, Margawse. *(He coughs a
little.)* Milords. I won't waste words. At last, I can tell you who
the next King will be. *(Reaction from all. Lot and Uriens exchange
confident glances, etc.)* But before I do, I must have your solemn oath
of allegiance to the rightful heir, no matter who it may be.

LOT: Your Majesty.

KING: Well?

LOT *(seems to be fishing)*: May we have the assurance that your choice
is of the noblest blood?

KING: Yes, you have my assurance. And now, Sir Lot, inasmuch as
you are my eldest son-in-law—*(He pauses a moment, and Lot, Margawse, and Morgan assume that Lot will be appointed King on the
spot.)* I call upon you to swear first.

LOT *(disappointed, but playing the obedient son)*: It is only right that
you do, Your Majesty.

KING: Bring in the sword.

LUCAN *(calls)*: His Majesty calls for the royal sword!

VOICE *(offstage)*: His Majesty calls for the royal sword!

VOICE *(further offstage)*: His Majesty calls for the royal sword! *(All
onstage look intently off. After a split-second pause, the Page comes
running on, with the magic sword on a pillow. He kneels in front of
the King, holding the sword up before him.)*

KING: Take your oath, Sir Lot.

LOT *(placing his hand on sword handle)*: I do promise on this royal
sword that I, Lot of Orkney, will defend the rightful heir to Britain's
throne.

KING: Well done, Sir Lot. *(Lot confidently resumes his place.)* Sir
Uriens, Sir Leodegrance, and Sir Bagdemagus, do you follow Sir Lot's
good example?? *(All three cross to sword and touch it, as they say)*:

URIENS, LEODEGRANCE, BAGDEMAGUS: We do. *(They return
to their places. Page gives sword pillow to Morgan, who places it
by the throne. Page stands off to side.)*

KING: I have your solemn promises. And now, milords, I can announce
for all the world my rightful heir to the throne. *(He turns to Lot, with
a beaming countenance. It is my eldest son—(Reaction from Lot and
his party.)* My only son, who was borne to Queen Igraine one week
ago today! *(Violent reaction from all. Lot is deflated as though by*

408

a sledgehammer blow, Uriens is confused, Leodegrance and Badge-magus are overjoyed, as is everyone except Margawse and Morgan. They are furious. Both fight to keep back their real emotions, but the audience must see the murder that is in their eyes.)

MORGAN: You mean, Your Majesty, the Queen—*(explosively)*—My Mother! has given birth to a baby?

KING: Yes, Morgan, your little brother.

LOT: Your Majesty, is this a joke?

KING *(coldly)*: I didn't call you together from the corners of the kingdom, to tell you jokes.

MARGAWSE: My husband means, Your Majesty, that it is difficult to believe.

MORGAN *(as though she doesn't know)*: Where is our mother now?

KING: In this castle, where she has been all the time. I was advised that she should see no one.

MORGAN: Advised? By whom?

KING: Someone who is supposed to be here right now. The royal physician, magician, and barber—Merlin.

ARCHBISHOP: Merlin!

MORGAN: You let that charlatan tell you what to do?

KING: Morgan!

MARGAWSE *(hastily)*: Dear Morgan, control yourself.

URIENS: Your Majesty, I apologize for my wife. She is inclined to crawl on the ceiling when she hears the name Merlin the Magician. Professional jealousy, I suppose. Admit it, dear wife. Merlin fooled you again.

MORGAN: Forgive me, my leige. The shock of hearing the news so suddenly—it has upset me. I can't wait to see my dear mother—and the baby. *(Ominously)*.

MARGAWSE: Yes, your Majesty. May we crave the favor of seeing our mother?

MORGAN: And perhaps taking care of the baby for her?

KING: Well ——

ARCHBISHOP: Your Majesty, if I may be forgiven for speaking, I am shocked that you listen to this Merlin so closely. It seems to me that his advice is strange indeed—to keep mother and daughters away from each other.

MARGAWSE: Thank you, your Grace. Your Majesty, please may we go see our mother, and the child?

ARCHBISHOP: How can your Majesty refuse such a request?

KING: I completely respect Merlin's judgment in such matters—but it does seem strange. Very well, you may go see your mother—but don't upset her.

MORGAN: Oh no, your Majesty. I can't wait to hold that little baby in my arms. *(As she and Margawse run down from the dais, where they were sitting by the throne.)*

MARGAWSE: Yes, it will be so much fun to take care of the child, your Majesty. *(So anxious to go get it, that she is practically running. Both girls turn to the King, bow deeply, and rush out. We must see that they plan to harm the child.)*

LEODEGRANCE: I hope your Majesty hasn't made a mistake. Merlin usually knows what he is about.

LOT: Are you trying to say that my wife will hurt the little prince?

LEODEGRANCE: I don't know what your wife would do, to make you a King.

LOT: I'll stand no more! *(He draws his sword, Leodegrance does likewise. They are able to parry for just an instant, before the King's command stops them. A Knight steps out, and hits their swords upward with his spear.*

KING: Put up your swords! How dare you draw in the King's presence? *(They both put swords in scabbards.)*

LOT: I crave pardon, Your Majesty, but this knave has worn my patience raw.

KING *(coughs)*: How can I die peacefully, while you two are enemies? I know you have wished to become King, Sir Lot. I know how you've plotted ——

LOT *(indignant)*: Your Majesty!

KING *(visibly weakened)*: Don't argue. You want to be a King, Sir Lot? Very well, I'll make you a King. *(All are astounded.)*

LEODEGRANCE: Your Majesty, the little prince!

KING: I didn't say King of what. I have resolved that I will confer upon you the title, King Lot of Orkney. *(As the King says the words, he points his mace at Lot.)*

LOT: What kind of trick is this? Are you trying to buy me off with a hollow title?

LEODEGRANCE: Watch your tongue, "King Lot".

URIENS: I think it's wonderful. Forgive his temper, Your Majesty. "King Lot"! *(He laughs.)*

KING: And I confer upon the rest of you the title "King". *(Repeats business of pointing mace as he speaks.)* But you are King only over your own domain, and owe higher allegiance to my son, the rightful heir.

URIENS: Well, think of that. Me, a king. King Uriens. Humph! And King Leodegrance. And even King Bagdemegus! Well, well.

LOT: May I ask if this is Merlin's idea?

KING: It is.

ARCHBISHOP: Your Majesty, it's dangerous to trust Merlin so much.

KING: Perhaps, your Grace. But he is always right. *(A woman's scream is heard affstage.)*

ARCHBISHOP: In Heaven's name, what was that? *(Lady in Waiting to the Queen comes rushing in.)*

LADY *(kneeling to the King)*: Your Majesty!

410

KING: What is it?

LADY: Something has happened to the baby. The little prince has disappeared!

KING: What? *(The entire company is shocked.)*

LADY: Someone has stolen the little prince!

LEODEGRANCE: Margawse.

KING*(over Leodegrance's speech)*: Search the castle! Search the castle! *(Great activity. Lot and Uriens exeunt the same direction as the Lady in Waiting, left. Lights dim during activity.)*

LEODEGRANCE *(to Bagdemagus, as they rush out, the same way.)* Find Morgan and Margawse, and we'll find the baby.

LUCAN: What about your Majesty?

KING: Leave me alone, you fool. Find that baby!

LUCAN *(to Guards)*: Search the castle. *(Lucan creaks out. The Knights follow. The King is alone. The magic sword must be lying at his side.)*

KING *(coughing weakly)*: Merlin was right. I should never have trusted Margawse and Morgan. *(Fit of coughing. Two figures appear stage left—Lot and Uriens.)*

LOT: He's alone.

KING: Who's that?

LOT: Me. King Lot.

KING: Have you found the baby?

LOT: What do I care about the baby. It's you I'm looking for. *(He brazenly circles around the throne so that he is standing on one side, Uriens on the other.)*

KING: Mind your place.

LOT: Where's your Guard to make me? Now, King Pendragon, I'll dictate a few terms.

KING: You can't touch me. It doesn't matter when I die.

LOT: But it matters when that baby dies! But he's not going to die, if you denounce him as a fraud, and declare me King! *(Lot has drawn his sword, and starts to advance toward the King. But Uriens steps in his way.)*

URIENS: Don't touch him, Lot!

LOT *(shaking him off)*: You fool, let me alone. *(King Pendragon picks up the magic sword.)*

URIENS: Get what you want, but don't harm the King.

LOT *(pushing Uriens out of the way)*: I knew I couldn't trust your tender soul. *(As Lot starts again for the King, Uriens draws sword, and confronts him.)*

URIENS: I'm with you, Lot, but I won't let you hurt the King.

KING *(stands holding magic sword)*. Thank you, King Uriens. But come ahead, King Lot. Since you can't best Leodegrance in a fight, perhaps you'll find me easy game.

LOT: Take your last breath! *(Lot starts for the King, after feinting*

Uriens out of position, but the King raises the magic sword, brandishes it. The lights blackout, and some sort of flash or cymbal crash near the King stops all activity. Lights come back immediately. Uriens and Lot hold their eyes a moment.) The magic sword!

URIENS: You can't touch him now, Lot. Come.

LOT: No! I've gone too far to stop. *(Leodegrance appears in the shadows left, unseen by anyone except the audience.)* You have two tricks on me—the third is mine. *(He is slowly advancing on the King, who feebly tries to lift the sword to defend himself. The previous effort was too much for him.)*

LEODEGRANCE: And mine, King Lot.

LOT *(whirling to face him)*: Leodegrance!

LEODEGRANCE: Now we'll settle up.

LOT: Come on, Uriens.

LEODEGRANCE *(as they start to fight)*: Two will make it interesting. *(Leodegrance starts to back them out, right.)* Your Majesty, we haven't found the baby yet, but we'll turn the earth upside down until we do. And now I'll give these knaves a haircut with my sword. *(He drives them offstage. We hear the clash of swords fade off. Alone, the King steps toward Leodegrance's exit as if anxious over the outcome. There is a cackle behind his throne, and a dim figure emerges, from the curtain which is draped behind the throne.)*

KING: Who is it? Morgan?

MERLIN: Well, Morgan Le Fay doesn't have a beard like this. *(He steps into the light. He has a bundle in his arms.)*

KING: Merlin.

MERLIN: Who else? And here's your baby. *(Gives him to the King.)* I got him before Morgan. *(The King has seated himself at the bench down right.)* Take your last look at him.

KING: Last look?

MERLIN: You must have been able to figure out by now that your cute little son's life isn't worth that—*(snaps fingers)*—around here now.

KING: He's not going to die!

MERLIN: Not if I can help it. But he can't stay here, and I'm sure of that.

KING: But he's the prince!

MERLIN: And he'll be a greater King than you someday. If you do what I say this instant.

KING: Well?

MERLIN: Give me the babe, and I'll take him to a lady I know who has just lost her little baby boy. She and her husband can rear him as their own son.

KING: But ——

MERLIN: We must hurry. Well?

KING *(with resolution)*: He must live, and be King. All right. *(Rises.)* But Magician, see that he lives. For if one hair of his head is harmed,

I vow vengeance, be you magician, devil, or demigod.

MERLIN: Give him to me. *(Takes baby.)* Take your royal locket. Break it in two. *(King does so, as Merlin tallks.)* Give me half, and give the other half to the Archbishop of Canterbury. Tell him nothing, except that he will know when to use it. *(Merlin takes locket.)* Goodbye, Your Majesty.

KING *(as Merlin leaves)*: Remember my vow.

MERLIN *(as he exits behind throne)*: Yes, your Majesty. *(The King siuks onto the throne, Leodegrance comes bursting in.)*

LEODEGRANCE: Your Majesty, Lot and Uriens went two different directions, and before I could decide which one to follow—*(He gestures helplessly with his hands.)* they both escaped!

ARCHBISHOP *(entering from left)*: Your Majesty, Margawse and Morgan have been found, but they don't have the baby.

KING: I know who has him. *(Leodegrance and Archbishop start to interrupt.)* Don't question me. Sir Leodegrance, and milord Bishop of Canterbury, I charge you act as regent to the realm, after my death, until my son can reign.

ARCHBISHOP: But your Majesty——

LEODEGRANCE: I don't understand.

KING: There will be wars in my kingdom, because Lot and Uriens won't accept you. But you must see that my son will have a kingdom. Take this locket, Your Grace, as symbol of your regency. You will know how to use it, when the time comes. Now leave me, and call my Guard. *(Leodegrance and Archbishop, very puzzled, bow to the King, and start toward exit, as the lights black out. The traveller is drawn, and music feathers in. Suggest Piston's "Incredible Flutist", Side 4, RCA Victor Album, DM-621.)*

INTERIM

(Merlin appears before the curtain.)

MERLIN: Poor King Pendragon died soon after I took his son from him, but he was able to see that the little baby was in a wonderful home. And the King was right about all the wars. As soon as Lot heard the King was dead, he set up a bellow that he should be King, and a lot of foolish people believed him, as they believe anyone who yells loud and long enough. But just as many others believed Leodegrance and the Archbishop of Canterbury, so soon people were fighting each other. All the lords called themselves king—King Lot, King Uriens, King Leodegrance, and King Badgemagus. Aren't those funny names? Well, things went on badly for fourteen years, and everybody got a little older—fourteen and a half years older. People soon tired of fighting, so the big lords made their castles into huge fortresses, and were suspicious of strangers. Everybody stayed close to home—and just between us, I think people got sick and tired of seeing the same faces every day. People weren't very happy those days. *(The music changes to a little sprightlier air. Suggest the latter part of the above record.)* Now, one of King Leodegrance's friends was named Sir Hector. He was a fine gentleman. Had two sons and a daughter. I want you to meet them—I think you'll find them interesting people. Why don't we see how they lived? *(During the above speech, the stage should be readied for the next scene. Merlin waves his hand, the curtains part, and—*

414

Act Two, Scene 1, of ARTHUR AND THE MAGIC SWORD
As presented by the University of Minnesota Theatre at Minneapolis

ACT TWO

SCENE 1. *We see Sir Hector's courtyard. Essential entrances are:*
(1) Into the Manor House, (2) the gate to the outer courtyard, through
which outside visitors come, (3) A stage entrance which appears as though
it is just a continuation of the inner courtyard. If a unit set is used, the
dais is now the platform in front of Sir Hector's manor door.

As Merlin waves the curtains open, Kay is shooting an arrow at an
offstage target. The arrows should be tipped with rubber—removable
pencil erasers work very well—and their flight should be stopped by an old
drape, burlap, or any substance that will deaden the noise. Strict offstage
discipline, to keep away from target area, should be observed during the
shooting scene. After Kay shoots, Arthur takes his place. He shoots just
before the first line of dialogue. Marion sits at one side.)

MERLIN: There is Sir Hector's courtyard, and there are Sir Hector's
    sons, shooting arrows. The taller one is named Kay. The other boy
    is Arthur—quite a boy, too. *(At this point, Arthur should be shoot-*
    ing.) And the girl's name is Marion. Sh, let's see what's going on.
MARION *(cheers loudly, for Arthur's shot)*: Yea, you beat him!
ARTHUR: There, how's that?
KAY *(with quiet frustration)*: All right. All right. So you win. *(He sits.)*
MARION: Kay is mad, and I am glad, and I know how to tease him.

(Note: None of this bickering should be nasty. Kay does not really become angry, until Arthur wins his bow.)

ARTHUR: Marion!

KAY: Well, don't turn to stone, Arthur. Go get the arrows, so we can shoot again.

ARTHUR: I got 'em last time. It's your turn.

KAY: It's not my turn. Besides, I'm older than you.

ARTHUR: What's that got to do with it?

KAY *(stands in his magnificence)*: You like to forget that I'll be a knight in a few weeks, and you'll be my squire. So you'd better start to learn how to serve me right now. You go get these arrows.

ARTHUR: You always bring that up. "I'm older than you." You might be older, but I'll bet you can't shoot any better than I can.

KAY: Pooh! I can shoot better than you, any day of the week.

ARTHUR: You want to bet?

KAY: Well—ah—no. Of course not. It's beneath me to bet with you.

MARION: Oh no it isn't. I'll go get the arrows. *(She starts off left, toward the inner courtyard. Kay catches her.)*

KAY: You come back here.

MARION: Hey!

KAY: I said I wanted Arthur to go get these arrows.

MARION: Let me go! *(She breaks away from him, and runs behind Arthur. Kay chases her, and they squirm around Arthur.)*

ARTHUR: Hey, stop making a Maypole out of me.

KAY *(as he catches Marion)*. Now—

MARION: Arthur, don't let him hit me!

KAY *(suddenly ashamed, when he sees how ridiculous he is acting)*. Oh, who's going to hit you? *(He lets her go. Arthur is embarrassed for Kay.)* I just wanted to make you behave.

ARTHUR: I'll go get the arrows, Kay.

KAY: No. I guess it's my turn. *(He starts off.)* Even if it isn't, I'll still get 'em. *(Exit.)*

MARION: He was going to hit me!

ARTHUR: Well, I don't blame him, Marion.

MARION: Don't you get mad at me.

ARTHUR *(laughs)*: I'm not mad at you. And if you didn't tease Kay so much, he wouldn't get mad.

MARION: But he's so much fun to tease!

ARTHUR: Well, that's not a very good way to have fun. Now be a good little girl.

MARION: That's impossible.

ARTHUR: Well, then, be pretty good. If you're nice to Kay, he'll be nice to you.

MARION: I'll try—for awhile. *(Kay enters with the arrows.)*

KAY: Well, here they are. Come on, let's shoot again.

ARTHUR: Go ahead. You got the arrows.

KAY: Very well. *(He takes an arrow, and resumes position.)* Move back, Marion. I can still see your face. *(She does so, making a face at him. Arthur pantimimes "Don't". Kay takes careful aim, and lets his arrow fly. A moment's pause. Kay's face lights up.)* Ha! Look at that!

MARION: Real good, Kay.

ARTHUR: That's a beauty! *(Kay is a little surprised at Marion's reaction.)*

MARION: Now aren't you sorry you bet with him, Arthur?

ARTHUR: What? *(Kay's eyes pop in surprise at Marion.)*

MARION: Don't tell me you're going to claim you didn't bet.

ARTHUR: You're addled. I didn't bet with Kay. He said it was beneath him.

MARION: Oh Arthur, he did too bet! You're just trying to worm out of it because he has a good shot.

ARTHUR *(a little stung)*: Who said I was worming out? I'll bet with him.

KAY: You will? What will you put up—your bow against mine?

MARION: That's a dirty trick, Kay. I mean—*(She gulps. She is getting in deeper than she thought.)* I didn't think you'd bet on anything like that. I thought you'd just bet for fun.

KAY *(superior)*: Nobody is speaking to you, child. *(Marion fumes.)* Well, Arthur—maybe you'd rather bet that old broken locket you wear.

ARTHUR: No. Merlin said I should always keep it.

KAY: Oh, so you're afraid you'll lose. *(He enjoys very much the unusual position of having a good chance of winning.)*

ARTHUR: I am not.

MARION: Don't let him talk you into it, Arthur.

KAY: Whose side are you on, anyway? Well, Arthur, I'll understand if you don't want to. I do have a rather good shot.

ARTHUR: Who said I didn't want to? I'll put up my bow. Look out of the way.

MARION: But Arthur, you've never played for keeps before.

ARTHUR: Be quiet, Marion. Move back, Kay. *(Kay is ill at ease, but still very confident. However he does his best to upset Arthur.)*

KAY *(just as Arthur is about to shoot.)* Are you sure you have the best arrow? A lot's at stake.

ARTHUR: I've got my best arrow. Now be quiet.

KAY: That goes for you too, Marion. *(The last is said as Arthur is getting ready to pull his bow up again. He gives Kay a dirty look, then takes careful aim. Just as he is shooting, Kay coughs, and Arthur lets the arrow fly wild, so that we see it is a bad shot.)* Ha! You didn't even hit the target.

ARTHUR: You coughed!

KAY: Give me the bow.

MARION: But you didn't win it fairly, Kay. You made him miss when

417

you coughed. And you did it on purpose.

KAY: I did not. Come on Arthur, Give me your bow. You lost.

ARTHUR: Here. *(He gives Kay the bow. Arthur must never sulk. Kay is a little non-plussed, and perhaps feels pretty cheap.)* I guess it's fairly yours.

MARION: Oh Arthur, it's all my fault. I was just doing what you said, and then look what happened.

KAY: What are you talking about? What did Arthur say?

MARION: He told me to be nice to you, so I am, only I didn't think you'd bet for keeps.

KAY *(hurt and mad)*: So you're telling people to be nice to me now!

MARION: If you were any kind of sport, you'd let Arthur keep his bow.

KAY: So now I'm a poor sport for keping what I won. All right. I'll show you what a sport I am. I'll let you have another chance, Arthur. Fair enough?

ARTHUR: What do you mean?

KAY: I'll put up my bow, and yours that I won, against that old locket.

ARTHUR: But Merlin said—

KAY: Merlin is an old fool. But if you don't want it—if you're afraid—

ARTHUR: I'm not afraid. I'll do it. Go ahead. Shoot.

KAY: Oh, no. I'll keep the same shot. I'm just giving you another one.

MARION: That's not fair.

ARTHUR: Shush, Marion. All right, Kay. *(Takes new bow from Kay.)* I'll let you keep your shot. You don't have good ones very often.

KAY: And don't get smart.

ARTHUR: Now be quiet this time. *(Arthur takes careful aim, and shoots. There is a moment's pause, then Arthur smiles, and Marion jumps up and down, shouting.)*

MARION: You beat him! You beat him!

ARTHUR *(quite amazed)*: I sure did.

KAY *(thoroughly crushed and burning inside)*. Well, you don't have to crow. *(Thrusts his bow at Arthur.)* Here.

MARION: You're mad again because you got beat.

KAY: You little scamp. Keep out of this. He didn't beat me fairly.

ARTHUR: I did too.

KAY: Humph! You had two chances against my one.

ARTHUR: But that was your fault. You coughed.

KAY: Quite by accident.

ARTHUR: Who said it wasn't?

KAY: You implied it wasn't.

ARTHUR: I didn't either, and if you're going to act like such a churl, I won't shoot with you again. *(Starts to exit toward target, with bow.)*

KAY: I won't let you, when I'm a knight, and you're my squire. You'll be beneath me then—you nobody. *(Malice consumes him.)* Because you're not even my real brother.

ARTHUR *(stops short)*: What did you say?

KAY *(sees Arthur's shock, and hastens to exploit his triumph)*: You heard me. You must know that my father and mother aren't really your parents. You're an orphan, and my mother and father took you in just because that old fool Merlin told them to. I heard 'em say so the other day.

ARTHUR: That's not true. And don't you call Merlin an old fool. He's best friend.

KAY: He's the only one who'd be your friend—you nobody.

MARION: Stop it, Kay! You're so mean that I don't think *you* could be our brother.

KAY *(stung)*: I—Arthur, I— *(He is about to say "I'm sorry and I didn't mean it and it isn't true", when a raucous laugh is heard offstage from the direction of the gate to the outside.)* Who's that—Merlin! *(The last word is said as Merlin enters from the direction of the outside gate.)*

MERLIN: Well, stop me if I didn't interrupt something. Hello!

ARTHUR: Hello, Merlin.

MERLIN: And what do you mean, Kay, by calling me an old fool?

KAY *(terrified)*: What?

MERLIN: That's not nice—and do you know what I do to people who aren't nice to me? I turn 'em into skarlarlomps! *(He approaches Kay, waving his hand magically.)* Do you want to be a skarlarlomp? *(He bites out the last word, and makes a mysterious pass at Kay, who lets out a ghastly shriek, and runs into the Manor entrance. Merlin and Marion laugh. Arthur alone is solemn. Merlin seats himself.)* Well now, Arthur my boy, what's the horrible thing that makes your face so long?

ARTHUR *(stoically, not whining)*: Nothing.

MARION: It is too something. Is it true what Kay said, Merlin, about Arthur being a nobody?

MERLIN *(laughing)*: What, did Kay say that? Well, I'll tell you a secret, Marion. *(Draws her to him, mock seriously:)* Arthur isn't a nobody, because he's sitting right there, see? And if you can see him, he's got a body, and therefore it must logically follow that he's not a nobody, understand?

ARTHUR *(standing)*: But he said that I'm not his brother, and that my father and mother—*(gulps)*—Sir Hector and Lady Lenore aren't really my father and mother. That's not true, is it, Merlin? *(No answer.)* Well?

MERLIN: I don't quite know the answer to that one.

ARTHUR: Then it's true.

MARION *(almost in tears)*: But you're still my brother.

ARTHUR: I'm nobody's brother.

MERLIN: Now see here, son—

ARTHUR: Don't call me that. It's all your fault. Kay said you told them to call me their son.

MERLIN: But Arthur—

ARTHUR—That's not even my name. I don't know who I am. *(He wanders offstage, muttering, with the bows in his hand.)* Stupid old world. Stupid old place. I'm just a stupid old nobody. *(Exits in direction of archery target.)*

MARION: Poor Arthur. *(Runs to Merlin.)* Is it true, what Kay said? Really true?

MERLIN *(very confidentially)*: Can you keep a secret?

MARION *(equally confidential)*: Yes.

MERLIN *(looks mysteriously around. Loud whisper:)* I won't tell you.

MARION: Oh! I think you're mean. *(She turns away, and stamps her foot.)*

MERLIN *(laughing)*: Don't worry, dear, because something wonderful is going to happen to Arthur in a few weeks—but you mustn't tell a soul. *(We hear Kay's voice offstage, within the Manor House, saying, "And he waved his hand at me", and Kay and Sir Hector enter. Merlin continues his speech without interruption.)* Now you run along and find Arthur, and cheer him up.

MARION *(leaving)*: All right, Merlin. *(Exit, in same direction as Arthur. and Sir Hector enter, from the Manor).*

KAY: And there he is, Father. He said he was going to turn me into something awful. A lump of something. *(Sir Hector is a ruddy-faced gentleman, immensely likable, we hope, with a semblance of a sense of humor.)*

HECTOR: Now Kay, you take life too seriously. By my beard. he'd be hard put. You're already quite a lump-head, eh, Merlin? *(Both laugh.)* Greetings, old friend.

MERLIN: And to you, Sir Hector. *(Hector suddenly remembers that he is supposed to have Guards to sound an alarm when strangers approach.)*

HECTOR: How did you get into my castle grounds without making a fuss? Was my Guard asleep?

MERLIN: No. I just made myself invisible, and walked past them.

HECTOR: Humph! Thank Heaven you're my friend. Now just what have you been doing to my boy Kay? He told me you were going to jinx him.

MERLIN: Just a little joke. I wanted to see you, and Kay thought this would be the best way to get you out here, eh, Kay?

KAY: Humph! *(Kay exits in the direction of the outside entrance.)*

HECTOR: Well, sir—

MERLIN *(imitating what Hector's inflection would be if Hector were speaking)*: To what am I indebted for this visit? *(Hector's mouth moves a little, then he stares at Merlin, who is not looking at him.)* I believe those are the words in your mind. I'll wait until the Archbishop and Leodegrance get here.

HECTOR: What?

MERLIN: They're coming to see you about making Kay a Knight?

HECTOR *(flabbergasted)*: Yes. But I thought it was a secret. You know everything!

MERLIN: Oh, it's nothing. A little magic, you know. *(Hector fumes. Merlin looks the other way, as if he were trying to see what has happened to Arthur. After a split-second pause, he speaks casually.)* Yes, it's a problem.

HECTOR: What's a problem?

MERLIN: That the Archbishop doesn't like me, and will be angry because I'm here.

HECTOR *(icily)*: Will you kindly stop reading my thoughts? *(Offstage male voices—"Sound the alarm!" Horsemen approaching the Castle!" "Raise the drawbridge!" "Man the parapets!" Music: a single trumpet call. (Suggest Victor Sound Effects Record 27676-A, Track 4.) Much noise and bustle offstage.)* Sounds like a raid! *(He exits in the direction of the outside entrance. Two or three extras rush across stage after him.)*

MERLIN *(as he dodges all the runners)*: No, just the Archbishop and Leodegrance. *(Lady Lenore enters. She is a very warm-hearted mother, as you would expect.)*

LENORE: Is it a raid? Where are the children?

MERLIN: They're safe, and it's not a raid, Lady Lenore.

LENORE *(a little frightened)*: Merlin. What are you doing here?

MERLIN: You'll soon know. *(Marion comes running, and goes to her mother.)*

LENORE: Where's Arthur and Kay?

MARION: I don't know about Kay, but Arthur's up on the parapets.

LENORE: That's dangerous.

MERLIN: There's nothing to be afraid of, Lady Lenore. It's just the Archbishop of Canterbury and Leodegrance. *(Voices offstage: "Peace Ho! It's the Archbishop of Canterbury and King Leodegrance. Lower the drawbridge!" A trumpet call.)* See?

LENORE: Dear me. I'll have to tell the steward to hurry the feast. Excuse me, Merlin. *(She exits into the Manor House.)*

MARION *(lingers behind a little)*: Are you sure you don't want to tell me who Arthur is?

MERLIN: Sh! *(He looks mysteriously around, shakes his head up and down affirmatively, then says, aloud:)* No!

MARION: Oh, you're mean! Mother! *(She runs after Lady Lenore.)*

HECTOR *(enters in a hurry)*: You're right as usual. They'll be here in a second. *(Hesitates a moment.)* Now Merlin—

MERLIN: No. I came to see the Archbishop, and see him I will. Tell him I'm an old friend of the family. *(Slight pause, and without looking at Hector.)* And don't swear at me so.

HECTOR: Will you kindly stop reading my thoughts. *(Kay runs in from outside gate.)*

KAY: They'll be here in a second. I wonder what they're coming for.

HECTOR: Well, I might as well tell you, son. They're here to see if you're ready to be made a knight.

KAY *(elated)*: What?

HECTOR *(laughs)*: I thought you'd like that. *(Offstage voice: "The Archbishop of Canterbury and King Leodegrance!" They come striding in. The Archbishop is dressed in a riding costume, or at least plainer dress than in the first scene. Leodegrance should wear suggestions of armor.)*

LEODEGRANCE: Greetings, Sir Hector.

HECTOR: King Leodegrance. Greetings, your Grace. We are honored. *(He bows to the Archbishop.)*

ARCHBISHOP: Sir Hector. *(Nods his head, and blesses him.)*

MERLIN: Hello, your Grace.

ARCHBISHOP: Merlin! What are you doing here?

HECTOR: He's just leaving. Aren't you Merlin?

MERLIN *(smiling sweetly at the boiling Sir Hector)*. No.

LEODEGRANCE *(laughs)*: Greetings, Merlin.

MERLIN: Hello, Leodegrance.

ARCHBISHOP *(ignoring Merlin's presence)*: Sir Hector, is this the boy? *(Indicating Kay)*

HECTOR: Yes, your Grace. This is my eldest son, Kay. *(Kay steps forward into the group.)*

ARCHBISHOP: He looks to be a fine boy.

HECTOR *(proud parent)*: He is, your Grace.

MERLIN *(with just a touch of irony)*: He certainly is.

HECTOR: Merlin!

MERLIN: I'm just agreeing with you.

ARCHBISHOP *(pointedly, at Merlin)*: Is there someplace we can talk to the boy—in private?

HECTOR: Yes, your Grace. Inside. I believe, though, that my wife has some refreshment for you first. Kay, run in and tell her that we'll be right in.

KAY: Yes, Father. *(Exits into Manor)*

HECTOR: I fear we are very informal in this Manor, your Grace.

MERLIN: In that case, I'm sure you won't mind if I speak to your guests a moment before they go in.

HECTOR: Of all the—

MERLIN: Nerve! Yes.

ARCHBISHOP: I would say that you have that in abundance.

MERLIN: Your Grace, I have something else in abundance which you have too.

ARCHBISHOP: Well?

MERLIN: Desire for peace in Britain.

ARCHBISHOP: Humph!

MERLIN: The time has come to place the crown on the rightful heir to Britain's throne.

LEODEGRANCE: What?

ARCHBISHOP: And just who is this King of yours?

MERLIN: I won't say, yet.

LEODEGRANCE: When will you say?

MERLIN: Four weeks hence, when the Archbishop calls a meeting of all barons, including King Lot and King Uriens.

ARCHBISHOP: Are you crazy? They'd never come to a meeting, unless with an army, to destroy us.

MERLIN: If your Grace makes quite clear that you have new evidence to indicate who the next King is, they will come, if only to see who it is.

LEODEGRANCE: What have we to lose, Your Grace. I vote for the meeting.

ARCHBISHOP: I'm still doubtful, but I'll try once more. Peace is worth my pride. All right, Merlin. Tell me what I must do.

MERLIN: When are you making Kay a knight?

ARCHBISHOP: Four weeks today.

MERLIN: Call a meeting for that day, in London Town, of all the barons. Tell them that a tournament will be held, that the new King will be chosen, and promise a miracle.

ARCHBISHOP: A miracle?

MERLIN: Well, maybe not your kind of miracle, but I'll cook up something.

ARCHBISHOP: And who will produce the rightful heir?

MERLIN: He will produce himself.

LEODEGRANCE: I wonder what would have happened if King Pendragon's little son had lived.

MERLIN: Nothing would be changed. Perhaps he did live.

LEODEGRANCE: Unlikely. Where could he be? *(Arthur enters, muttering, with his head down, at beginning of above speech, and bumps right into King Leodegrance.)*

ARTHUR: Old castle, stupid old bow, stupid old Kay—*(As he collides with Leodegrance, Arthur steps back, his eyes popping.)* Pardon me, Sire.

LEODEGRANCE: Isn't this your youngest son, Sir Hector?

HECTOR: Yes, my leige.

LEODEGRANCE: Well, the way he's going around with his head in the dirt, it looks as if he's training to be a professor.

ARTHUR: I can't train to be anything, Sire.

LEODEGRANCE: Huh?

HECTOR: Arthur, is that a proper manner of speaking? What are you talking about?

ARTHUR *(stepping toward him)*: You should know, Sir Hector.

HECTOR: What's that, sirrah? What did you call me?

ARTHUR: What else can I call you, Sire? You're not my father.

HECTOR *(visibly shaken)*: What in the—who's been telling you stories?

MERLIN: Careful, Sir Hector. Probably the lad heard servants gossiping. But if Arthur continues to talk like that, he'll be bewitched.

HECTOR: Humph! If he talks like that any more, I know he'll be switched. You're not to talk like that any more, understand?

ARTHUR: But sir—

HECTOR: I'll show you who your father is, if you keep on.

ARTHUR *(quelling his feelings, like a soldier)*: Yes sir.

HECTOR: That's better now. Oh, I apologize to your Grace, and to you, King Leodegrance. Perhaps we can go in now, and have some refreshment.

ARCHBISHOP: That will be nice.

LEODEGRANCE *(as they all start to move in, kindly, to Arthur)*: Come on Arthur. *(Arthur starts to respond to him, then turns back to Merlin. Manfully)*:

ARTHUR: I'm sorry if I said anything mean to you, Merlin.

MERLIN: Tush. Run along. I have work to do. I will see you all in four weeks—if I'm invited to Kay's knighting.

HECTOR *(smiles sickly at Archbishop, who nods. Very unenthusiastically, to Merlin:)* By all means, do come.

MERLIN: Thank you. Goodbye, gentlemen. *(The lights dim out, and the traveller curtain draws shut.)*

ARTHUR AND THE MAGIC SWORD

INTERIM

(When the lights come up, Merlin is standing before the curtain. Spot light up on Merlin. Music fades up as lights dim, and holds under Merlin's speech. (Suggest "Incredible Flutist", Side 4.)

MERLIN *(to the audience)*: Well, as you can see, I had two problems: First of all, poor Arthur was all confused about his mother and father. Wasn't that a mean thing of Kay to tell him? And second, what was to be done with the poor country of Britain. Well, I think you will find out that the two problems, who Arthur's parents were, and who was to be King of England, were related. Anyway, the Archbishop sent out his heralds with news of the meeting in London Town. Let's look in, just a moment, to see how King Lot of Orkney and his wife Margawse took the news. *(Merlin makes a pass with his hands, and—*

ACT TWO

SCENE 2. *The left-stage side of the curtain butterflies up to reveal Lot and Margawse. Lot holds a scroll. Lights are focussed on Lot and Margawse. Blackout on Merlin.)*

LOT: So there's to be a meeting on this matter of the King.
MARGAWSE: You'd be a fool to go.
LOT: I wonder. Do you believe I am the rightful King?
MARGAWSE: Of course.
LOT: Then what have we to fear? *(Looks at Scroll.)* A miracle will occur, it says in this message. But it doesn't say what kind of miracle.
MARGAWSE: What are you coming to?
LOT: Morgan le Fay is a sorceress. I wonder how she is at making miracles. *(He calls:)* Messenger! *(To Margawse:)* I think I'll send a little note. *(Messenger enters the area. One of the knights may double in this role.)*
MESSENGER: Yes, your Majesty.
LOT: I want you to listen carefully, and then ride to King Uriens' castle as quickly as you can. What I tell you must be given to Morgan le Fay, and not King Uriens. That's important, understand?
MESSENGER: Yes, your Majesty.
LOT: Now listen carefully.. *(As he starts to disclose his plot to the Messenger, the lights blackout, and the curtain drops.)*

425

INTERIM

(Spot light comes up again on Merlin, center stage, before the curtain. Music may be used again, if desired, to suggest the Courier's ride. (Suggest "Middle Ages", Side 3.)

MERLIN: And so Lot gave the Courier his message. As you see, King Lot didn't trust King Uriens. The messenger rode to King Uriens' castle, and found Morgan Le Fay, and delivered King Lot's message to her. Let's see how she takes the news. *(Lights fade on Merlin, as he makes a magical sign with his hands, and—*

ACT TWO

SCENE 3. *The right side of the curtain butterflies up, to reveal Morgan and the Messenger. A bench should be near the curtain. Lights are focused on Morgan and Messenger.)*

MORGAN: And I'm to concoct a miracle that will make Lot King of Britain, eh? . . . H'm . . . Anything else?

MESSENGER: Yes, your Majesty. He directs me to tell you that he will help your miracle, by having his army hidden in the outskirts of London, ready to capture all the barons.

URIENS *(offstage)*: He will, eh? *(Messenger draws sword, Morgan turns quickly.)*

MORGAN: What's that?

URIENS *(entering lighted area)*: Just your devoted husband, whom you seem to trust so much. *(To Messenger:)* You may go back to your Master. Tell him Uriens is still lord of his own domain, but that he too will have an army at London—to help King Lot.

MESSENGER *(looks toward Morgan)*: Is that all?

URIENS *(unusually stern)*: I said it was. Get out!

MESSENGER: Yes, Sire. *(He bows, and exits.)*

MORGAN: No one invited you to inquire into my affairs, with your big nose.

URIENS *(his urbane self again)*: Dear wife, I'm just trying to show my interest in your affairs. I'm going to be very curious to know if your magic works better than Merlin's. *(Uriens sits.)*

MORGAN: Merlin?

URIENS: Of course. Haven't you figured by now who must be behind the "miracle"? Ah, yes, it will be very exciting. Morgan Le Fay versus Merlin the Magician. The winner take the kingdom.

MORGAN: Yes, you're right. Who else would be clever enough to call a meeting, and then promise a miracle. Husband, you have greater sense than I thought.

URIENS: I would like to accept that as a compliment, dear wife, and I

426

will. *(He stands.)* But don't waste your time talking to me. You've got to get your formulas brewing. I'm going to place bets on the winner. The match of the century: Morgan Le Fay against the defending champion, Merlin the Magician! Do you quote any odds, dear wife?

MORGAN *(furious)*: Oh! *(She stalks off, Uriens looking after her, laughing, as the lights black out.)*

INTERIM

(Merlin's spotlight fades up, to disclose him before the curtain.)

MERLIN: Well, aren't they nasty people? Except Uriens. He is a good fellow, in a pleasantly obnoxious way. Well, four weeks passed, and the great day finally came. Kay had to stand guard over his armor all night—the vigil, you know—that was part of the ceremony. While everybody waited for the time to pass, poor Arthur sat by himself. *(The spot light blacks out on Merlin, and—*

Act Two, Scene 4, of ARTHUR AND THE MAGIC SWORD
As presented by the University of Minnesota Theatre at Minneapolis

ACT TWO

SCENE 4. *The traveller opens, as lights come up to reveal Sir Hector''s courtyard again. Arthur is sitting alone, thinking. He hears someone.)*

ARTHUR: Who is it?

MARION *(entering)*: May I be with you, Arthur?

ARTHUR: I don't care.

MARION *(hurt)*: Please don't be like that with me. We used to tell each other everything, now you hardly speak to me, or anybody.

ARTHUR: I guess I'm turning into a rock.

MARION: That old Kay. It's all his fault. He's so smart, now that he's going to be a big knight.

ARTHUR: He's got a right to feel good.

MARION: Well, he doesn't have a right to treat you so mean.

ARTHUR: Ah, he's just getting back at me for beating him in everything. He'll get over it after a while, or else I'll get used to it. It's just hard for me right now.

LENORE *((offstage)*: Marion! Marion—

MARION: Here I am, Mother.

LENORE *(entering from Manor)*: Darling, you mustn't be in the way during the ceremony. Arthur, why aren't you with the rest? Today's your brother's happiest day, and you should be celebrating with the others.

428

ARTHUR *(very polite and reserved)*: Yes ma'am.
LENORE: Oh, I do wish they'd hurry the ceremony. This waiting makes me nervous. *(Fanfare of trumpets. (Suggest Walton's music from the motion picture, "Hamlet", Side 3. Victor Album DM-1273. Must be repeated.)*
MARION: They're coming now.
LENORE: Take your place, Arthur dear. The way we rehearsed it. Hurry, Marion, you stand over here with me. *(During the last speech, the doors of the Manor open, and Sir Lucan and King Bagdemagus post themselves by the door, with crossed swords. Lenore and Marion stand to one side. The Archbishop of Canterbury, arrayed in all his vestments, enters next, very solemn. He is followed by the four knights, now dressed as priests. Arthur, holding Kay's sword on a pillow, stands center stage. The Archbishop goes to a place even with Arthur, but close to stage left, the priests behind him. King Leodegrance follows the Archbishop, placing himself close to him, and nearer Arthur. Merlin follows Leodegrance, and is the only one who isn't solemn. He has to duck his head to get through the crossed swords, and come down the steps winking at Marion. He crosses right to Lady Lenore and Marion. Kay enters, resplendent in white cape with a cross embroidered on his right shoulder. Otherwise, his costume may remain the same. Sir Hector follows Kay, and closes the door as he comes through. Sir Hector joins Lady Lenore and Marion. Arthur is kneeling, a little down right of Kay, ¾ closed position. Kay stands facing stage left, by Leodegrance. The music stops.)*
LEODEGRANCE *(bows to Archbishop, who acknowledges)*: Has the candidate been found worthy of this high estate?
ARCHBISHOP. He has cleansed his soul with a holy vigil, during the night.
LEODEGRANCE: Then Kay! *(Kay kneels.)* Son of Sir Hector and Lady Lenore, having found you worthy of the honor of knighthood, by right of birth and your own valiant deeds, and having found you to know the rules of chivalry, I present you before God and Man, for the honor of knighthood. Do any oppose this elevation? *(Kay looks nervously around, especially at Arthur. Leodegrance picks up sword from cushion held by Arthur, holds it in the form of a cross toward are Archbishop, who blesses it, then turns to Kay.)* Then by right of my knighthood, I hereby dub thee Sir Kay, by which name you shall be known henceforth. Hold high this mighty honor. *(He touches Kay's right shoulder with the flat of the sword.)* Rise, Sir Kay. *(Kay does so. Leodegrance lays sword across his left arm, handle facing Kay. Kay takes the sword from him. Then Leodegrance slaps him on the back with congratulations. Kay's teeth are jarred.)* Congratulations, Sir Kay.
ARCHBISHOP: May I add mine, Sir Kay. *(The moment Leodegrance congratulates the new knight, all crowd around him, leaving Arthur*

kneeling alone. Marion and Lenore go toward the Manor door, and after a moment, Lenore announces:)

LENORE: Please, gentle sirs, your feast awaits you. Come, your Grace. King Leodegrance. *(They start to join her. The rest follow.)*

LEODEGRANCE *(as Kay stands still)*: What about the new knight?

KAY *(all excited)*: I've got to get my armor ready. I'm going to the tournament today. Come, Arthur, we must get my armor. *(He sounds like a very new shavetail. Arthur takes it manfully, and follows Kay out. Marion breaks away from her mother, and follows Arthur. There is a moment of uncomfortable silence.)*

LENORE: Well, will the rest of you come in? *(She leads them in, except for Merlin, who is stopped by Sir Hector.)*

HECTOR *(as he closes the doors)*: Merlin, just a moment.

MERLIN: Yes, it is too bad, isn't it?

HECTOR: What's too bad?

MERLIN: What you were thinking.

HECTOR *(crisply)*: What was I thinking?

MERLIN: Now don't get so angry. You were thinking about Arthur, and how moody he's been.

HECTOR: How many times must I tell you—

MERLIN and HECTOR *(together)*: To stop reading my thoughts!

MERLIN: All right, Sir Hector. This is a serious matter, and I'm sorry if I made you angry.

HECTOR *(stalking down the steps)*: Don't be so infernally superior.

MERLIN *(following him down)*: I can't help it. I am.

HECTOR: I'm really concerned about the lad. He's been too quiet lately. Who told him he wasn't my son? *(He turns accusingly toward Merlin.)*

MERLIN: If you must know, it was Kay.

HECTOR: He couldn't be so unkind.

MERLIN: But really, it's time that Arthur found out.

HECTOR: What?

MERLIN: Arthur will find that he'll have an easier time if his shocks come gradually. He's going to find himself with more and more to think about.

HECTOR: You are so blamed obscure! Now tell me, whose son is Arthur?

MERLIN: I can only tell you that his parents were of much nobler blood than you can boast. *(He starts for the door.)* Now I'm hungry, and I believe you invited me to eat. Don't worry about Arthur. You'll find out who he is, soon enough.

HECTOR *(as they enter the manor, and close the doors)*: It's positively unsporting of you to hold off! *(Kay immediately enters, with part of his armor on. He has put on the breastplate during the above scene. Arthur follows, carrying the helmet and armpieces. Marion comes in with Kay's sword. Kay is carrying a shield, which he puts in a conspicuous place, probably against the steps, for use as a mirror.)*

430

KAY *(as he enters)*: Hurry up, you fool. I'll soon teach you to lag behind. *(After putting shield down, he stands center stage.)* Well, don't stand there gaping. Help me put it on. *(Arthur holds arm-pieces, while Kay slips his arms through. As they work, Kay says such things as "Hold it still, you clumsy oaf." "You're pulling too hard." After Kay gets the arm-pieces on, he goes over to the shield, to admire his reflection. This is more than Marion can stand.)*

MARION: Oh Kay, stop looking at yourself.

KAY: You be quiet, or I'll spank you.

MARION *(spiritedly)*: You just try.

KAY: I've been waiting for a long time, and if you don't keep quiet, I won't wait any longer. Arthur, get my helmet. *(Arthur gets helmet——should be beaver-type—and puts it on Kay. Kay has worn it before, of course, but is not very used to it, so he has trouble seeing out of the small slit. He gropes his way around toward the shield. Marion sneaks the shield away from its place, and Kay gropes blindly. Arthur has trouble keeping his face straight, and decides to halt things.)*

ARTHUR: Put it back, Marion.

MARION: Oh, why did you tell him?

KAY: Did you move my shield? You little scamp, now I *am* going to spank you! *(Kay starts after her, but he cannot see very well, and has to lift the visor. He bellows.)* Get me out of this, Arthur. Hurry up, or I'll beat you till your skin is raw! Hurry! *(Arthur takes the helmet off.)* Now, where are you, you little devil? *(He is really angry. Arthur sees this, and stops him.)* Get out of my way, churl.

ARTHUR: Kay, you're angry. You might hurt her.

KAY: I'm Sir Kay to you. Do what I say, you knave! *(He cuffs Arthur, who is caught off guard and sent sprawling. Kay is almost immediately remorseful, but before he can say so, Arthur is back on his feet. Kay turns to run after Marion, and Arthur jumps on his back. At that instant, Hector and the rest of the company come out to see what is going on.)*

HECTOR: Arthur! Kay! What is this?

KAY *(ashamed and surprised)*: Father.

HECTOR: What do you mean, Arthur, jumping on Kay when his back is turned, especially now, when you're his squire. Well, Kay, explain this.

KAY *(seeing that he will not be censured)*: I—I was just getting ready to ride to London with you, when Arthur—Arthur said he wished he was a knight—

MARION: Oh, Kay, that's not what—

KAY *(cutting her off)*: And so I said he would have to wait a few years till he was grown up. I laughed, and was leaving, when he jumped on my back. I was taken by surprise, and fell down, when you came out.

MARION: Father, he's not—

HECTOR: That will be enough, Marion. Arthur, I'm ashamed of you.

What have you to say?

ARTHUR: Nothing, sir.

HECTOR: Nothing?

ARTHUR: Well, sir, if you believe Sir Kay, what is there for me to say?

HECTOR: Oh, I'm disappointed in you, Arthur. You've been mooning around for the last four weeks, and I'm getting tired of it. You're not going to the council meeting with us.

ARTHUR: But—

HECTOR: Kay will use my squire in the jousts.

ARTHUR: But sir—

HECTOR: That will be all, Arthur.

LEODEGRANCE: Sir Hector, I suggest we leave now. It's rather late.

HECTOR: Yes, my leige.

LEODEGRANCE: Come, gentlemen. *(They all start to exit.)*

HECTOR *(to Kay)*: Come, Kay. You realize that you'll be the only knight in armor at the meeting. They'll wait until the tournament to put theirs on. Goodbye, my dear. *(He kisses Lenore.)* Come, Kay. *(Sir Hector exits. Kay picks up helmet and shield, but leaves his sword where Marion put it. All have gone except Arthur, Marion, Lenore, Merlin, and Kay.)*

KAY: Goodbye, Mother. *(He kisses her, crosses to gate, pauses by Arthur. He is genuinely sorry.)* I'm sorry, Arthur—honest.

ARTHUR: You'd better hurry, Sir Kay. Your father's waiting. *(Kay very contritely exits.)*

MERLIN: Well, boy, you've a talent for getting into trouble.

MARION: Arthur, it was all my fault. I'm sorry.

ARTHUR: It's nobody's fault, Marion.

LENORE: Now, just what happened?

MARION: Kay was going to spank me. Arthur wouldn't let him, and Kay knocked Arthur down. Kay was running away, when Arthur jumped on him.

LENORE: Is this true, Arthur?

ARTHUR: Yes ma'am.

LENORE: You mean Kay deliberately lied?

MERLIN: Seems he did.

LENORE: How unlike Kay! Arthur, you and Marion go in and get some food now.

MARION: Yes, mother. Come on, Arthur. *(They exeunt, into the Manor.)*

LENORE: Poor Arthur. He's going through such a change.

MERLIN: He's going to go through a much bigger one, I'm afraid.

LENORE *(quite apprehensive)*: What do you mean?

MERLIN: First of all, you've got to let him go to that Council meeting.

LENORE: But my husband ordered him to stay here.

MERLIN: Your husband is an old goat, which is beside the point. Arthur must go to that meeting.

LENORE: You've got something up that horrible sleeve of yours.

MERLIN: Lady Lenore, the time has come for me to take Arthur from you. You might as well know.

LENORE: Not so soon!

MERLIN: My gracious, woman, you've had him for over fourteen years!

LENORE: But he's still a child. Whatever do you want with him?

MERLIN: That you will find out before the day is over. I might say, though, you've made him into a fine boy. Well, I can't blubber all day Call him out.

LENORE (dispirited): Very well. (Crosses to doors, and opens them.) Arthur! Arthur!

MERLIN: If it's any consolation, you might know that you'll get to see him quite often, but the relationship will be somewhat changed.

LENORE: I wish you'd stop talking riddles.

MERLIN: Then who'd pay attention to what I say? (Arthur and Marion enter.) Oh, here's the lad.

ARTHUR: Yes, ma'am?

LENORE: Come here, Arthur. (He does so.) I've been thinking it over, and I've decided that you and Marion were right—so this is once I am going to change one of your father's orders. I want you to go to the Council meeting.

ARTHUR: But I thought—

MERLIN: Don't bother yourself, son. It's a woman's privilege to change her husband's mind.

ARTHUR: But I'll have to go alone.

MERLIN: You must get used to that, my boy. Before long, you're going to have to do a lot of things alone. Well, don't waste time. Better get on your horse and go.

ARTHUR (impulsively hugs Lady Lenore.) Thanks, Mother. You're wonderful! (He exits quickly toward outer gate.)

LENORE (close to tears): Dear me, I don't think I can bring myself to think of him not here.

MARION: What are you talking about, Mother?

MERLIN: She's talking nonsense. Don't pay any attention to her sentimental talk. (Takes handkerchief from sleeve, and blows his own nose loudly.) Besides, we're all going to the Council Meeting ourselves.

LENORE: What?

MARION: You mean us?

MERLIN: That I do. We'll wait until Arthur has a good start, then we'll follow him.

MARION: Let's go with him now!

MERLIN: Oh, I think he'll want to ride too fast for us. (Marion stamps her foot and walks away in disgust. She goes to where Kay's sword is lying.) You really ought to be there, Lady Lenore. You'll be very surprised, and very proud.

LENORE: Riddles, again. But all right.

MARION (seeing Kay's sword): Look, we'll have to go! (Brings the sword to Lenore.) Kay forgot his sword.

LENORE: Oh dear, and it's his very first day as a knight. He'll be so chagrined. We'll have to take his sword to him.

MARION: I bet he won't like it.

MERLIN: I daresay he won't. But we've got a long ride, and Arthur is well ahead of us by now. Come on, gracious ladies, let's go to London Town! (Blackout and curtain. There can be an intermission here, if desired, though it is not necessary.)

INTERIM

(Music should be sprightly and adventuresome. Suggest Hindemith's "Kammermusik", Side 4, Columbia Album, MX-VDT. Spotlight comes up on Merlin, standing before the curtain.)

MERLIN: Well sirs, if you think I didn't have fun riding to London with those ladies, you're right, because I didn't. That Marion was such a chatterbox. (Pantomimes talking with his two hands.) But she was a cute little chatterbox, and I didn't mind too much. And say, did you notice how much Lady Lenore and Sir Hector love Arthur—and how much he loves them? So I don't think it matters much whether they're his real parents—mind you, I'm not saying they aren't! (He laughs.) And I'm not saying they are! Well, here I am talking, and we should be seeing what's happening in London. You remember that King Leodegrance and his friends rode together. Well, someone else got to London before them. You remember Morgan Le Fay had promised Lot a miracle? Well, let's see her in London, getting ready for her miracle. And let's watch her husband, King Uriens, tease her—ah! (He waves his hand, and—

Act Three, from ARTHUR AND THE MAGIC SWORD
As presented by the University of Minnesota Theatre at Minneapolis

ACT THREE

SCENE: *The lights come up, as the curtains open on a Churchyard
in London. Important: The entrance to the church can be presumed to be
offstage, but a platform is necessary, approximately center stage, and a
sort of pulpit on the platform, in which the King's crown is concealed.
Underneath the platform, the magic sword is set into the anvil and the
stone, and a flash set up by it. Essential are entrances on either side of
the stage, one of which leads to the church. There should be a place where
Marion can logically hide. As the lights come up, Morgan Le Fay enters,
followed by her husband.)*

URIENS: Yes, sweet spouse, this is where the meeting will be held.

MORGAN: Good. Now leave me alone for a few minutes.

URIENS: Oh no, my dear. I love to watch you work. I won't disturb
you—and besides, I can sort of look to see if anyone is coming.

MORGAN: All right, if you insist. I don't have time to argue. We're
none too early. *(Uriens makes himself comfortable, and watches with
some amazement. Morgan wears a pouch on her costume, which has
fine powder in it. As she starts her incantation, the lights dim, and
she throws a little powder into the air. She must make a magic circle, as she chants. Weird lights should play across the stage: for
example, a color wheel revolving in front of a spotlight. Music may*

be used. (Suggest Sibelius' "Tempest", Side 14.)
    Huldra, Ouda, Henget, and Hosea,
    Send your magic through my torsa,
    Send your power as I sing
    That Lot of Orkney may be King!
    Oraye, oraye, Mauritinie,
    Oraye, oraye, Mauritinie.
(After the last line, there is a cymbal crash, and Morgan collapses on the steps of the platform. Lights should come up abruptly.)

URIENS *(rushing toward her, applauding)*: Magnificent, my dear. Good show! Are you all-right?

MORGAN *(panting)*: Just give me a moment. That takes it out of you. I'll be all right.

URIENS: Merlin might be a competent magnician, but he can't touch you for showmanship, my dear. And of course, you're a little prettier than he is. Oh, look who's coming. King Lot and his wife. *(Lot, Margawse, and Mordred enter from side opposite church entrance.)* Hail, royal sire. Margawse.

LOT: Greetings, King Uriens.

URIENS: What, and I do believe it's your son Mordred.

LOT: Well, Mordred, don't stand there with a frozen tongue. Say something!

MORDRED: Hullo.

URIENS: He's a brilliant conversationalist.

MARGAWSE: He's just shy. Mordred, run off and find something to do for awhile. We'll be busy here.

MORDRED: Yes, mother. *(Exits.)*

LOT: Is everything ready?

URIENS: Yes. Your miracle is in the oven, cooking.

MORGAN: Husband, you are speaking lightly of sacred things. Your miracle, King Lot, will appear when I desire it. *(She has recovered her strength now, and is up.)*

LOT: You'll not regret this, Morgan. I have great faith in your powers.

URIENS: Speaking of faith, are your armies ready to sweep in on this place, in the event your miracle doesn't work?

MORGAN: Husband!

LOT: That has nothing to do with faith. It is just a little added precaution. Yes, they are ready to come in on my signal. And your armies?

URIENS: Mine are ready to work with yours.

LOT: Good. Nothing can fail us this time.

MARGAWSE: Don't be too confident, my dear. There are one or two other people who might have different ideas from yours.

MORGAN: I have taken care of Merlin, if that's what you mean.

URIENS: Well, here comes King Leodegrance. I believe. A little older since I last saw him. *(Lot and his party should be grouped on the*

stage opposite the entrance to the church. Leodegrance, King Bagde-
magus, Hector, and Kay enter from the other. Leodegrance is reply-
ing to a speech of Kay's.)

LEODEGRANCE *(as he enters)*: You'll soon have your chance to joust,
Kay. *(He sees the rest of his company freeze, and turns to encounter*
Lot. There is a moment of charged silence. Remember, these people
have fought each other bitterly for 14½ years. Uriens finally breaks
the silence.)

URIENS: Well, I'm not going to stand on ceremony. *(Crosses a few steps*
toward Leodegrance.) How do you do, King Leodegrance, and greetings, King Bag!

BAGDEMAGUS: To you, sir, my name is Bagdemagus.

URIENS: What? Do you think I'd pronounce all of it, and take a chance
on spraining my tongue? *(He laughs.)*

LOT: Uriens! This is no time for your feeble jokes.

URIENS: On the contrary, it's just the time. Everybody looks so solemn, I thought I'd cheer you up.

MORGAN: Well, your effort is not appreciated.

URIENS *(crossing to her)*: Always my loving, understanding wife.

LEODEGRANCE *(stepping forward a little)*: I say, King Uriens, that
levity is welcome. *(Looks at Lot a moment, then laughs.)*

LOT *(very testily)*: What is so humorous?

LEODEGRANCE: I was just thinking. This is the first time I've seen
your face for fourteen years. I'm generally used to seeing your back
and heels. *(Leodegrance's party enjoys this. Lot's party freezes.*
Lot speaks with great self-righteousness.)

LOT: I came here to make peace, not to insult my former enemy.

URIENS: He touched you that time, Leodegrance.

LEODEGRANCE: Well put, King Lot. And if you meant what you
said, here's my hand. *(Leodegrance strides to the middle of the stage,*
thrusts his hand out. Lot glances at Margawse and Morgan, then
slowly steps to Leodegrance, and offers his hand. They shake.)

LOT: By this act, King Leodegrance, you signify your willingness to
make a truce, and dismiss your armies.

LEODEGRANCE: No need to dismiss them. They are far away at
Cameliard. And yours?

LOT: Mine are disposed of, also. *(They break the handshake. Lot can-*
not help looking at Uriens with a smile.) Perhaps after fourteen years
of war, they are tired of fighting.

LEODEGRANCE: Now there is only one thing left for us to do.

LOT: Well?

LEODEGRANCE: You, I, and all the rest should renounce our claims
to the throne, and someone be chosen who is acceptable to all of us.

LOT *(pulls quickly away)*: I see the trick! All your pious declarations
for peace—words to catch me off guard. My answer is no. I'll never
renounce my rightful claim to the throne!

LEODEGRANCE: Then there will never be peace on this land. Unless—

LOT: Well? Unless what?

LEODEGRANCE: Unless you are designated King by a miracle. And believe me, that's what it would take to convince me—a miracle! *(Leodegrance rejoins his group.)*

LOT *(smiles at Morgan)*: Don't be too shocked, then, King Leodegrance, if that is just what happens.

LUCAN *(offstage)*: The Archbishop of Canterbury! *(Music. Drums and trumpets play. The same procession music may be used as in Kay's knighting. The same priests that were in the knighting scene enter, carrying banners. They may be preceded by two page-boys, carrying banners. The Archbishop enters last, and takes his place at the top of the platform. Mordred slips in unobtrusively, and stands by his mother.)*

ARCHBISHOP: Milords! We meet to settle our differences peacefully *(Slight reaction from both groups, to whom this speech seems ironical, In light of previous action.)* If our hearts are honest, we shall find our King, and he shall be our symbol. *(The Archbishop is interrupted by a crash and/or a flash of smoke. If flash powder is used, place it by the platform, where the sword will be drawn out. There is a blackout for the split-second of the flash, during which a small section of the platform is opened up, so that the sword can logically be seen. The crowd reacts violently, with screams and shouts. Then as the lights come up, and smoke is seen rising, a hush falls over the group. Sir Lucan cautiously looks under the platform. Note: the sides of the platform may be draped, instead of the above, in which case Lucan can merely pull the drape aside.)*

LUCAN: Your Grace, there is a strange sight here.

ARCHBISHOP: What—what is it?

LUCAN: It looks like a sword.

ARCHBISHOP: A sword? Bring it out, for all to see. *(Sir Lucan and another knight drag out the huge stone, on which rests an anvil. Buried in the anvil is Uther Pendragon's magic sword. The crowd of course is intensely curious, and gather around, as Lucan and the knight pull the stone to center stage.)* Let me see.

LOT *(to Morgan)*: Is this your miracle?

MORGAN: Sh! No. It's Merlin's. But have no fear. See what it is.

ARCHBISHOP: By my faith, stand back, stand back! *(The crowd falls back.)* There's an inscription. This is the promised miracle.

LOT: What does the inscription say, your Grace?

ARCHBISHOP *(reading)*: Hear this: "Whosoever pulleth this sword out of this stone is of right born King of England." *(The crowd is amazed.)* A miracle has been sent to help us find the rightful King. *(The Archbishop steps back to the top of the platform. Lot steps forward.)*

LOT: I can't believe it.

438

ARCHBISHOP: You dare dispute my word? Read for yourself. You read Latin. *(Lot does not, but he bluffs. All eyes are on him, as he reads. Uriens and Morgan should be down right, and while Lot is reading, Uriens speaks:)*

URIENS *(to Morgan)*: You'd better pull your miracle now, darling. Sort of out-moracle this miracle.

ARCHBISHOP *(to Lot)*: Well?

LOT: That's what it says, all right.

ARCHBISHOP: We must begin immediately to draw the sword. *(Crowd immediately reacts. A hubbub. All eyes onstage must be on the sword. Morgan, without a pause, repeats the following words where she stands, making magical movements with her heads.)*

MORGAN:
>   Oraya, Oraye, Mauritinie!
>   Oraya, Oraye, Mauritinie!

(There is just a hint of the lights dimming, then there is a crash, lights up. We hear a slide whistle, or Frisco whistle, and all eyes focus on the same spot center stage, on top of the proscenium. Out of the heavens, thrown by someone on the bridge, a little parachute falls. Attached to it is a scroll.)

ARCHBISHOP: Another miracle! *(Crowd takes up the cry.)*

URIENS: Amazing, my dear.

LOT *(while crowd is focussed on scroll.)* Is this your miracle?

MORGAN: Yes. The scroll will say "Lot of Orkney is rightful King of Britain."

URIENS: How dramatic!

LUCAN *(who has taken the courage to pick up the scroll)*: Here, your Grace.

ARCHBISHOP: Heaven has sent us two miracles. Let me read this. *(All eyes on the Archbishop, Lot smiling confidently. Suddenly, the Archbishop bursts out laughing. All look puzzled.)*

LOT: What is the matter, your Grace? What does the scroll say?

ARCHBISHOP: Here, King Lot. Why don't you read it aloud. It must concern you. *(Lot is puzzled, but still confident. He takes the scroll, and reads quickly, before he realizes what it says.)*

LOT: It says—"Lot of Orkney is a fool." *(Double take.)* A fool! *(He rushes to Morgan, as the crowd roars.)* What is the meaning of this?

MORGAN: Something happened.

LOT: I'll say it did!

URIENS: As I said, my dear, you put on the best show, but Merlin is the better magician.

MORGAN *(muttering)*: Shut up!

MARGAWSE *(in low tones)*: Control yourselves. Everyone is watching you.

URIENS: The sword. Lot! the sword. You're not lost yet.

LOT: Oh, yes. *(Lot forces a smile, and steps toward the Archbishop.)*

Well, I admit the laugh is on me. No doubt Merlin has been having his little joke.

ARCHBISHOP: The sword awaits. Who shall draw first?

LOT: Your Grace, inasmuch as I believe I have prior claim to the throne, I should draw first.

LEODEGRANCE: Go ahead, Lot. If you are the rightful heir to the throne of Britain, I'll eat that sword.

LOT: Yes, you certainly will. *(He steps to the sword very cautiously. Morgan tries some incantations with her hands. Lot grasps the handle. He pulls. Nothing happens. The crowd buzzes, and Leodegrance laughs out loud.)* It won't move! *(Leodegrance laughs harder.)* All right, you try it, then.

LEODEGRANCE: I don't claim the throne, but I believe King Bagiemagus has some rights. Go ahead, King Bag. *(Bagdemagus objects strenuously, but Leodegrance and his party push him out. While he approaches the sword cautiously, the following two lines should be spoken.)*

MORGAN: What if he draws it?

LOT: My army is waiting for my signal. *(Indicating the horn around his neck. Bagdemagus touches the sword lightly, then tugs a little. Gives a quick tug, as if trying to take it by surprise.)*

URIENS: Try kicking it, King Bag. *(Everyone laughs.)*

LEODEGRANCE: Why don't you try, King Uriens?

URIENS: Me? Whatever do I want with that gaudy old sword? *(He tries to walk away, but Morgan and Lot stop him.)*

MORGAN: Go ahead, husband.

LOT: Yes, King Uriens, you try. *(Lot pushes him out. The crowd laughs. Uriens recovers his dignity, smiles, casually walks to the sword, and hardly looking at it, merely taps the handle with one hand. The crowd laughs.)*

URIENS: See, it won't budge. *(Jauntily walks back to his wife. Leodegrance laughs heartily.)*

LOT: Your Grace, no wonder we can't draw the sword. There are too many buffoons around.

ARCHBISHOP: The proper spirit is certainly not here. I command we adjourn for a time. I suggest you follow me to the church, where we can meditate. King Bagdemagus and Sir Lucan, will you volunteer to guard the sword. Cover it with my cloak. *(They immediately take it from him.)* The trumpet will sound the call to meet again. *(Music: The same as the entering procession of the Archbishop. The little pageboys exeunt first, followed by the priests and the Archbishop. As they are going, the following dialogue takes place.)*

MORGAN *(to Lot)*: Are you going into the church?

LOT: No. But Uriens, you and Margawse had better go. Morgan, you and Mordred stay with me.

MORDRED: What are we going to do, Father?

440

LOT: You'll find out. Sh! Go ahead, Margawse.

URIENS: Come, Lady Margawse. Let our spouses burn their fingers. *(They follow the procession. Sir Hector and Kay remain onstage until the tail of the procession. Lot, Mordred, and Morgan exeunt the opposite side from the church. As Morgan exits, Arthur comes bursting in, and bumps into her. She says—"You clumsy oaf!"—glares at him a moment, while he apologizes then leaves. Arthur sees Hector, and runs to him. Lucan and Bagdemagus sit on either side of the sword.)*

ARTHUR: Father! Father!

HECTOR: Arthur! What are you doing here?

ARTHUR: Well, I——

HECTOR: I told you to stay in the Manor.

ARTHUR: I know, sir, but my mother and Merlin told me to come.

HECTOR: Merlin.

ARTHUR: Yes, sir. But if you want me to go back, I'll go. *(He turns to leave.)*

HECTOR: Oh—no, no, you'd better stay, now that you're here.

ARTHUR: Where has everybody gone?

KAY: To church, if you must know.

ARTHUR: What for?

HECTOR *(starting off)*: Never mind. Come along with us.

ARTHUR: Are they going to have the jousts afterward?

HECTOR: I suppose.

ARTHUR: Well, Kay won't be able to be in them.

KAY: What are you talking about?

ARTHUR: You don't have a sword.

KAY *(feels, and notices the lack for the first time)*: I don't! Father, where's my sword?

HECTOR: Didn't you bring it with you?

KAY: No, I must have left it at the Manor. You hurried me so much, that I didn't have time to think about it. What'll I do?

HECTOR: Don't look at me, sirrah. I won't let you have mine. You'll have to go back to the Manor and get it.

ARTHUR: What?

HECTOR: That will be a good way to make up for the way you acted toward your brother, Arthur, and you'll be doing your duty as a squire.

ARTHUR *(without enthusiasm)*: Yes, sir.

HECTOR: Hurry now. We'll meet you here. Come, Kay. *(Hector and Kay exeunt. Arthur watches a moment, then starts off in the opposite direction.)*

ARTHUR *(muttering)*: Stupid old sword! Stupid old Kay! *(Marion enters, and finds Arthur.)*

MARION: Arthur!

ARTHUR: Marion! What are you doing here?

MARION: Merlin brought Mother and me.

ARTHUR: He did? Where are they?

MARION: I left them over by the pavillion where the tournament's going to be held. Mother met a friend, and told me to find you. Where are you going?

ARTHUR: Oh, Kay left his sword at home, and I've got to go clear back to the Manor house for it.

MARION: No you don't. Mother brought it for him.

ARTHUR: She did? Well, let's go find her.

MARION: I'm too tired, Arthur. I want to rest a while.

ARTHUR: Well, you stay right here, then. I'll look for Mother. *(Exit.)*

MARION *(as he goes)*: I'll lie down over here. *(Sees Bagdemagus and Sir Lucan).* May, I, Sir Knight?

BAGDEMAGUS: What? Oh, certainly, certainly, milady. Your couch awaits. *(Both Bagdemagus and Lucan rise, and Badgemagus indicates the "couch" with an expansive gesture.)*

LUCAN: Be very quiet, won't you.

MARION: Oh, I will. *(As she curls up)*: You won't even know I'm here. *(She should be logically hidden so that Morgan and Mordred will not see her when they enter.)*

LUCAN: Cute tyke.

BAGDEMAGUS: Quite.

LUCAN: Tiresome, this.

BAGDEMAGUS: Right.

LUCAN: Bother.

BAGDEMAGUS: Necessary.

LUCAN: I suppose.

BAGDEMAGUS: Boring.

LUCAN: Tedious.

BAGDEMAGUS: But necessary.

LUCAN: I suppose.

BAGDEMAGUS *(with a big yawn)*: Ho, hum!

LUCAN: What'd you say?

BAGDEMAGUS *(pointing to his yawning mouth)*: Ho, hum.

LUCAN: Quite right. *(Mordred runs in right, opposite Church entrance.)*

MORDRED: King Bagdemagus?

BAGDEMAGUS: Yes?

MORDRED: Here's a message from the Archbishop.

BAGDEMAGUS: A note.

LUCAN: How nice.

BAGDEMAGUS: Let me see. *(Reading)*: "I have changed my mind. I wish all who can to attend church. The sword will be protected."

LUCAN: How odd!

BAGDEMAGUS: First time the Archbishop has ever changed his mind.

LUCAN: How strange!

BAGDEMAGUS: Think we should?

LUCAN: Don't know.

BAGDEMAGUS: Let's do.

LUCAN: Very well. You first.

BAGDEMAGUS: After you.

LUCAN: I insist.

BAGDEMAGUS: Very well. *(Bagdemagus very smartly marches down-stage, turns abruptly toward left, and marches out, Lucan falls right in behind him, military style, trying to keep in step. Mordred looks after them, laughs, then beckons offstage in opposite directions. Lot and Morgan enter.)*

LOT: You acted your part very well. Keep watch now.

MORDRED: That was easy. *(Stations himself stage left, by Church entrance.)*

LOT: All right, Morgan. Lets see what we can do. *(Little Marion is aroused by this. We see that she hears what is going on. But Lot and his party do not see her.)*

MORGAN: Take off the cover. *(Lot removes the Archbishop's cloak, and places it on the platform.)* Now concentrate with me. I will break this stone with my most powerful formula. *(As she begins dancing around the stone, the same effects as were used for her first incantation may be used again. Music: Sibelius' "Tempest", Side 14. The lights flash weirdly.)*

> Oraye, Oraye, Mauritinie,
> Crack this stone a teeny-weeny,
> Huldra, Oura, horsa, hingst,
> Send your power, and break the jinx!

(There is a moment of silence, then Morgan quickly says:) Be quiet, something's going to happen. *(A Frisco or slide whistle is heard, as though something were circling, then there is a drum beat. Morgan and Lot, who have been bending over, straighten up on the beat, as though they had been kicked in the seat of the pants.)* Merlin, again. I could kill him! *(Another whistle, and another drum beat. Morgan reacts again as though she had been kicked.)* Ouch!

LOT: Be quiet! *(Uriens enters, unobserved.)* I'll call my armies. *(He lifts the horn about his neck, and starts to blow, but Uriens seems to interrupt deliberately.)*

URIENS: There you are. I thought I'd find you here.

MORGAN: We don't have any time to waste, listening to your prattle.

URIENS: Oh, but I've come to help you.

LOT: Humph. I suppose you're going to tell me how to get the sword.

URIENS: Yes, as a matter of fact, I am.

LOT: Well?

URIENS: I have two suggestions. First of all, have you thought of something like this? *(He produces a large wooden wallet and a chisel, from under his cloak.)*

LOT: A chisel!

MORGAN: Fool. People could see how you got the sword then.

URIENS: Very true, wife. But my second method is sure to succeed.

LOT: Well, what is it?

URIENS: Simply this. The sword appeared today. That indicates there will be someone to draw it. Now, unless I miss my guess, whoever draws that sword won't be anyone we know. It will be a person we have probably never seen. Undoubtedly, it will be the son of King Pendragon, a boy who should be about fourteen years of age by now.

LOT: You're crazy. The boy disappeared.

URIENS: Yes, but we don't know where to, nor if he's dead. I'll wager everything I have he will show up here.

LOT: I don't have time to waste, listening to you. I'm going to call in my armies, and settle the matter my own way. One blast in this horn, and in they come.

MORGAN (*as he lifts the horn again*): Wait, Lot. For once, I think my husband is right.

URIENS: An amazing concession.

LOT: I don't. We're letting our one chance slip.

MORGAN: Let's wait a little longer. What have we to lose? Think of what we gain if we find out who the boy is, then we'll know for sure. We can take care of him permanently this time—then you'll have a clear title to the throne.

LOT: Well—I still think you're wrong, but—

MORGAN: You go in to the church. Let me stay here to watch.

URIENS: Sounds like good advice, Lot.

LOT: All right. Come, Mordred.

MORGAN: Let him stay with me. You two should be seen in church.

URIENS: Very well, my sweet. Go along, Lot. (*Uses his mallet as a pointer. They exeunt toward Church.*)

MORGAN: Now Mordred, I want you to hide over there—(*Indicates where Marion is.*) and watch what happens to this sword. I'll be sitting on the lawn over there—(*Indicates offstage, opposite Church entrance. As she starts to exit, Mordred goes around behind platform, or wherever Marion is hidden, and sees her.*)

MORDRED: There's someone here! (*Marion is too frightened to move.*)

MORGAN: Who is it?

MORDRED(*seizing Marion*): It's a little girl.

MARION: Let me go. (*Mordred pulls her to Morgan.*)

MORGAN (*holding Marion*): What are you doing here?

MARION: Just taking a nap.

MORGAN: You were spying on us.

MARION: No I wasn't.

MORGAN: Don't lie to me. Mordred, you go and see that no one else is around. (*Mordred exits.*) Now, who are you?

MARION: Marion.

MORGAN: Do you know it isn't nice to spy?

MARION: I wasn't spying. I was just waiting for Arthur to come. Kay

444

left his sword, and Arthur—

MORGAN: Be quiet! *(Becomes very sweet.)* Now let's play a little game. You tell me just what you remember, what you heard—

MARION: I—

MORGAN: Oh, I won't hurt you. *(Then, savagely:)* Unless you don't tell me! *(Marion breaks loose from Morgan, as Arthur enters.)*

MARION*(running to Arthur)*: Arthur! Arthur!

ARTHUR: Marion, what's the matter? *(To Morgan.)* What are you doing to my sister?

MORGAN: Nothing, lad. We're just playing a game. So you're Arthur.

ARTHUR: Yes ma'am.

MORGAN: Who's your father and mother.

ARTHUR: Sir Hect—— I—— I——

MORGAN *(staring at him, fascinated).* What's the matter?

ARTHUR: I don't know who my father is.

MORGAN: What? Aren't you this little girl's brother?

ARTHUR *(dejected)*: No.

MARION: Yes you are, Arthur.

MORGAN: How—how old are you, boy?

ARTHUR: Fourteen and a half.

MORGAN *(becomes very intent)*: Fourteen and a half. That would be right.

ARTHUR *(Beginning to dislike her)*: What are you staring at me for? I don't think—

MORGAN: You look very much like someone I knew, once. Very much Amazing resemblance.

MARION: Arthur. Let's go.

ARTHUR: All right. I couldn't find the sword. *(Arthur and Marion start out.)*

MORGAN *(she should be standing by the magic sword.)* The sword. Oh, yes! Just a moment! *(Arthur and Marion stop.)* You're looking for a sword? Perhaps I can help you.

ARTHUR: What do you mean?

MORGAN *(as Arthur steps toward her)*: You're looking for a sword for your brother, and you can't find it, but your brother must have a sword, and a beautiful one. Why don't you take this one? *(She indicates the magic sword, very intent on Arthur. Morgan is standing behind the sword, on the platform steps.)*

ARTHUR: But it's not mine.

MORGAN: Oh, it belongs to anyone who can draw it.

MARION *(tugs at his sleeve)*: Arthur!

ARTHUR *(fascinated by sword)*: Just a minute, Marion. *(He walks toward the sword.)* But it's stuck in the stone.

MORGAN: That's to keep the blade sharp. Why don't you pull it out and use it?

MARION*(runs to Arthur, warningly.)*: Arthur!

ARTHUR: Sh! Just a minute, Marion.

MARION *(trying desperately to get his attention)*: But I have something to tell you.

ARTHUR: Wait'll I get this sword. *(Arthur grasps the handle, and easily pulls it out. As he does so, a sweep of the harp is heard. (Sug- gest Standard Sound Effect 930-B)* Well, it came right out!

MORGAN *(hatred welling up in her eyes)*: Yes, my little friend.

ARTHUR: Look how beautiful this is, Marion. Kay ought to like this.

MORGAN: Well, you may thank me, boy, for helping you.

ARTHUR: Oh, I forgot. Thank you very much.

MORGAN: I—I have a little nephew that I'd like very much to have you meet. I'll send him in. Just a moment. *(She exits right, opposite Church entrance.)*

MARION: Arthur, let's get out of here.

ARTHUR: We can't now, Marion. Didn't you hear what the lady said? She wants me to show someone the sword.

MARION: But she's wicked, Arthur. I heard her say things.

ARTHUR: What things?

MARION: Oh, they were talking about armies, and killing, and kings.

ARTHUR: Are you daft? Who's "they"?

MARION: Some people that were just here, and—*(Sees Mordred enter- ing, tries to whisper in Arthur's ear.)* Arthur-r-r.

MORDRED: Hullo.

ARTHUR: Hello. Marion, stop pulling my sleeve.

MORDRED: That's a pretty sword.

ARTHUR: Thank you. Marion, stop kicking me, and stop whispering in my ear. It isn't polite. *(Marion stamps her foot, goes behind Arthur, so she can be in position to trip Mordred.)*

MORDRED: Sword sure looks heavy.

ARTHUR: No, it isn't heavy. Lift it. Here. *(Mordred takes the sword.)*

MORDRED: No, it isn't heavy at all. Well, thanks very much, fool. *(He starts to run off with the sword, but Marion trips him. Arthur immediately follows, and they start to tussle.)*

ARTHUR: Give me back my sword. *(Offstage, we hear Kay's voice: "What's the commotion?" When Mordred hears someone coming, he runs off past Kay, toward the Church, with the intention of summon- ing his father. Kay enters as Mordred sweeps past him, and we see that Kay recognizes him.)*

KAY: What are you trying to do, Arthur, get us all in trouble? Do you know who that was? You were fighting with Mordred, King Lot's son. Go fetch him back this instant, and give him his sword.

ARTHUR: But it isn't his sword. I got it for you.

KAY *(sees Marion)*: And what are you doing here, you little snip? Wait till Father sees you!

ARTHUR *(giving the sword to Kay)*: Here's the sword.

KAY: Humph! I still wonder where you got it, though. Well, thank you. I'll go find father and—*(He glances at it, and sees what it is. Quick double take, from sword to stone, and back.)* E-e-e-e-e-ek! *(He draws in his breath.)*

ARTHUR: What's the matter?

KAY *(very weak and trembling)*: N-nothing. Nothing at all!

HECTOR *(offstage)*: Kay! *(He enters.)* Kay, did you find what the commotion was? *(Sees Arthur and Marion.)* Marion, what are you doing here?

MARION: Mother's here too. Merlin told us to come.

HECTOR: That old crow! I wish he'd keep his nose out of my family affairs.

KAY *(who has almost fainted, holding the sword as though it were a snake)* Father. Father, look what I've got.

HECTOR: Yes, I see. Arthur got your sword.

KAY: No. Look here!

HECTOR: Yes, I see——eeeee! *(And he double-takes, as he sees the sword, and the empty stone.)* By my beard, it's the magic sword!

ARTHUR *(to Marion)*: What does he mean? There's nothing magic about it.

KAY: Be quiet, Arthur.

HECTOR: How did you come by this, Kay?

KAY: I—it came from the stone.

MARION: Sure it did, but Kay didn't—*(Kay says "Marion!", as a hubbub wells up, and the stage fills with people from the Church. First it is Lot, with Mordred.)*

LOT *(to Mordred)*: You little fool! Why didn't you tell me quietly, instead of yelling it to the roof-tops? *(The entire cast, except Lenore, Merlin, and the Archbishop, are rushing onstage, and each reacts to the empty stone. Morgan creeps in, her eyes on Arthur. Marion sees her.)*

MARION *(tugs at Arthur, her eyes popping with fear)*: Arthur! Arthur!

ARTHUR: I said stop doing that, Marion! *(The above dialogue goes on, as the people enter. Finally, the Archbishop rushes in.)*

ARCHBISHOP: Who started this rumor that the sword has been drawn? Ah——*(Sees Kay, with the sword.)* Then it was true. And Sir Kay, the newest knight in Christendom is the next King of Britain, by virtue of his drawing the sword. *(Everyone starts to kneel. Hector has to tug on Arthur's sleeve, because the lad is staring with amazement at Kay. Before people get very far in the kneeling process, Lot interrupts.)*

LOT: Your Grace! *(The crowd turns to Lot, and quiets down.)* Milord Archbishop of Canterbury!

ARCHBISHOP: Yes, King Lot?

LOT: You, nor I, nor anyone saw him draw the sword. How do we know that some witchcraft or trickery hasn't been used? If he drew the sword once, why can't he draw it again? Fair enough? *(The crowd agrees with Lot.)*

LEODEGRANCE: Yes, that's fair. Go ahead, Sir Kay. Put the sword in, and pull it out again. *(Kay is almost ready to collapse. He timidly walks to the stone. All eyes are on him. In a fit of desperation, he tries to plunge the sword in, but it will not go. The crowd begins to buzz angrily, as Lot shouts:)*

LOT: Fraud! Treachery! *(And he starts to draw his sword, but Leodegrance draws his first, and confronts Lot.)*

LEODEGRANCE: Step back, Lot, or I'll run you through. Step back! *(Lot does so very slowly.)* Now Sir Kay, you had better explain fast. How did you get that sword?

KAY *(sees Arthur's hostile glance)*: I—I saw my squire Arthur wrestling with Mordred over the sword. I think Arthur took it away from Mordred.

LEODEGRANCE: I'll wager it was the other way around. Mordred was probably trying to get the sword from Arthur. *(Lot makes a move to draw his sword.)* Don't force yourself to an early death, Lot. Keep your hand away from that sword. *(Lot steps back again.)* Now come here, Arthur, *(He does.)* Tell me, did you draw the sword?

ARTHUR: Yes sir.

LEODEGRANCE: Do you think you could draw it again?

ARTHUR: Well, it came out easily enough. I'll try, sir. *(He takes the sword from Kay, and very easily slips it into the anvil again. Note: Harp music again: Standard Sound Effect 930-B. Crowd reacts with amazement.)*

LEODEGRANCE: Now, son, try to draw it out again.

LOT: Just a minute here. I'd like to try once more. I'll show you this was a fraud.

LEODEGRANCE: You can't stand to lose, can you? All right, go ahead, King Lot. Try. *(Lot walks confidently to the sword. He thinks it is loose now. He tries to pull it as though he expects it to come out, and of course it sticks. He falls on his back. The crowd laughs.)* Get up, King Lot. Now Arthur, draw the sword.

ARTHUR: I'll try, King Leodegrance. *(All eyes are intent on Arthur, who steps to the sword, and easily pulls it out. Harp music again, as he does so. The crowd cheers.)*

LOT: I've wasted too much time! *(He raises the horn to his lips, but before he can blow, Marion has run over, and kicked him in the shins.)* Ouch! You little vixen! *(He starts after her, with intent to kill. Kay stops him, and Leodegrance leaps to confront Lot.)*

KAY: Leave my sister alone!

MARION: Don't let him blow that horn! *(Lot tries again to blow, but Leodegrance knocks the horn out of his hand.)* I heard him say he has an army ready to attack, when he blows that horn.

LEODEGRANCE: Well, Lot?

448

URIENS: The little girl is quite right. There are two armies outside, mine and King Lot's.

LEODEGRANCE: Why, you—

URIENS: Ah—ah—there's nothing to worry about. My army is just as large as Lot's, and is here for one reason—to keep him out of London!

LOT: You traitor!

URIENS: That depends on your point of view. I'm sick of your dirty actions, Lot. It's time we had something decent in this country, and there he is—our rightful King! *(Points to Arthur. Leodegrance has firm hold of Lot.)*

LOT: No! There's fraud and magic in this.

ARCHBISHOP: One moment, milords. There is one more test. My son, let me see that locket you wear.

ARTHUR *(puzzled)*: Here, your Grace. *(Archbishop takes locket, fits it to his.)*

ARCHBISHOP: They fit! They fit! This is the royal locket that King Pendragon gave to me before he died. Now I know that Arthur is King Pendragon's son! *(There is a cymbal crash, or a light flash, and a momentary blackout. The lights come up immediately, revealing Merlin and Lady Lenore on stage with the others. Uriens is holding Morgan le Fay, the knights are guarding Lot's party. The Archbishop has placed Arthur on the platform, and put Uther Pendragon's crown upon him. The crown may be concealed on a pulpit on the platform. The crowd reacts to Merlin.)*

MERLIN: There's your boy, Lady Lenore. Well, folks, are you satisfied with your rightful heir? *(The crowd laughs and cheers.)*

ARTHUR: Father! Mother!

HECTOR: We're not your father and mother any more.

ARTHUR: I don't care what anybody says now. You are!

LENORE: Arthur, we'll always be near you, but you're the King now.

ARTHUR: I don't want to be King.

MERLIN *(goes up platform to Arthur)*: You have no choice, my boy.

ARTHUR: But I don't know anything about it.

MERLIN: You'll learn. You're smart, you know what it is to be a servant, you've a kind heart and a just mind—and besides, I'll help you.

ARTHUR: Oh* Well—maybe I can do it then—and I guess somebody has to be King.

MERLIN: Spoken like a statesman. And if you're a good King, most everyone will be happy—everyone but these people. *(He points to Lot, Morgan, and Uriens.)*

LEODEGRANCE: What does your Majesty suggest we do with them?

ARCHBISHOP: May I suggest that we banish them from the country, for a time?

ARTHUR: Very well. But King Uriens shouldn't be banished.

URIENS: Thank you, your Majesty. And if you will grant my wife pardon, I shall see that she becomes thoroughly domesticated! *(He* holds her arm tightly, to show who is master.)

ARTHUR: Very well.

ARCHBISHOP: Away with them! *(The knights escort Lot and his family out. As they exit, Kay kneels before Arthur.)*

ARTHUR *(highly embarrassed)*: What are you doing, Kay? Stand up.

KAY: I guess you'll have my head chopped off now.

ARTHUR: What for? You can't help it if—I forgive you everything.

MERLIN: Spoken like a King. He has forgiven everyone. Is there any doubt now? Hail to Arthur, King of Britain!

ALL: Hail to Arthur, King of Britain! *(All kneel, except Merlin and Arthur. As the curtain falls, music comes up. Suggest "Borie Goudonov", Side 3, about one inch.)*

CURTAIN

(Optional: If there is a curtain call, Merlin walks down the platform to center stage, waves his hand, and a puff of smoke comes up from the footlights, as the curtains close for the last time.)

Niccolo and Nicollette

or

The Puppet Prince

by

ALAN CULLEN

NICCOLO AND NICOLLETTE

By Alan Cullen

THE ANCHORAGE PRESS
Cloverlot
Anchorage, Kentucky 40223
U. S. A.

NICCOLO AND NICOLETTE

CHARACTERS

Nicolette
The Customer
Magnus the Magus
Seamus O'Shaughnessy
Niccolo, the Puppet Prince
The Duchess of Umbrage
Bugle, a Footman
The Leprechaun
The High Cockalorum
The Turk
Townsfolk
Dancers

SYNOPSIS

The premiere performance of this play was given in April, 1954, by the Bolton Little Theatre of Bolton, Lancashire, England.

SCENE 1.

The interior of a rather fantastic toyshop. Large dolls of different kinds, string and glove puppets, a model theatre, soldiers; very colorful but dark in the corners. A small counter with an account book and cash box. Among the toys a large, gaily-decorated upright box with a bolt on the outside. A chair and a stool or two. Dusk. A clock somewhere chimes musically the third quarter. Nicolette, a pretty girl in her 'teens, is sitting alone, stitching a doll. She finishes a stitch, bites off the thread and props up the doll on the counter.

NICOLETTE: There!—Almost finished, and very pretty too, although I do say it myself. Now all we want is for someone to walk right in and buy you on the spot, and everything will be just perfect!
(She looks up with a little frown.)
Which reminds me that I have sold very little this week. I don't know what Uncle Magnus will think, I'm sure, when he calls to check the accounts. However, I mustn't worry about that, and I *must* stop talking to myself, before it really becomes a habit.
(Footsteps are heard approaching the door.)
A customer!—Oh, I hope she buys lots and lots of things!
(Nicolette puts the doll down on the counter, then rapidly rearranges herself as the door bell jangles and the Customer comes in.—a woman, rather silly and affected.)
CUSTOMER: Oh, I'm so glad you're still open. It is getting late, though, is'nt it?

NICOLETTE: It is, rather. But we don't close until eight, you know.

CUSTOMER: Hasn't it been a wonderful day? I always think this is the best part of the year, don't you?

NICOLETTE: It has been nice. The evenings are drawing in, though.

CUSTOMER: Oh, now you've spoilt it. I hate people to say that. It makes it sound like winter already, and I can just *feel* my twinges beginning again. Do you get twinges?

NICOLETTE: No, I can't say I do. Not yet, anyhow.

CUSTOMER: You don't know how lucky you are. I'm a martyr to them, simply a martyr. But of course you shouldn't get them at your age. You're really very young to be looking after a shop all by yourself. Don't you find it tedious?

NICOLETTE: Not in the least. I love the shop and all the toys. I'm afraid I'm not a good saleswoman, though.—I hate parting with toys when someone buys them—they're like old friends. Uncle Magnus says I'm silly, but you *do* get fond of them, you know.

CUSTOMER: Is that the owner of the shop?

NICOLETTE: Uncle Magnus? —Yes, he's my guardian. I have no parents.

CUSTOMER: I'm sorry. Is he nice?

NICOLETTE: *(Doubtfully)* Ye-es. He's a little—sharp sometimes, but I don't think he means it. He's really been very good to me, letting me look after the shop and everything . . . . . . Can I—can I show you something?

CUSTOMER: Oh, of course—forgive me, I get carried away as soon as anyone mentions twinges . . . . . .Now what *did* I come in for? . . . . . I'm sure there was something. You know my husband is always telling me I should make a *list*—he's such a methodical man himself—his pockets are simply *full* of lists!

NICOLETTE: Really?

CUSTOMER: Quite full. But I can't live that way. Even a knot in my pocket handkerchief is worse than useless to me. I can never remember what I made it for. —Isn't it silly?

NICOLETTE: Was it a toy of some kind?

CUSTOMER: Was what a toy?

NICOLETTE: What you came in for.

CUSTOMER: Oh, that. I suppose it must have been, otherwise I wouldn't have come to a toyshop, would I? —That's logical, you can't deny. My husband is always telling me to be logical.

NICOLETTE: *(Patiently)* I'm sure he must be.

CUSTOMER: I'll tell you what we'll do. You tell me all the things you have in the shop, and I'll stop you when we come to it!

NICOLETTE: Isn't that going to take rather a long time? —It is getting late, you know.

CUSTOMER: Well, of course, if you are not prepared to take a little trouble over your customers . . . .

456

NICOLETTE: Oh no, please . . . . Was it a toy trumpet?
CUSTOMER: No. What would I want with a trumpet?
NICOLETTE: A skipping rope?
CUSTOMER: No, but it was something like that.
NICOLETTE: A top?
CUSTOMER: No.
NICOLETTE: Snakes and ladders?
CUSTOMER: Nothing like it.
NICOLETTE: A doll's house?
CUSTOMER: Now then, we're getting somewhere.
NICOLETTE: Was it a doll?
CUSTOMER: Yes it was!
NICOLETTE: This sort of doll?
CUSTOMER: How clever you are! That's exactly it.
NICOLETTE: Are you sure? We have others . . .
CUSTOMER: No, this is the thing . . . . It *is* lovely—did you make it?
NICOLETTE: Yes.
CUSTOMER: You are clever.
NICOLETTE: Shall I wrap it for you?
CUSTOMER: What for?
NICOLETTE: Well, I thought you came in to buy it.
CUSTOMER: Buy it? —Good Heavesns, no. I just wanted to see how it was made. I make my own, you see.
  (She gets up.)
  I *have* enjoyed our chat. Goodbye.
  (She goes out.)
NICOLETTE: Well! . . . Wanted to see how it was made indeed! . . . and just look what a mess she has made of it . . . now I shall have to fetch some more cotton from upstairs to put that right . . . .
  (She props the doll up on the counter.)
  Now you just sit there and wait till I get back.
  (She goes to the inner door.)
  Don't go away, will you?
  (She goes out. There is a pause, then suddenly the doorbell jangles and the Magician comes in. He is a smallish, dark man of about fifty, who tries hard to be fierce but without a great deal of success. At the moment he is just irritable. He looks around the shop suspiciously, goes to the upright box in the corner and examines it anxiously, then, apparently satisfied, turns away and calls.)
MAGNUS: Nicolette! . . . Nicolette! . . . Drat the girl. Never where she should be. Nobody looking after the shop, either. Anybody could walk in and take the lot, lock, stock and barrel. Nicolette!
  (Nicolette enters from the inner door. She stops and looks at him rather strangely and apprehensively.)
NICOLETTE: Yes, Uncle Magnus?
MAGNUS: How often have I told you not to leave the shop unattended?

NICOLETTE: I'm sorry. I only went for some more thread for my sewing. I .. I haven't been away half a minute—

MAGNUS: Don't start giving me a lot of excuses| I won't have the shop left for a minute—not for a minute, do you understand? You never know who might be prowling about. There are some very valuable things in this shop, and don't you forget it!

NICOLETTE: *(She is about to say something then stops herself.)* No, Uncle Magnus.

(She goes behind the counter and continues with the doll.)

MAGNUS: I'm pretty sure I saw that good-for-nothing pedlar, that Seamus, for instance, as I flew down the street.

NICOLETTE: *(She looks keenly at him.)* As you did what, Uncle Magnus?

MAGNUS: Eh?

NICOLETTE: I thought you said "flew" down the street!

MAGNUS: *(Testily)* Don't be absurd! —And don't change the subject. I won't have that mountebank hanging about the shop. Even if he was a friend of your parents, he's a bad influence—lazy, idle . . .

NICOLETTE: *(Bridling a little)* I think you're mistaken about Seamus, Uncle. He's not really all you say. After all, he does come and talk to me occasionally. He cheers me up.

MAGNUS: Cheers you up! . . . What do you want cheering up for? You ought not to need cheering up if your mind was on your work. No gratitude, that's what it is—no gratitude, after all I've done for you. —Are you listening to what I'm saying?

NICOLETTE: Yes, Uncle Magnus.

MAGNUS: Oh, give me the account book before I really lose my temper. *(She gives it to him from the counter.)* Let me see how business is this week. *(He turns over the pages.)* And if it isn't better than last week I shall have to reduce your allowance. I might tell you it isn't easy to keep this place going and my own cas— my own house as well. *(He begins to add up the accounts, somewhat laboriously.)*

NICOLETTE: *(Screwing up her courage.)* Uncle Magnus.

MAGNUS: What is it? —Can't you see I'm busy? —Four and six and eightpence is—

NICOLETTE: How far is your castle?

MAGNUS: *(Not looking up.)* Fifty miles as the crow flies—when he flies straight, drat him. Five and two and elevenpence is . . . .

NICOLETTE: Uncle Magnus . . .

MAGNUS: Don't keep interrupting! You're making me lose count. What do you want?

NICOLETTE: Why haven't you ever mentioned the castle before?

MAGNUS: Because I don't—Who said anything about a castle? I haven't got one. What are you talking about?

NICOLETTE: You said it just now. And you said it was fifty miles off. You *have* got a great castle, and you fly there and back every week

on the back of a great black crow. Don't you? *(He doesn't answer.)*
—I know you do, because I saw you arrive this evening from the upstairs window. You—you're a magician!

MAGNUS: *(Somewhat shaken by this.)* Rubbish! You're imagining
things. Castles and crows! *(He laughs a forced laugh, which ends as
an apprehensive cough.)*

NICOLETTE: *(Gaining courage.)* You're not being very convincing,
Uncle. I've wondered about you for a long time, and now I'm sure.
You *are* a magician, and you're . . . . . .

MAGNUS: *(In a great rage.)* That's enough! So you've been spying on
me, have you? Watching me from the upstairs window, have you? All
right, so now you know that much, you might as well know the rest.
I *am* a magician, and I *do* fly backwards and forwards from the castle
to the shop on the back of a big black crow. I only keep the shop going
to keep you out of my way and give you something useful to do.
(He looks at the box.)
And I find it useful sometimes to . . to dispose of things. I've been
very lenient with you, Nicolette, but if you go on prying into my affairs
I shall not be lenient any longer. I shall have to turn you into something—something that can't talk and spread gossip about me . . . like
a puppet, for example.

NICOLETTE: You don't mean you can turn people into puppets? —how
horrible!

MAGNUS: I thought that would shake you. Now remember—mind your
own business and look after the shop properly, otherwise . . . . . .
*(He picks up the doll she has been working on, looks at it ominously and
throws it back to her.)*
Now it's getting time I was back at the castle. I have a rather important
little spell on the stove, and I don't want it to boil over.
(He goes to the door.)
Rather interesting—gives everybody pins and needles over a range of
fifty miles.
(He turns to go.)

NICOLETTE: *(Firmly)* Uncle Magnus!

MAGNUS: *(Turning)* What is it now?

NICOLETTE: Now that I know you as you really are, I hope you realize
I can't stay here any longer. The first opportunity I get, I intend to
leave the shop and fend for myself, so—so I'm afraid you will have to
get yourself another assistant. I—I'm giving you notice of termination
of my appointment as from today. There!
(She stops and looks at him, defiantly.)

MAGNUS: Have you quite finished?

NICOLETTE: Yes, I have.

MAGNUS: Then I'll tell you something. I give *you* notice here and now
that if I have any more of your nonsense, you'll find yourself dangling

from a string like the rest of these marionettes—a puppet that can't give its notice.

(He turns to the door, then remembers something and turns back.)

One more thing that I almost forgot.

NICOLETTE: Well?

MAGNUS: That cabinet in the corner.

NICOLETTE: I've wondered about that. It came this week. You never told me the price.

MAGNUS: *(In alarm)* Price? It has no price. It's not for sale. It mustn't leave this shop on any account—not on any account!

NICOLETTE: But you never said anything about it. What is it here for then?

MAGNUS: Never you mind. You are not to touch it. What's in it is no concern of yours. It's very, very . . . . . precious. Yes, that's it— precious. And don't you think of opening it when I'm out of the way— *(Slowly)* not even if it asks you yourself! You understand?

NICOLETTE: Yes, Uncle. Not even if it asks me itself. Anyway, I'm sure I should be terrified if it did . . . . . When will you be back again?

MAGNUS: When I feel like it. *(He goes to the door.)* And don't forget— no spying from the upstairs window. *(He goes out.)*

NICOLETTE: Thank goodness he's gone. *(She goes over to the cabinet.)* I wonder why he told me that? If he hadn't told me there was something extraordinary inside I wouldn't want to look. I'm dying to know what it is. Something wonderful, he said. No, I mustn't open it. He would be terribly angry if he found out, and he frightens me so when he is angry. "Not even if it asks you itself", he said. I wonder if it will. Oh, I hope it does, even if I am a bit afraid of it. *(She goes away from it.)* I'd better leave it alone before something terrible happens. *(The door opens from the street, tinkling the bell as it does so, and Seamus O'Shaughnessy comes into the shop. He is a cheerfully eccentric character in a fantastic adaptation of Irish national dress, largely in tatters, and carrying a pedlar's pack.)*

SEAMUS: The top of the evening to you, me darling.

NICOLETTE: Seamus! You gave me such a start. I thought it was Uncle Magnus back again.

SEAMUS: The ould divil. He's after disappearin' down the street, mutterin' to himself as usual, and me concealin' myself till he was well out of it. Oh, he's a terrible man, that, with his skinny hands and his face like one o' the gargoyles on the top of the cathedral. But what call is there to be talkin' about him at all, when it's yourself I'm after callin' on to pay me respects?

NICOLETTE: I'm so glad you came, Seamus. I get so lonely in the shop except when you come to cheer me up with your nonsense.

SEAMUS: Nonsense, is it?

NICOLETTE: Beautiful nonsense. And I love it.

SEAMUS: That's better. But why did you jump when I came in at the door, —the way I was the banshee itself?

NICOLETTE: Oh, It's nothing really. Just—just the empty shop and everything—I get a bit jumpy sometimes.

SEAMUS: Och, it's a rich man I should be instead of a poor pedlar that has to live by his wits, such as they are. Then I could take you away out of this to a far country where you'd be a fine lady and never be bothered with that ould miscreant of an uncle, bad cess to him. But I don't know how it is—I can't sell as much of my Patent Panacea as will keep body and soul together, so I can't. I think the Sales Resistance of the local population is hardening against me more and more as every day goes by. Only yesterday for instance, I'm crying me wares as me custom is when an ould woman with a moustache pushes her way to the front of the crowd and says "Is it yourself" she says "that sold me a bottle for me corns a month ago?". "It is", sez I, "will ye come to the front here now and tell these lovely people what a power of good ye've had from it, and it only ninepence a bottle?". "I will indeed." sez she, and the wicked gleam she had in her eye— "I tried a thimbleful on the cow that's troubled the same way, and the poor creature lashed out so hard with her two hind legs that she lifted both me and the milking-stool into the duckpond". Ah, I'm thinkin' my physiognomy is getting a trifle too well-known in these parts.

NICOLETTE: (Laughing) I'm sorry Seamus. And I'm very grateful, too. I know you only stay near to keep an eye on me. I'm sure you would do much better if you went to another part of the country.

SEAMUS: And leave you with nobody but the ould spalpeen and a row of painted images? I may be only a pedlar, and a shady one at that, but the O'Shaughnessys have the blood of the Kings of Connaught in their veins and as long as there's a mouthful of breath in me body I'll be hanging about in case you need me.

NICOLETTE: Thank you, Seamus.

SEAMUS: Don't be after thankin' me till I'm able to help you properly. (He puts down his pack and in doing so sees the cabinet.) And what would the like of this be now? This was never here the last time I was in.

NICOLETTE: (Over to cabinet.) Oh, please don't touch it, Seamus. Uncle Magnus is terribly particular about its being left as it is.

SEAMUS: What could be inside it, I wonder? If he's so particular there must be something worth takin' a peep at.

NICOLETTE: I don't know what it is. He said I was not to open it on any account, even if it asked me itself.

SEAMUS: Now that was a queer way of putting it. Is there magic in it, would you suppose?

NICOLETTE: There must be. Boxes don't talk.

SEAMUS: That they don't. And they never will until somebody invents the wireless.

NICOLETTE: What's that?

SEAMUS: It's only an anachronism. Pay no attention to it. If there's something in there that he's not wanting people to see, that ould repobate is up to no good. I daresay it's a piece of loot from one of these mysterious jaunts he's always after going on. And wouldn't I like to know where he goes at the time, for he's never in the shop.

NICOLETTE: I don't know. But he did say it was precious.

SEAMUS: Precious. I'd swear by the Four Provinces 'tis a treasure he has locked away in there. Nicolette, me darlin', I think it's me duty as a citizen to open it. And me natural curiousity is even greater than me sense of duty, so stand back and we'll see.

(He makes to draw the bolt.)

NICOLETTE: No, Seamus. You're not to open it.

SEAMUS: Ah, where's the harm in one little peep? He'll never know.

NICOLETTE: No, Seamus.

SEAMUS: Not the teeniest, weeniest little peep?

NICOLETTE: No.

SEAMUS: No?

NICOLETTE: No, and that's final. Whatever we may think of Uncle Magnus it's his property, and we have no right to interfere with it.

SEAMUS: *(Affecting indifference.)* Ah, well, it's none of my business anyway. I'll be getting back to my peddling, Er . . . . You don't happen to have a drop of tay on the hob maybe, just to put a little life into me before sending me on my way, do you?

NICOLETTE: I suppose you won't leave until you get it. But only one cup, mind, because it's almost closing time. I'll go and put the kettle on—and don't touch the box, Seamus, please.

(She goes through the inner door. Seamus eyes the box curiously.)

SEAMUS: Ah, where would be the harm? If I was just quietly to draw the bolt and take a quick peep nobody would be any the wiser.

(He touches the bolt, then draws away again.)

O'Shaughnessy, you're a weak and vacillating character. Control yourself, now.

(He stands in an agony of temptation, then finally gives in.)

It's no use. I'll just *have* to take a look while she's in the kitchen.

(He stealthily draws the bolt, peeps in, and shuts the door again quickly.)

Holy St. Patrick!

(He opens it again fully this time so that the audience can see it.)

There's a wonderful piece of work, now. Ah, the hours that must have gone into the making of that!

(In the open box is revealed a life-size figure of a young man, gaily painted and splendidly dressed in uniform. In gazing at it, Seamus does not notice Nicolette return quickly into the room.)

NICOLETTE: Seamus! After all I told you!

SEAMUS: Ah, now don't be taking on at me, Nicolette me dear. I—I'm

462

not a very strong-minded sort of a man, and it's not fair to put temptation in the way o' the likes o' me.

*(Nicolette, meanwhile, has looked at the Puppet and stands gazing at it
with clasped hands.)*

And 'tis only another graven image after all the fuss. I—I suppose
I'd better be shutting it in again.

NICOLETTE: *(Enraptured)* Don't shut it just yet, Seamus. It was very
wrong of you, and I'm very angry with you, really, but it's *so* beautiful.
—Look! It has eyelashes and fingernails and everything. It looks so
real—it might almost be alive!

SEAMUS: I suppose for a doll it's human enough. But a doll it is.
(He lifts one arm and taps it, making a hollow wooden sound.)

NICOLETTE: Look! There's a key in its chest. Do you think it's
clockwork? Oh, I *must* see what happens. *(She winds it up, there is
a loud whirr of mechanism, and the head straightens. She jumps
away.)* Oh! It's moving! *(It opens its eyes with a click, then blinks
with a series of rapid clicks. It raises one arm, then the other, and
begins to walk out of the box.)*

SEAMUS: Did you ever see the like of that, now?

NICOLETTE: Sh! Let's see what it does now.
*(The puppet starts to dance, woodenly. Seamus draws a pipe from
his pocket and plays. The Puppet follows the rhythm and dances faster
until it gives a loud whirr and stops.)*
(Nicolette clapping her hands.)
It's marvellous, Seamus. I love it. We *must* make it dance again. I
can't imagine why Uncle Magnus did not want me to see it, though.
I think it was mean.

SEAMUS: Because he can't bear to see anyone enjoying themselves,
that's why, the miserable ould . . .

NICOLETTE: Seamus! There's someone coming! *(Over to window.)*
Oh, I hope it isn't Uncle Magnus. We must get it back to the box,
quickly.
*(SEAMUS hastitly gives the handle a few turns, and as the figure starts
to move he leads it back to the box. He has no time to close the door,
so he stands in front of it. The figure is still working and throughout
part of the following dialogue he is making desperate efforts to stop it
raising its arms and legs and walking out of the box.)*
Thank goodness! It's only a customer.
*(The DUCHESS enters with a footman in attendance and occupies the
only chair.)*

NICOLETTE: Good evening, Madam. *(Curtseys)* May I show you
something?

DUCHESS: *(Ignoring her and speaking to the Footman.)* Inform
this young person who I am.

FOOTMAN: Yes, your Grace. You are addressing Her Grace, the

Duchess of Umbrage. She never converses with anybody below the rank of Baronet, except through me.

NICOLETTE: That must make conversation rather difficult.

FOOTMAN: It would if she weren't such an impatient woman. She never keeps it up long.

NICOLETTE: Oh. Will you ask her Grace, please, if she has anything particular in mind, or if she just wishes to look round the shop first.

FOOTMAN: The young person, Your Grace, wishes to know what it is you have in mind, or whether—

DUCHESS: Tell the young person I want the best she has in the shop naturally.

FOOTMAN: Her Grace—

NICOLETTE: Never mind. Please tell her that these are our best line. They are very well made. They will last for years.
(Showing doll she has been finishing off.)

FOOTMAN: These are.. . .

DUCHESS: Nothing lasts for years in the hands of my daughter, Ermyntrude. Having had the most expensive possible education she is naturally completely uninhibited. She tears everything to shreds within an hour. Let me see that.
(Nicolette gives it to the Footman, who gives it to the Duchess.)
If that's the best you can do I am wasting my time.
(She gets up.)

NICOLETTE: Please don't go yet. I'm sure we have something your daughter would like.

DUCHESS: What's this?

NICOLETTE: That's Seamus, your Grace.

SEAMUS: I'm not for sale, your Majesty. I've no ambition to be torn limb from limb to find out if I'm stuffed.

DUCHESS: I mean this. *(Pointing past him to the box. Seamus hastily manages to get the door closed.)*

SEAMUS: You mean this box?

DUCHESS: Nonsense. I mean what's in the box.

NICOLETTE: The box belongs to the proprietor, your Grace. It is not to be opened.

DUCHESS: Of course it is to be opened. Boxes were made to be opened. Bugle, open the box.
(Bugle crosses to open the box.)
Stand aside, my good man. *(Seamus hastily scrambles out of the way.)*

NICOLETTE: *(Hastily)* But your Grace, you have not begun to look at the other things in the shop. I've a case full of things over here.
(Bugle has opened the door, and the Duchess now inspects the figure closely.)

DUCHESS: Ah! It seems to be mechanical. Just the thing! Ermyntrude will not rest for an instant until she has taken it apart, and it is large enough to occupy her for several hours. Ah, there's a handle here. Wind it up, and demonstrate it for me, please.

NICOLETTE: Your Grace, that is impossible. Now over here, I have a model theatre, and actors to go with it—

DUCHESS: Rubbish! Nothing is impossible. Do as I say.

SEAMUS: Will I dance for you instead, your Grace? I can do the Walls o'Limerick like nobody's business.

DUCHESS: I am a woman of exemplary patience, but unless you do as I say at once, I shall not be responsible for the consequences. Bugle, operate that contraption!

(As Bugle winds up the puppet, Nicolette wrings her hands.)

NICOLETTE: Oh Seamus, I knew we should never have opened the box. *(The figure comes out of the box, dances again, and then whirrs to a standstill.)*

DUCHESS: Wonderful! I've never seen anything so natural. I'll take it.

NICOLETTE: Oh no, your Grace!

DUCHESS: Wrap it up at once.

NICOLETTE: Your Grace, I—I'm very sorry, but it's not for sale.

DUCHESS: Nonsense. Wrap it up.

NICOLETTE: But it really isn't for sale, your Grace. We can't sell it.

DUCHESS: Why not?

SEAMUS: Ye see it—er—it isn't finished, your honour.

DUCHESS: What's the matter with it?

SEAMUS: Eh?—the matter with it? Oh, er—it's in the mechanism— yes, the mechanism's very delicate, you see. It has an eccentric differential turbo-sprocket, and—er—in fact it's so eccentric it can't differentiate properly, and the—er—the ratchet-stabiliser doesn't connect with the—er—

(He tails off ineffectually.)

DUCHESS: Very well. You will have it rectified immediately. The carriage will call for it tomorrow morning. See to it. Tell the young woman I wish her good evening. The other person you may ignore. *(She sweeps out.)*

NICOLETTE: *(To Footman)* You can't take it away. You mustn't. Can't she be persuaded that it isn't for sale?

FOOTMAN: Nobody has ever managed to persuade Her Grace of anything in her life. She'll have it if she has to buy the whole shop. Sorry. *(He goes after the Duchess.)* She's set her heart on it, if she has any.

NICOLETTE: *(Sits on the chair.)* What *am* I going to do? *(Seamus closes the box and goes to her.)*

SEAMUS: I don't know to be sure. It's the divil of a fix, so it is, and it's all my fault. I ought to have my big mouth stuffed with the Stone of Blarney for openin' it at all.

NICOLETTE: Oh, it's as much my fault as yours. More, because it's really my responsibility. If she sends for it tomorrow and Uncle

Magnus finds it's gone, I don't know what will happen, but it's sure to be something dreadful. *(A clock strikes eight.)* Eight o'clock. Oh, well. It's getting dark. I suppose I'd better shut the shop. *(She gets up to go to the door. As the last stroke sounds a knock is heard.)* What was that? *(Looks out)* There's no-one at the door. *(Knocking repeated)* There it is again.

SEAMUS: It's in the shop. *(Knocking again)* Listen.

NICOLETTE: It's from the box.

SEAMUS: The Saints preserve us, so it is. Shall I . . . shall I take a look inside, maybe? *(Without enthusiasm.)*

NICOLETTE: Not again. We are in enough trouble already through doing that. I won't have it open again—even if it asks me itself.

VOICE FROM THE BOX: Open the box. Please open the box.

(Seamus and Nicolette cling to each other.)

SEAMUS: It must have heard you, by all that's holy.

VOICE: Please let me out. Please. There is so little time. So little time. *(Knocking again.)* Open the box.

NICOLETTE: It's the puppet. I can't help it—I must let it out.

(She runs over and unbolts the box. Nikki, the puppet, comes quickly into the room. His painted face is now normal makup, but his costume is the same except for the handle in the chest which is not there now.)

SEAMUS: It really *is* alive!

NIKKI: Yes, alive again at last and human—for a few hours. I'm free! You don't know what a service you have done me Nicolette.

NICOLETTE: But I don't understand. A few minutes ago you were just a wooden puppet.

NIKKI: Please sit down and I'll explain. But there isn't much time for it. I must get away whilst I have the chance.

(She sits down and listens intently.)

My name is Niccolo, Prince Niccolo, really, but everyone calls me Nikki. Some time ago Magnus placed me under a spell and seized my lands and my castle. He is very powerful and very wicked. His magic transformed me into a mechanical doll, so that he could keep me and gloat over my misfortune.

NICOLETTE: But you're not like that now—you're alive.

NIKKI: Yes, for a short time. You see, the magic spell was not complete, and now every evening at sunset I regain my proper shape, but it only lasts until first cock-crow and then I become a puppet again.

NICOLETTE: That's why he kept you locked in the box!

NIKKI: Yes, and forbade you to open it. And that's why he brought me here—because he knows it is too far for me to travel to my castle between sunset and sunrise. He knows I should change back again before I got there, and try to stop him completing the spell.

NICOLETTE: Poor Nikki. We must do something to help, mustn't we, Seamus?

SEAMUS: We must indeed. But the divil knows what.

466

NICOLETTE: Uncle Magnus won't be back until tomorrow night. Surely we can think of something before then.

SEAMUS: But what about the Duchess? She'll be back for Nikki the first thing in the morning, so she said.

NICOLETTE: Oh dear. That only gives us a few hours.

NIKKI: I must get away from here and hide during the day. It's the only way.

NICOLETTE: *(Over to Nikki.)* But who will look after you? You can't go alone, and I can't stay here now that Nikki has come out of the box. Uncle Magnus would do something dreadful to me. Seamus—we shall have to run away together. Will you go with us? You know the roads better than we do.

SEAMUS: Go with you? On the contrary, you're both coming with me. I'll tell you what we'll do. Whenever we come to a town, Nikki can dance to attract the customers and then nobody will think it out of the way us travelling the road together. And you can help me sell me wonderful elixir.

NICOLETTE: Oh thank you, Seamus. I knew you would help us. Nikki! We're to be travelling showmen! What fun. I bet we sell more of your Panacea in a day than you've sold in the last month. Which way shall we go?

NIKKI: We must get to the castle. Once we are there I am sure I can do something to free myself forever. It's my only hope! I can't spend the rest of my life this way. But we must get there quickly. Magnus spends all his time there trying to perfect the spell—if he succeeds I shall remain a puppet all the time and never be free again.

NICOLETTE: It's going to take ages if we have to carry you during the day, Nikki. Can't we hold up the spell or something?

NIKKI: I'm afraid not.

SEAMUS: But we can! At least I think so.

NICOLETTE: Seamus! Can you do magic as well?

SEAMUS: No, but a friend of mine can. Now why did I not think of him before?

NIKKI: Who?

SEAMUS: The Luck of the O'Shaughnessys. Who else would an Irishman call on but a leprechaun? Ah, but I doubt if he'll come. They're queer chancy things, leprechauns, at the best of times, and if he's the wrong side out it would take the divil and all to fetch him out of the hills of Antrim.

NICOLETTE: Try, Seamus, please try. I've never seen a leprechaun.

SEAMUS: All right. But if he comes there'll be nobody more surprised than Seamus O'Shaughnessy. Now ye'll both have to help. 'Tis a powerful lot of concentration that's required to call the Luck of the O'Shaughnessys all the way from Connemara.

NICOLETTE: I thought you said Antrim.

SEAMUS: Did I now? Well, maybe it is. It's a long time since I called him and he might be anywhere. Now ye'll both have to close your eyes and think hard. Think all the magic you can muster, and keep all your fingers crossed.

(They put their hands out with fingers crossed and closed eyes.)

By the Beautiful Ones that live in the hills
Let the Luck of the O'Shaughnessys come if it wills.

(There is a gust of wind and a tinkle of the bell as the door flies open and the leprechaun bursts into the room. He is a tiny, wizened creature with a straggly beard, dressed (naturally) in green with a hammer in one hand and a tiny shoe in the other.)

LEPRECHAUN: *(Hopping about in a tearing rage and speaking in a high squeaking voice.)* Who is that drags me away from my last and me with the shoes of the Lord of Manahan to finish before moonrise? Who is it?

SEAMUS: 'Tis me, me darlint, and there's no call to take on like that. I won't be keeping you long.

LEPRECHAUN: Seamus O'Shaughnessy! You're a disgrace to your ancestors and a torment to me. You needn't be asking me any favours, for I've done with you. Do you hear me? I'm away back to my shoemaker's bench, and the back of my hand to you.

NICOLETTE: Don't go. I'm sure you can help us. It isn't for himself that Seamus called you, it's for Nikki and me. We're in terrible trouble and *we* persuaded Seamus to call you to help. Will you? Please? I'm sure you will, you have such a kind little face, really.

LEPRECHAUN: Little? I'm not little. I'm the biggest leprechaun of them all, so I am.

NICOLETTE: I didn't mean *you* were little. In fact you are much bigger than I expected. I just said you had a little face—but a very kind face.

LEPRECHAUN: You're trying to get round me with your female blandishments. Women! Hmmph! *(He is calming down a bit. He looks at them sharply with his beady eyes.)* What do you want anyway? —not that ye'll get it, mind.

NICOLETTE: It's Nikki—he's under a spell, which . . .

LEPRECHAUN: I know all about that. There isn't a spell or a charm or a piece of magic performed in the whole of the world but what I know about. What do you expect me to do?

NICOLETTE: Couldn't you stop it, or neutralize it or something?

LEPRECHAUN: *(Laughs)* What queer notions ye have about magic! Magnus is too powerful for the likes of me. There's only one thing I could do . . .

SEAMUS: That's more like it. I was wondering when ye'd *do* something instead of prating like an old hen.

LEPRECHAUN: But I won't. *(Stamps away in disgust.)*

468

NICOLETTE: Seamus! You've offended it again. Do be quiet.

SEAMUS: Me lips is sealed from now on. *(Turns away.)*

NICOLETTE: You will do it, won't you?

LEPRECHAUN: If I do it won't be on account of him. Besides I haven't said what it is yet.

NICOLETTE: Tell us then. Quickly.

LEPRECHAUN: Whenever the first cock crows, *he* changes into a puppet. Isn't that so?

NICOLETTE: That's right.

LEPRECHAUN: Well, suppose now the cock doesn't crow at all tomorrow? That'll give ye another twenty-four hours to be on your way.

NICOLETTE: Oh, thank you. If you can do that for us . . . if you can forbid the cocks to crow, we might be at the castle by tomorrow night.

LEPRECHAUN: I never said I could do it. Nor can I.

NIKKI: Then why did you tell us about it?

LEPRECHAUN: I'm coming to that, if ye'll just have a little patience. If you can get to the crossroads before dawn, you'll find somebody there that can do it for you. If he will, of course, which I doubt. Now I'm off. Good luck to you both, and the back of my hand to you, Seamus O'Shaughnessy.

(A gust of wind and he is out through the door leaving the bell jangling behind as the door slams.)

NICOLLETTE: Oh, but wait! . . . He's gone, and he never told us who we were to meet. Oh, I think we are as badly off as ever we were. Thank you for bringing him, Seamus, but I don't think he was much use.

SEAMUS: Now don't be thinking those things. He might be a bit sharp in the tongue, but he has a heart of gold, like all of his race. Anyway, it's our only chance.

NIKKI: Yes. I'm sure we should do what he said. Come. We must hurry if we are to be at the crossroads by midnight. *(They start to go.)*

NICOLETTE: I wonder who we shall find there? *(As they get to the door the Magician appears in it. They back downstage and he slowly advances.)* Uncle Magnus!

MAGNUS: Who will you find where, my dear? You are not planning to leave your kind Uncle Magnus, surely? With Nikki and Seamus? How nice. But I fear you will have to cancel your little plan.

NICOLETTE: The back door! Quick! *(They move to go.)*

MAGNUS: *(Makes a pass. There is a flash at the door.)* I don't think you will find it easy to get that way. It is now bolted from the other side. *(Nikki tries it. It is.)* You must not expect, Niccolo, to escape me as easily as that. You had better accept the fact, my dear Nikki, that you will never escape from me at all. *(The Leprechaun appears from behind the ample folds of Magnus' cloak.)*

LEPRECHAUN: Oh, yes he will.

MAGNUS: Who said that? *(He swings round, seeing the Leprechaun. With a screech of fear he jumps on the stool and gathers his cloak up in his hands.)* Take it away! Take it away! Leprechauns! Can't abide them. I've always been allergic to them. *(The Leprechaun hops across to him.)* Don't let it touch me! Ah, I shall faint in a minute. Keep it off!

(The Leprechaun dances round the stool and begins tapping one foot and then the other with his hammer, forcing the magician to dance on the stool.)

LEPRECHAUN: Now see how *you* like being made to dance when you don't feel like it. Naughty ould necromancer! *(He hits one toe.)* Wicked ould wizard. *(Hits the other.)* Miserable ould magician! *(Hits him again. The other three make their escape, as the curtain falls to the magician's cries of discomfiture).*

CURTAIN

SCENE 2.

A country road. Midnight, but a bright moon gives clear light. A smaller lane leads into the scene from the back. There is a fallen trunk somewhere to the rear also. Seamus, with his pack on his shoulder, and a lantern in his hand, comes in first followed by Nikki and Nicolette—hand in hand. They stop and look round. Nikki and Nicolette sit on the log.

SEAMUS: Well, here we are, unless me sense of direction fails me entirely, or me Leprechaun's leading me astray—which I wouldn't put past him. *(He puts down his pack.)* But there's divil a soul in sight except an ould hen scratchin' down the road yonder. And now I come to think of it, he never said who it was we were to meet, nor how we were to recognize him, even. The little varmint might have given us a password or a pink carnation for our buttonholes, or something. *(They are not listening to him.)* I might as well talk to myself. It's surprising what a fine night and a country walk can do in the way of improving human relations, as you might put it.

(With a glance at the other two who are looking fondly at each other. Seamus sits on his pack, takes a pipe from his pocket and starts to play softly.)

NIKKI: Are you tired, Nicolette?

NICOLETTE: Just a little. We must have been walking for hours. It must be nearly dawn—oh, I didn't want to think about that. I hate the thought of your turning back again into a horrid wooden figure. But somehow, sitting here in the moonlight, all that seems far away

471

and unreal. I feel safe, as though we weren't running away from anything . . . as though there was nothing in the world to be afraid of.

NIKKI: I know. As though the only real things were ourselves and the night. How close and comforting the night can be. I wish it could go on for ever like this, and the dawn never come.

(Tiny gleams of light begin to appear all over the stage, flickering among the trees and bushes by the roadside.)

NICOLETTE: How strange and beautiful the night is here. Look! It's as though all the fireflies and glow-worms for miles around were gathering on the road to light us on our way. I feel sure that something wonderful is going to happen.

NIKKI: Listen! There's someone coming.

SEAMUS: *(Stop playing.)* There is indeed. By the holy, I never saw the like in all my born days!

(Out of the lane upstage comes an enormous golden cockerel with shining plumage, looking very beautiful in the moonlight with scarlet and black tail and wing feathers and large jewelled eyes. He stops centre, flaps his wings and regards them majestically.)

NICOLETTE: What a beautiful creature. He must be the most splendid cockerel in the world.

SEAMUS: It's finest-looking fowl that ever came out of a shell, so it is. And it would make enough chicken broth to feed a battalion.

THE COCK: Broth? Don't mention that word in my presence.

SEAMUS: Save us! It can talk.

THE COCK: Naturally. I assure you I am no ordinary bird. I am the King of the Cocks and the Prince of Poultry, my usual title being High Cockalorum and my function Hereditary Herald of the Dawn. As mere mortals you must realize you are highly privileged in being granted audience. I must ask you not to scratch or cluck in my presence, and to fold your wings before you address me . . . if you can call them wings.

SEAMUS: Wings, is it? Sure, I was never issued with any up to the present, and I doubt if I ever will be in the future. However, I'll fold me arms if it makes your reverence any easier. *(He does so.)*

HIGH COCK: Irregular, but it will serve. For myself, I should be ashamed to own such featherless things. A recent moult, no doubt.

(He settles himself on the log vacated by Niccolette and Nikki, shakes his feathers and crosses his legs negligently.)

And now, before I receive you in audience officially, a little formality is necessary. It is time for the Dance of Dawn, a rather important ceremony which I cannot allow you to defer. Ah! here they come, punctual as always.

(Down the lane in pairs come the dancers dressed as an assortment of birds. They dance a ballet expressing the awakening of the world at dawn, and finish in a group around the High Cockalorum.)

472

And now I think we had better hear your request—and pray be brief—I must shortly perform my office of Heralding the Dawn, and I must on no account be late.

NICOLETTE: Please—how do you do that?

HIGH COCK: Do what?

NICOLETTE: Herald the Dawn—it is rather important to us.

HIGH COCK: It is important to everyone, I should imagine. I have the privilege of being the first cock to crow, a signal which is taken up by every cock throughout the world, thus announcing to a grateful universe that another dawn is about to begin.

NIKKI: You mean that no other cock can crow until you do?

HIGH COCK: They wouldn't dare. Only one ever tried it. A Buff Orpington, if I remember rightly.

NIKKI: What happened to him?

HIGH COCK: He was drummed out of the Buffs, of course. He has never crowed since. Who are you, by the way?

NIKKI: I'm Nikki.

HIGH COCK: You don't look very well. A spot of poultry spice in your mash would do you no harm.

NICOLETTE: His proper name is Niccolo—Prince Niccolo.

HIGH COCK: Ah! The aristocrarcy. I felt there was a certain nobility in your bearing, otherwise I would not have entertained you for a moment. You may be acquainted with a distant connection of mine, the Duchess of Rhode Island? No? A charming fowl and an excellent layer, if I may mention such matters. The Countess of Leghorn, perhaps? You *must* have met her—her picture is always in the Poultry Breeders' Gazette.

NIKKI: I can't say I have.

HIGH COCK: Pity, A *very* refined bird.

SEAMUS: What about the Cock o' the North? Are you related to him at all?

HIGH COCK: Certainly not. A mere barbarian. His crowing is invariably off-key. And now, what can I do for you?

NIKKI: You can help me a lot by not crowing this morning.

HIGH COCK: *(Rising in horror.)* Not crowing? Monstrous! Most unheard of. Why, that's what I'm *for*. It's an impossible suggestion, quite unthinkable. You realize what would happen if I didn't crow.

NIKKI: Of course. If you didn't start them all off, none of the other cocks would crow, either. And I should continue to remain free from enchantment, which only takes effect at cockcrow.

HIGH COCK: Enchantment? What enchantment?—This is all most unusual and quite distressing.

(He is very agitated and has lost all his dignity.)

NIKKI: Please listen. A powerful magician has cast a spell on me in order to take possession of my castle and lands. He changed me into a wooden puppet, and I can regain human shape from dusk until first

473

cock crow. If only I can remain free long enough to get to the castle, I may break the spell completely. Please say you'll help me.

HIGH COCK: My dear boy, you have obviously failed to realize the full enormity of what you ask. If I failed to crow and give the signal for dawn to break, the sun itself could not rise and the world would remain plunged in night and darkness for ever. *(Shudders at the thought of it.)* A terrible thing! An unthinkable thought! Oh, no, no. It's impossible. Quite impossible.

NICOLETTE: Nonsense!

HIGH COCK: What did you say?

NICOLETTE: I said nonsense. Even if you *are* the first cock to crow, which I very much doubt, you only *announce* the dawn, you don't *cause* it. The dawn will break whether you crow or not, you conceited thing!

HIGH COCK: Conceited! Me! I've never been so insulted since I was hatched. The audience is over. Leave my presence. *(Turns its back.)*

SEAMUS: Now it's offended too. We don't have an awful lot of success in our dealings with the supernatural.

NICOLETTE: I'm sorry, Nikki. I've probably spoiled everything by upsetting it, but it is the most irritating creature I've met.

NIKKI: It isn't your fault. Don't worry. We'll get to the castle somehow. I'll make one more last appeal to it. Can't you please hold things up for just a little while at least until we get a little further on our way?

HIGH COCK: *(Turns round again.)* Certainly not. I'm behind schedule as it is. *(Nikki turns away in despair and walks away.)* However, in view of your rank and so forth—noblesse oblige, you know—I will give you what help I can.

NICOLETTE: Nikki! He's going to help us after all. *(They go to him eagerly.)*

HIGH COCK: Under my right wing you will find a single silver feather among the gold. —anno domini, I'm afraid, but that's beside the point. If you pluck it out and hold it up and say "Jet propulsion"—

NIKKI: Jet propulsion? What's that?

HIGH COCK: How do I know? It's magic. It will carry you a long way in a very short time, and that's all you need to know. Now pluck it out. *(He lifts his wing. Nikki looks for the feather.)*

NIKKI: I can't see it.

HIGH COCK: *(Giggling)* Don't tickle me. I can't bear it.

NIKKI: I've got it. Stand still. *(He pulls it out.)*

HIGH COCK: Ouch! You might have been more careful. Now I really can't wait a moment longer. It's high time I crowed. You had better stand back if you don't want to be deafened for life. When I crow, I crow.

(The dancers hop away. The rest get well away from the High Cock. He starts to flap his wings and stretch his neck.)

NICOLETTE: Seamus! Call the Leprechaun again quickly.

SEAMUS: I doubt he'll come a second time, but I'll try.
(Crosses his fingers.)
   Come over the hills, come over the sea,
   O'Shaughnessy's luck come away to me.
(The Leprechaun leaps over the hedge.)

LEPRECHAUN: What d'ye want with me now? Ye have me leapin' about like a hare in March.

SEAMUS: There's no time for explanations. Can you stop this overgrown canary from singin' before he's the ruin of us all?

LEPRECHAUN: Of course I can. And so could you if you'd a mite of sense. Gimme yer kerchief. *(Plucks a large coloured handkerchief out of Seamus' pocket hops up to the log and whips the cloth over the cock's head.)* There! *(The Cock stops flapping suddenly. He struts, bewildered, for a few paces and comes down stage.)*

HIGH COCK: How very extraordinary! It's gone quite dark again. It mustn't be as late as I thought. I could have sworn it was nearly dawn. And I don't see anything of those impossible people either. Very odd! Oh well, if it's still the middle of the night I'll go back to sleep again.

(He goes to the log and roosts on it, settling himself comfortably.)

NICOLETTE: He's asleep. What a stupid creature to be taken in like that. And I thought he was so clever at first.

LEPRECHAUN: Stupid? Of course he is. You are all stupid or you would have thought of it yourselves. Now be off whilst you have the chance.

NIKKI: It's beginning to get lighter *(He feels his arm)*—and I'm still all right. It's working. Nicolette—it's working!

NICOLETTE: Oh, I'm so glad. Now we must be off. Come on, Seamus. *(He is picking up his pack.)*

NIKKI: Wait a moment. We've forgotten the feather. Hold on to me, both of you! *(He holds up the feather. They hold on to him at each side.)* Take us to the square in front of my castle. *(Pause)*

SEAMUS: Nothing happens.

LEPERCHAUN: Ye've forgotten the magic word. Hm! Amateurs! Ye're not fit to be entrusted with magic.

NIKKI: Of course. The magic word! What was it Nicolette?

NICOLETTE: Oh! I can't remember. Can you remember it, Seamus?

SEAMUS: Er . . . let me see now . . . er . . . begorrah, for the first time in my life I'm lost for a word. Was it something about compulsion? Emulsion?

NICOLETTE: No, it wasn't. Let's think. *(A shadow crosses the stage.)*

NIKKI: What was that?

SEAMUS: What?

NIKKI: Something just passed over our heads.

NICOLETTE: It's the crow with Uncle Magnus on its back. Look, it's circling round again!—He's seen us. We *must* think of the magic words before he finds us and spoils everything.

SEAMUS: Revulsion? No. It's on the tip of my tongue, so it is. *(He walks away from them thinking.)* You know, if it wasn't another anachronism, I could have sworn he said "jet propulsion!"
(Blackout as soon as he says it.)

NIKKI'S VOICE: Hold on Nicolette. *(Lights up. Nikki and Nicolette have disappeared.)*

SEAMUS: Begorrah, it *was* the right word! They've disappeared entirely.

LEPRECHAUN: No, they haven't. There they go, like a comet. *(Points upward.)* See them? They're almost out of sight already.

SEAMUS: So they are. *(Waves)* Goodbye. Goodbye. Now they've gone. *(Dismayed)* And left me behind.

LEPRECHAUN: Serve you right. You should have held on when he told you. Now you'll have to walk.

SEAMUS: Well, ye've no need to look so pleased about it, ye little varmint. *(Picks up his pack again.)* If ye had any sense of loyalty to the family at all, ye'd whisk me off in the twinkling of an eye, but I suppose that's too much to expect, for you're as contrary as you're high. *(As he speaks there is a flapping of wings.)* What's that? Don't tell me it's Magnus back again.

(Magnus comes down the lane. It is now full daylight. The Leprechaun slips out of the way.)

MAGNUS: Where are they? I know they are hiding somewhere about, because I saw them distinctly. If only that stupid crow would fly straight I could have dropped right on top of them. Where are they? You'd better tell me, O'Shaughnessy, or I'll shrivel you up to the size of an orange and use you as a pincushion.

SEAMUS: You must have passed them on the way. They were going up as you were coming down.

MAGNUS: Going up? Up where?

SEAMUS: Up in a beautiful parabola, like a rocket. They'll be at the castle by now.

MAGNUS: The castle! Witches and warlocks, just wait till I get my hands on them, I'll . . . but what's this? *(Seeing the Cock still perched on the log.)* So that's what you've been up to. I wondered why I heard no cocks crowing this morning. We'll soon settle that. We can't have our dear Nikki running about making mischief. *(He takes off the cloth.)* Wake up! Wake up you ridiculous creature and crow. Do you hear me?

HIGH COCK: *(Looks around and gets off the log.)* Good gracious! What a bright moon.

MAGNUS: Moon, you impossible fowl? It's the sun. It's daylight, and you should have crowed long ago. You're late.

HIGH COCK: Daylight! I don't believe it.

MAGNUS: Oh, get on with it. Of course it's daylight.

HIGH COCK: Then it is true what she said. I don't cause the dawn—
I only announce it.

MAGNUS: What are you waiting for? Hurry up and crow confound you.

HIGH COCK: No.

MANGUS: What do you mean, No?

HIGH COCK: I won't crow. I haven't the heart. It—it is a most
humiliating experience. I shall probably never crow again. I always
believed that there could be no day without me, and now . . . oh, it's
too much! Too much!

(He sits down and drops his head in utter dejection.)

MAGNUS: He's got to crow. I can't have Niccolo running about loooose.
No telling what he might be up to. *(To the Cock.)* Look, if I prove it
to you, will you believe you make the day?

HIGH COCK: I don't know. Perhaps.

MAGNUS: Right. Where's the cloth? *(Picks it up.)* Now then for a bit
of special sorcery. *(Covers the cock's head.)* Let me think a moment.
Spell for making a great black cloud to cover the sun. Ah, yes. I have it.

*(He crouches down and begins to gyrate widdershins, his cloak flying out
as he rises higher and highter, till he is whirling on tiptoe.)*

SEAMUS: What a performance for a grown man. It seems to be working
all the same.

(It is growing quite dark. The magician stops.)

MAGNUS: *(Staggering a little.)* Oh, my head. That always makes me
so dizzy, I'm nearly sick. *(Takes the cloth off the Cock.)* There. You
see it was the moonlight before. Now the moon is down and the world
is waiting for you. And for heaven's sake don't make any more fuss
about it.

HIGH COCK: *(Flaps his wings and lets out a terrific crow. Magnus,
behind his back, makes large passes. The lights come up again.)*

MAGNUS: There! Now are you satisfied?

HIGH COCK: Yes, I suppose so. But it was all very sudden. I have
a sneaking suspicion that something distinctly odd has been going
on. *(He is going off up the lane.)* Distinctly odd. Distinctly odd.

*(He is off. Seamus is tiptoeing off the stage, but Magnus sees him and
whips round.)*

MAGNUS: Where are you going?

SEAMUS: *(Turning round)* Oh, nowhere, nowhere. That is, I . . . . .

MAGNUS: Off to find those other two and make more mischief, weren't
you?

SEAMUS: Me? I wouldn't dream of it.

MAGNUS: Well you won't get the chance. *(He waves his arms at
Seamus's feet.)* Now move from that spot if you can.

SEAMUS: *(Trying to lift his feet.)* Bejabers, I've heard of people being
rooted to the spot, but I never thought it would happen to me! I
can't *(Pulls at his leg.)* stir *(Pulls again.)* an inch!

MAGNUS: *(Laughs uncontrollably.)* Ha, ha, ha, ha,! If you could only see yourself—ha, ha, ha! *(He goes off laughing.)*

SEAMUS: Now what am I to do? I can't stay here like a vegetable for the rest of my born days. I know one thing—I can save myself the trouble of calling on the Luck of the O'Shaughnessys—he'd only be laughing at me if he came. Now I wonder if that ould cockerel has another feather of silver that will carry me away the way it did the other two. It's worth a try—if I can attract his attention. *(Calling)* Your Majesty! Your Reverence! Your Fowlness! Wing Commander! *(He clucks like a hen.)* Cluck, cluck, cluck . . . . .

HIGH COCK: *(Appearing round the corner.)* Coming dear, coming. *(Sees Seamus.)* Oh, it's you. I thought for a moment it was my chief consort, the Great White Wyandotte. Frankly I'm quite relieved. She's such a masterful fowl. Excuse me.

SEAMUS: No don't go. You don't happen to have another silver feather about you, do you? The ould monster of a magician has me stuck to the ground by the soles of my feet, and I can't follow my friends.

HIGH COCK: I'm afraid not. But if you like I could probably carry you to them myself. In fact, a little trip would do me good. I have had such a trying morning.

SEAMUS: Thank ye, your Excellency.

HIGH COCK: But first we must release you from Mother Earth. Hold on to my tail feathers. Ready?

SEAMUS: I'm ready. *(The High Cock. pulls and straining forward, clucks and splutters and Seamus leans further and further forward.)* Pull, your Highness. Pull harder. Harder!

(There is a tearing sound and the Cock's tail is left in Seamus's hands Seamus looks at it in horror.)

HIGH COCK: What was that?

SEAMUS: What?

HIGH COCK: That tearing noise?

SEAMUS: *(Putting the tail behind his back.)* Nothing, your Majesty—only the wind in the bushes.

HIGH COCK: I thought I felt a draught. Tell me, can you feel it too?

SEAMUS: I can't say I do.

HIGH COCK: Well I do, it's—*(He turns round and realises his tail is gone.)* I've been robbed!

(He turns round in circles trying to look at his back. Seamus shame-facedly produces the feather from behind his back.)

SEAMUS: It came away in my hand.

HIGH COCK: Came away! Thief! Vandal!

SEAMUS: But it wasn't my fault, honest it wasn't.

HIGH COCK: Don't speak to me! Don't daré address me.

SEAMUS: But your Majesty . . .

HIGH COCK: Silence! This is the last straw—the ultimate humiliation. You have forced your way into my presence, you have pestered me with trivial petitions, deceived me, insulted me beyond measure, and now have despoiled me of my crowning glory—oh, my beautiful tail! My magnificent appendage! —Unless you repair the damage at once, I shall have you brought to justice on a charge of High Treason.

SEAMUS: High treason! But don't I keep telling you it was an accident?

HIGH COCK: And the penalty for that is Perforation.

SEAMUS: Perforation? And what in the name of injustice is that?

HIGH COCK: Perforation by pecking. I shall summon the birds and they shall peck you full of holes.

SEAMUS: Oh, now, this is getting fantastic. Be reasonable.

HIGH COCK: I am the most reasonable monarch in creation. It is the most lenient sentence I can possibly award. And you have the alternative—replace my tail and we will say no more about it.

SEAMUS: But how can I? Who can be expected to stick the feathers back on a plucked chicken?

HIGH COCK: You do not improve your case by referring to the Prince of Poultry as a plucked chicken. Come now, which is it to be? Will you replace the purloined plumage, or am I to summon the pecking squad?

SEAMUS: Have a heart, will you? —I can't put it back, nor can anyone else.

HIGH COCK: Very well. I have been just. I have been forbearing. I have given you every opportunity. Now you must take the consequences.

(He turns upstage and emits a loud crow. The Birds enter at once from upstage.)

Arrest that man! (They surround him.) This miserable mortal is arraigned on charges of High Treason, sarcilege, theft of the Royal Regalia, assault, battery, and—sabotage; not to mention unauthorized removal of State property. (He turns away. The Birds whisper and titter.) Silence! Being apprehended in flagrante delicto—

SEAMUS: I was perfectly sober!

HIGH COCK: Don't interrupt. Being, as I say, caught in the act you are hereby sentenced to the customary penalty—that of Perforation by Pecking. Have you anything to say before sentence is carried out? —and please be brief, because it will make no difference.

SEAMUS: If it's all the same to you, your Majesty, I'd like to make a last request.

HIGH COCK: You may certainly make it—I cannot guarantee that it will be granted.

SEAMUS: Do you mind if I recite a little poem before I die?

HIGH COCK: I think it most unseemly—but you seem to have no sense of the gravity of the occasion. However, as long as you make it brief I have no objection.

SEAMUS: Thank you, your Majesty. It's quite short and it goes like this:

Come over the hills, come over the sea,
O'Shaughnessy's luck come again to me.
(Pause. Seamus looks anxiously around, but the Leprechaun is nowhere in sight.) The little varmint's doing this on purpose.

HIGH COCK: Is that all? *(Seamus nods.)* It doesn't make sense. However, now we have got that over, we can proceed. Squad! Prepare to peck!

(The Birds take a pace forward and lower their beaks to Seamus.)

SEAMUS: Just a minute, your highness.

HIGH COCK: What is it? You're holding things up.

SEAMUS: I—I just remembered another verse. May I say it?

HIGH COCK: Oh very well, if you must. At ease! *(Birds relax.)*

SEAMUS: If this doesn't fetch him, I'm done for.

HIGH COCK: Fetch who?

SEAMUS: Nobody—nobody at all, your Grace.

HIGH COCK: I wish you'd get on with it—you're wasting my time.

SEAMUS: Certainly your Excellency—second verse:
Come over the hills, come over the sea,
O'Shaughnessy's Luck come away to me.

(Pause)

HIGH COCK: But that's exactly the same as the first.

SEAMUS: Yes; it's a very montonous poem.

HIGH COCK: Is there any more of it?

SEAMUS: No, I don't suppose it's any use saying the third verse—it's just the same, and I don't suppose it would have any better effect.

HIGH COCK: I am reluctant to believe this, but do you know what I think?

SEAMUS: What?

HIGH COCK: I think you are trying to delay this execution.

SEAMUS: I wouldn't dream of it. I'm a very law-abiding man.

HIGH COCK: That's enough! Squad! —Prepare to peck!

(The Birds advance again on Seamus.)

SEAMUS: Oh, I'll never trust a Leperchaun again.

HIGH COCK: You'll never trust what again?

SEAMUS: A Leprechaun.

HIGH COCK: I thought that's what you said. If you are relying on that to escape the due course of law, you are much deceived. There is no such thing as a Leprehaun.

(The Leprechaun arrives in the middle of them.)

LEPRECHAUN: Who says there isn't?

HIGH COCK: Good gracious. Is that a Leprechaun?

LEPRECHAUN: And what of it?

HIGH COCK: I don't believe it.

LEPRECHAUN: You don't believe I'm a Leprechaun?

SEAMUS: That's heresy, so it is.

LEPRECHAUN: Quiet, O'Shaughnessy. I'll deal with you later. Well?

HIGH COCK: For one thing you're too big for a Leprechaun.

LEPRECHAUN: Oh, I am, am I? Well you're too big for a cockerel, but I never said I didn't believe in you.

HIGH COCK: I am unique.

LEPPRECHAUN: And I'm hoppin' mad. It's bad enough to be ever at the beck and call of an irresponsible tribe of halfwits like the O'Shaughnessys without being informed to my face that I have no foundation in fact, and furthermore . . .

SEAMUS: Oh, be easy, will you and just come over here a minute.

LEPRECHAUN: I won't be easy, and if you want me you can just come over to me, for I'm sick and tired of traipsing around after ye.

SEAMUS: I can't.

LEPRECHAUN: Why not?

SEAMUS: I'm stuck fast.

LEPRECHAUN: Is that all?

SEAMUS: No it isn't. This refugee from a chicken-run is in the process of having me liquidated for pulling out his tail. He's totally devoid of a sense of humour if you ask me.

HIGH COCK: Humour? I see nothing amusing in the situation. *(He turns.)*

SEAMUS: You would if you were standing where I am.

LEPRECHAUN: Quiet the both of you. I can see I shall have no peace till I sort you out. Gimme those feathers! *(He takes them from Seamus.)* Come here, you. *(To High Cock.)*

HIGH COCK: What are you going to do?

LEPRECHAUN: Do you want your tail back or don't you?

HIGH COCK: Of course I do, but . . .

LEPRECHAUN: Then turn around. *(The Leprechaun takes a mouthful of nails from his pocket, pops them in his mouth, and raises his hammer.)*

HIGH COCK: *(Turning round)* I'm going to hate this, I know I am. *(The Leprechaun "nails" the tail on again with vigorous whacks of the hammer, to the audible discomforture of the Cock.)*

LEPRECHAUN: There. Now let anyone try to pull that off again.

HIGH COCK: *(Straining to look round at it.)* Why, it's as good as new!

SEAMUS: I hope you'll be more gentle with me—I'm very delicate.

LEPRECHAUN: I'll be gentle, O'Shaughnessy. Unbuckle your shoes.

SEAMUS: Unbuckle them?

LEPRECHAUN: That's what I said. It's only your shoes that are stuck to the ground, didn't you know that?

SEAMUS: Begorrah, I never thought of it. *(He bends to undo them.)* Ah, you're a broth of a wee man, so ye are, and me thinking all the time I should be stuck here and become a land mark for future generations to visit, and picnic by the side of me, I shouldn't wonder.

LEPRECHAUN: You talk too much. Are your shoes undone?

SEAMUS: They are.

LEPRECHAUN: Right. (*The Leprechaun gives him an almighty kick in the pants which lifts him out of his shoes, leaving them fixed to the ground.*)

SEAMUS: Ow! I told you I was sensitive.

LEPRECHAUN: I've been wanting to do that for a long time, O'Shaughnessy.

SEAMUS: I'm free again, anyhow. (*To the Cock.*) And now you have your feathers back, how about keeping your promise?

HIGH COCK: What promise?

SEAMUS: To carry me to the others—they'll be wondering where I am. I'm sure such an exalted personage as yourself won't be going back on a promise?

HIGH COCK: If you put it like that I suppose I can't refuse. Get on my back, then, and please be careful of my tail.

SEAMUS: Just a minute till I get my pack. (*He gets it.*) It's a pity to be leaving those shoes behind. They're the comfortablest pair I ever had in my life. (*To the Leprechaun.*) You don't happen to have a pair of size 9½ about you I suppose?

LEPRECHAUN: My shoes are made for fairies. Did you ever see a fairy in a size 9 shoes?

SEAMUS: I suppose not—only in Iolanthe. Oh, well, I'll go in my stocking soles. (*He gets on the back of the Cock.*) Giddup there.

HIGH COCK: You should think yourself lucky I'm doing this for you.

SEAMUS: You think yourself lucky I'm not wearing spurs. Giddup!
(*They gallop round the stage and off.*)

CURTAIN

SCENE 3.

Outside the castle. A large archway at the back is fitted with a great gate with a smaller door (practicable) inset in it. On either side are houses forming a small square. It is morning. Niccolo and Nicolette are discovered, Nikki holding up the silver feather and Nicolette is on his arm, as though they have just arrived.

NIKKI: We're here at last.

NICOLETTE: What a ride! I'm quite breathless. Is that the castle, Nikki?

NIKKI: Yes. But I wish I'd asked the silver feather to put us down inside instead of outside it. Now we have to get in and that's going to be quite a job.

NICOLETTE: But it's your castle, isn't it? Don't you know a back way in?

NIKKI: There isn't a back way. This is the only entrance. And Magnus has it well guarded night and day—by magic. The door only opens at his command. I've heard him say so.

NICOLETTE: Oh. But he's bound to be back sooner or later. Can't we wait until he opens it and then creep in behind him?

NIKKI: *(Doubtfully)* We might.

NICOLETTE: Oh, dear. We're as far off as ever we were.

NIKKI: We'll get in somehow—we've *got* to get in. Cheer up, Nicolette —I don't like to see you looking so sad. We're nearly there now, and with a bit of luck we shall soon both be free again. Seamus shall play a tune and cheer us both up. Seamus *(Looking round.)* . . . Nicolette, what happened to Seamus?

NICOLETTE: I'd forgotten all about him! We must have left him behind.

NIKKI: I only hope Magnus hasn't done anything dreadful to him.

NICOLETTE: Oh, so do I. I should hate anything to happen to him on my account. We'll have to wait for him, that's all.

NIKKI: Yes, but we're wasting time. If the golden cock should wake up and crow, I'd be powerless again. Oh, where *is* Seamus!

(Seamus rides in on the back of the Cock; the latter, much the worse for wear, sinks to its knees exhausted. Seamus steps off.)

SEAMUS: Here I am, what's left of me. *(Walks bow-legged.)*

HIGH COCK: *(Breathless)* What's . . . left . . . of me, you should say.

SEAMUS: Now I know how Dick Turpin felt when he arrived at Cork.

NICOLETTE: York, Seamus.

SEAMUS: Was it now? Perhaps so, but not according to my ould grandmother's version of the story.

HIGH COCK: And—Black Bess—can't possibly have felt any worse than I do at this moment. *(A cock-crow is heard off.)* There! —you see, we came faster than sound—that's me crowing half an hour ago.

(Nikki, his back to the audience, stands rigid at the sound—the others have not noticed.)

SEAMUS: Sure, we'll disguise you as a whippet and make a fortune on the track.

NICOLETTE: Seamus! *(Seeing Nikki.)*

SEAMUS: What is it?

NICOLETTE: It's Nikki—he's—he's changed back again.

SEAMUS: The divil take it! —just when we were beginning to get somewhere with all this taradiddle. And don't say what are we going to do now, for I was after asking you the same thing. *(To the Cock..)* This is all your fault, you perambulating eiderdown, you! Why couldn't you keep your big beak shut?

HIGH COCK: Oh, the ingratitude! The base ingratitude!

NICOLETTE: Don't scold it, Seamus. After all, it has done its best to make amends.

HIGH COCK: I should think so—more than enough for a personage of my position. And now I must leave—I have an investiture at nine, and one must be punctual.

NICOLETTE: An investiture?

HIGH COCK: I have to confer the Order of the Golden Yolk on an elderly rooster for Service to the State.

NICOLETTE: Service?

HIGH COCK: Quite. Goodbye. *(He struts off with great dignity.)*

NICOLETTE: Now we're stuck again. We can't do very much until Nikki changes back again at sunset. I think we must get him out of sight first. It's far too public here—people will be moving about soon, and he's bound to attract attention.

SEAMUS: Attract attention. Well, why not? Don't you remember saying last night that you were going to be travelling showmen? I'll set up my stall here and you and Nikki can help to sell my wares, like you said.

NICOLETTE: But what if Magnus sees him? He's sure to return before very long.

SEAMUS: Och, the ould spalpeen wouldn't dare to try any of his tricks with a crowd around us, in broad daylight.

NICOLETTE: I'm not so sure. I'd feel much happier if we were out of this square.

SEAMUS: We must stay near the castle. It's not fair to Nikki now he's got so far. Come on, wind him up and we'll put him in that bit of an archway over there.

(Nicolette winds him up and leads him to the niche in the wall of the house, where he sits. During the following business she also puts on his puppet mask, under cover of setting up the stall. Seamus takes his pack and opens it out into a small stall with several bottles and a gaudy placard reading "Seamus's Sirop—The Universal Panacea"—etc. Nicolette helps him.)

Here, put this on. *(Give her a colorful cloak and head-dress.)* And you can beat the drum whilst I do the barking. *(Gives her the drum.)* Quick—we're getting an audience already. *(One or two people and several children have begun to assemble, and are idly watching the proceedings.)* Now wind him up well—oh! he's going to be a great attraction.

(Nicolette winds up Nikki and he gets up, now in his puppet mask. Seamus plays the pipe and Nicolette beats the drum. Nikki begins to dance. Gasp from the children, who crowd closer, followed by the adults. Others enter and join them.)

NICOLETTE: Roll up, roll up, and come a little closer. This wonderful entertainment is provided at enormous expense solely to advertise a wonderful new remedy. Come a little closer—there is absolutely no charge. Are you stiff in the joints? Would you like to be able to dance about with joy? Seamus's Sirop will do it for you after only one dose of this amazing extract. *(To Seamus.)* How am I doing? *(Seamus winks and carries on playing.)* Are your corns killing you? One lavish application of Seamus's Sirop will banish them for ever and you too will dance like this wonderful marionette.

(The children are clapping and dancing in time to the music. Everyone is so occupied they do not notice a great shadow cross the square.) You'd better carry on, Seamus—I can't think of any more to say. *(Seamus stops playing, but the drum and clapping go on as Nikki continues to dance.)*

SEAMUS: You've done fine, Nicolette. Just keep Nikki going and we'll soon have half the town here. *(He steps forward to sell his wares to the crowd.)* Don't go away now without a bottle of the Universal Panacea. It doesn't matter what you suffer from—and who doesn't suffer from something nowadays—the Elixir of life, the Universal Panacea will cure you before you have time to swallow it. Have you fallen arches? Seamus's Sirop will give them the lift of their lives. Have you a wart or a bunion or an ingrown toenail? —Seamus's Siprop will make them vanish like the snows on the desert and leave your skin whiter than you ever dreamt it could be. Is your hair coming out by the handful? The Universal Remedy will grow it again overnight—you will be amazed and delighted, or I guarantee to replace the bottle absolutely free of charge. There is no end to the amazing properties of this wonderful product—it will remove stains from your carpets, mend broken china, and impart a delicious flavour to the most homely stew, making rabbit taste like pheasant, and yesterday's mutton like food for the fairies . . . Will ye try a bottle, ma'am? —Ah, ye will! — that'll be ninepence and the best of good fortune to ye. And what about you ma'am? You're looking powerful pale and drawn, so ye are—a dose or two of the Elixir will put the flush of the newblown rose in those cheeks of yours. Ninepence only, Ma'am, and ye'll bless the day ye parted with it. Now what about you, Sir? —Will it get rid of mice, says he—a drop or two of this extract on their toasted cheese and they'll be queueing up to get into the trap. Thank you, Sir—thank you . . . .

(Nikki runs down and stops. There is an "Oh" of disappointment from the children.)

CHILD: Make it dance again! Please make it dance again!

CHILDREN: *(Starting to clap in unison.)* We want the puppet! We want the puppet!

SEAMUS: All right, all right—you shall have it. Wind him up again Nicolette.

(She does so, and Nikki starts to dance again as Seamus continues to sell his wares. Presently Magnus appears. He comes in downstage. Seamus has stopped playing but the drum and clapping keep Nikki dancing as he sells the elixir to the people.)

MAGNUS: *(To the audience.)* Drat that crow! If he wouldn't persist in flying in circles I'd have been here hours ago. Ha! Quite a party going on—right in front of my gates, too. We'll soon settle that. *(Going upstage.)* Good morning, my dears, having a good time? *(The crowd shrink away from him and the rhythm stops.)* Oh, please don't let me interrupt you. Do go on playing. *(They stand apprehensive.)* Play, I tell you! Play! *(They strike up again, more subdued and rather frightened.)* That's better. But I rather think that Nikki's excellent dancing is wasted on you—he shall come and dance for me— *inside* the castle, and perhaps we'll soon have him dancing to a different tune. *(He turns to the door of the castle.)* Open! *(The door creaks open.)* This way, Nikki.

486

(Nikki still dancing, comes out of the group and dances into the castle. Magnus laughs as he follows him inside. As the door slams, the drum and clapping stop suddenly. Nicolette and Seamus run to the gate and hammer on it with their fists.)

NICOLETTE: } Uncle Magnus! Open the door! Nikki!
SEAMUS: { Open! Open, bad cess to you! Open.

(They turn away.)

NICOLETTE: It's no use. It's as firm as a rock.

SEAMUS: *(To the townsfolk.)* If ye'll all lend a hand, maybe we can break it down. We've got to get in. Will you help us now?

1ST WOMAN: I'm having nothing to do with magic.

2ND WOMAN: Nor me. Besides, I have a pie in the oven; I've just remembered. *(They go off.)*

SEAMUS: *(To a man standing near.)* Will you?

MAN: Not me. I've a wife and child to think about. I don't want to be bewitched. Besides, I'm late for work.

(Goes off. They all go, leaving Nicolette and Seamus despondent.)

NICOLETTE: It looks as though we've seen the last of Nikki—unless we can make one last appeal to the Leprechaun.

SEAMUS: He's our only hope—and if he doesn't come this time I'll—I'll change me name to McTavish.
Come over the hills, come over the sea,
O'Shaughnessy's Luck come away to me.

LEPRECHAUN: *(Entering immediately.)* I'd be glad if you would change your name to McTavish, for there's no other member of the family has me as much on the hop as yourself.

NICOLETTE: We're awfully sorry to keep troubling you.

LEPRECHAUN: Oh, *you* can trouble me as often as you please; 'tis *him* I was talking to.

NICOLETTE: Thank you, you are kind.

LEPRECHAUN: Not at all, at all.

SEAMUS: Would you two like me to play me pipe whilst you sing a duet?

NICOLETTE: Be quiet, Seamus. *(To the Leprechaun.)* Can you open the castle door for us, so that we can get in and rescue Nikki?

LEPRECHAUN: I told you before, I don't do magic. Never touch it.

NICOLETTE: Oh, don't tell me that even you can't help us.

LEPRECHAUN: I never said so.

NICOLETTE: Then you can help us.

LEPRECHAUN: I think I can bring someone here who can get you inside. Now be quiet till I concentrate and *will* her to come.

NICOLETTE: But won't that be magic?

LEPRECHAUN: Not at all. It's only common telepathy. Be quiet.

(He takes a deep breath, closes his eyes and puffs out his cheeks. The others look around expectantly. The Duchess of Umbrage, followed by her footman, enters downstage, talking as she comes.)

DUCHESS: . . . . . and then this afternoon I shall want the carriage

again in order to call on the Countess of Huff, Lord Sinecure and
. . . . . *(She puts her hands to her head and looks around.)* . . . . . what
on earth . . . . . now, why ever did I come out into the middle of the
town?

FOOTMAN: I couldn't say, your Grace, I'm sure. Shall I go back and
get the carriage?

DUCHESS: Don't be a fool. If I walked here, I can walk back.

FOOTMAN: Yes, your Grace.

DUCHESS: Bugle, do I look normal?

FOOTMAN: Oh, perfect, your Grace, quite perfect.

DUCHESS: You're such a comfort. I can always rely on you not to tell
me the truth. Ah, well, it's probably the strain of modern life beginning to tell on me. You must return at once, and remember—not a
word of this to his Grace.

NICOLETTE: Your Grace . . . . .

DUCHESS: *(Turning and seeing her.)* Hm? Gracious me, if it wasn't
beneath me to notice such people I should say I had met this young
person before. Bugle!

BUGLE: Yes, your Grace.

DUCHESS: Ask this young person if she is not—oh, never mind, I'll ask
her myself.

FOOTMAN: By all means, your Grace.

DUCHESS: Are you, or are you not, the female attendant in that very
ill-equipped toyshop?

NICOLETTE: Well, I . . . . .

DUCHESS: I thought so. What about my figure?

NICOLETTE: Oh, it's—it's a very good one, your Grace. I . . .

DUCHESS: The *mechanical* figure I ordered to be delivered first thing
this morning. My daughter has already wrecked the entire east wing
and has started on the west. Unless I have it by noon there will not be
a room in the house fit to live in.

SEAMUS: Magnus has it, your benevolence.

DUCHESS: Magnus? You mean the seedy-looking individual with the
absurd hat, who has recently moved into the castle? I should have
thought him a little old for dolls, myself. What does he want with my
property?

NICOLETTE: Nikki isn't a puppet, he's a Prince under enchantment,
and we have been trying so hard to break the spell—and—and everything seems to keep going wrong for us . . . *(She is almost in tears.)*

DUCHESS: *(Suddenly giving way to symphaty.)* Oh, come now, we
can't have you crying. Bugle, a handkerchief! *(Takes it.)* There now.
Cheer up and tell me all about it. I'm not really very fierce, you know.
It's just that I have to be with a child like mine.

NICOLETTE: There isn't much more to tell. We can't get in to rescue
Nikki, that's all.

DUCHESS: You are very fond of him, aren't you? *(Nicolette nods.)* I thought so. Ah, la belle jeunesse—l'amour, l'amour . . . . .well now, why can't you get in?

SEAMUS: Because that ould—saving your presence—that ould divil in there has the door bewitched till it won't open for anyone but himself.

DUCHESS: Nonsense. Is *that* all? I assure you, my good fellow, there is not a door in the country which dares stay shut to me for very long. Bugle!

FOOTMAN: Your Grace?

DUCHESS: Knock on that door.

FOOTMAN: Yes, your Grace. *(Goes to it.)*

DUCHESS: Not open, indeed! We shall see.

FOOTMAN: There appears to be no answer, your Grace.

DUCHESS: Let us have no more of its tomfoolery. Show it my card! *(Footman takes a card from his pocket and holds it up to the door.)*

FOOTMAN: With the compliments of Her Grace, the Duchess of Umbrage.

(The door creaks open.)

NICOLETTE: It worked! Oh, thank you, your Grace.

DUCHESS: Not at all. Any time, my dear.

NICOLETTE: Come on, Seamus, before it closes again!

SEAMUS: I'm right behind ye. *(They go inside.)*

DUCHESS: Come Bugle. I want to see the end of this. Besides I'm dying to see the inside of this place.

BUGLE: Yes, your Grace.

DUCHESS: But remember, not a word of this to the Duke.

BUGLE: No, your Grace. *(They go in and the door closes.)*

CURTAIN

SCENE 4.

A corridor in the castle. The Turk is on guard—a very fierce individual in outlandish garb and carrying a great curved scimitar. He parades the corridor once and then back, and gives a great yawn. There is the sound of a door closing in the distance. He is at once alert.

TURK: Who goes there? *(Silence)* Nobody.. Nobody ever comes. Nobody that I can slice into little pieces with Abdul. *(He runs his thumb along the blade of the scimitar.)* How I wish somebody would try to break into the castle, then I could just, *(he makes a slashing blow at the air)*—slice them in two; just *(he slashes again.)*—slice them in two . . . . But they are afraid to come—afraid of me and Abdul, beautiful wicked Abdul. All except the evil one—he comes and goes, and fixes me with his evil eyes and I am afraid. How I should like to slice him in two—just slice him in two! But his magic is too strong for me and Abdul—my sharp and terrible one. *(He yawns hugely.)* I am weary of this corridor. I think you and I sleep a little, Abdul, whilst the Evil One is away. *(He squats down on his haunches, with Abdul, the scimitar, across his knees, and yawns again.)* A-a-a-h!

(His head droops down and soon he is asleep. Presently Magnus enters the corridor leading Nikki, who walks mechanically beside him. There is a whirr. Nikki stops.)

MAGNUS: What is the matter now? Run down again, have you? I shall have to make sure there is a longer mainspring in the next one. *(He winds Nikki up again.)* There! . . . . . You still imagine your friends

490

will rescue you, don't you, Nikki? Well, they won't. As a matter of fact they are in the castle at this moment, although they think I don't know. Do you want to know why I allowed them to get in? Well I'll tell you. They will have to pass through this corridor to get into my study, as you very well know; and look what I have in store for them when they do—waiting to chop them to bits in the twinkling of an eye—my faithful guard, my Argus who never sleeps—*(He turns and sees the Turk fast asleep.)*—Death and destruction! . . . . . *(The Turk starts to his feet and lashes out widlly with his scimitar. The Wizard leaps out of the way.)* Stop it! Stop it at once, do you hear? *(The Turk stops it.)* You clumsy great fool! You almost cut my head clean off. What do you mean by sleeping on duty?

TURK: Pardon, Master. Me and Abdul, we dream—we dream that you are an intruder.

MAGNUS: Dream! . . . DREAM! ! . . . . . How dare you dream? You've no right to dream in my corridor.

TURK: We are sorry, Master. We are both sorry.

MAGNUS: What do you mean, both?—Who else have you got in here with you?

TURK: Only Abdul, Master. Abdul is sorry, too.

MAGNUS: Oh, he is, is he? Well you will be even more sorry by the time I have finished with you. I'll teach you to sleep on duty. Come here! *(The Turk trembles towards him. Magnus points a shinny finger at him and chants.)*:
Pains in the stomach! *(The Turk howls and clasps his middle.)*
Pains in the back! *(The Turk clasps his back.)*
Gripe him and twist him
Like one on the rack! !
That should keep you awake all right, you great lazy thing. Now you keep a sharp lookout and the first person that sets foot in this corridor, what do you do?

TURK: Slice him in two, Master, slice him in two.

MAGNUS: You see that you do it. *(Turns to Nikki.)* Come on you. Now I can settle with you without fear of interruption.
(They go off. The Turk groans and clutches his stomach, then his back, as he parades the corridor. As he gets back to the far end of it, Seamus and Nicolette creep fearfully into the corridor and peer about.)

TURK: *(Swinging round.)* Who is there?

NICOLETTE: Oh, Seamus! *(They cling together.)*

TURK: Stay where you are! At last! I have some one for Abdul. *(He raises his scimitar.)*

SEAMUS: Save us! What are you going to do?

TURK: Slice you in two!

SEAMUS: The saints preserve us! And me without even me shillelagh!

TURK: *(Suddenly clasping his stomach.)* Ouch!

NICOLETTE: What's the matter?

TURK: Ow! *(Clasping his back.)*

NICOLETTE: Are you in pain? *(The Turk nods and groans.)* Oh, poor thing!

SEAMUS: Never mind him, dodge past him before he recovers. *(They try to do so.)*

TURK: Stand back! Ouch! Or I'll strike off your head. Ow! Oh, if only I were rid of these pains, you would be mincemeat by now.

NICOLETTE: Please let us pass. We must get to Nikki. We must.

TURK: You will never get past Abdul. And you will never leave this corridor alive. Ow!

SEAMUS: Nicolette! I have an idea.

NICOLETTE: What? It had better be a good one.

SEAMUS: My elixir! I have a little here in my pocket.

NICOLETTE: But how will that help?

SEAMUS: Wait till you see! *(He goes to the Turk.)* Hark to me now. *(The Turk, between groans, aims a blow at him, which he dodges.)* I'll make a bargain with ye.

TURK: Stand still while I slice you.
  (He slashes at Seamus's feet. Seamus leaps over the blade, then ducks as the Turk sweeps it over his head.)

SEAMUS: For the love of heaven will you be easy now while I talk to ye.

TURK: What about? Ouch! Ow!

SEAMUS: About your pains and torments. If I can cure you of your stitches will you leave us be and let us pass?

TURK: You talk too much. Prepare to die. Ow! I shall not miss you this time. *(He raises his scimitar and is about to strike when the Duchess sweeps in, followed by Bugle.)*

DUCHESS: Put that thing down this minute! *(The Turk is so surprised he obeys.)* I'm surprised at a great big man like you threatening these poor defenceless people. *(The Turk hangs his head and fingers the handle of the scimitar.)* That's better. Now what is this all about?

NICOLETTE: Please don't stay here, your Grace. He is very fierce, and he has orders to kill anyone who tries to pass him. He'll kill you.
  (The Turk is meanwhile in the the throes of another attack, writhing in pain.)

DUCHESS: Nonsense. The man is obviously stupid. He only needs firm handling. Now listen to me, my man. *(The Turk groans.)* Good gracious! What ever is the matter?

NICOLETTE: Magnus has bewitched him with aches and pains. We have some of Seamus's medicine here, but he won't take it.

DUCHESS: He will. If I can make Ermyntrude take her medicine, believe me I can make him. Give it to me.
  (Seamus gives it to her, and she goes to the Turk. He shrinks from her.)

TURK: No. No, please. I hate medicine—so does Abdul.

DUCHESS: Rubbish. I'm having no fuss about it.

(Expertly she siezes him by the nose with one hand and pours the contents of the bottle down his throat with the other.)

TURK: Oh, it's horrible!

DUCHESS: I should hope so. Good medicine always is.

(The Turk straightens up and feels himself gingerly, then slaps his stomach hard and laughs.)

TURK: It has gone! The pain has gone. *(He throws himself at the Duchess' feet.)* Lady, your magic is greater than that of the evil one. I am your slave for ever. I kiss your feet.

DUCHESS: You'll do no such thing. This is the person you should thank—the concoction was his.

TURK: *(Transferring his attentions to Seamus.)* Master! May your shadow never grow less. Abdul and me we are your slaves for ever. *(He kisses the hem of Seamus's coat.)*

SEAMUS: *(Pulling his coat away.)* Here, here. That's enough of that, now. And what would I be doing with a slave, at all?

TURK: We will guard you, Master. Show me your enemies and I will slice them in two!

SEAMUS: Yes, of course, but put that thing away, now, there's a good fellow.

TURK: Yes, Master. To hear is to obey.

(He tucks the scimitar in his girdle.)

SEAMUS: And now for Magnus. Begorrah, we've collected quite an army! Forward the rescue party! *(They start towards the door.)*

DUCHESS: Stop! I can quite understand your anxiety to rescue your friend, but you will never do it this way.

SEAMUS: Why not? Isn't it four to one? We'll have him overpowered before you can say shillelagh.

TURK: Yes, and I will slice off his head before you can say Abdul.

DUCHESS: Mere bravado. We must, as the dear Duke would say, have a plan of campaign. Otherwise we shall find ourselves bewitched and turned into all kinds of revolting things. We *must* have a *plan*.

NICOLETTE: But we must hurry. We may be already too late.

DUCHESS: Right. You *(To the Turk.)* will stay here and guard the rear. If Magnus escapes us, you know what to do.

TURK: *(With a huge leer and fingering his sword.)* Abdul knows.

DUCHESS: Good. The rest of us will attack in two waves. Bugle!

BUGLE: Yes, ma'am?

DUCHESS: You and I will be the first wave. You will go first.

BUGLE: Me? Oh, but your Grace, I . . .

DUCHESS: *(Firmly)* Bugle!

BUGLE: *(Resignedly)* Very well, your Grace.

DUCHESS: Having effected an entry, we shall endeavour to distract the attention of Magnus long enough for you two to creep in unobserved.

SEAMUS: Wave two?
DUCHESS: Wave two, exactly.
NICOLETTE: And then what?
DUCHESS: After that it will be a question of Individual Initiative and Dogged Determination . . . . . Any questions?
SEAMUS: Er . . . . . no, your Grace.
DUCHESS: Right then Action stations! *(They take up positions.)* Advance!
(Bugle goes off, followed by the Duchess and the other two. The Turk remains.)

CURTAIN

SCENE 5.

Magnus' study. Fitted like an alchemist's workshop, it has a door, fireplace and bench littered with apparatus. Nikki stands in a box like his original one, with the door open. Magnus is closing the door of the room as the curtain goes up. He goes over to Nikki's box.)

MAGNUS: Now to settle with you once for all. You think your new friends are going to rescue you even yet, don't you, Nikki? I'm afraid not. As a matter of fact, they are probably in the castle already. But don't let that raise any false hopes, my dear boy. I have a nice reception committee of one waiting for them in the corridor below—waiting to slice them into little pieces. They will never reach this room alive. Did you say something?—How silly of me—you can't, of course, can you? Pity—your reactions just now might be well worth watching. However, we must get back to work. And this time there will be no mistakes—the spell will be final, irrevocable, and complete. No more midnight escapades for you, my friend. *(He goes to the bench.)* Where's my book of recipes? Ah, here we are. Now then. *(Rolls up his sleeves.)* Equal parts deadly nightshade and mandragora—yes— *(Selecting them and popping them into the mortar.)*—Friar's Balsam— yes,—Three dried toads—ugh! I always loathe this part. Toads— toads—none left, let's see *(Reading)* if no toads, bats will serve *(He shivers)*. Bats. Ugh! —can't bear 'em. *(Picks them up gingerly and drops them into the mortar.)*—Juice of a lemon and pepper and salt

495

to taste *(Puts them in.)* There! Now the magic formula as we stir it all up—

    Filthy brew
    Horrible stew,
    May it do
    What I want it to . . . . .

(During this the Leprechaun comes down the chimney and hides in front of the bench in view of the audience.)
What was that? . . . . . I could have sworn I heard something scrabble in the chimney.

(He goes to look. As he does so, the Leprechaun steals a small packet from the bench and hides again.)
H'm! Nothing there. Probably a bat. Ugh! Nasty things. *(Goes back to the bench.)* And now final ingredient—Dragon's Blood. Now where's the dragon's blood? *(Searches the bench top.)* It's gone! That's most peculiar—I could have sworn—Drat it! I shall have to fetch another packet from the tower. Vexation! *(He is going to the door. To Nikki.)* Don't go away till I get back will you?

(He laughs at his own joke and is going to the door when it opens suddenly and the Duchess sweeps in preceded by Bugle.)

BUGLE: Her Grace the Duchess of Umbrage. Wave one.

DUCHESS: Quiet, Bugle. Ah, my dear Dr. Magnus—it is Doctor, isn't it.

MAGNUS: Yes, but—Look here, Madam, I will not have people walking into my castle in this fashion.

DUCHESS: Oh, come, Doctor. I have been dying to meet you for ages. You have the reputation of being *such* a remarkable man. And now that I have finally penetrated to your sanctum sanctorum as it were, I hope you are going to tell me all about your wonderful experiments.

MANGUS: Some other time, Madam. I am extremely busy on important work, and I cannot be interrupted. I don't know how you got in here in the first place—somebody is going to smart for this—but I should be obliged if you would leave—at once.

DUCHESS: Dr. Magnus, I am simply not going to be intimidated by your manner. I'm sure you are a charming man, really in spite of your unprepossessing exterior. In any case, you can't let me go without offering me a cup of tea, at least.

MAGNUS: *(Exasperted)* Tea, Madam? —I—*(He suddenly has an inspiration.)* Tea. Of course. Of course. Of course you must have some tea. I hope you will forgive the ungraciousness of your reception.

(He goes to the bench and finds a cup and saucer, etc. and makes tea from an already boiling flask.)
—But you must understand that I am a very busy man, and a somewhat solitary one. I am not accustomed to receiving ladies of quality in my poor apartments. I have the things ready.

DUCHESS: *(Disappointedly)* So I see. *So* fortunate that you need not go out for them.

MAGNUS: Go out? Oh no, no. I have everything here. I practically live in this room.

DUCHESS: Pity. I mean how convenient.

MAGNUS: There you are, your Grace. *(He gives her the cup.)* And now *(He picks up a small bowl from the bench significantly and hands it to her.)*—sugar?

DUCHESS: Please. *(He puts a generous helping into her tea.)* How curious. It's a bright green.

MAGNUS: That's right—special sugar—very special. What about your footman? I'm sure he would like a cup as well?

BUGLE: *(Horrified)* Take tea with her Grace? Oh no, thank you. I hope I know my place.

DUCHESS: Nonsense, Bugle. Do as you are told.

BUGLE: Very well, if you say so, ma'am.

MAGNUS: Good. Excellent. *(Takes him a cup.)* There. That will settle you—refresh you, I should say. I hope the tea is to your liking, your Grace?

DUCHESS: Oh yes. Somewhat—curious, but not unpleasant. But it is beginning to have most odd effect. I feel as though I were floating away—floating gently on the breeze—a delightful feeling—quite delightful—floating away . . . . .

(She puts down her cup and drifts downstage.)

MAGNUS: Then float this way, madam—this way.

(And he leads her to a chair where she subsides gently into unconsciousness.)

BUGLE: *(Sliding slowly to the floor.)* Floating away—floating away— floating . . . . . *(And he is asleep too.)*

MAGNUS: Good. Very good. That's got them out of the way. Now where was I? Ah yes—the dragon's blood from the tower. But I think we'll have you locked in first, before we have any more unwelcome visitors.

(He locks the cabinet with Nikki inside and goes out, closing the door. The Leprechaun comes out of hiding, looks at the sleeping pair, and goes to the door. He opens it and whistles. Seamus and Nicolette creep into the room.)

SEAMUS: Where's his malevolence? Is he not at home?

LEPRECHAUN: He's away to fetch something from the tower. Ye'd better hurry, for he'll be back any minute and he's already disposed of your wave one.

SEAMUS: Wave one? *(Sees the Duchess and the Footman.)* Oh, my goodness, what a time to have a nap. I wonder if the Duchess knows she looks like that when she's asleep?

NICOLETTE: But where's Nikki?

LEPRECHAUN: He's in the box yonder. *(They go to it.)*

NICOLETTE: *(Struggling with the bolt.)* It's stuck fast. I can't open it. You try, Seamus. Oh, quickly.

LEPRECHAUN: *(At the door.)* I hear him coming back.

NICOLETTE: What shall we do? He mustn't find us here.

SEAMUS: Hide quick.

(They hide—Seamus in the chimney-breast Nicolette behind the box, Leprechaun under the bench. Magnus comes in with a small packet in his hand.)

MAGNUS: Dragon's blood. My last packet. Can't get any more, either, until next Beltane Day. If these interfering busybodies had kept away, I should have done by now, perish 'em all. *(He is at the bench.)* How much of this do I need? Let's see. As much as will cover a sixpence. Sixpence. *(He feels in his pocket.)*—Don't tell me I haven't one after all this. Thorns and nettles! I haven't. *(The Leprechaun hands one up to him.)*—Oh, thank you. *(He realises what has happened and looks over the bench. The Leprechaun dodges out of sight.)* How odd. Must be magic. Ah, well!

(He covers the sixpence and is about to drop it in the mortar when Seamus sneezes.)

SEAMUS: A-a-a-shoo!

MAGNUS: Bless you. I'm sure there's someone in this room besides me and those other two. *(He searches the room, Seamus and Nicolette dodging him as he does so. He comes back to centre stage.)* Nothing at all. That's the worst of being a magician, there's so much loose magic floating about in the air all the time . . . . .

BUGLE: *(Sleepily)* Floating—floating away . . .

MAGNUS: Who said that? Oh, it's you. I suppose it was you who sneezed as well. Yes—that explains it—that explains everything. Or does it? *(He shrugs and goes back to the bench.)* Now the final touch. This is the bit I like. *(He puts the ingredients in the bowl. There is a flash.)* Lovely. Now we'll see if it's done. *(Puts a finger in the bowl and licks it.)* Mm. Delicious. I must make this every week. *(The Duchess stirs and yawns delicately.)* So. Our unwelcome guests are beginning to wake up. That's very unfortunate for them. Who better to try out my spell on? This is going to be quite a pleasure. Wake up, Duchess! Bugle, wake up!

(They slowly wake up and look around.)

DUCHESS: Where am I?

MAGNUS: I knew she would say that. They always do. You are in my castle, Duchess. And in my power. This is the last time you will ever poke your aristocratic nose into other people's business.

DUCHESS: What do you mean, you revolting creature?

MAGNUS: I mean that shortly you won't have a nose to do it with—except a wooden one! *(He laughs)*

DUCHESS: I certainly won't stay here to be insulted. Come, Bugle. *(She is going to the door.)*

498

MAGNUS: Stop! *(They stop.)* Turn round! *(They turn.)* You will never leave this room again in human form. *(He grabs two handfuls of powder from the bowl and holds them oloft.)*
>Minikin, manikin,
>Wax and wane,
>Puppets become
>Puppets remain.

(He scatters the powder over them. They jerk once or twice, then fixed smiles appear on their faces and they flop together like dolls, holding each other up. Magnus laughs gleefully.) Perfect, perfect! Now we'll see how well you dance. *(Nicolette is meanwhile trying to open the box bolt.)* What's that? *She stops and shrinks behind the box.)* Nothing. I must be getting old; hearing things. Now a little music and we'll see you dance.

(He waves his hands and music is heard—quick music with a strong rhythm. He gets up on top of the bench and holds the imaginary strings of his new puppets. He walks them to the front of the bench and they dance a rapid, jerky, grotesque dance.)

MAGNUS: *(As they stop, and pretending to lower the "strings" as they collapse.)* Poof! That's enough of that. Makes my arms ache. *(A clock strikes somewhere in the castle.)* Eight o'clock. I must hurry before that Nikki comes to life again.

(He is clambering off the bench when the clock finishes striking. On the last stroke, Nikki hammers on the box lid, furiously.)

NIKKI: Let me out! Seamus! Nicolette! Let me out before it's too late.

NICOLETTE: *(Struggling with the bolt.)* Seamus! Help me! *(Seamus runs across to help her.)*

MAGNUS: What's this? The pedlar? The girl? —Stop that! Stop it, I say! before I shrivel you both to a cinder.

SEAMUS: *(Struggling with the bolt.)* Shrivel away, ye culd nannygoat. At least we'll go down fighting.

MAGNUS: *(Rushing to the door and flinging it open.)* Guard! *(As he does so the Leprechaun leaps on the bench and seizes a handful of powder from the bowl.)* Guard! Where are you, you fool.

TURK: *(Appearing in the doorway.)* Here master. *(The bolt is drawn on the box and Nikki rushes out.)*

NIKKI: Come on, Seamus! *(They make for Magnus.)*

MAGNUS: Stop! *(They stop.)* Cut them down! *(The Turk raises his scimitar and advances—toward Magnus.)* Not me, you fool—them! What are you doing? *(The Turk continues to advance.)* Go away! Leave me alone! *(As they all close in towards him, he backs to the bench and grabs the bowl.)* Not another step! One more and I finish you all. *(He laughs.)* Do you think you can get the better of me? It's really rather convenient to have you all together like this. It makes it so much easier than dealing with you one by one.

(He takes a handful of powder and holds it up as though to scatter it over them.)
> Minikin, Manikin,
> Wax and wane—
(The Leprechaun, on the bench behind him, scatters the powder over the Magician.)
LEPRECHAUN: Puppet become
> And puppet remain!
(The Magician gives a great cry as the powder fall on him, then collapses slowly in a heap. The Duchess and the Footman at the same time begin to straighten up. Nikki goes over to Magnus and lifts an arm, then lets it fall on the stage with a wooden click.)
NIKKI: We have beaten him at last . . . . . I mean you and your friends have, Nicolette.
(Nikki goes to Nicolette and takes her hands in his.)
NICOLETTE: If it hadn't been for the Luck of the O'Schaughnessys we could none of us have done anything.
SEAMUS: I think, Duchess, this would be a favorable opportunity to take our departure. —Me arm, Ma'am!
(He offers her his arm.)
DUCHESS: Certainly, Mr. O'Shaughnessy . . . . Come, Bugle.
(They go out, followed ceremoniously by Bugle and the Turk, leaving Nikki and Nicolette hand in hand in the centre of the stage. The lights begin to fade, and the Leprechaun tiptoes from the shadows unnoticed by them. He quietly takes the edge of one side of the front tabs and draws it across, fingers on lip, as the curtain music swells.)

FINIS

500

REYNARD THE FOX

Adapted from *Gestes de Renart le Goupil*

by

ARTHUR FAUQUEZ

Translation by Marie-Louise Roelants

*With Costume-Make-Up Designs by
IRENE COREY

*Introduction by
MOUZON LAW

*Included in the separate play-book only.

501

REYNARD THE FOX

By Arthur Fauquez

THE ANCHORAGE PRESS
Cloverlot
Anchorage, Kentucky 40223
U. S. A.

REYNARD THE FOX

by

Arthur Fauquez

Translation by Marie-Louise Roelants

CHARACTERS

Tiecelin, *the Crow*

Reverend Epinard, *the Hedgehog*

Brun, *the Bear*

Ysengrin, *the Wolf*

Noble, *the Lion*

Reynard, *the Fox*

Lendore, *the Marmot*

SYNOPSIS

The entire play takes place in the heart of the forest.

Prologue

Scene 1. Spring

Scene 2. Summer

Scene 3. Autumn

Scene 4. Winter

Epilogue

Reynard the Fox was first produced, under the title of "Le Roman de Renart", in 1958, by the Theatre de l'Enfance in Brussels, Belgium, under the direction of Jose Geal, and was subsequently toured across Belgium, in more than a hundred performances.

Translated from the French by Marie-Louise Roelants, an abridged version was presented in 1960 by the Madison, Wisconsin Theatre Guild, under the direction of Donald Von Buskirk.

The first full American premiere was presented in 1961 by the Department of Drama of the University of Texas, at Austin, Texas, under the direction of Mouzon Law. For this occasion, the costumes were designed by Lucy Barton, the set created by H. Neil Whiting. The stage photographs used in this book are taken from this production, and reflect their treatment of the play.

A subsequent production of *Reynard the Fox* was presented in 1962 by the Jongleurs of Centenary College, at Shreveport, Louisiana, under the direction of Orlin Corey. This was the first production to make use of the animal costume-make-up designs provided for the play by Irene Corey.

REYNARD THE FOX

by

Arthur Fauquez

PROLOGUE

(Tiecelin, perched in the crotch of a tree, practicing.)

TIECELIN: Caw! *(Higher)* Caw! *(Higher)* Caw!

(Brun enters, patch over one eye, his arm in a sling.)

BRUN: Stop that infernal racket!

TIECELIN: Caw! *(Higher)* Caw!

BRUN: Stop!

TIECELIN: You are interrupting my practice, Seigneur Brun. Caw!

BRUN: Stop this instant, and summon the King!

TIECELIN: *(notices him.)* The King? Good heavens, what has happened to you? Have you been caught in a bramble bush? Ha, ha, ha!

BRUN: Enough of your insolence! Call the King at once!

TIECELIN: Lord Bear, I am the King's Registrar. If you wish an audience with the King, you must state your reason to me.

BRUN: I have been beaten, do you hear? Look at me!

TIECELIN: Ha, ha, ha!

BRUN: I have been beaten, and it is all the fault of Reynard the Fox!

TIECELIN: Reynard did this to the mighty Bear?

BRUN: He tricked me. I want the King to punish him.

TIECELIN: Oh, if it was only one of Reynard's tricks —

BRUN: But look at me!

TIECELIN: I am. Ha, ha, ha!

(Ysengrin limps in, on a crutch, his head bandaged.)

YSENGRIN: Sound the trumpets!

TIECELIN: Baron Ysengrin!

BRUN: You, too?

TIECELIN: What a pair! Ha, ha, ha!

YSENGRIN: One more caw from you, Crow, and I'll wring your scrawny neck. Summon the King!

505

TIECELIN: The King is not to be called just because you stubbed your toe.

YSENGRIN: Stubbed my toe? I have been attacked by dogs. Look at me!

TIECELIN: Yes, I see. Ha, ha, ha!

BRUN: Who has done this to you?

YSENGRIN: It is all the doing of Reynard the Fox!

BRUN: Gr-r-r-r!

TIECELIN: Reynard did this to the powerful Wolf?

YSENGRIN: He tricked me.

BRUN: Me, too.

BOTH: Summon the King!

TIECELIN: *(climbs down.)* Gentlemen, if I were to summon the King every time Reynard played a trick, he would soon appoint a new Registrar.

YSENGRIN: But this is not to be borne!

BRUN: I intend to accuse Reynard in court.

YSENGRIN: Yes. We'll bring him to trial.

BRUN: And we shall demand his punishment.

YSENGRIN: I shall demand his hanging.

TIECELIN: Hanging?

BRUN: Yes! We have had enough of his tricks.

YSENGRIN: We are going to get rid of the Fox!

TIECELIN: If you have been unable to get rid of him in the field, how do you expect to get rid of him in Court?

BRUN: The King will do us justice.

YSENGRIN: Bring us to the King!

TIECELIN: Gentlemen, I am a man of law, and I will give you my best legal advice. Go home and lick your wounds. Reynard will trick you in Court, just as he has tricked you in the field. You have no evidence.

BRUN: Evidence? What of my black eye ? And my arm?

YSENGRIN: Look at my lame leg. And my head!

TIECELIN: Yes, ha, ha, ha! What a picture! Now you will excuse me. I must return to my practicing.

(He climbs up.)

BRUN: You miserable Crow! The King shall hear of your insolence!

YSENGRIN: If you had a little more meat on your bones, I should have a nice fat crow's wing for my supper!

TIECELIN: Caw!

BRUN: Save us from that deafening noise!

(Exit, holding his ears.)

TIECELIN: Caw!

YSENGRIN: Take care, Crow, that the Fox does not trick you.

(Exit, limping. Reynard enters, unseen by Tiecelin.)

TIECELIN: Ho, ho, ho! The Fox trick me? What a joke! I am too smart for that. Caw! Caw! Caw!

REYNARD: *(groaning with pain)* Oh-h-h-h-h!

TIECELIN: Can I never practice in peace? Caw-w-w-w — Good Heavens, it is the Fox himself!

REYNARD: *(weakly)* Tiecelin, my friend — Oh-h-h-h!

TIECELIN: What is your tale of woe? Do you wish to summon the King too?

REYNARD: No. I wish only to die in peace.

TIECELIN: To die?

REYNARD: Tiecelin, I have been poisoned.

TIECELIN: Poisoned?

REYNARD: Oh-h-h-h! It was an oyster I found. Sing me one of your sweetest songs, so that I may die with your music in my ears.

TIECELIN: You are not serious?

REYNARD: Sing, my good fellow

TIECELIN: Like this? Caw-w-w-w-!

REYNARD: Thanks, old friend.

(He gasps, then falls quiet.)

TIECELIN: Reynard? Reynard! Don't act the sleeping beauty. I know you. You are only faking. Oh, very well. I will rouse you. Caw! Caw! Caw! Not a wince. Not a quiver. He is very smart. Reynard? Is he really faking?

(He climbs down to look.)

My word, he sleeps like the dead. I can't even see him breathe. Good Heavens, he isn't breathing! Could he really be dead? What a release, Lord, if this is so!

(He moves Reynard's tail, which drops back, limp.)

But how could he be dead? This is too much to hope. He said an oyster. It is possible.

(He pokes the Fox with a long stick. Reynard rolls over, a dead weight.)

507

It's true! Brun! Ysengrin! No, I am the one who found him. It will win me the gratitude of the whole kingdom if I hint that I am a tiny bit responsible for this — oh, just a very tiny bit — just enough to make them think I am the one who liberated the world from this rascal. I should be hailed as a hero. I shall have my portrait painted in triumphant attire, crushing my vanquished enemy, and I shall sell his skin for a fur.

(He rests his foot upon Reynard, in a conqueror's pose.)

REYNARD: *(grasping his ankle)* Dear Tiecelin!

TIECELIN: Help! Help! He is not dead!

REYNARD: You had better learn, dear friend, never to sell Reynard's skin before you have killed him.

TIECELIN: What I said about it was only in fun. I — I only wanted to give you a laugh.

REYNARD: Well, you see, you succeeded. I am laughing. I am laughing with all my teeth, which in a few moments are going to gobble you up.

TIECELIN: You are not going to kill me like a simple chicken?

REYNARD: Why not?

TIECELIN: I am the Royal Registrar. And besides I am your friend.

REYNARD: Yes?

TIECELIN: Only a minute ago, I saved you from a Court trial.

REYNARD: I am very grateful, believe me. And because of that I'll swallow you in one gulp, without chewing.

TIECELIN: Let me go!

REYNARD: *(plucking a feather from Tiecelin's tail)* And moreover, I'll keep this to remember you by

TIECELIN: Aie! You have ruined my beautiful tail!

REYNARD: Never mind, Tiecelin. You will not be needing it any more.

TIECELIN: Oh-h-h, you monster! I am going to be eaten, and I can see no escape.

REYNARD: None whatever

TIECELIN: Then at least grant my last wish. If I have to be eaten, don't just gobble me down like a piece of cheese. Treat me as a delicacy, and prepare your stomach for this feast.

REYNARD: My stomach is always prepared.

TIECELIN: Oh, no. To enjoy a dainty morsel fully, it is necessary to warm your stomach and your head — like this.

(He rubs his stomach and his head.)

REYNARD: Why your head?

TIECELIN: To eat intelligently.

REYNARD: And why your stomach?

TIECELIN: To warm your appetite.

REYNARD: It is an odd method.

TIECELIN: But it works, I assure you.

REYNARD: Like this?

(He lets go of Tiecelin, to rub head and stomach.)

TIECELIN: Oh, harder than that.

REYNARD: It certainly does warm me up.

TIECELIN: *(clambering up to his perch)* The best way to digest well is to eat nothing.

REYNARD: Why, Tiecelin!

TIECELIN: You savage! Did you think I was going to let you eat me for lunch?

REYNARD: Eat you for lunch? I would have to be starving.

TIECELIN: I am going to denounce you to the King.

REYNARD: *(laughing)* Oh, Tiecelin, you take yourself so seriously.

TIECELIN: The King also will take me seriously. Trumpets!

(Trumpets.)

REYNARD: Caw! Caw! Caw! *(Mimicking)* Oh, Tiecelin, sing me one last song before I die.

(Exit, laughing. Returns immediately.)

By the way, keep this to remember me by.

(Tosses feather. Exit.)

TIECELIN: My feather! Monster! Thief! Cannibal!

(He climbs down to retrieve the feather.)

My beautiful feather! But this is evidence. Now we have him! Brun! Ysengrin! Bring the fox to trial! I have the evidence! Trumpets!

(Trumpets. Epinard enters quietly.)

EPINARD: My dear fellow, what are the trumpets all about?

TIECELIN: Reverend Epinard. Stand there. I am about to make a proclamation. Trumpets!

(Trumpets.)

509

We, Tiecelin the Crow, Royal Registrar, announce a great Court of Justice meeting, to put on trial the most infamous of all criminals, His Majesty's Own Knight —

(Drum roll.) Reynard the Fox!

EPINARD: Reynard, on trial? But will you explain —

TIECELIN: One moment. Whoever wishes to accuse the Fox is requested to give his name to the Registrar. I am the Registrar. Trumpets!

(Trumpets.)

EPINARD: What is this all about?

TIECELIN: It means, Reverend, that we are at last going to put Reynard on trial, and punish him for his misdeeds. Don't you yourself have some complaint to make against the Fox?

EPINARD: I?

TIECELIN: Yes, you. Has your religious robe protected you from his tricks?

EPINARD: Oh, no. Only last week, he got a duck-egg away from me.

TIECELIN: Well, then. You will lodge a charge against him?

EPINARD: Ahem! I should not wish it made public how I — ah — came by the duck-egg.

TIECELIN: As you wish. Sit over there. Here come two who will testify.

(Epinard sits and reads in his Bible. Brun and Ysengrin enter.)

YSENGRIN: You are bringing him to trial?

TIECELIN: I have the evidence.

BRUN: Where is the King?

(Noble the Lion enters, majestically, theatrically.)

NOBLE: Since when do the trumpets not greet my arrival?

TIECELIN: *(bowing)* Sire — your Majesty — I think — I thought — Trum — Trumpets!

(Trumpets.)

NOBLE: Let my arrival be announced to the Court.

TIECELIN: Yes, Sire. Trumpets!

(Trumpets.) Gentlemen, the King!

(All bow, as Noble seats himself.)

NOBLE: I declare the Court of Justice open. Now, Tiecelin, why have you assembled us all in Court?

TIECELIN: To hear charges against your Majesty's Knight, Sir Reynard the Fox.

NOBLE: Reynard? What charges?

YSENGRIN: I have been attacked!

BRUN: I have been beaten!

TIECELIN: My very life has been threatened!

NOBLE: Brun! Ysengrin! Where have you received these terrible injuries?
Have you been fighting again?

BRUN: Sire, it is Reynard!

YSENGRIN: We are the victims of Reynard's trickery!

TIECELIN: This is Reynard's doing!

NOBLE: If this is true, Reynard is a dangerous criminal indeed. Bring
him in.

TIECELIN: But your Majesty —

BRUN: We do not require his presence to recite his crimes.

YSENGRIN: We can tell you —

NOBLE: Where is Reynard?

TIECELIN: Knight Reynard thinks — he does not know — actually, I
think he thinks —

NOBLE: Enough thinking. Where is Reynard?

TIECELIN: He th — I mean, he believes — your Majesty, I will have him
brought before you.

NOBLE: Let this insolent character be called at once.

TIECELIN: Y-y-yes, Sire. S-s-s-sir Reynard the Fox! Trumpets!

*(Trumpets, resembling a hunter's call, ending with drum roll. During
this fanfare, each animal makes his own preparations for Reynard's entrance, reflecting his attitude toward this dangerous criminal.)*

YSENGRIN: Here comes the villain!

(Reynard enters, smiling, confident. Bows to the King.)

NOBLE: I greet you, Knight Reynard.

REYNARD: Good evening, Sire.

NOBLE: Just answer our questions.

REYNARD: Allow me, Sire, to wish that this day may not go by without
being the best one of your life.

NOBLE: Quiet. We have assembled the High Court of Justice, for the
express purpose of putting you on trial.

REYNARD: On trial? Me? The most devoted and faithful of all your
subjects? But why, Sire? What have I done to be tried for?

511

NOBLE: You shall know this very minute. Tiecelin, announce the first accuser.

TIECELIN: Master Ysengrin the Wolf.

NOBLE: We are listening, Ysengrin.

YSENGRIN: I accuse —

REYNARD: Cousin Ysengrin, you, my accuser?

YSENGRIN: I accuse! Do you deny that you led me into a farm-yard under the pretext of showing me a flock of nice, plump ducks?

REYNARD: Not at all. I did show you a flock of nice, plump ducks, Cousin. Is that a crime?

YSENGRIN: And do you deny that you fastened me in, and roused the dogs, so that I was so cruelly bitten, I barely escaped alive?

REYNARD: Oh, my dear Cousin, is that how you suffered those grievous wounds? Those dreadful dogs!

NOBLE: So you admit luring him into a trap where he almost lost his life?

REYNARD: Oh, no. Excuse me, Sire. I only took him to the farm-yard to show him nice, plump ducks, as he says. But when he saw them, he began to drool and slobber and lick his lips at the sight, and even started to chase them. I could not stay for this. I fled, and cried out for help. Was it my fault if the gate shut behind me, and locked Ysengrin in with the dogs?

NOBLE: If the story is as you tell it —

YSENGRIN: Allow me —

NOBLE: And I am inclined to believe you — the Marshal Ysengrin is as guilty as you are, and by the same token, deserves the same punishment. It is up to you, Lord Wolf, to fix Reynard's fate, since that fate shall be yours also. What punishment would you suggest?

YSENGRIN: Ah — uh — in that case — yes, in that case, I think it is better — and wiser — not to punish Reynard.

REYNARD: Thanks, dear Cousin, for your generous intervention.

NOBLE: This case is settled. Who is next, Tiecelin?

TIECELIN: Seigneur Brun.

NOBLE: It is your turn, Master Brun.

BRUN: I accuse!

REYNARD: You, my Uncle?

BRUN: Be quiet!

NOBLE: We are listening, Seigneur Brun.

BRUN: Your Majesty, I was taking a peaceful nap under an apple tree, when this creature —

REYNARD: Uncle.

BRUN: This mongrel —

REYNARD: Uncle.

BRUN: This rascal —

REYNARD: Uncle!

BRUN: For Heaven's sake, will you let me speak?

NOBLE: Proceed, Seigneur Brun.

BRUN: I was only sleeping, your Majesty, doing no harm to anyone —

REYNARD: He means, Sire, he was resting, after a large lunch. He had just stripped the apple tree, bare.

BRUN: It is not true! But this scoundrel found me there, and screamed for the farmer. Can you deny it?

REYNARD: No, not at all. I thought he was stricken, Sire. His belly was swollen till it looked like a barrel. I cried out in my grief. Could I help it if the farmer heard me? Uncle Brun heard me too, and tried to run away, but he was so full of apples, he couldn't even get to his feet.

BRUN: This is slander! He yelped for the farmer, your Majesty, and the farmer attacked me with a pitchfork. Before I could move from the spot, he gave me a black eye and four loose teeth, not to mention the hair and skin I lost in the fray.

NOBLE: If you had stolen his apples, Brun, it seems to me the punishment you received was justified. What do you think?

BRUN: I think — I think it was a very high price to pay for a few apples.

NOBLE: Forget it. Next one.

TIECELIN: The next one is myself: Master Tiecelin the Crow, Man of Law, and Royal Registrar.

NOBLE: What is your complaint against Reynard?

TIECELIN: I accuse!

REYNARD: Come, now.

TIECELIN: Yes! I accuse Reynard of trying, just a minute ago, to twist my neck and gobble me up, as simply as if I had been a chicken.

NOBLE: This is more serious. What have you to reply, Master Reynard?

REYNARD: One thing only. Look at this piteous carcass, and judge for yourself, Sire. Who would wish to gobble him up, skinny and emaciated as he is? And even if I did, am I any more guilty in this matter than my Cousin Ysengrin?

YSENGRIN: I protest!

REYNARD: Or my Uncle Brun?

513

BRUN: I deny it!

REYNARD: Or the cat, the dog, the sparrow, the vulture — or you yourself, Sire Lion, our very beloved King, as well?

(*Laughter.*)

NOBLE: Silence!

(*Nobody laughs any more.*)

Tiecelin, you over-estimate yourself. None of us wishes to eat crow.

TIECELIN: Reynard did. And here is the evidence. He pulled out one of my tail-feathers — this very feather.

REYNARD: Pouf! The wind plucks your feathers all the time.

TIECELIN: The wind!

(*General laughter.*)

NOBLE: Let's file this ridiculous case. Has anybody else any complaints against Reynard?

TIECELIN: Yes! The Reverend Epinard!

(*He prods Epinard, who has appeared immersed in his Bible.*)

EPINARD: Uh? Yes?

NOBLE: We are listening, Reverend Epinard.

EPINARD: You are listening to me? This doesn't happen every day.

(*He opens his Bible, and prepares to preach.*)

NOBLE: What charge do you wish to lodge against the red-haired Fox?

EPINARD: I?

TIECELIN: Remember — that duck-egg.

EPINARD: Duck-egg?

NOBLE: Look now, Reverend, has the Fox ever tried to harm you?

EPINARD: He wouldn't dare, Sire. My quills, you see.

NOBLE: If you have nothing to say, sit down. Is there any other accuser?

TIECELIN: Yes, Sire. There are countless ones. But they are not present.

NOBLE: Where are they?

TIECELIN: They are dead, Sire.

NOBLE: Dead?

TIECELIN: Yes, Sire. The rooster Chanticler, and his four hens. The drake, Halbran-des-Mares, and his three ducks. The guinea-fowl, Hupette. The turkey, Gloussard. And thousands of other winged creatures. All have met death and burial in the stomach of Reynard the Fox. Let's hang him, Sire.

YSENGRIN: Let's hang him upside down!

BRUN: Yes, he must hang!

NOBLE: That is a harsh judgement. Knight Reynard, can you think of any reason against it?

REYNARD: As many reasons as you have subjects, Sire. Doesn't my cousin Ysengrin himself devour innocent lambs and peaceful sheep? Doesn't my Uncle Brun treat himself to the honey he robs from the bees? Doesn't the Registrar Tiecelin eat the wheat and the grapes he steals from men? And you yourself, Sire, didn't you only yesterday have a gentle kid and half a deer for your supper?

YSENGRIN: We must hang him!

BRUN: Hang him!

TIECELIN: Hang him at once!

NOBLE: Do you hear?

REYNARD: I hear, Sire, and I don't worry too much, because I know there is more wisdom under a great King's crown than in the little brains of his courtiers. A very great King can forgive when need be.

NOBLE: A very great King can forgive when need be.

REYNARD: Mighty and gallant Majesty, I trust my fate to your hands.

NOBLE: I am a very great King, Reynard.

REYNARD: Without question, Sire.

NOBLE: You shall not hang.

REYNARD: Thank you, Sire.

TIECELIN: This is insane!

NOBLE: Who said that?

YSENGRIN: Sire, it is a mistake.

NOBLE: I pray you —

BRUN: If you will allow me, Sire —

NOBLE: I allow nothing! Silence, everybody, and let me render my sentence. You will not hang, Master Reynard. I grant you mercy for one more year.

TIECELIN: Mercy for one more year?

NOBLE: But this will be your last chance. In that year a record will be kept of your every crime.

BRUN: Of what use is a record, if he is left free to continue his crimes?

NOBLE: Twenty-four crimes we shall forgive you, without punishment.

YSENGRIN: Twenty-four crimes?

TIECELIN: Sire, this is proposterous!

NOBLE: Silence! We are all sinners, and hope for forgiveness. We shall forgive you twenty-four times.

REYNARD: You are a gracious King, Sire.

NOBLE: But take care. One crime more than twenty-four, and you shall be punished without mercy.

REYNARD: I understand, Sire.

NOBLE: One year from now, we shall hold court on this case again, and examine your record. Now you are free. Remember under what conditions.

REYNARD: Sire, you shall hear no further complaints from your humblest, most respectful servant, Reynard.

NOBLE: All right. Go.

REYNARD: I leave, Sire, broken-hearted to have earned the displeasure of so many esteemed friends.

(Exit.)

TIECELIN: Your Majesty, how can you —

YSENGRIN: Sire, this is madness!

BRUN: You have turned loose the greatest scoundrel in the kingdom!

TIECELIN: Who can keep track of all his crimes?

NOBLE: You will.

TIECELIN: I?

NOBLE: Yes. You are the Royal Registrar. I appoint you to keep a record book, and enter into it any crimes committed by Reynard.

TIECELIN: Thank you, your Majesty. It will give me pleasure.

NOBLE: I am very pleased with my judgement — stern, fair, but still merciful. Now, let each of you go peacefully back home, and recall my great justice.

TIECELIN: Trumpets!

(Trumpets.)

YSENGRIN: Hail to thee, Sire, Lion.

(Aside) What folly to let Reynard go free!

(Exit.)

BRUN: Hail, Sire.

(Aside) How foolish to forgive that redhair!

(Exit.)

516

NOBLE: You see, everybody is satisfied with my judgement. I am well satisfied myself. Good night, Tiecelin.

(Exit.)

TIECELIN: Good night, Sire.

(Aside) What a blunder, to leave that rascal at large!

(He goes to pinch Epinard's arm.)

EPINARD: Eh? Yes.

TIECELIN: It is all over, Reverend.

EPINARD: Yes, yes, I see. Moreover, it was very interesting. Very interesting indeed.

TIECELIN: I must say, you showed little interest in the cause of justice.

EPINARD: The cause of justice?

TIECELIN: Yes. Why didn't you tell the King about that duck-egg?

EPINARD: My dear fellow, I should not wish to earn Reynard's ill-will. The time might come when I should need Reynard on my side. Good night.

(Exit.)

TIECELIN: Good night, good night? How can I ever have another good night, after this? Reynard will make short work of me, if I give him the chance. My feathers rise with fear at the very thought.

(Lendore enters, half-asleep, pillow under her arm, bumps into Tiecelin, who freezes with terror.)

He has got me, already! Reynard?

LENDORE: What do you say?

TIECELIN: What? It is you? Lendore?

LENDORE: It's me.

TIECELIN: Why didn't you say something?

LENDORE: You didn't ask me anything.

TIECELIN: The Marmot. And I thought you were Reynard.

LENDORE: You didn't look at me very well.

TIECELIN: Where are you going?

LENDORE: To Reynard's trial. Is it here?

TIECELIN: The trial is over.

LENDORE: Already? I must have fallen asleep on my way.

TIECELIN: As usual.

LENDORE: How did it go?

TIECELIN: That rascal Reynard went scot-free, for a year!

LENDORE: Good!

TIECELIN: What is more, he is allowed to commit twenty-four crimes, without punishment.

LENDORE: Twenty-four? That will not take him long.

TIECELIN: But one crime more than twenty-four, and he shall hang! And I am appointed to keep the record.

LENDORE: The record?

TIECELIN: Yes. I am not the Royal Registrar for nothing. The King has appointed me to keep account of all his crimes. I shall make a book of them.

LENDORE: It is amazing how sleepy I still feel.

TIECELIN: Go to sleep, then. I intend to keep my eyes open, for the whole year.

LENDORE: *(settles to sleep, against a tree.)* Good night.

TIECELIN: It will be easy to accumulate twenty-five counts against him in a year. Ha, ha! I'll put an end to him, with my record-book.

End of Prologue

SCENE ONE — SPRINGTIME

(Lendore enters, yawning. Reynard bounds in.)

REYNARD: Ah, Lendore! You have come out of your shelter. Spring is truly here.

LENDORE: Is it?

REYNARD: Melted is the cold snow that kept my feet wet all winter.

LENDORE: So it is.

REYNARD: Gone is the bitter frost that kept the burrows closed.

LENDORE: Ah, yes.

REYNARD: Quiet is the freezing wind that pinched my nose.

LENDORE: Excuse me. I don't hear any quiet.

REYNARD: Welcome, Spring — welcome to you, who brings back the innocent young rabbit, and the tender birdies, not to mention the dainty little chickens.

LENDORE: Go somewhere else to sing your Spring Song, Reynard. I need a nap.

(Sleeps. Ysengrin enters, quietly.)

REYNARD: *(at the overlook.)* Ah, look, Lendore. See the fine rooster in the farm-yard over there. I see you, Seigneur Coincoin. I have given you all winter to get fat, and now I am saving a place for you in my bag.

YSENGRIN: So! You are up to your old tricks, Reynard.

REYNARD: Cousin Ysengrin! You always tip-toe.

YSENGRIN: Naturally.

REYNARD: I was just — ah — admiring the spring.

YSENGRIN: You were just plotting to gobble up that rooster. I heard you.

REYNARD: I have always admired your ears, Ysengrin.

YSENGRIN: Just dare to attack that rooster. The King shall hear of it.

REYNARD: Very well, Cousin. I leave Seigneur Coincoin to you. Happy hunting!

(Exit.)

YSENGRIN: Happy hunting, indeed. That wily Fox would beat me to the farm-yard, if I let him.

(Lendore stirs.)

Ah! Perhaps I won't have to go so far as the farm-yard.

(Drooling, he quietly creeps up on her, with obvious intentions.

519

Reynard returns.)

REYNARD: Ah, Cousin, you have found what you want without hunting?

YSENGRIN: What brings you back here?

REYNARD: To do you a good turn, Cousin. I have found you a hunting companion. Here comes our Noble King.

(Noble enters, with zest and majesty.)

Your servant, Sire.

YSENGRIN: The Marmot, Sire. The Marmot. She sleeps.

NOBLE: Lendore, indeed. She has come out of her shelter. This is the herald of spring.

YSENGRIN: As you say, your Majesty.

NOBLE: Ysengrin, we have had to keep under cover all winter. Now I feel like hunting. Come and join me.

YSENGRIN: I am honoured, Sire. And — ah — Reynard?

NOBLE: Reynard has given up hunting for a year. Let's go.

(Exit.)

YSENGRIN: I am coming, Sire.

(To Reynard) You — you schemer!

(To Noble, off) I come!

(Exit.)

REYNARD: *(laughs.)* Happy hunting, Cousin.

(To Lendore) Lendore, Lendore, wake up.

LENDORE: Eh? What? What do you say?

REYNARD: Wake up. It is not wise to sleep when the hunting season is open.

LENDORE: I am a Marmot. It is the nature of a Marmot to sleep, any time.

REYNARD: Find yourself a private spot, then. And don't trust Ysengrin.

LENDORE: I don't trust anybody, Reynard — not even you.

REYNARD: Lendore.

LENDORE: All the same — I like you.

REYNARD: Thanks, old friend.

LENDORE: By the way, don't sit there. It is a bumble-bee nest.

(Exit.)

520

REYNARD: A bumble-bee nest? Fortunately she warns me. Ah, and here comes my Uncle Brun. What a heaven-sent opportunity to play a joke on him! But if the King should find out, there would be one of my twenty-four chances gone. Shall I do it? Yes! It is too good a chance to miss.

(Brun enters, out of sorts.)

Good morning, Uncle. Still grumbling?

BRUN: Leave me in peace.

REYNARD: That is just what I offer you. Let's make peace, and forget our little misunderstandings. As a token of good faith, I offer you some fair honey-cakes left by the bees. What do you think of that?

BRUN: I think it is another of your fabrications.

REYNARD: How unfortunate I am! My uncle himself doubts my sincerity.

BRUN: I don't believe a word. Where are those honey-cakes?

REYNARD: Why show them to you, since you don't believe there are any?

BRUN: And why, if they exist, don't you eat them yourself?

REYNARD: I am on probation for a year, Brun. It would count against me if I should rob the bees. Heigh-ho! Since you don't care for it, that honey will be lost to everyone.

(He makes a subtle move toward the humble-bee nest.)

BRUN: *(to himself)* So there they are.

REYNARD: It's a shame.

BRUN: Yes. Too bad, isn't it? Well, I am off.

REYNARD: So am I. Good bye, Uncle.

BRUN: Good bye.

(Neither makes a move to go.)

Aren't you leaving?

REYNARD: Oh, certainly. And you?

BRUN: Me, too. So good bye.

(He pretends to leave.)

REYNARD: *(Pretending to leave also.)* Good bye.

BRUN: *(Comes back and finds himself in front of Reynard.)* I have lost something.

REYNARD: Can I help you look for it?

BRUN: Stupid of me. I left it at home. Good bye.

(Exit.)

REYNARD: Good bye, Uncle.

(Exit, but hides himself. Brun comes back.)

BRUN: *(Rushes to bumble-bee nest.)* Honey! That fool thought I was going to leave honey here to spoil!

(He puts his paw in the nest, withdraws it quickly.)

Bumble bees! The traitor!

(Bumble-bees come out in swarms and pursue him. Music. The flight of the bumble-bees can be suggested by light spots.)

Ah! Go away! My nose! Leave me alone! Ouch! My tail! A-h-h! it stings! My ears! Oh! Ah! It stings! Help, Help!

(Tiecelin enters.)

TIECELIN: Seigneur Brun! What is the matter?

BRUN: Out of my way, Crow! Ouch! My neck!

TIECELIN: Are you hurt?

BRUN: Am I hurt? I am eaten up! Aie! My leg! Stop blocking me! Oh, it stings! It stings!

(He runs off, followed by the bumble-bees. Tiecelin, pushed about, and stricken by fear, takes refuge on a tree. Reynard is convulsed.)

TIECELIN: Has he lost his mind?

REYNARD: Oh, no. He always acts that way, when the bees are after him.

TIECELIN: Well, he needn't be so rude about it. He nearly made me crush my camembert.

REYNARD: *(Nostrils wide open.)* Camembert? Ah, Master Crow, that cheese looks delicious. Will you give me a taste?

TIECELIN: No. I went to too much trouble to get it.

REYNARD: But cheese is bad for your voice. A singer should never eat cheese.

TIECELIN: Nonsense. It has never harmed me in the least.

REYNARD: Nevertheless, a fine voice should not be abused. If you were unable to sing any more, the animal kingdom would lose its best tenour.

TIECELIN: Do you think so?

(Crows.)

Do you really think so?

REYNARD: Sing, Tiecelin. Sing, and listen yourself.

(Tiecelin crows awfully.)

Ah! Very good, though a little low. I thought you could sing higher than that.

(Tiecelin croaks more shrilly.)

Better. One note higher . . . Ah! . . . More . . . Louder . . . Higher
. . . Splendid! . . . Go on! . . . Higher! . . . You are almost there! Keep
on! . . . More! . . . Now you have it!

(Tiecelin drops his cheese.)

And I have it too!

TIECELIN: My cheese!

REYNARD: Don't worry. It is in good hands.

TIECELIN: Give it back to me.

REYNARD: Come and get it.

TIECELIN: I know you.

REYNARD: We will share the cheese like brothers.

TIECELIN: If I come down, you will gobble me up first, and you will eat
the cheese for dessert.

REYNARD: No, no. Come.

TIECELIN: Cheese robber!

REYNARD: What a wonderful aroma!

TIECELIN: Rob — you like the smell?

REYNARD: Heavenly!

TIECELIN: When you close your eyes, you find the smell even better.

REYNARD: What's that?

TIECELIN: To get the full, rich, luscious flavour of a camembert cheese,
it is necessary to shut out all other senses, and enjoy it with your nose
alone. Your nostrils are much more sensitive when your eyes are closed.

REYNARD: Is this possible?

(He closes his eyes and sniffs.)

You are right. It is unbelievably richer.

TIECELIN: *(Taking advantage of the chance to climb down.)* Cheese
robber!

REYNARD: Tiecelin —

TIECELIN: This will go into my book!

REYNARD: Your book? What book?

TIECELIN: Aha! The King has appointed me to keep a record of all your
doings in a book. This will make a fine beginning.

REYNARD: Indeed.

TIECELIN: Keep on, Master Fox. The book will soon be full. Crime
Number One! Reynard stole my cheese! Cheese robber! Cheese
robber! Cheese robber!

(Exit.)

REYNARD: So, he is keeping a book! And on the very first day of spring, I have managed to spend one of my twenty-four chances, and get it recorded in the book. Oh, what a stupid, bungling Fox I am! That tattle-tale will cry the news aloud, all through the forest. I'd better get rid of the evidence.

(He hides cheese, as Noble enters, followed by Ysengrin.)

NOBLE: Did you see a pheasant fly over?

REYNARD: No Sire, but I can guide your Majesty toward some very attractive turkeys.

YSENGRIN: Oh, no. You are out of this hunt, remember.

REYNARD: I am talking about big, fat turkeys.

NOBLE: We can hardly afford to let such a chance go by, Ysengrin.

YSENGRIN: But Sire, Reynard has given up hunting for a year. You said so, yourself.

NOBLE: I think — ahem! — we may make an exception this time.

REYNARD: This way, Sire.

(Bows low. Noble and Ysengrin exeunt.)

Let's hope that Tiecelin will not find his cheese until I get back.

(Exit. Music. Ballet-mime for the hunt. Noble, Ysengrin, and Reynard chasing a turkey around the stage and off. Noble in the lead, graceful but heavy; Ysengrin lumbering along behind, eager but clumsy; Reynard nimbly outstripping both. The chase carries them offstage. Lendore enters.)

LENDORE: *(Crossing, pillow under her arm.)* Impossible to sleep with this infernal music.

(Exit. The ballet ends with the entrance of Reynard, who carries a turkey with head hanging limp. Noble and Ysengrin follow.)

NOBLE: Bravo!

YSENGRIN: You caught it right under my nose!

REYNARD: It is a matter of skill, Cousin.

NOBLE: Anyhow, now we must share.

REYNARD: *(Throwing the turkey at Noble's feet.)* Let's share, by all means.

NOBLE: You, my dear Ysengrin, may decide about each one's share.

YSENGRIN: In my opinion, it is fitting, first of all, to set aside the claim of this redhair, who had no right to be hunting anyway. The head, the neck, and one wing will be enough for me — and one leg. It is only right that you, being the King, should take all the other pieces.

NOBLE: *(Boxing his ears.)* You don't have the first instinct of a sportsman.

(To Reynard.) And you, how would you divide it?

REYNARD: It is easy. Take first what pleases you, Sire — the body and legs, for instance. Her Majesty Lioness the Queen, shall have the wings and the head. Your son, the Cub, will gladly practice on the neck, I'm sure. Ysengrin seems to have too much trouble with his teeth to eat anything. And when it comes to me, I don't really feel hungry.

NOBLE: This is what I should call a fine division. Who taught you to divide so fairly?

REYNARD: My Fox's wisdom, Sire — and most of all, the sight of your royal fist on Ysengrin's ears.

NOBLE: I congratulate you. As for you, Seigneur Wolf, take a lesson from Reynard. Well, good bye, my friends. Thank you for your company in the hunt.

(Exit, taking turkey.)

YSENGRIN: Take a lesson — take a lesson from Reynard! Ah-h-h-h! I don't know what keeps me from giving you the beating of your life, you scheming, mealy-mouthed rascal!

REYNARD: Is that not better than to have your jaw crushed under the Lion's paw?

YSENGRIN: I am mad. Oh, I am good and mad!

REYNARD: Cheer up. We don't lose much in this settlement. The turkey was so old that the King, the Queen, and the Cub face the risk of breaking their teeth on it. Anyway, I see a much better dinner coming than the King's.

YSENGRIN: Epinard?

REYNARD: Yes, the Reverend, carrying a wonderful ham! It will be ours.

YSENGRIN: Beware the quills.

REYNARD: Don't worry about the quills. Hide there, and be on the watch. I'll get Epinard to lay the ham down near your hiding place. You pick it up and wait for me. Afterward we shall divide it.

YSENGRIN: Agreed.

(He hides.)

REYNARD: *(Waiting for Epinard's entrance.)* Now is the moment. Oh, miserable fox that I am!

(Epinard enters, carrying ham.)

Shall I never be able to do anything but bad deeds? With the help of Heaven, let me find a holy man to hear my confession, and absolve me of my sins!

EPINARD: My son.

REYNARD: Reverend. Did you hear me?

EPINARD: Yes, my son.

REYNARD: I will go to Hades, won't I?

EPINARD: The one who repents will not go to Hades.

REYNARD: Ah, but I repent. I repent.

EPINARD: Very well, my son.

REYNARD: Heavens, what do I see?

EPINARD: What do you see?

REYNARD: It has gotten me again.

EPINARD: What has gotten you again?

REYNARD: My terrible sin of greediness. Ah, how wretched am I! The very sight of your ham makes me forget my pledge.

EPINARD: Be calm, my son. Be calm.

REYNARD: It is impossible, Reverend, as long as that splendid ham remains before my eyes. I shall be unable not to covet it.

EPINARD: My goodness! Have some will power.

REYNARD: It is Satan. It is Satan who tempts me. "Get thee behind me, Satan." Take that ham away from my sight, Reverend, and pray for me.

(Epinard puts his ham down.)

Take it away from my nostrils — farther — still farther, so that its wonderful aroma will not tempt my nose any more.

EPINARD: *(Puts the ham down near Ysengrin's hiding place.)* Kneel, my son, my dear Reynard. Kneel. I will pray for you.

(Ysengrin seizes the ham, takes a bite, makes his escape. Reynard, seeing this, cries out involuntarily.)

REYNARD: Aie! Wait for me, you thief!

(Recovers himself.)

Excuse me, Reverend. Save the prayer for another time. Right now I have — ah — other business.

(Exit hurriedly, in pursuit of Ysengrin.)

EPINARD: *(Discovering his loss.)* Pig! Rascal! Robber! My ham! My ham!

(Exit. In the distance are heard the joined cries of Tiecelin — "Cheese Robber!" — and of Epinard — "My ham!" Noble enters.)

NOBLE: This morning the forest is full of strange sounds. Don't I hear someone claiming a ham? And somewhere, this side, someone else shouting "Cheese Robber"? That joker Reynard must not be far away. Ham? Cheese? It is strange, but I fancy my royal nose thrills under the odor of a very near camembert.

(He searches, and discovers the cheese.)

Ha! But I am not mistaken. By jove, my royal nose is still in its prime. Ah, this suits me admirably. It makes up for that skimpy breakfast I had, eating that tough old turkey.

(He eats the cheese.)

It is truly fit for a King.

TIECELIN: *(Offstage, drawing nearer.)* Cheese robber! Cheese robber!

(Noble gulps down the last of the cheese hurriedly. Tiecelin enters.)

Sire, my cheese.

NOBLE: What cheese?

TIECELIN: My camembert.

NOBLE: So it was your cheese that — ah — which is missing?

(Brun enters, shaking off Reynard behind him.)

BRUN: Don't give me any of your sweet talk. I am stung all over.

TIECELIN: He stole it!

NOBLE: Who? Brun?

TIECELIN: No, Sire. Reynard.

NOBLE: Reynard, did you sneal his wheeze?

REYNARD: Wheeze, Sire? No, Sire, I did not wheeze.

TIECELIN: Cheese robber! Cheese robber!

REYNARD: I did not wheeze. Nor did I hear anyone else wheeze, nor sneeze, nor queaze, nor —

TIECELIN: Cheese robber!

REYNARD: Oh, cheese? Tiecelin has lost a cheese?

TIECELIN: Your Majesty will do me justice. He has stolen my camembert.

REYNARD: Oh, what slander!

TIECELIN: Punish that thief.

REYNARD: Your Majesty, this Crow is insane. Had I stolen his cheese, I should have eaten it at once, and you would all be able to smell it. Uncle Brun, be good enough to smell my moustache.

BRUN: You stay away from me.

REYNARD: But smell, and tell us all. Do you detect the very strong odor of a camembert cheese?

BRUN: *(Sniffing)* I wouldn't put it past you, you honey-fibber — but to tell the truth, I smell nothing at all on your breath.

TIECELIN: You have taken it away from me!

REYNARD: After all, the simplest way would be to ask everyone to submit to the test, would it not?

NOBLE: Do you think this necessary?

TIECELIN: I insist! I insist!

BRUN: It seems logical to me. So smell.

TIECELIN: *(Smelling Brun's breath.)* You smell more like a honey-robber.

BRUN: It is my natural fragrance.

REYNARD: You, Sire?

NOBLE: Although my royal eminence places me above all suspicion, I submit to your insulting request.

TIECELIN: *(Smelling Noble's breath.)* Sire! Sire! One would almost think—

NOBLE: What would one think?

TIECELIN: If I weren't afraid of hurting your Majesty's feelings, I should say — it's funny, but it smells more or less like —

NOBLE: More or less like what?

TIECELIN: Like camembert.

NOBLE: This exceeds the limits. Get out of here, and go fast. Let me not set eyes on you any more today, or it might be costly for you.

TIECELIN: But —

NOBLE: Get out, I say!

TIECELIN: Very well, then.

(Exit.)

BRUN: What a fool!

TIECELIN: *(Offstage.)* Cheese robber! Cheese robber!

REYNARD: He has a one-track mind.

BRUN: How absurd to think that your Majesty's moustache might smell like cheese!

NOBLE: Sniff yourself, Seigneur Brun, and give us your opinion, sincerely and honestly.

BRUN: *(Sniffing.)* Uh — ah —

NOBLE: Well?

BRUN: I don't believe I am mistaken, Sire, when I say that your moustache does have an odor —

NOBLE: What odor, I pray you?

BRUN: A very delicate perfume — ah — yes, very similar to the roses.

NOBLE: So that is your honesty! Lies and hypocrisy! Out of my sight. Bear without conscience!

BRUN: Well, then —

    (Exit, hastily.)

NOBLE: It is your turn, Reynard. What do you smell?

REYNARD: To tell the truth, Sire, I don't smell anything today. I have a cold in my head.

NOBLE: This is a cold that comes at a convenient time for you, doesn't it?

REYNARD: Yes, Sire.

EPINARD: *(In the distance.)* My ham! I claim my ham!

REYNARD: Sire, allow me to retire, and nurse my cold.

TIECELIN: *(In the distance, on the other side.)* Cheese robber! Cheese robber!

NOBLE: You are quite right. Let's both retire, and nurse our colds.

    (Exeunt. Epinard enters.)

EPINARD: My ham!

    (Tiecelin enters.)

TIECELIN: My cheese!

    (Brun enters.)

BRUN: I am stung all over!

    (Ysengrin enters.)

YSENGRIN: I am in the King's bad graces!

BRUN: So am I!

TIECELIN: So am I!

YSENGRIN: Whose fault is it?

TIECELIN: It is Reynard!

EPINARD: Reynard!

BRUN: Reynard!

TIECELIN: It is all the fault of that rascal Reynard!

EPINARD: Tiecelin, put all this down in your book against him.

TIECELIN: Don't worry. It shall go into my book, all right. H'm, h'm! We can almost be glad. This will make three crimes on the very first day. Ha, ha!

End of Scene One

(Appropriate music. Reynard is hidden behind a tree. Lendore and Epinard enter from opposite sides, both very thirsty, both looking for the spring. They collide.)

LENDORE: Oh, it's you?

EPINARD: As you see. Don't you think it's terribly hot?

LENDORE: Yes. Are you looking for the spring?

EPINARD: Where is it?

LENDORE: The hole is there, but the water doesn't flow any more. The brook has disappeared in the sand, the pond is dried up, and the fish, turned upside down, die in the sun.

EPINARD: May Heaven save us, dear Lendore! It is a dreadful summer.

(Ysengrin enters, brushes them aside.)

YSENGRIN: Out of the way, both of you!

(Epinard bristles. Lendore puts pillow on her head.)

Where is the spring? Who emptied the spring? You?

LENDORE: Certainly not. It is the sun.

YSENGRIN: I want a drink. Where is the water?

EPINARD: In the ground.

YSENGRIN: It must come out. I want it to gush, as it did before. Come out of your hole, water. I want a drink.

EPINARD: Don't shout so. Water doesn't hear. Each of us must be patient under our sufferings.

YSENGRIN: Don't preach your sermons to me. Go somewhere else.

(He pushes Epinard, stings himself.)

Thunderation!

EPINARD: As you wish.

(Exit calmly.)

LENDORE: He who plays with needles gets stung.

YSENGRIN: You think this is funny?

(Ysengrin strikes at Lendore, who pushes her pillow into his muzzle, and hurries off. Ysengrin fights alone with the pillow, as Brun enters, carrying a wooden bucket. He sets the bucket down, to watch Ysengrin in astonishment.)

BRUN: Here, don't upset my bucket!

YSENGRIN: What bucket?

(He throws the pillow down, and rushes to the bucket, kneeling in front of it.)

BRUN: *(Tumbles him down with a push.)* Don't touch!

YSENGRIN: Just a gulp.

BRUN: No.

YSENGRIN: I am thirsty.

BRUN: So am I.

YSENGRIN: I beg you.

BRUN: No.

YSENGRIN: One drop.

BRUN: No.

YSENGRIN: Only let me dip the tip of my tongue.

BRUN: No!

(He pushes Ysengrin back violently. Ysengrin tumbles down and rolls close to a tree, behind which Reynard is hidden. Brun drinks noisily. Reynard whispers a few secret words to Ysengrin, who then gets up and pretends to depart.)

Good bye, my nephew.

YSENGRIN: Good bye.

(He stops and pretends to gather honey, which he eats with delight.)

BRUN: *(Stops drinking to watch Ysengrin, then puts his bucket down and draws near.)* Is it honey?

(Reynard picks up the bucket and disappears.)

It is most probably honey?

YSENGRIN: No. I was just licking the wind.

(Exit, in pursuit of Reynard. Brun rushes for honey, finds none.)

BRUN: He *was* just licking the wind.

(Looks for his bucket.)

Ysengrin! Robber! Ysengrin! My bucket!

(Exit in pursuit. Reynard returns, drains the bucket, puts it back in place, then leaves. Ysengrin re-enters, rushes to the bucket, finds it empty.)

YSENGRIN: Scoundrel!

(Brun rushes in.)

BRUN: Give me that!

YSENGRIN: It is empty.

BRUN: *(Beating him.)* I'll teach you to rob your Uncle.

YSENGRIN: Uncle! Ouch! . . . Ouch! . . . I haven't — it isn't — oh, it is —

BRUN: Don't cross my path again, or you'll get twice as much.

(Exit. Reynard returns.)

REYNARD: Well? Do you have colic from drinking too much?

YSENGRIN: I have been beaten — through your fault. I am going to give you your share.

REYNARD: You are mistaken.

YSENGRIN: You have emptied the bucket, to the last drop.

REYNARD: Ah no! Is it my fault if there is a hole in the bucket?

YSENGRIN: Where?

REYNARD: Look!

(He puts the bucket on Ysengrin's head.)

YSENGRIN: Remove this bucket! I am smothering! Reynard, where are you?

REYNARD: I am here.

YSENGRIN: Get me out of this bucket at once!

REYNARD: Eat your way out. Remember, you ate Epinard's ham, all by yourself.

(Exit quietly.)

YSENGRIN: I'll strangle you! I'll pull out every hair of your moustache! I'll report this to Tiecelin to put in his book!

(Noble and Brun enter.)

BRUN: You see, Sire, the spring is dry.

NOBLE: Ah-h-h, yes.

BRUN: But I had the foresight to save back a bucket of water.

NOBLE: *(Panting.)* Where is it?

BRUN: That is what I am trying to tell you, Sire. I was tricked out of it.

NOBLE: Bah! Brun, I'm so thirsty I could drink the ocean.

BRUN: Drink the ocean?

NOBLE: I'd be willing to wager I could drink the ocean to the last drop.

YSENGRIN: *(Grapples with the King.)* Ah, villain, there you are!

NOBLE: *(Throwing him back so hard, it shakes the bucket.)* This will teach you to respect your King!

YSENGRIN: King? Oh, forgive me, Sire. I cannot see your Majesty.

532

NOBLE: Even if invisible, our Majesty is to be respected.

YSENGRIN: Take this bucket off my head, and I'll explain.

NOBLE: Quite unnecessary. I understand.

(Exit.)

YSENGRIN: Sire, I didn't rob Seigneur Brun. He jabbers a great deal lately.

BRUN: I, jabber?

(Gives him a mighty blow, and exit.)

YSENGRIN: Sire — your Majesty — will nobody help me?

(Lendore enters to pick up her pillow, notices Wolf. She knocks at the bucket discreetly.)

Who is there?

LENDORE: It's me, Lendore the Marmot, sir. And you, under the bucket, who are you?

YSENGRIN: I am the poor Ysengrin. For Heaven's sake, liberate me.

LENDORE: Promise first not to try to gobble me up again?

YSENGRIN: I promise anything, my sweet Lendore. I swear it a hundred times, a thousand times, if you wish. But remove this bucket. It is smothering me.

LENDORE: Don't move.

(She pulls at the bucket.)

YSENGRIN: You are pulling my ears off!

LENDORE: I have to.

YSENGRIN: *(Free, at last.)* You did hurt me!

LENDORE: It was unavoidable.

YSENGRIN: You deserve a thrashing.

LENDORE: Don't forget you swore —

YSENGRIN: Away with promises! Here is your reward.

(Trying to kick her, he misses, kicks the bucket instead. Lendore runs away. Ysengrin, in pain, hops on one foot. Tiecelin enters.)

Oh, I am in a rage — a rage — a rage!

TIECELIN: What is the matter with you? Have you lost one leg?

YSENGRIN: It is all the fault of that bounder Reynard!

TIECELIN: *(Eager, pencil poised.)* Reynard? What did he do? Tell me at once. I will put it in my book.

YSENGRIN: Your book? Your book? That for your book!

(He strikes the book from Tiecelin's hand.)

TIECELIN: *(Retrieving his book.)* Here, have a care!

YSENGRIN: Of what use is your everlasting book?

TIECELIN: It is a record of all his crimes, to bring against him at the trial.

YSENGRIN: Winter will be over before the trial. Are we to put up with his trickery till then?

TIECELIN: It is the King's judgement.

YSENGRIN: I want to deal with him now — right now!

TIECELIN: I, too. But how?

YSENGRIN: O, leave me in peace. I am lame for life!

TIECELIN: All the same, you needn't treat my book so lightly. This is legal evidence, sanctioned by the King. And it is getting full. He hasn't many chances left. If all else fails, this will bring him to account in the end.

(Exit.)

YSENGRIN: Prattling Crow!

(Reynard enters, but finding Ysengrin alone, conceals himself.)

It all goes back to the King's judgement. Leaving that Fox free for a year, to commit twenty-four crimes without punishment!

(Enter Brun.)

Uncle Brun!

BRUN: Don't speak to me, you water-thief!

YSENGRIN: But I beg you, listen to me. It was not I who emptied your bucket.

BRUN: Not you? Who, then?

YSENGRIN: It was Reynard.

BRUN: Reynard?

YSENGRIN: I swear it.

BRUN: Reynard, who drained my bucket dry?

YSENGRIN: And then stuck it on my head, and caused me to get a beating.

BRUN: The King shall hear of this!

YSENGRIN: Of what use is that? It was the King who set him free for a year, to perpetrate such tricks.

BRUN: And the year is not half over.

YSENGRIN: Exactly.

BRUN: It is not to be borne! We must put an end to this Fox!

534

YSENGRIN: If we are to get rid of the Fox, we must first get the King out of the way.

BRUN: The King is a fool. If I were King, now —

YSENGRIN: Or I —

BRUN: Why not?

YSENGRIN: Eh?

BRUN: Why should the Lion be King?

YSENGRIN: He always has been.

BRUN: Do you know any document that gives the title of King of the animals to the Lion?

YSENGRIN: All the school books say so.

BRUN: I know a way to topple him off his throne.

YSENGRIN: What way?

BRUN: Listen. This afternoon, his Majesty declared several times that he could drink the entire ocean, to the last drop.

YSENGRIN: That was only to express how thirsty he was.

BRUN: Of course. But what would happen if we should challenge him?

YSENGRIN: He would naturally be most embarrassed. I don't see how he could very well drink the ocean dry.

BRUN: Well, then! Do you think the animal kingdom will accept a King who is unable to keep his word?

YSENGRIN: No!

BRUN: No! Certainly not! We shall demand his abdication.

YSENGRIN: And take the throne ourselves!

BRUN: Tonight, my friend, we shall be Kings.

YSENGRIN: And we shall make an end of that rascal Reynard. Go and get him. I will gather the Court.

BRUN: Reynard has played his last trick.

(Exit.)

YSENGRIN: And that for you, Master Reynard. Trumpets!

(Trumpets. Reynard appears in the open, pretending to answer the trumpet call.)

REYNARD: Cousin, what is going on?

YSENGRIN: You'll see. Trumpets!

(Trumpets. Tiecelin enters.)

TIECELIN: Why are you calling a meeting when it is so hot? It must be most important.

(Trumpets. Enter Lendore.)

YSENGRIN: It certainly is. Trumpets!

LENDORE: There, there. Everybody has heard you. What is the matter now?

YSENGRIN: The King has made a very audacious boast, and he wants everybody present to see how he keeps it.

(Noble sweeps in, escorted by Brun.)

NOBLE: What is all this congregation for?

TIECELIN: The trumpets have called us to Assembly. I, as Royal Registrar, demand to know the business before the Court.

BRUN: You shall know it now. Sire, the animal kingdom, whose beloved sovereign you are, wishes to know if it is possible for your Majesty to keep a promise made by you this afternoon.

NOBLE: Why, certainly.

BRUN: Would you be willing to put your throne at stake?

NOBLE: Of course I would. I always keep my promises. What did I promise?

BRUN: To drink the ocean, Sire.

NOBLE: Ha, ha! It is true I made that statement, I was so thirsty.

YSENGRIN: The achievement you are going to perform thrills all your people, Sire.

NOBLE: You didn't take me seriously, I hope?

BRUN: We know your Majesty capable of accomplishing the greatest feats.

NOBLE: But you know very well —

YSENGRIN: Your people are looking forward to it, Sire.

BRUN: Gentlemen, your highly esteemed sovereign will, in a moment, lead you to the beach, and show you how, when one is a very great King, one can achieve things that would be impossible for his subjects.

YSENGRIN: His Majesty is going to drink the ocean.

BRUN: You will see how the strength of your sovereign, his bravery, his keen intelligence, his wit, and his determination will give him the power to drink the whole ocean. Our great King, gentlemen, is about to swallow the ocean. Sire, the ocean is waiting.

NOBLE: Did I actually say that I would drink the ocean?

BRUN: Indeed you did, Sire — to the last drop.

NOBLE: Did I say that?

BRUN: Those were your very words, Sire.

NOBLE: But — but I shall drown!

BRUN: Does your Majesty mean you cannot keep your promise?

NOBLE: I — ah —

YSENGRIN: A King always keeps his promises.

NOBLE: But it was only in jest —

REYNARD: Ah — your Majesty. Gentlemen.

YSENGRIN: You stay out of this.

REYNARD: Did the King also say that he would drink the water of all the rivers that flow into the ocean?

BRUN: Is this any business of yours?

NOBLE: No. I did not.

REYNARD: In that case, my dear Brun, will you stop all the rivers of the world, dam their flow, and prevent them from pouring their waters into his Majesty's soup? After you have done this, I'm sure his Majesty will gladly drink what is left.

BRUN: Stop up all the rivers of the world?

NOBLE: Exactly.

BRUN: How can anyone do that?

NOBLE: When you are able to do that, I will drink up all the waters of the ocean, to the last drop.

(General laughter.)

REYNARD: Bravo, Sire. It is easy to see that we have a wise King. Don't you agree, Cousin Ysengrin?

YSENGRIN: It is easy to see that the King has a clever counsellor.

BRUN: Counsellor? This redhair? Your Majesty, this is an outrage, that you should be taken in by this rogue!

NOBLE: Rogue? Are you referring to my trusted knight, Sir Reynard the Fox? Guard your tongue, Seigneur Bear.

BRUN: Only today he tricked me out of a bucket of water.

(Tiecelin writes busily.)

YSENGRIN: And then he inverted the bucket on my head, and caused me to get a beating.

(Tiecelin writes this down too.)

NOBLE: *(To Brun.)* You dare complain to me, when you have just tried to cheat me out of my throne?

(To Ysengrin.) And you, who just this afternoon, without provocation, assaulted your King? Let me hear not another word from either one of you. Come, Reynard. A rain is coming up. Let us seek shelter.

(Epinard rushes in.)

EPINARD: Sire! I beg — a matter of utmost importance!

BRUN: Save your important matters for the pulpit, Reverend.

EPINARD: Sire, give me leave to —

NOBLE: In good time, Reverend.

EPINARD: Your Majesty, it cannot wait. Does no one realize that a very serious danger threatens us all?

NOBLE: What danger can be greater than this wicked plot to overthrow my throne?

EPINARD: Men, Sire.

LENDORE: Men?

(The very word draws them together, in a tight little knot, glancing fearfully toward the overlook.)

EPINARD: Sire, I have just come from the farm. The farmer has his hunting dogs out on a leash, training them to pick up our scent.

NOBLE: How do you know this?

EPINARD: He led the dogs first to the hen-yard, where Reynard was careless enough to leave some tracks. Then he took them to the marshes, where I — ahem! — paid a brief call on some ducks recently. When I left, he was heading toward the pig-pen, where the dogs will easily pick up the trail of Seigneur Brun.

BRUN: The dickens!

EPINARD: From there, he will take them to the sheep-fold, where the smell of Wolf is very strong.

YSENGRIN: Oh, no!

EPINARD: Next they will go to the wheat field, where the Crow dropped a feather on his last visit.

TIECELIN: Aie!

EPINARD: And finally they will make for the pasture, where the Lion has left his traces.

NOBLE: Is this true?

EPINARD: Send Tiecelin to see.

NOBLE: Tiecelin, to the farm!

TIECELIN: A-a-a-alone, Sire?

NOBLE: Have we anybody else with wings?

TIECELIN: Y-y-yes, Sire. I mean — no, Sire.

NOBLE: Quickly!

TIECELIN: I — I'm going, Sire.

538

(Exit slowly, with obvious reluctance.)

EPINARD: Your Majesty, this is no time for nonsense. I know those farmers down there. They are all united in plotting our destruction. They want our bodies; the pelt of Seigneur Brun; Reynard's fur; Tiecelin's feathers; Ysengrin's skin and teeth; yours, Sire; my quills — and Heaven knows what else. Fall is coming, when all men go hunting for game. The dogs have our scent. Men are polishing up their weapons, oiling their rifles, filling their cartridges, sharpening their knives. It will be a fearful period for those of our kind. I make it my duty, Sire, to warn you that if we wish to survive, we must all band together against the common enemy — Man.

REYNARD: That, Reverend, is one of your very best sermons.

EPINARD: Thank you.

NOBLE: You agree, then?

REYNARD: Oh, unquestionably, your Majesty. Alone, we are each of us weak and vulnerable. United, we could resist the hunters and their dogs.

NOBLE: But how can we unite?

REYNARD: Ah! That, Sire, is the question.

NOBLE: It is always the question. I am going to require each of you to take an oath.

EPINARD: Excellent, Sire.

NOBLE: And I will expect you to be bound by this oath, no matter what the emergency.

YSENGRIN: Never fear, Sire. You can depend on us.

NOBLE: Hold out your right hands. Now, repeat after me. All for one. One for all.

ALL: All for one. One for all.

(Low, distant rumble of thunder. All are frozen.)

YSENGRIN: Listen!

(Tiecelin flies in, terrified.)

TIECELIN: Did you hear that?

YSENGRIN: It's gunfire.

BRUN: The hunters! The hunters are after us!

LENDORE: Merciful heavens! Already?

(A loud thunder-clap.)

TIECELIN: Hunters? That is cannon!

YSENGRIN: They've brought in the Army!

BRUN: The Army? Soldiers?

TIECELIN: The soldiers are coming!

LENDORE: E-e-e-ek!

REYNARD: It is only thunder, Sire.

BRUN: Thunder?

(Violent cracks, as the storm breaks.)

Sire, this redhair doesn't know the difference between gunfire and thunder.

YSENGRIN: It is the hunters!

TIECELIN: It is the soldiers!

REYNARD: Gentlemen, calm yourselves. It is simply thunder.

NOBLE: Hunters, soldiers, or thunder — I am taking no chances. Excuse me, gentlemen.

(Exit, hurriedly.)

TIECELIN: Your Majesty! Wait for me!

(Tiecelin, Brun, and Ysengrin collide in their scramble to run for safety.)

BRUN: Out of my way, Crow!

(Tiecelin exits in a panic.)

YSENGRIN: No you don't. Me first!

(Exit.)

LENDORE: Where is everybody going?

BRUN: It is the hunters! Save yourself!

(Exit, on the run.)

LENDORE: The hunters? Oh, help me!

(Clings fearfully to Epinard as he rushes past, on his way to the over-look.)

EPINARD: Help you? Each one help himself!

LENDORE: But we just promised — All for one. One for all.

REYNARD: Only when convenient, Lendore.

EPINARD: Ah! You were right, Reynard. It was only thunder, after all. And here comes the rain.

LENDORE: Rain?

REYNARD: Yes, Lendore. Use your pillow for an umbrella.

EPINARD: These thunder-showers bring out the snails. You understand? I must be on the watch for them.

(Exit hastily.)

REYNARD: Of course, Reverend.

LENDORE: But the Reverend is the one who said we must unite.

REYNARD: Ah, yes, Lendore. And yet, you see, at the first thunder-stroke, he goes off in his own interest, like everybody else.

LENDORE: But suppose it *had* been the hunters?

REYNARD: You and I would have been left to meet them, alone.

LENDORE: *(Hastening out)* Heavens! Not me!

(Exit.)

REYNARD: Then it is Reynard alone against the hunters. Let them come! Even the rain is on my side. It will wash away my tracks, so the dogs can no longer pick up my trail. Let it rain! Ha, ha! It is a good joke on Man!

End of Scene Two

(Music. Sounds of gaiety and merriment from the distant vineyard. Epinard stands at the overlook, peering off toward the farm. Lendore enters cautiously, carrying a basket.)

LENDORE: Greetings, Reverend. Is it safe to gather my supplies here?

EPINARD: For the present. Men are still busy celebrating.

LENDORE: Blessed be God who created the autumn.

EPINARD: It is the harvest season, my dear Lendore. You can see the wine-growers' dance from here. Men are full of joy, for the grapes are ripe.

LENDORE: So are the pears and apples, and the nuts and acorns. They will make a good crop to fill my attic.

EPINARD: As long as men are dancing, we are safe. But as soon as the harvest is over, they will take down their guns, call their dogs, and sound the horn. Then our only salvation will be to flee into the heart of the forest, and hide. May Heaven help us when they blow the horn!

LENDORE: Yes. Well, meanwhile, give me a hand in gathering my provisions.

(They start out, but encounter Brun coming in.)

BRUN: Do you have to take up the whole path?

LENDORE: No, but I wish you would watch where you step. You just crushed a chestnut.

(Exit.)

BRUN: You and your chestnuts! I have an appointment with the Royal Registrar.

EPINARD: Don't venture out into the open. Men are about.

BRUN: Men?

EPINARD: You can see them from there.

(Exit. Brun goes to the overlook. Tiecelin enters.)

TIECELIN: The Royal Registrar is not accustomed to be kept waiting, Master Brun.

BRUN: Look — Men!

TIECELIN: *(Looking.)* It is the wine-growers' dance.

BRUN: Don't let them see you.

TIECELIN: Do you take me for a dunce?

(Ysengrin enters.)

YSENGRIN: Brun! Tiecelin! I have been looking for you.

TIECELIN: Men are dancing, Ysengrin.

YSENGRIN: Men?

BRUN: They are celebrating the harvest.

TIECELIN: Don't show yourself. From now on, we shall have to stay under cover.

YSENGRIN: I will not be hedged into this forest all winter with that rascally Fox!

BRUN: Nor I!

TIECELIN: Gentlemen, take heart. Do you know how many counts I have accumulated against him in my book? Twenty-two!

YSENGRIN: But the year is only half over!

BRUN: Are we to suffer through the fall and winter, without any respite from his tricks?

TIECELIN: Do you have anything else to suggest?

YSENGRIN: Yes!

BRUN: Eh?

YSENGRIN: I have a new plan to dispose of the Fox!

BRUN: Now?

YSENGRIN: Now!

BRUN: Without waiting for Tiecelin's book to fill up?

YSENGRIN: Without waiting one more day.

BRUN and TIECELIN: We are listening.

YSENGRIN: Suppose I should convince the King that the lower classes — the pheasants, the ducks, geese, turkeys, chickens, rabbits, pigeons, and mice — have chosen me as their defender, and have charged me to challenge Reynard to a duel.

BRUN: Yes?

YSENGRIN: If you two should back me up, with all the prestige of your position, the King would not be in position to refuse the fight, and I should make a quick end to the redhair. You know me.

BRUN: Good! Eh, Tiecelin?

TIECELIN: Why didn't you think of this sooner? You could have saved me a lot of trouble.

BRUN: We'll help you. But if you give that Fox half a chance, he will turn the tables. I want all the chances to be on your side.

YSENGRIN: The chances *are* on my side. I am the best swordsman in the kingdom.

BRUN: Nevertheless, I will provide the swords. Reynard's will be so skill-fully made, that it will break at the first stroke.

YSENGRIN: I can win without such trickery.

BRUN: Some caution is necessary, my dear nephew. Follow my advice, and Reynard will be out of our way soon. I will go fix the swords. You inform the King.

(Exit.)

YSENGRIN: Do I need this treachery? Am I not stronger and braver than Reynard?

TIECELIN: You are, and without flattery, Seigneur Wolf. But nobody is as tricky as he is.

YSENGRIN: Tiecelin, you are a man of law. Give me your advice. Do you think it is honest and fair to allot him a faked weapon?

TIECELIN: As for being fair, certainly not. Honest — even less so. But as for being smart — ha, ha!

YSENGRIN: Do you think so?

TIECELIN: A trick is just what that Fox deserves!

YSENGRIN: But this one will cost him his skin.

TIECELIN: Isn't that what you wish? Besides, so do I.

YSENGRIN: Then consider it done. You may throw away your book, Tiecelin.

TIECELIN: Throw away my book? This book is going into history! Throw away my book, indeed!

YSENGRIN: As you wish. But we shall make an end of Reynard without it. I am going to arrange this matter with the King. As for you, not a word about this.

(Exit.)

TIECELIN: Count on me, Seigneur. This time Reynard shall definitely be punished.

(Epinard enters.)

EPINARD: Who is going to punish Reynard? You?

TIECELIN: That, Reverend, is a secret. I promised —

EPINARD: Oh, very well. I don't insist.

(Goes to the overlook to watch the wine-growers' dance.)

TIECELIN: Reverend —

EPINARD: Still dancing. Did you call me?

TIECELIN: If I told you that secret —

EPINARD: That wouldn't be very proper, would it? . . . I am listening.

TIECELIN: Ysengrin is going to challenge Reynard to a duel.

EPINARD: Is that a secret?

TIECELIN: No, but what is one — and it is this I beg you to keep secret — is that Reynard's sword will be faked.

EPINARD: Faked?

TIECELIN: It will break in two, at the first stroke.

EPINARD: That is certainly not fair, but it is fitting.

TIECELIN: Do you think so, too?

EPINARD: That scamp has tricked me out of a ham, and a duck-egg. He doesn't deserve any better.

TIECELIN: I couldn't agree with you more.

(Trumpet off.)

The King is calling me.

(He starts out.)

Not a word. It is a secret.

(Exit.)

EPINARD: *(Alone.)* It was bound to turn out this way. Reynard has so often fooled the rest of us. Now it is his turn to be fooled.

(Enter Lendore.)

LENDORE: See how much I have gathered?

EPINARD: We gather what we sow, and I pity — yes, I deeply pity the one who has sown bad seed.

LENDORE: Who has sown bad seed?

EPINARD: Reynard.

LENDORE: Has Reynard been planting seeds?

EPINARD: He has spread the spirit of trickery among the animals, and he will be destroyed by trickery.

LENDORE: Is someone going to destroy Reynard?

EPINARD: Ysengrin is calling for a duel with him.

LENDORE: The Wolf is strong, of course, but Reynard is shrewd.

EPINARD: He cannot escape this time. In fact, my dear Lendore, I will tell you — but for Goodness' sake, don't repeat it to anyone. Reynard will soon meet his end, for his sword will be faked. It will break in two at the first stroke.

LENDORE: Oh, no!

EPINARD: It is a secret, Lendore. Don't tell anybody.

(Exit.)

LENDORE: It is wrong just the same. Oh! They all agreed we should unite against Men — and that was right. But we should also unite against those who fake swords.

(Enter Reynard.)

REYNARD: Who fakes swords?

LENDORE: Reynard, I will tell you, because foul play is wrong.

REYNARD: Foul play?

LENDORE: Ysengrin is going to challenge you to a duel.

REYNARD: Ho! I am equal to that kind of trap.

LENDORE: That is not all. They will provide you with a faked sword. It will break in two at the first stroke. Ysengrin will kill you.

REYNARD: That remains to be seen.

TIECELIN: *(Offstage.)* Reynard! Reynard the Redhair! Where are you?

REYNARD: Here comes the messenger of death. Leave me, Lendore — and thanks, old friend.

LENDORE: Don't forget. It is a secret.

(Exit.)

TIECELIN: *(Offstage.)* Reynard the Redhair!

REYNARD: What do you want with me?

(Tiecelin enters.)

TIECELIN: Stay where you are. Trumpets!

(Trumpets.)

Royal message! By order of the King — stay there! His Majesty Noble the Lion — don't move! We, Tiecelin the Crow, Royal Registrar — stop! — request the Knight Reynard to hold himself at the disposal of the King, in order to meet in a duel the accuser, Ysengrin the Wolf, Marshall of the Court, and defender of the lower class. Let it be known! Signed, Noble the Lion, King of the animals. Trumpets!

(Trumpets.)

REYNARD: Is that all? Pouf, it is not much. Tell your master that Reynard is ready.

(Noble enters.)

NOBLE: Come, Tiecelin, if we have to have this duel, let's get it over. Sound the call.

TIECELIN: Yes, Sire. Trumpets!

(Trumpets. The offstage festival gaiety dies away.)

REYNARD: Hail, oh Noble Sire Lion, the wisest and bravest among us all.

NOBLE: Greetings, Knight Reynard. You already know the reason for my royal call.

REYNARD: I know, Sire.

(Ysengrin enters.)

YSENGRIN: I humbly greet your Royal Majesty.

NOBLE: Greetings, Seigneur Ysengrin.

(Epinard enters.)

EPINARD: God keep you, gentlemen.

NOBLE: Knight Reynard, Marshall Ysengrin has been chosen the champion of the lower class, and I am compelled — against my will, believe me — to grant him the duel he calls for. As weapon, your Cousin has chosen the sword.

(Enter Brun, with two swords.)

BRUN: Here are the weapons, Sire.

NOBLE: You have the choice, Ysengrin.

(Brun openly hands Ysengrin the sword prepared for him.)

YSENGRIN: *(Pretending to select.)* I'll take this one, the shorter.

BRUN: Here is yours, Reynard.

REYNARD: *(Takes the sword without looking at it.)* Your Majesty, I cannot accept this weapon.

BRUN: Why not?

YSENGRIN: What does this mean?

NOBLE: Do you refuse to fight?

REYNARD: I am not a champion, your Majesty. I am unworthy to fight Ysengrin with a sword.

(He breaks the sword across his knee.)

NOBLE: What do you mean?

REYNARD: Sire, Ysengrin represents the lower classes, and fights as their champion. I am defending nobody but myself, a poor Fox. I will be satisfied with a Fox's weapon. Attendant!

(Lendore enters, carrying a stick.)

Here, Sire, is my weapon.

NOBLE: This is not customary, but I don't think the Marshall will object?

YSENGRIN: I agree. But under the circumstances, I require the use of a shield.

NOBLE: Granted.
(Brun brings a heavy iron shield.)

REYNARD: My shield!

(Lendore hands him her pillow.)

NOBLE: Do you expect to fight in this attire?

REYNARD: It is good enough for me, Sire.

NOBLE: As you wish, though I think this whole thing is absurd. Gentlemen, take your places. The fight will start when I give the signal, after three trumpet calls. It is strictly forbidden for anyone to interfere in the fight. On guard, Knights, and let the noblest be victorious!

ALL: Let the noblest be victorious!

TIECELIN: Trumpets!

(Trumpets. The opponents eye each other.)

Trumpets!

(Trumpets. Each one raises his shield and gets ready.)

Trumpets!

(Trumpets.)

NOBLE: Go!

(Music. Ballet-mime. Long duel, during which Reynard's cunning is matched against Ysengrin's strength. Reynard uses the pillow as much as the stick. Ysengrin gets nervous and loses his balance. Any impulse on the part of spectators to take Ysengrin's side is sternly frowned down by the King. After several phases, Reynard, with a masterful pillow blow, tumbles Ysengrin to the ground. Immediately he puts his foot on Ysengrin's shield, as a token of victory, and greets the King with his stick. Ysengrin, taking advantage of this moment of inattention, lifts his shield violently, throwing Reynard down, and making him drop his stick and pillow. Ysengrin leaps up and puts his foot on Reynard's chest, threatening him with his sword.)

BRUN: *(Quickly.)* Ysengrin is the winner!

NOBLE: But only a moment ago —

EPINARD: Heaven has judged.

TIECELIN: His Majesty will declare Ysengrin the winner!

NOBLE: *(Reluctantly.)* Seigneur Ysengrin, I proclaim you Reynard's conqueror. His life belongs to you.

YSENGRIN: I want him to hang. But first of all, I want him humiliated in front of all — to beg forgiveness for his crimes. After that, he shall die.

REYNARD: Oh, Ysengrin, you are truly generous, to give me the opportunity to confess my sins, and beg forgiveness. Let me confess privately to each of you, and ask your blessing.

NOBLE: Granted, my poor Reynard. Come, gentlemen, let us make it possible for Reynard to unburden his conscience.

548

BRUN: That Fox will find a way to escape, if we give him such a chance.

NOBLE: If you are afraid of that, Seigneur Brun, you may keep watch on the east side, and Ysengrin will guard the west. I myself will take care of the north.

EPINARD: *(Indicating the auditorium.)* Do you wish me to watch the south?

NOBLE: It is not necessary, Reverend. The forest is impenetrable, this side. Who will be the first to hear your confession?

REYNARD: Lendore, if you will allow it.

NOBLE: Granted. Let's go, gentlemen. And keep watch.

(All leave, except Lendore and Reynard.)

LENDORE: My poor Reynard.

REYNARD: *(On his knees.)* Draw nearer, Lendore, and receive my confession.

(Whispers.) Look as stern as you can, and open your ears.

LENDORE: *(Loudly.)* Go on, wretched scoundrel. Unload your conscience, and don't dally.

REYNARD: *(Whispering.)* You must get me out of this fix.

LENDORE: All the roads of escape are guarded.

REYNARD: If I cannot run away, we must make *them* do it. Go out and find a loud instrument somewhere, to make a big noise. Imitate the barking of dogs. Make a monstrous uproar. If you can make them think the hunters are here, they will run away. Do you understand?

LENDORE: You can count on me.

REYNARD: Give me your blessing, good and loud, for their benefit. Thanks, old friend, and don't fall asleep on your way. Hurry back!

LENDORE: One for all, all for one.

(Exit.)

REYNARD: Next, Ysengrin.

(Ysengrin approaches.)

YSENGRIN: Well, Master Joker. Are you expecting you to receive our pardon?

REYNARD: Ysengrin, I acknowledge that I fully deserve the fate that lies in store for me.

YSENGRIN: Oh, yes?

REYNARD: Yes. And besides, if I had to lose, I'm glad to lose to so brave an adversary.

YSENGRIN: Enough hypocrisy!

REYNARD: I don't want to leave this world without proving that I hold no grudge against you for your victory. A short while ago, I spotted an easy and very appetizing prey. How would you like to benefit from it, since I shall not be here any more?

YSENGRIN: Is this your confession?

REYNARD: How would you feel about a plump hen?

YSENGRIN: Easy to catch?

REYNARD: Child's play. Every night she takes a walk right here, looking for her rooster. Just hide over there when twilight comes, imitate the rooster's cry, and the hen will come to you trustingly. You can make short work of her, if you strike her down with a heavy stick. Hit well and hit hard, for she is tough to kill, they say. That hen, Cousin, ought to be worth your benediction.

YSENGRIN: Yes. Pax vobiscum.

(Exit.)

REYNARD: Next, Uncle Brun.

(Enter Brun.)

BRUN: Not hanged yet?

REYNARD: In good time, Uncle.

BRUN: I shall not be sorry for it.

REYNARD: I will not beg your pardon, for I have done you too much wrong, but let me be remembered for one last good turn. Would you like a good meal?

BRUN: Is it another bumble-bee's nest?

REYNARD: Don't talk so loudly. It is a wonderful rooster. Each night, he strolls right here, looking for his hen. Just hide over there, and imitate her cackling to lure the rooster. It will be child's play for you to strike him down with a heavy stick. Hit well and hit hard, for he is tough to kill, they say.

BRUN: Is this not a new trap?

REYNARD: Uncle! How can you think I would play you a trick at the moment I am going to die? No. I wish you good appetite, and ask your blessing.

BRUN: Go in peace. And may the rope be quickly ready, so you may go soon.

(Exit.)

REYNARD: Thank you, Uncle. Don't forget. Over there, when twilight comes.

(To himself.) What the dickens can be keeping Lendore?

(Aloud.) Next, Sire.

(Noble enters.)

NOBLE: Reynard, I was maneuvered into this, and now I am powerless to help you.

REYNARD: Rest easy, Sire. I attach no blame to you. Let me only take this last chance to thank you, Sire, for your many kindnesses —

NOBLE: Oh, Reynard, how am I to do without you!

REYNARD: I am only a wicked Fox, Sire.

NOBLE: You are the only honest rogue among us all. Why did you let yourself in for this? Don't you know they will not rest until they have your life? See, here is Brun, with the rope.

(Brun enters, with tying-rope.)

BRUN: Sire, the time has come to tie him up.

REYNARD: *(To himself.)* And still Lendore has not come back.

(The company re-gathers on stage. Brun ties Reynard's hands.)

YSENGRIN: *(Brings hanging-rope, flings it over tree-limb.)* Next. You, Reynard.

REYNARD: *(Tied.)* Here I am. May God have mercy on me, a miserable Fox, who was led by demons to the most dreadful crimes.

BRUN: Hang him quick, and let us forget about it.

REYNARD: But where is Lendore?

BRUN: She is gone.

REYNARD: I would like to hug her one more time.

YSENGRIN: Don't let us wait any longer, Sire.

REYNARD: May I not see her once more?

BRUN: Can't you see he is only trying to gain time?

REYNARD: She was my true friend.

BRUN: Ah, well, let's put an end to this.

TIECELIN: Hang him!

(Ysengrin pulls the rope, experimentally. At this moment, there is the sound of a hunting-horn.)

BRUN: Men!

EPINARD: *(Rushing to look.)* They have stopped dancing!

(An outbreak of dog-barks, offstage.)

YSENGRIN: Dogs!

TIECELIN: Hunting dogs!

BRUN: On the chase!

(A dramatic explosion of rapid-fire, staccato bangs.)

EPINARD: It is the hunt!

NOBLE: The hunt is on! Take cover!

(Noble flees.)

TIECELIN: Escape if you can!

(Exit, flying. General flight.)

YSENGRIN: *(Holding Reynard's hanging-rope.)* Wait! Wait! We must hang him!

BRUN: Come! Do you wish to get pulled apart by dogs?

(Exit.)

YSENGRIN: *(Torn, he starts off, hesitates.)* But —

(Another burst of rapid-fire bangs, accompanied by barking.)

Farewell, Master Reynard. The dogs will take care of you.

(Exit.)

REYNARD: *(Alone.)* Lendore was a true friend.

(Lendore enters, beating a saucepan, blowing a hunting-horn, and barking.)

LENDORE: Woof! Woof! Bow-wow! Bow-wow!

(She laughs.)

Ha, ha, ha! I never saw them run so fast!

REYNARD: Thanks, my dear. It was high time.

LENDORE: *(Releasing him from the rope, and untying his bonds.)* You'll never know the trouble I had to find this horn, and this saucepan.

REYNARD: My good friend, I must be off.

LENDORE: Where will you go?

REYNARD: I will have to make for the outer edge of the woods.

LENDORE: *(Concerned.)* But that is where the men do their hunting.

REYNARD: If I can elude this pack of rascals, I can surely stay out of the reach of men.

LENDORE: Take care, Reynard.

REYNARD: I will need a little time to get away. If you will be good enough to keep up the music a few moments —

LENDORE: Oh, gladly!

REYNARD: Good bye, old friend.

(*Lendore gleefully beats, blows, and barks, though her barking turns a little plaintive, as she watches Reynard go. As she goes out the opposite side, her noise retreats, and soon gives way to the renewed sounds of celebration in the distant vineyard. Lights dim slowly, leaving the empty stage in twilight. Cautiously, Tiecelin peers around a bush, then creeps in.*)

TIECELIN: (*Alone.*) The rope is empty. Reynard is gone. But where is the hunt?

(*Music and laughter from the vineyard. Tiecelin runs to look.*)

They are dancing again. Ah-h-h! It was all a hoax! There were no hunters. There were no horns. There were no dogs. There was only noise. Reynard has fooled us once again. Oh, that wily Fox! He has out-tricked Ysengrin. He has out-tricked Brun. But he will not out-trick me. I still have my book. And this will make his twenty-third crime!

(*Exit. A moment of music. Night falls. Semi-darkness with light background, so that the following scene may be played in silhouette. Ysengrin enters, right side, with stick.*)

YSENGRIN: This is the place where Reynard told me to look for that hen. Kikikiki —

(*Brun enters, left side, armed with club.*)

BRUN: Cluck, cluck, cluck —

YSENGRIN: Kikiriki —

(*They advance slowly toward each other.*)

BRUN: Hold still, you rooster!

YSENGRIN: Rooster? How dare you call me a rooster! Take that, you miserable hen!

BRUN: Hen? Is this a hen stroke?

(*They fight in earnest, and quickly discover each other at the same time.*)

Ysengrin! So you want to fight, do you?

YSENGRIN: Brun! What are you beating me for?

BRUN: (*Chasing him.*) I'll show you what a beating is!

YSENGRIN: (*Fleeing.*) Help! Help!

(*From the distant vineyard comes a burst of laughter.*)

End of Scene Three

(Music. Wind. In the distance the howling of the Wolf can be heard. Stage lights come up slowly. Tiecelin, shivering, is stamping his feet.

Brun enters, muffled up in his fur.)

TIECELIN: It is winter, Master Brun.

BRUN: You don't have to tell me.

TIECELIN: Here we are, huddled together in a tight little circle, with fortifications all around us. We don't even have any place to run, to keep warm.

BRUN: Hug yourself with your feathers.

TIECELIN: I have tried that, but my feathers are cold, too. And the frost has made the ground so hard that it doesn't provide food any more. I am hungry, Seigneur Brun, and I am not the only one. Listen to the Wolf. What bitter cold! The pool is covered with ice, and even my tongue is frozen, and stiff as a stick.

BRUN: If you kept your mouth shut, this wouldn't happen.

TIECELIN: I would gladly shut it on some food, wouldn't you?

(Lendore crosses slowly, pillow under her arm, overwhelmed with sleep.)

Where are you going?

LENDORE: To sleep.

(Noble enters, overcome by a comic cough.)

NOBLE: Find me a doctor. Promise him a fourth, even half of my kingdom, but let him release me from this awful cough.

TIECELIN: A doctor? Where are we to find a doctor?

BRUN: We are holed up here like fugitives.

TIECELIN: Beyond the barricade, hunting dogs are waiting to pounce on us.

BRUN: And behind them are the hunters with their guns.

TIECELIN: None of us dares to stick our nose beyond the barricade.

NOBLE: But this is a matter of life or death.

TIECELIN: Your Majesty only has a bad cold.

NOBLE: Bad cold? Your King is dying of pneumonia, and there is no one here to lift a finger. Oh, where is Reynard!

TIECELIN: Reynard? The redhair!

NOBLE: Yes. Oh, my good Reynard, if you were only here!

TIECELIN: Your Majesty surely would not wish such a thing.

BRUN: He'd better not show his face around here.

NOBLE: Find him. Search the kingdom!

TIECELIN: Outside the barricade, where the dogs are lurking?

NOBLE: Even to the edge of the forest!

BRUN: The edge of the forest, where men are waiting with their guns?

TIECELIN: Would you have us risk our lives?

NOBLE: Yes! Bring me Reynard.

TIECELIN: Your Majesty, Reynard is in hiding. He would not dare to come.

BRUN: He knows a hanging is waiting for him.

NOBLE: Tell him I will forgive him everything, if he will only come back.

(Lendore exits quietly, but purposefully.)

BRUN: Forgive him?

TIECELIN: Forgive him all the crimes he has committed against us?

BRUN: Forgive him this rope?

TIECELIN: It is beyond your power, Sire. My book is full of indictments against him — twenty-four, to be exact.

NOBLE: Then I am doomed. Only Reynard can find a way to save me.

(Ysengrin enters, starving, violent.)

YSENGRIN: Give me something to eat — no matter what, but something.

NOBLE: I am sick, Ysengrin.

YSENGRIN: And I am hungry, Sire.

TIECELIN: Be patient, Sire. Don't die yet. When good weather returns, you will be well again.

NOBLE: I shall not last that long, my friends. My kingdom! Who will save my kingdom?

BRUN and YSENGRIN: *(At the same time.)* I! Me!

TIECELIN: Gentlemen.

YSENGRIN: *(Pushing Brun back.)* I can take your place, Sire. Don't be afraid to die.

BRUN: *(Elbowing Ysengrin away.)* I can do it, Sire. You may trust me.

TIECELIN: Don't die, your Majesty, or these two will kill each other to take possession of your throne.

NOBLE: Death is inexorable, my friends. There is only one who can help your poor, unfortunate King, and he is not here.

(Outbreak of savage barking.)

Listen!

BRUN: It is the dogs!

YSENGRIN: The dogs have broken through!

TIECELIN: The hunters have found us!

BRUN: They are coming!

YSENGRIN: We are trapped!

NOBLE: *(Struggling weakly to his feet.)* My friends, gather round me. We shall die together.

(Cowering together in a close huddle, they await the enemy's approach. Lendore enters, followed by Reynard, disguised as a Minstrel.)

LENDORE: Your Majesty —

NOBLE: Lendore!

TIECELIN: Lendore? It is not the hunters?

LENDORE: Hunters? It is only a poor Minstrel I found hiding beneath the barricade, to escape the dogs. I thought he might be able to help you.

BRUN: If he led the dogs to our stronghold, we are all done for.

TIECELIN: How did you get by the hunters?

REYNARD: *(Minstrel accent.)* Perdone, Senor. I no understanda very well.

YSENGRIN: Who are you, who plays the guitar while our King is dying?

BRUN: Cease your music, vagrant.

REYNARD: No de musique? Porque?

TIECELIN: The King is dying.

NOBLE: Let him approach. Who are you?

REYNARD: Un troubadour, from Andalusia d'Espagne, my gran Senor.

NOBLE: Can you play and sing?

REYNARD: Si. Very good player and singer. And very good doctor, too.

NOBLE: What? You are a doctor? Can you cure my pneumonia?

REYNARD: Si, Senor. I can cure anychosa.

BRUN: Beware. He is a spy.

REYNARD: I can save el gran Senor.

YSENGRIN: Get away.

REYNARD: I can kill la pneumonia, just like that — crac!

NOBLE: Do you really have a remedy?

REYNARD: Si, Senor, un gran remedia.

NOBLE: Relieve me of this cough, and you shall become my prime minister.

BRUN: Allow me, Sire —

NOBLE: I have spoken.

YSENGRIN: But your Majesty —

NOBLE: What remedy do you recommend?

REYNARD: *(Showing a bottle.)* Esta boteilla, gran Senor. Vino. Good vino. Vino grandissimo to kill la pneumonia.

NOBLE: Give it to me.

REYNARD: Ma, que, but it is not enough by itself. Needa still some otrechosa.

NOBLE: Some other things, such as what?

REYNARD: *(Makes gesture of pulling his moustache.)* Some chosa like this, but bigger, moocha bigger.

NOBLE: A big moustache?

REYNARD: Moustachio, si, yes. Yes, moustachio! Like that!
(Points to Brun.)

BRUN: My moustache?

REYNARD: Si, Senor. Si. Gracias.

NOBLE: Has it got to be cut?

REYNARD: Cut? Si, yes. That is of the most importance. It goes in la pocha —
(Shows his leather pouch.)
— and then on la cabeza, there.
(Indicates the King's head.)

NOBLE: Brun, your moustache.

BRUN: But Sire, it is impossible.

NOBLE: *(Stern.)* Your moustache.

BRUN: I shall be disgraced.

NOBLE: It is your King's life.

YSENGRIN: You cannot refuse, my dear Brun.

REYNARD: *(Scissors ready.)* Cut?

BRUN: Sire?

NOBLE: I am waiting.

YSENGRIN: Go ahead, troubadour.
(Reynard cuts off half of Brun's moustache.)

BRUN: Let Heaven be the witness of my disgrace!

NOBLE: It is for your King's welfare, Seigneur Brun.

REYNARD: It is truly un gran moustachio, Senor the Majesty. Half will be enough. No cut la otre. No wish to rob the fat senor.

BRUN: But Sire, I look ridiculous.

NOBLE: You will wear the half-moustache in remembrance of your self-sacrifice.

REYNARD: *(Putting moustache in his pouch.)* Ah, that is good, so far. But gran senor, that is not all.

NOBLE: You need something else? What is it?

REYNARD: A ball of white fur.

NOBLE: White fur?

REYNARD: Si. Oh, a very little ball. Perhaps no more than that.

(Points to Ysengrin's ears, which are lined with white.)

YSENGRIN: My ears? Oh, no!

(Frantically seeks a means of escape.)

REYNARD: Not the ears, senor. Only the white lining of them.

NOBLE: How lucky! Use your scissors, troubadour.

YSENGRIN: But Sire, I need my ear-linings!

BRUN: You cannot refuse, my dear Ysengrin.

NOBLE: This is for your King.

YSENGRIN: I shall never be the same!

NOBLE: Go ahead, Minstrel.

YSENGRIN: My ears! My ears!

REYNARD: *(Cutting.)* If the senor would only stand still — I do not wish to hurt the senor.

YSENGRIN: Ouch! He is taking my whole ear, Sire! Tell him to — Ouch!

REYNARD: Ah! Since the senor is so unhappy to lose a little bit of fur, we may content ourselves with this one piece.

(The ear he has trimmed has lost its erectness, hangs down ludicrously over one eye. The other ear stands up.)

YSENGRIN: But my ears will not match!

REYNARD: Small matter. We do not wish to ask too great a sacrifice of the senor.

YSENGRIN: I am lop-sided!

NOBLE: In the service of your King, Seigneur Wolf. You are sure you have enough white fur for the remedy, troubadour?

REYNARD: Oh, si, gran senor.

NOBLE: And now do you need anything else?

REYNARD: Only one otrechosa, Sire.

NOBLE: And what is that?

REYNARD: We must have three black feathers.

(Tiecelin starts creeping out.)

NOBLE: Tiecelin!

TIECELIN: You c-c-called me, Sire?

REYNARD: Ma, que, such beautiful, glossy black feathers!

NOBLE: Tiecelin, we have need of some feathers.

TIECELIN: But I have no feathers to spare, Sire.

REYNARD: Ah, si, si. On this side, too short. In front, too soft. On this side, the colour is not true. But ah, the back is just right.

(He seizes Tiecelin by the tail feathers.)

TIECELIN: Sire! He would not take my tail!

NOBLE: Do you find there what you require, troubadour?

REYNARD: Ah, si, si, Senor the Majesty.

TIECELIN: Help! Help! My beautiful tail!

YSENGRIN: Your tail is no better than my ear, Tiecelin.

BRUN: Or than my moustache.

REYNARD: *(Plucking.)* One!

TIECELIN: Aie!

NOBLE: It is for your King's life, Tiecelin.

REYNARD: Two!

TIECELIN: Aie!

YSENGRIN: At least you will not be one-sided.

REYNARD: Three!

TIECELIN: Aie! Oh, I am undressed! Sire, I shall take my death of cold.

(He does indeed look odd, with his stub tail.)

REYNARD: *(Placing feathers in the pouch.)* I regret any inconvenience this may cause the little senor. Now, your Majesty, all is ready. Gran senor. On la cabeza. There.

(He places the pouch inside Noble's crown.)

NOBLE: Are you sure this will cure me?

REYNARD: Oh, very sure, gran senor.

NOBLE: And if your remedy doesn't work?

REYNARD: Then we shall have to resort to extreme measures. But let us hope for the best.

NOBLE: No extreme measures. This will cure me. I can feel it. Give me that bottle.

REYNARD: Ah, si. This is the wine that gives life.

NOBLE: The moustache, what is it for?

REYNARD: Strength. It is the strength of the fat senor.

NOBLE: And the fur?

REYNARD: Warmth. It will dissolve the cough.

NOBLE: And the feathers?

REYNARD: It is a cover, to hold the strength and the warmth in. With the wine, it will spread through the body, and give new life. Drink.

(Noble drinks. All watch with suspense.)

TIECELIN: How does your Majesty feel?

NOBLE: To tell the truth, I don't feel any difference.

REYNARD: Ah, then, we shall have to use the last resort. For this I shall need three needles.

NOBLE: *(Alarmed.)* Needles? What for?

YSENGRIN: Needles? The Reverend!

BRUN: Of course. Epinard!

TIECELIN: I'll fetch him.

(Exit.)

NOBLE: What are these needles for?

REYNARD: Ah, Senor the Majesty is so very fortunate, to have such willing subjects to supply every need.

NOBLE: But what do you propose to do with these needles?

(Tiecelin returns with Epinard.)

TIECELIN: Master Troubadour, I have the honour to present the Reverend Epinard.

EPINARD: Peace be with you, Master Troubadour.

REYNARD: Ah, si. I can see that he has needles to spare.

EPINARD: *(Bristling.)* Needles? What is this about needles?

NOBLE: That is what I want to know.

560

REYNARD: We wish to request a small favour of you, Reverend, with your permission.

YSENGRIN: With or without your permission, his Majesty desires you to give up three needles to this troubadour here.

EPINARD: But my needles are my protection!

BRUN: Don't be stingy. You have plenty of them.

(Reynard has circled him, and selected three choice needles, between his ears.)

EPINARD: But your Majesty, I am not — Ow! Have some respect for my — Ow! Will you give me a chance to — Ow! Oh, I am unfrocked!

TIECELIN: It is for your King, Reverend.

REYNARD: Here are three needles, gran senor — nice and long and sharp.

NOBLE: Wait! I demand to know what you intend to do with these needles.

REYNARD: Why, if the first remedia has not cured you, it will be necessary to bleed you, Senor the Majesty.

NOBLE: Oh, no!

REYNARD: First in the arm —

NOBLE: Wait!

REYNARD: Then in the leg —

NOBLE: Stop!

REYNARD: And then, of course, in the — ah — underneath the — ah —

NOBLE: Enough! It is not necessary. I feel better now.

REYNARD: Ah, the remedia is taking effect?

NOBLE: I feel perfectly well. Throw those needles away.

REYNARD: My congratulations, Sire. The King is saved, gentlemen.

ALL: Long live the King!

NOBLE: Thank you. As for you, troubadour, I wish to reward you.

YSENGRIN: Are you going to make him your prime minister?

NOBLE: Did I say that?

BRUN: It is impossible, Sire. A Minstrel — a guitar-player —

NOBLE: Did I really promise it?

TIECELIN: According to law, Sire, a stranger cannot hold office in the animal kingdom.

NOBLE: Ah! You hear, Troubadour. The law prevents it.

REYNARD: The gran senor is cured, that is good. The povre Minstrel is not minister, that is also good. I ask only the gift of your royal favour in the country of los animalos.

NOBLE: Granted. Take this.

YSENGRIN: Your ring, Sire!

BRUN: The King's diamond!

TIECELIN: It is worth a million at least.

NOBLE: Is this too high a price for my life?

TIECELIN: No, indeed, indeed.

NOBLE: This ring will be the token of my royal protection. Whenever you show it to anyone in my kingdom, help and assistance will be granted you.

REYNARD: The senor is gran, gran como la luna. I am his servitor.

NOBLE: Do you wish anything else?

REYNARD: Only la pocha, there.

BRUN: My moustache!

NOBLE: Half of your moustache.

YSENGRIN: My ear!

NOBLE: The lining of one ear.

TIECELIN: My tail!

NOBLE: Three paltry feathers.

EPINARD: (*As Reynard tucks his quills into the pouch.*) My quills!

NOBLE: We wish you good luck, Minstrel.

REYNARD: Gracias, Senor the Majesty. Now I must go.

BRUN: Go? Out there?

TIECELIN: Sire, if he so much as snaps a twig going through the barricade, the dogs will be upon us in a flash.

REYNARD: Ma, que, Senors, the dogs will be upon me, not you. But have no fear, Majesty. I know how to escape the dogs.

NOBLE: Just the same, it would seem only wise for us all to take cover, until you are safely away. Follow me, gentlemen. Good bye, my good fellow.

REYNARD: The gran senor is good also. Viva, olle the gran senor. And gracias for the so beautiful ring.

(*Noble exits, followed by Brun, Ysengrin, and Epinard. Tiecelin pretends to follow, but lags behind, as Reynard prepares to leave. Lendore has fallen asleep.*)

TIECELIN: One moment, my friend.

REYNARD: The little senor said "my friend".

TIECELIN: I said "One moment". It is customary, in cases of audience with the King, to leave an expression of your thanks with me.

REYNARD: Ma, que, I did not know.

TIECELIN: Doubtless you do not know that I am the King's Registrar, and that I regulate, manage, and organize everything in the animal kingdom.

REYNARD: Hombre, que I, I thought the gran senor King did it all.

TIECELIN: He does what I command. When I say "Here comes the King", he comes. I say "The King sits down". He sits down. "The King drinks". He drinks. "The King gets up". He gets up. He can do nothing without my order. Without me there would be no King of the animals any more.

REYNARD: Ma, que, how about that! The little senor is a very important persona. It is a pity that he had to sacrifice his so beautiful tail plumage to the King's health.

TIECELIN: It is nothing less than a disgrace.

REYNARD: Ah, yes. Your costume is now a little lacking in dignity for a so important persona. Wait! I have a chosa in la pocha, to make him look more gran. Look. Would the senor do me the great honour to accept this, in place of the feathers he has lost?

(He takes out three peacock feathers.)

TIECELIN: They are peacock feathers, aren't they?

REYNARD: Si. The feathers del peacock. The very marvelosa bird que outshines the sun a hundred times, in his brilliance.

TIECELIN: He is a very beautiful bird indeed, but he is stupid.

REYNARD: Ma, que, but this is the tail, not the head. The little senor with the plumage del peacock, and his own gran intelligencio, will make the greatest bird of all, the very gran Phoenix of the occupantos of these woods.

TIECELIN: Do you think so?

REYNARD: Que, it is the truth. It is the thanks del troubadour to the gran persona del little senor.

TIECELIN: I accept the very humble present you give me. Now you may go.

REYNARD: Ah, si. Adios, senor.

TIECELIN: Take care, as you leave, not to draw the attention of the dogs.

REYNARD: Trust me, senor. Servitor, gran Phoenix. Servitor.

(Pretends to leave, but conceals himself on one side. Lendore stirs on the other side.)

TIECELIN: *(Listens tensely a few moments, for any possible disturbance caused by Minstrel's departure.)* Ah, he is safely away.

(Not noticing Lendore, he adorns himself with the peacock feathers.)

I can feel myself becoming very beautiful, very beautiful indeed. The King is far behind me when it comes to grace, charm, bearing, and elegance. I am really a Phoenix. The Minstrel said so. When the others see me, they will say "Look at the Crow!" And they will be green with envy. They will say "Look at the Crow!" And the echoes of the forest will endlessly repeat — "Look at the Crow!" Look at the Crow!"

REYNARD: *(Echoing.)* Oh! . . . Oh! . . . Oh! . . . Oh!

TIECELIN: How beautiful, beautiful, beautiful! How very beautiful! More beautiful than the Wolf, more beautiful even than the Lion.

(Shouts.) More beautiful than the King!

REYNARD: *(Echoing.)* . . . Ing! . . . Ing! . . . Ing! . . . Hee — hee — hee!

(Lendore takes it up, and the echo gradually changes into a laughter which is curiously prolonged.)

LENDORE: Hee — hee — hee — Hi — hi — hi —

TIECELIN: *(At first taken aback, stops and wonders.)* What? Hush, Echo.

REYNARD: Ho — ho — ho — ho —

LENDORE: Ho — ho — ho — ho —

TIECELIN: Instead of laughing, look at the Crow!

REYNARD: Ho — ho — ho — ho —

LENDORE: Ho — ho — ho — ho —

TIECELIN: *(In a rage.)* Are you almost through?

REYNARD: Hou — hou — hou — hou —

LENDORE: Hoo — hoo — hoo — hoo —

TIECELIN: You laugh at me?

REYNARD and LENDORE: Hee — hee — hee — hee —

(The laughter seems to come from everywhere at once.)

Ha — ha — ha — ha! Hee — hee — hee — hee! Look at the Crow! Ho — ho — ho! How beautiful is he! Hee — hee — hee! Ho — ho — ho! Ha — ha — ha! Hohoho! Hahaha! Hihihi! Hohohohaha-hahihi! Hohohohahahahihi!

(In shame Tiecelin divests himself of the peacock feathers, but the laughter continues to grow in volume.)

TIECELIN: *(Finally manages to top the laughter.)* Enough! Stop!

(Reynard stops, but Lendore, unaware of danger, continues, convulsed with genuine laughter.)

There is more to this than echoes.

(Creeping quietly across he discovers and seizes Lendore.)

Lendore! You were making fun of me!

LENDORE: I — I — Oh, Tiecelin, you were oh, so funny!

TIECELIN: Nobody is going to laugh at me, and live to tell it.

LENDORE: H — H — H — Stop! You are strangling me.

TIECELIN: *(Choking her.)* I am going to do more than that. I am going to feed you to the Wolf!

LENDORE: *(Struggling in his grasp.)* H-h-help! H-h-h-help!
(Reynard steps out of hiding, discarding his cape.)

REYNARD: Let her go.

TIECELIN: *(Frozen.)* I have surely heard that voice before.

REYNARD: Ma, que, senor, your costume is a little lacking in dignity —

TIECELIN: *(Trying shamefully to cover up his stub tail.)* Reynard! It is you!

REYNARD: At your service, Tiecelin.

TIECELIN: You, the Minstrel! I might have known it.

REYNARD: *(Placing peacock feathers at his tail and mimicking Tiecelin.)*

Am I not beautiful? The most beautiful of all? Am I not the great Phoenix of the deep woods?

TIECELIN: You will pay for this. It is your last trick. Everybody! Come! It is Reynard! It is his twenty-fifth crime! Trumpets! Trumpets!

REYNARD: Am I not splendid? Am I not the best-looking, the most intelligent —

(Trumpets. At the sound, Reynard breaks off short.)

TIECELIN: Everybody come! It is Reynard! Trumpets!

(Reynard runs desperately in all directions, seeking an escape. Trumpets.)

Twenty-fifth crime! Trumpets!

(Trumpets.)

VOICES: *(Off.)* Reynard! Twenty-fifth crime!

(The Epilogue follows immediately, without break.)

End of Scene Four

EPILOGUE

TIECELIN: By order of the King, his Majesty Noble the Lion —

REYNARD: All right. I know what is coming next.

(He tries to leave at right, but encounters Noble, entering, and has to bow.)

Sire.

NOBLE: Reynard.

(Reynard tries to leave at left, but Brun and Ysengrin enter there.)

REYNARD: Uncle Brun. Cousin Ysengrin.

BRUN: The rope is still in place.

YSENGRIN: We have kept it waiting for you.

REYNARD: I am in no hurry.

NOBLE: This time, Reynard, you have put the noose around your own neck.

LENDORE: Why did you let yourself get caught? Oh, Reynard, I cannot watch this!

(Exit. Epinard enters.)

EPINARD: What brings on this new disturbance? Ah, it is you, Reynard. You must be out of your mind.

NOBLE: Gentlemen.

TIECELIN: The King is about to speak. Trumpets!

(Trumpets.)

NOBLE: We are now at the end of the year of mercy granted to Reynard the Fox. What are the grievances charged against him now?

TIECELIN: A book full, your Majesty. Twenty-five crimes.
(He reads.)

The Knight Reynard, called Reynard the redhair, is accused —

NOBLE: Never mind, Tiecelin. You have all witnessed Reynard's misdeeds. So you will judge if he deserves to hang, or if he should be granted mercy. How do you feel about it?

YSENGRIN: I demand his hanging.

BRUN: Hang him!

TIECELIN: He must hang!

EPINARD: May Heaven forgive me, let him hang.

NOBLE: You hear, Reynard?

REYNARD: Nevertheless, your Majesty, I have the right to present my defense, I presume?

YSENGRIN: There is no defense.

TIECELIN: He has committed twenty-five crimes.

NOBLE: Have you any defender?

REYNARD: Yes, your Majesty.

NOBLE: Who is it?

REYNARD: You yourself, Sire.

NOBLE: I?

REYNARD: Doesn't this ring remind you of anything? *(Minstrel accent.)* The gran senor has lost la pneumonia. El troubadour has cured the gran senor.

NOBLE: So, it was you?

REYNARD: It was me, Sire, at your service.

(All the animals cry out with rage.)

BRUN: He has cut off half my moustache!

YSENGRIN: My ear!

EPINARD: My quills!

TIECELIN: *(Writing furiously.)* My feathers! And all this is going in the book!

BRUN: The bumble-bees have stung me all over!

EPINARD: He made away with my ham!

NOBLE: An end to this! Stop! Enough! Silence!

TIECELIN: Let the King speak.

(But the silence is broken by the sound of a hunting-horn, offstage. Lendore flies in, frantic.)

LENDORE: The hunters! The hunters are coming!

(The hunting horn is repeated from a different direction, and again from another. Everyone is electrified.)

They are closing in, from all sides of the woods!

BRUN: This has happened once before.

YSENGRIN: Is this rascal going to escape us again?

TIECELIN: The rope is ready.

BRUN: Let's not wait any longer. Hang him!

(Genuine rifle shots offstage.)

EPINARD: This is no joke!

NOBLE: We are caught!

(All make a grand rush for the left. The fanfare breaks out on that side, with renewed vigor.)

Tiecelin, go and see what is going on.

TIECELIN: B-b-b-but —

NOBLE: Go and see, I tell you.

EPINARD: It is no use, Sire. We are surrounded.

LENDORE: *(At right.)* There are more than twenty.

YSENGRIN: *(At back.)* They are coming this way, too.

BRUN: *(At left.)* And this way.

NOBLE: This time, my friends, we shall not escape the men. Let each one of you show your courage, and defend your life at a high price.

TIECELIN: Sire, I wish you a very gallant death. As for me, I have wings. Allow me to make use of them.

(Exit. His flight is hailed by shouts and rifle shots.)

BRUN: There goes our brave Phoenix.

YSENGRIN: What shall we do with the prisoner?

NOBLE: We are all prisoners, Seigneur Ysengrin.

REYNARD: I can save you, Sire.

BRUN: Don't listen to him. He is only trying to escape.

NOBLE: How can you save us?

REYNARD: Don't move from here. Stay under cover. I will go out of the woods. The fortifications will hold them until I can get out.

YSENGRIN: You see, he is only trying to get away.

REYNARD: I will let the hunters see me, willingly, in the open. The dogs will jump for me, and follow my tracks, and the men will follow them. I will lead them out of the woods, to the other end of the plain.

NOBLE: You will lose your life doing that.

REYNARD: It is possible — but it will save yours.

NOBLE: Release him. May Heaven help you!

REYNARD: Farewell, Sire. Farewell, my friends.

(He takes time to choose his exit point with care, then leaps out, to be greeted by furious dog-barking, men's shouts, and rifle shots. Ballet-mime, as the animals left onstage follow the progress of the chase. The cries, the barks, the shots, and the horn-calls intermingle. Cries and yells, close by at first — "The fox! The fox! Loose the dogs! Shoot! Shoot!" By some means, possibly by amplifying, there should be a noticeable difference between the human voices and the animal voices. At first the animals huddle together, frozen with terror, silent, distressed,

568

listening intently. As the offstage sounds retreat, they relax enough to register their fear, stopping up their ears, covering their heads, running for shelter, cowering under rocks, bushes, stumps. Eventually the noises fade away in the distance, indicating that Reynard is leading the chase far away. They begin to express their relief, and then their absolute joy, as the hunt moves further away, leaping with elation, embracing each other, dancing in triumph.)

LENDORE: *(Hopping up and down.)* He has done it! He has done it!

(One last, distant, terribly final shot, then a distressing silence.)

Oh, no!

(All are suddenly sobered.)

BRUN: And so, Sire, this is the end of Reynard.

EPINARD: May Heaven welcome his soul.

YSENGRIN: And the hunters his skin.

LENDORE: *(Who has rushed to the overlook.)* He is nowhere in sight.

YSENGRIN: Of course not. The dogs have got him.

NOBLE: He could outrun the dogs.

BRUN: But not the bullets, Sire.

YSENGRIN: The hunters have saved us the trouble of hanging him.

(Tiecelin returns, very cocky and proud.)

BRUN: Ah! Now that the danger is over, our valiant Crow returns.

TIECELIN: Sire, you are saved.

NOBLE: Where do you come from?

TIECELIN: From a tree, Sire. When I left here, I risked thousands of rifle shots — and look. Not a scratch.

LENDORE: Have you seen Reynard?

TIECELIN: He is dead. I saw him fall, covered with blood, and crawl under a hazelnut bush.

LENDORE: No!

NOBLE: The brave fellow!

TIECELIN: The dogs will catch up with him shortly. But they will find him dead. So will the hunters. I am the only one who saw his end.

YSENGRIN: Oh, stop your bragging. Reynard is dead, and that is all that matters.

LENDORE: *(Weeping.)* Poor redhair!

BRUN: We finally got rid of him.

EPINARD: Since he is gone, let him rest in peace.

NOBLE: At least he died like a hero — not by hanging.

(Reynard staggers in, tattered, exhausted, faltering, exaggerating his condition dramatically.)

REYNARD: Sire, my King —

TIECELIN: *(Hastily scrambling up his tree.)* What! You are not dead?

REYNARD: I . . . fulfilled . . . my promise —

(He staggers.)

NOBLE: Yes, good fellow. You have our undying gratitude.

LENDORE: Are you wounded?

REYNARD: No, it is nothing . . . no, nothing —

(He collapses.)

LENDORE: Reynard!

EPINARD: This time, Sire, beyond any doubt, he is really gone.

YSENGRIN: So much the better.

TIECELIN: Beware. He has more than one trick up his sleeve.

BRUN: Oh, no. Look.

(He lifts one leg, which falls back limply.)

TIECELIN: He did that to me once before.

(But he ventures down from his perch, nevertheless.)

EPINARD: *(Lifts one arm, which falls back, lifeless.)* He has undoubtedly passed away.

YSENGRIN: *(Lifts the tail, which falls back, a dead weight.)* There is no doubt indeed.

LENDORE: *(Sobbing.)* He was so good.

EPINARD: He was a rogue.

LENDORE: So witty.

YSENGRIN: He was a scoundrel.

LENDORE: So clever.

BRUN: He was a villain.

LENDORE: So full of fun.

TIECELIN: He was a cheese robber!

EPINARD: A ham robber!

BRUN: A moustache robber!

YSENGRIN: An ear robber!

TIECELIN: A tail robber!

EPINARD: A quill robber!

TIECELIN: And it is all down in my book. See, my book? Here are all his crimes.

NOBLE: Yes — and here is he. We live, because of him. Give me your book, Tiecelin. Let the accusations against him be buried with Reynard.

(He tears out pages, letting them fall on Reynard.)

TIECELIN: My book! My book!

(Silence. Reynard stirs.)

REYNARD: What gentle winds have blown this soft covering over my poor body? Ah, it is my noble King.

(He gathers loose pages and tears them across.)

What a relief it is to know that your royal person is safe from the hunters!

(He rises.)

BRUN: He lives!

LENDORE: Reynard, my friend!

YSENGRIN: He is alive!

TIECELIN: My book! My book!

REYNARD: Ah, you are concerned about your book, Tiecelin? Allow me to return it to you — at least a part of it. And a part for you, Uncle Brun. And some for you, Ysengrin.

(Gaily he pelts them all with torn fragments. Tiecelin, driven to despair by this desecration, scrambles about frantically, trying to gather them up.)

BRUN: Sire, he lives — and there goes all the evidence against him.

REYNARD: Indeed. Then we shall have no use for this grim thing. Let us use it for a gayer purpose.

(He snatches down the hanging-rope, jumps rope for a few steps.)

Come, my faithful friend Lendore, it is a moment to rejoice. If you will hold this end, perhaps the Reverend will be good enough to hold the other?

TIECELIN: *(Picking up torn pages.)* My book! My book!

YSENGRIN: Sire, he is free to start his crimes all over again.

NOBLE: Reynard, you are really a very bad fellow.

REYNARD: I know, Sire. We all have a little bad in us, don't we? Reverend, can't you turn a little faster?

EPINARD: Reynard, you have not changed one bit.

REYNARD: Faster, Lendore. Sire, won't you join me?

(He takes Noble's hand, and leads him into the game.)

LENDORE: Reynard is alive!

(And as the rope twirls faster, all take up the refrain.)

BRUN: *(Grumpy.)* Reynard is alive.

YSENGRIN: *(Bitter.)* Reynard is alive.

EPINARD: *(Resigned.)* Reynard is alive.

TIECELIN: *(In tears with frustration.)* My book! My book!

NOBLE: *(Amused.)* Reynard is alive!

LENDORE: *(Joyful.)* Reynard is alive!

REYNARD: *(Triumphant.)* Reynard is alive!

The End

JOHNNY MOONBEAM AND THE SILVER ARROW

*An adventure for
young people
in narration and mime*

by

JOSEPH GOLDEN

JOHNNY MOONBEAM AND THE SILVER ARROW

By Joseph Golden

JOHNNY MOONBEAM AND THE SILVER ARROW

by

JOSEPH GOLDEN

Cast

NARRATOR

JOHNNY MOONBEAM

MEDICINE MAN

RAIN GOD

FIRE GOD

EARTH GOD

JOHNNY MOONBEAM was first produced in August, 1957, by the Magic Circle Theatre, of Tufts University, at Medford, Massachusetts, under the direction of the author.

On this occasion, it was shown, in arena style, to the delegates assembled at Tufts University for the national Children's Theatre Conference.

For

DAVID

PRODUCTION NOTE

Although the narration and stage directions depict a fairly specific sequence of actions, it is hoped that the reader will find a wide margin permitted for the imaginative director. To such persons, the stage business provided in the text of the play becomes an *outline* for action rather than definitive business, and thus may be embellished and enriched to the limit of the director's and performer's capacity.

Furthermore, JOHNNY MOONBEAM may be treated as a *dance* and can be mounted for the stage by a choreographer as well as by a director. Music for the dance, beyond what is suggested in the text, may be specially contrived for the play or use be made of recorded music already available.

In regard to style and quantity of stage movement, size of cast (during instruction and final scenes) or treatment of Narrator, the director has considerable freedom of choice.

The stage effects called for in the play need not be, of course, as elaborate as indicated. The mood created by a response to even suggestive light or sound patterns by the performers is of primary importance. All sound effects are available for manual or recorded use. Lighting effects can be accomplished with almost any basic set up of red-green-blue circuits or strips and about a half dozen small, strong spots.

Johnny Moonbeam and the Silver Arrow

The curtain opens slowly, accompanied by a distant and incessant throb of drums. For a moment the stage is in darkness, with only the sound of the tom-toms breaking the emptiness. A sharp shaft of white light slowly dims up revealing the NARRATOR who is perched on the stage apron. His dress may be an odd combination of costumes. It is meant to suggest that while he is essentially a part of the stage picture, fully capable of thrusting himself into the heart of the action on Johnny's behalf, he is also identified with the audience. He is a virile, earthy character, but he can consort with moonbeams, moving nimbly among them, because he spins the dreams common to all boys. When the beam of light is up full he gestures to indicate that he is listening intently.

NARRATOR: Sh-sh! Listen!

(He listens intently again, turning his head fully to all sides to indicate that the sound of the drums is all around him.)

Ya hear that? Injuns! All around us. Ya can't take five steps in any direction but you'll run smack into an Injun standin' there with a head full of feathers, all proud and strong, with a tomahawk in his hand, and a quiver full 'o arrows. He'll be searchin' the night sky, or countin' stars, maybe, just like you do. Or he'll be settin' in a cool beam o' moonlight, like I'm doin' right now feelin'—oh, I don't know, sorta lonely maybe, but also feelin' kinda strong and proud 'cause he's got this beam o' moonlight all to himself. Like livin' in a small, round, white house with a great big dark outside.

(The drums stop suddenly. NARRATOR tries to peer into the darkness around him. Suddenly a voice, apparently from nowhere in particular, breaks the silence. It is a male voice, chanting a strange incantation. It is a powerful voice, rich and melodic.)

There. You hear? The ceremony's 'bout to begin. So hold on tight to your seats 'cause only Injuns are

579

supposed to know about this. It's a strange sort of ceremony . . .

(A blue light begins to dim up slowly at center stage, revealing a boy kneeling before a grotesquely ornamented MEDICINE MAN.)

. . . strange and powerful. Happens only once a year in this tribe and then only when the moon gets hooked on a crag of one of those steep cliffs out there on the horizon. And when the prairie is dark and cool on such a night, the chief Medicine Man sets up a lonesome kind of music— just like you hear him doin' right now . . .

(The MEDICINE MAN's arms are raised and are describing arcs in the air, slowly, eerily. On the circle of light are four — or any number — other persons, barely visible.)

What's it all about? Well, if you're not an Injun it might be hard to understand, 'cause you and me, well, we act and think different. But this is the night when Johnny Moonbeam's gotta go in search of the Silver Arrow!

(The chanting stops abruptly. The MEDICINE MAN is handed a small colored wooden bowl. During the following speech by the NARRATOR, the MEDICINE MAN holds the bowl aloft over JOHNNY's head, weaving intricate patterns with a free hand. He then places the bowl on the ground and begins to dance around the boy, shaking feathery sticks and rattles.)

Well, it's not exactly a search. But it's a way the tribe has of makin' a twelve year old boy prove he's ready to be treated like a man. The silver arrow is . . . well, it's sort of a symbol, kind of a sign you get if every-

580

thing's done all right. And this is the night for Johnny Moonbeam. It's gonna be a big night, a lonely night. A night full of danger for Johnny Moonbeam. He's got things to do. Not easy things like pickin' a quart of blueberries, or jumpin' off a tree, or wrasslin' with a tiger. Why any good Indian can do that! What Johnny's got to do is . . . Oh-oh! Watch. The Medicine Man's gonna give him final instructions.

(The drum starts again, slowly and softly at first, and gradually building up as the three assignments are given. The MEDICINE MAN *dips his hands into the bowl and scatters droplets of water up into the air. He repeats this three times whirling about each time he flicks the water off his fingers. Suddenly, he reaches out and snatches at an imaginary falling drop. He clutches it to his chest, bends over to conceal it, then turns and twists within the group to suggest that he has stolen something and is running away with it. He stops abruptly—as do the drums—and points at* JOHNNY.)

Oh-oh! 'Fraid of that. Johnny's gonna have to search the land, and the mountains, and behind all the clouds in the sky he can grab hold of. Johnny's gonna have to search all the dark corners of the night. He's gonna have to find the Rain God!

*(*JOHNNY *shakes his head "no" and rises to one knee, a fearful and perplexed look on his face.)*

Not only find 'im, but steal rain from the Rain God!

(The drums start again, a bit louder this time. The MEDICINE MAN *crouches opposite* JOHNNY *and begins to collect bits of wood from the*

Do ya think Johnny knows where the Rain God lives? Not a bit! Why, he could live where the water trickles out of the sides o' mountains, or up where icebergs melt, or where fierce dark clouds seem to hang like a scary roof at the tops o' trees. Anywhere at all. Wherever there's water. But Johnny's gotta find 'im and steal the rain away from 'im! It's a big thing to do for one Johnny's age . . . but it's only the first thing. To get the Silver Arrow is like learnin' to start your life all over again. Watch now. The M e d i c i n e Man is showin' Johnny the second thing he's gotta do.

(The MEDICINE MAN has finished assembling and stacking the wood for the "fire." He stands back slightly and sets a "torch" to it. With gestures and movements of his body, he indicates the upsweep of the flames, their heat and awesomeness. He stalks the fire, suddenly lunges at it, seems to encircle the flame with his arms, tears it from the wood, and runs off with it. He abruptly turns to JOHNNY and points. The drums stop.)

Whoever heard of such a thing? Whoever in this world! You saw it. You saw what that Medicine Man expects Johnny to do. That boy's gonna have to dig deep into the earth, or twist the tail of a lightnin' bolt or shut the blazin' sun up in a bottle. 'Cause he's gotta go out into the gloomy forest and find the Fire God!

(JOHNNY rises from his kneeling position, stumbles back a step and falls into a sitting position. Again shaking his head.)

582

JOHNNY MOONBEAM AND THE SILVER ARROW

And he's gotta *steal* the fire from the orangey scorching hands of the Fire God and bring it back. First the rain, now the fire. Why, that's like tryin' to steal the purr from kittens or the nose right off the elephant's face! But the Silver Arrow's mighty important to Johnny. And if it takes him all the days and all the nights and all the cool breezes that blow across the prairie, why he'll have to do it! And bring back the rain, and bring back the fire. And then he'll—

(Drums again. Stronger and more insistent. The MEDICINE MAN *starts by making wide gestures with his arms, as if indicating the shape of the earth. He is handed a second bowl. He follows this with movements suggesting the sowing of seeds. He traces the fall of a single seed, kneels beside it, and by a series of hand motions, urges it to sprout. It does, very quickly, and he follows its growth upward until it becomes a tall sturdy plant. He looks about furtively, takes the "plant" in both hands, wrenches it from the ground, and suggests that he is running off with it. He again turns to* JOHNNY *and points sternly. The drums have reached their climax here and stop suddenly.)*

Well, I never saw the like! Never since this old hat I got holdin' my hair down got dented and bent. And that was a long time before you got born. But there it is. The third thing Johnny's got to do to win the Silver Arrow. In every furrow a farmer turns in his earth, deep in the roots of giant trees, wherever a tiny seed warms itself and explodes in the brown soil, there Johnny will have to search for the Earth God!

(A man and a woman, apparently JOHNNY's *mother and father, kneel beside him to comfort him.)*

583

The Earth God! Wouldn't ya know it! There'll be a lot of stones to turn, Johnny, a lot of valleys and meadows and green slopes to climb. A lot of ups and downs, Johnny, 'cause the Earth God is wherever you are, and never all where you are. And when you find him, Johnny, you gotta steal the maize that grows in the earth!

(The drums again, to the rhythm of the following lines. The MEDICINE MAN *starts some gyrations. The man and woman raise* JOHNNY *to his feet. The boy is brought to Center and is gradually left alone, the pool of light slowly narrowing around him.)*

Wet is the Rain God—
Rain you must steal, Johnny.
Warm is the Fire God—
Fire you must steal, Johnny.
Green is the Earth God—
Corn you must steal, Johnny!

Where is the Rain God?
Rain God's above the earth.
Where is the Fire God?
Fire God's within the earth.
Where is the Earth God?
Earth God's around the earth.

(The drums stop.)

Darts and spears and rods of steel
Will fright the morning sparrow,
    Johnny,
And blades of wicked point will mark
    the warrior,
But a *man* holds the Silver Arrow,
    Johnny!

*(*JOHNNY *is now completely alone in the pool of light. A flute is heard distantly, playing a strange melody. Note: Debussy's Syrnx Suite for Solo Flute is suggested here.* JOHNNY *begins to turn slowly peering apprehensively into the darkness surrounding him.)*

JOHNNY MOONBEAM AND THE SILVER ARROW

Nothin' out there but the night and the forest, Johnny. And it's all waitin' for ya. Not much moon tonight to help. Just the one beam you're standin' in. That one's yours. And it'll be waitin' for ya when ya come back. So ya better get started.

(JOHNNY steps gingerly out of the protection of the moonbeam, is overcome by the darkness again, and hops back in.)

And don't be scared of shadows, Johnny. They're awful good to hide in. So go ahead, boy!

(The music stops. With a determined look JOHNNY darts off into the darkness. No sooner does he vanish than there is a low rumble of thunder, and a light flicker of lightning. The NARRATOR glances suspiciously off into the distance. He sets his hat a little more firmly on his head and turns up his collar.)

I wouldn't want to be Johnny Moonbeam tonight. No, sir! Not at all. Not for a free ride on a kangaroo! Hear that rumble up in the sky? Know what it is? Thunder, you say? I guess you're right, but it's more'n that. It's that ole Rain God. He must've been squattin' on his black cloud, thinkin' o' where to shake his wet hands on next. And he must've heard the Medicine Man tell Johnny to steal the rain. Now, I know the Rain God. He can be like your best friend, the kind you'd invite into your back yard for a cold drink on a hot day. But he can also be—

(There is a sudden clap of thunder, and another flicker of lightning.)

There! Hear that? He's got a temper, that Rain God! As fierce and

585

fearful as you ever saw or heard. And he's not one t' hide from the likes of a twelve year old boy. No, sir! He's movin' in, and he's mad . . . *(Thunder again)* and he'll set that black cloud o' his right down on Johnny's head so's that he like to swallow up Johnny!

(Sound of wind and rain are heard, faintly, but steadily growing louder during the ensuing scene. JOHNNY's moonbeam pool begins to fade.)

Hey, you Rain God! Leave that a-lone. Johnny needs that moonbeam t' find his way back! Move on! Move away! Leave the boy some light!

(He is answered by another clap of thunder and a brighter flash of lightning. The remaining pool of light snaps off.)

Well, looks like there's nothin' for a fella like me to do when it's rainin' but try to protect his own body a bit.

(He reaches behind himself and picks up an umbrella. Quickly opens it. He sets it into a slot, becoming a self-supporting c a n o p y against t h e "rain.")

Johnny! Where are ya now, boy? How're you doin'? We'll find you and watch you, Johnny! We'll go where you are, 'cause we got eyes like magic lanterns and we can flash a picture of you movin' through the shadows with all the color that drips from the trees and glimmers off the rivers. Where are ya, Johnny?

(Thunder. Suddenly the stage is bathed in blue light. It reveals two elevations on either end of the stage. Each is an irregularly stacked group of platforms representing a pile of boulders or small hills. At the peak

586

of each there is an opening, although not immediately visible to the audience. The opening should be large enough to permit a person to rise out of the "hills." JOHNNY enters from L. showing signs of straining against the mounting wind. The sound of rain has increased and the thunder and lightning c o n t i n u e intermittently. JOHNNY stumbles to C. and tries to study the terrain.)

Johnny, Johnny, why'd ya pick this place? Devil's Mountain just is no place for a boy! And the wind, Johnny, and all that thunder and lightnin'! Why, Satan himself wouldn't set foot on this spot!

(JOHNNY starts to move curiously toward the mound at stage R. Fighting the wind and rain, he comes to the foot of it, removes a small tomahawk from his belt, and starts to circle it cautiously and apprehensively.)

Careful, Johnny! Easy! That Rain God is everywhere! He'll streak down a gulley before you can count the ears of a rabbit. He lives in the sea and roams in the sky and visits the earth. He'll tickle the end of your nose and turn a brook into a wild thing at the same time!

(JOHNNY has started to mount the mound at R., his tomahawk poised. He reaches the top and looks around. He begins moving along the edge of the uppermost level, but moving gingerly, almost fearfully, carefully placing each step and looking down as if it were a long way to the bottom.)

Step easy, Johnny! Step easy! That's a mighty steep cliff.

(JOHNNY wavers a bit.)

Look out, boy! (JOHNNY *rights himself.*) Whew!

(JOHNNY *continues his perilous search of the hill. He has reached the summit when — suddenly—thunder, lightning, and rain cease abruptly. There is an ominous calm.* JOHNNY *drops to a kneeling position and looks fearfully around. From the hole in the L. hill, a bluish-white light appears, first faintly, then growing brighter.* NOTE: *it perhaps would be more effective if the light shone from inside the hill, but a shaft from above or behind would do equally well.*)

(*Whispering*) Johnny! Behind ya! He's here!

(JOHNNY *whirls and crouches on one knee.*)

Oh, the Rain God's a clever one! He made the rain drops stream down the side of the hill, knowin' all along you'd follow it up to the top. Ya got 'im now, Johnny—or he's got you. What'll ya do now, boy?

(JOHNNY *quickly returns the tomahawk to his belt and removes a hunting knife. He starts to move slowly down the side of the hill in the direction of L.*)

Don't ya be a little fool, Johnny! Go carve a piece of wood with that knife or clean a buffalo skin, but you try and cut water and all you got is a rusty blade! Throw it away, boy, before it's washed clean out of your hands!

(JOHNNY *hesitates, looks at the knife, He discards it. At that moment, there is a low steady rumble of thunder and the* RAIN GOD *begins to emerge from the top of the hill L. The* RAIN *GOD is a tall, slender, impressive crea-*

ture whose dress seems to sparkle and shimmer with droplets of water, all silver and blue. An expressionless mask covers his face. A glistening cape stands out from his shoulders as though in a perpetual state of being blown by a gust of wind. On his head a crown, with jagged lightning bolts as points. His hands are covered by gauntlet type gloves that come almost to the elbows. JOHNNY crouches low to avoid being seen. Suddenly the sound of thunder stops. JOHNNY looks around surprised and curious. The RAIN GOD actually turns away from JOHNNY. The boy rises slowly and starts moving cautiously toward the hill L.)

Careful! Careful! *(Whispering)* I told you he's a clever one! Playin' possum, that's all. He knows you're here. Think he turned off his lightnin' and rain just to make it easy for ya to sneak up on him? He's just not that kind, Johnny!

(JOHNNY pauses, then drops low on all fours and begins a deliberate and determined approach to the hill.)

I warned ya, Johnny. Can't say that I didn't boy! But go to it. And not a sound! Crawl without touchin' the ground. Move every muscle slow . . . slow, that's it! If ya let one eyelash bat against another, he'll soak ya, all over and right through, too. Make the body float on the earth, Johnny. Pull ahead again, boy . . . again, pull slow and soft!

(JOHNNY has reached the base of the hill and has started to pull himself up it.)

If ya gotta breathe, people, breathe, but don't open your mouth to make a sound.

589

(JOHNNY is almost at the top and could, if he wanted to, touch the heels of the RAIN GOD.)

It's that satchel, or bag, or whatever it is hangin' 'round his neck that you want, Johnny. That's the life and power of the Rain God. A million raindrops and more are in that satchel. Easy! Easy! First try to get that rod he's holdin'. When he points it up, there's lightning. If he points it down, there's rain.

(JOHNNY is making the last excruciating reach in the hope of snatching the pouch from the RAIN GOD. The reach seems to last forever. As his fingers are about to touch the rod, there is a sound of a sudden strong gust of wind, following by low rumbles of thunder which mount to a crescendo. The RAIN GOD whirls on JOHNNY, throwing his arms up and wide as he does so. The wind increases. As the RAIN GOD describes strange motions with the rod and seems to be rocking to and fro with laughter, the sudden gust of wind knocks JOHNNY off his perch and hurtles him, fighting all the way, to the opposite side of the stage.)

Now you'll have to fight it, Johnny! Why, he's even laughin' at you! I warned ya, Johnny! And I can't blame him for laughin'. What's a twelve year old boy doin' fightin' with the Rain God! Go home, boy! You still got time! You might be riskin' your life t' get that Silver Arrow. A whole basket full o' silver arrows wouldn't be worth it! Go home, Johnny!

590

(Johnny stares at the Rain God for a moment as if trying to determine his course of action. Out of the corner of his eye, he catches sight of the knife he threw aside. Suddenly, he lunges for the knife and, despite the strong wind, makes an effort to cross toward the Rain God.)

No, Johnny! Put the blade away. You can't fight him with steel! All you'll do is make him—

(As though to complete the sentence, there is a clap of thunder. The Rain God freezes into a position of defiance and anger. Slowly his arm sweeps around as he gradually brings the rod to point directly at Johnny. As the arm moves, the thunder quickly subsides and the sound of rushing water is heard.)

I told ya, Johnny! I told ya! He's boilin', rushin' mad, and he'll tear open the heavens and fill this place with water so deep you'll think you're a fish sleepin' on the bottom of the sea!

(The sound of water a little louder. Johnny looks around apprehensively and begins to slosh his way heavily through the quickly rising "water.")

It's gettin' deeper fast, Johnny! It's up to your belt already. I might have to be gettin' out of here pretty quick myself! Save yourself, boy! Climb up on that hill.

(Johnny is struggling against the rushing water, but instead of heading for the hill, "dives into" the water and tries to swim across toward the Rain God. His struggle is Herculean. With each sweep of the Rain God's arms and point of his rod, the sound of rushing water gets louder. The

blue light that bathes the stage flick-
ers, as though to reinforce the swell
and churning of the water. Johnny's
strokes are strenuous, he rolls, goes
under sometimes, but keeps thrash-
ing away, trying to reach the Rain
God's *hill.)*

If I ever tell the story of Johnny
Moonbeam and the Silver Arrow a-
gain, nobody'll believe me. That water's foamin', and churnin' and twist-
in' like a wild panther, billowin' and
kickin' like a horse stung by a bee!
And that boy's in there swimmin' for
his life just to steal the rain from that
ornery Rain God! Well, if you must,
then swim, boy, swim for your life!
He's got plenty of rain, but you got
the fight of a wild elephant!

*(*Johnny *continues the fight and is*
within two or three strokes of the hill
when—)

Johnny! Comin' down the gully behind ya! It's a big hunk of tree torn
out by the storm! Comin' at ya, boy!
Look out!

*(*Johnny *thrashes his arms to look*
b e h i n d him, sees what's coming,
starts to dive under the water, twists
and turns, but it's apparently too
late. After trying to ward off the tree
with his arms, he seems to be hit by
it, holds his head, moves dazedly,
crumples to his knees, then rolls onto
his back. He lies there motionless.
With a sharp gesture, the Rain God
lowers his arm. The sound of water
quickly diminishes. . Low distant
wind. A trace of thunder.)

Johnny! Johnny! Get up, boy. That
hunk o' tree! I thought it was going
to miss you, boy. Ya just gotta get

up, Johnny. I got more to say! This
story's not over yet! Johnny . . . you
all right?

(The RAIN GOD *starts moving down
the side of the hill toward the fallen
boy.)*

Look here, you Rain God! I don't
care if you're the god of puppy dogs,
or rattlesnakes or of all the Indian
gods rolled up into one big ball! If
you harmed that boy I'll just plain
stop talkin' and start doin'! Y'hear?

(The RAIN GOD *flicks his hand in the
general direction of the* NARRATOR
*and there is a sharp rumble of thun-
der.)*

Well, come ta think of it, I'm not
much good at doin'. But I'm boilin'
mad!

(The RAIN GOD *has reached* JOHNNY
and slowly kneels beside him.)

I'm sorry, Johnny. I know what that
Silver Arrow meant to you, boy. But
I'm proud just the same. You got
closer to that demon Rain God than
anybody ever did. Why you—

(As the RAIN GOD *is about to touch*
JOHNNY, *the boy suddenly rolls over,
snatching the rod from the* GOD'S
hand as he rolls.)

What—! Well, I'll be—! I knew this
story wasn't over yet! Now drive
him back, Johnny!

*(*JOHNNY *leaps to his feet, runs to
take up a position on the hill R. The*
RAIN GOD *starts to lunge toward the
boy, but* JOHNNY *brandishes the rod
at him.)*

Up, boy! Hold it up! Straight to the
sky! Make those black clouds gnash
their teeth together and spit a little
lightning!

(JOHNNY'S *arms shoot upward and he waves the rod frantically. The lights flicker and there is a sharp roll of thunder. The* RAIN GOD *stops abruptly and bends slightly as though in pain. He rubs his hands over his arms and shoulders and chest. He turns, bent a little further and begins to stagger and reel slightly in the direction of his hill. There is heard a crackling, breaking sound.)*

You got him goin', boy! And listen! Hear that? Why that Rain God is dryin' up inside, like a dried up old log! Ya beat him, Johnny!

(The RAIN GOD *is working his way up to the hole from which he emerged, stumbling and groping as he goes.)*

(Suddenly) Great serpent-tail comets, Johnny! Don't just stand there. That stick in your hand only *makes* the rain, but you ain't got the rain itself!

*(*JOHNNY *quickly lowers the rod and is ready for action again, but doesn't quite know where to act.)*

You think you can *drink* that stick you're holdin'? Or float a canoe on it? The Medicine Man said to get rain! Find it, boy, hurry up!

*(*JOHNNY *runs down off the hill toward the* RAIN GOD *and, somewhat apprehensively, tries to examine him at close range. The* GOD *has reached the peak of his hill and is starting to lower himself back into his hole.* JOHNNY *is becoming frantic. As the* RAIN GOD *is about half way down,* JOHNNY'S *hand suddenly comes upon the small raindrop-shaped pouch hanging from the* RAIN GOD'S *neck.)*

That's it! That's it! Snatch it off,
boy! If that Rain God gets swallowed up in the belly of that mountain,
you're done! He's not goin' *into* the
mountain, he's startin' to *be* the
mountain! Only his head and neck
are left. Get it, boy!

(JOHNNY *is struggling to remove the
pouch from around the* RAIN GOD'S
*neck but is having an awful time do-
ing it. The neck and then the head of
the* RAIN GOD *are slowly swallowed
up so that* JOHNNY *has to reach deep
into the hill, grunting and panting
and thrashing his feet. Finally, triumphantly, he pulls out his hand,
stands, and holds the pouch high.
The bluish-white light from the hill
vanishes.)*

Oh, Johnny, ya have no idea what it's
like for a mortal man like me to see
and tell what you just done! Stealin'
the rain from the Rain God. Imagine! Why, men have been scared
right out of their wits and washed
right out of their homes by the Rain
God. But you didn't scare, Johnny!
No, sir! Ya hunted 'im, ya found 'im,
and ya stole the rain from the Rain
God!

(*With an ecstatic leap,* JOHNNY *returns to the ground, leaping and skipping about like a twelve year old
might when something exceptional
has happened to him.)*

Whoa down, boy!

(JOHNNY *stops and cocks his head
to listen.)*

You stole the rain, sure enough. But
when you took it from the Rain God,
didn't ya steal it from *everybody?*

(JOHNNY *looks puzzled and a bit
confused. He studies the rod and
pouch a moment. He quickly rejects*

595

his troubled feeling. For a few moments he revels in what he has accomplished. He takes a little sip from the pouch, then a long drink, and it very obviously satisfies him. He enjoys the power of the rod by flashing it around, pointing to different parts of the heavens and causing lightning to flicker in the sky. And in a cocky display, he falls to the floor and holds the rod between his feet, pointing it and sweeping it across the sky.)

All right, boy. Enjoy it! Ya worked hard enough, dodgin' lightnin' bolts, swimmin' in that boilin' flood, bein' knocked around by a wind that slapped ya like a giant's hand!

(JOHNNY suddenly sits up, places the pouch around his neck, tucks the rod in his belt. He gets to his knees and looks around. Everything is silent. He wipes his forehead as though becoming very warm. He presses his hands against the earth, and withdraws them quickly as if the earth were hot to the touch. He rises and peers into the bluish darkness around him. A faint sound of crackling, as though from a distant fire, begins to be heard.)

You're right, boy. I feel it too. Like someone opened the door of a big furnace and you put your face near it. *(Mopping his brow)* Whew! All this umbrella is doin' is makin' the heat collect in one place! *(He takes it out of its socket and closes it.)*

(The bluish light begins to fade slowly and is gradually replaced by a reddish glow. JOHNNY moves left, examining the earth and rocks, still finds it hot and getting hotter.)

596

Hoo! I'm beginnin' to feel like a pancake ready to be flipped over and browned on the other side! Well, I suppose you know, boy. You know who's nearby.

(JOHNNY *turns abruptly and begins searching with more fear and energy. The reddish glow is becoming more intense.* JOHNNY *is looking everywhere.)*

It's the Fire God, Johnny! Fire and water don't mix. But these Indian gods stick together. You hurt one and the other'll come a runnin'. And you sure hurt one of 'em. Whew! I don't know if I can take much more 'o this! *(He picks up a fan and tries to cool himself.)*

(JOHNNY, *after searching L., is backing toward R.)*

This is why ya came out alone into the night, Johnny Moonbeam. Alone in this fearful dark forest. Ya got three of your gods to face. Ya ready for the second?

(JOHNNY *has backed up till he is at the foot of the hill L. At this moment, as the crackling sound becomes louder, the whole of the L. hill seems bathed in glowing red light, much more strongly than the rest of the stage. A torch, on a long black rod, is suddenly thrust from the hole on top of the hill. And as quickly, the* FIRE GOD *emerges. Of medium height, slender, wiry, the* FIRE GOD *seems clad in flame that is reaching upward. He is masked also and wears a crown with yellow, orange, and red points that seem to swirl together. In the center of his chest is a large red stone, hanging like a pendant.)*

Johnny, if ya move a muscle, he'll scorch your ears off!

(JOHNNY *freezes, afraid to look over his shoulder. The* FIRE GOD *bends and twists, as a flame itself might, to study the boy more closely. Slowly he raises his torch and points it at* JOHNNY *as though preparing to hurl a spear.*)

He's gettin' ready to throw fire at ya, boy. The heat of a dozen suns is in his torch. It'll turn a mountain into a boilin' stream of yellow jelly. You'll just go poof! and there won't be any more Johnny Moonbeam. He's rared back! Look out, Johnny! Duck!

(JOHNNY *ducks. The shaft goes over his head and lands in the center of the stage.* JOHNNY *scrambles away, then leaps to grab the torch for himself. He scarcely has his hands on it than the heat of the staff causes him to drop it. The* FIRE GOD *leaps from the hill and proudly reclaims the torch.*)

Try to tie the tails of wildcats or make an elephant sit on a teacup, but ya just can't hold fire, Johnny!

(*Pointing the torch at* JOHNNY, *the* FIRE GOD *moves gracefully yet menacingly toward him. Shielding his face with his arms,* JOHNNY *recoils, turns, stumbles in his efforts to escape the determined thrusts of the torch.*)

Keep away from it, Johnny! Bend and twist and jump for your life! Don't wave your arms, boy! You'll just fan the flame and make the Fire God hotter than before!

598

(JOHNNY continues to dodge the thrusts of the torch. He stumbles and falls at C., dazed and helpless from the heat. Weaving a simple pattern of encirclement, the FIRE GOD dances grotesquely around the fallen boy, touching the torch to different parts of the floor—stones or small mounds — causing glowing fires to start. JOHNNY looks up, sees what is happening, struggles to his feet and tries to beat out a few of the lesser blazes with his feet.)

Oh, Johnny, you're wastin' your strength! Those ain't little fires you're tryin' to beat out, that's all the fire on the earth, and all the fire in the earth. They're sunspots, Johnny, volcanoes, 12-alarm fires!

(The FIRE GOD has completed his circle of fire and starts to approach JOHNNY directly.)

You'll never get it now, boy! You'll never get that red stone that's hangin' in the middle of his chest. That's where the fire starts. That *is* fire. You just can't steal it from him!

(JOHNNY crouches and makes a determined lunge at the FIRE GOD. The GOD sweeps the torch near him, sending JOHNNY rolling away toward the hill L. A few whirls and leaps and the FIRE GOD has JOHNNY pinned down to the side of the hill.)

Keep movin', boy! You're gonna end up like a hotdog on the end of a stick unless ya keep movin'! Higher! Get up higher!

(Once again JOHNNY scrambles away from the FIRE GOD and stands breathlessly at the top of the hill. The FIRE GOD, now no longer playing with his prey, moves in.)

Oh, Johnny, your dream of that Silver Arrow is goin' to go up in a puff of smoke, and you're gonna go up with it! That Fire God made this earth, Johnny. He melted rock and caused mountains to split the crust of the earth and shove craggy shoulders into the sky! He burns and rages through the world with a fierce anger that makes whole cities tremble! There's nothin' to stop him, Johnny! Nothin' in the whole world!

(JOHNNY cowers on his knees at the top of the hill, his arms covering his face. The FIRE GOD is almost upon him and is ready to bring his torch down on his head.)

That Fire God is gettin' me all burned up too! There is somethin', Johnny. Drown him! You've stolen rain! Drown him! Douse him and his fire in a great ocean of water!

(JOHNNY just barely escapes the falling torch as he pulls the RAIN GOD's rod from his belt and waves it in circles in the air. Flashes of lightning and rumbles of thunder.)

Use your head, boy! before he singes your nose! Fire and lightnin' are old friends. Drown him! Point that stick down!

(Dodging another lunge by the FIRE GOD, JOHNNY points the stick down. The flashes and thunder stop. Abruptly, the sound of water is heard. The FIRE GOD hesitates, looks around fearfully. S o m e w h a t successful, JOHNNY continues to thrust the rod downward and the sound of water increases. The FIRE GOD dashes off the hill and by his chaotic movements we see him caught in an eddy of rushing "water." He flails about, trying to hold the torch aloft. Suddenly, we

hear a hissing sound, the sound of fire being quenched by water. The FIRE GOD *writhes in agony.)*

What a sweet sound! Hear it! That old Fire God is sputtering and sizzling, and burnin' out! You're drownin' him in the drops of the Rain God! Soak him, Johnny!

(JOHNNY *continues to point the rod down and finds he has to retreat to a bit higher on the hill to escape the water himself. The torch drops from the* FIRE GOD'S *hand and* JOHNNY *leaps into the water to grab it. With the sound of hissing continuing in the background, the* FIRE GOD *struggles to return to the top of the hill from whence he came.)*

Don't let him get too far, Johnny! That stone! That red stone on his chest! There'll be no Silver Arrow for Johnny Moonbeam without the red stone. Get it fast, boy, before he turns into a puff of purple smoke!

(JOHNNY *scrambles after the* FIRE GOD *and reaches him as he is about to re-enter the hole at the top of the hill. He places his hand on the stone and withdraws it abruptly, thrusting his fingers in his mouth to show that the stone is still hot.)*

He got a little fire in him yet, eh? You still got all the water in the world, Johnny!

(JOHNNY *leaps off the hill, scoops up a handful of water and returns just in time to spill it on the chest of the rapidly sinking* FIRE GOD. *As the water hits the stone, there is a large hiss, and the* GOD *disappears, leaving* JOHNNY *alone on the hill, holding the large red stone. The sound of hissing stops.)*

601

Johnny, you're holdin' in your hand
a fierce and frightful thing.

(JOHNNY *looks up curiously.*)

You stole the fire. It's just a little
stone to you . . .

(JOHNNY *looks at it proudly, then
hangs it around his neck.*)

but it's somethin' to read by, somethin' to warm up with, somethin' to
make great engines pound and heave
and turn a chunk of stone into a
great steel bird that makes the clouds
shiver. You stole fire, sure enough.
But when ya stole it from the Fire
God, didn't ya also steal it from *everybody?*

(JOHNNY *looks quizzically in the direction of the* NARRATOR. *A low, distant sound of wind is heard.*)

That wind, Johnny. It's blowin' over
all the earth now and pickin' up dry
leaves and velvety soft flowers turned all to dust. Rivers and lakes are
bein' sucked dry and all the oceans
from here to India and back are be-
comin' dusty fields. And it's a cold
wind, boy. 'Cause you stole the rain
and stole the fire. Not since the world
was made, Johnny, have t h i n g s
changed so much!

(JOHNNY *moves about, troubled. He
listens to the wind for a moment. He
looks at the rod and the torch. He
shrugs airily and ignites a small red
glow with the torch and indicates his
pleasure at this feat. He then points
the rod at it, and it goes out. Tucking the rod and torch back into his
belt,* JOHNNY *begins stalking a n d
searching for this third assignment.*)

One more thing to do. One more of
his Indian gods to track down, the
Earth God. So step easy, Johnny.

602

JOHNNY MOONBEAM AND THE SILVER ARROW

'Cause every step ya take brings ya closer to him. With every step, you're walkin' on him!

(There is a low rumble. The disturbance is strong enough to cause the NARRATOR's *stand to tremble and* JOHNNY *to stagger and drop to one knee. Another r u m b l e , throwing* JOHNNY *to the floor and making him hold on to the base of the hill L.)*

Hey! Hold on! Calm down! You're about to shake me clean off my chair. It's the Earth God, Johnny. You can bet he's hurt and angry. Without rain and fire, he's limpin' along but got enough fight to make a mountain sink or cause an—

(Another deep rumble.)

Like that! Cause an earthquake! He won't drown ya or burn ya! No, sir. That earth god is gonna rip open a seam down the side of the earth and swallow you up. Oh, that Medicine Man sure set you a task, Johnny. Playin' tag with a wild horse'll seem like baby stuff to ya after tonight!

(JOHNNY runs to R. in search of the EARTH GOD. As he peers into the darkness, the EARTH GOD appears from behind the hill L., accompanied by a low rumble. EARTH GOD is a sturdy creature, wearing deep green and brown, with seared branches and twigs growing out from all parts of his body so that, if motionless, he looks like a blasted tree. Around his neck, like a pendant, he wears a small ear of Indian corn. He carries a forked stick in his hands, like a divining rod. He sees JOHNNY and freezes, so that one might almost think him a peculiarly shaped and twisted tree standing on a double trunk. Continuing his search, JOHNNY

backs into the EARTH GOD, *getting prodded in the back by one of the protruding branches. JOHNNY whirls, stares at the figure, and studies him closely.)*

Funny trees grow in this forest, don't they, Johnny? Take that one you're starin' at. Looks so bleak and blasted, like a cold and dried up sassafras bush. Be careful, boy. Looks a little suspicious to me.

(JOHNNY takes hold of one of the branches on the EARTH GOD and is about to chop at it with his tomahawk, when the EARTH GOD suddenly breaks his position causing JOHNNY to be thrown off balance and fall to the ground.)

Look out for him, Johnny. He can tear open holes in the earth or make mountains crumble into little pieces and roll down on your head.

(JOHNNY scrambles to his feet and momentarily retreats. The EARTH GOD removes the corn from his neck and dangles it enticingly b e f o r e JOHNNY, moving in slow circles, provoking JOHNNY into action.)

He wants ya t' come after him, Johnny. Lookit what he's holdin'. That's what ya come for, boy. That ear o' corn. Of all that the Earth God holds, nothin's stronger or greater than his power to push green stalks of corn out of the ground and feed a million mouths. But watch that stick he's carryin'. Watch it, boy!

(Still taunting JOHNNY, the EARTH GOD moves in closer to the boy. JOHNNY's courage grows, and he moves into position for the battle. Now only a few feet apart, JOHNNY is set to lunge. As he does so, the EARTH GOD sweeps the stick in front

604

of him, close to the ground. There is a terrific rumble and JOHNNY *falls into a deep "pit." The* EARTH GOD *quickly steps aside and peers down at the boy triumphantly.)*

He did what I warned ya he'd do, Johnny. He made the earth open up and swallow a mouthful of Johnny Moonbeam. *(Straining forward on his stool.)* Can ya crawl out of there, boy? Hurry up or he'll make that mouth snap shut!

*(*JOHNNY *starts to climb out of the hole. The* GOD, *alert for more action, prepares himself for another earth splitting.* JOHNNY *makes a series of lunges, but all to no avail, for the rod of the* EARTH GOD *is swift and the boy falls into two or three crevasses. The* GOD *mounts one of the hills, tears loose a few "boulders" and hurls them at* JOHNNY *who frantically dodges each one.* JOHNNY *begins to back away, putting on a great act of being frightened by the* EARTH GOD.*)*

Johnny! Ya stole rain, and ya stole fire! You're not gonna let a few holes in the ground or a few rocks and boulders stop ya now, are ya? That Silver Arrow's not for cowards, boy! Ya gotta stand up, even if it means fallin' down a few times!

(But JOHNNY *continues to back away, running from the* EARTH GOD *first in spurts and then in long dashes, the* GOD *in hot pursuit. On one such dash,* JOHNNY *suddenly drops to his knees, causing the* GOD *to stumble and fall over the boy. Before the* EARTH GOD *can regain his stand,* JOHNNY *pounces on him and snatches the stick and ear of corn.*

With the prizes in his hand, JOHNNY runs quickly to hill L. to see what effect he has had on the EARTH GOD.)

Oh, that was clever and sly, Johnny! Even a God'll stumble on the prank of a twelve year old! Ya outdid him, and ya stole the maize. Don't stand around now. There are gulleys and hills and dark plains to cross before you get back to that Medicine Man and show him what ya done.

(But JOHNNY chooses to linger a moment and watch as the EARTH GOD, now stripped of rain, fire, and plant life, makes a feeble effort to regain his power. But it is useless. He seems to shrink, and plants protruding from his body bend and droop. As a last flourish of triumph, JOHNNY brandishes the stick at him and with a low rumble, the EARTH GOD staggers off. The green light snaps off, leaving the stage in a bluish white light. JOHNNY is exultant.)

He's gone now. And ya got no more gods to face. Rain, fire, and maize are in your hands, Johnny! All the things, all the forces that suck the breath of life. You're the strongest boy in the world, now, Johnny!

(In his glory, JOHNNY runs off the hill to bathe in his moonbeam, a shaft of light that has crept up at C. The sound of drums begins to be heard, faintly.)

You are rain and you are the fire, and you are the corn that ripens and points to the sun. You're all the gods rolled up into one. I just can't believe it! For a boy your age, Johnny, all those gods sure roll up nice and neat.

JOHNNY MOONBEAM AND THE SILVER ARROW

(The drums become a bit louder, attracting the attention of Johnny *and the* Narrator.*)*

They know, Johnny. Hear it? Medicine Man's waiting. Ya got rain, fire, and maize. But that Silver Arrow's still waitin'. So run, boy! A lot of night will seem mighty short when ya tell 'em about the gods ya faced. So run!

(With a quick look of triumph, Johnny *darts off L. His moonbeam remains.)*

(Looking up at the shaft of light) Just us two, huh? Left alone in this gloomy corner of the world, marvellin' at that boy. You know him better'n I do, moonbeam. You proud of him, too?

(The shaft of light blinks three times.)

Knew you would be! So am I. But aren't ya just a little worried?

(Again the light answers by three blinks.)

'Fraid of that. I know you can't say too much, moonbeam. Just yes 'n no. But tell me: think Johnny can handle all that power he's got? *(Pause)* Well, now, don't be afraid to answer. I only last long enough for this story to be told, and I sure won't tell anybody what you said. How about it? Can he handle it?

(The light blinks twice: no.)

Thought so. I don't think so either. But tell me . . .

(The light disappears.)

607

Hey, come back! No, guess you won't come back. That moonbeam may not agree with Johnny, but he's gotta go where Johnny is. Oh, that boy! Where are ya now, Johnny? Night, blink an eye and show us Johnny. Wind, clear all the fuzz and mist from space and show us Johnny Moonbeam.

(Drums have stopped. JOHNNY enters running. The stage, except for the NARRATOR's light, is very dimly illuminated. Music: (suggested) "Big Brave Dance" from "Reflections of an Indian Boy" by Fischer.)

There he is! Johnny, hold on tight to the things ya stole. Don't stop or stumble or even pause t' count fireflies. Move along, they're waitin'.

(JOHNNY starts to move away, when a sharp, small beam of light comes up quickly revealing a dark, cloaked figure huddled on the floor. There is nothing to identify the figure as even human except for an extended hand holding a bowl. It is the same bowl the Medicine Man used to describe the Rain God test earlier. JOHNNY stops to look at the figure, becomes curious, and moves closer to it, dropping to one knee.)

Don't pay it no heed, Johnny! Must be one of those beggars the forest is full of. Don't stop for him, boy! He can find water to put in that cup of his somplace else. Get along, hurry!

(JOHNNY starts to go, but stops again. The extended arm and cup are gesturing for water pitifully. The boy is struggling with a big decision. Suddenly, impulsively, he removes the Rain God's pouch from his neck, and drops it in the cup. The music surges up for a moment, and then drops.)

608

Oh, Johnny, that sure was a foolish
thing to do! What d'ya think that
Medicine Man is gonna say now?
Givin' all the rain to a beggar!

*(JOHNNY stands with his head bow-
ed, his fists clenched.)*

All right, all right! Maybe the Medicine Man won't mind so much. Af
ter all, stealin' the fire and maize
from those two fierce gods wasn't exactly like pickin' pansies. Ya still
might qualify, so get along, and
move, boy!

*(With a last glance at the dark fig-
ure, who is moving quickly off, JOHN-
NY sets out again. Another spot of
light comes up in another part of the
stage, revealing another huddled figure. The figure is shivering, and
holds out a stick of wood to indicate
he has no warmth. JOHNNY pauses
to look at him.)*

Johnny, everybody gets a little cold
at this time o' night! That's probably just one of your friends tryin' to
trick ya. Don't even look at him.
Let him rub a couple of trees together or scratch some stone. You need
that fire to win the Silver Arrow.

*(Again JOHNNY starts away, but a
glance back at the cold figure is too
much for the boy. He removes the
red stone and gives it to the figure.
The music swells up again, briefly.
The figure stops shivering and exits
quickly.)*

I just don't know what to say, boy.
All that terror and fright. Crawlin'
on an earth so blazin' hot it almost
fried your shoes. And you go givin'
it away to some lazy beggar who'd
probably jump at the name of the
Fire God. I hope you're thinkin' up
some mighty good excuses!

609

(The light spot vanishes, and John-ny *circles the stage and stumbles over a third crouched figure. A spot comes up on it. Again a dark and shrouded figure, with only one hand showing, holding an empty bowl.)*

Well, I guess that does it! You cut through the night and nearly got gulped down into the belly of the earth to tear the maize from the neck of the Earth God. And a hungry hand holds out an empty bowl and you . . . Go ahead, boy. Finish it up.

*(*Johnny *drops the ear of corn into the bowl. The music swells again for a moment. The third figure leaves.)*

Empty hands or full, Johnny, you gotta go back and face 'em. They'll listen, Johnny. Maybe they won't believe and maybe they won't like it, but they'll listen. All nature might have been your toy, your plaything. Ya could have made pools to splas around in when it pleased ya. Ya might have used fire to light up all the heavens when ya hunt at night. You might have had feasts and banquets the like of which a chief or king never saw, with all that corn— and ya might have won the Silver Arrow. But what might be never will! Ya held the earth in your hands, and ya let it roll away!

*(*Johnny *presses his fists to his face and, thus distraught, runs off. The music stops. His moonbeam quickly re-appears.)*

(Happily) Well, moonbeam, what'd ya think of *that?*

(The moonbeam flickers rapidly for a few seconds, then stops.)

610

Well, I guess I have to agree with you. That Johnny Moonbeam's not a *boy,* is he?

(Two blinks.)

If I never tell this story again, at least I'll have lived through it once. You know what's gonna happen now? Wait! Don't answer. He's comin' back!

(The moonbeam goes out. Drums start, low, in the background. Music: (suggested) "Squaw's Lament" from "Reflections of an Indian Boy." JOHNNY enters, despondent. He reaches the center and drops to his knees. He raises his head, then his arms slowly. Some light suddenly illuminates the top of hill L., revealing the Medicine Man. JOHNNY looks around and sees the figure and responds to the beckoning gesture by moving to the base of the hill. The MEDICINE MAN holds out the rain cup and asks if he has any rain to fill it. JOHNNY shakes his head. The MEDICINE MAN holds out the stick of wood and asks if he has fire to light it. Again "no" from JOHNNY. The maize bowl is extended. A third time a negative r e p l y . The MEDICINE MAN stares intently at the boy, then with a sudden gesture points off into the darkness behind JOHNNY. The boy turns quickly and sees the three shrouded figures moving in toward him from different directions. His first reaction is fear. When they arrive fairly close to the boy, each of the three figures, in turn, thrusts out an arm. The first holds the rod of the RAIN GOD, the second the torch of the FIRE GOD, the third the forked stick of the EARTH GOD. As each symbol is shown, the black cloaks drop from the figures, revealing the

three gods we have met before. They raise Johnny *to his feet and turn him to face the* Medicine Man. *Each god points his symbol of authority toward the sky in the area above the* Medicine Man's *head. The blue light returns, then the red, then the green. The* Medicine Man *holds both hands high above his head and there descends into them the large, glistening, Silver Arrow. He presents it solemnly to* Johnny. *The three gods back away and vanish into the darkness, their representative colored light leaving with them. The light on the* Medicine Man *also goes out and he, too, leaves. The Moonbeam returns at C. Music stops. Drums continue to throb in the background.* Johnny *is momentarily dazed by the arrow and slowly turns and re-enters his beam of light.*

Johnny's *parents or friends enter the frings of light. He kneels before them, proudly showing the arrow.)*

Ya see, Johnny. That old Medicine Man is a pretty smart fella. Stealin' the rain, and stealin' the fire, and stealin' the maize wasn't the real test. Why, that only got ya warmed up. Holdin' all the power of the earth is one thing, but how ya handle it is somethin' else. And you handled it right, boy! *(Looking up)* Didn't he?

(The beam blinks three times. Parents and friends move off, leaving Johnny *alone in the pool of light.)*
(Flute music is heard again.)

*(*Johnny *starts to rise slowly from the kneeling position, raising the arrow high into the beam of light, as if showing it to a dear friend. The light slowly fades out on the* Narrator. *Still holding both hands and the arrow high, the image of* Johnny

612

also fades slowly as the beam of moonlight diminishes and finally disappears. The flute continues in the darkness for a few seconds, then—

CURTAIN

Abe Lincoln of Pigeon Creek

OR

ABE GREW TALL

A Play in Three Acts

Adapted by

WILLIAM E. WILSON

from his novel entitled "Abe Lincoln of Pigeon Creek"

Introduction by

SAMUEL SELDEN

*Included in the separate play-book only.

Copyright 1962 by

THE CHILDREN'S THEATRE PRESS

ANCHORAGE, KENTUCKY

ABE LINCOLN OF PIGEON CREEK

By William E. Wilson

THE ANCHORAGE PRESS
Cloverlot
Anchorage, Kentucky 40223
U. S. A.

ABE LINCOLN OF PIGEON CREEK

CAST
(In the order of their appearance)

Sarah Lincoln	*Abe's sister*
Abe Lincoln	
Tom Lincoln	*Abe's father*
Mrs. Sarah Bush Lincoln	*Abe's step-mother*
Elizabeth Johnston	*Abe's step-sister*
Matilda Johnston	*Abe's step-sister*
John Johnston	*Abe's step-brother*
Dennis Hanks	*Abe's cousin*
Josiah Crawford	*a neighbor*
Mrs. Crawford	*Josiah's wife*
Anna Roby	*a girl whom Abe loves*
Allen Gentry	*a friend of Abe's*
Jim Gentry	*Allen's father*
Judge Pitcher	*a Rockport lawyer*
James Castleton	*a river-pilot*
A Negro Boy	*his slave*
Colonel Jones	*owner of a store in Gentryville*
Neighbors	*including Ogg and Cartwright*

ABE LINCOLN OF PIGEON CREEK

Synopsis of Scenes

ACT ONE

Scene One — Interior of the first four-sided cabin the Lincolns lived in after they moved to Spencer County, Indiana—January, 1820.

Scene Two — The same — April, 1821, a year and three months later.

Scene Three — The same — a Sunday morning in October, 1824, three years later.

ACT TWO

Scene One — The ferry-landing at the mouth of Anderson's Creek, on the Ohio River, near Troy, Indiana, about fifteen miles from the Lincoln cabin — Spring, 1825.

Scene Two — The same — a moonlit night, in the fall of the same year, 1825.

Scene Three — The same — a day in late summer, 1827, two years later.

ACT THREE

Scene One — Interior of the Lincoln cabin, same as Act One — a day in late autumn, 1828, a year later.

Scene Two — The same — a spring evening, 1829, several months later.

For

Sara Spencer

and

Richard Moody

The premiere performance of ABE LINCOLN OF PIGEON CREEK was presented in 1958 by the Indiana University Theatre at Bloomington, Indiana, under the direction of Richard Moody.

Subsequently this play was selected by the Southeastern Theatre Conference, for their New Play Project in the 1962-1963 season.

ABE LINCOLN OF PIGEON CREEK

ACT ONE

Scene One

The scene represents the interior of the first four-sided cabin the Lincolns lived in after they moved from Kentucky to Indiana. It is a small, poorly constructed affair. In places, the dim light of the winter day shines through great chinks between the logs. There are no windows. Across the one doorway, in the center of the rear wall, hangs a bearskin that flaps occasionally as the wind whips against it. To the right and the left of the doorway are gun-racks with pioneer rifles and powder horns. No other furniture adorns the room except two piles of brush and leaves, covered by skins, to the right and left of the fireplace, which is built into the wall at the right. The floor is of hard, packed earth, and the roof is a thatch of brush and poles, through which flakes of snow drift from time to time. The only light, besides the little that gleams through the cracks, comes from the fire on the hearth, where an earthen pot is set over the flame. A single skillet hangs beside the fireplace. Below it, on the floor, are two or three sticks of firewood.

Squatting before the fire, Sarah Lincoln, a thin, pale girl of thirteen, clad in a single garment of linsey woolsey, made like a sack, with holes for the arms and neck, is dipping a gourd into the boiling pot. Her hair hangs uncombed over her shoulders. Her forlorn, squatting figure adds to the air of abject poverty and despair that characterizes the scene. Behind her, stretched full length on a pile of brush, with a bearskin clutched to him and his shaggy head and bare feet exposed, lies her brother, Abe Lincoln. His feet are extended toward the fire, and, from time to time, he wiggles his toes. It is January, 1820, and in another month Abe will be eleven years old. Because of the great length of his body and the hardships that have already lined his thin, dark face, he seems much older. Abe is watching Sarah between half-closed eyelids.

SARAH: Come on now, Abe, get a hump on!

(Abe pretends to be asleep)

Abraham Linkern! You get up from there! You heard me!

ABE: *(Stirring slightly beneath the bearskin)* What — ? What is it?

SARAH: *(Contemptuously)* Like as if you didn't hear! *(Her anger rises)* Abe!

ABE: *(Still feigning confusion, but rising on one elbow)* Did somebody speak?

SARAH: You know good and well somebody spoke, and you know what the speaking was about and who it was for! If ever a girl had a lazy, no-count, good-for-nothing brother in this world . . . !

ABE: *(Collapsing on the brush bed again and drawing the bearskin over his shoulders)* Oh — *(In a tone of relief)* then it ain't for me.
(Sarah rises and, going to the bed, shakes Abe. A tussle ensues, but she finally succeeds in pulling the bearskin off him and leaves him sitting on his haunches in the middle of the disordered brushpile. He is clad in a deerskin shirt and deerskin pants that reach only halfway below his knees)

621

SARAH: (*Before the fire once more, still holding the bearskin, which drags on the floor*) Abe Linkern, I declare, you ain't no more help in this-here cabin than a dicky-bird — excepting you can't even sing.

ABE: (*Grinning and rubbing his eyes*) Aw, now, Sis . . !

SARAH: No, sir, you ain't! And that's a fact. Why, I do the cooking and the washing and the cleaning and . . .

ABE: (*Looking around the room*) What cleaning?

SARAH: (*Ignoring him*) . . . And all you do is just lay there, day in and day out, a-dreaming or something. I can't make out which.

ABE: I'm a-thinking, Sally.

SARAH: You're a-loafing, you mean.

ABE: No; I'm a-thinking . . . Like . . . (*He lifts himself on one elbow again and looks at the pot over the fire with the mock air of a gourmet*) . . . is it going to be boiled or fried today, I wonder. (*Pauses*) Well, I see it's boiled today again. (*He collapses again on the bed*)

SARAH: Well, a-thinking don't get me no firewood.

ABE: Where's Denny at?

SARAH: (*Contemptuously*) Who — ? Him — ? Like as not, he's off sparking him a girl somewheres this minute.

ABE: Well, it's his turn to fetch the firewood.

SARAH: When you're here, it's Denny's turn, and when Denny's here, it's yourn. Neither one of you two pitches into work like killing snakes — excepting I can't count on Dennis Hanks as much as I can on you even.

ABE: (*Laughing*) There's one thing you can count on with your cousin Dennis Hanks, Sally.

SARAH: I'd like to know what it is.

ABE: He'll go to heaven when he dies.

SARAH: How come?

ABE: They wouldn't have him in the other place. He's too unhandy with firewood.

SARAH: You just wait till Pappy gets back from Kaintuck.

(*At the mention of his father, the merriment goes out of Abe's face. He draws back and drops to his elbow in the bed*)

ABE: (*In a low but vehement tone, as if speaking to himself*) Let him stay there.

(*Sarah turns about suddenly and stares at Abe in astonishment. She is not quite sure that she has heard correctly. Abe keeps his head turned away from her. He is picking leaves out of the brush-pile and crumbling them in the palm of his hand*)

622

SARAH: *(In a hushed voice)* What did you say, Abe? *(When he does not answer her, Sarah gets up and walks halfway across the room toward him)* Abe . . . *(Still he does not answer, and Sarah comes the rest of the way)* Abe . . .

ABE: Huh?

SARAH: Abe, you just said you hoped Pappy wouldn't come back from Kaintuck.

ABE: *(Listlessly, still crumbling leaves in his palm and throwing the dust out on the earthen floor)* Uh-huh.

SARAH: Abe, you oughtn't to said that. *(Abe is silent)* It was wicked, Abe.

ABE: The truth ain't ever wicked, Sally.

SARAH: It is if it's a wicked truth.

ABE: *(He looks up at her long and earnestly before he speaks again)* Denny Hanks says most likely Pappy is sparking him another wife down there in Kaintuck.

SARAH: *(Drawing back with a start, and then speaking with a disdainful jerk of her whole body)* Oh, that Denny! Sparking is all he ever thinks about!

ABE: But what if it's true, Sally? *(Sarah is thoughtful for a moment. Abe continues to look at her searchingly)* What if it's true?

SARAH: *(Hesitantly, biting her lip)* Well, Pappy has been needing him another wife — *(Avoiding Abe's eyes)* — ever since Mammy passed on. *(Abe sits up and holds his head between his hands, resting his elbows on his knees. Sarah reaches out tenderly and touches his tousled hair. After a moment, she takes a deep breath and speaks as brightly as she can)* Looky-here, Abe. It's been more than a year now that Mammy has been gone, and Pappy needs him another woman bad. A man has got to have him a growed-up woman in this Indiana country. A little old girl like me ain't enough.

ABE: *(Looking up bravely and defiantly)* Oh, I don't mind all this-here, the way it is . . . *(He takes in the room with a sweep of his arms and then seems to have an afterthought)* . . . particular . . . I do get tired of boiled squirrel, and fried squirrel ain't much better. And there's times when I wish I had me more book-learning than I got in Kaintuck and at Andy Crawford's school up here in Indiana. But I ain't never complaining about you, Sally, or wanting another woman around this cabin. Why, for a little old girl like you with two good-for-nothing boys on your hands that won't even get you no firewood when you need it — *(He pauses and looks ruefully at the few dying coals of the fire, but he makes no move to go and fetch the firewood he has been speaking of)* — why, you're daggone good! *(Sarah moves toward him, overwhelmed by his praise. But Abe's tender mood does not last. He holds her off with a sudden stare that does not seem to see her)*

But — (*He clenches his fists on his knees and stares hard, past her*) — sometimes I wish the milk-sick would come to Little Pigeon Creek again — and take us all — the way it took Mammy.

SARAH: Abe!

ABE: (*Grimly*) It would be a heap better than this!

SARAH: Abraham Linkern!

ABE: (*Beginning to enjoy Sarah's horror, Abe looks up at the roof*) Last night I prayed that I was dead.

SARAH: (*Shocked*) Oh, Abe, — you didn't!

ABE: (*Still looking at the roof*) Yep, — that's what I prayed.

SARAH: (*Turning her back on him, suddenly sobbing*) You ought'nt to done it.

ABE: (*With bravado*) I don't care.

SARAH: (*Turning and facing him*) You'll go to hell, sure, for praying a prayer like that.

ABE: (*With somewhat less bravado*) I don't care. (*Trying to laugh*) Everybody but the Hardshells goes to hell, they say, and I never seen many Hardshells I'd hanker to set around on a cloud with for all eternity.

SARAH: (*Horrified*) Oh, Abe, don't talk like that!

ABE: I ain't scared. (*His voice weakens*) I ain't scared at all. Honest, I ain't.

SARAH: (*Beginning to cry again*) Oh, Abe, I don't want my own brother to die and go to hell. . . And all on account of me asking him to fetch me some firewood and not cooking his squirrel proper. . .

ABE: (*Getting up, but stopping awkwardly, just short of putting his arms about her*) Aw, I didn't mean it. Honest, I didn't. I didn't pray no such prayer. Don't take on so. (*Smiling*) Why, I reckon you can cook squirrel as good as any growed woman in Indiana — especially now that you always remember to take their guts out afore you put them in the pot. There ain't nobody can cook as good as you can, Sis. I didn't aim to hurt your feelings or scare you, Sis. (*Sarah runs to him, sobbing. He takes her in his arms and pats her shoulder awkwardly*) Don't take on so.

SARAH: (*Sniffling*) I'm all right now.

ABE: (*Looking over her head at the fire, which is going out*) Sure, you are. Why, you and me have got each other, Sis. We can get along just dandy — what with your good cooking and all. Now, you just set down, honey, and I'll run out and get you that firewood — maybe — after a while.

SARAH: (*Drawing back and looking up at her brother*) Abe, you know what?

ABE: What?

SARAH: You and me ought to be glad if Pappy brung us back a new Mammy from Kaintuck.

ABE: *(Stiffening and his arms falling to his sides)* Don't start that again.

SARAH: You and me both need a new mammy. That's just what's the matter with us now.
(Abe pushes her away)
Yes, it is, Abe!

ABE: *(Turning away suddenly)* I don't want no new mammy — never!

SARAH: *(Brightly)* But Pappy would pick us out a nice one. Look at what our real mammy was like. Pappy he . . .

ABE: *(Starting toward her, his fists clenched)* Sarah Linkern, you shut your mouth!

SARAH: But . . .

ABE: *(Threateningly)* Shut your mouth, I say! I don't want no new mammy. I don't never want none, and I don't want to hear you a-talking about one! *(Defiantly, shaking his fists)* If Pappy brung us home an angel outen heaven, I wouldn't have nothing to do with her! Ain't nobody can take the place of my real mammy. I'd hate any woman he brung into this cabin. I'd hate her!
(He stops abruptly when he sees Sarah staring at the door behind him. Tom Lincoln is standing there, holding back the bearskin doorflap. Tom is tall and dark, like his son, but heavy-set. He is dressed in deerskins, over which he is wearing a heavy coat of skins, with the hair still on them. On the shoulders of the coat and on his coonskin cap, there is a powder of snow. Behind him, offstage, there are voices and the sound of horses' hoofs stamping in the snow)

SARAH: Pappy!
(Tom looks at his children for a moment. Then he steps over the high doorsill and walks slowly into the room. Behind him, a woman and three children appear in the doorway)

ABE: *(Staring at his father, but hardly making a sound when he speaks)* Pappy.

SARAH: *(Stepping back, as Tom advances)* Why, Pappy! You . . .
(Tom walks up to Abe, still silent. Abe does not move)

ABE: Pappy!
(Suddenly Tom's long arm flies out and gives Abe a cuff on the head that sends him tumbling across the room and into the brush bed)
Oh, Pappy . . . !

TOM: *(To Abe)* Get up!
(The woman, who is Sarah Bush Lincoln, remains in the doorway, holding her three children, Elizabeth, Matilda, and John Johnston, behind her. Thirty-one years old, Sarah Bush Lincoln is lean and strong, but she is very much a woman. Her face is a study of blank incomprehension)

SARAH: *(To Tom)* Abe didn't mean nothing.

TOM: *(To Abe)* Get up on your feet, I say!

SARAH: We was just jimber-jawing, Pappy.

TOM: You heard me! Damn you!

(Abe lies still for another moment, rubbing his cheek, but when Tom steps toward him again, he gets up slowly)

ABE: Yes, sir.

TOM: *(To Abe and Sarah)* Now, you two come here.

(Sarah steps forward, full of curiosity, but Abe hangs back, sullen and aloof. Tom half-turns to Sarah Bush Lincoln, who stands now in the middle of the room, with her three children huddled behind her)

I want you two younguns to meet your new mammy, Mrs. Sarah Bush Johnston.

MRS. LINCOLN: *(Reproving him gently)* It's Sarah Bush Lincoln now, Tom. *(She moves farther into the room, followed by her children. Sarah approaches her new stepmother eagerly, and Mrs. Lincoln puts an arm about her, always, however, glancing toward Abe, who is still holding back)* Sally . . . *(She presents Sarah to the children)* This is your new sister. Sally, this is Elizabeth . . . and Matilda . . . and Johnny. . . .

(As the children greet each other, Mrs. Lincoln looks again at Abe. Then she crosses the distance that separates them)

And you are my new son . . . Abe . . . *(She holds out her hand. Abe hesitates a moment. Then he rubs his hands on his pants and, with a look of amazement at what he is doing, takes her hand, as THE CURTAIN FALLS)*

ACT ONE

Scene Two

The same. A morning in April, 1821, a year and three months later.

The structure of the cabin has not changed, but the interior is entirely different. The two brush beds are gone, and the floor is swept. A fire is burning on the hearth, and the bearskin flap has been taken down from the door, revealing a rail fence outside and a background of forest, just turning green. In the places of the brush beds are two mattresses set on logs and covered with colorful quilts. There is a puncheon table in the center of the room, with puncheon benches on each side of it. The other furniture consists of two chairs, a rocker, a stool, several hickory butts, and, in the corner, left, against the rear wall, a large walnut chest of drawers. About the fireplace, there are now numerous pots and pans. A grease-lamp hangs from the wall to the right of the door. The whole atmosphere of the room, in spite of its crowded appearance, is one of tidiness, cheer and comfort.

Mrs. Lincoln sits at the spinning-wheel to the left, forward, winding flax into a ball. The flax is being held by her daughter, Matilda Johnston, a child of ten. Sarah, Abe's sister, whose appearance is greatly improved by a new linsey-woolsey dress and red bows on her well-plaited pigtails, is removing breakfast dishes from the table and taking them to the iron kettle in front of the fire-place, over which there is now a clapboard shelf. She is assisted by Elizabeth Johnston, a handsome pioneer girl of fifteen. To the left of the doorway, tilted against the rear wall in a chair, Dennis Hanks is cleaning a rifle. He is a youth of twenty, of medium height, dark, and slow in his movements. From time to time, he looks up from his work and watches Elizabeth. On the end of one of the table benches, in the center of the room, Tom Lincoln is giving John Johnston, aged seven, a ride on his foot. From the enjoyment that Tom derives from the game, it is obvious that he is very fond of children.

TOM: *(Singing)* A frog a-courting he did ride,
With a sword and a pistol by his side.
Lallagung — lallagung — lallagung. . . .

JOHN: *(Laughing)* Do it again.

TOM: *(Singing)* Oh, where can the wedding supper be?
'Way down yonder in the holler tree.
Lallagung — lallagung — lallagung. . . .

JOHN: Again!

TOM: *(Puffing and laughing)* I can't son! I'm winded. I'm plumb flabbergasted!!

MRS. LINCOLN: *(Quietly)* Johnny, don't wear your pappy out today — afore he gets his yesterday's chores done.
(The girls giggle)

DENNIS: *(Gleefully)* I reckon that will finish taking the wind outen you, Tom!

TOM: *(Glancing round the room at everyone except Dennis and then speaking to John, as if he had not seen Dennis but had only heard his voice)*

There seems to be a big wind coming from the general direction of the door. I reckon I can use it if I run short.

MRS. LINCOLN: *(To Matilda)* Hold it a little higher, Matilda.

TOM: *(Tweaking John's ear and setting him down)* We menfolks can't have no fun at all, can we John, what with so many women cluttering up the cabin. Seems a shame a man can't have a little game with his younguns afore he sets off to work. *(Glancing at Mrs. Lincoln as he gives John an affectionate poke in the ribs)* And these is mighty fine younguns you brung me, too, Sarah Linkern — all of them except Matildy, of course. She's so noisy!

JOHN: *(To Mrs. Lincoln)* Can I go out and play?

MRS. LINCOLN: Yes, son. But stay around the house.
(Matilda smiles at Tom's teasing and hangs her head shyly. John goes out)

DENNIS: *(Looking at Elizabeth admiringly)* One of them is mighty fine, for sure.

TOM: *(Pretending to look around in search of Dennis)* There's that dang hurricane a-blowing again. How do you all reckon we can get shet of it?

DENNIS: They say love works powerful miracles with hurricanes — love and a kiss now and then.
(Elizabeth continues to carry dishes from the table, pretending not to notice. But Sarah stops midway between the table and the fireplace with both hands on her hips)

SARAH: *(To Dennis)* If kissing stopped hurricanes, Dennis Hanks, you'd have been blowing backwards long ago, you old tom-cat!

DENNIS: *(Laughing)* Why, Sally!

MRS. LINCOLN: *(Shocked)* Sarah Linkern!

TOM: *(Slapping his hams)* Give it to him, Sally! *(Turning to Mrs. Lincoln, chuckling)* Afore you came, Denny he made a great play for Sally. Always after her, though she wouldn't have no more to do with him than a polecat. There wasn't many girls in this country in them days, and poor Denny he just wasn't getting any at all. *(Proudly)* I tell you that girl of mine has got a tongue in her head quicker than a fly-catching toad's.

SARAH: *(To no one in particular)* Well, I said what I said.

DENNIS: *(With an air of mock virtue)* I give up all that lallygagging, Sally, about a year ago, when a certain angel of beauty come to grace these premises.
(Elizabeth giggles)

TOM: *(Looks at Elizabeth)* Now what is Elizabeth a-tittering about, I wonder. *(Turns to Dennis)* Don't sound to me like you give it up. You sound purty perfessional to me.
(John appears in the doorway and stands there, looking in. He has a ball in his hands, which he tosses up and catches idly)

DENNIS: *(Winking at Tom)* It's the inspiration, Tom. You got to have a right smart chance of inspiration. Then it comes easy.

JOHN: *(From the doorway)* What's inspiration?

TOM: Oh, I see.

JOHN: *(From the doorway)* What's inspiration?

DENNIS: *(Ignoring the question and addressing Tom again)* Spring weather like this here we've got now is a big help, too.

TOM: You don't say?

DENNIS: Yes, it kind of loosens up the muses in a feller, as Abe might say.

JOHN: *(From the doorway)* What's muses?

DENNIS: *(Noticing him at last)* Muses, Johnny — ? Why, they're the things that poets and such-like has to make out with in the spring, whereas fellers like me can get a fire up by ourselves.

MRS. LINCOLN: *(Looking up from her work)* Dennis Hanks . . . !

DENNIS: *(Innocently)* Ma'am?

MRS. LINCOLN: Big as you are, I'm going to wash your mouth out with lye soap one of these days. I heard you egging Abe on to tell one of them-there stories again the other day.

DENNIS: Abe don't require much egging, ma'am.

MRS. LINCOLN: Well, Abe's just a mite of a boy still, and you ought to be ashamed of yourself.

DENNIS: If that-there six-foot hoopole is a mite of a boy, I seen a giraffe a-setting under a toadstool!

JOHN: *(Calling from the doorway)* Mamma . . .

MRS. LINCOLN: *(Still to Dennis)* Abe's got too good a head on his shoulders for the likes of you to be spoiling it with what you got stored up in that gourd-shell of yourn, Denny Hanks!

DENNIS: *(With feigned meekness)* Yes, Ma'am . . .

JOHN: *(Calling again from the doorway)* Mamma . . .

TOM: *(Whose manner has changed to one of irritation at the mention of Abe's name)* Where is Abe at, anyhow?

MRS. LINCOLN: *(She has finished a ball of flax thread and is about to help Matilda arrange another skein on her hands. She answers John)* What do you want, Johnny?

JOHN: Can't Tildy come out now and play andy-over?

MRS. LINCOLN: *(Taking back the new skein of flax thread and looping it on the spinning wheel)* I reckon. *(To Matilda)* Run along, Matilda. *(Matilda curtsies to her mother. John disappears from the doorway, and Matilda runs out after him, calling "You git on the other side,*

629

Johnny." Their voices are occasionally audible outside thereafter, as they throw the ball back and forth over the roof)

TOM: Where is Abe?

MRS. LINCOLN: *(Standing by the spinning-wheel)* He's a-splitting rails over to Josiah Crawford's — him and that new boy.

SARAH: *(Alertly interested)* Aaron Grigsby?

MRS. LINCOLN: No — his brother, Natty.

SARAH: *(Losing interest and turning away)* Oh.
(Dennis quite audibly snorts)

TOM: I thought Abe finished up at Josiah's yesterday.
(Mrs. Lincoln pretends to be absorbed in disentangling the skein of flax thread)

ELIZABETH: *(Pausing at the table and looking at her mother)* Yes, Mamma, that's what I thought, too. I thought I heard you say —

MRS. LINCOLN: *(Quickly)* There was a misreckoning about his pay.

TOM: Is old Josiah Crawford pinching his cut-money again?

DENNIS: Old Josiah Crawford is watching his hired-help at work, if you ask me, and he don't hanker to get oratory when he's paying for walnut rails.
(Tom looks up angrily, then turns to Mrs. Lincoln)

MRS. LINCOLN: *(Defensively)* The men put Abe up on a stump again yesterday and made him give one of his speeches, and it just so happened that Mr. Crawford he come out of the woods and seen it all. Abe he's giving Mr. Crawford three hours of free work this morning to make up for his loss. Natty Grigsby offered to help.

TOM: *(Incredulous)* Free?
(Mrs. Lincoln nods)

DENNIS: Abe must be reforming.

TOM: *(Looking at his wife sharply)* Yeah, that don't sound like Abe. Did he get the idea of making up the work, or did Josiah?

MRS. LINCOLN: *(Evasively)* It wasn't Josiah's idea.

TOM: *(After regarding her for a long time)* And it wasn't Abe's neither, I reckon. *(Shakes his head disapprovingly)* It was yourn.

DENNIS: She'll be persuading Abe to eat with one of them-there new-fangled forks she brung up from Kaintuck, next thing you know.

TOM: If she can persuade Abe Linkern to give three hours of free work — why, she can persuade him to do anything.

MRS. LINCOLN: You can catch more flies with sugar than you can with vinegar.

TOM: *(Disgusted)* Sugar! *(He slams his fist down on the table)* What that boy needs is a larruping!

630

MRS. LINCOLN: *(Without looking at Tom)* What that body needs is education. *(She crosses the room to the fireplace, where the girls have started to wash the dishes. They step aside, and she dips her hands into the kettle. She addresses the girls)* 'Tain't hot enough. 'Tought to be scalding.

ELIZABETH: But it burns our hands Mamma!

SARAH: *(Wistfully)* When we used to didn't have dishes, we used to didn't have to wash them.

MRS. LINCOLN: *(Rolling up her sleeves)* I'll wash them then. You two dry. *(She sets the kettle back over the fire and then turns to Tom, who has been watching her warily from his place at the table)* What that boy needs, Tom Linkern, is more education, and he's going to get it!

TOM: *(Grumbling)* I can't get Abe to do his work proper now, what with him always sticking his nose between the covers of one of them-there books or always wanting to recite or speechify.

SARAH: I always did say Abe could talk a hound out of scratching.

TOM: Speechifying won't get him nowhere in this world. Look at what he's doing now for Josiah Crawford.

MRS. LINCOLN: *(She crosses the room to the table. Her manner is neither nagging nor pleading, but simply firm and convinced)* Speechifying will get Abe Linkern places that you and me will never get to, Tom. From the very first time I laid eyes on that boy, I knowed he wasn't cut out for the kind of work you and me was born to.

DENNIS: *(Looking up from his rifle)* Wasn't cut out for work? Why, Abe can already lick any growed man his own weight in Spencer County. Feller that can wrassle like Abe ought to be able to work.

TOM: Abe's just plain lazy. That's all.

MRS. LINCOLN: Abe looks lazy to you all, because he's working in his head all the time, in a way that you ain't fitten to do. He don't take kindly to using his legs and arms unless he has to, because he's tired from using his head.

DENNIS: *(With a snort)* Abe Linkern was born tired.

MRS. LINCOLN: *(She first quiets Dennis with a look. After he returns to his rifle-cleaning, she addresses Tom)* What Abe needs is to have that head of his given a chance, or else he'll come to no end of meanness. With some boys, to keep them outen trouble, you got to keep their arms and legs a-working all the time, because . . . *(She glances at Dennis)* . . . because there ain't enough in their heads to get plagued about. But with others, it's their heads you got to consider — or else —

TOM: *(Interrupting)* Abe's had a term with Andy Crawford here in Indiana, and he had a spell of schooling in Kaintuck afore we come here. He can't write, but he can read. That's enough.

MRS. LINCOLN: For you and me it is, Tom Linkern. It's more than enough for you and me, because you and me can't even read. But for Abe, it's different. There's a boy that can never get him enough.

TOM: He'll get it by hisself then.

MRS. LINCOLN: And that's just what I'm driving at. Abe he'll get something by hisself — sure. But will it be the right thing? That's the question. His head is just like that-there flowerbed Mrs. Reuben Grigsby planted this spring. *(She sits down at the other end of the bench)* I sot a spell over at Mrs. Grigsby's cabin yesterday. Mrs. Grigsby is as uppity as all get-out, what with their plunder and those china teeth she wears and all. But she has fixed up that clearing right pretty, I must say. Well, like I say, you take that flowerbed she has planted. Flowers can grow in it — the pinny and the pretty-by-night and the old maid's eyes and such like — or weeds can grow in it. But if Mrs. Grigsby wants flowers instead of weeds, even she has got to keep a-grubbing, uppity as she is.

SARAH: *(To Elizabeth)* You seen the Grigsby boys yet?

ELIZABETH: Sure' I've seen them. There's Reuben and Charles and Billy and Natty . . .

SARAH: *(Dreamily)* . . . and Aaron.

ELIZABETH: *(Mocking)* And Aaron!

DENNIS: Weeds or no weeds, there ain't a school in forty miles of here.

TOM: *(With an air of dismissal)* That's right. So I reckon there ain't no argument.

MRS. LINCOLN: *(Smiling victoriously)* Oh, yes, there is! Mrs. Grigsby told me that Mr. Azel Dorsey is hankering to start him up a school just four mile from here next fall. The Grigsbys is sending their Natty.

SARAH: And Aaron, too.

TOM: *(Taken aback, but undefeated)* Another blab-school like Andy Crawford's most likely. Learn them to take their hats off when they come into a cabin, and like of that. Hell, I paid Andy Crawford twenty dollars to learn my boy to take off his hat in the cabin, and what happened? Why, the boy never wore no hat to take off!

MRS. LINCOLN: Mr. Dorsey's school will be different. He has got grammar-books and a 'rithmetic and a *Bible*, Mrs. Grigsby says. *(She leans over the table, and Tom, looking at her, begins to smile sheepishly and yet tenderly. It is obvious that her strength does not lie in her superior will-power alone)* Please, Tom, say Abe can go.

TOM: *(Patting her hand)* A man that never makes a promise, Sarah Linkern, ain't fixing to tell no lies.

MRS. LINCOLN: But you'll be a-thinking about it between now and fall, won't you?

TOM: *(Smiling at her)* 'Twon't do no harm to think, I reckon.
(Mrs. Lincoln turns away and goes to the kettle over the fire. Sarah and Elizabeth have the dishes ready for washing now)
But it will be the ruination of the boy!

632

(Mrs. Lincoln dips the first stack of dishes into the kettle and begins to wash them, handing them out to the girls to dry)
He'll get as independent as a hog on ice!
(Mrs. Lincoln continues with her work)
And we'll never get no work done around this-here clearing!

MRS. LINCOLN: *(Quietly, without looking up)* While you're speaking of work, Tom, I mind you said you'd get started fixing up this cabin come the first real warm day.
(At the mention of work, Dennis rises quickly and beckons to Tom behind Mrs. Lincoln's back. Tom is startled by his wife's words. Dennis points to his own rifle and then to one on the rack above his head. Tom nods and, rising, starts stealthily toward the door) You said the first warm day you'd cut me a window in this cabin and lay me a puncheon floor and build me a loft and make a peg-ladder to reach it by. *(She turns about just as Tom is reaching for the rifle on the rack. At the same moment, Abe, carrying an ax, appears in the doorway)* Well, Tom, this-here is a real warm day.

TOM: *(As if he had not heard)* Here's Abe.

DENNIS: Come on Tom. *(He goes out with his gun)*

ELIZABETH: *(Seeing Dennis go out, she drops her towel and runs after him)* Denny . . . !

SARAH: *(Provoked, picking up Elizabeth's towel)* That girl . . . !

ABE: *(Leaning his ax against the wall and dropping wearily into the chair Dennis has just left)* That old Bluenose Crawford!

TOM: *(Amused in spite of himself)* *Bluenose* Crawford! That's good!

ABE: *(Sprawling)* You'd think that feller was a-fixing to set up a rail fence around all eternity.

TOM: You done the right thing, Abe, giving him that free work.

ABE: I had to — or else Mamma would have whupped the stuffing outen me, most likely. Anyhow, Natty Grigsby helped me.

MRS. LINCOLN: *(Finishing the dishes and wiping her hands on a towel)* I ain't never whupped you since I've been here and you know it, Abe Linkern.

ABE: *(Grinning slowly and looking down at his long legs)* I reckon there's too much territory for you to cover, Mamma. You wouldn't know where to start in at.
(Sarah stacks the dishes on the clapboard shelf above the fireplace)

MRS. LINCOLN: *(To Sarah)* Don't forget to hang up them towels, honey. *(She sees Tom slipping past his son and about to go out the door with his gun)* Tom!
(Tom turns about innocently)
Where you going, Tom?

TOM: *(Jerking his thumb over his shoulder)* Me and Denny . . .

ABE: They're plotting to gang up on a rabbit, Mamma. Pappy's got blood in his eye, I can tell. *(To Tom)* One of you two is going to get hisself killed one of these days — a-shooting at the same rabbit from both sides that-a-way.

TOM: *(To Abe)* You're getting too big for your breeches. How come you don't never do no hunting for this family?

ABE: Me and the rabbits have an understanding, Pappy.

MRS. LINCOLN: *(To Tom)* What are you a-going hunting for?

TOM: Turkey, maybe.

ABE: Maybe you could hit a turkey, but Denny couldn't hit one if it was tied on the end of his gun.

MRS. LINCOLN: You and Dennis had better give them poor turkeys a breathing-spell, Tom. Anyhow, we're having squirrel for supper tonight.

ABE: *(With a start)* Squirrel — ?

SARAH: *(As she passes Abe on her way out the door to hang up the dish-towels, she nods gleefully)* That's what she said — squirrel! *(She goes out)*

ABE: Maybe Pappy ought to go hunting after all, Mamma.

TOM: *(Edging toward the door)* Sure. Maybe we ought to have a couple more squirrels, Sarah. After all that work of his, Abe will be powerful hungry.

ABE: *(Making a face)* Not for squirrel, I won't.

MRS. LINCOLN: *(Firmly)* There's plenty already.

TOM: *(Temporarily defeated)* Well, I hope you're right. Anything I don't like, it's a chinchy meal.

ABE: *(Consoling him)* You can have my share, Pappy. I can't get into my breeches now from eating squirrel all the time. I'm growing a bushy tail.

TOM: *(Brightening)* See Sarah, Abe don't care for squirrel-meat. I ought to shoot a rabbit for him.

ABE: *(With a sigh)* Them poor rabbits!

MRS. LINCOLN: *(Looking at Tom steadily)* Tom . . .

TOM: Aw, shucks! *(He drops the butt of his rifle hard on the earthen floor. Suddenly he brightens again, inspired)* That's right. I plumb forgot. *(To Abe)* Abe, son, how would you like a little more schooling? *(Abe looks at him unbelieving. From the fireplace, where she is re-arranging the dishes on the shelf, Mrs. Lincoln smiles approvingly at Tom)*
I mean it, son. How would you like a little more book-learning?

ABE: *(Still incredulous)* Where would I get it at?

TOM: Your mamma tells me Azel Dorsey is fixing to start him up a school next fall.

634

ABE: *(Flatly)* Oh . . . next fall.

TOM: Well, you can't start up a school in the spring. There's too much plowing and planting to be done, and . . . *(He hesitates, glancing at Mrs. Lincoln)* . . . and some folks likes to fix up their cabins in the spring, too.

ABE: *(Screwing around on his chair and looking sharply at his father)* Just what you a-getting at, Pappy?

TOM: *(With an air of injured innocence)* Like I said, Abe — just more schooling for you. That's all.

ABE: But you was always dead-sot against schooling.

TOM: Not altogehter, I wasn't, boy. I always figured that whatever a boy is willing to earn he ought to get.

ABE: *(Losing interest)* Oh . . . *earn!*

TOM: *(Ignoring his attitude)* Now, your mamma here she was counting on having a thing or two done to this cabin.

MRS. LINCOLN: Tom!

TOM: *(Continuing breathlessly, pretending not to have heard her)* . . . and I ain't got too much spare time on my hands, so I figured maybe you . . .

MRS. LINCOLN: Why, Tom . . . !

ABE: *(Abruptly)* So you figured maybe you could get me to do some of the things you promised Mamma you'd do. That it?

TOM: *(Rubbing his chin)* Well, considering I'd be willing to pay for a term of schooling with Azel Dorsey next fall . . .

ABE: Is that a promise?

TOM: *(Somewhat taken aback by Abe's directness)* Well, now, I reckon maybe it ought to be put that-a-way, oughtn't it?

ABE: *(Looking steadily at his father)* All right then, Pappy. It's a bargain.

TOM: Now, I won't stand for no loafing or jimber-jawed nonsense on the job, you understand?

ABE: You and me never is very jimber-jawed when we're working together.

TOM: *(Startled) Together?*

ABE: Why, sure! You're aiming to help, ain't you? You're the best carpenter in Spencer County. You wouldn't want your own cabin fixed up all whopper-jawed by a amateur like me, would you?

TOM: *(Almost speechless)* Why, son, I . . .

MRS. LINCOLN: *(Sternly)* Tom . . . !

TOM: *(To Abe)* It's time you learned to do things by yourself.

MRS. LINCOLN: Tom Linkern!

TOM: *(Still to Abe)* You can start in on something simple at first and work up gradual. Now, I figure the puncheon floor ought to be easy. *(He urges Abe toward the door)* Take them puncheons out there in the clearing. They'd do to start in on. You can cut them to length.

(Abe goes out, first glancing at Mrs. Lincoln and then smiling craftily to himself. Tom, still carrying his rifle, is right on his son's heels)

MRS. LINCOLN: *(Raising her voice, but gently still, as if she were speaking to an irresponsible child)* Thomas Linkern . . .

TOM: *(Turning about innocently in the doorway)* Did you call me, Sarah?

MRS. LINCOLN: *(Quietly)* Yes, Tom. *(She moves to the middle of the room, and, without a word, Tom re-enters the cabin and comes forward, toward her. She puts her hands on her husband's shoulders and looks at him steadily for a few seconds. At first, Tom tries to outstare her with his look of puzzled innocence, but eventually he loses the contest and begins to grin)*

TOM: *(With a shrug of reluctant but half-amused surrender)* Aw, hell, Sarah!

MRS. LINCOLN: You promised.

TOM: *(He turns and hangs his gun on the rack. Then, without another look at his wife, who is watching him from the middle of the room, he goes out after Abe)* Wait a minutee, son. I reckon I'd better help you, after all.

CURTAIN

ABE LINCOLN OF PIGEON CREEK

ACT ONE

Scene Three

The Same. A Sunday morning in October, 1824, several years later.
There is a window to the right of the door now, with a greased news-
paper stretched across it, letting in a dull yellow light. The floor is laid with
puncheons, and a ladder of sassafras pegs driven into the rear wall above the
bed, right, leads to the newly-constructed loft.
Abe and his sister, Sarah, are seated at the table, eating. Just after the
curtain rises, Abe drops his fork on the floor under the table, and reaching
for it with a bare foot, picks it up with his toes, and sets it back on the table.

ABE: Danged if I can get the hang of these things!

SARAH: *(Eating stolidly)* Sure makes a heap of dish-washing.

ABE: Well, George Washington must have et with forks, so I reckon we can.

SARAH: I bet he used his fingers when his mam wasn't looking.

ABE: Last night, I was reading about George Washington again, in that
book old Bluenose Crawford loaned me. *(He glances up at the loft)*
Now that we finally got that new loft, I get a heap more reading done.

SARAH: Pappy will raise cain about the grease you're burning up there.

ABE: It will give Pappy a good excuse for more hunting and less clearing.
Take's bear's grease for night-reading, and Pappy's death on bears.

SARAH: *(Wistfully)* Well, at least you got you a loft, where you can get
away from this eternal family crowd.

ABE: Crowd? It's a regular public meeting. Ever since Denny and Elizabeth got married up, and moved in here with their young 'un, why,
there ain't hardly room in this cabin for a feller to wrassle with his own
conscience.

SARAH: I know.

ABE: *(Studying his sister a moment before he speaks)* You don't get much
chance, do you, Sis?

SARAH: Chance for what?

ABE: Sparkin'.

SARAH: Sparkin'? Me? If I had sparkin' in my head, Abe Linkern, I'd
find me a way to do it, never fear!

ABE: Not here in this cabin you couldn't, even with a sparkin' tube.

SARAH: *(Tossing her head)* There's other places.

ABE: *(Jolted upright)* Over at the Crawfords? Sally Linkern, you been
meetin' Aaron Grigsby over in the Crawford's settin' parlor.

SARAH: Who ever told you such a thing!

ABE: Nobody. They don't have to. So that's why you been stayin' so late
at the Crawfords', after your work is done. And then he don't even see
you home.

637

SARAH: He does, too — at least part way.

ABE: Part way? That ain't no way to do. Why don't he see you to your own door, like an honest man. I got a good notion to take a horsewhip to him!

SARAH: You mind your own business!
(Abe gets up and walks around the table to his sister's side. He stands there looking down at her thoughtfully before he speaks)

ABE: *(Slowly)* Sally, I don't want to meddle. After all, you're old enough to know your own business, and in another year or two, you'll be an old maid, if you ain't careful. Maybe Aaron Grigsby is a good man, but — *(He pauses, thrusting out his heavy lower lip, and scowling)* Well, it seems to me like he owes it to Mamma and Pa to put in an appearance here at our place now and then. Why don't he take you to church, say — like today?

SARAH: *(Evading the issue)* I'm goin' to church with the Crawfords, because Mamma took the family and went ahead, to be at that meeting.

ABE: *(Answering his own question)* It's that uppity mam of Aaron's that keeps him from doing it. His mam thinks us Linkerns ain't worth shucks. Aaron's scared to be seen courting you. Aaron Grigsby is a-wanting guts. That's what!

SARAH: *(Looking up at him steadily and putting her hand on his arm)* Listen, Abe. Aaron and me meets over at the Crawfords' only because it's quieter over there. There ain't so many folks. You understand? That's all. That's the only reason. You understand?
(Abe takes a deep breath and turns away from her)

ABE: *(Releasing the air from his lungs)* Well, the Grigsbys just better never make no trouble for my Sis. That's all!

SARAH: *(Quietly)* Abe Linkern, you stay outen this. I never tormented you about Anna Roby when she was sweet on you at Azel Dorsey's school, did I?

ABE: Oh, Anna Roby — that's different.

SARAH: How come?

ABE: Why, the Robys ain't uppity like the Grigsbys. Any anyhow, I just helped Anna with her spelling a time or two.

SARAH: *(With a short laugh)* Spelling! Now that her folks has gone off to Kaintuck for a visit, why'd she come up to Little Pigeon Creek to stay with the Gentrys? Her spelling broke down again?

ABE: Well, you wouldn't expect her to stay in that cabin down at Anderson Creek all alone, would you?

SARAH: Why didn't she go to Kaintuck with her folks? I reckon she figured the Gentrys' cabin was nearer Abe Linkern than Kaintuck. That's what she figured.

ABE: *(Trying to change the subject)* Pshaw! Now you take the Gentrys. They've got a heap more plunder than the Grigsbys have, but they ain't uppity at all.

SARAH: *(With a note of warning in her voice)* Abe —

ABE: *(Grinning affectionately at her)* Hokey day, Sis. I don't aim to torment you about Aaron Grigsby all the time. After all, I can't blame you for using the Crawfords' setting parlor for your sparkin'. You sure couldn't do it proper here. *(He pauses, growing thoughtful)* You know, Sally, after reading that book by Parson Weems about George Washington, I've been wondering what Washington would have come to if he'd been raised in a place like this-here. Washington's pa took powerful pains a-rearing him. He was always a-lecturing him about God and the truth and such-like and giving him object lessons. What do you reckon Washington would have come to without all that?

SARAH: *(Uninterested)* Same thing, like as not.

ABE: I bet nobody ever looked down on the Washingtons like the Grigsbys do on us.

SARAH: *(She gets up and goes to the fireplace, brings back a platter with one corndodger on it and offers it to Abe)* Corndodger?

ABE: *(Musing, he ignores the offer)* You reckon folks like us has got any chance to amount to anything?

SARAH: *(Indifferently)* If you don't quit your laughing and joking all the time, you won't amount to nothing. You can count on that.

ABE: *(Slyly)* Anna Roby thinks I will.

SARAH: *(Beginning to gather the dishes from the table)* If Anna Roby knows what's good for her, she won't tie up to no boy who's too lazy to help clean off the table when he's through eating. *(She stuffs the last corndodger in her mouth)*

ABE: *(Abstracted)* And Mamma thinks I'll amount to something, too. She's like George Washington's pa in that respect. *(Brightening)* It's funny about Mamma — the way I feel about her now. You remember the day she come from Kaintuck with Pa? It's been almost five years now.

SARAH: *(Setting the dishes down on the hearth)* Remembering something five years ago don't help me with these dishes now.

ABE: *(Unaware that she has spoken)* If it wasn't for Mamma, I wouldn't have gone to Azel Dorsey's school and learned to write. I owe Mamma a powerful heap. *(He stops abruptly and turns to Sarah)* Sally, do you ever feel like there was somebody else inside you?

SARAH: *(So startled she drops a wooden platter on the floor)* Great day in the morning, Abe! I should hope not!

ABE: *(Without noticing)* That's the way I feel sometimes. That's the only way I can describe it — just like there was two of me, instead of one. There's the one on the outside that folks see. He's always laughing and playing jokes, so's other folks will laugh, too — like the time I sewed up poor Pa's dog in a coonskin and Natty Grigsby's hounds chased it clean over to Gentryville and back and killed it. That outside feller is a loafer and a wastrel, and there's times when he gets an itch to do things that's plain ornery mean. But then there's the other one — the one that's inside of me. He likes to read and study and think. Nobody ever paid any attention to that inside feller till Mamma came along . . . *(He pauses and sighs)* Why, sometimes, when I was ciphering or reading at Azel Dorsey's school, I felt just like a old cow a-calving.

SARAH: *(Taunting)* And when singing class come along, you sounded like it too!

(Ignoring the remark, Abe stands up and, throwing back his head, begins to recite solemnly)

ABE: It is not, then, in the glare of public, but in the shade of private life, that we are to look for the man. Private life is always real life. Behind the curtain, where the eyes of the million are not upon him, and where a man can have no motive but inclination, no incitement but honest nature, there he will always be sure to act himself: consequently, if he act greatly, he must be great indeed. Hence it has been justly said, that, "our private deeds, if noble, are noblest of our lives. . ." *(He turns and looks at Sarah, who has had her back toward him throughout the recitation. Her indifference does not dismay him, however)* That's what that book about Washington says, and if it's true, then maybe there's some hope for me, because inside of me I think I am a decent feller, Sally. . .

(Sally continues to work over the dishes at the fireplace. Abe starts toward the peg-ladder)

Wait a minute. I'll get that book and read you some more. *(At the window, he stops abruptly and squints at the greased newspaper that has been put there as a window-pane. His voice rises in indignation)* Who ever told Pa he could use my newspaper to put in this-here window? Why, this is the Louisville *Journal* that I traveled clean down to Judge Pitcher's office in Rockport to get only last week! It's got Henry Clay's speech in it, and I was aiming to memorize it. *(He begins to tear the paper carefully out of the window-frame)*

SARAH: *(Finishing her work and taking off her apron as she turns about)* Pa'll raise Cain when he sees what you're a-doing.

ABE: I'm only going to set it around the other way. Pa put it in upside down, and I sure don't aim to memorize it a-hanging by my heels from the rafters.

(As Abe works at the window, Josiah Crawford and his wife, Elizabeth Crawford, appear in the doorway. Josiah is not yet middle-aged, but he appears so because of his pompous manner and carriage and the great size and purple color of his nose. His wife is a small, prim, pretty woman. Both are dressed in their pioneer best)

JOSIAH: Howdy, folks.

SARAH: Howdy. Come right in. *(To Abe)* Here's Mr. and Mrs. Crawford, Abe.

ABE: *(Still at the window, speaking over his shoulder, without interrupting his work)* Howdy, folks. I'll be with you in a minute — soon as I get Henry Clay sot right-side-up.

JOSIAH: *(Sententiously, as he steps over the sill)* Henry Clay is always right-side-up, I'd say, Abraham. And if the American people have any sense at all, they will elect him President of the United States.

ABE: *(Laughing)* Well, my Pa's such a Jackson man that, even though he can't read, he has sot Henry on his head here in this window.

JOSIAH: *(Ponderously)* John Adams would be a better man in the President's office than Old Hickory.

ABE: *(Turning about quickly)* Oh, come now, Josiah! You can't say that! You can't say a man like Adams. . .

MRS. CRAWFORD: *(Interrupting)* Don't get Josiah talking politics, Abe. It upsets his stomach, and he rumbles all during service. *(To Sarah)* You ready to go to church with us, Sally? Where's your folks at?

SARAH: Mamma and them set off early. There was a meeting of some kind afore the service. Elizabeth and Denny and the youngun went, too. I'll be ready in a minute. Won't you and Mr. Crawford set? *(They sit down, Josiah balancing his tall hat on his knee. Sarah goes to the bureau chest and begins to fix her hair)*

MRS. CRAWFORD: *(To Abe)* You're coming too, ain't you, boy?

ABE: *(With some embarrassment, which he overcomes as he proceeds)* Well, no, ma'am, I reckon not. You see, ever since the lizard hopped down inside the preacher's collar while he was reading the text, I ain't trusted myself in church. *(He digs his hand down inside his collar and goes into a squirming dance, imitating the preacher and quoting the text)* But God hath chosen the foolish things of the world to confound the wise: and God hath chosen the weak . . . *(Seeing that Josiah and Mrs. Crawford are definitely not amused, he breaks off his antics abruptly. After a pause, he speaks flatly)* Anyhow, I was aiming to read.

MRS. CRAWFORD: *(Solemnly)* Don't let your book-reading get in the way of your hereafter, son.

ABE: *(Meekly)* No'm.

JOSIAH: *(Clearing his throat)* Speaking of books, Abe, — I'm reminded. If you have finished with that book I loaned you. .

ABE: I've read it four times, Josiah.

JOSIAH: And you found it to your liking, no doubt.

ABE: *(Pulling thoughtfully at his lower lip)* Altogether, Josiah, I can't rightly say that I did. I got an idea Washington hisself wouldn't have cared much for it.

JOSIAH: *(Raising his brows in amazement)* I'm right sorry you didn't like the book.

ABE: Oh, I liked parts of it. Only, it would have been a heap better without the hogwash.

SARAH: *(Turning from the bureau, horrified)* Abe! You was just now quoting parts of that book that pleased you!
(Josiah raises his hand to silence her. It is obvious that he disapproves, but he is determined to hear Abe out)

ABE: *(Thoughtfully)* There was good parts to the book. But the bad parts pret' near spoil the whole thing. Parson Weems makes a powerful namby-pamby outen George, especially when he is a little feller. *(He assumes a sissified, simpering pose)* It's: Pa, do I ever tell lies ? Or it's: High! Ma! Ain't I a good boy — don't I always run to you soon as I hear you call? *(He assumes his natural manner again)* Now, you take that-there story about the cherry tree.

SARAH: Everybody knows George Washington chopped down the cherry tree and then told his pa about it. Master Dorsey learned us that in school.

ABE: Well, I don't believe it.

JOSIAH: *(Choking with incredulity)* You don't believe it?

ABE: *(Flatly)* Nope. I don't. Anybody that turned out later to be as smart as George Washington wouldn't have gone around chopping down fruit trees just because he had him a new hatchet. 'Tain't reasonable. And, furthermore, anybody that didn't have no more sense than to chop down a fruit tree wouldn't have had the moral gumption to tell the truth later when his pa asked him who done it. Why, if George Washington —

JOSIAH: *(Interrupting what is threatening to develop into an oration)* That's enough! We don't have time to listen to such nonsense. If you'll just give me back my book, Abraham . . .

ABE: Yes, sir. *(He climbs the peg-ladder)*

SARAH: *(To Josiah)* You mustn't mind, Abe, Mr. Crawford. He's always a-talkin'.

JOSIAH: *(Rising, with great dignity)* The boy gets some queer and contrary notions in his head. He's disrespectful — and — and unpatriotic!

SARAH: He don't never mean nothing by it.
(A thump and a muffled exclamation are heard in the loft. Mrs. Crawford rises and all three stare at the ceiling)

MRS. CRAWFORD: Land o' Goshen!

SARAH: *(Calling)* What's the matter, Abe? *(There is a silence. Sarah speaks then to Mrs. Crawford)* I reckon it's his growing-pains again. *(Abe's legs appear as he begins to descend the ladder, and they watch him in silence)*

MRS. CRAWFORD: *(Sympathetically)* Did you bump your head up there, boy?

ABE: *(Solemnly)* No, Ma'am. *(He comes forward, with the book covered by his large enveloping hands)* Josiah, how are you fixed for hired-hands over at your place now?

642

JOSIAH: *(Puzzled)* Pretty good, I reckon. Why?

ABE: *(After an inner struggle)* Oh, nothing . . . *(He goes to door and looks out. His profile is a study of indecision. Finally, he turns to Josiah with a shrug of dismissal)* I reckon, if you don't mind, I'll give you the book some other time.

SARAH: *(Astonished)* But you've got it there in your hand, Abe!

ABE: *(Frowning at her)* What? *(He pauses, and then improvises)* There's parts of it I want to read over again.

JOSIAH: *(Sternly)* You said you didn't care for the book.

ABE: *(Flustered)* Yeah, that's right. I did say that, didn't I? *(Brightening)* But maybe if I read it again, I'd like it better.

MRS. CRAWFORD: *(Arranging her skirts)* We'd better get a hump on, Josiah.

ABE: *(Eagerly)* Yes, you all had better get along afore you're late. I'll give you the book some other time. It would slow you down to have to tote it.

JOSIAH: I reckon I can tote a book without being bowed down.

SARAH: *(Looking closely at Abe's hand)* What's eating on you?

ABE: *(With renewed inner struggle)* You got plenty of hands on your place for the time being, you say, Josiah?

JOSIAH: *(Puzzled)* Why I'm hiring Natty Grigsby and Allen Gentry to help pull fodder next week.

ABE: *(Shaking his head dubiously)* Them boys don't really need the money. Anyhow, Allen Gentry is cornstob. He hurt his foot bad last week. He'll be as slow as the seven-year-itch.

JOSIAH: Allen Gentry won't be no slower than some I could name. He may be cornstob, but he ain't given to making stump speeches.

ABE: Well, if you could get that work done for nothing, now . . .

MRS. CRAWFORD: *(Impatiently)* Abraham Linkern, what you a-getting at anyway? You act like you got a burr in your breeches.

ABE: *(With great effort)* I got worse than that, ma'am. I figure I got another spell of free work coming on for Josiah. *(He thrusts out the book)* There! *(Josiah takes it and examines it)* I stuck that-there *Life of Washington* in a chink between the logs by my bed last night, and it come up a sudden rain in the night and spoiled it. I reckon the only thing I can do is to offer to pull fodder for you till it's paid for.

JOSIAH: *(Still examining the book ruefully)* I reckon that's all you *can* do.

ABE: *(With a sigh)* I was afraid that was what you'd reckon.

JOSIAH: *(Squinting at Abe)* Abe Linkern, it don't sound natural coming from you — offering free work without no prompting from your mamma. But there's one thing about you. You say you'll do a thing and you'll do it. I'll be looking for you tomorrow at sunup.

ABE: *(Dejectedly)* At sunup. *(Josiah, Mrs. Crawford, and Sarah exeunt. Abe, having an afterthought, calls)* Josiah . . . !

JOSIAH: *(Reappearing in the doorway)* What say?

ABE: Can I have the book to keep now?

JOSIAH: *(After some consideration)* I reckon. *(He hands the book to Abe and disappears; but in another moment, he is in the doorway again)* But that will cost you *three* days work instead of one. *(Abe looks after him, shaking his head dolefully, as Josiah disappears for the last time. Then Abe goes to the table and lays the book on it and sinks down to the bench, as if exhausted, holding his head between his hands. But as he sits there, he begins to gaze proudly at the book)*

ABE: *(To himself)* The labor pains was terrible — but the old cow calved. *(He picks up the book and thumbs its pages, finally pausing to read. While he is reading, Anna Roby appears at the door. She is a pretty girl of fifteen, dressed in her Sunday best; a plaid linsey-woolsey dress with bright ribbons at the waist and shoulders and a poke bonnet, from under which golden curls tumble down about her shoulders. Her motions are quick, nervous, like a young deer's, and she conveys somehow the innocence and wariness of a forest creature. Her face is flushed and she is out of breath. She has apparently been running. As she discovers Abe at the table, a look of delight comes into her eyes)*

ANNA: *(Speaking shyly)* Abe — *(Abe does not hear her and she steps lightly over the sill, glancing back over her shoulder before she speaks again)* Abe — *(Abe looks up with a start. As he recognizes Anna, his face brightens)*

ABE: Why, Anna Roby! Howdy! *(He gets up. She remains by the door)* I thought you'd be going to church with the Gentrys.

ANNA: I am. Leastwise, I'm supposed to be. With Allen Gentry. *(She glances out the door, then steps inside to be out of view of the road)* He's coming up the horse-path now. *(As she turns facing Abe now, she stands with her back to the wall, her hands spread out flat against the rough logs. She speaks breathlessly, giving Abe a bold look and then growing shy again)* I raced him.

ABE: *(Without thinking)* But Allen's cornstob. He can't run. *(He stops and looks at Anna quizzically)*

ANNA: *(Flashing a quick conspiratorial smile at him)* I know it. *(Her eyes widen)* I ran fast.

ABE: *(Suddenly overcome with shyness and unable to meet her gaze, he turns to the table. Anna utters a short laugh at his embarrassment and moves sidewise across the room, timidly but definitely approaching him. Abe picks up the book)* Look, Anna! I got me a book. *(He holds it out to her)*

ANNA: *(Taking the book, but looking at Abe still)* It's nice.

ABE: *(Still unable to meet her gaze)* Oh, 'tain't much of a book. It got wet in a chink in the wall last night. Furthermore, I still got three days

644

work to do for Josiah Crawford afore it's really mine. But then it will be mine to keep.

ANNA: *(Glancing over her shoulder at the door)* I saw them going down the road — the Crawfords and your sister. *(She turns back to Abe, handing him the book)* Abe . . .

ABE: *(Looking down at the book and not heeding her)* It's the first book I ever owned.

ANNA: Abe . . .

ABE: *(Still looking at the book)* I'm right proud to own it.

ANNA: *(Breathlessly)* Abe, you want to show me that place where the lilacs grow — the one you told me about in school?

ABE: *(Startled)* But you and Allen Gentry — I thought you was going to church.

ANNA: *(Vexed)* We was — but I thought — well, I —

ABE: What would Allen think?

ANNA: *(Brightening)* Allen is a slow-thinker. He wouldn't start thinking till next week probably. And I'd be gone by then.

ABE: *(Shaking his head with a grave smile)* The lilacs ain't in bloom now, Anna.

ANNA: *(Stamping her foot lightly)* Oh! Stupid — ! *(She bursts into tears briefly, but conquers them)* I didn't mean to be bold, Abe. I only thought . . . *(She breaks off and looks up at him with renewed eagerness)* Maybe you'd go to church with us then. There's just Allen and me.

ABE: *(Looking down at his bare feet)* I ain't dressed.

ANNA: You could put on your moccasins.

ABE: *(Still looking at his feet)* And anyhow — *(His eyes lift and meet hers and they stand gazing at each other for a moment, their hands slowly outstretched toward each other, almost touching but not quite. As they stand so, Allen Gentry appears in the dorway. He is big, humorless, heavy, somewhat older than Abe, dressed plainly but in new and well-fitting linsey shirt and jeans pants. He watches Abe and Anna without speaking for a moment, but his face reveals no comprehension of the situation)*

ALLEN: So you're in here.

(Abe and Anna turn about with a guilty start)

Dang near killed myself trying to catch up with you. This foot hurts like thunder. *(He comes in, eases a moccasined foot up on a chair, and looks at Anna reproachfully)* I thought you knowed I was cornstob, Anna Roby! *(To Abe)* Fool gal cut and run on me back there in the horse path, run like a deer.

ABE: I reckon you need a slippery-elm poultice, Allen.

ALLEN: Ot 'tain't nothing really. Only, I got to favor it. *(He rubs his leg tenderly. Then he speaks to Anna)* We better get a hump on, Anna. Pa won't like it if we're late.

ANNA: *(Without spirit)* All right. *(She moves slowly toward the door. Halfway she turns and looks back at Abe)* You coming?

ABE: *(Hesitates. Glances at his book, then at her, then at his bare feet. Gazing down at them, he speaks slowly and indecisively)* Well — I was aiming to read. Sunday morning is about the only daylight time I get. This cabin is so crowded with my folks that —

(While he is talking, Anna gives a shrug of despair and goes out, followed by Allen)

(Abe glances up and sees that they have gone. He looks at the book, then at his bare feet, then, searchingly, about the room. He speaks in quick decision and desperation) Where's them fool moccasins at? *(He finds them under the table, puts them on, and runs out, saying)* I reckon church can't hurt me no more than three days pulling fodder.

CURTAIN

ABE LINCOLN OF PIGEON CREEK

ACT TWO

Scene One

The ferry landing at the mouth of Anderson's Creek on the Ohio River, near Troy, Indiana, about fifteen miles from the Lincoln cabin. Spring, 1825.

The landing drops off downstage in a steep bank, with the Ohio River in the distance. Overhanging the landing is a great cottonwood tree, and more shade from the bright morning sunlight is afforded by a clump of willows, right. A rough dirt road leads off to the right and to the left.

As the curtain rises, Abe Lincoln is standing on the bottom of an upturned scow, concluding an oration he has been delivering to a group of young men from the neighborhood. They are sitting about on logs and treebutts, listening attentively. All are dressed, like Abe, in linsey shirts and jeans pants. One or two are wearing coonskin caps. Most of them are smoking corncob pipes, or chewing and spitting. In the road, right, among the willows, Judge Pitcher comes upon the scene as the curtain rises, and stands still while Abe finishes. Judge Pitcher is short of stature, a handsome man of thirty, wearing a black tailcoat and black trousers, which are tucked into well-polished boots. His hair is thick and black above a high forehead, and it is tied in short pigtails behind by eel-skin bows. He is holding a tall black hat in his hand.

ABE: *(Concluding his speech, which is Lord Chesterfield's oration delivered in the House of Lords in 1743, in opposition to the Gin Act)*
This man, who must be remembered by many of your lordships, was remarkable for vigor, both of mind and body, and lived wholly upon water for his drink, and chiefly upon vegetables for his other sustenance. He was one day recommending his regimen to one of his friends who loved wine, and urged him, with great earnestness, to quit a course of luxury by which his health and his intellects would be equally destroyed. The gentleman appeared convinced, and told him "that he would conform to his counsel, and thought he could not change his course of life at once, but would leave off strong liquors by degrees." "By degrees!" says the other, with indignation. "If you should unhappily fall into the fire, would you caution your servants not to pull you out but by degrees?"
(When Abe finishes, there is a round of applause from the group, and while the young men are speaking, Judge Pitcher draws nearer.)

FIRST SPEAKER: Hot diggety, Abe! You make me feel like I just busted all Ten Commandments in one dido! *(Takes a hearty chaw from a plug of tobacco)*

SECOND SPEAKER: Give us some more, boy.

THIRD SPEAKER: Go ahead, Abe. You're a-warmin' us up for a good log-rollin'!

ABE: *(Stepping down from the scow and approaching Judge Pitcher)* That's as far as I've memorized. Anyhow, I think Lord Chesterfield would have been smart if he'd stopped there. *(To Judge Pitcher)* Howdy, Judge Pitcher. Don't tell me you're going to the log-rolling today, too.

647

JUDGE PITCHER: *(Shaking Abe's hand)* I was over this way on business, and thought I'd look in on it. I suppose you're going.

ABE: Not just yet. I'm waitin' for the *General Pike.*

JUDGE PITCHER: The big passenger steamer, up from New Orleans?

ABE: Yep. She's due up river this morning.

JUDGE PITCHER: *(In a disciplinary tone)* Look here, boy, what are you up to? I thought you were supposed to be working for Jim Taylor this season.

FIRST SPEAKER: Oh, he's workin', all right, Judge. Don't you see that axe in his hand?
(Abe looks at the book he is holding, threatens good-naturedly to throw it at the speaker)

SECOND SPEAKER: You don't ever catch an industrious worker like Abe Linkern layin' down on his job.

THIRD SPEAKER: Not lessn' the boss ain't lookin'.

FIRST SPEAKER: Or lessn' there's too much noise for him to take a nap. *(All laugh)*

ABE: *(With good-natured spirit)* Listen, you pack of chuckleheads, you try workin' for Jim Taylor a spell. Why, between pushin' that ferry of his'n across the river, and plowin' and hoein' and maulin' rails, I ain't even found the chance to prop me a book up to read while I plow.

SECOND SPEAKER: Jim Taylor must have had a talk with Josiah Crawford, before he hired you.

ABE: *(Glumly)* Jim Taylor didn't have to talk to nobody. He was born that-a-way. He could get blood outen a turnip. Why, Judge, he's about to work the hide off'n me.
(The group of young men begin to gather in the road, left, talking among themselves, while the Judge pursues his conversation with Abe.)

JUDGE PITCHER: Looks like it, I must say. How can you find time to dawdle here on the river bank in the middle of the morning, waiting to see a steamer pass?

ABE: Why, Judge, I ain't dawdlin'. You see, if the *General Pike* blows her whistle, that means she wants to land a passenger. So I take this old scow and row out and bring the passenger ashore. Pick up a little extra money that way.

JUDGE PITCHER: On Jim Taylor's time?

ABE: He's got no kick comin'. I'm holdin' down two jobs for him. I work his farm, and run his ferry-boat — and long as I get it done, there's nothin' in our agreement says I can't make a little money on the side.

JUDGE PITCHER: Doesn't Taylor pay you?

ABE: Hah! Mighty chinchy pay, from that old skinflint!

648

JUDGE PITCHER: Well — I trust there are other compensations.

ABE: Other comfor — come again, Judge?

JUDGE PITCHER: I believe there are other attractions on Anderson's Creek besides money, aren't there?

ABE: *(Sheepishly)* Oh! So you know about that, do you?

JUDGE PITCHER: That didn't require much genius. You took this job over here so as to spend the summer near Anna Roby, didn't you?

ABE: We — yes sir.

JUDGE PITCHER: *(Keenly)* Look here, Abe, are you courting Anna Roby?

ABE: Confound it, Judge, I don't get a chance to. The way Jim works me, I got no time for it. You take the play-party tonight. Allen Gentry travelled all the way down from Gentryville, and got Anna's promise to go with him, afore I could get over to her cabin to ask her for myself. I'll just be a onlooker tonight.

FIRST SPEAKER: Come on, boys, let's go start the log-rollin'.

SECOND SPEAKER: The sooner we get it goin', the sooner the play party can begin.

FIRST SPEAKER: You goin' with us, Abe?

ABE: *(To the young men)* I'm goin' to wait till the *General Pike* passes, boys. You all go ahead.

FIRST SPEAKER: *(To Judge Pitcher)* You comin', Judge Pitcher?

JUDGE PITCHER: I'll be along soon.

FIRST SPEAKER: So long, then.

SECOND SPEAKER: See you there.
(The group leaves by the road, left, calling goodbyes)

JUDGE PITCHER: *(Turning to Abe)* I heard the end of that speech, Abe. You're improving. You aren't waving your arms about as much as you used to, and you have better control of your voice. Remember, simplicity is the thing.

ABE: I'm learning a heap from those books you're loaning me, Judge. I sure am obliged to you.

JUDGE PITCHER: You're welcome to anything in my library, Abe.

ABE: It's the best library I've seen in Spencer County.

JUDGE PITCHER: Well, I'm a lawyer. I've got to have books. They're all books that will stand you in good stead, when you become a lawyer.

ABE: *(He puts his foot up on the scow and rests his chin in his hands, gazing across the river)* Bein' a lawyer is a mighty fine thing, Judge. But I've just about concluded it ain't for me.

JUDGE PITCHER: *(Concerned)* Why, what's the matter, Abe?

ABE: I've decided I want to go on the river, instead.

JUDGE PITCHER: *(Scornfully)* And be a half-horse, half-alligator man?

ABE: *(Protesting)* Oh, no, not that! The keel-boats is done for, Judge. They won't last another year or two. I'm thinkin' of these new steamboats. There's a real future in steamboatin'.

JUDGE PITCHER: *(Scrutinizing him keenly)* I suspect you're not thinking of steamboats, Abe. You're thinking of Anna Roby.

ABE: *(Raising his hands in admission of the Judge's point)* Well, it's the only way I'll ever get her. I ain't got a chance if I don't do something soon to make myself independent. Be ten years afore I can make a living practicin' law — even longer afore I can make a livin' for two.

JUDGE PITCHER: How old are you now, Abe?

ABE: Sixteen.

JUDGE PITCHER: *(Smiling)* Only sixteen. Why, whatever you do, you've still got five years you have to work for your Pa. You can't do anything till you're twenty-one.

ABE: Four and a half years, Judge. Don't make it seem worse than it is. I'm countin' the days. There's exactly one thousand seven hundred and eighty-two left.

JUDGE PITCHER: *(Laughing)* You are looking ahead.

ABE: *(Bitterly)* Sometimes it seems like I just can't stand this way of livin' any longer. Plowin' and hoein' and maulin' rails. Livin' in that cabin of Pa's that's so crowded you can't cuss the cat without gettin' its hairs in your teeth. Folks like the Grigsbys lordin' it over the Lincolns like we was poor white trash. I don't aim for nobody to look down on the Lincolns. And yet if I try to improve myself, Pa thinks I'm killin' time. Pa's agin me, Judge.

JUDGE PITCHER: No man is against his own son, Abe.

ABE: Well, he sure gives a good imitation of it. If he catches me lookin' at a book, he thinks up a job for me to do. I'd run away, if it wasn't for Mamma. I come down here and took this job for the summer as much to get away from Pa, as to be near Anna Roby. But I've run into the same kind of life down here — plowin' and hoein' and maulin' rails, and no book-readin'. If anything, it's worse down here. Jim Taylor don't go off hunting, like Pa used to do every time he saw a squirrel track. And when Jim does go away, he leaves that son of his — Green Taylor — to watch me. Why, between the two of them fellers, I ain't had me a mid-day nap in a cornrow since I don't know when. And I never get a chance to stop plowin' long enough to spell myself with a chapter outen a book.

JUDGE PITCHER: *(Laughing)* Jim Taylor must have got wind of your reputation.

ABE: *(Suddenly earnest and eager)* Look, Judge Pitcher! If you'd just give me a recommend to go on the river, I wouldn't have to wait till I was twenty-one. I could get free of my Pa now, if I had your say-so.

JUDGE PITCHER: *(Becoming grave, and shaking his head)* And you would marry Anna Roby, and by the time you were twenty-one you'd have a cabin full of young 'uns — and then where would you be?

ABE: *(Brightly)* Why, I'd be on the river.

JUDGE PITCHER: *(With a tone of finality)* Abe, I will not give you a recommendation to go on the river. So you might as well stop asking me. You've got it in you to amount to something bigger than a steamboat pilot. If you tie yourself down to a wife and children now, you'll never rise above your present station in life. You'll be a farmer in Southern Indiana all your life, or, at best, a river-pilot who knows little else beyond currents and bends and towheads.

ABE: *(Sullenly)* Currents and bends and towheads is a heap better than plowing and hoeing and mauling rails.

JUDGE PITCHER: *(Emphatically)* No, I won't do it.

ABE: *(His voice rising)* But, Judge, I can't ask Anna Roby to wait five years!

JUDGE PITCHER: *(Correcting him slyly)* Four and a half, Abe. Just one thousand and seven hundred and eighty-two days. *(He pauses)* Anna Roby loves you, don't she?

ABE: *(Grudgingly)* I reckon. She ain't old enough to know better yet. At least, she sure don't act unfriendly. *(With an appeal in his voice)* But I can't bring myself to speak to the girl about love — knowing I've got nothing to offer her.

JUDGE PITCHER: *(With an air of knowing)* It wasn't so long ago that I was your age, and, if I remember correctly, there are ways of speaking of love without speaking of marriage.

ABE: *(Reverently)* Not with Anna Roby, there ain't. *(He looks down at the Judge's short stature)* Maybe it was because there wasn't so much of you to get het up, Judge.
(A steamboat whistle blows in the distance) There's the *General Pike.* She's got a passenger wants ashore.

JUDGE PITCHER: Abe, will you make me a promise?

ABE: *(Starting toward the river bank)* Depends on what it is, Judge.

JUDGE PITCHER: Will you promise me you won't marry till you're twenty-one?

ABE: *(Stopping and uttering a short laugh)* The way nature arranges those things Judge, maybe you'd better ask that promise of Anna Roby — not me. *(He starts toward the river bank again)*

JUDGE PITCHER: *(Following him)* I'm serious, Abe Lincoln. I don't know what it is about you. But it's something. I feel it's a promise I must exact. Before God, I must. Promise!

ABE: *(Turning and looking thoughtfully at him for a moment before he speaks)* I reckon it don't make no difference whether I promise or not. Even if I had the heart to ask her, Anna most likely wouldn't care to tie up with a slack-twisted gone-coon of a feller like me that's so poor he can't keep his tail in his breeches seat. So long as you won't set me up on the river, I got to work for my pa till I'm twenty-one anyhow. *(With a final shrug)* Sure, I promise. *(He holds out his hand, and Judge Pitcher shakes it. The steamboat whistle blows again)* I got to get a hustle on. *(He descends the bank, waving at Judge Pitcher)*

JUDGE PITCHER: *(Waving as he leaves by the road, right)* See you at the log-rolling.

CURTAIN

ACT TWO

Scene Two

The Same. A moonlit night in the fall of the same year, 1825, several months later.

As the curtain rises, Anna Roby and Abe Lincoln are entering by the road, left. Anna is walking a few paces ahead of Abe, looking back at him, scolding. Abe lopes along, grinning at her good-naturedly.

ANNA: You just stayed out there in the clearing all evening telling stories to the men, the way you did last spring at the log-rolling. You didn't come in to the play-party once, not *once!*

ABE: We was shucking corn. I was captain of my team and couldn't leave.

ANNA: The corn-shucking didn't last all evening. There was dancing in the cabin afterwards. The heard the men laughing outside. You kept half of them from coming into the dance — staying out there spinning them yarns of yourn.

ABE: Aw, shucks, Anna! You know I can't dance. I always bump my head on the rafters.

ANNA: *(Coyly)* Well, it wasn't all dancing. We played games, too. *(She dances along ahead of him, singing)* Who will shoe your pretty little foot? Who will shoe your pretty little foot . . . ?
(Abe runs after her, laughing, and takes her in his arms)

ABE: You know I don't care for kissing games — unless it's you I'm kissing. *(He kisses her)*

ANNA: *(She surrenders for a moment and then, breaking away, she goes to a log near the riverbank and sits down)* Well, anyhow, you're an old stick-in-the-mud! I don't know why I've wasted the whole summer on you.

ABE: *(Following her)* I don't count it a waste. *(Anna smiles up at him and takes his hand. Standing behind her, Abe looks out across the moonlit river and begins to recite)* Now glowed the firmament
With living sapphires: Hesperus, that led
The starry host, rode brightest; till the moon,
Rising in clouded majesty at length,
Apparent queen, unveiled her peerless light,
And o'er the dark her silver mantle threw . . .
But wandering oft with brute unconscious gaze
Man marks not thee, marks not thy mighty hand,
That, ever busy, wheels the silent spheres . . .

ANNA: *(Dreamily)* What's spheres, Abe?

ABE: *(Stroking her hair)* Things like the stars out there — and the moon, too, I reckon.

ANNA: And the poem means that God rolls the moon up in the sky every night, like a big yellow cartwheel.

ABE: *(Stepping over the log and sitting down beside her)* Yes, that's it. Only, of course, the moon ain't really rising out there at all, you know, Anna.

ANNA: *(Turning to him skeptically)* You're teasing me, again, Abe.

ABE: No, I ain't teasing. It's true. The moon don't rise. We're the ones that's moving.

ANNA: *(Laughing at him)* I don't feel nothing. I don't feel no wind in my face.

ABE: *(Protesting earnestly)* Honest. We're the ones that's moving. The moon is standing still.

ANNA: *(Giggling)* I don't know how you think up all them things. You can tell the biggest whoppers I ever heard.

ABE: *(Pursuing the lesson earnestly)* No, Anna. Look. It's like as if we were setting on a shelf here on the riverbank — a shelf that was dipping down and dipping down all the time — *(He demonstrates by bending forward)* — and letting us see more and more of the things that's shining down under us in the firmament.
(When he finishes, Anna looks at him for several seconds in silence. She has stopped laughing, but she is still skeptical)
It's true, Anna. I ain't fooling.

ANNA: *(Shaking her head in amusement and dismay)* It's hard for a girl ever to tell about you.

ABE: *(Earnestly and tenderly)* You know I wouldn't fool you, Anna. Never about the things that count — *(He kisses her lightly)* — like the moon. *(Anna puts her hands up to his cheeks and kisses him again, but just as his hands go up to her shoulders, she breaks away and stands up. Abe remains on the log, looking up at her)*
Daggone! You're the one it's hard ever to tell about.

ANNA: *(Gazing down at him thoughtfully)* Abe, you know what? You scare me, kind of, sometimes.

ABE: *(With a grin)* I ain't that ugly, am I?

ANNA: *(With an impatient toss of her head, dismissing such an idea)* I mean you know so much. You know a heap more than any of the other boys around Anderson's Creek.

ABE: *(Laughing)* That ain't sayin' much.

ANNA: *(Standing above him challengingly, her feet wide apart)* Abe Linkern, what you aiming to do with all the book-learning?

ABE: *(With a shrug)* I don't know. Something, I reckon.

ANNA: *(Teasing, but with a shade of contempt in her voice)* Be a schoolmaster, I bet, and wear green spectacles, like Azel Dorsey.

ABE: *(Nodding and grinning up at her)* Most likely — and hand out words you can't spell — like the time we had the spelling-bee and I had to help you get the "i" in "defied" by putting my finger over my eye.

ANNA: *(Tossing her head)* Pooh! I knew how to spell it all along!

ABE: *(Laughing at her again)* I suppose you was just hoping I'd poke my eye out.

ANNA: *(Serious again)* But what *are* you going to be, Abe?

ABE: *(Sticking out his lower lip)* Steamboat pilot, maybe. *(His face grows more serious)* Excepting I can't go on the river till I'm twenty-one. I've got to work for my pa till then. *(He pauses)* Judge Pitcher wants me to be a lawyer.

ANNA: And travel down to Boonville and try cases and wear your hair in eelskin bows.

ABE: *(Nods and rises, standing close to her, and looks down at her with great tenderness)* Boonville ain't shucks to where I'm a-going, Anna. As soon as I'm twenty-one . . . when I'm twenty-one and free, Anna . . .
(He lifts his hand to touch her and she waits expectantly but he does not touch her and he does not finish what he has started to say. His hands drop to his sides; and after a moment, seeing that he is not going to kiss her, Anna walks over to the edge of the bank and stands there looking down. She speaks in a lifeless voice, with her back half-turned to him)

ANNA: I know. You'll go to Illinois probably.

ABE: *(Without spirit)* Could be. Farther than that. To hell, maybe.

ANNA: *(Turning about suddenly)* Did you hear about Allen Gentry?

ABE: *(Looking up)* Who?

ANNA: Allen Gentry.

ABE: Oh, *him!* Naw, — what's happened to him?

ANNA: *(With a show of great interest)* His pa has just bought him a farm down this-a-way — a farm all for himself.

ABE: *(Feigning lack of interest)* Oh, is that all? Well, his pa is rich and can afford it, I reckon.

ANNA: *(Pretending great enthusiasm)* They was both down here this morning — Allen and his pa. They signed the papers in Rockport, and Allen he come over to our cabin, after, just to tell me.

ABE: *(Sullenly)* You don't say. *(Abe and Anna stand looking at each other awkwardly. Finally Abe shivers)*

ABE: Unreasonable cold, ain't it?

ANNA: *(Moving toward him)* Sure is.
(She wants Abe to put his arms about her, but there is a constraint upon Abe now. He speaks in a stilted formal way, as if she were a stranger)

ABE: Skim of ice on the rain-barrel at the Taylors' this morning.

ANNA: *(Waiting)* On ours, too.

ABE: Jim Taylor aims to start butchering next week. I figure he's making a mistake.

ANNA: Pa is waiting till after Christmas.

ABE: He's right. This-here weather won't hold. We've still got Indian Summer ahead of us. But, of course, you can't tell Jim Taylor anything. *(He looks down at Anna, and as he continues, his voice grows warmer)* Butchering so early means I'll be going back to Little Pigeon sooner than I thought I would. Means I won't be around these parts more than another week or two. Our summer is about over, Anna . . . *(Anna is silent but expectant, but again Abe is unable to speak what is in his mind)* I reckon all of Jim Taylor's hog-meat will spoil.

ANNA: *(Turning away from him quickly and uttering a little cry)* Oh! *(Abe looks at her helplessly. He speaks finally in a careful monotone)*

ABE: About Allen Gentry, — I'd heard his pa was looking for a place for him down this-a-way.

ANNA: *(Turning and looking at him sharply)* Then you knowed about it all along.

ABE: Not exactly. I didn't know he'd found a place.

ANNA: *(She waits again, but when she sees Abe is not going to continue, she speaks sharply)* Well, he has. *(She turns toward the road, right)* I better get along home now. It's late.

ABE: *(Following her)* Wait a minute. I'll see you up to your cabin.

ANNA: *(Turning upon him viciously. There is a sob in her voice as she speaks)* No! I don't want you to! You've got hog-butchering to do!

ABE: *(Stunned)* But, Anna —
(Anna runs down the road, leaving Abe by the log, looking after her. When she is almost out of sight, she turns and stands still, looking back at him)
Anna —
(Anna runs to him swiftly and, throwing her arms about his neck, kisses him long and hard on the mouth, clinging to him. Abe is startled at first; but, melted by her ardor, he quickly responds. Finally, she throws back her head and looks up at him)

ANNA: *(Passionately)* Abe —! Oh, Abe — !
(Abe struggles with himself for a moment and then becomes suddenly frozen with fright and frustration. His arms fall limply to his sides. When she comprehends, Anna turns and walks away up the road, right, her head down, leaving Abe standing motionless, looking after her, his face tortured by conflicting emotions)

ABE: Anna — !
(Anna stops but does not turn around)

656

I can't . . .
(Anna starts on)
I made a promise . . .
(As Anna exits, Abe finishes speaking more to himself than to her)
I made a promise to Judge Pitcher.

CURTAIN

ACT TWO

Scene Three

The same. A late summer day in 1827, two years later.

As the curtain rises, Allen Gentry is standing on the riverbank, looking down at the water and calling to Abe Lincoln, who is invisible below the bank, rear.

ALLEN: *(Calling down to Abe)* Throw me your line, Abe. *(A rope is thrown up from below the bank, and Allen, saying "I got it!" makes it fast to the cottonwood. He goes back to the edge and looks down again)* Need any help with that-there trunk?

ABE: *(His voice is audible, although he has not yet appeared over the edge of the bank)* Nope, — I got 'er, all right.

(Abe is seen then climbing up the bank carrying a leather trunk on his shoulders. Behind him appear a River-Pilot and a negro boy, whom Abe has brought ashore in a scow from a passing steamboat. The Pilot is a slim and dandified gentleman in his late thirties, dressed in pearl-gray, tight-fitting trousers, a bottle-green tailcoat, and a tall, fawn-colored hat. A gold watch-fob hangs from a pale blue ribbon at his waist. His cravate is of the material known as "ecorce d'arbre" and, below it, his waistcoat of white and purple silk shines respendently. As The Pilot appears, Allen Gentry steps back in open-mouthed admiration of his costume. The negro boy perches on the trunk as soon as Abe sets it down at the rear near the edge of the bank and remains there without speaking throughout the scene. As Abe sets the trunk down, The Pilot addresses Abe)

THE PILOT: Be careful of that trunk, son. It's got some of the best Madeira in it you ever tasted.

ABE: *(Glancing at him over the trunk)* Madeira — ? What's that?

THE PILOT: It's a wine, my boy, — the best you ever put in your mouth.

ABE: *(Straightening up and flexing his muscles before he walks away from the trunk toward mid-stage)* It ain't the best I ever put in my mouth, mister, because I ain't never had none in my mouth. What's more, if it's anything like blue-ruin whisky, I don't hanker to.

THE PILOT: *(Raising his brows in disapproval)* Oh — ! Free-Will Methodist, eh?

ABE: *(Grinning and shaking his head)* Nope, — touchy-livered Hoosier.

ALLEN: *(Solemnly, still over-awed by The Pilot, but hastening to defend Abe)* It's his stomach that's temperance, mister, — not his conscience.

ABE: *(Acknowledging Allen's defense with a smile)* I reckon that's a fact, Allen. *(To The Pilot)* This-here is a friend of mine — Allen Gentry.

THE PILOT: *(Ignoring the introduction)* It's hotter here in Southern Indiana than the *General Pike's* boilerdeck! *(He takes off his hat, and whipping out an enormous bright yellow handkerchief with a red border, wipes the sweat from his forehead)*

ABE: *(To Allen)* I just brung him ashore from the *General Pike.*

ALLEN: *(Staring at the handkerchief)* Great day in the morning! What flag is that?

ABE: *(To Allen)* That's a handkerchief. It's to save on sleeves. *(He makes a gesture across his nose with the back of his arm. To The Pilot)* Allen Gentry here owns a farm down in this neck of the woods, but he used to feel the same way I do about going on the river.

ALLEN: *(To Abe, while The Pilot continues to mop his head)* You been telling him about us, Abe?

ABE: I been telling him about me mostly. The river wasn't wide enough for me to get around to my friends. *(Gesturing toward The Pilot, who is still mopping)* He's a pilot. I just took him off the *General Pike.* He has come to take over that new boat they're a-building down-river.

ALLEN: *(Marveling)* You don't say!

THE PILOT: *(A vain man, brightening at this discussion of himself and his affairs)* James Castleton is the name, son. *(He extends his hand to Allen)* And yours — ?

ALLEN: *(Startled)* 'Tain't changed none since Abe just now told you — Allen Gentry.

THE PILOT: *(Shaking Allen's hand elegantly)* I'm taking this new boat — the *Pride of Indiana* — on her trial run to Natchez.

ABE: *(Dreamily)* Natchez — !

THE PILOT: *(Wiping his hand on the handkerchief after the handshake)* Regularly, however, I am with Captain Henry Shreve's boats.

ALLEN: *(Admiringly)* One of Captain Shreve's men!

ABE: *(Loyally)* You'll want to change over to the *Pride of Indiana* permanent, Mr. Castleton, once you see her. *(His enthusiasm waxing)* She's a hundred foot length and sixteen foot beam, and she's got that new hog-frame to stiffen her hull and slanting floats on her paddles that's sot just a mite aft to catch the second swell. And she's got —

THE PILOT: *(Interrupting, as he puts the handkerchief away, but tolerantly amused by Abe's enthusiasm)* You told me all that, son, while you were bringing me ashore.

ABE: *(Reluctant to abandon the subject)* Well, the *Pride* is a real horse of a steamboat.

ALLEN: She sure is!

THE PILOT: *(Stepping back and appraising Abe abstractedly, like an artist appraising a painting)* You take my interest, young man. What did you say your name was?

ABE: Lincoln — Abe Lincoln.

THE PILOT: *(Still appraising him)* Well, Mr. Abe Lincoln, you seem to have a genuine feeling for the river. You have the stuff that makes a good steamboatman. From the way you talk, I can see that you have the love in your heart which is greater than the love of women . . . *(He sighs romantically, with his hand over his heart)*

ABE: *(Drily)* I sure have better luck with the river than I do with women.

THE PILOT: *(Frowning at the interruption as he continues his posturing)* There is something about you . . . *(As Abe starts to interrupt again, The Pilot straightens up and speaks sharply)* Except that you talk too damn much! *(Abe subsides with a shrug and a grin, and the Pilot continues with a sigh)* Ah, there is so much to learn! A steamboat is very much like a woman. From her pilothouse to her boiler-decks there are things about her that you can not discover till you have spent a lifetime with her . . . And yet . . . *(He turns his head to one side and looks Abe up and down from head to toe. Embarrassed, Abe grins at Allen and shakes his head. Allen's face remains stolidly expressionless)* . . . and yet you have the right construction for learning. *(Advancing, the Pilot traces a forefinger delicately across Abe's chest)* Your hurricane deck now — it's on the small side perhaps; but there is power in your paddles, and you are not too broad in the beam. *(He frowns and ends abruptly)* But from the way you rowed me ashore, I judge you run on low pressure.

ABE: *(Laughing and wagging his head)* I judge you judge right, mister. Folks around Little Pigeon Creek would all agree that I run on low pressure, all right. My pa learned me to work, but he forgot to learn me to like it. Still and all, I can do a smart chance of work, over a stretch.

THE PILOT: *(Disapprovingly)* But low pressure —

ABE: The *General Pike* has low pressure.

THE PILOT: A crawfish in petticoats!

ABE: Well, she has been on the rivers ten years now and she ain't blowed her boilers yet.

ALLEN: *(Loyally)* Abe ain't blowed his neither — though he lets off a powerful lot of hot air around here at times.

THE PILOT: *(Resuming his appraisal by reaching forward and tapping Abe's forehead lightly with his finger)* What impresses me most about you is your pilothouse. It strikes me you have an uncommonly good pilothouse.

ALLEN: Abe's a powerful book-reader.

THE PILOT: *(Glancing at Allen and speaking with disgust)* Oh, — books!

ABE: *(Drily)* Hadn't been for a book, you wouldn't have got brung ashore. I was just coming back from borrowing that one in Rockport when I heard the *Pike* blow. *(He points to a book stuck in a crotch of the cottonwood tree)*

THE PILOT: *(After glancing at the book briefly)* Books will never teach you anything about the river. Experience is what you need — experience and instinct.

ABE: Well, you say I got the instinct. But I can't get the experience till I get on the river. Could you get me a job somewhere, Mr. Castleton? I figure if I don't get outen this country soon, my hide won't hold shucks.

ALLEN: *(To Abe)* I've heard about the mess of trouble you've worked up for yourself with the Grigsby family.

THE PILOT: *(To Abe)* How old are you?

ABE: Eighteen.

THE PILOT: Can you get your father's consent?
(Abe shakes his head ruefully)
Then you're too young.

ABE: *(Dolefully)* That's what Judge Pitcher used to say when I asked him to give me a recommend. I been working on Uncle Billy Wood up at Little Pigeon lately.

THE PILOT: And what does your uncle say?

ABE: Oh, Uncle Billy ain't my uncle by rights. That's just a manner of speaking round these parts. But he says the same thing Judge Pitcher used to say — too young.

THE PILOT: *(Nodding to his negro boy, who jumps down from the trunk and stands beside it waiting for his master to depart. The Pilot speaks then to Abe with an air of dismissal)* Yes, you're too young. You'll have to wait till you're twenty-one, if you can't get your father's consent. *(He turns to go, but Abe detains him)*

ABE: You will remember me, won't you?

THE PILOT: *(Romantically again)* Young man, a river pilot remembers everything — every snag, every sawyer, every planter —

ABE: *(With a grin)* Every beanpole?

THE PILOT: *(Acknowledging the joke)* Yes, and every beanpole. If you are ever in New Orleans, son, look me up. Just ask for James Castleton on Tchoupitoulas Street. Everybody knows me.

ABE: *(Delighted)* Much obliged, Mr. Castleton!

THE PILOT: I'll remember you if it's only because you have a weak stomach and don't drink. A man that don't drink on principle usually ain't worth his salt, but I've observed that a man with a weak stomach always goes a long way. *(He motions toward the trunk, and the negro boy picks it up)* By the way, boys, is there a good tavern round here?

ABE: Brown's Inn in Rockport is the best, I reckon. There's another just a mile down the road.

THE PILOT: Do your tavernkeepers still have both ears and their noses?

ABE: Far as I can recollect. Why?

THE PILOT: In a strange country, it is always wise to inquire. If a tavernkeeper's ears or his nose have been chewed off, it's a sign he can't take care of himself in a fight, and his place is not safe for a gentleman to drink in. *(He turns and starts off, motioning to his negro boy. Abe steps forward to lend the negro boy a hand with the trunk, but The Pilot restrains him, speaking sharply)* Don't spoil a good slave!

ABE: *(Protesting)* But he's just a young'un!

THE PILOT: He's still black, ain't he?

(Abe steps back reluctantly and watches the negro boy struggle offstage with the trunk, left. Just as the Pilot is about to disappear on the road, however, Abe is reminded of something and runs after him)

ABE: Hey, mister! You forgot something!

(The Pilot turns about, and Abe holds out his hand for his pay. The Pilot digs into his pockets)

THE PILOT: *(Smiling)* You'll get ahead, all right, Abe Lincoln. *(He hands Abe two coins and departs, left)*

ABE: Much obliged. *(He glances at the coins in his hand, is startled, and takes a second look)* Hokey day! *(Seeing Allen approaching to look at the money, Abe closes his hand over it quickly)*

ALLEN: How much did he give you?

ABE: Enough, I reckon. *(Hastily changing the subject, as he holds his clenched hand stiffly at his side)* Say, Allen, you reckon he will remember me?

ALLEN: Liker than not. *(Sidling round, he looks at Abe's closed hand inquisitively)* Was it two bits?

ABE: *(Ignoring the question)* Now, if I could just get down to New Orleans — *(Allen bends over to get a closer look into Abe's hand, but Abe ignores his curiosity. He looks dreamily across the river)* I've just got to get outen this country! I want to go on the river! *(He turns to Allen)* I'm gettin' in deeper and deeper up there at Little Pigeon. Ever since my sister Sally married Aaron Grigsby, there's been nothin' but trouble.

ALLEN: Well, look who started it!

ABE: Well, blame it, Allen, the Grigsbys all acted so high-and-mighty at the wedding, and did their best to spoil it for poor little Sally.

ALLEN: Even so, looks like you could have waited a day or so to pick a fight with 'em, 'stead of breakin' up the wedding party.

ABE: *(Angry)* No I couldn't. I wanted 'em to know what it was all about. I want everybody to know they can't treat the Lincolns that way. *(He moves toward the center of the stage, followed by Allen, who is still looking at his closed hand)* I am sorry about Natty, though. Natty Grigsby used to be one of my best friends, but now we ain't even on speakin' terms.

ALLEN: *(Without taking his eyes off Abe's hand)* I reckon Natty Grigsby ain't speakin' much to nobody these days, since you busted his jaw.

ABE: *(Abstractedly)* And the Grigsbys ain't the only ones. Josiah Crawford is down on me.

ALLEN: Well, why'd you want to go around callin' him Bluenose? His name was Josiah hereabouts, till you changed it to Bluenose. You can't expect him to love you for that.

ABE: Oh, it goes deeper than that. He's just like my pa, and everybody else. Thinks I'm lazy and shiftless an no 'count, cause I'd rather read than work. And there's Squire Carter — *(Ruefully)* Maybe they're right, at that. Anyway, nobody's got any use for me.

ALLEN: Well! Colonel Jones give you a job at his store.

ABE: Pshaw! The Colonel thinks more of dog-fightin' than he does of his store. I'm not cut out for clerkin' in Jones' store. And everybody that comes in to trade is my enemy, seems like.

ALLEN: I ain't your enemy, Abe.

ABE: *(Measuring him coolly)* I ain't so sure. You and me are after the same thing, and looks like you've got a good head start on me.

ALLEN: *(Not understanding)* Why, I'm your friend. I helped you get that pilot ashore, just now, didn't I? *(He waits a moment expectantly, turning his head to one side as he eyes Abe's closed hand again. Finally he gives up with a shrug)* Well, I ain't got time to stand around here till that money in your fist begins to draw interest. I got trading to do in the settlement.

(Abe, who seems not to hear Allen, remains motionless, gazing wistfully out across the river. Allen takes one last look at Abe's fist and then goes out, left. When he is safely gone, Abe opens his first slowly and cautiously looks down at the money)

ABE: A whole dollar! Two four-bit pieces! *(He begins to dance about awkwardly, singing in a high falsetto)*
The turbaned Turk
That scorns the world
And struts about
With his whiskers curled,
For no other man
But himself to see . . .

(He begins to juggle the two coins in the air, till finally one of them escapes him and disappears over the bank into the river. He runs to the edge of the bank and stands for a minute, looking down, scratching his head in frustration and dismay. Then he turns about, regarding the remaining coin in his hand disconsolately)
Easiest whole dollar I ever earned all at once, and I have to go and feed half of it to the catfish! *(He struggles for a moment to find a word that will express his disgust, but ends by saying flatly)*
Shucks!

(Putting the half-dollar in his pocket, he starts toward the edge of the bank again, but on his way his eye falls on the book in the crotch of the cottonwood. He pauses, looking at the book, and then takes it

down, as if he has remembered something he wants to read. Finding his place in the book, he begins to read standing up. As he becomes absorbed, he sinks gradually to the ground, without interrupting his reading. He is completely lost in the book by the time Anna Roby appears in the lane at the right. Anna is no longer the shy and elfin-like creature she was two years ago. Her mouth is set more firmly, even grimly at times, and her motions are slower, heavier, more mature. She approaches Abe, looks over his shoulder for a moment, glances round, goes to the edge of the bank and peers down at the water, and then looks up the road, left, shading her eyes with her hand. Coming back, she stands over Abe again. He remains absorbed in his reading and does not see her)

ANNA: Abe . . . *(He does not hear her)* Abe . . . ! *(Still he does not stir, and Anna approaches him and kicks the book out of his hands. Abe leaps belligerently to his feet, frowning and doubling up his fists; but when he sees who it is, he immediately melts with embarrassment and delight)*

ABE: Why, Anna Roby! Bless your heart! I didn't know you was anywhere around!

ANNA: That's always seemed to be your main trouble, Abe Linkern. You never seemed to know when a girl was around.

ABE: *(With awkward gallantry)* I generally did when it was you, Anna.

ANNA: *(Ignoring the compliment)* Have you seen Allen Gentry. I was to meet him in the settlement. I thought maybe he was down here.

ABE: *(Frowning)* Allen — ? Yes, he was here a minute or two ago. But he left . . . *(Eagerly)* How have you been Anna? I haven't seen you in a blue moon.

ANNA: *(With a toss of her head)* I've got along all right.

ABE: I don't get down this way much any more.

ANNA: *(Feigning surprise)* Don't you? I hadn't noticed. I thought I'd seen you places.

ABE: No, — I'm working at Colonel Jones' store in Gentryville, and I don't have much time off. *(Warmly)* But tell me about yourself, Anna. *(Laughing, with a trace of his old tenderness)* You got the moon and stars all figured out yet?

ANNA: *(Her mouth sets hard and she ignores the question)* You say Allen just now went into the settlement?

ABE: I don't recollect that I said where he went. *(With eagerness, trying to find a subject that will hold her interest)* Anna, there was a steamboat pilot here. I brung him ashore from the *General Pike* in my old scow down there. *(She shows no interest, but he continues)* That pilot is going to help me get on the river, Anna. At least, he says if I ever get down to New Orleans —

ANNA: *(Interrupting)* Allen Gentry was supposed to meet me a half hour ago.

664

ABE: *(Still talking about the pilot)* He took my name and promised to remember me. If I could only get a recommend, he'd take me on the river right now. *(Wistfully)* Remember how I always hankered to go on the river?

ANNA: *(Scornfully)* Oh, — the river! You still thinking about the river? That's all you ever think about!

ABE: *(Approaching her reverently)* Not exactly all I think about, Anna Roby. The river is only a means to an end.

ANNA: *(Evading him and picking up the book, she reads)* Lessons in Elocution . . . *(She drops the book carelessly)* What's elocution?

ABE: Oh, it's something politicians use when they ain't got nothing to say. *(He picks up the book, closes it, dusts it off carefully, and puts it in the crotch of the tree)* I just now borrowed that book off of Judge Pitcher in Rockport.

ANNA: *(Incredulously)* You mean you walked all the way from Gentry-ville to Rockport just for a book?

ABE: I hoped maybe I'd see you, too, Anna.

ANNA: *(Shaking her head in wonder)* Why, I know boys that wouldn't walk that far for a jug of ten-rod whisky!

ABE: *(Smiling and stepping toward her)* I'd walk a hundred miles to see you again.

ANNA: *(Evading him again)* You say Allen's coming back this-a-way?

ABE: I didn't say. *(Harshly)* But wherever that big lummox goes, I hope he takes his time!

ANNA: *(Angrily)* Well, don't get het up about it if he does, Abe Linkern. You'll be safe enough with me, I reckon!

ABE: *(Looking at her earnestly)* Anna, you've changed. You seem — I don't know — *(He steps toward her again, holding out his hand in an appeal)* Have you forgotten how we used to be — you and me?

ANNA: *(Rebuffing him)* Don't start that again!

ABE: *(Disconcerted, he is silent for a moment. Then his face brightens)* I heard in Rockport that Jim Taylor is a-throwing him a corn-shucking party tonight. Would you go with me, Anna? It would be like old times.

ANNA: No; I can't go with you.

ABE: Because you're going with Allen Gentry, I suppose.

ANNA: It's none of your business.

ABE: I could put Allen out of commission, if that would help.

ANNA: You leave Allen Gentry out of this.

ABE: Oh, I wouldn't do him no real harm. Just damage him up a little, so's he wouldn't be much interested in shucking corn tonight.

ANNA: I don't reckon you're man enough, Abe. *(Romantically)* Allen is strong.

ABE: *(Contemptuously)* Him! *(He changes the subject, not altogether without guile)* I forgot to tell you. That river-pilot gave me a whole dollar for bringing him ashore.

ANNA: *(Seeing through his intention)* You don't say?

ABE: A whole dollar . . . *(He speaks earnestly)* Anna, if you'll go to the corn-shucking with me, I promise I won't stay outside all night and spin yarns. I'll come inside to the play-party. I'll even dance.
(She stands off looking at him with a mocking smile. He hesitates, studying her, then continues)
I'll spend some of that dollar, too. I was going to get my sister a wedding-present. She's married to Aaron Grigsby now, you know. But I'll spend the money on you, instead.

ANNA: *(Bursting into cruel laughter)* Why, Abe Linkern, that's probably the best compliment you ever paid a girl! Everybody knows you ain't got much of the selfishness for the *git*, but you sure got a heap for the *keep*. *(She stops laughing abruptly, and her voice becomes hard)* But don't think you can buy now what you was never able to get for free.

ABE: *(Shocked by her crudeness)* Oh, Anna . . . !

ANNA: *(Advancing upon him, eyes narrowed)* By the way, let me see that dollar.
(Abe draws back, still shocked by her manner)
Let me see it.

ABE: *(Embarrassed, retreating)* Well, I . . .

ANNA: *(Abandoning her pursuit and looking at him victoriously)* That pilot never gave you a dollar, Abe Linkern. I knew it all along. You was too happy over the prospect of spending it on me.

ABE: Oh yes, he did.

ANNA: *(Imperiously)* Then let me see it.

ABE: *(Stammering)* Well, you see . . .

ANNA: No, I don't see. I don't see a thing.

ABE: I mean, I ain't exactly got it all here with me, Anna. All I've got is half of it. *(He pulls out the half-dollar. Anna takes it, examines it, and hands it back)*

ANNA: Where's the other half?

ABE: Well, it was like this . . . I . . . *(He hesitates, while Anna fixes relentless eyes on him, then he breaks into a broad grin)* I throwed it in the river.

ANNA: You did *what?*

ABE: *(His eyes twinkling with merriment, his grin broadening)* Throwed it in the river.

666

ANNA: I don't believe you did no such thing.

ABE: *(Letting his imagination take over)* Yep . . . After the pilot paid me, I got to thinking, "Why, that trip wasn't worth a whole dollar, Abe Lincoln!" I said to myself. So I throwed half of it into the river.

ANNA: *(Melting for a moment as she sees that he is teasing her)* Oh, Abe! You're terrible!

ABE: *(Earnestly now, overcome with emotion as he recognizes something of her old manner in her attitude and voice)* No, I really did have a dollar, Anna. Only, I got to sky-larking around and juggling it and half of it flew outen my hand into the river. *(He smiles at her tenderly)* And if you should ask me to, Anna Roby, I'd jump in the right right now and dig for that half-dollar till I'd muddied the water from here to Evansville, just to show you.

ANNA: *(Resuming her indifference, stepping round him and looking off up the road, left, she speaks absently)* You needn't trouble. Which way did Allen go?

ABE: *(He takes Anna unexpectedly by the shoulders and swings her about)* Look at me! *(He shakes her roughly)* You!

ANNA: *(Icily)* Let me go.

ABE: *(Fiercely)* You don't belong to Allen Gentry. You belong to me.

ANNA: *(The ice still in her voice)* Let me go.

ABE: *(Appealing)* I've tried and I've tried these last two years, but I can't get you outen my mind. I've told myself I was a gone coon. I don't have anything to offer you. I can't marry till I'm twenty-one. I've tried to leave you be — stay away from you — and now I see you again, and I go all slack-twisted inside.

ANNA: *(Meeting his eyes steadily and coldly)* Let me go, Abe.

ABE: *(His fierceness returning)* I love you, Anna Roby! *(He kisses her. She does not struggle but only remains wooden and cold in his arms)* Can you understand that? I've always loved you!

ANNA: *(Shaking her head slowly)* Let me go.

ABE: *(No longer dominating, or trying to, his voice breaking)* Oh, Anna. . . *(Murmuring lines from a poem)* Grace was in all her steps, heaven in her eye, In every gesture dignity and love . . . *(As he recites, Anna begins to struggle, but he holds her firmly)* Two years ago, you liked to hear me recite those words. Do you remember, Anna?

ANNA: *(Still struggling, she sobs)* Let me go! Let me go!

ABE: *(With a note of defeat)* I love you, Anna.

ANNA: *(She suddenly ceases struggling and with an effort gets control of herself and looks at him coldly again)* I'm going to marry Allen Gentry. We're promised.

ABE: *(Still holding her, shaking his head, unbelieving)* No, Anna . . . I won't let you.

667

ANNA: You! (*Her eyes widen in scorn and her fury rises, frozen and cruel. She pauses, trying to find the thing that will hurt him most*)

You're too ugly to love, Abe Linkern! You're the ugliest boy I've ever seen. You're too ugly even for hating.

(*Abe releases her. They stand facing each other, Abe with his arms limp at his sides, Anna horrified now at what she has just said. Abe closes his eyes against the pain that her words have caused him. His face is white and drawn. While they are standing thus, Allen Gentry reappears in the road, entering left. Seeing him, Anna hesitates at first, then runs to him. Abe, opening his eyes, remains where he is, looking at them dully*) Allen! (*Anna throws her arms about Allen's neck, sobbing, and Allen looks first at her and then at Abe. Finally, he takes Anna's arms down from his neck and approaches Abe, his fists clenched*)

ALLEN: (*To Abe*) I reckon I got to lick you for messing around with my girl.

ABE: (*Making no move to protect himself, he answers Allen wearily*) No, you don't. You don't have to do nothing. I'll never bother her again.

ALLEN: (*Obviously relieved that there is no need to fight Abe*) Well, you better not let me catch you ever trying to. (*As he turns away, Anna circles round and looks at him, appalled*)

ANNA: You ain't afraid of him, are you, Allen?

ALLEN: Hell, no! (*He swings suddenly at Abe, who, without raising his hands or moving his feet, dodges expertly so that the blow only glances off his shoulder*)

ABE: (*Quietly, with his arms still at his sides*) I wouldn't do that again, if I was you.

ANNA: He kissed me Allen. Abe kissed me. (*Allen swings again, and this time, Abe catches his arm, turns him about and in an instant has him doubled over with a hammerlock*)

ABE: (*To Allen, keeping him helpless with the hammerlock*) I warned you. (*Allen struggles, but Abe holds him. Abe speaks quietly*) Now, listen to me. Anna is your girl, and I did kiss her, against her will. It's true what she says. But . . . (*He pauses*) I only thought maybe . . . I kind of hoped . . . I . . . (*Desperately*) Oh, hell! (*He releases Allen, and gently pushes him away*) Go away . . . both of you. . .

(*Allen pretends still to be ready to fight, but Abe turns his back on him, ignoring his attitude, absorbed in his own thoughts*)

ALLEN: Come on, Anna. Let him stay here and rot.

(*They clasp hands and start away together. Anna turns and looks back once, seeming to hesitate, but Abe has his back turned and she goes on. Abe walks slowly over to the cottonwood and takes down his book. He looks at it a moment. Then he throws it viciously into the river*)

Too ugly. . . !

(*Standing under the cottonwood, his figure sagging with defeat and despondency, he looks out across the river*)

Too ugly. . . !

CURTAIN

668

ACT THREE

Scene One

The Lincoln cabin. A day in late autumn, 1828, a year later.

When the curtain rises, Mrs. Lincoln and Judge Pitcher are in the room. Judge Pitcher is seated on a chair near the door, holding his tall hat on his knee. He is wearing a black tailcoat and dark gray trousers, tucked into his boots. Mrs. Lincoln, facing him, is seated on one of the benches by the long puncheon table. She is knitting. On the table are several books and a roll of newspapers.

MRS. LINCOLN: It was right good of you to come so far outen your way, Judge Pitcher. Little Pigeon Creek is quite a ways off the road from Rockport to Boonville.

JUDGE PITCHER: Glad to oblige, Mrs. Lincoln. Anyhow, it gave me an opportunity to bring along that reading matter I've been saving for Abe. *(He gestures toward the books and newspapers)* I've been worried about Abe. He hasn't been down to Rockport to see me in a long time.

MRS. LINCOLN: *(Gravely)* I'm worried about Abe, too. That's why I was so bold as to ask you to come by up here, Judge.

JUDGE PITCHER: Abe isn't sick, is he, ma'am?

MRS. LINCOLN: He's worse than sick. For a year or more — ever since Anna Roby married Allen Gentry — Abe has had the devil inside him. And then Abe's sister died about the same time. *(She hesitates, re-arranges her skirts, and continues without looking directly at him)* You've heard about Abe's troubles with Sally's in-laws, I reckon.

JUDGE PITCHER: You refer to "The Chronicles of Reuben"? *(Mrs. Lincoln nods)* I reckon everybody in Spencer County has heard about "The Chronicles of Reuben". Understand it made quite a laughing-stock of the Grigsbys.

MRS. LINCOLN: Oh Judge, it was terrible! As hoity-toity as the Grigsbys are, I don't see how Abe could have brought himself to poke fun at their weddings.

JUDGE PITCHER: At their weddings?

MRS. LINCOLN: Oh yes, that's what it was all about — the Grigsby boys' double-wedding last spring. Ain't you read it?

JUDGE PITCHER: No ma'am. I only heard about it.

MRS. LINCOLN: Oh, mercy stakes, here 'tis. Read it.

JUDGE PITCHER: *(Reading)* It came to pass, when the sons of Reuben grew up, they were desirous of taking to themselves wives, and being too well known in their own country, they took a journey into a far country and there procured for themselves wives ... *(He laughs. While he has been reading, Dennis Hanks appears in the doorway, joining the Judge in repeating the last few words from memory. He laughs boisterously)*

DENNIS: That "far country" wasn't any further away than Anderson's Creek, where the girls came from. But the best part is about the welcome they got when they come home. *(He quotes)* "Some were playing on harps, and some on viols, and some blowing on rams' horns. And chief among them was Josiah, blowing his bugle, and making a sound so great the neighboring hills and valleys echoed" . . . *(Laughs uproariously, slapping his thigh)* Ain't that a good one! That's Josiah Crawford, of course, blowing his big blue nose.

(In spite of himself, the Judge chuckles)

MRS. LINCOLN: Denny, I thought you and Elizabeth was goin' to take the children and go down to the mill for the day, along with Squire and Matilda.

DENNY: *(Speaking over his shoulder as he goes to the gun-rack)* We are, Mamma. Just come back to get my rifle, in case we see some rabbits. *(Taking his gun, nods to the Judge as he heads for the door)* Good to see you, Judge. *(Reciting with chuckles as he goes out)* "Took a journey into a far country, and there procured for themselves wives" . . .

JUDGE PITCHER: Mrs. Lincoln, who all is living in this cabin?

MRS. LINCOLN: Why, besides me and Mr. Lincoln, there's Elizabeth and Denny and their four young'uns. And there there's Abe, and my John. And Squire Hanks and my Matilda have taken over the loft, and they're expectin' before Christmas.

JUDGE PITCHER: That will make thirteen in the cabin then, won't it?

MRS. LINCOLN: Fourteen. There's thirteen now, countin' Uncle John Hanks. It's hard to get them all outen the cabin at once. Today is one of them rare times.

JUDGE PITCHER: I reckon that's another thing wrong with Abe, Ma'am. It must be hard for him to study, with so many folks around.

MRS. LINCOLN: Oh, Abe don't study at all no more. But the crowdin' in this cabin don't keep him from writing them poems. He writ another one about the Grigsbys.

JUDGE PITCHER: He's really got it in for the Grigsbys, hasn't he? I suppose the whole trouble goes back to his sister's marriage to Aaron Grigsby.

MRS. LINCOLN: That's right. He picked a fight with 'em that very day. *(She chuckles)* He writ a poem about that day, too. He sure is the writin'est, fightin'est boy!

JUDGE PITCHER: But it was really through no fault of Aaron Grigsby that little Sally died last January, was it?

MRS. LINCOLN: No, sir. It wasn't Aaron's fault. Grigsbys haven't no more power over the ways of the Lord than anybody else. No — Aaron Grigsby done everything he could for poor little Sally when her time come. But Judge, right about the same time, Allen Gentry he married a girl Abe had had a claim on, named Anna Roby —

JUDGE PITCHER: *(Light begins to dawn)* Ah-h-h-!

MRS. LINCOLN: And Abe ain't been fit to live with ever since. He picks a fight with anybody, over nothin', at the drop of a hat, till he's got the reputation of a regular rounder. And he's so bitter about everything. *(Suddenly grave and wistful)* Abe is changed — changed.

JUDGE PITCHER: I suppose I have some responsibility in the matter of Anna Roby. I made Abe promise me once that he wouldn't marry till he was twenty-one.

MRS. LINCOLN: Abe told me about that. But, shucks, Judge, the boy wouldn't have got up enough fire to ask the gal even if you hadn't made him promise. He ain't exactly what you'd call a lady-killer. *(She smiles, and then adds loyally)* Still and all, you got to feel right sorry for him.

JUDGE PITCHER: *(Emphatically)* Oh, I do, Mrs. Lincoln! I do indeed! *(Musing)* It's a funny thing about Abe Lincoln. He can be his own worst enemy at times, and yet there's something about him that makes you want to push him ahead in spite of himself. He's a most remarkable boy.

MRS. LINCOLN: *(With emotion)* He's the best-behaved boy I ever knowed — most of the time. *(At this moment, Abe Lincoln appears in the doorway. When Mrs. Lincoln sees him, she is embarrassed at being found thus in conversation with Judge Pitcher)* Abe — ! Why, Abe, I thought you was over in Gentryville, at John Romine's.

ABE: I was. *(A half-amused, half-bitter smile plays over his mouth as he steps over the sill. He seems to be in a good mood, though cynical. He stands just inside the door looking at them in silence. Mrs. Lincoln grows more fidgety)*

MRS. LINCOLN: I thought Colonel Jones let you off for the whole day so's you could work there, at John's.

ABE: He did.

MRS. LINCOLN: *(Very nervous)* Judge Pitcher is here.

ABE: I see.

MRS. LINCOLN: He brung some books and papers for you. *(She points at the books and papers on the table. Abe looks at them, but says nothing)* Ain't you going to say much obliged, son?

ABE: Beware of Greeks bearing gifts. *(Mrs. Lincoln looks puzzled, but Judge Pitcher laughs)*

JUDGE PITCHER: It's not the Greeks, Abe. It's the Mountain coming to Mahomet. I was on my way up to Boonville, and I stopped by.

ABE: *(With a wry smile)* Well, the Mountain has found the Prophet without honor in his own country. *(He moves into the cabin at last, and reveals a large tear in his shirt)*

MRS. LINCOLN: Abe! You been a-fightin' again!

ABE: Not this time, Mamma. I'm real sorry I tore my shirt, though, after you mended it so nice.

671

MRS. LINCOLN: How'd it happen?

ABE: For once it was in the cause of peace.

MRS. LINCOLN: Abe Linkern, I've heard every excuse in Kingdom come for fightin' — but this is the first time I ever heard of fightin' in the cause of peace.

ABE: Honest, Mamma, I haven't been fightin'!. I broke up a fight.

JUDGE PITCHER: What happened, Abe?

ABE: I was comin' home from Gentryville, and just as I got to the Cartwright place, there come Mr. Ogg a-struttin' out of the hen-yard, mad as a hornet, carryin' an old gray goose under his arm. He was shoutin' all holler, and claimin' Cartwright had stole the goose from him. Cartwright was chasin' after him with a pitchfork, and callin' him a goose-thief. Time I drew up even with 'em, Ogg had let the goose go, and Cartwright had throwed down his pitchfork, and both men were squared away with their fists up, ready to light into each other. I separated 'em, that's all. The goose got away over the fence, and I marched Ogg home. Both men are still hoppin' mad about it, and Ogg says he'll have Cartwright's hide yet — but leastways I spoiled their fight for today.

MRS. LINCOLN: Well! I'm glad you put your strength to some good use, for once. I was beginnin' to think folks was right, you were nothin' but a trouble-maker.

ABE: Is that what you and the Judge were holdin' a committee meetin' about?

JUDGE PITCHER: Committee meeting? *(Protesting, with feigned innocence)* Why, your mother and I —

ABE: *(Laughing at him)* I haven't lived with Mamma most of my life for nothing. She wouldn't be wastin' her time in broad daylight passing the time of day even with you, unless it was on account of me ,or some other member of the family. I reckon it's about me. And you're not the only ones. You and Mamma are the second committee that's caught up with me today.

JUDGE PITCHER: All right. You've guessed it. We *were* talking about you. But before we say any more, maybe you'd better tell us about the other committee that caught up with you today.

ABE: That's exactly what I was aiming to travel down to Rockport to talk to you about. That's why I quit early at John Rowine's. *(Thoughtfully)* Seems like the whole of Spencer County is out today either to reform me or to get shet of me.

JUDGE PITCHER: I don't follow you.

ABE: Well, Colonel Jones did. Him and Jim Gentry and poor old Peter Brooner. Even old Bluenose Crawford. They followed me clean over to John Romine's place.

MRS. LINCOLN: *(Frightened)* Abe, they wasn't a posse of regulators, was they?

ABE: No, Mamma. These fellers didn't come to *get* me. They come to get *rid* of me. *(Turning to Judge Pitcher)* They told me they were a committee, Judge, and they'd had a meeting to discuss the troublesome case of one Abraham Lincoln, and you'll never guess what their verdict was.

MRS. LINCOLN: *(Frightened by the word)* Verdict — ?

ABE: *(Nodding)* Verdict. *(To Judge Pitcher)* It wasn't no hung, jury, neither. They decided unanimously to send me down to New Orlenas on a flatboat — *(He pauses for emphasis)* — with Allen Gentry.

JUDGE PITCHER: *(Coolly)* So you get to go to New Orleans, after all.

ABE: I said, *with Allen Gentry.*

JUDGE PITCHER: *(Undisturbed)* I heard you. When?

ABE: *(Somewhat disconcerted by his reaction)* Why, soon, I reckon. If we're going, it ought to be while there's good freshes in the river. But Allen says he won't leave till — *(His voice drops)* — till his wife has her baby.

JUDGE PITCHER: *(Still matter-of-fact)* That will be in December, I understand.

ABE: *(After looking at him quizzically for some time)* Now, why do you reckon Allen Gentry's pa wants me to go on this journey to New Orleans with him?

JUDGE PITCHER: Why, to man the gouger or the stern-sweep, I suppose.

ABE: *(Stepping closer to Judge Pitcher)* Surely you remember about me Allen Gentry's wife.

JUDGE PITCHER: *(Quietly)* You were sweet on Anna Roby at one time, I believe.

ABE: Well — ?

JUDGE PITCHER: Well — ?

ABE: Well, if Jim Gentry wants me to go to New Orleans on a flatboat with Allen, I'd say he was a durn fool.

JUDGE PITCHER: I wouldn't.

ABE: *(Amazed)* Then what would you say?

JUDGE PITCHER: *(Deliberately)* I'd say he was a smart man. It takes a thief to catch a thief. Maybe Allen Gentry's pa figures it takes a jilted lover to watch a traveling husband.

ABE: *(Taken aback)* You don't think Allen would — ?

JUDGE PITCHER: *(Raising a hand to silence him)* I don't think anything. Allen is a good, clean young man, like yourself. But New Orleans is a gay and fancy town and a long way from home, and Allen Gentry is a young man. *(He pauses, considering his next words)* I only know that if a son of mine was going to New Orleans, married or unmarried, there's nobody I'd rather have go along with him than Abe Lincoln.

ABE: *(Wryly)* I reckon you don't know me, Judge.

JUDGE. PITCHER: Oh, yes, I do! I've known you a long time. I've watched you grow up round here. *(He smiles)* You can be as ornery as they come, Abe Lincoln; but, most of the time, there's not another young man round this neck of the woods that can hold a candle to you for good common sense and good morals. *(He looks at Abe earnestly)* As I have just now been saying to your mother here, the only trouble with you is that you are your own worst enemy.

MRS. LINCOLN: That's true, Abe.

ABE: *(Sharply, to them both)* Now, don't go preaching at me!

JUDGE PITCHER: No one is preaching.

ABE: *(Heatedly)* Yes, you are! Everybody's preaching at me these days, trying to make me do this and make me do that. Look at Mamma — always telling me to love my enemies —

JUDGE PITCHER: *(Quietly)* What enemies, Abe?

ABE: *(At loss for a reply)* Why — why — everybody!

JUDGE PITCHER: *(Softly)* By enemies, do you mean a committee of the best men around Gentryville, who dropped their work just to have a meeting to see if they could help you? Do you mean Josiah Crawford, who served on that committee in spite of the fact that he has no cause to feel kindly toward you? *(He chuckles)* It must have hurt Josiah Crawford more than anybody else to give up a half-day's work on your account. He'll be asking you to pull fodder again to make the lost time good, the way he did when you ruined his book.

ABE: *(Sullenly)* I mean everybody. Even my own pa.

MRS. LINCOLN: Why, Abe, your Pa loves you!

ABE: *(Laughing bitterly)* He sure has a funny way of showing it.

MRS. LINCOLN: He loves you, Abe. He just don't understand you proper, is all. And, I must say, you don't do much to help him. I declare, you go out of your way to keep him from figuring you out, Abe Linkern!

JUDGE PITCHER: Everybody in Spencer County is your friend, Abe. You'd be surprised how many friends you have around here, how many people talk about you and wish you well.

ABE: *(Bitterly)* Meaning the Grigsbys, too, I suppose.

MRS. LINCOLN: *(Sniffing)* Well, of course, the Grigsbys is different. You've gone out of your way to offend them.

JUDGE PITCHER: *(Firmly)* Meaning the Grigsbys, too. Did you ever try to meet the Grigsbys halfway?

ABE: *(Contritely)* Oh, I know I've got friends. You, for one, have been mighty good to me, lending me books and all — and so have a heap of others, I reckon. Only — *(He clenches his fists)* — only, I'm sick and

674

tired of this backwoods country! I'm fed up with hoeing and mauling rails. I got to get away. I want to go on the river, where there ain't no Pa a-hounding me to do this and do that, where there ain't no Oggs and Cartwrights fighting over a silly goose — or uppity folks like the Grigsbys — or women and weddings — or *(His voice drops)* — or child-bearing, or milk-sick.

JUDGE PITCHER: *(Soothingly)* If you want to go on the river so bad, then maybe it would do you good to go away with Allen Gentry for a little while.

ABE: For a little while — ? *(He looks toward the door. Then he looks back at Judge Pitcher. There is a sudden resolution in his manner)* All right! I'll go! If Jim Gentry wants to take a chance on me a-slinging that son of his into the river, why, — I'll go! *(Grimly)* Only, it won't be for just a little while. I'll never come back! *(He goes out. Mrs. Lincoln rises in great alarm)*

MRS. LINCOLN: *(Calling after him, she steps out over the high sill, but remains visible)* Abe — !
(She re-enters the room and sits down disconsolately. Judge Pitcher is moved by her grief, but he makes no move to recall Abe. In a moment or two, Abe reappears in the doorway and tiptoes up behind Mrs. Lincoln. He leans over and kisses the top of her head)

MRS: LINCOLN: *(Turning about)* Abe.

ABE: I ain't gone yet, Mamma. I've got to wait for Anna and Allen's baby.
(Mrs. Lincoln turns and clutches at him, but he eludes her and goes out again)

CURTAIN

675

ACT THREE

Scene Two

The Lincoln cabin. A spring evening, 1829, several months later. Tom Lincoln and Jim Gentry are seated by the fireplace. Dennis Hanks stands at the doorway. Tom is gnawing artistically, round and round, at a raw turnip, examining the design left by his toothmarks after each bite. Jim Gentry is whittling with great concentration. A short, square-built man of fifty, Allen Gentry's father is a simple, unread man, but he has a shrewd intelligence that has made him the richest man in Spencer County. Dennis, smoking a corncob pipe, peers out the door at the moonlit night, apparently watching for someone. A pile of knitting is on top of the bureau. Tom swallows a large bite of turnip before he speaks.

TOM: Cousin John tells me you can plant fifty to a hundreds acres the first year, in that Illinois country across the Wabash.

JIM: *(Glancing up from his whittling and giving Tom a sharp look)* I reckon you can, most likely — if you're willin' to undertake the labor.

TOM: *(Speaking with his mouth full, after another bite of turnip)* Oh, the labor ain't nothin', compared to what we got here, Cousin John tells me.

JIM: I got a cousin over in that Illinois country, too.

TOM: *(Eagerly)* He like it over there, Jim?

JIM: *(Shakes his head and spits into the fire)* Says the soil over that-a-way is too dang rich. Says, take your wheat and oats, for instance — *(Spits again)* — says they grow so tall they break off of their own weight, and rot on the ground afore you can harvest 'em.

TOM: *(Taking another bite of turnip)* Well, I ain't makin' no headway here, choppin' down trees, and snakin' the big butts away, and grubbin' out the roots and sprouts — and nobody to depend on but that no 'count, worthless, book-readin' son of mine.

JIM: Ain't nothin' wrong with your Abe, Tom. Just likes book-readin' better than splittin' rails. Maybe I would too, if I knew how to read.

TOM: *(Contemptuously)* Shucks! What do the likes of need with book-readin'? If that boy don't come back from New Orleans, I'm a-going to give him a larruping!

DENNIS: *(With a taunting laugh)* How you a-going to do that, Tom, if he ain't here?

JIM: Abe'll be here, on the *Pride of Indiana*.

TOM: *The Pride* was due at Evansville yesterday. If he'd been on it, he'd 'a been here by now.

JIM: Boats don't always come on schedule, you know.

TOM: Anyway, he'd ought to a come on the fast boat, like Allen did. Allen got home a week ago.

JIM: Well, Allen had him a wife and baby to come home to. Reckon Abe figgered there warn't any call for him to hurry.

676

TOM: *(Threateningly)* If he got him a job on the river —

JIM: He couldn't do that. He's not twenty-one yet.

TOM: He's big enough to pass for twenty-one. All he'd have to do would be to lie about his age.

JIM: *(Pointedly)* Tom, your Abe is as full of meanness as any other healthy young man, but I'll say one thing for him. Abe Linkern don't lie.

DENNIS: *(Peering out the door)* Here comes old Bluenose Crawford up the horse path. Evenin' Josiah.
(Josiah Crawford appears at the door)

JOSIAH: Evenin', Dennis. Howdy, folks.

TOM: Come in, come in, Josiah, and set a spell.

JOSIAH: Ain't you all a-goin' to the law trial?

JIM: Are we? You don't think we'd miss it, do you?

TOM: We're just a-waitin' for Judge Pitcher. Ain't no use a-trailin' over to the meetin' house before the Judge gets here.

JOSIAH: Well, the crowd's a-gatherin'. Looks like the meetin house is goin' to be mighty crowded.

TOM: There ain't many folks goin' to miss this trial.

JOSIAH: You know what I just heard? The Cartwrights have got seven sure witnesses to swear that goose is theirs.

JIM: The deuce they have!

JOSIAH: That's what they tell me.

JIM: They must be seven geese, then. Ain't seven humans could tell one goose from another.

TOM: Well, I hear the Oggs ain't worryin' about witnesses. They claim that goose has got a mark on it the Oggs can tell it by. Nobody knows about the mark but Oggs.

DENNIS: *(Excited)* Here comes the Judge down the road, Tom!

TOM: Ask him in Denny. He'll want to stretch his legs.

JOSIAH: His horse'll need tendin', too, I reckon.

DENNIS: I'll look after it.
(Colonel Jones appears in the doorway)
Evenin', Colonel. Here's Colonel Jones.
(Dennis goes out as Colonel James comes in. He is a slim and somewhat dandified man of middle age, dressed more stylishly than the others. He wears a tailcoat and ruffled shirt and tight-fitting trousers. His manner is that of a man who has seen something of the world, and his speech is more cultivated than the others)

COLONEL JONES: Howdy, Tom, I closed the store up early tonight, to get over here in time for the trial.

TOM: Have a seat, Colonel. The Judge is just comin' now. We'll all go over to the meetin' house with him.

COLONEL JONES: Evening, Josiah . . . Jim.

TOM: *(On his way to the door)* Save that place by the table for the Judge. *(Steps outside the cabin to greet the Judge)*

JIM: Set here, Colonel. Reckon we won't be leavin' for a little while. *(Colonel Jones sits on a three-legged stool near the fire, and cuts a slice of chewing tobacco)*

JOSIAH: Well, Colonel, not keeping the store open tonight?

COLONEL JONES: No use. All my customers have come over here to this trial.

TOM: *(At the door, ushering the Judge in)* Come in, Judge Pitcher. We been a-watchin' for you.
(Judge Pitcher enters, carrying his portfolio, followed by Tom)
Denny'll see after your horse. Mrs. Lincoln thought you might need a little refreshment, after your trip. Make yourself comfortable. -*(Calls out the door)* Denny, bring in that jug of cider!

JUDGE PITCHER: Good evening, gentlemen. *(He puts his portfolio on the table, bows to the company, goes to stand before the fire. The men greet him in their various ways, reflecting the respect they have for him)*

JOSIAH: *(Formally)* Howdy, Judge Pitcher.

JIM: *(Whittling put away)* Evenin', Judge.

COLONEL JONES: *(Shaking hands with him)* Always a pleasure to see you, Judge.
(Denny brings in the cider, and he and Tom busy themselves dipping it into gourds and passing it around)

JUDGE PITCHER: Thank you, Colonel. Haven't seen you over my way for some time.

COLONEL JONES: No. Been tied down at the store since I lost my clerk. Thank you, Denny.

JUDGE PITCHER: Oh, yes. Abe Lincoln was clerking for you, wasn't he? Any news from Abe, Tom?

TOM: *(Glumly)* Only what I hear from Allen's pa. All that book-learing learned him was to write poems, I reckon. Have some cider.

JUDGE PITCHER: Thanks.

TOM: The boy said he warn't never coming back to Indiana, and I'm beginning to think he meant it. *(His voice sharpens)* But I'll tell you this. If he ain't back in time for the spring plowin', I'm a-goin' to get the law on him. He ain't twenty-one yet — only twenty — and he owes me another year of work.

JUDGE PITCHER: *(Smiling reminiscently)* Only nine-and-a-half months, Mr. Lincoln. Only two hundred and seventy-odd days.

(Tom gives him a puzzled look)

COLONEL JONES: I'll be glad to have Abe back. I miss him over at the store.

DENNIS: Don't know why. He sure never done much work over there, Colonel. All he ever did was lay on the counter with his long legs crossed in the air, like a danged well-sweep.

COLONEL JONES: *(Laughing)* That's the truth. I don't know as I ever had a clerk who took up as much room on a counter as Abe Lincoln.

DENNIS: Yes, sir. One time I went into your place to trade, and Abe like to kilt hisself gettin' out of waitin' on me. I never heard such snorin' and carryin' on in my life, the way he did, makin' out he was asleep, so's I'd go away and leave him be. I was scared he'd bust his bellows.

COLONEL JONES: *(Chuckling and speaking with affectionate remembrance)* You should have been more careful, Denny Hanks. You had no right to barge into a store like that where Abe Lincoln was trying to get his rest.

DENNIS: *(Laughing)* Oh, I high-tailed it right out again. Only — you know what he done, Colonel? Just as I was a-going' out, on tippy-toe like, Abe he riz up from that counter on one elbow and says, "Would you mind shettin' the door tight, Denny? If you don't, it'll blow open again, and I'll have to get up and shet it myself."

(All laugh except Tom and Josiah)

TOM: *(Spitting)* Ain't worth shucks.

JOSIAH: *(Looking dour at the thought of Abe's laziness)* Abe never loved his work, but he dearly loved his pay.

JIM: *(Slyly, looking at Josiah)* With some folks, he found his pay pretty hard to get, I reckon.

JUDGE PITCHER: Are both sides ready for the trial, Mr. Lincoln?

TOM: I reckon so. Though I hear the Cartwrights is right smartly worried. They tried to get Denny here to be a witness for 'em.

JIM: The deuce they did!

JUDGE PITCHER: What did they want him to testify to?

DENNIS: That's just it, Judge. One old gray goose looks just like another. How can I swear that's the goose I saw in Mrs. Cartwright's kitchen, time it got sick?

JIM: Who said it was sick? More like they was hidin' it there, where the Oggs couldn't find it.

JOSIAH: Jim Gentry, you take that back!

JIM: Take it back? Josiah Crawford, do you mean to stand there and claim that goose belongs to the Cartwrights?

JOSIAH: Everybody in Spencer County knows that goose belongs to the Cartwrights. Ogg stole that goose. He's a thief, and ought to be hung. *(All lean forward expectantly, watching Jim and Josiah. While their attention is thus concentrated, Abe Lincoln appears in the doorway, unnoticed, and stands there listening. When the men finally see Abe, they will get a shock, for he no longer wears backwoods clothes. He has on a dusty black tailcoat, a waistcoat, and tight black trousers — and most remarkable of all, a tall black hat)*

JIM: *(Half-rising to his feet, trembling)* Now you looky here, Josiah Crawford.

JOSIAH: *(Standing his ground)* I said Ogg stole that goose.

JIM: *(Clenching his fists)* I ought to make you swaller them words.

JOSIAH: You and who else?

JIM: Callin' a fine man like Mr. Ogg a goose-thief! *(As he finally rises to his full height, he knocks over the stool on which he has been sitting. Judge Pitcher starts toward them, in an effort to separate them)*

JUDGE PITCHER: Gentlemen! Gentlemen!

(At this point, Dennis finally spies Abe in the doorway, and cries out in surprise)

DENNIS: Great day in the morning!

(All turn and look at Abe, who grins back at them)

TOM: My God, what a get-up!

COLONEL JONES: *(Admiringly)* Store clothes!

TOM: And bought with my money, too!

ABE: *(Cheerfully)* Yep. Thought it was safer to spend it first, and ask you afterward. Hello, Pa.

COLONEL JONES: Abraham Lincoln! You look like a river-pilot — almost. *(He wags his head in delight)*
(Tom, after surveying him disgustedly, turns to the fireplace and spits)

JUDGE PITCHER: *(Stepping forward and shaking Abe's hand warmly)* Welcome home, Abe. Welcome back to Spencer County.

ABE: Howdy, Judge. *(Shaking Colonel Jones' hand)* Colonel Jones. How are things over at the store?

COLONEL JONES: I've missed you, boy.

ABE: *(Friendly)* Josiah.

JOSIAH: *(Shortly)* Howdy.

ABE: Well, Mr. Gentry. Reckon Allen got home safe.

JIM: Last week. We been expectin' you ever since.

ABE: *(Poking Dennis in the ribs)* And Cousin Denny. How's Elizabeth and the young 'uns?

680

DENNIS: Tol'able, Abe. 'Cept for the baby. He's got the janders.

ABE: Where's Mamma?

DENNIS: She ain't home yet from Peter Brooner's.

ABE: Peter Brooner got the shakes again? *(Not waiting for an answer, he addresses no one in particular, humorously, but with a note of sadness in his voice too, for his father has not welcomed him)* I see the neighborhood is still feudin' over that old gray goose of the Oggs and the Cartwrights. I kind of hoped that old goose would have died by now.

JUDGE PITCHER: Far from it. They've gone to law about it. The case is to be tried tonight.

ABE: You don't say! And you are aimin' to fight about it?

TOM: *(Without turning around)* You keep outen this.

ABE: *(Looks at his father's back, smiling wryly)* I aim to, Pa. But if Mr. Gentry and Josiah ever get goin', they're sure going to play hob with Mamma's furniture.

TOM: That's no business of yours.

ABE: *(With a shrug, he first sits on the table, then stretches out on it, with his hands folded under his head, the tall hat cocked over his eyes)* All right, Pa. Let 'em go ahead. *(He crosses his legs and swings one of them in the air)* I'm plumb tuckered out. I walked all the way from Evansville today.

DENNIS: *(Winking at Colonel Jones, and nodding toward Abe)* See what I told you?

COLONEL JONES: *(Amused)* Just like old times. *(To Abe)* Tell us about New Orleans, Abe. Did you go to the Big Bone Museum?

DENNIS: What were the women like, Abe? Did you get a job on the river, like you said you would?
(At this point, Jim raises his bent elbow and gives a false lunge at Josiah, and Josiah almost falls over the stool. He glares at Jim menacingly)

JOSIAH: Now you look-a-here, Jim Gentry!

ABE: *(Rising on one elbow and pushing his hat back on his head)* Mamma ain't going to like this.

DENNIS: *(At the door)* Here comes somebody.
(Allen Gentry appears at the door. He does not see Abe at first, and addresses Judge Pitcher)
Howdy, Judge. The whole crowd's a-comin', to take you over to the meetin' house. Are you ready for the — Abe! You old son of a gun!
(Judge Pitcher starts forward, but waits to watch the reunion between the two boys. Allen is obviously delighted. He starts toward Abe, but Abe has eyes only for Anna Roby Gentry, who at that moment appears in the doorway with Mrs. Crawford, behind Allen. Anna holds a baby in her arms, wrapped in a shawl)

ABE: Hold on, Allen. Ladies first. *(He leaps from the table and starts toward Anna. Halfway to the door, however, he pauses, uncertain. Then he approaches Anna more slowly, finally stops before her, and looks down at her in silence. Allen slowly withdraws his outstretched hand, waiting and watching uneasily. The room quiets)*

Anna —

(A gentle smile spreads over Abe's face. Anna, who has been constrained, begins to smile, too. Allen looks relieved, and relaxes. Mrs. Crawford reaches over and lifts the blanket from the baby, and Abe looks down at it. Finally, with a sudden motion, as if forcibly withdrawing from his thoughts, Abe turns and shakes Allen's hand)

Allen, it looks like you — *(He grins)* — Only, not so ugly.

(The word ugly startles him, reminding him of something, and he appears to repeat it in his mind. He is embarrassed for a moment, then he begins to laugh softly. To Anna)

Anna Roby Gentry, maybe you can't spell, but you're a smart girl. *(He nods solemnly)* You did the right thing, marrying Allen, here. You've got a *pretty* baby.

(Anna lowers her head shyly, and looks down at the baby. Allen looks fatuously pleased, not fully understanding Abe's remarks)

ALLEN: You come up on the *Pride*, Abe?

ABE: *(Nodding)* I hear folks coming up the horse path.

(Allen, Anna, Mrs. Crawford and Abe move away from the door, and downstage. Dennis peers out)

DENNIS: It's Mr. Ogg.

(Ogg a bustling, bantam-like little man, steps over the sill, past Dennis, and makes for the Judge, out of breath)

OGG: *(To Judge Pitcher, ignoring everyone else in the cabin)* Judge, I want to have a talk with you afore that feller Cartwright —

DENNIS: *(At the door)* And Mr. Cartwright.

(Cartwright, a little man, very much like Ogg, pushes his way into the cabin, out of breath)

CARTWRIGHT: *(To Judge Pitcher, ignoring the rest)* Judge, there's a few things I want to say afore Ogg starts a-lying —

JUDGE PITCHER: *(Raising his voice above theirs)* Gentlemen, gentlemen, you will have your turn in the witness box. Don't try to prejudice the court.

(At this point, Ogg pushes Cartwright, trying to stand in front of him, and Cartwright holds his ground. Outside, there are voices, and then a dozen or so neighbors crowd into the cabin, noisily taking sides in the quarrel)

Gentlemen — ! *(His voice is hardly audible above the noise)*

ABE: *(He is working his way through the disputing crowd, seeing that a fight is in the making. A grease lamp falls to the floor with a clatter, and a bench topples over. The voices rise)*

Hold on folks!

(He separates several pairs of wrestlers and sluggers on his way to Ogg and Cartwright and finally pushes his way between them. To Cartwright) Mr. Cartwright, hold on there! *(To Ogg)* That's enough, Mr. Ogg!

TOM: That's right, Abe! Tell him!

ABE: *(To All)* Ogg or Cartwright — I don't care which — the next feller that takes a swing at another feller in this cabin is going outside with me and get the worst thrashing he ever had in his life.
(The threat quiets the room, suddenly)

COLONEL JONES: *(He has remained aloof from the fight and is sitting on the end of the table casually swinging his leg. As he speakes, he looks at Abe admiringly)* Abe Lincoln, you've just busted up the sweetest little set-to Spencer County folks ever had the opportunity to enjoy. *(He stands up and addresses all)* Well, folks, you might as well get on with the trial. There's no use trying to have a fight with a peaceful feller like Abe Lincoln back in the neighborhood.

OGG: *(Blustering in front of Abe)* Young man, if I was twenty years younger —

ABE: *(Grinning down at Ogg)* Mr. Ogg, if you was twenty years younger, I'd be a two-months-old baby, and my Pa wouldn't let you try to scare me this-a-way.
(There is laughter, and a murmur of approval from Cartwright supporters)

CARTWRIGHT: That's right, Abe. Tell him! He's a thief! That's what he is!

ABE: *(Shaking his head, still grinning)* Mr. Cartwright, I'm afraid you misunderstand me. I ain't on your side, either.

TOM: Whose side *are* you on?

ABE: I'm for compromise, like Henry Clay.

TOM: Now, look-a-here, Abe, don't you try none of them ten-rod words on us! You just forget your book-learning and tell us where you stand. You hear!
(The crowd has quieted, to watch this direct conflict between father and son. Abe meets his father's eyes, then glances at Judge Pitcher, who nods approvingly. He walks, without haste, to the fireplace and mounts a tree-butt that serves the Lincoln household as a chair. Smiling, he begins to speak in a quiet voice)

ABE: Friends — including any Grigsbys that may be present — *(Laughter ripples through the crowd)* I've been away from these parts for several months now, and when I landed off the *Pride of Indiana* this morning I had a notion I was glad to be back. Walking home, up through Boonville and Gentryville, under the hickory and the ash and the oak trees, I was thinking how peaceful and quiet Indiana was, after the crowds of New Orleans — and then I entered my Pa's house. And what do I find? *(Rapidly, with sudden animation and many gestures)* Why, there was old Blue—I mean, Mr. Crawford—and Jim Gentry and they was squared away at each other like two bulldogs in a pit, and there was sparks flying and a lot of big talk in the air about chawing off noses and ears and like of that.

JOSIAH: I'd have done it, too, if Jim had so much as tetched me.

ABE: *(Nodding)* Sure, you'd have done it, Josiah — but I reckon Mr. Gentry would have done a little damage, too. *(To the crowd)* Why, folks, if they had kept on and the fight had spread, the way it looked looked like it was going to do a few minutes ago, all us Spencer County folks would have ended up looking like my Pa's cornpatch last summer after the squirrels got through with it. *(He pauses, and someone says, "How was that, Abe?" Abe drawls out the answer)* There wasn't a ear left.

(There is laughter, accompanied by a few good-natured groans, over the pun)

DENNIS: *(Shouting)* And everybody knows how much Abe Linkern likes squirrel-meat!

(The Neighbors laugh more freely)

ABE: But I ain't goin' to talk about squirrels. There's another critter I'd rather talk about just at present.
(There are cries of "What is it?" After they have subsided, Abe speaks in a comical, high-pitched voice, drawing out the words)
A o-o-ld gr-a-a-ay g-o-o-o-ose!
(The laughter is suddenly restrained, but it is there. Ogg and Cartwright, somewhat isolated from the rest now, begin to eye each other uncomfortably)
Yes, sir, a old gray goose. For many a year, we lived in considerable peace and some plenty on Little Pigeon Creek. Nobody bore anybody a real grudge or got careless in his fighting and really hurt anybody. Oh, there was one long, ugly, high-water feller that got too big for his britches a while back and caused a few busted noses till they send him off to New Orleans to cool off, but —
(The crowd laughs)

DENNIS: For a cooled-off feller, Abe, you come back with a powerful head of steam.

ABE: *(Pretending to be vexed)* Would someone kindly shut the door, to keep that big wind from blowing in here all the time?
(Laughter. Dennis slaps his thigh victoriously as if he had won in the exchange)
Folks, just afore I set off for New Orleans, something a whole lot worse than me come into the community and divided it into two camps, setting friend against friend and brother against brother. And do you know what it was? *(He pauses)* It was nothing but —
(The crowd joins in the refrain this time, Dennis' voice rising above the others) — a o-o-ld gr-a-a-ay g-o-o-o-se!
(The laughter is unanimous now. Even Ogg and Cartwright begin to grin foolishly. When the laughter subsides, Abe turns upon the two

684

men suddenly, shaking his finger at them. The crowd turns with him and watches the two men)

Now, you look here, you two! They tell me you're fixing to have a law-trial over that old gray goose tonight Well, when the trial is over, one of you will have the goose and the other won't. But that's all you'll have. Neither one of you will ever have the respect of this community again. Fact is, there won't be any respect left in this community. It's split right down the middle now over your argument, and after the trial is over it will stay split — *permanent. (He pauses for a moment and then appeals to the crowd)* Folks, an old gray goose ain't worth all this trouble. Nothing is worth it. A neighborhood divided against itself ain't fit to live in.

(For a few moments, the crowd is silent. Then there are growing murmurs of agreement with Abe, and attention is gradually turned expectantly to Ogg and Cartwright. The two men are manoeuvered into the center of the stage by shunting elbows and shoulders, and they face each other sheepishly. Finally, Abe leaps down from the tree-butt and goes to them, laughing)

All right, you two. Get it over with. *(They hesitate, but Abe's good nature begins to infect them)* Come on. Shake hands and forget it.

OGG: *(Rubbing his hand on his pants and extending it to Cartwright)* Well, I don't care if I do.

CARTWRIGHT: *(Shaking Ogg's hand)* All right with me, I reckon. You can keep the goose, Mr. Ogg.

OGG: *(With enthusiasm)* I tell you, Mr. Cartwright. You bring your folks over to my cabin tomorrow and Mrs. Ogg will cook it for supper.

ABE: *(To all)* There'll be no law-trial here tonight.
(Applause and cheering)

COLONEL JONES: *(Shouting)* Come on, folks! Let's celebrate. Let's all go over to my store and throw a dance!
(All, except Abe and Judge Pitcher, leave, singing, after much handshaking and peace-making)
Go tell Aunt Nancy,
Go tell Aunt Nancy,
Go tell Aunt Nancy,
Her old gray goose is dead . . .
(They can still be heard outside, their voices fading away, as Abe and Judge Pitcher look at each other for several seconds in silence)

JUDGE PITCHER: *(Smiling)* Young man, you did me out of my fee.

ABE: I'm sorry, Judge.

JUDGE PITCHER: I'm proud of you, boy. *(They stand in embarrassed silence for a moment before Judge Pitcher speaks again, making a move toward the door)* Are you coming to the Colonel's party?

ABE: *(He crosses the room and picks up Mrs. Lincoln's knitting, which has fallen from the bureau to the floor)* I think I'll wait here for Mamma.

JUDGE PITCHER: She'll be coming to the party, too.

ABE: Not without her knitting. *(He dusts it off and puts it back on the bureau)* She'll come back for it. She couldn't sit with her hands idle, even at a play-party.

JUDGE PITCHER: *(Smiling)* I reckon you're right. *(He goes to the bureau, takes his hat and puts it on)* Well, I'll see you at the Colonel's. *(He goes toward the door)*

ABE: Judge —
(Judge Pitcher turns about)
Judge, I owe you a lot. Everything you said before I left was true. Only, I had to learn it for myself, I reckon.

JUDGE PITCHER: I reckon we always have to learn things for ourselves.

ABE: *(Thoughtfully, as if he had not heard)* What I learned mostly was that folks are just about the same everywhere and there ain't no use in running away from trouble because you carry your trouble with you. *(He looks up at Judge Pitcher with a wry smile)* Oh, I reckon I'll have ornery spells again, Judge, like the one I was in when I left. I reckon a slack-twisted feller like me is made to be that-a-way — skylarking one day and black-hearted the next. I figure I'm in for trouble the rest of my life — a heap of trouble. *(After a brief pause, he speaks more hopefully, and with determination)* But from now on, Judge, I'm going to try never to set myself up as better than other folks. I don't care who they are. Ornery as we all are sometimes — and different, too — the Lord must love us all — the Oggs and the Cartwrights both — or He wouldn't have put us all here on the earth together.
(Mrs. Lincoln appears in the doorway)

MRS. LINCOLN: Abe!

ABE: *(He emerges, startled, from his thoughts; and then, seeing Mrs. Lincoln, he is suddenly overjoyed)* Mamma!
(Mrs. Lincoln steps over the sill and moves slowly downstage, her eyes fixed on Abe, oblivious of Judge Pitcher. Judge Pitcher moves quietly around behind her and exits. Abe starts toward Mrs. Lincoln; and then, remembering that he has his hat on, he stops, takes it off, and makes a low, sweeping bow. He straightens up)
Well, Mamma, I'm home.
(Mrs. Lincoln smiles faintly, holding back the tears and turns her head away. Abe smiles)
You don't seem very glad to see me.

MRS. LINCOLN: *(Running lightly toward him and into his arms, with a sob)* Oh, Abe . . . *(She draws back in his embrace and looks up at him)* It's them clothes. You don't look natural.

ABE: *(Glancing down at his new clothes)* I spent some of the money the Gentrys paid me. I figured I'd be smart to buy this outfit afore I saw Pa.

MRS. LINCOLN: *(Tersely)* You was. *(She examines the clothes, fingering the material, arranging the cravate, and finally taking the tall hat in her hands and admiring it as she blows off the dust in visible clouds. Putting the hat on the table, she looks up at Abe searchingly)* Abe, I hope these glad-rags don't signify nothing.

ABE: I ain't getting married, if that's what you're worrying about.

MRS. LINCOLN: *(She throws her arms impetuously about Abe again, and hugs him, resting her head on his chest)* Oh, Abe — son! I was sure I'd never see you again! *(Abe smooths her hair. After a moment or two, she looks up at him again searchingly)* There's a million things I've got to ask you, but there's one question that's got to be answered first.

ABE: What's that, Mamma?

MRS. LINCOLN: Did that pilot-feller offer you a job?

ABE: You mean Mr. Castleton — the one that gave me the dollar once?

MRS. LINCOLN: *(Impatiently)* You know I do.

ABE: *(Teasing)* Why, yes, ma'am, he did offer to take me on.

MRS. LINCOLN: *(Impatiently)* Well, what did you say?

ABE: Why, I thanked him, Mamma. I said, "Much obliged for the offer, Mr. Castleton," just like you taught me to do.

MRS. LINCOLN: *(Grasping the lapels of Abe's coat and shaking him)* Abraham Linkern, you quit tormenting me! You know what I've got to hear from you! Did that Captain — ?

ABE: *(Solemnly) Pilot,* Mamma — *not* captain.

MRS. LINCOLN: *(Exasperated)* Pilot or captain, I don't care which! Did you take the job?

ABE: *(Smiling down at her)* No, ma'am.

MRS. LINCOLN: *(Laying her head on his chest again and speaking with great relief and reverence)* Thank the Lord!

ABE: *(Stroking her hair and speaking slowly and distinctly as he leads her over to the table, where she sits on the bench)* . . . You see, Mamma, it was this way. The first day Allen and I were in New Orleans, we walked all over the city. We saw all the steamboats — hundreds of them — and the sea-going ships — hundreds more — and the Cathedral and the Cabildo and the Big Bone Meuseum. And finally we came to a slave-block — and that's where I saw Mr. Castleton. He was buying a slave at public auction. Now, I had never seen a man buy a slave before. Fact is, living in Indiana, I never thought much about slavery. But when I saw Mr. Castleton looking over this poor scared critter that first day in New Orleans . . . well, I knew then and there, I didn't want to work for him!

(He stops, turns and walks over to the door and stands there a long time looking out into the night. Finally, he turns about, his fists clenched at his sides)

Someday, Mamma . . . *(He pounds his right fist into the palm of his left hand)* Someday, by God's grace, I'm going to hit that thing and hit it hard!

687

(He stands a moment longer, absorbed in his thoughts. Then he looks at Mrs. Lincoln who is regarding him with a look of wonder, and he begins slowly to smile. Going to her, he bends over and kisses the top of her head. His manner changes suddenly to his normal gaiety) You got anything left over from supper, Mamma?

MRS. LINCOLN: *(Startled)* Why, yes, Abe . . .

ABE: What?

MRS. LINCOLN: *(Embarrassed)* I'm afraid it's squirrel.

ABE: *(With a grimace)* Boiled or fried?

MRS. LINCOLN: *(With considerable consternation)* It's boiled, Abe. *(Abe stands looking down at her, wagging his head)*

ABE: Boiled squirrel!
(Tom Lincoln appears in the doorway behind him)

TOM: Hey, you two! Ain't you coming to the shindig?
(Without warning, Abe turns about and grabs Tom by the elbows and begins dancing him about the room. Protesting, Tom is helpless in Abe's arms)

ABE: *(Singing as he dances)* The turbaned Turk
That scorns the world
"And struts about
With his whiskers curled . . .
(He sets Tom down on the bench at last beside Mrs. Lincoln and stands above him, addressing him with a mocking show of great enthusiasm) What do you think, Pa? Mamma's cooked a feast. I travel two thousand miles to get home to her, and sure enough, she's killed the fatted calf for me. Only it's a squirrel. *Boiled* squirrel!
(He puts his hands on Tom's shoulder, laughing. Slowly Tom gets the point and begins to laugh, too. Tom laughs harder. Abe shakes him again. Tom reaches up and pounds Abe's chest, the laughter coming out of him painfully in wheezes and chuckles, and finally in a roar)

TOM: *(Recovering, he finally turns to Mrs. Lincoln)* I be durned if that boy of yourn ain't the limit, Sarah Linkern! I be durned if there's anybody round these parts like him! You know, there was times while he was gone when I almost missed him! *(He turns and punches Abe again, affectionately)*

MRS. LINCOLN: *(Quietly)* He's *your* boy, Tom.

TOM: *(Nodding in agreement)* I be durned if he ain't! There's times I say to myself, I say, "Abe Linkern is just a chip off the old block." *(He stops chuckling suddenly after this speech and looks solemn. To Abe, reprovingly)* That reminds me, son. That woodpile out there is a-getting mighty low.

ABE: *(He is at first startled; then vexed; and finally amused as well as vexed. But as he turns his back and walks slowly toward the door, wagging his head in dismay, it is impossible to tell whether he is more vexed or more amused. His shoulders begin to shake as he nears the door and by the time he turns about, facing Tom and Mrs. Lincoln, his amusement has overcome his vexation. To Tom)*

Pa, I declare, you are the remindedest feller in Spencer County!

(Mrs. Lincoln sighs with relief. Tom starts to speak, but Abe interrupts him, once more in complete good humor)

Come on folks, let's go to the play-party. I'll chop wood tomorrow.

(Tom and Mrs. Lincoln rise and join Abe at the door. Abe steps aside to let them go out ahead of him. Tom exits first, followed by Mrs. Lincoln, who gives Abe an affectionate approving pat as she passes him. Abe starts to follow her out the door, but with one foot over the sill he stops, seeing Mrs. Lincoln's forgotten knitting on the bureau. He steps back into the cabin, quickly takes the knitting from the bureau, and goes out.

CURTAIN

End

THE MAN WHO KILLED TIME

by

ARTHUR FAUQUEZ

*Foreword by Esmé Church

*Included in the separate play-book only.

Copyright, 1964, by

THE CHILDREN'S THEATRE PRESS

CLOVERLOT

ANCHORAGE, KENTUCKY

THE MAN WHO KILLED TIME

By Arthur Fauquez

CAST

AMBROSIO, an inn-keeper

SPAZZINO, a street-sweeper

REGOLO, signalman, and night-watchman

PADRONA, mayoress of the village

FANTESCA, a servant-girl

ROMEO, a farmer

JULIETTA, a milkmaid

MOTHER, Julietta's mother

FATHER, Romeo's father

SYNOPSIS

The action takes place in the little Italian village of San Buco.

PROLOGUE: Night. The garden-arbour of Ambrosio's inn.

ACT ONE: Morning. The same.

INTERLUDE: Before the curtain.

ACT TWO: Inside the steeple of the clock tower.

INTERLUDE: Before the curtain.

ACT THREE: Mid-day. The garden-arbour of Ambrosio's inn.

This play was first presented by its French title, *Ambrosio Tue l'Heure,* in 1946, by the Theatre de l'Enfance in Brussels, Belgium, under the direction of José Geal.

Translated into English by Margaret Leona, it was presented in 1954 by the Northern Children's Theatre of Bradford, England, under the direction of Esmé Church.

It then crossed the Atlantic, and was presented in 1955 by the Holiday Theatre of Vancouver, Canada, under the direction of Joy Coghill Thorne.

Revised by the author in 1963, the English text was adjusted, and the new matter translated, by Marie-Louise Roelants.

The Man Who Killed Time

Three knocks. The lights dim in the Theatre while a tarantella is being sung. The curtains open slowly.

PROLOGUE

A ray of moonlight slowly lights up the singer, Ambrosio, in night-shirt and cotton nightcap, who sings as he swings lazily on a wooden flowertub suspended in his arbour. Suddenly a muted trumpet answers the song in the same tone.

(Spazzino enters, blowing his trumpet and carrying a lighted lantern. Seeing Ambrosio, he stops trumpeting).

AMBROSIO.   Good evening, Spazzino.

SPAZZINO.   Good evening, Ambrosio.

AMBROSIO.   I took you for an echo.

SPAZZINO.   Echoes sleep after nine o'clock in San Buco. Why are you singing after curfew?

AMBROSIO.   To please myself.

SPAZZINO.   You'll wake your neighbours.

AMBROSIO.   They will sing with me.

SPAZZINO.   Let them sleep since it pleases them.

AMBROSIO.   Let me sing, since it pleases me.

SPAZZINO.   Sing in the day time.

AMBROSIO.   Impossible.

SPAZZINO.   Why?

AMBROSIO.   Because of the train going by rattling the village like a bag of nuts, and the mill-whistle, and your sweeper's bell, and the church bells, and the noise of street carts, and the market criers, and the dogs barking and cats miouing . . .

SPAZZINO.   That doesn't stop you singing.

AMBROSIO.   O no, it would be a pretty song!

(He sings and mixes various noises with his song).

Lalalala lala lala - Bim bam bimbam - lalalala lala - ding diding diding - Sweeper! Lalalala - miouw, miouw, Wu - uuuuuu . . .

SPAZZINO.   Very queer, I must say.

695

AMBROSIO. Can't we do without these noises?

SPAZZINO. But we must have them. Each sound reminds us there is something to do.

AMBROSIO. Well, it's this that makes me sing at night.

SPAZZINO. Think of the people sleeping. I put a stopper in my trumpet so as not to wake them.

AMBROSIO. You'd do better still if you stopped trumpeting.

SPAZZINO. But it's a custom. I've been trumpeting every evening for the past 20 years, from nine till midnight. It's become a habit.

AMBROSIO. I have my habits, too.

SPAZZINO. Live as you like during the day. Swing as you like in the evening; but be reasonable, and don't sing when people are sleeping.

AMBROSIO. I'll do my best . . . if I must.

SPAZZINO. Goodnight, Ambrosio.

(He goes).

AMBROSIO. Goodnight, Spazzino.

(He swings silently and then starts singing again mechanically, at first softly and then getting louder and louder. Somewhere a window opens).

VOICE OF PADRONA. Oh, Ambrosio.

AMBROSIO *(Swinging).* Good evening, Padrona.

VOICE OF PADRONA. Can't you sing tomorrow morning?

AMBROSIO. It's more fun under the moon.

VOICE OF PADRONA. Your voice will be clearer under the sun.

AMBROSIO. Oh no, listen.

(He sings. Another window opens).

VOICE OF FANTESCA. Ambrosio . . .

AMBROSIO. What do you wish, Fantesca? Wine, noodles, macaroni, risotto?

VOICE OF FANTESCA. Only a little silence.

VOICE OF PADRONA. Yes, be good. Go to bed.

VOICE OF FANTESCA. Please be good, Ambrosio.

AMBROSIO. I can never refuse you anything.

VOICE OF PADRONA. Goodnight, Ambrosio.

AMBROSIO. Goodnight, Padrona.

VOICE OF FANTESCA. Goodnight, Ambrosio.

AMBROSIO. Goodnight, Fantesca.

(The windows close. Ambrosio swings dreamily and soon begins humming again. Then he remembers the time and stops. He stops swinging, comes off the swing, replaces the flowers in the tub of the swing and goes into the Inn).

ACT ONE

Little by little the light comes up on the set. The sun is rising. A cock crows a long way off. A dog barks. Another cock crows. The scene is Ambrosio's garden arbour—on one side the wayside inn with the sign "Ambrosio's Restaurant." At the back a vine. On the other side the garden with the suspended tub of flowers. A garden table and some stools, nearer the back, in front of the vine a trailing aerial wire across the stage.

VOICE OF SPAZZINO. Six o'clock, the market is open.

MARKET CRIES. Pumpkins, mushrooms, melons, fresh sea-fish, fresh river-fish, marrow, pimento, peppers, aubergines and onions.— Sweet, sharp, sweet smelling, fragrant. Grinder! bring out your knives, your scissors, your tools for grinding—Grinder! . . . Tomatoes, lovely tomatoes, the ripest, roundest, reddest, and best tomatoes . . .

FANTESCA *(Comes from the back and knocks at Ambrosio's, while the market goes on).*

AMBROSIO *(Puts out an arm with a jug for milk without being seen).* Three pints.

FANTESCA. Ambrosio.

AMBROSIO *(Still unseen).* I'll pay tomorrow.

(The jug disappears).

FANTESCA *(Knocks).* It's me . . . Fantesca.

AMBROSIO *(Opens the door).* It's not the milkman?

(He comes out of the house in his nightshirt).

What do you wish, my pretty one?

FANTESCA. Will you make some raspberry waffles for me, so that I can pick them up when I return from the market?

AMBROSIO. At this hour?

FANTESCA. They're for the school master's breakfast. He wants a dozen of them.

AMBROSIO. You shall have them . . . as a special favour.

FANTESCA. You are a curly lambkin.

AMBROSIO. Do you really think so?

FANTESCA. Yes.

(She goes out delighted).

AMBROSIO. For the school-master? What an absurd idea. How can a school-master eat waffles at sunrise, when he is too good to eat them at any other time of day—or even night?

(Pause).

. . . A curly lambkin . . .

(He looks in the mirror hanging on the outside wall. Yawns).

C-ur-ly . . . lam-bk-in . . .

(He notices wrinkles on his face, pockets under his eyes, his dim expression, his dirty tongue, his yellow teeth, his shiny nose, his soft ears, a tuft of hair coming out of his night-cap. He makes faces at himself, trying to look like a curly lambkin and does a . . .).

Bee-eee-eee.

(Finally he yawns, scratches his head and goes into the house with the obvious intention of getting back to bed).

Bee-eee-eeee-in my be-e-ed.

(Exits).

FANTESCA *(Comes back with an armful of flowers).* Ambrosio—Ambrosio—

(She knocks on the door with her heel).

AMBROSIO *(Coming out of the house, still in nightshirt, he receives a kick on the legs).* Ow . . .

(He has two enormous ear plugs in his ears).

FANTESCA. Have you made my waffles?

AMBROSIO. In my bed.

FANTESCA. In your bed? And the raspberries?

AMBROSIO. Nose in the air.

FANTESCA. Are you deaf?

(She shows her ear).

698

AMBROSIO. My ear?

(He touches his ear and understands. Takes out the plugs).

FANTESCA. What are those?

AMBROSIO. Ear plugs. To drown the noises that stop me sleeping.

FANTESCA. Have you cooked my waffles?

AMBROSIO. Sit down. I'll have them ready in two or three strokes.

(Goes in).

FANTESCA. Hurry up. I have promised them for half-past seven. The teacher is not an easy man. When he says half-past seven, he means half-past seven.

AMBROSIO *(Puts head out).* Don't worry. He will have them.

(Disappears. Sound of dishes).

FANTESCA. Don't break anything.

AMBROSIO *(Head out).* Never.

(Disappears. Sound of something breaking. Head out).

Hardly ever.

(Disappears).

(Offstage, very quick). One egg, two eggs, three eggs, four eggs, flour, sugar, vanilla.

(He enters beating the mixture in a bowl).

Why don't you make your own waffles?

FANTESCA. Yours are so much better.

AMBROSIO. Well, I get more practice.

(He disappears. We hear the sound of the mixture poured on the hot waffle-iron).

Shall I still be a curly lambkin?

FANTESCA. Yes, if I have my waffles for breakfast.

AMBROSIO *(Off).* And one—

(Sound of pouring the mixture on the waffle-iron more and more rapidly).

I will be—and two—a curly lambkin—and three—four—how many do you want? —and five—

FRANTESCA. Twelve.

AMBROSIO *(Off).* The raspberries. One, two, three—

(More and more quickly).

699

Four, five, six, seven, eight, nine, ten-eleven-twelve.

(He enters bearing the waffles, which he powders in a cloud of sugar, his nightcap fallen over his eyes, he collapses).

Here.

FRANTESCA. It's funny to see you make waffles in your night-shirt.

AMBROSIO. This is not living. It's the end of the world. The eggs go by like spinning stars, you mix the paste, you beat it like a merry-go-round, you put in the flour, it snows, the sugar, it showers, then the waffle iron snaps its jaws, you pour the paste, and you make little holes for the raspberries. It snows sugar, and you come out steaming from your pastry volcano, bruised, beaten, burned, skinned, amazed.

FRANTESCA. Amazed at what?

AMBROSIO. To be still alive after all that work.

FRANTESCA. If you started in time, this wouldn't happen.

AMBROSIO. Imagine cooking waffles at seven o'clock in the morning!

FRANTESCA. You get up a little earlier, you prepare the paste without hurrying, you cook the waffles at your convenience, I take them and go away.

(She starts out, leaving her flowers).

AMBROSIO. Your flowers.

FRANTESCA. I will come back and get them.

AMBROSIO. Am I a curly lambkin?

FRANTESCA. Curled and scented.

(She goes out).

AMBROSIO. Curled and scented.

(Tremblingly he takes a deep smell of her flowers).

Curled and scented.

(He starts to go back into his house).

ROMEO. *(A simple-minded peasant enters).* O, Ambrosio!

AMBROSIO. Hello, Romeo.

(He starts out).

ROMEO. Wait. I have to ask you something.

AMBROSIO. So early? I am hardly awake yet.

ROMEO. Me, I am up with the sun.

AMBROSIO. Me, at this hour, I prefer my pillow.

ROMEO. At the farm I have to get up. The animals demand it. That's why I'm going to marry.

AMBROSIO. Then your wife will demand it. Who is she?

ROMEO. Who is who?

AMBROSIO. Your intended.

ROMEO. Julietta.

AMBROSIO. All Romeos marry Juliettas.

ROMEO. Yes, but there is only one like mine. She is the milkmaid from San Marco del Piolo.

AMBROSIO. Congratulations, you lucky fellow. And now, let me go. I'm going to dress.

ROMEO. But wait. I have to ask you something.

AMBROSIO. Well, hurry up. I'm listening.

ROMEO. I can't think what it is.

AMBROSIO. It must not be important.

ROMEO. Oh, on the contrary, it's very important.

AMBROSIO. Well, then—tell me.

ROMEO. But I tell you, I cannot think what it is.

AMBROSIO. Come back tomorrow, you will think of it.

ROMEO. Tomorrow? Why?

AMBROSIO. Or day after tomorrow. Whenever you wish.

ROMEO. Day after tomorrow? What day will that be?

AMBROSIO. Wednesday.

ROMEO. Wednesday? That is my wedding day. The Padrona said she would marry us at eleven o'clock.

AMBROSIO. Very well. You can tell me on your way out of the city hall.

ROMEO. You think so?

AMBROSIO. It would seem to me simple.

ROMEO. You are probably right.

AMBROSIO. Good bye, Romeo.

ROMEO. Good bye, Ambrosio.

(He goes out).

AMBROSIO. Romeo and Julietta . . . ha, ha . . . Ambrosia and Fantesca—one day . . . perhaps . . .

(He goes back into his house).

701

FANTESCA *(Comes back)*. Ambrosio.

AMBROSIO *(Offstage)*. I'm dressing.

FANTESCA. You'll be a curly lambkin to the tip of your nose if you'll tell me what I'm to cook for lunch.

AMBROSIO. *(Offstage)*. Would you like some polenta?

FANTESCA. Not today.

AMBROSIO. *(Offstage)*. Some Risi-pisi?

FANTESCA. I have no fancy for it.

AMBROSIO *(Offstage)*. Ravioli?

FANTESCA. The master had that yesterday.

AMBROSIO *(Offstage)*. Canneloni?

FANTESCA. Don't you have anything else?

AMBROSIO *(Offstage)*. A chicken?

FANTESCA. Well, why not?

AMBROSIO *(Offstage)*. Would you like a young cockerel?

FANTESCA. Will you pluck it?

AMBROSIO *(Offstage)*. Yes.

FANTESCA. Promise?

AMBROSIO *(Offstage)*. Yes.

FANTESCA. And you won't be late?

AMBROSIO *(Offstage)*. I'm never late.

FANTESCA. To be quite sure, I'll give you a gadget that will remind you what to do.

AMBROSIO *(Offstage)*. I have my head.

FANTESCA. It's often in the clouds.

(Goes taking flowers).

AMBROSIO *(Comes on dressed and carrying a feathered cockerel)*. Look.

(Seeing he is alone).

Don't look.

(Puts the chicken on the swing).

FANTESCA *(Comes back with an alarm clock)*. Here's an alarm.

AMBROSIO. Here's your chicken.

FANTESCA. Look at the alarm.

AMBROSIO. Look at the chicken.

FANTESCA. You should hear it when it rings.

AMBROSIO. You should hear him when he sings.

FANTESCA. It has a hand for the seconds.

AMBROSIO. He has a comb as red as a tomato.

FANTESCA. Thanks to this you will never be late.

AMBROSIO. Thanks to him you won't be hungry.

FANTESCA. It's a precious alarm.

AMBROSIO. It's a precious chicken.

FANTESCA. It's more than a hundred years old.

AMBROSIO. And he is more than 200 . . . 200 days, of course.

FANTESCA. I give it to you.

(Puts it on the table).

AMBROSIO. I sell this to you.

(He holds out the chicken).

FANTESCA. It isn't plucked.

AMBROSIO. Alright.

FANTESCA. I'll have it by eleven?

AMBROSIO. Of course.

FANTESCA. Plucked?

AMBROSIO. Plucked.

FANTESCA. The alarm will remind you.

AMBROSIO. Do you think it will pluck the chicken?

FANTESCA. No, but it will help you not to forget.

(Moves to go).

AMBROSIO. You're going?

FANTESCA. I've so much to do: put the soup on the fire, peel the potatoes, clean the vegetables, dust the furniture, sweep the house, wax the parquet, and a hundred other things.

AMBROSIO. What a pity. I take such pleasure seeing you in my garden.

FANTESCA. So do I. I love your garden. It's full of flowers, and songs, and the sun, and colours, and lights and gaiety.

703

AMBROSIO. Stay, please. Enjoy it.

FANTESCA. I wish I could, but I haven't the time. Eleven o'clock, don't forget.

(She goes).

AMBROSIO. Hasn't the time. Hasn't the time.

(Picks up the alarm clock and looks at it).

Sixty seconds in a minute, and sixty minutes in an hour, 24 hours in a day, and thirty—or thirty-one—days in a month. Twelve months in a year, and many years in a life. That makes millions and trillions of seconds to spend—and yet some people haven't time. It's because of these gadgets. They need only produce more seconds and minutes and hours, and everyone would be happy. As for me, I arrange things easily.

(He puts the alarm in the flowertub, rolls up his shirt sleeves as though ready to start work, and takes out of the tavern window a bowl of soapy water with a clay pipe stuck in it. He blows soap bubbles, climbs on to a stool, then on the table. Finally he blows in his bowl and produces an enormous mousse of soap bubbles).

REGOLO *(Comes in peacefully smoking his pipe).*

AMBROSIO. Good morning, signalman.

REGOLO. Morning.

AMBROSIO. Pretty isn't it?

REGOLO. Euh . . .

AMBROSIO. No?

REGOLO. If you like.

AMBROSIO. Look, Regolo, see what fun this is. You blow and it goes. Pttt! It vanishes in the air. It's as pretty as a rainbow, light as an angel's feather, it swells with every colour in the world, it goes, it comes, it dances, it turns, it trembles, and . . . fwttt . . . it's gone . . . it's forgotten.

REGOLO. Like your promises.

AMBROSIO. What promises?

REGOLO. The oil for greasing my level-crossing gates.

AMBROSIO. True. You shall have it tomorrow.

REGOLO. That will be too late.

AMBROSIO. Too late, why?

REGOLO *(Looks at his watch).* Because at this very moment the train passes through the station of Tortorella in the plain, it whistles,

704

and bounds towards the mountain, and at eleven o'clock it will dash like a bullet through my level-crossing gates.

AMBROSIO. The same as every morning.

REGOLO. Yes, but today the gates will remain up.

AMBROSIO. Why?

REGOLO. Because I can't lower them without oil.

(Looks at chronometer).

AMBROSIO. Does it matter?

REGOLO. Do you know what could happen?

AMBROSIO. The train comes, it passes, it goes away.

REGOLO. And if there is at that minute, at that very minute, right in the middle of the track, a chicken or a duck or a dog or a goat, or a cow, or a man on foot, on a cycle, in a cart or in a car? Think, what a terrible accident . . .

(He looks at chronometer).

AMBROSIO. That's supposing . . .

REGOLO. It's a certainty. And who would be responsible for such a catastrophe? I would, because I had not closed the crossing . . . and you because you had not delivered the oil to grease the gates. And who would pay for the damage? I would. I would get a bad reputation, and I would lose my chance to ever be anything more than a simple train gate watchman.

AMBROSIO. Alright, alright, don't get so worked up. I'll go fetch it, your oil.

REGOLO *(Looks at chronometer).* Hurry up, time's getting on.

AMBROSIO. It's in the cellar.

REGOLO. You won't lose anything by doing me a good turn. When I become Stationmaster of San Buco . . .

AMBROSIO. There would have to be a station first.

(Goes into the tavern).

REGOLO. That'll come. I've already got the cap, and the whistle; the rest will come. And when I become Stationmaster of San Buco, I tell you, I'll order all the oil and grease for my fittings from you.

AMBROSIO. *(Returning with can of oil).* See, it didn't take long.

REGOLO. Why didn't you do that earlier?

AMBROSIO. Because I like to do things when I like and not when I must.

REGOLO. Yet it's so easy to do everything at the right time.

(Looks at chronometer).

AMBROSIO. Don't you ever enjoy anything else besides putting your gates up and down?

REGOLO. Yes . . . sometimes . . . when I have time.

AMBROSIO. What do you do?

REGOLO. Time calculations, to forecast where and when the moon will rise in the evening sky.

(Looks at chronometer).

Now it is time for oiling my gates.

(Goes out with can of oil).

AMBROSIO. Enjoy yourself, moontimer.

(He grasps his mandolin, plays and sings).

ROMEO *(Enters).* Ambrosio.

AMBROSIO. Yes?

ROMEO. I know what it is.

AMBROSIO. What what is?

ROMEO. What I wanted to ask you.

AMBROSIO. I thought you were coming to tell me on Wednesday.

ROMEO. Wednesday is my wedding.

AMBROSIO. Yes, I know. With Julietta.

ROMEO. Who told you?

AMBROSIO. You.

ROMEO. Me? When?

AMBROSIO. This morning.

ROMEO. Ah?

AMBROSIO. Yes, this morning. When you came to ask me what you are coming to ask me now.

ROMEO. Did I ask you something?

AMBROSIO. Not yet, but you are going to.

ROMEO. Why?

AMBROSIO. Because that's what you came for. Now, what is it?

ROMEO. What is what?

AMBROSIO. What you came to ask me?

ROMEO. I don't know.

AMBROSIO. In that case, you had better come back when you know.

ROMEO. You are right. I will come back. Good bye.

(He goes out).

AMBROSIO. Honest Romeo. He, at least, is no slave to time.

(Plays a few notes, Padrona enters, smiling. Ambrosio stops playing, takes off his hat, and salutes her with a big gesture).

Bless the heavens for making you so lovely, Padrona.

PADRONA. And who has made you so cheerful, Ambrosio?

AMBROSIO. Why shouldn't I be cheerful when I have two eyes to see the myriad beauties of the world, two ears to hear them, a mouth to sing them, and two legs to dance them?

PADRONA. And two hands to work with.

AMBROSIO. That's understood.

PADRONA. You're a very nice neighbour, but I want to give you a little advice: don't sing again in the middle of the night, think of people asleep.

AMBROSIO. Why don't they sing, like me?

PADRONA. They work hard during the day, they need rest during the night. And besides, think of me, Ambrosio. It's not easy, you know, to manage the business of a village like San Buco, to record the births, the marriages, and the whole life of each inhabitant.

AMBROSIO. You are right, Padrona. I won't sing any more. I promise.

PADRONA. On the contrary, sing the whole day long. I like your songs. They fly from your mouth and slip into my home like birds through the window. You cannot imagine how much pleasure they give me.

AMBROSIO. I ask nothing better. But each time I sing noises interrupt.

PADRONA. What noises?

(The Dustman's bell rings).

AMBROSIO. That's one.

SPAZZINO *(Enters, ringing his bell).* Sweeper, sweep . . .

(Seeing Padrona, he takes his cap off).

Good day, Padrona . . . day, Ambrosio.

PADRONA. Good day, Spazzino.

AMBROSIO. Good day, Sweeper.

707

PADRONA. The market is closed?

SPAZZINO. Yes, Padrona.

PADRONA. Aren't you sweeping it up?

SPAZZINO. Yes, Padrona, but I called in to warn Ambrosio to prepare his bin of peelings, orange skins, eggshells, vegetable parings, meatbones, chicken feathers, etc., etc.

PADRONA. You'll do it, Ambrosio?

AMBROSIO. I will do it.

PADRONA. That's a sensible arrangement. Good bye friends.

(She goes).

SPAZZINO. Good bye, Padrona.

AMBROSIO. Good bye, Padrona. Blessed be the heavens for making you so good.

SPAZZINO. Be good yourself, Ambrosio, and don't make me come back twice, like yesterday. I lose my time.

AMBROSIO. Why do you worry about time?

SPAZZINO. Because I've a lot to do and it must all be done.

AMBROSIO. Do you succeed?

SPAZZINO. By keeping to a strict timetable, yes. Six o'clock, I declare the market open.

AMBROSIO. You bray like a donkey.

SPAZZINO. Half past ten, Dustman. Sweep up.

AMBROSIO. You break my ears with your bell.

SPAZZINO. Eleven o'clock—collect the garbage.

AMBROSIO. You put everybody to a lot of trouble.

SPAZZINO. Midday, I eat.

AMBROSIO. It's the only time you leave us in peace.

SPAZZINO. Two o'clock, I am the Park keeper.

AMBROSIO. Your bell again.

SPAZZINO. Nine o'clock, I'm nightwatchman and sound the curfew.

AMBROSIO. And you trumpet loud enough to waken the dead.

SPAZZINO. Ten o'clock, eleven o'clock, midnight, I call the hours gently.

AMBROSIO. With your muted trumpet.

SPAZZINO. All these things must be done at their proper time.

708

AMBROSIO. I do everything when I feel like it.

SPAZZINO. I do everything at the right time.

(He rings his bell).

Sweeper . . . sweeper . . .

(He goes).

AMBROSIO. Poor Spazzino, his life is so mechanical, he knows every minute what he will do next.

(He goes toward the Inn, stops, looks at the flowers in the garden. Takes a little watering can and waters the flowers, nonchalantly humming . . . Suddenly the alarm goes off).

The alarm! Eleven o'clock. The chicken!

(Puts down the watering can, grasps the chicken, sits, and starts to pluck it with the speed of a madman while the alarm goes on ringing. He plucks, plucks, plucks and when he has finished the alarm has stopped ringing and Ambrosio is exhausted and covered in down).

FANTESCA *(Enters in a cloud of feathers).* Ambrosio, has winter come again?

AMBROSIO. True, it snows. It snows feathers. It's a storm of feathers, a whirlwind of feathers. I'm feathered, I'm a cock, a duck, an eagle, the Rock-bird of Sinbad the Sailor, I'm a feather broom, a feather-bed, I'm a quill, anything you like that's feathered, but I'm no longer a man.

FANTESCA. Have you plucked my chicken?

AMBROSIO. Here it is.

FANTESCA. Was it the alarm that reminded you?

AMBROSIO. It was.

FANTESCA. Don't forget to set it each morning.

(She goes taking the chicken).

AMBROSIO. Each morning? So that it can continue to divide my life into pieces and cut the hours into minutes like little "o's," and seconds into grains of sand?

(He shakes the alarm).

I don't want to know the time, do you hear? Stop that noise! I've enough of your hand grinding out the seconds . . . ticticticticic . . . like a chicken picking corn. I don't want to hear your wretched bell calling me. DRRR . . . quick, quick, quick, quick, hurry up . . . DRRRIN . . . pluck, pluck, pluck, time to pluck.

No. I want peace. I want to pluck when I want to pluck. I want to sleep when I want to sleep.

(Puts alarm on table).

I want peace and I shall have it.

(He goes, gets a pair of pincers, returns, opens the back of the alarm, takes out the ringer and other bits, wheel works, spring).

Your last hour has come. Your last minute. Your last second. It's done. From now on you'll not count every split second of my life.

(He hides the debris in the tub of flowers. He is about to go into the Inn, when he stops in front of his mirror, hanging on the wall by the door. He unhooks it, looks at himself, then plays catching the light in it, and throwing it into the eyes of the audience).

SPAZZINO *(Enters from the back of the audience, pushing his garbage cart and ringing his bell).*

AMBROSIO *(Throws light in his eyes).*

SPAZZINO. Stop it, I can't see.

AMBROSIO. Why worry? At a glance, the whole sun enters your head. Your eyes are full of the light and dust of the sun. Its heavenly gold entering your body, filling your chest, swelling your tummy, slipping down your arms and your legs. You are the richest man in the world. You are stuffed with sun.

SPAZZINO. Is your trash ready?

AMBROSIO. No.

SPAZZINO. You promised.

AMBROSIO. I prefer sunlight to garbage.

SPAZZINO. I've no time to fool about.

AMBROSIO. That's your mistake.

(He goes).

SPAZZINO *(Puts bell on table and starts sweeping the feathers).*

AMBROSIO. *(Comes back with a box of trash).* Here's your merchandise.

SPAZZINO. Pour it in.

(Ambrosio empties box into cart on wheels and notices the bell on table. Spazzino continues to sweep up. Ambrosio takes advantage of this to take out the bell-clapper).

(Sweeping). If only you had swept these feathers, I could have gone on my way.

710

AMBROSIO. Do you expect to sweep the sky after the angels have walked across it?

SPAZZINO. Angels or chicken feathers, all I know is: everything must be done at the right time.

AMBROSIO. Is that so amusing?

SPAZZINO. Amusing? No. Easy, yes. Six o'clock, I do this. Seven o'clock, I do that. Eight o'clock, this. Nine o'clock, that. Ten o'clock, go there. Eleven o'clock, here. Etc., etc., etc. I do everything on time and I never make a mistake.

AMBROSIO. It's the same for me. I do this, and this and that, go there, go there, etc., etc., etc. But always when I feel like it and never at fixed times. I never make a mistake either.

SPAZZINO. I've finished. Good morning.

AMBROSIO. Good bye, Spazzino. May you have sweet sweeping.

SPAZZINO (*Pushes his cart towards the exit while ringing his bell*). Put out your . . .

(*He stops, surprised at not hearing it ring. Shakes it violently once more then looks inside it*).

The clapper!

(*Comes back to Ambrosio*).

The clapper!

AMBROSIO. What clapper?

SPAZZINO. My bell clapper has disappeared.

AMBROSIO. Have you swallowed it?

SPAZZINO. It's not here.

AMBROSIO. Where is it?

SPAZZINO. It was inside when I came here.

AMBROSIO. Well surely, since you rang it.

SPAZZINO. Isn't it on the table?

AMBROSIO. No.

SPAZZINO. Nor underneath?

AMBROSIO. No, nor there either.

SPAZZINO. It can't have flown?

AMBROSIO. Flown? You said flown?

SPAZZINO. Yes, flown.

AMBROSIO. That's it. Just now, when you shook your bell the last time, I thought . . .

SPAZZINO. What did you think?

AMBROSIO. I thought I saw something come out. I wouldn't swear to it, but I thought so. It came out, and went up, and up, and up, and flew over there above the roof tops.

SPAZZINO. Is that so?

AMBROSIO. The more I say it, the more certain I am. It was as thick as this, as long as that, and it flew like a shot from a gun.

SPAZZINO. Over there?

AMBROSIO. Over there.

SPAZZINO. Thank you.

(He grasps his bell and cart, and goes out in great haste).

AMBROSIO *(Shows the clapper)*. As thick as this, as long as that. Another instrument that shall annoy me no more.

(He hides the clapper in the vine leaves).

ROMEO *(Enters)*. Now I have it!

AMBROSIO. What?

ROMEO. It has come back to me.

AMBROSIO. What you want to tell me?

ROMEO. Yes.

AMBROSIO. And that is what?

ROMEO. It is about the turkey.

AMBROSIO. The turkey?

ROMEO. For Wednesday.

AMBROSIO. For your wedding day?

ROMEO. Yes, that's right. It's Julietta who said to me—"Go to Ambrosio's and tell him." There, I have told you about it.

AMBROSIO. What? The turkey?

ROMEO. Of course. For Heaven's sake, you don't understand a word.

AMBROSIO. Oh yes, I understand that you want a turkey. I will get it for you.

ROMEO. Not now. Wednesday.

AMBROSIO. For your wedding?

ROMEO. For after the wedding.

AMBROSIO. Is that what you have been trying to say—for your wedding feast?

712

ROMEO. But naturally it is for that. My word, you're not very bright up there.

(He touches Ambrosio's forehead).

AMBROSIO *(Laughs).* Ah, but this time I get you. You can believe me. How many people will there be?

ROMEO. That's easy. There is Julietta.

AMBROSIO. That makes one.

ROMEO. Her mother, who is fat, like that.

AMBROSIO. Two.

ROMEO. And my father. He has sore feet, from his new shoes.

AMBROSIO. Three. And who else?

ROMEO. That's all.

AMBROSIO. And you?

ROMEO. What, me?

AMBROSIO. You will sit down to your own wedding feast, I suppose.

ROMEO. You think I ought to?

AMBROSIO. It seems to me indicated.

ROMEO. It's not a bad idea, that.

AMBROSIO. Then you will be four at the table.

ROMEO. Five.

AMBROSIO. Who is the fifth?

ROMEO. Me, of course.

AMBROSIO. I have already counted you.

ROMEO. No, you didn't. I eat enough for two. Good bye.

(He starts out).

AMBROSIO. Ah—when are you coming to fetch it?

ROMEO. What?

AMBROSIO. The turkey.

ROMEO. What for?

AMBROSIO. To eat it, probably.

ROMEO. But I am not coming to fetch it. We shall eat it at your restaurant.

AMBROSIO. Couldn't you have told me that in the first place?

713

ROMEO. You give me a headache with your questions. Till Wednesday, Ambrosio.

(Starts out).

AMBROSIO. Till Wednesday, Romeo. Don't forget your wedding.

ROMEO. And you, don't forget my turkey.

(He leaves).

AMBROSIO. Happy man. He goes, he comes, and life flows around him like a sparkling little brooklet that nothing can muddy up.

(Regolo enters, smoking his pipe peacefully).

And your train?

REGOLO. It passed half a second ahead of time.

AMBROSIO. Without accident?

REGOLO. My gates were closed.

AMBROSIO. Thanks to my oil.

REGOLO. Thanks to my way of oiling them.

AMBROSIO. You never forget to close them?

REGOLO. Never. I have my chronometer.

(He looks at it).

AMBROSIO. You never forget to look at it?

REGOLO. Never.

AMBROSIO. Is it ever slow?

REGOLO. Not a second. I can't do without it. In my job as a signal-man, I must be punctual and ready on time.

AMBROSIO. It must be maddening.

REGOLO. No, on the contrary, it's simple.

(Looks at chronometer).

You look at the chronometer and you know it's time to close the gates because the train is due. You close, it goes by. You open and finished: your work is done and well done. Thanks to the chronometer. This wonderful clockwork is the balm of my soul. Believe me, Ambrosio, there is only one thing in life, a good chronometer.

AMBROSIO. Is that so?

REGOLO. It's the secret of happiness.

(He turns to go).

714

AMBROSIO *(Accompanies him and sneaks his chronometer carefully)*.
A mandolin, Regolo, also has a little of the secret of happiness.

REGOLO. A chronometer, Ambrosio, has it all.

(Goes out).

AMBROSIO. Has it all.

(Looks at chronometer).

You've finished ordering the world to the sound of your tic-tac,
like the regular beat of marching feet: one-two, tic-tac, left-right,
tic-tac, tic-tac, tic-tac. I no longer wish to have my life sliced in
pieces. Tic, a chop, tac, a chop, tic, an arm, tac, a leg; tic, my eye,
tac, my nose. In the end there'd be nothing left of Ambrosio.

(He hides chronometer in the vine).

Chop up the minutes as much as you like, but don't force me to
eat them. To sum up, the alarm will ring no more; Spazzino's
bell has no clapper; Regolo's chronometer has disappeared. Who
else will come to trouble my peace?

(The sound of a radio station before an announcement).

RADIO. This is Radio Balbuziente. At the third stroke it will be
twelve o'clock.

AMBROSIO. Ah, no, no, no, no.

(He seizes pincers).

RADIO. Pip, pip, pip.

*(Ambrosio climbs on to table and cuts aerial in two pieces, winds
up the cut pieces and hides it in the vine)*.

VOICE OF PADRONA. Maria.

A WOMAN'S VOICE. Padrona?

VOICE OF PADRONA. Have you cut off the radio?

WOMAN'S VOICE. No I haven't.

VOICE OF PADRONA. I'll take a look at the aerial.

(Ambrosio disappears quickly into Inn).

PADRONA *(Comes in)*. Ambrosio, Ambrosio.

VOICE OF AMBROSIO. Coming.

PADRONA. Come quickly.

AMBROSIO *(Comes back)*. I was drawing the wine from my cellar.

PADRONA. Where is my aerial?

715

AMBROSIO. Your aerial? It's . . .

(Looks in the air).

Now where is it?

PADRONA. Did you cut it?

AMBROSIO. How could I? I was in the cellar.

PADRONA. You saw nobody?

AMBROSIO. No.

PADRONA. You heard nothing?

AMBROSIO. Nothing.

PADRONA. I wonder . . .

AMBROSIO (Suddenly). Oh!

PADRONA. What is it?

AMBROSIO. I remember.

PADRONA. What?

AMBROSIO. A man I met this morning, in front of the Post-Office.

PADRONA. What man?

AMBROSIO. As tall as this (very tall), as wide as that (very wide).
I don't know him. He wore a large black felt hat, that covered
his eyes. He had a black beard, and moustaches . . . very thick
ones . . . it's him.

PADRONA. Who?

AMBROSIO. The thief.

PADRONA. What thief?

AMBROSIO. The thief who stole the aerial. He had a roll of wire on
his shoulder, and some pincers in his hand. He was looking in the
air as if he was searching for something. The aerial wires likely.

PADRONA. Why should he steal the aerial wires?

AMBROSIO. Why? Yes, why? One meets so many weird people in
this life. But, come to think about it, what a cheek, to come and
cut your aerial in my garden.

REGOLO (Enters with a lost air). Ambrosio, you haven't seen . . .

(Ambrosio makes sign to him to acknowledge Padrona).

REGOLO (Bows). Padrona.

PADRONA. What makes you tremble like that?

REGOLO. My chronometer.

716

AMBROSIO. Has it stopped?

REGOLO. I've lost it.

AMBROSIO. But you had it a quarter of an hour ago.

REGOLO (*To Padrona*). That's true. I showed it to him.

PADRONA. Where did you lose it?

REGOLO. Here, I had it. On the pathway to the level crossing I didn't —I don't understand it.

AMBROSIO. Have you a hole in your pocket?

REGOLO. Certainly not.

PADRONA. Did you stop anywhere?

REGOLO. No. I came straight along the path as usual. When I got near the level crossing, I wanted to look at the time . . . as usual, too. No chronometer. I said to myself, I've lost it on the way back from Ambrosio's Inn, and I came back along the same path looking everywhere.

AMBROSIO. You must have looked badly.

PADRONA. Didn't you meet anybody?

REGOLO. I didn't notice.

PADRONA. Didn't you pass a man as tall as this . . . as wide as that . . . wearing a large black felt hat . . . black beard and moustaches . . . very thick ones . . . having a roll of wire on his shoulder?

REGOLO. I didn't see him.

AMBROSIO. You should have noticed.

REGOLO. Possibly.

AMBROSIO. It's him.

REGOLO. Who?

PADRONA. The bandit who stole my aerial. He stole your chronometer.

REGOLO. Do you really think so?

PADRONA. Absolutely certain.

AMBROSIO. Yes, absolutely certain.

REGOLO. All the same, I'll look again along the pathway and if I meet the thief . . .

AMBROSIO. Watch out, he's a big fellow.

REGOLO. For my chronometer, I feel strong enough to face a regiment.

(*Goes*).

AMBROSIO *(Calling after him)*. Call me if you want any help.

PADRONA. If you see him, call me at once. I'll have him arrested by Spazzino.

REGOLO. Yes, yes, of course. I'll let you know.

PADRONA *(Calling)*. Fantesca!

VOICE OF FANTESCA. Yes?

PADRONA. Can you come here a second?

VOICE OF FANTESCA. Coming.

PADRONA. She's a very attractive girl, Ambrosio.

AMBROSIO. She often says I'm a curly lambkin.

FANTESCA *(Enters)*. Curled to the tip of your nose.

PADRONA. Fantesca, will you do something for me?

FANTESCA. Whatever you like.

PADRONA. Someone has stolen Regolo's chronometer.

FANTESCA. What for?

PADRONA. Because he steals anything of any value, I suppose. He has also stolen my aerial, my radio's out of action, and I've no way of telling the time. Couldn't you lend me your alarm for a few days?

FANTESCA. I gave it to Ambrosio this morning, but he is kind, he'll lend it to you, won't you Ambrosio?

AMBROSIO. Yes . . . of course . . . naturally. Where is it? Where have I put it? It was here. Yes. Before I went down to the cellar, I put it there, on the table. What has happened? . . . It's him.

PADRONA. The thief?

AMBROSIO. Yes. Oh, how annoying, how annoying.

FANTESCA. Don't upset yourself, I still have an old cuckoo clock.

(To Padrona).

I'll go and get it.

(She goes out).

AMBROSIO. A cuckoo clock? How does it work?

PADRONA. With the help of two weights and a pendulum.

AMBROSIO *(Doing the pendulum swing with hand)*. Tic-tac?

PADRONA. Yes, and the cuckoo calls the hour.

FANTESCA *(Returns with clock)*. Here it is.

718

PADRONA. Let me see the bird.

AMBROSIO *(Hiding a little hammer behind his back)*. Does it need a little dusting?

PADRONA. He probably needs feeding.

FANTESCA. He only eats minutes.

AMBROSIO. Does he sing often?

FANTESCA. At the hour and at the half.

AMBROSIO. These little beasties need air and light. If I were you, Padrona, I would put him in front of my window.

PADRONA. That's an idea. And then you'll hear the time, too.

(To Fantesca).

I'll give it back as soon as my aerial has been mended.

(She goes).

AMBROSIO. Take care of him.

FANTESCA. You like birds?

AMBROSIO. Yes, when they're like you.

FANTESCA. And those made of wood?

AMBROSIO. Not so much.

FANTESCA. All the same they're nice.

AMBROSIO. Not as nice as you.

FANTESCA. Would you like a kiss?

AMBROSIO. Yes.

FANTESCA. Close your eyes.

(Ambrosio closes his eyes. Fantesca goes out on tip-toe, then we hear her gay laughter).

AMBROSIO. I haven't felt anything.

(He laughs).

The bird has flown. The bird, yes, but the other, the cuckoo? I must get rid of him, get rid of him for San Buco's sake.

(He takes a sling shot and picks up a stone in his garden).

My cuckoo friend, if you come out you will be shot.

CUCKOO. Cuckoo . . . bang . . . cuckoo . . . bang . . .

AMBROSIO. Beastly animal.

(He throws a stone. Noise of window breaking).

719

CUCKOO *(Continues)*. Cuckoo . . . bang . . . cuckoo . . .

AMBROSIO. A little more to the left.

(Throws another stone).

CUCKOO. Cuck— . . .

AMBROSIO. Nothing more to fear this time.

(He hides sling shot in vine).

The alarm has been taken down, the bell doesn't ring anymore, the radio is knocked out, the chronometer has disappeared and the cuckoo is out of order. No one, from now on, can break my ears telling me what time it is.

SPAZZINO *(Coming in)*. Do you want to know the time?

AMBROSIO *(Ironically)*. Yes, I was wondering what time it was.

SPAZZINO. Ten past twelve.

AMBROSIO. Who told you?

SPAZZINO. The church clock.

(He goes out).

AMBROSIO *(Squashed)*. The church clock . . . the church clock . . . the church clock . . .

(Curtains close).

END OF ACT ONE.

INTERLUDE

In front of the curtain. Night falls slowly. Regolo goes by looking for his chronometer.

FANTESCA *(Comes on)*. Regolo, what are you doing?

REGOLO. I'm looking for my chronometer.

FANTESCA. Don't worry. It will be found.

REGOLO. In the meantime, I dare not open my gates.

FANTESCA. Why?

REGOLO. Because I never know what time it is. And I am always wondering if the train is coming.

FANTESCA. Look at the time on the church clock.

REGOLO. The clock? That's right, my goodness! I'm so used to my chronometer that I did not think of the church clock.

FANTESCA. Spazzino thought of it first of all.

REGOLO. I'll re-open the level crossing, now that I know the time.

(Moves to go).

PADRONA *(Enters).* Have you found your chronometer?

REGOLO. Not yet.

PADRONA. Then how do you manage to tell the time?

REGOLO *(Importantly).* I look at the church clock.

(He goes).

Night has now fallen.

PADRONA. In the end nothing could be more simple.

FANTESCA. That's why nobody thought of it.

(Sound of Spazzino's trumpet).

SPAZZINO *(Offstage).* Nine o'clock, good people. Close your shutters, pull down your blinds. Nine o'clock, sleep in peace in sleeping San Buco. Nine o'clock.

(Trumpet).

PADRONA *(In a low voice).* Goodnight, Fantesca.

FANTESCA. Goodnight, Padrona.

(They go out quietly. Hardly have they gone when Ambrosio comes out of the center curtains. He moves quietly over to the Inn yard side when the muted trumpet blows behind him. Spazzino comes from the garden side, carrying a lighted lantern).

SPAZZINO *(Holding lamp up).* Who goes there?

AMBROSIO. Only me.

SPAZZINO. It's nine o'clock. I've trumpeted.

AMBROSIO. I'm not sleepy.

SPAZZINO. Nobody is sleepy at nine o'clock.

AMBROSIO. Then why do you sound the curfew?

SPAZZINO. Because it's an old custom.

AMBROSIO. Did everyone in San Buco go to bed at nine o'clock in the old days?

SPAZZINO. I don't know if they went to bed, but I know they went home.

AMBROSIO. I prefer to take a walk.

SPAZZINO. Thieves also walk at night.

AMBROSIO. I'm not a thief.

SPAZZINO.   I only mean you might very well meet one.

AMBROSIO.   What could he steal from me? I've only got my good nature, and one does not steal a good nature.

SPAZZINO.   All the same it is better to go home once night has fallen.

(He puts down his trumpet and opens the glass of his lantern to adjust the wick).

AMBROSIO.   You go for nice walks yourself.

SPAZZINO.   That's different, I'm nightwatchman and I call the hours.

AMBROSIO *(Coming to him).* Why do you call the hours when everyone is asleep in San Buco and can't hear you?

SPAZZINO.   Because it is a custom.

AMBROSIO. *(Pretends to sneeze and blows the lantern out).* Another cust . . . cust . . . cust . . .um . . .

(Complete darkness).

SPAZZINO.   That's a dirty trick.

AMBROSIO.   Wait, I've some matches.

(He grasps the trumpet).

SPAZZINO.   I've got some.

(He gets a terrific push and falls over).

Take care!

AMBROSIO *(Falls down).* Spazzino . . . Oh, I'm dead.

(Silence).

SPAZZINO.   Ambrosio . . . Ambrosio . . .

(He lights a match and with a trembling hand lights his lamp).

Ambrosio . . .

(He kneels and lifts lamp to Ambrosio's face).

Ambrosio . . .

AMBROSIO *(Pretends to come to).* Ah . . . Spazzino . . . Did you hit me?

SPAZZINO.   Of course not. You knocked me over.

(He gets up).

AMBROSIO.   It wasn't me; I got a bang on the head.

SPAZZINO.   And I in the stomach.

AMBROSIO.   It's the bandit.

(He gets up, hiding the trumpet behind his back).

722

SPAZZINO. What bandit?

AMBROSIO. The one that stole my alarm, and Regolo's chronometer, and cut the wire of Padrona's aerial, and broke Fantesca's cuckoo clock.

SPAZZINO. He nearly broke us up too.

AMBROSIO. Your lantern went out.

SPAZZINO. He must have been on the watch.

AMBROSIO. I seemed to have a tremendous man in front of me. I grabbed him . . . he had arms like trees . . . he knocked me about . . . then one bang on the head and I fell over . . . Thank goodness you were there.

SPAZZINO. I told you it was wiser to go home.

AMBROSIO. You were right. Let's go in.

SPAZZINO (Wanting to pick up trumpet). My trumpet?

AMBROSIO. What has it done?

SPAZZINO. Disappeared. Haven't you got it?

AMBROSIO (Back to audience who see the hand holding trumpet). No.

SPAZZINO. What are you hiding behind your back?

AMBROSIO. Nothing. I've a pain in my kidneys.

SPAZZINO. Show your hand.

(Ambrosio changes hands).

The other.

(Changes again).

AMBROSIO (Has managed to slip trumpet into his belt). It's wrong to suspect me, Spazzino; I'd never have thought you'd do that to a friend.

SPAZZINO. Forgive me. But so many queer things are happening in San Buco, one doesn't know what to believe. If it is not you, it is the bandit.

AMBROSIO. Let's go home.

SPAZZINO. You, yes. Me, no. I must watch over San Buco.

(The moon lights up the two men).

AMBROSIO. You'll only get knocked out again.

SPAZZINO. It's my duty to watch through the night. And here is the moon. I'm no longer alone. Goodnight, Ambrosio.

(He mimics the sound of his trumpet and goes out calling in a voice shaking with fright).

Sleep well, good people, sleep in peace in sleeping San Buco.

AMBROSIO.   Brave and courageous Spazzino.   Even without his trumpet he manages to carry out his duty, and watches over those who sleep.   I can't very well cut his head off to stop him imitating his trumpet.   Go my friend, do your round, for tomorrow a great surprise awaits you.   And you, San Buco, my little village, sleep your heart out, for tomorrow you will wake up bewildered.

(Darkness again).

The moon has flown.   This is the time to act.

(He is about to go and finds himself suddenly facing full face into an electric torch.   He is scared).

Ah?

PADRONA.   Ambrosio.

AMBROSIO.   Who? . . . Eh? . . . Please, lower your torch.

PADRONA.   It's me.

(She shows herself with torch).

AMBROSIO.   You frightened me.

PADRONA.   What are you doing here?

AMBROSIO.   I'm . . . looking for a bandit?   Are you?

PADRONA.   So am I.

(The moon comes out).

AMBROSIO.   Take care.   He prowls the place.

PADRONA.   You've seen him?

AMBROSIO.   No.   I've felt him.

(He shows his head).

I was talking to Spazzino.   Suddenly, the lamp was put out and he attacked us in the dark.

PADRONA.   He should have been knocked on the head.

AMBROSIO.   We were the ones who got knocked on the head.   I fought like a lion . . . you know me . . . But what can one man do alone . . . Spazzino had already been stunned . . . and against a person as big as a horse?

(The moon is veiled).

PADRONA.   Where is Spazzino now?

AMBROSIO.   He continues his rounds.

PADRONA.   He's a brave chap, but it's foolish to take useless risks.

AMBROSIO.   You are right.   We'd do much better to go home.

PADRONA. Yes. Let's go in. Goodnight, Ambrosio.

(She goes out with torch).

AMBROSIO. Goodnight, Padrona.

(The moon comes out. To the moon).

Go to bed. Do . . . Curfew sounded a long time ago. You ought to be in your bed of clouds and not come out before tomorrow morning. Be reasonable, go to your bed. If you walk through the night, you'll meet the bandit.

(He laughs).

As big as this, as large as that. He came all alive out of my head and now everybody sees him. Go on, old girl, one good spring and hop into bed. How do you expect me to get to the church without being seen if you obstinately spill your honey-moon light through the streets of San Buco? . . . Other villages, other countries, would like to have some, too. You must look after them. Hurry up; oh moon, oh round beloved. A lovely cloud is slipping towards you, like a soft pillow.

(Moon is veiled).

Sleep, sleep, my old moon, sleep.

(In a whisper).

Tonight I shall act for the happiness of San Buco.

(He goes out).

END OF INTERLUDE.

ACT TWO.

The curtains open partially showing the inside of the belfry tower. The bell and above this the clock mechanism. Several small openings in the steeple.

VOICE OF AMBROSIO. 143, 144.

(A lantern appears at floor level).

147, 148, 149.

(Ambrosio enters).

149 steps.

(Puts lantern down).

A church is higher than a mountain. If I climbed onto the weather-cock I could put out the moonlight. And this bell, what a paunch! One is devilishly well nourished here.

(He looks out through one of the openings).

725

San Buco rests her heart out beneath the caress of night. Not a light, sleep in peace, good people, sleep in peace in sleeping San Buco, as Spazzino would say. Your friend Ambrosio is arranging a new life for you. An hourless life, with no church clock, no alarms, no clocks. A life where all shall do their heart's desire, without jostling, peacefully. A life that each will lead with good will. San Buco, oh my old dear homeland, you will at last know true happiness.

(He climbs on to the bell framework and finds himself very unsteadily balanced).

Hola—ho—

(The bell machinery shakes in preparation for striking. It strikes. Ambrosio comes down rapidly from the framework and stops the bell).

I beg you . . . don't move again. You'll wake the whole world up.

(A noise makes him tremble, he listens).

VOICE OF SPAZZINO. 138, 139, 140.

(Ambrosio looks for a hiding place and slips into the bell, putting out his light).

141, 142, 143, 144.

(We see his lantern).

145, 146,.

(Spazzino enters lifting his lantern to arm's length, then in a very unassured voice).

Show yourself. I know someone is here. I heard the bell ring. Come on, come out of your hiding place. I warn you, I shall stay here until you come out.

(He searches about).

Don't think I'm afraid of you. Be sensible. Show yourself. Look here, I'll make you a proposition. Give yourself up without resistance and I promise you, if the Padrona has you put in prison, I'll come and play cards with you every evening, after the curfew . . . How obstinate you are. All the same you aren't going to force me to keep guard here all night . . . Remember I have to get up early in the morning to call the market open. I assure you . . .

(He stops and listens. Someone is mounting the tower. He hides behind the framework and veils the lamplight).

VOICE OF FANTESCA. 141, 142.

(A hand holding a lighted candle is seen at ground level).

143, 144, 145 . . .

(Fantesca enters, her head covered with a shawl).

726

SPAZZINO *(Blows out the candle and catches hold of her in the dark)*. Give yourself up!

FANTESCA. Let me go.

SPAZZINO. Don't move.

FANTESCA. I'm afraid.

SPAZZINO. You are my prisoner.

FANTESCA. Please, don't hurt me, Mr. Bandit.

SPAZZINO *(Unveiling his lantern)*. What are you doing here?

FANTESCA. What are you?

SPAZZINO. While doing my rounds in the village, I heard the bell ring.

FANTESCA. So did I.

SPAZZINO. I thought the bandit was hiding in the belfry.

FANTESCA. So did I.

SPAZZINO. I came here to catch him.

FANTESCA. So did I.

SPAZZINO. You aren't the bandit by any chance?

FANTESCA. Me? I was already in bed when I heard the bell.

SPAZZINO. All the same it's queer you should have had the same idea as I had.

FANTESCA. You found nobody?

SPAZZINO. No.

FANTESCA. Then you are the bandit!

SPAZZINO. Ah, no.

FANTESCA. All the same, he can't have flown out of the window, Spazzino, I'm frightened.

SPAZZINO. Let us go down.

FANTESCA. Yes.

SPAZZINO. Be quiet. Someone is coming up the stairs.

FANTESCA. It's him.

SPAZZINO. We'll arrest him. You hide there, I here.

(They hide. Complete darkness).

REGOLO. 136, 137, 138. What a job. 139, 140.

(He comes on and lights a match).

What a job.

727

(He climbs on to the bell framework, puts his head out of one of the peepholes, lights another match and looks outside).

Nearly midnight.

SPAZZINO *(Without showing himself).* Hands up!

REGOLO. Ah!

(Puts his hands up).

SPAZZINO *(Lights him with his lantern).* Regolo.

FANTESCA. Are you the bandit?

REGOLO. What bandit?

SPAZZINO. The trumpet thief.

REGOLO. What trumpet?

SPAZZINO. Mine.

REGOLO. I haven't stolen anything.

FANTESCA. Then what are you doing up there?

REGOLO. I came to see the time.

SPAZZINO. You can see the time perfectly well down below.

REGOLO *(Coming down).* During the day, yes, I look up at the church clock. But as soon as night comes I can no longer see it. I start thinking of my level crossing, of the train that might come, and I worry so much that I can't sleep. And to stop worrying I climb the belfry, put my head out of the peephole, I light a match and look at the hands of the clock. I can't live without knowing what time it is.

FANTESCA. And what time is it?

REGOLO. Just on midnight.

SPAZZINO. Midnight. The loveliest hour of the night. Midnight. The hour that is neither yesterday nor yet tomorrow. The hour I love announcing best. But I no longer have my trumpet.

FANTESCA. Let's ring the bell.

SPAZZINO. That's right, we can ring the bell.

REGOLO. You'll wake up all San Buco.

SPAZZINO. No. It has a solemn voice, like a kind father. It will give confidence to those who can't sleep.

FANTESCA. Let's go down.

(They go out).

(Darkness. Ambrosio's lantern shows in the bell. Ambrosio is about to go when the bell begins to swing, set in motion by

728

*those who have gone down, and strikes the twelve strokes of mid-
night, which Ambrosio punctuates by a cry of pain. Then the bell
becomes motionless and Ambrosio goes, bruised, beaten, battered
by the pitiless beating that sounded the twelve strokes and gave
him twelve others).*

AMBROSIO *(Feeling and tapping his body all over)*. Twelve beats, and
what beats. I'm ground finer than a bag of flour. Bim, on my
nose, bam, in the stomach. Bim, my arm; bam, my back. My
shoulder, my head . . . They have gone. Now to work, Ambrosio.

*(He prepares to mount the framework again, but changes his
mind).*

You, you'll not ring again to rouse the whole town.

(He takes out the bell clapper).

You mustn't wake up San Buco, old girl. Swing, if it pleases you
as I do on my swing, but don't ring again during the night. That's
a piece of advice from Spazzino; an order from the Padrona, and
Fantesca's wish.

*(He climbs on to the framework and puts his arm through the
little window and picks off the clock hands).*

Now you can grind the hours as much as you like, and you can
pound the minutes as you please. Nobody will see the time any
more. Without your hands you are a useless mill. San Buco will
at last live in peace without hearing every minute something saying "It's such and such a time, you must do so-and-so."

(He balances on the bell's axis).

I've killed the time. I've killed the time.

(He hums his Tarantella).

Curtains close.

END OF ACT TWO.

SECOND INTERLUDE.

In front of curtain.

SPAZZINO *(Comes in from back of audience, very agitated)*. Padrona,
Padrona!

PADRONA *(Comes on, her head covered in paper curlers)*. Spazzino?

SPAZZINO. Padrona!

PADRONA. What has happened?

SPAZZINO. The hands . . .

PADRONA. What?

729

SPAZZINO. The hands . . .

PADRONA. What hands?

SPAZZINO. The church clock hands. They've disappeared.

PADRONA. What are you saying?

SPAZZINO. As the cock crowed, I went off to call the market open. I
wanted to look at the time on the church tower . . . the hands had
disappeared . . . They've been stolen.

PADRONA. But why?

SPAZZINO. To stop us seeing the time I suppose.

FANTESCA *(Comes running in)*. The clock hands on the church tower
have been stolen!

PADRONA. Don't frighten us.

REGOLO *(Comes on)*. It's dreadful.

PADRONA. Yes, the hands have been stolen from the church clock.

REGOLO. What will become of us?

FANTESCA. It's aggravating.

PADRONA. I'll have an inquiry.

REGOLO. Now we shall never know the time.

SPAZZINO. Yes, we will.

ALL. How?

SPAZZINO. I've made a sundial.

PADRONA. It's true, a sundial can replace all the clocks in the world.

REGOLO. How have you made it?

FANTESCA. Where is it?

SPAZZINO. Go and look at the square by the church, you'll understand.

PADRONA. Come.

AMBROSIO *(Comes in)*. The hands of the church . . .

ALL. Have disappeared.

AMBROSIO. You know?

REGOLO. Everyone knows.

AMBROSIO. It does not seem to surprise you much.

PADRONA. No, because Spazzino has made a sundial.

  (She goes).

FANTESCA.   Are you coming, Regolo?

(She goes).

REGOLO.   A sundial, Ambrosio, just that.

(He goes).

AMBROSIO.   *(Astonished and shaken).*   I say, Spazzino, a sundial, what is it?

SPAZZINO.   It's a method, used in olden days, by people to tell the time.

AMBROSIO.   Does it work like a clock?

SPAZZINO.   No, the sun marks the hours.

AMBROSIO.   I don't understand.

SPAZZINO.   It's simple. Suppose the sun is there and the light falls on something immovable. Put yourself there and don't move. Do you see anything?

AMBROSIO.   No.

SPAZZINO.   And this?

AMBROSIO.   My shadow.

SPAZZINO.   I mark the place it falls and compare it with the clock. Suppose it is nine o'clock.

AMBROSIO.   You've got a clock?

SPAZZINO.   No. But when I made my sundial, yesterday, the church clock still had hands.

AMBROSIO.   Well, you were saying that here, where my shadow falls, it is nine o'clock. And after?

SPAZZINO.   Later, the sun is there. Where is your shadow?

AMBROSIO.   The sun is there?

SPAZZINO.   Yes.

AMBROSIO.   My shadow is here.

SPAZZINO.   I mark it *(marks the place)* and compare. It is two o'clock. If it is there, I mark here; if it moves there, I mark. In this way, I've marked each hour of the day.

AMBROSIO.   That's all very well, but if I move, the hour changes.

SPAZZINO.   That's why I chose something that does not move.

AMBROSIO.   What?

SPAZZINO.   A tree. I marked the hours by following the shadow of the big oak tree in front of the church. When the shadow of the tree is on the church tower it's, let us say, nine o'clock; when it's on the bake shop, ten o'clock; when it's on the schoolhouse, eleven o'clock. There twelve. And so, it follows on.

AMBROSIO. It's incredible how clever you are.

SPAZZINO. One only had to think of it. It's quite simple.

AMBROSIO. It's quite simple, one only had to think of it.

SPAZZINO. While waiting to find the thief and the clock hands, San Buco will look at my sundial.

AMBROSIO. It never gets out of order?

SPAZZINO. Impossible. To destroy it, one would have to knock down the tree, demolish the clock tower, or make the sun disappear. Good-day, Ambrosio.

(He goes).

AMBROSIO. Good-day, Spazzino.

(He is overwhelmed by this piece of news and sits).

The sundial. The tree, church, sun. Church, tree, sun. Tree, sun, church. Sun, tree, church. The sun? I can't put it out like a lamp, nor put it in my pocket. The belfry? I can't demolish it. The tree? . . . the tree . . . the tree . . . *(night falls slowly)* The . . . The tree . . .

(He goes out quickly and comes back with a saw).

To the two of us, sundial.

(He goes out. Sound of saw cutting tree, then music, and the curtains open slowly).

END OF THE SECOND INTERLUDE.

ACT THREE.

Same as Act One, brilliantly lit.

REGOLO *(Comes in running, very agitated, calling).* Patesca, Fanzino, Ambrona, Spatasio, Patrosio, Ambrotesca, Spata, Spasi, Ambri . . . Ah . . . . .

(Padrona, Fantesca Spazzino come from different sides).

REGOLO. The tree . . . the tree . . . the tree . . .

PADRONA. Calm yourself.

REGOLO. The dial . . . the sunset . . . the time—

PADRONA. The sundial.

(Spazzino goes out quickly).

REGOLO. Disappeared.

PADRONA. Explain yourself.

REGOLO. The tree, sawed off, cut down, the tree by the tower is felled.

(Fantesca goes out quickly).

PADRONA. What are you saying?

REGOLO. Cut down to the ground.

PADRONA. The tree?

REGOLO. The one that marked the time.

PADRONA. It's unbelievable.

REGOLO. I no longer know when to close the level crossing.

FANTESCA *(Returns)*. It's true, the big oak is cut down.

REGOLO. What time is it? Nobody knows, the train could come any minute.

(He goes quickly out).

PADRONA. Call Ambrosio. Ambrosio.

FANTESCA. Ambrosio. Ambrosio.

AMBROSIO *(Coming out of Inn)*. Alright, alright, alright. Here I am. Don't shout.

PADRONA. Do you know the sundial is destroyed?

AMBROSIO *(Pretending to be surprised)*. But how? tell me.

PADRONA. The big oak by the tower is felled.

AMBROSIO. Who did it?

PADRONA. I know nothing, but we must act.

(To Fantesca).

Go and get Spazzino and Regolo.

(Fantesca goes quickly out).

AMBROSIO. What a cheek . . . to saw the tree down.

PADRONA. This can't go on, Ambrosio. From to-day we must take strong measures.

(Fantesca returns with Spazzino and Regolo).

Gentlemen, I must speak to you. Take your places.

(She speaks with great solemnity. Spazzino is very proud to be invited to this conference. Regolo, conscious of his sudden import-ance, lights his pipe with due seriousness. Ambrosio sits on a bench, after taking his bowl of soap bubbles and clay pipe).

PADRONA *(In a very official manner)*. For the last few days we have been the victims of an unknown person. I will remind you of the the facts. Regolo's chronometer has disappeared; Spazzino has lost his trumpet and his bell clapper; someone cut and stole the aerial wire of my wireless; a stone broke the cuckoo clock belonging to Fantesca; the church clock has no hands; the church bell has no clapper; Ambrosio's alarm has been stolen; and now the sundial that Spazzino thought out has been destroyed. Someone, some being, some evil power, hangs over San Buco. We have all suffered; Regolo, Fantesca, Ambrosio, Spazzino and myself. We are without time. This cannot go on. We must remedy this and take steps to see that it does not continue. That is the reason I have called you here today, and I ask each one of you to say at once what you think is the best thing to do. I await your suggestions.

SPAZZINO. I propose . . . I propose to organize a patrol after nine o'clock at night.

AMBROSIO. Who will tell you it's nine o'clock?

SPAZZINO. I know we no longer know the time, but our patrol could very well start after night has fallen.

PADRONA. Who will be in command?

FANTESCA. Why not Regolo?

REGOLO. You know . . . I have nothing of the commander in me. A stationmaster, yes. But the commander of a patrol, no . . . I prefer not to, really.

SPAZZINO. What about Ambrosio?

AMBROSIO. Leave me to my waffles, my omelettes, and my kitchen, but don't ask me to patrol the night with a lantern, a trumpet, a rope and a gun.

(He puts his bowl of soap down on the table, near Spazzino).

SPAZZINO *(Convinced he will be appointed, swallows)*. Then who shall we ask?

FANTESCA. You, naturally.

(She waters the flowers).

SPAZZINO. Do you think so? Do you all think so?

REGOLO-AMBROSIO-FANTESCA. Yes, yes, that'll be fine.

PADRONA. I don't think so. Everyone should sleep at night and get rested, so that they can work in the daytime. We must find some other means.

REGOLO. I propose we put down wolf-traps in the belfry, and traps in the streets, false chronometers stuck with glue, so that the thief catches his fingers; electrified clocks, and . . .

734

PADRONA. That's too dangerous. Anyone might be caught.

(She looks at herself in mirror. Spazzino mechanically blows the soap bubbles).

FANTESCA. I wonder why we should go to so much trouble.

AMBROSIO. Fantesca is right.

REGOLO. All the same we should do something. We must get back to regular ways of living, and know the time.

AMBROSIO. And what good is that? Can't one live perfectly well without time? Look at Spazzino.

PADRONA. What tobacco are you smoking?

SPAZZINO. I don't know, but it's pretty. Look!

(He blows a bubble. Ambrosio breaks it on the tip of his finger).

REGOLO. You should have left it.

PADRONA. Why did you do that?

AMBROSIO. To show you what your plans are. They are here, hardly formed, frail, light, and pfft . . . a flick of my finger . . . they are forgotten. Yes, Spazzino, you dream of commanding a night-patrol in San Buco: soap-bubble! It only needs a bowl of soap and a clay pipe for you to forget everything. Instead of placing traps in every corner of the town . . . soap-bubble! Regolo smokes his pipe. You, Fantesca, ought to be preparing your master's dinner. Soap-bubble! . . . You water my flowers. And you, Padrona, you want to arrest the bandit: soap-bubble! . . . You mix in that mirror your beauty with that of the sun. You have forgotten the time.

PADRONA. It's true.

AMBROSIO. Is it less fun?

REGOLO. I get bored with nothing to do.

AMBROSIO. There is always something to do. You have a good voice. Sing us something.

PADRONA. Oh yes, sing something for us.

SPAZZINO. Go on, Regolo.

REGOLO. If you want me to.

(Tarantella. All dance. Spazzino goes out. While the music continues, one hears in the distance the roar of the traffic, of trucks, of horns blowing madly).

PADRONA. What is that noise?

SPAZZINO *(Returning joyously)*. There are at least fifty trucks, cars, carts, and dozens of people waiting for the level crossing gates to open.

735

REGOLO. Why can't they leave me in peace?

(He goes out).

FANTESCA. What about you, Spazzino? Have you swept the market place this morning?

SPAZZINO. No. I'm tired.

PADRONA. Tired of what? You've done nothing.

SPAZZINO. That's just the trouble. I'm tired of doing nothing.

(They all sit around comfortably).

AMBROSIO. One can always do something.

SPAZZINO. What?

AMBROSIO. Play, for instance.

FANTESCA. Play at what?

SPAZZINO. Play at chess.

PADRONA. Only two can play it.

AMBROSIO. What about a game of hide and seek?

FANTESCA. Yes, yes.

REGOLO *(Comes back).* I've opened the gates.

PADRONA. Will you play with us?

REGOLO. At what?

AMBROSIO. Hide and seek.

REGOLO. Its twenty years since I've played hide and seek.

SPAZZINO. One more reason why you should. It will limber up your legs.

PADRONA. Let's play.

FANTESCA. Who will be "It" first?

AMBROSIO. Let's choose him by a test. Now, we'll all do this. Tic, take a step forward with the left foot. Tac, step with the right. Tic-tac, tic-and-tac. Whoever goes wrong first will be "It."

PADRONA. Agreed.

SPAZZINO. Come on.

AMBROSIO. Ready? Tic-tac-tic-tac.

(Going quicker and quicker).

(Regolo uses the wrong foot).

FANTESCA. Regolo.

PADRONA. It's Regolo.

REGOLO. No, I didn't understand. Let's start again.

PADRONA. Start again, Ambrosio.

AMBROSIO. Are you ready? Tic-tac, tic-tac, and tic-tac-tic-tac-tic—
   (Regolo goes wrong again).

SPAZZINO. That's fair this time.

FANTESCA. You must look for us.

AMBROSIO. Hide your eyes, and you must slowly count tic ten times.

REGOLO. Ten times tic?

AMBROSIO. And ten times tac.

REGOLO. And ten times tac.

AMBROSIO. You stand here. This is "home." *(The swing)*.

REGOLO *(Counts)*. One tic, two tic . . . *(Up to ten)* one tac, two tac
   . . . *(Up to ten, then he looks for them. The others are hidden
   in various places)*.

FANTESCA *(Gets home and says)*. Tic-tac for Regolo.

SPAZZINO *(The same)*. Tic-tac.

PADRONA *(Gets home)*. Tic-tac, Regolo.

REGOLO *(Looks for Ambrosio in the audience)*. Where is he?

   (He sees him and races back to the swing).

   Tic-tac for Ambrosio. You're out.

PADRONA. Your turn, Ambrosio.

REGOLO. Ten times tic and ten times tac. Slowly.

SPAZZINO. And don't peep.

AMBROSIO *(At "home," counts steadily)*. One tic, one tac; two tic,
   two tac;—

SPAZZINO. You are peeping.

AMBROSIO. Oh, no. Three tic, three tac . . . *(faster and faster)* . . .
   four tic, and tac; five tic-tac; six tic-tac—tic-tac . . .

ROMEO *(Enters)*. Ambrosio.

AMBROSIO. Tic-tac . . . Oh, it's you . . . my congratulations.

ROMEO. For what?

AMBROSIO. Your wedding.

ROMEO. Exactly. It is about that . . .

AMBROSIO. Wait, let us finish our game.

JULIETTA (*Rushes in, a peasant girl dressed in her Sunday best*). Have you found her?

AMBROSIO. Hello, Julietta. You are a very pretty bride.

(*Then follows a scene where the speeches follow in rapid succession, overlapping and getting mixed up, until everybody is speaking at once, volubly and excitably*).

MOTHER (*A fat country-woman, enters, out of breath*). Julietta, don't run. You will ruin your dress.

FATHER (*Enters, walking with difficulty*). You run, you gallop, and you know that I have sore feet.

AMBROSIO. Sit down. I'm coming.

MOTHER. It's been more than an hour we've been waiting at the city hall.

JULIETTA (*In tears*). We are not yet married.

FATHER. These are new shoes. They pinch me there, and there.

ROMEO (*To Julietta*). Don't cry, we will find her.

MOTHER (*Pointing to Julietta*). And look at the result. This is no way to do.

FATHER. Next time, I'll wear my boots.

JULIETTA. It's always the same story. I never have any luck.

AMBROSIO. But good heavens, don't get yourselves into such a state.

MOTHER. If you think it's funny to see your daughter in this state . . .

FATHER. Not counting the two hundred francs I paid for them.

ROMEO (*To Ambrosio*). You have not seen her?

JULIETTA. I want to go back to my cows.

MOTHER. No. Calm yourself, wipe your nose, and be quiet.

(*At last they have run down, and return to normal rhythm*).

FATHER (*Who has sat down and removed his shoes*). Well, have you seen her, or have you not seen her?

AMBROSIO. Who?

ALL. The Padrona.

AMBROSIO. The Padrona? Why?

ROMEO AND JULIETTA. To marry us.

MOTHER AND FATHER (*At the same time*). To marry them.

738

AMBROSIO (*Calling out*). Padrona! . . . Come out! . . . I am stopping the game.

(*Padrona comes out*).

AMBROSIO. They are asking for you.

PADRONA. Good Heavens, the wedding . . .

MOTHER. We have been looking for you everywhere.

PADRONA. Oh, forgive me.

JULIETTA. We've been waiting at the city hall.

PADRONA. I forgot the time. Come, quickly.

(*She goes out, followed by Julietta and by her mother*).

ROMEO. Where are they going?

FATHER. Well, to the wedding, I guess.

ROMEO. Maybe I'd better go too, then.

(*He goes out*).

FATHER (*Rises, shoes in hand, to follow Romeo, then sees Spazzino, who is ambling across the stage with Fantesca and Regolo. To Spazzino:*) Ah, so there you are!

SPAZZINO. Hello, Mario.

FATHER. You know, in the market, there is almost a riot.

AMBROSIO. A riot? Why?

FATHER. They are absolutely enraged at him.

SPAZZINO. At me? I haven't done anything.

FATHER. Exactly, that's what they are mad about. You haven't swept up the trash.

(*He goes out*).

SPAZZINO. Oh, why do they have to be in such a hurry?

FANTESCA. Better get down there. We'll wait for you.

SPAZZINO. I'll be right back.

(*He goes out, wheeling his garbage cart*).

Sweeper . . . Sweeper—

AMBROSIO. We can continue without them.

FANTESCA. Just three of us?

REGOLO. Yes, why not?

THUNDEROUS VOICE (*Offstage*). Fantesca, where are you?

FANTESCA. It is the school-master.

THUNDEROUS VOICE *(Offstage)*. Fantesca, come here at once, or I will come get you.

FANTESCA. I'm coming.

(She runs off).

REGOLO. He doesn't sound very pleasant.

AMBROSIO. I don't understand people. They always find a way not to be happy, and yet it is so simple to take life easy, without troubling ourselves with—

(Shrill whistle and noise of approaching train).

REGOLO. My gates. The train. I forgot to close—oh, pray that nothing happens.

(Loud uproar, cries).

AMBROSIO. Aie!!

REGOLO. I have done it.

AMBROSIO. Let's go see.

REGOLO. I am a wretch.

AMBROSIO. But don't just stand there. Come on.

(He goes out).

REGOLO. I didn't do my job.

AMBROSIO *(Comes back)*. It is Spazzino.

REGOLO. I have killed my best friend.

(Spazzino enters, carrying one twisted wheel and some debris).

REGOLO. You are not dead?

SPAZZINO. Do I look like it?

REGOLO. My poor old friend, you are alive.

SPAZZINO. It's not my fault. Your train passed like that—vwouitt! —right before my nose.

AMBROSIO. Sit down, I'll go fetch you a drink.

(He goes out).

REGOLO. You had a narrow escape.

SPAZZINO. You can say that again.

REGOLO. I am glad, Spazzino.

SPAZZINO. Not I. This is all that is left of my cart.

REGOLO. Because of my gates . . .

SPAZZINO. Which were left open, yes.

REGOLO. I am an assassin.

SPAZZINO. Oh, no. Only careless.

REGOLO. This time, it is the end.

SPAZZINO. What?

REGOLO. My chance to be station-master.

AMBROSIO *(Returns and offers Spazzino a glass).* There. Swallow that. It will restore you.

SPAZZINO. Give it to him. *(Regolo)* He needs it more than I do.

AMBROSIO *(Hands the glass to Regolo).* You are not feeling well?

REGOLO. I am disgraced.

(He drains the glass. Music. The wedding party returns. This time, the Father has knotted the shoe-strings together, and wears the shoes around his neck).

SPAZZINO. Long live the bride.

AMBROSIO. Long live the bride.

REGOLO *(Feebly).* Long live the bride.

AMBROSIO. Congratulations to the bride's mother.

FATHER. Romeo.

ROMEO. Yes, Papa.

FATHER. I'm hungry.

MOTHER. Me too.

ROMEO *(To Ambrosio).* The turkey. Is it ready?

AMBROSIO. It is in the oven. A work of art, you will see. You will have a treat. Here, get settled.

(He goes into the Inn).

JULIETTA. I am so happy. May we invite Spazzino?

FATHER. Of course.

SPAZZINO. Thank you. You are very nice.

MOTHER. You too, Regolo.

REGOLO. I'm not hungry. Excuse me.

JULIETTA. But yes, Regolo. Eat with us.

ROMEO. It is a big turkey, like that.

741

(Ambrosio returns, very sheepish, bearing a turkey absolutely burned to a crisp).

FATHER. What on earth is that? Anthracite?

JULIETTA. The turkey . . .

AMBROSIO. It is a little overdone.

MOTHER. In place of playing games out here, you could have been watching it.

AMBROSIO. I forgot the time.

FATHER *(Rising)*. You are only a good for nothing.

ROMEO. Such a beautiful turkey.

JULIETTA *(In tears)*. This is all I needed.

MOTHER. It is a shame. This is a block of carbon.

FATHER. Romeo.

ROMEO. Yes, Papa.

FATHER. Let's go.

AMBROSIO. But Mario, wait. I will . . .

PERE. You will do nothing at all. We'll eat at home.

MOTHER *(To Julietta)*. Yes. Come.

AMBROSIO. I promise you that in half an hour . . .

FATHER. Half an hour?

(He draws a huge watch from his pocket).

Do you know what time it is?

AMBROSIO. I will fix you some hors d'oeuvres, a paella—

JULIETTA. I will not have my turkey?

AMBROSIO. A rizotto, if you wish.

FATHER. I told you, no. We'll never set foot in your inn again. Come everybody.

(He starts out).

AMBROSIO. Mario, listen.

FATHER. No.

(He leaves).

ROMEO. When he says something, he means it. Me, too. *(To Julietta)* Come.

JULIETTA. Yes, Romeo.

(They go out).

MOTHER. And you, you can eat it, your platter of carbon.

(Goes out).

AMBROSIO. What a fuss, over a turkey!

SPAZZINO. They are right, you know. Don't you think so?

REGOLO. It is uneatable.

AMBROSIO. There's no need to beat a dead horse.

PADRONA *(Enters).* Well, why have they all left?

SPAZZINO. The turkey is—

AMBROSIO. A little overdone.

REGOLO. A little, and a bit more. It is burned up, that is all the difference.

AMBROSIO. I didn't know it was so late.

PADRONA. Neither did I.

REGOLO. Which proves that you cannot get along without keeping time. Ah, when I had my chronometer—

AMBROSIO. Oh no, you are not going to begin that again.

PADRONA. He is right. I had set the wedding for eleven o'clock. I forgot it.

SPAZZINO. You, you had promised the turkey for noon. You, too, forgot it.

REGOLO. Result: you lose some good customers, and make your friends mad.

PADRONA. I will be reprimanded by the consul-general.

SPAZZINO. My cart is a total wreck.

REGOLO. I will never be station master of San Buco.

(Fantesca comes in, carrying a small bundle in her hand).

AMBROSIO. Where are you going?

FANTESCA. I've lost my job.

PADRONA. The school master?

FANTESCA. Yes. This morning, I woke him up too late. I didn't know the time.

AMBROSIO. And for that he fired you?

FANTESCA. He was late getting to school—later than the children. They made fun of him.

REGOLO. Another one who needs a chronometer.

743

Fantesca. "I have lost my authority," he said to me. "I cut a fine figure, coming to school last, when I punish them for being late." He cried, then he said, "And I have nothing to eat. For an hour and a half you have done nothing. Get out. I don't want you here any more."

Padrona. Don't cry. We will find you another job.

Fantesca (*Weeps, burying her head in the vine*). "A good for nothing," that's what he said . . . Look, a trumpet.

Regolo. A what?

Fantesca. A trumpet, there.

Spazzino (*Approaches*). But—that's mine.

Padrona. Your trumpet?

Spazzino. Yes, look. And there!

Regolo. My chronometer.

Padrona. The sling that killed the cuckoo.

Fantesca. My alarm clock—all smashed.

Regolo. The hands of the church clock.

Padrona. My antenna.

Spazzino. The bell clapper of the clock.

Regolo. The saw, that cut down the tree for the sundial.

Padrona. It was you.

Fantesca. Oh, Ambrosio, why did you do all this?

Spazzino. Yes, why?

Regolo. Explain yourself, chronometer thief.

Padrona. Easy, now. (*To Ambrosio*) It was really you?

(*Ambrosio nods his head, sheepishly*).

Padrona. Why?

Ambrosio. I thought I was doing a good thing, Padrona.

Spazzino. The robber with the black beard.

Regolo. It was him.

Ambrosio. I could not bear to see my life cut up into slices marked nine o'clock, ten o'clock, eleven o'clock, until the end of the day— only to start the same thing all over again the next day.

Fantesca. Cuckoo-killer.

744

AMBROSIO. It seemed to me that each of you would have no worries, no troubles, if only you could learn to live without the clock. I thought it would be possible to live without time, and I wished to prove it. I only did it for the happiness of San Buco.

PADRONA. Do you know that you deserve a severe punishment?

FANTESCA. He has done no harm.

PADRONA. He nearly caused Spazzino's death.

SPAZZINO. I was afraid so, true, when the train grazed my nose, but that is over. Let's say no more about it.

PADRONA. Regolo will possibly never be station master.

REGOLO. That's too bad, yes—but thanks to him, I have remembered that I can sing. That counts too.

FANTESCA. And you, Padrona, have you not recovered a little of your youth, dancing and playing hide-and-seek?

PADRONA. Well—yes. But you, you have lost your job.

FANTESCA. That's no reason to put him in prison.

AMBROSIO. I have another job to offer you, if you will take it.

FANTESCA. With a good master?

AMBROSIO. Yes. An honest chap who needs a smile like yours to forget the wrong he has done. Would you like to work in my inn?

FANTESCA. To pluck chickens, and cook waffles?

AMBROSIO. No. To become Madame Ambrosio.

FANTESCA. Me? Your wife? Oh, Ambrosio!

(She flies into his arms).

PADRONA. Eh, but this is excellent news.

SPAZZINO. I'm going to announce this marriage to all San Buco.

(He tries a toot on his trumpet).

REGOLO. I will give you a beautiful chronometer, like mine.

FANTESCA *(Drawing back)*. But . . . I have not said yes.

PADRONA *(With mild reproach)*. Fantesca!

AMBROSIO. You don't wish to . . .

FANTESCA. I will do it on one condition.

AMBROSIO. I accept, without knowing it.

REGOLO. Right. We accept without knowing it.

AMBROSIO. But even so, tell us your condition.

745

FANTESCA. You have made fun of us.

SPAZZINO. Only a little.

FANTESCA. You wanted to kill time . . .

PADRONA. That's true.

FANTESCA. That is why, if you wish to marry me . . .

AMBROSIO. I will do anything you wish.

FANTESCA. Until everything is put back to rights—the bell clapper, the hands of the church clock, Padrona's antenna, and everything —it is you who will be the clock for San Buco.

AMBROSIO. Me? The clock?

FANTESCA. You will balance yourself on your flower-tub . . .

(Regolo and Spazzino seize Ambrosio and set him on the swing).

FANTESCA. You will count the seconds like a pendulum.

SPAZZINO *(Gives the swing a push).* Tic-tac, tic-tac.

FANTESCA. And you will call out the hours, like the cuckoo you broke.

(Music. All sing, and Ambrosio, smiling, swings).

AMBROSIO. Tic-tac, tic-tac . . . Cuckoo—Cuckoo. It is time to . . . return to your homes . . . go ahead . . . go ahead . . . tic-tac, tic-tac . . . It is time . . . go ahead . . . go ahead . . . go ahead . . .

CURTAIN

746

ANDROCLES AND THE LION

Adapted by

Aurand Harris

A play for the young, based on the Italian Tale of "Androcles and the Lion," and written in the style of Italian Commedia dell 'arte.

ANDROCLES AND THE LION

By Aurand Harris

THE ANCHORAGE PRESS
Cloverlot
Anchorage, Kentucky 40223
U. S. A.

ANDROCLES AND THE LION

CAST

ANDROCLES

PANTALONE

ISABELLA

LELIO

CAPTAIN

LION AND PROLOGUE

SCENE

The improvised stage of a Commedia dell'arte troupe of strolling players. Sixteenth Century, Italy.

The play is in two parts.

The following is a copy of the programme of the first performance of
ANDROCLES AND THE LION, presented at the Forty-first Street
Theatre in New York City, 7 December, 1963:

Expore, Inc. Presents

Stan Raiff's Production of

ANDROCLES AND THE LION

A Play With Music in the Style of
Commedia dell 'Arte

by

AURAND HARRIS

Directed by Stan Raiff

Musical Score	*Choreography*	*Costumes and Settings*
Glenn Mack	Beverly Schmidt	Richard Rummonds

ANDROCLES	Joseph Barnaba
LION	Richard Sanders
PANTALONE	Leonard Josenhans
CAPTAIN	Eric Tavares
ISABELLA	Jacqueline Coslow
LELIO	Christopher McCall

Assistant Director: Montgomery Davis
Assistants to Mr. Rummonds: Maryet Ramsey and Charles MacNab

(Pictures used in this book were taken from this
production, and are reproduced here with the
permission of the photographer, Baruch Katz, of
New York City.)

750

For
Stan Raiff
who first produced and directed
ANDROCLES AND THE LION

MUSIC NOTE

The music for *Androcles and the Lion* covers a wide range of styles. In order to enhance the character of the Commedia dell' Arte form of the play, we chose to begin and end *Androcles* with music that is reminiscent of the early renaissance.

Thus, the Overture, Finale, and some of the incidental music utilize rythmic modes, short melodic fragments built from modal scales, and improvised percussion sounds executed by the players, on such instruments as hand drums, bells, and cymbals.

As each of the players is introduced, he is given a musical theme, to help emphasize his character in the play. Some of this material is then used in the songs.

The songs are simple, and were composed with the playwright's co-operation. Their purpose is to bring out the dramatic quality of various situations. They range from a work-song for Androcles, to a lament for Isabella, and a mock funeral march as the Captain and the Miser march Androcles into the pit.

There is also a chorus for everyone to sing. This, and the Lion's song, which end the first act, invite audience participation.

—Glenn R. Mack
New York City

Scene from New York production of Androcles and the Lion

Scene from New York production of ANDROCLES AND THE LION

Scene from New York production of ANDROCLES AND THE LION

ANDROCLES AND THE LION

ACT ONE

(The curtains open on a bare stage with the cyclorama lighted in many colors. There is lively music and the Performers enter, playing cymbals, flute, bells, and drums. They are a Commedia dell'arte group.

Arlequin, dressed in his traditional bright patches, leads the parade. Next is Lelio and Isabella, the romantic forever young lovers. Next is Pantalone, the comic old miser. Next is the Captain, the strutting, bragging soldier. And last is the Prologue who wears a robe and who later plays the Lion.

After a short introductory dance, they line up at the footlights, a colorful troupe of comic players).

PROLOGUE. Welcome!
  Short, glad, tall,
  Big, sad, small,
  Welcome all!

(Actors wave and pantomine "Hello").

We are a troupe of strolling players,
With masks, bells, and sword,

755

(Actors hold up masks, ring bells, and wave sword).

A group of comic portrayers
Who will act out upon the boards
A play for you to see—
A favorite tale of Italy,
Which tells how a friend was won
By a kindness that was done.
Our play is—"Androcles and the Lion."

(Actors beat cymbals, ring bells).

The players are: Arlequin—

(Arlequin steps forward).

Who will be Androcles, a slave.

(Arlequin bows, steps back, and Pantalone steps forward).

Pantalone, stingy and old.
Who thinks only of his gold.

(Pantalone holds up a bag of gold, bows, steps back; and Isabella and Lelio step forward and pose romantically).

Isabella and Lelio, two lovers
Whose hearts are pierced by Cupid's dart.

(They bow, step back, and Captain marches forward).

It is the bragging Captain's lot
To complicate the plot.

(Captain waves his wooden sword, bows, and steps back).

There is one more in our cast—
The Lion! He, you will see last.
Set the stage—

(Actors quickly set up small painted curtain backdrop).

Drape the curtains—raise the platform stand!
Here we will make a magic circle—
Take you to a magic land—
Where love is sung, noble words are spoken,
Good deeds triumph, and evil plots are broken.

(Holds up long scroll).

Our story is written on this scroll which I hold.
What happens in every scene here is told.

(Hangs scroll on proscenium arch at L).

Before we start, I will hang it on a hook
So if someone forgets his part
And has the need, he may have a look
And then proceed.

756

All the words in action or in song
We will make up as we go along.
All is ready! Players, stand within.

(Actors take places behind curtain).

For now I bow and say—the play—begins!

(He bows).

In ancient Rome our scene is laid,
Where the Emperor ruled and all obeyed.

(Points to curtain which is painted with a street in the middle and with a house on either side).

A street you see, two chariots wide,
With a stately house on either side.
In one lives Pantalone—rich, stingy, sour,

(Pantalone leans out the window-flap on the house at R and scowls).

Who counts and recounts his gold every hour.

(Pantalone disappears).

With him lives his niece, Isabella, who each day

(Isabella leans out the window).

Looks lovingly—longingly—across the way

(Lelio leans out the window of the house at L).

At the other house, where Lelio lives, a noble sir, who looks across lovingly—longingly—at her.

(Lelio sighs loudly. Isabella sighs musically, and they both disappear. Androcles enters from R, around the backdrop with broom).

And all the while Androcles toils each day.
A slave has no choice but to obey.

(Prologue exits at R).

ANDROCLES *(Music. He sweeps comically, in front of the door, over the door, then down the "street" to footlights. SINGS).*

Up with the sun
My day begins.
Wake my Nose,
Shake my toes,
Hop and never stop.
No, never stop until I—
Off to the butcher's,
Then to the baker's,
To and from the sandalmaker's.

Hop and never stop.
No, never stop until I—
Spaghetti prepare
With sauce to please her.
Dust with care
The bust of Ceasar.
Hop and never stop.
No, Never stop until I—drop.

Some masters, they say, are kind and good. But mine . . .! He cheats and he beats—he's a miser. Never a kind word does he say, but shouts, "Be about it!" And hits you a whack on the back to make sure. I'm always hungry. He believes in *under* eating. I'm fed every day with a beating. I sleep on the floor by the door to keep the robbers away. My clothes are patched and drafty because my master is stingy, and cruel, and crafty! When—oh when will there ever be a Roman Holiday for me!

(SINGS).

Will my fortune always be,
Always be such drudgery?
Will hope ever be in my horoscope?
Oh, when will I be free?

PANTALONE *(Enters around R of backdrop, counting money).*
. . . twenty-two, twenty-three, twenty-four, twenty-five . . .

(Androcles creeps up behind him, and playing a trick, taps Pantalone on the back with broom. Pantalone jumps).

Who is there?

ANDROCLES. Androcles.

PANTALONE. Be about it! Be off! Go! Collect my rents for the day. Everyone shall pay.

(Androcles starts R).

Lock the windows tight. Bolt the doors.

(Androcles starts L).

My stool! Bring me my stool.

(Androcles exits R).

Lazy stupid fool! There will be no supper for you tonight. Oh, I will be buried a poor man yet—without a coin to put in my mouth to pay for ferrying me across the River Styx.

(Androcles runs in R with stool).

My stool!

ANDROCLES *(Places stool behind Pantalone and pushes him down on it roughly. Pantalone gasps in surprise).*

Yes, my master.

PANTALONE.   Go! Collect my rents. Make them pay. Bring me—my gold. Away!

ANDROCLES.   Yes, oh master. I run!

(He starts "running" to L at top speed, then stops, looks back impishly, and then slowly walks).

PANTALONE *(Brings out bag and starts counting).*

Twenty-six, twenty-seven, twenty-eight, twenty-nine, thirty . . .

ISABELLA *(At the same time, she leans out the window, calls, stopping Androcles).*

Androcles . . . Androcles!

(He runs to her U.R. She gives him a letter).

For Lelio. Run!

(Androcles nods and smiles, pantomimes "running" to painted house on curtain at L, pantomimes knocking. There is music during the letter scene).

LELIO *(Appears at his window, takes letter).*

Isabella!

(Androcles smiles and nods. Lelio gives him a letter. Androcles "runs" to Isabella who takes letter).

ISABELLA.   Admired!

(Gives Androcles another letter. He "runs" with leaps and sighs to Lelio who takes it).

LELIO.   Adored!

(He gives Androcles another letter. He "runs" enjoying the romance, to Isabella who takes it).

ISABELLA.   Bewitched!

(She gives him another letter—they are the same three sheets of parchment passed back and forth—which he delivers. This action is continued with a letter to each lover, and with Androcles "running" faster and faster between them).

LELIO.   Bewildered!

ANDROCLES.   And she has a dowry. The gold her father left her.

("Runs" to Isabella with letter).

ISABELLA.   Enraptured!

LELIO.   Inflamed!

759

ISABELLA. Endeared!

(Holds letter).

LELIO. My dear!

(Holds letter).

ANDROCLES. My feet!

(Androcles sinks exhausted to ground. Isabella and Lelio disappear behind the window flaps. Music stops).

PANTALONE *(Picks up the dialogue with his action, which has been continuous).*

. . . One hundred three, one hundred four, one hundred five, one hundred six . . .

(Bites a coin to make sure).

one hundred seven . . . one hundred . . .

LELIO *(Enters from L, around backdrop).* Signor Pantalone.

PANTALONE *(Jumps from stool in fear).* Someone is here!

LELIO. A word with you, I pray.

PANTALONE *(Nervously hides money).* What—what do you wish to say?

LELIO. I come to speak of love. I come to sing of love!

(Reads romantically from a scroll he takes from his belt).

"To Isabella."

PANTALONE. My niece?

LELIO. "Oh, lovely, lovely, lovely, lovely flower,
Growing lovelier, lovelier, lovelier every hour . . .
Shower me your petals of love, oh Isabella,
I stand outside—with no umbrella."
Signor, I ask you for Isabella. I ask you for her hand in marriage.

PANTALONE. Marry—Isabella?

LELIO *(Reads again).*

"My life, my heart, revolve about her,
Alas, I cannot live without her."

PANTALONE *(Happy at the prospect).* You will support her?

LELIO. I ask you—give me, Isabella.

(Pantalone nods gladly).

Give us your blessing.

(Pantalone nods eagerly and raises his hand).

760

Give her—her dowry.

PANTALONE *(Freezes)*. Money!

LELIO. The gold her father left her.

PANTALONE. Gold! It is mine—to keep for her.

LELIO. But hers when she marries.

PANTALONE. How did he find out? No. She shall not marry you. Never! Part with my gold! Help! Androcles!

(Androcles runs to him).

LELIO. Part with Isabella? Help! Androcles!

(Androcles, between them, runs from one to the other as their suffering increases).

PANTALONE. My heart is pounding.

LELIO. My heart is broken.

PANTALONE. Quick! Attend!

LELIO. Lend!

PANTALONE. Send!

LELIO. Befriend!

ANDROCLES *(To Lelio)*. There is hope.

PANTALONE. I am ill.

LELIO. Amend!

ANDROCLES *(To Lelio)*. Elope!

PANTALONE. I have a chill!

LELIO *(Elated with the solution)*. Transcend!

(Exits around L of backdrop).

PANTALONE. I will take a pill!

(Exits around R of backdrop).

ANDROCLES *(To audience)*. The end!

(Comes to footlights and SINGS).

They are my masters and I obey.
But who am I? I often say.
"Androcles!" They ring.
"Androcles!" I bring.
But who am I?
A name—I am a name they call,
Only a name—that's all.

(Speaks simply and touchingly).

761

My father's name was Androcles. We lived on a farm by the sea. Free to be in the sun—to work the land—to be a man. One day when my father was away, a ship came in the bay. "Pirates," my mother cried. I helped her and my sisters hide, but I was caught and brought to Rome—and sold—for twenty pieces of gold. I thought I would run away! But when they catch a slave they decree a holiday. The Emperor and everyone comes to watch the fun of seeing a run-away slave being beaten and eaten by a wild beast. Personally I don't feel like being the meal for a beast. So I stay . . . just a name . . .

(SINGS).

"Androcles!" They ring.
"Androcles!" I bring.
But who am I?
If I were free
Who would I be?
Maybe . . . maybe . . .
A doctor with a degree,
A poet, a priest, a sculptor, a scholar,
A senator—emperor with a golden collar!
I want to be free
So I can find—me.

PANTALONE *(Calls off, then enters U.R.)*. Androcles! Androcles!

ANDROCLES. You see what I mean.

PANTALONE. Androcles!

ANDROCLES. Yes, my master.

PANTALONE. Quick! Answer the bell. Someone is at the gate.

(Androcles picks up stool and crosses to R).

Then come to me in the garden by the wall.

(Holds up a second bag of gold, different colors from the first).

I am going to bury—to plant—this bag of—stones.

ANDROCLES. Plant a bag of stones?

PANTALONE. Be off! To the gate!

(Androcles exits D.R. Pantalone holds up bag, schemingly).

Ah, inside this bag are *golden* stones! It is Isabella's dowry.

(There is a loud crashing of wood off R, announcing the entrance of the Captain).

Who is at the gate? I have forgot.

(Hurries to scroll hanging by the proscenium arch, reads—announcing in a loud voice).

762

"The Captain enters!"

CAPTAIN *(He struts in D.R., wooden sword in hand. His voice is as loud as his look is fierce).* Who sends for the bravest soldier in Rome? Who calls for the boldest Captain in Italy!

PANTALONE. I—Pantalone.

(Goes to him, speaks confidentially).

I will pay you well—

(Looks away. It breaks his heart).

—in gold—

(Then anxiously. Androcles peeks in at R).

to guard my niece. I have learned today she wishes to marry. You are to keep her lover away. Stand under her window. Station yourself at the door. Isabella is to be kept a prisoner forever more.

(No reaction from Captain).

ANDROCLES. A prisoner? She will be a slave—like me.

PANTALONE. What do you say?

CAPTAIN *(pompously).* I say—she who is inside is not outside.

ANDROCLES *(To audience).* I say—no one should be held a slave. This is treachery!

(Exits U.R. around backdrop).

CAPTAIN *(Struts).* I have guarded the royal Emperor. I have guarded the sacred temple. I can guard one niece—with one eye shut.

(Shuts one eye and marches L)

PANTALONE. No, no. The house is over there.

(Points R).

And that is her window.

(Isabella leans out of window).

CAPTAIN. Someone is there! Death to him when he tastes my sword!

(Advances with sword waving).

PANTALONE. No. No! It is she! *(Whispers).* It is—Isabella.

ISABELLA *(SINGS happily).*

Oh, yellow moon
Mellow moon
In the tree,
Look and see
If my lover
Waits for me.

PANTALONE *(Softly)*. Keep watch. Keep guard. She must not meet her lover.

(Captain salutes, clicks his heels, turns and with thundering steps starts to march. Androcles slips in from around backdrop U.L. and listens).

Sh!

(Captain marches with high, silent steps to window and stands at attention. Pantalone speaks to audience).

I must go to the garden! In this bag is the gold her father left her. I gave my oath to *keep* it—for her. To keep it safely—and for me. I will bury it deep, deep in the ground. Never to be found.

(He hurries off D.L.)

ANDROCLES *(To audience)*. More trickery that's wrong. The gold belongs to Isabella.

ISABELLA *(Aware someone is outside)*. Lelio?

CAPTAIN *(Laughs)*. Ha ha ha—no.

ISABELLA. Oh!

CAPTAIN. I am the Captain!

ISABELLA. Oh?

CAPTAIN. I guard your door. You cannot come or go.

ISABELLA. Oh.

CAPTAIN. Do not despair. I will keep you company. Observe how handsome I am—fifty women swooned today.

ISABELLA *(Calls softly)*. Lelio . . . ?

CAPTAIN. Know how brave I am—on my way to the barber two dragons I slew!

ISABELLA. Lelio . . . . . ?

CAPTAIN. Hear what a scholar I am—I say, "He who is sleeping is not awake."

ISABELLA. Lelio-o-o-o.

(Cries daintily. Captain makes a sweeping bow to her).

No!

(She disappears, letting the flap fall).

CAPTAIN. She sighs.

(Louder crying of musical "o's" is heard).

She cries. Ah, another heart is mine! Fifty-*one* women have swooned today!

(Poses heroically).

ANDROCLES. I must do something! She cannot be put in bondage. No one should be. Everyone should be free. But how—

(Beams with an idea, looks at scroll by proscenium arch and points).

Ah, look and see!

(He quickly reads scroll at side).

ISABELLA *(Appears at window, SINGS sadly)*.

Oh lonely moon,
Only moon,
Do you sigh,
Do you cry
For your lover
As—as I?

ANDROCLES. Yes, here is the plan I need!

(Clasps hands and looks up in prayer).

Oh, gods of the temple, please give me the courage to succeed.

(Makes a grand bow to Captain).

Signor Captain!

(Captain jumps).

It is said you are so fierce the sun stops when you frown.

CAPTAIN. That is true.

(Makes a frightening frown, turns, and frightens Androcles).

ANDROCLES. And that the tide goes out whenever you sneeze.

CAPTAIN. That is true.

(Screws up his face comically, puffs up and up his chest, then sneezes).

A-a-a-achew!

ANDROCLES *(Circling in front of Captain, going to R, toward window)*. Oh, brave and mighty Captain, I shake before you.

(Bows, back to audience, shaking).

CAPTAIN. Yesterday I swam five hundred leagues.

ANDROCLES. I heard you swam one thousand.

CAPTAIN. One thousand leagues I swam into the sea.

ANDROCLES. I heard it was into the ocean.

CAPTAIN. The ocean! To meet a ship—

ANDROCLES. A fleet of ships.

CAPTAIN. To meet a fleet of ships!

(Captain suddenly huffs and puffs as he starts pantomiming how he swam in the ocean, his arms pulling with great effort).

ANDROCLES *(At the same time, whispers to Isabella).* I have a plan to set you free, listen—carefully.

(Whispers, pointing to Captain. Pantomimes dropping handkerchief and fanning himself).

CAPTAIN *(Suddenly starts coughing and waving his arms).* Help! Help! I am drowning! Drowning!

ANDROCLES *(Rushes to him, hits him on back).* Save him. Throw out a rope. Man overboard!

CAPTAIN *(Sighs in relief, then dramatically continues with his adventure).* I was saved by a school of mermaids—beautiful creatures —and all of them swooned over me.

ANDROCLES. Then you swam on and on—

CAPTAIN *(Swimming on L, comically).* And on—

ANDROCLES *(Pushing him to exit).* And on—

CAPTAIN. And on—

ANDROCLES. And on—

CAPTAIN. And on—

(Exits L, "swimming").

ANDROCLES *(Quickly speaks to Isabella).* Do as I say and you can escape. We will trick the Captain. Wave your handkerchief. Get his attention. Then say the night is so warm—fan yourself. As he becomes warmer, he will shed his cap and hat and sword— and you will put them on. You will be the Captain.

ISABELLA. I?

ANDROCLES *(On his knees).* Try.

ISABELLA. The Captain's cape and hat will cover me, and I will be free to go—to Lelio.

CAPTAIN *(Re-enters at L).* After I had sunk the fleet of ships—

ANDROCLES. And brought the treasure back.

CAPTAIN. Treasure?

ANDROCLES. You awoke.

CAPTAIN. Awoke?

ANDROCLES. And found—it was but a dream.

(Isabella waves her handkerchief, then drops it coyly. Captain sees it and smiles seductively).

CAPTAIN. Ah! She signals for me to approach. Signora—your servant.

(Androcles, behind him, motions for Isabella to begin the trick).

ISABELLA *(Accepts handkerchief with a nod).* The night is so warm. The air is so still, so stifling. There is no breeze.

CAPTAIN. I will command the wind to blow a gale.

ISABELLA. The heat is so oppressive.

CAPTAIN. I will command the wind to blow a hurricane!

ANDROCLES. My nose is toasting.

CAPTAIN. I will call the wind to blow a blizzard!

ANDROCLES. My ears are roasting.

ISABELLA. The heat is baking.

(Captain, between them, looks at each one as each speaks. Captain becomes warmer and warmer. The dialogue builds slowly so the power of suggestion can take the desired effect on the Captain).

ANDROCLES. Sweltering.

ISABELLA. Smoldering.

ANDROCLES. Simmering!

ISABELLA. Seething.

(Captain begins to fan himself).

ANDROCLES. Stewing!

ISABELLA. Parching!

ANDROCLES. Scalding!

ISABELLA. Singeing!

(Captain takes off his hat, which Androcles takes, as Captain mops his brow).

ANDROCLES. Scorching!

ISABELLA. Smoking!

ANDROCLES. Sizzling!

ISABELLA. Blistering!

(Captain, growing warmer and warmer, removes his cape and sword which Androcles takes).

ANDROCLES. Broiling!

ISABELLA. Burning!

ANDROCLES. Blazing!

ISABELLA. Flaming!

CAPTAIN. Help! I am on fire! Blazing! Flaming! I am on fire!

(Captain goes in a circle, flapping his arms, puffing for air, fanning, hopping, and crying, "Fire! Fire!" At the same time, Androcles quickly gives hat, cape, sword to Isabella).

ANDROCLES *(Comes to Captain, who is slowing down).* Throw on water! Throw on water!

CAPTAIN *(Stops, dazed).* Where am I?

(Isabella dressed in Captain's hat, cape, and sword, marches from R and imitates Captain with comic exaggeration).

ANDROCLES *(Salutes her).* Signor Captain! What is your philosophy for the day?

ISABELLA *(Poses and speaks in low loud voice).* I say—he who is outside—is not inside.

ANDROCLES. Yes, my Captain.

CAPTAIN. Captain?

ISABELLA. I am off to fight a duel. Fifty-four I slew today. Fifty more I will fight—tonight!

ANDROCLES. Yes, my Captain.

CAPTAIN. Captain? Captain! *I* am the Captain.

(They pay no attention to him).

ANDROCLES. Your horse is waiting.

(Pantomimes holding a horse).

Your horse is here. Mount, O Captain, and ride away.

(Isabella pantomimes sitting on a horse, holding reins).

CAPTAIN. I am the Captain!

ISABELLA. Did you hear the wind blow?

CAPTAIN. I am the Captain!

ANDROCLES *(Listening and ignoring Captain).* No.

ISABELLA. I will ride a thousand leagues—

ANDROCLES. Two thousand—

ISABELLA. Three—

CAPTAIN. I am the Captain!

ISABELLA. Is that a shadow—there?

(Points sword at Captain).

ANDROCLES. A shadow . . . ?

(Takes sword and slashes the air, making Captain retreat fearfully).

No one is here . . . or there . . . or anywhere.

CAPTAIN *(Almost crying).* But I am the Captain.

ANDROCLES. To horse! Away—to the woods.

ISABELLA. To the woods!

ANDROCLES. But first, a bag of stones—by the garden wall, yours to take before you go.

ISABELLA. And then—to Lelio!

ANDROCLES. Yes, my Captain.

CAPTAIN *(Crying comically).* But I am the Captain. Look at me. Listen to me.

ISABELLA. To the woods!

(Starts pantomiming riding off L).

Ride, gallop, trot, zoom!

ANDROCLES. Hop, skip—jump over the moon!

(They "ride" off U.L.)

CAPTAIN *(Crying).* But I . . . I am the Captain.

(Then horrified).

If that is the Captain—then—who—who am I?

PANTALONE *(Enters D.L.)* Captain . . . Captain.

CAPTAIN. Some one calls. Oh, Pantalone . . . Pantalone! Can you see me?

(Waves his hands in front of Pantalone, then shouts in his ear).

Can you hear me?

PANTALONE. Yes.

CAPTAIN. Am I . . . I here?

PANTALONE *(Peers at him).* Yes.

CAPTAIN. Ah, I live. I breathe again.

(Breathes vigorously).

769

I am the Captain.

(Struts).

Look on my hat and shudder. Look at my cape and shiver. Feel my sword—

(Realizes he has no hat, cape, or sword).

It is gone! Ah, your slave took it. Androcles! It was a trick of his. After him!

PANTALONE.   My slave? Ha, ha, a trick on you.

CAPTAIN.   And another one dressed in my clothes!

PANTALONE *(Laughing, stops immediately)*. Another one?

CAPTAIN.   One who came from your house.

PANTALONE.   From my house?

(Runs to house U.R., then turns).

Isabella!

CAPTAIN.   Ha ha, a trick on you.

PANTALONE *(In a rage)*. Fool, stupid, simpleton! You have set Isabella free!

CAPTAIN.   I let Isabella free?

PANTALONE.   Fathead, saphead, noodlehead! It was she who left the house in disguise—and is off to meet her lover. Stop them! Which way? Which way?

CAPTAIN.   He said—

(Thinks, which is difficult).

to the woods!

PANTALONE.   Bonehead, woodenhead, block head! Quick! Save her! Before she is wed! To the woods!

(Starts R).

CAPTAIN.   He said—

(Thinks).

first, take a bag of stones by the wall.

PANTALONE.   A bag of stones—the gold! Muttonhead, pumpkin head, cabbage head! To the garden! Before he finds it.

(Starts to L, as Captain starts R)

Forget Isabella. Save the gold!

(Pantalone exits D.L. Captain salutes and marches after him. Lights may dim slightly. There is music as the Wall enters D.R.

and crosses to C. Wall is an actor (LION) with a painted "wall" hanging on his back and short enough to show his feet. The back of his head is masked by a large flower peeping over the wall. He stands at C, feet apart, back to audience. He puts down a bag of gold and then puts a rock over it.

Androcles, followed by Isabella, tiptoes in U.L. They circle around to D.R. Androcles starts feeling for the wall).

ANDROCLES. The gold is buried—by the wall—

(Flower on the wall nods vigorously).

buried under a stone—

(Flower nods again).

Look—feel—find a stone—a stone—a stone—

(Wall stomps his foot, then puts foot on top of stone, but Androcles passes by it).

ISABELLA *(Wall again taps foot and points it towards stone. Isabella sees stone and points to it).* A stone!

ANDROCLES. Ah, I see it! Pray that this will be it!

(Slowly lifts stone).

Behold!

(Holds up bag).

A bag of gold!

(Jumps up, sings and dances).

We've found it! We've found it! We've found the gold! Yours to keep! To have! To hold!

ISABELLA. Sh!

ANDROCLES. You are free—go! Off to Lelio, who implores you—adores you. Quick, do not hesitate. Run—before it is too late.

ISABELLA. Thank you. Some day may you be set free, too.

(Kisses her finger and touches his nose with it).

Good bye.

(Exits D.L.)

ANDROCLES *(Thrilled that she has touched him).* Fly—arrevederci.

(Sees he has the gold).

Wait! The gold! Isabella forgot the gold! Isabella! Isabella!

(He exits after her D.L. At the same time, Pantalone, followed by Captain, tip-toes in U.L., circling D.R. where they stop).

PANTALONE *(Peering and groping)*. It is so dark I cannot see.

CAPTAIN *(Also peering and groping)*. Wait . . . wait for me.

PANTALONE. The gold—by the wall—under a stone—find—find—

CAPTAIN. You look in front. I'll look behind.

PANTALONE *(He turns R, Captain turns L. Each peers and steps in the opposite direction on each word)*. Search—scratch—dig around it.

CAPTAIN *(Still peering, they now step backwards toward each other on each word)*. Feel—touch—crouch—

(They bump into each other from the back).

PANTALONE. Ouch!

CAPTAIN *(Grabs and holds Pantalone's foot)*. I've found it! I've found it!

PANTALONE. Knucklehead of soot! You've found my foot!

(Kicks free and creeps toward C).

Here . . . there . . . oh, where . . . where is my gold? The stone . . . the stone . . . where has it flown? Quick . . . on your knees . . . search . . . find . . . use your nose . . . and not to sneeze.

(He and Captain, on their knees, comically search frantically).

Pat . . . pound . . . comb . . . the ground . . . chase . . . race . . . find the place.

(He finds stone).

I have found it! Ah, to gods in prayer I kneel. The stone is here. My gold is back.

(Reaches between feet of Wall, then freezes in panic).

What do I feel? There is no sack!

(Rises in a frenzy).

I have been robbed! Thieves! The gold is gone!

CAPTAIN *(Rises)*. It was the slave who took it! Androcles!

PANTALONE. He is a robber. He is a thief! He will pay for this—with his life!

CAPTAIN. I will find him . . . bind him . . . bend . . . make an end of him!

PANTALONE. He has run away! To the woods! Catch him! Hold!

(Captain stomps to R).

To the woods! Before his tracks are cold.

(Captain stomps to L).

Follow! Follow! My bag of gold!

(Pantalone exits D.L. Captain salutes and follows him. Wall picks up stone, then he pulls the street scene curtain to one side, revealing another curtain behind it and painted like a forest. Over his shoulder, back still to audience, Wall announces, "The forest," and exits quickly at R.

Chase music begins. Isabella and Lelio run in from L, look about).

ISABELLA. The forest paths will guide us.

LELIO. The forest trees will hide us.

(They exit U.R. around the backdrop).

ANDROCLES *(Runs in front L)* Isabella! Lelio! I cannot find you. You have left the gold behind you.

(Exits off U.R. around backdrop).

CAPTAIN *(Enters D.L.).* After them! I say—follow me! This way!

(Exits U.R. behind backdrop).

PANTALONE *(Enters, wheezing, trying to keep up, from L).* We are near him. I can hear him—and my gold.

(Pantalone exits U.R. around the backdrop. Isabella and Lelio run in U.L. from behind the backdrop, start to R, but suddenly stop frightened at what they see offstage R).

ISABELLA. Oh, what do I see?

LELIO. It is a — quick! We must flee!

(Isabella and Lelio exit U.R. behind the backdrop. Captain enters U.L. around the backdrop, starts to R).

This way! This way! Follow me! Onward to—

(Stops horrified at what he sees off-stage R).

What is that behind a tree? It is a—Oh, no! We must never meet. The order is—retreat!

(Captain runs off U.R. behind backdrop. Pantalone enters U.L. around the backdrop).

PANTALONE. Find him. Fetch him. Catch him. My gold has run away.

(Stops and looks off-stage R).

What is that? Can that be he?

(Starts to call).

Andro—No! It is a—Help! It is a *lion*—coming after me!

(There is a loud roar off R. Pantalone sinks to his knees and quickly walking on his knees, exits L.

Music of Lion's song. Lion enters at R, a most appealing creature. he dances to C and SINGS).

LION. Have you roared today,
　　Told the world today how you feel?
　　If you're down at the heel
　　Or need to put over a deal,
　　Happy or sad
　　Tearful or glad
　　Sunny or mad,
　　It's a great way
　　To show the world how you feel!
　　Without saying a single word
　　Your meaning is heard,
　　"Good morning" is dull,
　　But a roar is musical!
　　Happy or sad
　　Tearful or glad
　　It's a great way
　　To show the world how you feel!

(He gives a satisfied low roar, then looks about and speaks).

The sun is up. It is another day—

(Yawns).

to sleep. Hear all! The King speaks. No birds are allowed over my cave—chirping and burping. No animals are allowed near my cave—growling and howling. Silence in the woods. The King is going to sleep.

(Actors off-stage imitate animal sounds, loud buzzing, barking, etc. Or actors may in simple disguise with masks enter as animals, dance and make sounds).

Silence!

(All noise and motion stops).

The King says, "Silence."

(Noise and motion increases, Lion becomes angry, puffs up and roars like thunder, stalking about in all directions).

R-r-r-r-r-roar!

(There is absolute silence. If actors are on stage, they run off).

You see—

(SINGS).

A roar's a great way
To show the world how you feel!

(He roars and exits majestically into cave—a split in the painted backdrop).

774

ANDROCLES (*Enters from around backdrop U.R. He runs to C. He looks anxiously to R and to L, and calls softly*). Isabella . . . ? Lelio . . . ? They are lost in the woods. *I* am lost in the woods. I have run this way—I have run that way—I have run—

(*A terrible thought strikes him*).

I have run—away! I am a run-away slave! No!

(*Calls desperately*).

Isabella! Lelio! Where will I go? My master will hunt me. He will track me down. He will take me back. I will be thrown to the wild beasts!

(*Sees bag he holds*).

The gold—my master will say I stole it. A run-away slave—and a thief! No, I was only trying to help.

(*calls*).

Isabella! Help *me*, Lelio.

PANTALONE (*Off L, loudly*). Oh, beat the bushes. Beat the ground. Find my slave. Find my gold!

ANDROCLES. My master! What shall I do? Where shall I go? Hide—

(*Runs behind imaginary tree R*).

Behind a tree—

(*Runs to imaginary bush U.L.*)

Under a bush—he can see.

(*Points at cave*).

What is that? Ah, a cave! I will hide—inside the cave and pray he never finds me.

(*Quickly he goes into cave, gives a loud "Oh!," and quickly backs out again*).

It is someone's house.

CAPTAIN (*Off*). Follow me. I say—this way!

ANDROCLES (*Knocks at cave in desperation*). Please! Please, may I come in? I am—

PANTALONE (*Off*). I think—I hear him!

ANDROCLES. I am—in danger.

(*Androcles quickly goes into cave. Pantalone enters U.L. followed by Captain. They are in hot pursuit*).

PANTALONE (*Crosses to R*). My gold! Find the slave. Bind him! Bring him to me.

775

CAPTAIN (*Circles D.C.*). I will look in every brook and nook and hollow tree!

PANTALONE. Fetch—catch my gold!

(*Exits D.R.*).

CAPTAIN. Follow me!

(*He exits D.L. From inside the cave, a long loud roar is heard, and Androcles calls, "Help!" Another and louder roar is heard. Androcles runs out of cave to D.L. and cries "Help . . . help!" Lion runs out of cave to D.R. and roars*).

ANDROCLES. It is a lion!

LION. It is a man! He will try to beat me.

ANDROCLES. He will try to eat me.

(*They eye each other. Lion springs at Androcles with a roar. Androcles backs away*).

I am sorry I disturbed you.

(*Lion roars. Androcles holds up bag*).

I—I will have to hit you if you come closer.

LION. Hit—hit until he kills—that is man.

ANDROCLES. Leap—eat—that is a lion.

(*Lion roars and then leaps on him. Androcles struggles and fights, but soon he is held in a lion-hug*).

Help! Help!

(*Lion roars. Androcles gets his arm free and bangs Lion on the back with bag of gold. Lion roars with surprise and releases Androcles. Androcles, thinking he is free, starts off, but Lion holds on to his pants. Androcles, at arm's length, runs in one spot. Androcles gets loose, turns, lowers his head and charges, butting into Lion's stomach. Lion roars. Androcles runs to L and hides behind imaginary tree. Lion, angry, roars and slowly starts to creep up on him. Androcles looks around "tree," one side, then the other, shaking with fearful expectation. Lion springs at him in front of "tree." Androcles leaps and runs back of "tree." Lion turns and runs after him. Androcles tries to escape, running in figure-eights around the two "trees." They stop, each facing opposite directions, and start backing toward each other. Androcles turns, sees Lion, jumps, then cautiously tip toes toward him and kicks the bent over approaching Lion. Lion roars and circles. Androcles laughs at his trick. Lion comes up behind him and grabs him, holding Androcles around the waist and lifting him off the ground. Androcles kicks helplessly. Lion throws Androcles on ground. Lion, above him, roars, raises his paw, and gives a crushing blow. But Androcles rolls over and the paw hits the ground. Lion immediately roars*

776

and waves his paw in pain. Androcles cautiously slides away and is ready to run. He looks back at Lion who, with tearful sob-roars, is licking and waving his paw).

ANDROCLES. He is hurt. I can run away.

(He starts, but stops when Lion sobs).

He is in pain. Someone should help. No one is here. No one but one—*I*—am here.

(Lion roars in frustration. Androcles turns away in fear. Lion sobs sadly. Androcles looks back at him).

If I go—I maybe can be free! If I stay—

(Lion growls at him).

he may take a bite out of me!

(Androcles starts to leave. Lion sobs. Throughout the scene the Lion "talks" in grunts and groans almost like a person in answering and reacting to Androcles. Androcles stops).

When someone needs your help, you can't run away.

(Trying to be brave, he turns to Lion, opens his mouth, but can say nothing).

I wonder what you say—to a lion?

(Lion sobs appealingly).

Signor—

(Lion looks at him. Androcles is afraid).

My name is Androcles.

(Lion roars, looks at his paw and roars louder).

Have you—have you hurt your paw?

(Lion grunts and nods).

If you—will sit still—I will try to help you.

(Lion roars defiantly. Androcles backs away).

Wait! If we succeed, we will need to—cooperate!

(Lion looks at him suspiciously and grunts).

You don't trust me—

(Lion roars).

and I don't trust you. But someone must take the first step— greet the other, or we will never meet each other.

(Cautiously Androcles takes a step sideways, facing audience. Lion cautiously takes a step sideways, facing audience).

That is a beginning—

(Lion roars. Androcles holds his neck).

But what will be the ending?

(Each raises a leg and takes another sideways step toward each other).

I don't want to hurt you. I want to help you.

(He slowly holds out his hand. Lion "talks" and slowly shows him his paw).

It's a thorn. You have a thorn stuck in your paw.

(Lion breaks the tension, crying with the thought of it and waving his injured paw).

I know it hurts.

(Talks slowly as if explaining to a small child).

Once I stepped on a thorn. My father pulled it out.

(Lion grunts and reacts with interest).

My father—on the farm—by the sea. I will pull it out for you— as my father did—for me.

(Lion grunts undecided, then slowly offers his paw. Androcles nervously reaches for it).

It—it may hurt a little.

(Lion draws back and roars in protest).

I thought a lion was brave—not afraid of anything.

(Lion stops, then grunts in agreement and with great bravery thrusts out his paw).

Now—hold still—brace yourself.

(Lion begins to tremble violently).

Get ready—

(Lion shakes more).

One—

(Lion shakes both of them).

Two—

(Lion cries and tries to pull away. Androcles is stern, with pointed finger).

Don't move about!

(Lion tries to obey, meekly).

778

Three!

(*Lion steps backwards*).

It's out!

LION (*Looks at his paw, looks at Androcles, then roars joyfully and hops about. SINGS*).

Let me roar today
Let me say today
We feel great!
Celebrate!
Exhilarate!
Congratulate!
It's a great way
To show the world how you feel.

ANDROCLES (*Lion rubs against Androcles and purrs softly. Androcles, being tickled by Lion's rubbing, giggles and pets him*). You—you are welcome.

LION (*To audience*). He looks tired. I will get a rock.

(*Quickly picks up a rock off R and holds it high*).

ANDROCLES. He is going to crush me!

(*He starts to defend himself, but Lion shakes his head and grunts, and shows Androcles that he should sit*).

For me?

(*Lion nods, trying to talk, and dusts the rock with his tail*).

He wants me to sit.

(*Lion, delighted, grabs Androcles to help him and seats him roughly*).

Thank you.

LION (*To audience*). He looks hungry.

(*Roars, shows teeth, and chews*).

ANDROCLES. He is going to eat me!

(*Lion shakes his head and "talks," points to Androcles and indicates from his mouth down into his stomach*).

He wants me to eat.

(*Lion agrees joyfully*).

I am hungry. I am always hungry.

LION. (*Thinking*). What was for breakfast today? A man's skull in the cave—his liver down by the river—

(*Embarrassed at what he has thought*).

779

Oh, I beg your pardon.

(Roars with a new idea, motions Androcles to watch. Lion hums and purrs lightly as he comically pantomimes picking fruit from a tree and eating and spitting out the seeds).

ANDROCLES. Fruit!

(Lion, encouraged, purrs happily and hops about pantomiming filling a basket with berries from bushes).

Berries!

(Lion, elated with his success, buzzes loudly and dances in ballet fashion like a bee).

What?

(Lion buzzes and dances bigger).

Honey from the bee!

(Lion agrees loudly).

Oh, that will be a banquet for me.

LION *(Speaks to audience).* A new twist in history! Man and beast will feast together. Celebrate! Sit—wait! I'll be back with cherries and berries for you—and a bone or two, before you can roar —e pluribus unum!

(Roars happily and exits R).

ANDROCLES *(Sits alone on rock, looks around, smiles, and speaks quietly).* I am sitting down. I am being served. I am being treated like a person. I—have a friend. This is what it is like to be free. To be—maybe—

(SINGS).

Maybe
A doctor with a degree,
A poet, a priest, a sculptor, a scholar,
A senator—emperor with a golden collar!
I want to be free
So I can find—me.

PANTALONE *(Off).* Hunt—hunt—search and find my slave. Find my gold!

ANDROCLES. My master has come. My freedom has gone.

PANTALONE *(Off R).* Ah, his footprints are on the ground! I have found him!

ANDROCLES *(Calls quickly).* Oh, Lion, I must be off before we have fed. I must run—or it is off with my head!

(He starts D.L. but sees Captain).

Oh! The Captain! Where will I hide? In the cave!

(Quickly hides in cave).

CAPTAIN *(Enters L with fishing net and a slap-stick).* Beware slave, wherever you are. I shall leap and keep and capture you. In this net—I will get you.

(Holds net out ready).

PANTALONE *(Enters R, peering at the ground, crosses to L).* His footprints are on the ground. Toe-heel, heel-toe. This is the way his footsteps go.

CAPTAIN *(To audience).* The trap is set.

PANTALONE. Lead on—lead me to him.

CAPTAIN. Ha, caught in the net!

(Throws net over Pantalone who has walked into it).

PANTALONE. Help! Help!

CAPTAIN. You stole my hat!

(Hits Pantalone over the head with slap-stick).

PANTALONE. Oh!

CAPTAIN. My sword.

(Hits him again).

PANTALONE. No!

CAPTAIN. My cape!

(Hits him again).

PANTALONE. Let me loose!

CAPTAIN. What?

PANTALONE. You squawking goose!

CAPTAIN. Who speaks?

PANTALONE *(Pulling off the net).* I—Pantalone.

CAPTAIN. Pantalone? Oh, it was my mistake.

PANTALONE. It was my head!

CAPTAIN. Where is the slave? The runaway? Where is Androcles?

PANTALONE. He is—with my gold.

CAPTAIN *(Struts).* I will drag him back to Rome. The Emperor will honor me—decree a holiday—so all can see the slave fight a wild and hungry beast. And after the fun is done and the slave is eaten, all will cheer the Captain of the Year.

PANTALONE. Before you count your cheers, you have to catch one slave—Androcles!

CAPTAIN *(They start searching, a step on each word. Captain circles to L and upstage. Pantalone circles to R and upstage).* Search.

PANTALONE. Seek.

CAPTAIN. Track.

PANTALONE. Trail.

CAPTAIN. Use your eyes.

PANTALONE. Scrutinize!

CAPTAIN *(Stops).* Think—if you were a slave . . . ?

PANTALONE. I?

CAPTAIN. Where would you hide?

PANTALONE. Inside.

CAPTAIN *(Sees and points).* A cave!

(They tip-toe to entrance, hold net ready, whisper excitedly).

Clap him.

PANTALONE. Trap him.

CAPTAIN *(Nothing happens).* The problem is—how to get him to come out.

PANTALONE. Poke him?

CAPTAIN. Smoke him?

PANTALONE. I have a great idea! You will call to him in a voice like Isabella.

CAPTAIN. I—I speak like Isabella?

PANTALONE. You will cry for help in a soft sweet voice. He will think you are her. He will come to Isabella.

CAPTAIN *(In high voice, comically).* Help! Oh, help me. I am Isabella.

(They look at cave entrance).

I heard—

PANTALONE. Something stirred.

CAPTAIN *(Falsetto again).* Andro-o-cles. Come out, ple-e-ese.

(They look at cave and excitedly hold net ready).

Ready.

PANTALONE. Steady.

(Androcles, behind backdrop, roars—long and loud!).

It is a lion in the cave!

(Runs D.R. and hides behind a "tree").

CAPTAIN *(Androcles roars again, up and down the scale, louder and louder. Even the backdrop shakes. Captain jumps and runs to Pantalone and hides behind him).* It is two lions in the cave!

(They stand shaking with fright).

ANDROCLES *(Peeks out of cave, then comes out).* They have gone. Ran away from a noise. I have learned that a roar is a mighty thing. No wonder a lion is a king.

(He enjoys another roar).

PANTALONE *(Still hiding).* We are undone!

CAPTAIN. Run! Crawl!

PANTALONE. I cannot move at all.

(Androcles roars again with joy).

I have an idea. You—you will call in a voice like a lion. He will think you are another lion—a brother.

CAPTAIN. I—roar like a lion?

PANTALONE. Our only chance is to answer back.

(Captain gulps, and then roars).

ANDROCLES *(He is startled. He hides behind "tree" at L).* It is another lion.

(Pantalone, helping, gives a roar).

It is two lions!

(With an idea, he roars back).

Ro-o-o-hello.

CAPTAIN *(He and Pantalone look at each other in surprise. Captain answers).* Ro-o-o-hello.

ANDROCLES *(Now Androcles looks surprised).* Ro-o-o-lovely-da-a-ay.

CAPTAIN *(He and Pantalone look at each other and nod, pleased with their success).* Ro-o-o-have-you-seen—ro-o-o-ar-a-runaway slave?

(Androcles is startled, then he peeks around "tree").

PANTALONE. Named-Andro—

(Captain nudges him to roar).

—roar—cles?

ANDROCLES. It is my master and the Captain. They have come for me.

(He roars loudly).

Ro-o-oar-he-went—roar-r-r-r-that-away.

CAPTAIN *(They nod).* Ro-o-o-thank-you.

(He and Pantalone start to tip-toe off R).

ANDROCLES *(Too confident).* Ro—o-ar. You are welcome.

PANTALONE. It is his voice. It is my slave, Androcles.

CAPTAIN. It is another trick of his.

PANTALONE. Nab him.

CAPTAIN. Grab him.

(They start back to get him).

ANDROCLES *(Unaware he has been discovered, continues to roar gaily).* Ro-o-oar. Goodbye. Ro-o-o-ar. Happy eating.

PANTALONE *(Confronts Androcles on R).* Eat, cheat, thief! I will beat you!

(Androcles turns to L and walks into net held by Captain).

CAPTAIN. Slide, glide, inside. I have you tied!

(Androcles is caught in the net over his head).

PANTALONE *(Grabs his bag of gold).* My gold!

CAPTAIN. My captive!

ANDROCLES. Help! Help!

CAPTAIN. You stole my hat!

(Hits Androcles over the head with slap-stick).

You stole my sword!

(Hits him).

You stole my cape!

(Hits him).

This time you will not escape.

PANTALONE *(Takes stick from Captain and swings it).* Robber, Traitor. Thief! Let me hit him.

(Pantalone, in the mix up, hits Captain several times on his head).

CAPTAIN. Help!

(He drops the rope of the net).

784

ANDROCLES *(Runs to R)*. Help!

PANTALONE. Help! He is running away!

CAPTAIN *(Quickly catches Androcles and holds the rope)*. Back to Rome. To the Emperor you will be delivered!

PANTALONE. Into the pit you will be thrown.

CAPTAIN. Where the wild beasts will claw, gnaw, and chew you!

(They start to lead him off, marching—Captain, Androcles, and last Pantalone).

Munch!

PANTALONE. Crunch!

ANDROCLES. I will be eaten for lunch! Help! Lion! Signor Lion, set me free. Come and rescue me! Oh, woods echo my cry for help. Echo so the Lion will know I am in trouble. Roar—roar with me. Echo from tree to tree!

(He roars and the Ushers—and the children—help him roar, as he is led off L).

Roar! Roar!

LION *(He leaps in at R and roars)*. Someone roars for help? Androcles!

(Off, Androcles cries "Help!")

He calls for help.

(SINGS).

Oh, roar and say
Shout out without delay,
Which way, which way, which way?
Oh, roar me a clue,
Roar me two.
I have to know
Which way to go before I start.
Oh, roar, please,
An-dro-cles.
Give a sigh,
Give a cry,
Signify!
I'll sniff—I'll whiff—
Smell *(Sniffs)* — Tell *(Sniffs)*
Fe, fi, fo, fum.
Here —

(Shouts).

I come!

(He exits L).

ISABELLA *(She and Lelio run in from R)*. Oh, Androcles, what has happened to you?

LELIO *(To audience)*. That you will see in Act Two. Now—we must bow and say, "Our play is half done." This is the end of Act One.

(They bow).

The Curtains Close.

A short intermission.

(Or if played without an intermission, omit the last speech of Lelio's and continue with his first speech in Act Two).

From New York production of ANDROCLES AND THE LION

ANDROCLES AND THE LION

ACT TWO

(Music: Reprise of "Oh, Roar and Say." The curtains open. The scene is the same. Isabella and Lelio stand in C. Music dims out).

ISABELLA. Androcles. What has happened to you?

LELIO. I heard his voice, calling in the woods.

ISABELLA. He has followed us to bring the gold—my dowry which I left behind.

(Calls).

Androcles?

LELIO. Androcles!

(Lion roars as he enters U.R. He sees the lovers and watches).

ISABELLA. It is a lion!

LELIO. Do not fear.

ISABELLA. Androcles is alone—unarmed. What if he should meet a lion? Androcles! Androcles!

LELIO. Androcles!

LION. Someone else roars "Androcles." I will stay and hear who is here.

(Lion hides his head behind the small rock).

ISABELLA. Androcles! Androcles!

LELIO. We are alone.

(Lion's head pops up behind rock).

Together. It is the time to speak—to sing of love!

(He turns aside, takes scroll from belt).

ISABELLA *(Not looking at him).* Please, speak no prepared speech, but sing true words that spring freely from your heart.

787

LELIO (*Looks surprised, glances again at scroll, then SINGS*).

Oh, lovely, lovely flower,
Growing lovelier every hour,
Shower on me, petals of love, Isabella—

(*Lion, enjoying the music, nods his head in rhythm*).

ISABELLA. So unrehearsed—so sincere.

LELIO (*SINGS*).

My life, my heart revolve about you.
Say yes, I cannot live without you.

(*Lion, unable to refrain, lifts his head and roars musically on Lelio's last note—unnoticed by the lovers—then hides his head behind the rock*).

ISABELLA. Oh, Lelio—

(*Turns to him and speaks or SINGS*).

My answer is—can't you guess?
Yes, yes, yes, yes, yes!

LELIO (*In ecstacy*). Oh, woods abound with joyous sound! Melodies sing in the trees—

(*Music sound. Lion raises up and listens to R*).

Bells ring in the breeze—

(*Music sound. Lion stands up and listens to L*).

Let the lute of the lily lying in the pond—

(*Music sound. Lion stands and begins to move his arms like an orchestra conductor*).

Let the flute of the firefly's fluttering wand—

(*Music sound. Lion motions to R*).

And let the flight of the nightingale—

(*Music sound. Lion motions L*).

Harmonize!

(*Music sounds blend together. Lion holds up paw ready to begin directing an orchestra*).

The moment we will immortalize!

(*Music of all sounds play a folk dance. Lion leads, dramatically, the unseen musicians. Isabella and Lelio do a short dance. At the conclusion, they hold their pose and Lion bows to audience*).

ISABELLA (*Points to ground*). Look! Footprints—boots and sandals.

LELIO (*Examines them*). The Captain's boots—Pantalone's sandals.

788

The Captain and Pantalone were here—following us—following Androcles.

ISABELLA. His cry was for help. He ran away. He is—a runaway slave! And they have found him—

LELIO. Bound him—

ISABELLA. Taken him back to Rome.

LELIO. To the pit!

ISABELLA. We must stop them.

LELIO. If we can.

ISABELLA. We must help him.

LELIO. All we can.

LION *(Jumps on rock heroically)*. And—we can!

(Roars).

ISABELLA. Help!

LELIO. Run!

(Lovers run off D.R.).

LION. Lead the way. I will follow you. To Androcles! To—the rescue!

(Lion roars, picks up rock, and runs off D.R. Chase music begins —repeated. But the running is reversed, going around in the opposite direction. Lovers enter from U.R. and run across. At C, they look back, "Oh!" and exit U.L. behind backdrop. Lion runs in U.R. At C, roars, and exits U.L. behind backdrop. Lovers enter U.R. from behind backdrop, running faster. At C, they look back in great fright, "OH!" and exit U.L. behind backdrop. Lion follows. At C, roars majestically, and shouts: "Andr—roar—cles! Here we come!" Lion exits after lovers. Lovers enter U.R. from around backdrop. Lelio pulls the curtain of the woods scene back to L, showing the street scene again. Chase music dims out).

LELIO *(Breathless)*. Safe at home—I hope. What does the scroll say?

ISABELLA *(Reads scroll on proscenium arch)*. The next scene is—a street in Rome.

LELIO. Ah, we can stay.

ISABELLA *(Reads, announcing)*. "The Captain enters."

(Clashing of slap-stick is heard off L, Isabella runs to C).

He will find us here.

LELIO. Do not fear. We will hide—behind a mask. Quick! We will hide behind another face, and re-appear in the Market Place.

(They exit R).

CAPTAIN (*Enters at L*). Make way, make way for the hero of the day! Bow, salute, kneel and gaze upon the hero. Raise your voice with praise for the hero. The hero passes by. The hero is—I!

(*Lelio and Isabella enter R. Each holds a long, sad beggerman's mask on a stick in front of his face. They walk and act and speak like beggars*).

LELIO. Help the poor. Help the blind.

ISABELLA. Alms for the cripple. Alms for the old.

CAPTAIN. Away beggars! The Emperor comes this way. It is a holiday!

LELIO. What Senator has died? What battle have we won?

CAPTAIN. None! We celebrate today the capture of a runaway.

ISABELLA. A slave?

(*They look at each other and speak without their masks; and at the same time, the Captain speaks. They all say together, "Androcles!"*).

CAPTAIN. Today all Rome will celebrate! A wild beast was caught outside the wall, clawing the gate as if he could not wait to come into the City. Now in the pit the beast is locked and barred, waiting to be released—waiting to eat a juicy feast.

LELIO AND ISABELLA (*They nod to each other and say:*) Androcles!

CAPTAIN. Ah, what a sporting sight to see—a fight—man eaten by a beast. Then I, who caught the slave, will appear. Women will swoon, men will cheer, and I will be crowned the hero of the year!

(*Shouts rapidly and marches quickly*).

Hep, hep, ho! Step, step, high. Hail the hero. I, I, I!

(*Exits R*).

ISABELLA (*They take their masks away*). Poor, poor Androcles.

LELIO. We must try and save him. Quick, before it is too late. We will go to the Arena—

ISABELLA. Yes!

LELIO. We will go to the Royal Box! Implore the Emperor with our plea!

ISABELLA. Yes!

LELIO. For only he by royal decree can save—our Androcles.

(*Lelio and Isabella run off L. There is music. Captain, leading Androcles by the rope, and Pantalone following, marches in from R. As they march, they SING*).

PANTALONE AND CAPTAIN. Off to the pit we three. Who will be left?

ANDROCLES. Just me.

PANTALONE AND CAPTAIN. Who will be left alone, shaking in every bone?

PANTALONE. Just—

CAPTAIN. Just—

ANDROCLES. Me!

CAPTAIN AND PANTALONE. Off to the pit we three. Who will be left?

ANDROCLES. Just me.

CAPTAIN AND PANTALONE. Who will the animal meet? Who will the animal eat?

PANTALONE. Just—

CAPTAIN. Just—

ANDROCLES (Shouts). Just a minute! I want to be an absentee!

(Music ends as he speaks).

I want to be free—to be—just me!

CAPTAIN. To the Arena! Forward march!

(Music: Reprise of Introductory Music of Act One. Captain, Androcles, and Pantalone march across the front of the stage or across down in the orchestra pit. At the same time, Lelio and Isabella, disguised with masks, dance in U.L. carrying colorful banners, one in each hand, and on stands. They set the banners down in a semi-circle in front of the backdrop to indicate the Arena. They dance off as the music stops, and the three marchers arrive in the middle of the scene).

CAPTAIN. Halt! We are at the Arena! The slave will step forward.

PANTALONE. Step forward.

ANDROCLES. Step forward.

(Frightened, he steps forward).

CAPTAIN. The slave's head will be covered.

(He holds out left hand to Androcles, who holds out left hand to Pantalone).

PANTALONE. Covered.

(He gives a cloth sack to Androcles, who gives it to Captain, who puts it over Androcles' head).

CAPTAIN (Trumpets sound). The Emperor's chariot draws near.

(Trumpets).

791

The Emperor will soon appear.

(Trumpets).

The Emperor is here!

(A royal banner is extended from the side D.L., indicating the Royal Box).

Bow!

PANTALONE. Now!

(Captain and Pantalone bow low toward Royal Box, facing D.L. Androcles groping with his head covered, turns and bows facing R).

Turn around!

(Androcles turns around).

To the ground!

(Androcles bows to ground).

CAPTAIN. Most noble Emperor—

(Pushes Androcles' head down, making him bow).

Most honored Emperor—

(Pushes Androcles, who keeps bobbing up, down again).

Most imperial Emperor—

(Pushes Androcles down again. He stays down).

The guilty slave stands before you. Stand!

(Androcles quickly straightens up).

As punishment for a slave who runs away, he will today fight a wild beast in the Arena for all Rome to see.

(Androcles shakes his head under the sack).

He will battle for his life—to survive. There will be but one winner—the one who is left alive.

(Androcles, courageously, draws his fists and is ready to strike. Captain, growing more eloquent, begins to strut).

I have fought and slain a hundred wild beasts.

(Androcles, visualizing the animals, starts hitting the air).

With fiery eyes, with gnashing teeth, they charged at me. Fight! The crowd cried, fight!

(Androcles, ready, starts to fight, hitting wildly for his life, hitting the Captain who is near and whom he cannot see).

Help! Stop! I am not the wild beast.

(At a safe distance, he regains his bravery).

792

I—I am the Captain, the boldest, bravest fighter in Rome—in all Italy! Go—stand at the side. Appear when you hear the trumpets blow.

(Captain points to L. Androcles starts to R).

No. The other way!

ANDROCLES *(He turns and starts to L. Loud trumpets blow. He stops, faces R, ready to fight).* The trumpets! Now?

PANTALONE. No!

(Androcles, groping, exits U.L. Pantalone bows to Royal Box).

Most Imperial Emperor, I am Pantalone, Master of the slave. From me he ran away. From me he stole. I am told you plan to reward me for this holiday with a bag of gold.

CAPTAIN. I tracked and captured him. I am sure you will confer a title of bravery on me.

(Trumpets blow).

ANDROCLES *(Enters U.L., ready to fight).* The trumpets! Now?

CAPTAIN. No!

(Androcles turns and exits).

Ah, the Emperor waves. It is the signal. Open the gates. Let the wild beast in!

PANTALONE. Let the entertainment begin!

(Captain and Pantalone quickly go D.R. where they stand. Drum rolls are heard. Then loud roars are heard off U.R. Lion, roaring, angrily stalks in from U.R.).

LION. Barred—locked—caged! I am—outraged!

(Roars and paces menacingly).

PANTALONE. What a big lion! I am glad he is below.

CAPTAIN. I could conquer him with one blow.

LION. Captured! Held in captivity! Robbed of my liberty! Only man would think of it. Only man would sink to it. Man—man—little—two legged—tailless thing. Beware man, I am a King!

(Roars).

The first man I meet I—will eat!

(Trumpets blow).

ANDROCLES *(Enters, head still covered).* The trumpets! Now?

LION *(Sees him).* Ah, a man! A chew or two and a bone to pick.

(Roars).

793

ANDROCLES (*Frightened and groping*). Oh! I am not alone. I must get out quick.

(*Drum starts beating in rhythm to the fight. Androcles starts walking, then running, the Lion after him. The chase is a dance-mime, fast, comic, with surprises and suspense. It ends with Lion holding Androcles in his clutches*).

LION. Caught! Held!

(*Shakes Androcles like a rag doll*).

Flip—flop. I will start eating at the top!

(*Takes off Androcles' headcovering*).

ANDROCLES. No hope ever to be free. This is the end of me!

(*Lion looks at Androcles, is surprised and roars questioningly. Androcles, frightened, freezes, then slowly feels his neck, his face and nose. He looks at Lion and he is surprised. Lion tries to "talk"*).

You?

(*Lion nods and roars, pantomimes pulling out a thorn from his paw, and points to Androcles who nods*).

Me.

(*Lion "talks" and points to himself*).

You!

(*Lion nods and roars happily*).

Signor Lion!

(*Lion "talks" and roars, and they embrace each other joyfully*).

PANTALONE. Let the fight begin! Beat him!

(*Lion stops and looks at Pantalone*).

CAPTAIN. The Emperor waits to see who wins. Eat him!

ANDROCLES. He is my master—who bought me. He is the Captain—who caught me.

LION. Slave makers! Taker of men! I will beat you! I will eat you!

(*Roars and starts to C*).

PANTALONE. Help! The lion is looking at me. Draw your sword!

(*Hides behind the Captain*).

CAPTAIN (*Shaking*). I am afraid his blood will rust the blade.

PANTALONE. Show you can do what you say—slay him with one blow!

CAPTAIN. I suddenly remember—I have to go!

794

(Starts off R. At the same time, Lion leaps with a roar and attacks the two).

PANTALONE. Help! Guards! Save, attend me!

CAPTAIN. Help! Someone defend me!

(There is an exciting and comic scramble, with Lion finally grabbing each by the collar and hitting their heads together. Then he holds each out at arms length).

LION. Listen and learn a lesson: only a coward steals and holds a man.

(Roars. Shakes Pantalone).

Only a thief buys and sells a man. And no one—can—own another man!

(Roars).

The world was made for all—equally. Nod your heads if you agree.

(Lion shakes them and makes their heads nod violently. Then he releases them, and the two drop to the ground).

The vote is "Yes"—unanimously!

(Trumpets sound. Off-stage voices shout, from R and L and from the back of the auditorium: "Kill the lion. The lion is loose. Club him. Stone him. Kill the lion. Kill! Kill! etc." Captain and Pantalone crawl to R. Hands appear off R and L shaking clubs and spears. This is a tense moment. The Arena has turned against the Lion. Lion is frightened. He crouches by Androcles who stands heroically by him).

ANDROCLES. Stop! Stop! Hold your spears and stones and clubs. Do not kill the lion. You see—he is not an enemy. He remembers me and a kindness which I did for him. Today that kindness he has returned. He did not eat my head, which would have been the end. Instead—he is—my friend.

(He offers his hand to Lion. Lion takes it. Music begins and the two start to waltz together. Pantalone and Captain crouch and watch in amazement. Hands and weapons disappear from the sides at R and L. Androcles and Lion waltz bigger, funnier, and happier. Trumpets sound. Music and dancing stop. Lelio enters D.L. by royal banner).

LELIO. The Emperor has spoken. His words will be heard.

(All bow low toward the Box as Lelio holds up a royal scroll).

The Emperor is amazed, astounded, and astonished—with delight —at this sudden sight. A fight unlike any in history. Indeed it is a mystery. Two enemies—man and lion—dancing hand in hand! To honor this unique occasion, the Emperor has issued this command: today shall be, not one of fighting, but of dance and revelry!

(Trumpets play and people cheer).

The Emperor gives to the Master of the slave—

PANTALONE. That is I, Pantalone. How much gold does he give?

LELIO. The Emperor gives this order; *you* will give twenty pieces of gold to Androcles.

ANDROCLES. To me!

LELIO. A sum he has well earned.

PANTALONE. Give twenty pieces of gold! Oh, I shall die a poor man. No. No!

(Lion starts toward him and growls loudly).

Yes—yes, I will pay.

(Quickly takes bag from pocket and begins counting).

One—two—three—

LELIO. Furthermore: the Emperor decrees to the Captain who caught the slave—

CAPTAIN. Ah, what honor does the Emperor give to me?

LELIO. You will command a Roman Legion in a distant land. You will sail to the Isle of Britain where even the boldest man must fight to keep alive, where it is so dangerous only the bravest survive.

CAPTAIN *(Shaking violently).* Danger? Fight? Me?

LELIO. Because of your boasted bravery.

CAPTAIN. I would prefer to stay, please. A cold climate makes me sneeze.

(Lion starts and roars loudly).

I will go.

(Lion follows him roaring).

I am going! I am gone!

LELIO. And to me—the Emperor has given me the lovely, lovely Isabella—

(Isabella enters D.L.).

and has blessed our marriage which soon will be.

ISABELLA. For me the Emperor decreed, Pantalone shall pay without delay my dowry which he holds for me.

PANTALONE. Pay more gold! Oh, no—no!

(Lion roars at him loudly).

796

Yes—yes. I will pay. It is here, my dear.

LELIO. And finally:

(Trumpets blow).

The Emperor has ruled that both lion and slave today have won a victory unequalled in history. So—both lion and slave are hereby —set free!

ANDROCLES. Free? I am free.

LION. The way the world should be!

ANDROCLES. Free—to find my family—to work the best I can—to raise my head—to be a man. To find out—who I am!

(Music. They all SING).

Let us roar today,
Let us say today
We feel great.
Celebrate!
Exhilarate!
Congratulate!

PANTALONE AND CAPTAIN *(Dejected).* We don't feel great.

ALL. It's a great way
To show the world how you feel.
When in need—find a friend.
Laws will read—have a friend.
We feel great.
Don't eat, but meet.
Why wait, make a friend.
Extend!
Do your part, make a start.
Roar today. Show the world today.
It's a great way
To show the world how you feel.

(All the actors bow, then Androcles comes forward).

ANDROCLES. Our story is told. The lovers are joined in happiness. The bragger and the miser are undone. And a friend was won by kindness. Our masks and bells and curtains we put away for another day. And we go our way—a group of strolling players. We say—

LION *(Points at audience).* Be sure you roar today!

ALL. Arreviderci!

(They all bow low and the music swells).

The curtains close.

797

TWO PAILS OF WATER

A PLAY FOR CHILDREN

INSPIRED BY AN OLD DUTCH NURSERY RHYME

by

A. E. GREIDANUS

Translated from the Dutch

by

BILL HONEYWOOD

TWO PAILS OF WATER

By Aad Greidanus

·

CHARACTERS OF THE PLAY

SANDRA . . . . The village constable's daughter

SIMPLINA . . . . Her sister

DOPHILIUS . . . . A poor shoemaker

ALFONSO GOLDPURSE . . A rich merchant

JORIS . . . . The constable himself

HODDEL DE BODDEL . . . A rag and bone man

Two Pails of Water was first presented in Amsterdam, Holland, in 1960, by Toneelgroep Arena, a professional Dutch theatre company for young people, who toured the play across the Netherlands in 170 performances.

Translated into English, it was presented in 1965 by the Unicorn Theatre of London, England, under the direction of Caryl Jenner.

The English-speaking world is indebted to the Netherlands Centre of the International Theatre Institute, at The Hague, for making this translation available.

TWO PAILS OF WATER

PART ONE

The scene is a village square, surrounded by houses.

On the left we see the fine white house of Alfonso Goldpurse, a rich merchant who is always so frightfully busy, and who possesses so much money that he doesn't know what to do with it.

Back centre stands the neat cottage of Joris, the village constable, who lives with his two daughters Sandra and Simplina.

To the right stands the tumble-down shack of Dophilius, the poverty-stricken shoemaker.

In the middle of the square is a round stone well, which is encircled by a wooden bench. Over the well is a wooden framework carrying a rope and pulley for drawing water.

The curtain rises at dawn, with the village awakening to life. Cocks clarion. From the open window of the houses the shuffle of people is heard, as they get up and begin to move about.

Sandra and Simplina enter from their house to draw water.

While they are lowering a pail, Dophilius enters sleepily. He is wearing his apron, and carries a hammer in one hand and a shoe in the other. He walks quickly to the two girls at the well.

DOPHILIUS (*To Sandra, hopefully*). Morning, Miss Sandra. Let me help you with that heavy bucket.

(*Sandra turns her back, sticks her nose in the air, and refuses to answer.*)

SIMPLINA (*Sweetly*). Hallo, Dophilius, are you already hard at work?

DOPHILIUS (*Coolly*). Hallo, Simplina. Yes, I've already started, not that it's any use. No-one wants to buy my shoes anyway.

(*Dophilius walks towards his house in a huff, angrily kicking at a stone. At this moment Alfonso Goldpurse opens his door, entering in a flurry, his pockets overflowing with cheques, letters and telegrams. He carries a bulging briefcase in one hand and a newspaper in the other. He is still chewing his breakfast*).

ALFONSO. No time to eat. No time to read the paper. No time to . . .

(*He hears the rattle of buckets, looks around and hurries toward Simplina*). . .

Good morning, dear, kind Simplina. What are you doing? YOU mustn't carry that heavy bucket! Wait a minute, and I'll call my servant, he'll carry it for you.

803

(Simplina turns her back on him, sticks her nose in the air and refuses to answer. She grabs her pail and hurries to house).

SANDRA *(Wistfully).* Hallo, Mr. Goldpurse. What a lovely velvet jacket you're wearing!

ALFONSO. Bah! I've got at least ten more like this.

SANDRA. How wonderful it must be to be so rich!

(She takes hold of pail).

This bucket's so heavy! I wish I had a servant to carry it for me.

(Telephone bell from Alfonso's house).

ALFONSO. There it goes again!

(Runs inside).

SANDRA. How fine to have a servant . . . and a telephone . . . and ten velvet jackets . . . How lovely it would be to be rich!

SIMPLINA *(Off).* Sandra! The wash is boiling over!

SANDRA. Oh! The wash!

(Sandra exits quickly, with pail. Enter Joris the constable, washed and dressed for the day).

JORIS. Aaaaaah! What a fine day for Joris the constable! Plenty of sun to make my buttons sparkle. No rain to make my moustache droop. No wind to blow my beautiful helmet off . . .

(Takes off helmet to admire it).

A jolly fine day to, er, to, er, to *do* something! I haven't got to worry about keeping an eye on the girls.

(Peeps through the keyhole).

They're too busy with the spring cleaning.

(Noises off of buckets tinkling, and splashing water).

And I don't have to keep an eye on Dophilius . . .

(Peeps through D's keyhole to the accompaniment of busy hammering). . .

Because Dophilius is too busy making shoes.

(Peeps through Mr. G's. keyhole, noises of rattling typewriters and ringing telephone bells). . .

And I never have to keep my eye on Mr. Goldpurse, because he's always so busy that he never has the time to get up to anything! So, so. Everyone's at work, and people at work are too occupied to get up to things, so in that case

804

(Looks around him carefully).

I think it would be best . . . if Joris . . . took a little nap. After all, it's been an early start, and who can tell what can happen before the day's out? Yes, I think it would be better if I took a little rest now, and then at least I'll be fit if anything should happen.

(He is just about to sit on the bench when Sandra and Simplina enter, Sandra carrying a tin with glue, and Simplina carrying a tin with paint).

S. & S. Father Joris! You've got to paper the kitchen walls.

JORIS. Paper the kitchen! Brrrrrr.

S. & S. And paint the bench.

JORIS. Paint! ME! Brrrrrr.

SANDRA. Come now! The sooner you begin, the sooner you'll be finished.

JORIS *(Stands up importantly)*. I . . . er . . . I've got no time.

SANDRA *(Firmly)*. Here is the glue.

JORIS. But I just said . . .

SIMPLINA. And here is the paint.

JORIS. But I told you . . .

SANDRA. And there's bubble and squeak for dinner.

SIMPLINA. And apple pie for afters.

(Exit).

SANDRA *(By the door)*. That is, if you're finished in time!

(Exit).

JORIS *(Helplessly)*. But I tell you . . . Hmm. Bubble and squeak! Apple pie!

(Takes ahold of the two tins, and walks around the bench, kicking it sulkily).

I've not got time to paint benches! Pai-i-i-int! And glu-u-ue! As though a constable hasn't anything better to do! I'll teach 'em! I'll . . .

(He grabs hold of the two pots as if to throw them away, but thinks twice about it) . . .

Hmm. Bubble and squeak, and apple pie! Just my cup of tea! *(He rolls up his sleeves).*

Now which was the paint, this, or that? This looks a bit like the glue, or the paint!

(Sticks his finger in, and can't get it out again).

It's the . . . glue!

(Finger shoots free).

And jolly good glue too! So, that must be the paint. Now don't let me get it mixed up. I know what I'll do! I'll put the paint on the floor, and the glue on the bench. Now I can't make a mistake.

(Sits).

Ooooh! First take the weight off my poor feet! Might as well; put them up for a moment.

(Yawns and falls back sleepily).

The . . . paint . . . on . . . the . . . floor . . . and . . . the . . . glue . . . on . . . the . . . bench . . . Aaaaah.

(Falls to sleep, snoring).

(A handbell is heard, off, approaching, and a melodious voice crying "Rags and bones. Any old rags and bones". Hoddel de Boddel enters with his handcart. He is rather remarkably dressed, but his attire stamps him as a happy character. He rings his bell,—Joris sleeps through it all—and sings:)

> Any old rags?
> Any old bones?
> Any old shirts,
> Or any old blouses;
> Any old breeches,
> Or any old trousers;
> Silks and laces,
> Pa's old braces;
> Furs and muffs,
> Or powder puffs;
> Boxes and crates,
> Broken down grates;
> Shawls and mittens,
> Unwanted kittens;
> Carpets and mats,
> And this's and that's;
> Shoes or nightshifts,
> Any old wedding gifts;
> Shift 'em and shake 'em,
> Hoddel will take 'em.

(Puzzled by the silence, he looks around, rings his bell.)

HODDEL. "Any old rags!" . . . Doesn't anyone live here?

(Rings).

Seems queer!

(Rings harder).

Perhaps the people around here aren't very inquisitive, that would seem stranger still!

(Rings harder).

I'll have a look.

(Peeps through Dophilius' keyhole, to the sound of busy hammering) ...

Hmm. Hard at work!

(To Joris' house, Sound of buckets and scrubbing brushes).

They're hard at work too!

(To Alfonso's house, Sound of typewriters and telephones. Surprised).

Hmmmm! Harder still! Everyone here seems terribly busy!

(Sees Joris lying on the bench asleep, laughs softly).

Ooooh, it's the constable! Just you wait, we'll teach him to sleep while everyone's hard at work!

(He tiptoes to his handcart and digs out a constable's tunic and helmet from among the rubbish, puts them on, and is about to return to the bench) . . .

Half — a mo'. A moustache! I almost forgot that!

(Digs out a false moustache and sticks it on his upper lip. He then takes a straw and begins to tease Joris by tickling the various parts of his face as if it is a fly. Joris slaps himself awake, but Hoddel ducks out of sight behind the well before he can be seen).

JORIS. Oh!

(As he pulls himself slowly upright, Hoddel's head appears at the other side of the well, the wooden framework over the well resembling the frame of a mirror. Joris' mouth falls open in amazement, Hoddel's follows suit. Hoddel simulates all Joris' movements like an image in a mirror. They stand up slowly).

Hey! That looks like a . . . How did that mirror get there! Ha, ha, ha, what a good mirror! A jolly fine mirror! Now I can have a good look at myself. At long last I can have a good look at my beautiful tunic.

(He pulls his tunic straight, twirls his moustache, and examines himself with great satisfaction. Then he first stands to attention

and begins to take on a variety of military positions. He giggles with satisfaction, and starts to act sillily, making faces and funny little hops. Once again he begins to examine his image carefully).

Hey! Am I seeing things? It looks as though . . . I think . . . *(He turns around, peering into the so-called mirror, turns left and right examining himself and feeling himself all over nervously).*

I really do believe that I am getting thinner! This tunic hangs a bit loose! See! Too loose. Much too loose. And now, if I look hard, very hard, I do believe that my helmet has grown bigger too!

(He shakes his head from side to side, Hoddel's helmet is indeed much too large, falling almost over his eyes).

Too big! My lovely helmet, much too big! And my handsome tunic! What will people say? Everyone will laugh at me, I must do something! But, what? Wait a minute! That mirror . . . .I suppose it is alright? I mean, it might be a magic mirror!

(He taps, his finger tips meeting those of Hoddel).

Hey! I tap and hear nothing!

(He punches, his fist meeting that of Hoddel).

A soft mirror! Never in my life have I heard anything like that. I'll have to look into this a little closer!

(He climbs on to the stone rim of the well itself. Hoddel too. They stand with their faces close together. Joris makes faces, and Hoddel copies him carefully).

It all seems to agree, but . . .

(He taps the mirror again) . . .

But if I tap the mirror it doesn't make any sound, and that doesn't seem to agree.

(He takes hold of the framework and looks around the edge of it).

I don't get the hang of this!

(He puts himself at the side of one of the supports and looks left and right of it, Hoddel naturally follows suit).

It all seems to be alright, and yet it doesn't.

(He walks around the well to the back of the 'mirror', Hoddel to the front. He bends forward and peers until their noses touch. They change helmets).

Still, I really do believe that it's a proper mirror. I am Joris, and that is Joris too. This is my helmet, and that one also.

(They change helmets again).

You see! That's alright. But I still don't understand it fully.

(He sits down on the rim of the well to think things out more clearly).

I still don't get the hang of it! When I twirl my moustache, he twirls his, naturally, because it's a mirror. When I take hold of my helmet, he takes hold of his, naturally, there's nothing extraordinary in that. And when I take hold of his helmet, he takes hold of mine . . . Hey! Ho! But that's not possible! A mirror can't take hold of a hat! But then, it can't be a mirror at all!

(Stands slowly up).

What . . . is . . . it . . . then . . . really! . . .

(Turns to well).

(Hoddel has meanwhile taken advantage of his meditation to run to the handcart, take off his uniform and moustache and hide them. He stands idly rummaging among the bits and pieces. Joris climbs back on to the well and discovers that the 'mirror' is no longer a mirror. He tries to tap it, walks around it, and finally steps through it).

Nothing! Absolutely nothing! Vanished into thin air. But by all the raindrops, I saw it! With my own two eyes, I saw it! I'm certain!

(He gets down from the well and looks searchingly around).

Hallo! What is that!

(Puts on his spectacles).

Who can that be?

(Takes out a telescope and looks again).

I'll have to look into this, and find out more about it!

(He puts away the telescope, pulls his tunic straight, pulls himself into an official posture, and ambles slowly toward Hoddel, his hands behind his back).

Ahem!

(Hoddel doesn't hear).

Aaaa-he-e-em!

(Hoddel starts, and begins calling).

HODDEL. Rags, Bones, Any old clothes!

JORIS. And who might you be?

HODDEL. Ah! Officer . . .

JORIS. I said: "Who might you be?"

HODDEL. What? You don't know me, constable? Everyone everywhere knows me! I'm Hoddel de Boddel, the junk man.

(Bows).

JORIS. Aha! And what might you be doing here?

HODDEL. Collecting junk.

(Cries).

Any old clothes!?

(Joris sleuths around the cart like a Sherlock Holmes).

JORIS. So! So! And what do you reckon to do with that lot?

HODDEL. Sell it.

JORIS. Aha! So, you sell things?

HODDEL. Anything you can think of, constable.

JORIS. Aha! So-o-o-o. Something of everything, huh? . . . Tell me, Mr. Junkman, er, you wouldn't perhaps have a mirror for sale, would you?

HODDEL. A mirror?

JORIS. Yes, a big one. You know, a sort of full length one that you can see your whole self in.

HODDEL. A mirror! Let me see now . . . No, that's something I haven't got just at the moment. Are you in need of one, officer?

JORIS. I? Well, er, I've sort of lost one, if you see what I mean. It was here only a moment ago, on the well.

HODDEL. On the well? I can't see a mirror on the well!

JORIS. No. That's it, you see! It disappeared!

HODDEL. Disappeared? That's strange!

JORIS. Very strange.

HODDEL. D'you need a mirror very badly, officer?

JORIS. Yes! I mean no. You see, I think . . . I - er - rather believe . . . Tell me, junkman, how do you think my tunic fits?

(Hoddel walks around Joris, pulling at his tunic here and there).

HODDEL. Hmm. Very smart. Very tidy. A little on the large side, perhaps.

JORIS. What's that? Too large? There! How about my helmet?

810

HODDEL. Mmmm. Smart. Very smart! Just a tiny bit too big, if I may say so.

JORIS. You think it's too big? I know it! Nothing fits me any more. I'm losing weight.

HODDEL. Perhaps you don't eat enough, constable.

JORIS. That's it! That must be it. I must eat more.

HODDEL. Or perhaps you work too hard?

JORIS. Yes, that's it too. I work too hard.

HODDEL. Perhaps you're overworked.

JORIS. Overworked? What's that?

HODDEL. That means that you work too hard, that you're always tired.

JORIS. Ay, that I am!

(Yawns).

Oooooh! How tired I am!

HODDEL. And then you just can't eat any extra.

JORIS. That I can't! Not one single extra spoonful can I get past my throat.

HODDEL. And you can't sleep enough, either?

JORIS. Sleep? Huh! Haven't shut my eyes in weeks! And I'm so tired!

HODDEL. There you are! And perhaps you see things that are not really there at all? For instance, you thought that you saw a mirror . . .

JORIS *(Glancing at well).* But that I did see! . . .

HODDEL. There you have it!

JORIS. Then I must be o, o, over . . . worked. What can I do?

HODDEL. DO? That's just it, you musn't DO anything! Just stay quiet, and rest, and sleep and eat.

JORIS. You've got it! I've got to get more sleep. I need plenty more sleep, because I'm terribly o, o, er . . .

HODDEL. Overworked.

JORIS. Yes. That's it, overworked. I'm going straight to bed!

(He moves toward the house, but stops halfway, remembering).

But I can't.

HODDEL. Why not?

811

JORIS. I've got to paint the bench.

HODDEL. But that's very dangerous, constable, for a man in your condition.

(Shakes head).

It always starts in the same way. First you start to see things that aren't really there, then to hear things, and to smell things.

JORIS. Hear things? And smell things? That aren't there at all! But that's terrible! I'm going straight to bed. I'm o, o, —

(Turns at door of house).

HODDEL. Overworked.

JORIS. That's it. Overworked!

(Exit).

HODDEL. Ha. Ha. Ha. The lazy constable! He's overworked! Ha. Ha. Ha. Ha. Ha. Ha.

(Alfonso enters, agitated).

ALFONSO. What's all the noise about?

HODDEL *(Pulls himself quickly together).* Rags and Bones!

ALFONSO. Who are you?

HODDEL. I'm Hoddel de Boddel the junkman. Have you any old rags to sell?

ALFONSO. Old rags! Me? I haven't got any old rags. Everything I've got is new!

HODDEL. Then perhaps you would like to buy something from me?

ALFONSO. No! I've got everything.

HODDEL. That's not possible. Have you got a hat like this, with such lovely feathers?

ALFONSO. I've got ten like it in the cupboard.

HODDEL. And this fine chinese jacket?

ALFONSO. I've at least a hundred jackets.

HODDEL. Oh! Then have you got . . .

ALFONSO. Yes. I've got that too. And that. And that. I've got everything, so you can stop it now, I've got to get to work.

HODDEL. To work? Why?

ALFONSO. Why? To make money, of course!

HODDEL. What do you do with your money then?

ALFONSO. Nothing.

HODDEL. Nothing! Don't you ever buy anything?

ALFONSO. Of course not! I've already got everything.

HODDEL. But if you've already got everything, what do you want to make more money for?

ALFONSO. For . . .

(Looks carefully around to make sure that no-one can overhear) . . .

For Simplina.

HODDEL. Who's that?

ALFONSO. Simplina? That's the girl I want to marry.

HODDEL. Why don't you then?

ALFONSO. She . . . she won't. She won't even talk to me.

HODDEL. Why not?

ALFONSO. Because I've got so much that I don't need anything more, and because I'm always so busy that I never have time for anything else.

HODDEL. Why work any more then?

ALFONSO. I just can't stop! People 'phone me. They write me letters, and send me telegrams. Money rolls in from everywhere. It's terrible! And it's all no use to me because I've already got everything and don't need anything more. Everything, that is, except Simplina. And I can't get her, because she just won't have anything to do with me.

HODDEL. It seems to me that Simplina might have more to do with you if only you could find some spare time, have some fun and learn to laugh now and then.

ALFONSO. But I can't laugh any more! I haven't laughed now for twenty years.

HODDEL. Try!

ALFONSO. Ha.

HODDEL. That's no good! Harder!

ALFONSO. Ha, ha.

HODDEL. Harder still!

ALFONSO. Ha, ha. Ha, ha. See! It's no use. I . . .

(Telephone rings).

Oooooooh! There it goes again!

(Runs inside).

(Dophilius enters to see what all the fuss is about).

DOPHILIUS. What's all the noise? What was that? Did I hear Mr. Alfonso laughing?

HODDEL. Poor Alfonso Goldpurse!

DOPHILIUS. Poor! He's the richest man in the whole world! He's got everything he wants, everything. And I've got nothing.

HODDEL. Nothing!

DOPHILIUS. Nothing at all, . . . except shoes, and no-one wants to buy them.

HODDEL. Why not?

DOPHILIUS. Because no-one needs them. Alfonso has at least a hundred pairs, and Joris never wears his out because he does nothing but sleep.

HODDEL. And Miss Simplina?

DOPHILIUS. She only wears slippers.

HODDEL. Then why do you make shoes?

DOPHILIUS. For Miss Sandra.

HODDEL. Aha! So there is some-one who wants them then!

DOPHILIUS. She doesn't want them! . . . But I haven't anything else to offer, and —

(He looks around carefully).

I want to marry her.

HODDEL. Why don't you then?

DOPHILIUS. Because she doesn't want to marry a man who has nothing but shoes to offer. Look out! They're coming. Perhaps Miss Sandra will speak to me this time.

(The girls enter. Each carries one corner of a carpet on high with one hand, and a carpet beater with the other. The carpet hides them from Dophilius and Hoddel. Dophilius walks as if to speak to them, but thinks better of it, and disappears into his house).

DOPHILIUS. It wouldn't be any use.

(As he exits).

SIMPLINA. I still think you're mean.

(Gives the carpet a smack with beater).

SANDRA. And I think you're mean.

814

(Smack).

SIMPLINA *(Looks around the carpet at Sandra).* In any case you might have thanked Dophilius.

SANDRA *(Looks around carpet at Simplina).* And you might have given Mr. Goldpurse an answer.

(They both disappear behind carpet).

SIMPLINA. Why should I answer Mr. Goldpurse!

(Angry slap at carpet).

SANDRA. He's got at least ten velvet jackets, and he likes you.

(Slap).

SIMPLINA. And Dophilius likes you.

(Two angry slaps).

(Hoddel, taken by surprise by this conversation, creeps nearer).

SANDRA. But Dophilius is so poor!

(Two slaps).

SIMPLINA. And Alfonso is rich.

(Three slaps).

SANDRA. Dophilius possesses nothing at all.

SIMPLINA. And Alfonso possesses too much of everything.

(Very hard slap).

(Hoddel, who has by now crept very close to the carpet, gives it an extra slap).

SANDRA. What are you doing now?

SIMPLINA. Nothing!

SANDRA. Dophilius is always discontented.

(Hard slap. Hoddel also gives a slap from his side of the carpet).

Hey! That's queer! Let's turn the carpet round.

(As they turn the carpet round, Hoddel ducks low, so that the girls come to stand on the audience side of the carpet, and Hoddel is concealed behind it).

SIMPLINA. There's nothing there!

SANDRA. We must have been imagining.

(She gives a slap, Hoddel gives another).

There you are! It is you!

SIMPLINA. No, it's not! The carpet's doing it itself!

(She gives it a slap, and Hoddel follows suit).

SANDRA. Then let's turn it this way.

(They walk around, the carpet stretched between them. Hoddel tripples with them).

SIMPLINA. There's nothing to see!

SANDRA. I don't understand it. Let's shake it out.

(They lay their carpet beaters down and take hold of the carpet by all four corners, then while Hoddel crouches underneath, they begin to shake it out. After a couple of shakes, Hoddel stands upright, the carpet hanging over his head).

SIMPLINA. What are you doing now?

SANDRA. Me? I'm not doing anything! I think you were right. The carpet's doing it itself!

(They drop the two D. S. corners, and lift the two U. S. corners on high, so that Hoddel once again is concealed behind it).

SIMPLINA. There's something very queer with this carpet!

SANDRA. Let's drop it suddenly. One . . . Two . . . Three . . .

(They let go of the two corners, but Hoddel forestalls them and catches hold so that the carpet remains hanging).

S. & S. *(Backing away)*. Hey!

SANDRA. It just stays hanging!

SIMPLINA. All by itself!

SANDRA. Let's creep underneath.

(As they begin to creep under it, Hoddel lets it fall over them. He then takes the other two corners and lifts them up high, so that the two girls are now behind the carpet).

SIMPLINA. Nothing!

SANDRA. It just hangs loose in the air!

(The girls now take hold of one side of the carpet, while Hoddel slides quickly to the other side, they hold one corner on high, he the other. As they look along the front of it, he steps behind, when they look behind, he steps in front. Then they begin to walk it around so that he becomes wrapped up in it).

SIMPLINA. Nothing!

SANDRA. It . . . It does it all by itself!

(The carpet begins to unroll itself. Hoddel walks around the two girls, wrapping them up in it).

SIMPLINA. Oh! What's happening now?

SANDRA. I . . . We . . . Oh!

(As they struggle to free themselves, Hoddel slips back to his handcart and busies himself with it).

SANDRA. That carpet's acting very strangely. It seems enchanted!

SIMPLINA. I wouldn't dare to touch it again, would you?

SANDRA. No, I wouldn't!

(Hoddel begins to ring his bell).

HODDEL. Any old rags! Any old bones!

SIMPLINA. Look! There's a ragman.

SANDRA. Let's give it to him.

SIMPLINA. Yes, let's.

(Calls).

Ragman!

HODDEL. Good morning ladies. Have you any old clothes or lumber for me?

SIMPLINA. We've got a carpet.

SANDRA. Here it is.

HODDEL. A carpet?

SIMPLINA. Yes. You can take it.

(As Hoddel goes to fetch it, the girls back away apprehensively).

HODDEL. But it's a very good carpet! It's in fine condition.

SANDRA *(Seeing Hoddel with the carpet in his hand).* Nothing's happened!

HODDEL. You can't call this old rags, or lumber.

SIMPLINA. Well, no-o-o. It's just an ordinary carpet. We ought to keep it.

(The girls come closer and touch it warily).

SANDRA. Look! Nothing happens.

SIMPLINA. Alright then, we won't give it away.

(She takes it back).

HODDEL. Pity. Have you got anything else?

SANDRA. No, ragman, we haven't. Come, Simplina.

HODDEL. Wait a minute! I've got lovely things for you to buy. Look.

SIMPLINA. We've got no money.

HODDEL. No money? You should ask your husbands for some, quickly.

S. & S. Ha, ha! We haven't got any husbands.

HODDEL. What! No husbands? Why not?

SANDRA. Well . . . because . . .

HODDEL. Ho, ho!

SIMPLINA. What do you mean, "Ho, ho!"?

HODDEL. Ho, ho, ho!

SANDRA. Is it so funny then that we haven't got husbands?

HODDEL. Funny? No, but, er . . .

SIMPLINA. Then why did you say, "Ho, ho, ho!"?

HODDEL. Well . . . Nice girls like you ought to get married, otherwise . . .

SANDRA. What do you mean, "otherwise"?

HODDEL. Well, I have heard it said that young girls who don't want to get married begin to see all sorts of strange things. Or hear them, or smell them.

SIMPLINA. What do you mean, "strange things"?

HODDEL. Oh, all sorts.

SANDRA. Ha, ha, ha. Don't let him kid you, Simplina.

HODDEL. Alright then! Only a little while ago I met a girl who gave me a carpet . . .

SIMPLINA. What of it?

HODDEL. She didn't want it any more because she saw it move of its own accord, with her own two eyes.

(The two girls give a scream and let the carpet fall).

HODDEL. What's the matter?

SANDRA. Was that girl married?

HODDEL. No. She didn't want to. She could have had either of two husbands, but one was too rich for her, and the other too poor.

SIMPLINA. I don't think I want that carpet anymore.

SANDRA. Neither do I. You can take it, ragman.

HODDEL. What's the matter with it then?

SIMPLINA. Oh, er, nothing! We just don't think that it's pretty any more. You take it, quickly.

HODDEL. Alright, if you really don't want it. Hoddel takes anything and everything. Have you anything else?

SANDRA. No, nothing. Come on, Simplina, let's get away quickly.

(Simplina follows her sister towards their house, but stops suddenly, and turns).

SIMPLINA. And what happened to that girl?

HODDEL. Oh, she got married since then.

SANDRA. And now?

HODDEL. Nothing! She's got her carpet back.

SIMPLINA. But . . . but then . . .

SANDRA. Oh! So what! It's nothing but gossip. In any case father Joris doesn't want us to get married . . .

SIMPLINA. . . . because then he'd have to do all the work for himself.

SANDRA. Yes, where is father Joris? He's not in the kitchen papering the walls.

SIMPLINA. And he's not painting the bench, either.

SANDRA *(To bench)*. The bench has not been touched!

(She walks around the well).

There's the tin of paint . . . and there's the glue! On the bench!

(She sees the closed curtains at Joris' window).

What's that? Has he gone back to bed again?

(Calls).

Father Joris!

SIMPLINA. Let's call together.

S. & S. Father Joris . . .!

(Dophilius enters).

DOPHILIUS. What's the trouble?

(He sees the closed curtains).

Wait, I'll help you to call, Miss Sandra.

(Sandra doesn't answer him).

819

SIMPLINA. That's very kind of you, Dophilius.

(Alfonso enters).

ALFONSO. What's very kind of Dophilius? Oh! I see it all. Shall I call him for you, Miss Simplina?

(Simplina turns her back on him).

SANDRA. How kind of you, Mr. Goldpurse! And you've such a fine voice for calling!

SIMPLINA. Perhaps Hoddel the ragman will help us too?

ALFONSO. Good then, all five of us together. Get ready, . . . one . . . two . . . three . . .

ALL. FATHER JORIS! ! ! ! !

JORIS *(Off)*. Hrrrr. Grrrr. Aaaah. Baaaah. Alright, alright!

(Puts his head out of the window).

Oooooh. Wha's er marrer?

SANDRA. What are you doing in there?

JORIS. Who me?

ALFONSO. Sleeping, as usual.

JORIS. Who? Me! No, I . . . I mean . . .

SANDRA. Were you sleeping or not?

JORIS. No . . . er . . . Yes. Just a little nap. I've hardly had time to shut my eyes.

SIMPLINA. And are the kitchen walls papered?

SANDRA. And is the bench painted?

JORIS. Yes . . . er . . . I mean, no . . . er . . . I mean, the "thinking it out" part's finished . . .

SANDRA. There's no bubble-and-squeak before the kitchen walls are well and truly papered!

SIMPLINA. And no apple pie before the bench is painted.

SANDRA. People who only sleep, need no food!

(The two girls and Joris exit).

ALFONSO. What an old lazy-bones! Poor Simplina.

DOPHILIUS. And poor Sandra.

ALFONSO. If only I could speak to Simplina, just once!

DOPHILIUS. And I to Sandra.

820

HODDEL. That can be done easily.

A. & D. How?

HODDEL. Just like that.

ALFONSO. But Simplina won't say one word to me!

DOPHILIUS. Nor Sandra to me!

HODDEL. There you have the answer!

ALFONSO. Where!?

HODDEL. Look. Simplina won't speak to you, and Sandra won't speak to Dophilius, so all you have to do is make a swap.

A. & D. Wh-a-a-a-t!

HODDEL. Make a swap! You take Dophilius' place, and Dophilius takes yours.

DOPHILIUS. What then?

HODDEL. It's all so simple. If you were Mr. Goldpurse, Sandra would speak to you, true?

ALFONSO. And then, if Simplina thought that I were Dophilius, she would speak to me too?

DOPHILIUS. That's right! I never thought of that! I'll do it.

ALFONSO. I too! What do we have to do?

HODDEL. First of all change clothes.

ALFONSO. What? D'you mean to say that I've got to put that filthy apron on?

DOPHILIUS. And d'you mean to say I've got to wear Alfonso's lovely jacket?

HODDEL. Of course! And his hat, too.

DOPHILIUS. Coo! Lumme!

(Takes his apron off in a hurry).

Here! Here's my apron.

(Alfonso takes the apron gingerly, and hands Doph. his jacket).

ALFONSO. And . . . here's my jacket. Careful with it. It's only for one day, remember!

DOPHILIUS. Oh! What a wonderful jacket. So soft and comfortable.

ALFONSO. Brrrrrrr. What a nasty old apron. It's all stiff and dirty.

HODDEL. That's good. And now you must give Dophilius your spectacles Alfonso.

821

ALFONSO. Yes, of course.

HODDEL. And Alfonso must have your pipe, Dophilius.

ALFONSO *(Takes pipe)*. Ooh, what a filthy pipe. It stinks!

HODDEL. Dophilius will have to have your briefcase too, Alfonso.

(He hands it over).

DOPHILIUS. Oy! This briefcase is heavy! What's in it?

ALFONSO. Money.

DOPHILIUS. Money? All money! Then I'm rich! Rich at last. Won't Miss Sandra be happy now!

HODDEL. Now, let me see . . . Oh! That's not good! You'll have to cut off your moustache, Dophilius.

DOPHILIUS. Of course! Alfonso doesn't have a moustache.

ALFONSO. What about me then?

HODDEL. You'll have to have one.

ALFONSO. But I haven't got one!

HODDEL. Aha! Finally something which Mr. Goldpurse hasn't got.

(He goes to his cart and brings back a false moustache).

Look!

DOPHILIUS. Hey! It's exactly like mine! I'm going to cut mine off straight away.

(He exits into his house).

(Hoddel sticks the false moustache onto Alf.'s upper lip).

HODDEL. There you are!

DOPHILIUS *(Enters clean shaven)*. Do we really look like one another?

HODDEL. Mmmmm . . . I think so. I don't think anyone will notice the difference.

DOPHILIUS. Ooh, I feel good with this jacket and this hat on, and a bag full of gold!

ALFONSO. It's only for one day, remember! I feel horrible in this nasty apron, and this moustache keeps tickling - atishoo - my nose - atishoo -, I'm going home.

(He walks towards his own house).

HODDEL. Wait a minute! You've got to go to Dophilius' house.

ALFONSO. What? Have I got to live in that hovel?

DOPHILIUS. And may I . . . may I really go into that beautiful large house?

HODDEL. Naturally! You're Mr. Goldpurse now, aren't you?

DOPHILIUS. What a joke! What a giant of a joke! I'll eat like a king!

ALFONSO. And what am I going to eat?

DOPHILIUS. Brown bread, and cold sausage. You'll find it on a shelf in the scullery.

ALFONSO. Brown bread! Ugh. And sausage! Just what I don't like.

DOPHILIUS. Oh, how I'll sleep tonight, between those silken sheets!

ALFONSO. And where have I got to sleep, then?

DOPHILIUS. On my straw mattress. You'll find it lying on the floor in a corner.

ALFONSO. A straw mattress! On the floor! How terrible. What have I done?

HODDEL. Hurry, you'd better go inside now before anyone comes.

DOPHILIUS. Don't worry, I'm off!

ALFONSO. Do we have to go in so soon?

HODDEL. Of course! As Dophilius you'll have to come out of his hut!

DOPHILIUS. And I, as the rich Mr. Goldpurse, will have to . . .

ALFONSO. Alright. Alright. We'll do it.

DOPHILIUS. Goodnight, Mr. Goldpurse.

HODDEL. You've got to say, "Goodnight, Dophilius"!

DOPHILIUS. Yes, of course. Goodnight, Dophilius.

(Alfonso moves disconsolately towards Dophilius' hovel).

ALFONSO. Goodnight, Dophilius.

HODDEL. And you've got to say "Goodnight, Mr. Goldpurse".

ALFONSO. Even that! But remember it's only for one day!

(Dophilius goes to Alfonso's house and opens the door).

DOPHILIUS. Oh! What a lovely house!

(Disappears inside).

ALFONSO *(Opens Dophilius' door and looks inside).* What a dirty, dark hole! What am I going to do? There's no telephone, not even a typewriter!

HODDEL. You don't need them any more. You're Dophilius, now! You've only got to make shoes.

823

ALFONSO (*Petulantly*). I won't! I can't make shoes at all.

HODDEL. Listen. If you want to marry Simplina, you've got to be prepared to make some sacrifice.

ALFONSO. Simplina! Of course I want to marry Simplina. Alright, I'll do it.

(*Turns back to Dophilius' hut*).

But I can't! I've never made a shoe in my life. I don't even know what a hammer looks like!

HODDEL. Don't worry, you'll learn soon enough. Come on, I'll help you for a while.

(*They both exit into Dophilius' hovel. Joris enters warily*).

JORIS. There's no-one about. Haha! I've slept like a log. But I'm hungry. I'm dying from starvation! I've got to eat something in a hurry.

(*Moves back toward house*).

(*Stops suddenly, remembering*).

Krrrriminy! Paint! Paper! If I don't get it finished I won't get any bubble-and-squeak or apple pie!

(*Rubs his middle sadly*).

And I could do with a hot plate of bubble-and-squeak and some nice fat sausages! And a plateful of apple pie with lots of sugar over it!

(*Moves slowly towards the bench*).

But first I've got to paint the bench. Bah! Now, how was it? Let me see! I put the glue on the bench, and the paint on the floor. So, that must be the paint, because it's on the floor. Then that must be the glue, because it's on the bench.

(*Sits*).

So, so. That's a bit of hard thinking! And now to get on with the work. What did that ragman say, again? I mustn't start painting, otherwise I'll begin to see things that aren't there. D'you think . . . d'you think I'll see anything else?

(*He looks around, his eye falling on Hoddel's handcart, and sees his carpet lying on it*).

Hey! What do I see there! It's . . . It's my own carpet!

(*He holds his hands before his eyes and takes them away again; looks through his fingers; turns away and looks back suddenly, to take it by surprise; puts his glasses on; takes a telescope out of his pocket and looks through this; finally he stands slowly up*).

824

That's my carpet! I can see it clearly.

(He creeps towards it).

It's still there . . . It . . .

(He has by now crept very close to it. He makes a spring and grabs it).

Aha! It IS my carpet. What is the ragman doing with it? Perhaps he's not a ragman at all! Perhaps he's really a thief . . . then it's my duty to catch him, after all I am the constable! And if I've got to catch him, then I've got no time at all to paint the bench. You know what I'll do? I'll wait here till he comes back. Here, on the bench. So.

(Yawns).

It wouldn't hurt if I had a little nap. Yes, I'd better do that, then at least I'll be fit when he comes.

(He falls back and begins to snore).

(Hoddel enters from Dophilius' hut).

HODDEL. No, I must go, now. It's nearly dark. But I'll be back tomorrow.

ALFONSO. Will you really come back?

HODDEL. You bet! I'm too curious to know how it will all work out!

(Alfonso closes the door).

So! Everything's in order. The men want to get married, the girls want to get married, and Joris is overworked. I think I can go now.

(Sees Joris asleep on the bench with the carpet).

Hahaha! The constable has found it. He thinks, naturally, that I'm a thief. Ssshh! I'll take it back.

(He tip-toes to Joris, takes the carpet, puts it back in Joris' house and comes out again).

Oh, ho! How Joris will look when he finds that his carpet's disappeared again! And how the girls will be surprised when they see that it's back! Now I'd better get away.

(Hoddel is about to ride away when he jogs the bell accidentally. The bell wakes Joris).

JORIS. Hey! Ho! Hold that thief!

HODDEL. Sorry, constable. Did I wake you up?

JORIS. Yes . . . no . . . I mean, of course you haven't awakened me. What on earth do you think, ragman, that a constable hasn't

825

anything better to do than sleep? An officer of the law is there to . . . catch thieves!

(Grabs Hoddel by the scruff of his neck).

And now he's got one! Hahaha. You hadn't thought of that, had you?

HODDEL. But I'm not a thief at all!

JORIS. Oh, no? Then how d'you come across my carpet?

HODDEL. Your carpet?

JORIS. Yes, my carpet. I've just taken it out of your barrow.

(Looks toward the bench).

Hey! Where's that now?

(Walks to bench).

I put it down here!

(He looks under the bench, around the well, and in Hoddel's handcart).

It's gone! Disappeared!

HODDEL. D'you know what, constable? I wouldn't be surprised if the carpet's lying in your own house.

JORIS. Impossible. I had it here, myself.

HODDEL. You're just imagining it, you know, like the mirror.

JORIS. But I'm absolutely certain . . .

HODDEL. Why don't you go in and have a look?

JORIS. Alright then, but . . .

(Walks slowly to his house and looks through the window) . . .

There . . . there it is! Lying on the floor. I HAVE imagined it!

HODDEL. Now do you see that I'm right, constable? You're overworked.

JORIS. I think you're right! That'll be it.

HODDEL. You ought to get some sleep.

JORIS. I've got to start painting.

HODDEL. But you can't go painting if you're sick!

JORIS. I must!

HODDEL. Who says so?

JORIS. The girls.

HODDEL. Why don't you let them get married? Then you won't have them to worry you.

JORIS. Let them get married? The girls! Never! Who would I have to do the work for me? No, ragman, that's out of the question. In any case, I don't believe in it. It's all a lot of nonsense.

HODDEL. About the carpet too?

JORIS. About the carpet too. I had it here.

(Walks to handcart).

Then I took it here.

(Walks to bench. While he does this Hoddel digs out his constable's uniform and the moustache, and slips them hurriedly on).
Then I sat here, and put it down there.

(He sits, stands up again, and then walks toward Hoddel) . . .

I know it! I'm certain of it! Hey! What's that! The mirror again! Then it's really true! I really am o . . . o . . .

HODDEL. Overworked.

(Joris yelps and runs off into his house).

Haha! Poor old Joris! I'm really curious to know how it will all work out.

(He takes the constable's clothing off, the bell pings).

Ssshhh! Don't give me away.

(He makes a circle with the handcart. The lights fade to blackout. Music).

End of the first part.

PART TWO

The scene is set the same as in Part One. It is early morning, and the cocks are crowing. Sandra and Simplina are busy at the well.

SIMPLINA. I'm sure that it's the same carpet that we gave to the ragman.

SANDRA. Yes, but now it's lying on our floor again!

SIMPLINA. I don't understand it.

SANDRA. Perhaps we're just imagining things.

SIMPLINA. Then the ragman was right after all!

SANDRA. So we've got to get married.

SIMPLINA. I think I'll be a little more friendly towards Mr. Gold-purse.

SANDRA. And I'll be more friendly towards Dophilius.

SIMPLINA. It's just possible that Mr. Goldpurse is quite nice when you get to know him.

SANDRA. Dophilius too.

(While they are busy at the well, Dophilius steps out of Alfonso's door. He is very satisfied with himself).

DOPHILIUS. Oh! What a night! What a bed! What blankets!

(The girls are struck dumb with amazement. They draw away from him as though they have seen a ghost, but eventually curiosity gets the better of them and they come closer by. Meanwhile Doph. carries on with his song of praise for all the blessings of this life).

What an awakening! What delicious cream-horns! What a day! A day to sing . . . tralalalala . . . a day to dance!

(Dances around).

A day to get married!

(Sees the girls).

With dearest Sandra!

(He walks to the girls, who fall back in surprise).

SANDRA. What did you say!?

DOPHILIUS. Oh, dear Sandra! If only you knew how wonderful it is to be rich!

SANDRA. But you always found it . . .

DOPHILIUS. To have everything that your heart could wish for . . .

SANDRA. But, I thought that . . .

DOPHILIUS. And to be in love . . . with a dewdrop . . . a cherry-blossom . . . an apple-turnover . . .

(The girls stand dead-still).

SIMPLINA. Some . . . something must have happened!

DOPHILIUS. Something happened, did you say? Haha! I feel like another man.

SIMPLINA. Yes, we've noticed it!

SANDRA. You're quite different from usual.

DOPHILIUS. How could it be otherwise, with such a life . . .

DOPHILIUS. Naturally! I feel different . . .

SANDRA. You look different than usual . . .

SIMPLINA. It looks as though you've grown . . .

DOPHILIUS. I have! I stretched out so much when I woke up, that I stretched myself longer.

SANDRA. And it seems as though you've got thinner.

DOPHILIUS. Of course I'm thinner. If you stretch yourself longer you must be thinner.

SIMPLINA. But it's the same jacket . . .

SANDRA. And the same hat . . .

SIMPLINA. But the voice is very much harsher . . .

SANDRA. And the hands much rougher . . .

SIMPLINA. And the feet are much bigger . . .

SANDRA. And the nose is much more pointed . . .

SIMPLINA. The eyes are darker . . .

SANDRA. And the hair longer . . .

SIMPLINA. But apart from that . . .

SANDRA. Yes, apart from that, you are Mr. Goldpurse.

DOPHILIUS (Who has been growing ill at ease). Of course! Of course I'm Mr. Goldpurse! Who other could it be? In any case you saw me come out of Alfonso's house yourself, didn't you?

SIMPLINA. Yes, that's true.

DOPHILIUS. Well, that's proof enough that I am Mr. Goldpurse, isn't it?

SANDRA. Yes, if you really live there then you must be him, but . . .

DOPHILIUS (Who is afraid that she will begin anew). And now I'll help you at once to draw the water, Miss Sandra.

SANDRA. What did you say!

SIMPLINA. Haven't you made a mistake?

DOPHILIUS. No, I . . .

(Fate comes to his aid and Alfonso staggers out of Dophilius' hovel, groaning. The girls are tossed from one amazement to another).

ALFONSO. Oooooooh! Oo-oo-ooh! Aaaaaaah! Horrible! What a night! What a bed! Oo-oo-ooh! What a house! And that bread! Ugh! Brown bread! And cold sausage! Oh, my back, my poor back! My arms! And my legs! Oh! Everything hurts!

(The girls had backed away, but it is too much for Simplina, who runs quickly to him).

SIMPLINA. What's happened, Dophilius? Have you hurt yourself? Are you sick?

ALFONSO. Oh! My back.

SIMPLINA. But what's happened?

ALFONSO. Happened? Oh! I'm a broken man.

SANDRA. We'd noticed that!

(She comes closer).

SIMPLINA. Come, Dophilius, tell us what's the matter. You're usually so different!

ALFONSO. Ooh! How could it be otherwise?

SANDRA. You even look different from usual.

ALFONSO. Yes, I can quite believe that!

SIMPLINA. It seems as though you've become smaller!

ALFONSO. I'm not surprised.

SANDRA. And as though you've become fatter . . .

ALFONSO. That's because of the pain . . .

SIMPLINA. Only your shirt remains the same . . .

SANDRA. And your cap too . . .

SIMPLINA. But your voice is much softer . . .

SANDRA. And your hands much finer . . .

SIMPLINA. And your feet are smaller . . .

SANDRA. And your nose is less pointed . . .

SIMPLINA. And your eyes are much lighter . . .

SANDRA. And your hair is shorter . . .

SIMPLINA. But further . . .

SANDRA. Yes, further, you're just Dophilius!

ALFONSO *(Makes a manly attempt)*. Yes, of course. And if I stretch out . . . Oooooohh! My back!

SIMPLINA. Oh, poor Dophilius. You really are sick.

ALFONSO. Ah! Simplina. I may be in pain, but all the same I'm very . . . Oooooh! . . . happy.

SIMPLINA. What d'you say? Are you happy that you're in pain?

ALFONSO. No. I mean that I'm . . .oh! . . . happy that you're speaking to me.

830

SIMPLINA. But Dophilius! I've always wanted to speak to you! I just didn't want to speak to . . .

(The girls exchange meaning glances, and look from Alfonso to Dophilius).

DOPHILIUS *(Butting in quickly)*. May I fill your pail for you Sandra?

SANDRA. Me! Oh, yes please, Mr. Goldpurse! Would you really do that for me?

DOPHILIUS. Of course. I couldn't think of anything I'd like better.

SANDRA. Simplina! Did you hear what Mr. Goldpurse just said?

ALFONSO. And I . . . Oh! . . . and I'll call my ser . . . I mean, I'll help Simplina.

SIMPLINA. What did you say? Will you really help me, Dophilius?

ALFONSO. Of course I will! I've always wanted to do that.

SIMPLINA. Sandra! Did you hear that! . . .

(Alf. and Doph. take the pails. Doph. is naturally quite at home with his, but Alf. fumbles terribly. It is the first time he has ever handled one).

SANDRA. Oh, Mr. Goldpurse! How handy you are at it!

SIMPLINA. No, Dophilius! Not like that! Anyone would think that you'd never drawn water in your life before! Look out! You'll drop the pail into the well! Let me do it. You really are a sick man, Dophilius.

ALFONSO. Ooooooooh!

DOPHILIUS. And now we'll carry that little bucket home for you.

SANDRA. Oh, Mr. Goldpurse! Aren't you strong!

DOPHILIUS. Strong? I can carry six buckets like this, and you as well, Sandra.

ALFONSO. Ooooooooh! This bucket's so heavy!

SIMPLINA. See, Dophilius? You are sick. You're going to bed now, and I'm going to look after you.

(She turns at the doorstep).

Thank you very much indeed, Dophilius. You've really been a wonderful help.

(She exits).

DOPHILIUS. There you are, Sandra. There's your bucket.

SANDRA. Oh, Mr. Goldpurse, I don't know how to thank you. I'm so happy that you wanted to help me.

DOPHILIUS. I'd like to do it always, Sandra.

SANDRA. Always?

DOPHILIUS. Always.

SANDRA (Entering the house). Simplina! Did you hear what Mr. Gold-purse said?

(The door closes behind them).

DOPHILIUS (Jumping for joy). Always, always, always!

ALFONSO. As Dophilius then! Not as Alfonso Goldpurse!

DOPHILIUS. What do you mean?

ALFONSO. I want to exchange again. I've had enough of it.

DOPHILIUS. Exchange? Enough of it? Enough of what?

ALFONSO. Of playing at being Dophilius, of course. I haven't been able to shut my eyes once last night on that hard straw! I haven't been able to get a mouthful past my throat, with that awful brown bread!

DOPHILIUS. Tell me, shoemaker, what are you going on about?

ALFONSO. Don't you understand? I want to be Alfonso Goldpurse again as agreed.

DOPHILIUS. You want to be Alfonso Goldpurse again? As agreed? Listen, shoemaker, I believe that Simplina was right, and that you really are sick!

ALFONSO. I'm not a shoemaker, and I'm not sick!

DOPHILIUS. You're very, very sick. You've got fever! You're de-lirious.

ALFONSO. I've not got a fever, only a pain in my back, and that comes only because I'm not Dophilius at all.

DOPHILIUS. Not Dophilius, Hahahahaha! That's a good one! Who are you then?

ALFONSO. Come on! Take my jacket off.

DOPHILIUS. Your jacket? It's my jacket.

ALFONSO. That's not true! It's mine. Give it here.

(Tries to grab the jacket).

DOPHILIUS. Look, shoemaker, no more jokes, if you please. Leave my jacket alone or I'll call my servant to give you a good hiding.

ALFONSO. Your servant! It's my servant!

DOPHILIUS. That's an impertinence! I'll not speak to you again!

832

(Dophilius turns majestically and strides towards Alf.'s door).

ALFONSO. But Dophilius . . . listen to me . . . Dophilius!

DOPHILIUS *(Turns quickly).* Tell me, shoemaker, how dare you call me Dophilius. Me! The rich Mr. Alfonso Goldpurse?

ALFONSO *(In despair).* Mr. Goldpurse, then. We did . . .

DOPHILIUS. We did nothing of the sort. I've got nothing to do with you. And now I'm going inside to eat a couple of cream-horns.

(Exit).

ALFONSO. Cream horns. My cream horns. Just what I could do with now.

(Feels in his pockets).

And all I've got is this filthy piece of cold sausage.

(He brings a piece of sausage out).

I daren't put my teeth into it.

(He goes to the well, and sits sadly on the bench. He puts the sausage to his mouth, but pulls away from it).

Ooooh! What a smell! I can't.

(He is about to throw it away, but thinks better).

Wait a minute, I'll hold my nose.

(He does so, but still hesitates).

Now, this time!

(Eyes and nose tight shut, he puts the sausage in his mouth, and takes a bite).

Hey! I can't taste it. Again.

(He repeats the last manoeuvre). (After a hesitant beginning, he starts to chew, warily. Slowly a light of astonishment begins to show in his eyes. His face clears up, and he takes his hand from his nose. He begins to savour it).

Mmmmm. Not bad. Not bad at all. It's better than I thought!

(Begins to enjoy it. Sniffs at it).

The smell's not bad either. It doesn't smell bad at all.

(Takes another good sniff at it).

It smells delicious! And it tastes good too. Very good.

(Takes a new bite). (With full mouth).

Good. Delicious. Spicy. And with body! A lot better than those sickly cream-horns. Healthy. That's the word for it, healthy!

(Takes the last mouthful).

It'd make you grow bigger, and stronger. I'm feeling stronger already! I'm going to try that bread. And then I'll be able to help Simplina, later. That's what I'm going to do. Boy, how strong I'll be!

(He stands up and walks towards Dophilius' house).

And Dophilius can keep those sickly old cream-horns!

(Exit).

(Enter Joris).

JORIS. Overworked, that's what I am. Completely overworked. And as if I wasn't enough overworked already, I have to go and do more work. I've got to paint the bench. And paper the kitchen walls. As if an officer of the law had nothing else to do!

(He looks all around).

Can I see anything that isn't there? No. Nothing.

(He listens).

Can I hear anything? No, I can hear nothing either. Perhaps I'm better. Perhaps I'm completely cured.

(Alfonso's door opens and Dophilius enters, singing and dancing).

DOPHILIUS. My bag. Where is my bag, folderol, where's my bag of money?

(Joris, struck with amazement and consternation, falls back, his unbelieving eyes following Dophilius' movements as he finds the bag and dances back into Alfonso's house. He shakes his head, shuts his eyes, puts his hands in front of his eyes, and then removes them quickly and looks).

JORIS. I've got it again! I've seen something else that isn't there. I've seen Mr. Goldpurse dancing. What's more I've heard something that doesn't exist, too. I've heard Mr. Goldpurse singing. I'm ill again. I'd better go straight to bed.

(During the last sentence the girls enter with a basket of washing).

SANDRA. You're not going to bed, you're going to paint the bench.

JORIS. But I'm overworked.

S. & S. Overworked! Where from?

JORIS. From . . . from . . . I don't know. I just see all sorts of things that aren't there.

SIMPLINA. What sort of things?

JORIS. A mirror . . ., and the carpet.

S. & S. *(Letting the basket fall with the shock).* The . . . carpet?

JORIS. Yesterday evening. It went all by itself into the house.

SIMPLINA *(Giving Sandra a meaningful look).* What did you see then?

JORIS. I saw the carpet . . . it came from over there . . . it passed close by me . . ., so, in the door.

SANDRA. But that's impossible.

JORIS. That's what I told you! I'm overworked.

SIMPLINA. Yes, that must be it.

JORIS. I've got to get some sleep. Lots of sleep.

SANDRA. Yes, you'd better go quickly to bed.

JORIS. And I've got to eat, too. A lot.

SIMPLINA. Yes, naturally, you've got to eat.

JORIS. So, first of all I'm going to sleep, then later, when I'm awake, I'll have something to eat. I'm overworked!

(Exit).

SANDRA. I don't understand a thing of this.

SIMPLINA. He evidently saw the carpet, too. Everything's so different from usual.

(They pick the basket of washing up, and go to the washing line which is hung between the houses of Dophilius and Joris. Dophilius enters from Alfonso's house).

DOPHILIUS. Oh! What a lot of cream-horns I've eaten! Perhaps too many. I've got a pain in my tummy from them.

(He sees the girls).

Oh, Sandra! Have you got to hang the washing up? Wait, I'll help you.

SANDRA. Ooh! Please, Mr. Goldpurse.

DOPHILIUS *(Bends over the basket)* Ooooooh!

(Stands quickly up again).

SANDRA. What's the matter, Mr. Goldpurse?

DOPHILIUS. I've eaten too many cream-horns.

(Alfonso enters from Dophilius' house).

ALFONSO. Ah! Simplina. Can I help you?

SIMPLINA. Are you quite better then, Dophilius?

835

ALFONSO. Quite! I've eaten some jolly good sausage, and a couple of delicious slices of brown bread and butter.

DOPHILIUS (*Dreamily*). Sausage!

SANDRA. Rich people never eat that, do they Mr. Goldpurse?

DOPHILIUS. No. Never.

(*Dreamily*).

Sausage!

SANDRA. They only eat cream-horns, don't they Mr. Goldpurse?

DOPHILIUS. Yes . . . cream-horns.

(*Ugh*).

(*The telephone rings*).

ALFONSO. The telephone's ringing, Dophi . . . I mean Mr. Goldpurse!

DOPHILIUS. Yes, the telephone's ringing. What d'you say? The telephone? Oh, yes, the telephone. Of course I'd better go to it.

(*Runs inside*).

ALFONSO. See! That's something a shoemaker never gets bothered by.

SIMPLINA. No. He's only got to make shoes, eh, Dophilius?

SANDRA. There you are then! The washing line is full.

SIMPLINA. Where are we going to hang the shirts up?

(*Dophilius enters again*).

SANDRA. Oh, yes! The shirts?

DOPHILIUS. Isn't there any more room? Then we'll have to make a new line for them.

SANDRA. That's a very clever idea of yours, Mr. Goldpurse. I'll fetch some rope.

(*She goes off for the rope*).

DOPHILIUS (*Looks around searchingly*). The best place to hang it would be here.

(*Straight across the fore-stage*).

SANDRA (*Back with rope*). What did you say, Mr. Goldpurse?

DOPHILIUS. I said . . .

(*Telephone rings*).

ALFONSO. The telephone's ringing!

836

SIMPLINA. Let Dophilius hang the line up.

ALFONSO. What? Me?

SIMPLINA. Of course. You can do that far better than Mr. Goldpurse.

ALFONSO. Me? Oh, yes. Naturally.

SIMPLINA. Go on then. Fetch a hammer and a couple of nails.

ALFONSO. A hammer? Oh, yes. A hammer.

(Disappears into house).

(Enter Dophilius).

DOPHILIUS. That's that. And now . . .

SIMPLINA *(Cattily)*. Dophilius is going to hang the new line up.

DOPHILIUS. That I will! . . . I mean, of course. Naturally. Dophilius.

(Alfonso enters with a last. The telephone rings).

ALFONSO. The telephone's ringing!

DOPHILIUS. Doesn't that thing ever stop?

(Disappears, sighing).

SIMPLINA. But Dophilius! Whatever have you got there? That's a last!

ALFONSO. Huh? What's that? A last? Oh, yes, of course. A last. I mistook myself. How silly.

(He goes inside again while the girls look at one another in astonishment). (Dophilius re-enters).

DOPHILIUS. That's that again, Sandra. Now I want to talk to you. Look, you know that I have got a very large house . . .

SANDRA *(Full of expectancy)*. Yes, Mr. Goldpurse!

DOPHILIUS. Two people could live in it comfortably.

SANDRA. Yes, Mr. Goldpurse.

(She sits on bench).

DOPHILIUS. And I've got a lot of money . . .

(Telephone rings).

SANDRA. Yes, Mr. Goldpurse.

(Alfonso enters).

ALFONSO. Hallo there! The telephone's ringing!

DOPHILIUS. Again! I'm not going.

837

SANDRA. You're not going? But you've got to earn money, haven't you?

DOPHILIUS. No . . . I mean yes . . . of course I've got to earn money. Oh, I'll go.

SIMPLINA. That's it! That's the hammer, Dophilius. Now bang a nail in here.

ALFONSO. What d'you say? A nail, there?

SIMPLINA. Yes. Go on then, Dophilius.

ALFONSO. Yes, alright. A nail . . . in that wall . . . there?

SIMPLINA. Well, that's not so difficult, is it?

ALFONSO. Yes, I mean no, I mean . . .

(He takes hold of the hammer and begins to bang at the nail with the wooden handle).

SIMPLINA. But Dophilius! Whatever are you doing now? The other way round!

ALFONSO. The other way round? Oh, of course. How silly of me.

(He holds the hammer against the wall, and begins to bang at it with the nail).

SIMPLINA. Now what are you doing? Not like that. Look, so!

(She shows him how to do it).

ALFONSO. Oh, yes. Very silly of me.

(Dophilius enters).

DOPHILIUS. Hey ho. Sandra, I was just telling you . . .

(Telephone rings).

ALFONSO. Telephone!

DOPHILIUS. That . . . telephone! I'm not going, I mean I am going, because I've got to make some more money.

SIMPLINA. Hm. That Mr. Goldpurse is always so frightfully busy.

ALFONSO. Not half! Terribly busy. He hasn't even got time to talk.

SIMPLINA. Life's much more agreeable for you, Dophilius.

SANDRA. But Mr. Goldpurse makes a lot of money.

SIMPLINA. What good is it to him?

SANDRA. He can buy everything he wants with it.

ALFONSO. That's not true, because he's already got everything.

SIMPLINA. And he hasn't even got the time to go shopping.

838

SANDRA. I can do that for him.

ALFONSO. Perhaps he hasn't even got the time to talk to you.

SANDRA. That's true! But I wouldn't like that! I'm going to tell him straight away that he's got to stop earning money.

ALFONSO. That won't help. He can't stop it now.

(Dophilius enters again. Alf. fumbles about with his hammer and nail).

DOPHILIUS. Here I am again, Sandra.

SANDRA. Mr. Goldpurse! I want you to stop all this business with the telephone. I don't want you to . . .

(Telephone rings).

ALFONSO *(Beginning on his second nail)*. Telephone!

DOPHILIUS. I . . . Oh, dear, . . . I've got to go and earn some money. I'm going.

(Exits).

SANDRA. Oh! How frightful. I can't even speak to him. He won't even let me finish! And I just don't want money any more.

ALFONSO. He'll never be able to stop it now. Never again. Ooooohhh!!!

(Hits his thumb with the hammer).

SIMPLINA. What's the matter, Dophilius? What's happened?

ALFONSO. Ooooooohhh!!!

SIMPLINA. Have you hit your thumb? Then why are you so careless? Wait a minute. I'll bandage it up for you quickly.

(She takes a clean handkerchief from the line and wraps it round his thumb).

ALFONSO. Oooooohhhhh!!!

SIMPLINA. There, there. Quiet now.

SANDRA *(Springing up)*. Pouf! A shoemaker who hits his own thumb with a hammer! That's something I've never seen.

(She hammers the nail home herself, makes the line fast, and hangs the shirts up).

ALFONSO. OOOOOOOhhhh!!!

(Joris appears at the window).

JORIS. What's that for a noise? Can't a person get a minute's rest? I've got to sleep! I've got to eat!

SIMPLINA. Oh, yes. The apple pie! I'll get it ready.

(The bandage is finished, and she runs inside).

SANDRA. And the bubble-and-squeak!

(She runs inside too).

(Simplina pokes head around door).

SIMPLINA. Hold your thumb up, Dophilius, and be careful now.

(Exit).

(Dophilius enters with the telephone under his arm).

DOPHILIUS. There you are Sandra, now I'll . . . Hey! Where's she gone?

ALFONSO. Whatever are you doing with the telephone?

DOPHILIUS. I'm fed up with it. I don't want it any more.

ALFONSO. But you've still got to make money!

DOPHILIUS. I don't want to. I don't want any money . . . or telephone . . . or cream-horns. I just want to make shoes again, and eat sausage. I want to be Dophilius again.

ALFONSO. Dophilius? But surely I'm Dophilius.

DOPHILIUS. No, you're Mr. Goldpurse.

ALFONSO. Tell me Mr. Goldpurse, I believe that you're ill, That you've eaten to many cream-horns.

DOPHILIUS. I have too! And that's just why I want to swap back.

ALFONSO. Swap back? Swap what back?

DOPHILIUS. I want my shirt back!

(Grabs Alf. by his shirt).

ALFONSO. Look here, Mr. Goldpurse, keep your hands off my shirt, otherwise I'll give you a smack with my hammer.

DOPHILIUS. Your hammer? It's my hammer. Here, take your telephone back.

(He thrusts the telephone into Alfonso's arms).

ALFONSO. What do I want with that thing? It rings and it talks, and it's nothing but a nuisance. Everyone's got to look after his own business. You after your telephone and your money, and I after my shoes.

DOPHILIUS. But they're my shoes!

ALFONSO. Mr. Goldpurse, I haven't the faintest idea what you're talking about.

840

(Shrugs his shoulders).

Anyhow, I'm going in to make a shoe for Simplina.

(Walks to his house).

DOPHILIUS. But Mr. Goldpurse! Mr. Goldpurse! Oh, he doesn't even answer his own name. Shoemaker!

(Alfonso stops by Doph.'s door and turns around).

ALFONSO. That's better. Now you know at last how to address me.

(Exits).

DOPHILIUS. Oooohh! How terrible. Now Mr. Goldpurse doesn't want to change back! I'll have to keep on earning money, and I'll never . . .

(Telephone rings. Dophilius starts, puts the telephone down on the well, and takes a couple of paces backwards. The telephone rings again).

No. Wrong number. I can't hear you.

(Telephone rings harder).

I'm not in, I tell you.

(He walks threatingly towards the telephone, but it keeps on ringing).

No!

(The telephone screams at him. Doph. moves back again).

No, no, no! I don't want to!

(The telephone rings again. He drops onto his knees and crawls in an encircling movement towards the apparatus, and as he gets close to it, it rings again).

Quiet!

(The anger in Dophilius' voice begins to give place to fright, especially when the telephone gives immediately a shrill answer to each command he gives it. He begins to beg).

Quiet now, please. Please keep quiet. It's me, Dophilius! Mr. Goldpurse isn't here.

(The telephone rings as though asking a question).

No, he's not here anymore.

(The telephone complains).

And I'm fed up with it all. I don't want to earn money any more.

(The telephone answers softly, understanding).

841

I just want to talk to Sandra.

(The telephone answers softer still).

I want to tell her everything.

(The telephone gives a slight whisper, and thereafter remains quiet. Dophilius wipes the perspiration from his brow. Joris door flies open and Sandra rushes onto stage).

SANDRA. Mr. Goldpurse! Mr. Goldpurse!

DOPHILIUS. Sssshhh!

SANDRA. Oh, there you are. I just thought I heard your telephone.

DOPHILIUS. Ssshhh! It's just become quiet again.

SANDRA. Have you already earned some more money then?

DOPHILIUS. No. Ssshh! I've got to tell you something, Sandra.

(He takes her hand and pulls her out of earshot of the telephone).

Ssshh. Now that it's quiet . . . I haven't got a big house at all, Sandra, and I don't possess a penny. I'm not Mr. Goldpurse at all. D'you know who I am? I'm . . .

(The telephone breaks the conversation).

There it goes again. It never stops.

(Ring).

I'll take it away. I'll take it inside.

(He grabs the telephone, which is still ringing shrilly, and runs off).

(Sandra gazes after him, astonished. She runs to her door).

SANDRA. Simplina! Simplina!

(Simplina enters in response to Sandra's call, with a string of freshly cooked sausages in her hand).

SIMPLINA. What has happened?

SANDRA. Did you know that Mr. Goldpurse is not Mr. Goldpurse at all?

SIMPLINA. What are you saying? Who is he then?

SANDRA. I don't know. I only know that I like him, and that I wouldn't marry with anyone else, even if he turned out to be Dophilius himself!

SIMPLINA. Dophilius? Then who's Dophilius?

SANDRA. Perhaps he's Mr. Goldpurse! Perhaps they've just exchanged!

842

SIMPLINA. Ye-e-es. That's quite possible. D'you know what? We've got to think out some way of finding out who is who.

SANDRA. Where did those sausages come from?

SIMPLINA. They're the sausages to go with the bubble-and-squeak. But father Joris isn't getting any sausage before that bench is painted and the kitchen walls are papered.

SANDRA. I know what! Let's hang them up here, somewhere.

SIMPLINA. Hang them up? Why?

SANDRA. Well, because Dophilius always eats sausage, and Mr. Gold-purse never does. Thus, the one who filches the sausages must be Dophilius!

SIMPLINA. That's a good idea! Let's hang them over the well.

(They go to the well).

Now look! Father Joris has put the tin of glue on the bench. He'll mistake himself next, and paint the bench with glue.

SANDRA. And here's the paint, on the ground. We'll change the tins round. That's that, and now for the sausages. Give them here, and look out that no-one comes.

(Sandra hangs the string of sausages on the hook, while Simplina keeps watch).

SIMPLINA. You alright?

SANDRA. Yes. They're hanging already.

SIMPLINA. Now we've got to hide ourselves.

SANDRA. Yes, but where?

SIMPLINA. Let's both of us creep into one of father Joris' nightshirts, then no-one will be able to see us.

SANDRA. Yes, that's what we'll do.

(Each girl creeps into one of the constable's nightshirts, which hang with the sleeves outstretched, and are so long and large that they are quite hidden).

SIMPLINA *(Poking her head out of the neck-opening of her shirt).* Pssssst!

(Sandra's head appears likewise from her shirt).

What if Mr. Goldpurse should really turn out to be Dophilius?

SANDRA. Well, then Mr. Goldpurse is Dophilius, that's all!

SIMPLINA. But I shall still want to marry him.

SANDRA. I too.

843

SIMPLINA. That's good then.

(They duck into their respective shirts).

(Dophilius' door opens and Alfonso enters. During this entire scene the heads of Sandra and Simplina pop out whenever anything interesting or strange occurs or is said).

ALFONSO. Hey ho, that's that. It's finished. My first shoe for Simplina. I'll wait here for her.

(Is about to sit on the bench, but stops half-way, sniffing).

I can smell something . . . hmmmmm . . . Sausage! I could just do with a bite of sausage.

(Sees them hanging).

Who could they belong to? Shall I . . . no, I won't. They're not mine. But whose are they then? Perhaps some-one's left them there for me. One little piece . . . One mouthful. I'll go and get a knife. No-one will notice.

(Goes inside).

SIMPLINA *(To Sandra).* Dophilius is Dophilius.

(Dophilius enters).

DOPHILIUS. Thank goodness I'm not troubled by that telephone any more. I wonder where Sandra is? I haven't yet told her. Hey . . . what's that? I believe I can smell sausage. Just what I could do with. Look, there it is, hanging over the well . . . Should I take a little mouthful, d'you think? Just for the taste. I'll get a knife, no-one will notice.

(Hurries inside).

SANDRA. Mr. Goldpurse is also Dophilius!

SIMPLINA. They're both Dophilius!

(Alf. and Doph. come out together, and walk to the well).

ALFONSO. Hallo, Mr. Goldpurse.

DOPHILIUS. Hallo, Mr. Goldpurse. What are you doing with that knife?

ALFONSO. And what are you doing with that knife?

DOPHILIUS. Who, me? Oh, nothing.

ALFONSO. Me too.

DOPHILIUS. Well . . . Goodbye, Mr. Goldpurse.

ALFONSO. Yes . . . Goodbye, Mr. Goldpurse.

(Both go back indoors).

844

SIMPLINA. They're both Mr. Goldpurse!

(Joris enters).

JORIS. Aaaaaaaah! That was a jolly good sleep. Wonderful. But . . . what do I see now? Looks like sausages. Sausages? On the well? I've got it again. I'm sick again. Seeing things that aren't there again. But I'm not going to be taken in. How can that be? Sausages on a well? No, Joris is too clever for that. That ragman can tell me another tale! I just can't see it. I don't want to see it. I'm just going to start painting, then I'll forget all about it. Let me see, how was it again? Oh yes, the paint was on the floor, and the glue was on the bench. This, then, is the paint, and I'm going to paint the bench with it.

(He starts painting madly, but gets slower and slower, until he finally stands up again sniffing).

I still smell sausage! Perhaps they're real sausages. Might even be the sausages to go with my bubble-and-squeak.

(He gives a last flourish with his brush).

There! In any case the bench is painted.

(He wipes his face off, worn out).

Hey! What's that now? I don't see any paint on the bench! D'you think that ragman was right after all? I just don't see any sign of paint on the bench, and I know that it's there, because I put it on myself! But I can see sausages that are not there at all. I can smell them too. And I'm going to get them. Careful, now. They mustn't hear me . . . I'll go and get a knife.

(Exits into house).

SIMPLINA. Look! What's he done now?

SANDRA. He's painted the bench with glue!

SIMPLINA. What shall we do?

SANDRA. We've got to get out of here.

SIMPLINA. But they mustn't see us. Look out!

(All three doors open at the same time, and Joris, Dophilius and Alfonso each creep out with a knife in the hand. They reach the well before they see one another).

JORIS. Hallo! What's all this?

DOPHILIUS. Oh, er, nothing.

(He backs to A's door, and disappears inside).

ALFONSO. Nothing at all. Just taking a little constitutional.

(Backs to D's door and disappears inside).

845

JORIS. Are my eyes deceiving me? Did I really see Mr. Goldpurse creeping! And Dophilius too! That's impossible. Just like those sausages. But I can still see them.

(He climbs very carefully, on to the bench, but can't reach the sausages).

I'll lower the hook. Hey! Let go of my foot! There's nobody here, yet someone's holding my foot fast. I'm stuck . . . on the bench . . . with my shoe! Wait a minute, if my shoe's stuck fast, then I'll take it off! Haha. Joris is not to be caught napping so easily as all that! Oh! help! Let me loose! Soppy! Now my sock's stuck. What am I going to do now? I know. If my sock's stuck, I'll just pull my foot out of it.

(He does so, careful this time to step with his naked feet onto the floor).

That was awful, it's made me really warm. Phew!

(He sighs and sits).

Ah, now I see it all. I've made a bad mistake. I've naturally painted the bench with glue instead of paint. But that's terrible. Now nobody can sit here anymore.

(He goes to stand up, but sits fast).

Now what on earth have I done? I've gone and sat on it myself! This time I really can't get out of it. Oh, what am I going to do now?

(The girls, who have followed Joris' antics all the time, can't contain themselves any longer, and burst out into laughter inside their nightshirts).

What's that now? It seems as if those nightshirts are laughing. I've never met anything like this in my life before. It looks as though I'm going to start hearing everything that isn't there too. Was that ragman really right after all? I don't want to see any more!

(He holds his hands in front of his eyes).

And I don't want to hear any more!

(Shuts the lobes of his ears with his thumbs).

And I don't want to smell any more either.

(Closes his nostrils with his two little fingers).

SIMPLINA. What shall we do?

SANDRA. He mustn't know that we've hidden ourselves here. Let's move up that way, then we'll creep out.

(The two nightshirts begin to glide along the line to the other side. Joris takes his hands away from his eyes).

JORIS. What now! The nightshirts are gone! They're not there at all! How can that happen? They were there just now. Hanging right there! Oh, I mustn't look any more.

(Hands before eyes again).

SIMPLINA. We'd better go back.

(She slides back, but Sandra stays).

(Joris takes his hands away from his eyes again).

JORIS. Oh, oh! Now there's only one. And the other one's over there! I don't understand anything any more. The ragman was right. I see, and smell, and hear things that just aren't there at all. It all started off with the mirror, and the longer it goes on the worse it becomes. I can't even rest any more. And here I sit! I can't get away, I . . .

(The nightshirts begin to glide towards one another; Joris slaps his hands in front of his eyes).

There they go again! I saw it clearly! Now there's only one. Now there are two again! Soon there'll be three, or even four! The ragman was right. Alright then, I'll let them get married. Where are they? Sandra! Simplina! Where are they now? Just at the moment when they've got to get married, they're not to be found!

(Alf. and Doph. come out).

JORIS. At last some-one's coming. Dophilius! Mr. Goldpurse! Come here a moment. Can you hear anything?

(They shake their heads).

Can you see anything?

(They shake their heads again).

Hold your eyes shut. Like this. Now. I'll count up to ten, and then we'll take our hands away from our eyes quickly. Ready?

(The girls take the opportunity to slip out of the nightshirts and disappear quickly indoors).

One, two, three, four, five, six, seven, eight, nine, ten! Now do you see anything?

DOPHILIUS. No, nothing.

ALFONSO. I can see two nightshirts.

JORIS. Aha!

ALFONSO. They're quite ordinary nightshirts, we **helped Sandra and** Simplina to hang them up ourselves.

(Goes over to them and shakes them).

847

There's nothing extraordinary about them, come and look yourself.

JORIS. I . . . I can't!

DOPHILIUS. Why not?

JORIS. I'm stuck fast!

ALFONSO. Stuck fast?

JORIS. Yes. I painted the bench with glue, and now I'm stuck to it!

ALFONSO. What did you say? With glue? Hahahahahahaha!

DOPHILIUS. And you stuck yourself . . . Hahahahahahahahahah!

ALFONSO. The constable's stuck! Hahahahahaha!

(Alf. and Doph. double up with laughter until they can't stand anymore and they fall on to the bench, one each side of Joris. He looks shocked at first, but begins to laugh too).

JORIS. What a joke! Hahahahahahaha!

ALFONSO. I'm sorry! I can't help laughing. It's giving me tummy ache. Haha!

DOPHILIUS. Hahahahaha! The constable! Haha!

(To Joris).

But why are you laughing?

JORIS. Because . . . Hahaha . . . you're stuck . . . too! Hahahaha!

ALFONSO. What! He's right! We are stuck!

DOPHILIUS. All three of us.

ALFONSO. What do we do now?

DOPHILIUS. Perhaps the girls will pull us off.

JORIS. The girls are nowhere to be seen.

DOPHILIUS. Where are they then?

JORIS. I don't know. I wish they'd get married to you two!

(To Doph.).

You can have Simplina,

(To Alf.).

And you can marry Sandra.

DOPHILIUS. But I don't want to marry Simplina!

ALFONSO. And I don't want to marry Sandra!

848

JORIS. I don't care two hoots about that! That's the way you've always wanted it, and that's the way it's going to be.

(Doph. makes a gesture of despair behind Joris' back, and signals that they ought to change again. Alf. gets it alright, and they begin to loosen their jackets).

Once and for all I want to make an end of all this nagging. A merry wedding feast is all that I need to make me forget my troubles. I know that they don't want it,

(Doph. and Alf. change jackets).

but if I say that Simplina is to marry Mr. Goldpurse, then that's what will happen.

(He looks at Doph. who has struggled into his own jacket).

Hey, Mr. Goldpurse, what are you doing with Dophilius' jacket on?

(Doph. gives Alf. his glasses back).

But it isn't Mr. Goldpurse at all! He wears glasses!

(Looks at Goldpurse).

He's wearing glasses!

(Alf. and Doph. change hats).

There's something wrong here!

(Alf. gives Doph. the false moustache).

Everything's going topsy-turvy for me again!

(He looks again at Dophilius).

Glasses gone! Hat and moustache belonging to Dophilius! It is Dophilius!

(He looks at Mr. Goldpurse).

And that is Mr. Goldpurse! Here we are, stuck to this seat, and still Dophilius—who was on this side of me—is now on that side of me! And Mr. Goldpurse who was on that side of me is now . . . HELP! SANDRA! SIMPLINA! HELP!

(They both enter hurriedly).

Oh! Thank goodness, there you are at last. Hurry up, you two have got to get married.

SANDRA. Get married? To whom?

JORIS. Get on with it. Simplina marries Mr. Goldpurse, and Sandra marries Dophilius.

SIMPLINA. But we don't want that at all!

(Seeing the bandaged thumb).

Oh, but you're not Mr. Goldpurse at all! You're Dophilius. I can see it by your thumb.

SANDRA. Then if he's Dophilius, you must be Mr. Goldpurse!

DOPHILIUS. I wanted to tell you all the time, Sandra, but I was kept so busy. I'm not Mr. Goldpurse at all. I'm Dophilius! We swapped around just for one day.

SANDRA *(flying to him).* So you're not rich? And you don't have to spend all your time earning money? Oh, Dophilius, I'm so very happy!

DOPHILIUS. But I am rich, and I will have to go on earning money, because Mr. Goldpurse doesn't want to swap back again.

SIMPLINA. What's that I hear? Is that true, Alfonso? Oh, how happy that makes me!

(Hoddel enters with his handcart).

HODDEL. Rags and Bones! Old rags! Look there, all together. You look very cosy sitting there.

JORIS. Cosy? Cosy! We're not sitting here cosily at all. We just can't get away!

HODDEL. What's that, constable? You can't get away?

JORIS. We're stuck. Fast!

ALFONSO. On the bench . . .

DOPHILIUS. With glue.

SIMPLINA. Can't you help them, Hoddel de Boddel?

SANDRA. Yes, please do, otherwise we won't ever be able to get married!

HODDEL. Tcha! Are you stuck very fast?

(He pulls, but it doesn't help).

I've got an idea! A plank,

(Gets a plank from his handcart).

And a block,

(Gets a large block of wood from the cart too).

We lay them down so,

(He sets them down like a see-saw, with the lower end of the plank under the bench).

Now get ready! Go to one side you two.

850

(The girls move away).

One . . . two . . . three!

(Hoddel jumps high into the air and lands on the other end of the plank. The three men catapult into the air).

Hooray!

SANDRA. Oh, Dophilius! How high you can jump!

SIMPLINA. Poor Alfonso. Have you hurt yourself?

JORIS. It worked! We're free again! I'm finished with everything. I don't want to have anything to do with anything any more. You'll have to sort it out yourselves who Mr. Goldpurse is, and who's Dophilius.

SANDRA. Dophilius is Dophilius. Everything's in order, except, who's going to look after the money, now?

DOPHILIUS. I know! Wait a minute, I've got it!

(Runs into Alf.'s house and brings out the bag).

Here, constable, this is for you!

JORIS. Hallo? What's this? What's in it?

DOPHILIUS. Money.

JORIS. Money?

(Looks inside).

Money! All that money! What am I going to do with it?

DOPHILIUS. You'll have to guard it. You're the constable!

JORIS. Guard it? Yes . . . yes, of course! Naturally! Who is there better for guarding things than the constable? That's important. I'll start work on it right away.

(Hoddel has put the wood back on to his handcart. He rings his bell, and begins to ride away).

HODDEL. Any old rags! Any old bones!

ALFONSO. Hey! Ragman! Wait a moment! Here, this is for you.

(Throws his fine hat on to Hoddel's cart).

And this too.

(Adds his jacket).

And very many thanks for all your help.

(Alf. exits with Simplina).

DOPHILIUS. Wait a minute! I've got something for you too.

(Runs inside and comes back with the telephone).

That's that! At least I can talk to Sandra without interruption.

(Hoddel sets off slowly again).

HODDEL. Any old junk! Any old lumber!

JORIS. And I . . .

(Yawns). . .

I just think I'll have a little . . . Oh! No. The bag. I've got to guard the bag of money! I've got work to do.

HODDEL. Old clothes! Any old bric-a-brac!

JORIS. But then . . . That means that I'll never be able to go to sleep again! Hey! Ho, there! You! Ragman! Stop a minute! I've got something for you too!

(Runs after Hoddel and throws the bag onto his handcart).

HODDEL. Any old rags! Any old rubbish!

(As Hoddel moves into the distance the constable yawns happily, and stretches himself, as the CURTAIN FALLS).

THE END

852

RAGS TO RICHES

A Musical Melodrama

by

AURAND HARRIS

Suggested by two stories
Ragged Dick and *Mark The Match Boy*
By Horatio Alger

Lyrics by *Aurand Harris and Eva Franklin*
Music, research and continuity by *Eva Franklin*
Additional music arrangements and manuscript
By *Glenn Mack*

RAGS TO RICHES

By Aurand Harris

RAGS TO RICHES

CAST

PoLICEMAN

RAGGED DICK, a shoeshine boy

MICKEY MAGUIRE, a news boy

MARK MENTON, a match boy

MR. GREYSON, a rich banker

MRS. FLANAGAN, an apple seller

MOTHER WATSON, an evil old crone

ROSWELL, an English butler

IDA GREYSON, a charming young girl

Singers, dancers, lamp lighter, firemen, rich
man, rich lady, children.

SCENES

The action takes place in the City of New York
in the late Eighteen Hundreds — on a street,
in a Fifth Avenue mansion, and in a tenement
room.

There are two acts.

MUSIC NOTE

Complete piano score for the music required
by this play is available, at extra cost, from
The Anchorage Press, Cloverlot, Anchorage,
Kentucky, 40223.

The music cue numbers used in the play-
book refer to this authorized score.

855

To

the members of

THE HARWICH JUNIOR THEATRE

The premiere production of *Rags to Riches* was given 2 August, 1966, by the Harwich Junior Theatre, in West Harwich, Massachusetts.

Two weeks following the Harwich run, on 18 August, 1966, a second engagement of *Rags to Riches* opened at the North Shore Music Theatre in Beverly, Massachusetts, where it was announced as their Prize-Winning Play for 1966.

RAGS TO RICHES

ACT ONE

(MUSIC, Cue 1, "Sidewalks of New York". SCENE, a painted
street scene of New York City in the late Eighteen hundreds. Unseen,
Dick, a young boy of the street, is asleep in a barrel which is spot lighted
D. R. Policeman enters R., glances at barrel as he passes, stops, does
a double take, steps back to barrel and raps on it with his stick).

POLICEMAN. Wake up there, youngster. Wake up!

(Dick's head appears above the barrel).

You can't sleep in an alley all day.

DICK (Yawning). Huh?

POLICEMAN. Wake up!

DICK. I'm awake.

(Stretches, eyes closed, then disappears into barrel).

POLICEMAN. You'd better be.

(Sees Dick disappearing into barrel).

And you'd better be on your way!

DICK (Rising). Who . . . who are you?

POLICEMAN. A policeman!

DICK (Opens his eyes and is looking straight at the law). Oh! Yes,
sir. Yes, sir! I'm getting right up.

(Steps out of barrel).

What time is it?

POLICEMAN. Seven o'clock.

DICK. Seven o'clock! I've missed my early shines.

(With funny business, he quickly fixes his ragged clothes).

Excuse me, while I fix my attire. My butler forgot to brush me
vest. You could do with a shine yourself, sir. No charge for
an officer of the law.

(Gives Policeman's shoes a quick wipe with a cloth).

POLICEMAN. Thank you.

(Aside).

I believe there must be some good in him . . . under those rags.

(To Dick).

857

Have you got money to buy your breakfast?

DICK. No, sir. But I'll soon earn some.

    (Aside).

If you've got some get-and-go, you can always get your breakfast.

    (Lights come up on full stage. MUSIC, Cue 2, "Sidewalks of New York." People on the street walk across. Dick exits L, soliciting shoeshines. Policeman removes barrel at R and exits. On Mickey's cue, people stop, holding walking postures as if a picture).

MICKEY *(Ragged newsboy, tough and a bully).*

        Paper . . . morning paper . . .
        Boss Tweed speaks.
        Latest news! Read the news!
        Building Brooklyn Bridge.
        Horace Greeley states his views.
        Paper . . . Paper . . .

    (MUSIC, Cue 3, resumes and people start walking. They stop again on Mark's cue, in suspended action, making a picture).

MARK *(Ragged, match boy, small and frail).*

        Matches . . . matches . . .
        Light your fires.
        Try . . . try a box?
        Light your lamps.
        Buy . . . buy a box?
        Matches . . . matches . . .

    (No one buys. MUSIC, Cue 4, resumes and people continue walking. Again on Dick's cue, they stop and hold their positions).

DICK.   Shine your boots, sir.
        Nobody better, nobody faster.
        Once shined the boots of Mr. Astor.
        No waiting in line.
        Start the day off . . . with a shine!

    (Mr. Greyson, a kindly rich banker, puts his foot on Dick's shine box. MUSIC, Cue 5, builds to a climax and people exit, as Dick finishes the shine).

GREYSON. How much for the shine?

DICK. Ten cents.

GREYSON. Isn't that a little steep?

DICK. Well, you know 'tain't all clear profit. There's the blacking and brushes.

GREYSON *(Laughs).* And you have a large rent to pay.

    (Takes out money).

858

I see I have nothing less than a two dollar bill. Have you any change?

DICK. Not a cent. But I'll get it changed for you.

(Calls).

Hey, Mickey. Mickey Maguire.

(Mickey enters L).

GREYSON. All right. And I will pay you five cents for your trouble.

(Starts off R).

Meanwhile I will try to hail a carriage.

(Exits R).

DICK. Can you change a two dollar bill?

MICKEY. Two dollars? Where'd you steal it?

(Takes bill).

DICK. Stealing ain't my style.

MICKEY. It's a counterfeit one.

DICK. I didn't know it.

MICKEY. You'd better beat it, or I'll tell a policeman.

DICK. Give it back to me.

MICKEY. So you can go and cheat somebody else?

(Plainly puts bill in left pocket).

DICK. Give it back. I say, give it back!

MICKEY. Big thieves have big mouths!

(Pushes him).

DICK. I'm not a thief. You are! Give it back!

(They start a fist fight, ad libbing. Policeman enters and separates them).

POLICEMAN. All right! Break it up. Break it up!

(Holds each by collar on either side of him).

What's the row?

DICK. I asked him to change a two dollar bill and he kept it.

MICKEY. It was a counterfeit one.

POLICEMAN. Let me see the bill.

MICKEY. The bill?

(Touches his left pocket, then smiles and takes out a bill from his right pocket and gives it to Policeman).

Here.

POLICEMAN. It *is* a counterfeit one.

GREYSON *(Enters quickly from R)*. Have you got the . . . What is all this?

POLICEMAN. Did you give the lad a two dollar bill?

GREYSON. Did he try to run off with it?

DICK. No, sir. I gave it to him.

MICKEY. It was a counterfeit one!

POLICEMAN. Do you remember what bank yours was on?

GREYSON. The Merchant's Bank of Boston.

MICKEY. Then he kept it . . . and gave me the bad one!

GREYSON. Or . . . you could have pocketed my bill and substituted the counterfeit one.

DICK. That's right! He put it in his *other* pocket.

MICKEY. That's a lie!

DICK. Search him!

MICKEY. I haven't got it!

POLICEMAN. Let's have a look in your other pocket.

MICKEY. I ain't got it! He's lying!

POLICEMAN. Put your hands up!

(Pulls bill from Mickey's pocket).

"Merchant's Bank of Boston."

GREYSON. That is mine.

MICKEY *(Threatens Dick)*. I'll get you!

POLICEMAN. Move along.

MICKEY. I'll get even with you . . . wait and see! I'll pay you off!

(Shows his fists then runs off L. Policeman follows him).

DICK *(Calls after him, fists raised)*. It'll be a pleasure to meet you any time, Mickey Maguire!

(Aside).

Stealing ain't my style.

GREYSON *(Interested in the plucky lad)*. What is your name, lad?

DICK. The name is Dick, sir. Well known as Ragged Dick, Esquire!

GREYSON. Well, Dick, you get the bill changed and bring the money to my office, Greyson, number 12 Fulton Street.

DICK. Yes, sir, Mr. Greyson.

GREYSON. Keep the dime . . . and fifty cents for your trouble.

(Starts R).

DICK. Yes, sir. Yes, sir! A fifty cent tip!

GREYSON (Aside). We will soon see if Ragged Dick is as honest as he says.

(Exits R).

DICK. Ten cents and fifty cents . . . I've made *sixty* cents before breakfast! I can go to Barnum's tonight and hear 'em sing "O, Susannah," and see the bearded lady, and the eight foot giant, the two foot dwarf, and other curiosities too numerous to mention!

(SINGS, Cue 6. Tune, "O, Susannah").

I'VE GOT MONEY IN MY POCKET

WHERE THE HOLES ONCE USED TO BE.

NOW I'M RICH AS MR. VANDERBILT,

I'LL LIVE IN LUX-U-REE!

MONEY! MONEY!

IT'S MUSIC TO MY EAR.

OH, A JINGLE IN MY POCKET

IS THE SOUND I LOVE TO HEAR!

I CAN EAT BEEFSTEW FOR BREAKFAST NOW,

FOR LUNCH AND DINNER, TOO.

THEN DROP IN TO DELMONICO'S

AND ORDER *OYSTER STEW!*

MONEY! MONEY!

IT'S MUSIC TO MY EAR.

OH, A JINGLE IN MY POCKET

IS THE SOUND I LOVE TO HEAR!

NO MORE SHIV'RIN' IN THE ICY RAIN

WHEN IT BEGINS TO POUR.

I CAN NOW BUNK IN A FIVE CENT BED

AND SNORE AND SNORE AND SNORE!

MONEY! MONEY!

IT'S MUSIC TO MY EAR

OH, A JINGLE IN MY POCKET

IS THE SOUND I LOVE TO HEAR!

(Mrs. Flanagan enters, a good natured Irish woman who sells apples. She speaks with a musical Irish brogue. Busy with her basket, she does not see Dick. He slips near her and speaks in a deep voice as he teases her).

Ah, Mrs. Flanagan! Have you paid your taxes for the year?

MRS. F. *(Surprised, but not turning around)*. Me taxes?

DICK. I've been sent by the mayor to collect your taxes. But I'll take it out in apples just to oblige. That big red one will be about the right size.

MRS. F. *(Turns and laughs)*. I'm thinking it will be the size of a good breakfast for you, Mr. Ragged Dick.

DICK. Oh, I can pay . . . but the smallest change I got is two dollars.

MRS. F. Two dollars!

DICK. Sixty cents of it is mine!

(SINGS, Cue 7).

I'VE GOT MONEY IN MY POCKET

WHERE THE HOLES ONCE USED TO BE . . .

MRS. F. *(Offers him apple. MUSIC continues as they speak)*. One . . . you say?

DICK. And one . . . to keep the Doc away.

(Take two apples and puts them into his pockets).

MRS. F. *(SINGS. Makes change with money)*.

MONEY! MONEY!

IT'S MUSIC TO MY EAR.

OH, A JINGLE IN MY POCKET

IS THE SOUND I LOVE TO HEAR!

DICK.   I CAN GO TO SEE A BOW'RY SHOW.

MRS. F.   JUST LIKE A REG'LAR SWELL.

DICK.   HISS THE VILLAIN . . .

MRS. F.   . . . CHEER THE HERO.

DICK.   WHEN HE SAVES POOR LITTLE NELL!

DICK AND MRS. F.

MONEY! MONEY!

IT'S MUSIC TO MY EAR.

862

OH, A JINGLE IN MY POCKET
IS A SOUND I LOVE TO HEAR!

(They dance. Dick exits L. Mrs. F. Looks after him fondly.)

MRS. F. Git along with ye, Dick. You're a scamp . . . and a good for-something boy.

(Villain MUSIC, Cue 8. Tune, "Kings of Bal Masque." Mother Watson enters R. She is a ragged, evil old crone).

MRS. F. *(Aside).* It's Mother Watson . . . up before noon. And already she's been tipping the bottle.

MOTHER W. I'm looking for him, the lazy little imp. Have you seen him?

MRS. F. Are ye meaning Mark the match boy?

MOTHER W. He's a lazy scalawag. Don't earn his keep. And I'm out of my medicine.

(Takes bottle from pocket).

MRS. F. Medicine, is it?

MOTHER W. It's for my cough.

MRS. F. *(Aside).* A cough never gave nobody that red nose.

MOTHER W. He'd better sell his matches . . . and have the money, or I'll . . .

MRS. F. What will ye be doing?

MOTHER W. I'll give him a taste of this!

(Pulls out a small whip).

MRS. F. May the Saints protect the little lamb!

(Looks off L).

And may they indeed . . .

(Points).

for here he comes now.

(Mark enters L).

MOTHER W. So here you are!

(Mark is surprised and frightened at seeing Mother W.).

Where have you been hiding?

MARK. I've been trying to sell my matches.

MOTHER W. How many have you sold?

MARK. Only three boxes.

MOTHER W. Three! You don't earn your salt. Give me the money.

(Fearfully he crosses and gives her a few pennies. She counts them).

There's a penny short! Where is it?

MARK. I . . . I was so hungry I bought a bit of bread.

MOTHER W. You little thief!

MARK. I didn't have any breakfast . . . or supper last night.

MOTHER W. You didn't earn it! But I have something for your appetite!

(Holds up whip).

I'll give you a taste of this!

(Starts after him).

I'll beat the laziness out of you!

MRS. F. *(Mark runs behind her).* Shame on you, Mother Watson! Leave the poor laddie alone.

MOTHER W. Buying himself a grand breakfast!

MRS. F. Sure and he was hungry.

MOTHER W. Beggar! Little beggar. That's what you are. Ah, and *that's* what you'll be! If you can't sell matches, you can beg for money.

MARK. Beg?

MOTHER W. Hold out your hand and beg from the kind hearted people.

MARK. I don't want to beg.

MOTHER W. Don't want to beg! Do you mind that now, Mrs. Flanagan? He's too proud to beg.

MARK. My mother told me never to beg if I could help it.

MOTHER W. Well, you can't help it! Do you see this?

(Raises whip).

Do as I say or you'll feel it! Now . . . get on the corner! And don't come back until you have twenty-five cents!

(Villain MUSIC, Cue 9, as she exits L).

MARK. I don't want to be a beggar.

MRS. F. Tell me, Mark darling, why are you living with her anyway? She ain't your mother, is she?

MARK. No. My mother was a good woman . . . and kind . . . and beautiful.

(Takes from pocket a small picture).

MRS. F. Is that a picture of her?

MARK. Yes. It is all I have left.

MRS. F. *(Aside).* Sure and he looks like her, he does. Anyone would know he was her son.

(To Mark).

When did she die?

MARK. A year ago. Mother Watson told me to come and live with her and she'd take care of me.

MRS. F. Ha! She's making you take care of her.

MARK *(Walks away).* Now I have to beg or she'll beat me.

MRS. F. Poor little laddie.

(SINGS, Cue 10. Tune, "After the Ball". As she sings, Rich Woman and Little Girl cross. Mark tries to beg from them, but cannot).

> POOR LITTLE ORPHAN LADDIE
>
> POOR LITTLE HUNGRY BOY.
>
> POOR LITTLE HOMELESS PADDY
>
> NO MOTHER'S PRIDE AND JOY.
>
> NO FATHER'S LOVE TO GUIDE HIM,
>
> NO ONE TO TAKE HIS PART,
>
> FACING THE WORLD WHILE HE'S HIDING
>
> HIS POOR, ACHING HEART.

(Song ends. Rich Man enters. Mark with great effort approaches him. MUSIC stops).

MARK. Sir, will you give me a few pennies, please?

MR. RICH. Pennies?

MARK. If you please, sir.

MR. RICH. I suppose your wife and your children are starving, eh?

MARK. No. I don't have a wife or any children.

MR. RICH *(Aside).* He hasn't learned his trade, but he will.

(To Mark).

Soon you'll have a sick mother starving at home.

MARK. My mother is dead.

MR. RICH. You'll get no money from me. Be off! Go home . . . go home.

(Exits).

MARK. Home . . . I haven't any home . . .

(Takes out picture).

or mother . . . nobody . . .

MRS. F. *(SINGS, Cue 11)*.

> POOR LITTLE ORPHAN LADDIE,
>
> POOR LITTLE HUNGRY BOY.
>
> POOR LITTLE HOMELESS PADDY.
>
> NO MOTHER'S PRIDE AND JOY.

(Mark exits slowly. Mrs. F. follows him, ending her solo on a dramatic note).

> NO FATHER'S LOVE TO GUIDE HIM.
>
> NO ONE TO TAKE HIS PART.
>
> FACING THE WORLD WHILE HE'S HIDING
>
> HIS POOR, ACHING HEART!

(She exits).

(MUSIC, Cue 12, changes to Tune, "Here We Go Round the Mulberry Bush." Roswell, a very English butler, enters L, turns the street flat at L around, showing a painted elegant room. On the second chorus he stands and sings).

ROSWELL *(SINGS)*.

> THIS IS WHERE THE RICH RICH LIVE
>
> THE RICH RICH LIVE
>
> THE RICH RICH LIVE
>
> THIS IS WHERE THE RICH RICH LIVE
>
> IN ALL THEIR BEE-U-TEE-FUL HOUSES.

(Music repeats as he brings on two small gold chairs, then a small Victorian table which he places between the chairs. He brings in a tea service which is handed to him. He stands behind the table, pours tea, and SINGS).

> THIS IS THE HOUR THE RICH HAVE TEA
>
> THE RICH HAVE TEA
>
> THE RICH HAVE TEA

THIS IS THE HOUR THE RICH HAVE TEA

AT FOUR IN THE AFTERNOON.

(Chimes strike four, as Ida, a pretty young girl, beautifully dressed, enters L and sits properly).

Your tea, Miss Ida.

IDA. Thank you, Roswell.

(SINGS, holding cup elegantly).

THIS IS THE WAY I DRINK MY TEA

PROPERLY

PROPERLY

WISHING, WISHING THAT I COULD BE . . .

(Speaks rapidly with conviction).

Shopping today, playing croquet . . . anything!

(SINGS).

BUT HAVING TEA ALL ALONE WITH ME.

(Dick enters R, pantomimes knocking at "door").

ROSWELL. Some one is knocking at the door.

(Crosses to "door").

DICK. Good afternoon, general.

(Walks past butler into "hall").

I've come to see the president . . . on business.

ROSWELL. Mr. Greyson is not at home, sir.

IDA *(Calls from L)*. Who is it, Roswell?

ROSWELL. Your name, sir?

DICK. Ragged Dick.

ROSWELL. It is Mr. Ragged Dick.

DICK. Esquire.

ROSWELL. Esquire.

DICK. Who is she?

ROSWELL. Mr. Greyson's daughter, Miss Ida.

IDA. Show him in, Roswell. And pour another cup of tea.

ROSWELL. Miss Ida requests the pleasure of your company at tea.

DICK. Tea?

ROSWELL (*Pantomimes lifting cup, with curved little finger, and sipping*). Follow me.

(*Dick follows butler, imitating his walk*).

Miss Ida. Mr. Ragged Dick, Esquire.

IDA (*Sweetly*). How do you do.

(*Curtseys*).

DICK (*Suddenly shy and ill at ease*). How d'do.

(*Uncertain, he bobs an awkward curtsey. Butler pours tea*).

IDA (*Aside*). His clothes are ragged, but his face is honest.

(*To Dick*).

How nice of you to come. I was wishing that Papa would come ... or someone ... and here you are! Like a genie out of a bottle.

DICK. Oh, no ma'am. I'm not a drinking man!

IDA (*Aside*). One good virtue in his favor.

(*To Dick*).

Won't you sit down?

(*She sits gracefully. Dick starts to, stops, brushes the seat of his pants, then sits awkwardly*).

ROSWELL (*At side of Dick, offers him tea*). Your tea, sir.

(*Dick starts to take saucer*).

May I take your hat?

DICK. My hat?

(*Dick takes off cap, is confused, starts to put saucer on his head, then gives saucer instead of cap to butler, finally keeps saucer and gives cap to butler. Dick looks at Ida hopefully. She stirs her tea gracefully. Dick stirs his tea vigorously*).

IDA. Drink it while it's hot.

(*Dick nods, wipes spoon on his pants, then puts it behind his ear, pours tea into saucer, blows on it loudly, then drinks it with a slurp, and wipes his chin on his cuff. Ida speaks aside*).

I have never had tea with a shoe shine boy before.

DICK (*Aside*). I've never had *tea* before.

ROSWELL (*Offers two plates to Dick*). Cakes or crumpets, sir?

DICK. I ain't got nothing against neither one.

(*He takes a handful from each, starts eating, putting some in his pockets. He smiles*).

Bully!

IDA. I'm glad you like them.

DICK. Yes, ma'am. Better than the peanuts at the Old Bowery!

IDA *(Rises excitedly)*. Have you been to the Old Bowery? Have you seen . . . a *play!*

DICK. Every night in the gallery when I got the price. This week I saw the "Demon of the Danube."

IDA. Oh, how exciting. Tell me all about it!

DICK *(As he tells the story, he starts acting it out with musical accompaniment. Cue 13. Or, if preferred, the scene may be danced with two dancers as a comic ballet)*. Well . . . you see . . . there's this Demon, and he's in love with a girl.

IDA. How romantic!

DICK *(MUSIC. If danced, Demon enters dragging girl, then a comic dance of protesting and conquering follows. If Dick tells the story alone, music accompanies his actions)*. He drags her by the hair up a cliff to his castle.

IDA *(Aside)*. What a strange way to show his affection!

DICK. She is in love with another chap, and when he hears that she is carried off, he swears an oath to rescue her.

(If danced, Dick becomes the hero and joins the ballet).

He gets to the castle . . . using an underground passage . . . he and the Demon fight it out! First one and then at the other . . . cut and slash and fight!

IDA. Who wins?

DICK. The young Baron draws a dagger and plunges it into the Demon's heart and says, "Die, thou false and prejured villain, die. The dogs of prey shall feast upon thy carcass." Then the Demon gives an awful howl and dies. The Baron seizes his body and throws it over the precipice. The girl kneels before her hero, who speaks these words: "So ends your life of captivity and begins a life of married bliss twix thee and me."

IDA. How wonderful!

(She applauds. If danced, Demon and Girl exit. Dick bows. MUSIC stops. Ida speaks aside).

He is quite a hero himself.

(To Dick).

Does your father let you go every night?

DICK. He ain't around to ask.

IDA. Where is he?

DICK. I don't know. They said he went off to sea. I expect he got wrecked or drowned.

IDA. And your mother?

DICK. She died when I was three. Some folks took care of me. But when I was seven I had to scratch for myself.

IDA (Aside). Out in the world at seven!

(To Dick).

What did you do?

DICK. Sold newspapers . . . sold matches . . . one night I was so cold I burnt all my matches to keep me from freezing.

IDA. Where do you live?

DICK. Last night I slept . . . at the Box Hotel.

IDA. The Box Hotel?

DICK. Yes, ma'am. I slept in a box behind a hotel.

IDA (Aside). Many of our greatest men were poor, but they climbed the ladder to success.

(To Dick).

I think you will, too . . . if you try.

DICK. Oh, I ain't lazy! But who'd hire Ragged Dick? I ain't had no learning.

IDA. I know a teacher . . . who will give you a free lesson every day . . . if you apply yourself.

DICK. You do? Who?

IDA (Goes to table, picks up book, and becomes a proper teacher). Our first lesson today will be in Reading.

(Reads).

"One befriends himself when he befriends another."

DICK. You?

IDA. I don't know too much, but I'll gladly teach you all I know.

DICK. Teach me? Ragged Dick?

IDA. I think you'll become a great man if you only get a little education.

DICK. Do you?

IDA. I am sure of it.

Dick. Then I've decided what I'm going to do. Starting today . . . with your help . . . I'm going to grow up respectable!

(They SING. MUSIC, Cue 14. Tune, "Glow Worm").

Ida *(Chorus).*

>EACH DAY WE'LL STUDY READING.

Dick. See-the-cat.

Ida. EACH DAY WE'LL STUDY GRAMMAR.

Dick. What is *that?*

Ida. YOU WILL LEARN TO WRITE WITH EASE . . .

>TO DOT YOUR I'S AND CROSS YOUR T'S, AND

>EACH DAY WE'LL STUDY HISTORY.

Dick *(Poses like Napoleon).* Na-po-le-on!

Ida. EACH DAY WE'LL STUDY NUMBERS.

Dick. Three-two-one.

Ida. STUDY HARD SO YOU WILL PASS!

Dick. I'LL BE THE HEAD OF MY CLASS!

Ida *(Verse).*

>WE MUST WORK ON ETIQUETTE.

Dick. I'LL DO MY BEST, YOU BET . . .

>IF YOU WILL SHOW ME.

Ida. DON'T FORGET TO BE POLITE . . .

>WITH TABLE MANNERS RIGHT . . .

Dick. MY FRIENDS WON'T KNOW ME.

Ida. YOU MUST GET SOME CULTURE, TOO,

>AND LEARN TO PARLEZ-VOUS.

Dick *(With a flat accent, rhyming with "concentrate").*

>LIKE S'IL VOOZ PLATE, MA'AM?

Ida. WHEN YOU'RE IN SOCIETY,

>ACT WITH PROPRIETY.

Dick. I'LL CONCENTRATE, MA'AM.

Ida. AT A PARTY

>OR A BALL,

>YOU MUST KNOW ALL THE DANCES.

SHOULD YOU MEET

A CHARMING GIRL

IT ALWAYS HELPS YOUR CHANCES.

(She dances to a phrase of music. Reprise chorus).

WHO WAS PRESIDENT NUMBER ONE?

DICK.   I know the answer. WASH-ING-TON!

IDA.   WHO DISCOVERED THIS LAND FOR US?

DICK.   That's easy, too. It was CO-LUM-BUS!

IDA.   IF I TAKE AWAY A FRACTION . . .?

DICK.   Take away? That means SUBTRACTION!

IDA.   KEEP IT UP AND YOU WILL PASS.

DICK.   I'LL BE HEAD OF MY CLASS!

(Mr. Greyson enters R and knocks at "door").

ROSWELL *(Enters L, crosses to "door").* Someone is knocking at the door.

(Admits Greyson, takes his hat).

IDA.   It's Papa!

(Runs to him). Papa!

(He embraces her).

Papa, you have a caller.

ROSWELL *(Announcing).* Mr. Ragged Dick, Esquire.

(Greyson and Ida enter "room").

DICK.   Good afternoon, sir.

GREYSON *(Surprised).* Good afternoon.

DICK.   I fetched your change. You wasn't at your office, so I walked up here.

GREYSON.   That was a long and an honest walk. Where did you learn the virtue of honesty?

DICK.   Nowhere.

(Aside).

I just know it ain't right to cheat or steal.

GREYSON *(Aside).* Then he is ahead of some of our business men.
(To Dick).

Do you read the Bible?

872

DICK. No, but I hear it's a good book.

IDA. He will be reading soon, Papa. I am going to teach him! He's promised to come every day and to study hard.

GREYSON. You want to learn to read . . . to improve yourself?

DICK. Yes, sir.

(Aside).

I'm awful ignorant.

GREYSON. You have an open and honest face. I believe you are a good boy. I hope you will prosper and rise in the world.

IDA. Does that mean . . . I can be his teacher? Oh, Papa, thank you.

GREYSON. I think I can teach you something, too. I have a Sunday School Class. Would you like to come?

DICK. Me go to church? Yes, sir!

(His spirits fall when he looks down at his ragged clothes).

No sir, I can't come.

GREYSON. Why not?

DICK. I'd shame you. This is my best . . . my only clothes I got.

IDA. Papa! I have an idea.

(She whispers excitedly in Mr. Greyson's ear).

GREYSON *(Aside).* Fortunately she has solved the problem.

(To Dick).

Young man, give your coat to Roswell.

DICK. Give away my coat!

GREYSON. And give him your shirt, and your shoes, and your trousers.

DICK. Me trousers!

GREYSON. And go into the next room and wash.
(Aside).

Clean clothes and dirty skin do not go together.

(To Dick).

Roswell will give you some of my son's clothing.

DICK. You're *giving* me . . . new clothes?

ROSWELL. This way, please.

DICK. Yes, sir! Yes, sir general!

(Takes off coat and holds it out).

So ends the life of Ragged Dick . . .

(Gives coat to Roswell who holds it far away from his nose).

. . . and begins the new life of Richard Hunter.

(Hero MUSIC, Cue 15. Tune, "American Patrol." Roswell exits L, Dick marches out after him. Music stops).

IDA. Oh, Papa, it's a Sunday School lesson coming true!

(Embraces him. Then Greyson strikes a solemn pose).

Papa . . . you look worried.

GREYSON. I am, my dear. I have a grave problem on my mind.

IDA. What is it?

GREYSON *(Aside).* Shall I tell her? Yes, I shall confide in her innocent ear.

(He motions to chair. Ida sits. He stands by her, hand on her shoulder in an old tin-type pose. MUSIC, Cue 16. Tune, "Flower Song.")

Many years ago your Grandfather disowned his second daughter, your mother's sister.

IDA. How cruel.

GREYSON. She was in love with a fine young man, John Talbot, who was a clerk. But your Grandfather wanted a marriage of wealth for his daughter.

(Moves).

The two lovers eloped and were secretly wed. Two years later, Irene appeared at your Grandfather's doorstep with a child in her arms. But he hardened his heart and cast her out of his life forever. A month ago he learned that both Irene and John Talbot were dead, but the child—a boy—is still living. Your Grandfather has repented. I am to find the boy, so he will come into his rightful fortune.

(He stands again, hand on her shoulder in the original picture pose. MUSIC stops).

IDA. Where will you look?

GREYSON *(Moves out of pose).* His mother died in New York a year ago. Probably the boy lives in a poor section and is making his own way in the world.

IDA. Like Ragged Dick . . . like Richard.

GREYSON. Yes.

(Aside).

874

She has given me an idea! Ragged Dick . . . Richard . . . can help me find the boy.

ROSWELL *(Enters L)*. He is dressed, sir. Mr. Richard Hunter.

(Hero MUSIC, Cue 17. Dick marches in at L, dressed in his new clothes. MUSIC stops).

IDA. Oh, how splendid you look!

DICK. I ain't sure it's me.

GREYSON *(Crosses to him)*. You have taken the first step in becoming respectable.

DICK. Yes, sir . . . and it sure feels good.

GREYSON. Mr. Hunter?

DICK *(Looks around)*. Mr. Hunter? Huh? *Me!* Yes, sir.

GREYSON. Would you like to become a detective?

DICK. A detective?

GREYSON. I must find a lost boy, probably living in New York and making his way even as you.

DICK. What's his name?

GREYSON. We think . . . John Talbott, after his father. Do you know such a boy?

DICK. No. 'Course some of the boys change their names. There's Fat Jack, Pickle Nose, Tickle-me-foot. Sir, if John Talbot's on the streets, I'll find him!

GREYSON. I have a man investigating, but I believe *you* will be more successful. Here is five dollars.

DICK. Oh, no sir.

(Looks at new clothes).

You've done enough.

GREYSON. It is your first payment as a detective.

(Dick takes money).

IDA *(On other side of Dick)*. You can rent a room . . . have a home!

DICK *(To Ida)*. Yes, sir . . . ma'am!

(To Greyson).

Thank you, ma'am . . . sir!

GREYSON *(Shakes Dick's hand, pumping bigger at the end of the speech)*. Remember in this country you can rise as high as you choose. Your future depends upon what you do for yourself!

(He exits L).

875

DICK. I'll start right now . . . detecting! **Goodby.**

(Nods to Ida, quickly exits at "door").

IDA *(Aside).* How true is what I read: **One befriends himself, when** he befriends another!

(She exits L).

DICK *(Comes from "door" to C. During the song, Roswell unob-trusively clears the stage and changes the scenery back to Street Scene. MUSIC, Cue 18. Tune, "O Susannah").*

(Verse).

> O-OH WHAT A CHANGE HAS COME TO ME!
>
> A CHANGE HAS COME TO ME.
>
> FROM NOW ON I AM RESPECTABLE
>
> AND THAT'S THE WAY TO BE.

(Reprise of verse).

> IN A COUNTRY THAT'S AS FREE AS OURS
>
> A POOR BOY HAS A CHANCE.
>
> IF HE WORKS HARD TO IMPROVE HIMSELF,
>
> HE ALWAYS CAN ADVANCE!

(Chorus).

> TAKE ABE LINCOLN . . .
>
> AS POOR AS HE COULD BE,
>
> BUT HE RAISED HIMSELF TO PRESIDENT
>
> AND MADE GREAT HISTORY!
>
> O-OH WHAT A CHANGE HAS COME TO ME!
>
> A CHANGE HAS COME TO ME.
>
> FROM NOW ON I AM RESPECTABLE
>
> AND THAT'S THE WAY TO BE.

(Chorus).

> WORK AND STUDY
>
> WILL TAKE YOU OFF THE SHELF!
>
> SO I'VE HITCHED MY WAGON TO A STAR
>
> AND I'LL DRIVE IT THERE MYSELF!
>
> O-OH WHAT A CHANGE HAS COME TO ME!

876

A CHANGE HAS COME TO ME.

FROM NOW ON I AM RESPECTABLE

AND THAT'S THE WAY TO BE!

(Dick exits L).

(MUSIC, Cue 19, changes to Tune, "Twinkle Twinkle Little Star." Lights dim slightly to early evening. Lamp Lighter enters R and lights street lamp C back. Policeman enters L).

POLICEMAN. It's going to be cold moon tonight.

(Lamp Lighter nods and exits L. Policeman looks after him. MUSIC stops).

A fine night to be home by the blazing fire . . .

(Mark enters R. He sees Policeman, looks for a place to hide, and quickly stands in a painted shop doorway. Policeman turns).

Who's there? Who's there? Speak out.

MARK *(Steps out, frightened).* It's me.

POLICEMAN. What are you doing?

MARK. Just standing . . . in a doorway . . . for shelter.

POLICEMAN. Get along with you. Get along home.

MARK. Yes, sir.

(Starts L).

POLICEMAN *(Exiting R).* Home's the place to be . . .

MARK *(Stops, wistfully).* Home . . .

POLICEMAN. Home with your family . . .

(Exits R).

MARK. Home . . . home . . . I haven't got a home.

(Takes out picture. MUSIC, Cue 20. Tune, "After the Ball." SINGS).

OH MOTHER, DEAREST MOTHER,

IF YOU COULD ONLY HEAR.

I AM SO COLD AND HUNGRY.

HOW I WISH YOU WERE NEAR.

BRAVELY, I TRY MY BEST NOW,

FACING LIFE ON MY OWN . . .

BUT WITHOUT YOU HERE BESIDE ME,

I'M SO ALONE.

(Puts picture in pocket, takes out money and counts slowly: Mickey enters R and sees money).

Five, six, seven . . . seven cents. She'll beat me. I can't go back.

MICKEY *(Aside).* Money! And mine for the taking!

(Slips up behind Mark who counts his pennies again. Mickey grabs Mark's arm, pulls it behind him, and twists it).

MARK. Let go of me!

MICKEY. Let go of the money.

MARK. It's mine!

MICKEY *(Twists Mark's arm harder).* Let go. Let go!

MARK *(Cries in pain, lets money fall).* Oh! Oh!

MICKEY *(Quickly picks up coins).* Finders Keepers.

MARK. Give it back to me.

MICKEY. Losers weepers.

MARK. It's mine. Give it back!

MICKEY *(Faces him, larger and tougher).* You going to make me?

MARK. Yes. Yes!

(Starts to hit and kick him).

MICKEY *(Laughs).* I'll give you something. Take this!

(Gives Mark a hard blow, which knocks him backwards and he falls).

DICK *(Enters L. Aside).* What's this? Mickey Maguire and his dirty fighting.

(Poses, fists ready).

MICKEY *(Sneers at the fallen Mark).* Next time pick on someone your size.

(Backs away toward Dick).

DICK. Why don't you?

(Mickey turns and is facing Dick).

MARK. He stole my money.

DICK. Give it back to him.

MICKEY. So *you* can steal it?

DICK. Stealing ain't *my* line.

MICKEY. You want to fight?

(Poses, fists ready).

878

DICK. Not 'specially. It's bad for the complexion, around your eyes and nose. They're apt to turn red, black, and blue.

MICKEY. What's wrong? You scared?

DICK. No! Give him his money back, or . . .

(With commanding authority).

I'll land you in the middle of next week at very short notice!

MICKEY. Like this!

(Gives Dick an upper cut, which Dick dodges).

DICK. Like that!

(Dick hits Mickey who stumbles).

MICKEY *(Down, cowardly).* Look out who you're hitting!

DICK. Give back his money!

MICKEY. Catch me first . . . if you can!

(Chase MUSIC, Cue 21. Tune "Midnight Fire Alarm." Mickey starts to run. Dick starts after him. It is an exciting chase with dodging and running around the street flats, or into the auditorium and back onto the stage, ending with a scuffle on the floor, Dick on top of Mickey, the winner. MUSIC stops).

DICK. Give it up. Give it up!

(Twists Mickey's arm).

MICKEY *(In pain, releases money).* Take the money.

(Dick quickly picks up money, as Mickey gets to his feet and cowardly backs away. Shouts, at a safe distance).

I'll get you. I'll get you yet!

DICK *(Makes a lunge at Mickey who exits quickly. Dick goes to Mark).* Here . . . here's your money. Seven cents.

(Gives Mark coins).

MARK. Thank you. It's all I have.

(He shivers).

DICK. You're cold. Come on. I'll help you home.

MARK. I don't have a home.

DICK. Ain't you got no folks? No place?

MARK *(Shakes his head).* She'll beat me.

DICK. Come on. I've got me a rented room . . . with a real bed! It ain't much, but it's better than a barrel. What do you say?

MARK. You want to take me . . . with you?

879

DICK *(Comically imitating Roswell)*. Mr. Richard Hunter requests the pleasure of your company to share his indoor lodgings. Come on!

(Mark stands by him).

Together we'll face the world . . . like in the play at the Old Bowery . . . we'll be the *two* Musketeers!

(Hero MUSIC, Cue 22, as they march. Suddenly Mark points off L. Music stops).

MARK. Look!

DICK. What's wrong?

MARK. It's Mother Watson. Looking for me with her whip!

(Villain MUSIC, Cue 23, as Mother Watson enters L, with whip in hand).

DICK *(Aside)*. My, she's a beauty, ain't she?

MARK. What will I do?

DICK. Leave her to me.

MOTHER W. *(Sees Mark. Aside)*. Ah, there he is.

(To Mark).

I see you! You little thief!

DICK *(Aside)*. My, ain't she polite?

MOTHER W. Try to run away, will you? Not from me you won't!

(Advances, swaying with drink).

DICK. Careful, madam. Your feet ain't steady.

MOTHER W. I'm not talking to you. I'm talking to him. Wait till I get my hands on you!

(Raises whip).

DICK. Stop! You ain't never going to get your hands on him again.

MOTHER W. What?

DICK. He ain't never going back to you and your whip. He's coming with me. *I* have adopted him!

MOTHER W. *(To Mark)*. Come here, I tell you. Come here this minute!

DICK. Stay where you are.

MOTHER W. *(Shouting)*. Do you hear me. Do you hear me!

DICK *(Shouting)*. I'm thinking they hear you in New Jersey!

880

MOTHER W. Don't give me your lip, you ruffian, or I'll give *you* the whip!

DICK. I ain't afraid of you! A whip is for cowards. You think because you're big you can hit little people. Lots of folks think 'cause they got a whip they can boss the world. That ain't right. And someone's got to stop them.

MOTHER W. I'll show you whose boss!

(Gives Dick a good lashing).

DICK. You ain't never going to use that whip again!

(Angrily he grabs whip. He and she struggle).

MOTHER W. Let go of me, you vagabond! Let go!

DICK. I'll show *you* how a whip feels!

MOTHER W. Give me back my strap! You scoundrel!

(He pushes her away. She turns and reels, bending over).

Help!

DICK *(Gives her exposed backside a whack).* There!

(Mother Watson jumps and screams. Dick laughs).

POLICEMAN *(Enters, shouting over their yelling).* What's going on? What's going on here?

MOTHER W. *(Aside, frightened).* The police!

DICK *(Aside, surprised).* The cops!

POLICEMAN. What's all the fighting? What's all the yelling about?

MARK *(Pause. He steps forward and speaks in a small voice).* Me.

MOTHER W. *(To Policeman, pretending to cry comically).* Oh, officer. I'm an old lady and . . . and my bad little boy, he's breaking my heart. Run away he did. But I'm willing to forgive him. All I want is my dear boy to come home.

POLICEMAN. Do you belong to her?

MARK. No, sir.

MOTHER W. Yes! Yes, he does!

(Remembers and becomes maudlin).

He's my own sweet little boy.

POLICEMAN. Is he your son?

MOTHER W. No.

MARK. I'm not any of her relation. She said she'd keep me after my mother died. But she starves me and beats me when I don't bring back money for her whiskey.

881

POLICEMAN. Whiskey? I thought I recognized you. You were drunk last week on Mott Street.

(Mother Watson looks at audience frightened, and gives an aside burp. To Mark).

Go along boy. You are free to go where ever you want.

MOTHER W. *(Aside).* Curses. Curses on them all.

POLICEMAN. Get along. Off the street with you and your bottle.

MOTHER W. Beware! Beware! I am not through with you scalawags!

(Aside).

I'll have my revenge. I'll have my revenge on both of them.

(Villain MUSIC, Cue 24, as she exits L. Policeman follows her off L).

DICK. Come on, Mark! We're on our way!

(Mark bravely stands by him).

We're going to climb . . . up . . . up the ladder of success! *(Aside).*

No matter how patched your pants are, you can still rise . . . to fame and fortune!

(MUSIC, Cue 25. Tune, "The Man Who Broke the Bank at Monte Carlo").

DICK *(Sings).*

> IF YOU WANT TO BE A MILLIONAIRE,
>
> IT'S AN EASY GAME TODAY.
>
> YOU CAN ALWAYS FIND A WAY
>
> IN THE GOOD OLD U. S. A.
>
> YOU CAN BE JUST WHAT YOU WANT TO BE
>
> IN THIS LAND OF OPPORTUNITY
>
> FOR WITH PLUCK AND LUCK
>
> YOU'LL GO FROM RAGS TO RICHES.

(As various people are mentioned, they enter, or some of them, and SING, making it a large chorus for a stirring finale. Dancing will also add to the scene).

> BE A SOLDIER . . . BE A SAILOR
>
> BE A RAILROAD ENGINEER
>
> BE A WEALTHY FINANCIER.

YOU MAY PICK YOUR OWN CAREER!

YOU CAN BE JUST WHAT YOU WANT TO BE

IN THIS LAND OF OPPORTUNITY

FOR WITH PLUCK AND LUCK

YOU'LL GO FROM RAGS TO RICHES.

DRIVE A CARRIAGE . . . DRIVE A TROLLEY

RIDE A HORSE OR RIDE A HACK,

BE A MAILMAN WITH A SACK,

BE A SLEUTH WHO'S ON THE TRACK.

YOU MAY LEAD A LAMB TO SLAUGHTER . . .

YOU MAY WED THE BOSS'S DAUGHTER,

AS WITH PLUCK AND LUCK

YOU GO FROM RAGS TO RICHES.

BE A DOCTOR . . . BE A LAWYER

BE A JOCKETY WITH A WHIP

OR A WAITER WITH A TIP

BE A CAPTAIN OF A SHIP.

WHILE OLD GLORY'S BANNER IS UNFURLED . . .

(A large American flag descends at back, to which they point).

ANY DAY MAY BRING A BRIGHT NEW WORLD . . .

(Straight line for curtain).

FOR WITH PLUCK AND LUCK

YOU'LL GO FROM RAGS TO RICHES.

(Musical tag).

YES, FOR WITH PLUCK AND LUCK

YOU'LL GO FROM RAGS TO RICHES!

CURTAIN

ACT TWO

(MUSIC, Cue 26. Tune, "The First Noel." SCENE: street. A group of Christmas carolers SING. A few shoppers with Christmas boxes and the Policeman cross during the scene. While Mickey calls the news, the Carolers hum).

MICKEY.   Paper . . . evening paper.
         Christmas Party at Mrs. Astor's.
         Mark Twain's latest story.
         New York sings Christmas glory.
         Paper . . . Paper . . .

(Carolers sing. Mrs. Flanagan enters selling apples. Mickey exits. Dick enters).

DICK.   Shine your boots, sir.
         Like I shine the rest, sir.
         Christmas time is the time, sir,
         To look your best.
         Shine . . . shoe shine . . .

(Dick exits. Carolers sing, then hum when Mark calls, entering L).

MARK.   Matches . . . matches . . .

(Puts hand to head and sways).

         Light . . . light your Christmas candles . . .

(Weakly. He is ill).

         Matches . . . mat--ches . . .

(He falls limply to ground).

LADY CAROLER.   The little boy . . . he fell!

(She and Mrs. Flanagan rush to Mark. Others group around, talking excitedly).

MRS F. *(Kneels by him, holding his head).* It's Mark the match boy. Poor little laddie.

POLICEMAN *(Enters).* What's the trouble? What's happened?

MRS. F. Poor laddie. Fainted, he did.

POLICEMAN. Let's have a look. He has a fever.

MRS. F. Starved he is and shivering with the cold.

POLICEMAN. Does he have a home?

MRS. F. Sure and Ragged Dick has took him in. They have a room on the top floor in the same house with me.

POLICEMAN *(Mark moves and tries to talk).* Are you all right?

MARK. Mother . . . mother . . .?

MRS. F. Out of his head. Delirious, he is!

POLICEMAN. I'll take him home.

(Picks Mark up in his arms).

DICK *(Rushes in).* What's happened! What's happened to Mark?

POLICEMAN. Toppled over . . . fainted.

DICK *(Shakes Mark).* Mark! Mark! What's wrong with him?

POLICEMAN. He's needing some rest. I'm taking him home. Lead the way.

DICK. Yes, sir. Yes, sir!

(Dick goes to R. Policeman carrying Mark, follows. Dick turns the street flat at R around, and the scene is a poor tenement room. He places a small cot with ragged covers at R. Carolers and Mrs. Flanagan SING, Cue 27, during scene change and exit, backing slowly away at L. Policeman puts Mark on bed and helps Dick take off Mark's coat and cap which he hangs on wall. MUSIC stops).

DICK. Is he going to be all right?

POLICEMAN. He's got a fever . . . and he's delirious.

DICK. But he'll be all right, won't he?

POLICEMAN. He needs to stay in bed and be cared for.

DICK. I'll look after him.

POLICEMAN. He needs a doctor.

DICK. I'll get a doctor.

POLICEMAN. If you need me, I'll be on duty.

DICK. Thank you, sir.

(Fixes cover on Mark).

I'll stay by him. I'll get him well.

POLICEMAN *(Aside).* A friend in need is a friend indeed.

(Exits R).

DICK *(Carolers SING softly off L, "Silent Night", Cue 28. Dick speaks tenderly to Mark).*

Mark . . . Mark . . . are you asleep, Mark? I . . . I'll get a doctor, Mark, and he'll give you medicine . . . and get you well . . .

(Singing stops. Dick walks away, counting money from his pocket).

885

Fifteen . . . twenty . . . thirty . . . forty . . . forty-five . . .
fifty . . . sixty . . . sixty-five cents. It ain't enough for a doctor . . . and medicine . . .

(Dick looks back at Mark).

But I'll make more money. I'll shine every boot in New York
City. You bet I will! Only . . . only you need a doctor now . . .
for the fever.

MARK *(Sits up, delirious).* Mother . . . mother . . .

DICK. What did you say, Mark? I'm listening.

MARK. Mother . . . mother . . .

DICK. No . . . no, your mother isn't here . . . just me.

(Mark leans back on pillows).

But don't you be afraid. I'm not going to leave you. I'll stay
right by you.

(Walks away worried).

and I'll help you . . . someway . . . somehow . . .

*(Off L, Carolers SING, Cue 29. Dick looks off L and listens, then
he smiles with an idea).*

I know a way, Mark. We'll get some help!

(He kneels and speaks earnestly).

God . . . I hope you're listening, God. I know I never talked
to you until I went to Mr. Greyson's church. But I . . . I never
thought you'd listen to Ragged Dick. If . . . if you are listening
and if . . . if you know even when a sparrow falls, then you
know that Mark fell in the street, and he's got a fever and he's
not talking straight. He hasn't anybody . . . nobody to help
him . . . but me. So what I'm asking is for your help. Please
. . . please help Mark get well.

(SINGING stops. There is a knock off R).

Someone is at the door.

(He rises as Ida enters R).

IDA. Hello.

DICK. Miss Ida!

IDA. I hope you don't mind my coming . . . uninvited. But it was
after four o'clock and you've never been late for your lesson
before and when you didn't come, I thought something had
happened. Has it?

DICK. It's Mark.

IDA *(Goes to bed).* Mark?

886

Dick. He's got a fever. He doesn't know me.

Ida. Delirious.

(Aside).

How fortunate I came!

(To Dick).

He must have a doctor right away. Go tell Papa and he will send Doctor Morrison.

Dick. A doctor! And I'll earn the money to pay your Papa back!

Ida. Run!

Dick. Yes. Mark's going to get well.

(Looks up).

Thank you.

(Carolers begin to SING off L, Cue 30. Mark sits up smiling).

Ida. He's trying to say something.

Mark. Singing . . . singing . . .

Ida. Yes. The Christmas Carolers.

Mark. Singing . . . like angels . . .

(Mark smiles and holds hand toward her).

angels . . . angels . . .

Dick. He thinks you are an angel.

Ida *(Aside).* Me?

Dick. And maybe . . . you are.

(Looks up again, gratefully).

I'll run!

(Dick exits quickly at R. Mark sleeps peacefully. Ida stands by bed, then slowly backs off at R, as Carolers end their song):

(Lights dim down on the "room" area at R, and come up at L. MUSIC, Cue 31, changes to the lively "Deck the Hall." Mother Watson enters L in a gay mood, wearing a bit of red and green for Christmas).

Mother W. *(SINGS comically with great joy).*

DECK THE HALL WITH BOUGHS OF HOLLY,

FA, LA, LA, LA, LA, LA, LA, LA, LA.

'TIS THE SEASON TO BE JOLLY

FA, LA, LA, LA, LA, LA, LA, LA, LA.

(Looks about, seeing no one, takes out bottle and SINGS wildly).

DON WE NOW OUR GAY APPAREL,

FA, LA, LA, LA, LA, LA, LA, LA, LA.

(Takes cork from bottle and smells bottle happily).

TROLL THE ANCIENT YULETIDE CAROL,

FA, LA, LA, LA, LA, LA, LA, LA, LA.

(Looks at bottle suspiciously, turns bottle upside down. Her joy changes to doubt. She shakes bottle, slowing down the song to rhythm of her shaking. Then stops. Bottle is empty. MUSIC stops).

DECK THE HALL WITH BOUGHS AND HOLLY,

FA, LA, LA, LA, LA, LA, LA, . . .

(Aside).

I hate Christmas!

MICKEY *(Enters L)*. Merry Christmas!

MOTHER W. Bah! Bah! Bah!

MICKEY. Have you heard? They're looking for a lost boy. They say there's a fortune waiting for some lost boy.

MOTHER W. Lost boy?

MICKEY. Limpy Jim told me and Pickle Nose told him and Little Runt told him that Ragged Dick told him.

MOTHER W. *(Aside)*. Ragged Dick! I have a score to settle with him!

MICKEY. They think the boy is on the streets.

MOTHER W. What's his name?

MICKEY. John Talbot.

MOTHER W. John Talbot? John Talbot!

(Aside).

Luck is with me!

(Laughs triumphantly).

MICKEY. Do you know him?

MOTHER W. *(Aside)*. Ha, I am the only person who knows who John Talbot is.

(To Mickey).

There is money waiting for him, you say?

MICKEY. A fortune!

MOTHER W. *(Aside).* They will never find him unless I tell who he is.

MICKEY. What are you mumbling?

MOTHER W. Hold your tongue! I'm thinking!

(Gives him a slap in the stomach. Aside).

John Talbot is . . . Mark the match boy. But he doesn't know it. His mother changed her last name. She told me that before she died.

MICKEY. Are you still thinking?

MOTHER W. Shut your lip, you vagabond!

(Gives him another slap. Aside).

Some *other* boy could get the fortune. I could prove *another* boy is John Talbot and cheat him out of the money. I must find me some stupid boy.

MICKEY. Can I help you?

MOTHER W. *(Aside).* Ah, ha! He can and he will!

(To Mickey).

You . . . you are going to help get the fortune.

MICKEY. Me?

MOTHER W. *(Suddenly bursts into loud SINGING).*

DECK THE HALL WITH BOUGHS OF HOLLY,

FA, LA, LA, LA, LA, . . .

MICKEY *(Aside).* I think she's been tipping the bottle.

MOTHER W. You . . .

(Dramatically).

You are John Talbot.

MICKEY. Me?

MOTHER W. *(Suddenly bursts into SONG again).*

TIS THE SEASON TO BE JOLLY,

FA, LA, LA, LA, LA, . . .

MICKEY *(Aside).* I know she's been tipping the bottle.

MOTHER W. *(Lost in reverlery).* Rich! Rich! We're going to be rich!

MICKEY. We are?

MOTHER W. *(Already acting elegantly rich).* Diamonds and jewels, capes and furs, and a feather fan.

MICKEY. And shoes without no holes?

MOTHER W. Horses and carriages . . . a house on Fifth Avenue and servants whenever I call.

(Claps her hands twice. Maid and Butler . . . dancers of "Demon of the Danube" and "Cakewalk" . . . enter and place two golden chairs U. L., exit).

Every day high society. And every night a show at the Old Bowery. We'll sit on the front row.

(She and Mickey sit on chairs).

MICKEY. And eat peanuts and watch them do . . . the Cakewalk!

(MUSIC, Cue 32. Tune, "At a Georgia Camp Meeting." Maid and Butler become performers and dance a lively cake walk. Mother Watson and Mickey react as if at the theatre and applaud when the dance is finished. MUSIC starts again. Dancers dance off, taking chairs with them. Mother Watson and Mickey try to dance a comic cake walk, but she soon collapses in Mickey's arms. Music stops).

MICKEY *(Back to reality).* First . . . we got to get the money.

MOTHER W. I'll get the fortune!

(Aside).

I must have the picture of Mark's mother which he carries in his pocket. The picture will be the proof that *my* story is true, and the boy who has it . . .

(Points to Mickey).

is John Talbot.

(To Mickey).

I have business to do. Be off! Steal a necktie. Look like an honest boy. Meet me here in two hours.

MICKEY. In two hours.

(He goes L. She goes R. Aside).

How fine it feels to have a fortune.

MOTHER W. *(Aside).* How sweet is revenge!

(Villain MUSIC, Cue 33, as he exits L and she exits R. MUSIC stops).

(MUSIC, Cue 34. Tune, "Emmet's Lullaby", played brightly. Lights come up on the "room" area at R. Mark is still in bed. Mrs.

Flanagan enters R, looks fondly at Mark. She tip-toes down and speaks an aside).

MRS. F.   Sleeping peaceful as a puppy he is. The fever is gone, praise be to the good doctor, and Ida, and Ragged Dick. All little Mark is needing now is a heap of caring for.

(Goes to bed. SINGS cheerfully, Cue 35. Tune, Emmet's Lullaby."

> GO TO SLEEP MY LADDIE,
>
> DEAR LADDIE, SWEET LADDIE.
>
> GO TO SLEEP MY LADDIE,
>
> HUSH-A-BYE, MY DEAR.

(Aside).

Some one is on the stairs. Is it you Dick?

MOTHER W.   *(Off).* No. It's Mother Watson.

MRS. F.   *(Aside).* Mother Watson! What could she be wanting?

MOTHER W.   *(Enters R, puffing).* Two flights of stairs make me short of breath.

(Too sweetly).

I heard that Mark is sick. I've come to cheer him up with a kiss.

(Faces audience and puckers lips).

MRS. F.   He's asleep.

MOTHER W.   Oh.

(Comically over-acting).

It's a lonely life I'm living since he left. I miss his footsteps coming home in the evening . . . his sweet voice calling in the morning . . . and his coat . . .

(Goes to coat hanging on wall).

His coat hanging by the door.

MRS. F.   *(Aside).* Faith, I'm believing she's had a change of heart, that she's sorry for the wickedness she's done.

MOTHER W.   *(Feeling the coat, comically searching for the picture).* His little ragged coat . . . too thin to keep him warm.

MRS. F.   Mother Watson, would ye be liking a cup of tea?

MOTHER W.   Oh, it would warm a body up.

MRS. F.   I'll step into my room and fix it. I have to be careful about the blaze in the stove. We almost had a fire in the house last week. If he gets restless, just sing a bit.

(Mrs. Flanagan sings softly the Irish song. Mother Watson nods, sings with her . . . nasal and comic. Mrs. Flanagan exits R. Mother W. ends the song with her true feeling of revenge).

MOTHER W. *(Aside)*. The picture is still in his pocket. All I have to do is take it.

(She tip-toes toward coat. Mark moves in bed. She stops. She begins singing the Lullaby urgently and comically. Stops when she is satisfied Mark is asleep).

Drat the little brat!

(As she puts her hand into pocket, Mark turns and mumbles loudly. She stops as if caught, starts singing Lullaby loud and fast; sees that he is asleep, stops singing. Cautiously takes picture from pocket and holds it up).

The picture is mine! You and Ragged Dick thought you could out-smart me, but Mother Watson has out-witted the two of you!

(Aside).

The fortune is mine!

(Laughs and exits R).

MARK *(Sits up, frightened)*. Mother Watson. I heard her voice. I heard her laugh. She's here!

MRS. F. *(Enters R, quickly)*. What is it, Mark?

MARK. Mother Watson!

MRS. F. Sure and you mustn't excite yourself. She's not going to harm you.

MARK *(Weakly lies down)*. I heard her . . . I heard her . . .

MRS. F. She's gone! Left in a hurry she did. But why? I'm thinking she is up to no good. Sure it was crocodile tears she was crying.

(Aside).

Everyone knows a crocodile weeps best when it is ready to bite!

(MUSIC, Cue 36. Tune, "Drill, ye Tarriers, Drill." Lights dim down on "room" at R. Mark and bed exit R. Mrs. Flanagan turns the room-flat so that it is the Street Scene).

(Mother Watson enters R. Mickey enters L. They both creep in sinisterly and in rhythm to music. He wears a new hat, comic on him, and a big bright necktie. They meet in C. The scene is played secretly and mysteriously. MUSIC stops).

MOTHER W. Are ye ready?

MICKEY. Ready. Stole the tie at Stewarts. Hooked the hat at City Hall.

MOTHER W. Listen carefully. Your name is John Talbot.

MICKEY. John Talbot.

MOTHER W. Named after your father.

MICKEY. After me father.

MOTHER W. This is a picture of your mother.

(Gives him picture).

MICKEY. Me mother.

MOTHER W. Her name was Irene.

MICKEY. Irene.

MOTHER W. He died first. She died last year.

MICKEY. Last year.

MOTHER W. Mother Watson has took care of you ever since.

MICKEY. Ever since.

MOTHER W. *And* I'm going to keep on taking care of you . . . and the fortune.

MICKEY. Me fortune!

MOTHER W. If you don't know the answer to what they ask you, think of your departed mother . . . and start crying.

(Show him how . . . comically).

MICKEY. Start crying.

(Cries comically).

MOTHER W. Then call me to explain it all.

MICKEY. Explain it all.

MOTHER W. Now be off!

MICKEY. Be off.

MOTHER. W. *(Starts L. Aside).* And the fortune will soon be . . . not his . . . but mine!

MICKEY *(Starts R. Aside).* And the fortune will soon be . . . not hers . . . but only mine!

(MUSIC, Cue 37, builds to climax as they exit).

(MUSIC, Cue 38, changes to "The Mulberry Bush." Roswell enters L and turns L. street-flat to show rich-room flat. Then he stands and SINGS).

ROSWELL *(SINGS)*.

IN THE PARLOR THE RICH RICH SIT

THE RICH RICH SIT

THE RICH RICH SIT

IN THE PARLOR THE RICH RICH SIT

WHEN NIGHT BEGINS TO FALL.

(Pantomimes turning on ceiling lights).

THE FIRE AND THE LAMPS ARE LIT

THE LAMPS ARE LIT

THE LAMPS ARE LIT

THE FIRE AND THE LAMPS ARE LIT

IN THE PARLOR AND THE HALL.

(Mickey enters R, knocks at "door." Aside).

Someone is knocking at the door.

(Opens "door").

MICKEY. I've come to get my fortune.

ROSWELL. Your name, sir?

MICKEY. Mickey Ma . . . John Talbot!

ROSWELL. I shall announce you, sir.

(Crosses to L, speaks off).

Excuse me, Mr. Greyson, but there is a gentleman who says his name is John Talbot.

GREYSON *(Enters L)*. John Talbot?

MICKEY. At your service, sir.

GREYSON. You?

MICKEY. I've come to receive my rightful fortune.

GREYSON. I assume you can prove you are the boy.

MICKEY. Yes, sir.

GREYSON. What was your mother's name?

MICKEY *(Thinking, which is difficult)*. Me mother's name? It was . . . was . . . Irene!

GREYSON *(Aside, amazed)*. That is true. It was Irene!

(Looks at Mickey with interest).

When did she die?

894

MICKEY. Me father kick off first, and she . . . departed . . . a year ago.

GREYSON. Where?

MICKEY. Where?

(He is desperate, then he begins to cry comically).

Excuse me, sir, but when I think of my departed mother, I . . . I . . .

(Cries louder).

GREYSON. Come now. You are a big boy.

MICKEY. When do I get the money?

GREYSON. *How* did your mother die?

MICKEY. How?

(Wild moment of panic, then he cries very loud and comically).

Oh, me poor mother . . .

GREYSON. I must have more proof that she was your mother.

MICKEY. Proof? Oh, I've got proof a-plenty. Here . . . here . . .

(Desperately feels pockets).

Here's proof. Here's her picture!

GREYSON. Her picture? Surely you don't think you can fool me with some faded photograph?

(Takes picture. Gasps. Aside).

It is . . . it is Irene!

(Looks at Mickey).

Could it be possible? Are you . . . John Talbot?

MICKEY. Yes, sir. Waiting for me fortune!

(Aside).

There ain't nobody that can stop me now!

(Hero MUSIC, Cue 39, as Dick enters R and knocks at "door." MUSIC stops).

ROSWELL *(Crosses and opens "door").* Some one is knocking at the door.

DICK *(Proudly hands Roswell book).* I have finished reading *Little Men* by Miss Louisa May Alcott, and I am returning it to Miss Ida.

GREYSON *(Aside, elated).* Richard! He has arrived at the right time.

895

MICKEY *(Aside, frightened)*. Ragged Dick! He's come at the wrong time!

GREYSON. Come in.

(Dick enters "room").

I believe we have found John Talbot.

DICK. Him?

MICKEY *(Trying to bluff)*. John Talbot . . . named after me father.

DICK. His name is Mickey Maguire and he never saw his father!

MICKEY. It's a lie!

DICK. It's the truth!

GREYSON. He has Irene's picture.

DICK. Then he stole it from somebody. Who'd you steal it from?

MICKEY. This time I'll pay you off!

(Fists ready).

DICK. I'll give you all you want!

(They grab each other and start wrestling. Mickey qucikly trips Dick. They fall . . . Mickey on top. As he pounds Dick, he shouts, "Liar . . . liar").

GREYSON. Boys! Boys! Stop them, Roswell!

(Dick is on top and shouts, "Thief . . . thief").

ROSWELL. Yes, sir. Gentlemen . . . please.

MICKEY *(In a helpless hold)*. Let me go!

DICK *(Sitting on Mickey, holding him down)*. I can prove to you, sir, he ain't . . .

(Aside).

isn't . . .

(To Greyson).

John Talbott. He is a forgery!

(Loud fire alarm and bells are heard).

GREYSON. What is that?

ROSWELL. The fire bell, sir, and the fire engine.

(Roswell goes to R and exits. Ida runs in from L).

IDA. There's a big fire, Papa. I can see flames and smoke from my window.

GREYSON. Fire!

896

ROSWELL *(Enters R)*. A big fire, sir, on Mott Street!

DICK *(Jumps up)*. Mott Street!

ROSWELL. The corner of Mott and Park Row.

DICK. The corner? It's *my* house. Mark is alone! Trapped on the top floor! I must help him. Mark must be saved!

(Dick rushes off R).

GREYSON. To the rescue!

(Fire MUSIC begins, Cue 40. Tune, "Petite Overture." Ida, Greyson, Mickey rush off R. Roswell turns the room-flat at L, so the Street Scene is shown).

(There is a cross-over of people. A stroboscopic light can help to give a fast running effect as people rush across the stage, ad libbing loudly and excitedly).

(Smoke starts to pour from one of the painted building fronts. The stage is lighted with a red glow. There can be a brief fast dance with bucket brigade, etc. Policeman blows whistle and pushes people back at L).

POLICEMAN. Stand back. Stand back! Let the firemen through!

(People shout, scream, etc. A Fireman enters from door of burning building, helping Mrs. Flanagan who is weak and coughing. MUSIC stops).

Stand back. Give them room. Are you all right, Mrs. Flanagan?

MRS. F. Yes . . . yes . . .

POLICEMAN. Is there anyone left? Anyone else inside?

MRS. F. Mark! The match boy! He is alone in the top room!

(Fire MUSIC starts again, Cue 41, and Dick, Ida, Greyson, Mickey, Roswell rush in from L).

DICK. It *is* my house!

(MUSIC Stops).

Mark! Where is Mark?

MRS. F. Inside . . . trapped . . . save him!

FIREMAN. Too late! The house is a blazing furnace!

DICK *(All look up as he calls)*. Mark!

POLICEMAN. No one can save him *now*!

DICK. I will.

POLICEMAN. You?

DICK. I will rescue him!!

(Hero MUSIC, Cue 42, as Dick shields his face with his arm and marches into the burning building. People call, "Come back . . . stop." MUSIC changes to, Cue 43, The Rescue Song, "Marguerite." All line up quickly at foot-lights, facing audience and sing dramatically).

ALL.   HELP! HELP! HELP!

OH LOOK . . . THE WALL IS FALLING!

HELP! HELP! HELP!

POOR MARK IS IN THERE CALLING.

SAVE HIM, DICK!

OH SAVE HIM FROM HIS FATE,

OH CARRY HIM TO SAFETY

ERE IT IS TOO LATE.

(All turn and look at burning building at back, except first soloist who faces audience and SINGS).

UP! UP! UP!

HE'S MADE IT THROUGH THE FIRST DOOR!

UP! UP! UP!

HE STAGGERS TO THE NEXT FLOOR!

UP! HE STOPS.

THE STEPS ARE ALL ABLAZE.

HE STUMBLES AND HE FALLS,

INTO THE SMOKY HAZE.

(First Soloist turns and faces building with others. Second Soloist faces front and SINGS. [Music changes to "Rumours."])

WILL HE . . . WON'T HE RESCUE MARK?

THE SITUATION'S MIGHTY DARK.

HE'S GETTING UP . . .

HE MOVES AHEAD . . .

HE'S IN THE ROOM . . .

THE FLAMES HAVE SPREAD.

HE CAN'T SEE MARK!

THE ROOM IS SMOKING . . .

MARK IS ON THE FLOOR . . .

HE'S CHOKING.

898

FIND HIM DICK . . . PLEASE LOOK HIS WAY.

THE LORD MAY HELP HIM IF WE PRAY!

(Second Soloist turns and faces building with others. Third Soloist faces front and SINGS).

THANK THE LORD

AT LAST HE'S FOUND HIM . . .

LIFTS HIM UP

WITH FLAMES AROUND HIM . . .

THROUGH THE SMOKE AND THROUGH THE FIRE,

WILL HE MAKE IT OR EXPIRE?

(All turn and face front and SING. [Music changes back to "Marguerite."])

DOWN, DOWN, DOWN,

BE CAREFUL OR YOU'LL DROP HIM.

STEP BY STEP . . .

OH WILL THE DANGER STOP HIM?

COURAGE, DICK . . . HAVE COURAGE AND YOU'LL WIN.

WILL HIS STRENGTH UPHOLD HIM

OR WILL HE GIVE IN?

(All turn and look at burning building in back, except First Soloist who faces front and SINGS. [Music changes to "Rumours."])

NOW THEY'VE REACHED THE SECOND LANDING.

CRASH! THE STAIRCASE ISN'T STANDING.

JUMP! OH TAKE A CHANCE. GO THROUGH IT.

WILL HE? WON'T HE? HE MUST DO IT!

(First Soloist turns and faces burning building with others. Second Soloist faces front and SINGS).

JUMP! HE DID AND CAUGHT A WIRE!

HELP! HIS COAT HAS CAUGHT ON FIRE!

ROLL BEFORE YOU BOTH GET TOASTED . . .

OVER . . . OVER OR YOU'RE ROASTED!

(Second Soloist turns and faces building with others. Third Soloist faces front and SINGS).

899

OFF HE SHEDS HIS COAT . . .

NO BURNING . . .

CRAWLING FORWARD

WITHOUT TURNING.

WEAK! HIS STRENGTH IS ALMOST GONE . . .

HE STOPS! HE FALLS! HE CAN'T GO ON!

(All turn and face front and SING very softly but intently. [Segue to "Marguerite" music]).

TRY! TRY! TRY! WITH ALL YOUR STRENGTH AND
POWER!

TRY! TRY! TRY! OR IT'S THE FINAL HOUR.

(All turn and face back, except First Soloist who faces front and SINGS).

LOOK! LOOK! LOOK! A MIRACLE'S IN VIEW . . .

(Second Soloist faces front and SINGS).

HE MOVES HIS ARMS . . .

(Third Soloist faces front and SINGS).

HE'S REACHED THE DOOR . . .

(All SING. The straight line breaks forming two lines, one on either side of the door. All point to the door and hold the last note triumphantly).

AND *HE'S COME THROUGH!*

(Door opens. Hero MUSIC, Cue 44, as Dick marches in, carrying Mark. Mother Watson enters at L).

GREYSON. Who . . . who is this boy?

(Aside).

His face has a familiar look.

MARK *(Points to photograph Greyson holds).* My picture! Where did you get my picture?

GREYSON. Your picture?

DICK. So . . . Mickey Maguire stole it from *Mark!*

(Mickey starts to exit R).

Stop him!

(Policeman grabs him).

MARK. It is the picture of my mother.

900

GREYSON. Your mother! Yes! It is Irene you look like. I know by your face you *are* her son!

MOTHER W. *(Aside, D. L.).* Curses! Curses!

MICKEY. Let me go. I ain't to blame. Mother Watson did it.

(Mother Watson starts L).

POLICEMAN. Mother Watson?

(Crosses and grabs her).

Halt!

GREYSON. Arrest that woman!

MOTHER W. Let loose of me, you rogue!

POLICEMAN. The law holds you now. You will be justly punished for the wickedness you have done.

DICK. Mark! *You* are the lost boy. You are rich!

MARK *(Aside).* Rich?

GREYSON. My nephew.

MARK. My uncle.

GREYSON. And you, Richard, you saved his life! You shall be richly rewarded. And I offer you a position in my bank!

DICK. A big reward! Work in a bank! It's come true, Mark. We've made our fortune. We've come from . . . rags to riches!

(Entire company lines up for the finale. MUSIC, Cue 45. Tune, "The Man Who Broke the Bank at Monte Carlo," reprise).

ALL. *(SING).*

IF YOU WANT TO BE A MILLIONAIRE,

IT'S AN EASY GAME TODAY.

YOU CAN ALWAYS FIND A WAY

IN THE GOOD OLD U. S. A.

YOU CAN BE JUST WHAT YOU WANT TO BE

IN THIS LAND OF OPPORTUNITY

FOR WITH PLUCK AND LUCK

YOU'LL GO FROM RAGS TO RICHES.

BE A DOCTOR . . . BE A LAWYER

BE A RAILROAD ENGINEER . . .

BE A WEALTHY FINANCIER.

901

YOU CAN PICK YOUR OWN CAREER!
WHILE OLD GLORY'S BANNER IS UNFURLED,
ANY DAY MAY BRING A BRIGHT NEW WORLD.
FOR WITH PLUCK AND LUCK
YOU'LL GO FROM RAGS TO RICHES.

(Musical tag).

YES, FOR WITH PLUCK AND LUCK
YOU'LL GO FROM RAGS TO RICHES!

CURTAIN.

THE GREAT
CROSS-COUNTRY RACE

or

The Hare and the Tortoise

An Entertainment for Children

by
ALAN BROADHURST

Proposed Production Plan by
IRENE COREY

*Included in the separate play-book only.

THE GREAT CROSS-COUNTRY RACE

By Alan Broadhurst

THE GREAT CROSS-COUNTRY RACE

Cast

MR. FLEET . . . . a Hare
MR. SETT . . . . a Badger
MRS. WARREN . . . . a Rabbit
MR. SPINEY . . . . a Hedgehog
MR. PADDLE . . . . a Water-Rat
MR. BRUSH . . . . a Squirrel
MR. SLOE . . . . a Tortoise
MRS. DARK . . . . a Rook
MR. BASKET . . . . a Dog
JACKIE . . . . a very nice young human
ROBIN . . . . another
A FISHERMAN . . . . the common variety
MAUDE . . . . one-half of a courting couple
GEORGE . . . . the other half
MR. URBAN NOTCOUTH . . . . . . a picnicker
MRS. URBAN NOTCOUTH . . . . . his wife
SOPHIA . . . . his daughter
BRANDO . . . . his son
FARMER BLACK . . . . an irate farmer
MRS. STAINER . . . . a near-sighted housewife

Note: *By doubling, the cast for this play can*
be reduced to 7 men, 5 women.

THE GREAT CROSS-COUNTRY RACE

The Action of the Play takes place in and about the Woodlands. Yesterday—if it was fine; or, even this very afternoon.

Basic are permanent Wings and Sky Cloth.
The ground rows are changed each time, and a central Set Piece keys the Scene.

The Continuity Scenes take place on the Apron and in the Auditorium. The Action is continuous but the Intervals may be arranged as desired.

To My Grandson

MARK RODERICK

who happily timed his arrival to
coincide with that of Mr. Fleet
and Company: August 1964.

THE GREAT CROSS-COUNTRY RACE was first produced, under the title of "The Hare and the Tortoise," for a six-weeks run in January-February, 1965, by the College Repertory Players of Doncaster Technical College, in Doncaster, England.

Producer	Vivien Wood
Settings	Charles Pym
	Walter Monks
Choreography	Nellie Stagles
Costumes	Dorothy Wilson
	Joan Robinson

Principal Players:

Mr. Fleet	George Wann
Mr. Sloe	Maurice Horsfield
Mr. Basket	Gerald Coley

MAKE-UP

PROPOSED

for

THE GREAT CROSS-COUNTRY RACE

Designed by Irene Corey

". . . The style of make-up devised for the purpose of this play is applied directly to the actor's face, resulting in a make-up mask, rather than a papier-maché mask."

—IRENE COREY

909

THE GREAT CROSS-COUNTRY RACE

by Alan Broadhurst

Included in the separate play-book are detailed instructions for make-up and costume, as well as a proposed production plan, designed by Irene Corey.

SCENE 1—FROG ROCK QUARRY

A Ground-row of boulders.

Centre—Frog-shaped rock.

Downstage of the Rock is a smaller rock of a regular mound shape. It is, in fact, Mr. Sloe, the Tortoise, in retreat.

Around him, puzzled and arguing, are Mr. Sett, Mrs. Warren, Mr. Paddle, Mr. Spiney, and Mr. Brush. Mrs. Dark is a little apart, Up-left.

RABBIT. Well, I'm quite certain that it wasn't here yesterday.

HEDGEHOG. It must have been. Rocks don't grow in the night.

BADGER. But is it a rock? That's the point.

RAT. What else can it be?

SQUIRREL. It's hard like a rock.

RABBIT. It's rough like a rock.

HEDGEHOG. It's round like a rock.

BADGER. All the same, I've never seen a rock like it. And look at this sticking out—surely that is a leg?

HEDGEHOG. Whoever heard of a rock with a leg!

RABBIT. Well, there seems to be three more—one at each corner.

RAT. Please—you'll be saying that this stubby bit is a tail next!

SQUIRREL. And there's something here that could be a head—if it had ears—which it hasn't.

BADGER. A most odd rock.

HEDGEHOG. It would be an even odder animal.

SQUIRREL. Of course, there are some very odd animals. Far be it from me to be personal, Spiney, but you yourself—prickles instead of fur!

HEDGEHOG. At least I live on the ground and don't make my home in the trees like a skyflyer.

BADGER. Now, gentlemen, live and let live. We all have our little peculiarities.

RAT. Shall we get on with the sports? After all that's the purpose of this meeting.

BADGER. Quite. We were side-tracked by this—uh—thing here. I suppose it must be a rock.

(He sits on it).

It's as firm as a rock, anyway. Now, then—you've all sent in your suggestions for the events so we just have to see who's going to compete in what, and the Sports Day can begin. First, the Grass Eating Competition. Who's going in for that?

RABBIT. Me.

BADGER. Yes, Mrs. Warren, it was your suggestion. Now, who's for Grass Eating?

SQUIRREL. Not me, for one. Nuts, yes: grass, no.

RAT. Grass—ugh!

HEDGEHOG. We all know that Mrs. Warren could nibble more grass in an afternoon than the rest of us in a week.

BADGER. Mrs. Dark?

ROOK. Wha'?

BADGER. The Grass Eating Competition?

ROOK. It chokes my craw.

BADGER. Oh, dear. Well, no other entries. It looks as though you've won that, Mrs. Warren.

RABBIT. Oh, good. Is there a prize?

BADGER. We'll have to see. Next. Mr. Brush proposes a tree climbing race. Twice up and down the Leaning Pine.

RABBIT. I couldn't possibly. I even get dizzy on top of our bank.

RAT. Much too cold up there for any civilized animal. Swimming now—twice across the river. That's the thing. Four times—ten times—hundred times, if you like. I'll take all comers.

BADGER. We'll come to that Mr. Paddle—but let's settle the Tree Climbing entries first.

HEDGEHOG. No thank you.

BADGER. Mrs. Dark?

ROOK. Wha'?

BADGER. Tree Climbing?

ROOK. Climbing's for morons. I soar.

SQUIRREL. Well, really!

BADGER. Quite. How about the Swimming Race? Would anybody like to challenge Mr. Paddle?—No? Nobody. Oh dear.—Well here's one you can all join in. A most novel idea from Mr. Spiney —a Curling in a Ball and Rolling Down Hill Race.

912

SQUIRREL. Most undignified.

RABBIT. I haven't done it since my bunny days. I'm afraid I'm much too matronly now for that.

RAT. Who can curl in a ball on land? Animal Bob Apple in the water, if you like.

BADGER. Oh, dear.—Mrs. Dark?

ROOK. Wha'?

BADGER. The Curling in a Ball and Rolling Down Hill Race?

ROOK. Deplorable.

BADGER. Then if nobody is going to enter these events, it just leaves the Cross Country Race. At least we have two competitors for that—Mr. Reynard and Mr. Fleet.

SQUIRREL. Reynard won't be entering, Mr. Sett. He asked me to say he was sorry but he sprained a paw yesterday on a hunt.

BADGER. Not badly I trust!

SQUIRREL. Nothing, really. But he's resting up today. Apparently there's another hunt at the week-end which he doesn't want to miss. The Horses and Hounds do look forward to it so, and he hates to disappoint them.

BADGER. What a kind fellow he is! Well, I'm sure we'll find plenty of others to give Mr. Fleet a run for his money.

RABBIT. Where is Mr. Fleet, anyway?

RAT. Late again—as usual.

HEDGEHOG. I've never known him be on time for an appointment yet.

RAT. He's certainly the dawdlingest animal.

BADGER. Something will have delayed him.

SQUIRREL. Food, most probably.

BADGER. Mrs. Dark?

ROOK. Wha'?

BADGER. Did you see Mr. Fleet on your way?

ROOK. Snoring in the straw.

BADGER. Sleeping again. It's too bad of him! Well, while we're waiting, who will enter for the Cross Country?

HEDGEHOG. Against Mr. Fleet! He's the fastest animal on earth.

RABBIT. I can do half a field quite quickly, but I'm afraid a Cross Country run would be far too much for me. I'd get dizzy.

SQUIRREL. Include a few trees as obstacles and I'd have a crack. But not Cross Country against a Hare. Oh, no!

BADGER. Mrs. Dark?

ROOK. Wha'?

BADGER. We must have somebody to race Mr. Fleet in the Cross Country.

ROOK. Circular tour?

BADGER. Yes. I've worked out an exciting course.

ROOK. All our family fly straight.

BADGER. This is most upsetting. We must have one race. How can we have a Sports Day if nobody competes against anybody!

ROOK. Warning! Warning!

(She hides in the wings. The others camouflage themselves to merge with the rocks, all curling motionless. Badger becomes an extension of Frog Rock.

The Dog bounds in.)

DOG. It's only me, Basket. Come on out.

(They uncurl. Rook re-enters).

BADGER. Why didn't you call?

DOG. Didn't want to make too much noise. *They* are with me. Or they think they are.

SQUIRREL. Slipped your lead again, eh?

DOG. No. We're hunting! What about that?

RABBIT. Hunting! Those two nice little doe humans? Oh, dear.

DOG. Not for you Woodlanders.

HEDGEHOG. Then what?

DOG. A new member of the family. Mr. Sloe. He got out of the garden.

BADGER. Mr. Sloe? What's his family name?

DOG. Tortoise.

BADGER. I don't think I know them.

DOG. This is the first one I've met. Came from a long way off, he says. What's a ship?

RAT. Like a floating log, I believe. But very big.

DOG. That's it then—he came from somewhere on a big floating log.

BADGER. What is he, a Woodlander?

914

Dog. I don't know exactly.

Rat. A Riverswimmer?

Dog. No. He'd sink for sure.

Hedgehog. A Skyflyer?

Dog. Impossible.

Badger. I suppose he is Animal?

Dog. Oh, yes—sort of.

Badger. Don't you know. How many legs?

Dog. Four—when you can see them.

Squirrel. Tail?

Dog. Sort of.

Squirrel. Head?

Dog. Sometimes.

Squirrel. Eyes?

Dog. I think so.

Rabbit. Ears?

Dog. Never saw any.

Hedgehog. What's his coat—fur or proper prickles?

Dog. Neither.

Badger. Then what? Feathers?

Dog. No. You won't believe this . . . Well, it seems to me to be rock.

Badger. Rock! — Stranger — dubious legs—no ears—rock? Oh my goodness!

(He leaps up).

I do believe . . .

Dog. That's him. See what I mean?

Squirrel. But it's not alive is it?

Dog. Oh, yes. Sleeps a lot.

Hedgehog. But what's he doing here?

Dog. Just having a look round. Said he'd explored our garden and wanted to meet you Woodlanders. My humans think he's run away. Run away! That's good!

Rabbit. Why?

DOG. Because he moves so slowly that sometimes you think he's going backwards.

BADGER. He seems to have reached here all right.

DOG. So he should have—he left last night.

SQUIRREL. Run away from the humans has he?

DOG. No more than me. But we both like a bit of intelligent conversation with friends. And poor old Mr. Sloe hasn't picked up any of the human language yet.

RABBIT. I'm sure I couldn't either. I do think you're clever, Mr. Basket—you understand every word they say.

DOG. True. The great thing, of course, is not to let on. Anyway today I'm with you. What's it to be?

BADGER. It was to have been sports—but no one will compete. I wonder if your Mr. Sloe would enter? He can't run fast, you say, so the Cross Country's out, but he might—uh—Swim . . .?

(All are surveying the Tortoise: All shake heads on each query).

Climb the Tree . . .? Roll Down the Hill . . .? Ah! Grass Eating!

DOG. He eats grass and such. Day before yesterday he ate a whole dandelion leaf. Started at sun-up and took the last bit to bed with him.—Still, perhaps he's good at something.

(He raps smartly on the shell).

Anyone at home? Heh. Torto—wakey, wakey! It's me, Basket. I want to introduce you to my friends.

(Tortoise emerges and rises slowly to his hind legs).

TORTOISE. Ah, it's you, Mr. Basket. Must have dropped off for a moment.

DOG. You found the Quarry, then.

TORTOISE. Just as you directed. There was no one about, so I waited.

DOG. Good for you. Well, we're all here now. Let's see . . . This is Mr. Sett, Leader of the Woodlanders, Chairman of the Winter Stores Committee, Secretary of the Sports and Pastimes, and all that sort of thing.

TORTOISE. How do you do, Mr. Sett.

BADGER. Very pleased to make your acquaintance, Mr. Sloe. You've been puzzling us a little. From over the Hill, are you?

TORTOISE. And beyond. My native home is over the sea.

BADGER. Sea?

RAT. Where all the rivers meet. Otter's been. Told me about it.

916

THE GREAT CROSS-COUNTRY RACE

They say there are Woodlands on the other side, but you can't see them, it's so big.

TORTOISE. Oh, there are, believe me.

DOG. This is Mr. Paddle.

TORTOISE. Delighted.

RAT. A pleasure.

DOG. And Mrs. Warren.

RABBIT. I'm so glad you're not a rock.

TORTOISE. My house? Yes, it's meant to look like a rock. Stops being pestered.

RABBIT. Do you take it everywhere?

TORTOISE. I find it convenient. It saves going home every night.

SQUIRREL. Ah, you're a relative of the Snails, I take it.

DOG. This is Mr. Brush.

TORTOISE. Pleased to meet you. Very distant cousins, the Snails. Very distant indeed. They haven't our swiftness of movement, you know. Our nearest relatives are the Turtle family.

BADGER. The Turtles?

TORTOISE. You don't know them? Pity. Charming creatures. The Turtles, the Terrapins and the Tortoise—we're quite a clan over the sea.

BADGER. And it's very nice to meet you. Mrs. Dark . . .?

ROOK. Wha'?

BADGER. This is Mr. Sloe. He has come to live with Mr. Basket and the little female humans. Thought he'd visit us.

ROOK. What for?

TORTOISE. Just to be sociable. It's very pleasant in the garden, but lonely. One pines for a friendly chat now and then.

SQUIRREL. I thought the humans were forever talking to the Garden Animals.

TORTOISE. They do. They do. But it's such gobble-di-gook, it makes my head swim. So if you don't mind, I would like to join you here in the Woodlands from time to time.

BADGER. Delighted to have you just whenever.

SQUIRREL. By all means. You must visit my Tree one evening: we'll have a bit of a crack.

TORTOISE. Thank you. Thank you.

917

(There is a commotion at the rear of the auditorium. Mr. Fleet has arrived. He charges down an aisle, and on to the stage).

HARE. Right, everybody, I'm here! Sorry to be a little late: Was delayed. Important conference.

(He is with them).

Are we all met? The Sports can begin. I'm here.

(He sees Tortoise).

Ah, who—what—is this?

BADGER. A new friend. Mr. Sloe. Mr. Sloe, meet Mr. Fleet.

TORTOISE. How do you do, Mr. Fleet.

HARE. Howdo. You competing in the sports?

TORTOISE. I had not really thought about it.

HARE. Just as well. Not much of a runner, I should say.

TORTOISE. I get where I want to be, you know.

HARE. Ah, but when?

TORTOISE. Slow and steady wins the race, they say.

HARE. Do they? Well, take it from me, they're wrong. 'To the Swift, the Lettuce'—my old school motto.

TORTOISE. I dare say you are right, Mr. Fleet.

HARE. I'm always right. And what's this on your back?

BADGER. Please, Mr. Fleet!

HARE. He don't mind me asking. You don't mind me asking, do you Mr.—uh . . .

TORTOISE. Sloe.

HARE. Slow. I should have remembered that easily enough.

TORTOISE. It is my back.

HARE. This great lump of whatever it is!

SQUIRREL. Shell. You know, Fleet—like Snails, only bigger. Terrapins and Turtles—same idea. Carry your house with you.

HARE. What's the point of that? He'd never get anywhere in a month of Sundays.

TORTOISE. You'd be surprised, Mr. Fleet, how we Tortoise do get around.

HARE. But not in athletic sports. I suppose we could use you as a finishing post.

(He turns away, rudely).

918

Why don't we start? I'll just win this race, then run over to Hambledon Hill for tea with the Moles—it's only ten miles. Where's Reynard?

SQUIRREL. Not coming. Laid up with a sprained paw.

HARE. That's what he says. Afraid of me beating him, more like it.

BADGER. I'm sure it's not that. Mr. Reynard is a very fine Cross Country runner.

HARE. Horse radish! I can beat Reynard with one paw strapped to my back! I can run faster and straighter and longer than any animal in the Woodlands. I can run so fast, that if I set out now to the Cabbage Field to fetch a head for dinner, I should meet myself coming back!

HDGEHOG. If you didn't stop for a nap on the way.

HARE. What's that! I could stop for fifty naps, and still beat any of you slow-coaches. And if you don't believe me, just enter for the Cross Country now. Come on—anybody.

RABBIT. You know we wouldn't stand a chance against you.

HARE. I tell you what, I'll give any of you five minutes start. What about it, Basket?

DOG. How d'you expect me to race you if my Greyhound cousins can't catch you? I'm not built for speed.

HARE. No good asking you, Paddle—you'd trip over your own tail.

RAT. I'll swim you a mile up the river.

HARE. Fiddle-di-de—swimming! I'm talking about real animal sport —running. And none of you are any good. Brush—he can't run for nuts. Nobody can beat me.

BADGER. That's the last event gone west. It is a shame. I've been to no end of trouble to arrange the course.

TORTOISE. Is it a long course, Mr. Sett?

BADGER. Three miles exactly. It starts here and goes to the Bramble Thicket, then to . . . Wait, I'll show you. Mr. Spiney and Mr. Brush, would you fetch the old gate I was working on, please?

(Hedgehog and Squirrel exit, to return with a solid gate on which is chalked a pictorial diagram of the Course).

HARE. Thinking of issuing a challenge, Mr. Sloe?

TORTOISE. Just interested. We often had Cross Country runs at home. Most enjoyable.

HARE. What did you use for legs!

TORTOISE. These I have served quite well.

(On comes the gate).

Ah.

BADGER (*Lecturing*). Now, here's the Start—Frog Rock. First check point—the Bramble Thicket. Then to the River Bank: From there to the Grassy Bank; then to Mr. Brush's Tree; half a mile to the Cornfield; then past the end of the Keeper's Cottage, and a straight run home to here again in the Old Quarry and Frog Rock, where the runners have to pass Frog Rock and do one more full lap of the Quarry to win—There will be judges at each point, and Mr. Basket will take short cuts and be general referee.

TORTOISE. Very, very interesting.

HARE. Too easy. Hardly worth running.

TORTOISE. Very similar to our courses at home. Not too short and not too long.

HARE. Well, you're wrong again, fat legs. This race is too short *and* too long for any animal—except me. And to me it doesn't matter. Short or long—Hares can't go wrong. We Hares are the fastest runners on earth.

TORTOISE. Mr. Sett . . .

HARE. We Hares are the most athletic creatures in creation.

TORTOISE. Mr. Sett, I think I will . . .

HARE. We Hares have the longest legs and longest ears of all animals.

TORTOISE. I think I will, if it's all the same to everybody . . .

HARE. We Hares are invincible—and bright and intelligent—and pretty—and witty—and charming—and no animal dares compete against us.

TORTOISE. I think I will enter for the Cross Country Race.

HARE. We Hares in general, and myself in particular—What!

BADGER. Are you sure, Mr. Sloe?

TORTOISE. Yes, I would enjoy a good run.

HARE. You! You want to race me?

TORTOISE. If you'd be so kind.

HARE. Ridiculous! I'd be past the winning post before you'd started.

TORTOISE. In that case, you would be the winner.

HARE. Winner? Of course I'd be the winner! No—I won't do it.

TORTOISE. Then I would be the winner. Mr. Fleet beaten at last.

SQUIRREL. That would be a tid-bit of news throughout the Woodlands.

HARE. But I can't be beaten if I don't run.

HEDGEHOG. And you can't win if you don't run.

920

SQUIRREL. Mr. Fleet refuses a challenge from a stranger!

HARE. I don't refuse a challenge. I just refuse to run against a fat-legged, hump-backed, earless old slow coach. I would be the laughing stock of the corn stukes!

DOG. You will be if my friend has a walk-over.

HARE. Walk-over! Crawl-over, you mean!

RABBIT. And he might win if you give him a good enough start.

HARE. Talk sense. He couldn't beat me if I gave him a half-way round start.

TORTOISE. Oh, I don't want a start.

HARE. You seriously think you can run faster than me?

TORTOISE. No.

HARE. Ah!

TORTOISE. But I'm sure I can win the Cross Country Race. In fact, I think any animal here could beat you, young Hare.

HARE. What!

TORTOISE. And, if I may say so, I think that some animal should have done it long ago.

HARE. Why, you . . .

TORTOISE. Because, I'm afraid you really need a lesson. You strike me as being just a little too proud of yourself—too boastful—not to say, cocky, young Hare.

HARE. Will you stop calling me 'young Hare'! I am three! And in the prime of my animalhood.

TORTOISE. Are you? I am twenty-four.

(A general gasp).

And am still a comparatively young tortoise. Now, do we race, or are you too scatter-brained even to start?

HARE *(Thumping his feet on the ground in temper)*. That does it! We race!

ROOK. Warning! Warning! Withdraw! Withdraw!

(The Animals freeze as previously, albeit with heads cocked until the last second. The Hare merely leans nonchalantly against a wing, confident that, if he is spotted, he can run from danger. The Dog listens and sniffs.

We hear human voices—but NOT intelligible speech. We are with the animals and can understand their speech: We cannot, therefore, reasonably expect to comprehend human speech as well. Only Dogs and some of the Birds are so bi-lingual. But we can

*sense general meanings from the expression of the human speech
. . . and it is the general sense of what the humans say that is
indicated in our play. The articulations with which they express
it are as incomprehensible in detail to us as they are to our
animal friends.*

*So: two young female voices approach, making calling sounds.
Jackie and Robin are seeking Basket . . . It might be written:
"Ah-skit! Ah-skit! Oo-ah-oo? Skit—good og. Ear oy! Whistle.
O air iz at aughty og! Ah-skit! Ood og. Whistle. Ear oy!" Etc.
This applies to all human speech tonight, and Producers and
Artistes will no doubt devise their own expressive—and amusing
—gobble-di-gook. Certainly no more will be phonetically illus-
trated).*

Dog. It's all right. It's only my humans. Keep still. They won't see
you.

Hare. Let 'em. They can't catch me.

Rabbit. Are you sure they won't, Mr. Basket?

Dog. I don't know how the humans manage—they have ears and
noses and eyes, but they can't hear or smell or see. Not what we'd
call hearing, smelling and seeing. You stay put: they'll walk
all round, and not know you're here. Just hark at them!

Badger. What are they saying?

Dog. They are calling me.

Squirrel. Oughtn't you to go?

Dog. Not yet. They don't really expect me to. Hear that? 'Good
dog.' Good dog!—It's funny: the more naughty a dog is, the
more the humans call 'Good dog.' Keep down now. I'll lead them
off. Back in a minute.

(He shouts—the Girls would say he was barking—off).

Here I am! Here I am! Just try to catch me!

Jackie's Voice *(Is saying that she has heard Basket. Come on).*

Robin's Voice *(Is saying that he is a good dog and must come to them).*

(They run on. Two very pleasant young ladies in jeans).

Dog. Hello, you two. Nice to see you. Follow me. This way.

(He exits and re-enters, inviting).

Jackie *(Is pleased to find him).*

Robin *(Wonders what he wants).*

Jackie *(Thinks he wants them to follow).*

Robin *(Is sure he's found Tortoise: clever dog).*

922

DOG. Come on, my pretties, I'll soon lose you for a while.—Back in a minute, Mr. Badger—Come on, then.

(He exits with the Girls following. The Animals unfreeze).

BADGER. Remarkable. I must say you garden dwellers seem to have the best of both worlds, Mr. Sloe.

TORTOISE. It is a comfortable life—with kindly humans—I agree.

RABBIT. How Mr. Basket can understand them, I don't know!

HEDGEHOG. It's all very well not being seen, but one of them nearly stepped on me.

HARE. I don't know why you bother to hide. I never care if humans do see me—I can always run away. They run like beetles.

SQUIRREL. I don't mind if I'm in my tree. They've no idea of climbing.

RAT. Or swimming.

ROOK. Or soaring.

BADGER. They can't do anything properly, and yet they rule the world. Remarkable!

(Dog re-enters).

DOG. Soon fixed that. Poor dears, they're properly lost now.

TORTOISE. Will they be all right?

DOG. Oh, yes—I'll pick them up later, and take them home.

HARE. Then we can start this Cross Country Race.

SQUIRREL. At last.

BADGER. Mr. Fleet: Mr. Sloe—are you quite clear? The first Point is the Bramble Thicket. Mr. Slither will be there to see you through and put you on the way to the next place. Now, line up please. The Start is here.

(Tortoise commences his very slow walk to the line. Hare runs through a series of limbering-up exercises and physical jerks. Then a couple of sprint dashes across and back. He jogs loosely to the line—and Tortoise arrives at the same time, having travelled all of three or four yards).

HARE. Some race! Go ahead, start it. I'll go when I'm ready.

RABBIT. Please, Mr. Fleet. I always think the 'Ready, Steady Go' is the most exciting part.

HEDGEHOG. You must start together.

HARE. Oh, all right. It's a farce, though.

DOG. The humans say 'On your marks' now.

923

BADGER. That's what I'm going to say: 'On your marks,' then, 'Ready. steady—Go!'—'On your marks!'

(Hare immediately snaps down into a thoroughly professional sprint-start crouch. Tortoise does the same in double slow motion. Hare watches him: the others are embarrassed).

Ready!

(Hare comes up: Tortoise too, but incredibly slowly).

Steady!—Go!

(To a cheer, Hare shoots off . . . A few high stepping paces, then he marks time, and turns to watch Tortoise who hasn't made any perceptible movement.—Check: he has now: one foot is just passing the other . . .

From this moment until the end of the Race he never stops, but for two notable exceptions, but he is excruciatingly slow.

Hare stops jog-trotting on the spot, and wanders back).

HARE. You all right, old Tortoise? Rheumatics? Twinges? Can I get you a couple of crutches?—You won't mind if I don't wait at the finish to see you arrive, will you? My Dam said I always had to be in bed by mid-night.

(Tortoise passes him and exits, to appear sometime later in the auditorium, an extension of our Quarry, where he progresses— if that is not too dynamic a word for it—up an aisle).

Well, I hope you're all satisfied. Cross Country Race, indeed! It's bad enough beating Foxy Reynard and the like, but at least they finish on the same day that they start!

HEDGEHOG. You won't beat him standing here.

SQUIRREL. He's just pacing himself. You see, he'll come strong at the end.

DOG. It's all right. Mr. Fleet's just giving him that start he promised.

HARE. Did I say 'half way'? I could let him sight the winning-post and still catch him.

(He lies down. Tortoise reaches the auditorium).

RABBIT. There he is! Run, Mr. Sloe! Go on, run! Give him a cheer. Go on, Mr. Sloe—go on!

SQUIRREL. Run up, old fellow!

HEDGEHOG. You're doing fine!

DOG. Thunder on, Torto! Keep it up!

He stamps twice and they sing:

> Thunder on, Old Torto, thunder on
> Thunder on, Old Torto, thunder on
> For we want you to be there
> At the post before the Hare,
> So, thunder on, Old Torto, thunder on.

924

Rook. Encore! Encore!

Hare. Idiots!

Badger. Oh, dearie me! Oh. I forgot!

Dog. What's that?

Badger. I meant to tell him—tell all the competitors. At the Grassy Bank, I've had the Shrews put an arrow to point the way. It's just near your place, Mr. Spiney, but you might not be there in time. They have to follow the arrow up the side of the hedge, otherwise they'll go straight on and go miles out of the way. Mr. Sloe! Mr. Sloe!

(They all call).

Rabbit. He can't hear.

Hare. No wonder—he's got no ears!

Badger. But we must tell him. Mr. Sloe!—Oh, Mrs. Dark?

Rook. Wha'?

Badger. Could you fly over and catch him and tell him . . .

Hare. Now, don't panic, Mr. Sett. Calm down. I'll tell him.

Badger. Would you really, Mr. Fleet! That's very kind of you. At the Grassy Bank there's an arrow which . . .

Hare. I know. I know.

(He dashes off, to re-appear immediately in the auditorium and, in no time flat, catches up with Tortoise within yards of an Exit Door. Tortoise keeps moving).

Message from the Officials. At the Grassy Bank look out for an arrow. Very important. Miss it and you'll go wrong. Got it?

Tortoise. Yes, indeed, Mr. Fleet. Yes, thank you very much.

Hare. Not at all. I was just passing.

(Tortoise exits. Hare runs back).

Dog. He's told him.

Badger. Good—Good Earthworks, he's coming back!

Squirrel. Keep going, Fleet!

Rabbit. Mr. Sloe's out of sight!

Hare (Regaining the stage). I told him. He says, 'thank you very much!'

Badger. But I didn't mean you to come back, Mr. Fleet.

Hare. I thought you'd like to know he understood.

BADGER. Yes. Yes, thank you very much. But the Race has started.

RABBIT. Oh do hurry, Mr. Fleet!

HARE. You think I ought to start?

RABBIT. Yes, yes!

HARE. I'm hungry.

RABBIT. You can't be!

HARE. I can be. I always am.

SQUIRREL. Hardly the time for a meal, I would have thought.

HEDGEHOG. He's well on his way now.

DOG. I'm off to the Bramble Thicket. Mr. Sloe will be there any minute.

HARE. I'll be there first, never fear.

BADGER. And you others should be getting to your positions. Mr. Paddle, the River Bank.

RAT. Right.

BADGER. Mr. Brush—your Tree.

SQUIRREL. Roger.

BADGER. Mr. Spiney—the Grassy Bank, and please make sure that they follow the arrow.

HEDGEHOG. I'll roll up in plenty of time. It's no distance across the Meadow.

BADGER. Mrs. Warren—see them through the Cornfield, but stay near to the hedgerow. Some very peculiar Humans frequent the fields now-a-days.

RABBIT. I'll slip into Mrs. Burrow's place and watch from there.

BADGER. Mrs. Dark?

ROOK. Wha'?

BADGER. You stay here with me. Perhaps you'd be good enough now and again to soar up and tell me if they are coming.

ROOK. Pleasure.

HARE. So you're all leaving me. And nobody's anything to eat?

RABBIT. Not here, Mr. Fleet—but if you'd like to pop in after the Race, I've some lovely turnip-tops fresh nipped this morning.

HARE. Where there's a fill—Hare's away! See you later. Right, let's start the race.

BADGER. I've already started it!

HARE. Just give me the 'Ready, Steady—Go' and I'll show you what a real start is.

BADGER. Oh, very well. It's all most peculiar. On your marks. Ready —Steady—Go!

(And Hare, indeed, goes like the wind: up the aisle, and out).
Well, that's that. Off you go.

SQUIRREL. I'll report back here as soon as they've passed me.

HEDGEHOG. And me.

RABBIT. If Mr. Sloe isn't too far behind, I should be able to scurry back for the Finish.

BADGER. See you all here about tea-time.

DOG. Yes. All except poor old Torto. If Fleet keeps that up, he'll pass him before the first check point. See you later.

(They have made their various exits. Badger settles against Frog Rock for a snooze).

BADGER. Well, what do you think of it, Mrs. Dark?

ROOK. Wha'?

BADGER. What do you think of our Race between a Hare and a Tortoise?

ROOK. Deplorable!

BADGER. Oh, I don't know. Mr. Sloe might win.

ROOK. Boars might soar!

BADGER. I expect you're right. Ah well, it's a pleasant afternoon.

(He nods off. Rook stands stonily).
Number One Tabs Close . . .

CONTINUITY SCENE ONE:

Jackie and Robin enter to Centre. They are looking for, and calling, Basket.

They hold a short conference, and arrange to circle in opposite directions.

All this, of course, in human gobble-di-gook.

Jackie exits right: Robin exits left.

Seconds later, Mr. Sloe starts his cross from right. He has travelled a yard, when Mr. Fleet dashes past him.

Mr. Fleet 'double-takes,' then circles him three times at speed and shoots off left, making motorbike noises.

Mr. Sloe has maintained his steady .001 m.p.h., and, eventually, he too exits left.

Number One Tabs open on Scene Two.

Scene 2. The Bramble Thicket

A Ground-Row of brambles. Centre—a large Bramble Bush.

Hare dashes on from right.

HARE. I'm here! I'm first! Check me through, Mr. Slither.

(But the Grass Snake is not to be seen).

Mr. Slither? Where are you? Come on—can't stop: this is a race. Mr. Slither?

(He nips round the bush, poking his head into it to see; getting tangled and scratched).

Oo-ah. Mr. Slither! Where are you?—Oo, these brambles!

(He extricates one ear, badly snagged).

Well, if you're not . . .

(He hears Mr. Slither in the very centre: we don't).

Oh, there you are. Come on out, you're supposed to be an Official.

What?—Oh, are there?

(He listens).

You're right—there are humans about. Yes, you stay hidden. I'm off—Uh-uh!

(The voices of the girls have neared, calling to each other. Now they enter: Jackie Up-Right: Robin Up-Left.

Mr. Fleet is balked, and he squats Centre below the middle of the thicket, making himself very small).

JACKIE *(Asks if Robin has seen Basket).*

ROBIN *(Hasn't. Has Jackie?).*

JACKIE *(No. He is a naughty dog).*

ROBIN *(Agrees. She is going to give him a good spanking when they do find him—Oh, what lovely blackberries).*

JACKIE *(Oh-yes! She's going to have some).*

ROBIN *(As well).*

They come Centre Up-Stage of the Thicket: pick, exclaim and eat. They work round, coming nearer and nearer to Mr. Fleet. He peers this way and that: becomes increasingly worried, and, when the Girls are half-way round each side, starts—hurt as it does— to work his way into the middle of the bush.

The last we see is his agony-wracked face as his body is completely hidden, and the Girls join up Down-Centre.

(Mr. Basket is heard off-Left).

928

DOG. Mr. Slither! Anybody arrived yet? Have the runners passed you?

(He bounds on).

Whoops! My humans!

JACKIE AND ROBIN *(Are saying that Basket is there. He's a good dog: he's a bad dog. He's to come here at once, etc.).*

(There is much dodging as Basket evades them. What to the humans are playful yappings, are in fact messages to any animals in the vicinity—and, of course, us).

DOG. It's all right, Mr. Slither. I'll lead them off.

HARE. Do! Then come back and get me out of these thorns!

DOG. You in there, Fleet?—Oops! Missed me, duckie!—Don't go away.

HARE. How can I go away when I'm stuck!

DOG. Won't be long—Come on, my dears—chase me!

HARE. Be quick. That Torto-mi-jig will catch me up!

DOG. Don't fret. Here we go!

(A final dodge, and he runs off with the Girls in full cry after him. There are upheavals and strugglings in the centre of the bush, and we can—if we are just a bit malicious, and who of us isn't?— enjoy Mr. Fleet's predicament).

HARE. Humans! Always poking about in the Woodlands where they've no right to be—Owch!—It's all right for you, Mr. Slither, you snakes are little and thin, and haven't got long fur and ears. Oh, my beautiful fur: it's coming out in great tufts! Oh, my lovely ears: they'll be cut to pieces!

(Mr. Basket enters left).

DOG. Here we are then. Lost them again. Now, what's to do?

HARE. Get me out of this tangle, that's what's to do! Come on, hold back some of these briars.

DOG. Right-ho.

(He essays).

Ooch, my paw!

(He tries again, but is defeated by the thorns).

Hold on, Fleet. Oo-ah! Heh, I'm getting caught up myself!

HARE. Will you get me out! Ow!

DOG. I'm doing my best. These thorns hurt. Yip!

HARE. I'm supposed to be in a race. D'ah!

DOG.   You'll beat him easily. A-a-ah!

HARE.   Not if I'm stuck in here. Gee-hup!

DOG.   Well, you shouldn't have gone in. Yi-yi-yi!

HARE.   I had to to escape from your humans. O-oo!

DOG.   They wouldn't have hurt you—Ah-no! It's no good, Fleet. I'm getting scratched to pieces. You'll have to get yourself out.

(He sits biting thorns out of his person).

HARE.   It's your fault, you get me out. Ee-ooo!

(Tortoise enters Down Right at the same sub-steady-pace).

DOG.   Here's Mr. Sloe, now.

HARE.   He can get me out. The thorns can't hurt him.

TORTOISE.   Hello, Mr. Basket. Check me through.

DOG.   Stop a minute, Torto. Mr. Fleet's stuck in the brambles.

TORTOISE.   Mustn't stop. It's a race. The only way to win races—or anything else—is to keep at it.

HARE.   But I'm stuck! Help!

DOG.   If you could just make a hole in the bush. Wouldn't delay you very long.

TORTOISE.   I have to keep going, Mr. Basket. I can't make up time like other creatures.

DOG.   But Mr. Fleet will die in there. This is an emergency.

HARE.   Please, Mr. Sloe. Nobody can get me out but you. Unless a male human comes along—and then I should be for the cooking pot!

DOG.   To oblige me, Mr. Sloe.

(Tortoise now left of Centre, circles to come below the bush).

TORTOISE.   If it is really a matter of life and death, then of course I will help if I can.

DOG.   Good for you. Can you force a tunnel through to him?

HARE.   Just stamp on the brambles. Hurry!

TORTOISE.   Very well.

(He opens up a hole with his fore feet and one hind foot, to the encouragement of the other two. Mr. Fleet attempts to come out but is still held).

HARE.   It's not big enough. I'm still caught up!

DOG.   Could you crash in backwards, Torto, and crush them down?

930

TORTOISE. That might do it. But if I get on my back, I cannot get up again. I'll manage this way. If at first you don't succeed, try, try again.

HARE. Do be quick, you silly old faggot! You're slower than a month of Sundays.

DOG. That's a fine way to talk to some-one who is doing his best to help you!

TORTOISE (*Amiably*). Slow but sure. Slow but sure, I hope, young Hare. Here we go.

(*He tramples well into the bush. With much scrambling and help from Basket, Mr. Fleet crawls out*).

HARE. I've done it!

DOG. That's it, then, now the race can go on.

HARE. I'm off!

DOG. Just a moment—you ought to let Mr. Sloe have a start.

HARE. He refused a start.

DOG. Yes—but now, if he hadn't stopped to help you, he would have been well away.

HARE. He should have thought of that! His trouble is, that he thinks about as slowly as he runs.

DOG. But it's not fair!

HARE. All's Hare in love and war! Ta-ta. I'll tell them he'll be late!

(*He runs off, Down-left*).

DOG. Of all the ungrateful selfish cheats!

TORTOISE. He's only young, Mr. Basket.

DOG. I'll 'young' him!

TORTOISE. Don't worry. The Race isn't over yet.

DOG. You did him a great kindness. He should reward you!

TORTOISE. If we only do kindnesses in hope of reward, they are no longer kindnesses—I'll just keep going. A lot can happen between here and the Winning Post.

(*He exits Down-left*).

DOG. I hope you do win, Mr. Sloe. I'll take the short cut to the River Bank. See you there.

(*He runs off Up-left*).

Number One Tabs Close.

CONTINUITY SCENE TWO:

Mr. Fleet enters from a rear auditorium door.

He makes his way down, unhurried but vigorous: jogging, doing training exercises, shadow-boxing and pausing to declaim at intervals . . .

HARE. I am the fastest runner on earth! I am also very beautiful . . . No animal can beat me. I can out-run and out-smart the lot of them . . .

I wish one of them had even half my prowess. It gets boring winning so easily all the time . . .

I can lick them all . . .

I can see further: hear further: and run further than the rest of them put together . . .

And I am pretty, too . . .

(And if he gets any understandable back-chat from his audience, he must ad-lib further conceits to full bent, stopping short only of promoting a full-scale riot.

Number One Tabs open on Scene 3).

And here we are, Check Point Two—first, as usual.

THE GREAT CROSS-COUNTRY RACE

A Bank Ground-Row.

A Fisherman, surrounded by paraphernalia and creature comforts, including a full picnic spread, is reclining asleep in his little canvas chair. His rod is propped, and the line dangles into the river.

Mr. Fleet makes his way on to the set with some caution, but soon realizes that this human is sound asleep.

HARE. Ah, a male human. The one that's always wetting worms.

(Mr. Paddle's head appears above the bank).

RAT. P-sst!—P-sst!

HARE. I wondered where you were, Paddle.

RAT. He's been here all afternoon, the nuisance. It's all right to pass through if you go softly.

HARE. No hurry. Old Fat-legs is miles behind.

RAT. You'd better not stop though. He might catch you up.

HARE. Let him. I can run rings round him. —What have we here?

(He investigates the picnic boxes).

Hello, hello—I do believe . . . Yes, lettuce sandwiches! And fresh tomatoes! Oh, very good! And what's this?

(Salad cream).

Milk?

(He sits).

RAT. No. They put it on their greens. It's pretty awful stuff—not fit for animals.

HARE. Have you tried it?

RAT. Once. One of them left a container lying around, and I had a lick. Made me quite ill.

HARE *(Sampling).* Oh, I don't know. Rather pleasant. Of course, you lower River Swimmers haven't the cultivated tastes of we Hares.

RAT. It won't do you any good.

HARE. Fiddle! If it's good enough for humans, it's good enough for me.

(He liberally smothers the sandwiches with salad cream—and salt—and pepper, and eats greedily).

RAT. What about the Race?

HARE. What race?—Ah delicious! I always knew we Hares should

933

eat something better than rabbit food—I can win that walking backwards . . . And special water in a container!

(Pop—which fizzes hugely when he un-stoppers it).

Oops!—Oh, very palatable!

RAT. I don't think that that is good for animals, either.

HARE. Not for you lower orders, certainly.

(Mr. Basket enters Right).

DOG. You're here, are you?

RAT. Not too loud—it's asleep.

DOG. Oh, him! What's his idea, wetting worms all the time?

RAT. He thinks the Under Water Swimmers will eat the worms and get caught.

DOG. Ridiculous!—Heh, Fleet, you ought not to hang around if you want to win.

HARE. Is Fat-legs still plodding on?

DOG. Yes. And he can't be far behind.

HARE. Plenty of time when he catches up. I'd give you one of these, but I'm afraid they're too delicious to waste on you.

DOG. Thank you very much!

RAT. He'll be ill.

HARE. Dry up, wet-head!

(He finds an apple—creams, salts and peppers it: then gobbles up).

RAT. Not that I mind his helping himself to the male human's food. Serve him right.

DOG. He's not doing any harm.

RAT. He would if I didn't stop him.

DOG. Stop him what?

RAT. Catching the Under Water Swimmers.

DOG. You mean to say that they really eat the worms?

RAT. Oh, yes. Especially the Tiddlers. You can't tell them. I spend half my day unhooking them, then tying on weeds, or sticking the hook under stones.

DOG. To stop him coming back?

RAT. Yes. But he doesn't seem to care. Comes back just the same. But I've a special surprise for him to-day.

DOG. What's that?

(Tortoise has entered the auditorium, and is coming down an aisle).

RAT. Here he is! Here's Mr. Sloe!

DOG. Come on. Torto—run up!

RAT *(To Hare).* You'd better be on your way.

HARE. I'll just finish this.

(A huge slice of cake which he also salad-creams, salts and peppers. He washes it down with the last of the Pop).

DOG. Come on! You've caught him up!

RAT. He's going to pass you here!

DOG. Thunder on, Torto!

RAT. Mr. Fleet, you must run now.

HARE. If you think so. But there's really no need.

(He rises—and is suddenly gripped by a tummy pain).

I can't.

RAT. Can't what?

HARE. Run. Oh, my stomach!

DOG. Come on, Torto! Come on!

RAT. Run, Mr. Fleet—run!

HARE. I don't feel very well!

RAT. I told you not to be greedy.

DOG. You've got him, Torto!

HARE. I'm dying!

RAT. No you're not. It's only tummy-ache with over-stuffing yourself. It'll work off. Run.

(Hare staggers a few paces, and stops again. Tortoise reaches the set, from right).

HARE. We ought to call a rest for a few minutes. All competitors.

(He rolls in agony).

RAT. Mr. Sloe, will you agree to a rest for a few minutes?

TORTOISE. Sorry, Mr. Paddle, must keep going. Check me through, please.

RAT. But Mr. Fleet—has a bad stitch.

HARE. It's not a stitch—it's my appendix! We Hares have more miles of appendix than any . . . O-oo! I'm dying!

935

Dog. Hard luck! On you go, Torto.

Tortoise. I expect he'll get over it.

Dog. See you at the Grassy Bank. Don't forget to look for the arrow.

Tortoise. I won't.

(He exits, Down-left).

Rat. Get up, Mr. Fleet. Keep moving and it'll wear off.

(He helps Hare move around).

If you'd kept running properly as I told you, this would never have happened.

Hare. I was hungry.

Dog. You have to eat after races; not while they are on.

Rat. That's better. Is it going?

Hare. A bit.

Rat. Fine thing if Mr. Sloe beats our champion! You'll never live it down.

Hare. I'll beat him. I can catch him and pass him, even if I am critically ill. We Hares are the bravest . . .

Rat. Never mind all that now—just get after him.

Hare. You watch me. I can beat him on two paws.

(He staggers off holding his tummy).

Dog. He's the boastingest animal in the Woodlands.

Rat. He can be very aggravating at times.

Dog. My little female humans' female parent says that 'Pride comes before a Fall' whenever they start swanking.

Rat. Well, he certainly swanks, does Mr. Fleet.

Dog. And if he doesn't beat Torto, he'll surely fall. Come on, let's cut across to the Grassy Bank.

Rat. You go on, Mr. Basket, I've a little job to do here.

Dog. With the male human?

Rat *(Tapping his nose significantly).* I'll cure him for good of wetting worms near my place—I'll see you at the finish.

Dog. Right—Oh, keep out of sight for a moment. My little female humans will be passing. Mustn't lose them altogether.

Rat. I'll pop in the river 'til they've gone.

(He nips over the bank, then his head re-appears. Dog calls right).

Dog. Heh, you two! Hello! I'm here—can you hear me? Come on.

(We hear the Girls distantly: their indefatigable calls and whistles. They approach. Dog exits Up-left. They run on, and check at the Fisherman).

JACKIE *(Wonders whether or not to ask him if he's seen a dog).*

ROBIN *(Thinks he looks as though he's been asleep a long time. He might be angry).*

DOG *(Off).* Come on! Come on! This way. Find me!

JACKIE *(He's over there!).*

ROBIN *(Yes. Come on!).*

They call and whistle as they run off.

Rat shakes his head, amused. He comes to the Fisherman's side and cautiously hauls—not reels—in the line as . . .

Number One Tabs close.

CONTINUITY SCENE THREE:

Tortoise enters the auditorium, and ploughs on steadily.

As he is nearing the Pass Door (or steps) to the stage, Hare reels in. To great groanings and puffings, he struggles on at nothing like his best pace but, even so, much faster than Tortoise.

Tortoise achieves the stage.

Hare passes him Down-Centre: his look of malicious triumph somewhat marred by grimaces of pain.

He may not be the most lovable of Hares—but at least he's game.

He exits Down-Right.

Tortoise, unmoved, follows to exit some long seconds later.

Number One Tabs open on Scene 4.

Centre—a Grassy Bank.

Stuck on the top is a crude stick arrow pointing Left.

Waiting and enjoying the afternoon sun, is Hedgehog.

Groans presage the entrance Down-Right of Hare.

HEDGEHOG. Somebody coming!—This way: here's the arrow.—You, Mr. Fleet. Well, I'm not surprised, I must confess.

HARE. Oo-oh!

HEDGEHOG. What's the matter?

HARE. I've been poisoned!

HEDGEHOG. Poisoned!

HARE. That rat Paddle. Made me eat some human-type food.

HEDGEHOG. But why?

HARE. How should I know why! Doesn't want me to win, I suppose.

HEDGEHOG. This is dreadful! It's your tummy?

HARE. Tummy, and all over.

HEDGEHOG. Could you manage a raw egg?

HARE. Would it help?

HEDGEHOG. Very good for settling an upset tummy. Not only that, all the best runners suck raw eggs.

HARE. Is that a fact!

HEDGEHOG. Oh yes. Makes them go like the wind.

HARE. Does it?

HEDGEHOG. Most assuredly. Luckily, I have one. Found it by the hay-stack, freshly laid this morning. Very hard to come by these days with all the hens living in blocks of flats. Years since I found a full clutch of eggs in the open.

HARE. I'll try anything once.

HEDGEHOG. Better come to my house. You are all right for time, I expect. Mr. Sloe will be miles behind.

HARE. He's not! I've only just managed to pass him.

HEDGEHOG. I am surprised! How does that come about?

HARE. First he pushed me in the Bramble Thicket, then he wouldn't agree to a halt when I was nearly dying.

HEDGEHOG. Most unsporting. Well, come on quickly and have this raw egg, and you'll be as right as rain and twice as fast. Oh—do you suck or dip?

HARE. Do I what?

HEDGEHOG. Suck the egg through a hole, or break it and dip your paw in it and lick it? I suck myself.

HARE. How do I know? I've never had a raw egg.

HEDGEHOG. A treat in store. You'd be a dipper, I should think. You haven't got a sucking face.

HARE. It's a very pretty face, let me tell you!

HEDGEHOG. Oh, yes, yes, quite. Nothing personal. But I'm sure you're a dipper. I'll open it for you. Come on.

(He leads off Up-Left. Hare sees the arrow, has a thought, and calls . . .).

HARE. Ow-ch! Be with you in a minute, H. H. Got a thorn in my paw.

HEDGEHOG *(Off)*. You are in the wars.

HARE *(Lifting the arrow and reversing it)*. And that will do more than slow old Fat-legs down—it'll send him backwards!

(He dusts his paws, and treats us to a few well-chosen, self-laudatory observations).

Not only are we Hares gay, open and frank—we are extremely cunning! . . . If you can't beat 'em—cheat 'em! There are two sorts of animals in the Woodlands: the Hares and the Squares . . . You may have noticed that besides being fantastically fast and incredibly clever, I am also preternaturally pretty! . . . We Hares . . .

HEDGEHOG *(Off)*. It's ready, Mr. Fleet. Come along.

HARE. Coming old friend.

(To us).

Sucker!—Coming, no great hurry

(To himself).

—now!

(He exits, Up-Left. Dog bounces on Up-Right calling).

DOG. Anybody about? It's me—Basket!

HEDGEHOG *(Off)*. I'm here, Mr. Basket.

(His head appears).

I'm just giving Mr. Fleet some nutricious raw egg.

DOG. Oh. Mr. Sloe gone through?

HEDGEHOG. Not yet.

939

(His head withdraws).

Come in for a bit. We will hear him.

DOG. Right.

(He 'takes' the arrow: weighs it up . . .).

Those dreamy Shrews! They can't see for looking! Give them the simplest job and they get it wrong! Good thing I spotted it— Mr. Sloe would be sent back!

(He turns the arrow to point in the original and correct—Left).

And that Hare can't afford to hang about if he wants to win. Where are you?

(He exits Up-Left.

Tortoise enters Down-Right. He has ample time to study the arrow as he approaches it . . .).*

TORTOISE. Mr. Spiney? Mr. Basket? I'm checking through.

HEDGEHOG *(Off)*. It's Mr. Sloe!

(He enters).

DOG *(Off)*. He's here! He's here!

(He enters).

Come on, Torto! Thunder on! Everything all right?

TORTOISE. Doing very nicely, thank you. Have just got my second wind.

HEDGEHOG *(Calling)*. He's here, Mr. Fleet! Hurry!

HARE *(Off)*. Has he followed the arrow?

HEDGEHOG. Yes. He's on his way. You must get running again!

DOG. Go on, Torto—you've passed him again.

(Tortoise exits Down-Left).

HARE *(Off)*. Don't fuss, H. H. It's a walk-over.

HEDGEHOG. But it won't be if you just sit there!

HARE. Coming.

(He enters quite slowly: yawns, stretches and goes through his limbering exercises).

Ah, I feel much better now. Very hospitable of you. Your only egg, too!

HEDGEHOG. That's quite all right—but do hurry.

HARE. Followed the arrow, did he?

DOG. Of course. Mr. Sloe may take his time, but he's not soft.

HARE. Oh, I agree. Hard as rocks, in fact. Especially his head!

HEDGEHOG. You really must try to catch him, Mr. Fleet. You'll be beaten!

HARE. First catch your Hare.

DOG. What?

HARE. Nothing. Family joke. Right, then—start me off.

DOG. You've already started.

HARE. Well, this is a fresh start. Just watch me fly. Hare to-day and gone to-morrow.

DOG. Mad as a May Queen!

HEDGEHOG. Do be quick!

HARE. So old Fat-legs followed the arrow, did he!

HEDGEHOG. Yes, yes! Hours ago!

HARE. Set me off then.

(He studies the arrow, and takes up a sprint-crouch-facing the wrong way).

DOG. You're facing the wrong—

HEDGEHOG. Onyourmarks—readysteadygo!

(Hare dashes off—Down-Right! The others stare, appalled).

DOG. He's gone the wrong way!

HEDGEHOG. Oh dear! Oh, dearie me!

DOG. He's going back!

HEDGEHOG. Oh my pins and needles!

DOG. He'll end up at the River Bank again!

HEDGEHOG. Mr. Sloe will win! Turn him back, Mr. Basket! Turn him back!

DOG. I'll try, but if he keeps up that speed, I'll never do it. What was in that egg!—Heh, Fleet! Fleet! You're going the wrong way!

(He dashes off in pursuit).

HEDGEHOG. Oh dear, oh dear! I don't know what Mr. Sett will have to say about all this! Whatever made Mr. Fleet make a mistake like that!

Number One Tabs close.

CONTINUITY SCENE FOUR:

Hare rushes across from Down-Left to exit Down-Right (or steps), and up the aisle, taking the reverse route of Continuity Three.

Dog follows breathlessly, calling on him to stop, turn back, etc.

Number One Tabs open on Scene 5.

SCENE 5. THE RIVER BANK AGAIN

The Fisherman is still asleep.

All is peaceful.

The Girls wander on from Left, disconsolate.

JACKIE *(Is upset because they've lost touch with Mr. Basket again).*

ROBIN *(Is tired: doesn't know where to look now).*

JACKIE *(Where are they, anyway?).*

ROBIN *(Thinks they should wake the Fisherman and ask).*

JACKIE *(You do it).*

ROBIN *(No, you).*

JACKIE *(Doesn't like to).*

ROBIN *(Dares her).*

JACKIE *(Shall she?).*

ROBIN *(Yes).*

After much to-ing and fro-ing, Jackie reaches the point of shaking the Fisherman's shoulder.

A little bell at the top of the rod rings sharply. The line runs out.

The Girls retreat.

The Fisherman wakes, and plays the line, exclaiming with excitement and anticipation.

He eventually reels in—an old boot.

He is furious, and turns to see the Girls stifling their giggles.

Rat's head pops up above the bank. He is chortling.

The Fisherman throws the boot from him, and re-baits the hook.

Rat's head goes down.

The line is cast. Almost immediately: another bite.

He reels in an old frying-pan.

Rat's head pops up.

The Fisherman hurls it away: rebaits.

Rat's head goes down.

Another bite. An old push-chair wheel.

Rat up.

The Fisherman stamps on it, and it is a good thing that we cannot understand human gobble-di-gook as some of the words are not quite nice.

942

The Young Ladies have covered their ears.

Still grumbling, he throws the rod down and decides to take solace in food.

He finds the sandwiches—pop—cake—gone; getting angrier each time. He accuses the Girls who make vehement denials.

He has no proof, and is waving his finger before their noses when Hare dashes on, and cannons into him, sending him sprawling.

Hare is up first, darting round in amazement).

HARE. Great hairy hind-legs—I'm going the wrong-way!

(He belts off, passing Dog who skids on.

The Fisherman rises, raging. He grabs his landing-net. Dog manages to halt and change direction. The Girls exclaim and give chase.

The Fisherman succeeds in getting the net over Mr. Basket's head, but Mr. B. doesn't take kindly to it. He tears round in a circle, and centrifugal force spins the Fisherman to the River's edge where he teeters, unbalanced.

Mr. Basket runs off, followed by the Girls.

The Fisherman topples into the River. There comes a most satisfactory, amplified splash.

Rat comes over the bank, crosses to the spot and peers down . . .

Number One Tabs close quickly.

CONTINUITY SCENE FIVE:

On the now familiar auditorium track.

Mr. Fleet rushes through, followed by Mr. Basket, followed by The Girls.

Number One Tabs open on Scene 6.

SCENE 6. THE GRASSY BANK AGAIN

Mr. Spiney is just sitting.

Mr. Fleet tears across.

HEDGEHOG. Where . . . wha! . . . Mr. Fle . . .

(Mr. Basket tears across).

I say . . . wha! . . . who . . . eh . . .

(The Girls tear across).

Who! What . . . wait . . . I don't . . .

(He is alone again).

They've *all* been eating raw eggs!—Do you know, I do believe they must have found a clutch of eggs back there—perhaps a whole clutch of clutches!

(His little nose wrinkles avidly, and he sets off to explore, Down-Right).

Number One Tabs close.

CONTINUITY SCENE SIX:

Tortoise enters from the Auditorium door furthest from the stage, and undulates on.

He is not visibly distressed although he does mop his brow, but without, however, faltering in his ponderous rhythm.

As he nears the stage, Number One Tabs open on Scene 7.

(If the interval is taken here, Continuity Six may be omitted.)

SCENE 7. MR. BRUSH'S TREE

Ground Row—distant hedge.

Centre—the Tree. It has a very wide trunk, well scarred with old initials, hearts and arrows and the like.

Squirrel is Right of the Tree, looking off Down-Right.

George and Maude, young rustic humans, are taking their first 'walk out.'

Maude enters first, demurely scuffing the ground. George follows a few paces behind. He picks up a stoutish stick and, with an effort, breaks it.

Squirrel starts, sees them, and disappears Up-stage of the Tree. In a flash his head pokes round the trunk some feet up, observing them.

Maude gazes at George admiringly.

MAUDE *(Thinks he's ever-so strong).*

GEORGE *(Is duly modest, but suggests she feel his biceps).*

MAUDE *(Does. O-oo!).*

(George hurls a stone into the far distance. Then he does a hand-stand—(a cart-wheel? . . . at least a few vigorous press-ups)

Maude isn't looking—but she is.

Squirrel is rather exasperated.

Tortoise enters Down-Right, sees the humans, and sinks to the ground.

Maude sits at the foot of the Tree, and commences to make a chain of flowers. George, to one side, digs the ground with his toe.

There is a bit of an impasse all round.

Finally, George catches Maude's eye and absentmindedly—he's only been thinking about it all day—sits by her.

And there they sit. Not even any gobble-di-gook.

A very concerned Squirrel at last takes a chance).

SQUIRREL. P-sst!

TORTOISE. That you, Mr. Brush?

SQUIRREL. Yes. I'm up here. I think it would be safe if you crept across very quietly.

TORTOISE. Are you sure? I don't want to land up in a strange garden.

SQUIRREL. I don't think this sort of human is very interested in gardening.

945

TORTOISE. Well, if you're sure . . .

(He Indian-crawls on all fours across the stage. And we thought he was slow before!).

SQUIRREL. Go ahead. I must say I'm surprised and quite delighted to see you here first. Where's Mr. Fleet?

TORTOISE. I'm not sure. He tends to get diverted.

SQUIRREL. Good luck. Only two more check points, and then the finish.

TORTOISE. Thank you, Mr. Brush.

SQUIRREL. Press on. They are a bother, this sort of human, but I've never seen them harm a Woodlander.

TORTOISE. No?

SQUIRREL. But they do terrible damage to my Tree.

TORTOISE. Oh?

SQUIRREL. They cut the bark to pieces. Mr. Basket says they are marking their names.

TORTOISE. On a tree!

SQUIRREL. Yes, with knives.

TORTOISE. They are the oddest creatures, humans.

SQUIRREL. As a matter of fact, I think these are what Mr. Basket calls 'Soppy Dates'. It's a word he got from his little female humans. They are a special kind, anyway.

TORTOISE. They haven't moved—yet they must have seen me.

(He is three-quarter way across).

SQUIRREL. I doubt it.

(George has a clasp-knife out, and is repeatedly throwing it into the ground).

TORTOISE. I say, I don't like this! He has a weapon!

SQUIRREL. I thought as much! It means he's going to start cutting my Tree any second! Oh, I do wish the young humans wouldn't cut trees and break branches and rob nests! They just don't think you know.

TORTOISE. Well, I'm glad the knife is not for me.

SQUIRREL. It's all right now. I should get on your hind legs.

TORTOISE. Yes.

(He does so).

That's better: now I can break into a trot again.

946

(Well . . . all speed is comparative).

Goodbye for now, Mr. Brush. Thank you for your help.

(He is nearly off).

SQUIRREL. See you at the finish. Good show.

(George rises and starts carving a heart and arrow. Maude, quite oblivious—yeah!—chains on.

Hare dashes through the auditorium on to the set, and falls exhausted).

HARE. I'm here! Check me.

(He pants madly).

Oo! Ah! Ooo—what a run! Mr. Brush?

SQUIRREL. Here, Fleet.

HARE. Ah, up there, eh? Has old Fat-legs passed?

SQUIRREL. Mr. Sloe has just this minute gone.

HARE. That's all right. I've caught up. I knew I could. Can stop for a breather. Mind if I rest against your Tree?

(He turns to the Tree, and for the first time sees George and Maude. They take not the slightest notice of him, But . . . he does a cartoon nip behind the trunk. There he was: there he isn't. His head, now directly below Mr. Brush's, looks out and round).

HARE. Why didn't you warn me?

SQUIRREL. No need, they can't see you.

HARE. What are you? Some kind of nut! I nearly squatted on the long-haired one!

SQUIRREL. Wouldn't have made any difference. They've no senses, that sort. As a matter of fact, the long-haired one is sitting on Mr. Croaker at this very moment!

HARE. Old Froggy Croaker! What's he doing here?

SQUIRREL. Came to watch the Race go by.

HARE. A fine view of it he's going to get from there!

SQUIRREL. Talking of the Race, hadn't you better get cracking?

HARE. I can catch old Fat-legs anytime. Let's watch these two a bit. We Hares are very interested in manology.

SQUIRREL. What in trees, is that?

HARE. Study of the humans. They are very simple, of course—you can lift things from under their noses—but interesting.

(Dog arrives, breathless).

947

DOG. There you are! I'll give it to you, Fleet, you can certainly move when you do run. My poor little female humans are miles behind again—What's the hold-up now?

HARE. Just observing the antics of these humans.

DOG. Oh, Soppy Dates. No need to worry about them. Watch.

(He bounds up to Maude, and about George's legs. They carve and chain on: from time to time staring into each others eyes, and then turning away bashfully).

Heh, Soppy Dates! I'm here. Give us a pat, then. Throw a stick— I'll bite you! Have a piece out of your leg! G-rr!

(He returns to the others).

Oh, a real pair of Soppy Dates, these two! You see?—Reynard and his Horses and Hounds could charge through here. These humans wouldn't notice: not when they're like this.

HARE. Well, course me up the Downs! Blind as Bunnies!

(He moves to George and peers into his face).

How d'ye do!

(No reaction.

Maude has finished her chain, and puts it on her head.

She joins George who stands back from his handiwork.

More bashful simpers.

Mr. Fleet studies the markings).

HARE. What's this, then?

DOG. It'll be their names.

HARE. What for?

DOG. I don't know. It's just something Soppy Dates do.

SQUIRREL *(Joining them)*. Well, I wish they wouldn't! My poor trees! How would they like it if we scratched our names on them!

(Maude and George re-sit).

HARE. She's squatted on him again!

DOG. On who?

HARE. One of the Frogs.

SQUIRREL. I hope he had the sense to get under a root.

HARE. What happens now?

DOG. You watch. This is the bit that makes my little female humans wag their tails.

SQUIRREL. They haven't got tails!

Dog. Just a saying. They do it with their mouths. It's called giggling. Watch.

(The Three Animals squat Up-stage above the Pair. The five heads are in a group: Hare Up-centre between George and Maude: He has squeezed between them and the tree-trunk).

George *(Suddenly asks Maude to give him a kiss).*

Maude *(Won't: and thinks he's awful!).*

George *(Go on).*

Maude *(Perhaps just one, then).*

(She proffers her cheek. George closes his eyes and plants a smacker on it).

Hare. What in bunny-burrows is he doing!

Squirrel. Washing her . . .?

Hare. Isn't she big enough to wash herself!

Dog. That's the tail-wagging bit.

Hare. But why does he do it?

Dog. Because she's pretty.

Hare. Pretty! That creature! She's got no proper nibbling teeth to start with!

Squirrel. And no tail!

Hare. Nor any ears worth mentioning!

Squirrel. She's as bald as old Croaker!—I do hope he's all right.

Hare. No fur at all except this bit of mane. Pretty! Old Fat-legs isn't what I'd call pretty, but compared with humans, he's beautiful!

Dog. Yes, but she's pretty to him. Only one human can possibly think that another human is pretty.

Hare. Well I'll be jugged! Pretty—these specimens!

(He leans between them to have a last incredulous examination just when, two pairs of eyes closed in ecstasy, they turn to exchange a mutual kiss.

Hare gets kissed on both cheeks.

He leaps up).

Jumping buck-rabbits—I've been washed!—That does it! No more manology for me. I'm off.

Squirrel. About time, too.

Dog. Mr. Sloe will be at the Cornfield by now. If you waste any more time, he's going to win.

HARE. Win! Him! Don't make me wag my tail! We Hares are not only the . . .

SQUIRREL. Oh, do go, Fleet!

HARE. I'm off. Give me a start.

DOG. Great Danes preserve us! On your mark. Ready—steady—Go!

(Hare exits at speed.

Poor Jackie and Robin: we hear their calls and whistles for Mr. Basket).

DOG. Me too. I'll be glad when this race is over. My little humans are very tired. It's time I took them home. See you.

(He goes).

(Squirrel climbs behind his Tree.

George kisses Maude's cheek. The Girls enter. They giggle quietly. They cough. George and Maude shoot to their feet, and leap apart).

JACKIE *(Excuses herself and asks have they seen a dog?).*

ROBIN *(A large, playful, brown—or whatever—dog?).*

GEORGE *(Hasn't seen any dog. Has Maude?).*

MAUDE *(No, she hasn't. Have they lost one?).*

JACKIE *(Yes: sort of).*

ROBIN *(They've been looking all day).*

MAUDE *(Is very sorry, but they haven't seen him).*

GEORGE *(Says that they will keep a sharp look out).*

JACKIE *(Is very sorry to have bothered them).*

ROBIN *(Thank them very much).*

MAUDE *(No bother).*

GEORGE *(We weren't doing anything important. Goodbye).*

MAUDE *(Hopes he'll turn up. Goodbye).*

JACKIE AND ROBIN *(Thanks again. Goodbye).*

(With a last look back and a suppressed giggle, they exit Down-Left.

George and Maude are back in square one—toe scuffing. But not for long.

Maude suddenly sits again.

Mr. Brush grimaces: 'Oh, no'! Poor old Froggy Croaker.

Number One Tabs close.

THE GREAT CROSS-COUNTRY RACE

Tortoise enters the auditorium.

Hare runs in immediately, passes him, halts and returns to him.

He strolls ostentatiously by Tortoise's side.

HARE. Still think you can win, Fat-legs?

TORTOISE. A race is never won until it's lost.

HARE. You'll be telling me next that a carrot in the paw is worth two in the garden.

TORTOISE. I might well. We also have a saying at home—'Do not count your turtles before they are hatched.' Had you thought about that?

HARE. Frankly, no, old Egg-head. 'Hares not to reason why: Hares but to do them in the eye!'—Herrick.

TORTOISE. Herrick?

HARE. Bob-Bob Herrick—the finest of our harey poets—Ah well, it's a nice day for a stroll, but I'd better be getting on.

TORTOISE. Yes. And, if you'll take my advice, don't dawdle anywhere. Remember curiosity killed the cat.

HARE. Horse radish! Care to start me off?

TORTOISE. Certainly, if you wish.

(They are about two-thirds down the Theatre. Hare stops, and limbers up. Tortoise moves on. Between each word, he takes several steps; he is not deliberately holding up—it's just his speed of speech).

On . . .

HARE *(With whimsical superiority to those around him: although we can all hear).* He hasn't forgotten. It just takes the poor old thing a bit of time to articulate.

TORTOISE. . . . your . . .

HARE. I told you he'd get around to it. He'd be all right in Sunday School telling a story—you wouldn't get out until Friday!

TORTOISE. . . . marks.

HARE. Ah, now we're getting somewhere! I'd better think about it, I suppose. He'll give the 'Ready' in the next ten minutes.

TORTOISE. Ready.

(He has reached the Apron).

HARE. There we are, what did I tell you! It's a good job he doesn't stutter.

951

(He calls out).

Right-o-, Flash—I'm ready.

TORTOISE. Steady.

HARE. 'Steady,' no less! If I stay 'Steady' any longer, I'll take root. This is it—any half-hour now, and we're off. Wait for it . . . wait for it . . .

TORTOISE *(Two-thirds across the stage).* Go!

HARE. We're off!

(He belts down the aisle, flies across the stage passing Tortoise, and off Down-Left).

Tortoise continues, and finally goes from view.

Number One Tabs open on Scene 8.

SCENE 8. THE CORNFIELD

Ground-row—a Stone Wall.

Centre—a stuke or bale of straw, with two others Up-stage of it, RC and LC.

All is peaceful.

From over the wall come the sounds of a flock of sheep engaged in desultory conversation. On differing frequencies, and over-lapping each other, we can make out some of the chit-chat. All the 'a' vowels are in triplicate.

VARIOUS SHEEP *(Off).* Marvelous day, Martin.
Marvelous.
Ma-mma! Mamma-a-a!
Drat that lamb! Here, darling.
Ah, basking, Grandpa?
Admiring the panorama, lad. Just admiring the panorama.
Barbara! Barbara—don't stray too far!
Yes, Ma.
Fancy Agatha's Bartholomew being half-black!
Mark! Where is that lamb? Mark!
Here Ma, gamboling with Sam.
Afternoon, Arthur. Balmy again.
Balmy as Bath, Bartrum. Balmy as Bath.
Pappa, Pappa—can we play in the straw?
Nay, lad! Whatever would Farmer Black say!
Ah, Pa-a-a! Etcetera-a-a- . . .

A raucous car-horn, door slams and human gobble-di-gook, off Left.

Silence over the wall: then:—

Alarm! Alarm! Mark! Barbara! Ma! Ma! Alarm! Mark! Ma! Back! Back! Barbara! Ma! Ma! A car—no harm! Ma! Ma! etc.

The Urban-Notcouths descend on the Cornfield. Mr. U-N in T-shirt and jockey cap: Mrs. U-N in eye-searing slacks—'slacks', no man-made fibre was ever intended for this strain.

Miss U-N, a teen-age peroxide brunette, and Master U-N. We can tell Brando from Sophia: Brando wears the three-inch heels and the hair net.

They express their various satisfactions with the Sylvan spot— and dump their gear. Picnickers!

Brando jumps over the stuke Up-Right, and wrecks it. He looks over the wall.

He says that there is a load of crazy sheep. He yells at them. He throws stones: throwing further as the panic stricken flock— we hear—rush down the hill.

953

Various Sheep *(wildly off)*. 'Alarm! Alarm! Back! Back! Martin! Barbara! Paronoia, that's what it is! Martin! Ma! Ma! Go far! Far!!

Brando follows with a few 'Pows!' from his imaginary six-shooter, then joins the others who are going to eat—or have a quick 'Nosh-Up' as they are so quaintly phrasing it, if only we understood English—before pitching the tents.

The—perhaps it is a good word, at that—'Nosh' is spread. Sandwiches, cake, chocolate all tastefully wrapped in newsprint, tissue and polythene: all manner of tinned stuff which U-N Senior struggles to open; fruit; bottles of beer and pop. And, to prove how genteel we really all are, Mrs. U-N is issuing paper plates and napkins.

However, as these seem to stand between him and the actual 'Nosh,' Brando's first action is to skim the plates around the field, crumple the napkins into balls and kick them.

They all start and, as they don't want to fill their nice car with rubbish, throw the wrappings over their shoulders.

And so it goes on. Bottles, cans, paper, skins, cores: all are strewn in profusion during the Scene.

But back to the beginning . . .

Sophia can't eat without music: she can't do anything without music, if it comes to that, and, with a half stripped banana held delicately between her neon-pink tinted lips, tunes her transistor.

'If music be the food of love'—then this is the very stuff for a Nosh-Up.

The Young Urban-Notcouths dance. And even the Urban-Notcouth Seniors seem to derive some stimulous. The Tempo of noshing, discarding of hygienic wrappers, and handing out of goodies, speeds up.

Hare rushes on, and takes cover behind the RC stuke. He has not been seen. His head pops up to reconnoitre. He tip-toes in double-time to above the stuke LC. Up comes his head again.

The music and the dancing fascinate him. It was only by an oversight that he forgot to mention that Hares are the nimblest, the most rhythmic, indefatigable etc., etc. . . . But as we knew this from our animal books, and are about to see it proven beyond doubt, nothing is lost.

Mr. Fleet dances. He achieves a remarkable union of his own Moonlight pas de Hare and the current rave as executed by Sophia and Brando.

He is so 'sent' that he actually joins them. They are so 'sent' that he is accepted. In his turn, he absently takes and eats various delicacies which Mrs. U-N is handing up as they near her.

Mr. U-N is engrossed in food, drink and his paper.

There is a break in the programme and Mr. Fleet, first to reach a state of 'un-Sent,' nips behind a stuke.

The music re-starts, but Brando has seen something off Down-Right. He exits to re-appear struggling with Tortoise.

He dumps Tortoise on his back, helpless.

Brando pokes and prods. Sophia is 'sent' again. Mrs. U-N won't have anything to do with such a creature: she can't bear Wood-lice and Ear-wigs. Mr. U-N walks over, has a look, and returns. Mr. Fleet pops up, and is delighted. He does a 'boxer's' salutation.

Dog runs on: sniffs Tortoise and speaks to him, but this is not audible above the transistor.

Brando backs away and threatens him. Mr. U-N hurls a bottle.

Dog runs off Left. Brando plagues Tortoise anew.

Mr. Fleet reaches over the stuke and intercepts a cake intended for Sophia. Then a banana . . .

Mr. U-N sees this. He tells Mrs. U-N casually that he is just going to the car, picking up a tent sack on the way, and exits Down-Left.

Mr. Fleet intercepts a cup of pop.

Mr. U-N enters Up-Left, and creeps up on Mr. Fleet. A struggle and uproar in which Brando joins, and Mr. Fleet is in the bag. They tie the mouth. The bag thumps and jumps around a bit, but Mr. Fleet is well and truly trapped.

What with one thing and another, this rural spot now resembles a battle field—or a popular beach at the end of a fine Summer Sunday.

Dog leads on the Girls. They exclaim over the plight of Mr. Sloe, and while arguing—they are too incensed to be over-awed by the U-Ns—put him on his feet.

Whilst the discussion rages, Mr. Sloe resumes his old rhythm and exits Down-Left.

Farmer Black, carrying a shot gun, comes over the wall.

He takes command. His first action being to put the butt of his gun into the transistor.

He takes no back-gobble-di-gook from any of them.
It is a monologue. He tells the Un-Ns that:—
  they are trespassing
  they've frightened his sheep
  they've no respect for the Country Code
  they have disgusting habits
  and he'll give them two minutes to clear up the mess!

The U-Ns set to, prompted and threatened by the Farmer.
Every last little toffee paper: every last straw back on its bale.

Finally: what's in this sack?

The sack convulses. Poaching too! Open it!

Mr. U-N unties the neck, and out shoots Mr. Fleet. Twice round, between Mr. U-N's legs, and knocking Brando down, he gets direction, and darts off Down-Left.

Mr. Basket follows.

The Girls, with a word to Farmer Black, run too.

Farmer Black, gun in support, is going to prosecute.

Got a car, have they? Good. It'll save a walk to the village Police Station.

On the litter-laden and dejected exit of the Urban-Notcouths . . .

Number One Tabs close.

CONTINUITY SCENE EIGHT:

Tortoise is crossing the Apron from Left to Right.

Hare passes him, turns and runs backwards pulling 'fat-bacon' at him.

They are going to exit through the auditorium via a previously untravelled aisle, if we still have one.

Half-way up Mr. Fleet again delivers himself: this time of:—

HARE. Not only am I the nimblest and most graceful dancer of all the Woodlanders, but I am the most dexterous escapologist . . . The trap has yet to be invented that can hold me . . . Hares laugh at Snares! . . . Ah well, I'd better saunter to the winning post. If you're still here when old Fat-legs totters past, give the old thing a cheer or two. He's trying his best.

Ta-ta. Here we go again. Will you start me off?

(If our Hare has so alienated our affections, he may have to call his own start, but we doubt it. Some, if not all of us, will oblige with 'On your marks etc.'—and off he goes.

Tortoise storms in pursuit, to thunderous encouragement).

On his exit, Number One Tabs open on Scene 9.

SCENE 9. THE COTTAGE GARDEN

This time the Ground Row is Down-stage. It is the Stone Wall.

Above it, in the Garden, stretching across the stage with no visible supports other than a central prop, is a washing line.

Mrs. Stainer, a buxom good-wife, is hanging out her wash. She wears thick glasses.

The job complete, towels, shirts and what-not flapping gently, she exits.

Mr. Fleet, at a comfortable lope, enters Down-Right.

Centre, a familiar scent strikes his nostrils.

HARE. Carrots!
(He peers over the wall).

O-oo, beauties! Young and tender.

(He whistles nonchalantly; walks, cranes and looks).

Nobody guarding them. Very remiss. If I grew carrots like that I should watch them night and day. If people don't guard their carrots, they jolly well deserve to lose them.

(He looks over again).

Wouldn't take two minutes. Old Fat-legs is way behind—and this is the last point. Better just make sure he hasn't got a lift on a hay-wagon. Sort of mean trick he would get up to.

(He looks off Right).

No, not out of Nobbet's Spinney yet. Not only are we Hares in general, and myself in particular, the fastest, most intelligent and prettiest of the Woodlanders, but I am also the agilest vaulterer-rer of garden walls in the country.

(He has several dummy attempts employing different approaches, none of which look like being successful. So . . .).

I might damage the carrots if I land on them from too great a height.

(He climbs the wall. Even now his second leg is caught, and he falls inelegantly from view. However, his head soon pops up. He is eating a carrot).

Delicious!

(He bobs down.

Mr. Basket enters, hot on the trail. Sniffing, he follows Mr. Fleet's confusing tracks; realizes that he has not gone through: returns to Centre and starts a prolonged exploration of the wall. Mr.

Fleet, looks over, munching, and surveys him. Their faces meet. Basket leaps back).

DOG.   What in old slippers are you doing there!

HARE.   Vitamins. Very good for the eye-sight. Have one. Oh, there are only six left. Sorry.

DOG.   The old female human here will give you vitamins if she catches you.

HARE.   She can't see for bilberries. I expect that's why she has grown these perfectly delectable carrots.

DOG.   You're supposed to be in a Race! Not stopping stealing carrots.

HARE.   Race! I could hop on one leg from here and win! As a matter of fact, I think I will—would be very spectacular. Not only do I run, dance and box magnificently, but I am quite the hottest hopper-rer in the kingdom.

DOG.   You're quite the loudest boasterer-rer!

HARE.   Please—no petty envy.

DOG.   Well, you'd better hop back quick—here's the old female human!

HARE *(Choking)*.   What!
(He makes an ineffective scramble, falls back, panics).

DOG.   Quick! Come on! She'll catch you!

(Mr. Fleet fails again. What to do?

He runs to a gap between the clothes on the line and, fore-legs stretched in a Y holding the line he 'makes-like' a piece of washing.

Mrs. Stainer works down the line from Left feeling each piece to see if it is dry.

Mr. Basket ducks below our side of the wall.

Mr. Fleet trembles.

Mrs. Stainer puts extra pegs in a towel. She reaches Mr. Fleet, and feels him. It tickles: one 'leg' involuntarily lets go of the line. Repeat.

She thinks this is a bit rum, and pegs it securely: then the other 'leg,' and finding his ears dangling—pegs those too.

She completes her examination, and re-adjusts the prop. Singing rurally, she exits Left.

Mr. Fleet is spread-eagled on tip paw.

Mr. Basket cautiously stands against the wall and looks over).

DOG.   Fleet? Fleet—you all right?

HARE.   No, I'm not all right! Get me down!

Dog. Where are you?

Hare. Here!

Dog. Where? I can smell you, but I can't see you.

Hare. You're looking straight at me, bat eyes!

(He wriggles).

Here!

Dog. Behind the washing?

Hare. I *am* the washing! The third shirt from the left!

Dog. Ye Danes and little litters! This is no time to be drying yourself off. Come down!

Hare. I can't come down! I'm pegged up! Lower the line. Unpeg me quick!

Dog. How can I lower lines? I couldn't unpeg you, anyway.

Hare. You domesticated, bottle-fed, hand-reared, kennel-housed renegade from the real animals! I'll see that you don't play in our Woods any more!

Dog. Now don't get shirty—as my little female humans would say. Likewise: keep your hair on!

Hare. Well, do something! Quick—here's Fat legs! He'll win! He'll win!

(Mr. Sloe crosses from Down-Right).

Dog. Heh, Torto! It's Mr. Fleet in trouble again. He's fastened to the clothes line.

Tortoise. Oh dear. What is he now—the whiter than white Rabbit?

Hare. Get me down! Stop! Not fair to Hare!

Dog. Can you help, Torto?

Tortoise. Sorry, I really cannot stop this time. Only two fields to the finishing post. Must keep moving. Can't win races if you stop.

(He leaves the stage, and is on his way up an aisle).

Hare. I've been framed!

Dog. My little female humans call it being taken to the cleaners. I never did understand what they meant before.

Tortoise *(Calling back from the auditorium).* You'd best fetch them, Mr. Basket. They could get him down.

Dog. My little female humans. Of course!

Hare. They'd put me in a hutch!

DOG. Not they. They won't keep any animal that prefers the woods. I'll find them.

(He exits Down-Right).

HARE. Hurry! It's the last lap!

(He yells after the retreating Tortoise).

I'll catch you! You can't beat me! You see—as soon as I am free, I'll catch you up and win by a mile . . . Hare will be there!

(Tortoise leaves us, well on his way).

I'll show him! This is the return I get for letting him keep up with me! And offering him a start! And distracting those humans in the Cornfield so that he could get away!—Some animals can only win by cheating!

(Mr. Basket enters and paws the wall. The Girls follow).

DOG. Here we are, then. Come on, little friends, look where I'm pointing.

JACKIE *(Wonders what's up with Mr. Basket).*

ROBIN *(Thinks he's trying to show them something).*

JACKIE *(Perhaps a cat in the garden).*

ROBIN *(He knows he's not to chase cats. He must come down).*

DOG. Oh, come on! Come on! You're not usually so slow as this. Look—hanging up like a piece of washing! Hare. Third shirt from the left.

JACKIE AND ROBIN. ?

HARE. You mole-eyed, cow-snouted, fly-brained little human sub-does—I'm here! Get me down!

DOG. It's no use you screeching like that: they can't understand you.

(But they have heard).

JACKIE *(Is startled. She looks and points).*

ROBIN *(Can it be? It is—a hare, pegged to the line!).*

DOG. That's it! You've seen him! Get him!

(He shouts and bounds against the wall).

ROBIN *(Says he is to get down. He is a bad dog. He is not to touch the poor hare. She cuffs him).*

DOG. Ow! Ow! Ow-ow!

HARE. You all right?

DOG. Yes. She thinks I want to chase you. Fine thing getting a clip when you're just trying to help!

960

JACKIE *(Thinks it's terribly cruel. What can they do?).*

ROBIN *(Set him free, of course).*

JACKIE *(How? Old Mrs. Stainer might see).*

ROBIN *(Has an idea).*

JACKIE *(Yes. Who is going to do what?).*

HARE. What are they on about?

DOG. Making a plan. One of them is going to ask the old female human for a drink of water, and then the other one is going to climb over and set you free.

HARE. Well, I wish they'd HURRY!

JACKIE *(Poor thing, he's in terrible pain! Listen).*

ROBIN *(She'll tackle Mrs. Stainer).*

JACKIE *(All right, she'll go over the wall).*

DOG. Won't be long now.

(Robin takes a deep breath and exits Down-Left. Mr. Basket follows to the wings. Jackie watches and waits.

We hear a knock and faint conversation. Mr. Basket returns to Centre).

Go on, now. She's busy at the door.

JACKIE *(Tells him to be quiet. She essays the climb).*

HARE. Just as I thought. About as athletic as a worm!

DOG. Quiet. She's doing her best.

JACKIE *(Ss-sh. He's a bad dog! Mr. Basket implores the Heavens.*

He puts his back conveniently under a dangling foot and bunks her over.

The next few minutes are hectic.

Jackie scrambles to the prop and lowers the line fully. The clothes and Mr. Fleet disappear for a moment. Then up he comes, still attached to the line, squirming.

There is some furious milling around as Jackie pulls the pegs.

Mr. Basket keeps cave on the Cottage Door (Off Left).

HARE. About time—Ow—my ear! The other peg!

JACKIE *(Is telling him to keep quiet, and that she won't hurt him).*

DOG *(At the wall).* Shut up, Fleet, and stay still. The old female human will hear.

(Robin rushes back, speaking).

Quick! She says the old female human has gone in to see to the washing!

(Mr. Fleet is free. He scales the wall, and is off up the aisle . . . Jackie lifts the line on the prop, and scrambles back to our side).

The clothes are in a shocking state: soiled, crumpled and paw-marked. (Second pre-set line).

Mrs. Stainer has appeared. She exclaims over the debacle.

The Girls and Mr. Basket huddle at the foot of the wall.

Mrs. Stainer just glimpses the bobbing tail of Mr. Fleet on his way out.

She shouts and gesticulates, and exits Left to re-enter immediately with a shot-gun.

She blazes away over our heads, as . . .

Number One Tabs close.

CONTINUITY SCENE NINE:

The furthest auditorium door bursts open and Mr. Sloe enters the stadium.

Down he comes, but not one whit faster than previously.

He is about half-way down when . . .

Number One Tabs open on Scene 10.

THE GREAT CROSS-COUNTRY RACE

Scene 10.   Frog Rock Quarry Again

Present All the Animals (except possibly Water Rat who, if he has been playing Mrs. Stainer, may be a little late)—plus any Cubs, Does, Leverets etc., who may have come to see the Finish of the Great Cross Country Race.

They all raise a tremendous cheer as they spot Mr. Sloe.

Badger.   Well done, Mr. Sloe! Well done indeed!

Rook.   Encore! Encore!

Squirrel.   Splendid fellow! Come on, keep it up!

Rabbit.   I am surprised!

Rat *(Or who-ever)*.   Come on, old Sloe! Come on!

Hedgehog.   Thunder on, Mr. Sloe! Thunder on!

Badger.   Once round the quarry, and you're home!

Squirrel.   Where's Hare?

Hedgehog.   He's not in sight yet! He's not in sight!

Rabbit.   I'm quite dizzy with excitement!

Squirrel.   I said he could do it! Stout fellow!

Badger.   One last effort, Mr. Sloe.

Rook.   Hoo-raw! Hoo-raw! *(And so on . . .*
Mr. Sett displays the back of the gate on which is chalked Last Lap with an arrow pointing Right.

Mr. Sloe reaches the stage from Left, and continues to exit Right and start on a complete tour of the auditorium—the stadium lap).

Rat.   Just once round the Quarry, and you're home!

Rabbit.   Oh, do hurry, Mr. Sloe!

Rook.   Once more! Once more!

Hedgehog.   He's still not in sight! You're going to win!

Squirrel.   Young Fleet licked at last! Go on, Sloe!

Badger.   We'll get out the tape. Keep it up!

(Mr. Sloe is approaching the back-straight).

Rabbit.   Hurry!

Rook.   Hoo-raw!

Hedgehog.   Hare's nowhere!

963

SQUIRREL. Keep it up!

RAT. Faster, Mr. Sloe. Put on a spurt!

BADGER. Run up! Run up!

HEDGEHOG. Hare couldn't do it even if he came now!

SQUIRREL. Go, Sloe, go! You're home and dried!

RAT. Only half a lap to go!

RABBIT. Quickly! Quickly!

BADGER. On, on, on!

HEDGEHOG. More speed!

ROOK. More! More!

SQUIRREL. It's in the bag!

RABBIT. E-eee! He's here!

> (*Mr. Fleet crashes in at tremendous rate. He simply flies down the aisle whizzing past Mr. Sloe, who is, of course, on his last few yards.*
>
> *The din is terrific. All the Animals repeating what they've said and ad-libbing—which we will drown anyway with our own support.*
>
> *Mr. Fleet rushes on, breasts the tape—only it isn't being held out yet—heroically, and collapses just managing a Victor's handclasp.*
>
> *Mr. Sloe lumbers relentlessly on.*
>
> *They all yell together . . .).*

BADGER. There's another lap! You haven't finished!

HEDGEHOG. Round the Quarry again!

SQUIRREL. Another lap! Run, Fleet, run!

RABBIT. Oh! Oh! Oh! I think I'm going to faint!

RAT. Go on! Again! You can just make it!

HEDGEHOG. Round again!

RABBIT. Hurry! Oh, do hurry!

ROOK. I implore! I implore!

BADGER. You must finish the course! Round again!

SQUIRREL. Up, Fleet up!

> (*Truth dawns on Mr. Fleet—and off he goes.*
>
> *Mr. Sloe is mounting to the stage.*

964

Mr. Sett and Mr. Brush hold the tape taut).

Come on, Fleet.

HEDGEHOG. Come on, Sloe!

RABBIT. Come on, Somebody!

BADGER. Run up! Run up!

ROOK. A draw! A draw!

(And it nearly is . . . but Mr. Sloe surges into the tape—First: as Mr. Fleet bursts past him—Second.

He again collapses, this time into the arms of Mr. Paddle and Mr. Spiney. He is trying to utter protests and objections and explain the dire plots that have delayed him. But he hasn't the breath to be intelligible and they are all talking at once again, anyway).

BADGER. Mr. Sloe wins!

SQUIRREL. Great show, Sloe, Congratulations!

TORTOISE. Thank you. Thank you!

HEDGEHOG. The Winner!—Hold up, Mr. Fleet.

RABBIT. Mr. Sloe wins! Mr. Sloe wins! Oh—I'm quite dizzy!

ROOK. Hoo-raw! Hoo-raw!

RAT. I thought he'd do it. Very well run, Mr. Sloe—You feeling all right, Mr. Fleet?

BADGER. What a splendid race!

HEDGEHOG. You must challenge Mr. Reynard now.

TORTOISE. That would be very different, I feel.

SQUIRREL. Mrs. Dark, let all the Woodlanders know.

ROOK. Sure, sure.

HEDGEHOG. They will be surprised.

BADGER. You'll join me for a bite of tea, Mr. Sloe?

TORTOISE. If you'll excuse me, Mr. Sett, I really must get back to the garden. It has been most enjoyable.

BADGER. I quite understand.

HEDGEHOG. We ought to get Mr. Fleet a drink. He's quite exhausted.

SQUIRREL. He'll revive.

BADGER. A worthy Woodland Champion.

TORTOISE. Any of you could have done it. I'm afraid our young friend lacks concentration.

SQUIRREL. Grass Hopper minded.

HEDGEHOG. Won't stick at things.

RAT. Too easily diverted. Always said so.

RABBIT. But he can run fast.

(Mr. Basket reaches the stage from the auditorium).

DOG. Here I am. Who won?

BADGER. Mr. Sloe—by a neck.

DOG. Good old Torto! Three cheers for Mr. Sloe. Hep, hep—etc.

(The Animals, especially if there are young ones, dance and sing "Thunder on," altering the lyric to 'We are glad that you were there, at the post before the Hare!

The Girls enter the Auditorium).

ROOK. Warning! Warning! Withdraw! Withdraw!

(The Animals freeze as previously, with the exception of Mr. Fleet who has had a relapse. He lies on his back, panting and kicking feebly.

The Girls reach the stage).

DOG. It's all right, they won't hurt. I've just brought them to pick up Mr. Sloe. Come on, you two, here's your pet.

(He sniffs Mr. Sloe, who emerges).

JACKIE *(Why, here he is! Clever dog!).*

ROBIN *(Here all the time! This is where they started!).*

JACKIE *(Thinks it would be wise to tie his string on and lead him).*

ROBIN *(Yes).*

(She sees the prostrate Hare. They both bend over him compassionately).

JACKIE *(Poor thing! Nearly run himself to death!).*

ROBIN *(That terrible Mrs. Stainer, tying him to a washing line!).*

HARE. What are they saying?

DOG. That you're a poor weak animal who's run himself to death because you were frightened.

HARE. They are probably right!

DOG. And that you are squeaking with terror. Now they are planning to take you home and keep you in a hutch.

HARE. I knew it!

DOG. And feed you on bread and milk.

966

HARE. I hate bread and milk!

DOG. Then take my advice—nip off quick.

(Jackie cuffs him, and tells him not to worry the poor hare).

Ow! She's done it again! Every time I talk to you, I get a smack!
—Go on, hop it! I'll give you a start. On your mark—Ready.
Steady Go!

(Mr. Fleet goes with what alacrity he can muster.

*The Girls are relieved. He can't be so ill, and it's for the best—
But Basket is a bad dog for frightening him).*

DOG. I didn't frighten him! Oh dear, you're very nice but I wish
sometimes you had the sense to understand what I say.

(Robin speaks to him, and pulls his lead).

No, I won't stop barking! Barking! I'm talking to my friends—
Cheerio, all of you. Been a grand days sport. What's on tomorrow?

BADGER. We're not sure yet. But Mr. Paddle thinks we should have
the Swimming Gala.

DOG. Good idea!

BADGER. We're meeting on the River Bank.

DOG. Right. We'll be there.

(To Robin who is yanking him off).

All right, love, don't choke me! I'm coming—Bye, all.

(A little chorus of 'Goodbyes'

The Animals start to uncurl.

*The Girls turn back: they freeze again—the Girls exit and
the Curtain Falls).*

CURTAIN CALL

The Curtain Rises on the same still picture.

*In order, Mrs. Dark—Mrs. Warren—Mr. Paddle—Mr. Spiney—
Mr. Brush uncurl and take a bow.*

Mr. Basket runs on to Centre, and bows.

Jackie and Robin join him and bow.

Mr. Sloe runs—at speed—from Left.

Mr. Fleet enters from Right—on crutches.

*All wave 'Goodbye' and the hair-raising adventures of the Hare
and the Tortoise are over for another night.*

THE HUMAN SPEECH—GOBBLE-DI-GOOK.

In the original production Back Slang, or Dog Latin, was used most effectively, and is recommended to any Company which has a member or associate who knows its simple formula, and who could instruct.

(The initial letter or sound is placed at the end of the word, and EH added. Small words beginning with a vowel: merely add the EH.

Thus:—'Basket, Basket, where are you? Here, boy. Good dog. Would be:—'Askitbeh, Askitbeh, erewhey areh ouyeh? Ereheh oybeh. Oodgeh ogdeh.' etc.)

Another idea would be to use a foreign language such as French in an English production: English to a young French audience. It is important that the Gobble-di-gook has some linguistic discipline, otherwise a slack and dreary succession of vowel sounds will result in an unauthentic speech form.

Trudi and the Minstrel

A Neo-Gothick Extravaganza

By

ALAN CULLEN

*With Music by Roderick Horn

*Score included in separate play-book only.

TRUDI AND THE MINSTREL

By Alan Cullen

Trudi and the Minstrel

Cast

TRUDI, a country girl

PETER PUMPERNICKEL, strolling minstrel

SENTRY

SIEGFRIED, the Magnificent

BARONESS, his mother

ROTHBART, a troll

SCHLAFNICHT, a dragon

WEISSBART, an ancient troll

OTHER TROLLS

ROM, a gypsy

ROMOLA, his wife

OTHER GYPSIES

KING'S HEAD

BARON GROSSKOPF

BROTHER INNOCENT

SEA KING'S DAUGHTER

Following is a copy of the programme of the first performance
of *Trudi and the Minstrel,* as presented at the Sheffield Playhouse,
Sheffield, England, 21 December, 1965:

The Sheffield Repertory Company Limited
(In association with the Arts Council of Great Britain)

Presents

Trudi and the Minstrel

By ALAN CULLEN

PETER PUMPERNICKEL	Roderick Horn
SENTRY	Wilfred Harrison
SIEGFRIED	Peter Penry-Jones
ROTHBART	Anthony Douse
SCHLAFNICHT	Christopher Wilkinson
WEISSBART	Barrie Smith
TROLL 1	Ray Callaghan
TROLL 2	John Hartley
TROLL 3	Brian Huby
TROLL 4	Michael Graves
ROM	John Hartley
SERGEI	Barrie Smith
DIMITRI	Brian Huby
VALENTI	Michael Graves
HEAD WAITER	Alan Cullen
BARON GROSSKOPF	Wilfred Harrison
BROTHER INNOCENT	Ray Callaghan
TRUDI	Marilyn Taylerson
BARONESS	Rosemary Towler
ROMOLA	Dorothy Vernon
OLGA	Sharon Duce
SEA KING'S DAUGHTER	Myra Frances

Directed by COLIN GEORGE
Settings by EDWARD FURBY
Incidental Music by GILBERT KENNEDY
Songs and Dances by RODERICK HORN
Costumes designed by SARAH MORTON
Executed in the theatre wardrobe by MADGE D'ALROY
Stage Manager for this production,
and Acting Stage Director BRIAN HUBY

972

Scenes

The action takes place in, around, and
under a medieval German state.

ACT ONE

1. Haystack................................Full stage
2. Castle Gates.........................Apron, before plain trailers
3. Baroness' Room.....................Full stage
4. Echoing Rocky Passageway.........Apron, before rocky frontcloth
5. Dragon's Cavern....................Full stage
6. Another Passageway................Apron, before rocky frontcloth
7. Trollheim............................Full stage

ACT TWO

1. Gypsy Camp.........................Full stage
2. A Portion of the Baroness' Room Apron, before plain trailers
3. Gypsy Camp.........................Full stage
4. King's Head Inn....................Apron, before plain trailers
5. Castle Seeblick.....................Full stage

ACT THREE

1. Seashore............................Full stage
2. Passageway........................Apron, before rocky frontcloth
3. Dragon's Cavern...................Full stage

PROGRAMME NOTE

"Trudi and the Minstrel" is a somewhat distorted version of an old folk tale, originally placed in England, but here transferred to somewhere vaguely Germanic, for no other reason than that such a transference might, it was hoped, adequately conceal the liberties taken with the original. Besides, Trolls seemed to offer better dramatic possibilities than boggarts and hobs, and German names might be more amusing than English ones.

The tale has no moral. It is not intended to imply that marriages are made in heaven, or even that Baronesses should not try to interfere with fate, or anything serious of that sort. Nor is it inferred from it that the guitar was invented by an obscure troubadour with a foolish name. Every fantasy should be allowed one or two slight anachronisms—and who plays the lute nowadays, anyway?

ALAN CULLEN

974

Act One

A fine summer's morning in the country. The remains of a small haystack in which TRUDI, half-hidden, is asleep. When she appears, she is a pretty country girl with some independence of spirit, simply dressed in the style of the early 16th century.

PETER PUMPERNICKEL appears at the back. He is a strolling minstrel in shabby hand-me-down finery from some great patron, easy-going and cheerful. He strums a stringed instrument, inventing a song as he goes.

PETER *(Singing)*. Says I to myself one morning
Says I to myself one day
It's a wonderful day for minstrelling
It's the very first of May;
With the bluebells all a-ringing
Adown along the way
Ring-a-ling ting-a-ling, no time for lingering
Time to be on your way.
So I hitches up my britches
And I saddles up the bay
And I nods to all neighbours
As I passes by the way;
And I hears them all a-singing
As I bids each one good-day
Ring-a-ling ting-a-ling, no time for lingering
Time to be on your way.

(TRUDI sits up, makes a face and lies down again).
And I travels all the morning
And I travels all the day
And I—

(TRUDI sits up, annoyed).

TRUDI. Do you mind?

PETER *(Surprised)*. What?

TRUDI. I said do you *mind.*

PETER. Mind what?

TRUDI. Not making quite so much noise when people are trying to sleep.

PETER. What people?

TRUDI. Me.

(TRUDI flops down again).

PETER. Oh.—Hey!

TRUDI. What?

975

PETER. I resent that.

TRUDI. I beg your pardon?

PETER. I should think so, too, if you can't tell the difference between music and noise.

TRUDI. There isn't any difference.

PETER. What? What are you, an ignoramus?

TRUDI. If it wakes me up, as far as I'm concerned, it's noise. Now would you mind going and doing it somewhere else?

PETER. All right, I will go somewhere else.

(He crosses and turns).

People pay good money to listen to my noise, I might tell you.

TRUDI. *Good* money?

PETER. Well, money . . . sometimes.

TRUDI. You're a minstrel! You sing for a living!

PETER. If you can call it a living. Mostly it's not even money—mostly it's a chunk of bread and a cut off the joint if I'm lucky.

TRUDI. What's your name?

PETER. Peter—Peter Pumpernickel.

TRUDI. How funny. Where are you going?

PETER. There's a castle of some sort close by. I expect they'll let me sing for my supper.

TRUDI. D'you think they'd let me sing for mine?

PETER. Why, do you sing too?

TRUDI. Not so you'd notice. I mean they might give me a job.

PETER. You're looking for a job. Have you no home?

TRUDI. No. Well, I have and I haven't.

PETER. Turned you out, did they?

TRUDI. No, they didn't. They're not like that. I just left.

PETER. Oh. What for?

TRUDI. Because there were too many mouths to feed and not enough to feed them with. I'm the eldest, so I left.

PETER. I see. Well, we can but try. Come on, then.—By the way, what's your name?

TRUDI. Trudi.

PETER. Trudi what?

TRUDI. Just Trudi. We're not important enough to have a surname.

PETER. It's nice.

(They set off to walk, talking as they go. The haystack moves off).

I like it. You should have a song about it.

TRUDI. Will you make one up?

PETER. Perhaps. I'll have to think about it.

TRUDI. Sing the other one.

PETER. Which one?

TRUDI. The one you were singing when you woke me up.

PETER. "Says I to myself"?

TRUDI. Yes, that one.

(They sing as they walk around the stage. As they reach the end of a section of the song, they come to a SENTRY standing guard. He is an uncertain young man with a cross-bow).

SENTRY. Halt!

(They halt).

Just a minute.

(The SENTRY takes out a red book of rules).

Er — Who Goes There?

TRUDI. Me and him.

SENTRY. What?

TRUDI. Him and me.

SENTRY. You can't say that, you know.

TRUDI. He and I, then, if you are so particular.

SENTRY. I don't mean that. I mean it's the wrong thing.

TRUDI. Oh. Well, what's the right thing?

SENTRY. Just a minute.

(The SENTRY consults his book).

Er — Friend. You should say Friend.

TRUDI. Oh. I didn't know.

SENTRY. Would you mind awfully going back and doing it again?

TRUDI. All right, if you say so.

SENTRY. Thanks.
> *(They retire).*
> Just a minute.
> *(He puts his book away, and turns away from them).*
> I'm ready.
> *(They advance towards him).*
> Halt!
> *(They halt).*
> Who goes there?

TRUDI. Friend?

SENTRY. That's it!

PETER. What now, then?

SENTRY. Eh? — Oh, just a minute.
> *(He consults his book).*
> Er — Advance one and be recognized.
> *(They both step forward).*
> Wait! It says advance *one* and be recognized. Would you mind awfully doing it again?
> *(They shrug and step back).*
> Thanks. Now, advance one and be recognized.
> *(They nudge each other. PETER steps forward).*
> That's it!

PETER. What now?

SENTRY. Eh? — Just a minute.
> *(He studies the book, mouthing the words silently).*
> *(Stepping close to PETER, and peering in his face).*
> Do I know you?

PETER. I don't think so.

SENTRY. I thought I didn't. That makes it awkward.

PETER. Why?

SENTRY. Because if I don't know you, I can't say Pass, Friend, All's Well, can I?

PETER. Can't you?

SENTRY. No. And that's what I should say next, d'you see, according to this. It's very awkward.

PETER. I do see your difficulty, of course.

SENTRY. Do you? How nice of you!

PETER. But what do we do?

SENTRY. I'll tell you what.

PETER. What?

SENTRY. You come back tomorrow.

PETER. Tomorrow? What difference will that make?

SENTRY. Well, tomorrow I'll recognize you because I'll have seen you before, won't I? Then it'll be all right, d'you see?

PETER. Will it?

SENTRY. Oh, yes.

PETER. But we want to go in today.

SENTRY. I know you do, but you see when I say "advance and be —"

PETER. All right, all right.

SENTRY. You do understand, don't you?

PETER. Oh, yes, I understand. It's the Regulations.

SENTRY. That's it, it's the Regulations. I'm terribly sorry.

PETER. That's all right.

(To TRUDI).

Come on, we'll try somewhere else.

(They move to go. The SENTRY hastily takes out his book and consults it).

SENTRY. Halt!

PETER. What's the matter now?

SENTRY. Halt or I shoot!

TRUDI. What?

SENTRY. That's what it says here.

TRUDI. But we're not doing anything.

SENTRY. Oh, yes you are. You're trying to escape.

PETER. But you told us to go away.

SENTRY. Ah, no I didn't. I said come back tomorrow.

PETER. Well how on earth can we —

SENTRY. Now please. Please don't get excited.

PETER *(Taking TRUDI's arm and moving away)*. Oh, come on, I'm getting out of here.

SENTRY. Halt or I shoot!

(They halt).

PETER. You said that before.

SENTRY. Yes. Now I've said it twice. If I say it a third time, I shall have to shoot. It's in the Regulations. Look, I'm awfully sorry, but don't try to escape, will you? I can't bear shooting people.

PETER. Well, if we can't pass, and we can't go back, what *can* we do?

SENTRY. That's none of my business, is it?

(He turns away).

TRUDI. What are we going to do, then? We can't sit here till to-morrow.

PETER. Not if I can help it. They might change the guard and we can try again. Let's sit down anyway.

(They sit down).

SENTRY. Excuse me.

PETER. What now?

SENTRY. You can't sit there, you know.

PETER. Why not?

SENTRY. Private property. I'm terribly sorry.

(They get up).

I say.

PETER. What?

SENTRY. May I say what a pleasure it is when the public is so co-operative?

PETER. Don't mention it.

SENTRY. It makes one's job so much pleasanter.

PETER. How nice for you.

(The SENTRY turns away, humming. A pause. Suddenly, a very splendid young man enters and walks across, ignoring Peter and Trudi).

SENTRY. Halt! Who goes there?

SIEGFRIED *(passing him)*. Don't be a damn fool.

980

SENTRY *(Coming to attention)*. Sir!

SIEGFRIED *(Stopping and turning)*. Who are these peasants?

SENTRY. Strolling minstrels, sir.

SIEGFRIED. Get rid of them.

SENTRY. Sir!

> *(He raises his crossbow. TRUDI and PETER cling together and close their eyes).*

SIEGFRIED. Just a minute. Minstrels, did you say?

SENTRY. Sir!

SIEGFRIED. They might amuse the Baroness. They might even amuse me. Let them in.

> *(SIEGFRIED goes off).*

TRUDI. Who was that?

SENTRY. *(Admiringly)*. That was Siegfried. He's the son and heir, you know. Siegfried the Magnificent they call him. Oh, he'll be a great aristocrat one of these days. Did you notice how he said "Don't be a damn fool?" It's a pleasure to be called a fool by a man like that.

PETER *(Unimpressed)*. Can we go in now?

SENTRY. Of course. *He* said so.

> *(PETER and TRUDI cross to go in).*

Whether you ever come out again is another matter altogether.

> *(They look at each other and follow Siegfried. The lights fade). (The lights go up on a room in the castle, used as a bower by the Baroness. A dark, heavily-draped apartment. At a tapestry-covered table with a mirror on it sits the BARONESS. She is an eccentric old woman in rich clothes untidily thrown on, with masses of jewelry jingling as she moves. She lifts a couple of strings of beads from a box on the table and holds them against her chest, peering at her reflection in the glass.*
> *Crouching half-asleep at her side is a Troll, ROTHBART. Excessively ugly, he is not much more than a grotesque face in a mass of long red hair.*
> *There is a knock at an unseen door).*

BARONESS. There's someone at the door, Rothbart.

> *(Another knock).*
>
> *(The BARONESS digs ROTHBART in the ribs with a stick from the side of her chair).*

Rothbart! Answer that door!

(ROTHBART stirs and yawns, shambles across and disappears in the drapes. Noise of a heavy door opening. PETER and TRUDI come hesitantly into the light. Noise of the door closing. ROTHBART re-appears, crossing PETER and TRUDI to crouch by the BARONESS. They shrink from him as he passes them).

Don't be afraid of Rothbart. He's perfectly harmless.—Down, Rothbart! — He's a Troll.

(To TRUDI, suddenly).

Do you like beads?

TRUDI. I — yes, ma'am.

BARONESS *(Flinging a necklace at her).* Have those.

TRUDI *(Catching them).* Thank you, ma'am.

(TRUDI hesitates, then puts on the necklace).

BARONESS. I've had him since he was a pup. Haven't I, Rothbart?

(ROTHBART grins a hideous grin).

He's very useful, but he has to be beaten twice a day or he gets depressed. Don't you, Rothbart?

(ROTHBART cowers).

He thrives on it. What did you say your name was?

TRUDI. Trudi, ma'am.

BARONESS. Pretty, but common. Those garnets don't suit you. Have these.

(She flings two more necklaces at Trudi).

And you?

PETER. Peter, ma'am. Peter Pumpernickel.

BARONESS. Well don't *stand* there. Play something.

PETER. Yes, ma'am. Certainly ma'am. What would your grace like me to play?

BARONESS. How on earth should I know? I'm tone deaf. But Rothbart is very musical. Aren't you, Rothbart?

(Excited reaction from ROTHBART).

What would you like?

(ROTHBART capers).

Something to dance to, I gather.

PETER. Yes, ma'am.

(PETER plays. ROTHBART dances).

982

BARONESS. Come here, girl.

(TRUDI goes to her).

What did you say your name was?

TRUDI. Trudi, ma'am.

BARONESS. That's pretty. In fact, you are very pretty altogether. But why on earth do you wear all that jewelry? Take it off.

(TRUDI takes off the beads).

Why don't you dance with Rothbart? I'm sure he'd love it.

(Without much enthusiasm, TRUDI dances with the Troll, doing her best to follow his shambling steps.
Suddenly, the door bangs, and SIEGFRIED comes in. The dance stops. ROTHBART quails, and scuttles round to the Baroness. SIEGFRIED takes TRUDI's hand).

SIEGFRIED. Don't stop playing.

(SIEGFRIED and TRUDI continue the dance to the end).

Thank you. You dance very well.

BARONESS. Her name's Mitzi.

TRUDI. Trudi, ma'am.

BARONESS. Trudi, Mitzi, what's the difference?

SIEGFRIED *(Looking at her).* Trudi . . .

BARONESS. I think we'll put her in the Blue Room, overlooking the herb garden.

SIEGFRIED. We'll put her in the Pink Room.

BARONESS. No, we won't. It has no view.

SIEGFRIED. We'll put her in the Pink Room.

BARONESS. The Blue Room.

SIEGFRIED. The Pink Room.

BARONESS. The Blue Room!

SIEGFRIED. The Pink Room.

BARONESS. The Pink Room's too pink.

SIEGFRIED. The Blue Room's too blue.

BARONESS. It has a *chandelier.*

SIEGFRIED. I *hate* you!

(SIEGFRIED goes out in a huff).

983

BARONESS. That's sons for you. Why did I ever have a son? What did you say your name was?

TRUDI. Trudi.

BARONESS. It's very common. Who did you say was your father?

TRUDI. I — I didn't. But his name is Albrecht.

BARONESS. That's common too.

TRUDI. He has a — a smallholding in —

BARONESS. Smallholding?

TRUDI. Well, a cottage and a cow.

BARONESS. You're a peasant!

TRUDI. He's always worked hard for his living, at least!

BARONESS. You'd better sleep over the stable. You can find a bench in the hall, Apfelstrudel.

PETER. Pumpernickel, ma'am. Peter Pumpernickel.

BARONESS. I shall call you Apfelstrudel.

PETER. Yes, ma'am. It's very kind of you, but we shall have to be going.

BARONESS. Going? But you've only just come.

PETER. Yes, but I have to — to play at a wedding in the village.

BARONESS. What village?

PETER. The one just — just down the hill.

BARONESS. Don't be absurd. You will stay till I'm tired of you. Besides, I haven't told your fortune yet. You can't go till I've told your fortune, can you? And there is no village anyway. The Von Grubelsteins live, and have always lived, in splendid isolation. We are a very ancient family. Rothbart, my wrap.

(She has no wrap, but ROTHBART mimes taking up a shawl and putting it round her shoulders. She sweeps upstage and poses.
The door bangs. SIEGFRIED strides in).

SIEGFRIED. All right. She can have the Blue Room. But I shall hate you for ever.

(SIEGFRIED flings a tortured look at TRUDI and goes out).

BARONESS. You see? He does it only to torment me. But I always win in the end. — Now we shall see what the future holds for you, my dear.

TRUDI. The future?

BARONESS. Didn't I tell you? I'm clairvoyante. I am the seventh daughter of a seventh daughter — I was born with the Second Sight. Rothbart, serve tea.

(ROTHBART scuttles out).

TRUDI *(Questioningly, to Peter).* Tea?

(PETER shrugs).

BARONESS. You won't have heard of it, of course; — it's a rare herb from Cathay. It soothes the nerves and foretells the future. I wouldn't be without it.

(ROTHBART returns with two china tea-bowls on a tray. PETER and TRUDI take one each).

Drink it up.

(They drink and pull faces).

TRUDI. I don't like it very much.

BARONESS. An acquired taste, of course. Finish it.

(TRUDI drinks).

Now give me the cup.

(The BARONESS swirls the cup round three times and empties the dregs. She stares at the cup. She blanches).

No!

(She stares in horror at Trudi).

TRUDI. What is it? What can you see?

BARONESS. Never! — Never, never, never! — But I must be sure. I must be quite sure. Rothbart, the crystal.

(ROTHBART takes the cups, scutters to the table, and brings her a crystal ball).

Why, I'd rather see him dead first!

(She snatches the crystal from Rothbart, and stares into it).

Oh!

TRUDI. But what is it? What can you see? Oh, please tell me.

BARONESS *(Horrified).* It's true. It's unmistakable. But I will be sure. I will be absolutely sure. Rothbart, the Book.

(She goes to her chair, and sits, drawing herself up very straight, with a hand on each arm).

The Book.

(ROTHBART, having removed the crystal, goes behind the chair and emerges with an object wrapped in a silk cloth, which he places on the Baroness's lap).

Light the candles.

(ROTHBART lights two tall candles either side of the back of her chair. The BARONESS unfolds the silk cover, revealing a huge book bound in black and gold).

In this book, for those with eyes to see, is written the fate of every man, woman, and child who has ever lived or who ever will live. What has been, has been; and what will be, will be. Place your right hand on the book.

(TRUDI hesitates).

TRUDI. Do I have to?

BARONESS. Do as I tell you.

(TRUDI puts her hand on the book. The BARONESS places both her hands over TRUDI's, and looks her in the eyes. Then she takes her hands away).

Step back.

(TRUDI steps back. There is a mysterious sound as the BARONESS opens the book. It glows with a strange light).

BARONESS *(Staring at the book).* NO!

(She shuts the book, and stands up, eyes staring).

Never!

(She flings the book to the ground).

Never in a thousand years!

(She glares at TRUDI and goes out wildly.
PETER kneels by the book, and opens it. He stands up and shows the blank white pages).

PETER. It's blank. There's nothing there at all. She's crazy.

TRUDI. Unless she saw something there that we can't.

(ROTHBART takes the book from Peter and hugs it, jumping up and down. PETER and TRUDI draw apprehensively together).

PETER. Come on, we're leaving — now!

TRUDI. But can we get out?

PETER. We can try — come on!

(PETER pulls her away, and they hurry out. As soon as they are out, the BARONESS re-enters).

BARONESS. Where are they?

(ROTHBART indicates that they have left).

Fetch them back.

(ROTHBART goes after them. The BARONESS picks up the book and opens it).

"Within a space of seven and nine
She shall marry the heir of Von Grubelstein".

(She shuts the book).

My son? The heir of Von Grubelstein to marry a peasant? I'll see her dead first!

(There is a peal of thunder. She quails, and drops the book. She raises her fist, recovering).

I'll see her dead!

(This time there is no response from the heavens. She picks up the book, and returns it to the table).

But we must be cunning. We must not be obvious. Rothbart!

(ROTHBART returns, with PETER and TRUDI).

Rothbart! Ah, there you are — you found them. I'm so glad. — My dears!

(She gushes over to them).

But surely you weren't thinking of leaving?

TRUDI. Well, it *is* getting late, and we —

BARONESS. Nonsense, I won't hear of it. You must stay at Grubelstein for a few days at least — stay a week — stay a month — there's plenty of room. You can see for yourself that Siegfried hates me, and as for Rothbart, he isn't even human. So I have nobody.

(She moves away, dabs her eye, and sniffs).

Stay a little.

(She pretends to brighten up bravely).

Stay to supper at least.

TRUDI *(To PETER).* Well?

(PETER shrugs helplessly).

(Aside to him).

I'm hungry.

PETER *(Aside to her).* All right, but we leave straight afterwards.

TRUDI. We — we'd quite like to stay to supper, ma'am.

BARONESS. Splendid! — Supper, Rothbart!

(ROTHBART scuttles out).

Now I'll tell you what we'll do. While supper is preparing, Apfelstrudel can stay here and think of something nice to play, and you and I, my dear, will look over the castle. How about that?

TRUDI. Oh, but — can't Peter come too?

BARONESS. No, dear. Just you and I. I want to talk to you. Come.

(The BARONESS picks up one of the lighted candles. ROTHBART re-enters).

You'll keep Wienerschnitzel company, won't you, Rothbart?

(ROTHBART nods and grins).

(The BARONESS takes TRUDI out. PETER makes to follow, but ROTHBART steps quickly in his way and grins. PETER grins back, and makes another attempt at the other exit, with the same result. PETER gives up and sits. He plucks at the guitar).

PETER. Do you play?

(ROTHBART shakes his head).

Perhaps you play something else?

(ROTHBART nods vigorously).

What do you play?

(ROTHBART mimes playing a keyboard instrument).

Harpsichord!

(ROTHBART shakes his head and repeats the mime).

The organ!

(ROTHBART nods vigorously).

What a pity there isn't one.

(ROTHBART nods).

There is?

(ROTHBART goes to the table, sweeps back the clutter on it, and very grandly throws back his hair, poising his hands over the table-top).

Oh, yes. Very funny. Quite the maestro.

(ROTHBART plonks his hands down on the table. There is a deafening chord of organ-music. PETER is stupefied. ROTHBART plays a brilliant short passage, swings off the chair, and bows).

988

Tremendous! Can you play anything else?

(ROTHBART grins and nods, jumping up and down).

What?

(ROTHBART comes centre front, and mimes taking a cloth off a non-existent glockenspiel. He takes up imaginary sticks, flourishes them, and plays a scale).

Marvellous! — May I?

(ROTHBART bows, gives him a second pair of sticks).

Move over, then.

(They stand side by side).

Ready?

(ROTHBART nods. They play a duet).

PETER. You know, you're quite good.

(ROTHBART looks modest).

What shall we play now?

(ROTHBART thinks. He mimes picking up the glockenspiel and throwing it into the wings. There is a jangling crash. They laugh. ROTHBART mimes picking up a set of bagpipes off the ground, and tucking them under his arm. He nudges PETER to do the same. They blow up the bagpipes, start the drones, ROTHBART stamps on the ground to give the time, and as they blast off an ear-splitting march, they go round in step to it. They march round the furniture. As the march comes to an end, PETER peels off and goes out after TRUDI, leaving ROTHBART still marching. There is a slam of a door, and a noise of bolts. ROTHBART stops, throws down the bagpipes in disgust. Blackout).

(Front cloth of an echoing, rocky passageway. The BARONESS comes in, carrying a lighted candle, and followed by TRUDI).

BARONESS. Isn't it fascinating? *(ECHO: Fascinating, fascinating . . .).* These galleries and passageways below the castle go on for ever — simply for ever. *(ECHO: Simply for ever . . .).* Of course we usually charge our visitors to come down and see them, but I'm making an exception in your case, my dear. *(ECHO: your case, my dear).*

TRUDI. Don't you think it's time we turned back, Ma'am?

BARONESS. Oh, but you haven't seen anything yet. We have to go down, and down, and down before it becomes really interesting.

(ECHO: Oh, so interesting . . .).

TRUDI. But we're an awfully long way down already.

BARONESS. Yes — isn't it exciting? And deep, deep down is — something wonderful. *(ECHO: wonderful, wonderful . . .).*

TRUDI. Something wonderful? What?

BARONESS. You'll see . . . you'll see. Come along, my dear — this way down . . . *(ECHO: This way down, way down, way down . . .).*

(They go off.

PETER appears, following).

PETER. Trudi . . . Trudi . . . where are you? It's so dark down here . . . Trudi . . . Trudi! . . . *(ECHO: Trudi . . . Trudi . . . Trudi . . .).*

(PETER goes off).

(Front cloth rises on a weird cavern. It is full of shifting lights, and there is a steady musical sound of dripping water echoing through it. It has no obvious entrances. The BARONESS and TRUDI appear).

BARONESS. Here we are at last . . . There now! Didn't I say it was wonderful?

TRUDI. Yes. I — I've never seen anything like it.

BARONESS. Listen!

(There is a splashing sound, and someone singing a scale).

TRUDI. There's someone singing.

BARONESS. Yes.

TRUDI. Who is it?

BARONESS. Schlafnicht.

TRUDI. Who?

BARONESS. Schlafnicht, singing in his bath. He's a very *clean* Dragon.

TRUDI. Dragon!

BARONESS. Yes, didn't I tell you? He lives here. Such a pet of the household. Ah, Schlafnicht has seen hundreds of generations of Von Grubelsteins come and go — but Schlafnicht goes on for ever.

TRUDI. I — I don't think I care for Dragons.

BARONESS. The point is, will Schlafnicht care for you?

TRUDI. What?

BARONESS. He is rather particular, you know.

TRUDI. What do you mean, particular?

BARONESS. About his food, of course.

TRUDI. His food!

BARONESS. But he'll be very hungry, poor dear. It must be all of a week since he ate the under-gardener. I do hope he likes you. Well, goodbye, my dear. Now I must fly.

(The BARONESS disappears, preferably going up on a wire, but otherwise with a flash and blackout).

TRUDI. Baroness! Baroness! — She's gone!

(There is a noise of water running out of the bath. The scales cease. A noise of heavy shuffling and breathing. TRUDI looks round apprehensively. The shuffling steps come nearer. PETER appears, timorously).

PETER. Trudi!

TRUDI. Peter! Oh, I'm so glad it's only you!

PETER. What's happened? Where's the Baroness?

TRUDI. She's gone — disappeared. Peter, we must get away from here.

PETER. Isn't that what I kept telling you?

TRUDI. I know, but I didn't realize I was going to be fed to a Dragon.

PETER. What! A Dragon! Where?

TRUDI. Here.

PETER *(Spinning round, terrified)*. Here!

(Clinging to Trudi).

Where? No, don't tell me, I don't want to know.

TRUDI. Listen!

(The shuffling and breathing are heard).

That's him. He's called Schlafnicht.

PETER. I don't care what his name is. I'm off. Come on, Trudi.

(They turn to go off the way they came. They stop suddenly and back away as the Dragon SCHLAFNICHT appears. He is bright blue, with gilt tips to his scales, and has a bath-towel round his neck. He is somewhat fat and heavy, and wheezes a good deal. He lets out a hiss like a steam engine. TRUDI gives a little shriek, and clings to Peter).

SCHLAFNICHT. Ah, breakfast!

TRUDI. Oh, Peter!

PETER. Oh, Trudi!

TRUDI. He means us.

PETER. I know.

SCHLAFNICHT. Or is it supper? So difficult to tell the time of day down here.

TRUDI. Peter, what shall we do?

PETER. Pray. That's all there is left.

SCHLAFNICHT. Now I don't know how you feel, but I would very much appreciate it if you would have a bath before my breakfast — or supper, as the case may be. I'm a little particular, you see. Water's nice and hot. Now who's first?

TRUDI. Peter, *do* something!

(PETER kneels down and puts his hands together).

Oh, Peter!

SCHLAFNICHT. You'll find two kinds of bath-salts there — lavender for me, and brown sauce for you. Now I don't want to hurry you, but I *am* hungry.

PETER *(Getting up)*. All right. I'll go first.

TRUDI. Peter, don't leave me!

SCHLAFNICHT. Now it's all right — I won't eat you till he comes back.

PETER *(To TRUDI)*. I'll — er — I'll wipe the bath when I've finished.

TRUDI *(Frustratedly)*. Oh!

PETER. I'll take as long as I can.

(PETER crosses and turns).

Excuse me.

SCHLAFNICHT. Did you want something?

PETER. Er — little boats.

SCHLAFNICHT. What?

PETER. I always have little boats in my bath. You wouldn't have any, I suppose?

SCHLAFNICHT. There's a rubber duck there somewhere, I think.

PETER. Thank you.

(He turns to go).

SCHLAFNICHT. Just a minute. What's that you're wearing?

PETER. This? It's a musical instrument.

SCHLAFNICHT. You'll have to take that off. It will give me indigestion. What did you say it was?

992

PETER. A musical instrument.

SCHLAFNICHT. Is it really? I make music, you know.

PETER. Do you?

SCHLAFNICHT. Yes. Listen.

(Singing a scale).

Ah - ah - ah - ah - ah - ah - ah - ah!

PETER. You're flat.

SCHLAFNICHT. I'm what?

PETER. You're flat. Listen.

(He plays a note).

(Singing). Aaah.

SCHLAFNICHT *(Flat).* Aaah!

PETER. No, listen. Aaah.

SCHLAFNICHT. Aaaah!

PETER. That's it. You've got it!

SCHLAFNICHT. Aren't you good? I must have been flat all these centuries and never knew.

PETER. Yes. Well, so long.

SCHLAFNICHT. Wait. I don't think I'll eat you. Not just yet anyway. I'll eat her first, and then we'll have some more music, eh? — She's thin, though, isn't she? I do like them a bit fatter, I must say. Just wait there, I shan't be long.

(He shuffles towards Trudi).

TRUDI. Oh, my goodness!

TRUDI *dodges behind a lump of rock, the Dragon shuffling after. They circle round, the Dragon wheezing and shuffling).*

TRUDI *(As she comes round).* Why don't you *do* something?

PETER *(Helplessly).* But what?

TRUDI. Oh, play your fiddle.

(She dodges the Dragon, and they go round again).

PETER *(As she passes him a second time).* I don't know what to play!

TRUDI. Play anything.

(She dodges the Dragon. He follows her round the rock, wheezing).

PETER (*Thoughtfully*). I could play Greensleeves, I suppose. But he might not like that. Or then again there's Here We Come A-Wassailing, only it isn't Christmas. I wonder if he'd like this?

(PETER plays a lullaby. The chase slows down until the Dragon and Trudi are moving to the music, drifting slowly round, and it is no longer a chase. They dance together, swaying gracefully to the music. As the lullaby comes to an end, the Dragon sinks gently asleep by the rocks).

He's asleep.

TRUDI. Thank goodness for that. Now come on, before he wakes.

PETER. Oh, yes, of course. Wait a minute, where's the way out?

TRUDI. I don't know. Look round that side.

(They go different ways and return).

PETER. There's no way that side.

TRUDI. There's none that side either. Oh, what an infuriating place. What shall we do?

PETER. I don't know. We could always take a bath.

TRUDI. Oh, you're impossible.

(SCHLAFNICHT stirs and wheezes).

He's waking up!

PETER. I don't think so. He's just turning over.

TRUDI. He's bound to wake sooner or later. Haven't you any suggestions at all?

(There is a whistle off).

What's that?

(ROTHBART appears).

PETER. It's Rothbart!

TRUDI. Oh, no. As though we haven't enough to put up with.

(ROTHBART jumps up and down, and gestures off).

I wonder what he means?

PETER. I think he's trying to tell us the way out.

TRUDI. No thank you. I don't trust him.

PETER. It's either him or the Dragon.

(To Rothbart).

That way? — Is that the way?

994

(ROTHBART nods).

What did I tell you? Come on.

(PETER pulls TRUDI. ROTHBART stops them).

What now?

(ROTHBART makes complicated gestures).

I haven't the faintest idea what he means.

(The DRAGON stirs and yawns).

TRUDI. He *is* waking up. What are we waiting for?

PETER. I can't tell what Rothbart means us to do!

TRUDI. Oh, why on earth can't he speak?

ROTHBART. Shoes. Off.

PETER. Shoes off? — You *can* talk!

ROTHBART. Of course.

TRUDI. Then why don't you, for goodness sake?

ROTHBART. Because ninety per cent of what people say isn't worth saying anyway.

(The DRAGON wheezes).

Sh! Shoes off.

(They take off their shoes).

Hats off.

(PETER takes off his hat, TRUDI her headscarf).

PETER. What are we doing this for?

ROTHBART. Sh!

PETER *(Whispering).* What are we doing this for?

ROTHBART. He's very stupid, even for a Dragon. If there's no sign of you, he'll think he hasn't eaten you yet, and follow you. On the other hand, if he sees your shoes and things, he'll think he has. Then he won't bother.

PETER. Rothbart, I've underestimated you.

ROTHBART. People do it all the time. Now come on. Sh!

(They creep out after Rothbart.

Flash. The BARONESS appears. She examines the shoes, and the sleeping Dragon).

BARONESS *(Smugly).* How about that, then?

(A peal of thunder. She quails).

(Another passageway. ROTHBART enters first, and beckons. TRUDI and PETER follow, treading gingerly).

PETER. Oh, my feet.

TRUDI. Mine, too.

PETER. It's all very well for a Troll. They've got built-in springs, but I can't go much further on these rocks without shoes.

(ROTHBART motions them to hurry).

TRUDI. I think I can see daylight. Are we nearly outside?

(ROTHBART nods, and points off).

ROTHBART. There's Trollheim, then outside.

PETER. Trollheim, what's that?

ROTHBART. Well, I'll tell you —

(A bell rings).

That's the Baroness. No time to tell you. Must go.

(He crosses them to go back).

PETER. Wait. Are there more Trolls down there?

ROTHBART. More Trolls. Watch it. And keep your hearts whatever you do.

(A bell rings).

TRUDI. You mean keep our heads, don't you?

ROTHBART. No time. The Baroness — big stick. Goodbye.

(The Troll darts off).

PETER. Hey, Rothbart! — What do you mean —? He's gone. I don't relish the idea of more Trolls, I must say.

TRUDI. Well, we can't go back. We'll just have to go on.

PETER. I suppose so. Come on then.

TRUDI. Oh, my feet.

PETER. Mine, too.

(They go off).

(TROLLHEIM. It is another cavern with no apparent entrances. On top of a rock sits WEISSBART, an ancient Troll who is just a face in a mass of white hair. In a half-circle below him sit four other TROLLS, of various colours. They have a bowl of soapsuds between them, and a loop of wire each. In unison, they dip in

996

*the bowl and blow out a stream of bubbles. Having done so, they
jump up and down in great excitement, uttering a stream of high-
pitched chatter. They repeat the process. TRUDI and PETER
enter, and stand watching them).*

PETER. Excuse me.

(The TROLLS take no notice).

(Louder).

Excuse me!

(The TROLLS look round sharply, as one).

TROLLS *(Together).* People!

*(They put their pieces of wire into the bowl, one of them gives
it to WEISSBART, and they get swiftly into line facing Peter and
Trudi).*

TROLL 1 *(Intoning).* How d'you do?

TROLL 2 *(Higher).* How d'you do?

TROLL 3 *(Higher).* How d'you do?

TROLL 4 *(Higher).* How d'you do?

WEISSBART *(Very deep).* How do you do?

(WEISSBART blows a stream of bubbles).

PETER. How do you do?

TROLL 1 *(Intoning).* Who are you?

TROLL 2 *(Higher).* Who are you?

TROLL 3 *(Higher).* Who are you?

TROLL 4 *(Higher).* Who are you?

WEISSBART *(Deep).* Yes, *who* are *you?*

(WEISSBART blows a stream of bubbles).

PETER. This is Trudi, and I'm Peter — Peter Pumpernickel.

TROLL 1. How d'you do?

*(He intones it, and the others repeat, as before, WEISSBART
blowing bubbles).*

PETER. Er — how do you do?

(Aside to Trudi).

This could go on for ever.

(To the Trolls).

I'm — I'm sorry to intrude and everything, but we would be obliged if you would let us pass through your — er — territory, and find our way out.

TROLL 1 *(Spoken, high-pitched)*. But of course.

TROLL 2 *(Likewise)*. Why not?

TROLL 3 *(Likewise)*. Yes, indeed.

TROLL 4 *(Likewise)*. By all means.

WEISSBART *(Deep)*. Why, certainly.

PETER *(Surprised)*. You mean — just like that? We can go?

TROLL 1 *(As before)*. But of course.

TROLL 2. Why not?

TROLL 3. Yes, indeed.

TROLL 4. By all means.

WEISSBART. Why, certainly.

PETER *(Incredulously)*. Well, thanks very much. Come on, Trudi.

(They cross the Trolls to go. Suddenly, the four TROLLS dash in front of them and line up, barring the way).

WEISSBART. When you've paid the toll.

TROLL 1 *(Intoning)*. The toll.

TROLL 2 *(Higher)*. The toll.

TROLL 3 *(Higher)*. The toll.

TROLL 4 *(Higher)*. The toll.

WEISSBART *(Deep)*. — You've paid the toll.

TRUDI. The toll?

TROLLS *(Together, pointing at Peter and Trudi)*. You must pay the toll!

PETER. I'm afraid we — we have no money. How much is the toll?

WEISSBART. One thousand marks.

TRUDI. A thousand marks! — I've never *seen* so much money.

WEISSBART. Or . . . your heart.

TROLL 1 *(Intoning)*. Your heart.

TROLL 2 *(Higher)*. Your heart.

TROLL 3 *(Higher)*. Your heart.

TROLL 4 *(Higher)*. Your heart.

998

WEISSBART *(Deep)*. Or else your *heart*.

TRUDI *(Pulling Peter aside)*. I don't understand. What do they mean, my heart?

PETER. I think I do. If you let a Troll take your heart, you also become a Troll.

TRUDI. What?

PETER. Yes. So I've heard people say. I don't want to be a Troll. Do you?

TRUDI. I should think not. A lot of hair and a few springs — that's all they are, you know.

PETER. I know. Listen. If we go back, it's the Dragon or the Baroness. Right?

TRUDI. Right.

PETER. If we try to go on, it's the Trolls.

TRUDI. So?

PETER. So either way we're in a mess, unless —

TRUDI. Unless what?

PETER. Unless we fight our way out.

TRUDI. Who — you?

PETER. All right, I know I'm no hero, but they *are* only hair and springs. I'm going to have a go.

(PETER takes his lute by the neck, holding it like a club).

Keep behind me.

TRUDI. Peter, I don't want you to get hurt.

PETER. Quiet, before I lose my nerve.

(To the TROLLS).

I'm sorry, but our hearts are not for sale. We're coming through. Stand aside.

TROLLS *(Pointing at him)*. Your heart!

PETER. All right, then!

(PETER makes a dash at the TROLLS, swinging his guitar. The TROLLS, as one, each thrust out an open hand towards him. There is a shrill sound, and Peter is spun round and away from them. He falls to the ground, and TRUDI runs to him. The TROLLS fall about in shrill laughter. On his rock, WEISSBART hops up and down in glee).

999

TRUDI. Peter, what happened?

PETER *(dazed)*. I don't know. It was like — like a lot of red-hot needles all over me.

TROLL 1 *(Intoning)*. Your heart.

TROLL 2 *(Higher)*. Your heart.

TROLL 3 *(Higher)*. Your heart.

TROLL 4 *(Higher)*. Your heart.

WEISSBART *(Deep)*. We'll have your *heart*.

PETER. I think they will, too.

WEISSBART *(Pointing at Peter)*. Now!

(The TROLLS, in a line, move towards Peter with extended arms and pointing fingers. TRUDI backs away. The TROLLS surround Peter, still on the ground. They swoop on him, two taking each arm, pull him to his feet, whirl him round, and take him across to the rock where WEISSBART stands. They stand him up with his back to it, and group around him. They make a big movement away and back, each pointing a forefinger at his chest).

TROLLS. Your heart!

PETER. It's a bit further to the left, actually.

(A loud double thumping begins to be heard).

I say, is that me? I don't know what you want with my heart anyway. What will you do — pickle it?

(The TROLLS begin to make large movements in time to the heartbeats, as though trying to draw the heart out of Peter's body. The sound increases in pace, and the TROLLS' movements become a dance in time to the beats, like a drum working them up to a frenzy. They pull PETER into the midst of them, whirl him around, and take him out of sight behind the rock on which WEISSBART stands.

The drumming subsides to a new low beat, with some excited Troll chatter. WEISSBART, now unconcerned, blows bubbles).

TRUDI. What are they *doing*?

WEISSBART. Taking out his heart.

TRUDI. Will it — will it hurt very much?

WEISSBART. Hurt? Not in the very least. In fact, it's rather pleasant. I'm told it tickles.

(He blows bubbles).

PETER *(Off, laughing)*. Ha, ha. . . Ha, ha, ha. . . Ha, ha, ha, ha, ha!

WEISSBART. There, what did I tell you? Won't be long now.

(WEISSBART puts down the bowl of soapsuds, and turns round. The laughter of PETER continues. The drumming reaches a climax and stops. There is a cheer from the TROLLS).

TROLLS. Hooray!

(An object is thrown up from behind. WEISSBART catches it and turns round. It is a rather large and impossibly heart-shaped heart. The four TROLLS file out and stand in line).

TROLL 1 *(Intoning)*. His heart.

TROLL 2 *(Higher)*. His heart.

TROLL 3 *(Higher)*. His heart.

TROLL 4 *(Higher)*. His heart.

WEISSBART *(Deep)*. Behold his *heart!*

(PETER emerges. He has on a Troll wig, ginger-coloured. He carries a bowl of soapsuds and a bubble-wire. He blows a stream of bubbles. The TROLLS collapse in high-pitched laughter, and all disappear abruptly).

TRUDI *(Dismayed)*. Oh, Peter! You're a Troll!

(PETER blows a stream of bubbles, and goes off after the Trolls).

Peter! Oh, of all the stupid things!

(TRUDI looks around, anxious and irresolute. There is a rumbling noise, as of a great door opening. A stream of daylight pours in from the side. She goes towards it, hesitates, and turns back. ROTHBART suddenly appears).

ROTHBART. What are you waiting for?

TRUDI. Peter — I — I don't know what to do.

ROTHBART. Nothing you can do. Go while you have the chance. Quickly.

TRUDI. But what will happen to him?

ROTHBART. He's safe enough, but you're not. Go *on.*

(ROTHBART sees Peter's heart on the rock where Weissbart left it. He grabs it and gives it to Trudi).

Here — take this. Now go!

(ROTHBART pushes TRUDI off, into the light).

1001

Trudi (*Off*). Peter! — Peter!

(*The daylight narrows and disappears, with a rumbling sound*).

(*The bell rings. ROTHBART shrugs, and goes off the opposite way*).

CURTAIN

Act Two

(The following morning. A small Gypsy camp. Under a half-open tent ROM and ROMOLA are asleep on a pile of rugs.

On the other side of the stage, TRUDI also lies asleep, clutching Peter's heart wrapped in her apron.

A cock crows. ROMOLA, a matter-of-fact Gypsy woman, yawns, stretches, and wakes up. She sits up, looks at ROM, and gives him a dig with her elbow).

ROMOLA. Hey!

(ROM grunts).

Rom!

ROM *(Without moving)*. What?

ROMOLA. Get up.

(ROM grunts).

Get up.

ROM. What for?

ROMOLA. It's daylight.

(He grunts).

(Yawning). The birds are singing.

(He grunts).

The sun's shining.

(He grunts).

And there's nothing for breakfast.

(ROM grunts. ROMOLA looks at him, makes a face, reaches for her guitar, and sits strumming it). (Singing).

> Rum-tiddle-um-a-diddle-um-a-diddle-um
> Rum-tiddle-um-a-diddle-um-a-diddle-um.
> Sun is shining, rum-tiddle-um;
> Birds are singing, rum-tiddle-um;
> To this conclusion I must come
> My husband is a lazy bum
> Rum-tiddle-um-a-diddle-um-a-diddle-um.

(ROM grunts).

> He lies a-snoring, rum-tiddle-um,
> His wife ignoring, rum-tiddle-um;
> If I don't shift him, rum-tiddle-um,
> He'll lie in the hay till Kingdom come.
> Rum-tiddle-um-a-diddle-um-a-diddle-um.

(ROM yawns and sits up).

ROM.   All right. What's for breakfast?

ROMOLA.   Nothing.

ROM.   No use getting up then, is it?

ROMOLA.   That's one way of looking at it.

(She goes on strumming).

> Rum-tiddle-um-a-diddle-um-a-diddle-um —
> My mother told me, rum-tiddle-um
> Don't marry a Gypsy, rum-tiddle-um;
> They're not very clean and they're awful dumb —

(Meantime, ROM has got up, put on his boots, and shambled across the stage).

ROM.   Romola!

ROMOLA.   What?

ROM.   Come here.

ROMOLA.   What for?

ROM.   Come here.

(ROMOLA gets up and moves over).

Sh!

ROMOLA.   It's a girl.

ROM.   I know it's a girl.

ROMOLA.   Asleep.

ROM.   Yes.

ROMOLA.   Fast asleep.

ROM.   I know.

ROMOLA.   She's not dead, is she?

ROM.   I don't think so. She's breathing. They don't breathe when they're dead.

ROMOLA.   No. Rom.

ROM.   What?

ROMOLA.   Poor little thing.

ROM.   Why?

ROMOLA.   Look at her feet.

ROM.   Oh, yes.

1004

ROMOLA. Poor thing. All scratched and dirty.

ROM. That's because she has no shoes on.

ROMOLA. No, she hasn't. Rom.

ROM. What?

ROMOLA. We shall have to do something about it, shan't we?

ROM. I suppose we shall.

ROMOLA. Isn't she pretty?

ROM. Is she?

ROMOLA. Of course she is. She's beautiful.

ROM. She's very blonde.

ROMOLA. That's because she's not a Gypsy.

ROM. We can't leave her there.

ROMOLA. No.

ROM. I'll put her in the tent.

(He picks TRUDI up).

ROMOLA. I was wondering when you were going to think of that.

(ROM puts TRUDI on the pile of rugs).

Now go and get some milk.

ROM. I don't like milk.

ROMOLA. Milk for the girl.

ROM. Oh.

ROMOLA. And some eggs. She's half-starved.

(ROM goes off. ROMOLA makes TRUDI comfortable, then sets about reviving the fire by putting some kindling on the ashes, and blowing. TRUDI stirs and sits up).

TRUDI. What am I doing here?

ROMOLA. Now don't worry. We'll look after you, Rom and me.

TRUDI. Rom?

ROMOLA. He's my idle husband. He's gone for some milk. How do you feel?

TRUDI. I don't know. A bit weak. How did I get here?

ROMOLA. You must have wandered here in the night.

(TRUDI remembers the bundle she carries, and clutches it to her).
What have you got there?

TRUDI. Nothing. It's — it's something I'm looking after. What's your name?

ROMOLA. Romola.

TRUDI. I'm Trudi.

ROMOLA. What you need is a good feed and a good rest. You want building up. Now just lie down and rest till Rom comes back.

(TRUDI obediently lies down. ROMOLA picks up the guitar, and sings softly).

> Rum-a-diddle-um-a-diddle-um-a-diddle-um
> Bees are a-buzzing, rum-a-diddle-um
> Grass is a-growing, rum-a-diddle-um
> To this conclusion I must come
> Winter's gone and summer's come;
> Rum-a-diddle-um-a-diddle-um-a-diddle-um.

(ROMOLA looks at Trudi, who is already asleep, puts down the guitar, and comes to look at the fire).

If I don't find some more kindling, that fire will be out.

(ROMOLA goes out. PETER appears silently, peering round a tree or whatever. He is still a Troll).

PETER *(Softly)*. Trudi . . . Trudi . . .

(ROM appears with the milk. PETER darts away. ROM puts down the milk, and crosses, looking off. ROM turns back to Trudi, and notices the bundle which has fallen out of Trudi's hand as she sleeps. He picks it up and opens it. ROMOLA returns).

ROMOLA. Rom, what are you doing?

ROM. Sh, look!

ROMOLA. What is it?

ROM. It's a heart.

ROMOLA. It's a heart.

ROM. That's a very strange thing to have.

ROMOLA. Yes. But it's none of our business, Rom. Put it back.

(ROM puts it back. ROMOLA breaks an egg into the milk and starts to beat it up).

ROM. Do you know what I saw just now?

ROMOLA. What?

ROM. A Troll.

ROMOLA. You didn't!

ROM. Yes, I did.

ROMOLA. Where?

ROM. Over there.

ROMOLA. It's not there now. What a pest.

ROM. They're a pest.

ROMOLA. They shouldn't be allowed.

ROM. They should be exterminated.

ROMOLA. Got rid of.

ROM. Eradicated.

ROMOLA. Rooted out.

ROM. Yes.

ROMOLA. This is ready now. I'll give it to her.

(ROMOLA takes the egg-and-milk to TRUDI).

Trudi . . . Trudi . . .

(TRUDI sits up).

Have this. It'll do you good. It's an egg beaten up in milk.

(TRUDI eats. They watch her).

ROM. She's enjoying that, isn't she?

ROMOLA. Of course she is. It's good stuff.

(PETER appears, furtively half-hidden).

ROM (Quietly). Romola.

ROMOLA. What?

ROM. It's there again.

ROMOLA. What is?

ROM. That Troll.

TRUDI (Jumping up). A Troll? Where?

ROMOLA. Nowhere. It's nothing, Trudi.

TRUDI. But it might be —

(Seeing Peter).

— it is! — It's Peter!

(PETER disappears. She runs across, and stops).

Peter, come back! Peter!

(The GYPSIES watch her).

He's disappeared.

1007

Rom. They're very quick.

Romola. Quick as lightning.

Rom. You'll never catch one.

Romola. I've never even seen one.

Trudi. I'm sure it was him — I'm sure it was.

Romola. Who?

Trudi. Peter. He's not a Troll really. I mean he is, but he shouldn't be.

Romola. Poor thing, she's rambling.

Trudi. I'm not rambling. Listen. If a Troll takes your heart, you become a Troll yourself. You know that, don't you?

Rom. Oh, yes, I know that.

Romola. Everybody knows that.

Trudi. Well, the Trolls took Peter's heart, so now he's a Troll. Only — only I managed to get his heart back.

Romola. Fancy.

Rom. She got his heart back.

Romola. I know she did. I heard her say so.

Trudi. Well, somehow, I've got to see that it's returned to him, and then he'll stop being a Troll.

Rom. How can you do that?

Trudi. I don't know. I thought you might know.

Romola. How should we know?

Trudi. I thought — well, I thought Gypsies would know things like that.

Romola. He doesn't know anything.

Rom. Yes, I do.

Romola. What do you know?

Rom. Well, snaring rabbits . . . tickling trout. That's something, isn't it?

Romola. How many trout have you tickled this week?

Rom. Well, I —

Romola. How many rabbits have you snared?

Rom. Well, it's —

Romola. You're all talk, you.

1008

Rom. I'm not all talk. I know how to catch a Troll, anyhow.

Trudi. You do? How?

Romola. How, then?

Rom. I'm not going to tell you.

Romola. You see. He doesn't know.

Rom. I do know.

Romola. Then why don't you tell her?

Rom. You'll laugh at me.

Trudi. Oh, I won't. I promise I won't.

Rom. Well, *she* will.

Romola. Oh, don't be so soft. Tell her.

Rom. Well, you get a bit of mistletoe, and you hold it up, and you
say "Mistletoe, mistletoe,
    Show, Troll, show;
    Troll, Troll, near or far,
    Come out, come out, wherever you are."

(ROMOLA giggles).

Romola. What a daft thing to say.

Trudi. Is that all?

Rom. No. When it comes, you grab it by the hair.

Romola. Sooner you than me. I wouldn't touch one of those things.

Rom. And then it does whatever you tell it.

Trudi. Are you sure?

Rom. Well, that's what my grandmother used to say.

Romola. And a crazy old thing she was, too.

Trudi. We'll do it. Now. Can you find me some mistletoe?

Romola. You mean you believe it?

Trudi. Yes, I do. I think.

Romola. Then you're just as daft as him.

Trudi. Please. Get me some mistletoe. It's very important to me.

Romola. All right, if it makes you feel any better. But it'll never
work.

(To ROM).

Come on, we'll both go.

1009

(ROM and ROMOLA go out. As soon as they have gone, TRUDI looks about the stage).

TRUDI. Peter! — Peter, are you there?

(There is no response. Trudi gives up, and sits down, holding the heart. Presently, PETER quietly appears at the side).

PETER. Have they gone?

TRUDI *(Jumping up).* Peter! — Yes, there's only me. Listen, there's nothing to be afraid of. I have your heart.

PETER. I know.

TRUDI. If we can find out how to put it back, you'll be all right again.

(PETER stands motionless).

You — you want to be yourself again, don't you?

PETER *(Flatly).* Yes.

TRUDI. So when the gypsies come back, you must stay here, do you understand?

PETER. Yes.

TRUDI. And we'll help you, somehow.

PETER. Yes.

(A slight pause).

TRUDI. Come and — come and sit down over here.

(PETER moves mechanically across, but doesn't sit down).

PETER. I'm a Troll now.

TRUDI. Yes, but not for much longer, Peter.

PETER. I'm a Troll. It's good being a Troll. You must be a Troll, too.

TRUDI *(Afraid).* Peter . . .

PETER. You must be a Troll.

TRUDI. But I don't —

PETER. You must be a Troll. We want your heart.

TRUDI. No, Peter —

(The four TROLLS spring out from four corners of the stage, surrounding her).

TROLLS. Your heart!

TRUDI. No!

TROLL 1 *(Pointing).* Your heart.

1010

TROLL 2 *(Pointing)*. Your heart.

TROLL 3 *(Pointing)*. Your heart.

TROLL 4 *(Pointing)*. Your heart.

PETER. We'll have your heart!

(The four TROLLS whirl round once and stop, their arms extended towards Trudi).

TROLLS. Give us your heart!

(ROM and ROMOLA re-enter, each with a branch of mistletoe).

ROM. Trolls!

ROMOLA. Hundreds of them!

(ROM and ROMOLA dash at the TROLLS, swiping at them with the mistletoe. Pandemonium. The Trolls, terrified of the mistletoe, scatter in panic with high-pitched squeals of terror).

ROMOLA. Catch one!

ROM. Why don't you?

ROMOLA. Get them by the hair!

ROM. I'm trying, but they're too quick.

(PETER hesitates which way to escape, and TRUDI seizes him by the hair. ROM and ROMOLA, having chased off the TROLLS, return).

ROMOLA. She's got one!

ROM. Is that him?

TRUDI. Yes, it's Peter.

ROM. Don't let go of his hair, then.

PETER. Make her let go of me, and I'll make you rich. I'll tell you — I'll tell you where all the gold of the Trolls is hidden — I'll tell you — I'll tell — I'll tell — I'll tell . . .

(PETER's voice fades out. He goes limp, and sinks to the ground, kneeling, his head lolling, TRUDI still holding his hair).

TRUDI. What's happened? What's the matter with him?

ROMOLA. I don't know.

ROM. I do, his spring's run down.

TRUDI. What? What spring?

ROM. The spring where his heart should be. It wants winding up again.

TRUDI. Like a clock?

Rom. That's it — like clockwork. They're all like that — they have springs instead of hearts.

Romola. Well, now's your chance then.

Trudi. Chance? What chance?

Romola. Take the spring out and put his heart back.

Rom. Screwdriver!

(He goes to the tent).

Trudi. What?

Rom *(Rummaging).* I've got one somewhere.

Trudi. But what do you want —

Rom *(Holding up a screwdriver).* That's it! Now hold him up while I have a look.

(TRUDI and ROMOLA lift PETER to his feet, head lolling and arms hanging. ROM opens Peter's coat).

That's it! See that? Three screws. Now hold him still.

(Business of unscrewing. Appropriate sound).

That's one. Hold it.

(He gives Romola something. Repeat business).

That's two.

(Repeat business).

And that's the last.

(A loud twang, and a large mainspring uncoils from Peter's chest).

Romola. Good heavens! Fancy having that in your insides.

(ROM pulls the spring off ,and throws it aside).

Rom. Give me the heart.

(TRUDI gives it to him. He stuffs it under PETER's jacket).

Right. Screws.

(ROMOLA gives him the screws, ROM rapidly mimes the replacing of them, with suitable noise).

One . . . two . . . three . . . And that's it.

(PETER begins to straighten up. TRUDI and ROMOLA, who are still holding him, contrive to remove his Troll wig as he does so, so that he appears to shed his Troll appearance in one movement).

Peter. What's going on?

1012

ROMOLA. You've just been repaired.

PETER. What?

ROM. We've put your heart back.

TRUDI. Well, aren't you glad about it? What have you got to say?

PETER. My feet are killing me. Where are my shoes?

TRUDI. Is that all?

PETER. Eh? Oh, thanks very much. I wish I had my shoes, though.

ROMOLA. Rom will get you both some, won't you, Rom?

ROM. Eh? Oh, all right, I'll try.

ROMOLA. And get me a chicken or something at the same time. I'm famished, if they're not.

ROM. I'll do my best.

(ROM goes out).

TRUDI. You keep sending him for things. Where does he get them all from?

ROMOLA. Well, he is a Gypsy, you know.

TRUDI. Oh, I see. He borrows them.

ROMOLA. That's right.

PETER (Seeing the guitar). Do you play?

ROMOLA. Of course. Do you? Well, you're bound to, aren't you, I mean, being a minstrel and all. Let's have a song till Rom comes back.

PETER. All right. What do you know?

ROMOLA. Do you know "Foxey, Foxey"?

PETER. Yes! I know that!

(They sit down and sing).

PETER & ROMOLA (Together, singing).

> Foxey, foxey, where are you going to—
> Foxey, foxey, oh, won't you stay?
> "I'm off for a chicken or a duck for my dinner,
> And I can't let anything stand in my way
> We will go a-walking, Madam, some other day."
>
> Foxey, foxey, homeward returning—
> Foxey, foxey, what did you find?
> "I found me a chicken, and I ate all but the wing of it
> And you may have it, ma'am, if you've a mind,
> Then we'll go a-walking, for I feel so inclined."

Foxey, foxey, I do not care for it—
Foxey, foxey, keep it, I pray.
I found me another fox who is more of a gentleman,
And so, dear foxey, I bid you good day.
You can keep your chicken wing, I bid you good day.

(The BARONESS's bower. She sits in her chair, trying on tiaras).

BARONESS. Rothbart!

(She rings a little bell).

Rothbart!

(ROTHBART appears).

You're getting very slack, Rothbart. I think we shall have to beat you more often. Bring me my harp.

(ROTHBART brings in a full-size harp without strings. The BARONESS arranges herself at it, and begins to sweep the non-existent strings, with great panache. Harp music, as she gives her virtuoso performance).

(Suddenly, the door offstage bangs, and SIEGFRIED bursts in).

SIEGFRIED. What have you done with her?

(She ignores him, and goes on playing).

What have you done with Trudi?

BARONESS. I can't imagine what you are talking about.

SIEGFRIED. You know perfectly well. I went down to have a look at Schlafnicht just now, and I found — this!

(He produces Trudi's scarf).

It's Trudi's.

BARONESS. Who or what is Trudi, as if I cared?

SIEGFRIED. Will you stop pretending! And please stop playing that awful harp, it sets my teeth on edge.

BARONESS *(Stopping).* You always had good teeth, Siegfried. You get them from my side of the family, of course. Now what is it you want?

SIEGFRIED *(Looking at the scarf).* She was the sweetest girl I ever met, and I shall never forgive you.

BARONESS. Every girl that comes along is the sweetest girl you've ever met. It's getting to be a bore, Siegfried.

SIEGFRIED. Mitzi was different.

BARONESS. You mean Trudi.

1014

SIEGFRIED. Do I? Well, she was.

BARONESS. Rubbish. It's all in the mind.

SIEGFRIED (*Sadly*). And now she's gone, and I hate you more than ever. Why must every girl I meet finish up inside a dragon? It's so — so inconsiderate.

BARONESS. Because none of them was good enough for you. It's simple.

SIEGFRIED. I shall go away. As far away as possible.

(*The BARONESS resumes playing*).

Did you hear what I said? I shall go away.

BARONESS. You'll be back.

SIEGFRIED. Never. I shall go away and become a hermit, and I shall keep her scarf always.

BARONESS. As I said, you'll be back.

SIEGFRIED. Not this time. I shall never forget her.

BARONESS. Of course you won't — not until you meet the next pretty girl, Siegfried.

SIEGFRIED. Goodbye, mother. I shall hate you for ever.

(*SIEGFRIED rushes out. The BARONESS plays on, then stops, thoughtfully*).

BARONESS. Never be a mother, Rothbart.

(*She plays a little more, then stops*).

Something has just occurred to me. Did you actually see Schlafnicht eat those two?

(*ROTHBART shakes his head*).

Of course you didn't — you weren't there — and neither did I, now I come to think of it . . . That girl may still be alive!

(*The BARONESS rises*).

Rothbart, bring me the glass.

(*ROTHBART goes out returning at once with a sizeable looking-glass, its face covered with a black velvet cloth*).

BARONESS. Wherever she is, whatever she does, the glass will show.

(*ROTHBART crouches before her, holding the glass. She throws back the cover*).

Wherever she is, whatever she does, show, glass, show!

(*She peers into it intently*).

. . . Nothing . . . nothing but darkness and swirling fog. . . . Oh, come on, you infuriating thing . . . show me . . . show me . . . Ah! — that's better . . . it's clearing . . . A tent . . . a fire . . . Gypsies . . . Gypsies dancing . . . and yes — there she is. It's she! Dancing with them. How dare she dance!

(Pointing suddenly).

I know that place!

(She whips the cover back over the glass).

Take it away . . . Wait! We must think, Rothbart, think. . . . I have it! Rothbart, my number three disguise, quickly.

(ROTHBART scutters out with the glass).

I'll write a letter — a letter to my brother Grosskopf.

(Goes to the table, getting ink and paper).

A letter she shall deliver for me — yes — a letter which says —

(Writing).

— "Dear Grosskopf: Immediately on receipt of this letter, you will strike off the bearer's head — and oblige. Your loving sister, Gudrun von Grubelstein." — There, that should do it . . . Good.

(Seals the letter. ROTHBART has entered with a cloak, a large hat, and a big false beard).

Rothbart, prepare me.

(ROTHBART helps her into the disguise).

The letter.

(ROTHBART gives her the letter).

My cane.

(ROTHBART gives her her cane).

Thank you. I shall not be in for dinner, Rothbart.

(The BARONESS sweeps out, making no attempt to characterize the disguise).

(The Gypsy camp. TRUDI and PETER are just finishing a dinner of rabbit stew. ROMOLA is watching them. ROM lies flat on his back, a straw in his mouth).

TRUDI. Oh, that was so good, Romola. And I've eaten so much.

PETER. Mm. Lovely.

ROM. She's a very good cook, is Romola.

ROMOLA *(Taking the bowls from Peter and Trudi).* What do you know about it? I send him for chicken and he comes back with rabbit.

(ROMOLA takes the dishes round behind the tent. PETER takes up his guitar, and picks idly at it).

PETER *(To Trudi, who is staring into the fire)*. What are you thinking about?

TRUDI. Nothing . . . there's a face in the fire . . . Peter . . .

PETER. Yes?

TRUDI. What did you think of Siegfried?

PETER *(Shrugging)*. He's a lord, isn't he?

TRUDI. What does that mean?

PETER. He's no worse than most of them, I suppose.

TRUDI. He's rather splendid, though, isn't he?

PETER. Splendidly spoilt, if you ask me.

TRUDI. I wonder if we shall ever see him again.

PETER. You're not —

TRUDI. Not what?

PETER. You're not getting fond of Siegfried, are you?

TRUDI. I don't know. Why shouldn't I?

PETER. No reason, only — only it might mean trouble for you, that's all.

TRUDI. I like you, Peter — you're so funny.

PETER. Funny?

TRUDI. Yes — you've a funny face when you're serious. And Pumpernickel is such a funny name.

PETER. I'm glad it amuses you.

(He gets up).

TRUDI. Now you're offended.

PETER. No, I'm not. Trudi, how long will you stay here?

TRUDI. I don't know. Romola says I can stay as long as I like.

PETER. I think I'd better leave.

TRUDI. Do you have to go?

PETER. It's time I earned some money, anyway.

TRUDI. Peter . . .

PETER. What?

TRUDI. Nothing.

1017

PETER. The best of luck, Trudi. I hope everything turns out all right for you.

(ROMOLA returns).

PETER. I'm just leaving, Romola.

ROMOLA. What? But you can't go yet. Rom's told all his cousins and things about you — they'll be coming to have a look at you — you can't go.

PETER. But I do have a living to make, I —

ROMOLA *(Kicking Rom).* Rom, tell him he can't go yet.

ROM *(Waking up).* Eh? What do you say?

ROMOLA. There you are, Rom says you have to stay!

PETER. But I —

(Four GYPSIES enter from the back, a girl and three men. They greet Romola enthusiastically).

OLGA. Romola!

ROMOLA. Olga! Sergei! Dimitri! Valenti!

(The GYPSIES invade the place, greeting Peter and Trudi, pulling ROM to his feet. Music begins almost at once).

It's ages since I saw you. This is Trudi — and this is Peter — and this is Sergei and Dimitri and Valenti.

TRUDI. Kosko bokht.

SERGEI. Kosko bokht! She's a Romani!

(They laugh).

She can rokra Romani!

GYPSIES. Kosko bokht!

(OLGA begins to dance. The MEN join in).

PETER. What does that mean?

TRUDI. It means good luck in Romany.

PETER. I'll remember that. Kosko bokht.

(The dance continues. TRUDI is swept into it. As it finishes, there is general applause and conversation. One of the men produces a bottle of wine and circulates it as they settle down).

ROMOLA. Quiet now! Quiet a minute — shut up, Rom. — Now Peter's a minstrel.

SEVERAL. A minstrel!

ROMOLA And he knows hundreds of songs —

PETER. Well, one or two.

ROMOLA. So just be quiet while he sings one. What will you sing?

PETER. What sort of song do you want?

SERGEI. Something we can all sing.

PETER. How about the Queen of Sheba?

SERGEI. Never heard of it.

PETER. Right, then. The Queen of Sheba.

(Sings).

> Look through the window
> Who goes riding by?

PETER & TRUDI. Oh, the beautiful Queen of Sheba, Sheba, she goes riding by.

ALL. Oh, the beautiful Queen of Sheba, Sheba, she goes riding by.

PETER. Look through the window
Who goes riding by?

TRUDI. On an elephant!

ALL. Oh, the beautiful Queen, etc.

(The song continues to the end. Note: the song is additive; i. e. a new line is added on at each repetition, in the manner of "The Twelve Days of Christmas", each of the Gypsies contributing a line).

> Look through the window —
> Who goes riding by?
> With a golden crown
>   ermine gown
>   jewel in her nose
>   red silk hose
>   diamond ring
>   bells in her ears going ring-a-ding-ding;
> On a pink silk cushion
> On a golden throne
> On a bearskin rug
> On a how- how- howdah
> On an elephant!
> Oh, the beautiful Queen of Sheba, Sheba,
> She goes riding by.

(As they finish, and applaud themselves, the BARONESS, in her disguise, appears at the side. As the GYPSIES gather in a group, PETER and TRUDI are left to themselves. The BARONESS catches Trudi's eye, and beckons to her).

TRUDI (Quietly). Peter.

1019

PETER. What?

TRUDI. Who's that?

PETER. Who?

TRUDI. Over there.

PETER. I don't know. I've never seen him before.

TRUDI. I think he wants something. He's very odd.

PETER. Pay no attention.

BARONESS *(Aside)*. What a stupid girl she is.

(The BARONESS beckons to Trudi, waving the letter).

TRUDI. Peter.

PETER. What?

TRUDI. It's a false beard.

PETER. How do you know?

TRUDI. It keeps slipping. I must go and see what he wants.

(TRUDI crosses to the Baroness).

Did you want something?

BARONESS. Sh! Walls have ears.

TRUDI. What walls?

BARONESS. Don't be silly. You know what I mean. Sh!

(The BARONESS draws Trudi further away).

If your name is Trudi, I have a message for you . . .

TRUDI. My name is Trudi.

BARONESS. —from the Lord Siegfried.

TRUDI. Siegfried! But how does he know —

BARONESS. Sh! The Von Grubelsteins know everything.

TRUDI. What is the message?

BARONESS. You are in danger of your life.

TRUDI. Me? Why?

BARONESS. Don't ask so many questions. You are, that's all. Can you read?

TRUDI. No, I'm afraid I can't.

BARONESS. All the better. Now take this letter . . . hide it . . . and go at once to Castle Seeblick.

1020

TRUDI. Seeblick?

BARONESS. Yes. Give it personally to the Baron, and he will — see that you are taken care of.

(She laughs).

Sh! You will be safe there. Quite safe.

TRUDI. Safe from what?

BARONESS. None of your business. Go at once. And remember — not a word to a living soul. Sh!

(The BARONESS goes off).

PETER. What was all that about?

TRUDI. A message from Siegfried.

PETER. Siegfried? What about?

TRUDI. He said not to tell. I must go — straight away.

PETER. Go? Where to?

TRUDI. Castle Seeblick. Don't ask me any more — I'm not supposed to tell anybody.

PETER. I'm coming with you.

TRUDI. What for? I can look after myself.

PETER. All the same, I'm coming.

TRUDI. Please yourself, but I must go now.

(TRUDI runs off. PETER looks irresolutely at the Gypsies, then follows her. The Gypsies, unaware, begin to sing).

(A road. An inn-sign, "The King's Head", hangs from nothing over a table covered with a white cloth which reaches to the floor. In the centre of the table is a large dish-cover. There is nothing else. PETER and TRUDI come in together).

TRUDI. Do you think it's much further to Castle Seeblick?

PETER. Quite a way yet, I imagine.

TRUDI. I could do with something to drink. Look, there's an inn-sign.

PETER. The King's Head, it says.

TRUDI. How peculiar. I don't see anyone about.

PETER *(Going to the table).* Nor do I. Wait a minute — here's a little notice. "Ring for service" it says. Where's the bell, then?

TRUDI. I can't see one. Look under there.

(PETER lifts the cover. There is a hand-bell under it).

PETER. How odd. Shall I ring it?

TRUDI. That's what it's for, I imagine.

(PETER rings it, and puts it back under the cover. They wait).

PETER. No signs of anybody. It's the oddest inn I ever saw.

TRUDI. Ring again.

PETER. Do you think I should?

TRUDI. Yes, go on.

(PETER lifts the cover. The bell has disappeared, and in its place is a cheerful-looking crowned HEAD, rather like the king on a playing-card).

HEAD. Good afternoon. Nice day.

PETER. Oh yes, very nice.

(He puts the cover back hastily. Trudi and he look at each other in amazement, then Peter slightly lifts the cover to see if the Head is still there. It is, so he lifts the cover off and puts it down by the side of the Head).

HEAD. Welcome to the King's Head. What can we do for you?

TRUDI. We — we'd like something to drink, if it's not too much trouble — sir.

HEAD. Trouble? My dear madam, nothing can be too much trouble at the King's Head. Now what would you like to drink? We have a very cheerful little sparkling white wine I can recommend. I'm sure you will like it.

TRUDI. Th-Thank you. I'm sure it will do very well.

HEAD. If you wouldn't mind lifting the cover? We are having a little staff difficulty at the moment.

(PETER lifts the cover, putting it down in another place. An opened bottle of wine is revealed, with two goblets. PETER pours out the wine).

I think you'll find it's just about the right temperature. I don't care for a sparkling wine to be too chilled, myself.

(They drink).

TRUDI. It's very nice.

HEAD *(Smugly)*. I thought it would have a modest success with you. And now — a little something else?

TRUDI. I — I don't think so, thank you.

HEAD. A cheese souffle, perhaps?

1022

TRUDI. Not — not at the moment.

(To PETER).

Peter, have you got any money?

PETER. About two marks fifty, I think.

TRUDI. It looks a very expensive place. Will that pay for the wine?

PETER. I don't know.

TRUDI. Oh, dear. I wish we'd never come.

HEAD. Do have a stuffed olive, at least.

PETER. I don't think so, thank you.

HEAD. They're on the house, of course.

PETER. Oh, that's different.

(PETER lifts the cover, and finds some stuffed olives and cheese straws).

HEAD. Well, if there should be anything else, you know where to find me.

(Looking at the dish-cover).

Do you mind?

PETER. What? Oh, certainly.

(PETER puts the cover over the Head. TRUDI and he nibble olives thoughtfully).

Trudi.

TRUDI. What?

PETER. That letter.

TRUDI. What about it?

PETER. How do you know it's from Siegfried?

TRUDI. Well, the old man said it was.

PETER. Yes, but — may I see it?

TRUDI. Of course.

(Giving it to him).

There it is.

PETER. It has the Von Grubelstein seal on it all right.

TRUDI. There you are then — what are you worrying about?

PETER. I don't know — it just seems odd, that's all.

(A discreet cough issues from under the cover. They look at each other).

HEAD *(Underneath).* Excuse me.

(PETER lifts the cover, showing the Head).

I don't wish to intrude, but did I hear the name Von Grubelstein?

PETER. Yes, that's right.

HEAD. How strange. We have so few guests at the King's Head, but we had the pleasure of a visit from a Von Grubelstein not half an hour ago.

PETER. You did? Who?

HEAD. The heir, I believe. A rather imperious young man by the name of — er — let me see now — I've such a head for names —

TRUDI. It wasn't Siegfried, was it?

HEAD. Do you know, I believe it was. Yes, Siegfried.

TRUDI. Which way did he go?

HEAD *(Nodding).* That way, I think.

TRUDI. I wonder if — Peter, I wonder if we could catch him up?

PETER. What do you want to do that for? He might not like it.

TRUDI. I could ask him if — if he really did send that old man with the message. I'm going.

PETER. But, Trudi —

TRUDI. If I run, I might catch him.

(TRUDI runs off. PETER stands irresolute, with the letter).

PETER. She's forgotten the letter.

HEAD. I was just about to say, I should be very careful about any dealings you have with the Von Grubelsteins, if you'll forgive my saying so.

PETER. I'm only too well aware of it.

HEAD. You're dying to know what's in that letter, aren't you?

PETER. Yes, I am. I think it's some sort of trick.

HEAD. Why don't you open it, then?

PETER. I will.

(PETER opens the letter and reads it).

Well, of all the — !

HEAD. Bad news?

1024

PETER. The worst. Listen. "Dear Grosskopf; Immediately on receipt of this letter, strike off the bearer's head, and oblige — your loving sister, Gudrun von Grubelstein".

HEAD. That's just like her. She always had a twisted sense of humour.

PETER. What shall I do? I can't let Trudi deliver it.

HEAD. I know what I would do.

PETER. What?

HEAD. Get my own back. — Lift the cover, will you?

(PETER lifts the cover. There is a sheet of paper, ink, pen, and a sand-box).

Write a substitute letter.

PETER. What shall I say?

HEAD. Anything, as long as it turns the tables on the Baroness Gudrun Von Grubelstein.

PETER. You don't like her much, do you?

HEAD. I'm almost certain that it's because of her that I'm here, dear boy. I've often wondered what she did with the body. It seems to me to be an excellent opportunity to turn this to the young girl's advantage.

PETER. Yes . . . I know what I'll put!

(PETER writes, sands the paper, and folds it).

There. I've no seal for it, but I'll have to risk that.

HEAD. Look under the cover.

(PETER looks. There is wax, and a seal).

PETER. It's the Grubelstein seal! How did you get it?

HEAD. One has one's little secrets, you know.

(PETER seals the letter).

PETER. Thank you. If there's anything I can do for you at any time —

HEAD. There is.

PETER. What is it?

HEAD. Scratch my left ear, will you? It's driving me mad.

(PETER scratches his ear).

Thank you so much.

PETER. Anything else?

HEAD. Yes. Two marks fifty.

PETER. What?

HEAD. For the wine, you know.

PETER. Oh, of course.

(He pays).

HEAD. By the way, what did you put in the letter?

PETER. One has one's little secrets, you know. Goodbye, and thanks.

(He covers the Head, and runs off).

*(Castle Seeblick. A terrace overlooking the sea. BARON GROSS-
KOPF and BROTHER INNOCENT are sitting on the parapet,
eating cherries and flicking the stones into the sea.
Sea-gull noises).*

BARON. Do you know what I'd like to do more than anything in the
world, Brother Innocent?

INNOCENT. Wh-what, Baron?

BARON. Fly. Fly like a bird.

INNOCENT. If m-men had b-been intended to fly, they would have
b-been b-born with w-wings.

BARON. Fiddlesticks. You might as well say if men had been intended
to ride horses they would have been born with spurs.

INNOCENT. It isn't qu-quite the s-same.

BARON. Or if they had been meant to swim, they would have been
born with fins. — Look at that! Look at that sea-gull there, sailing
down over the water — it's so easy. Now if a stupid creature like
that can do it, why can't I? Tell me that, Innocent.

INNOCENT. B-because you haven't got wings. B-besides, if you'll
p-pardon my s-saying so, you haven't got the f-figure for it either,
Baron.

BARON. Some geese are quite fat, but geese fly, don't they?

INNOCENT. N-not the fat ones. Besides, they have w-wings.

BARON. Shall I tell you a secret, Brother Innocent?

INNOCENT. Wh-what's that?

BARON. Strictly between ourselves, you understand?

INNOCENT. Oh, of c-course.

BARON. You won't tell a soul?

INNOCENT. I p-promise I won't.

BARON. Well, I *have* got wings.

1026

INNOCENT. What?

(Looking round the Baron's shoulders).

I c-can't see any.

BARON. Sh! I haven't shown them to anybody yet. Would you like to see them?

INNOCENT. Oh yes, Baron. V-very much ind-deed.

BARON. Wait there, then.

(The BARON goes off, and returns at once with a pair of wings, rather crudely made).

There, what about that?

INNOCENT. Oh, false ones. B-but they're r-rather splendid, aren't they? Have you t-tried them out yet?

BARON. Not yet. I've been sort of saving it up.

INNOCENT. I think they're b-beautiful, B-baron. S-simply beautiful. They d-do work, of course?

BARON. Oh, I'm sure they do.

INNOCENT. B-baron —

BARON. What?

INNOCENT. I d-don't like to ask.

BARON. What?

INNOCENT. Y-you'll only say n-no.

BARON. How can I say no till I know what it is?

INNOCENT. Well, d-do you th-think I could have a go?

BARON. What, before I've tried them myself?

INNOCENT. Oh, p-please. I'd be v-very c-careful with them. P-please, Baron.

BARON. Well, as a very special favour, and only because it's you — you can put them on for five minutes. But only five minutes, mind.

INNOCENT. Oh yes, only f-five minutes, Baron. I w-won't keep them a s-second longer.

BARON. All right, then.

INNOCENT. Wh-what do I do?

BARON *(Helping him)*. Put your arm through there — that's it — and your other arm through there. Now you tie these tapes round there — like that. And that's it.

1027

INNOCENT. H-how do I l-look?

BARON. Very well. You'll make a very creditable angel in due course, Innocent.

INNOCENT. W-will I? How m-marvellous! — Baron.

BARON. What?

INNOCENT. C-can I f-flap them?

BARON. Oh, I don't know whether I can let you go as far as that, Innocent.

INNOCENT. Oh p-please, Baron. L-let me flap them j-just once. Please.

BARON. All right then.

INNOCENT. Th-thank you.

(INNOCENT flaps his wings).

Oh, isn't it lovely. I f-feel j-just like a b-bird.

BARON. You've had your five minutes now, Innocent.

INNOCENT. Oh, B-baron, I c-can't have!

BARON. Yes, you have. Take them off.

INNOCENT. ˉB-baron.

BARON. What?

INNOCENT. C-could I just try one j-jump off the b-balcony with them? — Please? — Oh, please let me.

BARON. Now, Innocent, I made them and I ought to go first, you know.

INNOCENT. I know, b-but I have got them on, haven't I? And it's all right, it isn't Lent or anything.

BARON. Well — because it's you, and because it isn't Lent, and as a very special favour — all right. But be very careful how you land. I don't want them scratched.

INNOCENT *(Going to the parapet).* Oh, I'll b-be ever so c-careful of them, Baron.

(He gets on the parapet).

BARON. Ready?

INNOCENT. J-just a minute. L-let me get my balance.

(Looks down).

— B-baron!

BARON. What?

1028

INNOCENT. It's an awfully l-long way down, isn't it?

BARON. You're not going down, you're going up.

INNOCENT. I kn-know, but it *is* a long way down . . . B-baron . . . I d-don't know whether I want to d-do it now.

BARON. Don't be silly. Start flapping.

INNOCENT. M-my kn-knees won't keep still.

BARON. Never mind your knees. Flap your arms.

INNOCENT *(Flapping)*. Oh, Baron!

BARON. Go on, flap. Flap harder!

INNOCENT. I-I'm scared, Baron.

BARON. Keep flapping.

INNOCENT. I'm s-scared. I c-can't do it!

BARON. Yes, you *can*. I'm going to count three.

INNOCENT. Oh, no!

BARON. One . . . Two . . . Three . . . and away!

> *(He pushes Innocent off the parapet. A long wail as Innocent disappears).*

Flap, Innocent! Flap your wings! You're losing height! You're —!

> *(Loud splash).*

Oh, the idiot. — Innocent! — Innocent!

INNOCENT *(A long way off)*. B-baron?

BARON. Can you swim?

INNOCENT *(Faintly)*. I d-don't know. I n-never tried.

BARON. Well now's your time to find out.

> *(Makes swimming action).*

Do this! Innocent — like this, look — no, like *this*. — Oh, he *is* a fool! Innocent, watch me!

> *(SIEGFRIED enters).*

Turn over on your back . . . on your back . . . oh, he's so stupid!

> *(The BARON turns and sees Siegfried).*

Why, Siegfried . . .

SIEGFRIED. What's the matter? What are you doing?

BARON *(Turning back)*. Oh, nothing really. Teaching Innocent to fly — or rather, swim, that's all.

SIEGFRIED. Oh . . . Uncle Grosskopf, I've left home.

BARON. Really? — That's better, Innocent — now splash with your legs — with your *legs* . . .

SIEGFRIED. It's on account of the Baroness.

BARON (*Preoccupied*). Oh yes . . . Keep it up, you're doing fine! — What an idiot . . . you're doing fine!

SIEGFRIED. I'm afraid she's getting quite impossible.

BARON (*Not looking at him*). Always was, dear boy . . . *That's* the way, you're actually moving, Innocent!

SIEGFRIED. So I've come to stay with you.

BARON. Oh yes. — Siegfried, be a good fellow and give him a hand, will you?

SIEGFRIED. Who?

BARON. Brother Innocent. He's down there, look, in the sea.

SIEGFRIED. In the sea? Can he swim?

BARON. I don't think he can, really.

SIEGFRIED. He'll drown.

BARON. Yes, he very well might.

SIEGFRIED (*Shouting*). Hold on, I'm coming down!

(*SIEGFRIED runs out*).

BARON. You can't imagine how funny you look down there, Innocent. — I said you can't imagine — Oh, never mind. Swim!

(*A knock*).

Come in!

(*Turning away from the parapet*).

Well, it's proved one thing, at least. You need something more than a pair of wings if you're going to fly.

(*TRUDI and PETER enter*).

Yes?

TRUDI. I am to deliver this letter to the Baron Grosskopf.

BARON. A letter? For me? How simply splendid. Do you know, I don't think I've had a letter in years. What's it about?

TRUDI. I'm afraid I don't know.

BARON. You mean you haven't read it?

TRUDI. I can't read.

BARON. Neither can I. Isn't it a small world? Never mind, Innocent can read it for me when he gets back.

(To Peter).

What's that you have there?

PETER. This? It's called a guitar. It accompanies the voice, like a lute.

BARON. How very interesting. And how very apposite, because I've just written a sonnet. I'll tell you what — I'll say it, and you can accompany me. Will you?

PETER. I'll try.

BARON. Good. It goes like this . . .
>   When I consider that I cannot fly,
>   Whilst many another lesser creature can,
>   And sadly watch them flit about the sky —
>   The pigeon, partridge, peacock, pelican —
>   And see them lift and swoop and dip and glide,
>   I ask myself why I was born a man,
>   Condemned to walk through this dark world and wide
>   On his flat feet, an earthbound also-ran.
>   But whilst my sorry state I do beweep,
>   This thought to me occurs to cheer me up
>   (Like golden shafts of sunshine that do creep
>   Through fog, and help to keep one's pecker up)
>   Were I a bird, I'd feed on worms and such;
>   Oh, Grosskopf, wouldst thou like that very much?

There. What do you think about that?

TRUDI. I'm sure it's very good. What a pity you can't write it down.

BARON. Oh, but I have.

TRUDI. I thought you said you couldn't.

BARON. I said I couldn't read. I didn't say I couldn't write. What do you think I am? Illiterate?

(INNOCENT returns, wingless and draped in seaweed).

Why, Innocent, you're even wetter than usual.

INNOCENT. I'm so s-sorry, Baron.

BARON. What for?

INNOCENT. I s-spoilt your b-beautiful wings.

BARON. Well, let it be a lesson to you.

INNOCENT. Y-yes, Baron. M-may I go and d-dry myself now?

BARON. Not just yet, Innocent. Where are the wings, by the way?

INNOCENT. The y-young man is b-bringing them up.

BARON. Good. Perhaps we'll let you jump again tomorrow.

INNOCENT. Oh, no, please!

BARON. Well, we'll see. Now I want you to read a letter for me.

INNOCENT. R-read the l-lesson? But it isn't Sunday.

BARON *(Taking a bit of seaweed out of Innocent's ear)*. Letter, not lesson.

INNOCENT. Oh. Oh, of course.

BARON *(Giving him the letter)*. There you are then. Read it — and be quick before you smudge the ink — you're dripping all over it.

INNOCENT. Y-yes, Baron. It s-says: "D-dear G-grosskopf —"

BARON. That's me! It *is* for me. How delightful! Go on.

INNOCENT. "Immediately upon receipt of this l-le-l-le-l-le—"

BARON. Letter?

INNOCENT. "Letter," yes, "you will s-see that the b-be-b-be-be"

BARON. What's the matter with you? You're stammering worse than usual.

INNOCENT. It's b-because my t-teeth are ch-chattering as w-well.

BARON. All right, but do get *on*.

INNOCENT. Y-yes, Baron. — "You will s-see that the b-be-b-be-b-be-b-be—"

BARON. Best bedroom?

INNOCENT. No, the b-be-b-be-b-be-b-be—

BARON. Belltower?

INNOCENT. No, the b-be-b-be-b-be-b-be-b-be—

BARON. Birdcatcher.

INNOCENT. No, the "b-bearer of this letter —"

BARON. Oh. That's her. What about her?

INNOCENT. — "is m-ma-m-ma-m-ma-m-ma-m-ma—"

BARON. Manacled?

INNOCENT. No, m-ma-m-ma-m-ma-m-ma—

BARON. Murdered?

INNOCENT. No, m-ma-m-ma-m-ma-m-ma—

BARON. Marinated — manumitted — manslaughtered — matriculated — machicolated — made into marmalade —

1032

INNOCENT *(Stamping his foot)*. No, m-*married*. — "m-married forth-with to L-lord Siegfried."

(SIEGFRIED enters, carrying the remains of the wings).

TRUDI & SIEGFRIED *(together)*. What?

BARON. Sh! Don't interrupt, or he'll never get through it.

INNOCENT. "— and oblige, your loving sister, G-gudrun von G-grubel-stein."

BARON. Is that all?

INNOCENT. Th-that's all.

TRUDI. Oh, my goodness!

BARON. Well, what are you waiting for, Innocent? Take them away and marry them!

INNOCENT.   But I —

TRUDI.   *(together)*. But he —

SIEGFRIED.   But she —

BARON. Don't shilly-shally! You *can* marry people, can't you?

INNOCENT. Well, y-yes, but —

BARON *(Taking Trudi by one hand and Siegfried by the other, and hustling them off)*. Off you go then, all of you — Off! — Off! — Off! — I won't hear a word! Off!

(The BARON hustles off INNOCENT, TRUDI & SIEGFRIED and comes back).

Now where were we? Oh yes, your catarrh.

PETER. Guitar.

BARON. That's what I said. Now listen. I'll make a deal with you. You teach me the guitar, and I'll teach you how to fly. How's that?

PETER. It's very kind of you, but I'm not very interested in flying.

BARON. Between you and me, nor am I now. I'll tell you what I'll do then — you teach me a new song, and I'll give you a new suit of clothes.

PETER. It's a deal!

(PETER begins to teach the Baron a song. They have not got very far through it when the BARONESS sweeps in).

BARONESS. Grosskopf!

PETER *(Seeing her)*. Oh, Lord!

(He hides his face behind his guitar, and stands behind the Baron).

BARON. Gudrun, what an unpleasant surprise.

BARONESS. Did you get my letter?

BARON. Oh, yes — such as it was.

BARONESS. Well?

BARON. Well what?

BARONESS. Where is it?

BARON. Where's what?

BARONESS. The head, of course.

BARON. Head? Whose head?

BARONESS. Grosskopf, I know you are a congenital idiot, but please don't repeat everything I say. Where is the head of the girl who delivered my letter?

BARON. At the end of her neck; where should it be?

BARONESS. You mean she is still alive?

BARON. Well, of course. She could hardly get married if she was dead, could she?

BARONESS. Married? What do you mean?

BARON. I mean married, espoused, wedded, given in matrimony.

BARONESS. What! Who to?

BARON. You mean to whom. Why, to Siegfried, who else?

(PETER begins to tiptoe across the back to get out of it).

BARONESS. Oh, you fool!

BARON. Well, wasn't that what you said in the letter?

BARONESS. Of course it wasn't. I ordered you unequivocally to remove her head. —

(PETER is almost at the door).

Apfelstrudel, stay where you are! I will deal with you presently.

(PETER freezes. At the same time, SIEGFRIED, TRUDI and INNOCENT re-enter. They stop on seeing the Baroness).

Come here, girl.

(TRUDI comes forward hesitantly).

So the Book was right after all, and you have married the heir of Von Grubelstein.

SIEGFRIED. Now, mother, you —

BARONESS. Silence! — Show me your wedding-ring.

(TRUDI extends her hand).

I might have known. The fire-opal I gave to Siegfried on his seventeenth birthday. Siegfried, how could you?

SIEGFRIED. But it was all I —

BARONESS. Don't speak to me!

(The BARONESS takes hold of Trudi's hand, and pulls off the ring).

TRUDI. Oh!

SIEGFRIED. Mother, how dare you?

BARONESS. Silence! You may have married my son, but you shall never be his wife in the eyes of the world.

(She goes to the parapet).

And unless you wear this ring on your finger, you shall never come within sight of him again, or he of you.

(Throws the ring in the sea).

If you want it — there it is — at the bottom of the sea. — Now go!

(Strikes her cane on the floor. Flash & blackout. TRUDI and PETER disappear).

BARON. Good gracious. She's vanished. How on earth did you do that?

(SIEGFRIED goes to the door).

BARONESS. Siegfried! Where are you going?

SIEGFRIED. To find her, of course. She's my wife, isn't she?

BARONESS. Don't be stupid, Siegfried. Don't you understand? Unless she has the ring on her finger, you may search for a thousand years and never see her.

SIEGFRIED. Then I'll search for a thousand years, and if I never see her again, you may rest assured I shall never see you again either.

(SIEGFRIED goes out).

BARONESS. Siegfried!

BARON. I suppose it's none of my business, but where have they gone?

BARONESS. Who?

BARON. The girl and the minstrel.

BARONESS. Out of my sight, that's all I care.

BARON. Well, they won't leave it at that, you know.

BARONESS. What do you mean?

BARON. I mean, if they have any sense, they'll go and look for the ring.

BARONESS. Don't be ridiculous. How can they possibly find something as small as that at the bottom of the sea?

BARON. It's surprising how things turn up sometimes. I'm sure they'll try anyway. I know I would.

BARONESS. You may be right, Grosskopf. But we can easily settle that, I think.

(She raps on the floor with her cane. WEISSBART appears).

INNOCENT. Oh, B-baron!

(He retreats behind the Baron for protection).

BARONESS. Weissbart, I have a job for you.

(WEISSBART grins foolishly).

Now try to concentrate. You remember the girl Trudi?

(WEISSBART nods vigorously).

Find her. Follow her. If you value your hide, you'll prevent her from putting on the wedding ring. Off with you.

(WEISSBART goes out).

Not that she will ever find it, of course.

(Thunder. The BARONESS looks up, shrugs, and goes out).

INNOCENT. B-baron.

BARON. What?

INNOCENT. I hope she does find it, don't you?

BARON. Of course I do.

(He goes to the balcony).

I thought she was a very nice girl — much too good for Siegfried. Oh, look!

INNOCENT. Wh-what, Baron?

BARON. There's a mermaid.

INNOCENT *(joining him)*. A m-mermaid? Where?

BARON *(pointing)*. There.

(Waving).

Good afternoon! You see, Innocent, that's the way to swim.

INNOCENT. Y-yes, Baron. B-but she was born with a tail, wasn't she?

1036

(The BARON goes to cuff him, loses his balance, and falls off the balcony with a yell. There is a distant splash).

B-baron, can you swim?

BARON *(at a distance).* I don't think I can.

INNOCENT. Well, now's the time to find out.

(He chuckles and eats a cherry as the curtain falls).

CURTAIN

Act Three

(The seashore. The SEA-KING'S DAUGHTER is sitting on a pile of rocks. She is knitting a strangely-shaped garment in brilliantly coloured wool, and singing to herself).

S. K. D. *(Singing).*

> Fa la la la, and derry down dee
> There's nothing like living at the bottom of the sea;
> Hey nonny no, and hi tiddly-i-ti,
> It's better by far to be too wet than too dry;
> Fol de rol lol, and fol de rol dee
> O won't you take a dip in the ocean with me.

(Calling, not very urgently).

Help . . . Rescue . . . Help . . .

(PETER enters).

PETER. Was that you? Calling for help?

S. K. D. Yes it was. I'm stuck.

PETER. Oh, I am sorry. In what way?

S. K. D. I'm wedged in these rocks. I could wait for the next high tide, and hope to be floated off, I suppose; but if you could possibly unwedge me, I'd be very much obliged.

PETER. Well I'll try. What do you think would be the best way? I mean, which end shall I pull?

S. K. D. Try this end.

PETER *(Holding under her arms)*. Is this all right?

S. K. D. Oh yes.

PETER. Tell me if I — If you —

S. K. D. Oh, I will.

PETER. Here goes then.

(PETER lifts. She gives a little shriek).

S. K. D. Oh!

PETER *(Dropping her hastily)*. Oh, I'm terribly sorry!

S. K. D. Never mind, what's a few scales, anyway? Perhaps you had better try the other end.

PETER. Oh, all right.

(PETER comes round to the front).

S. K. D. Try the narrow bit, where my ankles would be if I had feet.

1038

PETER. Ah, yes. Do say if I —

S. K. D. Oh, I will.

PETER. Here goes then.

(*PETER pulls*).

PETER. You *are* wedged in, aren't you?

S. K. D. Yes, I'm afraid I am.

(*PETER pulls*).

PETER. Really stuck.

S. K. D. Yes.

(*PETER pulls a third time*).

PETER. I'm sorry, I just can't shift you at all.

S. K. D. Oh well, you tried. I'll just have to wait for somebody stronger — I mean, not that you're not quite strong and everything, but thanks all the same.

PETER. I've never seen a mermaid before.

S. K. D. Haven't you?

PETER. No, never.

S. K. D. We don't often emerge, as a matter of fact.

PETER. You've got a sort of crown on. Are you something special?

S. K. D. Well in a way. I'm the Sea King's Daughter.

PETER. You're a sort of princess then?

S. K. D. Sort of. But the Sea King has fifty daughters, so I'm not all that special.

PETER. My word . . . What's that you're making?

S. K. D. It's for Daddy. It's a tail-cosy.

PETER. A what?

S. K. D. A tail-cosy. It's to keep his tail warm in the winter.

PETER. Oh. I see. Like bedsocks.

S. K. D. Yes. Sea-bed socks.

(*She giggles. PETER smiles politely*).

It's a peace-offering really.

PETER. Oh? Is he angry with you?

S. K. D. Well, I *am* in disgrace rather. For talking to sailors . . . if he knew I was talking to you he'd be livid.

1039

PETER *(Looking over his shoulder).* Would he? What would he do?

S. K. D. Drown you in a tidal wave or something. But I shouldn't worry. He's almost certainly in the Caribbean just now, organizing the Gulf Stream.

PETER. Oh, good.

S. K. D. It gets sluggish every now and then, and he has to give it a shove. Do you often come down to the beach?

PETER. No. I was looking for something.

S. K. D. Oh? What?

PETER. A ring. It was lost in the sea near Castle Seeblick, and it's rather important it should be found.

S. K. D. Sentimental value?

PETER. In a way.

S. K. D. A young lady perhaps?

PETER. Well, yes. Anyhow, we must get it back. Everything depends on it.

S. K. D. What's it like?

PETER. It's gold, with a fire-opal in it.

S. K. D. Oh, they probably wouldn't bother with that, then.

PETER. Who wouldn't?

S. K. D. The lobsters.

PETER. The lobsters? What have they got to do with it?

S. K. D. *(Rummaging in her jewel-box).* Oh, they're always bringing me little things they pick up. But there's all sorts of junk gets lost in the sea, you know, — garnets, opals, they wouldn't bother with those. No, I don't think it's here. — I could always get them to keep a look out for it if you like.

PETER. Could you?

S. K. D. Oh yes. They like to have an objective. They live such aimless lives, poor things. I'll do it the minute I get back.

PETER. You couldn't do it now?

S. K. D. My dear, how can I till somebody unwedges me?

PETER. Of course, I forgot. I'll have another go.

(PETER pulls at the tail. SIEGFRIED enters. He sees the mermaid, but not Peter).

S. K. D. Do try to be careful.

1040

SIEGFRIED. I beg your pardon?

S. K. D. *(To Peter)*. Look, I'll tell you what. Go down to the sea and find one of the lobsters.

SIEGFRIED. What?

S. K. D. One of the lobsters. Tell him I sent you, and what they have to look for.

(PETER nods and goes off).

SIEGFRIED. I'm afraid I don't follow you.

S. K. D. *(Seeing him)*. Where did you spring from?

SIEGFRIED. What's this about lobsters?

S. K. D. Oh, I was talking to the other gentleman.

SIEGFRIED. What other gentleman?

S. K. D. That one over there. Didn't you see him?

SIEGFRIED. Do you ever get the feeling that all this has happened to you before?

S. K. D. What?

SIEGFRIED. Never mind. Look, perhaps you can help me. I'm looking for a certain ring.

S. K. D. Gold, with a fire-opal?

SIEGFRIED. Yes, How did you know?

S. K. D. I'm psychic.

SIEGFRIED. It's very important it should be found.

S. K. D. So I gather.

(Resumes her knitting).

Well, I shouldn't worry. The lobsters will find it, I expect.

SIEGFRIED. Oh, will they?

S. K. D. Though why there should be all this fuss over a mere opal I can't understand.

SIEGFRIED. It's — what's that you're knitting?

S. K. D. A tail-cosy.

SIEGFRIED. Oh . . . You see if my wife doesn't get the ring back, we shall never see each other again.

S. K. D. Really? What a peculiar arrangement.

SIEGFRIED. But I shall find it if it takes me a thousand years, and we shall be together whether my mother likes it or not.

1041

S. K. D.   Ah. You're quite sure you're not doing all this just to spite your mother?

SIEGFRIED.   Perhaps I was at first, but not now. I really love Trudi, and I know I can make her happy.

S. K. D.   Well, I hope it all turns out all right.

(PETER returns, sucking his thumb).

Oh, you've been quick. What's the matter with your thumb?

PETER.   Have you ever tried arguing with a king-size lobster?

S. K. D.   Oh, I am sorry. I must speak to him about it. Did you get the ring?

PETER.   It won't give it to me.

S. K. D.   But it has it?

PETER.   Oh, yes, it has it. It says you must come and fetch it yourself.

S. K. D.   But I'm still wedged.

PETER.   So you are. What can we do, then?

S. K. D.   I think both of you might manage it.

PETER.   Both of us?

S. K. D.   Yes. You and the man over there.

PETER.   What man? — Oh, it's all right. I know what's happened. — Siegfried!

(SIEGFRIED looks round).

You take the top end.

SIEGFRIED.   What? Who's that?

PETER.   Oh, never mind. Take her shoulders.

(SIEGFRIED wonderingly takes the mermaid's shoulders).

SIEGFRIED.   What's happening? I don't understand.

PETER *(At the tail).* Now heave.

SIEGFRIED.   What?

PETER.   Heave!

(They heave).

S. K. D. *(A squeak).* Aah!

PETER.   That's it! She's free! Now help me down to the sea with her.

(They begin to carry the mermaid off).

S. K. D.   Oh, I feel such a fool!

SIEGFRIED. But I can't *see* anybody.

PETER. It's me — Peter. I can't see you either, but it doesn't matter.

SIEGFRIED. Well why can't I see you?

PETER. The ring — the spell — your mother; don't you understand?

SIEGFRIED. Oh, you mean —?

PETER. Yes, we're all invisible to each other — you and me and Trudi.

SIEGFRIED. How perfectly absurd. But it's just like her.

PETER. Wait a minute. She's heavier than I thought.

S. K. D. Do you mind?

(TRUDI enters, taking no notice of the others. She carries a large lobster in and puts it on the rock vacated by the mermaid).

PETER. Put her down a minute till I get my breath back.

(They put the mermaid down on a pile of seaweed).

TRUDI *(To the lobster)*. There. Now you will give it to me, won't you?

(The lobster squeaks. The others look round).

SIEGFRIED & PETER. Trudi!

TRUDI *(To the lobster)*. I know, but you see it *is* mine, really.

(The lobster squeaks).

No, I can't prove it, but I assure you it is. It's my wedding ring.

(Squeak from the lobster).

Yes. And if I don't have it I shall never see my husband again.

(Squeak).

No, never.

(Squeak).

So you will give it to me, won't you — Please —

(She holds out her hand)

— Please —

(Drawing her hand back).

— Oh, it bit me!

(Angry jabber of squeaks from the lobster).

S. K. D. I'm afraid it's being very awkward, because it doesn't know you. You'd better let me handle it.

TRUDI. Oh, would you? It doesn't seem to like me.

1043

(TRUDI gingerly takes the lobster over to her).

S. K. D. Now don't be obstinate. Give.

(Squeak).

Yes, I know, but give.

(Squeak).

This very minute. Give.

(Squeak. She takes the ring from it).

That's more like it. Thank you.

(Squeaks).

Yes you may.

(Puts lobster down on the ground).

Go on, go home.

(The lobster scuttles off).

Well, there we are, then. I suppose this *is* it?

TRUDI. Oh yes, I'm sure it's mine.

(WEISSBART enters unnoticed and creeps behind).

SIEGFRIED. Yes, it is.

PETER. I recognize it too.

TRUDI. What? Who said that?

PETER. Me.

SIEGFRIED. I did.

TRUDI. I don't understand. It sounds like Siegfried and Peter.

SIEGFRIED & PETER *(Together).* It is.

TRUDI. But I can't see you.

SIEGFRIED. Put the ring on and we'll all be able to see each other.

TRUDI. Oh . . . Oh, I *see!* — May I have it, please?

S. K. D. Of course.

(She hands it to Trudi. As she does so, WEISSBART pops up behind them, and snatches it).

WEISSBART *(Very deep).* Thank you.

SIEGFRIED.   Weissbart!

S. K. D.   What was that?

TRUDI   *(Together).* The Troll?

1044

PETER. He's got the ring!

(WEISSBART hesitates a few seconds, wondering which way to run).

PETER & SIEGFRIED. After him!

(The TROLL dodges them around the Mermaid and the rocks. They can see him but not each other; business of colliding with each other. The Troll is chased around the stage and the auditorium, and off).

(The passageway under the castle. WEISSBART runs in, and stops, panting, to get his breath back. SIEGFRIED enters after him).

SIEGFRIED. Weissbart!

(WEISSBART jumps, and is about to make off).

Wait!

(WEISSBART stops).

Give me the ring, Weissbart.

(WEISSBART shakes his head).

. . . . Look, it belongs to me, it's mine . . . Weissbart, you don't wish me any harm, do you?

(WEISSBART shakes his head).

. . . . well then, listen. It means everything to Trudi and me — and you don't wish her any harm either, do you?

(WEISSBART shrugs).

. . . she's my wife, Weissbart, but we can't ever be together again till I get the ring back, do you understand?

(WEISSBART shifts uneasily).

. . . Come on, now, you'll give it to me, won't you? Won't you, Weissbart?

(WEISSBART is in an agony of indecision).

VOICE *(Of the BARONESS, over the speakers).* Weissbart, don't you dare!

(WEISSBART shrinks, jumps and makes off).

SIEGFRIED. Weissbart!

(PETER runs in and collides with Siegfried).

Who's that?

PETER. It's me.

SIEGFRIED. I do wish you'd look where you're going.

PETER. I am looking.

(Putting his hands out).

Where are you?

SIEGFRIED. Here.

PETER. Oh yes, so you are.

(TRUDI enters).

TRUDI. Peter? . . . Siegfried?

PETER. We're here.

TRUDI *(Putting her hands out).* Where?

PETER. Here.

(He touches her hand).

TRUDI. Oh, yes . . . Siegfried?

(She touches Siegfried's hand).

SIEGFRIED *(Taking her hand).* Trudi!

TRUDI. Siegfried!

PETER. Now look, we haven't time for that. It looks as if he's gone down to Trollheim, so if we're to get anywhere, we'd better stick together. Are you listening?

TRUDI. Oh, yes, I'm listening.

PETER. Come on, then — and watch out for Schlafnicht.

(The Dragon's Cavern. The sound of SCHLAFNICHT practicing his scales to the accompaniment of sloshing water. WEISSBART dashes in and leans against a rock to get his breath. The singing comes nearer, with the dragon's squelching footsteps.

WEISSBART reacts, and runs round behind the rocks as SCHLA-FNICHT appears, with a towel and a shaker of talc).

SCHLAFNICHT *(Singing).* Ah-ah-ah-ah-ah-ah-ah!

(Stops).

That's odd. I'm sure I heard somebody . . .

(wipes out his ear, and then listens).

. . . H'm. Tummy rumble, it must have been. Can't remember when I last had a decent meal, so it's no wonder . . .

(TRUDI, PETER and SIEGFRIED enter, hand-in-hand, and stop short on seeing SCHLAFNICHT).

1046

Ah, food! Breakfast, dinner and tea all at once. How very thoughtful of somebody.

(TRUDI and company step back three paces in unison).

No, don't go. There's room for three more inside.

(They turn. Clang of a heavy door shutting).

Interesting thing about this place; easy to get in, but hard to get out, I'm thankful to say. Now I'll tell you what I'll do. I'm very peckish, so I'll let you do without a bath this time. Isn't that considerate of me?

(Wiping himself).

Be with you in a minute.

TRUDI. Peter — play something. Soothe him as you did last time.

PETER. All right.

(Feels for his guitar).

— I can't!

TRUDI. What? Why not?

PETER. I've lost my guitar.

TRUDI. Peter, you haven't.

PETER. Yes, I have.

TRUDI. Oh, Peter, what can we do?

SCHLAFNICHT *(Dusting talc over himself).* Sorry to keep you waiting but I won't be a moment — Dream of Geranium, this is —

(Sniffing).

Mmm — heavenly . . .

SIEGFRIED. Schlafnicht!

SCHLAFNICHT. Yes? Shan't be a minute.

SIEGFRIED. You don't propose to eat me too, do you?

SCHLAFNICHT. Why not?

SIEGFRIED. But it's me — Siegfried. You've known me since I was that high.

SCHLAFNICHT. What's that got to do with it?

SIEGFRIED. Well, you couldn't — you wouldn't. Would you?

SCHLAFNICHT. Ah yes, I would. I always intended to one of these days. I've been saving you up.

SIEGFRIED. Schlafnicht!

SCHLAFNICHT. But I'll tell you what I'll do if you like. Just for old time's sake, I'll leave you till the last.

SIEGFRIED. No, you won't. You'll tackle me first.

SCHLAFNICHT. What do you mean, tackle?

SIEGFRIED. I mean this.

(He draws his sword).

If you want to eat Trudi, you'll have to kill me first.

SCHLAFNICHT. Dear me. Oh dear, dear, dear, dear me! You'll never get through my hide with that, dear boy.

SIEGFRIED. Well it's all I've got, so we'll see, shall we?

(They circle round, looking for an opening. SIEGFRIED attacks by making slashes at the Dragon, then getting out of the way of his swiping claws. SIEGFRIED slips and falls, losing his sword).

TRUDI. Peter, help him!

PETER. What, me?

(SIEGFRIED rolls out of the way, and gets up).

TRUDI. Yes, help him!

PETER. But I can't even see him.

TRUDI. Look, there's his sword. Get it!

PETER. What's the use? I might hit him instead.

(SIEGFRIED recovers the sword and carries on).

TRUDI. Oh, you're so useless. Can't you twist his tail or something?

PETER. Well, I'll try.

(The combatants are dodging about, so that PETER has difficulty in grabbing the tail).

TRUDI. What are you doing now?

PETER. I'm trying to get hold of his tail, but he won't keep still while I do it.

(SCHLAFNICHT, with a grunt, knocks the sword out of SIEG-FRIED'S hand and seizes him. At the same moment, PETER seizes the tail).

SCHLAFNICHT & PETER *(Together).* Got you!

(PETER twists the Dragon's tail).

SCHLAFNICHT *(In agony).* Aaaaaaooooooh!

(The Dragon releases SIEGFRIED).

1048

TRUDI. Siegfried, where are you?

SIEGFRIED. I'm here.

TRUDI. Are you all right?

SIEGFRIED. I think so. Where are you?

TRUDI. Here.

(They find each other).

Oh, I'm so glad you're safe.

(PETER, meanwhile, is twisting the tail so that the DRAGON is face down on the ground, beating the floor like an all-in wrestler submitting. PETER, with one foot on him, struggles to keep him there by twisting the tail every time he moves).

PETER. Wh-what do I do now?

TRUDI *(To SIEGFRIED)*. You were so brave, so wonderful.

PETER. What do I do now?

TRUDI. — and I was so afraid. I couldn't see what was happening to you.

PETER. What do I *do*?

(WEISSBART appears round the rock).

TRUDI. Weissbart!

SIEGFRIED. Where?

TRUDI. There.

(Turning Siegfried round).

After him!

(WEISSBART jumps, and sets off. SIEGFRIED and TRUDI chase him around the rock, and then around Peter and the Dragon).

PETER. I can't keep this up much longer. Siegfried — wherever you are — you'll have to take over.

SIEGFRIED *(Stopping)*. What?

PETER. Take over.

SIEGFRIED. Oh, all right.

(SIEGFRIED takes the tail, and PETER joins TRUDI in trotting after WEISSBART. They go round once or twice more, and PETER stops, taps SIEGFRIED on the shoulder, and takes over again).

Thanks.

1049

SIEGFRIED joins the chase. Next time round, WEISSBART stops, taps Peter, and takes the tail).

PETER. Thanks.

(Peter joins the run-around. WEISSBART drops the tail, gives SCHLAFNICHT a kick; SCHLAFNICHT gets up; they both join the chase, so that all five are now trotting round.

ROTHBART comes in, strolls across to the rock, and leans on it, watching the five of them trot round, more slowly now. They all disappear behind the rock. Then WEISSBART appears, very weary. ROTHBART casually trips him. WEISSBART falls, picks himself up, looks at his empty hands, and starts to search around the floor for the ring. As he moves away, ROTHBART picks it up. WEISSBART goes on looking. SIEGFRIED appears, stops, and starts looking. PETER does the same, and TRUDI. The DRAGON goes on chugging round, chasing nobody, as ROTHBART watches the others search the floor. The BARONESS enters).

BARONESS. Weissbart, what is going on here?

(WEISSBART points to his finger and the floor, and shrugs).

What? Oh, you fool! ·

(The BARONESS joins the search. TRUDI, looking on the floor finds herself near Rothbart).

ROTHBART. Psst!

TRUDI. What?

ROTHBART. Sh!

(He holds up the ring).

TRUDI. You've found — !

ROTHBART. Sh ! !

(ROTHBART takes her by the hand, and brings her to the front).

Here, put it on.

TRUDI. At last. Now we shall see what we shall see!

(She puts on the ring. Flash and blackout. When the lights go up all have vanished except TRUDI, PETER, and SIEGFRIED).

What an extraordinary thing! Siegfried! . . . Peter! . . . What's happened?

PETER. I'm not quite sure.

TRUDI. I can see you again! Can you see me?

PETER. Yes, I can.

TRUDI *(Turning to SIEGFRIED)*. Siegfried!

SIEGFRIED. Trudi!

(*They embrace*).

PETER. So that's that then. Everything would seem to be all all right now, wouldn't it? I even have my guitar back.

(*They pay no attention*).

I said everything would . . .

(*He shrugs, and turns away*.

The BARONESS *enters, followed by* ROTHBART *with a large travelling-bag*).

BARONESS. And be very careful with it, Rothbart.

SIEGFRIED. Mother, where are you going?

BARONESS. I am leaving Grubelstein for good.

TRUDI. Leaving?

BARONESS. If you are to be the mistress of Grubelstein, what else can I do?

TRUDI. Mistress of Grubelstein? Me?

BARONESS. Naturally.

SIEGFRIED. Of course.

TRUDI. Good gracious.

BARONESS. I have done my best to prevent it, but there you are. What is written in written, it seems.

(*Takes out keys*).

That's the key of the linen-cupboard, and that's for the pantry. Come, Rothbart.

(*She leads the way.* ROTHBART *picks up the suitcase, whistles sharply, and follows. The rest of the* TROLLS *enter in line, with travelling-bags, and cross, following him. Lastly comes the* DRAGON *with a large carpet-bag. He crosses and follows the others*).

PETER (*After watching them go*). I suppose I'd better be on my way too.

(*SIEGFRIED and TRUDI are not listening, being too occupied with looking into each others' eyes*).

I said I suppose —

(PETER shrugs, and begins to sing as he strolls off).

> "Says I to myself one morning
> Says I to myself one day . . . ."

(The song fades out as he goes.

TRUDI and SIEGFRIED are left together).

CURTAIN

Don Quixote

of

la Mancha

Taken from the epic of Cervantes

By

Arthur Fauquez

Translation from the French by
MARGARET LEONA

Introduction by ORLIN COREY

DON QUIXOTE OF LA MANCHA

By Arthur Fauquez

Characters

DON QUIXOTE

THE HOUSEKEEPER

NICOLAS, a barber

CARRASCO, a scholar

INNKEEPER

MARITORNE

SANCHO

THE ARCHER OF ST. HERMANDAD

GINES, a galley-slave (later, Master Pedro)

GALLEY-SLAVES

SHEPHERDS

A YOUNG BOY

*ROSSINANTE, Don Quixote's horse

*GRISON, Sancho's donkey

> *Optional

Scenes

DON QUIXOTE OF LA MANCHA

DON QUIXOTE OF LA MANCHA was given its world premiere, in English, 4 November, 1965, at the Marjorie Lyons Playhouse, of Centenary College, in Shreveport, Louisiana. Following is a copy of the programme: *

THE SPEECH AND DRAMA DEPARTMENT

presents

THE JONGLEURS OF CENTENARY COLLEGE

in the world premicre of

DON QUIXOTE DE LA MANCHA

Adapted for Stage by Arthur Fauquez

Translated by Margaret Leona

Orlin Corey, Director   Irene Corey, Designer

Donald Musselman, Technical Director

THE PLAYERS

ROCINANTE	Jimmy Journey
DON QUIXOTE	Allen Shaffer
NICHOLAS	Steve Murray
MARITORNES	Sandra West
SANCHO PANZA	Charlie Brown
MASTER PEDRO	David Kingsley
NARRATOR	Terry Turner
GRISSON	Russell Johnson
DONA BELISA	Dorothy Bradley
CARASCO	John Goodwin
INNKEEPER	Gary Ball
ARCHER	Jim St. Amand
PUPPETEERS	Ken Holamon
	David Kingsley
GUITARIST	Philip Rosheger
GALLEY SLAVES, SHEPHERDS	Gene Cagle
	Nancy Nichols
	Jim St. Amand
	Bobbie Culpepper
	Terry Turner
	David Kingsley

The scene is laid in Spain of the early sixteenth century.

* *Note: The sketch on the front cover of this play-book is taken from this programme, designed by Irene Corey.*

1057

INTRODUCTION

"Ars longa, vita brevis," Hippocrates observed.

And what an agony of living is expended upon art! Nearly four and a half years have passed since I first learned about Arthur Fauquez' stage version of DON QUIXOTE, then in the early throes of translation. Only M. Fauquez can say how long before that time he had been toiling on his play. Since then playwright and publisher, translator, designer and producer have all laboured again and again. Two cycles of writing and translation gave us a vehicle for staging at the Marjorie Lyons Playhouse in 1965. The crucible of production altered the play in subtle ways, initiating a still more painful reappraisal of the play by all of us. Another full year was required for a third cycle of anguish to give us the latest and final version.

The ultimate tribute to the play is that at no time in the labyrinth of labour has anyone had the slightest doubt about the worth of the work. From M. Fauquez' imaginative vision of Cervantes' masterpiece, all found fuel for enthusiasm.

Our first surge of excitement at the Marjorie Lyons rose when we tried to gauge the Fauquez achievement by turning to the original of Cervantes. DON QUIXOTE! The very words are a bright cry, shivering the air with echoes. This rollicking extravaganza is the world's most widely translated and read book after the Bible. A great many people, not all of them Spanish, believe it is the greatest prose fiction ever written. And if such praises require vindication, the most irrefutable proof lies beneath the covers of the title that sounds like trumpets.

On a canvas vast as Spain, and at a pace calculated to encompass all the dynamism and somnolence of a people, Don Quixote, mad Knight of La Mancha, rides on pilgrimage to better the world. His touching idealism and cadenced language is balanced against the garlic-humor and earthy proverbs of Sancho Panza. The most noble fool of literature is accompanied by the most foolish realist on the planet. Astride the faithful Rossinante, this self-styled Knight becomes Everyman on horseback, his head full of phantasm. At a nag's pace he moves from adventure to adventure among peasants and scholars, rogues and imposters, wenches and ladies, demons and visions. In all the noisy activity, out of his bruises, defeats and triumphs, Don Quixote discovers mankind and, inevitably, himself. From illusion he progresses through paradox and puzzle, toward reality. As his romantic dreams recede he bestows a sense of wonder upon the commonplace. Courtesy and kindness bloom in the wasteland after he has passed. Even gullible, cowardly Sancho is moved by beauty, constrained to loyalty, and acts in honour.

Perhaps the most appropriate epitaph for the lean and serious Knight was written by his young friend, Carrasco, graduate of the University of Salamanca:

"Here lies the noble fearless knight,
    Whose valour rose to such a height;
When Death at last had struck him down,
    His was the victory and renown.

"He reck'd the world of little prize,
    And was a bugbear in men's eyes;
But had the fortune in his age
    To live a fool and die a sage."

No book ever contained more of the authentic stuff of great entertainment.

But can it be caught on the stage? How can anyone compress one of the longest and most formless books ever written into the relentless limits of stage traffic? Others have entered the mansion of Cervantes to remove a noble staircase, or a partition, and so construct a lesser cottage, worthy in itself. This is genuine flattery. Inevitably derivative works, in opera, story, musical or play, are measured against the original. And well they should be when they purport to contain plot and flavour of a masterpiece. Can Cervantes' two volumes and 122 chapters be honestly represented in Fauquez' three acts?

New enthusiasm was generated when we read the play. DON QUIXOTE OF LA MANCHA is indeed true to Cervantes. Notwithstanding the incredible achievement of compression and the difficult demands of dramatic form, this play has very few of the faults and almost all the virtues of the original. The sense of adventure and lofty idealism is present. Within the limits of eighteen or twenty performers the essence of Cervantes' humanity is revealed. And in the noblest tradition of the great Spanish writer, M. Fauquez creates and maintains awareness of many levels of reality, such as the obvious, the sensual, the poetic, the ideal, the metaphysical and the spiritual with many of the nuances of overtone and contradiction interplaying across these planes. Most of the more famous events of spectacle are presented, arranged in a theatrically valid order of expanding and heightened importance. Perhaps M. Fauquez' finest achievement is his dramatic unification of the unstructured original novel. On the surface the play retains the wandering aimless appearance of the book. Closer study reveals, and performance confirms the subtle ties that invisibly weave across the diverse and scattered incidents, making a web of interest and involvement.

There is a developing relationship between each character, one that grows in understanding and breadth of sympathy, gradually linking each to all. Furthermore there is a progression of illusion within the confusions of the Knight. These move from the barber basin to himself and the mirror, then outward to himself and the inn and the Innkeeper, to Maritorne and her lantern by the well at night, to the Knighting ceremony, and at last to the spectacular attack on the windmills. In the second act Quixote's illusions have broadened to mankind in general as he frees the galleys, to Spain itself as he fights against a horde of horned demons who threaten the land. Even in his handstands the Don shows that he is capable of the ludicrous for the sake of his ideal. The climactic defeat of the fictional enemy Caraculiambro suggests how far his courage and madness have taken him. We find him wiser and weaker in the third act, saddened by the loss of his books. He sees himself the victim of fate, a force he now recognizes as greater than his own. Curiously he leaves on his second mission less for himself than for the sake of Sancho to whom he has promised a governorship. M. Fauquez thus deepens the implication of the story. The puppet scene is brilliant. As a "play-within-the-play" device it summarizes Quixote's illusions, making minescule satire of romantic chivalry while it enables the Don to display loyalty and daring for his cause against the imagined onslaught of Moslem soldiers. From a theatrical point of view this is the most masterfully drawn scene for its contrasts, and its comment on the theme and character of Quixote. When the Don confronts his last illusion, the Knight of the White Moon, he is looking at a youthful caricature of himself, a reductio-ad-absurdam of chivalry's clap-trap. He stands before this challenge without self-delusion, except that he believes his love of the ideal makes his warfare as invincible as his cause is lofty (but is this an illusion?). Defeat destroys even this. He becomes a mere man, aged, broken, but fiercely proud within his now defenceless ideals. For these he can do no less than die. When he is most helpless he is most noble. All that the playwright has to do is to gently carry him forward to that human end which is so inevitable after the joust. We watch the gallant old Knight, saner, sadder, speaking gently of himself as a man, of his lost hopes, making his peace with man even as he already has with God. The final Fauquez touch is to allow the Hidalgo, like a latter Moses, to glimpse his immortality. For a moment he knows that his crusade for a gentler, nobler world is not in vain. He is assured that he may continue to sally forth against the cowardly, the ignoble, the mean and the evil of the earth on the pages of the book of his pilgrimage. Then he dies.

Our excitement burned higher when we realized that beyond the requirements of adaptation—a faithful reflection of the greatness of the original—this script deserves to be judged on its own terms as a play. Of necessity it is less than the novel. To our delight it proved to be more than just another play.

Characterization and pageantry are present in abundance as the previous appraisal suggests. A unified play has appeared. Performance established the rest. This play is an actor's vehicle. And this is as it should be, for acting is the center of theatrical fascination. That this production will fly or falter according to the versatility and verve of the performers is only just. That so much may soar so beautifully justifies the risk of failure. Seek out your very best actors. This is worth their mettle.

Pageantry is an essential. A fundamental resource of all theatre, here is a production demanding the most spectacular effects imagination can create. They may be as simply realized offstage and by mime as M. Fauquez suggests. Or they may be as elaborate as your theatre can create. But they must be imaginative, and exciting.

Our chief resource in the production was Cervantes himself. We carefully studied each of the stories chosen by the adapter, examining them in the fullest context of the original. Even the color of the hat worn by Carrasco, and the silk eye-patch of the rascal puppeteer, were borrowed from Cervantes. Many elements of Cervantes' theatricalism were used. The final scene, for example, was amplified by Cervantes' somber spectacle of the Priests, the solemn ritual of laying out the dead, sword on breast, amid the lofty music of the mass. In this way we were able to prolong what Fauquez had created on stage—an intense sense of the spirit of the Don, romantic and profoundly religious, magnificently triumphant even at death.

Another major source of inspiration for the production and its pageantry came from the illustrations of Gustave Doré. These suggested the designs for the study of the Knight, his armour and visage, as well as the portrayal of the common people.

The production at the Marjorie Lyons Playhouse sought to cope with the gradual progression of illusion and spectacle within the confused world of Quixote, as opposed to the substantial actual world in which he exists. Our first decision was to give the play a firm basis in southern Spain. Simple unit sets of selected realism were employed, drawn from authentic architectural forms of sixteenth century Spain. These were washed in the warm ochres and sienas of that landscape. The fantastic illusions—the assault on the windmills, the battle against the stampeding goats, the destruction of the puppet play and theatre, and the climactic joust on horseback, and many others—were created by theatricalistic means: floor-mounted spotlights casting vast shadows, altering real places beyond recognition; projections of grotesque, enormous goat forms leaping across the sky (actually puppet goats); the horizon filled with ominous windmills, whirling across the breadth of a Spanish morning, projected 40 feet high and 70 feet wide. The solid commonplace reality dissolved in the fevered imagination of the Don, enabling the audience to participate in the dual levels of Cervantes' creation.

The playwright wisely recognized that an indispensable part of the great saga is played by the two animal companions of the Knight and his Squire. The result is the creation of Rossinante and Grison, two of the most famous mounts in literature. They have ample opportunity to serve as beasts of burden in the world of reality, and as spirited associates in the fantastic spectacles. Two wonderful creatures of wood and wire were constructed, drawn by an actor in each, his legs forming the forelegs of the caparisoned horse or donkey, while the arms, adorned with elaborate trappings, made the bridle.

Music is another major resource for this play. The playwright's suggestions are most appropriate. Indeed, production experiments with music and mime may create imaginative variations to the original solutions for spectacle, even the animals themselves. Nothing, however desirable in itself, must impede the rhythm of this production. Of course the play lends itself to open staging, too. Mime and musical bridges may be devised to sweep the action forward between scenes.

Perhaps our greatest source of enthusiasm about DON QUIXOTE OF LA MANCHA was discovered in the production itself—its limitless capacity to creatively stimulate the imagination of artists and actors, no less than the audience. This play is not for children, nor is it for literary types. It belongs to everybody, including children and lovers of books.

This is a final high mark of the Fauquez achievement. His theatrical midwifery gives us Cervantes' creation anew. DON QUIXOTE belongs to all of us. Sharing his quest makes everyone a little bit larger, a little bit wiser, and leaves each a lot more delighted. Anyone who climbs up behind the Don onto Rossinante will be different thereafter. A year after our presentation we still hear tales of its impact on those who met the Knight of la Mancha at the Marjorie Lyons. If he were revived next season we would pack out before the play opened, not because of what we would be doing on stage, but because Don Quixote is already among the audience, doing exciting things in their imaginations.

In 1966, at the Children's Theatre Conference convention in Tempe, Arizona, Mr. Robert Radnitz, producer of such films as ISLAND OF THE BLUE DOLPHINS and AND NOW MIGUEL, gave the keynote address. His remarks about films belong to the theatre in general, particularly when he said:

"Unfortunately, what we dole out too frequently today to our youngsters, is . . . a sickly, syrupy concoction that passes in the guise of children's entertainment, visual fare which allows them to sit there, like non-reacting sponges. Furthermore, as is sometimes the case with contemporary children's literature, motion pictures for children are guilty of over-simplification. The situation is analogous to those authors who are too interested in children and insufficiently interested in themselves. These authors are all sure they all know how to adapt their ideas to those of average children in a so-called given age bracket. Happily, neither Mark Twain, Robert Louis Stevenson, Dickens . . . ever possessed these qualities. They thought out of themselves, out of their own sense of the surprisingness of life, never once asking whether they were overstepping the young readers' experience."

He was not talking of Cervantes and Fauquez, but he could have been. This is why DON QUIXOTE OF LA MANCHA is such an enchantment for *all* of us. Long may the lanky Knight of la Mancha canter against the sky! Long may we ride along, too, side-saddle with dear old Sancho! Steady, lances lowered, and away!

Orlin Corey, Chairman
The Speech and Drama Department
Marjorie Lyons Playhouse
Centenary College
Shreveport, Louisiana

November, 1966

AUTHOR'S NOTE

Don Quixote must never, at any moment, appear ridiculous. He believes intensely in his mission, and is in reality far less crazy than one imagines. He is not a comic character. Even when he sprawls in front of everyone, he must remain dignified. Through the laughter his downfall provokes, one must feel the bitterness he suffers to find himself in such a pass. Some of his speeches are treated in an alexandrine or octosyllabic rhythm. Here one must feel that Don Quixote does not speak in the usual manner, and that his way of expressing himself is strongly influenced by the style of the books he has been reading.

Sancho, too, is neither a comic nor a ridiculous character. No one should force the tune, no one overplay his character. These are human beings, whom we find on the stage.

For music, I suggest Ravel, de Falla, Debussy, Turina, any of the great Spanish musicians. Perhaps Lalo. Or an original composition, provided always it is in the Spanish classical style.

ARTHUR FAUQUEZ

Maleves Sainte Marie

October, 1966

THE TRANSLATION

The delights and difficulties of translating this enchanting play from the French, were manifold. Arthur Fauquez uses language in a telling poetic rhythm. Many times in Don Quixote's own speeches, he has come close to the original Spanish of Cervantes, whilst avoiding the archaic expressions of the original. It is always graceful and easy on the ear.

French words are sonorous, and double syllables add to beauty of tongue. But where words of numerous syllables are charming in French, these must be translated into short and harder terms for English speech. Some of the fineness of the French script may be lost. I have tried to be as faithful as I could, and still keep the language lively for actors. The alexandrine and octosyllabic speeches were especially difficult.

With the full agreement of the author, I have tried to convey a variation of speech in the pastoral characters, to give a country flavour without specifying any particular locality—a speech that all English-speaking players can use.

Details of translation have been carefully worked over with Arthur Fauquez and his charming wife Elizabeth. My thanks are also due to Mme. Olga Cieflinska, who checked the whole translation with me, and to Tom Sellars, who first read it.

MARGARET LEONA

London

October, 1966

Don Quixote of la Mancha

ACT ONE

(Three beats on the gong. Music. Light on the curtain).

VOICE *(Off)*. "In a village of la Mancha, somewhere in the very heart of ardent Spain, there lived an hidalgo, thin of face, and even thinner pursed."

(On these last words the curtain opens).

SCENE 1—DON QUIXCTE'S BEDROOM

(A table, a high-backed armchair, well-stocked bookshelves, A cheval mirror, Don Quixote's arms, one guesses a four-poster bed. A door leads to other parts of the house. A window opens onto the courtyard. A roof-top may be seen through the window.

Don Quixote is seated at his table, badly lit by a single candle placed in the lowest branch of a five-branched candelabra. He is lost in reading a romantic story of Chivalry, which is placed beside his plate of eggs and bacon. He holds his fork in his right hand, but does not eat.

Soft music. In the distance the ringing sound of glorious trumpets.

Off).

"When the Giant, standing so arrogant, saw him fearlessly draw near, he said insolently, 'I am amazed, little man, to see you approach death with so much confidence. And so saying, he brandished with fury the heavy iron hammer which commonly served him as weapon. Then, full of valour, standing up in his silver stirrups like a fighting-cock, Amadis raised his shining sword high, and cried—

(Suddenly Don Quixote springs up, brandishing his fork, and holding the book in his left hand).

DON QUIXOTE *(In a thunderous voice)*. " 'Caraculiambro, O fabulous loathsome-headed Giant, this time I'll put an end to your foul deeds, and I'll—

(Unable to decipher what follows in the text, he brings the book nearer the candle and goes on, almost without a break).

—" 'and I'll slit you through the middle of your body—

(With a back stroke of his right hand, he flings plate and all to the floor, but unaware of what he has done, he takes up his position again, and goes on without looking at the book).

—" 'Through the middle of your body!' "

HOUSEKEEPER (*Enters holding up a candelabra with five lighted candles in it*). Sir—what's going on?

DON QUIXOTE (*Automatically taking advantage of this new light, goes on with his reading*). " 'Your dark soul shall descend to Hell, and your fearful head, severed from your shoulders, shall bear witness to my high courage!' "

HOUSEKEEPER (*Putting the candelabra down*). Calm yourself.

DON QUIXOTE (*Looks into her eyes without seeing her and murmurs*). Caraculiambro—

HOUSEKEEPER. I am your housekeeper.

DON QUIXOTE. Dona Belisa . . . after all she might be . . . Don Quixote's housekeeper . . .

(*Exultantly*).

Don Quixote of la Mancha, last of Knights-errant. He, who will rid Spain of the detestable race of evil Giants . . . Have with you Caraculiambro . . .

HOUSEKEEPER (*Gently makes him lower his arm*). . . . . Mind what you're doing.

DON QUIXOTE. What am I doing?

HOUSEKEEPER. You've spoilt your eggs and bacon.

DON QUIXOTE. What does an omelette matter to the life of a hero? What does eating matter, when glory is the hunger of our heart? Doesn't this book say, Amadis of Gaul alone in the loneliness of a lone mountain, armed from head to heel, from heel to head, standing proudly with invincible lance, watched for four days and four nights, without food, for love of his lady?

HOUSEKEEPER. These stories are confusing your brain.

DON QUIXOTE. Without food do you hear?

HOUSEKEEPER. I hear. But you are ruining your health.

DON QUIXOTE. Four days and four nights . . .

HOUSEKEEPER (*Shrugging her shoulders and pointing to the mirror*). Look what a sight you are.

DON QUIXOTE. O shining face of Prince Galaor . . .

HOUSEKEEPER. You're as thin as a rake.

DON QUIXOTE. O marvellous image of paladin Roderigo.

HOUSEKEEPER. Look at your clothes. They are rags and tatters.

DON QUIXOTE. O peerless beauty of Amadis of Gaul.

HOUSEKEEPER (*Kneeling and picking up the plate*). One day this nonsense will be the death of you, if it hasn't driven you out of your mind already.

DON QUIXOTE. Nonsense, you call these deeds of courage and daring, these glorious achievements?

HOUSEKEEPER. Do you think it's glorious to fling your omelette on the floor?

DON QUIXOTE. Madam, that accident was only due to my blazing valour.

HOUSEKEEPER. And is it equally due to your blazing valour that your walls are decorated with the hop-pole?

DON QUIXOTE. My battle-lance.

HOUSEKEEPER. The saucepan lid?

DON QUIXOTE. My shield of brass.

HOUSEKEEPER. And the preserving pan?

DON QUIXOTE. My breast-plate. Zounds, Dona Belisa, your lack of respect for a Knight-at-arms . . .

HOUSEKEEPER. Put that book down and be reasonable. Nicolas is downstairs, waiting to shave you.

DON QUIXOTE. I'm glad to hear it. He's a sensible man. I'll put the argument to him, and I'm sure he will agree with me.

HOUSEKEEPER (*As she goes out carrying the plate etc.*). That would surprise me!

DON QUIXOTE (*Alone*). O woman of little faith. How different are you from the simplicity and noble wisdom gracing ladies of old. Come in Master Barber.

NICOLAS (*Enters*). And how is your Honour?

(*He puts his things on the table*).

DON QUIXOTE. My honour would be doing well, Nicolas, if it were not being constantly challenged by my block-headed housekeeper . . .

NICOLAS. She was just telling me . . .

DON QUIXOTE. Don't give an ear to that demon of slander, judge for yourself, I beg you, why we are at loggerheads. Do you know this?

(*He takes his place in the armchair and Nicolas knots a towel round his neck*).

NICOLAS. By Heaven, a fine book. The binding alone is worth a crown at least.

DON QUIXOTE. Do you know what it's about? The most thrilling story in the world. The stupendous adventures of the invincible and valorous knight, Amadis of Gaul. Listen to a little of this. "The reason for the unreason that my reason gives you, so weakens my reason, that I have reason to pity myself for your beauty." What do you think of that?

NICOLAS. I can't say I really understood it.

DON QUIXOTE. But it's so clear, so enlightened. 'The reason for the unreason . . . that my reason gives you . . . so weakens my reason . . . that I have reason to pity myself for your beauty . . .' What do you say to that?

NICOLAS. That it's a pity such a lovely binding, and it is lovely, covers so much twaddle.

DON QUIXOTE. What do you say?

NICOLAS. It's stuff and nonsense.

DON QUIXOTE. What have you said?

NICOLAS. Tripe. One can't understand a word . . .

DON QUIXOTE. What have you dared say?

NICOLAS. These romances are stupid. Don't you think so?

DON QUIXOTE. Take back those words without delay.

NICOLAS. But . . .

DON QUIXOTE. Take them back, I say, and quickly . . .

NICOLAS. Don't you agree with me?

DON QUIXOTE. Take back those words or I'll stuff them down your throat with my sword.

NICOLAS. I did not mean to offend you.

DON QUIXOTE. Amadis of Gaul, the most generous hero the world has ever known. And you dare to call this twaddle, stuff and nonsense, and tripe. Thunder and lightning!

NICOLAS. Calm yourself, sir. I'm going to shave you.

DON QUIXOTE. I give you ten seconds.

NICOLAS. I'll fetch some water for shaving.

(He goes out).

DON QUIXOTE. Tripe. Will no one understand the wealth hidden in these superb adventures? Do I alone recognise their meaning? Poor old devil of a barber . . . what a sad world we live in.

(Amongst the barber's materials his eye falls on the shaving-bowl).

Ye heavens! What catches my eye? By what strange chance amongst the bits and pieces belonging to this doer of beards . . .? The Helmet of King Mambrino, no mistake . . . that's it. So described in my romances. Bright as the sun.

(He puts it on his head and struts in front of the mirror).

. . . The magic helmet making one invulnerable.

NICOLAS *(Returns, carrying a jug of hot water which he places on the table. He comes to Don Quixote, touches his arm, and points to shaving-bowl on his head).*

. . . Allow me . . .

DON QUIXOTE. It is Mambrino's helmet.

NICOLAS. Ah—pardon . . . it belongs to me.

DON QUIXOTE. Fashioned of purest gold.

NICOLAS. Sir, it is brass.

DON QUIXOTE. Rogue, coarse crafty churl, full of impertinence. Don't you recognise the marvellous headpiece?

NICOLAS. Well at a pinch, yes, it could be a headpiece—But please give it to me, so that I can make my lather.

DON QUIXOTE. Have you fallen so low, O Master Nicolas, that you have lost respect for this priceless thing? Do you know where it came from?

NICOLAS. I bought it on Thursday in the market at Salamanca.

DON QUIXOTE. In the market at Salamanca . . . what a bitter mockery . . . amongst the potatoes, the eggs, the tomatoes.

NICOLAS. The water is getting cold.

DON QUIXOTE. It shall never be said, that with soap for my beard, I should ever defile the miraculous helmet of the greatest nobleman of Islam.

NICOLAS. One more time, if you want me to shave you, give me back my bowl.

DON QUIXOTE. Never.

NICOLAS. But I must shave you.

DON QUIXOTE. To the devil with my beard. It does very well at the end of my chin. Let it stay there.

NICOLAS. In that case, sir, I see no point in remaining. Give it me.

DON QUIXOTE *(Unhooks his sword).* By my faith, as a Knight-errant, I will not permit further ridicule of King Mambrino's helmet. I'll buy it from you, villain. How much?

NICOLAS. I need it.

DON QUIXOTE. How much, I say?

NICOLAS. Er—since you insist—three crowns.

DON QUIXOTE. It is worth a thousand, but as you say, you don't deserve more than three. Be paid by my housekeeper. Take away your tools, and don't enter my presence till you are ready to eat humble-pie and bow the knee. Then only shall you shave me.

NICOLAS (Gathering his things together). . . . My towel . . . I am going, Sir, but let me tell you, you're a bit touched in the head. The days of chivalry are long past.

DON QUIXOTE. I will renew them.

NICOLAS. Hang up your sword. You'll do yourself an injury. Goodnight.

(He goes out).

DON QUIXOTE. Go, Master Nicolas, and don't bother your head about my fate. By the grace of Mambrino's helmet from now on I am invulnerable.

(He gives himself a terrific whack with his sword on his helmet and sits suddenly in his chair.

Very soft music of mounted horses).

HOUSEKEEPER (Enters). Sir . . . Now what have you done? Are you hurt?

(She puts the sword back on the wall).

DON QUIXOTE. I am invulnerable.

HOUSEKEEPER. You'd better go to bed.

(She puts her hand out for the bowl).

Give it to me.

DON QUIXOTE. Destiny has charged me to guard it. Have you paid Master Nicolas three crowns?

HOUSEKEEPER (Putting the book in the book-case). I have. But I must say it's too big a price for an ordinary brass basin.

DON QUIXOTE. It's Mambrino's helmet. Bright as the sun. Fashioned of gold, the purest gold of the Atlas Mountains.

HOUSEKEEPER. Go to bed quickly, and don't talk any more nonsense, and before you sleep remember tomorrow you will have to sell your horse.

DON QUIXOTE. Rossinante? But you don't know what you're saying. Has one ever heard of Paladin selling his charger? None of these books tell of such ingratitude.

1070

HOUSEKEEPER. It's the only way to pay my wages. Goodnight.

(She goes out carrying the candelabra. Lights fade. Only the one candle of Don Quixote remains).

DON QUIXOTE. Rossinante, companion of my glory? Rather sell my bed, the chair, the table, or the house. Rossinante, never!

(He takes a book, installs himself in the chair, and reads. Soft music. Reading).

"For the glory of the world, and the love of his lady, Prince Galaor donned his armour, took up his arms, mounted his charger, and sallied forth to seek his fortune."

(Dreamily).

For the glory of Spain, and the love of my lady Dulcinea, O Dulcinea of Toboso, fairest of the fair—

(He goes and stands in front of the mirror).

Knight Don Quixote of la Mancha, the Spanish world awaits your deeds of valour. What are you doing here in your chamber? Are you not the last of the Knights-errant? Isn't your mission to travel the world? To purge the mountains of the brigands that infest it? To subdue all enchanters and giants? Don Quixote . . . Don Quixote of la Mancha, the time has come for you to seize your sword and go your way.

(Briskly he makes up his mind, and puts on his armour, takes up his lance, his sword, his shield, and shaving-basin helmet).

Go, fair Knight. Play your part. Do not deprive the world of your famous deeds. Go down to the stable, saddle your charger and sally forth to fortune.

(Music.

After a last look in the mirror Don Quixote grasps his candle and is about to exit but is so cluttered in his armour that his lance collides with the door-post, and he drops his shield in the confusion. He hides quickly, and blows out the candle.

A pause. The door opens slowly and the Housekeeper appears holding her candelabra high).*

HOUSEKEEPER. Sir . . .

(Pokes head through).

DON QUIXOTE *(Hiding)*. . . . I'm in bed. What more do you want?

HOUSEKEEPER. Did you hear?

DON QUIXOTE. It's coming from below. In the stable. It's Rossinante.

HOUSEKEEPER. It was the sound of clanging-irons.

DON QUIXOTE. I told you, it's Rossinante. Go back to bed.

HOUSEKEEPER. Don't forget you must sell him tomorrow. Goodnight.

DON QUIXOTE. To bed Madame, to bed and let me sleep.

HOUSEKEEPER. You owe me six months' wages. Sleep well.

(She goes out and closes the door . . . It is dark. Only the window lights the scene. There is moonlight outside).

DON QUIXOTE. Sleep well.

(Muffled music of martial march. Don Quixote opens the window. Silhouette on the clear night).

O gentle moon . . . that watches o'er the world . . . behold your dauntless hero whom fortune awaits . . . Light my road, protect my deeds, lead me to triumph, and crown my glory. The door is too narrow. There lies the window . . . The way to adventure.

(He passes his lance through the window, straddles the ledge, and quickly climbs out, disappearing with renewed clatter.

Music).

VOICE *(Off)*. . . . The way to adventure.

(Neighing).

THE CURTAIN CLOSES.

SCENE 2. IN FRONT OF THE CURTAIN.

(Full light on the curtain.

Enter Nicolas and Carrasco).

NICOLAS. He puts it on his head, he struts about, he waves his arms, and then starts to shout something about a marvellous helmet that makes him invulnerable.

CARRASCO. It was a jest.

NICOLAS. No. I wanted to take it back to prepare my lather. He refused. He got angry. He seized his sword. He was in such a state I had to sell it to him to keep him quiet.

CARRASCO. How much?

NICOLAS. Three crowns.

CARRASCO. It wasn't worth two.

NICOLAS. Frankly, no. It only cost me a crown in the Salamanca market. But if it lends magic to Don Quixote, it could well be worth three.

CARRASCO. Frankly Master Nicolas, you are a rogue.

HOUSEKEEPER *(Enters, in tears)*. Good day, Senor Carrasco. He has gone. I thought the horse was stamping in the stable, but it was Don Quixote.

CARRASCO. Let's understand each other Dona Belisa. I suppose Don Quixote wasn't stamping about the stable?

HOUSEKEEPER. No, but he has left . . . he's gone . . . God knows where and his hop-pole and his sword and the preserving pan . . . and the horse too. This morning, everything had disappeared.

NICOLAS. My shaving bowl?

HOUSEKEEPER. Likewise. He was to sell the horse today to pay me my wages, and now he's gone as well. Ah, what will become of me if you don't help me?

CARRASCO. Just a minute, Dona Belisa. Is it absence of the animal or Master that's worrying you?

HOUSEKEEPER. Both. Don Quixote's health isn't so good he can afford to go careering over the countryside in the boiling sun harnessed as he is.

CARRASCO. He'll come back, don't worry.

HOUSEKEEPER. Sick, battered, covered with sores and vermin . . . God knows in what state. He's bound to have broken the back of his scruffy old nag. It will be no use for selling, and once again I'll have to wait for my wages.

CARRASCO. Still he has some money.

HOUSEKEEPER. Don't you believe it. We live on a shoe-string. He spends the little money he has in buying rusty arms and rubbishy romances of chivalry. Those confounded books are driving him mad.

CARRASCO. They're nothing but a lot of nonsense.

NICOLAS. I was nearly run-through for saying less than that.

HOUSEKEEPER. All his troubles spring from them—if we don't take away those wicked works, Don Quixote will go out of his mind.

CARRASCO. From what you say, he's not far from it.

HOUSEKEEPER. That's what frightens me Senor Carrasco. I beg you both, will you help me?

NICOLAS. You know, I'd do anything for you.

CARRASCO. What do you want us to do?

HOUSEKEEPER. Help me burn these cursed books and bring my Master and Rossinante home safely. I know how fond you are of him. Save him, I pray you, before it's too late.

NICOLAS. We'll do it.

(To Carrasco).

Won't we?

CARRASCO. Of course. We'll share our labour. Nicolas will help you burn the romances. I will go and look for him.

NICOLAS. You'll find him easily. Capped with my shaving bowl. He can't go around unnoticed.

HOUSEKEEPER. Bring him back, Senor-Scholar, and see he forgets Knight-errantry, and all the Dulcineas in the world.

CARRASCO. He'll come back, Madame. Count on it.

NICOLAS. Do you really think we should burn . . .?

HOUSEKEEPER. It's our only hope. Come . . .

(They go out.

Flame light on the curtain. Sound of burning fire).

CARRASCO *(Dramatically).* "Into flames of war go Galaor and Tirant,
Amadis of Gaul and his son Esplandian,
The Knight of Platir, and Lisuart of Greece,
Florizel of Nicea, and a thousand paladins——"

VOICE *(Off).* While Don Quixote rode out, Knight of la Mancha,
Astride his spiney Rossinante.
From dawn to dusk, without halt nor respite,
Overcome with the heat, and choked with dust,
They rode straight ahead, as destiny beckoned.
A little way yonder, beyond the next road-bend,
Seeming so close, yet they never drew near.

(The curtain begins to open slowly. Carrasco leaves the scene).

Slowly the sun sank on the horizon, when an Inn appeared in front of their eyes, and our Knight whose head had baked the whole day beneath his large, scorching brass bowl, saw a fortress flanked with six turrets, with its drawbridge, its moats and walls. Then suddenly, as the hills turned blue in the evening light, echoed three times the deep call of a horn.

THE CURTAIN HAS OPENED.

SCENE 3. THE COURTYARD OF THE INN.

(A large doorway, or gate, gives on to the countryside. In the middle of the yard, a water-trough for animals. On the left, the Inn).

(Maritorne, her back turned, standing in the gateway, blows three times feebly into a trumpet).

INNKEEPER *(Coming through the doorway).* Blow harder if ye wants pigs to hear thee.

MARITORNE. Blow thyself, since thee be so clever.

INNKEEPER *(Takes the horn)*. Ye'll not get pigs coming in by doing peu - peu - peu.

(He gives a tremendous blow and produces a deafening false note).

MARITORNE. For a success, that be a knock-out, no doubt about it. But thou'lt have to change thy tune fer pigs. What's comin' seems to be a horse and on it a packet of ironmongery with man in the middle.

INNKEEPER. A traveller. Put a smile on thy face, and don't show thou hast two teeth missing.

MARITORNE. And ye, go and put on thy apron.
(She takes back the horn and blows. Innkeeper goes back into the Inn).

DON QUIXOTE *(Mounted on Rossinante appears in the doorway)*. O gentle damozel . . .

MARITORNE *(Two fingers over her teeth)*. Beg pardon?

DON QUIXOTE. I said damozel.

MARITORNE. Don't follow ye.

DON QUIXOTE. I heard the sound of a horn.

MARITORNE. It be trumpet for calling pigs in.

DON QUIXOTE *(Angrily)*. I said the sound of a horn, and I beg you not to contradict me.

MARITORNE. There, there, no need to lose temper.

DON QUIXOTE. Some valet will look after my steed?

(He dismounts).

MARITORNE. Thy scruffy dobbin? I'll put it in stable myself.

DON QUIXOTE. What? . . . You, damozel?

MARITORNE. Ah, go on, I know how to do't. Same as a man.

(Innkeeper comes peacefully out of the Inn, his belly tied round with an apron, more or less clean, and a long wooden spoon stuck in his belt).

DON QUIXOTE. Who is this gentleman?

MARITORNE. Him! Lorks-a-mercy — our master.

DON QUIXOTE. Have the goodness to tell him, that the Knight Don Quixote of la Mancha requests his hospitality.

(Innkeeper stops in the middle of the courtyard, and puts on an air of tremendous self-importance, and puts his hand on handle of wooden spoon).

MARITORNE *(To Innkeeper)*. Lord love us, he be a bright one, thy traveller, asking so many things . . . I don't know what he's a-talkin' of: he must be foreign. See if thou canst make head or tail of what he say.

(She goes out of the doorway leading Rossinante off).

DON QUIXOTE. My lord of the castle—

INNKEEPER *(Looks at him stupefied, and as Don Quixote salutes him, he bows)*. . . . Come in, Sir.

(Music of a glorious March.

Don Quixote advances, trips over his lance and falls flat. Recovers with noise and dignity).

INNKEEPER *(Goes to help him)*. Let me help thee.

DON QUIXOTE. A Knight always gets up by himself, my lord.

INNKEEPER. I be'unt lord, Sir, I be innkeeper and farmer both at once. My name be Ferdinand.

DON QUIXOTE. You are lord of the Castle. I can see by your noble bearing, lord Ferdinand, and by the sword that hangs by your side.

INNKEEPER. It be my spoon for stirring soups.

DON QUIXOTE. Don't you believe it, my lord. You, like me, are the victim of an invisible enchanter, who is jealous of your glory. He is the one that gave me that vicious kick just now, that made me stumble.

MARITORNE *(Returning by the gateway)*. The beast has his oats.

INNKEEPER. And pigs? Be thou forgettin' them?

MARITORNE. I brought them in at same time.

DON QUIXOTE. My lord of the castle.

MARITORNE. Now he be callin' thee my lord of the castle . . .

INNKEEPER *(Aside to Maritorne)*. Say what he do . . . he's a bit touched . . . and hide thy teeth.

MARITORNE. Perhaps thou art thirsty, Sir?

DON QUIXOTE. The road to glory is long and hard. In fact I have a great thirst.

INNKEEPER. I have wine from Galicia . . .

DON QUIXOTE. Just a plain draft of fresh water.

MARITORNE. Thou be a fine sort of guest, thou be.

INNKEEPER. Hold thy tongue. Have some wine Senor. I have some Carinena, if you prefer it . . .

DON QUIXOTE. I cannot, my lord. And you will understand why if I tell you that, though I am lord of my estate, I have not yet been received officially into the Order of Knighthood. I can eat nothing, drink nothing but water, until I am dubbed Knight according to the rules of chivalry. Therefore, I beg your Grace to swear me in as Knight in this magnificent castle.

MARITORNE. Lorks! Thou friend, I can say thou be a blasted . . .

INNKEEPER. Go and prepare thy soup and leave me to deal with this lump of conceit. I'll find way to make him sup.

(Maritorne goes into the Inn).

INNKEEPER. Sir, I will swear thee in . . . what thou asked me to do.

DON QUIXOTE. To knight me, my lord, neither more nor less.

INNKEEPER. Aye at once. I will and all. That way thou'lt be able to drink wine and eat as thou pleaseth. Mustn't ye be on thy knees for this?

DON QUIXOTE. It would be a great pity to hurry things that way. In fact, the rule requires, my lord, before being received into Knighthood, the suppliant—that's me—fulfills his vigil-of-arms. Where is your chapel?

INNKEEPER. My chapel?

DON QUIXOTE. Belonging to your castle?

INNKEEPER. My castle? My chapel? O aye, for sure. Well . . . ye see . . .

DON QUIXOTE. Will it not be available?

INNKEEPER. Nay, that's it . . . it be needin' a thorough patch-up . . .

DON QUIXOTE. Well, do not let that upset our plans at all. I read . . . now where the devil did I read it? In one of my romances no doubt . . . but which? I read, I say, that instead of the chapel, any other place would do; a mountain, a desert, a deep forest, a terrace, a dungeon, or even a well like this.

INNKEEPER. That be only horse-trough. But I hire rooms by th'night. That should serve purpose of thy vigil I'm thinking. Hast thou money?

DON QUIXOTE. Not a centimo. The romances of chivalry are silent on that subject. You will never read of a Knight-errant wanting money.

INNKEEPER *(Calling)*. Maritorne!

(To Don Quixote).

If thy stories don't tell of it, it's because it be so plain it's took for granted.

1077

(Maritorne comes from the Inn peeling a potato).

Go and take away oats from horse. The gentleman has no money.

MARITORNE.   No money? I be saying same to myself with such a skinny carcass . . .

(As she goes out of the doorway, she returns and considers Don Quixote with pity, and then she goes out shaking her head from side to side).

INNKEEPER.   The next time thou seekest adventure, take a well-lined purse with thee. That's a piece of advice I'm givin' ye. With a hundred crowns thou couldst go any place. For now, since thou hast nothing, watch in courtyard. It don't bother me, none will disturb thee and thou wilt disturb none. Tomorrow morning . . .

DON QUIXOTE.   At daybreak . . .

INNKEEPER.   I gets up at cock-crow. I'll make more honour of Knighthood for thee alone, than what belongs to all Knights of Castille and Aragon rolled into one.

(Night falls slowly and darkens the scene).

DON QUIXOTE.   You have the sword, but have you the book?

INNKEEPER.   What book?

DON QUIXOTE.   The one that contains the formal ritual by which all Knights receive their title.

INNKEEPER.   O aye, course I have it.

DON QUIXOTE.   And the sacred flame?

INNKEEPER.   Us has everything. Watch in peace. It will all be right and proper.

DON QUIXOTE.   From lips such as yours, my lord Ferdinand, these words give me much comfort. I will mount my guard this night, in front of this mysterious well.

INNKEEPER.   Horse-trough.

DON QUIXOTE.   The horse-trough, then.

INNKEEPER.   Well guard it, since ye've set thy heart on it, but don't be drinkin' it all up; I need it for beasts. And for lord's sake, I pray thee, no songs. I be going to sleep. Good-night.

MARITORNE *(Passes by, coming from doorway)*.   Good-night, Sir Horseman.

DON QUIXOTE.   May the night be quiet and peaceful for you, my lord of the castle, and for you, gentle damozel. Don Quixote of la Mancha, watches o'er your rest.

(Innkeeper and Maritorne go into the Inn, leaving Don Quixote in front of the water-trough . . .

*The moon rises just above the courtyard wall. Don Quixote takes
a book out of his pocket; thumbs it, and not seeing clearly enough,
perches on the water-trough to get a better light. He reads . . .).*

"Each Knight, on the eve preceding his sacred dedication, shall
watch bare-headed, without sword, and standing . . ."

(He comes off the trough and places his sword on it).

"Bareheaded . . ."

*(He takes off the shaving basin. His silhouette is seen against the
clear circle of the moon. Music. Lance at the ready, he kisses
his shield, and poses, an immobile figure in front of the water-
trough).*

Ah how fortunate are those who soon will read of my incredible
deeds inscribed on great parchments, who will contemplate the
figure engraved artistically in ever-lasting bronze, cut in marble
or painted on wood; or whose ears will be filled with delight when
the minstrels sing my praise and glory.

(Pause).

. . . O Dulcinea . . . O Dulcinea . . . of Toboso, most fair, amongst
the fair the fairest . . . your humble suitor, alone in the loneliness
of a lone night, dreams of your image and lets forth sad sighs, from
a heart torn in sorrow at your absence. May the shadows of night
fold my thought in a luxurious mantle of black velvet and may
a shaft of moonlight like an arrow of silver, carry it to you, O
my Queen, and my idol. O Dulcinea of Toboso.

(A shadow comes from the Inn and approaches the trough).

Halt . . . Who goes there?

MARITORNE. I needs water for pigs.

DON QUIXOTE. Ghostly creature, come not near this well.

MARITORNE. Move over, please.

DON QUIXOTE. Withdraw, infernal being. Whoever you are, you
shall not touch this that I guard with my life.

MARITORNE. Take away thy scrap-iron.

DON QUIXOTE. O fly, rash monster from this sacred plot, or you will
feel the strength of my lance.

MARITORNE. Hogs be thirsty.

*(She knocks off the shaving-bowl and sword and they fall with
a clatter).*

DON QUIXOTE. Heavenly stars, fire my fury and admire my combat.

*(He attacks Maritorne, who drops her pail and flies screaming.
She disappears behind the Inn. Don Quixote returns quietly to
the water-trough).*

Here, I dare swear, lies my first victory. O Dulcinea, my beauteous lady, my heart, my soul, receive this first token, from him who is nothing but your devoted slave.

INNKEEPER (*Comes out of the Inn in his night-shirt, grasping a candle*). What's up? What hast thou knocked over?

DON QUIXOTE. A fearful demon, straight from Hell, came towards the well . . .

INNKEEPER. Horse-trough.

DON QUIXOTE (*Irritated*). . . . The horse-trough then, if you like . . .

(*He resumes*).

But conscious of your commands and strong in the trust put upon me, I defended the approaches . . .

MARITORNE (*Behind the Innkeeper*). I be needing water for beasts.

DON QUIXOTE. Diabolical shade . . .

INNKEEPER. Softly, Sir Knight . . .

DON QUIXOTE. Abominable demon . . .

INNKEEPER. Thunder and lightning, come to thy senses. This be Maritorne, my servant.

DON QUIXOTE. A thousand pardons, O gentle damozel, your figure appeared near the well . . .

INNKEEPER. Horse-trough, once and for all.

DON QUIXOTE (*Raging*). Alright . . .

(*Going on without a break*).

A fantastic creature took on your presence, your walk, your face . . .

INNKEEPER. Just a minute, Sir Knight.

(*To Maritorne*).

Go fetch cooking-spoon, lantern, book, it don't matter which. I be a-going to confer his Knighthood on him in less time than it takes to tell, and then I be going to throw him out, otherwise he be keeping us up all night.

MARITORNE. Lantern, should it be lit?

INNKEEPER. 'Course, it be sacred flame.

(*Maritorne goes back into the Inn*).

INNKEEPER. To the two of us, Sir, prepare thyself. I be a-going to appoint thee forthwith in the disorder of Knight-errantry.

DON QUIXOTE. Doesn't it say one should await day-break?

INNKEEPER. Nay, nay, it don't matter. After thy last unsurpassed victory the law commands me to stick a Knighthood on thee without more ado.

DON QUIXOTE. For the glory of Spain.

INNKEEPER. And for our own peace and quiet.

DON QUIXOTE. I am your faithful servant.

(Maritorne enters with the spoon, the book and a lighted lantern).

INNKEEPER *(Takes the book).* Hold up sacred flame, so as I can read ritual. Thou shalt answer 'Amen'. On thy knees, Don Quixote. I will pour Knighthood upon thee in one stroke.

(Don Quixote kneels. During the following scene he remains in an ecstasy, quite unconscious of what is being said around him).

INNKEEPER *(Opens the book, and reads at random)....* "Twenty-sixth August: By wagoner Lopez . . ."

(To Maritorne).

. . . these be farm accounts.

MARITORNE. Amen. It be all I could find.

INNKEEPER. Don't matter.

(He goes on).

. . . "By wagoner Lopez, sent two boars to Marquess of Santa Cruz. For carriage paid ten pesetas and a few cents."

DON QUIXOTE. I swear it.

MARITORNE. Amen.

INNKEEPER. Twenty-eighth at noon, soup and sausage for three men who come from mountain. Received eight pesetas and a quarter.

DON QUIXOTE. I swear it.

MARITORNE. Amen.

INNKEEPER. Third September, bought two goat skins of red wine from Juan Benediz of Priego's hamlet; paid six crowns, three chickens, and half a pig of twelve kilos. What a thief . . .

DON QUIXOTE. I swear it.

MARITORNE. Amen.

INNKEEPER. Fifth, received from Marquess of Santa Cruz, for two pigs noted above; twelve crowns precisely.

MARITORNE. That be thieving too.

DON QUIXOTE. I swear it.

INNKEEPER. Look after thine own affairs.

MARITORNE. Amen.

INNKEEPER. By the power of my sword . . .

(To Maritorne).

. . . my spoon. Once, twice, three times, dubbed. I give thee Knight-errantry and all it stands for. There!

MARITORNE. Amen.

INNKEEPER. The whole thing be in boiling pot.

(A pause).

. . . Get up . . .

(Getting no response from Don Quixote he shakes him).

. . . Hey . . . Sir Knight . . . day-break be come even as ye desired it. If thee wants to go and slaughter, time be come for ye to pass on thy way.

DON QUIXOTE. Truly. Here is the radiant sun of Spain turning for the first time his golden gaze on my new-born Knighthood.

(He puts on the shaving basin).

INNKEEPER *(To Maritorne)* Go saddle horse . . .

(Aside).

. . . and haste ye, I've seen enough of what serves him for face.

MARITORNE. Well, Sir Horseman, as the sun be rising thou wilt simmer up there like turnip in pot. I be going to saddle thy horse.

(She exits).

DON QUIXOTE. Allow me, my lord, to say I am more than astonished to see a maiden so high born having the care of my steed. In all the books I've read, and God knows I've read many, a Knight's mount is always, and without exception, saddled, groomed, combed, and fed by his squire. May the Heavens and the love of my lady, guide me soon to him who will be my squire.

SANCHO *(Appears in the doorway and attaches his donkey to a ring).*

O Ferdinand, thou art in uniform.

INNKEEPER. It's just — my friend, I've been giving a Knighthood

SANCHO. Thou don't have any work—

(To his donkey). Quiet, you.

(To Innkeeper). — nothing too hard, to keep me busy?

(To Don Quixote). Excuse me, your worship.

1082

(To Innkeeper). It be more than a month I be idle, and Theresa

(To Don Quixote). that's my wife—

(To Innkeeper). she spent the last crown yesterday.

DON QUIXOTE. Crowning did you say? Could you be a squire?

SANCHO. What's he a-talking of?

DON QUIXOTE. Heaven has guided you to this castle.

SANCHO. Which castle?

INNKEEPER *(Aside)*. Say same as he do. Mebbe he'll take thee into his service. He's looking for someone.

(He goes into the Inn).

SANCHO. Alright about the castle, your worship, but as for being what thou sayest . . .

DON QUIXOTE. Squire.

SANCHO. I don't really know what that be.

DON QUIXOTE. You are one. It's as plain as a pike-staff. What is your name?

SANCHO. Sancho . . . Sancho Panza.

DON QUIXOTE *(Laying his arms on the water-trough, and sits)*. . . . What can you do?

SANCHO. Most anything . . . as long as it's not too much.

DON QUIXOTE. You could be invaluable to me.

SANCHO. If thou sayest so, must be true.

DON QUIXOTE. Do you know who I am?

SANCHO. Might I speak honest?

DON QUIXOTE. That is your duty as a knight's squire.

SANCHO. Right. For me thou be just a queer fish.

DON QUIXOTE. I am the Knight Don Quixote of la Mancha.

SANCHO. Never heard of him.

DON QUIXOTE. You will hear of me soon enough, for my deeds are about to shake the world.

SANCHO. Shake the world if it's thy pleasure, but not too much all same. If thou shakest fleas off others, sooner or later thou'lt catch them thyself.

DON QUIXOTE. You are made to be my squire, you rascal, for your speech is gold.

SANCHO. Contrary to thee Sir Knight, who never speak of it, how much wilt thou pay me for being what thou sayest?

DON QUIXOTE. A Knight-errant pays neither gold nor silver to his squire, you should know that.

SANCHO. If that be so, excuse me.

DON QUIXOTE. Know that the calling I follow consists of conquering provinces, kingdoms and empires.

SANCHO. All that? All by thyself?

DON QUIXOTE. Yes. And if you give yourself to my service, I will make you Count, perhaps Marquess, . . . in less time than you'll take to write it.

SANCHO. That'll be a long time. I don't even know my A B C.

DON QUIXOTE. You will only need to serve me properly. I will look after the rest, and I warrant you, before the week is out, I shall reward you by a post as Governor of a prosperous and sunny isle.

SANCHO. Be there wine?

DON QUIXOTE. More than you need.

SANCHO. And hams?

DON QUIXOTE. In abundance.

SANCHO. And cheese?

DON QUIXOTE. Without a doubt.

SANCHO. I could take Theresa, my wife?

DON QUIXOTE. It's your absolute right.

SANCHO. From now on, Sir Knight, I be thy squire. But between thee and me, I would much prefer a little province with Count's title, for I don't very well see how my Theresa, who be washer-woman by trade, can jump from washing into skin of Governor's wife, all at once. She might pass for countess, or marquise, or duchess, maybe—but Governor's wife, no.

DON QUIXOTE. Leave it to me to give you the honour and title best suited to you. You have the profile of a Governor, you shall be Governor.

SANCHO. That, Sir Knight, since thou be at present my master shall be as thou thinks fit.

DON QUIXOTE. The matter then is closed. And from now on, call me, not Sir Knight, but rather Your Grace, or Sir, or my lord Don Quixote as you think best. And if by chance you speak of me to someone else, you will say to him; it is my Master the Knight Don Quixote of la Mancha.

1084

SANCHO. Don't worry thyself on that score. About stories of thy titles and lordships. I will serve thee in a manner that will astound thee. I worked for three days in the stables of the Marquess of Santa Cruz, over there behind those hills, so seest thou . . .

MARITORNE (*Comes back through the doorway leading Rossinante*). . . . Thy old crock be ready.

SANCHO. Holy mother! What on earth be that?

(*Maritorne, finger on her lips, discreetly indicates Don Quixote with thumb*).

DON QUIXOTE. Gentle damozel . . .

MARITORNE. Seems to be me.

DON QUIXOTE. Have the goodness to give my noble mount to my faithful squire.

SANCHO (*To Maritorne*). And that seems to be me.

DON QUIXOTE. And will you warn my lord of the Castle of my desire to bid him farewell again, ere I resume my quest.

SANCHO. Where do he want to go?

MARITORNE. Don't ye ask questions, squire, and hold bridle.

(*She goes into the Inn*).

SANCHO (*Eyeing Rossinante*). Well, old man, you're no fat dumpling.

DON QUIXOTE (*In the gateway turns to the outside*). . . . Our journey beckons us radiantly ahead, friend Sancho. Fair Phoebus . . .

SANCHO. Who be he?

DON QUIXOTE. Phoebus—

SANCHO (*Designating Rossinante*). That's him?

DON QUIXOTE. No. He is Rossinante. That's Phoebus up there, the king of heaven, whose golden rays caress the country-side. A light mist veils the far-off mountains, the spider is happy in the middle of her web, and the lark above—Oh, Heavens, what catches my eye? Sancho—there on the hill—

SANCHO. Whereabouts?

DON QUIXOTE. Just at the end of my finger. What do you see?

SANCHO. Windmills.

DON QUIXOTE. Giants, you blind dunderhead. An army of monstrous big-bellied giants, drunk with blood and carnage, about to assault us.

SANCHO. I assure you, My Grace.

DON QUIXOTE. Your Grace.

SANCHO. Thine or mine it be all same.

DON QUIXOTE. They are waving their arms about . . .

SANCHO. Those be sails the wind whirls around.

DON QUIXOTE. Pest of my life . . . you are . . . you poor Sancho too, the victim of a magician who persecutes us, and who makes you see windmills over there where the warring giants advance.

(Innkeeper comes out of the Inn, spoon in hand).

DON QUIXOTE *(Equipping himself in haste)*. . . . My lord, they are approaching.

INNKEEPER. Who?

DON QUIXOTE. They. Look! Barricade your doors, raise up your drawbridge, put all your archers at their posts on the battlements, sight the cannons, prepare the mortars.

INNKEEPER *(To Maritorne who comes back)*. So, thou be calling me out for this?

SANCHO. My master, thou be mistook.

(To Innkeeper).

Thou, talk to him.

DON QUIXOTE. For mercy's sake, listen. Get your fortress ready for defence. Prepare boiling-oil, and stone cannon balls. As for me I will attack these monsters as my destiny demands. In open country, alone against one and all.

INNKEEPER. May the devil grill me if I understand a word of his jabber.

SANCHO. Don't go, my lord. Thou'lt break his bones.

(Pointing to Rossinante).

DON QUIXOTE. Duty calls me, loud and clear.

MARITORNE. Boiling oil sir, be it for frying?

DON QUIXOTE *(Making his horse rear and crying)*. . . . For Dulcinea and for Spain!

(He disappears at a gallop.

Music of a charge).

SANCHO. Sir, my Master, your Grace, and everything thou art. Turn back—

INNKEEPER. But where be this madman going?

SANCHO. To attack windmills.

MARITORNE. He'll break his bones—

1086

SANCHO (*Crying out*). They don't be giants, Sir.

(*To Innkeeper*). He takes them for giants . . .

(*Crying out*). They be windmills—turn back, turn back . . . O Saints in Heaven!!

INNKEEPER. I've never come across his like—He be plain daft.

MARITORNE. Holy Mother, now he be throwing hisself at them.

SANCHO. Ah, my Master . . .

INNKEEPER. Take care . . . look out . . .

(*All scatter from doorway, through which Don Quixote returns in a backward somersault, unarmed and unconscious. The Innkeeper places his spoon on the water-trough, and like the others, hurries to the inanimate Don Quixote*).

SANCHO. My Master, your Grace, Don Quixote of la Mancha.

MARITORNE (*At the same time*). Lorks-a-mercy what a pounding— And poor old dobbin, flat on his back.

INNKEEPER. He be dead. In my courtyard. Water—Bring some water.

(*Maritorne draws a bucket of water from the water-trough*).

SANCHO. That be just my luck—I found a Master, then he goes and breaks head on windmill—

INNKEEPER. We can't be leaving him like that. To do such a thing to me. Us must lift his head up. As though he couldn't find something better to attack.

MARITORNE. Lift thy head up—Not thine—But thine. Gentle now.

(*Helped by Sancho she forces Don Quixote to drink*).

INNKEEPER. Not for drinking. To bring him round.

MARITORNE. Should'st have said so.

(*She upsets the whole pail on Don Quixote*).

INNKEEPER. Oh, nay . . .

SANCHO. Stop, his eye moved.

MARITORNE. Thou bring him round. I go to give hand to beast.

(*She goes out by the doorway*).

SANCHO. Ferdinand . . . thy apron.

(*Maternally he sponges Don Quixote's face with apron*).

. . . Your Grace . . . it's me Sancho . . . thy squire.

DON QUIXOTE (*Feebly*). How many? How many did I exterminate?

SANCHO. Put thy mind at rest, master. They be windmills for sure.

INNKEEPER. They been on that hill over thirty years.

DON QUIXOTE. I understand.

INNKEEPER. It be none too soon.

DON QUIXOTE. I've undergone a new enchantment. When the giants . . .

INNKEEPER. Nay, thou be'unt starting all over?

DON QUIXOTE. When they saw with what tremendous strength I fell on them . . .

INNKEEPER (Shrugging his shoulders). He won't let up.

(Goes out of doorway).

DON QUIXOTE. As soon as they realized Sancho, they were going to perish beneath the touch of my invincible lance, they changed themselves suddenly, into so many windmills, knowing very well that one man . . . whatever Knight he be . . . can do nothing against walls of stone and sails turning in the wind.

SANCHO. Thou be mistook. They be truly windmills, my master. I've known them since I were born. The biggest one caught thee badly, sending by same stroke, my Governorship and my isle flying sky-high, God knows where.

DON QUIXOTE. Console yourself, friend Sancho, and have patience. Nothing is lost and soon a time will come—I give you my word—when, by the force of my arms, it won't be an island I'll bestow on you, but a whole archipelago.

MARITORNE (Enters carrying several fragments of the broken lance, the dented shaving-basin and his shield, bent in two). Only these be left.

DON QUIXOTE. My battle-lance.

MARITORNE. Some pieces of wood and spear-head.

DON QUIXOTE. My shield of brass.

MARITORNE. Folded like pancake.

DON QUIXOTE. King Mambrino's helmet.

MARITORNE. It got a good bonk.

DON QUIXOTE. And Rossinante? Where is my charger?

MARITORNE. Flat on his back. Our master be getting him up. I couldn't manage to do it.

DON QUIXOTE. Come, Sancho. Let us find our valiant friend and quit this place, where I have been the victim of an enchanter, jealous of my success, twice, already.

SANCHO. Where be we going?

DON QUIXOTE. To the mountain.

(He takes his sword from the water-trough).

At least this remains unconquered. Pick up my arms and follow me.

SANCHO. All this stuff?

DON QUIXOTE. All of it. When in imitation of Amadis of Gaul, alone in the loneliness of a lone mountain, I have watched without food, four days and four nights, I shall truly have earned my title of Knight-errant, and thereby gained strength and daring.

(Maritorne, after listening to him open-mouthed, goes into the Inn).

SANCHO. Four days, four nights, without eating?

DON QUIXOTE. So it is written in the books.

SANCHO. If that be what books say, and that's what thy service be, without offending Your Grace, I'd as soon resign right now.

DON QUIXOTE. It does not concern you. On the contrary, while I keep my lonely watch—I told you—I would be bestowing on you a mission of the greatest importance. Come.

(He goes out by the doorway, walking painfully.

Sancho, encumbered with the shield, the shaving bowl, and the pieces of the lance, tries to climb on to his donkey.

Maritorne comes from the Inn with a package in a knotted handkerchief).

SANCHO *(To his donkey).* My poor Grison! Dost see all that's needed to be a Governor?

MARITORNE *(Slides the parcel into Sancho's leather saddle-bag).* There be some meats. Some wine. Look after him. He be a good one.

(She helps Sancho to mount on Grison).

SANCHO. Thanks be to thee from him . . . and from me.

(He goes out by the doorway).

MARITORNE *(Watching him go).* Gentle damozel . . . it be a little like he were calling me Madame.

INNKEEPER *(Coming back through the doorway).* . . . . What be that?

MARITORNE. What be what?

INNKEEPER. The package.

MARITORNE. What package?

INNKEEPER. Come off thy high horse. What didst thou slip Sancho? Thinkest thou I did not see? . . .

MARITORNE. Some cold meats and some wine. And so?

INNKEEPER. Hath he paid?

MARITORNE. Nay, but he were hungry.

INNKEEPER. Thou be doing well, thou be. Dost ye think meats fall from sky? And the wine, do ye know how much it costs?

MARITORNE. Ye can doff it off my wages if it bothers thee.

INNKEEPER. Nay, no question. But I don't be a Count of This nor That, no more than Marquess of Bazaadir nor Bazaadar to hand out goods to all who come.

MARITORNE. Go on with ye.

INNKEEPER. Go on with ye, forever, go on with ye . . . where do ye get thy notions? Thou throwest my hams, my roasts, my stews, and my leather wine-bottles, to all the riffraff who pass, without asking my leave. What dost thou take me for?

MARITORNE. For what ye be.

INNKEEPER. And what be I, and please ye?

MARITORNE. A cross old bear . . . with a devilish good heart, big as this.

INNKEEPER. Ah!

(Pleased with the compliment, relaxes a second, then furiously). . . . That be no reason . . .

(A pause . . . Softly while putting on his apron). Did ye give enough?

MARITORNE. If Sancho hath any sense, aye, they be having sufficient for three days.

INNKEEPER. And the beast?

MARITORNE. What about beast?

INNKEEPER. In the state he be in, he'll not be able to go three days on empty belly.

MARITORNE. Don't fret thyself. I gives him oats too.

INNKEEPER *(Exploding).* . . . And what beside? I've told thee already . . . thou'lt drive me to drink.

(He shuts up, smiles, shrugs his shoulders). Much good it be doing them, anyways. Give me . . . my sword.

(For a short instant he considers the spoon thoughtfully that Maritorne holds out to him—Music. Then he lifts his head proudly looking towards the doorway. Perhaps he dreams of glory and adventure too. Then he returns a little sadly to the reality of day).

1090

I be going to stir soup.

(He puts the spoon through his apron belt, and looks at Maritorne, and says affectionately to her . . .).

And hide thy teeth . . . damozel . . .

(He goes proudly towards the Inn and enters).

MARITORNE. Gentle damozel . . . that be a true Knight.

CURTAIN

END OF ACT ONE

ACT TWO

Scene 4. In The Countryside.

(Quixote and Sancho asleep in the shadow of a bush. A few bars of bucolic music, then mingled with the music, a rather harsh galley-chant which gradually builds until it predominates).

Archer's Voice *(Off)*. Advance, rogues. Pick up thy feet, thou. Go on, hurry, scum!

(Whip-lashes off. Groans. Don Quixote wakes up with a start—).

(Off). Thee, in front, are slowing down others.

(Whip.

Don Quixote shakes Sancho, who wakes up).

Don Quixote. Listen!

Archer's Voice *(Off)*. Advance, I say, or I'll tear the skin off thy back.

Sancho. The skin off their back?

Don Quixote. My helmet.

Archer's Voice *(Off)*. Into line with thee.

(Whip).

Don Quixote *(Standing, with helmet on)*. Either I am greatly mistaken, friend Sancho, or my lucky star is sending me a golden opportunity to come to the aid of the suffering. My sword.

Sancho. Mistrust what thou hearest.

Archer *(Enters, leading the galley-slaves, who are linked together by chains to Gines)*. March.

Sancho. And above all, what thou see'st.

Don Quixote *(Plants himself squarely in their way)*. No one's to move.

Archer. What do you want, you?

Don Quixote. To know why you ill-treat these people.

Archer. My good man—

Don Quixote. I am not your good man. I am the Knight Don Quixote of la Mancha.

Archer. Oo—ay. And I, Mr. Hurlburly, I am the Archer of St. Hermandad. Which means armed constable in case you don't know.

1092

SANCHO *(Aside)*. This stinks. This stinks.

DON QUIXOTE. Does this give you the right to bully these poor devils as you're doing?

GINES. Aye, it's terrible Sir, he beats us something terrible.

ARCHER. Silence, thou.

(Whip).

GALLEY-SLAVES. Aye, Sir, Aye, it be terrible.

ARCHER. Thee too.

(Whip).

DON QUIXOTE. Another move from you, and I'll cleave you open from head to foot.

SANCHO. My Master . . .

ARCHER. Enough of this folly. Make way!

SANCHO. Sir Archer . . .

DON QUIXOTE. Stand aside. This is my concern.

(To Archer).

Are you a Knight?

ARCHER. Archer, I've told you.

GINES. Your Worship, free us.

ARCHER. Thou, holdst thy tongue.

(He pushes them roughly).

SANCHO. My Master, thou canst see the senor be an armed constable and he be taking condemned to galleys.

DON QUIXOTE. They are poor wretches, persecuted by a monster.

GALLEY-SLAVES. Aye, that be true, sir. Ah, it be true, he be monster. Look at these scars. He done it. And that one. He's marked me for life.

DON QUIXOTE. Fear no more. I am here.

(To Archer).

If your courage, sir, equals the cruelty you use to ill-treat these worthy men—

ARCHER. I've had enough of your tongue. Make way.

(He seizes his sword).

DON QUIXOTE. By St. James . . . For me, Spirit of Galaor!

(He kisses his sword).

GALLEY-SLAVES. Go to it, sir! Cut him to ribbons! He's asked for it. Split his head open!

(Sancho hides beneath the shield).

ARCHER. Keep off!

(Rapid engagement. Gines goes on all fours behind the Archer, who, pressed by Don Quixote, falls backward in a somersault and drops his sword. A Galley-Slave takes possession of the whip. Gines picks up the sword. Another Galley-Slave takes the keys from the Archer's belt).

GALLEY-SLAVES. Bravo, sir! Finish him off.

DON QUIXOTE. Silence, pray. A Knight does not strike a disarmed enemy. Rise.

GINES. Stand up.

(To the others).

Chain him up.

(The Galley-Slaves who have freed themselves from their chains, try to master the Archer. But he pushes them off and runs away. The others are about to follow).

DON QUIXOTE. Ho there, sirs! Just a moment.

SANCHO *(Who has got up).* Thou hadst better let them be. Look at those ugly mugs.

DON QUIXOTE. It is the mask of suffering.

(The Galley-Slaves make a group behind Gines).

GINES. Be quick. We're in a hurry. They're waiting for us at home.

DON QUIXOTE. Though I find you too impatient, my friends, I will make an effort to understand you, and I readily admit that naturally, like birds freed from their cage—

GINES. Cut the high-faluting.

GALLEY-SLAVES. Come to the point.

SANCHO. Aye, leave them alone. It be better.

DON QUIXOTE *(Stamping his foot).* Zounds! I will speak. I admit, I say, gentlemen, you must have had a great longing to take your leave, in this liberty my valourous arm has won for you. But—

GINES. How much longer will this go on?

DON QUIXOTE. Long enough to tell you, Mr. Impertinent, that in gratitude for what I have done for you, my express will is to see you go immediately, without further delay, to my Lady Dulcinea, in the city of Toboso, to whom you will recount in detail, without adding or taking away one jot, the adventure from which I have delivered you.

1094

GINES. That, old cock, is like looking for a pumpkin in a nut-tree. We have better things to do.

DON QUIXOTE (Furious). Great Heavens! I swear, you will do as I command—

GINES. Oh, oh, oh . . .

GALLEY-SLAVES. Command? What dost take us for? Who be giving commands around here? We've had enough of that.

SANCHO. Take care!

DON QUIXOTE (Pushes him aside and speaks to Gines). Yes, you will do it. And it is yourself, blockhead, who shall go alone, with the chains on your back, to bow low in Toboso, before her whom I love.

GINES. Come on.

(The Galley-Slaves throw Don Quixote and Sancho to the ground).

DON QUIXOTE. Cowards! . . . Blackguards! . . .

GINES. Shut him up.

(Galley-Slave whips Don Quixote vigorously. He tries in vain to get up).

DON QUIXOTE. I'll make you pay—

GALLEY-SLAVE (Whipping him). We're paying. We're paying, you fool.

GINES. Enough compliments. Let's go. Farewell, my lord, and thank you for sparing us the galleys.

(He helps himself to Sancho's leather bag, then they make a swift exit).

SANCHO. My satchel!

DON QUIXOTE. Scoundrels—

SANCHO. Did you see him?

DON QUIXOTE. Yes. Outcasts from hell!

SANCHO. The one you called blockhead?

DON QUIXOTE (He lifts himself up painfully). Go and fetch Rossinante.

SANCHO. He's took our satchel.

DON QUIXOTE. I know. Let us press on.

(Sancho goes out).

Whipping me, me, the Knight Don Quixote of la Mancha! 'Sdeath! If I held you at my sword's point—

(He makes big sword sweeps in the air).

SANCHO *(Returns with Rossinante)*. Your Grace—

DON QUIXOTE. I wouldn't give a centimo for your worthless skin.

SANCHO. My Master . . .

DON QUIXOTE. This insult to my dignity, as Knight, shall be washed in a cataract of blood.

SANCHO. Pull thyself together.

DON QUIXOTE. You tell me to pull myself together, when they were a hundred, to pull me apart . . . and whip me.

SANCHO. A hundred? Sayest thou?

DON QUIXOTE. I saw them . . . I counted them . . . Thunder and lightning!

SANCHO. I warned thee not to put thy trust in them. They've took my leather-bag.

DON QUIXOTE. And scoffed at my honour.

SANCHO. The meats and the bread.

DON QUIXOTE. My glory.

SANCHO. The wine. There was some. There is none.

DON QUIXOTE. My fame. And yours.

SANCHO. Here be we, with naught to eat.

DON QUIXOTE. How can you talk of food when my shame is beyond everything?

SANCHO. Indeed Sir, at the moment, thou cuts a pretty sad figure.

(He goes to fetch Grison).

DON QUIXOTE *(Alone, speaks to himself)*. Sad figure. Here is the title that from now on I shall add to my name, as a reminder of this painful adventure. Nor shall I change it till the day I finally achieve a success worthy of my sword.

(Seeing Sancho come back with Grison on his last words).

For now I see, Sancho, nothing in my profession as a Knight-errant will succeed until like Amadis of Gaul, alone in the loneliness of a lone mountain—

(He straddles Rossinante).

SANCHO. O aye, four days, four nights, without eating.

DON QUIXOTE. I shall drink spring-waters and gnaw the bark of trees.

SANCHO. For myself, I prefer, by a long shot, a full table.

1096

DON QUIXOTE. You shall have better still.

SANCHO. In mountain?

DON QUIXOTE. No. There where I shall send you as my ambassador.

SANCHO. Ambassador, me, where be this?

DON QUIXOTE. I will explain to you up yonder. Come.

(He goes out).

SANCHO *(Mounts Grison).* So I be ambassador already. From there to Governor can't be more than three paces.

(Before going out, Sancho urges his donkey forward, saying "Hue da!" He exits).

THE CURTAIN CLOSES.

SCENE 5. IN THE MOUNTAIN.

(Some rocks. A tree.

Don Quixote casts off his armour and hangs up the various parts on the tree).

SANCHO *(Repairing the lance).* But seest thou, my Master, I can't go longer than an hour without food.

DON QUIXOTE. Don't worry. You will be treated more than royally where I am sending you as an ambassador of love.

SANCHO. An ambassador of love? That be a good one that be! Me, with my face? Thou can'st not mean it?

DON QUIXOTE. All will go well, I promise you. While alone in this lonely place—I've told you already—I shall be keeping watch and fulfilling the commands of the law of Knight-errantry, you will go for me, straight-on, without looking left or right, carrying this letter here, to her whom I adore, the fairest of fair, Dulcinea of Toboso.

SANCHO. I know Toboso, and all its folk. There be fewer than my fingers and toes gathered together. But Dulcinea as thou callest her, I don't know who she be, truly, I don't.

DON QUIXOTE. You must understand, Dulcinea is a romantic name— as those Knights give their lady—a name that I myself forged in the flame of my love, for her whom I adore and who, Princess of my heart, is in fact called, Aldonza Lorenzo.

SANCHO. The herdsman's daughter?

DON QUIXOTE. An enchanter keeps her as such.

SANCHO. By my Faith! She be a fine slip of a girl! Built like battle-axe, as broad above as below!

DON QUIXOTE. Poor Sancho, who believes all that your eyes see, whereas in one's heart everything is so wonderful. A simple village becomes a new world, and a peasant girl a gracious lady.

SANCHO. I admits then, since thou sayest so, she must be seen in a different fashion—which seems mighty hard. But there be one thing I must warn thee about. That is, she don't like to be made fun of. And thy letter, I be wondering at time, in what temper she will take it.

DON QUIXOTE. My answer to that is, very well indeed. To convince yourself, listen to a little of this.

(He reads).

Most gracious and sovereign lady, O dulcet Dulcinea of Toboso, thou whose pale visage surpasses the beauty of the noonday sun . . .

SANCHO. I must stop thee there. She be redder than a poppy.

DON QUIXOTE. Thou whose fingers are as fine as spindles . . .

SANCHO. Let me laugh. She can knock thee out with one slap of back of her hand.

(He leans the lance he has just repaired against the tree).

DON QUIXOTE. Thou whose tresses are a heavenly torrent . . .

SANCHO. Verily, I tells thee she wears bun.

DON QUIXOTE. Cease interrupting me at every turn, incorrigible babbler.

(He resumes).

. . . are a heavenly torrent, thou whose gentle looks . . .

SANCHO *(With his fingers shows that Aldonza squints).* She be . . .

DON QUIXOTE. Silence . . .

(Sancho goes to get Grison, returns at once).

. . . are a snare for love, thou whose moist lip is a fruit of delight, O peerless thou, fairest of fair, receive my squire, the faithful Sancho, who shall tell thee without needless detail—I stress—the glorious feats I have performed for thee. O lovely Dulcinea, Princess of my heart, my soul's gentle sun, I offer you my Fate, my deeds and my life . . . to thee, thine who loves thee, Don Quixote of la Mancha, the Knight of the Sad Figure.

(He closes the letter and returns it to Sancho).

I commit it to your care.

(A pause).

You may speak.

SANCHO. God bless me, Your Grace! For a well plastered letter, that be well plastered and as ye charges me to recount thy deeds, trust to my vivid imagination. I shall tell Aldonza Lorenzo . . .

(While he is speaking he poses the letter between two branches of the tree and finishes saddling the donkey).

DON QUIXOTE. Dulcinea . . .

SANCHO. Aye . . . such a tale of thy chivalry, as goes far beyond any in the books from which thou drums my ears.

DON QUIXOTE. I count on your memory to omit none of my great deeds.

SANCHO. My Master, heed Sancho, even though maybe at times he more or less loses his head, he don't never forget what's been committed to his care. A word to the wise be sufficient. I go to carry out thy embassy of love.

(As Don Quixote examines lance).

It be'unt quite as straight as should be on neck, but I guarantee it be unbreakable this time. With it, thou'lt be able to pierce an army of enchanters and conquer my isle and my kingdom, with no more waiting about. I salute thee, My Master.

DON QUIXOTE. Wait. See, first of all what a perilous thing I am going to perform in her honour and go and tell Dulcinea to what lengths my daring goes.

(He does a hand-stand on his head and hands).

SANCHO. Aye, I be seeing, it turns thy head upside-down . . .

(Don Quixote falls back heavily).

SANCHO. . . . And biffs thy bottom on ground.

DON QUIXOTE. Now go, my faithful squire, to fulfill your mission.

SANCHO *(Straddling Grison).* Quick as lightning, since I be getting something to eat there. Look after thyself till I come back. Hue, ambassador's donkey, thou be trotting out on a mission of love.

(Exits.

Music. Don Quixote tries in vain to do a perfect hand-stand.

Night falls. He gets up, puts on the shaving-bowl, takes up his lance and goes out slowly.

The sound of bells ringing. The Shepherds enter and immediately set about lighting a fire).

DON QUIXOTE *(Re-enters).* Stay . . . Who are you?

SHEPHERD. Shepherds, Sir. Or rather, Goatherds. Be ye lost in mountain?

DON QUIXOTE. Lost? No. This mountain is mine.

SHEPHERD (*Ironically*). Then would ye be the King of Spain?

(*Night has slowly fallen. The men are lit from below by the fire-light*).

DON QUIXOTE. Not at all, but only his humble servant. I am Don Quixote of la Mancha, Knight of the Sad Figure.

SHEPHERD. Sad or no, thy figure can no be seen in this night. As for us it's no matter, I tells thee. Will ye share supper with us?

DON QUIXOTE. Well you see, the rule is, a Knight must keep his watch alone.

SHEPHERD. Knights, goatherds, it be all one. And while ye be among us, since thou be sole-living-creature of thy sort, thou wilt be alone, and canst watch as ye please.

DON QUIXOTE. For the Glory of Spain and the love of my lady, I accept.

SHEPHERD. For anything thou likes, Sir . . . come ye close to fire.

(*Aside to the others who are roasting acorns and chestnuts while Quixote puts the shaving-bowl back in the tree*).

Make place for him; he be a crack-pot. Sit ye down, Sir Knight.

DON QUIXOTE. I will remain standing as the law commands. Bare-headed, without sword, and upright.

SHEPHERD. Just as thou pleases.

(*He takes his place near the others. A porringer passes from hand to hand . . .*

Nocturnal music played by a goat-herd).

DON QUIXOTE (*Standing, leaning on his lance*).
O Dulcinea of Toboso,
O thou fairest of fair,
Princess of my heart, planet of my sky,
See thy fearless hero, standing beneath the quiet stars,
Guarding the mountain and sleeping Spain.
Close thy pretty eyes yonder in Toboso, and dream thy golden
    dreams.
Nothing can befall thee, save that I adore thee, my sweet queen.

SHEPHERD (*Holding the bowl out to him*). These be acorns and chest-nuts.

DON QUIXOTE. I cannot.

SHEPHERD. They be thy share. Take some, Sir.

DON QUIXOTE. Thank you.

(*He eats*).

1100

All this is strange. In most of the romances that were my daily pittance, Knights dying of hunger—as in my case—are succoured by a bird—generally an eagle—who brings them something to eat at the very last moment. So this, Gentlemen, is not usual. And it is but just, for, after all, neither is my destiny usual.

(Shepherd holds out a horn in which he has poured wine from a leather bottle).

DON QUIXOTE. I can only drink water.

SHEPHERD. That's what it be, Sir, don't ye worry.

DON QUIXOTE. It smells like wine and tastes like it.

SHEPHERD. And that be all the better, be'unt it, for if wine tasted like water it'd be a terrible how d'yer-do.

(Laughter.

Music. A Spanish tune. A shepherd scrapes his guitar. Then the music takes a dance-rhythm. A man gets up and dances in front of the fire. The others do the same and soon Quixote joins the dancers. Then he becomes the centre of the dance, while the others clap their hands. Although being slightly clumsy, Don Quixote is never ridiculous.

The dance must be a moment of musical and visual beauty. At the end of the dance the goatherds fete Quixote).

Bravo! This be done in true knightly fashion.

DON QUIXOTE. Give me some more of this marvellous water tasting like red wine.

(Shepherd holds out the horn for him to drink. Don Quixote brusquely pushes it back).

There, look.

(The horned shadows of three goats are seen in profile on the back-cloth).

My lance. Withdraw.

SHEPHERD. Sir . . .

DON QUIXOTE. Fear not. I am here. Back! This mountain is under my guard. Withdraw, dread spirits.

SHEPHERD *(Laughing).* Those be our goats.

DON QUIXOTE. They are devils, I see, horned demons, with cleft feet and flaming beards.

SHEPHERD. Woa . . . Woa . . .

DON QUIXOTE *(Beating the goats).* By St. James, you shall return to Hell.

SHEPHERD. He be going to kill them. Thy staves!

(*They thrash Quixote*).

DON QUIXOTE. Gentlemen . . .

SHEPHERD. He be killing two of them.

DON QUIXOTE. Have you too come out of Hell?

SHEPHERD. Thou crack-pot! Lay about him.

DON QUIXOTE. Curses on you.

SHEPHERD. Thou, rescue beasts.

DON QUIXOTE. Hear me . . .

SHEPHERD. Come on.

DON QUIXOTE. I die . . .

SHEPHERDS (*Gathering the goats together*). Djick hoa, djick hay hay hoa.

SHEPHERD. Away.

SHEPHERDS (*Going off*). Djick hay, djick djick hoahoa hoa.

DON QUIXOTE. I die . . . for Spain.

(*He collapses*).

(*Music*).

THE CURTAIN CLOSES.

SCENE 6. ANOTHER PLACE IN THE MOUNTAIN.

(*Full lights.*

Enter from D. R. Carrasco, enveloped in a large embroidered cape, and Maritorne, richly dressed. She walks with bare feet, carrying elegant shoes in her hand. They stay at the extreme R. of scene).

MARITORNE. Thou makest me do things, thou dost.

CARRASCO. It's got to be done if you really want to help me save him.

MARITORNE. O' course I do. But must us push out of his head all notions of chivalry?

CARRASCO. The time is past for these tom-fooleries.

MARITORNE. More's the pity.

CARRASCO. Behave yourself. Someone's coming.

(*Sancho enters L. on his donkey. Seeing the couple he stops and puts foot to ground*).

SANCHO (*to Grison*). Behave yourself. Someone's coming.

1102

MARITORNE. It be'unt somebody, it be Sancho.

SANCHO *(Approaches)*. Sir, Madam, I . . . but it be Mr. Carrasco . . . and thou? Nay, it be'unt thou. Aye, it be thee . . .

CARRASCO. Her.

MARITORNE. Him.

SANCHO. There be no Fiesta on now.

CARRASCO. I'll tell you all about this later. Where is your Master?

SANCHO. Above, up there. He be doing a hand-stand and biffing bottom on ground, for love of his lady.

MARITORNE. Poor body. He must hurt hisself.

CARRASCO. You left him alone doing these antics?

SANCHO. I don't see for why I be having to do same, besides, he wanted to do it. He be stopping, to keep his watch, he said, four days, four nights, without eating. That be no way to please my belly, so, says I:—I be going. Aye, says he, go, but I post thee as an ambassador of love, and send thee to my lady Dulcinea, before I name thee Governor.

MARITORNE. That one, who be she?

SANCHO. His fairest of fair, says he. Ye must see letter he charged me bring her.

(He searches, becomes uneasy, and suddenly starts to beat himself on the forehead with his fists).

Devil take it, Devil take it, O Lord, O Lord.

CARRASCO. Here, here, stop.

SANCHO. I've lost it. I been and gone and lost letter.

MARITORNE. Thou'lt do thyself harm, dearie.

SANCHO. I slipped it in here—or there—or in shirt—I don't recall no more. Mebbe in cap? Nay.

MARITORNE. Keep thy wits about thee.

SANCHO. Keep my wits about me? That be a prize one, that be. A letter like that, and I gone and lost it. She-ass, donkey-on-two-feet that I be . . . Such a pearl of a letter, Senor Carrasco, so well plastered.

CARRASCO. But who is this Dulcinea, deserving your care and attention as an ambassador of love?

MARITORNE. Aye. Who be she? I'd much like to know and all.

SANCHO. As for that, thou's going to laugh thyselves in stitches. Art ready? It be Lorenzo's daughter.

1103

CARRASCO. The herdsman in Toboso?

SANCHO. Aye.

MARITORNE. Aldonza?

SANCHO. Aye, her very self.

MARITORNE. Lorks-a-mercy, where do he get his notions? She be great lump.

SANCHO. Whether she be or whether she don't, my trouble be, I've lost letter. I be dishonoured.

CARRASCO. What's the good of breaking your head? Aldonza can't read.

SANCHO. Be that so?

CARRASCO. I'm absolutely certain, and this settles everything.

SANCHO. How?

CARRASCO. If she doesn't know how to read, it's useless to bring her the letter. And, if it's useless to bring her the letter, it is even more so to hammer your nose, eyes, and ears because you have lost it.

MARITORNE. Besides, it be better this way.

SANCHO. Such a fine letter, all the same, saying such lovely things.

CARRASCO. Come, come, take heart, and lead us to your master. You will tell him you have met the Queen of Micomicon.

(He points to Maritorne).

SANCHO. The Queen of what?

CARRASCO. Of Micomicon.

SANCHO. Her?

CARRASCO. Yes. She will hold a fan to hide her teeth.

SANCHO. I must say, thou hast just the right air.

MARITORNE. As much as thou hast, to be ambassador of love.

CARRASCO *(Putting on a false beard).* You will introduce me as her Prime Minister.

SANCHO. I shall have to hold-myself-in, not to laugh, when I sees thee covered in beard like this, and her in her majesty.

CARRASCO. Go before and announce our arrival.

SANCHO *(To Grison).* Best not to cross them, my beauty. Art coming? Giddup.

(He goes out, followed by Grison).

MARITORNE. Be we going?

CARRASCO. Let him prepare the way, and you, get ready to play your part as well as you know how.

MARITORNE. Well, I'll do what I can, but I don't be used to masquerades, I don't.

CARRASCO. You will put on your shoes.

MARITORNE. I'd rather let them be, I tell you that.

CARRASCO. You must, Maritorne.

MARITORNE. They catch me bad, on bunions.

CARRASCO. You are a Queen, don't forget that.

MARITORNE (*Tries a few wavering steps*). Lorks, I pity them, the queens I mean, if they must do all things thou makest me do. And besides, they pinch me . . . they pinch . . .

CARRASCO. You suffer for him.

MARITORNE. For him? He be laughing at me. He be sending letters by messenger to that silly donkey Aldonza.

CARRASCO. When he sees you walking so exquisitely, he'll change his mind.

MARITORNE. Do it make me quality, do'st think, to squeeze my toes into such-like?

CARRASCO. It gives you an air of royalty you haven't got with bare feet.

MARITORNE. I be going to trip and fall flat, I can feel it.

CARRASCO. You'll carry it off. You will see. It's much better already. Come.

(*He goes out*).

MARITORNE. Aldonza, this be 'twixt the two of us. Tomorrow, it be to me he be sending his ambassador of love.

(*She is about to go out, walking painfully, then changes her mind*).

Oh, bother!

(*She takes off her shoes and goes out, holding them in her hand*).

THE CURTAIN OPENS.

SCENE 7. THE MOUNTAIN. (Same as Scene 5)

(Don Quixote is sunk against the tree).

SANCHO *(Enters with Grison)*. My master . . .?

DON QUIXOTE. There you are.

SANCHO. Be it doing thy acrobatics thou art come to such a pass?

DON QUIXOTE. No Sancho. It was much worse. Terrifying. The cursed enchanters . . .

SANCHO. What, again?

DON QUIXOTE. Let me speak. Jealous of my success . . . sent me twelve thousand horned devils and thirty treacherous shepherds to seize the mountain under my guard. Midnight rang from the village belfry . . .

SANCHO. What belfry? What village? The nearest be four leagues away.

DON QUIXOTE. I know it. But I know as well, it always rings at midnight in a village belfry, when the demons burst out of hell. They were an army. You know my valour. I met them with a firm foot. I stabbed, cut down, hewed, split, resplit, split through, cut in pieces, shattered, massacred, I opened heads and shaved off horns; I sliced, resliced, sliced again, struggling in a terrible battle —terrible against unequal odds. When day came, at cock-crow, a trumpet-call rang out, there, beneath the ground, and in-the-twinkling-of-an-eye, arms, heads, legs, ears and noses—in short, all I had cut down with my valorous sword, in this horrible carnage, all I say, disappeared by enchantment, leaving me here alone, exhausted, panting . . . but victorious.

SANCHO. And I weren't there to lend thee a strong arm.

DON QUIXOTE. To each his duty, friend Sancho. Yours was as ambassador. And speaking of that, tell me, did you give my letter to Dulcinea?

SANCHO. Yes . . . O' course . . . I gives it. Why don't I be giving it, since thou gives it me to give and charged me to.

DON QUIXOTE. How did she take it? Did she read it at once?

SANCHO. At once, be saying too much. It be a long tale. I be telling thee later about it, my Master, for here come folk I must announce to thee; the Queen of Mirlitons with her scholar . . . her minister I mean—her Prime Minister.

DON QUIXOTE. Help me . . . and leave me, I will receive them.

SANCHO. They be nice folk, thou'lt find . . . and in some ways, bit comical.

(He goes out with Grison).

1106

CARRASCO *(Bearded, advances)*. Is it my great good fortune that brings me to the presence of the very noble and mighty Knight Don Quixote of la Mancha?

DON QUIXOTE. I am he you seek.

CARRASCO. Permit the humble person that I am, to present to your Honour, the warmest greetings of my Imperial Mistress, the Queen of Micomicon.

DON QUIXOTE. Sancho told me: Mirliton.

CARRASCO. Micomicon, my lord.

DON QUIXOTE. Whichever it is, Sire, I am immensely flattered by your admirable introduction. I am your servant.

CARRASCO *(To Maritorne who advances with her shoes on and walking painfully)*. Madame, heaven showers us with its favours. Here, in person, is the man we seek.

(Aside).

Go on, hold yourself straight and hide your teeth.

MARITORNE. Sir; my lord Don Quixote . . .

(Kneeling).

Behold I be the Queen . . . the Queen of . . . Ah, but I don't recall no more, I don't.

(She takes her shoes off).

DON QUIXOTE. Madame, Your Majesty, I am but a poor Knight-errant.

CARRASCO. My Mistress is the Queen of Micomicon.

(To Maritorne).

Your shoes.

MARITORNE *(To Don Quixote)*. Aye, that be it.

(To Carrasco).

They hurts too bad.

DON QUIXOTE *(Kneels facing Maritorne)*. Arise, Madame, for it would be unjust and unseemly for you to prostrate yourself there, when I am not worthy to kiss the soles of your royal feet.

MARITORNE. O I don't be taking them off fer that.

(She points to her shoes).

DON QUIXOTE. Arise, I conjure you, for it is I, Madame, who am your humble slave.

MARITORNE. I be thy servant.

DON QUIXOTE. I kiss your hands.

MARITORNE. Lord love us!

DON QUIXOTE. Arise, Madame.

MARITORNE. Thou first, Sir.

DON QUIXOTE. I shall do nothing of the kind.

MARITORNE. Neither shall us.

CARRASCO. Your Majesty should arise, since this is the desire of the very noble Don Quixote.

MARITORNE (Getting up). Kneeling or standing, it be all the same to me. Thou told'st me to do it.

(To Don Quixote).

CARRASCO. You, Sir Knight, could arise honourably too.

MARITORNE. Aye, to that. Everbody standing be much better. Be'unt it?

DON QUIXOTE (Getting up in pain). Excuse my stiffness. The bloody battles fought here, have dislocated my limbs.

CARRASCO. Reveal to my lord Don Quixote the reason for our coming, Madame.

MARITORNE. Oh, Aye, I will and all. Well, I comes with him . . . Us be climbing for hours in mountain. And he says to me that, as to giant, thou'lt be able to settle whole matter.

(To Carrasco).

How do ye call him again?

CARRASCO. Who?

MARITORNE. Giant o' course.

CARRASCO. Caraculiambro.

DON QUIXOTE. Who? Repeat it.

MARITORNE. Aye, be just like he says.

CARRASCO. Caraculiambro.

MARITORNE. That be it.

DON QUIXOTE. Majesty, are you certain of this name?

MARITORNE. Well, he a-told me . . .

CARRASCO. Yes my lord, it is indeed that terrifying monster.

DON QUIXOTE. My mortal enemy.

MARITORNE. Ye knows him, dost thou?

Don Quixote. He is much talked of in all the books I've read, and I am eager to do battle with him.

Maritorne. That be a good thing. Be'unt it minister?

Carrasco. It's more than we hoped for my lord.

Don Quixote. I'm your man.

Maritorne *(With a sigh)*. As for that, aye, thou be'st my man.

Don Quixote. Ho there, my squire. Bring me my charger.

(To Maritorne).

Lead me Madame, to my terrible adversary, put your shoes on again, and I give you my word as a Knight-errant your kingdom will be freed forever from the infamous Caraculiambro. Ho there, Sancho.

Maritorne *(Forcing herself to put on her shoes)*. Drat the plaguey things. Who under the sun hatched such miserable toe-trippers without sweeping them right away.

(Sancho enters with Rossinante).

Carrasco *(Aside, to Maritorne)*. Watch your language . . . Your Majesty.

Maritorne. I repeats to thee Minister, I be going to fall flat with such-like and there be end of Queen.

Don Quixote. If you please?

Maritorne. I've a pain in my pads with . . .

Carrasco. Her Majesty's shoes vilely pain her little royal feet.

Don Quixote. I don't want to hear another word. Madame, here is Rossinante. For him, to carry your gracious person will be a feather in his cap.

Maritorne. Lordy, Sir Knight, there be a bright notion.

(She climbs on to Rossinante helped by Sancho who exits immediately afterwards).

Carrasco. Can a Knight-errant go on foot?

Don Quixote. Must one be on horse-back to travel?

Carrasco. But, my lord, do you think . . .

Don Quixote. I don't think anything; I've spoken.

(To Sancho who returns with Grison).

Your donkey will carry His Excellency.

Sancho. And us?

Don Quixote. Pedibus cum jambis.

SANCHO. If thou be talking French, call me goose.

DON QUIXOTE. That's just what I shall do.

(To Maritorne).

Let your Majesty deign to lead the Royal retinue. We will stay and bring up the rear. After you, Madame.

(Maritorne, on Rossinante, goes out, followed by Carrasco on Grison. Sancho goes to follow them).

DON QUIXOTE. Just a minute, old fellow. There is one thing, above all, I want to clear up.

SANCHO. Dost need me to serve thee as lantern?

DON QUIXOTE. Yes. As you alone know why I am in the dark.

SANCHO. And what be this darkness perplexing thee?

DON QUIXOTE. You have not yet told me what my tender Dulcinea was doing when you arrived in Toboso. Was she combing the heavenly gold of her beautiful hair? Or weaving with deft fingers the figures on a marvellous tapestry?

SANCHO. She don't be doing that exactly . . . Nay . . . wait . . . She be winnowing corn, aye, and chasing chickens, kicking them in backside, I recall. That be what I sees when I arrive in Toboso.

DON QUIXOTE. Which proves once again, you were the victim of enchanters who pester me ceaselessly. There they showed you a vulgar scene where anyone but you would have looked upon a delightful picture. What did she say when you gave her my **letter?**

SANCHO. O, Aye . . . but it be O Nay, more like . . . I prefers to tell thee all. I don't be giving her letter, my Master. I gone and lost it . . I begs pardon.

DON QUIXOTE. I am glad you have told me the truth, Sancho. There is my letter.

(He takes letter from branch of tree).

There in the same place where you foolishly forgot it.

SANCHO. Thank goodness. That be all straightened out, for it'd been a thousand pities to be losing such a lovely speech.

DON QUIXOTE. But if you didn't deliver this message to Dulcinea, at least did you speak to her?

SANCHO. For sure . . . O' course I did . . . I says . . . O aye, what be I a'saying to her? Well, I tells her I be losing thy letter, but it be no great matter, since she can't read.

DON QUIXOTE. Can't read, Dulcinea, who said that?

SANCHO. Carrasco.

DON QUIXOTE. Have you seen Carrasco?

SANCHO. Aye . . . yonder . . . thereabouts. I don't recall now where it be. He be walking and he asks me where I be going.

DON QUIXOTE. All this seems very odd to me.

SANCHO. Like as not it be more of thy enchanters.

DON QUIXOTE. Is that all you did in Toboso?

SANCHO. O nay. I promised thee I be telling of thy great deeds. I done so, and how? I been and told in what sovereign manner thou didst hurl down, with one blow of thy lance, even though they be transformed into windmills, twenty three giants, tall as towers.

DON QUIXOTE. Twenty-three? Are you sure?

SANCHO. Like thee, I gone and counted them. I be telling too, how, with one thrust of thy rusty sword, thou didst overthrow a whole regiment of archers, of the St. Hermandad. And puts to rout, more than a thousand galley-slave-robbers-of-saddle-bags.

DON QUIXOTE. You exaggerate a little. But I must recognize that your manner of presenting these things is that of an admirable ambassador.

SANCHO. I be telling moreover of all acrobatics thou be doing in her honour to the great damage of thy bottom, which be making her split with laughing.

DON QUIXOTE. This time you lie. Dulcinea cannot laugh at what I do in her name.

SANCHO. When I be saying—split with laughing—I be still exaggerating. She be smiling . . . with satisfaction, for sure. She be even more pleased when I reports how one terrible night thou astounded, pestered, and cut off a hundred thousand devils on thy mountain.

DON QUIXOTE. Stop there. For this last battle took place in your absence and you had no knowledge of it when you departed. Sancho, you rascal, I have a strong feeling you are telling more and more lies and that you did not go to Toboso at all.

SANCHO. What be good denying it? That be truth, my Master, and I humbly asks thy pardon. But when all be said and done, what do it matter if I be going or no, since this be way I be telling her when I goes really?

DON QUIXOTE. You are right. Moreover you won't forget my letter this time—and as a token of my deeds, you will carry to Dulcinea Caraculiambro's head, for in a few days I shall decapitate him. Follow me.

(He starts out, walking painfully).

SANCHO *(Grabbing his back)*. Aie!!

DON QUIXOTE. Now what's the matter?

SANCHO. Shooting pains at bottom of spine.

DON QUIXOTE. Sign of rain, Sancho.

(He goes out).

SANCHO. Sign of rain, thou sayest? Aye. I fears hailstorm of bruises, scrapes, and blows. O, for skin so tough it do be storm-proof!

(He goes out).

THE CURTAIN CLOSES

SCENE 8. THE INN COURTYARD.

INNKEEPER. Thou and thy plots . . . the Lord knows how this'll end.

CARRASCO. Let me do it, I say. Tomorrow I'll take him away.

INNKEEPER. Thou promise'st me thou weren't going to bring him back.

CARRASCO. To make him go all that way to his home without a break, would be enough to kill him. The blows he has received have made him a dying man.

INNKEEPER. I be no better pleased for that.

CARRASCO. Be quiet, here he is. All will be well.

INNKEEPER. Easily said.

DON QUIXOTE *(Enters with Sancho)*. My lord of the castle, I offer you my homage.

INNKEEPER. Sir . . . Sir Knight . . .

SANCHO. Say 'Your Grace' to him.

(He puts the arms down and goes out).

INNKEEPER. 'Your Grace' . . . my dwelling be thine. Come in, but Lord Almighty, get thee some rest.

CARRASCO. The lord of the castle speaks wisely, Sir Knight. Your last combats and the superhuman deeds you've accomplished have left you in such a bad way, it would seem better you stay here and recover your strength, ready for the mighty battle you will undertake in the very near future, with the giant Caraculiambro.

INNKEEPER. By Gum! Sir, them words be well-knit together, and say well what they say.

(To Quixote).

The gentleman talks sense. I be going to make-up thy bed.

1112

Don Quixote. I cannot accept it. My calling as a Knight-errant forbids it. But if, in your generosity my lord, you will give me a corner of your barn and throw in a handful of straw, I will gladly stretch out my weary bones.

Innkeeper. Thou'lt do much better . . .

Carrasco. Do what the Knight desires.

(Whispers).

I will pay you the price of a room.

Innkeeper. Whatever next! . . . Well, be it just as thou pleases.

(He calls).

Maritorne.

Maritorne (Still richly dressed, comes in wiping her hands). Here I be.

Carrasco. Your Majesty is mistaken. The lord of the castle called 'Maritorne' and not the Queen of Micomicon, which, on his part, would have been very bad manners.

Maritorne. I tells thee, her or me, it be all one. We be together, having a gossip and scrubbing kitchen-pots. So with all that din . . .

Innkeeper. Come Madame. Since that labour seems to please thee, I'll give thee a few more pans to add to thy fun.

Maritorne. They must have a good shine on, mustn't they, minister?

(She goes out with Innkeeper).

Don Quixote. Mr. Prime-Minister, permit me to say how surprising I find the strange pleasure your Gracious Sovereign takes in mixing with the servants and scrubbing out the kitchen pans.

Carrasco. It's a self-inflicted penance she has voluntarily undertaken, until she sees her kingdom freed from the infamous Caraculiambro.

Don Quixote. God give me help, Sir, and in a few days, this monster will cease to live.

(To Sancho who returns).

How is Rossinante?

Sancho. He be as usual.

Don Quixote. What do you mean?

Sancho. Like rider, like horse.

Don Quixote. Make yourself clearer. What is he doing?

SANCHO. He be giving, in horse-talk, endless and wordy speeches to my Grison, who don't take a word in, but who wise-like—same as me—wiggles ears while munching peck of oats.

DON QUIXOTE. That's what you do, is it?

SANCHO. Don't mistake me, again. What I say is, there be two good and noble beasts, just like thou and me.

INNKEEPER (*Returns carrying a bedcover*). Come, my lord, Sir Knight, I've seen hay be put in barn, since thou prefers it to a good bed.

DON QUIXOTE. I follow you.

(*To Carrasco*). Mr. Prime-Minister.

(*To Sancho*). Behave honourably, and at the slightest danger, the slightest alarm, call me.

SANCHO. Sleep in peace. I be watching over thee.

DON QUIXOTE. Thank you, my son.

(*He goes out behind Innkeeper*).

SANCHO. Poor Devil, he can't hardly stand up.

CARRASCO. That's why we are taking him back home. Dona Belisa will know how to look after him.

SANCHO. But if he be no longer Knight, I'll no longer be squire and I be losing my place.

CARRASCO. No. He will keep you for all the services you have given him when he was in trouble.

SANCHO. Thou can'st well say that, for there be no lack of trouble where he be. He gets hisself in tangles up-to-the-neck, at the slightest provocation, and each time his efforts misfire—he gets a right royal walloping. What thou be saying, be too true, Sir, the rate he be going, he soon won't have whole bone left in body, and if I wants to keep him as master, he must be took home, even if us has to sit on him to keep him there. I'll give thee a hand.

INNKEEPER (*Returns with bedcover*). He won't take bedcover. I be putting hay over and under him. That makes a good litter, 'twixt my corn bags and barrel of sardines, and just below, two skins of wine hanging from joists. He fell asleep like stone at bottom of pond.

SANCHO. Because he be wore-out, poor soul. It be eight days now he be sleeping in open, on ground and pebbles. Even then he don't sleep nighttimes, for he spends all of them mounting guard under the stars.

CARRASCO. That's what comes of the romances of chivalry.

INNKEEPER. Have a care, Senor Scholar. There be good ones, just as there be bad ones. Don't be lumping them together.

1114

CARRASCO. They do a deal of harm.

INNKEEPER. Not if ye catch their proper meaning, they don't. Since Don Quixote come here to be knighted, I be reading from these books myself . . . some of them . . . the best ones.

CARRASCO. They are nothing but an unbelievable collection of gibberish and very apt to confuse your brain.

INNKEEPER. O but nay. Take for instance Amadis of Gaul.

SANCHO. Art thou too going to start?

INNKEEPER. Be it for thee to tell me what I can do? If I hadn't be making thy master a Knight, thou'dst not have had title of squire and thou'd still be running after work like sun after moon.

SANCHO. Thou callest this work, dost thou? Trotting behind Rossinante's tail; lifting my master back each time he falls off his scruffy nag; taking half the blows meant for him; eating nothing but fresh air two out of three times; drinking rainwater or streamwater, when Spain be covered in vines; sleeping with one eye, and doing sentry duty with t'other, watching for an enemy who never comes when one be waiting for him, and only shows hisself when one don't. And all this for why? A'cause he made me fair promise of an isle and a government that don't come neither.

INNKEEPER. Not so fast, it takes time.

SANCHO. I'm for justice. Something promised, something due. He told me I'd be Governor; let him make me Governor and no more talk of it.

CARRASCO. Still, it would have to be proved you possessed the required qualities for the Governor of an isle.

SANCHO. Ah but, it hath been proved, I has all qualities required. Laugh, if thou likes. I've got profile; he a-told me. I knows how to speak, and at length if need be, certain sure. I holds myself honourably at table and quietly drinks my six pints a day with the best. What more be needed to be Governor?

CARRASCO (*To Innkeeper indicating the bedcover*). Is it tough?

INNKEEPER. I thinks so.

SANCHO. And see if this be'unt the proper walk for commanding a large sunny isle.

(*He walks proudly back and forth*).

CARRASCO. Chin up . . . Stretch your leg out.

(*Aside to Innkeeper*). Call someone, we'll give him a blanket-toss.

(*Innkeeper goes to call Maritorne*).

(*To Sancho*). Perfect. The very thing. There is really little missing to make you a first class Governor.

(The Innkeeper puts Maritorne up-to-date with Carrasco's plan).

SANCHO. And what and please thee, be still missing?

CARRASCO. Only an item. We'll tell you directly, under a veil of secrecy. Come.

SANCHO. A secret? That be my strong point. Bury it in my head; I won't let on.

(They all go out by doorway.

Music, then Sancho's dummy can be seen tossing up and down behind the wall).

SANCHO *(Off).* Nay . . . nay . . . ah . . .

CARRASCO. Oops!

(Mixed shouts of four people off).

CARRASCO. Ho, the Governor; higher—and oops—and oops! Again. Higher. Oops!

MARITORNE *(At the same time, laughing generously).* Oops—and oops, brother Sancho—and oops, my fat turkey—oops!

INNKEEPER. Oops—up in the air—to the moon—oops, to the moon—to the moon!

SANCHO. Nay—nay—Help—my master—stop—rescue me—ohohohoh . . .

(The game stops, laughter).

Wretches . . . I be bust-in-two.

(He comes in).

Everything be all topsy-turvy inside my inside.

DON QUIXOTE *(Off, in a thunderous voice).* For me, Spirit of Galaor: by St. James . . . Caraculiambro!!!

(Fearful uproar. Stupour of the four).

MARITORNE. Holy Mother! the Knight!

SANCHO. Something be hotting-up.

INNKEEPER. May the Lord protect my sardines.

CARRASCO. Don Quixote! Don Quixote!

DON QUIXOTE *(Enters, in a long nightshirt, helmeted, brandishing his sword which pierces an empty goatskin).* I have triumphed, my friends, I have triumphed.

INNKEEPER. He hath run through goat-skin.

SANCHO. My Master . . .

1116

CARRASCO. Senor . . .

MARITORNE. Ohlalalala . . .

DON QUIXOTE. Here is the head of Caraculiambro.

INNKEEPER. It be my wine.

(He runs out to the barn).

DON QUIXOTE. Madame, your kingdom is freed.

CARRASCO. My lord, Sir Knight . . .

DON QUIXOTE. Do not thank me.

INNKEEPER *(Returns)*. My corn—my wine all over the place—the sardines . . .

DON QUIXOTE *(Kneeling, lays the wine-skin at Maritorne's feet)*. Here is your enemy's head.

INNKEEPER. Corn in the sardines—Wine spilt all over . . .

DON QUIXOTE. The monster is dead, Madame. His blood flows in great torrents.

INNKEEPER. It be my wine. He be busting two goatskins. Get up, get up, out with thee . . . get out.

SANCHO. But Ferdinand, he be in nightshirt.

INNKEEPER. Don't matter. Get out.

MARITORNE. What a mess! What a mess! . . .

CARRASCO. Steady, steady.

INNKEEPER. I've had enough. I'm going to make trouble.

DON QUIXOTE *(Gets up with dignity)*. Is there something else . . . ?

INNKEEPER. I be going . . .

DON QUIXOTE. Don't congratulate me. It was a pleasure.

INNKEEPER *(Seizes his cooking spoon and attacks Quixote)*. There be door. Out with thee.

DON QUIXOTE *(Defending himself with his sword against the cooking spoon)*. My lord, take heed. You are enchanted.

MARITORNE. They be going to tear each other to pieces.

INNKEEPER. Thou art ruining my Inn.

CARRASCO. Listen to me. What the devil.

INNKEEPER. Peace, to thee.

DON QUIXOTE. I am Don Quixote . . .

INNKEEPER. Thou be nothing but calamity.

1117

SANCHO. Ferdinand, stop it.

INNKEEPER. Ye, leave me alone. I've had all I can stand from this crack-pot.

MARITORNE. Ferdinand . . .

CARRASCO. I'll pay for the wine.

INNKEEPER. And corn? And sardines?

DON QUIXOTE. I've conquered Caraculiambro.

ARCHER *(Coming through the doorway)*. In the name of the St. Hermandad.

SANCHO. The Constable.

(He takes refuge behind the water-trough).

INNKEEPER. Thou arrives just in the nick.

ARCHER. One can hear ye yelling down to cross-roads . . .

(Recognizing Don Quixote).

Ah, but you, I know you. Devil take it, this time I'll arrest you.

DON QUIXOTE. A moment, young man.

INNKEEPER. Aye, aye, arrest him. He's done damage enough.

MARITORNE. O, but nay.

CARRASCO. Excuse me. What do you want him for?

ARCHER. For a matter concerning this desperado and the Law.

MARITORNE. Law or no, what do ye wants to nab him for?

INNKEEPER. Why be ye poking thy nose in?

DON QUIXOTE. I believe I know you too.

ARCHER. Ah, so you've tumbled have you? Come on, follow me.

CARRASCO. Senor Archer, allow me . . .

ARCHER. I don't know who you are, Sir, but let me tell you: mind your own business.

MARITORNE. Thou no can'st take . . .

INNKEEPER. Shut up.

ARCHER. Thou, young lady, I advise thee . . .

DON QUIXOTE. Boor! This young lady is the Queen of Micomicon.

ARCHER. The Queen of what?

CARRASCO. I will explain it all.

INNKEEPER. She be my sarvant.

1118

(To Maritorne).

Push off to thy kitchen.

MARITORNE. That I won't.

ARCHER. Leave me in peace with your stories. And you, go get dressed.

DON QUIXOTE. I take orders from no-one.

(Sancho comes back prudently).

ARCHER. By the St. Hermandad!

MARITORNE. Thou, don't ye touch him.

INNKEEPER. Wilt thou have done?

SANCHO. Nay, she be right.

(In the ensuing quarrel, the six characters are drawn into a perfect circle, Quixote blaming Carrasco, who berates Sancho, who disputes with Innkeeper, who scolds Maritorne, who prevents the Archer from arresting Quixote).

CARRASCO *(To Sancho).* Get back behind the cattle-trough.

DON QUIXOTE. Mr. Minister, pay attention please, to your Ministry, and not to my squire.

ARCHER. Art coming, at last, or must I knock you on the head?

MARITORNE. Dare, if thou darest.

INNKEEPER. Thou, thou quits here at same time he do.

SANCHO. Ferdinand, that don't be fair.

CARRASCO. . . . Leave him alone.

DON QUIXOTE. Take your paws off me, I said.

(Music. Uproar. The row turns brusquely into a brawl where each beats the other in a circle. At a certain moment the whole circle turns the other way and the blows fall on the other side with equal vehemence. This becomes in fact, more of a ballet than a brawl. Various exclamations, beats on tambours, drum, cymbals, and other percussion instruments. A bolero is in the air. Suddenly Don Quixote comes out of the infernal circle, one is not quite sure how, perches on the water-trough and thunders).

Stop! By St. James stop!

(Silence).

Can't you see you are, once again—and you even more than I—the victim of the mad ravings of a magician? Come to your senses. We are all suffering from a malicious enchantment.

ARCHER. What's he burbling about now?

1119

MARITORNE. Give him chance.

INNKEEPER. Be quiet.

DON QUIXOTE. Wake up. Come out of your dream. Shake yourselves free, and see things right way up, and not wrong way round.

ARCHER. Enough speechmaking.

MARITORNE. Go on, Sir.

INNKEEPER. Nay. Give us peace.

SANCHO. Shut up, Ferdinand.

DON QUIXOTE. This cursed enchanter who mocks you, is showing you things that only exist in your imagination. He is jealous of my triumph. Caraculiambro's head! . . .

INNKEEPER. It be my wine-skin.

CARRASCO. I'll pay you for it, I say.

DON QUIXOTE. Caraculiambro's head!

ARCHER. Enough of heads and rubbish. Go, get dressed and follow me.

SANCHO. Let go of him.

DON QUIXOTE. Caraculiambro's head!

ARCHER. Come.

CARRASCO. My lord. . . .

INNKEEPER. My wine, my sardines . . .

SANCHO. My Master, hear me . . .

(*Renewed laying hold of each other. Carrasco shakes the Innkeeper. Sancho engages with the Archer*).

DON QUIXOTE. The head . . . the head of Caraculiambro . . . the head . . .

(*He falls into the water-trough*).

MARITORNE (*Helps him to get up*). Sir . . . Sir . . .

DON QUIXOTE (*Recovers, with his feet in the cattle-trough, his nightshirt soaking, brandishing his sword, yells*). Caraculiambro . . . my first victory!

(*The others brawl with a will. The Innkeeper kneeling on Carrasco. The Archer kneeling on Sancho. Music of glory*).

CURTAIN.

END OF ACT TWO.

1120

ACT THREE

SCENE 9. DON QUIXOTE'S ROOM.

(The bookshelves are empty.

Don Quixote in indoor clothing, profile on the sunlit window which he is opening).

HOUSEKEEPER *(Enters and closes the window).* You are unreasonable.

DON QUIXOTE. I've had enough of this couch, these broths and ointments . . .

HOUSEKEEPER. The doctor says . . .

DON QUIXOTE. I know my health better than he.

HOUSEKEEPER. A pinch of this powder . . .

DON QUIXOTE. Flea-dust.

HOUSEKEEPER. A little of this ointment . . .

DON QUIXOTE. Bacon fat . . .

HOUSEKEEPER. This medicine will do you good.

DON QUIXOTE. I don't want any more. I'm fed up. Am I Don Quixote, yes or no?

HOUSEKEEPER. You are, but if you want to remain so, bow to the doctor's orders.

DON QUIXOTE. Taratata . . .

HOUSEKEEPER. You were picked up in a burning fever, roaring your head off, in a fury to make the heavens shake, spitting out words that a sailor would blush at, and how? I daren't think.

DON QUIXOTE. In a state coach, Madame.

HOUSEKEEPER. In a frightful cage, Sir. One of those filthy cages used for hogs, when taken to the butcher's.

DON QUIXOTE. Rubbish to all that.

HOUSEKEEPER. How disgraceful! I cried my eyes out to see you housed like this, and yelling like mad.

DON QUIXOTE. You don't know what you are talking about.

HOUSEKEEPER. On the contrary, I know only too well. Since your return—you have been in bed—three weeks and two days—I have not ceased to care for you in the way the doctor ordered.

DON QUIXOTE. I am cured.

1121

HOUSEKEEPER. You are still weak.

DON QUIXOTE. I'm firmer than a rock.

HOUSEKEEPER. A bird could topple you.

DON QUIXOTE. That's what you say. Look at this.

(He does a hand-stand).

HOUSEKEEPER. For Heaven's sake, don't start your acrobatics again.

(Don Quixote collapses).

Blood goes to your head and there you are, down on the floor.

(She helps him up).

DON QUIXOTE. Your drugs and broths have taken away all my strength.

HOUSEKEEPER. You don't understand a thing.

DON QUIXOTE. I need air, Madame.

(He opens a window).

HOUSEKEEPER. Close that window.

(She closes it).

DON QUIXOTE. Space . . .

HOUSEKEEPER. Stay in bed.

DON QUIXOTE. Combats . . .

HOUSEKEEPER. Go to bed and sleep.

DON QUIXOTE. No, no, I've had my fill.

HOUSEKEEPER. At least, don't thrash about like that. You'll fall to pieces.

DON QUIXOTE. I'm bored Madame. This lack of action kills me. Then give me a book.

(He looks at the bookshelves).

Where are they? Who has taken my books? What has been done with them? Tell me, my books, my romances of chivalry? Amadis? Tirant? Galaor? Lancelot? Where have you put them?

HOUSEKEEPER. Yes, I must tell you.

DON QUIXOTE. What must you tell me? Speak, Madame. By Heaven, I want to know.

HOUSEKEEPER. You had hardly been gone two days, when, one night . . . I was sleeping peacefully up there, as usual . . . I heard a terrible uproar coming from your room. I thought you had come.

1122

back and I came down. Ah, my lord, what did I see on opening this door?

DON QUIXOTE. What did you see?

HOUSEKEEPER. The bookshelves empty and the window open.

DON QUIXOTE. And my books, my books? Go on, speak.

HOUSEKEEPER (*Close to the window*). There in the middle of the courtyard, you see those blackened cobbles. Your books—all—in a heap, ablaze, in dreadful flames.

DON QUIXOTE. But who? Thunder and lightning, who did such a thing?

HOUSEKEEPER. Three demons with horns and claws, yelping and stinking, armed with forks, stirred the blaze, while planted there, near the entrance, draped in a black cloak hanging from his heels, an immense creature, bearded and moustached, loomed terrifyingly, cackling away, as he eyed the disaster.

DON QUIXOTE. What did you do?

HOUSEKEEPER. I fainted.

DON QUIXOTE. Why wasn't I here to defend my possessions?

HOUSEKEEPER. Nothing was left, but a few cinders the wind scattered to the four corners of the courtyard.

DON QUIXOTE. And you let them do it?

HOUSEKEEPER. O Sir. It was an enchanter and three devils from Hell. I am only a woman. You can well imagine how frightened I was.

DON QUIXOTE. All my books destroyed.

HOUSEKEEPER. They've done you enough harm. When you have recovered, instead of reading this gibberish, you would do better to gather some money together to pay me my wages. That would be more useful.

DON QUIXOTE (*Crucified in front of his empty bookshelves*). Be quiet. Don't hit a man who has lost all his friends, in one single blow.

(*Sancho pushes the door open*).

HOUSEKEEPER. Ah, you, go away.

DON QUIXOTE. Come in, Sancho. And you Madame, get out of my sight.

HOUSEKEEPER. I won't leave you with that scamp who brought you back in a hog's cage.

DON QUIXOTE. I said: get out of my sight. Don't you understand?

HOUSEKEEPER. I . . . but . . . ah this . . .

SANCHO. Which means: Go away lady. And leave two men of honour in peace.

HOUSEKEEPER. I will not allow you to stay.

DON QUIXOTE. Go.

SANCHO. Go, go.

(Housekeeper goes out, slamming the door).

SANCHO. She don't agree with us, I'd say. I be coming a hundred times, my Master, and a hundred times this . . .

DON QUIXOTE. Sancho.

SANCHO. She slammed door in my face. It be good to see thee up.

DON QUIXOTE. Is it true you brought me back in a cage?

SANCHO. I had to. Thou'dst have killed all and sundry and was yelling and screaming fit to wake the dead.

DON QUIXOTE. Did I talk so much rubbish?

SANCHO. More than enough. But thou was't in fever; which excuses thee. How art feeling today?

DON QUIXOTE. Wonderful, I dare say it.

SANCHO. And thy notions, in there, be clear?

DON QUIXOTE. Of course, why?

SANCHO. Because I be come to ask thee if at times thou give'st a mind to Governorship thou promis'st.

DON QUIXOTE. I think of it, yes, I think of it. Just a little more patience please.

SANCHO. Give a mind to this, my Master. Patience be a lovely quality, I agrees. But, put it on platter with pepper and salt and sprig o' basil, and tell me if thou canst eat it?

DON QUIXOTE. What does this new invention, eating patience, mean?

SANCHO. While I waits to be a well-fed, rich-paid Governor, like thou promis'st—I be always a big-nothing-at-all, poor Sancho, who swallows fine words and indigestible idle-talk.

(Night falls slowly outside).

DON QUIXOTE. In a few days, my good friend, we shall set out again along the road to new victories. You shall have your isle. It will be vast, enormous, limitless.

SANCHO. I be far more took by tiny islet, that be very pretty and doing well, now at once, rather than gigantic isle, I don't be seeing, except in thy fancies and my dreams.

1124

DON QUIXOTE. You shall have it, I swear.

SANCHO. Something promised something due.

DON QUIXOTE. Truly, I've waited too long.

SANCHO. It be too late to run after it, if we don't be going at right time.

DON QUIXOTE. That's just what we're going to do.

SANCHO. At once?

DON QUIXOTE. At once.

(He gives him a purse).

Here is wherewithal to fill your leather bag. Go and get your Grison, and join me secretly and without delay at the village gateway.

SANCHO *(Going toward door)*. I be going.

DON QUIXOTE. Not that way.

(He opens the window).

SANCHO. Eh? You want—? Me? Through there?

DON QUIXOTE. It's the way to adventure.

SANCHO. I be going to break my—

(Joyful neighing).

DON QUIXOTE. It's Rossinante. It is a good omen.

SANCHO. Do'st think so?

DON QUIXOTE. Darius owed his Persian crown to his horse's neighing. You will owe your isle to Rossinante's.

(Neighing).

Out you go, my friend.

SANCHO. I don't know what thou's talking of—but I believes thee, my master.

(He straddles the window, and helped by Quixote, lets himself down. He disappears. Uproar).

DON QUIXOTE. Ssh—ssh—

(He stays a minute leaning out of the window, while fresh neighings re-echo. Music).

THE CURTAIN CLOSES.

Scene 10. The Courtyard of the Inn.

(In addition a puppet booth, its curtains closed.

Maritorne and Innkeeper are busy when Quixote and Sancho appear in doorway).

Maritorne.   The Knight.

Innkeeper.   It be going to start all over. Go, shut up barn. Put key in thy pocket.

(Maritorne goes out.

Sancho enters and dismounts).

Innkeeper.   Ah, thou, I be having bone to pick with thee.

Sancho.   Ferdinand, don't vex thyself.

Innkeeper.   I be asking thee, all same . . .

Sancho.   We be just passing by.

Innkeeper.   Why didn't ye take him further off? On t'other side?

Don Quixote *(On horseback)*. My lord, I am happy Rossinante's footsteps have, of their own accord, retraced the path to your much admired castle.

Sancho.   Dost see? It's Rossinante.

Innkeeper.   So be it, come in, since thou canst hardly do aught else.

Don Quixote.   I am bound to you for your hospitality.

Innkeeper.   No need.

(Quixote gets down from his horse. Sancho goes out by doorway leading the two mounts. Maritorne comes back hiding her teeth).

Innkeeper.   Take all his ironmongery off of him, so he don't start wrecking whole place again.

Maritorne.   Sir Knight . . .

Don Quixote.   I place at your feet my faith and my ardour, O gentle damozel.

Maritorne.   Better give me thy trappings.

Don Quixote.   I cannot.

Maritorne.   For sure. They must tire thee.

Don Quixote.   Nothing tires me but people who speak badly.

(He sees the puppet booth).

What's that?

DON QUIXOTE OF LA MANCHA

INNKEEPER. A puppet theatre.

MARITORNE. The man be inside with Storyteller. They be having soup.

DON QUIXOTE. Is he putting on something merry, tragic, or very moral?

INNKEEPER. As for that, Sir, ask him thyself. Here be Master Pedro and his valet.

(Pedro comes from the Inn. He is no other than Gines, the Galley-Slave who has put a patch over his eye and a very impressive false moustache. He gives a start when he sees Quixote, but only the audience notice this. He goes towards his booth, followed by a young boy).

DON QUIXOTE. Senor allow me. Your reputation has just reached my ears and I shall be happy to become acquainted with your talent.

PEDRO. It's three crowns a seat, pay in advance, few folk or many.

DON QUIXOTE. What remarkable story are you about to show us?

PEDRO. If Your Grace be giving me leave, I'll show him the very moral tale of the Princess Melisandre and her beloved husband, the very noble Knight Gaiferos.

DON QUIXOTE. The title is promising.

(Sancho comes back).

PEDRO. The story be true. It be taken, without changing a word, from the Spanish romances and the great chronicles of French knighthood.

DON QUIXOTE *(To Sancho).* Three crowns.

SANCHO *(Laying out money).* That be dear.

DON QUIXOTE. Art has no price, my son.

(To Pedro).

Sir, we are ready.

PEDRO. In a moment, Very Honourable lord.

(He disappears inside the booth with the boy, while Maritorne and Innkeeper place a bench in front of the theatre).

INNKEEPER. Not here, there.

MARITORNE. It be too far.

INNKEEPER. Nay, too near.

MARITORNE. I loves puppets, I does.

INNKEEPER. Sit down, Sir.

1127

DON QUIXOTE. Not in front of a Princess, my lord.

SANCHO. A Princess?

INNKEEPER. Where be that?

DON QUIXOTE. The one who will appear, in a moment, poor nincompoops. The Princess Melisandre. The three of you sit down. I will remain standing.

(Sancho and the Innkeeper take their places on the bench sandwiching Maritorne. Uproar in the booth. Gong, trumpet, rattle, then three knocks).

THE BOY *(Comes in front of the theatre and bows)*. Honourable assembly, Madame, my lords. Here is the true story and faithful account of the love of the very valiant Lord Gaiferos and his very gracious wife Melisandre, the Princess of big eyes and very small feet. Let it be told.

(Trumpet. The curtain opens on a Gothic interior).

THE BOY. The first part. This is the castle of the Emperor Charlemagne. Don Gaiferos, whom you see on the right, is lamenting and beating his head against the immovable walls. What is the reason for this deep despair? You are about to learn.

GAIFEROS. Alas, alas, a thousand and a thousand times alas: how huge is my sorrow and vast my distress. Melisandre, O my radiant wife, where art thou now? What have King Marsilio's horsemen done with thee? Where have they taken thee? In what muddy dungeon have they imprisoned thee, O my tender love! Ah, how heavy my fate, poignant my disarray.

(He beats his head on the wall.

Enter Charlemagne).

THE BOY. You will recognize—the one who enters now—It's the Emperor Charlemagne, Melisandre's father.

CHARLEMAGNE. Quiet now, quietly, my son. You will spatter your brains on the wall and that is no better for your spirit, than for my tapestries.

GAIFEROS. O, let me perish.

CHARLEMAGNE. Nay, do not perish, for King Marsilio's retreat is discovered.

GAIFEROS. Where is this jackal, that I might disembowel him?

CHARLEMAGNE. In his town of Saragossa and it is there in his invulnerable fortress, he holds captive and trembling with sorrow, your lovely Melisandre, my daughter.

GAIFEROS. Thundercracks! Give me the wonder-sword of Roland the Knight that rends in twain rocks and mountains, and I fly in haste to the rescue of my adored wife.

1128

CHARLEMAGNE. Go, don thy helmet, my boy, and be on thy guard, for with the sally thou hast in mind, more sword-blows will fall, than raindrops.

GAIFEROS. I go, Sire, and knight's faith, I will bring back thy daughter or I will perish utterly, before the walls of Saragossa.

(He goes out).

CHARLEMAGNE. Ah, what a brave and valiant person I have as son-in-law. What a comfort for my flourishing beard.

(He goes out).

THE BOY. While Gaiferos equips himself, see how easily we pass from the Emperor's Castle to the moat in the town of Saragossa.

(Pedro turns round the base of his theatre which now shows the crenelated walls on which Melisandre appears).

THE BOY. The second part: The beautiful person who appears, walking so sadly, there, on the battlements is—as you have guessed—the peerless Melisandre who is crying like a cataract.

MELISANDRE. Ah, how distant is sweet France, and my husband Gaiferos, and my father the Emperor Charlemagne.

(Enter a frightful Moor. Puppet).

THE MOOR. Ah, ah, ah, come to mee, preety leetle zewel:

(He throws himself on Melisandre).

MELISANDRE. Oh . . . Oh . . . Help . . . I die . . .

THE BOY. Ho there, ho, Master Pedro. Stop. That one don't belong to the story.

(The Moor disappears).

PEDRO *(Passes his head through).* Let the honourable audience be good enough to pardon this interruption. The frightful fellow you have just seen, has nothing, as a matter of fact, to do with this play, and I will punish him as he deserves.

DON QUIXOTE. Do not let this break-up your scene in any way. Continue Sir, I beg you, for the whole thing is too well handled and too well done for it to stop, merely on account of a coarse and vulgar creature.

PEDRO. Thank you, my lord.

(He disappears).

THE BOY. We will resume our story. The beautiful Melisandre burst into renewed tears, when here comes the very esteemed King Marsilio, great enemy of Charlemagne, but very generous knight, he too, is much in love with the charms of the noble princess.

MARSILIO. Delicious and sweet lady, have you no thirst?

MELISANDRE. No, none.

MARSILIO. Perhaps you are hungry?

MELISANDRE. No, neither.

MARSILIO. Do you not desire something I could give, except liberty of course, for prisoner you are by the pitiless laws of war, and prisoner you will remain, despite my ardent desire to please you.

MELISANDRE. Then there is naught I need. Leave me to weep alone on the walls of Saragossa, as I gaze at the sky of France, all blue on the horizon.

MARSILIO. I understand, Madame, and I retire with dignity, on tiptoe, leaving you, as you desire it, to empty your full heart of its bitterness.

(He goes out).

THE BOY. And Melisandre, hearing this advice, took once more to bitter weeping. See, how she shakes with sobs, when, approaching the walls, an unknown traveller draws near.

(Gaiferos, enveloped in a long cloak, appears).

THE BOY. Melisandre has seen him and leans towards him.

MELISANDRE. Ah, Sir, do you come from France, as I think I can tell by your cloak? And can you tell me what in this terrible war has become of my husband, Don Gaiferos, and my beloved father, the Emperor Charlemagne?

GAIFEROS. Madame, the Emperor is alive and well, and Don Gaiferos, hold fast, is no other than myself.

THE BOY. Sensation. Melisandre has grown pale. You cannot see this, but that's the truth, I swear it. Is her heart pounding up and down? Will she faint? Fall from the walls and break her head at her husband's feet? No, she recovers, stretches her arms out to her beloved and cries:

MELISANDRE. Ah, save me, Sire, for I die being so far from you.

GAIFEROS. Come Madame, quickly jump into my arms and let us return to France.

THE BOY. Without a pause, as soon said as done. Melisandre has passed the walls and falls into her husband's arms. As they should —and it's quite natural—they started to embrace many many times to crown their happiness at finding each other. But, Don Gaiferos brusquely tears himself away from his lady's kisses.

GAIFEROS. Come away Madame. We shall embrace each other better in France. But now it is time to flee, if you do not want King Marsilio to recapture you, and perhaps me, as well.

MELISANDRE. Come, my dear husband, and let us return to France.

1130

THE BOY *(They draw away)*. Just in time, for already, in Saragossa, a watchman had signalled their flight.

(Trumpet).

King Marsilio has come to the battlements. In the distance, he sees, running in the dust rising from the road, Melisandre and her husband, hastening towards France.

MARSILIO. To arms! to arms! Bring them back dead or alive.

(Saracen soldiers come out in packets and throw themselves in hot pursuit of the fugitives).

CRIES. Death to Gaiferos! For us Melisandre!

DON QUIXOTE *(Throws himself with big sword slashes on the puppets, massacring them and breaking open the decor)*. Stop scoundrels! Gaiferos, here I come!

(General confusion. The Innkeeper and Maritorne get up with a bound. The bench see-saws and Sancho finds himself seated on the ground. Everybody talks at the same time).

By St. James! Leave this to me. For me, spirit of Galaor! For me, Florizel and Tirant, Amadis, Esplandian—to my side! Strike, heroes, strike! And cut and thrust. Destroy Saragossa and save Melisandre!

INNKEEPER *(At the same time)*. He be starting again. My lord . . . Stop! They be puppets. Run to Inn. He be putting our eyes out. Come away and close door.

MARITORNE *(At the same time)*. Mother of Heaven, it's took him again. Sir, Sir . . .

(To Sancho). Get up. Stop him. He'll break-up everything.

(To Innkeeper). I come, I come.

SANCHO *(Removes himself on all fours to get himself out of the line of battle)*. My Master . . . listen . . . my Master . . .

PEDRO *(In his booth. At the same time)*. Aie. What's the matter with you? Stop.

(The Innkeeper and Maritorne go into the Inn. The boy flies swiftly through the doorway. The booth falls in a heap of scenery and broken lathes. Quixote trips over and sprawls in the ruins).

PEDRO *(Extricates himself. He no longer has the patch over his eye, his moustache has come unstuck on one side)*. My theatre . . . you are mad . . . you are going to pay . . .

SANCHO. Hullo, thou hast found thy second eye.

PEDRO. My patch . . . dost see, I've lost patch.

SANCHO *(Tearing the false moustache off Pedro)*. And art losing thy moustache too . . . my galley-slave.

PEDRO. What dost think art doing?

SANCHO (*Seizes Quixote's lance*). It be my turn to lead dance, saddle-bag thief.

(*He pursues Pedro who runs away through doorway*).

DON QUIXOTE (*Gets up and calmly shakes the dust from his clothing*). Let no one come and say to me now, this isn't a victory.

INNKEEPER (*Coming back*). What more have ye done?

DON QUIXOTE. I've rescued Melisandre.

INNKEEPER. See that. Where be Master Pedro? Thou hast drove away my best guest.

SANCHO (*Coming back*). Dost know who it be, thy best guest? A galley-slave, Ferdinand. One of galley-slaves my Master . . .

DON QUIXOTE. Don't exaggerate.

SANCHO. . . . that my Master gives thrashing to, some time back.

DON QUIXOTE. Good.

MARITORNE (*Who has come back*). Thou art not in bad shape?

DON QUIXOTE. Not a scratch. I am a Knight-errant and all Knights-errant would have acted as I did.

INNKEEPER. God preserve me.

DON QUIXOTE (*Vexed*). It pleases me, however, to look upon this event as a new and unquestioned victory. And since you, my lord, seem to doubt it—

INNKEEPER. That be putting it mild.

DON QUIXOTE. —I declare your ears will soon tremble at the sound of my deeds.

INNKEEPER. Do hundreds and thousands of them, as many as please thee, but in Lord's name, once and for all, not here.

DON QUIXOTE. You shall no longer have that honour. Come Sancho.

SANCHO. Where to?

DON QUIXOTE. Where destiny awaits me.

(*He bows*). Farewell, Madame.

(*He goes out, eyeing Innkeeper from top to toe*).

INNKEEPER. Let him fall over.

SANCHO. O, nay. He hath my Governorship in 's pocket.

(*He goes out*).

INNKEEPER. One be as mad as t'other.

MARITORNE. Less than thou thinkst.

INNKEEPER. What dost need to convince thee? Be'unt this sufficient? Nay, then, look at that.

MARITORNE. He be brave.

INNKEEPER. Against puppets, and for pole-breaking and for tearing down canvas, aye.

MARITORNE. Thou dost not understand.

INNKEEPER. That's right. I'm an idiot.

MARITORNE. I don't be saying it.

INNKEEPER. I be the one that's crackpot. He be one that's right. Damn it, thou'rt in love.

MARITORNE. And what beside?

INNKEEPER. Be it true?

MARITORNE. Do it matter to thee?

INNKEEPER *(The last thing he expects)*. Knock me down with a feather.

MARITORNE. I have a right, don't I?

INNKEEPER. Thou don't ask much.

MARITORNE. What dost thou know about it? And anyway, shut-up.

(She goes back into the Inn).

INNKEEPER *(Watches her go. Affectionately)*. With her broken teeth and all . . .

(He busies himself picking up the debris of booth).

NICOLAS *(Enters)*. O Ferdinand.

INNKEEPER. O Nicolas!

(Carrasco enters, dressed in impressive armour, over which he wears a short tunic decorated with a large crescent moon. He has a helmet on, crested with feathers. His visor is up).

INNKEEPER. Now another one. No and nay. I want no more. Make thyself scarce and get out.

NICOLAS. It's Carrasco.

INNKEEPER. Thou? Be thou starting to smash up everything as well? Be it catching? This sickness?

CARRASCO. No. Fear nothing. This is of no consequence to you. Is he here?

INNKEEPER. Who?

CARRASCO. Don Quixote.

INNKEEPER (*Indicating debris*). He been here. A real demon.

(*Showing the doll Melisandre*).

To be saving her, he massacred whole theatre. Thou hast only just missed slaughter.

(*Maritorne comes to the Inn doorway*).

NICOLAS. Where is he?

MARITORNE. What more dost want with him, thou, with thy fiesta dressings-up?

CARRASCO. No ill, merely to return him back home.

MARITORNE. Thou's done it once. He be going again.

CARRASCO. We took him by force.

MARITORNE. In cage . . .

CARRASCO. That was an error on our part. A man of his metal refuses to be bound. This time, we will take him by an appeal to his reason.

INNKEEPER. Not a grain hath he.

MARITORNE. He hath.

NICOLAS. More than you think.

INNKEEPER. That's right. Thou be all against me.

CARRASCO. I plan to play him at his own game. By it, he will take himself.

INNKEEPER. I don't know what thou hast a mind to—and little I care. Meantimes, if he heeds thee and be returning by home-path—which—allow me—I do be doubting—make sure, by Grace of God, he don't be coming no more to my inn. He leaves nothing but ruins and regrets.

MARITORNE (*With a sigh*). Thou canst not tell, thou, what it be like to have broken teeth, and somebody calling thee: "Madame".

THE CURTAIN CLOSES.

SCENE 11. BEFORE THE CURTAIN.

(*Sancho comes in front of the curtain. He eats a sausage from which he cuts slices with the aid of his knife*).

NICOLAS (*Enters, with an enormous grotesque cardboard nose, scarlet in colour, he speaks to Sancho with a frightful accent*). Ah, zir . . . per-aps ah mak-ze meestak? Viz dat stomack—oh budt yez, budt —andt deez andt deez—budt no—budt orl ze zame—no meeztak— ze aarmes, ze leggzes, ze frunt, ze backt, andt everydingt andt

1134

everydingt—ah, hah, zare eet eez se beeg eenormuz bulbuz Sancho Pendzundt—Panza. Zat's eet, zat's eet. Do ah meeztak orr do ah nodt meeztak?

SANCHO. Senor, it be true I be Sancho Panza, but thou, there, with that . . .

NICOLAS. Caarfool, caarfool off ma noze, yung mann. Caarfool. Don'dt zay eef someting eez eider deez or dat. Ah verree badt temperr eef zu larf adt ma zo beeg noze.

SANCHO. I say—nay, don't lose thy temper—I say, to thee . . . with that nose . . .

NICOLAS. Caarfool.

SANCHO. That . . . sweet nose . . . I don't know thee.

NICOLAS (Bowing). Pedrooleeno el Tambourino, squire off zuperioreezt dknight off zee Vite Moon.

SANCHO. Don't be knowing him neither. But if he be what thou sayest—as much as I follow thy jargon—my master be the miraculous Don Quixote of la Mancha, the Knight of the Sad Figure. Ah.

NICOLAS. Off la Mancha?

SANCHO. Just that. And if that upsets thee, let me add, my little man, that with one brush of his sleeve, he be wiping out thy master's moon.

NICOLAS. Ohoh—ahah—eheh—

SANCHO. Add some hee hee and some hehew and take it as done he'll be gobbled up in one mouthful.

(With a nimble gesture he pierces a round of sausage).

NICOLAS. Vere vill ee? Vere eez dis fabooliss dknight?

SANCHO (Showing the curtain). There.

NICOLAS. Deadt? Keeldt? Burreedt?

SANCHO. Neither one nor t'other. He sleeps. He dreams. And from his dreams will rise, I swear it, hundreds of stories, each more cock-eyed than last, as he hurls hisself anew into fresh adventure.

NICOLAS. Yez, yez, ee eez a verree queerr lordt andt I vill varn mah dknight off de Vite Moon.

SANCHO. That's it, that's it. Thou warns him, thou, to keep away from my Master, it be much better for him and for us. And take away thy . . .

NICOLAS. Caarfool, yung mann, caarfool.

SANCHO. Well then, Senor, be it said, without offending thee, thy nose dost so overshadow me, I prefers to know it be at t'other end of Spain, rather than in neighborhood of my sun. Go away, farewell and a good journey.

NICOLAS. Orrlrrighdt, I zaludt zee, zquire Zanchoo.

(He goes out).

SANCHO. Zanchoo???

(He watches him go, wants to carry a piece of sausage to his mouth and, absentmindedly, carries it to his nose).

NICOLAS *(Off).* Caarfool, caarfool.

(Sancho very simply, without forcing it, throws a look at sausage and bites it with one clever snap of the teeth).

THE CURTAIN OPENS BEHIND HIM

SCENE 12. A WOODED PLACE.

(Don Quixote sleeps at the foot of a tree).

SANCHO. My Master . . . my Master Don Quixote, dost hear me? Hoohoo, Knight of the Sad Figure and all sorts of things, dost hear me?

(Anguished). Thou art not dead, art thou? Not wounded neither? Say something. Open an eye. Just one, wilt do. It don't matter which. Move thy nose, a finger, thy moustache, anything thou likes, but show me thou art alive. My Master, wake up.

(He seizes the sword and bangs with heavy blows on the shield. Don Quixote, without opening his eyes, scratches his head).

Wake up. Say something.

DON QUIXOTE *(Opening his eyes).* Double . . . triple ass.

SANCHO. Why these compliments? Please?

DON QUIXOTE. Foolish creature, why did you take me out of that dreamy paradise?

SANCHO. Thou wert asleep.

DON QUIXOTE. Enchanted, o triple destroyer. You have broken my enchantment. The most beautiful enchantment Spanish knight ever knew.

SANCHO. Thou canst not fool me with thy enchantments and thy comic inventions. Thou wast deep in sleep, that be all.

DON QUIXOTE. What you say wrongs me and we shall come back to this, later. Give me something to eat.

SANCHO. Thy dream, if I am to believe thee, hast not cut thy appetite.

DON QUIXOTE. Give me some bread.

DON QUIXOTE OF LA MANCHA

SANCHO. It's er . . . seest thou . . .

DON QUIXOTE. Again? Can't you control your greed?

SANCHO. Let's come to an understanding, Your Grace. I think—aye, I think, it were by enchantment, that my bag be empty.

DON QUIXOTE. That explanation hardly satisfies me.

SANCHO. Hear me, if I must myself, accept as daily bread thy magical stories, it be only fair, thinks I, to grant me mine.

DON QUIXOTE. Let it go. Isn't there a piece of cheese left?

SANCHO. It hath disappeared too . . . by enchantment. But wait. I saw farm behind hill, not so far away. I'll find something good there, to please thee.

(He takes the barber's basin and goes out).

DON QUIXOTE *(Dreamily)*. The most beautiful enchantment of my life . . . in a marvellous scene of castles and full of wonders, Dulcinea . . . smiling, gracious . . . I, at her feet . . .

(Nicolas enters with his grotesque nose, and Carrasco dressed in his armour, visor up).

NICOLAS. Here he is. Do not destroy him.

CARRASCO. Leave this to me.

(He lowers his visor).

NICOLAS. He is looking at us.

CARRASCO *(Advances and bows ceremoniously)*. To judge by your equipment and your presence, I have a presentiment, we must, my lord, exercise the same profession.

DON QUIXOTE. I am a Knight-errant. Are you?

CARRASCO. I am. I am the Knight of The White Moon and I am surprised that you did not recognize my arms. My renown is such, that the whole of Europe, and Africa, and Asia, know of my great deeds. I have decimated three hundred and eighteen giants—not a scratch. I have vanquished six of the most fearful dragons—not a bruise. I exterminated no less than twenty two complete regiments of Arab horsemen, in a very brief combat—without losing a single one of my feathers.

DON QUIXOTE *(Without enthusiasm)*. That's good work.

CARRASCO. That's nothing, however, to my remarkable succession of victories over most Spanish Knights.

DON QUIXOTE. Ohoh.

CARRASCO. You were saying?

DON QUIXOTE. I say—ohoh.

1137

CARRASCO. What means your ohoh?

DON QUIXOTE. That I find it odd, Sire, that you fought your fellow members in chivalry.

CARRASCO. It fulfills a promise made to my lady.

DON QUIXOTE. And what have you promised?

CARRASCO. To make all the Knights in the world, beginning with those in Spain, admit that she is the fairest of the living fair.

DON QUIXOTE. May one know, my lord, who is this beauty?

CARRASCO. The incomparable Cassildea of Vandaly.

DON QUIXOTE. Don't you think, my lord Knight, that your lady, however incomparable she be, is nevertheless eclipsed by the more than ideal Dulcinea of Toboso?

CARRASCO. Certainly not.

DON QUIXOTE. You will allow me to doubt that.

CARRASCO. I hold in undeniable proof that her servant-Knight, the very esteemed Don Quixote of la Mancha, has himself recognized the superiority of Cassildea.

DON QUIXOTE. What are you saying?

CARRASCO. The strict truth. I vanquished, as a matter of fact—and it is not the least of my deeds—I vanquished, I say, just over eight days ago, in single combat, the very valiant and more than renowned Don Quixote of la Mancha.

DON QUIXOTE. Are you sure?

CARRASCO. If my word, my lord, does not satisfy you, this steel shall convince you.

(He puts his hand to his sword).

DON QUIXOTE. I accept this challenge, for I am the one you pretend to have vanquished. I am Don Quixote of la Mancha.

CARRASCO. What?

DON QUIXOTE. The Knight of the Sad Figure, yes. And the one you took for me can only be an imposter, or some person magically enthralled by an enchanter to confuse you.

CARRASCO. Be that as it may, I maintain what I said. Cassildea of Vandaly is the fairest.

DON QUIXOTE. As for me, I confirm, that your error on this point is flagrant. The fairest without doubt, is Dulcinea of Toboso.

CARRASCO. Our lances shall decide.

DON QUIXOTE. I am your man.

CARRASCO. I shall make you, as one must, admit before the whole world, that Dulcinea, the uncontested beauty of Toboso, is but an ugly duckling, compared to my lady.

DON QUIXOTE. I shall never say other than I think, and this reason, Sir, suffices for me to accept your challenge.

CARRASCO. I desire, however, to put another condition to this encounter. If I come out the victor—in which there is no shadow of doubt—I demand, you lay down your arms for the length of a year; you retire to your home, without looking for more adventure; moreover, without reading a single romance of chivalry. If, against all likely odds, you triumph over me, my arms and my fortune will be yours and you may add my deeds to the list that already make you famous.

DON QUIXOTE. Be they as big as mountains, I have no need of your deeds. My own suffice for my renown. For the rest, I say: Get ready, my lord, for in three minutes, you will have bitten the road's dust.

CARRASCO. We shall see.

DON QUIXOTE. However, before we begin a fight which, I predict, will be as courteous as superhuman, may I ask you my lord, to raise that visor and allow me to glimpse the glory of your generous visage?

CARRASCO. I cannot satisfy your wish, and you will understand when I tell you, I made a promise to my fair Casildea, the strange promise, never to unmask before combat.

DON QUIXOTE. In that case, Sir, let us tarry no longer.

(They salute ceremoniously. Carrasco, aside, lifts his visor and speaks to Nicolas.

Sancho returns with barber's bowl).

DON QUIXOTE. My helmet.

SANCHO *(Holds out the bowl distractedly as he is looking at Carrasco).* Who be this well-feathered bird?

DON QUIXOTE. The Knight of . . .

(He puts the basin which Sancho has filled with cream cheese on his head).

SANCHO. What art thou a-doing?

DON QUIXOTE. What is it?

SANCHO *(Wiping Quixote's face and the empty basin).* Some cream cheese.

DON QUIXOTE. O, deadly omen. Cream cheese in Mambrino's helmet. What for, in God's name?

SANCHO. It don't be, for sure, to put on thy head. What art to do?

DON QUIXOTE. The Knight has challenged me.

SANCHO. Another battle? Wilt thou never have done?

DON QUIXOTE. Combat is my daily bread.

SANCHO. If today's bread be delivered by that baker, thou'rt making bad bargain. Hast thou taken good look at White-Moon? Three like thee can be put in his armour.

DON QUIXOTE. If a regiment were inside, I would do the same, as he scorns Dulcinea. Be ready to clear up the mess I am about to make.

SANCHO. Do as thou thinkst best. That's thy right. But call to mind, as far as I be concerned, I stoutly refuses to be stuck with his squire, whose nose I can't abide.

NICOLAS (In the distance). Caarfool, Caarfool.

DON QUIXOTE. My charger.

(Sancho goes out).

CARRASCO (To Nicolas). He wants to fight on horseback.

NICOLAS. That was to be expected.

(Sancho comes back with Rossinante).

CARRASCO. What's to do? . . .

(To Quixote). My Lord, one word more.

DON QUIXOTE. I am listening, young man.

CARRASCO. I see you mistake me. I have no mount.

DON QUIXOTE. A strange thing, Sir, a Knight without horse.

CARRASCO. Mine is dead, my lord.

DON QUIXOTE. God keep his soul.

CARRASCO. Killed beneath me in my last combat.

DON QUIXOTE. It does not matter. Sancho, your donkey.

SANCHO. Grison? Thou be'unt thinking of him?

DON QUIXOTE. This will tarnish my victory, but it must be.

SANCHO. Thou'lt be boning poor brute.

DON QUIXOTE. Don't worry. He will not lose a hair in the affray. With one blow—you know me—I will overthrow this audacious fellow and all will be done.

SANCHO. It's my bread and butter.

DON QUIXOTE. If the slightest harm comes to him—these gentlemen are witness—I will replace him with two other colleagues—I swear it.

SANCHO. So be it. I wants to believe thee, once again, but this be last time. And for love of God, go carefully. There be no telling where blows'll fall with thee.

(He goes to get the donkey and introduces it to Carrasco, who perches on it, helped by Nicolas).

Take care of him, sir. He be like brother to me.

(To Grison).

Be brave, my Grison, and if fighting gets too hot, just turn tail, don't hesitate. I wouldn't blame thee for saving thy skin.

(He goes to help Don Quixote).

Can'st tell thee what I think?

DON QUIXOTE. Speak, but be brief.

SANCHO. To see ye two together, looks like grasshopper in front of fortress.

DON QUIXOTE. That's not very flattering, friend Sancho, but I will show you.

SANCHO. Were I in thy shoes, I wouldn't be too sure.

DON QUIXOTE. My honour is at stake.

SANCHO. My donkey, too. Spare him!

DON QUIXOTE *(With Sancho's help climbs on Rossinante and grasps his lance).* Knight of the White Moon, I await your command.

CARRASCO. Knight of la Mancha, I await yours.

DON QUIXOTE. If you please. On Guard!

CARRASCO. On Guard! For Casildea of Vandaly!

DON QUIXOTE. For Dulcinea of Toboso!

(Sancho and Nicolas stand apart).

SANCHO. My Grison! Don't forget!

(Combat. Carrasco, with lowered lance obviously waits for Don Quixote's charge. Don Quixote hurls himself, with lance mid-height. Carrasco prudently puts his lance aside so as not to wound Quixote. After several passes Carrasco pushes his lance between Rossinante's paws, who sprawls on the ground. Don Quixote falls without much injury. At once Carrasco points his lance at Quixote. Sancho and Nicolas hurry forward).

SANCHO *(Bending over Quixote).* My master—

NICOLAS *(To Carrasco)*. You've wounded him.

CARRASCO. No. He has not been touched.

(He dismounts).

SANCHO. Your Grace—

DON QUIXOTE. Leave me.

(To Carrasco). I am vanquished, Sir.

(He gets up with difficulty.

Sancho overcome, steps aside and lifts up Rossinante whom he takes away, whilst Nicolas follows him with Grison).

CARRASCO. While admiring your courage, my lord, I am forced to ask you to acknowledge my superiority.

DON QUIXOTE. I acknowledge it.

CARRASCO. And the beauty of my Lady as well?

DON QUIXOTE. Never. Were she queen of the world, the sky and the stars, I would declare—even if my life depended on it—that Dulcinea of Toboso surpasses her in beauty, in wisdom, and gentleness. Kill me, my lord, for I shall never say contrary.

CARRASCO. God forbid, that I should ever commit so base an act, I declare myself, that Dulcinea must be the fairest, since she is worthy of such steadfast love. No, Sir Knight, let this be. I want but one thing to mark my victory. You shall return to your home, as we have agreed, and stay there one whole year.

DON QUIXOTE. I have promised, I will do it.

CARRASCO. And you will read no books of chivalry.

DON QUIXOTE. On my honour, I swear it.

CARRASCO. Then I am satisfied and I leave you your arms and your life. Farewell, very dear and valiant Don Quixote. Never in the memory of Knight-errant, have I met a more courageous and honest adversary. So much do I admire you, that no one—I promise you—shall learn that I vanquished you. Farewell, incomparable hero.

(He bows in a dignified manner and goes out, followed by Nicolas).

DON QUIXOTE. Farewell, too generous friend.

(Sad music. It is defeat.

Sancho picks up the arms).

THE CURTAIN CLOSES

1142

DON QUIXOTE OF LA MANCHA

(Enter Don Quixote and Sancho).

SANCHO. No need to be so down in dumps.

DON QUIXOTE. I'd like to see you in my place.

SANCHO. When all be said and done, what art thou losing?

DON QUIXOTE. Everything.

SANCHO. 'Course not. Dulcinea be still fairest in the world. Thou keepest thy arms, and not a soul be knowing White Moon hath settled thy account in less than two minutes. Take heart. For once, I'll hold my tongue. So thou be'unt losing much. Quite the contrary, thou be gaining something, since thou be finally going to get some rest, certain sure for one year thou'lt not risk more thrashings like thou's had in past.

DON QUIXOTE. I am dishonoured.

SANCHO. Badly shook-up, that's all. In fact, I be worse off than thee, as all my hopes of getting, one day, county, kingdom, or empire, be gone up in smoke.

DON QUIXOTE. I can only counsel you anew, to be patient, for, I warrant you, in a year and a day, I shall go back to campaigning with the firm intention of satisfying you.

SANCHO. I wants very much to believe thee, anew, as thou sayest, but thou knowest as well as I, much water flows under bridges in twelve months, and many donkeys goes on top.

DON QUIXOTE. Great is my despair, Sancho. After so many victories, this ridiculous defeat. It's so stupid, so stupid.

(He cries with rage).

SANCHO. Don't weep, my Master. Don't ye weep, I beg you. Each of thy tears be big enough to drown me. A repulse ain't mortal. Thou art hurting thyself. Never mind. Come along.

DON QUIXOTE. You are right. The bitterest tears will never heal the terrible wound to my honour. Let us return home, to fulfill our promise. For one year—no more adventures, no more deeds of courage, no more feats of valour. It will be hard, Sancho, very hard.

SANCHO. What be we going to do?

DON QUIXOTE. What else is left for us to do?

(They go out).

THE CURTAIN OPENS

CARRASCO. I promised to bring him back. I have done it, but not without trouble. He fought like a lion.

HOUSEKEEPER. Is he really so strong?

CARRASCO. Strong, no, but with a matchless courage. He never gave a thought to the blows he might receive, but dreamt only of those he was going to give.

HOUSEKEEPER (*Looking out of the window*). Isn't it pitiful to see him walking round and round the courtyard thus, like a caged animal. Do you feel we were right to tear him from his dream of chivalry?

CARRASCO. One day or another—you said so yourself—he would have come back dangerously wounded, a broken arm, his head split open, perhaps dying. Wasn't that just what you were trying to avoid?

HOUSEKEEPER. Yes, of course. But don't you, yourself, feel distressed, to see him so miserable and downcast?

CARRASCO. With time, this will pass, believe me.

(*Don Quixote enters*).

My lord Don Quixote, how are you?

DON QUIXOTE. As a vanquished person is.

CARRASCO. What are you saying? A vanquished person? When the whole country prides itself on your glittering victory, over the Knight of the White Moon? He himself, so they say, never stops singing your praises for valour and the sovereign way you overcame him.

DON QUIXOTE. Do me the pleasure, Carrasco, to contradict that news. White Moon is an honourable fellow, but an arrant liar. You know that better than I.

CARRASCO. I don't understand you.

DON QUIXOTE. Don't play with words. He vanquished me. It is good that the world should know it.

CARRASCO. But, noble Knight . . .

DON QUIXOTE. And let everyone cease to drum my ears with these ridiculous titles: Knight, Lord, Your Grace and all the litany of these absurd names. I am Don Quixote, full stop, that's all.

(*To the housekeeper*).

Madame.

HOUSEKEEPER. My lord . . .

DON QUIXOTE. I have just said: Don Quixote, Madame. Nothing more. Call Sancho.

HOUSEKEEPER. Again? What are you going to do?

DON QUIXOTE. Call him. Fear nothing. I promise not to set out with him again. And, as you go out, tell Master Nicolas too.

HOUSEKEEPER. To come and shave you?

DON QUIXOTE. To shave me, yes.

(He watches her go out, then, anxiously).

My armchair.

CARRASCO. Are you alright?

(He slides the chair rapidly behind Don Quixote).

DON QUIXOTE *(Sits with difficulty, but with dignity. Bitter).* My armchair . . .

CARRASCO. You're ashen.

DON QUIXOTE. My last battle has just begun.

CARRASCO. What are you saying?

DON QUIXOTE. The truth. This is between ourselves. I have your word?

CARRASCO. You have it.

DON QUIXOTE. Your word as a Knight?

CARRASCO. Yes.

DON QUIXOTE. Thank you. This morning, this old tic-toc, beneath my doublet, gave me full warning.

CARRASCO. Your heart?

DON QUIXOTE. My heart, yes. My heart is bursting, and will soon stop.

CARRASCO. Call a doctor.

DON QUIXOTE. This is no matter for a doctor. My story is finished, that's all. Don Quixote has lived, Don Quixote has committed a thousand follies, Don Quixote has dreamed that chivalry could be revived in this poor world . . .

CARRASCO. It will be revived, my lord.

DON QUIXOTE. The world has such great need of it.

CARRASCO. Men will always be born who, by your example will fight injustice and defend honour.

DON QUIXOTE. Then, I have succeeded, you think?

CARRASCO. Yes, Sir. You will see, it's certain . . .

DON QUIXOTE. I shall not see anything more.

CARRASCO. Don't talk like that.

DON QUIXOTE. Don Quixote will depart, Carrasco. For the third and last time.

SANCHO *(Enters)*. My master . . .

DON QUIXOTE. Come in Sancho.

SANCHO. Dost know something, don't fret any more about my governorship. I be finding work as waggoner; it be all one.

DON QUIXOTE. Brave and faithful friend. The only one really who understood me.

NICOLAS *(Enters with the housekeeper)*. Your Grace . . .

DON QUIXOTE. No, barber. Simply, Don Quixote. Leave our follies aside.

HOUSEKEEPER. Sir, you are pale . . .

DON QUIXOTE. It's fatigue. Isn't it Carrasco?

CARRASCO. Fatigue, yes, Sir.

NICOLAS. Am I to shave you?

DON QUIXOTE. Not just now. Dona Belisa, my friends, listen. Gather around me. You know that I am not rich . . .

SANCHO. There be two crowns left in purse of chivalry.

DON QUIXOTE. Keep them, they are yours. My fortune, you know consists of this house, and what it contains, of Rossinante—

HOUSEKEEPER. Why are you talking like this? What's happening?

DON QUIXOTE. I happen to be listening to wisdom, Madame, who wishes me to say to each one . . .

(He screws his face up in pain).

CARRASCO. Sir . . .

HOUSEKEEPER. What is the matter?

DON QUIXOTE. A remorse. Rossinante is too old. He no longer is worth the wages I owe you. You shall have the house.

HOUSEKEEPER. Senor Don . . .

CARRASCO. Enough, Madame.

DON QUIXOTE *(Makes a sign to Carrasco who unhooks the barber's basin and gives it to him)*. You, Nicolas . . .

(He looks a second at the basin and holds it out to Nicolas).

1146

Take back your barber's basin. You were right, it is not Mambrino's helmet. In a moment you will prepare my lather in it.

NICOLAS (*To hide his emotion puts the basin on his head*). It sits less well on me than on you, doesn't it?

DON QUIXOTE. My lance to Sancho, with my shield and Rossinante.

(*Carrasco executes the order*).

SANCHO. What for?

DON QUIXOTE. So that one lance at least, still watches over Spain. To you, Carrasco, my sword. White-Moon certainly deserved it. Here you are, all armed for my last combat.

(*Timidly Maritorne and the Innkeeper, who carries his cooking spoon in his belt—enter*).

DON QUIXOTE. Come in Ferdinand, Maritorne. You were missing from the picture.

INNKEEPER. I've come to offer thee . . . how be I saying? . . . this . . .

DON QUIXOTE. I've given my word. Not one more romance of chivalry.

INNKEEPER. Really, it don't be a romance.

(*To Maritorne*).

Thou tells him, thou—

MARITORNE. It be . . . don't vex thyself—it be thine own tale—

INNKEEPER. The most moving story in th' world.

DON QUIXOTE (*Dreamily*). The most moving story in the world. Mine.

(*To Sancho*). Ours.

(*He looks at the cover*).

"The Adventures of Don Quixote of la Mancha"—

SANCHO. Do it really speak of me?

INNKEEPER. Of thee, yes. And of your Grison.

MARITORNE. Of us all.

DON QUIXOTE. Listen.

(*He reads*).

In a village of la Mancha . . .

(*He screws his face up in pain*).

. . . in the very heart of ardent Spain . . . lived . . .

(*He lets the book slide and stands up*).

1147

HOUSEKEEPER. Sir . . .

CARRASCO. My lord . . .

DON QUIXOTE. Don Quixote of la Mancha . . .

(He falls back, dead).

HOUSEKEEPER. Sir.

MARITORNE. Sir Knight . . .

SANCHO *(Approaches, understands, and in his despair breaks into a
clamour shaking with sobs).* My master . . . no . . . my master
. . . my master . . .

(Music).

THE CURTAIN CLOSES SLOWLY.

Appendix I

PLAYS FOR SUPPLEMENTARY READING

appearing in chronological order

A Midsummer Night's Dream: William Shakespeare
Rip Van Winkle: Joseph Jefferson
Peter Pan: James Barrie (1907)
The Blue Bird: Maurice Maeterlinck (1907)
The Silver Thread: Constance D'Arcy Mackay (1910)
Snow White and the Seven Dwarfs: Jessie B. White (1912)
Treasure Island: Jules Goodman (1915)
The Forest Ring: William DeMille and Charles Bernard (1921)
Rackety Packety House: Frances Hodgson Burnett (1926)
Alice in Wonderland: Eva LeGallienne and Florida Friebus (1932)
Toad of Toad Hall: A. A. Milne (1932)
Aladdin: Theodora DuBois (1932)
The Emperor's New Clothes: Charlotte B. Chorpenning (1938)
A Christmas Carol: Martha Bennett King (1941)
Greensleeves Magic: Marion Jonson (1951)
The Magic Horn: Anne Nicholson and Charlotte Chorpenning (1951)
Beauty and the Beast: Nicholas Stuart Gray (1951)
The Prince and the Pauper: Charlotte B. Chorpenning (1954)
Abe Lincoln — New Salem Days: Charlotte B. Chorpenning (1954)
King of the Golden River: Margery Evernden (1955)
The Red Shoes: Hans Josef Schmidt (1955)
Winnie the Pooh: Kristin Sergel (1957)
Indian Captive: The Story of Mary Jemison (1961)
The Snow Queen: Suria Magito
William Tell: W. Vosco Call (1963)
The Dragon: Eugene Schwartz (1963)
The Adventures of Harlequin: William Glennon (1964)
Dr. Graymatter's Dilemma: Cynthia Zievers (1964) (Unpublished)
Young Dick Whittington: Alan Broadhurst (1964)
King Patch and Mr. Simpkins: Alan Cullen (1964)

The Dancing Donkey: Erik Vos (1965)
Big Klaus and Little Klaus: Dean Wenstrom (1966)
The Ice Wolf: Joanna Halpert Kraus (1967)

Major anthologies or collections prior to the scope of this volume

PORTMANTEAU PLAYS: Stuart Walker (1917)
MORE PORTMANTEAU PLAYS: Stuart Walker (1919)
A TREASURY OF PLAYS FOR CHILDREN: Montrose Moses (1921)
ANOTHER TREASURY OF PLAYS FOR CHILDREN: Montrose Moses (1926)
PLAYING THEATRE: SIX PLAYS FOR CHILDREN: Clare Tree Major (1930)
RING UP THE CURTAIN: Montrose J. Moses (1932)

Note: All published titles that remain in print are available from The Drama Book Shop, 150 W. 52nd St., New York City 10019.

Appendix II

OTHER PUBLICATIONS FROM
THE ANCHORAGE PRESS

As of August, 1967

Aladdin and the Wonderful Lamp: Norris
Ali Baba and the Forty Thieves: Atiyeh
Ali Baba and the Forty Thieves: Masters
Alice in Wonderland: Miller
Big Klaus and Little Klaus: Wenstrom
THE BOOK OF JOB: Corey
The Brave Little Tailor: Harris
Buffalo Bill: Harris
CHILDREN'S THEATRE MANUAL: Seattle Junior Programs
A Christmas Carol: King
The Christmas Nightingale: Groff and Kelly
Cinderella: Chorpenning
The Dancing Donkey: Vos
The Dancing Princesses: King
Daniel Boone: Baptist
The Elves and the Shoemaker: Chorpenning and MacAlvay
The Emperor's Nightingale: Miller
Flibbertygibbet: Chorpenning and MacAlvay
Fox in a Fix: Dean
The Good Witch of Boston: Borgers
Hans Brinker and the Silver Skates: Chorpenning
Hansel and Gretel: Miller
Heidi: Miller
Hiawatha: Norris
King Midas and the Golden Touch: Chorpenning
King Patch and Mr. Simpkins: Cullen
Little Lee Bobo: Chorpenning and Lee
Little Red Riding Hood: Chorpenning
Little Women: Spencer
The Man in the Moon: Cullen
Marco Polo: Siks
The Marvelous Land of Oz: Thane
The Merry Pranks of Tyll: Fleischhacker
MINIATURE PLAYS: Miller
Mr. Popper's Penquins: Mitchell
Mystery at the Old Fort: Musil

1151

No Dogs Allowed (or "Junket"): Harris
The Nuremberg Stove: Siks
Oliver Twist: Browne
The Panda and the Spy: Heinlein
Pegora the Witch: Wright
The Pied Piper of Hamelin: Miller
Pinocchio: Miller
The Plain Princess: Harris
Pocohontas: Harris
Prince Fairyfoot: Siks
The Prince and the Pauper: Chorpenning
The Princess and the Swineherd: Miller
Puss in Boots: Miller
Rapunzel and the Witch: Melanos
Rip Van Winkle: Ruthenburg
Robin Hood: Norris
Robinson Crusoe: Chorpenning
Robinson Crusoe: Miller
The Sandalwood Box: Siks
Simple Simon: Harris
Sinbad the Sailor: Melanos
The Sleeping Beauty: Chorpenning
Snow White and Rose Red: Miller
STORIES TO DRAMATIZE: Ward
The Three Bears: Chorpenning
THEATRE FOR CHILDREN: Ward
THEATRE SCENECRAFT: Adix
The Tinder Box: Broadhurst
TWENTY-ONE YEARS WITH CHILDREN'S THEATRE: Chorpenning
Treasure Island: Drew
The Unwicked Witch: Miller
The Wizard of Oz: Thane
The Wonderful Tang: Bruestle
Young Dick Whittington: Broadhurst

INDEX

Printed in the United States of America
by The Kentucky Printing Corporation,
Louisville, Kentucky.